Elements of
Language

First Course
Annotated Teacher's Edition

Lee Odell

Richard Vacca

Renée Hobbs

Judith L. Irvin

Grammar, Usage, and Mechanics
Instructional Framework by
John E. Warriner

HOLT, RINEHART AND WINSTON

A Harcourt Education Company

Austin • Orlando • Chicago • New York • Toronto • London • San Diego

STAFF CREDITS

EDITORIAL

Executive Editor
Robert R. Hoyt

Program Editor
Kathryn Rogers

Project Editors
Randy Dickson
Eric Estlund
Anne Michelle Gibson

Copyediting
Michael Neibergall, *Copyediting Manager;*
Mary Malone, *Copyediting Supervisor;*
Elizabeth Dickson, *Senior Copyeditor;*
Christine Altgelt, Emily Force,
Julia Thomas Hu, *Copyeditors*

Project Administration
Marie Price, *Managing Editor;*
Lori De La Garza, *Associate Managing
Editor;* Christine Degollado, Janet
Jenkins, *Editorial Coordinators*

DESIGN

Book Design
Joe Melomo, *Design Director;* Candace
Moore, *Senior Designer;* Rina May
Ouellette, *Design Associate*

Image Acquisitions
Curtis Riker, *Director;* Jeannie Taylor,
Photo Research Supervisor; Rick
Benavides, *Photo Researcher;* Sam
Dudgeon, *Senior Staff Photographer;*
Victoria Smith, *Staff Photographer;*
Lauren Eischen, *Photography Specialist*

Media Design
Richard Metzger, *Design Director*

Cover Design
Bill Smith Studio

EDITORIAL PERMISSIONS

Susan Lowrance

PRODUCTION

Carol Trammel, *Production Manager;*
Belinda Barbosa Lopez, Michael Roche,
Senior Production Coordinators

MANUFACTURING

Shirley Cantrell, *Senior Manufacturing
Supervisor;*
Mark McDonald, *Inventory Analyst;*
Amy Borseth, *Manufacturing Coordinator*

Printed in the United States of America
ISBN 0-03-068673-3
1 2 3 4 5   048   05 04 03 02

LEE ODELL helped establish the pedagogical framework for the composition strand of *Elements of Language.* In addition, he guided the development of the scope and sequence and the pedagogical design of the Writing Workshops. Dr. Odell is Professor of Composition Theory and Research and, since 1996, Director of the Writing Program at Rensselaer Polytechnic Institute. He began his career teaching English in middle and high schools. More recently he has worked with teachers in grades K–12 to establish a program that involves students from all disciplines in writing across the curriculum and for communities outside their classrooms. Dr. Odell's most recent book (with Charles R. Cooper) is *Evaluating Writing: The Role of Teachers' Knowledge about Text, Learning, and Culture* (1999). He is Past Chair of the Conference on College Composition and Communication and of NCTE's Assembly for Research.

RICHARD VACCA helped establish the conceptual basis for the reading strand of *Elements of Language.* In addition, he guided the development of the pedagogical design and the scope and sequence of skills in the Reading Workshops. Dr. Vacca is Professor of Education at Kent State University. He recently completed a term as the forty-second President of the International Reading Association. Originally a middle school and high school teacher, Dr. Vacca served as the project director of the Cleveland Writing Demonstration Project for several years. He is the co-author of *Content Area Reading; Reading and Learning to Read;* and articles and chapters related to adolescents' literacy development. In 1989, Dr. Vacca received the College Reading Association's A.B. Herr Award for Outstanding Contributions to Reading Education. Currently, he is co-chair of the IRA's Commission on Adolescent Literacy.

RENÉE HOBBS helped develop the theoretical framework for the viewing and representing strand of *Elements of Language.* She guided the development of the scope and sequence; served as the authority on terminology, definitions, and pedagogy; and directed the planning for the video series. Dr. Hobbs is Associate Professor of Communication at Babson College in Wellesley, Massachusetts, and Director of the Media Literacy Project. Active in the field of media education, Dr. Hobbs has served as Director of the Institute on Media Education, Harvard Graduate School of Education; Director of the "Know TV" Project, Discovery Networks and Time Warner Cable; and Board Member, The New York Times Newspaper in Education Program. She works actively in staff development in school districts nationwide. Dr. Hobbs has contributed articles and chapters on media, technology, and education to many publications.

JUDITH L. IRVIN also helped establish the conceptual basis for the reading strand of *Elements of Language.* Dr. Irvin taught middle school for several years before pursuing graduate studies in Reading-Language Arts. She now teaches courses in curriculum, middle school education, and educational leadership at Florida State University. She chaired the Research Committee of the National Middle School Association and was the editor of *Research in Middle Level Education Quarterly* for six years. Dr. Irvin writes a column, "What Research Says to the Middle Level Practitioner," for the *Middle School Journal.* Her many publications include *What Research Says to the Middle Level Practitioner* and *Reading and the Middle School Student: Strategies to Enhance Literacy.*

JOHN E. WARRINER was a high school English teacher when he developed the original organizational structure for his classic *English Grammar and Composition* series. The approach pioneered by Mr. Warriner was distinctive, and the editorial staff of Holt, Rinehart and Winston have worked diligently to retain the unique qualities of his pedagogy. For the same reason, HRW continues to credit Mr. Warriner as an author of *Elements of Language* in recognition of his groundbreaking work. John Warriner also co-authored the *English Workshop* series and was editor of *Short Stories: Characters in Conflict.* Throughout his long career, however, teaching remained Mr. Warriner's major interest, and he taught for thirty-two years in junior and senior high schools and in college.

The program consultants reviewed instructional materials to ensure consistency with current research, classroom appropriateness, and alignment with curriculum guidelines.

Ann Bagley
Senior Administrator for
    Secondary English
Wake County Public Schools
Raleigh, North Carolina

Vicki R. Brown
Professor of Education
Grambling State University
Principal, Grambling Middle School
Grambling, Louisiana

Max Hutto
Supervisor of Middle School
    Language Arts
Hillsborough County Schools
Tampa, Florida

Beth Johnson
Supervisor of Language Arts
Polk District Schools
Bartow, Florida

Kathleen Jongsma
Associate Professor,
    Department of Education Chair
Texas Lutheran University
Seguin, Texas

Kaye Price-Hawkins
Language Arts Consultant
Abilene, Texas

Lanny van Allen
Consultant, Texas Center for Reading
    and Language Arts
The University of Texas at Austin
Austin, Texas

The critical reviewers read and evaluated pre-publication materials for this book.

Pupil's Edition
Jennifer Bassin
Otto Shortell Middle School
Oneida, New York

Margaret Batig
Marshall Middle School
Beaumont, Texas

Judy Champney
Science Hill High School
Johnson City, Tennessee

Amy Duke
Frostproof Middle-Senior High School
Mulberry, Florida

Raffy Garza-Vizcaino
Brooke Elementary School
Austin, Texas

Katherine Grace
Labay Middle School
Houston, Texas

Gail Hayes
South Florence High School
Florence, South Carolina

Heidi Huckabee
Mesa Middle School
Roswell, New Mexico

Thomas F. Lathinghouse
Bruner Middle School
Fort Walton Beach, Florida

Nancy Levi
Oakland High School
Murfreesboro, Tennessee

Mary Alice Madden
Lathrop Intermediate School
Santa Ana, California

Constance M. Solheim
Corporate Landing Middle School
Virginia Beach, Virginia

Betty Templeton
Riverside High School
Greer, South Carolina

Catherine Wagner
Willow Creek Middle School
Rochester, Minnesota

Nell Waldrop
T. H. Harris Middle School
Metairie, Louisiana

Michael J. Wallpe
Metropolitan School District
Indianapolis, Indiana

Annotated Teacher's Edition
Mary M. Goodson
Pershing Middle School
Houston, Texas

Mary Alice Madden
Lathrop Intermediate School
Santa Ana, California

Constance M. Solheim
Corporate Landing Middle School
Virginia Beach, Virginia

Elizabeth Wallin
Dripping Springs Middle School
Dripping Springs, Texas

The following teachers and students worked with HRW's editorial staff to provide models of student writing for the book.

Teachers

Karen L. Gamble
Labay Middle School
Houston, Texas

Karyn Gloden
Wake County Public School System
Raleigh, North Carolina

Susan Gordon
Randolph Middle School
Randolph, New Jersey

Bonnie Hall
St. Ann School
Lansing, Illinois

Belinda Small
Davidson Middle School
Crestview, Florida

Beverly E. Sparks
Chemawa Middle School
Riverside, California

Students

Jenna Arndt
Labay Middle School
Houston, Texas

J. D. Brannock
Davis Drive Middle School
Apex, North Carolina

Chris Cheung
Davidson Middle School
Crestview, Florida

Artemese C. Evans
Chemawa Middle School
Riverside, California

Matthew Hutter
St. Ann School
Lansing, Illinois

Stephanie Pearl
Randolph Middle School
Randolph, New Jersey

David Stamas
Oak Bluffs Middle School
Oak Bluffs, Massachusetts

FIELD TEST PARTICIPANTS The following teachers participated in the pre-publication field test or review of prototype materials for the *Elements of Language* series.

Nadene Adams
Robert Gray Middle School
Portland, Oregon

Carol Alves
Apopka High School
Apopka, Florida

Susan Atkinson
O. P. Norman Junior High School
Kaufman, Texas

Sheryl L. Babione
Fremont Ross High School
Fremont, Ohio

Jane Baker
Elkins High School
Missouri City, Texas

Martha Barnard
Scarborough High School
Houston, Texas

Jennifer S. Barr
James Bowie High School
Austin, Texas

Leslie Benefield
Reed Middle School
Duncanville, Texas

Gina Birdsall
Irving High School
Irving, Texas

Sara J. Brennan
Murchison Middle School
Austin, Texas

Janelle Brinck
Leander Middle School
Leander, Texas

Geraldine K. Brooks
William B. Travis High School
Austin, Texas

Peter J. Caron
Cumberland Middle School
Cumberland, Rhode Island

Patty Cave
O. P. Norman Junior High School
Kaufman, Texas

Mary Cathyrne Coe
Pocatello High School
Pocatello, Idaho

Continued on page T6

Geri-Lee DeGennaro
Tarpon Springs High School
Tarpon Springs, Florida

Karen Dendy
Stephen F. Austin Middle School
Irving, Texas

Dianne Franz
Tarpon Springs Middle School
Tarpon Springs, Florida

Doris F. Frazier
East Millbrook Magnet Middle School
Raleigh, North Carolina

Shayne G. Goodrum
C. E. Jordan High School
Durham, North Carolina

Bonnie L. Hall
St. Ann School
Lansing, Illinois

Doris Ann Hall
Forest Meadow Junior High School
Dallas, Texas

James M. Harris
Mayfield High School
Mayfield Village, Ohio

Lynne Hoover
Fremont Ross High School
Fremont, Ohio

Patricia A. Humphreys
James Bowie High School
Austin, Texas

Jennifer L. Jones
Oliver Wendell Holmes Middle School
Dallas, Texas

Kathryn R. Jones
Murchison Middle School
Austin, Texas

Bonnie Just
Narbonne High School
Harbor City, California

Vincent Kimball
Patterson High School #405
Baltimore, Maryland

Nancy C. Long
MacArthur High School
Houston, Texas

Carol M. Mackey
Ft. Lauderdale Christian School
Ft. Lauderdale, Florida

Jan Jennings McCown
Johnston High School
Austin, Texas

Alice Kelly McCurdy
Rusk Middle School
Dallas, Texas

Elizabeth Morris
Northshore High School
Slidell, Louisiana

Victoria Reis
Western High School
Ft. Lauderdale, Florida

Dean Richardson
Scarborough High School
Houston, Texas

Susan M. Rogers
Freedom High School
Morganton, North Carolina

Sammy Rusk
North Mesquite High School
Mesquite, Texas

Carole B. San Miguel
James Bowie High School
Austin, Texas

Jane Saunders
William B. Travis High School
Austin, Texas

Gina Sawyer
Reed Middle School
Duncanville, Texas

Laura R. Schauermann
MacArthur High School
Houston, Texas

Stephen Shearer
MacArthur High School
Houston, Texas

Elizabeth Curry Smith
Tarpon Springs High School
Tarpon Springs, Florida

Jeannette M. Spain
Stephen F. Austin High School
Sugar Land, Texas

Carrie Speer
Northshore High School
Slidell, Louisiana

Trina Steffes
MacArthur High School
Houston, Texas

Andrea G. Freirich Stewart
Freedom High School
Morganton, North Carolina

Diana O. Torres
Johnston High School
Austin, Texas

Jan Voorhees
Whitesboro High School
Marcy, New York

Ann E. Walsh
Bedichek Middle School
Austin, Texas

Mary Jane Warden
Onahan School
Chicago, Illinois

Beth Westbrook
Covington Middle School
Austin, Texas

Char-Lene Wilkins
Morenci Area High School
Morenci, Michigan

CONTENTS IN BRIEF

CONTENTS

CHAPTER 1

Witnessing an Event

Informational Text

Narration/
Description

CHAPTER

2

Explaining a Process **48**

Informational Text

Exposition

Informational Text

Exposition

Finding and Reporting Information

Informational Text

Exposition

Parts of Speech Overview
Verb, Adverb, Preposition, Conjunction, Interjection

CHAPTER 12

Complements

CHAPTER 13

Direct and Indirect Objects, Subject Complements **384**

The Phrase

CHAPTER 14

Prepositional and Verbal Phrases **400**

The Clause
Independent and Subordinate Clauses **422**

Kinds of Sentence Structure

Simple, Compound, Complex, and
Compound-Complex Sentences **438**

Agreement

Subject and Verb, Pronoun and Antecedent **456**

Contents   **T21**

Using Verbs Correctly

Principal Parts, Regular and Irregular Verbs,
Tense, Voice **484**

Using Pronouns Correctly

Nominative and Objective Case Forms 510

Using Modifiers Correctly

Comparison and Placement 530

A Glossary of Usage

Capital Letters

Punctuation

End Marks, Commas, Semicolons, and Colons **596**

Punctuation

Underlining (Italics), Quotation Marks, Apostrophes, Hyphens, Parentheses, Brackets, and Dashes **626**

Spelling

Correcting Common Errors

Key Language Skills Review **684**

PART 4 Quick Reference Handbook 718

MODELS

Features

Grammar Links

Writing Test-Taking Mini-Lessons

Connections to Literature/Life

Designing Your Writing

Viewing and Representing/Speaking and Listening

STUDENT'S OVERVIEW

Elements of Language is divided into four major parts.

PART 1   Communications

This section ties together the essential skills and strategies you use in all types of communication—reading, writing, listening, speaking, viewing, and representing.

Reading Workshops In these workshops, you read an article, a story, an editorial—a real-life example of a type of writing you will then try on your own. In addition, these workshops help you practice the reading process through

- a Reading Skill and Reading Focus specific to each type of writing,

- Vocabulary Mini-Lessons to help you understand unfamiliar words, and

- Test-Taking Mini-Lessons targeting common reading objectives

Writing Workshops In these workshops, you brainstorm ideas and use the writing process to produce your own article, story, editorial—and more. These workshops also include

- Writing and Critical-Thinking Mini-Lessons to help you master important aspects of each type of writing

- an organizational framework and models to guide your writing

- evaluation charts with concrete steps for revising

- Connections to Literature and Connections to Life, activities that extend writing workshop skills and concepts to other areas of your life

- Test-Taking Mini-Lessons to help you respond to writing prompts for tests

Focus on Speaking and Listening
Focus on Viewing and Representing

This is your chance to sharpen your skills in presenting your ideas visually and orally and to learn how to take a more critical view of what you hear and see.

PART 2   Sentences and Paragraphs

Learn to construct clear and effective sentences and paragraphs—what parts to include, how to organize ideas, and how to write these essential parts of compositions with style.

PART 3   Grammar, Usage, and Mechanics

These are the basics that will help you make your writing correct and polished.

Grammar   Discover the structure of language—the words, phrases, and clauses that are the building blocks of sentences.

Usage   Learn the rules that govern how language is used in various social situations, including standard versus nonstandard and formal versus informal English.

Mechanics   Master the nuts and bolts of correct written English, including capitalization, punctuation, and spelling.

PART 4   Quick Reference Handbook

Use this handy guide in and outside school any time you need concise tips to help you communicate more effectively—whether you need to find information in a variety of media, make sense of what you read, prepare for tests, or present your ideas in a published document, a speech, or a visual.

Elements of Language on the Internet

Put the communication strategies in *Elements of Language* to work by logging on to the Internet. At the *Elements of Language* Internet site, you can dissect the prose of professional writers, crack the codes of the advertising industry, and find out how your communication skills can help you in the real world.

As you move through *Elements of Language,* you will find the best online resources at **go.hrw.com.**

Student's Overview   xxxi

Elements of Language

Designed for the Information Age

While reading and writing have been traditional topics of instruction for centuries, *what* and *how* students read and write have changed dramatically. Personal computers have become a staple in most homes and classrooms, and the variety of communications coming through television, radio, movies, and the Internet demands that students process information in a number of ways. That's why Holt, Rinehart and Winston has created *Elements of Language*.

Professional Development

To help you make the most of the book and all its parts, Holt offers a comprehensive and systematic training program to complement *Elements of Language,* providing high-quality and accessible professional learning opportunities designed to relate to the unique needs of the educator. For more information on professional development services provided by Holt, email us at **holtinfo@hrw.com**.

Structured for Teacher Flexibility

Elements of Language is comprehensive in scope yet structured to give you flexibility in choosing the most appropriate instruction for each class. Each book opens with a special section on preparing for standardized tests. Parts 1, 2, and 3 develop instructional topics in depth, and Part 4 provides a comprehensive reference tool.

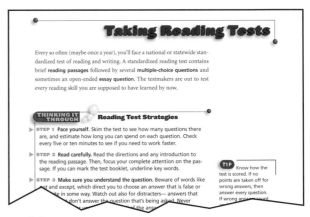

Taking Reading Tests

Every so often (maybe once a year), you'll face a national or statewide standardized test of reading and writing. A standardized reading test contains brief **reading passages** followed by several **multiple-choice questions** and sometimes an open-ended **essay question**. The testmakers are out to test every reading skill you are supposed to have learned by now.

THINKING IT THROUGH   **Reading Test Strategies**

▶ **STEP 1 Pace yourself.** Skim the test to see how many questions there are, and estimate how long you can spend on each question. Check every five or ten minutes to see if you need to work faster.

▶ **STEP 2 Read carefully.** Read the directions and any introduction to the reading passage. Then, focus your complete attention on the passage. If you can mark the test booklet, underline key words.

TIP Know how the test is scored. If no points are taken off for wrong answers, then answer every question. If wrong answers count

▶ **STEP 3 Make sure you understand the question.** Beware of words like *not* and *except*, which direct you to choose an answer that is false or ... in some way. Watch out also for distracters— answers that ... don't answer the question that's being asked. Never ...

Taking Tests: Strategies and Practice

If you are like most teachers, you and your students are concerned about state tests. This chapter helps your students build test-taking skills in reading and writing and provides hands-on practice with the types of tests given in most states.

Part 1

Communications

Part 1: Communications is dedicated to an intensive study of a variety of literacies—reading, writing, speaking, listening, viewing, and representing—with an emphasis on reading and writing. Each chapter uses nonfiction texts and real-world documents to explore different modes of communication.

Part 2

Sentences and Paragraphs

Part 2: Sentences and Paragraphs gives students focused instruction in how to revise and improve their sentences. After mastering the skills of structuring sentences, students then learn the basics of good paragraphs, including how to achieve unity and coherence and how to use effective transitions between paragraphs in a longer piece of writing.

Part 3

Grammar, Usage, and Mechanics

Part 3: Grammar, Usage, and Mechanics is organized in the classic and effective Warriner's format—rule, followed by example, followed by exercise. Part 3 also contains spelling instruction with spelling rules and an extensive list of words that are often confused.

Part 4

Quick Reference Handbook

Part 4: Quick Reference Handbook gives students an efficient way to access information to help them write, do research, hone speaking and listening skills, learn strategies for studying and taking tests, and develop visual literacy. The **Handbook** also includes "Grammar at a Glance," a concise overview and reference tool.

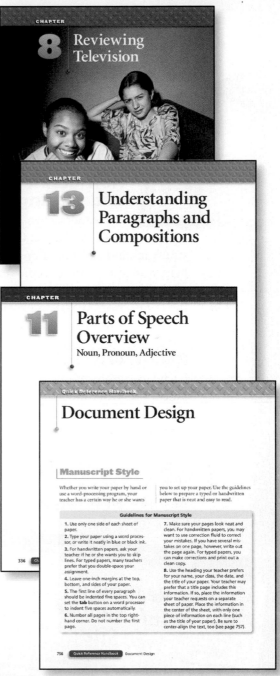

The Reading Workshop
Connecting Reading and Writing

Holt Connects Reading and Writing

All readers, even the best, sometimes struggle. **Part 1: Communications** offers strategies and skills developed by the experts to help you address the specific reading needs of your students. Reading skills are also strengthened by the connection to **Writing Workshop**, in which students write a piece related to their reading.

Real-World Focus

Each Communications chapter opens with a **Reading Workshop** that focuses on a reading skill students need to become effective communicators. Each **Reading Workshop** features nonfiction texts drawn from real-world sources—such as magazines, newspapers, brochures, or Web sites—to model for students the different ways ideas are communicated through writing.

Reading Skills for Life

The **Reading Workshops** teach students strategies for reading and for understanding different kinds of texts.

| READING SKILL

Each **Reading Workshop** targets one essential reading skill, demonstrating the strategies active readers use to maximize comprehension.

| READING FOCUS

Each **Reading Workshop** focuses on a unique element characteristic of the informational or persuasive text students are studying.

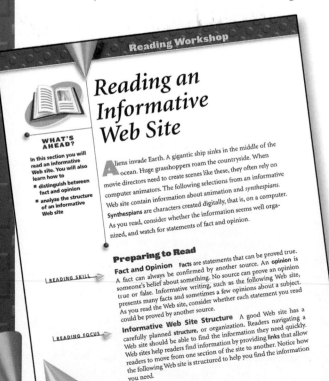

Reading Workshop

Reading an Informative Web Site

WHAT'S AHEAD?

In this section you will read an informative Web site. You will also learn how to
■ distinguish between fact and opinion
■ analyze the structure of an informative Web site

Aliens invade Earth. A gigantic ship sinks in the middle of the ocean. Huge grasshoppers roam the countryside. When movie directors need to create scenes like these, they often rely on computer animators. The following selections from an informative Web site contain information about animation and *synthespians*. Synthespians are characters created digitally, that is, on a computer. As you read, consider whether the information seems well organized, and watch for statements of fact and opinion.

Preparing to Read

Fact and Opinion Facts are statements that can be proved true. A fact can always be confirmed by another source. An **opinion** is someone's belief about something. No source can prove an opinion true or false. Informative writing, such as the following Web site, presents many facts and sometimes a few opinions about a subject. As you read the Web site, consider whether each statement you read could be proved by another source.

Informative Web Site Structure A good Web site has a carefully planned **structure**, or organization. Readers navigating a Web site should be able to find the information they need quickly. Web sites help readers find information by providing **links** that allow readers to move from one section of the site to another. Notice how the following Web site is structured to help you find the information you need.

| READING SKILL

| READING FOCUS

Exposition: Reporting Your Research

Expert Advice

Dr. Richard Vacca, past president of the International Reading Association and author of *Reading in the Content Areas*, established the conceptual basis for the reading strand in *Elements of Language*. He was pivotal in shaping both the instructional design and the content of the program, and his classroom experience informs the program's practical, real-world strategies for improving communication.

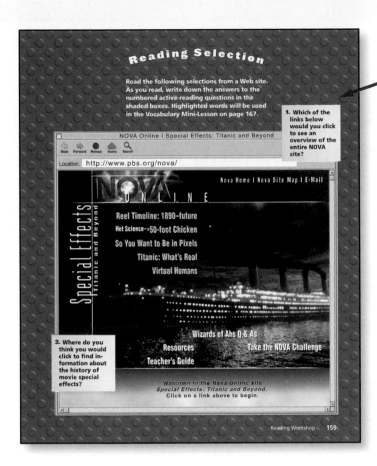

Reading Selection

Read the following selections from a Web site. As you read, write down the answers to the numbered active-reading questions in the shaded boxes. Highlighted words will be used in the Vocabulary Mini-Lesson on page 167.

1. Which of the links below would you click to see an overview of the entire NOVA site?

NOVA Online I Special Effects: Titanic and Beyond

Back Forward Reload Home Search

Location: http://www.pbs.org/nova/

NOVA ONLINE

Nova Home I Nova Site Map I E-Mail

Special Effects
Titanic and Beyond

Reel Timeline: 1890–future
Hot Science–>50-foot Chicken
So You Want to Be in Pixels
Titanic: What's Real
Virtual Humans

Wizards of Ahs Q & As
Resources   Take the NOVA Challenge
Teacher's Guide

2. Where do you think you would click to find information about the history of movie special effects?

Welcome to the Nova Online site
Special Effects: Titanic and Beyond.
Click on a link above to begin.

Reading Workshop   159

Active-Reading Questions model the thinking and questioning students need to acquire strong reading skills.

Mini-Lessons demonstrate strategies for acquiring an extensive vocabulary and scoring well on standardized tests.

MINI-LESSON VOCABULARY

Words with Multiple Meanings

When you read an informative text, you may see a word that has a different mean-

■ I ran a *lap* around the track at school.
■ My dog will *lap* water out of my hand.

MINI-LESSON TEST TAKING

Fact vs. Opinion

Reading tests often ask you to identify facts and opinions in reading passages.

substitution shot is a crude and awkward technique, but it was exciting to

Thinking It Through walks students through the steps needed to analyze a task and identify the critical path to success.

THINKING IT THROUGH   Finding an Implied Main Idea

To find an implied main idea of a piece of writing, use the following set of steps.

▶ **STEP 1** Read the whole piece carefully. Ask yourself what the piece covers. That is its topic.

▶ **STEP 2** Write a summary of each major section of the piece. To summarize, condense the information in each section into the smallest number of words that still give a complete picture of the section. For examples, see the three section summaries in the diagram on the previous page.

▶ **STEP 3** Look at your section summaries, and infer a main idea by writing an "umbrella" sentence that brings them all together. This sentence will be the implied main idea. You can write this as an equation:

topic + main point = implied main idea

Life in the town is calm, quiet, and relaxing—especially in contrast to life in the big city.

TIP Sometimes a passage or piece of writing begins with a question. The unwritten answer to that question is often the implied main idea.

YOUR TURN 2 Identifying an Implied Main Idea

First, look back at "The Sounds of the City" and use a graphic organizer like the one below to summarize the supporting details in each section of the article. Then, based on your summaries, write an umbrella sentence that reflects the main idea the writer is trying to convey. Write the main idea in the oval at the bottom of your graphic organizer.

Section 1 Introduction   Section 2 Imagination Takes Flight   Section 3 Sounds of the New Day   Section 4 Farewell to the Day

Reading Workshop   23

Expert Advice

Judith L. Irvin helped establish the conceptual basis for the middle school reading strand of *Elements of Language.* Dr. Irvin teaches courses in curriculum, middle school education, and educational leadership at Florida State University. She is also chair of the Research Committee of the National Middle School Association and was the editor of *Research in Middle Level Education* for six years.

The Writing Workshop
Connecting Reading and Writing

Writing by Design

A blank page can be one of the most terrifying things any writer faces. *Elements of Language* recognizes that fear and through its **Writing Workshops** guides students step by step through the writing process with focused exercises for prewriting, writing, revising, and publishing.

Reading/Writing Connection

The *Pupil's Edition* provides clear connections between reading and writing, easing the transition from reading "writing" to writing "reading." In the **Reading Workshop** at the start of each chapter, students learn how to read a real-world text and identify the techniques authors use. This instruction prepares students to write a similar piece in the **Writing Workshop.**

Visual Delivery of Instruction

The step-by-step instruction is enhanced by its visual presentation. Throughout the **Writing Workshop,** abundant, colorful graphics convey information and key concepts. A writer's model and a student model—both clearly structured and labeled— provide strong instructional cues for putting pen to paper or fingers to keyboard.

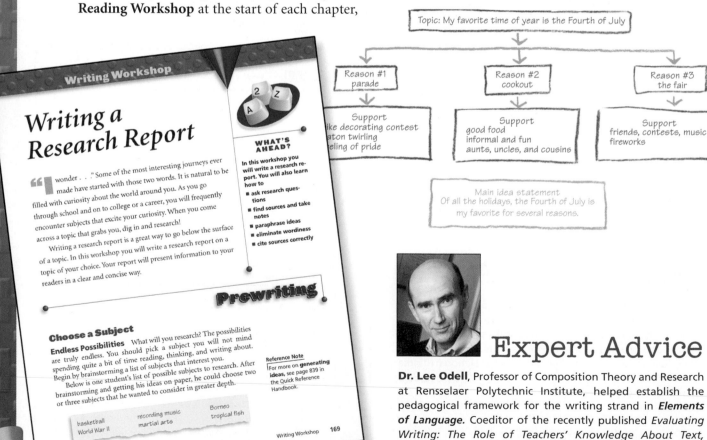

Topic: My favorite time of year is the Fourth of July

Reason #1
parade

Reason #2
cookout

Reason #3
the fair

Support
like decorating contest
baton twirling
feeling of pride

Support
good food
informal and fun
aunts, uncles, and cousins

Support
friends, contests, music
fireworks

Main idea statement
Of all the holidays, the Fourth of July is
my favorite for several reasons.

Writing Workshop

Writing a Research Report

WHAT'S AHEAD?

"I wonder . . ." Some of the most interesting journeys ever made have started with those two words. It is natural to be filled with curiosity about the world around you. As you go through school and on to college or a career, you will frequently encounter subjects that excite your curiosity. When you come across a topic that grabs you, dig in and research!

Writing a research report is a great way to go below the surface of a topic. In this workshop you will write a research report on a topic of your choice. Your report will present information to your readers in a clear and concise way.

In this workshop you will write a research report. You will also learn how to

■ ask research questions
■ find sources and take notes
■ paraphrase ideas
■ eliminate wordiness
■ cite sources correctly

Prewriting

Choose a Subject

Endless Possibilities What will you research? The possibilities are truly endless. You should pick a subject you will not mind spending quite a bit of time reading, thinking, and writing about. Begin by brainstorming a list of subjects that interest you.

Below is one student's list of possible subjects to research. After brainstorming and getting his ideas on paper, he could choose two or three subjects that he wanted to consider in greater depth.

Reference Note
For more on **generating ideas,** see page 839 in the Quick Reference Handbook.

basketball
World War II

recording music
martial arts

Borneo
tropical fish

Writing Workshop   **169**

Expert Advice

Dr. Lee Odell, Professor of Composition Theory and Research at Rensselaer Polytechnic Institute, helped establish the pedagogical framework for the writing strand in *Elements of Language.* Coeditor of the recently published *Evaluating Writing: The Role of Teachers' Knowledge About Text, Learning, and Culture* (1999), Dr. Odell guided the development of both the scope and sequence and the instructional design of the **Writing Workshops.**

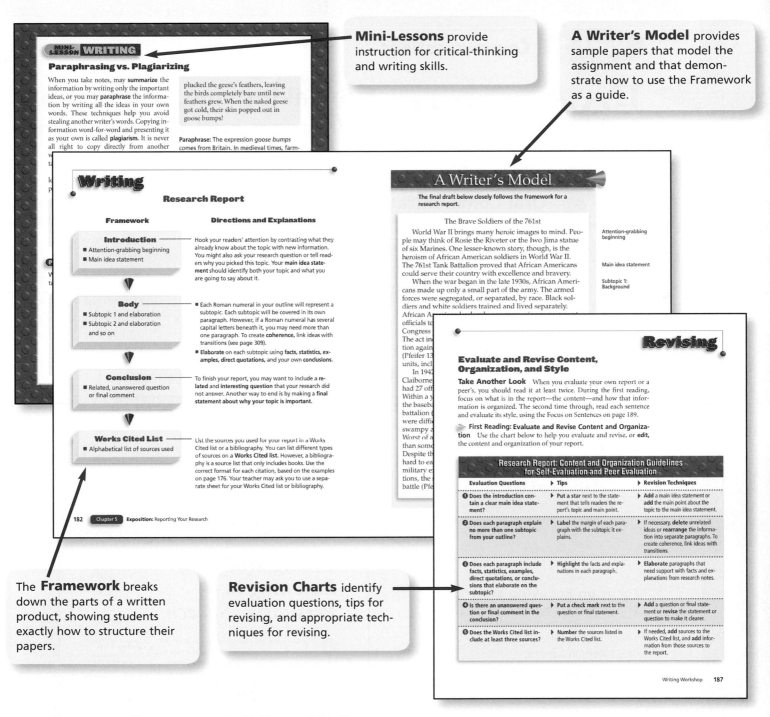

Mini-Lessons provide instruction for critical-thinking and writing skills.

A Writer's Model provides sample papers that model the assignment and that demonstrate how to use the Framework as a guide.

The **Framework** breaks down the parts of a written product, showing students exactly how to structure their papers.

Revision Charts identify evaluation questions, tips for revising, and appropriate techniques for revising.

Features for Developing Style

WORD CHOICE or SENTENCES

Additional instruction and practice help students refine one aspect of their writing style, such as revising wordy sentences or eliminating clichés.

Grammar Link

Instruction and practice show students how to identify and correct common grammatical problems.

Designing Your Writing

This feature teaches students about the visual aspects of writing, helping them choose the most effective design and layout and select the best graphics to convey their message.

Focus on
► **Speaking and Listening**
► **Viewing and Representing**

Media Literacy and Oral Communication

Today's teenagers are often delighted by the variety and frequency of media. Stimulated from all directions by a multitude of messages, from magazine and television advertising to billboards, movies, and the Internet, students must learn how to understand the power of these messages, how to evaluate them, and how to produce their own messages in a variety of formats. Teaching students to view the media with an analytical eye is a serious responsibility. Students must also learn to receive and interpret verbal messages and to organize ideas and communicate them orally. *Elements of Language* is here to help.

At the end of each Communications chapter, one or more extensive lessons highlight speaking and listening or viewing and representing skills, offering meaningful instruction on ways students can learn to take advantage of the power of the media.

Focus on Viewing and Representing helps students become savvy, critical viewers and creative, responsible media communicators.

Focus on Speaking and Listening encourages students to improve the ways in which they receive and convey oral communications.

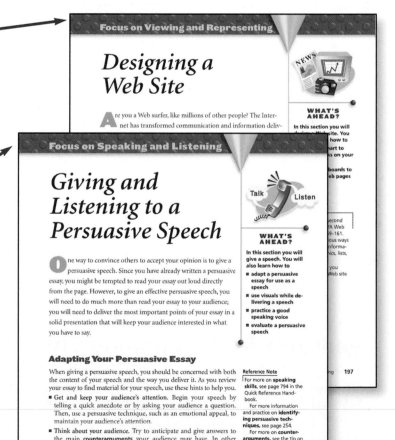

Focus on Viewing and Representing

Designing a Web Site

Are you a Web surfer, like millions of other people? The Internet has transformed communication and information deliv—

WHAT'S AHEAD?

In this section you will

Focus on Speaking and Listening

Giving and Listening to a Persuasive Speech

One way to convince others to accept your opinion is to give a persuasive speech. Since you have already written a persuasive essay, you might be tempted to read your essay out loud directly from the page. However, to give an effective persuasive speech, you will need to do much more than read your essay to your audience; you will need to deliver the most important points of your essay in a solid presentation that will keep your audience interested in what you have to say.

WHAT'S AHEAD?

In this section you will give a speech. You will also learn how to

■ adapt a persuasive essay for use as a speech
■ use visuals while delivering a speech
■ practice a good speaking voice
■ evaluate a persuasive speech

Adapting Your Persuasive Essay

When giving a persuasive speech, you should be concerned with both the content of your speech and the way you deliver it. As you review your essay to find material for your speech, use these hints to help you.

■ **Get and keep your audience's attention.** Begin your speech by telling a quick anecdote or by asking your audience a question. Then, use a persuasive technique, such as an emotional appeal, to maintain your audience's attention.

■ **Think about your audience.** Try to anticipate and give answers to the main **counterarguments** your audience may have. In other words, tailor your speech to appeal to your listeners. Every story, point, example, and visual you choose should be directed to them.

■ **Adjust the tone of your speech.** Delivering your speech from a simple outline—a list of your main points written on paper or note cards—will help your speech sound more conversational than an essay.

Reference Note

For more on **speaking skills**, see page 794 in the Quick Reference Handbook.

For more information and practice on **identifying persuasive techniques**, see page 254.

For more on **counterarguments**, see the tip on page 217.

Focus on Speaking and Listening **233**

YOUR TURN 13 — Delivering a Persuasive Speech

Adapt your persuasive essay for use as a persuasive speech. Then, practice your speech before presenting it to your entire class.

Evaluating a Persuasive Speech

TIP As you listen to a classmate's persuasive speech, evaluate the speaker's **credibility**. Begin by interpreting the speaker's **perspective**, or bias. What is the speaker's relationship to the topic? Does the speaker have personal motives for wanting to persuade you? Listen for the speaker's use of fact and opinion. Credible speakers use facts and other types of evidence to support an opinion. However, speakers who lack credibility fill their speeches with unsupported opinions and let their bias overwhelm the speech.

To evaluate the effectiveness of an essay, you only have to consider the words on the page. However, evaluating a speech is a little more complicated. After all, a speech involves not only words but also a speaker. To help you decide if a classmate's persuasive speech is effective, answer the questions in the chart below as you listen to the speech.

Content	▪ What is the purpose of the presentation? ▪ What is the topic? What is the speaker's verbal message about the topic? Does the speaker clearly state his or her opinion? ▪ Does the speaker include convincing reasons and enough strong support for those reasons?
Use of Visuals	▪ Does the speaker use visuals that make important ideas easy to understand? ▪ Are the visuals easy to see? ▪ Does the speaker explain the visual thoroughly? ▪ Overall, do the visuals add to the effectiveness of the presentation?
Delivery	▪ Is the speaker's tone conversational? ▪ Does the speaker speak loudly and slowly enough? ▪ Does the speaker make eye contact with the audience? ▪ Do the speaker's nonverbal messages (such as gestures and facial expressions) match the verbal message?

Reference Note

For more information on **listening to evaluate**, see page 807 in the Quick Reference Handbook.

For more on **distinguishing fact from opinion**, see page 779 in the Quick Reference Handbook.

YOUR TURN 14 — Evaluating a Persuasive Speech

As students in your class deliver their speeches, use the chart above to help you evaluate each speaker's message and delivery. Then, compare your evaluations with the evaluations of one of your classmates. In what ways were your evaluations different or similar?

Expert Advice

Renée Hobbs, one of the nation's leading authorities on media education, guided the development of the Viewing and Representing lessons in *Elements of Language.* As the director of the Media Literacy Project at Clark University in Worcester, Massachusetts, Dr. Hobbs works with school districts to develop programs that build the media literacy of students across the nation.

Your Turn puts students' new knowledge to work in real-world situations with hands-on activities.

Features That Connect to Literature and Life

Connections to Life

Giving an Informative Speech Using a Web Site as a Visual

When researchers present their findings, they often do so in a **multimedia presentation**, a speech that includes visuals and gives audience members the opportunity to ask questions. While charts or overhead transparencies can be helpful visuals, Web sites can grab an audience by including sound and motion. The links on Web pages also allow a presenter to switch quickly from one page of information to another in a way that traditional videotapes or audiotapes do not. **Note:** If you do not have access to the Internet, you can still give a research presentation. Read the following section, and use visuals such as illustrations, charts, or video segments. (For more on **creating visuals**, see pages 77–80.)

Adapt Your Report Even though your report is about an interesting topic, simply reading it aloud will not keep your audience interested. You will need to adapt your report in order to use it as a short speech (under ten minutes). Follow these steps.

▪ Make notes about the most important points of your report. One way to organize your speech is by making one note card per category of information. Make sure you include evidence, examples, and elaboration to support and clarify your main points.

▪ Use your Works Cited list to tell listeners the sources for statistics, quotes, or unusual facts you use in your speech. If your audience knows where the information comes from, they will consider it more trustworthy. To credit your source simply say something like, "According to *World Book Encyclopedia*, the Armed Forces were segregated until...

Choose a Web Site Once you have created your speech, pick a Web site to use as a visual. Ask your teacher if your school has the tools needed to allow an audience to view a Web site. You might use an overhead projector (Liquid Crystal Display, or LCD) to project the site onto a screen, or could also print and photocopy pages for your class.

Choose a Web site with a strong connection to your topic. For example, look for pictures of important people, places, or things you will mention in your speech, or for charts that show data supporting the ideas in your speech. You can use one page that addresses a key point, or several pages that illustrate ideas in your speech. If the pages you choose are only weakly connected to your ideas, though, they will confuse your audience.

Connections to Literature

Writing a Short Story That Persuades

Although pigs cannot write, they can be very persuasive—at least when they are characters in a *fable*. **Fables** are short stories that teach lessons about life.

A Fabulous Recipe Fables generally follow a formula. Using this formula helps make a persuasive point in just a below. The main ingredients of a below.

	Definition	Example
	usually animals that talk and act like humans	an ant who saves food all summer and a grasshopper who relaxes all summer
	the problem the characters face	In winter, the ant has food because he prepared, but the grasshopper has none.
Moral	the lesson	Be prepared.

A Lesson for Us All The most important part of a fable is its *moral*. The moral, or lesson, is like the opinion statement of a persuasive essay. It expresses what the writer wants readers to do or believe.

Read the following fable by Aesop, retold by Anne Terry White.

The Dog and His Shadow
by Aesop

Curly the Dog was happily trotting home. It wasn't every day that the butcher gave him a juicy bone with meat on it! The Dog was carrying it very carefully in his mouth.

On the way he had to cross a little stream. He looked down from the footbridge into the clear water. And, to his surprise, he saw another dog under the water. Yes, and that other dog also had a bone in his mouth! It seemed to Curly that it was a bigger bone than his own.

With a growl he dropped his bone in order to grab the other dog's bone too. But he had no sooner done that than the dog under the water also dropped his bone.

For a moment Curly stood looking angrily down at his shadow. He couldn't understand it. All he knew was that he had lost his bone and must now trot home without it.

MORAL: Grasp for all and lose all.

Aesop's is a dog named Curly. The conflict is that Curly wants more than what he has. The moral is that greed will only cause unhappiness.

The steps on the next page will show you how to write a fable of your own.

Connections to Life/ Connections to Literature features connect chapter concepts to the students' own lives, to the literature they may be reading, and to the communities in which they live.

Foundations for Writing

Part 2 ## Sentences and Paragraphs

In **Part 2: Sentences and Paragraphs,** *Elements of Language* focuses on the nuts-and-bolts knowledge students need to become successful writers.

The *Pupil's Edition* presents easy-to-follow instruction on writing complete and effective sentences, combining sentences, and correcting common errors such as fragments, wordiness, and lack of parallel structure.

Students also learn to develop strong paragraphs, focusing on unity and coherence. In grades 10, 11, and 12, students focus on composition structure.

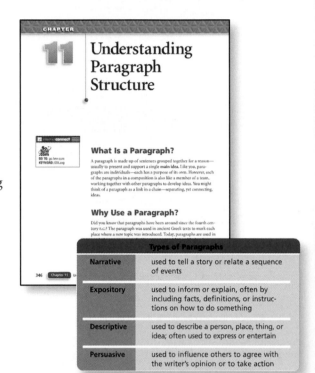

Types of Paragraphs	
Narrative	used to tell a story or relate a sequence of events
Expository	used to inform or explain, often by including facts, definitions, or instructions on how to do something
Descriptive	used to describe a person, place, thing, or idea; often used to express or entertain
Persuasive	used to influence others to agree with the writer's opinion or to take action

Part 3 ## Grammar, Usage, and Mechanics

A confident control of grammar, usage, and mechanics helps to ensure clear and effective communication. In **Part 3: Grammar, Usage, and Mechanics,** *Elements of Language* delivers a comprehensive language skills curriculum that's accessible and effective. Diagnostic Previews give opportunities for diagnosing students' strengths and weaknesses. Reviews A and B provide cumulative assessment, and Chapter Reviews offer additional exercises for ongoing assessments.

Time-Tested Model

Part 3 of *Elements of Language* is based on John Warriner's logical model of instruction—teach students the rule, show examples of the rule in action, and provide immediate practice to reinforce the skill or concept. This time-honored approach has been the authoritative standard for teaching grammar, usage, and mechanics skills for over fifty years.

Common Conjunctive Adverbs		
also	incidentally	next
anyway	indeed	nonetheless
besides	instead	otherwise
consequently	likewise	still
finally	meanwhile	then
furthermore	moreover	therefore
however	nevertheless	thus

Common Transitional Expressions		
after all	even so	in fact
as a result	for example	in other words
at any rate	for instance	on the contrary
by the way	in addition	on the other hand

Warriner's Model for Instruction

"Practice makes perfect," and a multitude of exercises, both written and oral, offer students ample opportunities to practice each rule and learn one concept at a time.

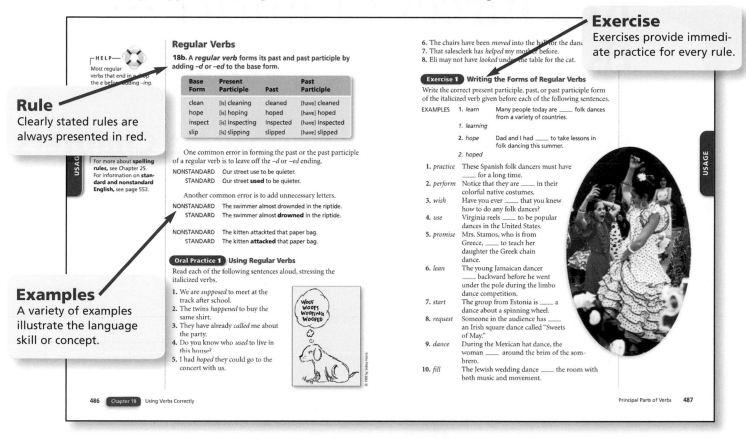

Rule
Clearly stated rules are always presented in red.

Examples
A variety of examples illustrate the language skill or concept.

Exercise
Exercises provide immediate practice for every rule.

Grammar Expert

John E. Warriner, English teacher for thirty years in junior and senior high schools and college, developed the original organizational structure that serves as the basis for the Grammar, Usage, and Mechanics instruction in *Elements of Language*. His well-known and respected pedagogical concept, a clearly stated rule followed by examples and then immediate practice, continues to stand as the ideal model for authoritative grammar, usage, and mechanics instruction.

 **Quick Reference Handbook**

Designed to give students quick and convenient access to key communication concepts, this handbook covers the following topics:

- ▶ **The Dictionary**
- ▶ **Document Design**
- ▶ **The History of English: Origins and Uses**
- ▶ **The Library/Media Center**
- ▶ **Reading and Vocabulary**
- ▶ **Speaking and Listening**
- ▶ **Studying and Test Taking**
- ▶ **Viewing and Representing**
- ▶ **Writing**
- ▶ **Grammar at a Glance**

Resources to Enrich the Learning Process

Support for Communications Chapters

The wide array of print, visual, and technological resources included with *Elements of Language* gives you the visual and academic support needed to make learning come alive for students.

The **Communications** booklet provides support and practice for the Reading and Writing Workshops with graphic organizers, teaching transparencies, and student worksheets. It includes

- writing prompts
- journal warm-ups
- revising charts
- proofreading practice
- fine art transparencies
- guidelines for peer evaluation and self-evaluation
- additional practice

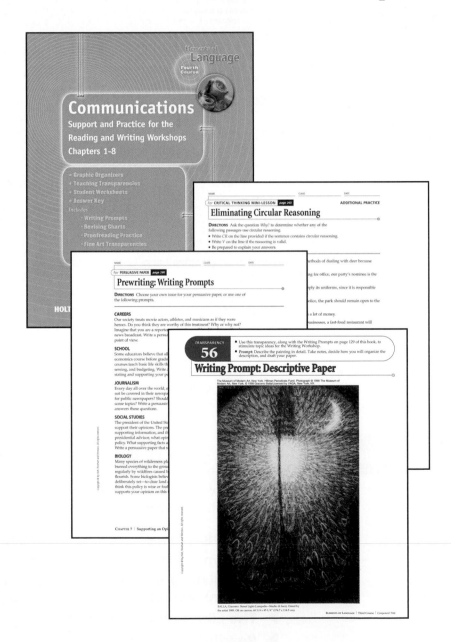

Designing Your Writing transparencies and worksheets model effective techniques for presenting writing. They teach and demonstrate how the choice of formatting, graphics, and other design elements can affect the intended message.

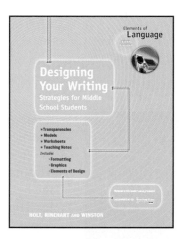

Alternative Readings booklet benefits struggling readers by offering an easier **MiniRead®,** including active-reading questions, for each **Reading Workshop.** Additional reading strategy options target struggling readers and provide tools they can apply to a range of texts.

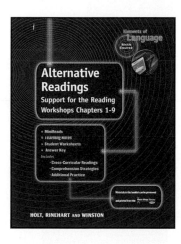

Media Literacy and Communication Skills provides chapter-by-chapter support for speaking, listening, viewing, and representing skills. The package includes videocassettes, *A How-to Handbook,* a set of *Support and Practice* transparencies and worksheets, and *A Teacher's Guide* that pulls these materials together. For more information, see **Technology Resources** on page T49.

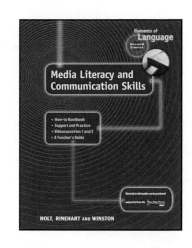

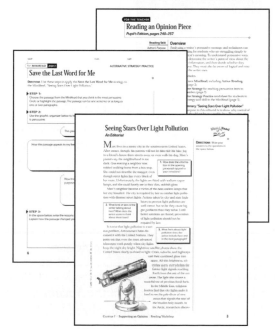

Language Skills

Elements of Language is a comprehensive program of language skills instruction that gives students a solid foundation for effective communication.

Grammar, Usage, and Mechanics: Language Skills Practice provides additional practice for all grammar, usage, and mechanics rules in **Part 3** of the *Pupil's Edition*. Based on Warriner's rule-example-practice model, this invaluable workbook features exercises, proofreading applications, writing applications, and literary-model activities.

Spelling Lessons and Activities (Grades 6–8) focuses on both sound patterns and word analysis strategies. Analysis and additional practice are included for each word list.
Holt Interactive Spelling CD-ROM engages students with lively animation. (See T49.)

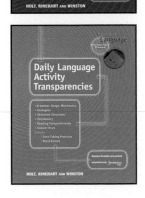

NEW!

Developmental Language Skills and ***Developmental Language Skills Answer Key*** includes remedial worksheets for guided instruction, practice, and reinforcement of lessons in **Part 3**. It targets those students who have not yet mastered specific grammar, usage, and mechanics concepts.

Daily Language Activity Transparencies binder includes test-taking practice in analogies, sentence completion, and reading comprehension. Practice is also included for proofreading in grammar, usage, and mechanics; sentence combining; vocabulary building; and word games.

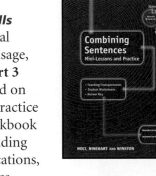

Combining Sentences provides instruction, models, and practice in sentence-combining strategies. This instruction addresses all the basic techniques, such as inserting prepositional or appositive phrases and using compound subjects and verbs.

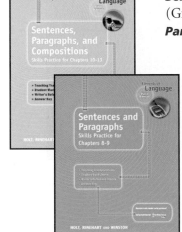
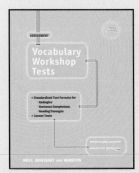

Sentences and Paragraphs (Grades 6–9) and ***Sentences, Paragraphs, and Compositions*** (Grades 10–12) provide up to two pages of additional practice for every exercise in **Part 2** of the *Pupil's Edition*.

Additional Resource

Vocabulary Workshop helps students build their vocabularies and simultaneously prepare for standardized tests. Concepts and skills include analogies, context clues, prefixes, suffixes, roots, synonyms, antonyms, and etymologies.

Vocabulary Workshop Tests assess knowledge of the words and concepts taught in the ***Vocabulary Workshop*** and provide practice in standardized test formats.

Planning and Assessment

Elements of Language provides several options for planning and assessment, giving you more flexibility for today's diverse classroom.

One-Stop Planner® CD-ROM with ExamView® Test Generator for Macintosh® and Windows®

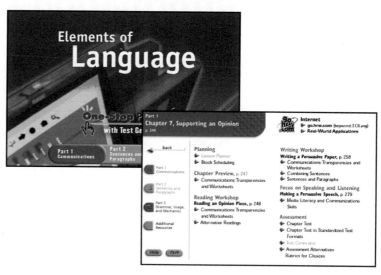

Planning and managing lessons has never been easier than with the ***One-Stop Planner CD-ROM.*** This convenient, all-in-one planning software program includes all the teaching resources for *Elements of Language,* plus valuable planning and assessment tools. The ***One-Stop Planner*** provides

- editable lesson plans
- previews of teaching resources
- an easy-to-use test generator

To preview a video segment or transparency or to print out tests and worksheets for your students, simply select and click.

The ***Lesson Planner*** focuses on both classroom time and the independent working time needed for the reading, writing, speaking, listening, viewing, and representing lessons in the *Pupil's Edition.*
Teaching Strategies for English-Language Learners provides suggestions for using lessons with students who are not native speakers of English.

Chapter Tests provides short-answer questions in traditional formats for each chapter in the *Pupil's Edition.* The tests include assessment for the **Reading and Writing Workshops** in **Part 1**; for the sentences, paragraphs, and compositions instruction in **Part 2**; and for the grammar, usage, and mechanics skills in **Part 3**.

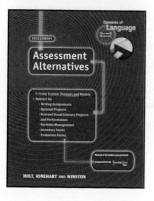

Assessment Alternatives includes inventory and evaluation forms for both teachers and students in writing, reading, listening, speaking, viewing, representing, working in groups, and working on projects. Scoring models demonstrate the use of both holistic and analytic rubrics and scales for assessment.

Chapter Tests in Standardized Test Formats offers an additional test for each chapter in the *Pupil's Edition.* Using a range of formats from the most commonly used standardized assessments, these tests include all of the content listed under ***Chapter Tests.***

Technology
The Key to Learning in the Information Age

The wide range of dynamic and interactive resources available with *Elements of Language* gives students the opportunity to learn and retain more.

Elements of Language Online Textbook

The *Online Edition* of *Elements of Language* sets your students free to pursue language learning any time, anywhere.

Elements of Language Online Edition provides so many convenient options, including online versions of the textbook pages, an instant grading feature, and interactive versions of textbook activities, exercises, and tests. Of course, the *Online Edition* includes the Warriner's grammar model, the authoritative standard for teaching grammar, usage, and mechanics skills, leading students logically through lessons—from rule to example to exercise.

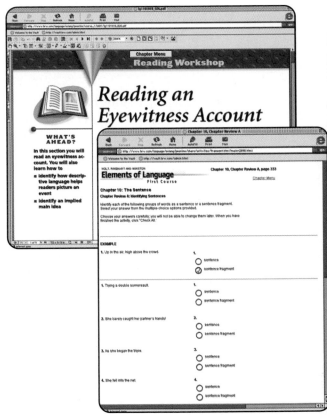

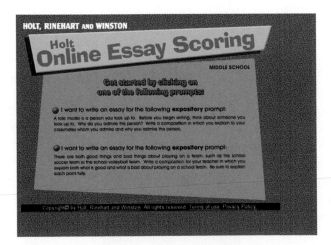

Holt Online Essay Scoring

Looking for more time to enjoy the parts of teaching that you love the most? **Holt Online Essay Scoring** can help carry the paper load. With prompts and rubrics like those found on state assessments, our computer scoring system uses the latest technology to analyze and provide a holistic score for your students' writing.

Additional links connect the student to more specific **Analytic Feedback,** a **Model Essay,** and **Writing Activities** based on the prompt and the student's score.

Holt Interactive Spelling

This exciting computer program can help students improve spelling and vocabulary skills. The interactive CD-ROM allows students to work at their own pace and is adaptable to a wide range of classroom settings. It begins with a diagnostic pretest to determine which areas need work and provides clear, instructive feedback and printable progress reports. Lively animation encourages students' interest in learning.
Levels 1, 2, and 3.
(Recommended for grades 6, 7, 8.)

go.hrw.com

Internet references throughout the *Student Edition* direct students to a Web site for users of *Elements of Language*. This site links students to activities and projects for each **Communications** chapter and allows them to put their reading, writing, speaking, and listening skills into action in real-world situations.

Media Literacy and Communication Skills

Designed to support the speaking, listening, viewing, and representing lessons in *Elements of Language*, this package contains videocassettes, a *How-To Handbook, Support and Practice,* and a *Teacher's Guide.*

Language Workshop Interactive Multimedia CD-ROM Software

This award-winning CD-ROM gives your students a complete course of study in grammar, usage, and mechanics.

Writer's Workshop Interactive Multimedia CD-ROM Software

This award-winning interactive CD-ROM program guides students through the eight most common writing assignments, such as writing a personal narrative, preparing an informative report, or composing a persuasive essay.

All CD-ROMs are available for both Macintosh® and Windows®.

The Reading and Writing Processes

Do these situations sound familiar? While reading, you suddenly realize you have read the same sentences several times without gaining any meaning from them. While writing, you stare at the single sentence you have written, unable to think of anything else to write. When you find yourself stuck, step back and look at the processes of reading and writing.

Reading

The reading you do in school requires you to think critically about information and ideas. In order to get the most from a text, prepare your mind for the task before you read, use effective strategies while you read, and take time to process the information after you read.

- **Before Reading** Get your mind in gear by considering your purpose for reading a particular piece of writing and by thinking about what you already know about the topic. Preview the text by skimming a bit and considering headings, graphics, and other features. Use this information to predict what the text will discuss and how challenging it will be to read.

- **While Reading** As you read, figure out the writer's point about the topic. Notice how the text is organized (by cause and effect or in order of importance, for example) to help you find support for that point. Connect the ideas to your own experiences when you can. If you get confused, slow down, re-read, or jot ideas in a graphic organizer.

- **After Reading** Confirm and extend your understanding of the text. Draw conclusions about the writer's point of view, and evaluate how well the writer communicated the message. Use ideas in the text to create a piece of art, to read more on a related topic, or to solve a problem.

Writing

A perfect text seldom springs fully formed from your mind; instead, you must plan your text before you write and work to improve it after drafting.

TIP Reading and writing are both recursive processes—that is, you can return to earlier steps when needed. For example, you might make new predictions while you are reading a text or you might develop additional support for ideas when you are revising a piece of writing.

- **Before Writing** First, choose a topic and a form of writing, such as a poem or an editorial. Decide who your readers will be and what you want the text to accomplish. Develop ideas based on your knowledge and on research. Organize the ideas, and jot down your main point.

- **While Writing** Grab attention and provide background information in an introduction. Elaborate your ideas to support your point, and organize them clearly. Then, wrap things up with a conclusion.

- **After Writing** To improve a draft, evaluate how clearly you expressed your ideas. Ask a peer to suggest areas that need work. Then, revise. Proofread to correct mistakes. Share your finished work with others, and reflect on what you learned.

You may have noticed that the reading and writing processes involve similar strategies. The chart below summarizes these similarities.

The Reading and Writing Processes

Reading		Writing
Determine your purpose for reading. Consider what you already know about the topic. Review the text to make predictions about what it will include.	— Before —	■ Identify your writing purpose and your audience. ■ Draw upon what you know about the topic, and do research to find out more. ■ Make notes or an outline to plan what the text will include.
Figure out the writer's main ideas. Look for support for the main ideas. Notice how the ideas in the text are organized.	— While —	■ Express your main ideas clearly. ■ Support them with details, facts, examples, or anecdotes. ■ Follow prewriting notes or an outline to organize your text so readers can easily follow your ideas.
Evaluate the text to decide how accurate it is and its overall quality. Relate what you have read to the world around you by creating something, reading further, or applying ideas. Reflect on what you have read.	— After —	■ Evaluate and revise your text. Use peer editors' comments to help improve your work. ■ Relate your writing to the world around you by publishing it. ■ Reflect on what you have written.

The Reading and Writing Workshops in this book provide valuable practice for strategies that will help you effectively use these related processes.

Communications

Communications   1

Taking Tests: Strategies and Practice

PREVIEWING THE CHAPTER

■ As standardized tests become increasingly important for promotion and graduation, students must become more comfortable with the types of test items they will most often see. In this section students will learn and practice strategies for effectively taking standardized tests of reading and writing skills, both in multiple-choice and essay format. You may want to use this chapter periodically during the school year, first having students use the reading selections, questions, and writing prompts here and later having them apply the strategies in this chapter to other passages and prompts.

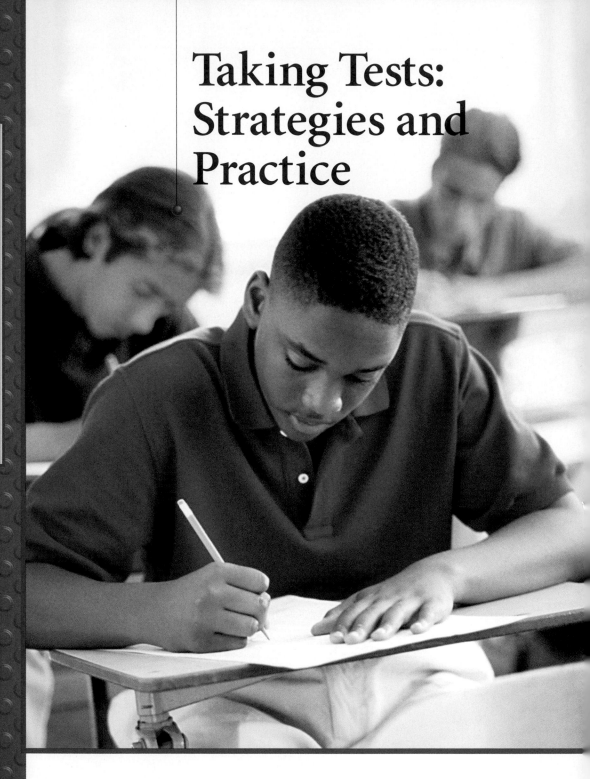

Taking Reading Tests

Every year or so, you're probably asked to show what you know about reading and writing by taking a **standardized test.** A standardized reading test contains **reading passages** followed by **multiple-choice questions** and sometimes an open-ended **essay question.** In this section, you'll find strategies and practice to help you boost your scores on the reading sections of standardized tests.

THINKING IT THROUGH   Reading Test Strategies

▶ STEP 1 **Watch your time.** Divide the test time by the number of questions to estimate how long you can spend on each question. Check every five or ten minutes to see if you need to speed up.

▶ STEP 2 **Concentrate.** Carefully read the directions and introduction to the reading passage. As you read the passage, don't let your attention wander. If you are allowed, underline or circle key words.

▶ STEP 3 **Understand the question.** Look for words like *not* and *except;* they require you to choose an answer that is false or opposite in some way. Don't be fooled by answers that make true statements but don't answer the question that's being asked. Never choose an answer until you've read *all* of the answer choices.

▶ STEP 4 **Make educated guesses.** To narrow your choices, eliminate answers you know are wrong. Then, from the remaining answers, choose the one you think is most likely to be right.

▶ STEP 5 **Keep going.** Skip difficult questions you can't answer. You can go back to them later if you have time at the end.

▶ STEP 6 **Don't lose your place.** Before you bubble in an answer, match each question to the number on the answer sheet. If you skip a question, be sure to skip that number on the answer sheet.

▶ STEP 7 **Take a last look.** Finally, try answering any questions you skipped. Check your answers, and erase any stray marks.

TIP Ask about how the test is scored. If no points are taken off for wrong answers, plan to answer every question. If wrong answers count against you, answer only questions you know and those you can answer with an educated guess.

Read the following passages carefully. Then, choose the **best** answer to each question.

WHEN DISASTER STRIKES!
by Lynne Roberts Key

Would you know what to do if a tornado were sighted near your home? What if you were out riding your bike in the country when a violent thunderstorm rolled in? How would you prepare if you learned a hurricane were headed your way? . . .

Bolts out of the Blue

Each year lightning causes an average of 300 injuries and 93 deaths—that's more deaths than are caused by tornadoes, tropical storms, or hurricanes. Lightning strikes the earth about 100 times a second. One bolt of lightning contains more power than is produced by all the power plants in the United States at that same instant. A lightning bolt may be several miles long, travels about 60,000 miles per second, and is about 50,000 degrees Fahrenheit—that's five times hotter than the sun.

Here are a few tips on how to stay safe from lightning:

- If you feel your skin tingle or your hair stand on end, lightning may be about to strike. The American Red Cross recommends making yourself the smallest target possible. Minimize your contact with the ground. Squat close to the ground on the balls of your feet. Place your hands on your knees with your head between them.

- Get inside a sturdy building or a hard-topped automobile. Small metal sheds and convertibles are not safe shelters.

- Get away from water. If you're boating or swimming as a storm approaches, get away from the water as quickly as possible.
- Drop anything metal. That includes fishing gear, rifles, bikes, metal baseball bats, racquets, or golf clubs. It's also a good idea to take off shoes with cleats.
- Never take shelter under a tall tree. Lightning often strikes the object that is the highest in the area, then arcs to another. If you are standing near a tall tree, the lightning may travel down the tree, then arc to you. Instead, look for a low area with very short trees or bushes. If you are in an open area with no trees, look for a ravine or ditch to lie in.
- Avoid using the phone and electrical appliances. Lightning has been known to injure and even kill a person when it has struck a phone or electrical line, traveled through the wire, then hit the person.

Twisters

Producing winds that exceed 250 miles per hour, tornadoes, defined as violently rotating columns of air extending from a thunderstorm toward the ground, are considered nature's most violent storms. The American Red Cross reports that each year 800 tornadoes are reported nationwide. They cause an average of 1,500 injuries and 80 deaths.

If a tornado warning is issued in your area, follow these safety tips:
- Get to a safe place. Mobile homes, cars, and sheds are no protection from a tornado's powerful winds. Instead, take shelter in the basement of a sturdy building. If you don't have access to a basement, go to an interior room, like a bathroom.
- Stay away from windows.
- Get under a piece of heavy furniture. It can serve as an extra layer of protection.

- If there is no way you can get inside, lie flat in a ditch or depression.

Hurricanes

Hurricanes, with their deadly combination of powerful winds, heavy rains, and storm surges, are among nature's most destructive storms. The best thing about hurricanes is that there is usually ample warning for people to prepare and evacuate. If a hurricane is headed your way, be prepared.
- Listen for local weather updates.
- Prepare a disaster supplies kit.
- Refill prescriptions so that you have at least a two-week supply of any medications.
- Clear your yard of anything that could become flying debris (lawn chairs, potted plants, bikes, and trash cans).
- Fill your car's gas tank and check the oil, water, and tires—in case you need to evacuate.
- Have plenty of cash. Without electricity, ATMs and credit cards don't work.

After Storms Pass

. . . It's pretty clear that it's important to follow common sense safety rules after the storm, too. Here are some tips on how to stay safe after a storm:
- Avoid low hanging wires and anything touching them.
- If you are burning charcoal or wood, be sure the area is well ventilated. Deadly carbon monoxide will build up in an enclosed area.
- In flooded areas, snakes, animals, and insects will seek dry, warm areas like piles of debris. Never pick up debris with your bare hands. Wear gloves, long pants, and a shirt or jacket with sleeves. Use rakes and shovels.

- If traffic lights are not working, treat every intersection as a four-way stop.
- Check all food for spoilage before eating.
- After a major storm, the water supply may be contaminated. Drink only bottled or disinfected water. You can disinfect water by boiling it for at least five minutes or by adding eight drops of chlorine bleach (without scent or additives) per gallon. Let the water sit for at least 10 minutes before drinking. Use only disinfected water for brushing teeth, washing hands, and even cleaning contact lenses.

1. Which sentence **best** states the main idea of this article?
   A. Lightning, tornadoes, and hurricanes are dangerous and unavoidable.
   B. Surviving natural disasters requires a lot of expensive equipment.
   C. Preparation and common sense can save lives during disasters.
   D. It is more important to be careful after a disaster than during one.

2. The writer's main purpose is to provide
   F. unusual facts
   G. vivid details
   H. amusing anecdotes
   J. useful advice

3. For all three disasters, the safest place to be is
   A. indoors
   B. under a tree
   C. in a car
   D. in a shed

4. Why does the author compare a bolt of lightning to power plants?
   F. to emphasize how much power one bolt of lightning can produce
   G. to clarify that power plants are much safer than lightning
   H. to show that lightning is deadlier than tornadoes or hurricanes
   J. to illustrate that a lightning bolt is about 50,000 degrees Fahrenheit

5. You can infer that tornadoes are called *twisters* because of
   A. the way they twist metals
   B. the destruction they cause
   C. the speed at which they travel
   D. the rotating winds they produce

6. In the sentence "Minimize your contact with the ground," *minimize* means to make
   F. as short as possible
   G. as tall as possible
   H. as small as possible
   J. as large as possible

7. You can infer from the article which of these reasons for staying away from windows during a tornado?

A. glass windows attract high winds

B. wind and debris may break the glass

C. seeing the tornado will terrify you

D. furniture might fly out the window

8. Why should you avoid talking on the phone during a lightning storm?

F. Emergency workers need access to the phone lines.

G. Telephones are destroyed when lightning hits them.

H. Phone service is often out during lightning storms.

J. Lightning can travel through phone lines and cause injuries or death.

9. Why does the writer use bullets (•)?

A. to identify each piece of advice

B. to decorate the article

C. to show how each disaster differs

D. to distinguish facts from opinions

10. Write several paragraphs in response to the following question:

A hurricane (or a tornado) is headed your way soon. Tell how you will prepare for this disaster. Describe what you experience and how you feel during the storm and afterward. Use details from the article for information, and make up sensory details.

Trying to Reason with Hurricane Season

by W. E. Butterworth IV

First Class Boy Scout Jamie Perez watched television news pictures of the wind-whipped Florida seashore. Waves whacked the beach. Boats bobbed like bathtub toys. Trees bent double, many snapping like giant toothpicks.

"This could be it," Jamie said last June 5. "Allison could be another Andrew. Any hurricane can become another Andrew."

Jamie, 13, worried for good reason. He lives in Coral Gables, Florida. Just a few months earlier, he and his troop heard a lot about hurricanes during a visit to the National Hurricane Center near their home.

He also remembered, as did a lot of other South Floridians, the record destruction and deaths Hurricane Andrew caused there and in Louisiana in 1992.

From *Boys' Life*, vol. 85, no. 10, October 1995. Copyright © 1995 by **W. E. Butterworth, IV.** Published by the **Boy Scouts of America.** Reprinted by permission of the author and the publisher.

Wicked Wind and Water

Dr. Richard Pasch and Dr. Ed Rappaport, two of five hurricane specialists at the National Hurricane Center in Miami, spoke to the scouts in March. Just three months later, Hurricane Allison shot across the Gulf of Mexico at the start of hurricane season. (The season runs June 1 to November 30.)

Everything the hurricane specialists told the scouts was still fresh in their minds.

The scouts had learned that hurricanes are what scientists call tropical cyclones. *Tropical* comes from the warm part of the world where they occur. *Cyclone* means a rotating storm.

Hurricanes spin fast.

Hurricanes begin as tropical depressions (less than 39-mile-per-hour winds), and then become tropical storms (39 to 73 m.p.h.).

"Seventy-four miles an hour is a baby hurricane," Dr. Pasch said.

Major storms have hit 174 m.p.h. As heat builds from condensing water vapors,[1] winds on the ocean surface spin. The heat released may be equal to the energy burned by some countries in one year. And the wind spins faster and faster.

They cut a terrible path of destruction up to 125 miles wide. Deadly tornadoes spin off. Severe thunderstorms can let loose 10 inches of rain daily. Widespread flooding follows. . . .

One of the worst parts of a hurricane is its storm surge.[2]

"Wind makes the storm surge," said Dr. Pasch. "Blow on water and you'll see how it'll rise. Hurricane Andrew had a 16.9-foot storm surge in [Miami's] Biscayne Bay."

Wind-driven waves on top of the surge cause most of the damage to coastal areas. These places, only a few feet above sea level, have many homes, businesses—and people.

---

1. **condensing water vapors:** visible water particles that are changing to a denser form.
2. **storm surge:** a large mass of water blown ashore by a storm.

Predictions and Warnings

Although Allison was not aimed toward southern Florida, that did not mean it could not go there.

Even experts admit hurricanes are hard to predict.

"How accurately can you say where a hurricane will hit?" Life Scout Steven Tonkinson, 15, had asked the hurricane specialists.

"Every six hours we have to tell where the hurricane will be in the next 24 and 36 hours," Dr. Pasch replied. "We're off 100 to 150 miles. So we issue a warning two to three times that size because we're not sure. That's why it's so important that people move to a safe area."

By Sunday, June 4, a hurricane warning told people from north of Clearwater to Pensacola to find safe shelter inland. Police in Florida's Big Bend area evacuated thousands before rising water cut off roads to beach resorts.

Keeping Track

Dr. Rappaport explained to the scouts how hurricanes are tracked.

"We have two geostationary satellites,"[3] he said. "They stay in the same place—22,000 miles above the Equator; one over the Pacific Ocean,

the other over Key West—and send us pictures to study."

The images show the storm's location, size, and intensity.

"We also have hurricane hunters who fly special airplanes into the storm," said Dr. Pasch. Scientific instruments aboard the aircraft measure the hurricane's humidity, temperature, pressure, and wind.

As the storm reaches shore, the hurricane specialists said, land-based Doppler weather radar creates detailed tracking information.

Still Dangerous

Allison came ashore June 5 at 10 A.M. It hit the Big Bend area with an eight-foot storm surge. It caused flooding and blew down power lines but killed no one.

The National Hurricane Center had done it again.

Allison had not become another Andrew. But, as Jamie noted, the next hurricane could be a deadly one too.

---

3. **geostationary satellite:** a satellite that is always above the same place on the earth's surface.

---

11. Why did the author include the Boy Scouts in the article?
    A. to convince readers to join the Boy Scouts
    B. to present a vivid account of a hurricane's effects
    C. to make the article sound more scientific and scholarly
    D. to show that hurricanes affect young people more than adults

12. If you live very near the coast and a hurricane is headed your way, your greatest danger will be from
    F. traffic accidents during evacuation
    G. flooding from a storm surge
    H. wind-driven debris
    J. thunderstorms and tornadoes

continued

20. This written-response question should take fifteen to twenty minutes to complete. Answers should be one hundred to two hundred words long.

Strategies for Answering the Question Tell students that the types of information in each passage provide clues to the author's purpose. Before they begin writing, have them list the differences they find—for example, the first article's use of bulleted, practical advice versus the second article's heavy use of quotations.

Description of a Top-Score Response Using information and details from the passages for support, a top-score response will note that the purpose of the first passage is to provide tips for surviving various kinds of weather disasters, while the purpose of the second is to provide information about hurricanes and the work of the National Hurricane Center.

13. Tornadoes, like hurricanes, always
- **A.** develop first over water
- **B.** can be precisely predicted
- **C.** have violent rotating winds
- **D.** create storm surges

14. The author divides the article into meaningful chunks by using
- **F.** headings
- **G.** graphics
- **H.** footnotes
- **J.** ellipses (. . .)

15. During a hurricane, what is the **main** goal of the National Hurricane Center?
- **A.** to prevent hurricane damage to homes and businesses
- **B.** to track and record a hurricane's precise location and speed
- **C.** to provide people with safe shelter until they can return to their homes
- **D.** to predict where a hurricane may hit and alert people to move to safety

16. Why does the author compare trees during a hurricane to toothpicks?
- **F.** because the trees bend and snap easily
- **G.** because the trees sway violently from side to side
- **H.** because the trees break into tiny pieces
- **J.** because the trees stand sturdily without moving

17. Lilya is researching Hurricane Andrew. Which is the **best** source of information?
- **A.** the *Hurricane* entry in a 1990 encyclopedia
- **B.** an interview with a Miami survivor of Hurricane Andrew
- **C.** a 1993 article about hurricanes by a Miami TV weather forecaster
- **D.** the National Hurricane Center's Hurricane Andrew Web site

Comparing the Passages

18. The structure of the two passages differs. The second presents information through a story about Boy Scouts. The first passage organizes ideas in what way?
- **F.** in chronological order
- **G.** in spatial order
- **H.** by causes and effects
- **J.** in logical categories

Write several paragraphs in response to *one* of the following questions:

19. The first passage states, "The best thing about hurricanes is that there is usually ample warning for people to prepare and evacuate." Use details and information from the second passage to explain *why* there is usually ample warning before a hurricane.

20. Both passages provide information about storms, but the authors have different purposes for writing. How do the authors' purposes differ? Use details and information from the passages to support your response.

Taking Writing Tests

Standardized tests measure your writing skills in two ways:

- An **on-demand writing prompt** gives you a situation and asks you to write a coherent, well-developed **essay** in a limited time, often less than an hour. The prompt may ask you to write a narrative, expository, or persuasive essay.

- **Multiple-choice questions** test your knowledge of sentence construction and revision as well as paragraph content and organization.

Use the following strategies to write any type of essay. You'll recognize these steps as the steps in the writing process.

THINKING IT THROUGH — Writing Test Strategies

▶ **STEP 1** **Read the writing prompt very carefully.** You need to find out exactly what you're supposed to write. Underline key verbs (such as *analyze, argue, explain, discuss*) that tell you what to do. (Before the test, review the chart of **key verbs that appear in essay questions,** pages 779–80.) Many writing prompts ask you to do two or three different things. Make sure you cover all parts of the prompt, or you'll lose points. Identify your audience.

▶ **STEP 2** **Think before you write.** If you have forty-five minutes, take ten minutes or so for prewriting. Use scratch paper to brainstorm ideas, make a cluster diagram or a rough outline, and gather details. Before you start writing, decide on your main idea statement and how you'll support it. Plan how you'll organize your essay.

> **TIP** Don't skip this prewriting step. Using prewriting strategies will result in a stronger, more interesting essay.

▶ **STEP 3** **Draft your essay.** Spend about two thirds of your time drafting your essay. Express your ideas as clearly as you can. Write a strong opening paragraph and a definite closing, and add many specific details to support and elaborate your main points.

▶ **STEP 4** **Edit and revise as you write.** Leave enough time at the end to re-read your draft. Try to use transitions or combine sentences to make the ideas flow together more smoothly. To add a word or a sentence, use a caret (∧) and insert it clearly and neatly.

▶ **STEP 5** **Proofread your essay.** Find and correct all errors in grammar, usage, mechanics, and spelling. Your score partly depends on how well you follow these conventions of standard English.

Narrative Writing

Sample Writing Prompt *Think about something important you learned and how you learned it. Write it as an autobiographical incident that tells a story. Include dialogue and details of setting and characters.*

Reference Note

For more on writing an **autobiographical narrative,** see pages 27–40.

A story map like the one below can help you plan a short story or an autobiographical incident. Be sure to do what the prompt asks you to do—add dialogue and details of setting and characters. (See **punctuating dialogue,** page 39.)

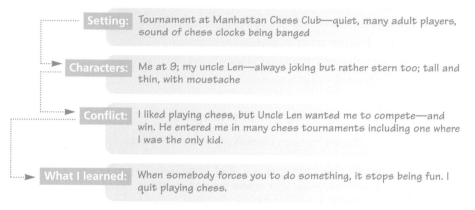

Setting: Tournament at Manhattan Chess Club—quiet, many adult players, sound of chess clocks being banged

Characters: Me at 9; my uncle Len—always joking but rather stern too; tall and thin, with moustache

Conflict: I liked playing chess, but Uncle Len wanted me to compete—and win. He entered me in many chess tournaments including one where I was the only kid.

What I learned: When somebody forces you to do something, it stops being fun. I quit playing chess.

Expository Writing

Sample Writing Prompt *Choose a single invention (telephone, computer, or TV, for instance), and imagine that it was never invented. Describe what the world would be like without that invention, and then tell how your own life would be different, too.*

This prompt asks you to write a cause-effect essay. What is the cause, and what are the two different kinds of effects you need to explain in your essay? One writer gathered ideas by using a chart:

Invention that doesn't exist: telephone

What the world would be like: no long distance, no Internet, no telephone solicitations, no radio call-in contests. People would have to communicate in person or by writing letters.

How my life would be different: I'd have a lot more free time. I'd try to spend that time with friends in person. I'd really miss the Internet and e-mail—I'd have to go to the library to do research. I'd have to write letters!

Reference Note

For more on **analytical writing,** see pages 91–106.

Persuasive Writing

Sample Writing Prompt *Your principal is considering enrolling your school in the President's Challenge, a physical fitness program for students between six and seventeen. Students can win Presidential awards for demonstrating fitness with curl-ups, pull-ups, an endurance run, and other exercises. Write a letter to the principal, clearly stating your opinion and supporting it with reasons and evidence.*

You probably don't have to think very long before making up your mind about this proposal. (With some issues, you need to carefully consider both sides—the pros and cons—before you decide what you think.) Here's a cluster diagram by a student who thinks her school should join the President's Challenge program. She is trying to think of reasons and evidence to support her view.

Reference Note

For more on writing a **persuasive essay,** see pages 211–226.

Multiple-Choice Writing Questions

In addition to a written essay component, multiple-choice writing questions like the ones below are another way to test your understanding of sentence and paragraph structure and the conventions of standard English (grammar, usage, punctuation, capitalization, and spelling).

Read the following paragraph. Then, choose the best answer for each question.

(1) Imagine being swamped by waist-high water, while everything you own is washed away. (2) This happens somewhere in the world almost every week. (3) Floods also destroy crops and increase the risk of disease. (4) Flooding is a natural occurrence and can be useful. (5) For example, in tropical countries such as Bangladesh, monsoon floods spread silt that fertilizes fields. (6) But most floods are harmful, and their effects are getting worse. (7) One reason for this is that more people now live in areas prone to floods. (8) Another is that the world's climate is changing, making floods more severe.

(9) Countries near the Equator have wet and dry seasons instead of hot and cold ones. (10) In southern Asia, the wet season, or monsoon, starts with violent thunderstorms that can drop more than 12 inches (30 centimeters) of rain in a day. (11) These downpours make it difficult to get around, particularly in low-lying places where the water drains slowly.

From *Earth Watch* by David Burnie. Text copyright © 2001 by David Burnie; copyright © 2001 by *Dorling Kindersley Ltd*. Reprinted by permission of the publisher.

1. Sentences 7 and 8 elaborate on sentence 6 by explaining why floods are
   A. useful
   B. natural occurrences
   C. harmful
   D. getting worse

2. The subject of sentence 5 is the word
   F. *countries*
   G. *Bangladesh*
   H. *floods*
   J. *fields*

3. Where is the **best** place to add this sentence?

   In Egypt, too, the flood plain is fertilized each fall when the Nile overflows its banks.

   A. after sentence 1
   B. after sentence 3
   C. after sentence 5
   D. after sentence 6

4. The word *One* in sentence 7 is

   F. a pronoun

   G. a noun

   H. an adverb

   J. an adjective

5. Which sentence is worded correctly?

   A. The growth of some crops is aided by annual flooding.

   B. The growth of some crops, which are aided by annual flooding.

   C. The growth of some crops, being aided by annual flooding.

   D. The growth of some crops are aided by annual flooding.

6. In sentence 9, the indefinite pronoun *ones* refers to which antecedent?

   F. *Countries*

   G. *wet and dry*

   H. *seasons*

   J. *hot and cold*

7. What is the **best** way to combine these two sentences?

   Egyptians used flood waters from the Nile for irrigation. They did this in 4,000 B.C.

   A. Egyptians used flood waters from the Nile for irrigation, they did this in 4,000 B.C.

   B. In 4,000 B.C., Egyptians were using flood waters from the Nile for irrigation.

   C. Although Egyptians used Nile River flood waters for irrigation, they did this in 4,000 B.C.

   D. In 4,000 B.C. for irrigation flood waters from the Nile were used by Egyptians.

8. How should this sentence be corrected?

   Hoover Dam on the Colorado river provides hydroelectric power and also helps to control floods.

   F. Change *river* to *River.*

   G. Change *provides* to *provide.*

   H. Change *and* to *however.*

   J. Change *floods* to *flood's*

9. Which word is misspelled?

   Hoover Dam, an <u>enormous</u> structure
               A

   <u>biult</u> in the 1930s, is 726 feet high
   B

   and 1,244 feet in <u>length</u>. NO ERROR
               C   **D**

10. Zach is using the Internet to find myths about floods from many different cultures. What **keywords** are likely to yield the best results?

   F. U.S. floods

   G. stories about floods

   H. floods AND world history

   J. world myths AND floods

ANSWERS

  1. D

  2. H

  3. C

  4. J

  5. A

  6. H

  7. B

  8. F

  9. B

10. J

Reference Note

For more on preparing for reading and writing tests, see the **Test-Taking Mini-Lessons** in each Part 1 chapter and **Studying and Test Taking** on pages 774–783.

Witnessing an Event

Use this guide to create an instructional plan that suits the individual needs of your students. Assignments marked by an asterisk (*) may be completed out of class. Times given for pacing lessons are estimated. See pp. 16–17 for chapter-wide resources. Resources listed in this guide are point-of-use resources only.

Curriculum Connections

Connections to Literature *pp. 41–43*
- Writing a Descriptive Essay
- Writing a Descriptive Poem

Choices *p. 47*
- Crossing the Curriculum: Art
- Connecting Cultures
- Writing
- Drama

internet connect

go. hrw .com
GO TO: go.hrw.com
KEYWORD: EOLang 7-1

All resources for this chapter are available for preview on the *One-Stop Planner CD-ROM with Test Generator.* All worksheets and tests may be printed from the CD-ROM.

		Chapter Opener *pp. 16–17*	Reading Workshop: Reading an Eyewitness Account *pp. 18–26*
DEVELOPMENTAL PROGRAM		**30 minutes** • Your Turn 1 *p. 17*	**80 minutes** • Preparing to Read *p. 18* • Reading Selection *pp. 19–20* • First Thoughts in groups *p. 21* • Descriptive Language *p. 21* • Your Turn 2 *p. 22* • Implied Main Idea *pp. 22–24* • Your Turn 3 *p. 24* • Test Taking Mini-Lesson *p. 26*
CORE PROGRAM		**20 minutes** • Your Turn 1 *p. 17*	**80 minutes** • Preparing to Read *p. 18* • Reading Selection *pp. 19–20* • First Thoughts *p. 21* • Descriptive Language *p. 21* • Your Turn 2 *p. 22* • Implied Main Idea *pp. 22–24* • Your Turn 3 *p. 24* • Vocabulary Mini-Lesson *p. 25* • Test Taking Mini-Lesson *p. 26*
ADVANCED PROGRAM		**15 minutes** • Your Turn 1 *p. 17*	**60 minutes** • Preparing to Read *p. 18* • Reading Selection *pp. 19–20* • First Thoughts *p. 21* • Descriptive Language *p. 21* • Your Turn 2 *p. 22* • Implied Main Idea *pp. 22–24* • Your Turn 3 *p. 24* • Vocabulary Mini-Lesson *p. 25*
RESOURCES	**PRINT**	• *Communications,* TP. 10, WS. p. 6	• *Alternative Readings,* Ch. 1 • *Communications,* TPs. 11, 12, WS. pp. 7–14
	MEDIA	• *One-Stop Planner CD-ROM*	• *One-Stop Planner CD-ROM*

TP.=Transparency   WS.=Worksheet

Writing Workshop: Writing an Eyewitness Account
pp. 27–43

🕐 **210 minutes**
- Choose an Experience; Your Turn 4 *pp. 27–28*
- Think About Purpose and Audience; Your Turn 5 *p. 29*
- Gather Events and Details; Your Turn 6 *pp. 29–30*
- Framework; Models; Your Turn 7* *pp. 32–35*
- Evaluate and Revise *pp. 36–37*
- Focus on Word Choice in groups *p. 38*
- Your Turn 8 *p. 38*
- Proofread, Publish, and Reflect *pp. 39–40*
- Grammar Link *p. 39*
- Your Turn 9 *p. 40*

🕐 **160 minutes**
- Choose an Experience; Your Turn 4 *pp. 27–28*
- Think About Purpose and Audience; Your Turn 5 *p. 29*
- Gather Events and Details; Your Turn 6 *pp. 29–30*
- Writing Mini-Lesson *p. 31*
- Framework; Models; Your Turn 7* *pp. 32–35*
- Evaluate and Revise *pp. 36–37*
- Focus on Word Choice *p. 38*
- Your Turn 8 *p. 38*
- Proofread, Publish, and Reflect *pp. 39–40*
- Grammar Link *p. 39*
- Your Turn 9 *p. 40*
- Connections to Literature (Descriptive Essay); Your Turn 10* *pp. 41–42*

🕐 **120 minutes**
- Choose an Experience; Your Turn 4 *pp. 27–28*
- Think About Purpose and Audience; Your Turn 5 *p. 29*
- Gather Events and Details; Your Turn 6 *pp. 29–30*
- Writing Mini-Lesson *p. 31*
- Framework; Models; Your Turn 7* *pp. 32–35*
- Evaluate and Revise *pp. 36–37*
- Focus on Word Choice *p. 38*
- Your Turn 8* *p. 38*
- Proofread, Publish, and Reflect *pp. 39–40*
- Grammar Link *p. 39*
- Your Turn 9* *p. 40*
- Connections to Literature (Descriptive Poem); Your Turn 11* *p. 43*

- *Communications,* 🖱
  TPs. 13–16,
  WS. pp. 15–25
- *Designing Your Writing*

- *One-Stop Planner CD-ROM* 💿

Focus on Viewing and Representing: Examining News
pp. 44–46

🕐 **60 minutes**
- Look at the News *pp. 44–45*
- Your Turn 12 *p. 45*
- TV News Versus Newspaper News *pp. 45–46*
- Your Turn 13* *p. 46*

🕐 **45 minutes**
- Look at the News *pp. 44–45*
- Your Turn 12 *p. 45*
- TV News Versus Newspaper News *pp. 45–46*
- Your Turn 13* *p. 46*

🕐 **40 minutes**
- Look at the News *pp. 44–45*
- Your Turn 12 *p. 45*
- TV News Versus Newspaper News *pp. 45–46*
- Your Turn 13* *p. 46*

- *Media Literacy and Communication* 🖱
  Skills
  —*Support and Practice,* Ch. 1
  —*A How-to Handbook*
  —*A Teacher's Guide,* Ch. 1

- *Media Literacy and Communication*
  Skills 📺
  —Videocassette 1, Segment A
- *One-Stop Planner CD-ROM* 💿

Witnessing an Event

CHAPTER OBJECTIVES

- To read an eyewitness account and analyze the characteristics of narrative and descriptive writing
- To write an eyewitness account
- To examine television and print news stories

Chapter Overview

One of the best ways for someone to share an event he or she has experienced is to give an eyewitness account. In this chapter, students will learn to recognize and evaluate eyewitness accounts and to write one of their own. The Reading Workshop (pp. 18–26) provides students with an original eyewitness account to read and to study for its use of descriptive language. The Writing Workshop (pp. 27–43) guides them through the steps in the writing process as they create their own eyewitness account. The Focus on Viewing and Representing shows students how eyewitness news accounts are chosen and compares television and print news. While the sections of the chapter can be taught separately, they work together to give students a thorough understanding of how eyewitness accounts are formulated.

Why Study Eyewitness Accounts?

Studying eyewitness accounts will teach students to identify and use the elements of narrative and descriptive writing to share their own experiences. Recognizing descriptive language and narrative techniques will help students appreciate and evaluate all types of narrative and descriptive writing. Also, students who can use descriptive language will communicate more effectively with their readers. Examining eyewitness accounts will help students understand that narrations or descriptions of events are interpretations created by writers who choose the details to include. This understanding will help students to be discerning readers and listeners.

Teaching the Chapter

Option 1: Begin with Literature

You could begin by exploring how writers narrate events in literature. Point out descriptive language such as sensory details in novels and short stories. Show students how writers use narrative techniques such as chronological order to help readers follow the story. Then, have students read the eyewitness account in this chapter (pp. 19–20) and identify its organizational structure and descriptive language. After students have analyzed descriptions of events, they will be ready to work on their own eyewitness accounts in the Writing Workshop (pp. 27–43).

Option 2: Begin with Nonfiction and Writing

To familiarize students with narrative and descriptive writing before you turn to literature, begin with the material in this chapter. The eyewitness account in the Reading Workshop (pp. 19–20) can show students how writers use narration and descriptive language to help readers picture events. Then, direct students through the process of writing their own eyewitness account in the Writing Workshop (pp. 27–43). Once students have learned to identify and use narrative techniques and descriptive language, they will be better prepared to evaluate those elements in works of literature. See also **Connections to Literature** on pp. 41–43.

Making Connections

■ To the Literature Curriculum

In narrative literature, descriptive details set a mood and capture the reader's interest. For example, the morbid details and figurative language in "The Naming of Names" by Ray Bradbury help set a mood of foreboding, while the comical descriptions in "Fish Cheeks" by Amy Tan create humor.

Lesson Idea: Descriptive Language in "Fish Cheeks" by Amy Tan

1. Introduce students to the elements of description. Then, have students divide a sheet of paper into three columns labeled "Sensory Details," "Exact Words," and "Figures of Speech." Ask students to write examples from the narrative of each type of description. A sample response is given.

Sensory Details	Exact Words	Figures of Speech
black veins	littered	Squid, their backs criss-crossed with knife markings, resembled bicycle tires.
slimy rock cod	raw food	Tofu looked like wedges of rubbery white sponges.

2. Next, ask students about the mood that the writer creates with these descriptive details. How might she have altered the mood by describing the food differently? [by describing the food in an appealing way] What details capture readers' interest? [the comparisons between the food and everyday objects] What

details of the dinner does the author leave out? [She leaves out descriptions about how the food tastes. She omits most of the dialogue that occurs during the dinner.] How do these omissions affect the atmosphere? [Omission of details about taste causes readers to focus on the food's grotesque appearance; omission of dialogue causes readers to concentrate on the narrator and identify with her distress.]

3. Have students read the eyewitness account in the Reading Workshop and identify the types of description in it. Then, help students understand that in both fiction and nonfiction, descriptive details set the mood and capture the interest of the reader.

■ To Careers

Point out that workers in many careers, such as medicine and sales, need to provide clear descriptions. Ask students to interview someone to find out how the person uses descriptive language in his or her job. Have students report their findings to the class. You may want to obtain permission from parents or guardians and from the parties students will contact before you begin this assignment.

■ To the Community

In the Focus on Viewing and Representing in this chapter, students will find out how news stories are chosen. Explain that local newspapers and TV news broadcasts include stories of community interest. Have students look through copies of local newspapers or watch the local TV news to identify stories that deal with community issues. Help students develop a list of questions to send to a local newspaper editor or TV news producer about how stories with community appeal are chosen and developed. Discuss any replies the class receives.

■ To the Art Curriculum

Ask students if they have ever seen a painting that was so vivid they could imagine the taste, feel, or smell of the objects in it. Invite an art teacher or local artist to speak with your class about how artists can suggest sensory details that appeal to all five senses, not just the sense of sight. The speaker might display works of art and encourage students to describe how the works appeal to each of their senses.

CHAPTER

1

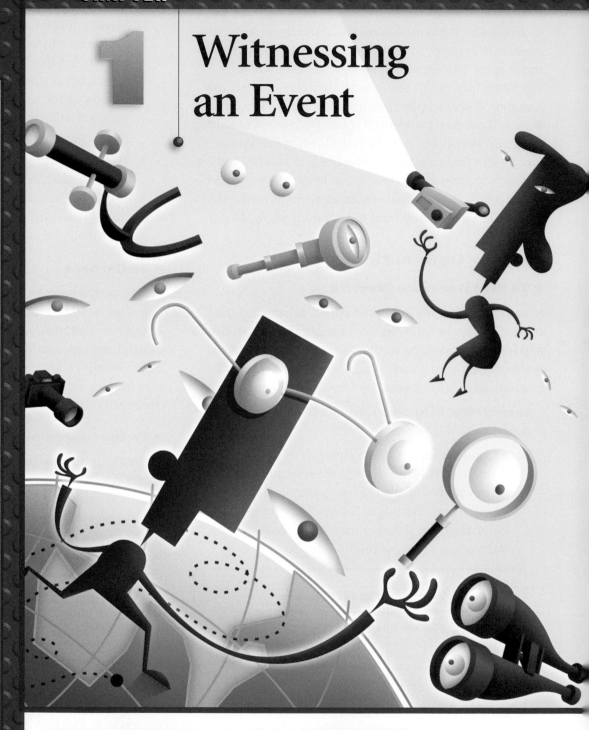

Witnessing an Event

PREVIEWING THE CHAPTER

■ The three workshops in this chapter focus on eyewitness accounts of events. The workshops can be taught separately, but taught together they can help students develop a clearer understanding of narrative and descriptive writing. Reading and analyzing an eyewitness account prepares students to write their own eyewitness accounts. After reading and writing eyewitness accounts, students will be better able to examine representations of events in television and print media. To integrate this chapter with grammar, usage, and mechanics chapters, see pp. T311A–T311B.

INTRODUCING THE CHAPTER

■ To introduce the chapter, use the Journal Warm-up, Transparency 10, in *Communications.*

VIEWING THE ILLUSTRATION

■ Ask students to describe how the illustration relates to the title of the chapter, "Witnessing an Event." [The objects in the illustrations, such as the eyeglasses, the telescope, the magnifying glass, and the numerous pairs of eyes, all relate to viewing and "witnessing."] Discuss how color and shape contribute to the illustration's startling effect. [The contrasting colors and the exaggerated, geometric qualities of the objects and the human figures tend to make the individual objects in the illustration jump out at the viewer, creating a jarring effect.]

CHAPTER RESOURCES

Planning
■ *Lesson Planner, ELL Strategies,* Ch. 1
■ Block Scheduling, p. T15A (this book)
■ *One-Stop Planner CD-ROM*

Practice
■ *Communications,* Ch. 1

■ *Media Literacy and Communication Skills*

Reinforcement
■ *Communications,* Ch. 1
■ *Alternative Readings,* Ch. 1

Reading Workshop

Reading an Eyewitness Account

Writing Workshop

Writing an Eyewitness Account

Viewing and Representing

Examining News

Narration/Description

Have you ever seen huge explosions of fireworks at a festival? Have you watched a famous Hollywood director shutting down the streets of your hometown to make a new film? Even if you have not seen events like these, someone somewhere has, and has probably written about them in an *eyewitness account.* An **eyewitness account** is a **narrative,** or story, that tells about something interesting, unusual, or exciting that the writer has seen. It gives facts and details about an event so that the reader can picture it clearly.

Reading an eyewitness account can put you at the scene of the action. You can also write your own eyewitness account that will pull a reader into your world. Writing an eyewitness account is one of the best ways you and other writers can share what you have seen with the rest of the world.

YOUR TURN 1 — Discovering an Eyewitness Account

Think of an exciting or unusual event you have seen lately, and then briefly discuss it with a partner. Answer these questions.

- What was the event?
- Why does this event stand out in your mind?
- What details of the event can you recall most easily? Why do you think you can recall these details?

internet connect

GO TO: go.hrw.com
KEYWORD: EOLang 7-1

Connecting Reading and Writing **17**

Motivate

Ask students to close their eyes and visualize an event. Suggest that students consider an event that happens around school grounds, such as the arrival of school buses each morning. Then, ask students to write down words that describe the event and appeal to the five senses—sight, hearing, touch, taste, and smell. Ask individual students to share their details aloud while the rest of the class tries to guess the event. Discuss with the class how the sensory details help listeners picture what each speaker describes.

ELEMENTS OF *Literature*

Descriptive Language in Narrative Literature. In *Elements of Literature,* First Course, see the excerpt from *Homesick,* pp. 105–116, and the excerpt from *Barrio Boy,* pp. 125–129, for examples of narrative works of literature that feature descriptive language.

YOUR TURN 1

Possible events include a plane trip, a sporting event, or a storm. Encourage students to use specific details and vivid language in discussing the event with their partners.

- *Daily Language Activity Transparencies*
- *Vocabulary Workshop* and *Tests*
- *Spelling*

Evaluation and Assessment

- *Test Generator (One-Stop Planner CD-ROM)*

- *Assessment Package*
  —*Chapter Tests,* Ch. 1
  —*Chapter Tests in Standardized Test Formats,* Ch. 1
  —*Assessment Alternatives,* Ch. 1

Internet

- go.hrw.com (keyword: EOLang 7–1)

Reading Workshop

OBJECTIVES

Reading and Writing Connection

- To read an eyewitness account in preparation for writing one

Reading Skills

- To identify three types of descriptive language in a reading selection

- To identify and map an implied main idea

- To use parts of speech and context clues to determine the meaning of unfamiliar vocabulary

Quotation for the Day

"I have always paid a good deal of attention to painting. . . . I tried to capture the same effect in words."

(John Dos Passos, 1896–1970, American writer and poet)

Write this quotation on the chalkboard and explain to students that words are a writer's paintbrush. Writers use specific, imaginative, and vivid details to create a picture for the reader.

TEACHING TIP

Preparing to Read
The two concepts, descriptive language and implied main idea, will be the instructional focus of the Reading Workshop and will be taught in more detail on pp. 21–24. The Reading Selection **"Hopi Snake Ceremonies"** illustrates both of these concepts.

RESOURCES

Reading Workshop Reinforcement
- *Alternative Readings*, Ch.1

WHAT'S AHEAD?

In this section you will read an eyewitness account. You will also learn how to

- identify how descriptive language helps readers picture an event

- identify an implied main idea

Reading an Eyewitness Account

You are hiking along a path when you hear a distinctive sound, like bacon sizzling in a pan. It could be a camper cooking breakfast, but more likely it is a rattlesnake. You look down and see the long, legless creature, whose body—marked with a blotched diamond pattern—coils tightly around itself. Bright yellow eyes with vertical slits gaze out at you, and the snake shakes its rattle as if to say, "Watch out! I don't want to have to use my fangs!"

Snakes may scare you or fascinate you. People's views of snakes may differ, but these creatures always seem to create a strong reaction. The author of the following eyewitness account saw an extraordinary event involving snakes. As you read the selection, try to picture the event she is describing.

Preparing to Read

READING FOCUS

Descriptive Language   Author Jennifer Owings Dewey wants to do more than give a list of the events she witnessed. She wants to create in your mind a clear picture of those events. As you read, look for ways the author uses language to create a picture for you.

READING SKILL

Implied Main Idea   The main idea in a reading reveals the point that the writer is trying to make. The author of "Hopi Snake Ceremonies" never clearly states the main idea of her eyewitness account. Instead, the main idea is *implied*. The author gives the reader clues to figure out the main idea by supporting and building on the idea throughout the account. Watch for clues as you read to decide what you think the main idea is.

18   Chapter 1   **Narration/Description:** Witnessing an Event

READING PROCESS

PREREADING
Build Background. Inform students that they will get more out of what they read if they have some background knowledge to help them contextualize events in a selection. Consider telling them the following facts about the account they are about to read. After students have read the selection, have them consider how background information helped their understanding of it.

Read the following article. In a notebook, jot down answers to the numbered active-reading questions in the shaded boxes. The underlined words will be used in the Vocabulary Mini-Lesson on page 25.

from Rattlesnake Dance

HOPI SNAKE CEREMONIES

BY JENNIFER OWINGS DEWEY

1   **D**eath is not the automatic result of a snakebite. I learned this when I was nine. But the mystery of snakebite and venom, and the human response to these, deepened for me when I was ten and my father took me to the Hopi snake ceremonies in Arizona.

1. What do you think this piece will be about?

2   For more than two weeks in August the Hopi Indians held secret <u>rituals</u> that concluded with the snake dance. On those days non-Indians were allowed to watch the dance, although they probably understood little of what they saw. My father did his best to explain what he knew.

3   The Hopi live in a bone-dry region of the desert Southwest. They depend on rain to water their crops. The Hopi believe snakes have unique powers, that they are messengers between humans and spirits—especially the spirits that bring the rain.

4   For the Hopi, the snake ceremony is a time to make a <u>plea</u> to the spirits for the water the Indians badly need to survive. . . .

5   The dancers, all men, filed into the dance plaza of the town. They had shoulder-length hair as sleek and black as raven wings. Bunches of eagle feathers were tied into the thick strands.

6   The men were painted black and white, with zigzag lines to represent lightning. They wore knee-length kilts and woven belts. Each of the dancers had a tortoise-shell rattle tied to his right leg below the thigh.

7   The men moved in a shuffling circle, their buckskin moccasins kicking up puffs of white dust. Their movements were accompanied by a chant, a low, humming sound that rose and fell like the wind. With this came the rattling of the tortoise shells, not unlike the noise a rattlesnake makes when it shakes the hinged buttons at the end of its tail.

2. How does the author help you see the dancers?

Hopi life includes many ceremonies. Those held in the fall center around crops. The Snake Dance honors snakes, whose movements suggest lightning and rain. First, Hopi men gather wild snakes. Then, during the dance, attendants stroke and calm the snakes, which are carried by dancers. The ritual concludes with returning the snakes to the wild.

Active-Reading Questions

The purpose of the active-reading questions is to focus students' thinking on the details that support the implied main idea and on descriptive language that shows readers an event, rather than just tells about it.

ANSWERS

1. Students may think that the writer will tell about a time she learned interesting information about snakes and snakebites at Hopi snake ceremonies.

2. The author uses descriptive language such as "hair as sleek and black as raven wings" and "zigzag lines"—to help readers picture the scene.

TEACHING TIP

Have students buy spiral notebooks to use as learning logs. As they read the **Reading Selection**, they can write their answers to the active-reading questions in their learning logs.

3. Students may say that the author wants to emphasize that no one, including the dancer, seems concerned that he had been bitten.

4. The author believes that the Hopi keep mysterious secrets because she saw a Hopi survive a rattlesnake bite, and she knows that many Hopi rituals cannot be known to outsiders.

8   After several turns around the dance area, a few of the dancers reached into a hole in the ground, a pit that had a shelter of cottonwood boughs over it. They came up with serpents in their hands. They gave these to other dancers, who put them in their mouths and carried them that way, moving in rhythm with the chant. . . .

9   Many of the snakes were <u>coachwhips</u>, bull snakes, and other harmless reptiles. Some were full-grown rattlesnakes, their rattles buzzing furiously. . . .

10   For a long time I kept my eyes on one dancer, a short, <u>stocky</u> man with hair that flew up when he moved. As he made his circle he faced me for as long as a minute. He came close, and I could plainly see the sun shining on the scales of the snakes he carried. On one turn he had a rattlesnake in his mouth.

11   I stared in horror as the snake arched itself around and attached its jaw to the dancer's cheek. The man went on dancing.

> **3.** Why do you think the author includes the detail about the snake biting the dancer?

12   When it came time to change snakes, the man following with the prayer stick unhooked the rattlesnake's mouth from the dancer's face. Two spots of blood remained.

13   "Did you see?" I asked my father in a whisper. "Did you see what that snake did?"

14   "Quiet," my father said. "No talking now."

15   Later, when the dance was over, the two of us sat in the cab of the truck watching fat drops of rain spatter the windshield. . . .

16   "Did you see what that rattlesnake did? How it bit the dancer on the cheek?"

17   "Yes," my father said. "I saw it. It's a mystery, how they do it. . . . Perhaps the dancers have a special way with snakes. The Hopi are protective of their rituals. There are questions we can't answer, because we're not Hopi."

18   We drove across the desert <u>obscured</u> by sheets of rain. My mind returned to what I'd seen that afternoon.

19   Figures of Hopi dancers, snakes of all kinds dangling from their mouths, passed through my imagination like the rain sweeping across the land. I believed the Hopi kept mysterious secrets in their hearts, knowledge of how to <u>cajole</u> a rattlesnake into withholding its venom.

> **4.** Why do you think the author believes the Hopi keep "mysterious secrets"?

READING PROCESS

READING

Make Personal Connections. Explain to students that making personal connections with what they are reading will help them make meaning from a selection by relating what they already know to what they read. Ask students to note passages in **"Hopi Snake Ceremonies"** that remind them of a cultural experience or social event in their lives. Have students work with partners to share one of these connections. Then, ask students to discuss how making these connections helped them understand the narrative.

Descriptive Language

READING FOCUS

Do You See What I See? Do you see anything when you read the following list of events? "We camped. . . .We saw some people dance with snakes. . . . It rained. . . .We were interested." You probably do not see much because this list lacks descriptive language. The writer of an eyewitness account uses descriptive language to help the reader experience an event. Three types of description that a writer relies on are **sensory language, figures of speech,** and **precise words.**

The following chart defines these three types of description and provides examples of how they can be used to help a reader "see" an event.

Types of Descriptive Language		
Types of Description	**Definition**	**Example**
Sensory Language	words and descriptions that appeal to one or more of the five senses—sight, hearing, touch, taste, smell	The fire crackled and the smell of pine filled the air as I watched the sparks leave trails of light.
Figures of Speech	words or phrases that describe one thing by comparing it to something else—*similes* and *metaphors* are two common figures of speech	**Simile:** The snow fell *like* a whisper. [a comparison that uses the word *like* or the word *as*] **Metaphor:** When he is embarrassed his face *is* a ripe tomato. [a direct comparison that says one thing *is* another thing]
Precise Words	specific words that make a description as clear and sharp as possible	**Inexact words:** He walked across the court to receive the trophy. **Precise words:** The 6'4" basketball player strutted across the court to receive the MVP trophy.

Reading Workshop **21**

EXTENDING

Apply What You Read. Explain to students that applying the reading focus they studied in this chapter (see the PE feature **Descriptive Language,** above) to their writing will help them better understand descriptive language when they read it. Ask students to create an artistic interpretation, such as a poem, that uses descriptive language to express personal connections to **"Hopi Snake Ceremonies."** Then, ask them to think about how the Hopi snake ceremony relates to U.S. society at large.

Critical Thinking

Metacognition. Ask students to write a journal entry that discusses how their own social or cultural background affects their understanding of the selection **"Hopi Snake Ceremonies."** Use the following as a springboard:

• What aspects of **"Hopi Snake Ceremonies"** remind you of events you have read about or experienced? Explain.
• What do you think the narrator's father means when he says "There are questions we can't answer, because we're not Hopi"?
• How can cultural or social background affect a person's understanding of a ritual or tradition?

Meeting INDIVIDUAL NEEDS

LEARNERS HAVING DIFFICULTY
Remind students that figures of speech do not mean exactly what they say; similes and metaphors use comparisons to create pictures in readers' minds. Point out that the metaphor in the descriptive language chart does not really mean the boy's face becomes a tomato. Have students explain the sentence in their own words. Then, ask them to brainstorm other similes and metaphors. [His heart was a sunshine factory; The crumpled sleeping bags looked like giant raisins.]

Some examples of descriptive language are listed below.

sensory language: puffs of white dust; rattling; buzzing

figures of speech: hair as sleek and black as raven wings; humming sound that rose and fell like the wind

precise words: shoulder-length hair; knee-length kilts; a tortoise-shell rattle

You might have groups contribute their answers to a class list of descriptive language on the chalkboard. Students may say that the writer's use of sensory language helps the readers experience the event, the figures of speech create vivid images of hair and sound, and the precise words make the descriptions clear and sharp.

Reference Note

For more on **descriptive language,** see page 31.

TIP The details and description in a reading may help you understand the main idea, but they do not state the main idea directly. To understand the main idea, you must add up all the details and descriptions in the entire passage.

- Re-read "Hopi Snake Ceremonies" on pages 19–20 and find at least two examples each of sensory language, figures of speech, and precise words.

- In a small group, tell what examples of descriptive language you found and discuss how they helped you picture the events clearly.

READING SKILL

Implied Main Idea

What Does It All Mean? Suppose you want to tell someone that you are afraid of snakes. You could state your main idea, "I am afraid of snakes." You could also **imply** it by explaining your reaction to seeing a snake: "When I saw the snake, I froze; my heart was pounding and echoing in my ears. My hands were damp and clammy, and sweat was running down my back. My friends were carefully walking around the snake, but I still could not move." To figure out an implied main idea, you need to *read the entire passage* and then put the clues together.

When a writer implies a main idea, he or she gives clues throughout the reading to help you find the main idea.

In the following paragraph, the main idea is implied. Can you identify it? If you have trouble, use the steps on the next page.

When I visited northern Arizona I went to the Hopi Indian Reservation. I visited a very old village; many of the houses had been built more than four hundred years ago. The houses sat around a central plaza, which served as a meeting place as well as the site of ceremonies and celebrations. One of the houses that I saw was falling apart, but the villagers were working to rebuild it. Newer houses were made of stone carved so the pieces fit together, a traditional Hopi construction technique. Solar panels located on the roofs of the houses provided their power. Solar power allowed the people to have modernized homes, but it did not disrupt the villagers' traditional way of life.

RESOURCES

Your Turn 2
Practice
- *Communications,* WS. p. 7
Reinforcement
- *Communications,* TP. 11, WS. p. 8

THINKING IT THROUGH

Identifying the Implied Main Idea

Follow these steps to find a paragraph's implied main idea:

▶ **STEP 1** Read the paragraph. Ask yourself, "What is the general topic?"

The paragraph tells me about a Hopi village.

▶ **STEP 2** Look at the details and descriptions to decide what points the writer is making about the general topic.

The village is old. There are celebrations and ceremonies in the village. The houses have solar panels.

▶ **STEP 3** Sum up the details in a statement that tells what the paragraph is about. This is the **implied main idea.**

The Hopi villagers live in traditional homes with modern conveniences.

▶ **STEP 4** Confirm the implied main idea with details from the paragraph.

I know tradition is important because the Hopi have ceremonies in the village and use old ways to build new homes. They use solar panels for electricity, which is a modern convenience.

TIP Not every paragraph that you read will have a main idea, but you can still figure out the point an author is making by looking at several paragraphs instead of one. These same steps can help.

Mapping It Out   The steps for figuring out the implied main idea of a paragraph can also help you find the implied main idea of a longer reading selection. Follow these steps.

1. Divide the reading selection into multi-paragraph sections.

2. Look at the details in each section and ask yourself, "What is the general idea of this section?"

3. Use the ideas from each section to figure out the implied main idea of the whole reading selection.

4. Compare your main idea with the details to confirm your answer.

When you are hunting for the implied main idea of a passage, you need a place to keep track of information. A graphic organizer can help you keep the information in order and see how it all fits together. Suppose the paragraph about the Hopi village on page 22 were part of a longer selection. The following graphic organizer

Reading Workshop   **23**

Wrap It Up

Metacognition. Encourage students to reflect on what they have read by asking them the following question:

1. While reading **"Hopi Snake Ceremonies,"** which type of descriptive language did you find most difficult to pick out? Why?

Then, ask students this question:

2. How do writers help readers feel, see, hear, taste, smell, and understand what is described? [with sensory language, figures of speech, and precise words]

YOUR TURN 3

A main idea for each section of the selection is suggested below, followed by a main idea statement for the whole reading.

1st Section: While watching the snake dance ceremony, the author learned from her father that the Hopi believe snakes will bring rain.

2nd Section: The male dancers chanted, wore rattles, and danced with snakes carried in their mouths.

3rd Section: A rattlesnake bit one of the dancers, who paid no attention and continued dancing.

4th Section: One of the Hopi secrets is how they persuade snakes to withhold their venom.

Whole Reading: The Hopi have a mysterious, special relationship with snakes that non-Hopi can appreciate but never fully understand.

---

shows how ideas throughout the longer selection would add up to the implied main idea.

Implied Main Idea for a Multi-paragraph Selection

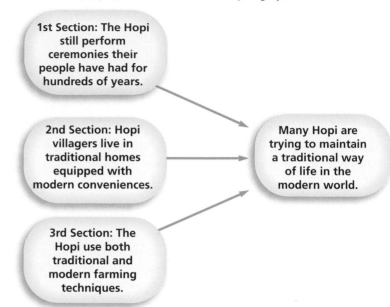

YOUR TURN 3 Mapping the Implied Main Idea

With three other students, find the implied main idea of "Hopi Snake Ceremonies" by completing the following steps. It may help to create a map like the one above.

- Assign each group member one of the following parts of the selection: Paragraphs 1–4, 5–9, 10–14, 15–19. Some of the paragraphs in the reading have main ideas, and some do not. Each group member should use the steps in Mapping It Out on page 23 to come up with a main idea statement for his or her section.

- As a group, look at all of your main idea statements. What do they say about the Hopi snake ceremony? Sum up these main ideas into one overall statement that tells the main idea of the whole reading. This is the reading's implied main idea.

- Confirm the overall main idea your group has identified by checking it against details from the reading.

MINI-LESSON VOCABULARY

Parts of Speech and Context Clues

As you read eyewitness accounts, you may find words you do not know. To figure out a word's meaning, you can think about what is happening in the story and look at other words around it—its **context**. Context clues can come from all the sentences around a word, not just the sentence in which the word appears.

You can also use a word's **part of speech** to understand the word's meaning. The part of speech tells you the word's job in a sentence.

If the word . . .	you know it is . . .
names a person, place, thing, or idea	a noun
shows an action or state of being	a verb
describes something	an adjective

The steps below can help you figure out a word's meaning.

THINKING IT THROUGH — Using Parts of Speech and Context Clues

The following example uses the word *plea* from "Hopi Snake Ceremonies."

Context: "For the Hopi, the snake ceremony is a time to make a *plea* to the spirits for the water the Indians badly need to survive."

▶ **STEP 1** Identify the word's part of speech.

The sentence says, "to make a plea." You make things, so a plea is probably a noun.

▶ **STEP 2** Get clues about the word's meaning from its context.

The plea is made "to the spirits." The Hopi are making a plea because they need rain.

▶ **STEP 3** Use what you may already know to figure out the word's meaning. Check your definition by plugging it into the original sentence.

The Hopi are having a ceremony to ask the spirits for rain. A plea must be a very serious request.

PRACTICE

Use the parts of speech and context clues to find the meanings of these words. They are underlined in "Hopi Snake Ceremonies."

1. rituals (page 19)   2. coachwhips (page 20)   3. stocky (page 20)   4. obscured (page 20)   5. cajole (page 20)

MINI-LESSON VOCABULARY

Parts of Speech and Context Clues

ANSWERS

Possible answers are given below.

1. The sentence says they "held secret rituals." You hold things, so rituals are things, which means *rituals* is a noun. The rituals are secret and one of them is the ceremony called the snake dance. Rituals must also be spiritual or religious ceremonies.

2. The sentence says "many of the snakes were coachwhips." Whips are things people used to drive coaches pulled by horses, so *coachwhips* must be a noun. *Coachwhips* might be snakes that look like those whips.

3. The sentence says "short, stocky man." *Stocky* is an adjective that describes the short man. One of the meanings the word *stock* has is a trunk of a plant. *Stocky* must mean thick and strong just as a trunk is.

4. The sentence says "the desert obscured by sheets of rain." *Obscured* must be an adjective because it modifies the noun *desert*. It tells something about the desert. I know sheets of rain make it dark and hard to see outside. Maybe the word *obscured* means "to hide something or make it hard to see."

5. The sentence says "knowledge of how to cajole a rattlesnake." *Cajole* is a verb because it is what you do, an action. To get a rattlesnake to withhold its venom, you would have to do something to it. The Hopis are gentle with snakes. Maybe they talk to them or persuade them with their secret rituals. *Cajole* could mean "persuade."

RESOURCES

Your Turn 3
Practice
■ *Communications,* WS. p. 9
Reinforcement
■ *Communications,* TP. 12, WS. p. 10

Vocabulary
Practice
■ *Communications,* WS. p. 11

Looking Ahead to Writing

In the Writing Workshop for this chapter (pp. 27–43), students will be asked to narrate an experience using details and descriptive language. As they work to show, rather than tell, events in their narrative, students can refer to the definitions of sensory language, figures of speech, and precise words included in the chart on p. 21 of the Reading Workshop.

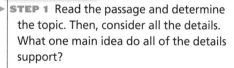

MINI-LESSON TEST TAKING

Identifying an Implied Main Idea

When taking a reading test, you will often be asked to identify a reading selection's main idea. Read the following passage and the test item after it. How would you respond to this item on a reading test?

I have had close encounters with snakes. Most snakes are shy and do not want to be around people; however, sometimes they come around houses looking for water. Snakes hide in rock piles, broken logs, or areas with tall grass. When I am walking in an area I think may have snakes, I take a long stick with me. I go slowly and hit the ground with the stick to make noise, so the snakes know I am coming. Then the snakes can get out of the way or warn me that they are there. I have seen many snakes. Many of them are poisonous, but I've never been bitten.

The main idea of this paragraph is that

A. snakes come to houses to find food and water

B. if you shake a stick at a snake, it will not bite you

C. if you take precautions, you do not need to fear snakes

D. people should be terrified of snakes

THINKING IT THROUGH — Identifying an Implied Main Idea

▶ **STEP 1** Read the passage and determine the topic. Then, consider all the details. What one main idea do all of the details support?

The topic is snakes. I think the writer is saying that snakes are not always dangerous.

▶ **STEP 2** Find the answer choice that best matches the main idea you have decided on. Confirm your answer choice by checking to see whether details in the passage support it. Remember that details will help you confirm the main idea, but the answer itself should not be a specific detail.

A. This answer is mentioned in the passage, but it is only a detail.

B. The passage doesn't say this, so it can't be the answer.

C. I think this is the best answer. The writer talked about precautions to take when you think snakes may be around.

D. The writer did not seem to be afraid of snakes at all. This is not the answer.

RESOURCES

Test Taking
Practice
■ *Communications,* WS. pp. 12–14

Writing an Eyewitness Account

An account of the *Titanic* disaster in the words of a survivor…The story of a calf being born, told by the 4-H member who witnessed it…These firsthand observations are called *eyewitness accounts.* Through an **eyewitness account,** a writer can share an experience with someone who has never seen the event. A writer's vivid retelling of an experience can create something like a movie in the reader's mind, allowing him or her to imagine every detail and action.

It is your turn to create a mental movie for your reader. In this workshop you will write a **letter** giving an eyewitness account of a memorable event. You will use detail and sensory language to show your reader an event.

WHAT'S AHEAD?

In this workshop you will write an eyewitness account. You will also learn how to

- narrate an experience by using details and chronological order
- describe by showing rather than telling
- choose exact nouns and adjectives
- punctuate dialogue

Prewriting

Choose an Experience

Seeing the World   Have you ever had an experience like this? You are walking through the park when you come across a dog show. You are thrilled to be seeing dogs of every breed. Mainly though, you wish someone were there to witness the event with you. If you have ever witnessed something that you wanted to share with a friend or family member, write about that experience now. Choose an event that you think is interesting. Your goal will be to communicate your interest and enthusiasm to your reader.

OBJECTIVES

- To use the writing process to write an eyewitness account
- To narrate an experience by using details and chronological order
- To describe events by showing them rather than telling about them
- To choose exact nouns and adjectives
- To punctuate dialogue

Quotation for the Day

"If every time you sat down, you expected something great, writing would always be a great disappointment."

(Natalie Goldberg, American writer, poet, and teacher)

Ask students to discuss their reactions to this quotation. Remind students that even prewriting efforts they discard can give them valuable practice in writing.

TEACHING TIP

Choose an Experience
Make sure students understand that they do not have to limit their choices to spectacular events. Let them know that accounts of more ordinary experiences, such as their baby sister feeding herself for the first time, can be just as interesting and entertaining to the reader if told with detail, originality, and enthusiasm.

An eyewitness account takes the form of a **narrative,** or story. Therefore, **choose an event you saw from beginning to end and can recall clearly.** Your reader should be able to see the account as you did, so be sure you can remember plenty of details.

| KEY CONCEPT

TIP When choosing experiences, focus on events that you observed rather than participated in. For example, you would write about the soccer game you saw instead of the basketball game you played in.

THINKING IT THROUGH — Choosing an Experience

Use these steps to choose an event for your eyewitness account.

▶ **STEP 1** Brainstorm a list of events you have witnessed. You might consider
- sports events such as a soccer game or track meet
- school events such as a science fair or art exhibit opening
- natural events such as a flood or sunset
- neighborhood events such as a parade or street festival

▶ **STEP 2** Decide which events
- you find most interesting
- you remember most clearly
- you saw from beginning to end
- you observed without participating in

▶ **STEP 3** Choose the event you most want to write about.

The writer whose example appears below chose the snowboarding exhibition because she had the most fun watching it and remembered the most details from that event.

state championship track meet	Cinco de Mayo parade
my brother's soap-box car race	snowboarding exhibition ✓

YOUR TURN 4 — Choosing an Experience

Use the Thinking It Through steps above to brainstorm and evaluate events you have seen and to choose an experience for your eyewitness account.

YOUR TURN 4

Have students state their topics and tell you their reasons for choosing them. If students have chosen events they did not actually witness or that may be difficult to describe, assist them in making better choices.

RESOURCES

Your Turn 4 and 5
Practice
- *Communications,* WS. pp. 15, 16

Think About Purpose and Audience

Share Your Vision   Your **purpose,** or reason for writing, is to share a memorable experience. You would not need to write a letter describing a snowboarding exhibition to a friend who saw it with you. Instead, you would want to tell a friend who was not there about the thrill of watching people glide on the snow and flip through the air.

YOUR TURN 5 Identifying Your Audience

To identify the audience for your eyewitness-account letter, think about a person who would be interested in the event but who did not get to see it.

Gather Events and Details

What Happened?   You are thinking about the snowboarding exhibition and all you can remember is the woman who amazed you by flipping through the air. Your mind may jump to the most exciting moments or to your favorite part of the experience. However, there is more to an eyewitness account than the big moments. You are telling a story, so **think about and list the small events that made up the experience from beginning to end.**

Who, What, Where, How   A good eyewitness account will give plenty of specific information to create a complete picture of the event for the reader. You can flesh out details from the events by asking yourself these four questions.

Who?	questions about **people,** such as *Who took part in this event? Who caught my attention?*
What?	questions that get at **sensory details,** such as *What did I hear* (including **dialogue**), *see, smell, feel, or taste?*
Where?	questions about **places,** such as *Where did this event take place?*
How?	questions about **feelings,** such as *How did I feel watching this event?*

KEY CONCEPT

TIP Check your list for unnecessary events— those that don't really add to the narrative. Think about these questions: *Does each event add something to my story? Can I make each event vivid for my audience?*

Writing Workshop   **29**

As you list details, you may include terms or information that your reader may not know. Support your descriptions and details with definitions or background information.

Order Up Once you list the events and details involved in your experience, you'll need to put them in order. **The best order for an eyewitness account is chronological** (or time) **order.** Tell the events in the order they happened—first, second, third, and so on. Chronological order helps the reader follow the story.

To make the chart below, the writer first listed the events that made up the experience. Then, for each event, she listed details that answered the Who, What, Where, and How questions.

| KEY CONCEPT →

Snowboarding Exhibition

Events	Details: Who, What, Where, How?
1. arrived and waited for the competition to begin	who: crowd of people what: cold; people stamping feet to keep warm; crunchy snow where: around the exhibition area; overlooking the half-pipe how: surprised at how many people were there definition: a half-pipe is a U-shaped snow structure, about 10 feet high and 360 feet long; it is like a pipe cut in half
2. half-pipe jam session	what: cheers of the crowd and crunch of the snow how: amazed by the skill of the athletes
3. big air session	what: a woman doing an inverted 720; riders framed by the sky when they were in the air how: impressed by the tricks; want to take more lessons background info: riders fly off a jump and do tricks in the air
4. drove home	how: asked Dad to let me take more snowboarding lessons

YOUR TURN 6 — Gathering and Organizing Ideas

- Create a chart like the one above for your event. In the first column, write the events of your experience in chronological order.
- In the second column, include details for each event. Use the questions on page 29 to find details.

Showing Instead of Telling

The stomach flu keeps you away from the state championship basketball game. Later, when you ask a friend about the game, he says, "It was fun. We won." "That's it?" you think. "I want to hear more!"

What you want is a dazzling **description.** You want to hear the stomping of the crowd's feet, smell the sweat of the packed gym, and sense the thrill of cheering your team on to victory. You want your friend to *show* you the victory, not tell you, "We won."

Showing rather than telling allows your **style,** the way *you* express ideas, to come through. Showing lets the reader see through your eyes and hear your **voice,** which indicates your attitude toward the event.

There are several ways to show an event rather than tell it. Show by adding

- **dialogue**—actual words of the people involved in the events
- **precise words**—strong verbs, vivid adjectives, precise nouns

You can also show details through **figures of speech,** expressions that describe one thing in terms of another. Two figures of speech you can use are *similes* and *metaphors.*

A **simile** uses *like* or *as* to compare two unlike things.

The runner looked as graceful as a cheetah.

A **metaphor** says directly that one thing *is* another thing.

Her eyes were a well of disappointment.

Here is an example of the difference showing can make.

Telling: Betsy is a clumsy girl.

Showing: Betsy usually trips through a doorway, her arms flailing toward any object that might keep her from falling. "My mom keeps telling me to wear more sensible shoes," she says to cover up the near fall. She then teeters along, looking like a flamingo with a twisted ankle.

This example *shows* by using strong verbs (*trips, flailing, teeter*), a simile (*looking like a flamingo*), and dialogue.

PRACTICE

Turn the following *telling* statements into descriptive *showing* passages.

1. I look forward to lunch every day.
2. Anna-Marie was fascinated as she watched the play.
3. Jordan was angry that his parents had taken him to the symphony.
4. My dog misses me when I am at school all day.
5. Paco looks happy today.

Rather than reviewing all the "showing" passages students have written, ask students to put a check mark (√) next to their favorite "showing" passage and an (X) next to the one they found most difficult to do. Discuss these two passages with them individually or as a class.

MINI-LESSON .... **WRITING**

Showing Instead of Telling

ANSWERS

Sample answers appear below.

1. About 11:40 A.M. every day, pictures of food begin dancing around my brain. I shift restlessly in my seat. Time slows to a crawl. Then—oh, joy!—the bell rings. I whip by my locker, throw my books inside, and race to the cafeteria.

2. For two hours, Anna-Marie was a statue, hardly breathing as she stared with wide-open eyes at the figures on the stage.

3. "Why did *I* have to come? You know I can't stand this symphony stuff," Jordan grumbled to his parents as he kicked at the velvet padding on the seat in front of him.

4. I can hear her whining as I get off the school bus. The whines change to barks as I near the front door. When I finally step inside, two furry paws land with a "thud" on my chest, and a slobbery pink tongue laps at my face.

5. Paco's eyes twinkle like diamonds, and a wide grin splits his face.

Quotation for the Day

❝I even have loved spending an entire day seeking the buried treasure of one right word.❞

(Ralph Schoenstein, 1933– , American author)

Use the quotation to emphasize the importance of selecting precise words in writing an eyewitness account. Name various nouns and ask students to give a single word that best describes each noun.

Meeting
INDIVIDUAL NEEDS

MULTIPLE INTELLIGENCES
Interpersonal Intelligence. You might consider having students work in pairs to collaborate on a letter. Instruct them to work collaboratively to complete the following tasks.

1. Choose an event.
2. Agree on a purpose and choose the audience.
3. List events and gather details by answering the *who, what, where,* and *how* questions.
4. Compare events and details. Decide which ones are important.
5. Organize events in chronological, or time, order.
6. Write a collaborative draft of the letter. Partners should write alternating paragraphs.
7. Exchange drafts with another pair of students. Read the other pair's draft and collaboratively make suggestions for revision.

 YOUR TURN 7

If you want to assign a length to students' letters, 500 to 700 words is appropriate. Check that students are following the framework on this page.

Writing

Eyewitness Account

Framework	Directions and Explanations

Introduction
- Salutation
- Attention-grabbing opener
- Statement of the event

- Open with a greeting, or salutation. (For more on letter form, see page 798 of the Quick Reference Handbook.)
- Use a question, a story, or a personal note to get your reader's attention. Try two different attention grabbers. Then, ask a peer which is better.

Body
- First event and details
- Second event and details and so on

- Put each event of your experience in a paragraph. Combine two or more short events into one paragraph.
- **Elaborate** on each detail from your prewriting chart by using descriptive language that **shows, rather than tells,** what the experience was like. Provide additional **background information,** including definitions, for anything that might be unfamiliar to your audience.

Conclusion
- Your feelings or questions about what you observed
- Importance of the event
- Closing for the letter

- Leave your reader with an understanding of the importance of the event. You might summarize why you liked the event and wanted to share it. Remember the reason you decided to write this letter. Then, close with a **personal note** to your reader.

YOUR TURN 7 Writing Your Eyewitness Account

Now it is your turn to write a letter about an eyewitness account. As you write, refer to the framework above and the Writer's Model on the next page.

RESOURCES

Writing
Writing Prompts
- *Communications,* TP. p. 13, WS. p. 19

Your Turn 7
Practice
- *Communications,* TP. 14, WS. p. 20

A Writer's Model

The final draft below follows the framework for a letter relating an eyewitness account.

1825 E. Avenue B
Salt Lake City, UT 84103
January 21, 2000

Dear Jake,

    Have you ever seen a snowboarding exhibition? I have been wanting to see one ever since I took a lesson a month ago. This past Saturday, my dad and I went to see a competition. I had a great time, and I got to see some of my favorite professional riders.

    When we arrived, we were surprised by how many people were there. We worked our way through a crowd around the exhibition area and waited for the first session to begin. People were stamping their feet to keep warm in the twenty-degree weather. The gray snow crunching under our feet sounded like pieces of plastic foam rubbing together. My skin felt tight and prickly, and I could see my breath in puffs of fog on the chilly air. As we waited, we talked about how good the half-pipe looked. A half-pipe is snow packed into a U-shape, about 10 feet high and 360 feet long. It is like a big pipe that has been cut in half. Riders drop in from the top at one side and glide down and then up the other side and perform tricks in the air above the pipe. The tricks involve twisting and flipping in the air, usually while grabbing the board with at least one hand.

    As the half-pipe jam session began, I could sense a rush of excitement from the crowd. The whooshing and crunching sounds of the boards in the snow were soon muted by the whooping cheers of the crowd. We were all amazed by how graceful the athletes looked. Once in a while, a rider would fall. One rider missed the edge of

(continued)

Salutation
Attention-grabbing beginning

First and second events

Descriptive language
Details (sensory)

Definition

Precise words

Third event
Details (sensory)

Detail (feelings)

Connecting Reading and Writing

Have students refer again to the information on implied main idea on pp. 22–24 in the Reading Workshop. Then, ask them to identify the implied main idea of **A Writer's Model** on this page. [A snowboarding exhibition is an exciting event.] Remind students that when they write their own letters, they should make sure that all the sentences and paragraphs support one main idea.

(continued)

Detail (dialogue)
Fourth event

Detail (sensory)
Descriptive language

Last event

Importance of
experience

Closing

the pipe and fell to the other side of the wall. "Ouch!" Dad said, "Did you see that fall? You know that hurt."

The second part of the competition was a "big air" session. In this event, riders go off a jump to perform tricks in the air. Sometimes the riders would hang in the air with one arm extended. It looked like they were holding on to a handle in the sky. The last woman in the exhibition performed an inverted 720, which means she rotated twice in the air while flipping!

I was so excited that I talked the whole ride home, trying to convince my dad to let me take more snowboarding lessons. He must have been impressed, too, because he is going to let me. Next winter when you visit, I will show you what I have learned.

All my best,

Samantha

PEANUTS reprinted by permission of United Feature Syndicate, Inc.

A Student's Model

When you write an eyewitness account you want to *show* the event to your reader. Matthew Hutter, a student from Lansing, Illinois, uses vivid descriptions and dialogue to pull readers into a snowy morning event. The following excerpts are from a letter he wrote.

It was 6:30 in the morning, and I was in dreamland. Suddenly, my dad threw open my bedroom door with a loud bang and started tickling me until I got all tangled up in my covers and fell out of bed.

First event

"Gosh Dad, how can you be so energetic at 6:30 on a Monday morning?" I asked with a bit of an attitude.

Detail (dialogue)

"Look outside and that will answer your question," he said. It was amazing! There were snowflakes of every imaginable size. Some were as big as two inches, and some were as small as an eraser on a pencil. I could hear the wind howling past my window, as the snowflakes flew in every direction. . . .

Second event

Descriptive language

Dad drove slowly to the school because he couldn't see. On the way we saw fallen trees and damaged houses. About a block away from school we saw a tree that had fallen on a car. The whole back of the car was smashed. As we turned the corner to school, I noticed that the whole east side of the school was covered with snow and ice. . . .

Third event

Descriptive language

I put my book on my desk and sat down. I kept the lights off because I liked to listen to the silence of an empty school.

Fourth event

For some odd reason, I was counting the lines on the chalkboard when all of a sudden I heard a buzzing sound and a green glowing light filled the room. I whirled around and to my astonishment, I saw a power box outside, exploding. After about four seconds, the explosion stopped as abruptly as it had started. I walked to Mrs. Hall's room where it was also dark. She was sitting at her desk.

Fifth event

Details (sensory)

"Pretty cool huh," I said. . . .

"Very cool," she said. . . .

Connecting Reading and Writing

Consider providing each student with a copy of **A Student's Model** without the marginal labels. Tell students that it will help them in their own writing if they pay attention to descriptive language as they read. Divide the chalkboard into three columns. Label the first column *Sensory Details,* the second *Precise Words,* and the third *Figures of Speech.* Then, read the model to the class and ask volunteers to write examples from the narrative of each element of description in the appropriate column. Direct students to the chart on p. 21 of the Reading Workshop if they need help identifying descriptive elements. [Possible examples follow. Sensory Details: "loud bang," "wind howling," "buzzing sound," "green glowing light"; Precise Words: "threw open," "tangled up," "energetic," "damaged houses," "whirled around"; Figure of Speech: "small as an eraser on a pencil"]

Quotation for the Day

❝I don't write easily or rapidly. My first draft usually has only a few elements worth keeping. I have to find what those are and build from them and throw out what doesn't work, or what simply is not alive.❞

(Susan Sontag, 1933–   , American writer)

Ask volunteers to explain how Sontag's quotation relates to their own methods of evaluating and revising. [Some writers draft in pencil so they can erase. Others prefer to write on the computer so they can delete and insert easily. Many writers like to wait a while before evaluating so that they can approach the material with fresh eyes.]

TEACHING TIP

Checking It Twice

Remind students that they should use standard usage in their letters, even though they might be tempted to use nonstandard usage if the addressee is a close acquaintance. Review the **Glossary of Usage** on pages 552–571 with students and provide examples of nonstandard usage to help learners distinguish between the two types of writing.

▶Elaboration

To help students elaborate with descriptive language, suggest that they select a sentence that could benefit from a comparison between two unlike things. For example, a sentence about trees with colorful autumn leaves could incorporate a figure of speech, such as a simile or metaphor comparing the trees to giant bouquets of flowers.

Revising

Evaluate and Revise Content, Organization, and Style

Checking It Twice When revising your first draft or evaluating a peer's, read through it at least twice. In the first reading, look at the content and organization of the letter, using the guidelines below. In the second reading, examine the letter at the sentence level, using the Focus on Word Choice on page 38. As part of each reading, try **collaborating** with a peer or having a **writing conference** in order to make your evaluation more effective.

▶ **First Reading: Content and Organization**   Use the chart below to evaluate and revise your eyewitness account so it is clear and interesting.

Guidelines for Self-Evaluation and Peer Evaluation		
Evaluation Questions	**Tips**	**Revision Techniques**
❶ Does the introduction include an attention-grabber?	**Underline** the personal note, question, or story that grabs the reader's attention.	**Add** an interesting question or brief story, if necessary.
❷ Does the account provide background information to help the reader understand unfamiliar terms and ideas?	**Put stars** next to terms that might be unfamiliar to readers. **Circle** information that helps the reader understand the terms.	**Add** information or **replace** unclear information with more helpful details.
❸ Are the events retold in chronological order?	**Number** each event in the letter. Check that the numbers match the order in which the events happened.	**Rearrange** events in the order they happened, if necessary.
❹ Are there enough details to make the experience real for the reader?	With a colored marker, **highlight** details and vivid descriptions.	**Elaborate** on the experience by adding descriptive language to help the reader "see" it.
❺ Does the letter's conclusion show why the experience was important?	**Put a check mark** next to statements that explain why the event was important.	**Add** thoughts or feelings that will show the importance of the event.

RESOURCES

Revising
Practice
■ *Communications,* TPs. 15, 16, WS. pp. 21, 22, 23

ONE WRITER'S REVISIONS This revision is an early draft of the letter on page 33.

> People were stamping their feet to keep warm in the
> *gray*
> twenty-degree weather. The ~~snow was~~ crunching under
> *sounded like pieces of plastic foam rubbing together.*
> our feet. My skin felt tight and prickly, and I could see my
> *in puffs of fog*
> breath on the chilly air. As we waited, we talked about how
>
> good the half-pipe looked. A half-pipe is snow packed into
> *It is like a big*
> a U-shape, about 10 feet high and 360 feet long.
> *pipe that has been cut in half.*

add

add

add

add

Responding to the Revision Process

1. Why do you think the writer added a sentence to the end of this passage?
2. What is the effect of the other additions the writer made to the passage?

▷ **Second Reading: Style** You have already evaluated and revised *what* you say in your letter. Now look at *how* you say it. Look closely at each of your sentences to polish your writing. For this assignment, focus on using precise nouns and adjectives to create clear and descriptive writing.

When you evaluate your letter for style, ask yourself whether your writing includes precise nouns or adjectives that clearly describe the event. As you re-read your letter, draw a wavy line under precise nouns and adjectives. Then, if you see only a few wavy lines, look through your letter for dull nouns or adjectives and replace them with descriptive ones. The Focus on Word Choice on the next page can help you learn to use precise nouns and adjectives.

PEER REVIEW

If you are evaluating a peer's eyewitness account, ask yourself:
- Can I picture the events the writer is describing?
- Does the order of the account make sense?

Reference Note

For more on **precise words,** see page 31.

TEACHING (TIP)

One Writer's Revisions
Students may not be familiar with standard editing and proofreading marks. You may want to refer them to the **Symbols for Revising and Proofreading** chart on page 809 of the **Quick Reference Handbook**.

Cooperative Learning

Group Revision. Divide the class into groups of five for peer revision. Tell students to attach a blank piece of paper to each letter to be used for evaluation. Have students pass their letters to the person on the left. Evaluators should read the paper in front of them for the first question in the content and organization guidelines on p. 36. They should write an answer to the question and suggest a revision technique. Then, students should pass the letters to the left again, and evaluators should repeat the process for the second question. Have students continue reading and evaluating until they have addressed all five questions. This exercise will allow each student to receive feedback from several other students.

Responding to the Revision Process
ANSWERS

1. The writer added a simile to the end of the passage to compare the halfpipe to a big pipe cut in half. This comparison helps the reader envision a halfpipe.

2. By adding sensory details and precise words, the writer helps the reader see and feel the scene.

Evaluating Student Writing

The ancillary *Assessment Alternatives* contains a variety of assessment forms, including Inventories and Evaluation Forms and rubrics: Six-Point Scales, Four-Point Scales, and Six Trait Scales.

Focus on

Word Choice

TIP If you cannot think of the precise noun or adjective for what you are describing, use a **thesaurus.** Look up the word you want to change and you will find many *synonyms*— different ways of expressing a similar idea.

Precise Nouns and Adjectives

"How was that thing you went to?"

"It was nice."

That brief dialogue did not tell you much, did it? Nouns like "thing" and adjectives like "nice" are *vague*. **Vague words**—words that are not clear or precise—cannot give the reader of an eyewitness account enough information to understand what happened. Precise words quickly tell a reader exactly what a writer means.

■ **Precise nouns** illustrate *particular* persons, places, or things. A *noise* can become a *clank, squeak, clatter, shriek,* or *rattle.*

■ **Precise adjectives** describe nouns specifically. A *fun* amusement-park ride can be transformed into a *thrilling, exhilarating, pulse-pounding* ride.

Do not settle for vague, dull words in your eyewitness accounts. Make an impression with precise words.

ONE WRITER'S REVISIONS

whooshing and crunching
The ~~loud~~ sounds of the boards in the snow were soon
whooping cheers   crowd.
muted by the ~~loud sounds~~ of the ~~people.~~

Responding to the Revision Process

How did adding precise words improve the sentence above?

YOUR TURN 8 — Evaluating and Revising Your Eyewitness Account

■ First, evaluate and revise the content and organization of your letter following the guidelines on page 36.

■ Next, use the Focus on Word Choice above to help you use more precise nouns and adjectives.

■ Finally, have a peer evaluate your paper. Think carefully about your peer's comments as you revise.

Proofread Your Eyewitness Account

Second Opinions Errors in your final letter will distract your reader. If you ask another person to proofread the letter after you have gone through it, you will be more likely to find all the mistakes.

Grammar Link

Punctuating Dialogue

You may include **dialogue,** exact words spoken by people, in your account. Punctuate dialogue correctly so your reader can tell the dialogue from the rest of the text.

Use quotation marks to enclose a person's exact words.

Incorrect	Ouch Dad said did you see that fall?
Correct	"Ouch!" Dad said. "Did you see that fall?"

- A direct quotation begins with a capital letter. Commas, a question mark, or an exclamation point can separate the dialogue from the rest of the sentence.

  Examples:
  The weather person said**,** "There is a seventy-percent chance of snow today."

  "Should I wear boots**?**" Grace asked.

- When the expression identifying the speaker interrupts a quotation, commas set off the expression. The second part of the quotation then begins with a small letter.

  Example:
  "I like to ski**,**" Ian said**,** "but I don't like to wait in the lines."

- A period or comma always goes inside the closing quotation marks.

  Examples:
  "The snowboarding exhibition begins at 9:00 A.M.**,**" said the ticket taker.

  Dad remarked, "We have time to get some hot apple cider**.**"

PRACTICE

Punctuate the dialogue in each of the following sentences.

1. It's too bad that snowboarding can be expensive said Henry.

2. When you think about it Isabel sighed everything can be expensive.

3. Do you think individual lessons are less expensive Naomi wondered.

4. Let's take lessons during the winter break Roshanda suggested.

5. I really like the clothes snowboarders wear Cesar added especially the hats.

For more information and practice on **punctuating dialogue,** see pages 630–635.

Quotation for the Day

"If you do not write for publication there is little point in writing at all."

(Bernard Shaw, 1856–1950, playwright, critic, and social reformer)

Discuss whether students agree or disagree with Shaw's statement. Those who disagree may feel that the act of writing itself is enjoyable and therapeutic.

Grammar Link

Punctuating Dialogue

ANSWERS

1. "It's too bad that snowboarding can be expensive," said Henry.

2. "When you think about it," Isabel sighed, "everything can be expensive."

3. "Do you think individual lessons are less expensive?" Naomi wondered.

4. "Let's take lessons during the winter break," Roshanda suggested.

5. "I really like the clothes snowboarders wear," Cesar added, "especially the hats."

RESOURCES

Grammar Link
Practice
- *Communications,* WS. p. 25

Wrap It Up

Metacognition. Ask students to reflect on their writing processes by answering the following question:

1. What part of the writing process was most difficult? Why?

Then, ask students this question:

2. Why is it important to use descriptive language when writing an eyewitness account? [so that the reader can visualize the event]

PORTFOLIO

Publish Your Eyewitness Account

Show the World   It is finally time to send your letter. You can now put it in an envelope and mail it, or you can e-mail it in a flash. However, with a few changes you can also use your letter in other ways. Take off the salutation and cut out any direct references to your audience, and you simply have an eyewitness account. What are some things you can do with an eyewitness account?

- Submit your eyewitness account to your local or school newspaper as an article describing the event.

- Submit it to your school's yearbook as a historical record of events in your area, or include it in a class chronicle of the year's events.

- Narrative and descriptive writing are often read aloud. You might read your eyewitness account to classmates.

Reflect on Your Eyewitness Account

Building Your Portfolio   Take time to reflect on your finished letter. Reflecting will help you strengthen your narrative and descriptive writing skills. Think about how you can use this kind of writing for other projects.

- What was the best description in your paper? Why do you think it was effective?

- How did you use sensory language, precise words, dialogue, and figures of speech in your writing? How could you use these types of descriptive language in other forms of writing?

- In what other forms of writing could you use narration? In what kinds of writing assignments would chronological organization be helpful?

YOUR TURN 9

Proofreading, Publishing, and Reflecting on Your Eyewitness Account

- Correct any grammar, usage, and mechanics errors. Be especially careful to punctuate dialogue correctly.

- Publish your eyewitness account.

- Answer the Reflect on Your Eyewitness Account questions above. Write your responses in a learning log, or include them in your portfolio.

Connections to Literature

Writing a Descriptive Essay

Eyewitness accounts and descriptive essays are both based on observation. A descriptive essay focuses on an object, such as a statue or car; on a place, such as a room or park; or on a person.

Two important skills to master in preparing to write a descriptive essay are making **observations** and using **spatial organization.**

What You See Is What They'll Get

Close, accurate observation is essential to writing a descriptive essay. After all, how can you describe something unless you know exactly what it looks like? Once you choose the subject of your essay, you should spend at least twenty minutes observing it.

When you write the essay, you'll want to use **descriptive language:** sensory details, figures of speech, and exact words. You will *show* your object rather than tell about it. Asking questions about your subject can help you **develop** and **record** specific details for your essay.

- What colors do you see?
- What size is the object, person, or place in relation to the surroundings?
- What shape or shapes do you see?
- What specific adjectives describe the object, person, or place?
- Can you create a simile or metaphor by comparing the object, person, or place to something else?

As you observe, focus on the special characteristics that draw your attention to the object, person, or place.

Filling Up Space An effective way to organize a descriptive essay is by describing items according to their location. Using this **spatial organization** technique, you will start your description at a certain point and then move in a logical way around your subject. For example, if you were describing a dog, you might start with the dog's face and then move along his body to his tail. Organize the description in your essay so that it moves

- from top to bottom or bottom to top
- from near to far or far to near
- from left to right or right to left
- from inside to out or outside to in

Words Showing Spatial Organization		
next to	across from	between
down	up	around
close	far	near

Picture This As you read the description on the next page, notice how author Jamaica Kincaid uses specific details and spatial organization when describing a child's bedroom.

ENGLISH-LANGUAGE LEARNERS
General Strategies. Because students will be using adjectives and adverbs in their descriptive writing, you may want to review comparative forms. Draw a grid with three columns, labeling them with √, √+, √++. Start by writing *good* in the first column, and have students fill in *better* and *best*. Have students continue with other words, either from Kincaid's description (*old, beautiful, happy*) or from their own writing. Ask students to explain comparative forms. You could also point out that one- and two-syllable words use *–er* or *–est* and words with three or more syllables use *more* or *most*.

YOUR TURN 10

To help students observe their subjects, have them answer each of the following questions and then include the responses in their drafts.

Object
What does the object's surface feel like?

Does the object have any special features, such as decorations?

Place
What do objects in the place look like?

What is the overall mood or atmosphere of the place?

Person
What do the person's clothes, accessories, hair, face, and body look like?

What mood or feeling do you associate with the person?

Description of important objects in room	Lying there in the half-dark of my room, I could see my shelf, with my books—some of them prizes I had won in school, some of them gifts from my mother—and with photographs of people I was supposed to love forever no matter what, and with my old thermos, which was given to me for my eighth birthday, and some shells I had gathered at different times I spent at the sea. In one corner stood my washstand and its beautiful basin of white enamel with blooming red hibiscus painted at the bottom and an urn that matched. In another corner were my old school shoes and my Sunday shoes. In still another corner, a bureau held my old clothes. I knew everything in the room, inside out and outside in. I had lived in this room for thirteen of my seventeen years. I could see in my mind's eye even the day my father was adding it onto the rest of the house. Everywhere I looked stood something that had meant a lot to me, that had given me pleasure at some point, or could remind me of a time that was a happy time. But as I was lying there my heart could have burst open with joy at the thought of never having to see any of it again.
Description moves from wall down to corner	
Description moves from corner to corner	
Explanation of the room's meaning to the writer	

Jamaica Kincaid, *Annie John*

Now You Try Think of the object, person, or place you want to describe. Choose a subject with plenty of details.

After you have written a first draft, revise your essay by following the suggestions in the next column.

- Add details about the subject's shape, size, or color.
- Include information about its overall appearance or atmosphere.
- Rearrange information to make the spatial organization clearer.

YOUR TURN 10 **Writing a Descriptive Essay**

Before you write your descriptive essay, observe your subject for at least twenty minutes and record details. Then, use spatial organization to organize your observations and write your essay. Finally, revise your essay to make it clearer and more descriptive.

Choices

Choose one of the following activities to complete.

▶ CROSSING THE CURRICULUM: ART

1. Create a World Closely observe an object, such as a machine, a leaf, or a coin, and make a **drawing** of it. You might draw the object you observed for your descriptive essay, an element from your haiku, or another object. Be sure to include as many of the details of your subject as you can.

▶ CONNECTING CULTURES

2. Once upon a Time Folk tales, fairy tales, and other narratives from the **oral tradition** show up in all cultures, often as different versions of the same story. The story "Cinderella," for example, is "Aschenputtel" in Germany and "Yeh-Shen" in China. Think of a folk tale or fairy tale that you enjoy, and research similar stories in other cultures. In a **presentation,** share the stories with your classmates and describe the differences.

▶ CAREER: JOURNALISM

3. On the Beat Think like a reporter for a week. Carry a notebook with you and go out looking for an interesting story that you could write for your school newspaper. Get together with a few other students, compare observations, and write a **collaborative news article.**

▶ WRITING

4. Do You See Eye to Eye? With a partner, choose an event or object to observe. Observe it at the same time, but do not talk to each other. Write separate **descriptions** of the event or object. Compare your two essays to see if your partner's observation is different from your own. Talk about your differences, and write a **summary** of your discussion.

▶ DRAMA

5. The Way I See It Communicate the events of your eyewitness account in a **dramatic interpretation** or short **play.** Assemble a cast to act out the events from the experience you wrote about in the Writing Workshop, or star in a monologue presenting your descriptive essay aloud.

PORTFOLIO

Choices **47**

▶ CONNECTING CULTURES

Tell students that an informative presentation, just like an informative essay, includes an introduction, a well-organized body, and a conclusion. Explain that in the introduction students should name the folk tales that they will be comparing and give some background about each story. In the body of their presentations, students should use comparison-and-contrast order to show the similarities and differences among the stories. You might suggest that students share a passage from each narrative to highlight similarities or differences. Finally, students should summarize the main points of comparison in the conclusion.

▶ CAREER: JOURNALISM

Have groups compare observations and choose a common topic. Then, to ensure that students work together collaboratively and that all students contribute to the writing process, have each group member choose one of the following roles: reader, compiler, scribe, or proofreader. Once students have chosen roles, the reader reads aloud students' observations on the topic, as the compiler organizes them in chronological order. The scribe writes the words and sentences the group composes. Then, the proofreader checks the draft for grammar, spelling, and punctuation errors. Finally, students should work together to revise their story.

CHAPTER 2

Explaining a Process

Use this guide to create an instructional plan that suits the individual needs of your students. Assignments marked by an asterisk (*) may be completed out of class. Times given for pacing lessons are estimated. See pp. 48–49 for chapter-wide resources. Resources listed in this guide are point-of-use resources only.

Curriculum Connections

Choices *p. 79*
- Crossing the Curriculum: Art
- Crossing the Curriculum: History
- Crossing the Curriculum: Science
- Creative Writing

GO TO: go.hrw.com
KEYWORD: EOLang 7-2

All resources for this chapter are available for preview on the *One-Stop Planner CD-ROM with Test Generator.* All worksheets and tests may be printed from the CD-ROM.

		Chapter Opener pp. 48–49	**Reading Workshop: Reading Instructions** pp. 50–58
DEVELOPMENTAL PROGRAM		🕐 **20 minutes** • Your Turn 1 *p. 49*	🕐 **90 minutes** • Preparing to Read *p. 50* • Reading Selection *pp. 51–52* • First Thoughts in groups *p. 53* • Identifying Author's Purpose *pp. 53–55* • Your Turn 2 *p. 55* • Order of a Process *pp. 55–56* • Your Turn 3 *p. 56* • Test Taking Mini-Lesson *p. 58*
CORE PROGRAM		🕐 **15 minutes** • Your Turn 1 *p. 49*	🕐 **75 minutes** • Preparing to Read *p. 50* • Reading Selection *pp. 51–52* • First Thoughts *p. 53* • Identifying Author's Purpose *pp. 53–55* • Your Turn 2 *p. 55* • Order of a Process *pp. 55–56* • Your Turn 3 *p. 56* • Vocabulary Mini-Lesson *p. 57* • Test Taking Mini-Lesson *p. 58*
ADVANCED PROGRAM		🕐 **10 minutes** • Your Turn 1 *p. 49*	🕐 **60 minutes** • Preparing to Read *p. 50* • Reading Selection *pp. 51–52* • First Thoughts *p. 53* • Identifying Author's Purpose *pp. 53–55* • Order of a Process *pp. 55–56* • Your Turn 3 *p. 56* • Vocabulary Mini-Lesson *p. 57*
RESOURCES	**PRINT**	• *Communications,* TP. 17, WS. p. 26	• *Alternative Readings,* Ch. 2 • *Communications,* TPs. 18, 19, WS. pp. 27–34
	MEDIA	• *One-Stop Planner CD-ROM*	• *One-Stop Planner CD-ROM*

TP.=Transparency   WS.=Worksheet

Writing Workshop: Writing Instructions *pp. 59–75*	Focus on Listening: Following Oral Instructions *pp. 76–78*
🕐 **240 minutes** • Choose and Evaluate a Topic; Your Turn 4 *pp. 59–60* • Reflect on Audience and Purpose; Your Turn 5 *p. 61* • Gather and Organize Information; Your Turn 6 *pp. 62–63* • Framework; Your Turn 7* *p. 64* • Writer's Model and Student's Model *pp. 65–67* • Evaluate and Revise *pp. 69–71* • Focus on Sentences in groups *p. 71* • Your Turn 8 *p. 71* • Proofread, Publish, and Reflect *pp. 72–73* • Grammar Link *p. 72* • Your Turn 9 *p. 73* • Test Taking Mini-Lesson *p. 74* • Connections to Life; Your Turn 10 *p. 75*	🕐 **60 minutes** • Learning to Listen *pp. 76–77* • Taking Notes *p. 77* • Asking Questions *pp. 77–78* • Your Turn 11 *p. 78*
🕐 **180 minutes** • Choose and Evaluate a Topic; Your Turn 4 *pp. 59–60* • Reflect on Audience and Purpose; Your Turn 5 *p. 61* • Gather and Organize Information; Your Turn 6 *pp. 62–63* • Framework; Your Turn 7* *p. 64* • Writer's Model and Student's Model *pp. 65–67* • Critical-Thinking Mini-Lesson in groups *p. 68* • Evaluate and Revise *pp. 69–71* • Focus on Sentences *p. 71* • Your Turn 8* *p. 71* • Proofread, Publish, and Reflect *pp. 72–73* • Grammar Link; Your Turn 9 *pp. 72–73* • Test Taking Mini-Lesson *p. 74* • Connections to Life; Your Turn 10* *p. 75*	🕐 **45 minutes** • Learning to Listen *pp. 76–77* • Taking Notes *p. 77* • Asking Questions *pp. 77–78* • Your Turn 11 *p. 78*
🕐 **100 minutes** • Choose and Evaluate a Topic; Your Turn 4 *pp. 59–60* • Reflect on Audience and Purpose; Your Turn 5 *p. 61* • Gather and Organize Information; Your Turn 6 *pp. 62–63* • Framework; Your Turn 7* *p. 64* • Writer's Model and Student's Model *pp. 65–67* • Critical-Thinking Mini-Lesson *p. 68* • Evaluate and Revise *pp. 69–71* • Focus on Sentences *p. 71* • Your Turn 8* *p. 71* • Proofread, Publish, and Reflect *pp. 72–73* • Grammar Link *p. 72* • Your Turn 9* *p. 73* • Connections to Life; Your Turn 10* *p. 75*	🕐 **40 minutes** • Learning to Listen *pp. 76–77* • Taking Notes *p. 77* • Asking Questions *pp. 77–78* • Your Turn 11 *p. 78*

• *Communications,*
  TPs. 20–23,
  WS. pp. 35–46
• *Designing Your Writing*
	• *Media Literacy and Communication Skills*
	  —*Support and Practice,* Ch. 2
	  —*A How-to Handbook*
	  —*A Teacher's Guide,* Ch. 2

• *One-Stop Planner CD-ROM* 💿	• *One-Stop Planner CD-ROM* 💿

Explaining a Process

CHAPTER OBJECTIVES

■ To read a chapter from a "how-to" book and analyze its organizational structure

■ To write instructions for a process

■ To listen actively and follow oral instructions

Chapter Overview

This chapter is designed to teach students to read, write, and listen to instructions effectively. In the Reading Workshop (pp. 50–58), students read a chapter from a "how-to" book and analyze the order of the steps in the process that is being explained. The Writing Workshop (pp. 59–75) allows them to write their own instructions.

Finally, Focus on Listening teaches students strategies for listening actively to oral directions. The three workshops can be taught as separate units, but taught together they complement one another and help give students a thorough understanding of process writing.

Why Study Instructions?

Understanding how to give and follow instructions will prepare students to meet challenges in the real world. Learning to recognize chronological patterns in instructions will help students make sense of written and oral directions. Students who can follow instructions will acquire new skills quickly, and those who can give clear instructions will be able to communicate what they know.

Teaching the Chapter

Option 1: Begin with Literature

If you use literature to introduce reading and writing concepts, nonfiction is often a good place to find examples of "how-to" writing. As you examine instructional passages, point out characteristics such as the use of technical terms, chronological order, and transition words like *first, next, then,* and *last.* Then, have students read the excerpt in this

chapter (pp. 51–52) and ask them to identify the characteristics of "how-to" writing. Once students have analyzed the techniques used to write instructions, they will be better prepared to write instructions of their own.

Option 2: Begin with Reading and Writing

To acquaint students with the techniques used in instructional writing, start by having them complete the Reading Workshop on pp. 50–58. Then, have them apply what they learned as they write their own instructions in the Writing Workshop (pp. 59–75). With this understanding of process writing, students will be better able to follow the order of a process in literary fiction and nonfiction.

Making Connections

■ To the Literature Curriculum

Instructions can be found woven into the narrative of fiction. For example, as the narrator in "Antaeus" describes the boys' efforts to build a rooftop garden, he provides readers with a set of instructions for creating their own gardens. Dougal Robertson's account from *Survive the Savage Sea* gives instructions on how to survive on the open seas.

Lesson Idea: "How-to" Writing in "Antaeus" by Borden Deal

1. Have students working in groups create flowcharts showing the steps for creating a rooftop garden. They should use the sample flowchart shown on p. 63 as a model.

2. Tell students to place steps in chronological, or time, order and use arrows and numbers to indicate the order. A sample flowchart appears below.

Topic: Building a rooftop garden

Materials: Potting soil, seeds

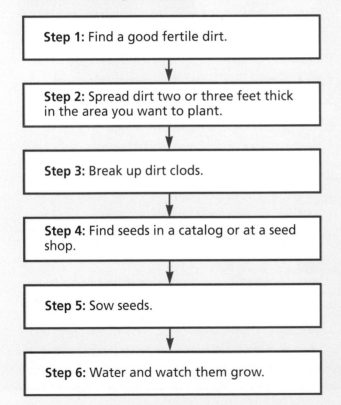

Step 1: Find a good fertile dirt.

Step 2: Spread dirt two or three feet thick in the area you want to plant.

Step 3: Break up dirt clods.

Step 4: Find seeds in a catalog or at a seed shop.

Step 5: Sow seeds.

Step 6: Water and watch them grow.

3. After students complete their flowcharts, have group members evaluate the instructions. Are any steps missing? Do any steps need more explanation? Could you create a garden by following these instructions?

4. Then, introduce students to the excerpt from the "how-to" book in this chapter (pp. 51–52). Have them compare the two sets of instructions. Which instructions are easier to follow? Why?

5. Finally, discuss with students why instructions in a "how-to" book might be more detailed than those in a short story. Lead students to understand that since the two authors have different purposes for writing (to inform and to entertain), the way in which they write is different.

■ **To Careers**

Relate what students are learning in the classroom to the world of work by talking to them about your job—teaching. Inform students that teachers impart knowledge by giving and writing instructions every day. Model for them the process of creating a lesson plan that teaches students how to do something, or give another teacher the background information in this chapter and have him or her speak to your class about creating a set of step-by-step instructions for students. You could even let students experience "a day on the job" by dividing them into groups and having them write a lesson plan for teaching the class a simple skill, such as how to find a book on a specific topic in the school library. See also **Connections to Life** on p. 75.

■ **To the Community**

Encourage students to contact their local fire department to learn the steps that people should follow in case a fire breaks out in their house or apartment building. Then, students should write the proper procedure in the form of instructions. These instructions could be shared with family members. You may want to obtain permission from parents or guardians and from parties students will contact before beginning work on this assignment.

■ **To the Music Curriculum**

Explain that instructions are not always spoken or written. Ask your students if they have ever seen a conductor of a band or an orchestra in action. A conductor uses his or her hands to give musicians instructions. Ask a music teacher in your school or a student who plays in the school band to demonstrate some of the signals that a conductor uses.

2 Explaining a Process

PREVIEWING THE CHAPTER

- The three workshops in this chapter teach students to read, write, and listen to instructions for a process. Although the workshops may be taught separately, taught together they can help students develop a complete understanding of the techniques used to instruct others. Reading a chapter from a "how-to" book in the Reading Workshop prepares students for the writing assignment in the Writing Workshop. Once students have practiced reading and writing instructions, they can practice following oral directions in the Focus on Listening workshop. For help in integrating this chapter with grammar, usage, and mechanics chapters, see pp. T311A– T311B.

INTRODUCING THE CHAPTER

- To introduce the chapter, use the Journal Warm-up, Transparency 17, in *Communications*.

VIEWING THE ILLUSTRATION

- The illustration might indicate that anyone can follow directions if the steps are clear and logical. Explore with students the artistic elements and style that make the illustration interesting and that contribute to its meaning. [Bright, playful colors and the use of varied textures give the illustration a childish appeal.] Ask students to identify the instances of contrast in the illustration. [contrasting colors of the sky, the creature, the buttons, and the dials; a contrast between the setting (a spaceship) and the creature's reliance on handwritten notes]

CHAPTER RESOURCES

Planning
- *Lesson Planner,* Ch. 2
- *ELL Strategies,* Ch. 2
- *Block Scheduling,* p. T47A (this book)
- *One-Stop Planner CD-ROM* 🔘

Practice
- *Communications,* Ch. 2

- *Media Literacy and Communication Skills*

Extension
- *Designing Your Writing*

Reinforcement
- *Communications,* Ch. 2
- *Alternative Readings,* Ch. 2

Reading Workshop

Reading Instructions

Writing Workshop

Writing Instructions

Focus on Listening

Following Oral Instructions

he blue light blinks at you: "12:00, 12:00, 12:00." With VCR manual in hand, you try to follow the instructions for setting the clock. You punch buttons until, finally, you have completed every step in the directions. You have conquered the VCR! No, wait! It is still blinking "12:00, 12:00, 12:00." In frustration, you howl, "My little sister could write better instructions!"

Instructions are all around us. They come with the electronic gadgets, frozen dinners, and games we buy. When you tell a friend how to bait a fishhook or how to get to your house, you are giving **instructions**. Reading and listening to instructions helps you learn new skills. Writing your own instructions lets you share what you know.

Informational Text

Exposition

Looking at Instructions

Find several examples of instructions that tell how to do something or how to make something. Look in manuals, books, or magazines. Then, working with a partner, discuss the following questions.

- Do the instructions tell how to *do* or how to *make* something?
- Which instructions are the clearest and easiest to follow? Why?
- In general, do you think it is easier to tell how to *do* something or how to *make* something? Why do you think so?

internetconnect

go. hrw .com

GO TO: go.hrw.com
KEYWORD: EOLang 7-2

Connecting Reading and Writing   **49**

Motivate

Explain to students that they follow processes throughout their lives. For example, learning to ride a bicycle and to print their names both involve processes. Focus students' attention on the "how-to" process by asking them to follow your instructions for making a paper airplane or for completing some other hands-on procedure that can be easily explained. Then, discuss with the class what made the instructions easy or difficult to follow.

ELEMENTS OF
Literature

Explaining a Process in Literature. In *Elements of Literature,* First Course, see "When the Earth Shakes," by Patricia Lauber, pp. 435–439, for an explanation of a process in a nonfiction narrative.

Looking at Instructions

Check that partners evaluate at least three sets of instructions and that they include reasons for their conclusions. You might lead a discussion of "how-to" writing by having volunteers share their answers with the class.

- *Daily Language Activity Transparencies*
- *Vocabulary Workshop* and *Tests*
- *Spelling*

Evaluation and Assessment

- *Test Generator (One-Stop Planner CD-ROM)*

- *Assessment Package*
  —*Chapter Tests,* Ch. 2
  —*Chapter Tests in Standardized Test Formats,* Ch. 2
  —*Assessment Alternatives,* Ch. 2

Internet

- go.hrw.com (keyword: EOLang 7–2)

Reading Instructions

WHAT'S AHEAD?

In this section you will read part of a book chapter that gives instructions. You will also learn how to

- identify an author's purpose for writing
- map out the order of events in a process

You hear the sound faintly at first, but gradually it becomes louder. It sounds like a voice, but it is coming from . . . the chimney? People have been amazed and confused by ventriloquism for centuries. In the following reading selection, Ormond McGill explains how to "throw" your voice so that it sounds like it is coming from an attic or chimney. The selection is a chapter from a book on *ventriloquism,* the art of disguising the real source of a voice.

Preparing to Read

READING SKILL

Identifying Author's Purpose   Every time a writer sits down to write, he or she has a *purpose* in mind. **Purpose** is the reason for writing a particular article or paper. As you read the following chapter from Mr. McGill's book on ventriloquism, think about his purpose for writing.

READING FOCUS

Order of a Process   In order to learn a process, you need to know what to do and when to do it. As you read the selection and learn how to "throw" your voice, notice the **order** of steps that the author uses. If you drew a map of the steps in the chapter, it might look something like this:

As you read, see if you can identify the separate steps in the process and figure out how they fit together.

50   Chapter 2   **Exposition:** Explaining a Process

READING PROCESS

PREREADING
Make Predictions. Explain that readers tend to read more efficiently and understand better when they are curious about the information they will find in a text. The introduction on p. 50 gives students an idea about what follows in the Reading Selection. Challenge students to skim the selection and make predictions about the content of the Reading Selection. One way they can do this is to preview a text by using the title of a reading and other features that stand out,

Read the following selection about ventriloquism. In your notebook, jot down answers to the numbered active-reading questions in the shaded boxes. Underlined words will be used in the Vocabulary Mini-Lesson on page 57.

from **VOICE MAGIC**
◆

The Voice in the Attic

BY ORMOND MCGILL

You look up at the ceiling and call out to an imaginary person in the attic. The person answers you! To the amazement of the audience, you carry on a conversation with this mysterious person.

1. What activity is the author describing?

You can choose to direct your conversation toward someone up in the attic or toward someone down in the basement, if you like. The key to this performance is that you stand with your back to the audience. Your mouth movements can then be less restricted when you speak in the voice of the distant person.

Be sure to direct the audience's attention to the attic by pointing to the ceiling and looking up at it. Call out loudly and distinctly in your natural voice. Ask some questions, as though you know there is a person up there. Remember that the success of the illusion depends on convincing the audience you believe in this imaginary presence.

2. What is the main point of this paragraph?

Now, in exactly the same tone and pitch of voice, make the distant voice answer. But, this time, form the words at the back part of the roof of your mouth. Draw your lower jaw back and hold it there. Keep your mouth open. Inhale deeply before you speak. Then, as you speak, exhale in little jerks, using a bit of air for each word. This action will produce a sound that is subdued and muffled, just a little louder than a whisper.

3. Do you have any trouble following each step? Rewrite the steps in your own words.

You can make this distant voice appear to come gradually nearer, too. To do this, call loudly in your natural voice and say, "Come down here!" At the same time, gesture downward with your hand to increase the illusion.

4. What two actions happen at once in the second-to-last paragraph? How do you know?

Have the voice answer, "I'm coming" or "I'm getting closer now," being sure to speak a little louder as

such as headings, illustrations, annotations, and boldface words. Have them write down their predictions and revise the predictions as they read.

Active-Reading Questions

The purpose of the active-reading questions is to encourage students to think about the order the author uses to explain the steps in the process and the clarity of his instructions. Possible answers follow.

ANSWERS

1. The writer describes the act of ventriloquism.

2. The point of this paragraph is to explain how to "throw" one's voice and create the illusion of a conversation with an imaginary person.

3. If students are having difficulty following the steps, have a student paraphrase each step aloud for the class.

4. The writer instructs the reader to call to the distant voice and point at the ground. The phrase "At the same time" tells the reader that the two happen at once.

TEACHING (TIP)

Active-Reading Questions

One way of using the active-reading questions is to have each student read silently to the first question and determine the answer to the question. Then, lead a brief class discussion in which students share and discuss their answers to the first question before you have them go on to the next question.

5. The sample conversation gives the reader some lines to use for practice. The conversation also adds humor to the chapter.

6. Since some of the vocabulary words in these two paragraphs may be difficult for eight-year-olds, the author would probably need to include extra information to explain the meaning of the following words: "ventriloquial," "seemingly," "supposed," "alter," "cavity," "degrees," and "drawn."

7. Some students might say that the paragraph seems to be a good conclusion to the selection because it tells the reader what to do as the mysterious person finally enters the door.

---

the imaginary person approaches.

Here is an example of a conversation you might have with a person who is up inside a chimney:

You: (Look up the chimney.) *Are you up there?*
Voice: *Yes, I'm up here sweeping the chimney.*
You: *What for? The chimney has already been cleaned.*
Voice: *I'm looking for birds' nests.*
You: *That's ridiculous! There aren't any birds' nests up there. . . . Now, come down out of there. . . .*
Voice: *All right. I'm coming . . . . I'm coming.*

> **5.** Why do you think the author includes a sample conversation?

You can then continue your ventriloquial conversation with the voice as the person seemingly comes down the chimney. At every supposed step closer, alter the place from which the person's

> **6.** If the author were writing for eight-year-olds, what changes in vocabulary might he need to make here?

voice comes. Gradually open the cavity of your mouth and produce the sounds closer to your lips. You will create a larger space inside your mouth so that the voice will appear to come nearer and nearer by degrees.

By the time the person reaches the bottom of the chimney, your lips should be drawn into a circle, as though you were whistling. This movement enlarges the cavity of your mouth as much as possible.

Here is another conversation you could have with a person on the roof. Start by directing the attention of the audience upward.

You: *Are you up there on the roof, Frank?*
Voice: *Hello down there! What did you say?*
You: (shouting louder) *I said, are you up there on the roof?*
Voice: *I sure am. I'm putting on some shingles.*
You: *Good. Are you almost finished?*
Voice: *I'm just putting on the last one now.*
You: *Fine. Please come on down then. I want to see you.*
Voice: *Okay. I'll come right down.*
You: *Which way are you coming, Frank? . . .*

Keep the conversation going as long as you wish. Make the voice get closer and closer, and use gestures to show that Frank is descending. Finally, as the voice approaches the door, speak in the near ventriloquial voice that you learned in the previous section. Practice hard, and the illusion will be complete.

> **7.** Is the last paragraph a good wrap-up for this selection? Why or why not?

READING PROCESS

READING

Self-Check. Tell students that skilled readers realize when they are off track and change their reading speeds, slowing down or stopping to re-read when they are confused. As students read **"A Voice in the Attic,"** ask them to place a sticky note next to places in the selection where they slowed down and re-read portions of the text. After students finish reading the selection, discuss with

First Thoughts on Your Reading

1. What is the main idea or focus of this selection?

2. Based on the selection you have read, for whom do you think Mr. McGill wrote *Voice Magic*? Young people? Ventriloquists?

3. Do you think you can learn ventriloquism by using the steps in the selection? Why or why not?

PEANUTS reprinted by permission of United Feature Syndicate, Inc.

Identifying Author's Purpose

Tell Me Why   No piece of writing happens by accident. Whenever you write a report, story, or essay, you have a *purpose* in mind. An **author's purpose** for writing is the reason he or she writes a particular piece. Sometimes the author's purpose is obvious. After all, the author of an owner's manual for a CD player is not writing to express a love of electronics. That author's purpose is to give information about how to use the CD player.

At other times, the author's purpose will not be as clear. In every kind of writing, however, there are clues to help readers determine the author's purpose (or purposes) for writing. The chart on the next page explains each of the four main purposes for writing and gives examples of clues that point to each purpose.

TIP   Sometimes authors have more than one purpose. For example, an author who writes a story about tigers may write both to entertain readers and to inform them that tigers are endangered.

First Thoughts on Your Reading
ANSWERS
Sample answers appear below.

1. The focus of this selection is to explain the steps involved in creating a ventriloquial voice that appears to be coming from an attic or a chimney.

2. Mr. McGill probably wrote his book *Voice Magic* for young people.

3. Yes, the steps and explanations are clear and easy to follow.

them how strategies like varying reading speeds can help them improve their understanding of a selection.

Purpose for Writing

As you discuss the chart on this page with students, have them cover up the clues in the far right column. Read the purposes for writing and their explanations aloud to the class. Ask students to think of the clues that help them determine each purpose for writing. Compare their responses to the clues listed in the chart. Discuss any clues they did not mention.

Purpose for Writing	Explanation	Clues
To inform	Informative writing may teach *how to* or it may teach *what, how,* or *why.* The author's purpose in **"how-to"** writing is to teach readers how to do or make something. **"What-how-or-why"** writing may explain what a paramecium is, how bees make honey, or why the Egyptians built pyramids.	*"How-to" Writing* ■ step-by-step instructions ■ numbered steps, lists, or diagrams ■ words such as *first, next,* and *last* *"What-how-or-why Writing"* ■ facts, statistics, examples, or definitions explaining what, how, or why ■ illustrations, diagrams, maps, charts ■ headings and subheadings
To express	This type of writing expresses an emotion or belief, but does not try to change your beliefs. Poems and personal essays are written to express.	■ emotional words and expressions ■ frequent use of the word *I* ■ words that show value, such as the adjectives *worst, best, terrible, great*
To entertain	Entertaining writing often tells a story, uses drama or humor, or features playful language. Stories, novels, poems, and plays are all written to entertain.	■ a story that has a beginning, middle, and end ■ dialogue ■ rhymes ■ drama or humor
To influence	Persuasive writing tries to convince the reader to share the writer's opinion.	■ statements of opinion, backed up by facts, statistics, and examples ■ words like *should, must,* and *have to* ■ words that show value, such as the adjectives *worst, best, terrible, great*

Try identifying the author's purpose in the following paragraph. If you get stuck, use the Thinking It Through on the next page.

> Over two thousand schools use peer-mediation programs. How does peer mediation work? Starting as early as the third grade, students can be trained to mediate, or help work out, other students' conflicts. Student mediators help peers to understand the source of the conflict, to listen to each other, and to arrive at a "win-win" solution.

READING PROCESS

EXPLORING

Evaluate the Order of a Process. Tell students that they can better appreciate the importance of order in explaining a process (in informational texts) by evaluating the function of clue words in **"The Voice in the Attic."** Students should answer the following questions.

1. Identify four words or phrases in the selection that signal chronological order. ["now," "then," "at the same time," and "finally"]

Identifying an Author's Purpose

▶ **STEP 1** Read the passage carefully, and look for clues to the author's purpose. Narrow the possible purposes based on the clues.

I see a statistic, "Over two thousand schools. . . ." The purpose could be to inform or to influence.

▶ **STEP 2** Re-read the passage. Look for specific statements to help you confirm the author's main purpose. Make a final decision about purpose.

The statistics don't seem to back an opinion. They seem to explain peer mediation, because the author also says, "How does peer mediation work?" I think the writer is mainly trying to inform me about what and how.

Identifying an Author's Purpose

Using the chart on page 54 and the Thinking It Through steps above, jot down your thoughts as you figure out the author's purpose in "The Voice in the Attic." Then, complete these sentences:

The author's purpose is _____. I know this because _____.

A possible response follows.

The author's purpose is to teach the reader how to "throw" his or her voice so that the reader can appear to have a conversation with a mysterious person in the attic or the chimney. I know this because the author clearly explains each step.

Order of a Process

◀ **READING FOCUS**

Take It One Step at a Time   Have you ever taught a young child to do something? If you have, you probably had to show the child how to proceed step by step—explaining the first step first, the second step second, and so on, to the end. When you explain something this way, you are following **chronological order** (or **time order**). Most "how-to" writing uses chronological order because it is the clearest way to explain a process.

As you read "how-to" explanations, certain clue words let you know that the steps are listed in chronological order. Some of these clue words appear below.

as	before	finally	next	then
at the same time	during	first	second	while

Cooperative Learning

Step-by-Step Instructions. Help students experience the importance of step-by-step instructions by having them work together in randomly assigned groups of three to create a "how-to" explanation for making something. Then, have students cut these instructions into separate strips for each step and give the strips to another group. The second group should then put the instructions back in order.

2. Find two passages where the author did not use clue words to signal chronological order. [Paragraphs one and three] Was the order of the steps clear to you? Why or why not?

RESOURCES

Your Turn 2
Practice
■ *Communications*, WS. p. 27
Reinforcement
■ *Communications,* TP. 18, WS. p. 28

Wrap It Up

Metacognition. Ask students to use the following questions to reflect on their own reading process.

1. While reading **"A Voice in the Attic,"** where did you get confused? What did you do to get back on track?

Then, ask students to answer the following question.

2. What is the purpose of "how-to" writing? [to teach readers how to do or make something]

YOUR TURN 3

ANSWERS

In the sample response below, each step would be a cell in a flow-chart. Steps with the same number would occur simultaneously.

Topic: "Throwing" your voice

Step 1: Stand with your back to the audience.

Step 2a: Point to the ceiling.

Step 2b: Call out a question loudly.

Step 3: Before you answer, inhale.

Step 4a: Hold your lower jaw back.

Step 4b: Keep your mouth open.

Step 4c: Exhale in jerks as you speak.

Step 4d: Form the words at the back of your mouth.

Step 5a: Call out in a natural voice, "Come down here!"

Step 5b: Gesture downward.

Step 6: Have the voice answer, speaking louder as it approaches.

Step 7a: To make the voice sound closer, enlarge the cavity of your mouth.

Step 7b: Make sounds closer to your lips.

Step 8: Use near ventriloquial voice as voice nears the door.

Charting a Path   One way to make sure you understand the order of instructions is to create a *flowchart*. A **flowchart** is a map that shows the steps in a process. Flowcharts use arrows to indicate the order of steps. Read the following paragraph and the flowchart below it. Notice how you can use a flowchart to show that two steps happen at the same time.

> Veggie pizza is a tasty, nutritious snack. First, you need to make or buy pizza dough. Then, pre-heat the oven. While the oven heats, put toppings like tomato sauce, mushrooms, onions, and cheese on the dough. Pop it in the oven, and soon you'll have a great snack to share with your friends.

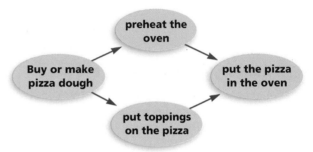

TIP   Some instructions can be hard to follow. Occasionally, writers *omit,* or leave out, details or entire steps because they assume that readers already know them. In the example above, the writer did not tell you to take the pizza out of the oven. However, you would know that in order to eat the pizza, you need to remove it from the oven. Missing steps can be frustrating, but if you draw on your experience, you can often figure out what to do.

YOUR TURN 3   Mapping the Order of a Process

- Re-read "The Voice in the Attic" on pages 51–52. Then, make a flowchart like the one above. Use clue words like those on page 55 to help you figure out the order of the steps necessary to "throw" your voice. Fill in each step as it is listed in the reading selection.

- Would you have added any steps or details about steps? If so, what types of information would you have added? Write your additions below your flowchart.

RESOURCES

Your Turn 3

Practice
- *Communications,* WS. p. 29

Reinforcement
- *Communications,* TP. 19, WS. p. 30

Identifying Greek and Latin Word Roots

Instructions may define unfamiliar words. If they do not, you can figure out the meanings of some words by using common *word roots*. The **word root** is the main part of a word. Many English roots come from ancient Greek and Latin.

Greek Root	Meaning	Examples
–bio–	life	biology
–cycl–, –cyclo–	circle, wheel	bicycle
–graph–	writing	biography
–ton–, –tonos–	sound	monotone

Latin Root	Meaning	Examples
–aud–, –audi–	hear	audible
–cav–, –cava–	hollow	cave
–lud–, –lus–	trick	elude
–strict–	draw tight	constrict

THINKING IT THROUGH — Identifying Greek and Latin Word Roots

The steps below show how word roots can help you define the word *ventriloquial* from "The Voice in the Attic."

▶ **STEP 1** Separate any roots from the rest of the word, and define them.
–Ventri– means "stomach" or "belly," and –loqui– means "speaking."

▶ **STEP 2** Use the meanings of the roots to guess the word's meaning. Then, see if your meaning makes sense in the word's original context.
–Ventri– plus –loqui– means "belly speaking." The reading selection is about talking without moving your lips, which seems like speaking from the belly.

PRACTICE

Based on their roots, define these words from "The Voice in the Attic."

1. audience (page 51)
2. restricted (page 51)
3. illusion (page 51)
4. tone (page 51)
5. cavity (page 52)

Reference Note

For more on **word roots,** see page 754 in the Quick Reference Handbook.

RESOURCES

Vocabulary
Practice
■ *Communications,* WS. p. 31

Identifying Greek and Latin Word Roots

ANSWERS
Possible answers appear below.

1. –*Aud*– means "hear." An audience is a group of people who hear something. In this selection, an audience listens as you "throw" your voice.

2. –*Strict*– means "draw tight." To restrict means to limit something. The instructions say to stand with your back to the audience so that you don't have to limit your mouth's movements.

3. –*Lus*– means "trick." An illusion is a trick. A ventriloquist tricks an audience into believing that he or she is speaking to another person.

4. –*Ton*– means "sound." The tone of your voice refers to a particular pitch or sound. You use sound when "throwing" your voice.

5. –*Cav*– means "hollow." A cavity is a hollow space. When "throwing" your voice, you use your mouth, which is hollow.

Taking a Second Look

Identifying Greek and Latin Word Roots. Have students use context clues instead of word roots to determine the meaning of the words in this exercise. Students should read the sentence containing the vocabulary word, examining the meaning of words around the unfamiliar word and the way the word is used in the sentence. Ask them to replace the unfamiliar word with another word or phrase they know that fits the context of the sentence. Then, have them check the dictionary to see if their meaning matches the dictionary definition.

Identifying Sequence of Events

When you take reading tests, you may find questions about the **sequence,** or order, of events in a reading selection. Read the following passage and the question after it. If this were a reading test, how would you go about answering this question?

When you use your imagination, you can create an exercise program for yourself that is fun and healthy. First, decide whether you want to work out for a particular sport or just for overall improved health. If you want to focus on one sport, talk to the coaches at your school to find out which kind of exercises are best for that sport. Then, think about how much time you would like to spend exercising each week. After you have determined when and how often to exercise, try to add a little variety. For example, if you usually work out in a gym, try taking your exercise routine outside. Adding variety to your workout will help you stick with it and be a happier, healthier person.

According to the reading passage, what should you do after you decide when and how often to exercise each week?

A. Choose a type of workout to do.

B. Add variety to your workout.

C. Talk to your coach.

D. Stick with your workout routine.

THINKING IT THROUGH — **Identifying Sequence of Events**

> **STEP 1** Look for clues in the question to figure out what it is asking.

The question asks what step comes <u>after</u> another step. "After" tells me it is asking about chronological order.

> **STEP 2** Scan the passage, looking only for chronological-order clue words or phrases.

I found "first," "then," and "after."

> **STEP 3** Re-read the text around each clue word to find the part of the passage referred to in the question.

"<u>After</u> you have determined when and how often to exercise, try to add a little variety." There's my answer.

> **STEP 4** Match your response to one of the answer choices available.

Answers **A** and **C** both happen before you decide when and how often to exercise. **D** is the last step mentioned. **B** matches my response best. It must be correct.

Looking Ahead to Writing

In the Writing Workshop, pp. 59–75, students will write instructions to teach someone how to do something. They will need to explain the steps of the process in chronological order. Suggest that students refer to the flowchart on p. 56 for a system that they might use to explain the steps of their processes in the correct order.

RESOURCES

Test Taking
Practice
- *Communications,* WS. pp. 32–34

Writing Instructions

"Show me how to shoot a free throw," a little boy says to his older sister. To him, she is an expert. Like the boy's big sister, you, too, are an expert on something, no matter who you are or where you live. You have unique skills and talents. Do not keep all of that knowledge to yourself—share it with the world!

One way to share what you know is by writing instructions that teach your reader how to do something. In this workshop you will explore your expert knowledge to write instructions for a process. As you develop your ideas, you may learn even more about that process than you knew when you started.

WHAT'S AHEAD?

In this workshop you will write instructions that tell how to do something. You will also learn how to

- **map the sequence of your activity**
- **identify relevant and irrelevant details**
- **use transitional phrases**
- **use commas after introductory phrases**

Prewriting

Choose a Topic

How to . . . What? You know how to do so many things. To write your instructions, however, you need to choose just one thing to explain. Instructions can either tell how to make something or how to do something. For example, a recipe for banana bread tells how to make something, while a Web site on dog training tells how to do something.

In this workshop, you will focus on writing instructions for an activity or process that you *do*, rather than for something you *make*. **The topic you decide to write about should be something you know how to do well enough to explain.** After all, you cannot tell someone else how to play the guitar if you have never played a note yourself.

 KEY CONCEPT

OBJECTIVES

- To use the writing process to write instructions
- To map the sequence of an activity
- To identify relevant and irrelevant details
- To use transitional phrases
- To use commas after introductory phrases

Quotation for the Day

"We are wiser than we know."

(Ralph Waldo Emerson, 1803–1882, American poet, essayist, and philosopher)

Write the quotation on the chalkboard. Ask students to discuss how Emerson's observation is useful to a writer during prewriting. Remind students that each day they complete many processes that have become automatic. Ask them to list a few processes they go through regularly. The students' lists can be used to help them select topics for their "how-to" essays.

TEACHING TIP

Choose a Topic
Point out that topics such as how to play tennis are too complex to write about in a one- to two-page paper. Instead, students should narrow the topic and explain how to serve or how to volley. Have students practice narrowing some other topics, such as playing baseball, swimming, or playing a video game, to a more specific focus.

Writing Workshop **59**

Brainstorm about things you enjoy doing. If you need help coming up with ideas, think about these questions.

- If I could do any activity I wanted to right now, what would it be?
- Am I proud of any special skill, talent, or trick? If so, what?

Evaluate Your Topic

Testing the Water   Before you begin writing, make sure you have picked the right topic. The chart that follows shows how one student evaluated three topics based on these questions.

- Is the topic something I *do* or something I *make*?
- Do I know how to do it? How well?
- Is the topic interesting or unusual?

Topic	Something I do or make?	Can I do it? How well?	Is it interesting or unusual?
✓Flying a kite	Do	Yes. I won third place in a kite contest.	Yes. It's a lot of fun.
Making bread	Make	Kind of. I only made it once.	Yes. Fresh bread tastes great!
Tying my shoes	Do	Yes, I've been doing it since I was four or five.	No. I tie my shoes all the time.

Because the assignment calls for something to *do,* not *make,* the student chose not to write about making bread. He settled on flying a kite as the more interesting topic of the two remaining.

YOUR TURN 4   Choosing and Evaluating a Topic

Make a list of possible topics for your instructions. Then, evaluate your topics by making a chart like the one above. Choose a topic that is something you know how to do well and find interesting.

Reflect on Your Audience and Purpose

Who and Why   Before you start writing, think about your audience and your purpose. First, ask yourself, "Who will be reading my instructions?" It may be your classmates, a teacher, or a younger brother or sister. In any case, you should write for readers who do not know how to do the activity you have picked but want to learn.

Next, think about your purpose. Your purpose answers the question, "Why am I writing?" You are writing for a very specific reason: to teach someone how to do something. **To make your instructions effective, make them as clear and simple as possible.** Notice how the student writing about kite flying analyzed his audience in the Thinking It Through below.

TIP   Be sure that your **voice,** or the sound of your writing, is clear and straightforward. Use vocabulary that your audience will understand, and avoid humor that may not come across in writing.

◀ **KEY CONCEPT**

THINKING IT THROUGH

Writing for a Specific Audience

STEP 1   Ask yourself:

- Who is my audience?

  students my age who have no experience with kites

- What is my purpose?

  to explain how to fly a kite

STEP 2   Consider any special words or names that go with your topic. Decide how you might make these ideas clear to a beginner.

There aren't any special words or names I know of in kite flying. Someone might need to know where to get a kite, though.

STEP 3   Identify any parts of this activity that are easier to show than tell. Decide how you can make these parts clearer to your audience.

It's easier to show than to tell how a kite takes off. I can write down the steps as I imagine getting a kite off the ground to make this action clear.

YOUR TURN 5 — Thinking About Your Audience and Purpose

With your topic in mind, consider the audience for your "how-to" paper and the purpose for which you are writing it. To figure out how to match your instructions to your audience, use the Thinking It Through steps above.

Writing Workshop   **61**

Meeting INDIVIDUAL NEEDS

MULTIPLE INTELLIGENCES
Interpersonal Intelligence. Tell students that explaining and discussing their topics with another person can help them clarify and further define their topics. As they complete **Your Turn 5,** have students work in pairs to explain to each other the audiences and purposes of their papers. Students can imagine themselves as a person from their partners' target audiences (a first-grader, a peer, or a parent) and offer feedback as to what they would find interesting or unimportant.

YOUR TURN 5

To check students' work, have them state their topics and read their answers to **Step 1** of **Thinking It Through** to a small group of classmates. Each student should tell the group why the audience he or she selected is likely to be interested in the topic. Then, the group members can decide whether or not the specific audience chosen is the best target for the topic.

RESOURCES

Your Turn 4 and 5
Practice
- *Communications,* WS. pp. 35, 36

Gather and Organize Information

To help students find more information about their activities when revising and editing their final drafts, you may discuss key word and phrase searches. Tell students that they should use very specific key words or phrases to find the information more efficiently at the library or on the Internet. Ask students to look in the index of any textbook to see how key words work to assist readers in finding information. *You need to be aware that Internet resources are sometimes public forums, and their content can be unpredictable.*

Meeting INDIVIDUAL NEEDS

MODALITY

Visual Learners. Have students visualize themselves actually doing the process to help them remember the materials and the steps of the process. Have students close their eyes, imagine themselves in the place where they would perform the steps, see the materials laid out on a table or floor, and imagine the steps one by one. As students finish their visualization, they can start writing the steps. They might also find it helpful to use very simple drawings to storyboard their processes.

STUDENTS WITH SPECIAL NEEDS

For students who may not remember an activity done in the past, suggest that they write about a process they used in the last day.

TIP Since you already know each step of the process, you probably have all the information you need. However, if you have any questions, use **reference materials and resources,** such as books, articles, videotapes, or the World Wide Web.

Gather and Organize Information

Pretend You Are Talking to a Two-Year-Old   Even if your audience does not include young children, pretend for a moment that it does. Then, jot down every single thing a small child would need to know. Make two lists: one for the materials needed to complete your activity and the other for the steps. Later, as you put the steps in order, you can decide whether you have included more steps than your audience will need.

Order Put Directions In   Re-read the heading to the left. It does not make sense because it was written in the wrong order. Putting steps in the correct order helps your audience successfully follow your instructions. Most instructions are written in **chronological** (or time) **order.** They explain what comes first, what comes second, and so on.

You can organize your list of steps by numbering each step to show its place in the process. To decide the order of your steps, ask yourself the following questions.

- Is one step a better place to start than the others? What is the very first thing a beginner should do? Make this step the first step.
- Is there any step on which other steps depend? If so, this step must come before the ones that depend on it.

The following example shows one student's list of steps and materials. First, the student wrote down all the steps. Then, he added numbers showing the correct order of the steps.

> **Topic:** how to fly a kite
>
> **Materials:** a kite and string
>
> **Steps:** 2. Hold the kite so the wind can pick it up.
> 3. When the wind catches the kite, let out string so the kite won't crash.
> 1. Find out what direction the wind is blowing.
> 5. Walk backwards to keep the string tight.
> 6. When you're done, roll up string slowly and the kite will come down.
> 4. As the kite gets higher, gradually let out more string.

A Student's Model

Stephanie Pearl wrote these instructions as a student at Randolph Middle School in Randolph, New Jersey. Notice that the following excerpt from her paper gives clear, step-by-step instructions in chronological order.

How to Choose a Puppy

Everyone knows that puppies are cute. What some people don't know is that a puppy requires planning and responsibility, even before you bring it home. By following the steps below, you can find the puppy that is right for you and make a home that is right for your puppy.

Before adopting a puppy, you must prepare for one. Make sure you have a crate or area set aside in your home for the puppy to stay in when you are not around. Have all the supplies you will need before you bring the puppy home. You should have a collar and leash, some toys, and puppy food. You may want to consider fencing in a part of your yard.

After you have decided to get a puppy, and you are prepared and have all necessary supplies, you need to decide where to get one. The best place to go adopt a puppy is an animal shelter. Animal shelters usually have a wide variety of puppies that people have abandoned.

When choosing a puppy, you should look for one with good qualities. The puppy should not be too timid or too aggressive. It should respond to noises and allow you to pet it. It should appear healthy and have all necessary vaccinations.

After picking out a puppy you like, take that puppy into a separate room. Sit down on the floor, and call it. The puppy should come, or at least look at you. If it does not come, walk over and pet the puppy, letting it smell your hand first. If it cringes or snarls, you may want to think twice about adopting it. Overly aggressive or submissive puppies require a lot of patience to train. . . .

Interesting opening

Statement of topic

Step 1
Explanation

Step 2
Explanation

Step 3
Explanation

Step 4

Explanation

Connecting Reading and Writing

After students read **A Student's Model,** have them identify the author's purpose for writing and point out the clues that helped them determine the author's purpose. If they need assistance, refer them to the chart in the Reading Workshop on p. 54.

MINI-LESSON CRITICAL THINKING

Relevant and Irrelevant Details

ANSWERS

1. R

2. I

3. R

4. I

5. R

MINI-LESSON CRITICAL THINKING

Relevant and Irrelevant Details

"So then, at the end of the movie, the aliens landed on earth, and they had these really spiffy spaceships, but they weren't shaped like flying saucers. They were more like garbage cans. Oh, I got grounded today because I didn't take out the garbage. Anyway, the aliens came down and…"

Have you ever had friends who rambled this way about anything that popped into their heads? People ramble when they talk or write because they can't separate relevant and irrelevant details.

A **relevant detail** is one that gives information about the main idea. In instructions, relevant details are ones that help explain the process and provide **logical support** for ideas and explanations. **Irrelevant details** are just fluff. They do not give necessary information, and they may distract and annoy your reader. Look at the examples in the following paragraph.

There *is* a right way to make a peanut butter sandwich **(main idea)**. First, you should use a butter knife or some other dull knife so that you can easily spread the peanut butter without cutting yourself **(relevant detail)**. Once, when I made a sandwich, I almost cut my hand, but I didn't **(irrelevant detail)**.

To identify relevant and irrelevant details, ask yourself these questions.

- What is the main idea of the paragraph?
- Does this detail help me understand the main idea?

For instructions, you should also ask,

- Does this information tell me how to do the task better?

Reference Note

For more on **main idea**, see page 289.

PRACTICE

The following sentences are instructions for shooting a basketball free throw. On a piece of paper, number from 1 to 5. Write *R* if the sentence following the number in brackets contains relevant details. Write *I* if the sentence contains irrelevant details.

> You can shoot free throws much better if you learn the technique. [1] Before you shoot, help yourself relax by following a routine, such as bouncing the ball or taking a deep breath. [2] My brother likes to play basketball, but he's a lousy free-throw shooter. [3] Hold the ball out in front of you with your hands on the sides. [4] Basketball is one of the most popular sports in America today. [5] As you release the ball, push the ball off your hands with a flip of your wrist.

RESOURCES

Critical Thinking
Practice
- *Communications,* WS. p. 40

Evaluate and Revise Content, Organization, and Style

Doing a Double Take   Whether you are evaluating and revising your own paper or evaluating a peer's, read the paper twice. The first time, look at big issues, such as content and organization. The second time, ask whether each sentence is as clear as it can be.

➤ First Reading: **Content and Organization**   Use this chart to evaluate and revise your paper so your instructions are effective and easy to follow.

Guidelines for Self-Evaluation and Peer Evaluation		
Evaluation Questions	**Tips**	**Revision Techniques**
❶ Does the introduction clearly state what the activity or process is?	**Put a star** next to the statement that tells what activity or process will be explained.	If needed, **add** a sentence telling what the activity or process is.
❷ Does the introduction give the reader a reason to learn the activity or process?	**Underline** the reason for learning the activity or process.	**Add** a reason why the reader should learn to do the activity or process.
❸ Do the steps show a logical progression of ideas?	**Write a number** in the margin next to each step and compare the numbers to the flow chart from prewriting.	**Rearrange** steps that are confusing or out of order, if necessary.
❹ Do any steps need additional explanation?	**Use a highlighter** to mark any explanation that follows a step.	**Elaborate** any step that needs more explanation.
❺ Are all details relevant to the instructions?	Look at the highlighted explanations. **Write** an *R* by relevant details and an *I* by irrelevant ones.	**Delete** all irrelevant details, and **replace** them with helpful, relevant details and examples.
❻ Does the conclusion restate the reason for learning this process and end with advice?	**Put a check mark** next to the sentence that restates the reason for learning the process. **Draw a wavy line** under the advice for using the process.	**Add** a restatement of the reason for learning the process. **Add** some advice for using the process successfully.

Writing Workshop   **69**

RESOURCES

Revising
Practice
- *Communications,* TPs. 22, 23, WS. pp. 41, 42, 43

1. The writer took out irrelevant details that do not relate to the main idea of the paragraph.

2. The writer added a sentence to elaborate on how to begin flying a kite.

Meeting
INDIVIDUAL
NEEDS

ENGLISH-LANGUAGE LEARNERS
General Strategies. English grammar may be difficult for some students when revising their essays. Provide students with a grammar checklist that includes guidelines on subject-verb agreement, fragments and run-on sentences, capitalization, and punctuation. You may preview students' drafts and guide them to work on specific grammatical elements.

Evaluating Student Writing

The ancillary *Assessment Alternatives* contains a variety of assessment forms, including Inventories and Evaluation Forms and rubrics: Six-Point Scales, Four-Point Scales, and Six Trait Scales.

ONE WRITER'S REVISIONS Study this revision of an early draft of the essay on pages 65–66.

> Before flying your kite, figure out which way the wind is blowing. You can do this by observing the way the trees are bending or by throwing a few blades of grass into the air. ~~I like the grass method because when I throw the blades in the air, my dog jumps up and tries to catch them. It is very funny to watch.~~ To begin flying your kite, stand with your back to the wind and hold the kite up so the wind can catch it. Let out about three feet of string or else your kite will just crash after the wind hits it. *If the day is not very windy, you may need to get your kite started by running while holding the kite up with a little string let out.*

delete

elaborate

PEER REVIEW

As you read a peer's instructions, ask yourself, Does this paper make me want to try out the activity or process it explains? Why or why not?

Responding to the Revision Process

1. Why do you think the writer deleted two sentences?
2. Why do you think the writer added a sentence?

Second Reading: Style Now you are ready to begin fine-tuning the individual sentences in your instructions. One way to improve your sentences is by using **transitional phrases,** phrases that connect ideas.

When you evaluate your instructions for style, ask yourself whether your writing contains phrases that act as signposts and help the reader move from one step to another. As you re-read your instructions, circle each transitional phrase. Are there any paragraphs with few or no transitional phrases? If so, add transitional phrases to paragraphs that need them.

Prepositional Phrases

Some transitional phrases are *prepositional phrases*. A **prepositional phrase** consists of a preposition followed by a noun or pronoun and any modifiers of the noun or pronoun. Prepositional phrases can help you show the order of steps involved in a process. Prepositional phrases help you improve the **coherence,** or connectedness, of your instructions by showing how all of your ideas relate to one another. Using a tightly knit style will help you achieve your purpose for writing instructions.

Below are a few examples of prepositional phrases. In each example, the preposition is in boldface.

about 3:00	**at** the same time	**during** this step
after lunch	**before** finishing	**until** dawn

Focus on

Sentences

Reference Note

For more on **coherence,** see page 297.

Reference Note

For more information and practice on **prepositional phrases,** see page 371.

ONE WRITER'S REVISIONS

> Once the wind catches your kite, gradually let out more and more string so the kite can climb higher into the air. *At the same time,* Walk backwards a few steps to keep the string tight.

Responding to the Revision Process

How did adding a prepositional phrase improve the instructions?

YOUR TURN 8

Evaluating and Revising Your Instructions

- First, evaluate and revise the content and organization of your essay using the guidelines on page 69.
- Next, use the Style Guidelines on page 70 and the Focus on Sentences above to help you add transitional phrases to your instructions.
- If a peer evaluated your paper, think carefully about each of your peer's comments as you revise.

Publishing

Proofread Your Instructions

Reference Note

For more on **proofreading,** see page 13.

Catching Your Mistakes   Errors in the final draft of your instructions will be distracting to your readers. Mistakes may even steer your readers in the wrong direction as they try to learn from your instructions. Have a peer help you find mistakes.

Grammar Link

Commas with Introductory Prepositional Phrases

A **prepositional phrase** includes a preposition, a noun or pronoun, and any modifiers of the noun or pronoun. An introductory phrase is one that comes at the beginning of a sentence.

You need a comma after two or more introductory prepositional phrases.

Example:
At the ends of the basketball court, you should see the two backboards.

Use a comma after a single introductory prepositional phrase only if you need the comma to avoid confusing your reader.

Example:
After breakfast, sausage production begins.
[A comma is needed so that the reader does not read "breakfast sausage production."]

Reference Note

For more information and practice on using commas with **introductory prepositional phrases,** see page 613.

PRACTICE

Decide whether a comma should follow any of the introductory prepositional phrases in each sentence. Rewrite the sentence on your paper with the comma in the correct place, or write C on your paper for correct sentences. The introductory prepositional phrases have been underlined for you.

Example:
1. By the mid-twenties advertising was a mainstay of American society.
1. C

1. After World War I soldiers returned home to a booming economy, and advertising became a billion-dollar business.

2. To many consumers in the twenties a product endorsement by a famous person was as good as a guarantee.

3. At this time even Eleanor Roosevelt promoted a breakfast food.

4. Across the nation during this decade new stores were built to fill the demand created by the advertisers.

5. In the mid-twenties one grocery chain had 14,000 stores.

Designing Your Writing

Using illustrations Illustrations can make your instructions clearer for your audience. You can draw diagrams, maps, or illustrations by hand and add them to your final draft.

If you prefer, you can take photographs of a friend following your instructions. Then, paste the photos onto your final paper. If available, use a scanner to put photos into a computer file, or use a digital camera. Using any of these techniques will help you create an impressive, illustrated final draft.

Reference Note

For more on **illustration,** see page 789 in the Quick Reference Handbook.

Publish Your Instructions

Putting It All Together Now your instructions are ready to be used. How can you get those instructions into the hands of people who need them?

■ Make an illustrated book of your instructions to present to your school library. You might get together with several classmates and combine your instructions into one handy manual.

■ Give your instructions to a class in a different grade. Arrange a demonstration of your activity or process for the class.

Reflect on Your Instructions

Building Your Portfolio Finally, it is time to reflect on your instructions. Reflecting can help you improve on future assignments.

■ Which details and explanations in your instructions are the most effective? Why do you think they are more effective than others?

■ Think about how you planned the order of steps in your instructions. Did you use any techniques that you might use in another type of writing? What are these techniques?

◀ **PORTFOLIO**

YOUR TURN 9 — Proofreading, Publishing, and Reflecting on Your Instructions

■ Proofread to correct grammar, usage, and mechanics errors. In particular, look for comma errors.

■ Publish your instructions so that they can be used.

■ Answer the Reflect on Your Instructions questions above. Record your responses in a learning log, or include them in your portfolio.

TIP As you proofread your instructions, you may find **reference materials,** such as language handbooks, dictionaries, and Part 3 of this book, helpful.

Writing Workshop **73**

Explaining "How-to" for Tests

Sometimes a prompt on a writing test asks you to explain how to make something or the process involved in doing something. The essay that you write for this type of prompt is called a **"how-to" paper.** To the right is a "how-to" prompt from a writing test. How would you answer this prompt?

Making arts and crafts is a popular hobby. Think about something you like to make, such as a model airplane or tie-dyed T-shirts. Write a letter to a friend explaining how to make your favorite craft. Be sure to include examples and specific details to explain your steps.

THINKING IT THROUGH   **Explaining "How-to" for Tests**

▶ **STEP 1**

- First, decide exactly what the prompt is asking you to do.
  I need to explain how to make a craft, such as a model airplane.
- Then, figure out who the audience for your paper is.
  The audience is a friend.
- Finally, decide on the form of your paper.
  The form is a letter.

  (For more on **letters,** see page 798 in the Quick Reference Handbook.)

▶ **STEP 2** Decide the topic of your "how-to" paper.

▶ **STEP 3** Brainstorm a list of the steps that readers will need to follow or understand. Then, put the steps in order by using a flowchart or some other graphic organizer.

▶ **STEP 4** Use your brainstorming notes to write your "how-to" paper. Write an introductory paragraph that tells readers what to expect from your paper. Then, write other paragraphs that thoroughly explain each step. Make each major step its own paragraph, and include a list of the materials needed.

▶ **STEP 5** Re-read your "how-to" paper, and add details and explanations if you need to make steps clearer.

TIP When writing a process explanation for a test, do not use illustrations to explain your steps. Also, write in essay format, without numbered lists. Your essay will be evaluated only on the way you express yourself in words, not numbers or illustrations.

RESOURCES

Test Taking
Practice
- *Communications,* WS. p. 46

Connections to Life

Giving Directions

Oral Directions Have you ever given someone directions to get somewhere and wound up explaining the steps over and over again to a confused listener? Giving directions orally is difficult because you usually do not have an opportunity to plan what you will say. Remembering a few steps can make you a better guide when someone asks for your help.

- Ask questions to make sure you understand where the person asking for directions wants to go.
- Visualize the route in your mind and explain it step by step.
- Mention well-known landmarks to help the lost person get oriented. A landmark does not have to be an important building or historical place. Often, the best landmarks are signs for businesses, colorful buildings, or places with odd names.

Written Directions Of course, many times you need to give written directions. For example, if you throw a birthday party for your best friend, you might include directions in the invitation to help your friends find your house. When you give written directions, you should follow the same steps for oral directions, with the following additions.

- Write the instructions in numbered or bulleted steps or other manageable chunks instead of in paragraph form.
- Write legibly. You may choose to write **cursive** or **manuscript**, but be sure that your audience will be able to read the directions.
- Draw a map on the same page. The combination of written directions and a map will make it more likely that people will easily find your party.

YOUR TURN 10 Giving Directions

Think of a place close to your home or school, and explain to a classmate how to get there. Then, write down directions to the same place and show them to your classmate. Switch roles, and then discuss these questions with your partner.

- Which was easier: giving oral or written directions? Why?
- Which is more effective when you ask for directions: getting them orally or having them written down? Why?

OBJECTIVES

- To follow oral instructions
- To practice active listening skills
- To take notes while listening
- To ask questions for understanding

Quotation for the Day

❝Then I want to sit and listen and have someone talk, tell me things—. . . . Not to say anything—to listen and listen and be taught.❞

(Anne Morrow Lindbergh, 1906–   , American author, married to the aviator Charles Lindbergh)

Write the quotation on the chalkboard. Then, ask students to reflect on their own listening skills. Do they pay close attention when someone is speaking, or do they find themselves "tuning out"? What do they do to help themselves stay focused when listening?

TEACHING TIP

Learning to Listen
As you discuss verbal and nonverbal cues, demonstrate some of the cues listed in the chart on p. 77 or have students demonstrate them to the class.

WHAT'S AHEAD?

In this workshop you will learn how to follow oral instructions. You will also learn how to

- **practice active listening skills**
- **take notes as you listen**
- **ask questions for understanding**

Following Oral Instructions

❝**A**ttention, students! All students with last names beginning with A through M should report to Room 206 at 10:15 A.M. for school pictures. Students with names beginning N through Z report to Room 208 at 10:45 A.M. Afterwards, please turn in order forms in Room 315.❞

Do announcements like this make your head spin? You probably hear oral instructions every day. For example,

- in class when your teacher gives an assignment
- when your sister explains how to get to the museum
- when your uncle explains how to bait a hook and clean a fish

You can improve your ability to follow oral instructions by learning to listen.

Learning to Listen

The ability to follow oral instructions is a skill you need for life. Why is it sometimes hard to follow spoken instructions? Maybe you "tune out" for a minute, only to realize later that you have missed something important. Maybe the speaker uses terms that you do not understand.

Most people *hear* what is being said, but they may not really *listen*. Listening is an active process. It involves trying to interpret the main points, as well as *verbal* and *nonverbal cues*. **Cues** are hints or clues a speaker gives to help listeners follow speech. **Verbal cues** are spoken hints, while **nonverbal cues** are unspoken hints such as movements, facial expressions, and gestures. The chart on the next page shows some common verbal and nonverbal cues.

76　　Chapter 2　　**Exposition:** Explaining a Process

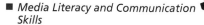

RESOURCES

Focus on Listening
Practice
- *Media Literacy and Communication Skills*
 —*Support and Practice,* Ch. 2
 —*A How-To Handbook*

Teaching Notes
- *Media Literacy and Communication Skills*
 —*A Teacher's Guide,* Ch. 2

Verbal Cues	Nonverbal Cues
clue words such as *first, next, last,* and *in conclusion* to help the listener follow along	"body language," or movements and facial expressions that show the speaker's mood or attitude
repetition of important phrases or ideas	demonstrating the activity or using hand movements to emphasize important points
emphasis on important information, such as speaking more loudly or stressing certain words	facial expressions or movements that ask for questions or encourage the listener's participation

Tricks for Tuning In   In addition to using verbal and nonverbal cues, you should focus on the speaker to get the main points. You will miss important information if you are gazing out the window or doodling instead of taking notes. To keep yourself from "tuning out," try to avoid such distractions.

Taking Notes

As you listen to oral instructions, you may need to take notes. Jotting down a few key phrases and steps can help you remember what was said. As you take notes, keep the following points in mind.

- Do not try to write down every word. Instead, focus on key words and phrases.
- Abbreviate frequently used words or phrases. Just remember to make a key so you do not forget what your abbreviations mean.
- Jot down questions or put question marks by steps that confuse you. Look back to your notes if the speaker asks for questions.

Asking Questions

As you listen, think about whether you are understanding what you hear. Ask questions to clarify anything you do not fully understand. You ask questions all the time, but you might not realize that there are "dos and don'ts" when it comes to asking questions. The chart on the next page lists some of the most important "dos and don'ts" to remember when you need to ask a question.

Reference Note
For more on **eliminating barriers to effective listening,** see page 767 in the Quick Reference Handbook.

TIP   Ask the speaker to listen to you summarize his or her instructions to ensure that you have understood them.

If it is not possible to confirm your understanding through summarizing or questioning, take a moment to organize your notes. Remember, it is much easier to organize your notes while the instructions are still fresh in your mind than it will be if you put if off.

Focus on Listening   **77**

Meeting INDIVIDUAL NEEDS

STUDENTS WITH SPECIAL NEEDS
To help students who may have difficulty listening and taking notes simultaneously, give them a copy of written instructions. Then, ask a volunteer to read the instructions aloud. As students listen to the volunteer reading, have them work with a helper to highlight key words and phrases and to put question marks next to confusing sections.

Critical Thinking

Analysis. Present students with a simple set of instructions in which you give both verbal and nonverbal cues. Ask students to take notes about the material they hear. Then, have students compare notes and share note-taking techniques. Discuss with students the verbal and nonverbal cues they noted, and have them share the strategies they used to analyze the cues.

What to Do	What Not to Do
Wait until the speaker pauses before you ask a question.	Do not blurt out a question while the speaker is still talking.
Ask specific questions that show you have been listening.	Do not ask vague questions such as "What are you talking about?"
Ask in a clear, loud voice.	Do not mumble the question.
Read notes back to the speaker to make sure they are correct.	Do not assume you can figure out anything you did not understand.

YOUR TURN 11 Following Oral Instructions

For this activity, work in groups of three or four students. Each of you will need several sheets of paper and a pen or pencil.

1. Draw a simple picture. Do not let anyone else in your group see it.

2. Describe your picture. Each of the other group members should listen, take notes, ask questions, then draw the picture.

3. Share your picture with the group. Discuss the similarities and differences of the pictures each group member created.

4. Complete the steps above using a picture and oral instructions from each member of the group. Then, talk about what group members learned about giving and listening to instructions.

Reference Note

For more on speaking and listening in a **group discussion,** see page 763 in the Quick Reference Handbook.

YOUR TURN 11

ANSWERS

Possible answers to step 4 follow.

4. When I give oral directions, I need to use clue words more carefully and emphasize them as I speak. When I follow oral directions, I need to ask more specific questions and read my notes back to the speaker so I can be sure I understood what I heard.

Wrap It Up

Metacognition. Ask students to answer the following question to reflect on their own listening process.

1. Do you find it difficult to follow oral instructions? Why or why not? [Students who have difficulty following oral instructions may feel they do not pay attention to verbal or nonverbal cues, they fail to take notes, or they do not ask questions. Students adept at following oral instructions will probably be successful at the above tasks.]

Then, ask students to answer the following question.

2. What three things can you do to listen more actively? [pay attention to body language, take notes, and ask specific questions]

2 *Choices*

Choose one of the following activities to complete.

▶ CROSSING THE CURRICULUM: ART

1. That Covers It Create a **cover for a "how-to" video** based on the paper you wrote. Remember that a cover should catch people's attention and give them information about the video. Include pictures, eye-catching headlines and titles, and a brief summary of the contents of the program.

▶ CAREERS

2. What Goes on in Your Mind? Do you ever wonder how your favorite author develops ideas for his or her books? Get together with two or three classmates and write a **letter** asking an author about his or her creative process. Compare the response you receive with those received by your classmates.

▶ CROSSING THE CURRICULUM: HISTORY

3. How It Was Done Choose an activity, such as mummification or shipbuilding, and find out how it was performed in an ancient civilization. Research the step-by-step process used in the activity. Create a **flowchart** of the process, including important steps and explanations. Share what you have learned with a small group of classmates.

▶ CROSSING THE CURRICULUM: SCIENCE

4. What Makes It Tick? Are you the kind of person who likes to figure out what makes things work? Choose a simple mechanical device like a doorknob or a kitchen tool, and figure out what makes it work. Explain the process in a **technical drawing,** or present a short **demonstration** explaining how this device works.

▶ CREATIVE WRITING

5. How to Create a Snicker Poetry is a form of writing that is meant to entertain or express, often through humor. A process with missed steps, or a simply ridiculous process, can be funny. Tickle someone's funny bone by writing a **humorous "how-to" poem.**

◀ PORTFOLIO

▶ ART

To get students started, bring in some sample video covers for them to use as models. Discuss how pictures and headings are designed to appeal to viewers.

▶ CAREERS

Before groups write their letters, ask members to discuss the kinds of problems they think published writers face. Next, members should think of how they might overcome these obstacles if they were professional writers. Groups may use the results of their discussions to write the letters. Tell students that their letters should include specific questions about the writers' processes and should have a polite and formal tone. Group members should work together to compose, evaluate, and revise the letter. For correct letter format refer to pp. 798–800.

Groups may present their response to the class on the overhead projector. Have each group share with the class the professional writers' strategies and similar strategies students might use in their own writing.

▶ CREATIVE WRITING

Suggest to students that they think of an ordinary, everyday process, like brushing their teeth or tying their shoes, to write about. Once they think of a process, have them write down in their notebooks metaphors or similes that describe their processes. Students may also jot down hyperboles or alliterative phrases to make their processes humorous. To create their poems, have students choose the ten best similes, metaphors, or phrases from their notes and combine them in a way that makes sense.

CHAPTER 3

Looking at Both Sides

Use this guide to create an instructional plan that suits the individual needs of your students. Assignments marked by an asterisk (*) may be completed out of class. Times given for pacing lessons are estimated. See pp. 80–81 for chapter-wide resources. Resources listed in this guide are point-of-use resources only.

Curriculum Connections

Choices *p. 115*
- Consumer Education
- Crossing the Curriculum: Art
- Speech
- Crossing the Curriculum: History

GO TO: go.hrw.com
KEYWORD: EOLang 7-3

 All resources for this chapter are available for preview on the *One-Stop Planner CD-ROM with Test Generator.* All worksheets and tests may be printed from the CD-ROM.

	Chapter Opener pp. 80–81	Reading Workshop: Reading an Advantages/Disadvantages Article pp. 82–90
DEVELOPMENTAL PROGRAM	**🕑 30 minutes** • Your Turn 1 *p. 81*	**🕑 100 minutes** • Preparing to Read *p. 82* • Reading Selection *pp. 83–85* • First Thoughts in groups *p. 86* • Advantage/Disadvantage Structure *pp. 86–87* • Your Turn 2 *p. 87* • Making Inferences: Drawing Conclusions *pp. 87–88* • Your Turn 3 *p. 88* • Test Taking Mini-Lesson *p. 90*
CORE PROGRAM	**🕑 20 minutes** • Your Turn 1 *p. 81*	**🕑 90 minutes** • Preparing to Read *p. 82* • Reading Selection *pp. 83–85* • First Thoughts *p. 86* • Advantage/Disadvantage Structure *pp. 86–87* • Your Turn 2 *p. 87* • Making Inferences: Drawing Conclusions *pp. 87–88* • Your Turn 3 *p. 88* • Vocabulary Mini-Lesson *p. 89* • Test Taking Mini-Lesson *p. 90*
ADVANCED PROGRAM	**🕑 10 minutes** • Your Turn 1 *p. 81*	**🕑 75 minutes** • Preparing to Read *p. 82* • Reading Selection *pp. 83–85* • First Thoughts *p. 86* • Advantage/Disadvantage Structure *pp. 86–87* • Your Turn 2 *p. 87* • Making Inferences: Drawing Conclusions *pp. 87–88* • Your Turn 3 *p. 88* • Vocabulary Mini-Lesson *p. 89*
RESOURCES — PRINT	• *Communications,* TP. 24, WS. p. 47	• *Alternative Readings,* Ch. 3 • *Communications,* TPs. 25, 26, WS. pp. 48–55
RESOURCES — MEDIA	• *One-Stop Planner CD-ROM*	• *One-Stop Planner CD-ROM*

TP.=Transparency   WS.=Worksheet

Writing Workshop: Writing an Advantages/Disadvantages Essay *pp. 91–110*	Focus on Viewing and Representing: Making a Documentary Video *pp. 111–114*
🕐 **210 minutes** • Topics; Purpose and Audience; Your Turn 4 *pp. 91–93* • Main Idea; Advantages and Disadvantages; Your Turn 5 *pp. 93–94* • Gather Support; Your Turn 6 *pp. 94–95* • Plan Your Essay; Your Turn 7 *p. 97* • Framework; Models; Your Turn 8* *pp. 98–101* • Evaluate and Revise *pp. 102–104* • Focus on Sentences in groups *p. 104* • Your Turn 9 *p. 104* • Proofread, Publish, and Reflect on Your Essay *pp. 105–106* • Grammar Link; Your Turn 10 *pp. 105, 106* • Test Taking Mini-Lesson *p. 107*	🕐 **75 minutes** • Identifying Stereotypes *pp. 111–112* • Your Turn 13 *p. 112* • Making a Documentary *pp. 113–114* • Your Turn 14 *p. 114*
🕐 **180 minutes** • Topics; Purpose and Audience; Your Turn 4 *pp. 91–93* • Main Idea; Advantages and Disadvantages; Your Turn 5 *pp. 93–94* • Gather Support; Your Turn 6 *pp. 94–95* • Critical-Thinking Mini-Lesson in groups *p. 96* • Plan Your Essay; Your Turn 7 *p. 97* • Framework; Models; Your Turn 8* *pp. 98–101* • Evaluate and Revise *pp. 102–104* • Focus on Sentences in groups *p. 104* • Your Turn 9 *p. 104* • Proofread, Publish, and Reflect on Your Essay *pp. 105–106* • Grammar Link; Your Turn 10 *pp. 105, 106* • Test Taking Mini-Lesson *p. 107* • Connections to Life: Comparing TV and Real Life; Your Turn 11* *pp. 108–109*	🕐 **60 minutes** • Identifying Stereotypes *pp. 111–112* • Your Turn 13 *p. 112* • Making a Documentary *pp. 113–114* • Your Turn 14 *p. 114*
🕐 **150 minutes** • Topics; Purpose and Audience; Your Turn 4 *pp. 91–93* • Main Idea; Advantages and Disadvantages; Your Turn 5 *pp. 93–94* • Gather Support; Your Turn 6 *pp. 94–95* • Critical-Thinking Mini-Lesson *p. 96* • Plan Your Essay; Your Turn 7 *p. 97* • Framework; Models; Your Turn 8* *pp. 98–101* • Evaluate and Revise *pp. 102–104* • Focus on Sentences; Your Turn 9* *p. 104* • Grammar Link; Your Turn 10 *pp. 105, 106* • Proofread, Publish, and Reflect on Your Essay *pp. 105–106* • Connections to Life: Comparing Informative TV or Video Presentations; Your Turn 12* *p. 110*	🕐 **45 minutes** • Identifying Stereotypes *pp. 111–112* • Your Turn 13 *p. 112* • Making a Documentary *pp. 113–114* • Your Turn 14 *p. 114*

• *Communications,* 🎮
  TPs. 27–30,
  WS. pp. 56–68
 • *Designing Your Writing*
	• *Media Literacy and Communication* 🎮 *Skills*
	  —*Support and Practice,* Ch. 3
	  —*A How-to Handbook*
	  —*A Teacher's Guide,* Ch. 3

• *One-Stop Planner CD-ROM* 💿	• *Media Literacy and Communication Skills* 📼 —Videocassette 1, Segment B • *One-Stop Planner CD-ROM* 💿

CHAPTER

3

Looking at Both Sides

CHAPTER OBJECTIVES

- To read a magazine article to analyze advantage/disadvantage pattern and draw conclusions

- To write an advantages/disadvantages essay

- To classify how teens are shown in the media and create a documentary video

Chapter Overview

Classifying the pros and cons of issues helps people make sound decisions. This chapter is designed to help students recognize and use methods of classification when they read, when they write, and when they view and create media. In the Reading Workshop (pp. 82–90), students analyze a magazine article that presents the advantages and disadvantages of a topic. The

Writing Workshop (pp. 91–110) guides students to write their own advantages/disadvantages essays. The Focus on Viewing and Representing helps students learn how to classify media messages. Although the three sections of the chapter can be taught independently, they also work together to give students practice classifying information from a variety of media.

Why Study Classifying Information?

Students who can group or classify information are better able to organize material and make sense of it. Classifying also helps students relate new information to what they already know by means of identifying familiar aspects in new ideas. Finally, classifying advantages and disadvantages can help students evaluate the elements of a subject and make more informed decisions.

Teaching the Chapter

Option 1: Begin with Literature

You might introduce this chapter after having students analyze the advantages and disadvantages of a character's decision or action in a drama, novel, or short story.

Afterward, introduce students to the magazine article in this chapter (pp. 83–85) and discuss how reading about the advantages and disadvantages of a topic can help readers make informed decisions. Once students are aware of writing about advantages and disadvantages, they can write their own advantages/disadvantages essays.

Option 2: Begin with Nonfiction and Writing

The Reading Workshop (pp. 82–90) introduces students to the structure of advantages/disadvantages writing. The Writing Workshop (pp. 91–110) guides students through the process of writing and revising their own advantages/disadvantages essay. The concepts introduced in these two workshops will help prepare students to examine advantages and disadvantages in fiction.

Making Connections

■ To the Literature Curriculum

Readers can evaluate the decisions of fictional characters by weighing advantages and disadvantages. For example, refer students to "Amigo Brothers" by Piri Thomas, in which two friends weigh the pros and cons of fighting fiercely when they meet in the boxing ring. The following lesson idea guides students through the process of weighing the advantages and disadvantages of a character's actions in a short story, "The No-Guitar Blues."

Lesson Idea: Weighing Advantages and Disadvantages in "The No-Guitar Blues" by Gary Soto

1. Help students identify decisions that Fausto must make. [Fausto has to decide how to get enough money to buy a guitar, whether or not to lie about the dog's whereabouts, and what to do with the twenty-dollar bill.]

2. Divide the class into groups. Ask each group to create a diagram showing the advantages and disadvantages of one decision in the story. A sample diagram is shown below.

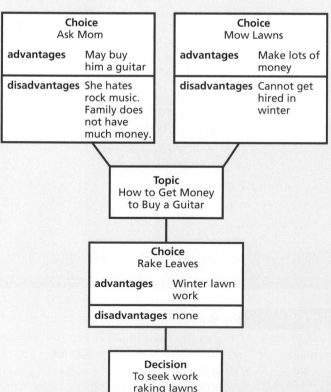

3. Once students have completed their diagrams, have group members discuss why Fausto made the choice he did. Then, suggest that students discuss whether Fausto made the right decision.

■ To Careers

Have students research a career choice that interests them and then report on its advantages and disadvantages. For example, a student interested in becoming a doctor might identify helping others, interesting work, and financial security as advantages. Disadvantages might include a long, expensive period of education; long hours; and high stress. Students might use library sources or interview someone in the field. If students conduct interviews, you may want to obtain advance permission from parents or guardians and from the parties students will contact. See also **Connections to Life** on pp. 108–110.

■ To the Community

Suggest that students apply their understanding of how to weigh advantages and disadvantages of an important issue in their community. Invite to class two speakers who have differing opinions about a community issue, such as closing a city park. One speaker should talk about the advantages of the choice and the other about the disadvantages. Then, allow students to weigh the pros and cons and make their own judgments.

■ To the Curriculum

You might have students investigate how classification systems are used to organize information in various disciplines, such as language arts, social studies, science, and mathematics. For example, literature may be categorized chronologically, by genre, or by style. Students should work in groups to identify classification systems in at least three subjects. Once students have done this, they might discuss the advantages and disadvantages of each classification method.

CHAPTER

3

Looking at Both Sides

PREVIEWING THE CHAPTER

■ The three workshops in this chapter focus on ways to classify information. They can be taught separately, but taught together, they reinforce one another and can help students develop a thorough understanding of methods of classification. After reading and writing advantage/disadvantage pieces, students will classify information presented through the medium of video. To integrate this chapter with grammar, usage, and mechanics chapters, see pp. T311A–T311B.

INTRODUCING THE CHAPTER

■ To introduce the chapter, use the Journal Warm-up, Transparency 24, in *Communications*.

VIEWING THE ILLUSTRATION

■ Ask students to describe the scene. [Two images of the same Dalmatian with a red kerchief, suspended in blue sky. The right image is upside down and rotated 180 degrees.] Invite students to identify clues that suggest the art was created by computer. [The images are precise and appear three-dimensional, yet not lifelike.] Explain how the illustration relates to the chapter's title. [Both "sides" of the dog are visible to the viewer.]

Representing. Have students prepare two sketches of an ordinary object, each from a different side or angle. Ask students to comment on the differences between the two images.

CHAPTER RESOURCES

Planning
■ *Lesson Planner,* Ch. 3
■ *ELL Strategies,* Ch. 3
■ Block Scheduling, p. T79A (this book)
■ *One-Stop Planner CD-ROM*

Practice
■ *Communications,* Ch. 3

■ *Media Literacy and Communication Skills*

Extension
■ *Designing Your Writing*

Reinforcement
■ *Communications,* Ch. 3
■ *Alternative Readings,* Ch. 3

**Reading
Workshop**

*Reading an Advantages/
Disadvantages Article*

**Writing
Workshop**

*Writing an Advantages/
Disadvantages Essay*

**Viewing and
Representing**

*Making a
Documentary Video*

W hen you walk into a supermarket, you know that similar types of foods are grouped together. For example, if you need an orange, you know that you should go to the produce section. Sorting items into different categories is known as **classification.** The supermarket organizes the items in a way that makes sense so you can find them quickly and easily.

Classification is a good way to sort not just things but also ideas. For example, when you need to make a decision, you can sort out the pros and cons, or advantages and disadvantages, of a topic.

**Informational
Text**

Exposition

YOUR TURN 1 **Understanding Classification**

On your own paper, brainstorm the pros and cons, or advantages and disadvantages, of being a seventh-grader or of having an older/younger sibling. Here is an example.

Having a Little Brother

Advantages	Disadvantages
Someone looks up to me.	Sometimes I have to baby-sit instead of being with my friends.

Compare your responses with those of another student.

GO TO: go.hrw.com
KEYWORD: EOLang 7-3

Connecting Reading and Writing **81**

Motivate

To get students thinking about classifying information, ask them how they make choices. Students may say that they think about the pros and cons of each choice and then choose the option for which the pros outweigh the cons. Ask them if they could make a more informed decision if they first read about the advantages and disadvantages of each choice. Explain that in this chapter they will weigh the advantages and disadvantages of a topic and come to their own conclusions.

ELEMENTS OF
Literature

Classifying Information in Literature. In *Elements of Literature,* First Course, see the short story "Song of the Trees" by Mildred D. Taylor, pp. 29–40, and the essay "Names/Nombres" by Julia Alvarez, pp. 145–148, for characters who must weigh advantages and disadvantages in order to make decisions.

YOUR TURN 1

To assess quickly students' ability to classify, have students review their partners' entries and put a check next to any entry that is in the wrong column.

- *Daily Language Activity Transparencies*
- *Vocabulary Workshop* and *Tests*
- *Spelling*

Evaluation and Assessment

- *Test Generator (One-Stop Planner CD-ROM)*

- *Assessment Package*
  —*Chapter Tests,* Ch. 3
  —*Chapter Tests in Standardized Test Formats,* Ch. 3
  —*Assessment Alternatives,* Ch. 3

Internet

- go.hrw.com (keyword: EOLang 7–3)

Reading Workshop

OBJECTIVES

Reading and Writing Connection

■ To read an article about the advantages and disadvantages of a topic in preparation for writing an essay

Reading Skills

■ To identify the pattern of advantage/disadvantage pieces

■ To draw conclusions based on information in an article

■ To use denotation and connotation to determine the meaning of unfamiliar words

Quotation for the Day

❝So before writing, learn to think.❞

(Nicolas Boileau-Despréaux, 1636–1711, French critic and poet)

Ask students how the quotation relates to reading and writing advantages/disadvantages essays. [Students may say that before they can write about the advantages and disadvantages of a topic, they must learn how to classify information. Others might point out that reading about and recognizing bias will help them write more balanced essays.]

TEACHING (TIP)

Preparing to Read
This section introduces advantage/disadvantage structure and drawing conclusions. Both concepts will be taught in depth on pp. 86–88. The Reading Selection **"For Girls Only?"** illustrates advantage/disadvantage structure and provides an opportunity for students to apply what they learn about drawing conclusions.

RESOURCES

Reading Workshop
Reinforcement
■ *Alternative Readings,* Ch. 3

WHAT'S AHEAD?

In this section you will read an article about the advantages and disadvantages of a topic. You will also learn how to

■ **identify the pattern of advantage/disadvantage pieces**

■ **draw conclusions based on information in an article**

Reading an Advantages/ Disadvantages Article

Would you like to attend an all-girls or all-boys school? The article on the next page investigates the advantages and disadvantages of all-girls schools. The writer's goal is to present a balanced look at the topic of single-sex schools. Once you have read about the advantages and disadvantages of all-girls schools, you can make your own decision about the topic.

Preparing to Read

READING FOCUS ➤ **Advantage/Disadvantage Structure** The author of the following article organizes her discussion of **advantages** and **disadvantages,** or pros and cons, in a certain way. As you read, watch for clues the author gives to let you know whether she is discussing an advantage or a disadvantage.

READING SKILL ➤ **Making Inferences: Drawing Conclusions** Sometimes, instead of fully explaining *every* point in an article, an author leaves some "blanks" for the reader to fill. In order to fill in these blanks, the reader must *draw conclusions*. Readers **draw conclusions** by combining the details found in an article with what they already know about the topic. As you read the following article, look for places where the author leads you to draw your own conclusions.

READING PROCESS

PREREADING
Make Predictions. Explain that readers tend to read faster and understand the material better when they have an idea of, or can predict, what they will find in a text. Have students preview the title and headings of the Reading Selection on pp. 83–85 for clues about its structure and subject matter. Ask them to write down predictions about the structure of the article and what

Read the following magazine article. In your notebook, jot down answers to the numbered active-reading questions in the shaded boxes. You will refer to the underlined words when you complete the Vocabulary Mini-Lesson on page 89.

from Junior Scholastic

FOR GIRLS ONLY?

Do girls get a better education in all-girls schools? Would you want to go to a school where there were no students of the opposite sex?

by Alexandra Hanson–Harding

1   Thirteen-year-old Maryam Zohne used to be shy. "I always used to try to sneak out of giving presentations in school," she says. In sixth grade, she never spoke up in class. Not any more. Now in the eighth grade, she is the president of the student body at her school. What made the difference? For the past two years, Maryam has gone to an all-girls public school—the Young Women's Leadership School of East Harlem, in New York City. "I feel more open," says Maryam. "The girls here are like sisters."

2   Nicole Flores, who goes to the same school, agrees. "You gain more confidence in this school," she says. "We've learned how to speak in a strong, respectful way."

3   In 1992, the American Association of University Women (AAUW) published a study called *How Schools Fail Girls*. It said that girls often do not get the same educational opportunities as boys. When boys and girls are in the same classroom, the report said, boys speak out more and teachers call on them more often to answer questions.

4   What can be done? One solution, say some experts, is to establish more single-sex public schools—such as the Young Women's Leadership School. Today, however, there are only a handful of such public schools. By contrast, there are hundreds of private and

> **1. How does the writer get your attention in the first few sentences?**

Active-Reading Questions

The purpose of the active-reading questions is to help students think about the advantage/disadvantage structure in the article and to help them draw conclusions from their reading. Use students' answers as an informal assessment of their understanding of these concepts. Possible answers follow.

ANSWERS

1.   The writer grabs the reader's attention by introducing a character and telling about the character's problem. A story is a valuable device for attracting the reader's involvement in a magazine article.

---

kind of information they expect to find in each section. [Students may say, for example, that since the title is in the form of a question, the article will probably contain more than one point of view.] Advise students that the headings may be especially useful in helping them predict information that might be included in a section.

As students read the selection, suggest that they return to their predictions to confirm or adjust them.

2. According to this paragraph, being called on in the classroom is a good thing. The reader can infer this because the fact that girls are called on less often in coed classes is presented as a negative.

3. This section describes the advantages of single-sex schools. The heading, "Yes! Single-Sex Schools Help," and words such as "good" indicate that the writer is discussing advantages.

4. The words "opposed," "against," "unconstitutional," and "discrimination" let the reader know that this paragraph discusses the disadvantages of single-sex schools.

Critical Thinking
Analyzing Problems and Solutions. Point out that problem-solution relationships lie at the heart of many persuasive texts (essays and advertisements) and some informative texts. To help students analyze the implicit problem and its possible solution in the informative article "For Girls Only?" ask the following questions:

- What problem(s) do you think inspired the author to write the article? [low test scores for girls in the subjects of math and science; lack of confidence and opportunity for girls in classrooms shared with boys]

- What is the main solution the author discusses in the article? [separate schools for girls]

- Does everyone mentioned in the article agree with the solution? Give examples from the article to support your answer.

- What solution would you offer? Explain.

---

parochial (church-related) schools just for girls or just for boys.

Changed Its Mind

5 Last month, the AAUW released a new study. It said that girls in single-sex schools tend to be more confident in traditionally male subjects such as math and science. The new study found, however, that girls in single-sex schools do not make higher test scores in those subjects.

6 As a result of this study, some people are changing their minds about the benefits of single-sex schools. As Janice Weinman of the AAUW says: "What the report says is that single-sex education is not the silver bullet [magical solution that solves a problem]."

7 Are single-sex schools a good idea—especially for girls? Or is there a better solution? Here are some of the arguments on both sides.

Yes! Single-Sex Schools Help

8 Many experts say that single-sex schools are a good thing, especially for girls. They point to studies that show that teachers tend to call on boys more and take the work of girls less seriously. "Too often, girls receive praise for how they look and how they behave rather than for

> **2.** According to this paragraph, is being called on in the classroom a good thing or a bad thing? Why do you think so?

what they accomplish and what ideas they have," says Whitney Ransome, executive director of the National Coalition of Girls Schools.

9 All-girls schools can make girls more confident at crucial times of their lives, says Ransome—especially during the middle school and high school years.

10 Maryam Zohne agrees. "This school isn't for all girls," she says. "It's for girls who want the confidence to move on in life. Some girls have the tools they need already."

> **3.** Is this section discussing advantages or disadvantages? How do you know?

11 Whitney Ransome says that all-girls schools work because, "When there are all girls in the classroom, the culture changes. You're not a second-class citizen because of your gender. . . . You're surrounded by people who look like you, think like you, and empower you."

No! Not the Solution

12 Chris Dunn, a lawyer for the New York Civil Liberties Union (NYCLU), is opposed to the idea of single-sex public schools. The NYCLU fought against the opening of the Young Women's Leadership School. Dunn says that the idea of "separate but equal" schools is unconstitutional.

> **4.** What word(s) tell you that this paragraph discusses the disadvantages of single-sex education?

READING PROCESS

READING
Make Personal Connections. Explain to students that making personal connections will help them relate what they are reading to something they already know so that they

can gain meaning from their reading. Ask students to write down one or two ways the Reading Selection on pp. 83–85 connects to their lives. [Girls may recall feeling confident on an all-girls sports team or being reluctant

"If a person can't go to a public school just because he's a boy, that's discrimination," he told JS. When the government runs schools, it needs to provide an excellent educational environment for *all* students."

13 Would the NYCLU still object if New York City opened a separate all-boys school with equal facilities? Yes, says Dunn. "If a school district has four hundred buses and they won't let white students on ten of them, that's still discrimination," he says.

> **5. Would the NYCLU object if New York City opened a separate all-boys school? Why or why not?**

14 Some educators say that single-sex schools fix only part of the problem. "What the research shows is that boys and girls both <u>thrive</u> when the elements of good education are there—elements like smaller classes, focused academic curriculum, and gender-fair instruction," says the AAUW's Janice Weinman.

The problem of unequal treat-

ment will not be solved by putting girls in all-girls classes, say these educators. The solution, they say, is to make the classroom a better place to learn for everyone. Since 95 percent of all girls in the U.S. are in mixed-sex classes, that is where the problem should be solved. 15

How? By emphasizing "<u>equality</u>, better coeducation, and an end to discrimination against girls in the classroom," says Ann Connor of the National Organization for Women (NOW). "To be a leader, you have to interact with both sexes. You have to learn to be a leader of both men and women." 16

> **6. Based on this paragraph and on what you know, are boys and girls treated differently in the classroom? Explain your answer.**

What Kind of School for You?

Students at the Young Women's Leadership School think that they are learning plenty about leadership. "I've learned to speak up for myself, voice my opinion, and not to be negative," says Melique Birks, thirteen. 17

Contrary to what students in coed classes may think, Melique does not feel that she is missing out on the chance to meet people of the opposite sex. "You're <u>focused</u> on your work during the day, and after school you can meet boys," she says. 18

Nicole Flores agrees: "The school's not responsible for your meeting boys—it's responsible for teaching you to learn." 19

Active-Reading Questions
ANSWERS continued

5. The NYCLU would object if New York City opened a separate all-boys school because the NYCLU believes that the "idea of 'separate but equal' schools is unconstitutional."

6. Students may think that boys and girls are sometimes treated differently. For example, students may have observed that sometimes boys are expected to be better than girls at math and science. Some students may think that such treatment depends on the teacher—some teachers call on boys and girls equally, while others more frequently call on boys.

to speak out in a coed classroom. Boys may recall being in a leadership role in a coed club or encouraging a female friend to speak out.] Have volunteers share their examples with the class. Then, lead students in a discussion about how making personal connections can help them better comprehend what they are reading.

First Thoughts on Your Reading

1. Is the order in which the author discusses the advantages and disadvantages in this article clear? Why or why not?

2. Now that you have read the article, what is your final decision about all-girls schools? How did you arrive at this decision?

ANSWERS
Possible answers follow.

1. The order of the advantages and disadvantages is clear. The author groups all the advantages together in one block and all the disadvantages together in another block. Headings indicate whether the text that follows discusses advantages or disadvantages. Also, within each section, clue words signal an advantage or a disadvantage.

2. Students may say that all-girls schools are not the solution. The unconstitutionality of "separate but equal" schools is a powerful dissuader—this disadvantage outweighs the advantages.

Critical Thinking

Evaluation. Reinforce the importance of structure in advantages/disadvantages writing by having students answer the following questions.

- In what ways is the author's use of advantage/disadvantage structure (block structure) effective? [clear presentation of topic; easy to distinguish advantages from disadvantages]

- In what, if any, ways is it ineffective? [seems unbalanced until reader completes entire article]

- What other approach might the author have used to present the information? How well would it have worked? [Point-by-point method—countering each advantage with a disadvantage—makes it difficult to separate advantages from disadvantages.]

READING FOCUS

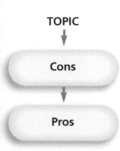

TOPIC

Cons

Pros

TIP One way to decide quickly whether the writer is going to discuss an advantage or a disadvantage is to look at any **headings** included in the piece. These headings may include **clue words** that hint at a paragraph's purpose.

Advantage/Disadvantage Structure

What Are the Pros and Cons? The purpose of advantages/disadvantages writing is to present both the advantages *and* the disadvantages of a topic so that a reader can get information to make a decision. To help the reader, the writer **classifies,** or groups, the advantages and disadvantages in a pattern that makes them easy for the reader to understand.

Many writers choose to discuss all of a topic's advantages together in one block and all of its disadvantages together in another block. Just as the drawers in your dresser separate your socks from your shirts, this block structure helps the reader separate a topic's advantages (pros) from its disadvantages (cons).

"Cluing" In How does the reader decide whether the writer is discussing an advantage or a disadvantage? One way is to look for **clue words.** Words such as *benefit, pro, positive,* and *plus* point to advantages, while words such as *drawback, con, negative,* and *downside* point to a topic's disadvantages. Look at the following sentences and decide whether the writer is discussing an advantage or a disadvantage in each one. How do you know?

> Another benefit of teaching at an all-boys school is that I have more opportunities to boost a young man's self-confidence.

> The downside to teaching boys only is that the boys miss out on the opportunity to hear girls' views on certain subjects.

Mapping the Advantages and Disadvantages Writing the ideas from an article into a graphic organizer will help you understand the relationships between those ideas. The **fishbone** is a graphic organizer you can use to list advantages and disadvantages. Notice how the sample fishbone on page 87 clearly organizes the pros and cons of the topic "coed sports."

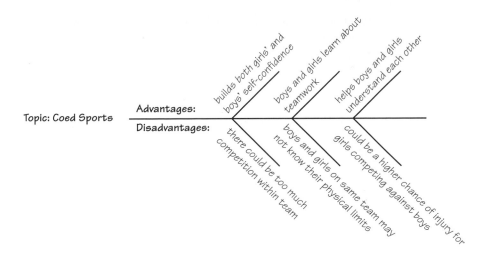

Topic: Coed Sports

Advantages:
- builds both girls' and boys' self-confidence
- boys and girls learn about teamwork
- helps boys and girls understand each other

Disadvantages:
- there could be too much competition within team
- boys and girls on same team may not know their physical limits
- could be a higher chance of injury for girls competing against boys

YOUR TURN 2 — Mapping the Advantages and Disadvantages

On your own paper, draw a fishbone organizer like the one above. Fill in the advantages and disadvantages discussed in "For Girls Only?" on pages 83–85. If you have trouble locating the advantages and disadvantages, look for clue words such as those on page 86.

Making Inferences: Drawing Conclusions

I Think . . . While reading about a topic's advantages and disadvantages, you may have to fill in information that the writer has left out. You fill in those "blanks" in the text by making *inferences*. An **inference** is an educated guess about information in the text. A **conclusion** is a type of inference based on details in the text *and* on what you already know. A conclusion applies only to the text on which it is based.

> **What you read:** Mara passed the ball to Howard, who scored the winning basket.
> + **What you already know:** I know that passing a ball and shooting a basket are things you do when playing basketball.
> _____
> **Conclusion:** Mara and Howard are playing basketball on the same team.

◁ READING SKILL

TIP A conclusion applies only to the text on which it is based. A **generalization** is an inference based on a text that applies to the world in general. From the details about Mara and Howard, you might generalize that girls and boys sometimes play basketball on the same teams.

Reading Workshop **87**

INCLUSION

To approach **Your Turn 2** in smaller steps, give each student a copy of a fishbone organizer with the lines on the top (advantages) labeled *1–3* and the lines on the bottom (disadvantages) labeled *4–6*. Then, pass out sticky notes and have students label them *1–6*. Ask a helper to read aloud the article. As students follow along, they should place in the text the notes labeled *1–3* next to where they locate advantages and the notes labeled *4–6* next to disadvantages.

Then, have students fill in their organizers by referring to their corresponding sticky notes.

YOUR TURN 2

Sample answers for students' fishbones are shown below.

TOPIC: Single-Sex Schools
Advantages:
- girls taken seriously by teachers
- can make girls more confident during the middle school and high school years
- girls empowered in single-sex classrooms—no longer second-class citizens

Disadvantages:
- single-sex schools discriminate, which is unconstitutional
- only address part of what is wrong with schools
- to be a leader, you need to be able to interact with both sexes

RESOURCES

Your Turn 2
Practice
- *Communications,* WS. p. 48

Reinforcement
- *Communications,* TP. 25, WS. p. 49

Wrap It Up

Metacognition. Ask students to reflect on their reading processes by answering the following question:

1. Which information on advantage/disadvantage structure did you find most useful?

Then, ask this question:

2. What is the purpose of advantages/disadvantages writing? [to present both aspects of a topic so that a reader can make an informed decision]

ANSWERS

Here are possible answers.

- The article states that leaders need to interact with both sexes. I know that leaders in government and in business lead people of both sexes. In coed schools, boys and girls learn to interact with one another. A coed school would help a student become a leader.

- Melique states that she focuses on schoolwork during the day, and that later on she can meet boys. When I focus on schoolwork during the day, my work is better than when I also pay attention to other things. Based on what I know and what she says, I can conclude that Melique values focusing on schoolwork during the day.

What conclusion could you draw from these lines found in "For Girls Only?" If you have trouble, use the Thinking It Through steps following the passage to help you.

> Many experts say that single-sex schools are a good thing, especially for girls. They point to studies that show that teachers tend to call on boys more and take the work of girls less seriously.

TIP Usually, the author of an expository advantages/disadvantages article like the one on pages 83–85 will not favor one side of an issue over the other. However, after hearing both the pros and the cons, most readers will like one option better than the other. For example, after reading "For Girls Only?" you may decide that the disadvantages to single-sex schools outweigh the advantages.

THINKING IT THROUGH

Making Inferences: Drawing Conclusions

▶ **STEP 1** Re-read the passage. Identify its topic and look closely at the details about the topic.

Topic: single-sex schools. The first sentence says that single-sex schools are good. The second sentence says that teachers in coed schools call on boys more.

▶ **STEP 2** Think about what you already know. What are your experiences with the topic or the details?

I know that in many of my classes, some boys are called on a lot because they raise their hands first or even shout out answers to the teachers' questions. So, in a way, boys get more attention.

▶ **STEP 3** Connect your experiences from Step 2 with the details in Step 1 to draw a conclusion about the topic.

Girls might get more attention—participate more and be taken more seriously—if there were no boys in class.

YOUR TURN 3

Making Inferences: Drawing Conclusions

Working in pairs, use the steps in the Thinking It Through above to answer the following questions about "For Girls Only?" For each question, explain what led you to your conclusion.

- Read paragraphs 15 and 16 on page 85. Which type of school would help a student become a better leader?

- Read paragraph 18 on page 85. Is Melique for or against focusing on schoolwork during the day?

READING PROCESS

EXTENDING

Connect to the World. Point out to students that in their independent reading they often draw conclusions based on details in a text and on information they already know. Ask students to read a magazine or newspaper article and write down one or two conclusions they make as a result of their reading. Students should explain how they drew their conclusions. What details from the material did they use? What did they already know about the topic?

MINI-LESSON VOCABULARY

Denotation and Connotation

Advantages/disadvantages writing has one purpose—to inform the reader by giving the facts. Even when you are reading for facts, be aware that some words can influence your feelings. In addition to a **denotation,** or dictionary definition, many words have strong *connotations*. A word's **conno-** tation includes the feelings and associations connected with that word. For example, you know the denotation of the word *leader:* someone who is in charge. The connotations of *leader* may include *power, pride, strength, role model, determination,* and *wisdom*.

THINKING IT THROUGH — Understanding Denotation and Connotation

Take a look at this example using the word *equality* from "For Girls Only?" to understand how a word's connotations can affect a reader.

Context: ". . . make the classroom a better place to learn for everyone . . . [by] emphasizing 'equality, better coeducation, and an end to discrimination against girls in the classroom.'"

▶ **STEP 1** Write down the word's **denotation.** Use your own definition, or check the word's definition in a dictionary.
Equality means "fair treatment for everyone."

▶ **STEP 2** Think about the word's **connotation.** What feelings or ideas do you associate with this word?
The word equality makes me think of freedom and fairness. In the excerpt above, it tells me girls need to be treated fairly in the classroom so they can succeed.

▶ **STEP 3** Ask yourself, "What if the author had used a synonym? What are its connotations?"
Sameness is a synonym with more negative connotations. "Emphasizing sameness" doesn't sound very attractive.

PRACTICE

Use the Thinking It Through steps above to figure out the denotations and connotations of these words from "For Girls Only?" Each word has been underlined in the article.

1. respectful (page 83) **2.** second-class (page 84) **3.** empower (page 84) **4.** thrive (page 85) **5.** focused (page 85)

MINI-LESSON VOCABULARY

Denotation and Connotation

ANSWERS

1. *Respectful* means "showing high regard or esteem for something." It makes me think of correct behavior and decency. *Polite* is a synonym with less positive connotations.
2. *Second-class* means "below the best, of an inferior status." *Second-class* makes me think of people without rights and of racism and sexism. *Inferior* is a synonym with more negative connotations.
3. *Empower* means "to give authority or power to someone." It makes me think of gaining strength, courage, and self-esteem. *Enable* is a synonym with less powerful connotations.
4. *Thrive* means "to flourish." *Thrive* makes me think of growing in a healthy way. *Prosper* is a synonym that does not create as vivid a picture in the reader's mind.
5. When people are *focused,* they are paying close attention to something. *Focused* makes me think of someone concentrating on one thing without distractions. *Concentrate* is a synonym with less positive connotations.

RESOURCES

Your Turn 3
Practice
■ *Communications*, WS. p. 50
Reinforcement
■ *Communications*, TP. 26, WS. p. 51

Vocabulary
Practice
■ *Communications*, WS. p. 52

Drawing Conclusions

When taking a reading test, you may be asked to draw conclusions about a selection. Read the following passage and the test item that follows it. How would you tackle this test question?

Last weekend Isabell's service club helped rebuild a home destroyed by floods. Over two days, the group made noticeable progress in restoring the family's home. In just a few days, six young men and women made a great difference to a family who had lost nearly everything. In addition, club members learned to work together as a team.

You can tell from the passage that the service club members

A. will help rebuild other homes in the future

B. found that teamwork can be rewarding

C. encouraged the family to participate in the rebuilding

D. helped repair other homes in the same town

TIP The answer to a conclusion question will not be in the passage word-for-word. You will have to use details in the passage and your own knowledge to figure out the correct answer.

THINKING IT THROUGH **Drawing Conclusions in a Reading Test**

▶ **STEP 1** See what information you can get from the question.

The question tells me that I need to make a decision about the service club. I should look for details in the passage.

▶ **STEP 2** Use what you know and the details from the passage to examine each answer choice.

Choice A is wrong; they may rebuild more homes, but the passage does not mention what they will do next. Choice B sounds reasonable; the passage said they learned to work together as a team and they made a difference, and I know that can feel good. Choice C is not right because there is no mention of the family working. Choice D is not supported. Other homes may have been destroyed by floods, but the passage doesn't mention other homes.

▶ **STEP 3** Choose the answer that is supported by details from the passage *and* that makes sense.

Choice B makes sense and can be supported by details in the passage. Choice B must be the answer.

Drawing Conclusions in a Reading Test
Model the think-aloud process for your students by following the steps in **Thinking It Through** to arrive at the correct answer to the sample question.

Looking Ahead to Writing

In the Writing Workshop for this chapter (pp. 91–110), students will be asked to write their own advantages/disadvantages essays. As they plan their essays, students will need to make a fishbone organizer. They may wish to refer to the fishbone organizer on p. 87 of the Reading Workshop for guidance.

Students will also need to use clue words in their essays to signal whether they are discussing an advantage or a disadvantage. Use the words in the **"Cluing" In** section on p. 86 of the Reading Workshop as well as those students come up with to create a list of clue words. Post the list in the classroom for students to refer to as they are preparing their papers.

Students may also benefit from re-reading a professional model. Direct students to the Reading Selection on pp. 83–85 as a model for their advantages/disadvantages essay.

RESOURCES

Test Taking
Practice
■ *Communications,* WS. pp. 53–55

Writing an Advantages/Disadvantages Essay

W hen you decide which electives to take, what helps you settle on fine art instead of industrial technology, or Spanish instead of band? Chances are, you investigate the advantages and disadvantages of each class to see which one better suits your needs. When you group ideas into categories, such as "advantages" and "disadvantages," you are **classifying** information.

Classifying information not only helps you make decisions, but also gives you the opportunity to help someone else make a decision. When you write about advantages and disadvantages, you provide readers with the facts they need to make well-informed decisions.

WHAT'S AHEAD?

In this workshop you will write an essay about advantages and disadvantages. You will also learn how to

■ choose and evaluate a topic
■ evaluate support
■ identify balance and bias
■ eliminate stringy sentences from your writing
■ correct run-ons when combining sentences

OBJECTIVES

■ To use the writing process to write an essay about advantages and disadvantages

■ To choose and evaluate a topic

■ To evaluate support

■ To identify balance and bias

■ To eliminate stringy sentences

■ To correct run-ons when combining sentences

Quotation for the Day

"A writer needs three things, experience, observation, and imagination, any two of which, at times any one of which, can supply the lack of the others."
(William Faulkner, 1897–1962, American novelist)

As students begin to think about topics for their essays, write this quotation on the chalkboard and point out to them that their own experiences and observations are often the best sources for topic ideas.

Prewriting

Think of Possible Topics

What Do You Know?   Finding a topic for your advantages/disadvantages essay can be a snap if you stick with what you know. Think about topics that relate to your school, hobbies, or home life. Following are more suggestions for discovering a topic for your essay.

■ Think of a time when you made a big decision. List the pros and cons that you thought about in order to make your decision.

Writing Workshop   **91**

■ Refer to **resources,** such as TV news programs, local newspapers, magazines, or the World Wide Web for current topics. Then, freewrite about the topics, answering these questions: What topics are familiar to me? Can I list these topics' advantages and disadvantages?

| KEY CONCEPT ➤

As you search, **remember that you are looking for topics with both advantages *and* disadvantages.** To help keep your essay focused and informative, you should look for topics that are specific and narrow. For example, instead of discussing the advantages and disadvantages of owning pets, investigate the advantages and disadvantages of adopting a pet from the local animal shelter.

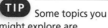

TIP Some topics you might explore are
■ a school dress code
■ summer vacations
■ after-school jobs, such as baby-sitting or paper routes
■ a particular hobby or sport

Evaluate Your Topics

Finding the Right One   Which topic will work best for this essay? To find out, ask yourself these questions: Can I think of at least three advantages and three disadvantages for this topic? Are the advantages and disadvantages balanced?

A topic with advantages or disadvantages that are too obvious will not tell your reader anything new. On the other hand, a topic that has advantages but no disadvantages (or vice versa) will result in a lopsided essay. Instead of discussing the advantages of getting regular exercise, explore the pros and cons of exercising at an indoor gym.

Consider Your Purpose and Audience

| KEY CONCEPT ➤

Discovering the "Why" and the "Who"   You know your purpose for writing this essay: to inform your audience about the advantages and disadvantages of an important topic. Since your purpose for writing is to provide information, you can assume your audience's purpose for reading will be to get information, possibly to make a decision. It is up to you to give the audience the whole picture. That means you will have to **be careful not to leave out an important advantage or disadvantage.**

The next step is to think about your audience. Ask yourself who can use information about the advantages and disadvantages of your topic to make a decision: your classmates? younger students? your teacher? After you have identified your audience, answer the following questions to help you think about their needs.

■ What will this audience need to know to get a balanced picture of the advantages and disadvantages of my topic?

■ What does this audience already know about my topic?

A Matter of Style Once you know your audience, consider your writing **style.** Different readers understand different levels of writing. For example, when writing for teachers, sentences can be longer and more complex, and your words can be more difficult. For an audience of third-graders, however, you would have to use shorter, simpler sentences and easier words.

 Evaluating Possible Topics and Considering Your Audience

Jot down several topics that you might write about in your advantages/disadvantages essay. Then, evaluate each possible topic, and choose one that is interesting and has a balance of advantages and disadvantages. Next, identify your target audience. Make notes about the audience you have identified using the questions on page 92.

State Your Main Idea

The Game Plan Tell your reader early on what your essay will discuss. A **main idea statement** gives your topic and your plan for discussing it. Your main idea statement may be a single sentence or a few sentences. Here is how one student developed his main idea statement.

Topic: extracurricular activities

Plan: to discuss the advantages and disadvantages

Main idea statement: Deciding whether or not to participate in an extracurricular activity can be a challenge. Before signing up to sing in the choir or play on the volleyball team, first consider the advantages and disadvantages of such a decision.

List the Advantages and Disadvantages

Getting the Picture You chose a topic with at least three advantages and at least three disadvantages. Making a fishbone graphic organizer like the one on the next page will help you list those advantages and disadvantages and any others you can think of for your topic. Later you will evaluate these advantages and disadvantages to see which ones you will use in your essay.

TIP Remember that your job in this essay is to present the facts so your reader can make a decision. Do not let your own feelings about the topic become part of your main idea statement.

 YOUR TURN 4

Check that students have chosen topics with a balance of advantages and disadvantages and that they have a realistic grasp of their audience's awareness of the topic.

State Your Main Idea
To give students additional examples of main idea statements, write the following statements on the chalkboard and then ask volunteers to generate others.

- Before trying out for a school play, consider whether the benefits will be worth the many hours you will spend on rehearsals and other preparation.

- When you see that cute puppy, be aware that there are several pros and cons to owning a dog.

Meeting INDIVIDUAL NEEDS

MULTIPLE INTELLIGENCES
Interpersonal Intelligence. Have students work with a partner to help them compose main idea statements. One student should state his or her topic and plan for discussing it in one or two sentences, while the other student writes down what was said. Next, have students switch roles. Students can use their statements as a basis from which to write their main idea statements.

RESOURCES

Your Turn 4
Practice
■ *Communications,* WS. p. 56

To help you assess students' graphics, have pairs of students exchange papers and then check their partners' graphics for at least three advantages and disadvantages. Next, have students write their reactions to one another's graphics on separate sheets of paper and attach them to the graphics. They might answer these questions: Do the advantages and disadvantages make sense? Should any be eliminated? Are there any that might be added?

Cooperative Learning

Examples of Support. To ensure that students understand the three types of support, give them practice in finding examples of each type. Have students form randomly selected groups of three. Provide several magazines and newspapers and ask each group to find two examples of facts, expert opinions, and anecdotes. Each member should find examples of one type of support and share results. These examples could be circled and labeled and placed in a central spot in the classroom for students to consult.

Meeting INDIVIDUAL NEEDS

INCLUSION

Provide students with individual research guidance to help them find support for their essays. Pair students with helpers to assist them in the school library or media center. Helpers can discuss with students where they might find the best information on their topics. For example, if the topic is owning a dog, a simple book on dog ownership may provide a clear explanation of pros and cons. The helper or school librarian could also locate a few sources for a student and then focus on helping the student find information within each source.

Topic : Extracurricular Activities

Advantages:
- makes lasting friendships
- helps students do better in school
- looks good on school records

Disadvantages:
- too much stress in a busy life
- may take time away from schoolwork
- possibly can't participate if you ride the bus

YOUR TURN 5 Listing Your Advantages and Disadvantages

Make a fishbone organizer like the one shown above. List at least three advantages and three disadvantages that relate to your topic.

Gather Support

Finding the Facts To help your audience make a decision about your topic, you will need to provide support for each pro and con. Support can take the form of

- **facts:** statements that can be proved true
- **expert opinions:** opinions of people with expert knowledge in a field
- **examples or anecdotes:** instances or brief stories that illustrate a point

To find support for your advantages and disadvantages, you may brainstorm examples or anecdotes from your own life that show a specific advantage or disadvantage; research in your school or public library; look in magazines, newspapers, or school databases; and interview experts for their opinions or read about what they think.

Making the Right Choices Your support will help you choose which advantages and disadvantages to keep and which to cut. Specifically, **favor advantages and disadvantages with strong support and eliminate advantages and disadvantages not supported by facts, expert opinions, or examples.**

| KEY CONCEPT →

RESOURCES

Your Turn 5
Practice
- *Communications,* WS. p. 57

Your Turn 6
Practice
- *Communications,* WS. p. 58

TIP Good support for your pros and cons requires **elaboration.** When you elaborate on a point, you extend it a little bit more, often by giving an example. See how elaboration helps the following point.

> **Advantage:** Extracurricular activities help students get to know certain teachers better.
> **Support:** I got to know Mrs. Ashton, the art teacher, better through the Art Club.
> **Elaborated Support:** Mrs. Ashton helped me work on my entry for an art contest even though I was not in her class.

Mapping It Out Study the partial **conceptual map** below on which one student recorded the support for each advantage listed in his fishbone organizer. Notice that he decided *not* to use one advantage. See if you can figure out why.

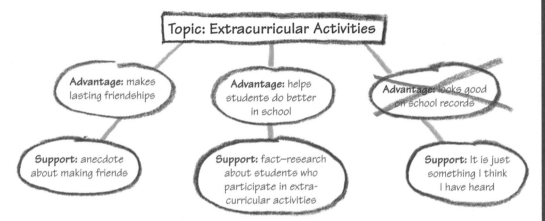

YOUR TURN 6 Choosing the Advantages and Disadvantages

- Refer to the fishbone organizer you made in Your Turn 5 on page 94. List each advantage and disadvantage in a conceptual map like the one above. Add the support you found for each advantage and disadvantage. Note whether each piece of support is a fact, an expert opinion, an example, or an anecdote.

- Look over the information and cross out any advantage or disadvantage you could not support well.

Writing Workshop **95**

Meeting INDIVIDUAL NEEDS

**MULTIPLE INTELLIGENCES
Bodily-Kinesthetic Intelligence.**
To help students check the support they have for each point, have them create a system for organizing their support notes. Suggest that they write advantages on index cards of one color and disadvantages on cards of a different color. Then they should write each support note on a plain white index card and file it behind the appropriate colored card. Students can use these card files to complete their concept maps.

YOUR TURN 6

Have students work in pairs to evaluate each other's conceptual maps. Students should check that their partners have found, and identified as to type, strong support for each advantage and disadvantage listed and that they have eliminated advantages and disadvantages that have no support.

ENGLISH-LANGUAGE LEARNERS

General Strategies. To check for and correct bias in their essays, have students highlight words that they think may be loaded words and words or phrases that they think show an opinion. Work with students individually to discuss whether the words and phrases actually do show bias and, if so, how students can revise the sentences so they are less biased.

MINI-LESSON   **CRITICAL THINKING**

Telling the Difference Between Balance and Bias

ANSWERS

1. The writer includes more discussion of the advantages of summer vacation than of the disadvantages. The writer also uses stronger support for the advantages than for the disadvantages.

2. The following words or phrases show bias: *I think, fabulous, a long,* and *a lot.*

MINI-LESSON   **CRITICAL THINKING**

Telling the Difference Between Balance and Bias

What would you think if you were reading an advantages/disadvantages essay and you came across the following passage:

> Another disadvantage of owning a pet is that it is too much work. Who wants to clean up horrible messes all the time? I can think of better things to do with my day!

You may have noticed that the writer made a decision about the topic for you. That's because the writer let his or her *bias* show. **Bias** is the writer's attitude about a topic. All writers have a bias, and in persuasive writing the bias will be clear. In informative writing, though, writers try to conceal their biases by presenting a balanced picture of their topic.

To check for balance in your essay, look for a roughly equal number of advantages and disadvantages. Also, check your support. Balance may be lacking if you have included strong support for the disadvantages but only weak support for the advantages.

Also, read your writing aloud and listen to the **voice,** the way the writing sounds. Your writing voice can reveal your bias. For example, if you hear many sentences beginning with *I think* or *I prefer,* you are trying too hard to push the reader toward your opinion. Another element of voice is your choice of descriptive words. **Loaded words** are words charged with positive or negative meanings, such as *worn-out, disastrous, super,* or *incredible.* Eliminate opinion words and loaded words to keep your writing balanced.

PRACTICE

Read the following essay excerpt about the pros and cons of a long summer vacation, and answer the questions below the excerpt.

> I think summertime is fabulous. Children and parents can use a long vacation to participate in educational activities. Every summer, my family and I learn a lot about our city's history and culture.

> Sometimes, over a summer, students forget what they learned during the last school year. When school starts, teachers have to refresh the students' memories.

1. Find two ways in which the writer's discussion of the advantages and disadvantages of summer vacation is unbalanced.

2. Jot down the words or phrases in the passage that show bias.

RESOURCES

Critical Thinking	**Your Turn 7**
Practice	**Practice**
■ *Communications,* WS. p. 59	■ *Communications,* WS. p. 60

Plan Your Essay

Arranging Information   When you write your essay, should you discuss the advantages or the disadvantages first? If a topic has obvious advantages or disadvantages, you may choose to discuss what the reader is familiar with first. Your reader will want to read the entire essay to find out what he or she *does not* know. **The key point is to discuss *all* the advantages together and *all* the disadvantages together.** These separate chunks of information make it easier for the reader to navigate your essay.

 KEY CONCEPT

Order in the Court   Get organized by jotting down the advantages and disadvantages in the order in which you would like them to appear in your essay. In the example below, notice how one writer organized the advantages and disadvantages of his topic.

Order of My Essay

I'll discuss the advantages of extracurricular activities first because they are more familiar to my audience.

Advantages	Disadvantages
1. helps students do better in school (a strong advantage with good impact—will grab the reader's attention)	1. too much stress in a busy life (begin with an unexpected disadvantage—this is unexpected because the reader may not think this is stressful)
2. makes lasting friendships (put second—not as strong as first advantage)	2. possibly can't participate if you ride the bus (place second—has less impact on reader)

YOUR TURN 7   Organizing Your Essay

Answer the following questions. Use the information from the graphic organizer you created for Your Turn 6 on page 95.

- Will I discuss advantages or disadvantages first? Why?
- In what order will I discuss each advantage and disadvantage *within* the paragraphs? Why is this a good order?

COMPUTER TIP

You may need to try several different orders for the advantages and disadvantages in your essay before you find the order that makes the most sense. To make your job easier, type your prewriting notes into a word-processing program. Then, use the program's cut and paste commands to try out different orders for your advantages and disadvantages. When you finally decide on an order, you can use the prewriting notes document to help you write your first draft.

YOUR TURN 7

Assess students' responses by checking that their arrangements make sense and will lead to coherent paragraphs.

Timesaver

To save time assessing students' understanding of the framework, ask them to highlight their main idea statements. Then, have them select pens or pencils of two different colors and underline each advantage with one color and each disadvantage with the other. Next, have them label the various parts of their essays in the right-hand margin in the manner shown in **A Writer's Model** on page 99.

Writing

Advantages/Disadvantages Essay

Framework	Directions and Explanations

Introduction

- Attention-grabbing opening
- Main idea statement

To grab reader interest, give your essay a **title** that creatively and accurately reflects your topic. Include an **engaging quotation** or piece of **dialogue** that makes the reader curious about your topic. In a **main idea statement**, state your topic and inform readers that you plan to discuss advantages and disadvantages. This statement may be one sentence or more.

Body

- *First paragraph:*
  Advantage (or disadvantage) #1
  Support for #1
- *Second paragraph:*
  Advantage (or disadvantage) #2
  Support for #2 and so on
- *Third paragraph:*
  Disadvantage (or advantage) #1
  Support for #1

  and so on

For each paragraph, be sure to

- clearly state and explain the advantage or disadvantage
- support the advantage or disadvantage with a fact, an expert opinion, or an anecdote
- **elaborate** by extending your support with examples

Conclusion

- Restatement of an advantage and a disadvantage

Pick a strong advantage and a strong disadvantage from the body of your paper. **Restate both** in a way that allows your reader to draw his or her own conclusions about the topic. **Do not include your opinion.**

YOUR TURN 8

Drafting Your Advantages/ Disadvantages Essay

It is your turn to draft an advantages/disadvantages essay. As you write, refer to the framework above and the Writer's Model on page 99.

RESOURCES

Writing	Your Turn 8
Writing Prompts	**Practice**
■ *Communications,* TP. 27, WS. p. 61	■ *Communications,* TP. 28, WS. p. 62

A Writer's Model

The final draft below closely follows the framework for an advantages/disadvantages essay on the previous page.

To Join or Not to Join?

"Hey, Juan, did you hear about the new multicultural club? Why don't you come with us?"

"I don't know—I have to finish my homework, practice the saxophone, *and* do my chores. It sounds like a great club, but I already have so much to do! I'll have to get back to you about it."

Many students are overwhelmed by all the things they have to do. Can students juggle their time between school, home, friends, and extracurricular activities such as sports or clubs? Deciding whether or not to participate in an extracurricular activity can be a challenge. Before signing up to sing in the choir or play on the volleyball team, first consider the advantages and disadvantages of such a decision.

Participating in extracurricular activities has many advantages. Students are successful when they participate in many activities. They do well in their classes and feel more connected to school. Research shows that students in extracurricular activities have better attendance and grades. Research also shows that these students have higher goals for their education after high school.

Extracurricular activities also help students make new friends and lasting relationships. I met my best friend when we were on the YMCA swim team. We were both in the eight-and-under age group, and we swam on the same relay team. Even though we became friends a long time ago, we are still close today.

While these activities have many advantages, students should consider the negative side as well. One drawback to participating in extracurricular activities is the stress it

(continued)

Attention-grabbing opening

Main idea statement

Advantage #1

Support (fact)

Advantage #2

Support (anecdote)

Disadvantage #1

Connecting Reading and Writing

Remind students that in the Reading Workshop on pp. 82–90 they learned that writers often leave out information so that readers have to draw conclusions based on details from the text and what they already know. Ask students to identify places in **A Writer's Model** where they filled in "blanks" in the text by drawing conclusions. Students should state their conclusions and explain what details in the text and what information they already knew helped them draw these conclusions. [Here are some possible conclusions students can draw from **A Writer's Model:** (1) The author thinks that having higher goals for education after high school is a good thing. (2) The author thinks that lasting friendships are important for students. (3) Students who are not good at budgeting their time will not do as well in school if they have too many extracurricular activities.]

(continued)

can add to a student's life. Extracurricular activities can be too much for students who do not practice good time management. Students need to be good at budgeting their time between different activities, such as homework, instrument practice, and sports. Kathleen Glenn Doyle, a family therapist, says that a child needs a healthy balance between structured time (time spent in class or in extracurricular activities) and free time (time spent with friends or family or time to unwind).

Support (expert opinion)

Disadvantage #2

Another downside to extracurricular activities involves transportation. What if you ride the bus to school, or a parent picks you up right after school? Some clubs or sports meet before or after school. This situation limits students' extracurricular choices to those outside of school and closer to home. A few of my classmates joined the school's multicultural club. They later discovered that it met after school. These students dropped out of the club after the first meeting because they had to catch their buses.

Support (anecdote)

Restatement of advantage and disadvantage

Only you can decide if extracurricular activities are right for you. Activities outside of school can help you be successful in many areas of your life. However, you need good time-management skills to avoid stress that comes with a busy life. Are you up for a challenge?

FOR BETTER OR FOR WORSE

FOR BETTER OR FOR WORSE © Lynn Johnston Productions Inc./Dist. by United Feature Syndicate, Inc.

A Student's Model

Jenna Arndt, a student at Labay Middle School in Houston, Texas, wrote about the advantages and disadvantages of being a teenager. Below are excerpts from her essay.

Advantages and Disadvantages of Being a Teenager

. . . One significant asset of being a teen is having fewer worries. "When I was a teenager, I didn't have the family's needs to take care of," claims my uncle Bob Arndt. "I also didn't have bills to pay." Having fewer of these problems to worry about results in more overall free time, extra-curricular activities, and additional time to spend with friends. When I asked my mother and brother if they would like to ride bikes, my brother immediately agreed to join. My mother, on the other hand, shook her head no because she was "much too busy sorting out the bank books." Besides having to worry about paying the bills, adults constantly have to worry about how much they spend. They are usually very resourceful shoppers, so as not to spend more money than they need to. Having fewer worries is a definite plus of being a teenager.

Although there are benefits of being a teenager, there are also drawbacks. One certain disadvantage is the fact that we get fewer privileges than the average adult. One of the significant privileges teens miss out on is voting. Not being able to vote is like being blocked from the political world. Because teens have not been introduced to politics sooner, many make mistakes when they *can* vote. Another privilege that the younger teens miss out on is driving. Since I am not able to drive, I constantly have to bother my parents. Just the other night I had to get to soccer practice. With my father at work and my mother at a party, I was in a tight spot. I had to wait until my father arrived home and was over a half hour late. Having fewer privileges is definitely a minus to being a teenager. . . .

TIP Jenna used the acronym SCORE to support and elaborate on her ideas. SCORE stands for *source/statistic, compare, outcome, relate,* and *example.*

Source

Outcome
Relate

Example

Compare

Outcome

Relate

Connecting Reading and Writing

Before students begin reading **A Student's Model,** review the material on clue words in the **"Cluing" In** section on p. 86 of the Reading Workshop. Then, as students read the model, have them look for clue words that signal whether the writer is discussing advantages or disadvantages. [Clue words are *one significant asset* and *drawbacks.*] Students can then check their own essays to make sure they have used words that make it clear whether they are discussing advantages or disadvantages.

TEACHING **TIP**

▸**Elaboration**
Peer reviewers can use a questioning strategy to check for sufficient elaboration in their partners' essays. Have them look for places in a paper that lead them to ask *How?* or *Why?*

When a question arises, students should check whether the rest of the sentence or a following sentence answers it. If not, students should write the question word in the margin of their peer's paper. When students are revising, they can add a sentence or sentences to answer the question.

Evaluating Student Writing
The ancillary *Assessment Alternatives* contains a variety of assessment forms, including Inventories and Evaluation Forms and rubrics: Six-Point Scales, Four-Point Scales, and Six Trait Scales.

Revising

Evaluate and Revise Content, Organization, and Style

Play It Again, Sam   As you evaluate your own essay or a peer's, make sure to read the essay twice. In the first reading, keep an eye out for content and organization problems, using the guidelines below. During your second reading, focus on strengthening each sentence by using the guidelines on page 103.

▶ **First Reading: Content and Organization**   Use the following chart to evaluate and revise your essay so the advantages and disadvantages of your topic are clear to your reader.

Guidelines for Self-Evaluation and Peer Evaluation		
Evaluation Questions	**Tips**	**Revision Techniques**
❶ Does the introduction include a main idea statement?	**Circle** the main idea statement.	If needed, **add** a sentence or two to state the topic and explain that the topic's advantages and disadvantages will be discussed.
❷ Are all the advantages together? Are all the disadvantages together?	**Put a star** next to each advantage and **put a check mark** next to each disadvantage.	**Rearrange** the advantages and disadvantages so that all the advantages are together and all the disadvantages are together.
❸ Is each advantage and disadvantage explained and supported?	**Highlight** the explanation and support for each advantage and disadvantage.	**Elaborate** on advantages and disadvantages with facts, anecdotes, or expert opinions.
❹ Does the conclusion include a restatement of both an advantage and a disadvantage?	**Put brackets** around the restated advantage and disadvantage in the conclusion.	**Add** a restatement of the strongest advantage and disadvantage from the essay, if needed.
❺ Does the essay present a balanced discussion of the topic?	**Put exclamation points** next to statements of opinion and biased words. Count the advantages and disadvantages.	**Delete** personal opinions and biased language. If necessary, **add** more advantages or disadvantages.

RESOURCES

Revising
Practice
■ *Communications,* TPs. 29, 30, WS. pp. 63, 64, 65

ONE WRITER'S REVISIONS Study this revision of an early draft of the essay on pages 99–100.

> Another ~~really big~~ downside to extracurricular activities involves transportation. What if you ride the bus to school, or a parent picks you up right after school? Some clubs or sports meet before or after school. This ~~pitiful~~ situation limits students' extracurricular choices to those outside of school and closer to home. A few of my classmates joined the school's multicultural club. They later discovered that it met after school. *These students dropped out of the club after the first meeting because they had to catch their buses.*

delete

delete

elaborate

Responding to the Revision Process

1. Why do you think the writer cut out words in the first and fourth sentences?
2. Why do you think the writer added a sentence to the passage? How does it improve the passage?

> **Second Reading: Style** Now, take a look at your sentence style. Your readers can become confused if you include long, drawn-out sentences, called **stringy sentences.** Improve your style by eliminating stringy sentences from your writing.

When you evaluate your essay for style, ask yourself whether your writing contains any long sentences made up of strings of ideas. As you re-read your essay, draw a wavy line under each sentence that connects more than two ideas using *and, but, or,* or *so.* If necessary, break one or more stringy sentences into separate sentences. The Focus on Sentences on the next page can help you learn to revise stringy sentences.

PEER REVIEW

As you evaluate a peer's essay, ask yourself the following questions:

- Which advantages and disadvantages were presented clearly? Which were not?
- How many advantages and disadvantages were discussed?

Responding to the Revision Process
ANSWERS

1. The writer eliminated the words "really big" and "pitiful" because they show bias.

2. Adding a specific example to the anecdote provided strong support for transportation difficulties as a disadvantage to participating in extracurricular activities.

Meeting
INDIVIDUAL
NEEDS

LEARNERS HAVING DIFFICULTY
Some students may have difficulty differentiating between the acceptable uses of the conjunction *and* (to connect compound subjects and verbs or parts of speech such as adjectives, adverbs, and prepositions) and its use to connect several ideas in a stringy sentence. Write the following sentences on the chalkboard.

- Luis <u>and</u> Jeff ride the subway to school.

- Luis gets off <u>and</u> runs part of the way.

- Both are athletic <u>and</u> studious.

Explain that these are acceptable uses of the word *and.* Suggest that students check that the word *and* is used in one of the acceptable ways shown above. If not, have them see if it is a stringy sentence that requires revision. You may wish to have students work with partners.

Focus on Sentences

Stringy Sentences

The reader of an advantages/disadvantages essay should not have to pick apart sentences to get to the meat of the topic. Having many ideas in a sentence connected with *and, but, or,* or *so* results in a **stringy sentence.** Stringy sentences don't give the reader a chance to pause before each new idea. One way to fix a stringy sentence is to break it up into separate sentences as in the example below.

> **Stringy:** I have to finish cleaning my room so we'll have to wait to go to a movie, but I will call you when I'm done.

> **Revised:** I have to finish cleaning my room, so we'll have to wait to go to a movie. I will call you when I'm done.

TIP When you break apart a stringy sentence, you may need to add punctuation or a word to make the new sentence clear.

ONE WRITER'S REVISIONS

I met my best friend when we were on the YMCA swim team, and we were both in the eight-and-under age group, and we swam on the same relay team.

Responding to the Revision Process

How did breaking the stringy sentence above into two parts improve the flow of the writing?

YOUR TURN 9
Evaluating and Revising Your Advantages/Disadvantages Essay

- First, evaluate and revise the content and organization of your essay, using the guidelines on page 102.
- Next, use the Focus on Sentences above to see if you need to revise any stringy sentences in your essay.
- If a peer evaluated your essay, think carefully about each of your peer's comments as you revise.

RESOURCES

Focus on Sentences
Practice
- *Communications,* WS. p. 66

Publishing
Extension
- *Designing Your Writing*

Grammar Link
Practice
- *Communications,* WS. p. 67

Proofread Your Essay

Striving for Perfection Avoid including any errors in the final draft of your essay. Remember, your goal is to inform the reader. Edit your essay to eliminate grammar and spelling errors. Enlist the help of a peer to read your essay and check for mistakes.

Reference Note
For more on **proofreading**, see page 13.

For more on **proofreading**, see page 13.

Grammar Link

Correcting Run-ons When Combining Sentences

An **independent clause** expresses a complete thought and can stand alone as a sentence. However, when you identify a pair of advantages or disadvantages, you may find that you want to combine sentences. Be careful, though. Combining two sentences without proper punctuation or a conjunction results in a **run-on sentence.**

Run-on: One benefit of bringing your own lunch to school is that you have more control over what you eat another benefit is that you may save money.

You can correct a run-on sentence by inserting a semicolon or a comma and a conjunction between the independent clauses.

One benefit of bringing your own lunch to school is that you have more control over what you eat**;** another benefit is that you may save money.

One benefit of bringing your own lunch to school is that you have more control over what you eat**, and** another benefit is that you may save money.

PRACTICE

Decide whether each sentence below is a run-on sentence. If it is a run-on, revise it by inserting a semicolon or a comma and a conjunction in the correct place. If the sentence is not a run-on, write C on your paper.

Example:
1. The bell rings at noon the students fill the cafeteria.
1. *The bell rings at noon; the students fill the cafeteria.*

1. I start to smell cafeteria food my stomach begins to growl.
2. I packed a big and nutritious lunch.
3. We have only twenty minutes for lunch I eat very quickly.
4. The cafeteria serves fresh fruit and sandwiches until they sell out.
5. Lunch is fun I enjoy spending the time with my friends.

For more information and practice on **punctuating independent clauses,** see page 618.

For more information and practice on **punctuating independent clauses,** see page 618.

TEACHING   TIP

Correcting Run-ons when Combining Sentences

Tell students not to connect two independent clauses with a semicolon unless the ideas in the clauses are closely related. Only then will a sensible compound sentence result. Write the following sentence on the chalkboard.

The characters in the sitcom were farmers this comedy appeared on TV for the first time in the 1950s.

Point out that ideas in these independent clauses are not closely related enough to become a compound sentence. Each should stand alone in a separate sentence.

Grammar Link

Correcting Run-ons when Combining Sentences

ANSWERS

1. I start to smell cafeteria food, and my stomach begins to growl.
2. C
3. We have only twenty minutes for lunch; I eat very quickly.
4. C
5. Lunch is fun, and I enjoy spending the time with my friends.

106   Exposition: Looking at Both Sides

TEACHING TIP

Publish Your Essay

If students submit handwritten final drafts, remind them to write legibly in either cursive or manuscript style. Illegibly written essays are distracting and confusing to readers. Encourage students to have a peer read over their final copies to check that they are legible.

TEACHING TIP

Reflect on Your Essay

When students review their portfolios, have them look for consistent patterns of errors in grammar, usage, and mechanics and for style problems. Then, ask them to create a T-chart of strengths and weaknesses in their writing and to think of a plan to improve their writing. For example, they can use a dictionary or spellchecking feature to improve their spelling, a thesaurus to find vivid verbs, and a peer editor to improve punctuation.

YOUR TURN 10

You may wish to have students submit their answers to the **Reflect on Your Essay** questions with their final drafts.

Wrap It Up

Metacognition. Ask students to reflect on their essays and to answer the following question:

Did you find it difficult to avoid bias in your essay? Why or why not?

TIP   Before you make design decisions, such as adding boldface heads, check with your teacher to be sure that your choice is acceptable.

PORTFOLIO

Designing Your Writing

Boldface Heads   In an advantages/disadvantages essay, it is sometimes hard for readers to tell whether you are discussing the advantages or the disadvantages of a topic. To help readers, you can use **boldface heads** that include clue words.

Advantages   The Pros of Participating in Extracurricular Activities
Disadvantages   Why You Should Not Join

Publish Your Essay

Sounding the Trumpets   It is time to share your work with an audience. Try one of these ideas.

■ Add your essay to a class collection of advantages/disadvantages pieces, and post the collection on a school bulletin board or Web page. Invite students and teachers to view your class's essays.

■ Make a quick-reference booklet for readers. Fold a piece of paper in half. On one side, print the advantages from your essay. On the other side, print the disadvantages.

Reflect on Your Essay

Building Your Portfolio   We all learn from our experiences. Reflecting on your advantages/disadvantages essay gives you a chance to think about what you wrote and how you wrote it.

■ What was the strongest support in your essay? Why?

■ How did you find the best topic ideas for your essay?

■ Review your writing portfolio. What strengths and weaknesses do you notice? Set goals to use your writing strengths and improve upon your weaknesses in future assignments.

YOUR TURN 10   Proofreading, Publishing, and Reflecting on Your Essay

■ Correct grammar, usage, and mechanics errors in your essay.

■ Publish your essay so that others can learn more about your topic.

■ Answer the Reflect on Your Essay questions above. Record your responses in your learning log, or include them in your portfolio.

Explaining Advantages and Disadvantages for Tests

An essay test may ask you to discuss the advantages and disadvantages of a specific topic. Some tests may ask you to discuss what is good and bad about a topic. "The good points and bad points" is another way of saying "the advantages and disadvantages." How would you respond to the prompt to the right from a writing test?

Your school is considering adding girls' field hockey to its athletic program. Write an essay for your principal that reports the good points and bad points of adding a new sport to the school's current athletic program. Include solid support for each advantage and disadvantage you discuss.

THINKING IT THROUGH

Explaining Advantages and Disadvantages for Tests

▶ **STEP 1** Analyze the test prompt to identify the

- topic [the good and bad points of adding a new sport to the school athletic program]
- audience [the school principal]
- format [an essay]

▶ **STEP 2** To find out what you know about the topic, ask yourself the following questions.

- Have I seen or read anything positive or negative about the topic on TV or in magazines?
- What do I know about the pros and cons from firsthand experience?
- What are some of the good and bad things about the topic that I can figure out for myself? (**MoTiV**ate yourself to find the pros and cons by thinking about **m**oney, **t**ime, and hidden **v**alues relating to the topic.)

In a fishbone organizer, jot down the good and bad points of the topic.

▶ **STEP 3** Use an outline or a conceptual map to organize your good and bad points. Support the points with examples or anecdotes from your own experiences or experiences of people you know.

▶ **STEP 4** Write your essay. Then, verify that you have supported each good point and bad point, and check your essay for correct grammar and spelling.

RESOURCES

Test Taking
Practice
- *Communications*, WS. p. 68

Connections to Life

Comparing "TV Life" to "Real Life"

The classification skills you learned by writing an advantage/disadvantage essay can help you with many other types of writing and thinking. For example, comparing and contrasting also requires you to place information into two categories. In the following activity, instead of pointing out pros and cons, you will examine similarities and differences between life on television and life in the real world.

It Looks Like . . . What you watch on television is not real life. That may sound obvious, but it is an important point for you to remember as a knowledgeable, critical viewer of television. What you watch on television is created by people who choose *what* activities and events to show and *how* to show them.

For example, think of hospitals on television. TV hospitals are exciting places brimming with extremely young and attractive doctors and patients. These TV hospitals might not match your own experience of hospitals, where perhaps you found that you spent a lot of time waiting, that most of the patients were older, and that your doctors were no more attractive, on average, than anyone else. On the other hand, perhaps you have never been in a hospital. TV hospitals might have shaped your idea of what a hospital is like.

Get Real This is the question: Is TV life realistic? You may get many answers to this question. People have different **points of view,** or ways of seeing "real life," so people also have different ideas about whether events on TV are realistic. After all, everyone has had different experiences and ways of doing things. Your experience with hospitals may be limited to your trip to the emergency room of a small community hospital. Perhaps you know someone who volunteers at a large city hospital (with many young interns) and sees more of what goes on behind the scenes. *Your* ideas are based on *your* experiences, just as your friend's ideas are based on his or her experiences.

Call It As You See It To explore the differences between TV life and real life, you will compare how an activity such as doing homework or eating dinner looks on TV with how it happens in your own life.

In the example on the next page, one student compared a classroom discussion on TV to classroom discussions from his own experiences. The student watched a television program and made a Venn diagram based on what he saw. On the left side, he recorded how the activity looked on TV. On the right side, he recorded how the activity looks in his class. In the center, he listed similarities between the two. The student used the information in the diagram to make a decision about how realistic the TV activity was.

Program: Junior High Blues   Activity: a classroom discussion

TV   Similarities   My Experiences

- The students sat in neat rows.
- All students paid attention.
- All students raised their hands.
- Every student that spoke sounded smart.

- Some students get really involved during discussions.
- Most students raise their hands and wait to be called on.
- Some students add something intelligent to a discussion.

- We sit in grouped tables.
- Not all students participate in discussions.
- Some students shout out comments during a discussion.

The class discussion on TV was not realistic. It was too smooth and orderly. While my class does have good discussions, sometimes we are not as focused as the show's class, and we do not always raise our hands.

YOUR TURN 11 — Comparing an Activity on TV to an Activity in Your Life

Pick an everyday activity or event from a TV show and think about what it looks like. What point of view about that activity is reflected? Next, think about what that same activity looks like in your own life, from your point of view. (You should choose an activity you are comfortable sharing.) In a journal make a Venn diagram like the one above to compare the TV activity to your own experience. Then, answer the following questions in a **journal entry.**

- Was the activity portrayed on TV in a realistic way? Explain.

- Remember that someone chooses the way you see things on TV. Why do you think the show portrayed the activity as it did?

Meeting INDIVIDUAL NEEDS

ADVANCED LEARNERS
Remind students that sometimes point of view must be inferred. Using the notes in the Venn diagram on this page, discuss with students the perspectives or biases of the TV producer of *Junior High Blues* and those of the student viewer. [Students may say that the somewhat unrealistic version of school in the TV program is probably a sign that the producer has not been in school for many years. The student's view is based on his or her experience of school today.]

YOUR TURN 11

Some students may not have access to television at home. You can re-create a similar assignment by substituting magazine or newspaper advertisements that depict an activity.

You can assess students' understanding by asking them to share with the class their responses to the following question: *Why is what you watch on television not realistic, even though it appears to be?* [Possible responses: It can never be the viewer's own experience; real life has to be altered on TV to move a plot forward.]

Connections to Life

Comparing Informative TV or Video Presentations

When you compare and contrast, you place information into categories, much as you organized your advantages/disadvantages essay. Comparing and contrasting requires you to look at the similarities and differences between two subjects. To compare two informative television or video presentations, you might use the following points of comparison:

Video: What do you see? Do the producers include documentary (or actual) footage, animation (cartoons), or still photography? Does the program use actors in dramatizations (pre-scripted scenes)?

Audio: From whose **point of view** is the "talk" delivered? Is there an unseen narrator, or do people on-screen do the talking? How is music used?

Overall Effect: How do the audio and video add up? Does the program succeed in informing? Does it have any other purposes or goals besides informing?

Study the following comparison.

Bugs are everywhere, even on your TV screen. Two good television programs about bugs are "The Giant Bug Invasion!" (*Kratt's Creatures*, 1995) and *Insect* (Eyewitness Video, 1994). Each program uses different techniques, resulting in different overall effects.

Insect features rapid cuts of stills, animation, and documentary footage. The producers used 3-D animation. These visuals force the viewer to look at the insect world in a fresh, new way. For the audio, narrator Martin Sheen stays off-screen and remains in the background, accompanied by soothing background music.

Like *Insect*, "The Giant Bug Invasion!" uses rapid editing to present documentary footage of bugs. The program entertains as it informs by mixing facts with funny scenes involving the hosts. Music plays a big role. Different styles of upbeat dance music accompany each image, creating an energetic mood.

Both programs are informative and highly entertaining.

YOUR TURN 12 — Comparing Informative TV or Video Presentations

View two informative TV or video presentations about the same subject, and make notes about the audio and video elements used in each. Then, write a comparison-contrast essay like the one above.

Making a Documentary Video

You are watching a TV show when one scene makes you do a doubletake. It shows a school hallway full of teenagers. At first it seems normal, but then you notice something: These students do not look like the students at your school. First, they seem older. They are also gorgeous and dressed in the trendiest clothes. In fact, these "students" do not look like students at all.

Is this portrayal of teenagers typical of what you see on TV and in movies or magazines? Are the teens you see in the media like you, your friends, or the people you see at school? How realistically do the media portray groups of people? You will answer this question by examining how TV classifies teenagers, just as you classified advantages and disadvantages in your essay.

Identifying Stereotypes

The way groups of people are portrayed by the media is often *not* realistic. More often, what we see on TV and in movies or magazines are *stereotypes*. **Stereotypes** are limited, fixed ideas about groups of people. For instance, the media often imply that all teens can be classified as one of a few "types." Some of these types are

- the bully
- the popular kid
- the troublemaker
- the lonely, sensitive kid
- the "good kid"
- the jock
- the outcast
- the brain

What is the purpose of media stereotypes? Stereotypes are a kind of shortcut, a quick and easy way to introduce the characters in

WHAT'S AHEAD?

In this section you will make a video about how teens are shown in the media. You will also learn how to

- identify stereotypes
- classify the way teens are shown
- create a documentary video

TIP Think of a TV or movie character who fits one of these "types."
? What makes that character a stereotype?

OBJECTIVES

- To create a documentary video about how teens are shown in the media
- To identify stereotypes
- To classify the way teens are shown

Quotation for the Day

"There's nothing the world loves more than a ready-made description which they can hang on to a man, and so save themselves all trouble in future."

(W. Somerset Maugham, 1874–1965, English novelist and playwright)

Copy the quotation on the chalkboard. Have students write journal entries explaining what they think this quotation means and how it might relate to stereotypical roles in the media. For example, students might say that ready-made descriptions, while easy to grasp, actually leave out individual and cultural diversity. In the media, this simplistic way of portraying people can misinform by passing these descriptions off as real and so create stereotypes.

RESOURCES

Focus on Viewing and Representing
Practice
- *Media Literacy and Communication*
  Skills
  —*Support and Practice,* Ch. 3
  —*A How-to Handbook*

Teaching Notes
- *Media Literacy and Communication*
  Skills
  —*A Teacher's Guide,* Ch. 3

To help students stay aware of media stereotyping, have a student who is especially knowledgeable about computers input the rating scale for stereotypes and a chart like the one on this page for *Jimmy's World*. Throughout the school year, have students continue to record their observations and ratings of characters on the form. You may occasionally print out the form for students to discuss.

TEACHING TIP

Classifying TV Teens
To explore this topic further, you may want to use the videocassette that comes with this program. It contains video segments that students can use for this activity.

YOUR TURN 13

Ask volunteers to use the charts to give a short presentation of their responses to the TV show. Decide with the class if the specific details support the conclusions about the characters.

TIP To evaluate the purposes and effects of stereotypes in TV shows or movies, discuss these questions with your classmates. When is it all right to use stereotypes? When is it not all right? How do media stereotypes influence viewers? What are the effects of having stereotypes in media?

a TV show or movie. Viewers quickly recognize the jock, the brain, and the bully in a typical TV or movie classroom scene. When showing students in stereotypical roles, the media are saying, "You know people like these." Real people, however, are well-rounded and much more complex than stereotypes. For example, a real teen can have a sense of humor, be intelligent, *and* rule the basketball court at the same time.

Many TV and movie characters fall somewhere between the stereotype and the complex people you know in real life. Think about rating TV and movie characters on a scale such as this one.

1 2 3 4 5 6 7 8 9 10

| Stereotypical | Less Stereotypical | More Complex | Realistic |

You may give a "one" to the "brain" character who wears glasses, always carries books, and does homework for all the other students. On the other hand, you may give a "seven" to the "bully" character who is occasionally kind. A "ten" would go to the character who seems real to you—like someone you might know.

YOUR TURN 13 Classifying TV Teens

Watch one or two TV shows with several teenage characters. If possible, record the shows on a VCR as you watch; you will use the recording in Your Turn 14. As you watch the shows, decide which characters are stereotypes and which are more complex—like real teenagers. Use a scale like the one above to rate the characters. Record your observations in a chart like the one below.

TV Show: Jimmy's World

Character	Rating and Type of Character	Why I Think So
Steve	1—stereotype (a "jock")	Steve's attitude, his muscles, and the fact that he wore sweats all the time made him a stereotype. Not all athletes look like athletes, have an attitude, and always wear sweats.
Ling	9—well-rounded character	Ling was both smart and popular. She also had friends from several different groups.

112 Chapter 3 **Exposition:** Looking at Both Sides

RESOURCES

Your Turn 13
Practice and Reinforcement

■ *Media Literacy and Communication Skills*
—*Support and Practice,* Ch. 3
transparencies and worksheets

Making a Documentary

A **documentary film** or **video** explains or interprets some aspect of reality. It creatively presents and analyzes a topic through words and through images related to the topic. For example, a documentary may explore the life of the first astronaut, the Brazilian rain forests, or how teens are shown in the media.

In a group, you will create a documentary to discuss how teens are shown on television. Your group will select and analyze a short scene (two to three minutes) from one of the TV shows you and other group members watched for Your Turn 13. Your video will show a narrator standing next to a television set. As a recording of the scene plays (with its sound off), the narrator will present your group's analysis of the scene.

Put It on Film   Making a documentary video requires planning and preparation. The chart below shows the first steps for creating an informative documentary video.

Preproduction (everything you do before using the camera)	
Step	**Helpful Hints**
❶ **Make decisions** about the main idea your group wants to communicate to your audience.	Answer these questions: ■ Who will make up our audience? ■ What do we think about how teens are shown on TV? ■ How can we support our ideas?
❷ **Select** a scene from the TV show you taped.	■ Look for a scene with a variety of characters. ■ Look for a scene that will help you support your ideas.
❸ **Storyboard** the scene.	■ Draw a sketch of each shot in the scene. Under each sketch, write notes on the events, actions, and language in the shot.
❹ **Analyze** the scene.	■ What types of characters are present in the scene? Discuss what those characters reveal about how teens are shown in the media.
❺ **Write** a script.	■ Use your storyboard to match your words to the action. Remember to introduce the TV show you are discussing.
❻ **Choose** roles for group members.	■ Narrator: presents the group's analysis and conclusions while discussing the selected scene ■ Cameraperson: shoots the video ■ Producer: directs the narrator and the cameraperson; signals the cameraperson when to start and stop shooting

Focus on Viewing and Representing   **113**

Making a Documentary
Students can collaborate to create forms to assist their project planning. To get them started, draw the outline of a simple T-chart on the chalkboard. In a class discussion, suggest students include in the left-hand column items such as *main idea statement, audience, TV program title, scene analysis, character analysis,* and *documentary title.* Suggest that as each group reaches a consensus in its discussion, the group's recorder can fill in the right-hand column of the chart and read it aloud at group meetings. You may also want to provide students with the chart below, which group members can use to sign up for the roles they choose.

You may want to have students show you their group charts and their scripts before they begin recording.

ROLES	NAME(S)
Recorder	
Storyboard Sketch Artist(s)	
Scriptwriter(s)	
Script Editor(s)	
Script Proofreader	
Music Technician	
Cameraperson	
Narrator	
Producer	

Critical Thinking

Evaluation. Have each group keep notes on the revisions made during the production phase of their documentaries. The notes should briefly explain what kinds of revisions are made. After the video has been produced, ask groups to consider how revision affected the final version of their documentaries. Did they revise the script? the taping technique? gestures? If so, why? How did these revisions to language, medium, and presentation affect the message of their videos?

Metacognition. Ask students the following question:

1. What part of the project did you find the most difficult? Why?

Then, ask students the following question:

2. What are stereotypes? [limited, fixed ideas about people or groups of people]

It is action time! Once your group has finished planning the video, you can begin producing the final product.

Depending on your school's policy, you may need to use your school's video equipment during class time, or you may be able to check it out to record your documentary. Either way, be sure you understand how to operate the equipment before you begin. Ask your teacher, librarian, or someone else experienced with using the equipment to show you how to use it. If no video equipment is available, skip step 3 in the chart below.

Production	
Step	**Helpful Hints**
❶ Rehearse your documentary video.	Rehearsing gives you a chance to work out problems and polish a performance. Rehearse off-camera first. Have the **narrator** practice speaking at the proper volume for recording. The **cameraperson** should decide the correct distance for recording to get a clear image of both the narrator and the television program being analyzed. The **producer** should hold cue cards to help the narrator with the script and practice signaling the cameraperson when to start and stop shooting. Then, using the video camera, record one rehearsal.
❷ Revise the documentary, if necessary.	As a group, evaluate your taped rehearsal. Decide whether you should revise your script to make your main idea easier to understand. Then, consider other elements of the video, such as the narrator's voice and gestures and the quality of the recording. Note where improvements are needed.
❸ Record the video.	Most video cameras allow you to view what you have just recorded. Look for problems with the sound or camera work in your recording. Reshoot your documentary if you find problems.

YOUR TURN 14 **Making a Documentary Video**

Use the guidelines on pages 113–114 to create a documentary. Then present the documentary to your class, and discuss these questions with your audience:

■ How well did the script fit the video images?

■ Could the same information have been presented as effectively through a medium other than video? Why or why not?

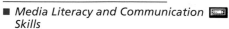

Choices

Choose one of the following activities to complete.

▶ CONSUMER EDUCATION

1. Do You Buy This? Think of a product that interests you, such as a game or stereo equipment. List the advantages and disadvantages of buying this particular product. Then, write a brief **review** of the product. Explain in detail why you would or would not buy the product. With other students, create **database records** of product reviews for the class to use.

▶ CROSSING THE CURRICULUM: ART

2. Picture This Create a **chart** using pictures rather than words to represent the advantages and disadvantages of your essay topic. Use symbols such as + or – to label the columns on your chart. In each column, draw or paste pictures showing the good and bad points of your topic.

▶ SPEECH

3. Hear Me Roar Present a **speech** about the topic of your advantages/disadvantages essay. This time, however, include a persuasive slant. Try to convince your audience that one option *is* better than the other. See page 758 for information on formal speaking.

▶ CROSSING THE CURRICULUM: HISTORY

4. From the Past Making comparisons requires you to categorize information, just as considering advantages and disadvantages does. Compare two accounts, or perspectives, of a historic event. For example, you might read about the sinking of the *Titanic* from a survivor's standpoint and from a rescuer's standpoint. List the similarities between the two accounts, and then list the differences. In a **paragraph,** explain the similarities and the differences between the accounts.

▶ CAREERS

5. The Results Are In Pick a workplace topic such as shorter work hours, longer lunch breaks, or a change of the dress code. Discuss its advantages and its disadvantages in an **oral report.** To research your topic, ask an adult how such a change might affect his or her workplace.

 ◀ PORTFOLIO

▶ CONSUMER EDUCATION

To assist students in reviewing a product, have them generate a list of evaluation criteria, such as *Cost, Age Appropriateness, Packaging, Durability,* and *Guarantees.* They can then rate the product's performance according to each criterion as an "advantage" or "disadvantage." Students may collaborate to create records for their database. Have one student be responsible for composing a record template—a table with column headings that reflect the criteria and row headings for "Advantages" and "Disadvantages." "Fields" (blanks to be filled in) for the product name and for recommendation should appear at the top of the template. Once the template is created, another student can complete records for each product based on the group's previously brainstormed list by filling out the table's fields, using either database software or photocopies of the template. A third student can revise the records for consistency. Finally, students can publish their records by loading the database on a class computer or binding the records for others to read.

▶ SPEECH

Remind students that in the **Critical Thinking Mini-Lesson** on p. 96 of the Writing Workshop they learned how to avoid bias. Inform students that in a persuasive speech, however, it is acceptable to use loaded words or words and phrases that signal an opinion, such as *I think* or *I prefer.* Encourage students to choose strong adjectives rather than overused adjectives like *good* or *bad.* Remind students to establish eye contact with the audience and use gestures and an emphatic tone of voice to emphasize main points. Humor is also a very effective tool for winning an audience.

RESOURCES

Looking at Both Sides
Assessment
- *Assessment Package*
  —*Chapter Tests,* Ch. 3
  —*Chapter Tests in Standardized Test Formats,* Ch. 3
  —*Assessment Alternatives,* Ch. 3

- *Test Generator (One-Stop Planner CD-ROM)*

Choices
Rubrics
- *Assessment Package*
  —*Assessment Alternatives,* Ch. 3

Previewing a Novel

Use this guide to create an instructional plan that suits the individual needs of your students. Assignments marked by an asterisk (*) may be completed out of class. Times given for pacing lessons are estimated. See pp. 116–117 for chapter-wide resources. Resources listed in this guide are point-of-use resources only.

Curriculum Connections

Connections to Literature
pp. 144–147
- Writing a Short Story
- Analyzing a Poem

Choices *p. 155*
- Speaking
- Drama
- Crossing the Curriculum: Science

internet connect

GO TO: go.hrw.com
KEYWORD: EOLang 7-4

 All resources for this chapter are available for preview on the *One-Stop Planner CD-ROM with Test Generator.* All worksheets and tests may be printed from the CD-ROM.

T115A

	Chapter Opener pp. 116–117	**Reading Workshop: Reading a Novel's Book Jacket** pp. 118–127
DEVELOPMENTAL PROGRAM	🕐 **30 minutes** • Your Turn 1 *p. 117*	🕐 **75 minutes** • Preparing to Read *p. 118* • Reading Selection *pp. 119–121* • First Thoughts in groups *p. 122* • Preview Information *pp. 122–124* • Your Turn 2 *p. 124* • Questioning and Predicting *pp. 124–125* • Your Turn 3 *p. 125* • Vocabulary Mini-Lesson *p. 126* • Test Taking Mini-Lesson *p. 127*
CORE PROGRAM	🕐 **25 minutes** • Your Turn 1 *p. 117*	🕐 **60 minutes** • Preparing to Read *p. 118* • Reading Selection *pp. 119–121* • First Thoughts *p. 122* • Preview Information *pp. 122–124* • Your Turn 2 *p. 124* • Questioning and Predicting *pp. 124–125* • Your Turn 3 *p. 125* • Vocabulary Mini-Lesson *p. 126* • Test Taking Mini-Lesson *p. 127*
ADVANCED PROGRAM	🕐 **15 minutes** • Your Turn 1 *p. 117*	🕐 **40 minutes** • Preparing to Read *p. 118* • Reading Selection *pp. 119–121* • First Thoughts *p. 122* • Preview Information *pp. 122–124* • Your Turn 2 *p. 124* • Questioning and Predicting *pp. 124–125* • Your Turn 3 *p. 125* • Vocabulary Mini-Lesson *p. 126*
RESOURCES — PRINT	• *Communications,* TP. 31, WS. p. 69	• *Alternative Readings,* Ch. 4 • *Communications,* TPs. 32, 33, WS. pp. 70–77
RESOURCES — MEDIA	• *One-Stop Planner CD-ROM*	• *One-Stop Planner CD-ROM*

TP.=Transparency   WS.=Worksheet

Writing Workshop: Creating a Jacket for a Novel
pp. 128–147

🕐 **220 minutes**
- Select a Novel *pp. 128–129*
- Purpose and Audience; Your Turn 4 *p. 129*
- Front Cover Image; Back Cover Quotation; Your Turn 5 *pp. 130–132*
- Plan Your Summary; Your Turn 6 *pp. 132, 134–135*
- Research the Author; Your Turn 7 *p. 135*
- Framework; Models; Your Turn 8* *pp. 136–138*
- Evaluate and Revise *pp. 139–141*
- Focus on Sentences in groups *p. 141*
- Your Turn 9 *p. 141*
- Proofread, Publish, and Reflect *pp. 142–143*
- Grammar Link; Your Turn 10 *pp. 142, 143*

🕐 **160 minutes**
- Select a Novel *pp. 128–129*
- Purpose and Audience; Your Turn 4 *p. 129*
- Front Cover Image; Back Cover Quotation; Your Turn 5 *pp. 130–132*
- Critical-Thinking Mini-Lesson in groups *p. 133*
- Plan Your Summary; Your Turn 6 *pp. 132, 134–135*
- Research the Author; Your Turn 7 *p. 135*
- Framework; Models; Your Turn 8* *pp. 136–138*
- Evaluate and Revise *pp. 139–141*
- Focus on Sentences *p. 141*
- Your Turn 9* *p. 141*
- Proofread, Publish, and Reflect *pp. 142–143*
- Grammar Link; Your Turn 10 *pp. 142, 143*
- Connections to Literature; Your Turn 12* *pp. 146–147*

🕐 **100 minutes**
- Select a Novel *pp. 128–129*
- Purpose and Audience; Your Turn 4* *p. 129*
- Front Cover Image; Back Cover Quotation; Your Turn 5 *pp. 130–132*
- Critical-Thinking Mini-Lesson *p. 133*
- Plan Your Summary; Your Turn 6 *pp. 132, 134–135*
- Research the Author; Your Turn 7* *p. 135*
- Framework; Models; Your Turn 8* *pp. 136–138*
- Evaluate and Revise *pp. 139–141*
- Focus on Sentences; Your Turn 9* *p. 141*
- Proofread, Publish, and Reflect; Your Turn 10 *pp. 142–143*
- Connections to Literature; Your Turn 11* *pp. 144–145*

- *Communications,* 📠 TPs. 34–37, WS. pp. 78–89
- *Designing Your Writing*

- *One-Stop Planner CD-ROM* 💿

Viewing and Representing: Book Cover; Speaking and Listening: Dramatic Reading *pp. 148–154*

🕐 **75 minutes**
- Illustration; Color; Font *pp. 148–149*
- Put It All Together *pp. 149–150*
- Your Turn 13 *p. 150*
- Design Your Cover *p. 151*
- Improve Your Drafts *p. 151*
- Your Turn 14* *p. 151*

🕐 **60 minutes**
- Choose Your Selection *p. 152*
- Prepare for Reading *pp. 153–154*
- Practice Delivery *p. 154*
- Your Turn 15 *p. 154*

🕐 **60 minutes**
- Illustration; Color; Font *pp. 148–149*
- Put It All Together *pp. 149–150*
- Your Turn 13 *p. 150*
- Design Your Cover *p. 151*
- Improve Your Drafts *p. 151*
- Your Turn 14* *p. 151*

🕐 **45 minutes**
- Choose Your Selection *p. 152*
- Prepare for Reading *pp. 153–154*
- Practice Delivery* *p. 154*
- Your Turn 15 *p. 154*

🕐 **30 minutes**
- Illustration; Color; Font *pp. 148–149*
- Put It All Together *pp. 149–150*
- Your Turn 13* *p. 150*
- Design Your Cover *p. 151*
- Improve Your Drafts *p. 151*
- Your Turn 14* *p. 151*

🕐 **30 minutes**
- Choose Your Selection *p. 152*
- Prepare for Reading* *pp. 153–154*
- Practice Delivery* *p. 154*
- Your Turn 15 *p. 154*

- *Media Literacy and Communication* 📠 *Skills*
  - —*Support and Practice,* Ch. 4
  - —*A How-to Handbook*
  - —*A Teacher's Guide,* Ch. 4

- *Media Literacy and Communication Skills* 📺
  - —*Videocassette 1, Segment C*
- *One-Stop Planner CD-ROM* 💿

Previewing a Novel

CHAPTER OBJECTIVES

- To read a book jacket and learn to preview through predicting and questioning
- To create a book jacket that includes illustrations and text
- To analyze and design book covers
- To perform a dramatic reading

Chapter Overview

This chapter lets students discover how examining a book jacket can help them make informed reading choices. In the Reading Workshop (pp. 118–127), students learn to preview, predict, and question as they explore a novel's book jacket. The Writing Workshop (pp. 128–147) has students create a book jacket for a novel of their choice. In the Focus on Viewing and Representing, students analyze book cover art and then finalize the book covers they began in the Writing Workshop. The Focus on Speaking and Listening gives students an opportunity to perform a dramatic reading from a novel. Although the sections of the chapter can be taught independently, teaching them together gives students a well-rounded view of previewing a novel.

Why Study Previewing a Novel?

Understanding how to preview a novel can help students enhance their reading experiences. In this chapter, students will learn what the elements of a book jacket can tell them about a novel. By creating a book jacket, students can share their excitement over a favorite novel— and learn the elements that go into book jacket design. Students who understand the purpose of book jackets and how to interpret them will be well equipped to preview and evaluate other types of texts, such as magazine covers.

Teaching the Chapter

Option 1: Begin with Literature

If literature is the starting point of your instruction, you could introduce the chapter after students first preview several short stories or a novel. Students should make and modify predictions and ask questions as they read these works of literature. Afterward, have students read the book jacket in this chapter (pp. 119–121) and identify how making predictions and asking questions can interest them in reading a novel. Then, students will be ready to design and write their own book jackets in the Writing Workshop (pp. 128–147).

Option 2: Begin with Nonfiction and Writing

To familiarize students with previewing, predicting, and questioning before turning to literature, begin with the material in this chapter. The Reading Workshop (pp. 118–127) will enable students to understand how book jackets help readers make predictions and ask questions. Next, have students create book jackets in the

Writing Workshop (pp. 128–147). When students return to literature, they will be better prepared to use previewing techniques. See also **Connections to Literature** on pp. 144–147.

Making Connections

■ To the Literature Curriculum

A book jacket summary should intrigue potential readers without disclosing the story's climax or resolution. To create a book jacket, students need to distinguish the climax and resolution from other plot elements. Have students practice identifying a plot's introduction, complications, climax, and resolution in such short stories as "A Day's Wait" by Ernest Hemingway.

Lesson Idea: Previewing, Predicting, and Questioning in "The Smallest Dragonboy" by Anne McCaffrey

1. After students have read the story, ask them to set up a story map like the one for Critical Elements (p. 145) but to complete only the character and setting sections. A sample response is given below.

> **Characters:** Keevan, the smallest boy eligible to be a dragon's partner; Beterli, an older and tougher classmate; Keevan's supportive foster mother
>
> **Setting:** A fantasy world where dragons and humans fight together for just causes; around dragon-hatching time

2. Ask students to list five plot events, including an early event, the final event, and three important events that occur between the opening and closing actions.

3. Next, have students evaluate their plot events with a partner and decide which event is the latest one that could be divulged without eliminating all suspense. They should write *omit* next to events that cannot be divulged, as in the sample below.

> **Plot Event:** Boys eligible to be dragonriders visit the hatching cavern.
>
> **Plot Event:** Beterli teases Keevan about his size.
>
> **Plot Event:** A suggestion is made to drop small boys from eligibility.
>
> **Plot Event:** Beterli starts a fight with Keevan just before the eggs start hatching. (omit)
>
> **Plot Event:** Beterli is not allowed to go to the hatching, and a dragon chooses Keevan. (omit)

4. Remind students that the wording of a theme statement can also affect a reader's predictions. Ask them why "Character's size causes conflict" would be a better way to phrase the theme in a book jacket than "Good character is rewarded." [The first statement leaves room for a prediction.]

■ To Careers

A book jacket is partly a marketing device designed to entice potential customers. Invite individuals in marketing, advertising, or design professions to talk to your class about predicting and questioning, summary writing, quotation selection, presentation, or package design for their products. Ask them to bring appropriate samples of their work. Students will be able to see that what they are learning about addressing specific audiences has broad application.

■ To the Community

The skills needed to create a successful book jacket are similar to presentation and persuasion skills used in the larger community. Suggest that students identify issues of importance to the community by scanning local newspapers, viewing community cable television programs, or locating flyers placed around the community. You may want to obtain permission from parents or guardians before beginning work on this assignment. Have students work alone or in pairs to select one issue and analyze the way it is being presented. They might identify the audience being addressed, the way in which the issue is presented, and methods of persuasion used.

■ To the Art Curriculum

Many of the questions raised in the Focus on Viewing and Representing are fundamental to analyzing art. Have an art teacher bring examples to class and speak about works of art that show a wide range of media, color, and composition. Then, provide art books that students can examine. Suggest that groups of students discuss the purpose and effect of media, color, and arrangement in several of the works depicted. Such an activity can help students appreciate the complexity of creating a work of art as well as its impact on its viewers or audience.

Previewing a Novel

PREVIEWING THE CHAPTER

- The goal of the four workshops in this chapter is to help students understand how the information on a book jacket can contribute to making informed reading choices. Although they can be taught separately, if they are taught together, these workshops complement one another. Reading a novel's book jacket prepares students to preview, make predictions, and ask questions about the novel. After writing and illustrating a book jacket, students learn how a dramatic reading can offer a preview of a novel and how a cover illustration can increase a book jacket's effectiveness. To integrate this chapter with grammar, usage, and mechanics chapters, see pp. T311A–T311B.

INTRODUCING THE CHAPTER

- To introduce the chapter, use the Journal Warm-up, Transparency 31, in *Communications*.

VIEWING THE ILLUSTRATION

- Point out that the details in the background of the illustration come from the novels on which the boy is reclining. Ask students why the artist used short, thick brush strokes and a mixture of light and dark colors to create the lifelike textures of the boy's pillow and clothes and the background scenery. [The colors and textures make the details of the novels spring to life.]

Representing. Have students sketch details from a book they have read. Ask students to think about images and colors that best represent the books they choose to illustrate.

CHAPTER RESOURCES

Planning
- *Lesson Planner,* Ch. 4
- *ELL Strategies,* Ch. 4
- Block Scheduling, p. T115A (this book)
- *One-Stop Planner CD-ROM*

Practice
- *Communications,* Ch. 4

- *Media Literacy and Communication Skills*

Extension
- *Designing Your Writing*

Reinforcement
- *Communications,* Ch. 4
- *Alternate Readings,* Ch. 4

Reading Workshop

Reading a Novel's Book Jacket

Writing Workshop

Creating a Jacket for a Novel

Viewing and Representing

Analyzing and Designing a Book Cover

Speaking and Listening

Performing a Dramatic Reading

Imagine that you are standing in the library with a book in each hand. You read the back cover of each book. You look at the writing on the inside flaps. Then, you put one book back on the shelf and confidently tuck the other under your arm as you walk toward the check-out desk.

How did you decide which book to take and which to leave on the shelf? When you read the book jackets, you used a method called *previewing*. **Previewing** is an activity that helps you gather information about a book. After previewing a book, you can predict what the book is about and decide whether you want to read it. Writers and editors create book jackets to let readers preview books—in the hope that those readers will buy (or borrow) the book.

Informational Text

Exposition

YOUR TURN 1 Previewing a Book

Go to the library and check out a book with a book jacket that has flaps. Only hard-backed books will have an entire book jacket. Bring the book to class and discuss it with a few classmates. Be sure to

- decide what the image on the cover says about the book
- read the back cover and inside flaps and see if they change what you thought about the book based on the cover image
- tell whether the book jacket makes you want to read the book

internetconnect

GO TO: go.hrw.com
KEYWORD: EOLang 7-4

Motivate

To get students thinking about the purpose and effect of book jackets, show them a hardback novel or non-fiction book without its jacket. State the title of the book, and give students one minute to guess what plot developments or information the book might include. Then, show the front of the book jacket and have students change their first impressions or add predictions.

ELEMENTS OF *Literature*

Previewing in Literature. In *Elements of Literature,* First Course, see "The Frog Who Wanted to Be a Singer" by Linda Goss, pp. 172–177, and "Bargain" by A. B. Guthrie, pp. 231–239, for examples of literary works well suited to previewing, predicting, and questioning.

YOUR TURN 1

Make sure students examine all four parts of the book jacket—front cover, back cover, front flap, and back flap. You might suggest that students jot down notes about the book jacket they are reviewing before they discuss it with classmates.

- *Daily Language Activity Transparencies*
- *Vocabulary Workshop* and *Tests*
- *Spelling*

Evaluation and Assessment

- *Test Generator (One-Stop Planner CD-ROM)*

- *Assessment Package*
  —*Chapter Tests,* Ch. 4
  —*Chapter Tests in Standardized Test Formats,* Ch. 4
  —*Assessment Alternatives,* Ch. 4

Internet

- go.hrw.com (keyword: EOLang 7–4)

Reading Workshop

OBJECTIVES

Reading and Writing Connection

- To read a book jacket in preparation for creating a book jacket for a novel

Reading Skills

- To preview a novel
- To generate questions and make predictions about a novel
- To use context to unlock the meanings of multiple-meaning words

TEACHING (TIP)

Preparing to Read

This material reminds students to question and predict as they read a book jacket. These skills, covered on pp. 122–125, can help students make informed reading choices. Previewing, questioning, and predicting will be the focus of the Reading Workshop, and students will be reminded to use both experience and printed details while they preview the novel *Crash*.

Quotation for the Day

❝**Man is like an iceberg—the more important part is hidden under the water. It interests me to dive down to the most hidden places.**❞

(Fernando Arrabal, 1932–   , Moroccan-born Spanish poet and author)

Use this quotation to prepare students for the character study suggested by the book jacket for *Crash.* After students read the book jacket, ask them what "more important part" of the main character will be revealed if students "dive down" into the book. [Crash's family life and the conflicts he faces]

RESOURCES

Reading Workshop
Reinforcement

- *Alternative Readings,* Ch. 4

Reading a Novel's Book Jacket

J ohn "Crash" Coogan is the star athlete of his seventh-grade class and is a better athlete than most eighth-graders, too. He is the high-energy main character of the novel *Crash,* whose covers and inside flaps appear on the following pages. As you look at the cover and flaps of *Crash,* try to notice what information you can learn about a novel just by looking at its jacket.

WHAT'S AHEAD?

In this section you will read a novel's book jacket. You will also

- **learn how to preview a novel**
- **learn how to generate questions and make predictions about a novel**

Preparing to Read

READING FOCUS

Preview Information   When you take stock of the details on a novel's jacket, you are *previewing.* **Previewing** happens before you read or view something, and it helps you decide whether you are interested in the story. For this lesson, you will preview a novel—a long, fictional story. You will gather information from the book jacket of *Crash* to help you guess about the plot of the novel and decide whether you would like to read it.

READING SKILL

Questioning and Predicting   As you gather information from a book jacket, you can make some educated guesses about what might happen in the novel and what the characters might be like. You can also draw upon your own experience and knowledge of stories to ask questions such as, "What will happen to the main character?" To the left is a picture of what a book jacket looks like when laid flat.

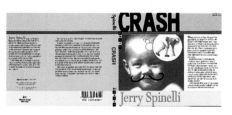

118   Chapter 4   **Exposition:** Previewing a Novel

READING PROCESS

PREREADING

Set a Purpose. Point out to students their purpose for reading the book jacket for *Crash* on pp. 119–121—to preview a novel and to make educated guesses about its

characters and outcome. Remind students that they will get more out of their reading when they read for a purpose.

Tell students that although the purpose is often set by the teacher, they also need to

CRASH

KNOPF

Jerry Spinelli

FRONT COVER

Look at the covers and inside flaps of *Crash*. In your notebook, answer the numbered active-reading questions that appear in the margins. The underlined words appear in the Vocabulary Mini-Lesson on page 126.

1. What is unusual about the photo and drawing that appear together on the front cover?

2. What sort of expression does the baby have? What do you think the expression says about his character?

Active-Reading Questions

The purpose of the active-reading questions is to encourage students to think about questioning and predicting as they explore the content in the Reading Selection. Use students' answers to assess informally their comprehension of book jacket analysis.

ANSWERS

Possible answers are suggested below.

1. The baby has a mustache. Also, babies do not think about playing football.

2. The baby looks mischievous. The expression suggests that he will probably be funny and playful.

find their own purposes for reading. In reading a book jacket, for example, they might adjust their previewing strategy depending on whether their purpose is to get a sense of the author's style, an overview of the book's content, or biographical information about the author.

3. Students may identify with Crash's love of sports, his humor, or his flippant attitude. Many students may know peers who show extreme behaviors.

My real name is John. John Coogan. But everybody calls me Crash, even my parents.

It started way back when I got my first football helmet for Christmas. I don't really remember this happening, but they say that when my uncle Herm's family came over to see our presents, as they were coming through the door I got down into a four-point stance, growled, "Hut! Hut! Hut!" and charged ahead with my brand-new helmet. Seems I knocked my cousin Bridget clear back out the doorway and onto her butt into a foot of snow. They say she bawled bloody murder and refused to come into the house, so Uncle Herm finally had to drag his whole family away before they even had a chance to take their coats off.

Like I said, personally I don't remember the whole thing, but looking back at what I do remember about myself, I'd have to say the story is probably true. As far as I can tell, I've always been crashing—into people, into things, you name it, with or without a helmet.

3. What aspect of Crash's character makes him interesting to you? Is he like anyone you know?

51600>

9 780679 879572

ISBN 0-679-87957-9   NB21

BACK COVER

4. This book seems to be about a boy who likes to play jokes but who is suddenly forced into a situation in which the jokes do not seem funny anymore.

5. It seems as if Crash might disapprove of one of Mike's pranks. Maybe Crash will have to decide whether or not to still be Mike's friend.

6. Jerry Spinelli must be an experienced writer; he has written more than fifteen books.

---

4. What does this novel seem to be about?

6. Is Jerry Spinelli an experienced writer? What makes you think so?

What's it like to be Crash Coogan? You might think you know him already—the big jock, star of the football team. Huge shoulders, smallish brain. Basically <u>mows</u> down everything in his path, including kids like Penn Webb, the dweeby, puny, button-wearing vegetable-eater who moved onto Crash's block when they were little—and has been a <u>prime</u> target ever since.

But there's more to Crash than the touchdown-scoring kid every seventh grader sees. And it's not the predictable sob story that's supposed to make you feel sorry for the poor bully. It's the story of a kid with overworked parents, an ecology-minded smart-aleck little sister, a <u>crush</u> on an activist cheerleader, and a best buddy named Mike Deluca, who helps Crash pull off hilarious pranks at Webb's <u>expense</u>.

Until one day <u>Mike</u> goes too far, maybe even for Crash, and the football hero has to choose which side he's really on.

5. What do you think will happen to make Crash "choose which side he's really on"?

Jerry Spinelli won the Newbery Medal for *Maniac Magee*, the sixth of his more than fifteen acclaimed books for young readers, which include *There's a Girl in My Hammerlock* and *Who Put That Hair in My Toothbrush?* Growing up, he played no less than five different sports—from football and track to basketball. He wanted to be a shortstop in the majors long before it occurred to him to be a writer.

Crash came out of his desire to include the beloved Penn Relays of his home state of Pennsylvania in a book. And, of course, to show the world a little bit of what jocks are made of.

http://www.randomhouse.com/

Jacket illustration © 1996 by Eleanor Hoyt
Jacket photo © 1996 by Stan Reis

Also available in Gibraltar Library Binding
Printed in the United States

Alfred A. Knopf
New York

FRONT FLAP

BACK FLAP

Reading Workshop **121**

READING PROCESS

READING

Make Personal Connections. Remind students that making personal connections will help them relate what they are reading to what they already know. Have them read the front flap of the book jacket and then think about people, either real people or characters in books or movies, who have had to draw the line when a friend pushed them too far. Ask students to discuss how people know when to draw that line and what the consequences of drawing the line might be.

First Thoughts on Your Reading

ANSWERS

Possible answers are suggested below.

1. Crash may have trouble talking his friend Mike out of some cruel trick. He might have to stand up for Penn Webb.

2. What is the prank that Crash might think is not funny? How does his crush on the cheerleader turn out? How does his family influence Crash's decision?

TEACHING TIP

Preview Information

Looking closely at the jackets of novels checked out from the library can help students assimilate information in the chart on this page. Ask students to locate on their book jackets examples of the types of information described in the chart. For instance, a student might point out the summary and critic's assessment on the back cover. Students might use self-stick notes to label the kinds of information they locate on the book jackets. Allow time for students to share their findings.

| READING FOCUS

TIP Movie previews are called **trailers.** Like a novel's book jacket, a movie trailer will summarize the story and give you an idea of who the characters are.

Preview Information

You *Can* Judge a Book by Its Cover! The first step to understanding a novel is gathering information from its front and back covers and inside flaps. The information you gather from a book jacket will help you decide whether you want to read the novel. Reading the book jacket to get an idea of the contents is a technique that works for any type of book—novels, photography books, sports books, or cookbooks. Use this chart to see what the parts of a book jacket can tell you about a novel.

Part of the Book Jacket	Information You Might Find
Front Cover	■ Title ■ Author ■ An illustration or picture that tells something about the novel ■ Awards the novel has received
Back Cover	■ Quotations from the novel ■ Summary of the novel ■ Reviews of the novel or reviews of other novels by the same author
Front Flap	■ A summary of the novel ■ A reason for people to read the novel
Back Flap	■ Information about the author

The text from parts of the jacket of another novel, *Where the Red Fern Grows* by Wilson Rawls, is shown on the next page. Read over the information, and look at the chart on page 124 to see how one reader recorded the information he found.

Back Cover:

My eyes were wide, my throat dry, and my heart thumping. One judge stopped in front of Little Ann. My heart stopped, too. Reaching over, he patted her on the head.

Turning to me, he asked, "Is this your dog?"

I couldn't speak. I just nodded my head.

He said, "She's a beautiful hound."

He walked on down the line. My heart started beating again.

There were eight dogs left. Little Ann was still holding her own. Then there were four. I was ready to cry.

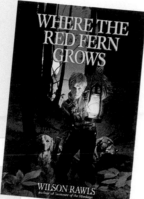

Front Flap:

Growing up in the Ozark Mountains of northeastern Oklahoma, Billy Colman wants nothing more than to own the pair of coonhound pups he saw advertised in a sportsman's magazine. Although the sum is tremendous, Billy is determined, and after two years of hard work and saving, the two puppies become his.

Billy's pups are his "shadow," following his every move through the dark hills and icy river bottoms in search of the elusive raccoons. The three gain a fine reputation as an inseparable team when they win the coveted gold cup in the annual coon-hunt contest, capture the deceptive ghost coon, and, in the most difficult battle of all, put up a fierce struggle against a mountain lion.

But the victory over the mountain lion turns to tragedy, and Billy's days of freedom and innocent boyhood rapidly end. Yet much remains for Billy: He not only has his wonderful memories, but he learns a beautiful old Indian legend which gives them sacred meaning.

As it has for generations, this modern classic is sure to warm the hearts of young and old alike.

Part of the Book Jacket	Information I Found
Front Cover	The book is Where the Red Fern Grows, written by Wilson Rawls. The front cover shows two dogs and a boy who is carrying a lantern.
Back Cover	The long quotation tells me that a character enters his dog in a contest. The judge praises the dog.
Front Flap	The front flap tells me about Billy Colman, a boy who saves his money and buys two puppies. Billy and the puppies win a gold cup in a hunting contest and go on many adventures. The flap mentions an Indian legend, which makes me curious to read the book.

YOUR TURN 2 **Gathering Preview Information**

In your notebook create a chart like the one above. Then, using the book jacket from *Crash* on pages 119–121, fill in the chart. (Note: You will need to add a row titled "Back Flap" to your chart.)

READING SKILL

Questioning and Predicting

What's Happening?   Previewing a book leads a reader to **ask questions**. After looking at a book jacket, you probably find yourself asking several questions. For example, you may ask why a character acts a certain way, or you may wonder what will happen next.

What Happens Next?   Once a reader begins to ask questions, he or she also begins to make *predictions*. A **prediction** is an educated guess about what will happen in the future based on what you have read and what you know. When reading a book jacket, you base your predictions on the parts of the novel you have examined closely. You also draw from your own life experience and your knowledge of how stories generally work.

124   Chapter 4   **Exposition:** Previewing a Novel

YOUR TURN 2

Possible responses are given below.
Information I Found

Front Cover The book is <u>Crash</u> written by Jerry Spinelli. The front cover shows a baby dreaming about playing football.

Back Cover The quoted passage on the back cover is John Coogan's memory of receiving his first football helmet; the recollection includes his tackling his cousin Bridget.

Front Flap The front flap tells me about the main characters and the conflict in the novel. The flap mentions that there is more to the main character than just being a football star.

Back Flap The back flap states that one of Jerry Spinelli's novels won a Newbery Medal. It also says that he played five different sports in school.

Timesaver

To check quickly on students' understanding of the book jacket content in **Your Turn 2,** have them highlight the two most interesting pieces of information they found.

READING PROCESS

EXTENDING
Read Other Works. Tell students that they can extend what they have learned about previewing a novel by examining the jacket of another novel by Jerry Spinelli. As they review the jacket or paperback cover of the novel they select, they might jot down predictions about the plot and characters. Suggest that students read the book, revising their predictions as appropriate. After reading, students might evaluate the value of the jacket or cover in conveying information about the book.

text: what you read

+ prior knowledge: what you already know based on your life

prediction: an educated guess about what will happen

Asking questions and making predictions will give you a **purpose** for reading. As you read, you will look for answers to questions and see whether your predictions are correct.

THINKING IT THROUGH • **Questioning and Predicting**

Here is how one student used the book jacket of Rawls's novel to generate questions and make predictions.

STEP 1 Review the information you gathered while previewing the book jacket, and ask questions about what you want to know.
Why are the dogs and the boy out in the woods at night with a lantern? Will something bad happen to the dogs or to the boy?

STEP 2 Think about your own experiences that relate to your questions.
I know that people hunt in the woods and that some people, like my uncle, bring their dogs. Also, it seems like a lot of the stories I've read about dogs, like Old Yeller, end with something bad happening.

STEP 3 Make predictions that answer your questions by considering preview information and your own experiences.
I bet the boy and his dogs are hunting for the "ghost coon" or the mountain lion mentioned on the front flap. I also think the dogs will get hurt saving the boy's life because the front flap says "the victory over the mountain lion turns to tragedy."

STEP 4 Confirm or revise your predictions as you read the novel.

YOUR TURN 3 **Questioning and Predicting**

Using the Thinking It Through steps above, ask questions and make predictions about *Crash*. Use the information you gathered from the book jacket in Your Turn 2 and your own experience to help you.

> **TIP** You can ask questions and make predictions *before* you read a novel by previewing its jacket, but you can also do so *as* you are reading a novel. These questions and predictions can be about the characters' personalities, the events in the story, or problems the characters may face.

Wrap It Up

Metacognition. To have students reflect on their own reading processes, ask them the following question:

1. What did you learn about how to use the information on a book jacket?

Then, ask students this question:

2. For what reasons would a book jacket include an illustration about the novel and information about the author? [The visual appeal of an illustration might intrigue a potential reader; author information might include other titles to interest readers.]

YOUR TURN 3

ANSWERS
Here are sample questions and predictions.

Step 1 The front cover shows a baby thinking about football. Why is a baby thinking about football?

Step 2 If the baby is already thinking about football, it must be important in his life.

Step 3 I bet that the main character is a good football player.

Step 4 The front flap confirms that Crash is a great football player, but it also hints that there is more to Crash than just football. I predict that Crash will turn out to be more than just a big jock.

RESOURCES

Your Turn 2
Practice
■ *Communications*, WS. p. 70
Reinforcement
■ *Communications*, TP. 32, WS. p. 71

Your Turn 3
Practice
■ *Communications*, WS. p. 72
Reinforcement
■ *Communications*, TP. 33, WS. p. 73

Multiple-Meaning Words
ANSWERS
Possible answers are given below.

1. *Stance* can be a standing posture or an attitude. Getting down in "a four-point stance" may refer to squatting in a football position. It works to say, "I got down into a football position . . . and charged. . . ."

2. *Mow* means to cut or to cause to fall. The sentence states that Crash "mows down everything in his path." He often runs into people and knocks them down. Here, *mows* means "charges recklessly."

3. *Prime* is an adjective in the sentence. It means first in importance. The passage indicates that Webb is "a prime target." I think *prime* here means "most frequently selected." It works to say, "Penn Webb has been the most frequently selected target."

4. *Crush* is a noun in the sentence, and it means an infatuation. The passage states that Crash has "a crush on an activist cheerleader." Here, *crush* seems to mean "to be intensely fond of someone." "A kid who is intensely fond of an activist cheerleader" works in the sentence.

5. *Expense* means a cost or sacrifice. The passage states that Crash pulls off "hilarious pranks at Webb's expense," meaning that everyone laughs at Webb. *Expense* seems to mean "at the cost of someone's feelings." The passage makes sense when it reads, "Crash pulls off hilarious pranks at the cost of Webb's feelings."

Multiple-Meaning Words

Sometimes when you read, you find familiar words used in ways you do not understand. Such words are **multiple-meaning words.** For instance, the word *bank* often means a place that keeps money, but what does it mean in the following sentences?

> We all sat on the *bank* of the river.

> The basketball player made a *bank* shot.

When you see a multiple-meaning word, you have to decide which meaning is the right one.

TIP The difference between word meanings can depend on a word's part of speech. For example, many of the words we recognize as nouns may also be used as verbs. *Elbow, staple,* and *ice* are examples of nouns that have meanings as verbs, too. The following sentences show how the same word can be used as a verb and as a noun. Note how the meaning changes.

> She *cut* her hand. [the *action* of cutting, which is a verb]

> It was a bad *cut*. [the *result* of the cutting, which is a noun]

THINKING IT THROUGH Multiple-Meaning Words

The following steps can help you find the correct definition of multiple-meaning words. The example is a word from the book jacket of *Crash.*

Example: *bawled*

▶ **STEP 1** Consider all meanings of a word. Rule out definitions that are not the correct part of speech. You may need to use a dictionary.

(1) v.: to shout out noisily; (2) v.: to weep loudly (3) n.: an outcry. The word is a verb in the sentence, so definition #3 is wrong.

▶ **STEP 2** Examine the context of the word or passage.

"They say she bawled bloody murder. . . ." She does not sound sad, so #2 must be wrong.

▶ **STEP 3** Substitute your definition into the sentence. You may have to adjust the wording of your definition.

"They say she shouted noisily bloody murder . . . ." It works!

PRACTICE

These words are underlined on the book jacket of *Crash.* Follow the steps above to define the words as they are used on the book jacket.

1. stance (page 120)
2. mows (page 121)
3. prime (page 121)
4. crush (page 121)
5. expense (page 121)

RESOURCES

Vocabulary
Practice
- *Communications,* WS. p. 74

Test Taking
Practice
- *Communications,* WS. pp. 75–77

Making Predictions About Future Outcomes

On many reading tests, you will find questions that ask you to predict future actions or events. You will not find answers to the questions in the selection, but you will find hints. You can also draw on your own experience and knowledge to predict the future event. Read the following passage and answer the question after it.

> Karen, a seventh-grader, was very nervous on the first day that she went to tutor a group of third-graders. She did not know how they would respond to her. With a queasy feeling in her stomach, she knocked on the door to Mrs. Warren's classroom.
>
> Mrs. Warren opened the door and led her inside. Karen could see that most of the third-graders were sitting quietly at their desks with their books open.
>
> "Class, this is Karen," Mrs. Warren announced. "She will be helping you with your math problems. Who would like Karen's help?"
>
> Several students quickly raised their hands. Karen was glad she had an hour to spend with them.

During the next hour, the children will

A. argue about who gets to go first

B. work with Karen only because their teacher expects it

C. be glad Karen is helping them with their math problems

D. convince Karen that she does not want to tutor them after all

THINKING IT THROUGH **Predicting Future Outcomes**

▶ **STEP 1** Read the test item and turn the incomplete sentence into a question, if necessary.

"During the next hour, the children will . . ." becomes "During the next hour, what will the children do?"

▶ **STEP 2** Gather clues about what will happen from information in the text and from your own experience.

In the passage, the children were working quietly. Many of them raised their hands so they could work with Karen. In my experience, a lot of children welcome help on math problems.

▶ **STEP 3** Eliminate answers that are obviously wrong, and choose the answer to which the clues in the passage lead you.

The children seem ready and willing to work with Karen, so answers B and D must be wrong. The children seem well behaved, so choice A is probably wrong, too. I choose answer C. It matches the information in the passage.

Looking Ahead to Writing

In the Writing Workshop for this chapter (pp. 128–147), students will be asked to design and write a book jacket for a novel. As students make choices for each section of the jacket, have them refer to the chart on p. 122 that shows the parts of the book jacket.

Writing Workshop

OBJECTIVES

- To use the writing process to write copy for a book jacket
- To choose a front cover image and a back cover quotation
- To identify the elements of a novel
- To plan and write a summary of a novel
- To combine sentences
- To use hyphens correctly

Quotation for the Day

"The reader will be drawn into our stories if we are drawn into characters."

(Lucy M. Calkins, 1952–   , American author, speaker, and professor)

Share this quotation with students. Discuss what kinds of characters make a novel seem interesting when they are pictured in an illustration on a book cover or described in a novel summary on the book flap.

TEACHING TIP

Select a Novel
To help students select novels, provide lists of good novels from your school or public library, lists of award-winning novels, or district grade-level reading lists. Such lists will help remind students of novels they have read and will be resources for students who do not read widely.

WHAT'S AHEAD?

In this workshop you will create a book jacket. You will also learn how to

- choose a front cover image and a back cover quotation
- identify the elements of a novel
- plan and write a summary of a novel
- combine sentences
- use hyphens correctly

Creating a Jacket for a Novel

Do you remember the last time you liked a book so well that you told someone else about it? Creating a book jacket is a way to promote the book to hundreds of people at once. Professional publishers and designers create book jackets as *marketing* tools. **Marketing** is the process of promoting and selling a product.

In this workshop you will create a book jacket for a novel you have read. You will give readers important information about the novel and help them decide for themselves whether they want to read it.

Prewriting

Select a Novel

TIP Make sure you read the novel you choose before you start the project, even if you have read it before. Otherwise, you might not be able to remember important details needed to create a good book jacket.

Find Your Inspiration For this workshop you need to choose a novel that you really like or that you think you will like. Your enthusiasm for the novel you choose should come through in your writing. The best way to make sure that happens is to write about a novel you enjoyed reading. You can also choose a new novel based on your interests.

To select a novel, complete these sentences.

My favorite kinds of novels are about _____.

The most exciting moment I remember from a novel is _____.

One student chose a novel this way:

> The most exciting moment I remember from a novel is . . . the scene where Ponyboy gets his head held underwater by a member of the Socs. That was in a novel called <u>The Outsiders</u>. I would like to read that novel again. I think I'll use it for my book jacket.

Think About Purpose and Audience

Be Reasonable If you think about your reasons for creating this book jacket, you will realize that you really have three goals:

- to tell people what the novel is about
- to give your audience a **reason to read** the novel
- to attract the readers' attention

Since you are writing a book jacket for a young-adult novel, young adults are your primary audience. To create an effective book jacket, you will need to include information that will appeal to readers your own age. Keep in mind, however, that parents and librarians also select novels for young adults to read. Include for this secondary audience information such as awards the novel has received.

> My primary audience will be young adults. They would be interested in the rivalry and what happens between groups of teens who think they are tough. I will include information about that for them.
>
> My secondary audience will be parents and librarians. They might worry about the rivalry, so I will mention on the jacket that the book is really about how violence is bad.

TIP Since you have two audiences for your book jacket, you should avoid words and phrases that sound too formal as well as words and phrases that are considered to be slang. In other words, make sure the **tone** of your writing **voice** fits both your primary *and* secondary audiences.

 YOUR TURN 4 **Selecting a Novel and Thinking About Audience**

To select a novel and target your audience, complete the following.

- Think of possible novels by completing one of the sentences at the bottom of page 128. Choose a novel you would be interested in reading or re-reading.
- Identify information you should include to get your primary and secondary audiences interested in the novel.

Think About Purpose and Audience
Concern about reaching primary and secondary audiences is critical when the content of a novel may be controversial. Since many of the students may not have read *The Outsiders,* discuss some differences between gangs in the mid-1960s and now. Inform students that while there was a certain amount of violence in the old gangs, as this novel depicts, most fights were considered fair because everyone agreed upon and obeyed certain rules. Weapons were rarely used, and people were rarely killed.

Critical Thinking
Evaluation. Have students read the front flap for the novel *Crash* on p. 121 of the Reading Workshop. Ask whether language such as "dweeby," "sob story," and "poor bully" helps create a voice appropriate for young adults. Have them discuss the effect of vocabulary replacements—*studious, sorrowful tale, pitiful habitual teaser*—on the same audience.

YOUR TURN 4

Have students turn in sheets listing the titles of their novels and any information they plan to include to get the attention of their audiences. That way you can check that students have chosen appropriate young adult novels and that they have considered their purpose and audience.

RESOURCES

Your Turn 4
Practice
- *Communications,* WS. p. 78

Cooperative Learning

Short-Story Book Jackets. Many students may gain confidence by cooperatively producing an original book jacket before creating one individually. Have the class read a short story. Then, divide the class into groups of four students. Ask groups to assign one of the following to each member: cover design, quotation selection, summary, or biography. Have students create a book jacket for the short story, and allow them to share their jackets with the class.

Critical Thinking

Analysis. Ask students why an unusual or exciting incident in a novel could provide a good cover idea. They might say that a crisis or predicament attracts immediate interest. Have them compare an unusual incident with other, less dramatic possibilities in the novel they have selected, such as a scene that is typical of a character's everyday life or a scene showing a character relaxing in scenic surroundings. Then, ask students why the unusual incident is better for the cover. [It looks more exciting or intriguing and may make a potential reader curious enough to read the book.]

TIP Your goal is to create an entirely *new* jacket for a novel, not to copy the original one. If you choose a novel that already has a jacket, look for a chance to show your unique views about the novel. You will pick the characters and scenes *you* like best for your jacket, not the ones another person chose.

Select the Front Cover Image

A Picture Is Worth a Thousand Words Which book are you more likely to pick up from the shelf: a plain book with the title written across it, or a book with a big picture on the cover? No contest, right? The picture on the front cover makes the book instantly interesting. Deciding on the picture for your book jacket may be difficult because there are so many images that come to mind. How do you pick just one?

Think about the story. Make a list of all the times the main character runs into trouble or does something unusual. Briefly describe the scene. For example, the student writing about *The Outsiders* chose the following scenes. Notice that he was careful to make sure the scene did not give away too much of the story. After completing the chart, the student ranked the scenes to determine which one would make the best cover for the novel.

Rank	Scene	Analysis
3	A member of the Socs dunks Ponyboy's head in a fountain and holds it there.	I think this would be a bad choice because you can't see the main character's face, and it gives away a big surprise in the story.
1	Ponyboy and Johnny run away to an abandoned church and wait for Dallas to come and help them.	I like this one because it shows that these "tough guys" are really just scared kids, and it does not give the story away.
2	Ponyboy saves several children in a burning church.	I like this picture, but it has lots of characters that aren't important. Plus, the fire was less important than some of the other events.

Just Close Your Eyes When you have decided on a scene to use for your cover, sit back for a minute with your eyes closed and get a clear picture of it. Then, start describing the scene on paper. Take a pen or pencil, and write down everything you can about the picture in your head. After deciding which scene to illustrate, the student whose example is shown above used the steps on the next page to decide which elements to include in his cover image.

Choosing the Elements for the Cover Image

▶ **STEP 1** Determine who or what the major focus of the scene is.

The major focus of the scene is on the characters Ponyboy and Johnny.

▶ **STEP 2** Identify the action that takes place during this scene.

They are sitting on the steps of an abandoned church.

▶ **STEP 3** Think about the emotions or feelings that are present in this scene.

They must be experiencing feelings of fear, uncertainty, and disbelief.

▶ **STEP 4** Identify the setting of the scene. What does the place look like?

It is sunrise as the boys sit on the old, stone steps outside the church. The church is crumbling and sitting in the middle of a field.

Once you have a good idea of the elements you will include in your scene, you can draw a rough sketch of it. Decide where you will place the title of the novel and the name of the author. Also decide where you will list any awards the book has won. Because this is only an early sketch, stick figures are fine. You will create your final cover image later in the chapter.

Reference Note

For more on **analyzing and designing book covers,** see page 148.

Select the Back Cover Quotation

Listen to the Characters   A common element on the back cover of a novel is a quotation. **Quotations help readers learn more about the story and the characters in the novel.** To select a quotation for the back cover, you need to remember important things that the characters or narrator said. A sentence from the book that reveals something important about the novel's conflict or about one of its main characters makes a good cover quotation. Use sticky notes to mark potential quotations as you read or re-read the novel. Looking back at the novel will help you decide on a good quotation. Notice how the writer of the example on the next page chose a quotation from *The Outsiders.*

 **KEY CONCEPT**

TEACHING (TIP)

Choosing the Elements for the Cover Image
Although this section does not go in depth on how to create the cover, the **Writing** section (pp. 136–138) provides a detailed framework for students. There is also a helpful section on how to illustrate a cover in the Focus on Viewing and Representing on pp. 148–151.

TEACHING (TIP)

Select the Back Cover Quotation
To give students a chance to consider audience appeal when choosing quotations, have them create a simple two-column chart and list several favorite quotations from their novel in the left column. Remind them to write the number of the page where the quotation appears in the novel. Have them circulate their lists around the classroom. Ask students to place two tally marks to the right of the quotation they find most intriguing, and one tally mark to the right of the second most appealing quotation. Students can review this peer response to their quotations before making a final decision.

MODALITY

Auditory Learners. Hearing dialogue passages may help students select a quotation. Have students work informally with partners. First, they should bookmark several pages in their chosen novels that contain key dialogue. Then, ask them to exchange books so that one student can read the other's dialogue passage aloud. The second student can then listen for the best quotation from the passage.

YOUR TURN 5

Give students the opportunity to evaluate their own progress at this point. Let them rate their cover image ideas on a scale of 1–5 with 5 being very satisfied by the cover idea at this point and 1 being unsure about the effectiveness of the idea. Have them make the same self-assessment of their quotation selection. Then, work individually with students who are unsure about the effectiveness of either their cover image or their quotation selection.

There are two big moments in the book—when Ponyboy meets a Soc girl who is actually nice to him and when Ponyboy and Johnny are confronted by the girl's boyfriend late at night. I don't see a good quotation during the scene with the boyfriend. I'll use this quote from the scene with the girl.

"I figured it was all right to be sitting there with them. Even if they did have their own troubles. I really couldn't see what Socs would have to sweat about—good grades, good cars, good girls, madras and Mustangs and Corvairs—Man, I thought, if I had worries like that, I'd consider myself lucky. I know better now."

When you pick a quotation, consider whether your audience will understand it. Some quotations make sense only as part of a longer passage. Be sure you choose a quotation that people will understand without knowing what happened before and after it.

TIP When choosing a cover quotation, consider whether a quotation gives away too much of the story. Make sure the quotation you choose sparks the audience's interest without giving anything away.

YOUR TURN 5 **Selecting a Cover Image and a Quotation**

Use the following suggestions to select a front cover image and a quotation for the back cover.

- List possible scenes and determine which would work best.
- Use the Thinking It Through steps on page 131 to determine what to include in your cover image.
- Create a mental picture of the scene, and sketch it on paper.
- Choose a quotation from one of the most important moments in the book. Choose carefully, and do not give away the whole story.

Plan Your Summary

Make a Long Story (or Novel) Short The front flap of your book jacket will contain a *summary*. When you write a **summary,** you briefly state the main ideas of a piece of writing. Because a novel is a special type of writing, its summary is special, too. **The summary for a novel must include details about characters, setting, plot, and theme.** The Critical Thinking Mini-Lesson on the next page will explain these key elements of novels and other fictional pieces.

| KEY CONCEPT

RESOURCES

Your Turn 5
Practice
- *Communications,* WS. p. 79

Critical Thinking
Practice
- *Communications,* WS. p. 80

Elements of Fiction

Even though novels can be about many different kinds of characters and subjects, all novels share four key elements: character, plot, setting, and theme. These key elements appear not only in novels but also in other types of stories, such as short stories and fairy tales. The following chart lists, defines, and gives an example from the fairy tale "Cinderella" for each element.

Element	Definition	Example
Character	A person or animal that takes part in the action. This includes the main character, called the **protagonist.**	Cinderella, prince, stepmother, stepsisters, fairy godmother
Setting	Setting is the time and place in which the events occur.	A kingdom long, long ago
Plot	Plot is the series of events that make up a story. The plot events of a story indicate the **conflict** (the problem the main character faces), the **climax** (the highest point of action), and the **resolution** (the solution of the problem). Note: Leave the resolution out of your book jacket summary—you want your readers to enjoy reading the novel's ending themselves.	**Event 1:** Jealous of her beauty and kindness, Cinderella's cruel stepfamily leaves her at home to do housework on the eve of the ball (conflict). **Event 2:** However, Cinderella's fairy godmother magically cleans the house and helps Cinderella get to the ball. **Event 3:** At the ball, the prince falls in love with Cinderella, but at midnight Cinderella disappears (climax). **Event 4:** The prince conducts a search and finds her. They marry (resolution).
Theme	A **theme** is the author's message about life that is revealed in the story.	Kind people will be rewarded.

PRACTICE

Choose a novel you have read or a familiar fairy tale such as "The Three Little Pigs." Then, identify the characters, setting, plot, and theme of the story.

Cooperative Learning

Group Evaluation. You may want to have students compose formal evaluations of the novels for which they create jackets. Divide the class into small groups. Then, have each group generate evaluation criteria that center on these elements: plot, character, and language (dialogue, figurative language, and so on). Groups can generate these criteria by brainstorming to identify what each of these elements are like in a good novel.

Encourage group members to give support for their statements about plot, character, and language by citing examples from novels they have read. Then, have each group member complete this sentence starter: In a good novel, the plot is_____, the main character is _____, and the language is _____.

After generating and discussing criteria in a group setting, group members can work individually to write an evaluation by applying their criteria to the novel chosen for their book jacket. Before students write, have them consider what the context and audience for the evaluation will be and what the purpose of the evaluation is. Each paragraph should be devoted to the discussion of a single criterion. Each paragraph should explain what the criterion is, tell whether the novel meets the criterion, and then elaborate with examples from the text on why the novel does or does not meet the criterion.

Have students write their introduction last, stating what their overall judgment is and what criteria they used to make that judgment. After writing, each student can share the evaluation with his or her original group.

Put It All Together   To write a summary of a novel, you must include information about all the important elements of the novel—characters, setting, plot, and theme. In addition to a summary, your book jacket's front flap should begin with a piece of information to "hook" your reader, and end with a reason to read the novel. The questions in the following charts will help you identify the information your readers will want as they read your summary. Be sure to include all these elements. In the right column are the notes one reader took about the novel *The Outsiders.*

Hook	
What small bit of information would make the reader want to know more about the novel?	*Ponyboy's friends often get mugged.*

Summary		
Characters	Who is the main character? What is he or she like? What is that character interested in or concerned about?	*Ponyboy is the main character. He's a tough member of the greasers but a good guy overall. He's worried about the conflict between the greasers and the Socs.*
Setting	Where does the story take place? Is it set in the past, present, or future?	*The setting is a big town in the mid-1960s.*
Plot	What major problem does the main character face? In general, how does he or she respond to that problem? (Be careful; do not give away too much of the plot.)	*Ponyboy gets in trouble when he talks to a Soc cheerleader, and her boyfriend wants to get back at him.*
Theme	What idea about life do you think the author is trying to give you? What does he or she want readers to learn from this novel?	*Violence is senseless.*

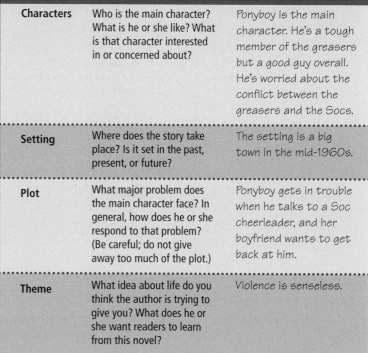

Reasons for Reading	
Why should people read this novel? What will they get out of it?	Readers will understand that the novel's message about violence is as important to today's readers as it was to readers in the 1960s.

YOUR TURN 6 **Writing the Front Flap**

Create charts like the ones on page 134 and the one above to help you gather information for your summary and front flap.

Research the Author

"Let Me Introduce You to . . ." The back flap often includes a short biography or other information about the author of the novel. If you have read other novels by the same author, you can say a little bit about the topics about which he or she likes to write. The back flap often includes interesting information about the author. To find author information, visit a library or use the Internet.

- **Library** In your school or local library, you will find many books that tell you about authors. One source is *Contemporary Authors*, a book that tells about authors' lives, careers, and awards. Some books such as *The Junior Book of Authors* and *Authors of Books for Young People* are geared toward young-adult readers. Also, the library's catalog will list other books, stories, and articles the author has written.

- **Internet** The World Wide Web offers many Web sites about authors. Browse on a search engine using the author's name or keyword combinations, including the words *young adult, literature, authors,* and *biographies.* You may even find an author's personal Web page.

◀ KEY CONCEPT

TIP As you read about authors, think about what other people will want to know about them. Look for details that surprise or interest you. Other people will want to know that information, too.

Reference Note

For more on **searching the World Wide Web,** see page 740 in the Quick Reference Handbook.

YOUR TURN 7 **Researching the Author**

Conduct a search for information about the author of your novel. Take notes on any important or interesting details that you can use in creating your book jacket.

YOUR TURN 6

Ready-made handouts of the chart on pp. 134–135 may help to encourage note taking in the writing process. You might want to count completed charts as a portion of the final grade for the front flap.

TEACHING TIP

Research the Author
To promote sound research techniques, distribute a few index cards to each student. Tell students that they should list the source and page number or Internet address for any new information they find about an author. Have them jot down on the cards quoted material that they can paraphrase later. *If students use the Internet to research their authors, you need to be aware that Internet resources are sometimes public forums, and their content can be unpredictable.*

YOUR TURN 7

Before students write from their notes or turn them in, have them highlight in one color the pieces of information that they consider basic about the author. Ask them to use a contrasting color to highlight author facts that are new or especially interesting. Such distinctions may help students create a final draft within space limitations.

Quotation for the Day

"Writing is a difficult trade which must be learned slowly by reading great authors . . ."

(André Maurois, 1885–1967, French writer)

Write the quotation on the chalkboard, and explain that each time a student reads, he or she is also gathering ideas about how another author works with words. Ask students to freewrite for five minutes about what makes an author great. Have volunteers share their thoughts with the class.

TEACHING TIP

A Writer's Model ◄
Students may need a definition of the word *madras.* The word refers to a lightweight cotton plaid or striped material from India. Madras shirts were popular during this time with some boys. Tell students that authors often include details like this to add to their character descriptions.

Framework

Back Flap
- Author biography *or*
- Information about the author

Back Cover
- Catchy quotation or passage

Directions and Explanations

Show your audience what makes this writer interesting. Tell them about other books by the author, the author's career, or where the author lives.

Choose a **quotation** or **passage** that grabs the reader's attention. A good quotation or passage usually introduces an important character or conflict in the novel.

A Writer's Model

The Outsiders was published when S. E. Hinton was just seventeen years old. The New York Herald Tribune named it one of the two best novels for teenagers in 1967. Since then Hinton has written many books for young adults. The list includes That Was Then, This Is Now, which is an American Library Association Notable Book, Rumble Fish, and Tex. She lives in Tulsa, Oklahoma, with her husband, David.

"I figured it was all right to be sitting there with them. Even if they did have their own troubles. I really couldn't see what Socs would have to sweat about—good grades, good cars, good girls, madras and Mustangs and Corvairs—Man, I thought, if I had worries like that, I'd consider myself lucky. I know better now."

RESOURCES

Writing
Writing Prompts
- *Communications*, TP. 34, WS. p. 83

Book Jacket

Front Cover	**Front Flap**
■ Author and title	■ Hook
■ Meaningful image	■ Summary and reason for reading

Be sure to include the **author** and **title** of the book. You will create the cover in detail later. For now, use your rough sketch.

Begin this section with a quotation or phrase that will **hook** the reader. Your **summary** and **reason for reading** should not give away the novel's ending.

Have students refer to the section on questioning and predicting on pp. 124–125 in the Reading Workshop while they preview **A Writer's Model.** Then, have them write their questions and predictions about *The Outsiders.* Suggest they share their responses to the book jacket with a partner.

Connecting Reading and Writing

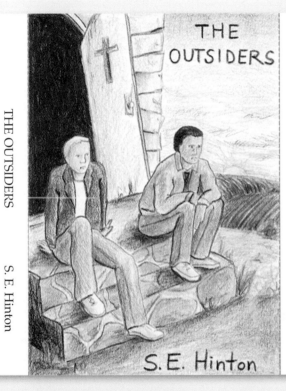

THE OUTSIDERS

S. E. Hinton

Ponyboy cannot walk home from the movies without being mugged. He is one of the greasers and an enemy of the Socs, the rich kids from the other side of town. Most people think that the only thing the greasers and Socs have in common is their hatred of each other. When Ponyboy meets a Soc cheerleader, Cherry Valence, he begins to wonder whether greasers and Socs are really so different after all.

When Cherry's boyfriend finds out about her innocent conversation with a greaser, he sets off a frightening chain of events that adds to Ponyboy's anger at the Socs. It also leads Ponyboy to get over old grudges. He learns that people are pretty much the same and that things are rough all over.

The Outsiders is set in the mid-1960s, and it deals with the senselessness of violence. The novel is as important today as it was in 1967, when it was first published.

Connecting Reading and Writing

To help students create an effective book jacket, direct them to review the parts of a summary on pp. 134–135. Ask them to review **A Student's Model** to see how one student answered those questions.

To evaluate students' drafts, you may want to use a rubric such as the following:

Contains a front cover, back cover, front flap, and back flap	40 points
Grabs audience's attention	20 points
Contains sufficient information to help readers preview the book	20 points
Does not reveal too much of the plot	20 points

A Student's Model

Here is the front cover and flap text of a book jacket created by Artemese C. Evans, a student at Chemawa Middle School in Riverside, California.

Setting
Character

Hook

Summary

Setting

Theme
Reason for reading

During the twelfth century, a young boy named Muna yearns to know his father, a proud samurai warrior. When his mother dies, Muna has only one clue to his father's identity: a chrysanthemum tattoo on his father's left shoulder.

Muna stows away on a ship and goes to the capital city of Japan, where he meets a swordsmith named Fukuji. Muna becomes a servant for the well-known swordsmith and has to fight temptations such as the temptation of stealing a sword from Fukuji. However, Muna never gives up his dream of claiming his father's name and becoming a man.

The Sign of the Chrysanthemum tells about a boy with fantastic goals and courage. Muna dreams about finally belonging in the world, but he realizes there are more important things in life. This story will teach its readers to overcome their fears and become individuals.

YOUR TURN 8 **Creating a Book Jacket**

As you create your book jacket, keep both your primary and secondary audience in mind. Also, refer to the framework and Writer's Model on pages 136–137.

RESOURCES

Your Turn 8
Practice
■ *Communications,* TP. 35, WS. p. 84

Revising

Evaluate and Revise Content, Organization, and Style

It's as Easy as One, Two . . . Read over your draft at least twice. In the first reading, follow the guidelines below to check content and organization. In the second reading, work on the style of your writing by following the instructions on page 140.

▷ **First Reading: Content and Organization** Use this chart to evaluate and revise your book jacket so the message is clear.

Guidelines for Self-Evaluation and Peer Evaluation

Evaluation Questions	Tips	Revision Techniques
❶ Does the cover image grab the audience's attention?	**Use sticky notes** to mark three things in the illustration that would interest readers.	**Elaborate** with details to make the illustration more interesting, or choose a more interesting scene for the cover.
❷ Does the front flap hook the reader?	**Circle** a statement that should make readers want to read the entire novel.	If needed, **add** a hook to the beginning of the summary.
❸ Does the summary include details about character, setting, plot, and theme?	**Underline** these details in the summary and label the element each describes.	If necessary, **add** details about character, setting, plot, or theme to the summary.
❹ Does the summary provide a reason for reading that will encourage people to read the novel?	**Place a star** by the reason for reading, and consider whether you would read the novel based on the information provided.	As needed, **elaborate** with additional information that will help readers understand how the novel will relate to them and why they should read it.
❺ Does the back cover quotation make sense, and does it make audiences want to read the novel?	Ask a friend who has not read the novel to **evaluate the quotation.**	If necessary, **replace** the quotation with one that is easier to understand or more interesting.
❻ Does the biography include interesting facts and details about the author?	Review the biography and **highlight** each of the interesting facts or details.	**Elaborate** with more details about the writer's books, career, or life, if needed.

Writing Workshop **139**

Quotation for the Day

❝I am under the spell of language, which has ruled me since I was 10.❞

(V. S. Pritchett, 1900–1997, British critic)

After writing the quotation on the chalkboard, ask students to freewrite about its meaning. A few volunteers might read aloud from their responses. Explain to students that the purpose of evaluation and revision is to make their papers as clear and powerful as the work of the professional authors they admire.

TEACHING TIP

▶ **Elaboration**
To help students add elaboration to their drafts, have randomly selected partners exchange drafts. Then, ask partners to read each other's drafts and write responses to the following questions:

1. Does the cover include all the information that you want to know? Is that information interesting? Why or why not?

2. Does the front flap contain enough information, and does it get your attention?

3. Does the summary provide all the details about character, setting, plot, and theme that you want to know?

4. Does the summary help you to understand how the novel will relate to you? Why or why not?

5. Does the biography include enough interesting information about the author?

Then, have partners read each other's responses.

Responding to the Revision Process

ANSWERS

Possible answers are provided below.

1. Showing Ponyboy in action is a more interesting hook than just identifying him.

2. The added information helps the reader understand why Ponyboy changes his views about greasers and Socs.

Critical Thinking

Metacognition. Ask students to reflect on their own typical sentence style. Ask them to consider whether they prefer shorter sentences, longer sentences, or varied sentence lengths. Present the following questions as journal or discussion starters:

1. Which sentence length may better communicate moods or feelings? [long]

2. Which sentence length may better create action or suspense? [short]

3. Which sentence style may best maintain reader interest? [varied]

4. What strategies help to make the writing more concise and varied? [combining sentences]

Then, ask them the following question:

5. Why is it important to vary sentence style? [to keep readers engaged with the text]

ONE WRITER'S REVISIONS Examine this revision of an early draft of the book jacket on pages 136–137.

add

cannot walk home from the movies without being mugged. He
Ponyboy is one of the greasers and an enemy of the Socs,

the rich kids from the other side of town. Most people

think that the only thing the greasers and Socs have in

common is their hatred of each other. When Ponyboy

elaborate
a Soc cheerleader,
meets Cherry Valence, he begins to wonder whether

greasers and Socs are really so different after all.

PEER REVIEW

As you evaluate a peer's book jacket, ask yourself these questions:

- Does this jacket make me want to read the novel? Why?
- What parts could be made more interesting?

Responding to the Revision Process

1. Why do you think the writer added a sentence to the beginning of the passage?

2. Why do you think the writer elaborated on information in the third sentence?

Second Reading: Style The writing on a book jacket is somewhat like a movie preview, or trailer; an interesting preview can make viewers want to see the movie that the trailer advertises. However, a dull preview can sink a good movie. Likewise, the writing on a book jacket needs to be interesting to encourage people to read the inside of the book. One way to interest potential readers is to make sure your writing has a lively and interesting rhythm.

When you evaluate the rhythm of your book jacket's text, ask yourself whether your writing contains short, choppy sentences. Read the sentences on your book jacket aloud. Put an X by each sentence that contains only five to eight words. Then, combine some of the short, choppy sentences—if they are clearly related to each other.

Be sure to punctuate your combined sentences correctly. You can combine them by joining them with a semicolon or by putting a comma and a conjunction between them.

Combining Sentences

Since your purpose for creating a book jacket is to inform potential readers quickly and clearly, your book jacket has to read smoothly. One way to improve the flow of your writing is to vary your sentence length. Too many short, choppy sentences will make your jacket less readable.

Example:
The Pearl was written over fifty years ago. Its message is still true today.

Revised:
The Pearl was written over fifty years ago, but its message is still true today.

Short sentences that have the same subject can be combined to form a compound sentence. To create a compound sentence, place a comma after the first sentence and add a conjunction such as *and*, *but*, or *or*.

Focus on Sentences

TIP When you combine your sentences, be careful not to create a *run-on sentence*. A **run-on sentence** is actually two complete sentences punctuated as one sentence. In a run-on, the thoughts just run into each other.

Reference Note
For more information on **combining sentences,** see page 273.

ONE WRITER'S REVISIONS

The Outsiders is set in the mid-1960s. ^{, and it} It deals with

the senselessness of violence.

Responding to the Revision Process

Why do you think the writer combined the two sentences above?

YOUR TURN 9 — Evaluating and Revising Your Book Jacket

- First, use the guidelines on page 139 to evaluate and revise the content and organization of your book jacket.

- Next, use the Focus on Sentences section above to help you decide whether you need to combine any choppy sentences.

- If a peer evaluated your jacket, think carefully about those comments and how they might help you improve your jacket.

Combining Sentences
Point out to students that they can combine sentences that contain different subjects and verbs, as long as the ideas are closely related. Write the following sentences on the chalkboard, and ask students how they would combine them.

Ponyboy is a greaser. The rich boys in the Socs consider him an enemy. [Ponyboy is a greaser, so the rich boys in the Socs consider him an enemy.]

Responding to the Revision Process
ANSWER
Here is a possible answer.

The writer combined the two sentences to make it easier to understand the connection between the two ideas and to improve the flow of the writing.

YOUR TURN 9

Let students exchange work and act as peer editors. You might have them use self-stick notes to make organization and content suggestions. Ask peer editors to sketch any alternative cover design suggestions on a separate sheet of paper, not directly on the original cover image.

Evaluating Student Writing

The ancillary *Assessment Alternatives* contains a variety of assessment forms, including Inventories and Evaluation Forms and rubrics: Six-Point Scales, Four-Point Scales, and Six Trait Scales.

Publishing

Proofread Your Book Jacket

The Home Stretch   Before you finalize your book jacket, proofread by reading your entire book jacket out loud slowly. Make **edits**, or corrections, as you find errors in spelling and grammar in the draft. If possible, repeat the same exercise with a classmate's book jacket.

Grammar Link

Hyphenation

Have you ever noticed how narrow the inside flaps of a book jacket really are? To make good use of that cramped space, you may need to divide some words at the end of a line by using **hyphens**. It is important to learn how to use hyphens properly. Read each rule below, and notice how *not* following the rule makes a sentence hard to understand. For more on **hyphenation**, see page 646.

■ Never divide a word that has only one syllable.

Incorrect
Ponyboy cannot walk home from the movies without being mug-ged.

Correct
Ponyboy cannot walk home from the movies without being mugged.

■ Divide a word only between syllables.

Incorrect
When Ponyboy meets a Soc cheerle-ader, Cherry Valence . . .

Correct
When Ponyboy meets a Soc cheer-leader, Cherry Valence, he . . .

■ Make sure you do not divide a word so that one letter stands alone.

Incorrect
Since then she has written many books for young adults. . . including an A-merican Library Association Notable Book.

Correct
Since then she has written many books for young adults. . . including an American Library Association Notable Book.

PRACTICE

Show how you would divide the following words if they did not fit on the end of a line.

1. different
2. movies
3. conversation
4. important
5. through

6. practice
7. following
8. innocent
9. consider
10. amend

Publish Your Book Jacket

Check It Out!   To make your book jacket available to people who will benefit from it, try one of these ideas.

- Help put all the information from your classmates' book jackets into a book-preview *spreadsheet*. A **spreadsheet** is a document that is arranged into rows and columns. See the tip to the right.

- With your classmates, talk to the school librarian about laminating your book jackets and displaying them in your library.

COMPUTER TIP

To start a spreadsheet, create columns labeled "title," "author," "summary," "quotation," and "author information." Then, have your classmates type in their book jacket information.

Designing Your Writing

Book Jacket Layout   After you have finished writing and editing the text for your book jacket, you will need to create the final version. You can do this either by hand or on a computer. The diagram to the right shows you how to place your covers and flaps on paper so that it will fold into a book jacket. You will need two sheets of 8½- × 11-inch paper and tape.

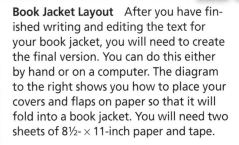

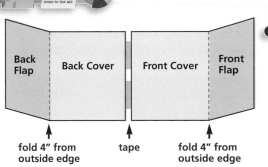

Back Flap | Back Cover | Front Cover | Front Flap

↑ fold 4" from outside edge   ↑ tape   ↑ fold 4" from outside edge

Reflect on Your Book Jacket

Building Your Portfolio   Reflect on your work by answering the following questions.

- How well did you achieve your purpose for creating a book jacket? Explain.

- What did you learn while writing your summary? How could you use those summary-writing techniques in other types of writing?

YOUR TURN 10   **Proofreading, Publishing, and Reflecting on Your Book Jacket**

- Correct grammar, usage, and mechanics errors.
- Publish your book jacket so that it will reach your target audience.
- Answer the questions from Reflect on Your Book Jacket above. Record your responses in a learning log, or include them in your portfolio.

PORTFOLIO

Writing a Short Story

In a novel like the one you read for this chapter, readers spend a long time with the characters and follow a complex plot. The novel's elements, which you used in the summary for your book jacket, are spread out over many chapters. A **short story** includes the same elements as a novel. In the case of a short story, however, the **characters, plot, and setting** of the story are given in only a few pages. In this workshop, you will write a short story using all of these fiction elements.

Read the first few paragraphs of the short story "The No-Guitar Blues" by Gary Soto. Notice how quickly he introduces the main character and sets the plot events in motion.

The No-Guitar Blues
by Gary Soto

The moment Fausto saw the group Los Lobos on *American Bandstand*, he knew exactly what he wanted to do with his life—play guitar. His eyes grew large with excitement as Los Lobos ground out a song while teenagers bounced off each other on the crowded dance floor.

He had watched *American Bandstand* for years and had heard Ray Camacho and the Teardrops at Romain Playground, but it had never occurred to him that he too might become a musician. That afternoon Fausto knew his mission in life: to play guitar in his own band; to sweat out songs and prance around the stage; to make money and dress weird.

Fausto turned off the television set and walked outside, wondering how he could get enough money to buy a guitar. . . .

The main **character** of this story is Fausto. The **plot** begins with him wondering how he will be able to buy a guitar. You have a hint at the **setting** for the beginning of the story—he is at home watching television.

A Flash of Inspiration Before you write a short story of your own, you must come up with an idea for the story. Some-times a story idea springs into your mind immediately, but other times you have to search for one. You might try

- writing about a person you know who is interesting or unusual
- telling about an experience you have had

One student decided that his friend's desire to play hockey might make a good story. He decided to change parts of the story to create **suspense,** the uncertainty a reader feels about what will happen.

Critical Elements   Once you have a story idea, consider each of the fiction elements and decide how they will take shape in your story. Creating a story map like the one below will help you. Do not forget that your plot events should indicate the conflict, climax, and resolution of your story. (For more on the **elements of fiction,** see page 133.)

Characters: John, his mom

Plot event: Mother is looking for John and finds him at a skating rink watching a hockey team. (setting)

Plot event: He explains that he really wants to be on the team. She won't let him because she thinks it's dangerous. (conflict)

Plot event: A game is about to start, and John convinces his mom to watch.

Plot event: She gets very excited cheering for the team. (climax)

Plot event: She decides hockey might be a good thing for John to do after all. (resolution)

YOUR TURN 11 Writing a Short Story

Brainstorm a story idea, and fill in a story map like the one above. Then, use the information in your story map to write a short story.

Put It in Words   Once your story map is complete, you are ready to begin writing a draft of the story. Remember to use **dialogue** to show character and to use concrete **description** to explain your setting. (For more on **dialogue,** see page 31. For more on **description,** see page 21.) The following is the beginning of the student's story about his friend.

John lived for hockey. Every day after school, he would walk to the town's only ice rink and watch the local youth teams practice. Often when the teams were packing up, he would borrow some skates and a stick and zoom around on the ice, perfecting his turns or slamming the puck into the net.

"Come on, John!" someone would almost always say. "Why don't you join the team?"

"Naw," he would answer. "My mom's scared I'll get hurt. She won't sign the papers."

Meeting

INDIVIDUAL NEEDS

MODALITY

Visual Learners. Simple sketches can help students understand the term "concrete description." Using a novel, read one or two sentences that describe setting. Then, have students think of specific nouns and adjectives that they heard. Invite a student to do a simple sketch on the chalkboard. Point out that a concrete description helps the reader easily visualize the scene.

YOUR TURN 11

For assessment, check that students have included all the critical elements of a short story. You might use a rubric such as the one below.

Story map was followed	30 points
Characters are believable and engaging	20 points
Plot includes conflict, climax, and resolution	20 points
Setting is described adequately	10 points
Dialogue is included	10 points
Theme is clear	10 points

Analyzing a Poem

When you made the cover of your book jacket, you created a picture that quickly gave readers an idea about the novel you chose. Poets also create pictures for their readers by using descriptive language.

Figuratively Speaking   A **figure of speech** is a descriptive word or expression that is not meant to be taken literally. Two figures of speech commonly used in poetry are *simile* and *metaphor*.

A **simile** is a comparison between two unlike things, using a word such as *like* or *as*.

> The windblown children dashed across the field like scattered leaves.

A **metaphor** is a comparison between two unlike things in which one thing is said to *be* another thing.

> Our feet became hot potatoes roasting in the sand.

Sense or Sensibility   While figures of speech describe by making comparisons, **imagery** uses vivid language to help the reader feel like a part of the poem. Imagery appeals to the senses—sight, touch, hearing, taste, and smell.

> The buzzing of bees in the garden broke the morning's silence.

Read the poem "Construction" by Patricia Hubbell, paying attention to its descriptive language.

Construction
by Patricia Hubbell

The house frames hang like spider webs
Dangling in the sun,
While up and down the wooden strands
The spider workers run.
They balance on the two-by-fours,   5
They creep across the beams,
While down below, the heap of wood,
A spider-stockpile, gleams.
The spider-workers spin the web
And tack it tight with nails.   10
They ready it against the night.
When all work ends.

A Closer Look   When you analyze a poem, you should read it several times and take notes on what you find. The notes below were taken by a student who analyzed the descriptive language in "Construction."

- simile—house frames compared to spider webs (line 1)
- imagery—"Dangling in the sun" (line 2)
- imagery—"They creep across the beams" (line 6)
- metaphor—workers compared to spiders spinning a web (line 9)

146   Chapter 4   **Exposition:** Previewing a Novel

The Big Picture Next, decide what message the poem's descriptive language seems to support. You will use this message as the main idea of your paper.

Put It in Words Before writing your essay, you will need to organize your ideas. Your poem analysis should include the parts listed in the following chart.

Introduction	<ul><li>the author and title of the poem</li><li>the types of descriptive language used</li><li>the writer's message</li></ul>
Body	<ul><li>examples of descriptive language</li><li>explanation of how the descriptive language points to the writer's message</li></ul>
Conclusion	<ul><li>restatement of the descriptive language used and the writer's message</li></ul>

Here is one student's analysis of the poem "Construction." Notice that the student summarizes significant events and details in the poem for readers who might not be familiar with it. She also includes quotes from the poem when discussing examples of figurative language. According to the essay, what is the poet's message?

> In her poem "Construction," Patricia Hubbell uses similes, metaphors, and imagery to show the similarities between workers building a house and spiders spinning a web.
>
> Hubbell uses a simile and a metaphor to compare the workers with spiders. In this poem, the "house frames hang like spider webs." She also describes "spider-workers" who "spin the web." The imagery supports these comparisons as well. The
>
> house frames are "dangling in the sun." The description of the workers is spiderlike: "They creep across the beams." All these descriptions help the reader picture the workers and spiders at the same time.
>
> The figures of speech and imagery point to the message that a construction site is very similar to a spider web. The workers and spiders work the same way and both build houses.

YOUR TURN 12 Analyzing a Poem

Find a poem you like that contains figures of speech and vivid imagery. Follow the guidelines in this lesson to write an essay analyzing the poem's descriptive language. If you wish, present your ideas as an oral, rather than written, response to literature.

ENGLISH-LANGUAGE LEARNERS
General Strategies. Students who have difficulty with the concept of sensory words can work in pairs to create a sensory word map. Have students draw a circle on a piece of paper and write "Sensory Words" in the middle. Then, have them draw five "arms" extending out, attach a circle to the end of each arm, and label each circle with one of the senses: sight, touch, hearing, taste, and smell.

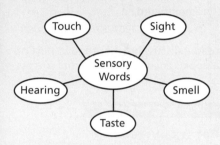

Then, have students brainstorm words that appeal to each sense and write them next to the appropriate arm. Here are some examples.
Sight: dazzling, rosy, murky
Touch: soft, scratchy, smooth
Hearing: howl, chirp, squeak
Taste: salty, sweet, bitter
Smell: fresh, sharp, musty

YOUR TURN 12

Five hundred to seven hundred words is an appropriate length for a student essay. For assessment, check that students correctly identify figures of speech and imagery and that they explain how the figurative language supports the poem's message. Students should use quotations from the poem when they discuss examples of figurative language.

OBJECTIVES

■ To recognize the effects of color, font, and illustration on a book's cover

■ To analyze a cover for its effectiveness in revealing content

■ To finalize a book jacket using appropriate media, color, and type

Quotation for the Day

❝Some books are undeservedly forgotten; none are undeservedly remembered.❞

(W. H. Auden, 1907–1973, British poet)

Lead a discussion about the impact of a book's cover on its potential success.

TEACHING TIP

Get It Covered
Book catalogs of various kinds are often available to classroom teachers. Have randomly selected small groups of students informally browse through several book catalogs and select the three covers they think are the most appealing. Then, ask students to explain their choices to other group members or to the entire class.

WHAT'S AHEAD?

In this section you will analyze book covers and design your own. You will also learn how to:

■ recognize the effect of color, font, and kind of illustration on a book's cover

■ analyze a cover for effectiveness

■ finalize your book jacket using appropriate media, color, and type

TIP *Media* is the plural form of *medium.*

Reference Note
For more on **illustration,** see page 789 in the Quick Reference Handbook.

Analyzing and Designing a Book Cover

Can you judge a book by its cover? People do all the time. Sometimes a person will read or buy a book simply because of the cover, so the cover can be very important. If you know how to analyze a book cover, you can gather much more information than the title and author's name. A good book cover presents images, colors, and words in a way that reveals something about the book's content.

To analyze and interpret a book's cover, pay attention to three important elements: illustration, color, and font.

Illustration

Tools of the Trade An illustration is an image; a **medium** is the way an artist chooses to present that image. An artist has many media to choose from when presenting an illustration. For instance, an artist who wants to show a sailboat on an ocean could draw it with pencils, paint it with acrylic paint, use a computer-generated design, or take a photograph of a real sailboat. The artist could also use scraps of paper to create a collage of a sailboat.

Get It Covered No matter what medium an artist uses, the illustration on a book's cover should tell readers something about the book. It can reveal something about the characters, setting, or action.

■ **Characters** Are they male or female, young or old, rich or poor?

148 Chapter 4 **Exposition:** Previewing a Novel

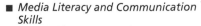

RESOURCES

Focus on Viewing and Representing Practice

■ *Media Literacy and Communication Skills*
  —*Support and Practice,* Ch. 4
  —*A How-to Handbook*

Teaching Notes

■ *Media Literacy and Communication Skills*
  —*A Teacher's Guide,* Ch. 4

- **Setting**   Is the story set in the past, present, or future? Is it set in the city, the country, the United States, or somewhere else?
- **Action**   Is there a chase scene or an important discovery?

Color

Color is an important element of an illustration. Colors can be described as warm or cool. Warm colors, such as red or yellow, tend to create a feeling of excitement. On the other hand, cool colors, such as blue or green, often create feelings of calmness or moodiness. The feeling an artist creates through his or her use of color is part of the artist's own style. Artists can also use color, however, to tell the reader something about the mood of the novel. An artist might also use a combination of warm and cool colors to emphasize important information. For example, in an illustration full of cool colors, the artist can use a warm color to draw the reader's eye to an important aspect of the novel. For more on **color,** see page 728 in the Quick Reference Handbook.

Examine the covers in the right margin and decide whether the colors are warm or cool. What do you think the artist is trying to achieve by using these colors?

Font

Most computers allow you to change the **font,** or the size and design of the type. Fonts can look like newsprint or handwriting. The font can look heavy and dark or light and thin. In addition, most fonts are available in styles such as bold or italic, and come in any number of sizes. Like colors, different fonts can suggest different meanings. For more on **font,** see page 726 in the Quick Reference Handbook.

Look at the examples below. What makes each font match the subject?

Romance   **Old-fashioned**
Children   **FUN!**
SCARY   `Technology`

Put It All Together

Using illustration, color, and font, the artist gives a general understanding of a book's content. Read the example on the next page of how one student analyzed the cover of the book *Hatchet*.

Color

As students examine the covers in the margin, you may want to provide the following examples:

- *Tuck Everlasting*—The warm colors that swirl together and disappear suggest mystery.
- *The Call of the Wild*—The cool colors of silver, white, and ice blue suggest distance and trouble.
- *The Adventures of Tom Sawyer*—The warm, vivid colors suggest emotion, fun, and adventure.

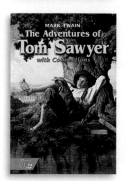

LEARNERS HAVING DIFFICULTY
As students work to determine whether the covers shown on p. 149 and on this page are literal or symbolic, point out that the covers for *Hatchet* and *The Adventures of Tom Sawyer* depict characters in actual settings, while the cover for *The Call of the Wild* shows only an image of a dog and the cover for *Tuck Everlasting* includes an image of a forest and a pair of eyes. Students should say that the covers for *Tuck Everlasting* and *The Call of the Wild* are symbolic, and the covers for *The Adventures of Tom Sawyer* and *Hatchet* are literal.

Critical Thinking

Evaluation. After they have completed **Your Turn 13**, have students read the books whose covers they interpreted and then evaluate the book covers. In groups, students should develop criteria by reviewing the questions about cover elements and deciding what qualities each of the elements should exhibit. (Example: *A book cover's color should reflect the mood of the novel.*) Using these criteria, students should write evaluations supported by evidence from the cover. They should conclude with an overall rating.

Have students exchange papers with peers who evaluated the same book covers. Remind students that as they receive feedback, they should consider alternative viewpoints openly and then revise their evaluations.

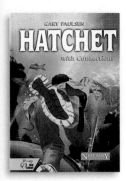

GARY PAULSEN
HATCHET
with Connections

NEWBERY

TIP You might classify an illustrator's style as *literal* or *symbolic*. A more **literal** style of illustration might show actual scenes from the book. A more **symbolic** style of illustration may hint at an important idea or emotion in the book, rather than show an actual scene.

How would you describe the style of each cover shown on page 149 and on this page?

Illustration

Does the illustration clearly show the main character, setting, and action?	The illustration shows a boy—maybe the main character. The setting seems to be underwater, since there are fish and bubbles. The action is pretty clear—the boy must be trying to get to the surface.
What medium was used, and how does that medium help convey meaning?	The medium could be paint or computer. Bright painting or computer-generated art like this looks clean and crisp. It shows the setting, character, and action clearly.

Color

Are the colors in this cover warm or cool? What emotions could they represent?	The purple and green (cool colors) make me think that the novel might be moody and emotional. Because the boy's shirt is yellow, it really stands out against the green water. The ripped shirt might be important. Maybe the boy faces a dangerous or difficult situation.

Font

What meanings do the font styles reveal?	The word "hatchet" has pointed edges, just like a blade. The hatchet must be an important part of the story. I think the hatchet is going to help the boy.

YOUR TURN 13 Interpreting a Book Cover

Make a chart like the one above to interpret the cover of a book. If you have trouble, review the information on pages 148–149.

YOUR TURN 13

Ask students to explain their interpretations and allow for a variety of responses about what the illustration, color, and font suggest.

RESOURCES

Your Turn 13 and 14
Practice and Reinforcement
■ *Media Literacy and Communication Skills*
—*Support and Practice,* Ch. 4 transparencies and worksheets

Design Your Cover

Now that you know how book covers provide information about a book, you should create your own. Look at the rough sketch of the cover you began earlier in the chapter. To complete your cover, use the same elements other artists use: illustrations, color, and font. Remember, the cover should convince people to read the novel. Make sure it gives readers interesting hints about the action, characters, or setting of the novel you have chosen.

A Rave Review   Do you think that the characters, setting, and action you have chosen to illustrate represent the novel well? Review your choices in the chart you created on page 150. Once you are sure about the content of your image, pick the medium that best helps you express something important about the novel.

The mood of the novel will help you decide on the colors to use. Determine the primary emotions portrayed in the novel, and use warm or cool colors to emphasize those emotions.

Finally, decide how the title should look on the page. Experiment with different fonts on a computer or flip through a magazine, tracing any fonts that fit the subject or mood of your novel.

Improve Your Drafts

Like writers, artists need to make drafts before they create a finished product. Few cover illustrators convey the true meaning of a book on their first try. Experiment with different images, media, colors, and fonts until you feel you have captured the point of the novel. Sketch several ideas, and choose one that you will fully develop as your final cover image.

YOUR TURN 14   Designing Your Book Cover

Follow the guidelines beginning on page 148 to finalize the book cover you began as part of your book jacket project. Remember to include the title of the book and the author's name on the cover. After you complete a rough sketch of your cover design, ask a classmate to look at it and give you suggestions for improving it.

Reference Note

To review how to get ideas for your cover illustration, see the Thinking It Through on page 131.

Wrap It Up

Metacognition. Ask students to reflect on their analysis by answering the following questions:

1. What did you learn from this activity about why certain book covers appeal to you?

2. How will having done this activity affect the way you choose a novel?

Then, ask students this question:

3. What elements of a book cover should give the reader a general understanding of the book's content? [illustration, color, font]

TECHNOLOGY TIP

Computers have simplified many stages of publication, including the generation of cover ideas and the consideration of final arrangement. Students can work with cover images and title styles, as well as with text. Allow them to experiment with fonts, type style, graphic elements, and color and to print out two or three trial versions to consider as they make final decisions about medium.

YOUR TURN 14

Have them turn in self-evaluations in which they analyze their choices of medium, color, and font. Rather than marking errors on the students' covers, you may prefer to use a comment sheet for the correction of mechanics or grammar not caught in the draft stage.

Focus on Speaking and Listening

OBJECTIVES

- To choose a reading selection
- To edit a selection for a dramatic reading
- To analyze a selection for its mood and the personalities of its characters
- To use facial expressions, gestures, and different voices to portray different characters

Quotation for the Day

"There was still some heavy booing when I arrived at the microphone, and I made a deep English-actor type of bow, with princely flourishes and flutters, and they laughed, and then they were mine all the way. I held on to them for dear life for the next two minutes."

(Garrison Keillor, 1942–   , host of the radio show "A Prairie Home Companion")

Read the quotation to students and suggest to them that their purpose in a dramatic reading is to cast a spell on the audience within a limited time frame.

WHAT'S AHEAD?

In this section you will perform a dramatic reading. You will also learn how to

- choose a reading selection
- edit a selection for a dramatic reading
- analyze a selection for its mood and the characters' personalities
- use facial expressions, gestures, and different voices to portray different characters

TIP You may also choose a dramatic reading from a play. Be sure the scene you choose still follows these guidelines.

Performing a Dramatic Reading

You are in an auditorium. On stage, a young man begins to speak, but he does not sound like a young man. He stomps his foot, and in a little girl's voice he demands a snack. Then, suddenly, his tone changes: "Honey, you can't have a snack now. It'll spoil your dinner." You are watching a *dramatic reading*. A **dramatic reading** is a presentation of a reading selection in which the reader acts out the characters and action as he or she reads aloud.

In one way, a dramatic reading from a novel is just like a novel's book jacket. They both give audiences a taste of a longer piece of literature. A dramatic reader brings the reading to life by using voices, facial expressions, and hand gestures. In this section you will have the opportunity to become a dramatic reader by dramatizing a scene from a novel.

Choose Your Selection

Choose Wisely   Use these questions to help you pick a passage for your dramatic reading.

- **Is it interesting?** Avoid long, descriptive passages. They are not easy to dramatize, especially for a young-adult audience. Instead, choose a passage with interesting dialogue or action. Focus on scenes that are full of suspense, action, or emotion.

- **Is it easy to understand?** If you have trouble understanding your passage, your audience will, too. Make sure your reading will make sense to people who have not read the whole book.

- **What is your time limit?** Make sure you know what your time limit is, and stick to it. Test the length of your passage by reading it slowly.

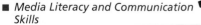

Prepare for Reading

From the Page to the Stage   After you choose a selection, you need to adapt it for performance. Follow these three steps.

- **Edit the Selection.** Some parts of a novel do not sound right in performance. To keep your reading interesting, cut dialogue tags such as "he said" and "she said," long descriptive passages, and references to characters and events that are not important to the passage you selected. All these things break the flow of your performance and distract your audience. To make editing easy, make a copy of your selection. Then, cross out the parts that will not sound right in a performance.

> "Honey, you can't have a snack now. It'll spoil your dinner."
> ~~Maggie's mother said firmly.~~

  After you have crossed out unnecessary parts, you can add background information from other parts of the novel as needed. Sometimes this is necessary to make sure the audience understands what is happening in the passage.

- **Analyze the Selection.** What happens in your selection? How do the characters feel? Is the tone of the piece happy, sad, or suspenseful? Go through the passage and make notes on the overall scene and on each character. You can show what the characters are like in general, as well as how they act in your selection.

> <u>Maggie</u>: She is stubborn and likes to get her own way. In this passage about the snack, she's having a temper tantrum. She pouts. She takes her anger out on her brother.
>
> <u>Maggie's mother</u>: She is gentle, but firm. She has a soothing voice.
>
> <u>Little brother</u>: He is afraid. He seems to get picked on by Maggie a lot.
>
> <u>Overall tone</u>: The tension rises when Maggie confronts her brother.

- **Plan Your Delivery.** Have you ever noticed that when you are happy or excited, the **pitch** of your voice gets higher and your speaking **rate** gets faster? If you are serious or sad, the pitch of your voice becomes lower and your speaking rate gets slower. Using your notes, figure out what kind of voice will fit the moods of the narrator and each of the characters. Most important, keep a character's voice consistent until the selection is over or until his or her feelings change. Also, use gestures. When people

TIP   Use your voice to help listeners follow along. Speak louder to **stress** important words, and raise your pitch to connect, or show **juncture** between, related ideas.

Focus on Speaking and Listening   **153**

If you plan to have students practice before their peers, offer the following guidelines for constructive criticism.

1. Say what you think is working well.
2. Avoid criticism of physical appearance or attire.
3. Make suggestions about voice or gesture changes in the form of questions, such as "Could you speak louder here?" and "Should you shake your head when you say that?"

Wrap It Up

Metacognition. Ask students to focus on the tasks they performed to prepare for their dramatic readings. Give them a few minutes to answer these questions:

1. Which task gave you the most trouble? Why?
2. What did you discover about your strengths and weaknesses during your practice sessions?

Then, ask these questions:

3. For what reason would you recommend doing a dramatic reading? [to bring a story to life]
4. What elements make a passage good for a dramatic reading? [dialogue, action]
5. What tools do you need to use for an effective delivery? [voice, gestures]

YOUR TURN 15

Depending on students' oral reading ability, you may want to weigh selection choice, editing, and analyzing more heavily than performance.

---

speak, they move. Most people emphasize their words with gestures. Some even have certain mannerisms, like raising their eyebrows or waving their hands. Your reading will look more realistic if you act out unique gestures for each character.

To figure out the best way to add voices and actions to your reading script, you can add notes to remind you how to perform your edited selection. Retype or rewrite your edited reading selection with the acting notes in parentheses.

Example:
(Maggie's mom, medium-low voice, soft but firm)
"Honey, you can't have a snack now. It'll spoil your dinner."

(Maggie, high voice, yelling. Face in a pout.)
"But I want a snack NOW!" (stomp)

Practice Delivery

Practice Makes Perfect To make your reading the best it can be, you need to practice many times. Think of practicing as a series of steps, each one a little different from the one before it.

Step 1	Practice reading until you are comfortable and familiar with the characters and story.
Step 2	Practice your delivery several times, each time adding another element, including ■ voice changes, pauses, and adjustments in how fast or slow you talk ■ gestures and facial expressions (practice with a mirror)
Step 3	Rehearse in front of a friend or relative, or tape your rehearsal with a video camera or a tape recorder. Ask your listener for feedback, or play back the tape, noting parts you need to improve. Watch especially for how fast you are reading, how you use gestures, and how your facial expressions change.

YOUR TURN 15 Performing a Dramatic Reading

Prepare for a performance of your own dramatic reading by
■ choosing a scene with few characters and clear action
■ editing the scene to remove any unnecessary parts
■ analyzing the scene to get a feel for the characters and their voices and gestures
■ practicing the scene until you know it well

RESOURCES

Your Turn 15
Practice and Reinforcement
■ *Media Literacy and Communication Skills*
—*Support and Practice,* Ch. 4, transparencies and worksheets
—Videocassette 1, Segment C

Choices

Choose one of the following activities to complete.

▶ **SPEAKING**

1. Lights, Camera, Action!
Imagine you are a movie director and want to make a movie from a book. Just as your book jacket previewed a book, you will need a preview for the movie. Use the book you read earlier in the chapter for your **movie preview.** Use the same information as you did for your book-jacket summary—character, setting, plot, and theme. This time, however, make a three-minute presentation of your summary as if you were the narrator for the preview. You may want to include a few visuals showing scenes that you would include in your preview.

▶ **DRAMA**

2. Acting Out Choose a poem and give a **dramatic interpretation** of it. Read it for an audience, using gestures, pauses, and voice changes to dramatize the poem. Ask your teacher or librarian for assistance in finding the perfect poem to read aloud.

▶ **LITERATURE**

3. Two for One Choose selections from two different **genres,** or types of writing—for example, a science fiction short story and a piece of realistic fiction. Examine the plot, conflict, theme, and characters in both selections, and then choose the most interesting one of these elements to compare and contrast in depth in a **short essay.** You might write an extended character analysis, comparing and contrasting the personalities, actions, and situations faced by the main character in each work.

▶ **CROSSING THE CURRICULUM: SCIENCE**

4. Experience Laboratory Life Choose an experiment by reading a science book for young adults or by asking your science teacher for ideas. Study how the experiment works. Then, write a **hypothesis,** or a prediction about what will happen when you conduct the experiment. Then, conduct the experiment with a teacher or other adult and record the results. Write a **paragraph** explaining why your hypothesis was or was not correct.

PORTFOLIO

▶ **SPEAKING**
To help students prepare their movie previews, have them create oral summaries of their books first. Refer students to the procedure on pp. 132–135 for writing a book-jacket summary. Explain that students might want to organize information for their oral book summaries in the same order novel summaries follow—setting, characters, plot, theme—and focus on presenting to listeners interesting information in a logical order. Then, have partners work together to transform the summaries into movie previews, creating scripts for narration and storyboards for visuals. Have students present their previews to small groups.

▶ **DRAMA**
To assist students in selecting a poem, encourage them to review the procedures for choosing a dramatic reading and practicing the reading on pp. 152–154. Then, to help students develop a dramatic interpretation of the poem, you might write the following suggestions on the chalkboard:

- Consider your audience. Make eye contact. Read slowly enough for them to understand.
- Use gestures to emphasize dramatic emotions and actions.
- Change your voice's tone, pitch, and speed to help the audience comprehend the poem.
- Include graphics, costumes, puppets, sound effects, or music to help make the reading effective.

After students have performed their poems, you could have the audience use the above suggestions to evaluate each presentation.

RESOURCES

Previewing a Novel
Assessment
- *Assessment Package*
  —*Chapter Tests,* Ch. 4
  —*Chapter Tests in Standardized Test Formats,* Ch. 4
  —*Assessment Alternatives,* Ch. 4

- *Test Generator (One-Stop Planner CD-ROM)*

Choices
Rubrics
- *Assessment Package*
  —*Assessment Alternatives,* Ch. 4

CHAPTER 5

Finding and Reporting Information

Use this guide to create an instructional plan that suits the individual needs of your students. Assignments marked by an asterisk (*) may be completed out of class. Times given for pacing lessons are estimated. See pp. 156–157 for chapter-wide resources. Resources listed in this guide are point-of-use resources only.

Curriculum Connections

Choices *p. 199*
- Crossing the Curriculum: Social Studies
- Crossing the Curriculum: Math
- Drama

internet**connect**

GO TO: go.hrw.com
KEYWORD: EOLang 7-5

All resources for this chapter are available for preview on the *One-Stop Planner CD-ROM with Test Generator.* All worksheets and tests may be printed from the CD-ROM.

	Chapter Opener *pp. 156–157*	**Reading Workshop: Reading an Informative Article** *pp. 158–167*
DEVELOPMENTAL PROGRAM	**30 minutes** • Your Turn 1 *p. 157*	**90 minutes** • Preparing to Read *p. 158* • Reading Selection *pp. 159–161* • First Thoughts in groups *p. 162* • Textbook Features *pp. 162–163* • Your Turn 2 *p. 164* • Summarizing Information *pp. 164–165* • Your Turn 3 *p. 165* • Test Taking Mini-Lesson *p. 167*
CORE PROGRAM	**20 minutes** • Your Turn 1 *p. 157*	**75 minutes** • Preparing to Read *p. 158* • Reading Selection *pp. 159–161* • First Thoughts *p. 162* • Textbook Features *pp. 162–163* • Your Turn 2 *p. 164* • Summarizing Information *pp. 164–165* • Your Turn 3 *p. 165* • Vocabulary Mini-Lesson *p. 166* • Test Taking Mini-Lesson *p. 167*
ADVANCED PROGRAM	**15 minutes** • Your Turn 1 *p. 157*	**60 minutes** • Preparing to Read *p. 158* • Reading Selection *pp. 159–161* • First Thoughts *p. 162* • Textbook Features *pp. 162–163* • Your Turn 2 *p. 164* • Summarizing Information *pp. 164–165* • Your Turn 3 *p. 165* • Vocabulary Mini-Lesson *p. 166*
RESOURCES — PRINT	• *Communications,* TP. 38, WS. p. 90	• *Alternative Readings,* Ch. 5 • *Communications,* TPs. 39, 40, WS. pp. 91–98
RESOURCES — MEDIA	• *One-Stop Planner CD-ROM*	• *One-Stop Planner CD-ROM*

TP.=Transparency   WS.=Worksheet

Writing Workshop: Writing a Report of Information
pp. 168–190

🕐 300 minutes
- Choose and Focus a Subject; Your Turn 4 *pp. 168–169*
- Audience, Purpose; Ask Questions; Your Turn 5 *pp. 169–171*
- Find and List Sources; Your Turn 6 *pp. 171–172*
- Take Notes; Your Turn 7 *p. 174*
- Plan Your Report; Your Turn 8 *p. 175*
- Mapping It Out; Your Turn 9* *pp. 175–177*
- Write Your Main Idea Statement; Your Turn 10 *p. 177*
- Framework; Models; Your Turn 11* *pp. 178–182*
- Evaluate and Revise *pp. 183–185*
- Focus on Sentences; Your Turn 12 *p. 185*
- Proofread, Publish, and Reflect *pp. 186–187*
- Grammar Link; Your Turn 13 *pp. 186–187*
- Test Taking Mini-Lesson *p. 188*

🕐 200 minutes
- Choose and Focus a Subject; Your Turn 4 *pp. 168–169*
- Audience, Purpose; Ask Questions; Your Turn 5 *pp. 169–171*
- Find and List Sources; Your Turn 6 *pp. 171–172*
- Critical-Thinking Mini-Lesson in groups *p. 173*
- Take Notes; Your Turn 7 *p. 174*
- Plan Your Report; Your Turn 8 *p. 175*
- Mapping It Out; Your Turn 9* *pp. 175–177*
- Write Your Main Idea Statement; Your Turn 10 *p. 177*
- Framework; Models; Your Turn 11* *pp. 178–182*
- Evaluate and Revise *pp. 183–185*
- Focus on Sentences; Your Turn 12 *p. 185*
- Proofread, Publish, and Reflect *pp. 186–187*
- Grammar Link; Your Turn 13 *pp. 186–187*
- Connections to Life; Your Turn 14* *pp. 189–190*

🕐 160 minutes
- Choose and Focus a Subject; Your Turn 4; Audience, Purpose; Ask Questions; Your Turn 5 *pp. 168–171*
- Find and List Sources; Your Turn 6 *pp. 171–172*
- Mini-Lesson; Take Notes; Your Turn 7 *pp. 173–174*
- Plan Your Report; Mapping It Out; Your Turn 8, 9* *pp. 175–177*
- Write Your Main Idea Statement; Your Turn 10 *p. 177*
- Framework; Models; Your Turn 11* *pp. 178–182*
- Evaluate and Revise *pp. 183–185*
- Focus on Sentences; Your Turn 12* *p. 185*
- Proofread, Publish, and Reflect *pp. 186–187*
- Grammar Link; Your Turn 13 *pp. 186–187*
- Connections to Life; Your Turn 14* *pp. 189–190*

- *Communications,* 📖
  TPs. 41–44,
  WS. pp. 99–114
- *Designing Your Writing*

- *One-Stop Planner CD-ROM* 💿

Speaking and Listening: Informative Speech; Viewing and Representing: Graphics and Web Sites *pp. 191–198*

🕐 60 minutes
- Adapting a Report for a Speech *pp. 191–192*
- Using Visuals in a Speech *p. 192*
- Listening to an Informative Speech *p. 193*
- Your Turn 15 *p. 193*

🕐 60 minutes
- Interpreting Information from Graphics *pp. 194–196*
- Your Turn 16 *p. 196*
- Interpreting Web Sites *pp. 197–198*
- Your Turn 17 *p. 198*

🕐 45 minutes
- Adapting a Report for a Speech *pp. 191–192*
- Using Visuals in a Speech *p. 192*
- Listening to an Informative Speech *p. 193*
- Your Turn 15 *p. 193*

🕐 50 minutes
- Interpreting Information from Graphics *pp. 194–196*
- Your Turn 16 *p. 196*
- Interpreting Information from Web Sites *pp. 197–198*
- Your Turn 17 *p. 198*

🕐 40 minutes
- Adapting a Report for a Speech *pp. 191–192*
- Using Visuals in a Speech *p. 192*
- Listening to an Informative Speech *p. 193*
- Your Turn 15 *p. 193*

🕐 40 minutes
- Interpreting Information from Graphics *pp. 194–196*
- Your Turn 16 *p. 196*
- Interpreting Information from Web Sites *pp. 197–198*
- Your Turn 17 *p. 198*

- *Media Literacy and Communication* 📖
  Skills
  —*Support and Practice,* Ch. 5
  —*A How-to Handbook*
  —*A Teacher's Guide,* Ch. 5

- *Media Literacy and Communication Skills* 📼
  —*Videocassette 2, Segment D*
- *One-Stop Planner CD-ROM* 💿

Finding and Reporting Information

CHAPTER OBJECTIVES

- To read an article for information using textbook features and summarizing skills

- To write a report and a personal narrative

- To prepare an informative speech

- To interpret information contained in graphics and on Web sites

Chapter Overview

This chapter is designed to help students understand and convey information. The Reading Workshop (pp. 158–167) helps students use textbook features to identify and comprehend information. The Writing Workshop (pp. 168–190) guides students as they do research and then write a report. Focus on Speaking and Listening (pp. 191–193) emphasizes speeches—how to adapt a report into a speech and how to listen to one. In Focus on Viewing and Representing (pp. 194–198), students learn how to interpret information in print graphics and on the Internet. Chapter sections may be taught independently, but together they give students a basic knowledge of how to locate and share information.

Why Study Finding and Reporting Information?

In learning to think for themselves, students need to know how to ask questions and find answers. By reading for information and by writing informative reports, students will gain experience in interpreting and presenting information. They will be better prepared to comprehend issues and to express convincing opinions.

Teaching the Chapter

Option 1: Begin with Literature

If literature is the focus in your classroom, you might introduce the chapter after reading works of literature to obtain information, for example, about a time or place.

After students have explored information as an aspect of literature, introduce them to the informative article in this chapter (pp. 159–161). Point out that reading for information is the primary purpose for reading nonfiction. Once students have analyzed the article, they will be ready to write their own informative report.

Option 2: Begin with Nonfiction and Writing

Use this chapter to help students comprehend the purpose of informative articles and develop expertise in reading and writing them. The article in the Reading Workshop and its accompanying instruction (pp. 158–167) help students understand how to use textbook features and summarize information. This experience will help students write informative reports in the Writing Workshop (pp. 168–190). When students return to literature, they may better understand the research a writer must do to write a story.

Making Connections

■ To the Literature Curriculum

Discuss how some literary works can be sources of information. In the excerpt from *Survive the Savage Sea* by Dougal Robertson, for example, students can learn about the contents and uses of a survival kit. "Homesick," Jean Fritz's memoir of her childhood in China, includes informative details about China.

Lesson Idea: Finding Information in "Homesick"

1. Divide the class into four groups. Assign each group one fourth of the story "Homesick."

2. As groups read each section, have them fill in a chart like the one below. The features in the left-hand column are typically found in nonfiction. Sample responses have been provided from the first section of "Homesick."

Features	Examples from "Homesick"
Information (details, ideas, or events new to you)	Chinese words are not printed on a page from left to right, but top to bottom.
Vocabulary (words new to you)	*amah,* which means "nanny"
Words in italic or bold-face type (for emphasis)	The author's letters to her grandmother are in italic type, indicating that they are asides to the main story.
Important quotations	The author re-creates conversations with her nanny, teacher, and schoolmates.
Illustrations or visuals	The illustrations show aspects of China.

3. After groups have filled out their charts, ask them questions such as What information did you learn from reading "Homesick"? What questions did you ask while reading? Where could you find the answers? Discuss the questions that interested students and suggest resources, such as encyclopedias, that they might consult for answers.

4. After discussion, introduce students to the informative article on pp. 159–161. Suggest that they note similarities to and differences from the way that information is presented in "Homesick."

■ To the Community

To help students understand that research reaches beyond the classroom, encourage them to think about their neighborhood, town, or city and to ask questions such as What is the history of my neighborhood, town, or city? How is my community organized or run? What changes have been made in the last decade? What brought about these changes? Invite a local official or historian to class to answer students' questions and to suggest ways that they might do research about their community.

■ To Careers

Ask students to list careers in which people find and report information. Students may suggest police work, medical practitioners and researchers, lawyers, and journalists. Ask individuals in one or more of the careers listed by students to speak with the class about the role of research in their work.

■ To the Music Curriculum

Point out that information is sometimes embedded in folk songs. Listen together to a recording of Huddie Ledbetter (better known as Leadbelly) singing "The Boll Weevil Song," and then discuss ways that the song informs listeners about the effects of this insect on the cotton-growing South. Have students work in small groups to research other folk songs that include information, such as those created or recorded by Woody Guthrie or Pete Seeger, and report on their findings.

5 Finding and Reporting Information

CHAPTER

5

PREVIEWING THE CHAPTER

■ The four workshops in this chapter focus on communicating information. The workshops can be taught separately, but together they reinforce one another and help students appreciate the many ways they can find and share information. Reading an informative article provides students with a model of how to write a report. Then, students will practice how to deliver and listen to an informative speech. Finally, they will interpret information presented graphically and on Web sites. To integrate this chapter with grammar, usage, and mechanics chapters, see pp. T311A–T311B.

INTRODUCING THE CHAPTER

■ To introduce the chapter, use the Journal Warm-up, Transparency 38, in *Communications*.

VIEWING THE ILLUSTRATION

■ Have students identify what the objects in the illustration may represent. [The objects are sources of information.] Point out to students that the variety of colors in the illustration may suggest that information can come from a "rainbow" of sources—there are as many sources of information as there are colors in a rainbow.
■ **Representing.** Have students create illustrations of themselves seeking information by using a variety of shapes, colors, and textures in their artwork to represent the variety of sources available.

CHAPTER RESOURCES

Planning
■ *Lesson Planner, ELL Strategies,* Ch. 5
■ Block Scheduling, p. T155A (this book)
■ *One-Stop Planner CD-ROM*

Practice
■ *Communications,* Ch. 5
■ *Writer's Workshop 1 CD-ROM*

■ *Media Literacy and Communication Skills*

Extension
■ *Designing Your Writing*

Reinforcement
■ *Communications* Ch. 5
■ *Alternative Readings,* Ch. 5

Reading Workshop

Reading an Informative Article

Writing Workshop

Writing a Report of Information

Speaking and Listening

Giving and Listening to an Informative Speech

Viewing and Representing

Interpreting Graphics and Web Sites

Who decided that people need to go to school? What does a manatee eat? How do computers work? Questions like these probably run through your mind all the time.

You may begin finding answers to the questions *Who? What? When? Where? Why?* and *How?* by doing research. Look around and you will find many sources of informative writing to help you answer your questions: textbooks, newspapers, and other media sources such as the Internet and documentaries. When you have a question about a particular topic, look for informative books or articles to help you find the answer.

Informational Text

Exposition

YOUR TURN 1 Exploring Informative Articles

Find an informative article on a topic that interests you. After you read it, answer the following questions.

- Where did you find the article?
- Did the article give you all the information you wanted? Explain.
- Was the information in the article easy to understand? Explain.
- Where else might you look for information on this topic?
- How might you share what you have learned?

internet connect

GO TO: go.hrw.com
KEYWORD: EOLang 7-5

Motivate

Tell students that locating and reporting all sorts of information is part of their daily lives. Ask them to think of a question that puzzles them. It might be a question with a concrete answer, such as "What is global warming?" It might be more abstract, such as "Why is music so important to teenagers?" Have students record their questions and brainstorm for a few minutes about sources they might consult to find answers.

ELEMENTS OF
Literature
....

Finding and Reporting Information in Literature
In *Elements of Literature,* First Course, see "A Mason-Dixon Memory" by Clifton Davis, pp. 206–211, for a memoir that conveys factual information of a historical and sociological nature.

YOUR TURN 1

Students may consult with a school or local librarian for help in searching for an informative article. Encourage them to look until they find an article that provides the information they need.

- *Daily Language Activity Transparencies*
- *Vocabulary Workshop* and *Tests*
- *Spelling*

Evaluation and Assessment
- *Test Generator (One-Stop Planner CD-ROM)*

- Assessment Package
  —*Chapter Tests,* Ch. 5
  —*Chapter Tests in Standardized Test Formats,* Ch. 5
  —*Assessment Alternatives,* Ch. 5

Internet
- go.hrw.com (keyword: EOLang 7-5)

Preview   **157**

OBJECTIVES

Reading and Writing Connection

- To read an informative article in preparation for writing a report

Reading Skills

- To identify features of a textbook
- To summarize information
- To use prefixes and suffixes to understand unfamiliar vocabulary

Quotation for the Day

"If we lived on a planet where nothing ever changed, there would be little to do. There would be nothing to figure out."

(Carl Sagan, 1934–1996, American astronomer and Pulitzer Prize-winning author)

Ask students to freewrite for a few moments about what they imagine a world without change would be like. Would there be a need for research in an unchanging world?

TEACHING TIP

Preparing to Read
The material on this page introduces concepts that will be taught in more depth on pp. 162–165. Using textbook features and summarizing information will be the instructional focus of the Reading Workshop. The Reading Selection, **"The Body's Defenses,"** illustrates both of these concepts.

RESOURCES

Reading Workshop Reinforcement
- *Alternative Readings,* Ch. 5

Reading an Informative Article

WHAT'S AHEAD?

In this section you will read an excerpt from a science textbook. You will also learn how to

- identify textbook features
- summarize information

Have you ever wondered why people sneeze, or why some people seem to get sick all the time while others never do? Our bodies have several ways to defend themselves when germs and viruses are around. In the following textbook selection, you will read more about the human body's defense system. As you read, notice how the author makes the information in this section easy to understand.

Preparing to Read

READING FOCUS

Textbook Features   Imagine that you are writing a letter to your best friend (during lunch, of course), and you really want to get a certain point across. What do you do? You probably underline it, circle it, or draw a big arrow pointing to it. Without realizing it, you have used some of the same types of features that textbook authors use to communicate their points. **Textbook features** include bold or italic print, definitions and notes in the side and bottom margins, and special headings. As you read the following textbook selection, pay attention to the way the author uses text features to present information.

READING SKILL

Summarizing Information   Textbooks are loaded with information. Even when you read a short selection, you may feel like you are experiencing an information overload. Putting information in your own words by *summarizing* can help you get a handle on it. When you **summarize** information, you state only the most important ideas. Summarizing a reading selection is a great study strategy that can help you remember what you read.

158   Chapter 5   **Exposition:** Finding and Reporting Information

READING PROCESS

PREREADING
Set a Purpose for Reading. The **Preparing to Read** section on this page explains that the students' purpose for reading **"The Body's Defenses"** is to gather information. The section also explains that using textbook features and summarizing will help students identify and retain the information that they read.

Tell students that they also need to set

Read the following textbook selection. In your notebook, jot down answers to the numbered active-reading questions in the shaded boxes. The underlined words will appear in the Vocabulary Mini-Lesson on page 166.

from **SciencePlus**

THE BODY'S DEFENSES

The boy in the photo to the right has spent his entire life inside a plastic bubble. He is not allowed to touch anyone, not even his mother or father, because he was born with no natural defense against <u>infectious</u> diseases. As a result, even a simple cold could endanger his life. Fortunately, most of us have a defense system that automatically fights off most of the bacteria and viruses that could harm us. This system consists of several lines of defense.

> **1. Which sentence indicates the main idea of this selection?**

The First Line of Defense
Skin and Mucus

Under normal conditions, the skin stops microorganisms from entering the body. However, when the skin is broken, cut, or damaged, germs can enter. That is why it is very important to clean cuts and scrapes. But skin does not cover every surface of the body.

> **2. What role does skin play in your body's defense system?**

Mucus stops germs from attacking tissue not covered by the skin. For example, the inside of the nose is covered by tiny hairs and mucus. These hairs and mucus trap dust and germs from the air you breathe. Sometimes extra mucus is made by the body in response to the presence of foreign substances such as dust, pollen, or germs. . . . Blowing your nose and sneezing help remove trapped microorganisms. It

> **3. What is your body doing when you sneeze?**

Mucus A thick, sticky fluid covering many surfaces inside the body and its natural openings.

Active-Reading Questions

The purpose of the active-reading questions is to get students thinking about how to read an informative article. Use students' answers to these questions as an informal assessment of their grasp of the information provided in **"The Body's Defenses."** Possible answers follow.

ANSWERS

1. The fourth sentence: "Fortunately, most of us have a defense system that automatically fights off most of the bacteria and viruses that could harm us."

2. The skin forms a protective barrier against germs.

3. By sneezing, the body rids itself of microorganisms.

---

their own purposes for reading to help make the selection more meaningful. Suggest that they skim the selection, noticing headings and boldface type. Using this information, students should ask themselves what they want to learn from the selection. Explain that the questions they ask can help them decide what they want to learn from their reading.

4. White blood cells protect you by killing germs and allowing healing.

5. An invader is a microorganism or foreign substance.

is important to cover your mouth and nose when you sneeze to <u>pre</u><u>vent</u> the spread of these microorganisms. . . .

The Second Line of Defense
White Blood Cells

What happens if you cut your skin and germs enter the cut? Then your second line of defense, the *white blood cells*, becomes active.

White blood cells are one part of your blood. They are made inside some of your bones. Many of them are found in structures called lymph nodes and in the tonsils.

It is believed that damaged tissue, such as a cut, and invading germs both release chemicals. These chemicals attract white blood cells. At the same time, the area around the cut becomes warm and appears red, indicating that the cut has become infected.

White blood cells, like the one shown here, are the body's second line of defense.

White blood cells surround and destroy germs and damaged tissue. This action is similar to the way that an amoeba surrounds its food. The activity of white blood cells stops infection and cleans the area so that proper healing can take place.

> **4. How could you put the main details in this paragraph in your own words?**

The Third Line of Defense
The Immune System

. . . Some kinds of white blood cells make special chemicals called **antibodies.** Antibodies help in the destruction of microorganisms and other foreign substances. Your body is capable of producing antibodies for just about every kind of germ or foreign substance that exists on earth.

The <u>production</u> of antibodies is a relatively quick process. A few days after an <u>invader</u> has entered the body, a large number of antibodies can usually be found in the blood. This process of antibody production

> **5. What does "invader" refer to in this paragraph?**

Antibodies Chemicals that are made by the body and that fight germs or other foreign substances.

READING PROCESS

READING

Self-Check. Explain to students that checking their understanding as they read can help them avoid missing important points that the author makes. Have students work in pairs as they read, using a "Think-and-

Share" strategy. Partners should sit together and read the article silently. After both complete a section, one partner should summarize it by saying, "What I think is going on in this paragraph or section is _____. Do you agree?" Then, the other partner should

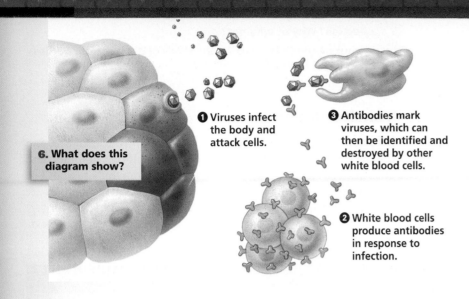

1 Viruses infect the body and attack cells.

3 Antibodies mark viruses, which can then be identified and destroyed by other white blood cells.

2 White blood cells produce antibodies in response to infection.

6. What does this diagram show?

6. The diagram shows how antibodies mark viruses so that white blood cells will destroy the viruses.

7. It is in bold print to help readers to notice it, pause, and look for its definition at the bottom of the page.

is a function of the immune system, the body's third line of defense.

Soon after a disease is successfully stopped, the level of the antibody that fought against it drops. For example, a person who has recovered from chickenpox will have only a small amount of chickenpox antibody left in his or her bloodstream. But a few of the white blood cells that made the chickenpox antibody remain in the bloodstream to fight the chickenpox virus if it returns. These white blood cells "remember" how to make the antibody for

chickenpox. If the virus that causes chickenpox enters the body again, these cells will make a lot of new antibodies in a very short time. They will eliminate the virus before it can do any damage and before you become ill. That is why a person usually gets diseases like measles, mumps, whooping cough, scarlet fever, and chickenpox only once. This resistance to a disease is called acquired immunity. Acquired immunity to some diseases lasts a lifetime.

7. Why is "acquired immunity" in bold print?

Immune system Body system that uses antibodies to seek out and destroy invading microorganisms.

Acquired immunity Resistance to reinfection by a disease after the body has recovered from the original infection.

evaluate the summary. If both agree, they should continue reading. If they disagree, partners should re-read the section together and agree on a summary. Students should alternate roles and jot down the agreed-

upon summaries. This activity will help students answer the active-reading questions and respond to **First Thoughts on Your Reading.**

First Thoughts on Your Reading

1. Did the headings and definitions help you understand this selection? Why or why not?

2. In your own words, describe the types of defenses our bodies use against infection.

First Thoughts on Your Reading
ANSWERS
Possible answers follow.

1. Students might find the headings useful because they provide clues to the organization of the article. The definitions aid in understanding because they provide an explanation of unfamiliar terminology.

2. There are three types of defenses: skin and mucus, which protect; white blood cells, which attack invaders and clean the body; and the immune system, which marks viruses and patrols the body against an invader's return.

TEACHING TIP

Textbook Features
Remind students that they have been using textbook features for as long as they have been reading textbooks. After students review the chart on this page, suggest that they look through this textbook, or one from another subject area, for examples of each type of feature.

READING FOCUS

Textbook Features

Information, Please Imagine opening up your textbook and finding out that all bold words, headings, definitions, graphics, and other *textbook features* had been removed. Do you think it would be easier or harder to understand your textbook? **Textbook features** are designed to help you easily locate and understand important information. The following table lists and explains some common textbook features.

Types of Features	Examples	What They Do
Features within the main reading (or chapter)	• titles, subtitles, headings, and subheadings	• break information into chunks to make it clearer
	• boldface and italic type	• point to important ideas or add emphasis
	• charts, graphs, and diagrams	• present information found in the text in a visual way
Features in the margins	• definitions	• provide meanings of important words
	• questions	• give readers clues to important information
	• reference notes	• tell readers where to find more information about a topic
Features after the main reading	• end-of-selection questions	• emphasize information from the main text

Using Textbook Features Recognizing textbook features is important. However, textbook features are meaningless unless you use them to help you learn. Learning to use textbook features before, during, and after you read will make informative writing easier to understand and remember.

162   Chapter 5   **Exposition:** Finding and Reporting Information

Before You Read   If you spend a few minutes making predictions about the chapter *before you read*, you will find that the details of the chapter will easily fall into place *as you read*. For example, after reading the chapter title "The Body's Defenses," you could predict that the chapter is about how the body defends itself. Then, if you studied the first main heading (The First Line of Defense) and the subheading beneath this heading (Skin and Mucus), you could conclude that skin and mucus are part of the first line of defense.

As You Read   As you read a textbook, pay close attention to boldface and italic type. **Boldface** and *italic* type call attention to important vocabulary you will need to know to understand a certain concept. When you read a word in boldface or italics, look for the meaning or definition within the passage or in the margin.

Many textbooks also include questions or reference notes in the side or bottom margins. The questions help you check your understanding. If you cannot answer a question, you should re-read the passage or ask your teacher for help. The reference notes tell you where to find more information about an important idea.

After You Read   Answering end-of-chapter questions is a great way for you to check your understanding. If you are able to answer these questions correctly, you can be confident that you understand the main points of the chapter. After you have successfully answered end-of-chapter questions, you can use text features to make a *study guide* to help you remember what you have read. A **study guide,** like the partial example below, contains only the most important information from the selection, such as the main headings and important vocabulary.

TIP   Some textbooks provide questions at the beginning or end of a chapter. If so, you should take a moment to read them. These questions often stress the main points of the chapter. Of course, when you first read these questions, you might not know the answers. However, you will be surprised to find that some of the answers may "jump out" of the book as you read.

TIP   If a book does not have end-of-chapter questions, you might want to make your own. You can do this by turning headings or subheadings into questions. For example, for the heading "The First Line of Defense," you would ask "What is the body's first line of defense?"

Chapter Title: The Body's Defenses

Heading one: The First Line of Defense

Subheading one: Skin and Mucus

Relationship of heading to subheading: The first line of defense is the skin and mucus.

Boldface or italicized words with definitions: Mucus is a sticky substance that helps keep germs out of the body.

Explanation of graphic: no graphic in this section

Summary of information in subheading one:

ANSWERS

Sample responses for the second and third headings appear in italics.

Heading two: *"The Second Line of Defense"*

Subheading two: *"White Blood Cells"*

Relationship of heading to subheading: *White blood cells are the second line of defense.*

Boldface or italicized terms with definitions: "White blood cells" *are cells that surround and destroy germs and damaged tissue.*

Explanation of graphic: *The graphic shows a white blood cell.*

Heading three: *"The Third Line of Defense"*

Subheading three: *"The Immune System"*

Relationship of heading to subheading: *The immune system is the third line of defense.*

Boldface or italicized terms with definitions: "Antibodies" *help in the destruction of germs and other foreign substances. The* "immune system" *uses antibodies to seek out and destroy invading microorganisms.* "Acquired immunity" *is resistance to reinfection by a disease after the body has recovered from the original infection.*

Explanation of graphic: *The graphic shows how viruses are marked by antibodies so that white blood cells can identify and destroy the viruses.*

Using Textbook Features to Make a Study Guide

Make a study guide like the one on page 163 for the second and third headings of "The Body's Defenses." Be sure to use the chapter's textbook features to help you. (Do not fill in the "summary" section for either heading. You will do this in Your Turn 3.)

| READING SKILL

TIP Summarizing as you read will help you remember what you have read.

Summarizing Information

Say It Your Way You have probably heard teachers and librarians say this a thousand times: "Put it in your own words!" When you **summarize,** you put only the most important information you have read or heard into your own words.

A good summary covers the main ideas of a selection, not every detail. For this reason, a summary is always much shorter than the original material. Think of a summary in terms of a sportscast: A summary includes only the highlights, such as the key plays and final results; it does not include a lengthy play-by-play account with every name and statistic.

How would you summarize the following passage? If you have trouble, use the Thinking It Through steps on the next page.

> . . . Some diseases, such as various types of heart disease and arthritis, are caused by malfunctions of the immune system. Like other systems in the body, the immune system can malfunction or even break down altogether. Such a breakdown is called an immune disease or disorder. There are three basic types of *immune disorders:* allergies, autoimmune disorders, and immune deficiency disorders.
>
> An **allergy** is a condition in which the immune system reacts to a normally harmless foreign substance, such as pollen or certain foods. In an allergic reaction, the immune system produces antibodies that attack the foreign substance, causing a variety of symptoms: runny nose, sneezing, red and watery eyes, swelling, rashes, and so on. In a few cases, severe allergic reactions can be fatal.
>
> "The Body's Defenses," *SciencePlus*

RESOURCES

Your Turn 2	**Your Turn 3**
Practice	**Practice**
■ *Communications,* WS. p. 91	■ *Communications,* WS. p. 93
Reinforcement	**Reinforcement**
■ *Communications,* TP. 39, WS. p. 92	■ *Communications,* TP. 40, WS. p. 94

Summarizing Information

STEP 1 Find the main idea of each paragraph. For each paragraph, ask yourself, "What do all of the sentences have in common?"

STEP 2 In your own words, write the most important supporting details necessary for understanding each main idea. In other words, explain what the author is saying about each main idea. Do not include most examples, anecdotes, or sensory language in your summary.

STEP 3 Check that you did not copy any sentences or long phrases from the original text. If you did, replace them with original words and phrases that have the same meaning as those you copied.

In the first paragraph, all of the sentences are about the immune system.
The second paragraph is about allergies.

Diseases are sometimes caused by problems with the immune system. When the immune system stops working right, it's called an immune disorder. One type of immune disorder is an allergy. An allergy is a reaction to something that is normally harmless. Antibodies attack this substance, which causes an allergic reaction. Allergic reactions are usually minor, but they can be deadly.

Reference Note

For more on **identifying implied main ideas,** see page 745 in the Quick Reference Handbook.

YOUR TURN 3 Summarizing Information

■ Re-read "The Body's Defenses" on pages 159–161. Then, working with a small group, orally summarize the section titled "The First Line of Defense." Be sure to state the main idea and only the most important supporting details.

■ On your own, write summaries for the two remaining sections of "The Body's Defenses," and add these summaries to the study guide that you began earlier. Remember to write your summaries using your own words.

YOUR TURN 3

ANSWERS

A possible summary for each section appears in italics.

Section one: *Skin and mucus keep microorganisms out of our bodies. Mucus traps them and blowing your nose or sneezing helps get rid of them.*

Section two: *If microorganisms invade the body, chemicals are produced that attract white blood cells. These cells surround and attack invaders and allow the body to heal.*

Section three: *The immune system ensures that certain white blood cells release antibodies when microorganisms invade the body. After the invaders are destroyed, some antibody-producing white blood cells stay in the blood to protect the body against future attack.*

Wrap It Up

Metacognition. Ask students to reflect on their reading process by answering the following question:

1. How did the Reading Workshop change your reading habits?

Then, ask students the following questions:

2. What textbook features help you understand information as you read? How do they help? [Headings, boldface and italic print, graphics, marginal questions, and definitions call attention to important vocabulary and concepts.]

EXTENDING

Apply What You Read. Tell students that they can use textbook features when reading different types of material. Have students explore the use of textbook features in advertisements, instructions, maps and signs, and Web pages. After looking at several examples, ask students the following question: Are the features similar to those in textbooks or different from them? [Words in boldface on a Web page may indicate a "hot link."] *You need to be aware that Internet resources are sometimes public forums and their content can be unpredictable.*

MINI-LESSON · VOCABULARY

Prefixes and Suffixes

ANSWERS
Possible answers follow.

1. The root *infect* means "to invade a body part and produce injury." The suffix *–ous* means "characterized by." *Infectious* must mean "characterized by a bodily invasion that produces injury." Since the article describes a boy "with no natural defense against infectious disease," the definition works.

2. The root *vent* means "to come." The prefix *pre–* means "before." The article says "to cover your mouth and nose when you sneeze to prevent the spread of these microorganisms." One meaning of *prevent* is "to keep from happening," which implies taking advance measures against something happening. This definition works.

3. The root *produce* means "to manufacture." The suffix *–ion* means "action or result." *Production* must mean "the action of being manufactured." The article describes "the production of antibodies." It makes sense to say that the body is manufacturing the antibodies.

4. The root *invade* means "to enter or spread over." The suffix *–er* means "doer." In the article, an invader enters the body. It makes sense that an invader is one who, or something that, enters the body.

5. One meaning of the root *cover* is "to guard from attack." The prefix *re–* means "back or again." *Recover* must mean "to guard again from attack." The article describes a person who "recovered from chickenpox" or was, in a sense, back to a state of being guarded from attack.

MINI-LESSON · VOCABULARY

Prefixes and Suffixes

When reading a textbook, you may come across unfamiliar words that are not defined for you. Learning to take these words apart can help you determine their meanings.

The main part of a word, the root, contains the word's core meaning. When a prefix or a suffix such as those shown in the charts below is added to a root, the meaning of the word changes.

Prefix	Meaning	Example
anti–	against	antibiotic
pre–	before	preview
re–	back, again	replay

Suffix	Meaning	Example
–ion	action, result	selection
–ous	characterized by	joyous
–er	doer, action	catcher

THINKING IT THROUGH — Using Prefixes and Suffixes

Here is how to use a word's parts to understand its meaning.

▶ **STEP 1** Separate word parts until you get to a word you know.

resistance = resist + –ance

▶ **STEP 2** Find the meaning of each part.

Resist means "to oppose."
The suffix –ance means "the condition of."

▶ **STEP 3** Combine the meanings to define the unfamiliar word.

Resistance means "the condition of opposing something."

▶ **STEP 4** Adjust your definition to fit the context of the sentence.

Sentence: "This resistance to a disease is called acquired immunity." Resistance is "the condition of being able to oppose diseases."

PRACTICE

Use the charts and steps above to define these words, which are underlined in "The Body's Defenses."

1. infectious (page 159)

2. prevent (–vent: to come) (page 160)

3. production (page 160)

4. invader (page 160)

5. recovered (page 161)

RESOURCES

Vocabulary
Practice
■ *Communications,* WS. p. 95

Answering Questions That Include Graphs

Like textbooks, many reading tests include graphs. However, a graph on a reading test usually does not have a paragraph that explains it. Instead, the reading test will probably ask you to answer a series of questions about the graph. Study the graph below and the question that follows it.

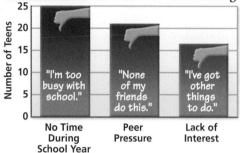

Reasons Teens Give for Not Volunteering

Number of Teens

- "I'm too busy with school."
- "None of my friends do this."
- "I've got other things to do."

No Time During School Year · Peer Pressure · Lack of Interest

How would you answer the question?

A local charity is starting a campaign to get more teens to volunteer for its program, which builds housing for families in need. According to the graph at left, which of the following approaches might be most successful in attracting teenage volunteers?

A. Have "Teen Volunteer Days" during the summer.

B. Hold training classes for volunteers.

C. Distribute informational videos to get teens interested.

D. Start a "Be Brave—Don't Cave" program to combat negative peer pressure.

THINKING IT THROUGH — Answering Questions That Include a Graph

▶ **STEP 1** Read the question to determine what it is asking.

It is asking how the charity can get more teens to volunteer.

▶ **STEP 2** Read the title of the graph.

It is about why teens don't volunteer.

▶ **STEP 3** Find and interpret each of the inter-sections of the graph. An **intersection** in a bar graph is the point at which the top end of a bar rising from the floor of the graph meets with a number from the left side.

25 teens decline to volunteer because they don't have enough time during the school year; about 21 because of peer pressure; and around 17 because of a lack of interest.

▶ **STEP 4** Use the question and the graph to find the correct answer.

Most (25) don't volunteer because they have no time. Because they might have more time in the summer, answer "A" is the best choice.

Looking Ahead to Writing

In the Writing Workshop of this chapter (pp. 168–187), students will be writing an informative report. As students organize their reports, remind them of how textbook features help readers identify and remember important pieces of information. Encourage students to refer to pp. 159–164 and to use subheads, bold and italic print, definitions, and graphics to emphasize important information in their own writing.

RESOURCES

Test Taking
Practice
■ *Communications*, WS. pp. 96–98

WHAT'S AHEAD?

In this workshop you will write a report of information. You will also learn how to

- focus a subject
- find and evaluate sources
- take notes
- add sentence variety to your writing
- format sources

Writing a Report of Information

If you have ever sought answers to the questions *Who? What? When? Where? Why?* or *How?* you have done research. After all, seeking answers to questions is the whole point of doing research. In this workshop you will write a report of information. The subject of your report is up to you, but it should be something that sparks your curiosity. Finding information and writing a report about it is your chance to answer your own questions about your subject as well as the questions of your readers.

Prewriting

Choose and Focus a Subject

I Wonder . . . What will you write about in your report of information? If you have ever said, "I wonder," about something, that something might be a good subject for research. After all, the best subject for a research report is one that really interests you.

You may already know what you want to research. However, if you still need a subject, try one of these ideas and see if you become inspired.

- Thumb through an informative magazine to get ideas. Scientific discoveries and historical events make good research subjects.
- Think about your favorite class. Then, list the subjects from this class that you like. Choose one of these subjects to explore.

At the top of the next page is one student's list of possible subjects.

> Favorite class: (science,) math, history, English
>
> I like when we talk about (animals,) volcanoes, and inventions.
>
> Animals that interest me: elephants, wolves, tigers, (eagles)

Get Focused   From avalanches to zebras, you can choose almost anything for a subject. However, unless you plan on pitching a tent and living in the library for the next year or two, **you should limit your subject. You can do this by focusing on something specific about your subject.** For example, instead of writing everything about zebras, you could limit your report to how zebras raise their young.

◄ KEY CONCEPT

Begin focusing your subject by making a **conceptual map.** Draw an oval in the center of a piece of paper and write your subject within it. As you think of specific topics, write them in connecting ovals.

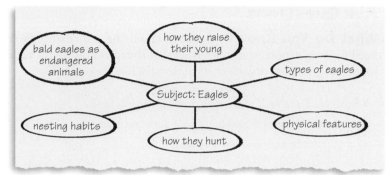

TIP   Once you start researching, you may not be able to find enough information on your specific topic. If so, you might have focused your subject too narrowly. On the other hand, if you find *too much* information about your specific topic, it may still be too broad. Talk to your teacher about getting the best focus.

YOUR TURN 4   Choosing and Focusing a Subject

Choose a subject and focus it by making a map like the one above. Then, choose the specific topic that is most interesting to you.

Think About Audience and Purpose

What's My Motivation?   Every time you write, you should remind yourself why you are writing. **The purpose of a report of information is to find information and share it with other people.** Who are those people? Your audience will probably include your teacher and

◄ KEY CONCEPT

YOUR TURN 4

If students choose topics that still seem too broad, suggest that they make another map with the chosen topic in the center oval.

TEACHING TIP

Think About Audience and Purpose

To help students focus on audience, arrange them into randomly selected small groups. Have students take turns asking other group members every question in the chart on p. 170. You may want to ask students to take notes on group members' responses for use in their research.

RESOURCES

Your Turn 4
Practice
■ *Communications,* WS. p. 99

ADVANCED LEARNERS

Some students may have quite a bit of experience writing reports. To help motivate students, suggest that they set a challenging goal for this project. For example, students may familiarize themselves with a new resource for research or design their writing as a magazine article for publication. Students should write their goals as checklists that may be turned in with their final papers.

Cooperative Learning

Category Conferences. Explain to students that scholars and other professionals often develop ideas for articles during conferences with their peers. Students can help one another generate questions about their topics by talking with students who are interested in the same general subject category. Write every student's topic on the chalkboard. Then, with input from the class, separate the list of topics into categories, such as science, nature, history, music, art, or literature. Have students form groups based on these categories. Each student can ask fellow group members to provide *5W-How?* questions about his or her topic.

TIP Be sure to write in your own **voice.** Because your purpose is to inform, you should be as clear as possible by using standard, formal English. However, you should avoid trying to sound like an adult scientist or someone you are not. In other words, your writing voice should sound like you—a knowledgeable and serious you.

| KEY CONCEPT

TIP Your list of research questions may change as you do your research. As more questions occur to you, add them to your list.

classmates, but anyone who is interested in your topic could be your audience. Ask yourself the following questions about the audience you identify.

Question	Explanation
What do my readers already know about my topic?	If you repeat information that your readers already know, they might become bored with your report.
What do my readers need to know about my topic?	Give your readers enough information to understand your topic by thoroughly explaining important ideas.
What can they do with the information?	Explain why the information is important for readers to know.

Ask Questions

What Do You Know?   To think about the information you need for your report, start with what you already know about your topic. Use a graphic organizer, or make a list like the one below.

- There are fewer bald eagles now than there used to be.
- I know that there are laws to protect other animals.
- I think bald eagles used to be hunted.

What Do You Need to Know?   After brainstorming what you already know about your topic, make a list of the questions you still have. **These questions will guide your research later.** Also, write down questions your audience might have. Start with the **5W-How?** questions: *Who? What? Where? When? Why?* and *How?*

Who is trying to help endangered eagles?

What are they doing to help endangered eagles?

Where are bald eagles most endangered?

When did bald eagles first become endangered?

Why are they endangered?

How many bald eagles are living today?

YOUR TURN 5

Thinking About Audience and Purpose and Asking Questions

- Think about your purpose and audience. Answer the questions in the chart on page 170 to identify your audience's needs.

- List the information you already know about your topic. Then, write a list of questions that you still have or that your audience might have. Title this list "Research Questions."

Find Sources

Get the Facts! Start finding answers to your questions by re-searching sources. A **source** gives you information about your topic. Where can you find sources?

The Library The library is a great resource for print sources such as encyclopedias, books, magazines, and newspapers. Many libraries also contain nonprint sources such as videotapes, audiotapes, slides, microfiche, CD-ROMs, and Internet access. Try to use both **primary** sources, such as letters and diaries, and **secondary** sources, such as biographical sketches.

Television Some TV channels broadcast informative documen-taries and biographies as well as programs about science and nature. To find programs about your topic, check a television guide.

The Web The World Wide Web is a resource for information on almost any subject. If you use a Web site, be sure it is a reliable source of information. A reliable Web site should include informa-tion on the author's professional background, the date the site was last updated, and a list of the sources the author used.

Experts You may find experts on your topic at a local museum, university, hospital, or government office. If you arrange an **inter-view** with an expert, be sure you prepare for it by bringing a list of questions and paper on which to write down all of the answers.

Make a Source List

Hey, Where Did You Get That? You will need to make a **source list,** which includes information about all of the sources you use for your report. There are several styles for listing sources. The next page shows the style the Modern Language Association recommends.

Writing Workshop **171**

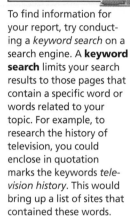

| COMPUTER TIP

To find information for your report, try conduct-ing a *keyword search* on a search engine. A **keyword search** limits your search results to those pages that contain a specific word or words related to your topic. For example, to research the history of television, you could enclose in quotation marks the keywords *tele-vision history*. This would bring up a list of sites that contained these words.

Reference Note

For more on **evaluating Web sites,** see page 742 in the Quick Reference Handbook. For more on **interviewing,** see page 772 in the Quick Refer-ence Handbook.

YOUR TURN 5

If students need help writing a list of research questions, remind them to refer to the *5W-How?* questions listed on p. 170.

Critical Thinking

Metacognition. After students have generated their research questions, have them answer the following questions:

- Are your research questions chal-lenging enough for you and for your readers? How do you know?

- Which research question do you think will be the most difficult to answer? Which one will be the easiest?

TEACHING TIP

Find Sources

Students may have difficulty finding relevant sources from which to take notes. The **Library/Media Center** sec-tion on p. 735 explains how to use a library's card catalog (print and online) and the *Readers' Guide to Periodical Literature.* Encourage students to use these tools and to work with a media specialist to find relevant sources.

You may also need to help students understand the concept of authority: an authoritative source is a reliable source from which to take notes; its author has credentials, such as a degree in the field about which he or she writes; or he or she has published an article in a magazine or newspaper that has a good reputation. Help stu-dents understand that magazines, newspapers, and publishers act as a fil-ter for unreliable writing; a library acts as a second filter; therefore, most books, magazines, and newspapers found in your school can be consid-ered fairly reliable. Anyone can pub-lish anything on the World Wide Web, so it is important to evaluate carefully the authority of material from Web sites by using the guidelines on p. 742.

ENGLISH-LANGUAGE LEARNERS

General Strategies. Some students may find that sources are difficult to understand due to vocabulary and complexity. Suggest that they restrict sources to print media. To help students clarify basic concepts or vocabulary, suggest that they first consult simple texts that are heavily illustrated.

TECHNOLOGY TIP

Students may be confused about whether to add a period when a sentence ends with an Internet address. Explain that a period *should* be added. The final period in such a sentence is the punctuation for the sentence; it is not part of the Internet address. One way to avoid confusion is to put the entire address within greater than/less than signs, < >, with the end punctuation following.

YOUR TURN 6

Have students work in pairs and exchange papers to check source lists against the **MLA Guide for Listing Sources.** Suggest that partners highlight parts of citations they feel are incorrect. Then, you can quickly check the highlighted areas and discuss common errors with the class.

MLA Guide for Listing Sources

Book

Author/editor. <u>Title</u>. City: Publisher, year.

Grambo, Rebecca L., ed. <u>Eagles: Masters of the Sky</u>. Stillwater, OK: Voyageur Press, Inc., 1997.

Electronic Sources

Online: Author (if known). "Document Title." <u>Web Site or Database Title</u>. Date of electronic publication. Name of Sponsoring Institution. Date information was accessed <url>.

Martell, Mark, and MaryBeth Garrigan. "Bald Eagle." <u>The Raptor Center</u>. Sept. 1994. U of Minnesota. 18 Nov. 1998 <http://www.raptor.cvm.umn.edu/>.

CD-ROM: Author (if known). "Title of Article." <u>Title of Database</u>. Title of Medium (CD-ROM). City of Electronic Publication: Electronic Publisher, Date of electronic publication.

"Eagle." <u>1997 Grolier Multimedia Encyclopedia</u>. CD-ROM. Danbury: Grolier Interactive, Inc., 1997.

Encyclopedia Article

Author (if known). "Title of Article." <u>Name of Encyclopedia</u>. Edition (if known) and year.

Grier, James W. "Eagle." <u>The World Book Encyclopedia</u>. 1998.

Interview

Speaker. The words *Personal interview, Telephone interview,* or *Guest speaker*. Date.

Sullivan, Vanessa. Personal interview. 17 Nov. 1998.

Magazine or Newspaper Article

Author. "Title of Article." <u>Publication Name</u> Date: page number(s).

Gerstenzang, James. "Eagle May Fly From Nest of Endangered." <u>Los Angeles Times</u> 6 May 1998: A1.

Movie or Video Recording

<u>Title</u>. Name of Director or Producer. The words *Videocassette, Videodisc, or Movie*. Name of Distributor, year released.

<u>Amazing Birds of Prey</u>. Dir. Ann Neale. Videocassette. DK Vision, 1997.

Television or Radio Program

<u>Title of Program</u>. Name of Host (if any). Network. Station Call Letters, City. Date of broadcast.

<u>Jaws & Claws: Flying Assassins</u>. Discovery Channel. DISC, Austin. 26 July 1998.

YOUR TURN 6 — Finding Sources and Making a Source List

Find at least three different types of sources for your report of information. Then, make a source list, and number each source on your list. You will need these numbers when you take notes.

RESOURCES

Your Turn 6

Practice

■ *Communications,* WS. p. 101

MINI-LESSON CRITICAL THINKING

Evaluating Sources

Newspapers, magazines, books, the Internet, and television shower us with information every day. Unfortunately, not all of the information available is reliable. Use the following guidelines to evaluate the reliability of the sources you find.

- **Identify the writer or creator of the source.** Look for an "About the Author" page that lists the writer's qualifications. In general, the more experience and education a writer has on the subject, the more reliable he or she will be. Also, sources that are endorsed by reputable nonprofit or educational organizations are generally reliable.

  Preferred source: *a book on endangered animals written by an environmental scientist and endorsed by the World Wildlife Federation*

  Less reliable source: *a Web page created by a nine-year-old as a class project on endangered tigers*

- **Locate the date the information was published.** Although older sources can be helpful for historical topics, up-to-date information is usually best for a report, especially one on a scientific topic.

  Preferred source: *a recent magazine article on the state of endangered animals in Guatemala*

  Less reliable source: *a book about Central American animals published in 1934 by an explorer and hunter*

- **Identify the purpose of the source.** Look for factual material that is written to inform. If a source includes too many opinions and too few facts, don't use it as a main source. However, two equally reliable sources may present different perspectives on a topic. Try to discover various viewpoints on your topic.

  Preferred source: *a newspaper article citing statistics on endangered animals*

  Less reliable source: *a fund-raising brochure describing the plight of a certain species*

PRACTICE

Below are several descriptions of sources for a research paper on the moon. Identify each description as either a **preferred** source or a **less reliable** source. Be prepared to defend your answer.

1. a book published in 1910 on the geography of the moon
2. a Web page on moon rocks published by the National Aeronautics and Space Administration (NASA)
3. a 1999 edition encyclopedia article on geographical formations on the moon
4. a book of poetry about the moon
5. a report on the moon published on the Web by a high school student

RESOURCES

Critical Thinking
Practice
- *Communications,* WS. p. 102

TEACHING TIP

Evaluating Sources
You may remind students about acceptable sources of information. Point out that students should not use sources that contain inconsistencies, irrelevant facts, too many extraneous details, and poor organization. Also, explain that tabloids, reality shows, infomercials, and hearsay or gossip are not reliable sources. Reinforce the idea that not everything students read or view is necessarily true.

MINI-LESSON CRITICAL THINKING

Evaluating Sources

ANSWERS

1. **Less reliable:** A book published in 1910 would not have information obtained by more powerful telescopes and, in particular, from the actual walks on the moon by astronauts in later years.

2. **Preferred:** NASA is an expert source of information about the moon.

3. **Preferred:** The 1999 edition would contain current information.

4. **Less reliable:** This source will probably not contain factual information.

5. **Less reliable:** This source is not written by an expert in the field.

Take Notes

Take time to talk to students about plagiarism and its consequences. Explain that plagiarism is not difficult for readers to detect and is a serious offense. Keep in mind the following common signs of plagiarism when reading and grading students' papers.

- The writer uses sophisticated language that is not quoted or cited.
- Several sentences or paragraphs are written in distinctly different styles.
- Concepts, opinions, or ideas that are not commonly known are discussed in the paper without citation.

Unforgettable

Although parenthetical citation is widely used by many publications and accepted by universities, footnotes and end notes are two additional ways students may identify sources.

- Explain to students that footnotes are consecutively numbered citations that appear at the bottom of a page. The information in the body of the paper is given a number that corresponds to the footnote. End notes are essentially footnotes that are grouped together on a page or pages at the end of the report.
- The format required for footnotes and end notes depends on the style that is used and is similar to the style for the Works Cited entries. The footnote below uses the style recommended by the Modern Language Association.

EXAMPLE:
[3]Sandra H. Torres. <u>Black Holes: Fact or Fiction?</u> Bayview: Scientific Press, 1990.

For more on footnotes and parenthetical citations, follow the MLA's style guide.

YOUR TURN 7

Check that students used a variety of sources. You may ask to see the actual source materials. Make sure that students have used the note-taking format shown on this page.

Take Notes

Unforgettable   The Great Lakes have an area of 94,600 square miles. Light travels at 186,000 miles per second. Jasmine is a plant in the olive family. So many facts and ideas can be hard to remember. To remember the facts and information you gather while researching, you should write them down.

Use note cards, small sheets of paper, or computer files to record your notes. Here are some suggestions for taking notes.

- Write a short label on the top line of each card, sheet of paper, or computer file to identify the subject of the note.
- Make sure that each note contains only one main idea.
- Summarize information, using your own words. If you do write an author's exact words, use quotation marks. Using an author's words or ideas without giving credit is called *plagiarism*. **Plagiarism** is a form of cheating and can result in disciplinary action.
- Write the source number you are using in the top right corner of your card, file, or piece of paper. For example, if you are using source five from your source list, write "5" in the top right corner.
- Write the number of the page where you found the information at the bottom of your card, file, or piece of paper.

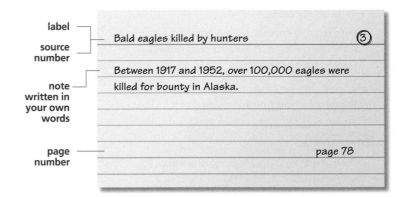

TIP   Sometimes a quotation from a writer or speaker lends interest and believability to your report. If you use a quotation, give the person credit by using the person's name or the title of the book in which the quotation appears.

Example:
In an interview Babbitt said, "The eagle is doing splendidly. It's making a wonderful comeback everywhere."

TIP   If your teacher asks you to show your sources in the body of your paper, use **parenthetical citations.** A parenthetical citation includes the author's last name or, if no author is given, the first major word of the source title followed by the page number.

Example:
The territory of Alaska paid a bounty for every eagle that was shot (Grambo 78).

The Writer's Model on pages 179–181 includes parenthetical citations.

YOUR TURN 7 Taking Notes

Read your sources to find answers to your research questions. Take notes when you find useful information. Refer to the suggestions for taking notes above, if necessary.

RESOURCES

Your Turn 7
Practice
- *Communications,* WS. p. 103

Your Turn 8
Practice
- *Communications,* WS. p. 104

Plan Your Report

Get It Together   Making an early plan and an outline can help you make sure none of the information you gathered falls through the cracks.

Early Plan   First, group the notes that deal with similar information into separate sets. Then, give each group of notes a **heading**—a word or phrase that describes the information in that set. **The headings for your groups are the main ideas of your report.** Here is a list of headings for a student's report on bald eagles. Notice that each of her headings represents a single idea. In what order would you discuss the following headings?

◄ KEY CONCEPT

- General facts about endangered eagles
- Reasons eagles were endangered
- Eagles' recovery
- Ways eagles were helped

YOUR TURN 8   Making an Early Plan

Sort your notes into sets and give each set a heading. Then, decide the order in which you will discuss each heading in your report.

Mapping It Out   Before you begin writing your report, you should make an *outline* using the headings you created for your early plan. An **outline** shows how the ideas in a composition are related to each other. Study the following excerpt from a student's outline. Notice that she listed related details beneath her heading.

II. Reasons eagles were endangered

   A. Belief that eagles were destroying crops and livestock

   B. Bounties that encouraged hunting

   C. Loss of trees

   D. New homes and businesses

The main heading in the example above is "Reasons eagles were endangered." The specific causes for their low numbers are underneath the heading. These are called **subheadings.**

TIP   You can also use a graphic organizer, such as a **conceptual map** or a **time line,** to organize your notes into groups or categories. For more information on these and other graphic organizers you can use for prewriting, see page 806 in the Quick Reference Handbook.

TIP   When making your outline, you may notice that some of your subheadings can be grouped together. If this happens, think of a word or phrase that describes these subheadings. This word or phrase will become your new subheading. Compare Roman numeral two in the example to the left with the Roman numeral two in the outline on the next page.

MODALITY

Visual Learners. Some students may prefer to use a graphic organizer for their outline. Offer them the spider map below. Each spider map represents the equivalent of a main heading or section (I, II, and so on) of a formal outline. The diagonal lines are the subheadings (A, B, C, and so on). Details can be written on the horizontal lines (1, 2, 3 in an outline).

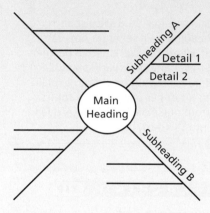

Kinesthetic Learners. Students may prefer to create their outlines on index cards, with each main heading of the outline on a separate index card. Subheadings and details can go on other cards and can then be placed behind the corresponding main heading. Students can lay out the cards and arrange them in the correct order. Suggest that students use different colored cards for the different sections of the outline.

TIP If your outline does not have at least three Roman numeral headings with two subheadings each, you probably need to **evaluate your research.** Take another look at your notes. You may be able to seek fuller answers to your research questions or frame new questions. In either case, hit the books (or the Web) to find more information.

TIP Since the Roman numerals from your outline will be the main sections of your report, you might want to include these headings in your final draft. Providing a clear heading before each major part of your report can help the reader understand the organization of your report.

To make your own outline, use the following steps. If you have trouble, study the outline that follows.

- Write your main headings on a sheet of paper in the order you want to discuss them. Label each heading with a Roman numeral.
- Under each main heading, write subheadings. Label each subheading with a capital letter. Number each detail that explains a subheading.

Bald Eagles as Endangered Animals

I. General facts about endangered eagles
  A. Drop in numbers in the 1940s and '50s
  B. Enormous decline in 1960s

II. Reasons eagles were endangered
  A. Hunters
    1. Belief that eagles were destroying crops and livestock
    2. Bounties that encouraged hunting
  B. Demand for lumber and land
    1. Lumber mills
    2. New homes and businesses
  C. Pesticides
    1. Effect on eagles' food
    2. Effect on offspring

III. Ways eagles were helped
  A. Laws
    1. 1940—the Bald Eagle Protection Act
    2. 1972—banning of DDT
    3. 1973—the Endangered Species Protection Act
  B. Captive breeding programs
    1. Description of program
    2. Effect on eagle population

IV. Eagles' recovery
  A. Statistics about recovery
  B. Eagles' removal from the endangered species list

YOUR TURN 9 Outlining Your Report

Create an outline for your report based on your notes and on the headings you created in Your Turn 8. Use the example outline and the instructions on pages 175–176 to help you make your own outline.

Write Your Main Idea Statement

What's the Big Idea? Now that you have done your research and taken notes, you are ready to write a main idea statement about your specific topic. **The main idea statement, also known as a *thesis statement*, appears in the introductory paragraph of your report and tells what you will say about your topic.** A good main idea statement serves as an umbrella for the main headings from your outline.

KEY CONCEPT

Focused Topic: Eagles as Endangered Animals

Headings from outline:

I. General facts about endangered eagles

II. Reasons eagles were endangered

III. Ways eagles were helped

IV. Eagles' recovery

Main idea statement: Although bald eagles were in danger of becoming extinct in the 1950s, the efforts of many groups over the last ten years have helped them make an amazing comeback.

Anyone who reads your report should understand what it is about after reading the main idea statement. In the example above, the reader could guess that the report would cover eagles as endangered animals, the reasons eagles were once endangered, and how people helped them to recover.

YOUR TURN 10 Writing Your Main Idea Statement

Use the example above to help you write your main idea statement. Remember that this statement should serve as an umbrella for the Roman numeral headings of your outline.

YOUR TURN 9

Outlines should reflect the information included in the students' notes. Students may notice areas in which they need to do more research to complete their outlines.

TEACHING TIP

Write Your Main Idea Statement

You may write additional examples of main idea statements on the chalkboard to give students other models to refer to when creating their own. The following are two examples:

- Good movies share similar features that make them winners.
- Many changes have taken place since the Olympic games first began.

Timesaver

Have students highlight the major headings in their outlines. That way you can quickly verify that their main idea statements reflect the information that they considered important in their outlines.

YOUR TURN 10

Students' statements should include elements of all main idea outline headings, in the order in which they appear in the outline.

RESOURCES

Your Turn 9
Practice
- *Communications*, WS. p. 105

Your Turn 10
Practice
- *Communications*, WS. p. 106

Writing

Report of Information

Framework

Directions and Explanations

Introduction
- Attention-grabbing beginning
- Main idea statement

To catch the reader's interest, start with an **attention-grabber,** or hook, such as an interesting fact, quotation, or question. Then, state the **main idea,** or **thesis,** of your paper.

Body
- Heading #1
  Supporting details
- Heading #2
  Supporting details
  and so on

- Use the information from your outline and notes to write the body of your report. In general, each paragraph should address one heading or subheading from your outline. However, you may need to use more than one paragraph to explain a particular heading or subheading.

- Make sure that the main point in each paragraph has **logical support,** including all of the relevant **details** (facts, examples, and statistics) you found during research. **Elaborate** on each detail by asking yourself, "Why is this detail important?" or "What does this detail mean?" Be sure to distinguish your own ideas from those of others.

Conclusion
- Restatement of main idea

In your conclusion, sum up the ideas in your report. **Restate your main idea** and bring your report to a close. You can bring your report to a close by drawing a conclusion about your research or by referring to something specific in your introduction.

Works Cited
- List of sources used

End with a list of the works you used. In this list, show your sources in alphabetical order by the author's last name. If there is no author for a source, alphabetize by the first word in the title of the source. If you did not use nonprint sources, such as videos or sound recordings, your teacher may ask you to title your list of sources "Bibliography," rather than "Works Cited."

178   **Chapter 5**   **Exposition:** Finding and Reporting Information

A Writer's Model

The final draft below closely follows the framework for a report of information on the previous page.

Flying High—Again

You see its picture every time you look at a quarter. You even see it when the letter carrier delivers your mail. The bald eagle has symbolized the United States since 1782. Not long ago, though, the bald eagle seemed headed for extinction. Although bald eagles were in danger of becoming extinct in the 1950s, the efforts of many groups over the last ten years have helped them make an amazing comeback (Bald).

In the 1950s, nature watchers noticed there were fewer bald eagles in the skies. Charles Broley, a volunteer eagle watcher, was one of the first to notice the decline of eagles in Florida. Broley counted one hundred fifty eaglets, or baby eagles, in 1939. In 1952, he counted only fifteen in the same area. Broley thought something was keeping adult birds from raising babies (Grambo 82).

Broley was right. The National Foundation to Protect America's Eagles estimated that 10,000 nesting pairs of eagles lived in the continental United States in the 1950s. In the 1960s, the number of eagles fell to fewer than 500 pairs. Eagles moved closer to extinction every day (Bald).

Many things caused the decline of the bald eagle. One of the most obvious was hunting. Farmers once thought of eagles as pests. They believed that bald eagles harmed livestock and crops (Tucker 58). To decrease its number of eagles, the territory of Alaska paid a bounty for every eagle that was shot. It is estimated that more than 100,000 bald eagles were shot while this policy was in effect (Grambo 76–78).

The demand for lumber and land also hurt eagles. When America was first being settled, it had over a billion acres of forest land where eagles and other animals could

(continued)

Attention-grabbing beginning

Main idea statement

Heading #1: General facts about endangered eagles

Heading #2: Reasons eagles were endangered

Connecting Reading and Writing

Students may notice that this report does not contain subheadings, as the Reading Selection on pp. 159–161 does. (In the margins, though, students may see that the subheadings are implied.) Creating subheadings for texts is a useful reading strategy because it helps the reader understand how the information is organized. Suggest that students cover the margin notes as they read the model and invent their own subheadings for the report. For example, paragraphs 2 and 3 might have the subheading "Signs of Trouble."

TEACHING TIP

Remind your students of the proper format for a research paper. In this book, **A Writer's Model** and **A Student's Model** have not been double-spaced, due to space considerations. Most writing guides, however, recommend double-spacing for both the body and the list of sources in a research paper.

(continued)

make their homes. However, as lumber mills cut more and more trees, eagles lost their forest homes. Eagles also suffered as people built houses, roads, and businesses in their nesting areas. As early as 1930, much of America's forest land was becoming unsuitable for many animals (Tucker 62–69).

The major cause of the eagles' endangerment was the use of pesticides such as DDT. Farmers used pesticides to kill unwanted insects and plants. Sadly, other animals and plants also absorbed the poisons. When bald eagles ate the poisoned animals, they became poisoned too. Eagles that consumed DDT laid thin-shelled eggs that broke easily when the mother sat on them (Dudley 54–55).

Heading #3: Ways eagles were helped

Fortunately, lawmakers realized that eagles could become extinct. In 1940, Congress passed a law to protect bald eagles: the Bald Eagle Protection Act. Under this act, people who killed eagles could be punished by a fine and time in jail (Tucker 69). The bald eagle was also helped by the Endangered Species Act of 1973. Under this act, the government protected millions of acres where bald eagles could live without being threatened by hunting or construction. The passage of these laws, along with the ban of the pesticide DDT in 1972, provided much-needed protection for the bald eagle (Tucker 75; Bald).

Scientists also helped bald eagles. To help increase the number of mature eagles, scientists developed a captive breeding program. In this program, injured eagles that could not survive in the wild laid eggs in a laboratory. After hatching, the eaglets were returned to the wild. Captive breeding successfully increased the number of bald eagles (Tucker 85).

Heading #4: Eagles' recovery

With the help of many people all over the United States, eagles are slowly recovering. From a low point of fewer than 500 nesting pairs in the 1960s, the numbers have grown to an estimated 4,500 nesting pairs in the continental United States. If you count eaglets and young adults, there are about 55,000 bald eagles in the United States today (Bald). In 1998, Secretary of the Interior Bruce Babbitt took steps to remove the bald eagle from the endangered species list. In an interview, Babbitt said, "The eagle is doing splendidly. It's making a wonderful comeback everywhere" (qtd. in Gerstenzang).

The bald eagle is not completely out of danger yet, but its future looks better every day. If eagles keep making a comeback, our national symbol should be around for a long time to come.

Works Cited

Bald Eagle: The U.S.A.'s National Symbol. 1997. The National Foundation to Protect America's Eagles. 16 Nov. 1998 <http://www.eagles.org/moreabout.html>.

Dudley, Karen. Bald Eagles. Austin: Raintree Steck-Vaughn, 1998.

Gerstenzang, James. "Eagle May Fly from Nest of Endangered." Los Angeles Times 6 May 1998: A1.

Grambo, Rebecca L., ed. Eagles: Masters of the Sky. Stillwater, OK: Voyageur Press, Inc., 1997.

Tucker, Priscilla. The Return of the Bald Eagle. Mechanicsburg, PA: Stackpole Books, 1994.

Restatement of main idea

TIP Reports of information and their *Works Cited* lists are normally double-spaced. Because of limited space on these pages, A Writer's Model and A Student's Model are single-spaced. The *Elements of Language* Internet site provides a model of a report of information in the double-spaced format. To see this interactive model, go to **go.hrw.com** and enter the keyword **EOLang 7-5**.

YOUR TURN 11 Writing Your Report of Information

Write the first draft of your report of information. Be sure to

- put information you gathered from sources into your own words
- write each paragraph using a separate heading or subheading from your outline
- support each paragraph with details, such as facts and statistics
- refer to the Writer's Model on pages 179–181 and framework on page 178

YOUR TURN 11

If you wish to assign a length to the students' writing assignment, 500 to 700 words is appropriate.

RESOURCES

Your Turn 11
Practice
- *Communications*, TP. 42, WS. p. 108

Connecting Reading and Writing

Remind students that they can check their understanding of information they have read by summarizing it. Refer them to the information on summarizing on pp. 164–165 in the Reading Workshop. Suggest that they follow the steps in **Thinking It Through** on p. 165 to summarize the information in **A Student's Model.** One possible summary is shown below.

> Spelunking, or exploring caves, is a popular pastime. If you are interested in exploring caves, you may want to know something about them. Caves are usually formed when surface water eats away at rocks over the centuries. A cave might be a single large chamber or a series of chambers that are connected. Many caves contain stalactites—pillars that protrude from the ceiling.

A Student's Model

Writing a research report is your opportunity to be a teacher. In the following report excerpt, J.D. Brannock, a student at Davis Drive Middle School in Apex, North Carolina, teaches his readers about the interesting subject of caves.

Caves

Attention-grabbing beginning

In Mark Twain's book <u>The Adventures of Tom Sawyer</u>, Tom and Becky spend three dreadful days in a winding, confusing cave. No matter how they try, they cannot find a way out until the last minute. Today spelunking, the American word for exploring caves, is a popular pastime around the world. Experienced guides lead adventure-seeking groups of people through these mystifying underground worlds, pointing out anything of interest and leading them to magnificent caverns. Before you dive headfirst into these wonderlands, you might want to know a little bit about them.

Main idea statement

Fact

Caves are usually formed out of limestone by surface water leaking through cracks in the rock.

Elaboration

Above the surface the water gathers carbon dioxide from the air, making a weak acid that eats away at the rock. Over the centuries the water hollows out the rock, leaving behind a cave.

Example

The largest cave chamber in the world is the Sarawak Chamber in the Gunung Mulu National Park in Malaysia.

Elaboration

It is 2,300 feet long, has an average width of about 985 feet, and at no point is it less than 230 feet high.

Fact

Some caves are one chamber. Other caves consist of a series of chambers that are all connected in some way, known as a cave system.

Example

The longest known cave system is the Mammoth-Flint Ridge cave system in Kentucky.

Fact

When people think of caves, they think of caverns filled with pillars protruding from the floor and ceiling. The pillars protruding from the ceiling are stalactites.

Elaboration

Stalactites form when water droplets containing limestone sediments drip from the ceiling. . . .

Revising

Evaluate and Revise Content, Organization, and Style

"Making a list and checking it twice . . ." Whether you are evaluating a peer's paper or revising your own report, it is a good idea to read the paper twice. The first time, think about both the content, or information, and the organization of the draft. Use the guidelines below to help you. During your second reading, focus on each sentence using the Focus on Sentences on page 185.

> **First Reading: Content and Organization** Use this chart to evaluate a peer's report or to evaluate and revise your own paper.

TIP Use reference materials to help you edit your draft. Dictionaries and reference handbooks (like Part 4 of this book) can help you improve your writing.

Guidelines for Self-Evaluation and Peer Evaluation		
Evaluation Questions	**Tips**	**Revision Techniques**
❶ Does the main idea statement cover all of the report's important ideas?	**Match** each part of the main idea statement with a paragraph or section of the report.	**Revise** the main idea statement so that it covers the important ideas of the report.
❷ Is the main point in each paragraph clear? Does all the information in the paragraph support that main point?	**Write** each paragraph's main point in the paper's margin. **Write N** next to information that does not support the main point.	If needed, **add** a sentence that states the main point. **Delete** or **rearrange** information that does not support the main point.
❸ Is the information in each paragraph properly summarized or quoted?	**Circle** sentences that sound as if someone else wrote them. **Underline** quoted information.	**Revise** by summarizing information or adding quotation marks.
❹ Does the conclusion restate the report's main idea?	**Put a check** next to the restatement of the main idea.	**Add** a restatement of the report's main idea if needed.
❺ Does a list of sources in the correct form end the report?	**Check the format and punctuation** by referring to the guide on page 172.	**Add** correct format and punctuation as needed.
❻ Does the list of sources contain at least three different types of sources?	**Count** the number of different types of sources on the list.	**Add** information from another reliable source to the report if needed.

Writing Workshop **183**

Quotation for the Day

"... Plato is said to have written the introduction to his *Republic* seven times, differently modified."

(Arthur Schopenhauer, 1788–1860, German philosopher)

Ask students why a piece of writing is worth revising to get a certain result.

TEACHING **TIP**

Evaluate and Revise Content, Organization, and Style

As students evaluate and revise the content of their reports, they may find that they need to do further research to find support and elaboration. Plan to make the library available to them at least once during the revision phase so that they can select and use the additional reference materials they need.

To help students learn to select their own resource materials, provide a variety of types. For example, thesauruses, which students may use as they edit their reports to improve word choice, come in different organizations. Explain the differences between *Roget's International Thesaurus* and *Roget's II*, for example, so students know how to use each but can select the organization that they prefer. [In the first, words are grouped in associated categories; in the latter, words are arranged alphabetically.]

TEACHING **TIP**

▶ **Elaboration**
To help students elaborate by inserting a quotation as a piece of supporting evidence, suggest that they lead up to the quotation in the previous sentence or embed the quotation in another sentence.

One Writer's Revisions
You might wish to provide students some of the following strategies for selecting and using reference materials when revising and editing final drafts.

For help with spelling:

- Select a dictionary. First, sound out the word and divide it into syllables. Then, at the top of a dictionary page, find a guide word close to your spelling. Once you locate the word on the page, check the accuracy of your spelling.

- Check your textbook for spelling rules and a list of commonly misspelled words.

- If you have access to a computer, use the spellchecking software.

For help with grammar, usage, and mechanics:

- In the index of any grammar handbook, you will find after each concept, pages listed that explain that concept and give examples. For instance, if you have an error in verb tense, look up *Verb, tense* for the pages in the grammar handbook that teach that concept.

Responding to the Revision Process
ANSWERS

1. As a detail, the sentence is out of place in the first paragraph. It makes more sense in the second paragraph, which discusses the effects of construction on eagles.

2. The addition provides a clear statement of the paragraph's main idea.

PEER REVIEW

As you read your classmate's report, ask yourself these questions:

- What part of the report is the best?
- What new information did I learn about the report's topic?

ONE WRITER'S REVISIONS Study this revision of an early draft of the report on page 179.

> To decrease its number of eagles, the territory of Alaska paid a bounty for every eagle that was shot. It is estimated that more than 100,000 bald eagles were shot while this policy was in effect. Eagles also suffered as people built houses, roads, and businesses in their nesting areas. *The demand for lumber and land also hurt eagles.* When America was first being settled, it had over a billion acres of forest land where eagles and other animals could make their homes. However, as lumber mills cut more and more trees, eagles lost their forest homes. As early as 1930, much of America's forest land was becoming unsuitable for many animals.

rearrange

add

Responding to the Revision Process

1. Why do you think the writer moved a sentence from the first paragraph to the second paragraph?
2. Why do you think the writer added to the second paragraph?

> **Second Reading: Style** One thing you can do to make sure your report flows smoothly is to vary how your sentences begin. Adding variety to your sentence beginnings can also help ensure that the reader will remain interested in what you are saying.

When you evaluate your report for style, ask yourself whether your writing contains a variety of sentence beginnings. As you re-read your report, draw a wavy line under the first five words of each sentence. Do several sentences begin the same way, perhaps with the same subject? If so, revise one or more of these sentences by moving a phrase from the end of a sentence to the beginning of a sentence.

Varying Sentence Beginnings

To add variety to your writing, look for places where you can move a phrase from the end of the sentence to the beginning. When you move a phrase to the beginning of a sentence, you may need to add a comma after the phrase. The following chart gives some examples.

Original Sentence	Revision Strategy	Revised Sentence
People depended on candlelight *before the invention of the light bulb.*	Move the *prepositional phrase* to the beginning.	*Before the invention of the light bulb,* people depended on candlelight.
You need skill *to repair a watch.*	Move the *infinitive phrase* to the beginning.	*To repair a watch,* you need skill.

ONE WRITER'S REVISIONS

Scientists also helped bald eagles. Scientists developed a captive breeding program to help increase the number of mature eagles.

Responding to the Revision Process

How did the revision above affect the flow of the sentence?

 **Evaluating and Revising Your Report of Information**

Use the guidelines on page 183 to revise the content and organization of your report. Next, add variety by using the Focus on Sentences above. Finally, consider feedback from your peers as you revise your report.

Sentences

Reference Note

For more information and practice on **prepositional phrases** and **infinitive phrases,** see pages 402 and 415.

RESOURCES

Focus on Sentences
Practice
■ *Communications,* WS. p. 112

TEACHING TIP

Varying Sentence Beginnings

Students may have trouble understanding why sentence beginnings matter. Explain that varied sentence beginnings make reading more interesting. You may have students look through newspaper articles, instructions, or books for examples of varied sentence beginnings.

Responding to the Revision Process

ANSWER

The changes make the ideas clearer and the paragraph more interesting.

YOUR TURN 12

Suggest that students work in peer-revision pairs, using the guidelines to respond to their partner's report. Students can write suggestions for revisions on a separate piece of paper and attach it to the original. Remind students to comment on parts they especially like, too.

Evaluating Student Writing

The ancillary *Assessment Alternatives* contains a variety of assessment forms, including Inventories and Evaluation Forms and rubrics: Six-Point Scales, Four-Point Scales, and Six Trait Scales.

Publishing

Proofread Your Report

Get It Right   Before you write your final draft, proofread your paper for mistakes in spelling, usage, or punctuation. Having a peer **edit** your report will help you find and correct errors that might distract your readers.

Grammar Link

Formatting Sources

One of the most difficult parts of research is correctly formatting your sources on the Works Cited list. Not only do you have to indent your sources a certain way, but you also have to mark titles correctly and use correct punctuation.

- **Periods:** Place a period after the author's name and after the title of the book or article. The end of the entry is also punctuated with a period.
- **Titles:** Titles of books, magazines, newspapers, encyclopedias, television or radio programs, or Web pages are underlined if handwritten and usually *italicized if typed on a word processor*. Titles of magazine, newspaper, or encyclopedia articles are placed in quotation marks.
- **Indentations:** Always indent the second and all following lines of a citation five spaces.

Here is the correct format for citing a book.

Horton, Casey. Eagles. Tarrytown, N.Y.: Benchmark Books, 1996.

PRACTICE

Each of the following citations has two or more problems. Refer to the guide on page 172, and rewrite each citation with the correct punctuation and format.

1. (Book)

MacGuire, Spunky Baseball's Favorite Heroes. Boston: Home Base Publications, 1983.

2. (Magazine article)

Aliki, Malik, Watch Out for the Bird Lady. Birdwatching Today. August 1998: 67–70.

3. (Online source)

Wark, Lori. Mummies in the Midst Discovery Channel Online 16 Oct. 1998. 5 Apr. 1999. <http://www.discovery.com/stories/history/mummies/mummies.html>.

Designing Your Writing

Text features If you have access to a word-processing program, you can use **text features** to help you create interesting, eye-catching reports.

    Fonts: Use a **text font,** such as Times or Palatino, for formal papers. Decorative fonts, such as *Mistral,* are often difficult to read.

    Size: For your report, make sure your print size is set at twelve points. Experiment with larger sizes for headings, if your teacher allows.

    Numbering or Bulleting Features: Most word-processing programs can automatically number lists. If you have a list that does not require numbers, consider using a decorative "bullet," such as a point (•) or check mark (✓) to separate items in the list.

Publish Your Report

Spread the News Now, share what you have learned. Here are some ideas for publishing your findings in a variety of formats.

- Publish your report on a personal or school Web page.
- Turn your report into an illustrated book for children.
- Send your report to a teacher with an interest in your topic.

Reflect on Your Report

Building Your Portfolio Think back on the process of researching and writing your report. Reflect on what you wrote and how you wrote it by answering the questions below.

- What information did you not include in your paper? Why? What information was the most difficult to find?
- What research techniques did you use? Would you use them again?

YOUR TURN 13   **Proofreading, Publishing, and Reflecting**

- Correct grammar, usage, and mechanics errors.
- Publish your report for your target audience.
- Answer the Reflect on Your Report questions above. Record your responses in a learning log, or include them in your portfolio.

Reference Note

For more information on **text features,** see page 162.

TIP Your teacher might ask you to create a title page for your report. A **title page** tells your name, the title of the report, and the date. Also include any other information your teacher recommends.

 PORTFOLIO

Writing Workshop   **187**

TEACHING TIP

Reflect on Your Report
Explain to students that unless they reflect on ideas in their writing, as well as overall quality, their written work will not improve significantly over time. To help students ensure that their portfolios will gradually improve, suggest that they reflect by answering the following questions after completing a written work.

- Are the ideas communicated clearly?
- Are the ideas supported?
- Are the ideas communicated in a way that is appropriate for the audience?
- Are the style, content, and organization effective?
- Are the grammar, usage, punctuation, and spelling correct?
- Does the writing engage the reader?
- In what ways should future writing projects be different? Why?

YOUR TURN 13

Ask students to prepare a brief statement explaining the grade they feel they deserve for their reports. The statements should address the level and variety of sources used and the care they took in writing and revising the reports.

Wrap It Up

Metacognition. Ask students to write a brief answer to the following question:

1. What did you learn about evaluating sources in this workshop?

Then, ask students this question:

2. What is the purpose of the Works Cited page? [to let readers know the sources used in a report]

MINI-LESSON TEST TAKING

Writing to Explain

Some writing test prompts ask you to inform your readers by explaining your thoughts on a topic. The informative essay that you write for such a prompt is sometimes called a **clarification essay**. The best thing about writing this kind of essay is that you get to explain what a topic means to you. Read the following prompt and think about how you would answer it.

> Think about your favorite food. Then, write an essay that explains why that food is your favorite. Be sure to explain each of your reasons fully.

THINKING IT THROUGH · Writing an Informative Essay to Explain

▶ **STEP 1** Read the prompt and decide what it is asking you to do.

The prompt asks me to think about my favorite food and write an essay that explains why it is my favorite.

▶ **STEP 2** Identify your answer to the prompt.

My favorite food is Chinese food.

▶ **STEP 3** Brainstorm a list of reasons that tell why you chose your answer.

Reason 1: Chinese food is sometimes spicy.
Reason 2: It is so different from what I usually eat.
Reason 3: You also get good soup.

▶ **STEP 4** Think about the support you will give for each of your reasons. Ask *What do I mean? How do I know?* You can use examples, descriptions, and facts.

Support for Reason 1: I could explain why I like spicy food. I could also give an example of a spicy Chinese dish, like garlic chicken with peppers, and I could describe the taste of it.
Support for reason 2: I could explain that Chinese food contains ingredients that I normally don't eat, such as bamboo shoots.
Support for reason 3: I could list different kinds of soup. Then, I could describe my favorite soup, which contains tofu and seafood.

▶ **STEP 5** Write your essay, making sure that you thoroughly explain your answer to the prompt. After you complete your essay, read it at least once to check for errors.

RESOURCES

Test Taking
Practice
■ *Communications,* WS. p. 114

Connections to Life

Writing a Personal Narrative

Everybody has a story to tell. In fact, you probably have a good story to tell about writing your research report. You might think at first that you have nothing else to say about your topic. After all, you *did* just write a report about it. However, for this assignment, you will not focus on the facts you learned about your research subject. Instead, you will write a *personal narrative* about the experiences you had while writing the report. A **personal narrative** is a true story with a beginning, middle, and end, told from your point of view. The writer's purpose in a personal narrative is to **express** his or her thoughts and feelings and to **reflect on ideas.**

Less Is More? When you write a narrative about writing your research report, you might be tempted to include everything. However, by focusing on a single event, you can make your narrative more interesting. To help you focus the **topic** of your narrative, think about an event associated with a specific person or place. You can also think about a particular problem you solved.

- **Person:** Who helped you with your report? A librarian? A friend? How did he or she help? Did you interview an interesting expert? Can you tell about an interaction with this person?
- **Place:** Where did you go to get information for your report? Did you have a funny or interesting experience at the li-

brary? Did you go somewhere unique, such as a museum? Did you get information by sending e-mail?

- **Problem:** Did you experience a problem while you were writing or researching your report of information? How did you solve this problem?

Express Yourself After you have focused the subject of your personal narrative, think about the **thoughts and feelings** you experienced while writing your research report. Were you glad? relieved? frustrated? confused? excited? One way to relate your thoughts and feelings to the reader is to state them **directly.** For example, the student whose example is given below directly states that he experienced panic and a sense of defeat on finding the library closed.

> I tried to go to the library to get the sources I needed. However, when I got there, it was closed. Needless to say, I began to panic. I felt defeated because I thought that I would never get my research report done.

A more interesting way to express your thoughts and feelings is to do so **indirectly** through action and dialogue. In the following example, the same student uses action and dialogue to reveal his thoughts and feelings.

On reaching the entrance, I realized that the library was already closed. I desperately shook the immovable doors. The only thing separating me from the sources I needed was a thin sheet of glass! "How can I do research without books?" I murmured as I walked from the building with my head down.

The following excerpt from another student's personal narrative focuses on one important event: choosing a research subject. Does the student express feelings about this topic directly, indirectly, or both?

The Research Subject That Swooped Down from the Sky

. . . I went to school the next morning with a sense of dread at showing up for English without the assignment. As a last effort, I tried to come up with a subject during free time that morning while the rest of my science class watched a video on birds. Then, just as I was about to give up and choose something like "the history of yarn," it happened. I looked up at the television screen just in time to see a majestic bald eagle swoop down and grab a fish out of the water with its talons. What an awesome sight! The eagle made catching a fish look so easy. Suddenly, all sorts of questions began to pop into my head. "How can they swoop down like that and grab fish out of the lake?" "Do eagles eat anything else besides fish?" "How big do eagles get?" "Why don't we see more bald eagles?" I was so excited that I accidentally exclaimed "Woo-hoo!" during the video. I had to stay after class because of the disturbance, but I finally had a good subject for my report.

I was happy to go to English class that day with my homework in hand. I was even happier to discover that I had chosen a subject that I really wanted to research. Over the next few weeks, I worked hard on the report. I went to the library several times and even spent a couple of hours after school talking to my science teacher, Mr. Newton. He let me borrow a book about birds of prey. He also helped me understand an article I found on the Internet about eagles. Researching was hard, but I am glad I did it.

YOUR TURN 14

Suggest that students work in pairs and practice telling each other about the key events and problems of doing reports before actually writing their narratives. This would remind them of parts of the process and also help them develop the more casual tone a personal narrative requires, as compared to the formal reports they wrote earlier. The listener could note parts he or she found especially interesting. Then the students could work independently to write their narratives.

YOUR TURN 14 **Writing a Personal Narrative**

Write a personal narrative about your research report. Be sure to focus on key events or problems as the topic of your narrative. Also, make sure to express your thoughts and feelings on your topic directly, indirectly, or both. If you wish, plan and present an **oral narrative** of your experience instead.

Giving and Listening to an Informative Speech

Talk **Listen**

Ahush falls over the crowd as you approach the podium. You can feel the tension in the audience as everyone waits for you to begin. Delivering a speech can be a nerve-racking experience. However, if you prepare well, delivering a speech can also be fun. After all, when you deliver a speech, you are the center of attention. The audience is in your control.

Adapting a Report for a Speech

What makes a good speech? As you get ready to make a speech based on the topic you chose in the Writing Workshop, focus on these elements:

- **Think about the purpose and occasion.** Are you giving an informal speech to your class, or is your speech part of a formal evaluation? Think about how these factors affect your word choice and delivery.

- **Limit your speech to your report's major ideas and the evidence you need to clarify and support** those ideas. When giving evidence, make sure you tell your audience where you found that information.

- **Adjust your word choice** so that your audience can easily understand your ideas and learn from your speech.

- **Use a simple outline** to deliver your speech, rather than simply reading your report. Speaking from a simple outline will make your speech sound more conversational and natural.

- **Avoid speaking too fast or too slow or too loud or too soft.** In other words, use an effective **rate** and **volume** for your audience.

WHAT'S AHEAD?

In this workshop you will give an informative speech. You will also learn how to

- adapt a research report for a speech
- use visuals
- listen to get the most out of an informative speech

TIP Use elaborations to explain your main ideas. **Elaborating,** or explaining your points in more detail, will make your speech easier to understand.

Reference Note

For more information and practice on **elaboration,** see page 304.

OBJECTIVES

- To adapt a research report for a speech
- To create visuals to support an informative speech
- To deliver an informative speech
- To listen for information in a speech

Quotation for the Day

"The secret of being interesting is to move along as fast as the mind of the reader (or listener) can take it in. Both must march along in the same tempo."

(Brenda Ueland, 1891–1985, American writer, editor, and teacher)

Ask students if they agree with the quotation. How does one know what the pace of a reader or listener is? [by analyzing the audience] How do listeners, in particular, let speakers know if the speakers are talking too fast or too slow? [by showing frustration or lack of interest]

TEACHING TIP

Adapting a Report for a Speech
Suggest to students that speeches take between three and five minutes.

You may also remind students to use the narratives they wrote for **Connections to Life** on pp. 189–190 as a source of anecdotes for their speeches.

TIP Running through your entire presentation—visuals and all—a few times will help you avoid making mistakes on speech day. Practice delivering your speech as if you were in front of the class. If you are using note cards or visuals, practice using them, too. Improve your speech through **self-evaluation,** or ask a peer to **collaborate** or **confer** with you about your content, visuals, and delivery.

Reference Note

For more on giving a **formal speech,** see page 758 in the Quick Reference Handbook.

■ Use the pitch, or the highs and lows, of your voice to create an enthusiastic tone. If the tone of your voice suggests that you do not care about your speech, your audience is likely to feel the same.

Using Visuals in an Informative Speech

Avoid getting caught up in "chartmania," the mysterious disease that affects speakers who use too many visuals. Having one or two well-chosen visuals is better than having too many. Whatever the number of visuals you decide to use, each one should have the same purpose: to complement and extend the meaning of an important point.

Hand-held Visuals If you decide that using a poster, picture, chart, graph, or prop is essential to your presentation, follow these tips.

■ Make sure all words and pictures are large enough to be seen clearly from the back of the room. Consider passing around props.

■ Be sure to describe in words what the visual means.

■ When explaining a visual, face the audience.

Overhead Projectors or Presentation Software One of the best ways to use visuals that everyone can see is to use a projector. By creating transparencies of your visuals, you can make them large or small by moving the projector away from or closer to the screen. Some projectors even project images from a word-processing program or presentation software. If you choose to use a projector, consider these tips.

■ Use dark colors for your text and pictures.

■ Make your graphic simple. A cluttered design is confusing.

■ Have a backup plan in case the projector breaks or is unavailable.

Video- or Audiotaped Segments Sometimes the best way to demonstrate your point is by using a video- or audiotaped segment. Here are some tips for using a video or audio clip.

■ The clip should be fairly short; it should support your presentation, not replace it.

■ Have your tape cued up before you speak so that the audience does not have to wait for you to rewind or fast forward it.

■ Test your equipment before your audience arrives.

Listening to an Informative Speech

An informative speech often contains so much information that you might have trouble absorbing it all. To make the most of the informative speeches you hear, follow these steps.

Before the Speech

- **Determine your purpose.** Identify what you want to learn from listening to this speech.
- **Make predictions.** Identify two or three points you expect the speaker to cover.
- **Get ready.** Have pen or pencil and paper ready for taking notes.

Reference Note

For more on **listening purpose** see page 767 in the Quick Reference Handbook.

During the Speech

- **Devote your full attention to the speaker.** Looking around the room or doing another assignment is discourteous and will prevent you from learning all you can.
- **Listen for cues that signal main points,** such as the speaker's slightly changing the volume or tone of his or her voice. Cues can also include these words and phrases: *first, second,* and *finally; there are many reasons* or *causes; the most important thing is;* and *in conclusion.* Hearing these cues is the key to understanding, interpreting, and organizing the information you hear in the speech.
- **Summarize the main points of the speech.** As you listen, take notes by summarizing the speaker's main points and supporting details.

Reference Note

For more on **eliminating barriers to effective listening,** see page 767 in the Quick Reference Handbook.

After the Speech

- **Monitor,** or note, your understanding of this speaker's message by asking yourself if the speaker covered all of the points you expected. If not, what did he or she leave out? Ask the speaker to clarify.

Reference Note

For more on **summarizing,** see pages 164–165.

YOUR TURN 15 — Giving and Listening to an Informative Speech

Now it is your turn to make an informative speech with visuals.

- First, adapt your report, using the suggestions on pages 191–192.
- Next, choose a visual that will help your audience understand your topic and practice with it. Use the guidelines on page 192.
- Finally, practice your listening skills when your classmates present their speeches.

Focus on Speaking and Listening   **193**

Interpreting Graphics and Web Sites

- To interpret information provided in graphic form
- To find information on a Web site

Quotation for the Day

❝Original details are very ordinary, except to the mind that sees their extraordinariness.❞

(Natalie Goldberg, American writer, poet, and teacher)

Invite students to quickwrite for a few minutes about some object or event that they saw and thought was amazing. What made the object or event special? How would hearing about the object or event have compared to actually seeing it?

Meeting **INDIVIDUAL NEEDS**

STUDENTS WITH SPECIAL NEEDS

Some students may need assistance in completing this workshop. Consider asking another student to describe the graphics in this workshop and to help summarize the information contained in them.

WHAT'S AHEAD?

In this workshop you will learn how to

- understand data contained in graphics
- use a Web site as a source of information

How are compact discs made? Who was the first female astronaut? The answers to these and many other questions await you in books, on the Internet, and even on TV. However, just knowing where to find information is only half of the battle. You must also understand how to interpret the graphics and other features, such as hyperlinks, that writers use to communicate information. That way, you can compare your findings to get a complete view of a topic.

Interpreting Information from Graphics

I See! When words alone are not enough, writers often use tables, maps, and other graphics to help you visualize difficult concepts and ideas. Most graphics contain the elements in the table below.

Element	Use
Title	gives the subject or main idea of the graphic
Body	presents the main information in the form of a chart, map, graph, time line, or other graphic
Legend	includes special symbols, codes, and other features needed to understand the graphic
Source	lists where the information is from

RESOURCES

Focus on Viewing and Representing

- *Media Literacy and Communication* *Skills*
  —*Support and Practice,* Ch. 5
  —*A How-to Handbook*

Teaching Notes

- *Media Literacy and Communication* *Skills*
  —*A Teacher's Guide,* Ch. 5

Maps Maps give geographical information, such as the streets and landmarks in a city, state, or country. However, some maps contain other useful information. To read a map, such as the one to the right, first study the title. Then, study the legend for special symbols and definitions or color codes. By studying the title and the symbols of this map, you learn that one of the colonial products in the 1700s was fish. By looking for the symbol of the fish on the map, you can determine that fish was an important product from the Boston and Portsmouth areas in the 1700s.

Tables Tables organize written information into categories, or groups. Textbooks often contain tables that organize and summarize important ideas. Whenever you see a table, such as the one on the previous page, first look for the capitalized or boldface words that identify the categories. The two categories in this table are "Element" and "Use." By reading from left to right, you can easily identify each element and its use.

Line Graphs Line graphs usually show how something changes over time. For example, the line graph to the right shows how the reindeer population of Saint Paul Island changed over a period of forty years. The first step in reading this graph is to find the intersections. An **intersection** is the point at which a number from the bottom of the graph intersects, or meets with, a number from the left side of the graph. By finding the first intersection in the line graph to the right, you learn that the reindeer population in 1940 was about two thousand. Once you find and interpret all of the intersections of a line graph, you can usually draw a conclusion from the data. What trend occurred between 1925 and 1940?

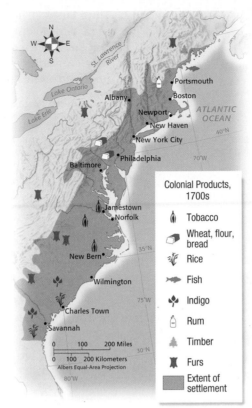

Colonial Products, 1700s

- Tobacco
- Wheat, flour, bread
- Rice
- Fish
- Indigo
- Rum
- Timber
- Furs
- Extent of settlement

The Population of Reindeer on Saint Paul Island Between 1910 and 1950

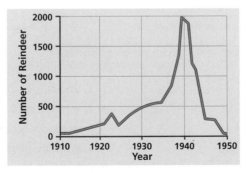

Critical Thinking

Evaluation. Explain to students that they should be critical of graphics, just as they should be critical of anything they read. As students look at the graphics shown here, ask them to consider the following questions:

- Is the graphic well organized and clearly labeled?

- Is it easy or difficult to interpret the information in the graphic? Why?

- How could the graphic be improved? With better organization or a different format? With different colors or symbols?

Time Lines   Time lines illustrate when important events occur in time. Time lines usually have a beginning date and an ending date. You know when things occur by their placement on the time line, which is read from left to right. The following time line shows some important events that occurred between 900 and 1500.

The Age of Discovery

	Crusades		Commercial Revolution

900	1000	1100	1200	1300	1400	1500

982
Eric the Red founds settlement on Greenland

1000
Vikings reach America

1095
Crusades begin

1271
Polo travels to China

1488
Dias sails around southern tip of Africa

1492
Columbus sails to America

YOUR TURN 16
Interpreting Graphics

Study the following graphics. Then, answer the questions at the bottom of the page.

Major Rivers of the World

River and Location	Length (mi)
Nile (Africa)	4,145
Amazon (S. America)	4,000
Mississippi-Missouri (N. America)	3,740
Yangtze (Asia)	3,720
Yenisey-Angara (Asia)	3,650
Amur-Argun (Asia)	3,590
Ob-Irtysh (Asia)	3,360
Plata-Paraná (S. America)	3,030
Huang (Asia)	2,903
Congo (Africa)	2,900

Source: U.S. Dept. of Commerce, National Oceanic and Atmospheric Admin., Principal Rivers and Lakes of the World

Unemployment,* 1925–35

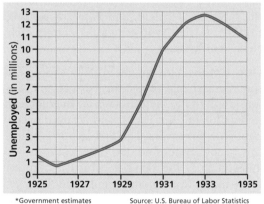

*Government estimates   Source: U.S. Bureau of Labor Statistics

1. What are the categories in the table to the left?
2. Which continent has the greatest number of major rivers?
3. Around what year was unemployment at its lowest point?
4. What trend do you see taking place between 1926 and 1932?

YOUR TURN 16

ANSWERS

1. River and Location and Length (mi)

2. 3,720 miles

3. 1926

4. There was a rise in unemployment.

RESOURCES

Your Turn 16

Practice and Reinforcement

■ *Media Literacy and Communication Skills*
—*Support and Practice,* Ch. 5, transparencies and worksheets

Interpreting Web Sites

Where Is It? How would you go about finding information on plant reproduction in your biology book? One way would be to turn each page, one-by-one, until you found it. Of course, the more efficient way would be to look in the **index,** which is a listing of the major topics in a work. An index—whether for a book or for a Web site—can help you find answers to your questions more efficiently.

A Web site's index can usually be found on the site's home page and is usually a list of *hyperlinks.* A **hyperlink** might look like a button, or it may be an underlined word, phrase, or sentence. In the home page below, the underlined words and phrases are all hyperlinks.

Critical Thinking

Evaluation. Students may benefit from a discussion evaluating the types of information that are best shown through print graphics and through Web sites. Lead them to see that the information in print graphics must be complete and clear. Each graphic can contain only limited information and must tie closely to the text it is enhancing. Charts, maps, and time lines are some graphics that work well in printed matter.

Web graphics, on the other hand, can extend information by using hyperlinks. An illustration of a rain forest tree, for example, could contain links to information on the tree, animals that live in the tree, and the rain forest in general. A Web graphic does not need to have complete information in one place. In addition, Web graphics might be interactive, such as a graph that allows the user to input information and click for a result. Web graphics can also employ media such as sound and animation.

Wrap It Up

Clicking on a hyperlink in the index will take you to another page that contains more information on that subject; it can also take you to a page that contains another, more specific index.

Making good predictions about the hyperlinks in an index can help you narrow the number of links to explore. After all, when you have a question, you want to get the answer as soon as possible. To make predictions about where the hyperlinks in an index will take you, follow these steps.

■ Read each hyperlink in the index.

■ Ask yourself if the information you want could logically fit in the category of the hyperlink.

■ If your answer is "yes," explore the link until you find your answer. If you run into a dead end, go back to the home page and try another link.

For example, a student who wanted biographical information about former astronaut Alan Shepard visited the NASA home page that appears on the previous page. He studied the home page index and decided to explore two hyperlinks, "Human Exploration and Development of Space" and "History." Both of these links seem as if they might contain information about Alan Shepard. However, after clicking on the "Human Exploration and Development" link, the student found that it only led to a page that explained NASA's purpose. He then returned to the home page and clicked on the "History" link, which eventually led him to a page with a link to astronaut biographies.

YOUR TURN 17 **Interpreting Information from a Web Site**

Use the NASA home page on page 197 to complete the following.

1. If you were trying to find information on how NASA began, which hyperlink(s) would you follow? Why?

2. If you wanted to find general information about space, which two links might you follow? Why?

Choices

Choose one of the following activities to complete.

▶ **CAREERS**

1. Get a Job! Pick a career you would like to have ten years from now. Then, write a **letter** to someone who has this career to discover how much education you will need and what the daily activities are. After getting a response, pretend that ten years have passed and that you have just finished your first day on the job. Write a **journal entry** describing your work activities and the way you feel about landing your dream job.

▶ **CROSSING THE CURRICULUM: SOCIAL STUDIES**

2. Where Did I Come From? Do some family research to find out more about your relatives. Create a **family tree** to share with your class that includes information you find about your relatives. Then, write a **memoir** about a special event you experienced with one or more of the relatives on your tree.

▶ **CROSSING THE CURRICULUM: MATH**

3. Learning to Count Find out about different methods of counting that have existed, or research the "invention" of mathematical symbols and ideas such as zero, percentages, and signs. Then, report your findings in an **oral report** for your math class.

▶ **DRAMA**

4. Let's Put on a Show Many children's programs use puppet shows to break down difficult concepts into easy-to-understand "edutainment." Adapt the information you learned in your research project into a **puppet show** for young children. Then, create your own puppets and arrange for a show at a local elementary school or day-care center.

▶ **CONNECTING CULTURES**

5. You Say Potato Pancake, I Say Latke All over the world, people love to celebrate, but we all celebrate in different ways. Read about how people in other cultures celebrate birthdays and holidays. Make a **report** that compares and contrasts the celebrations of other cultures with your own culture's celebrations.

PORTFOLIO

▶ **CAREERS**

Remind students that keeping a journal offers one of the best opportunities to write to discover. Explain that in writing a journal entry, students can explore and develop their personal responses to ideas and everyday encounters. Encourage them to record ideas, emotions, and ambitions about their chosen career.

▶ **CROSSING THE CURRICULUM: SOCIAL STUDIES**

Explain to students that in a memoir, a writer shares a biographical or an autobiographical account of personal experiences. To help students focus on a topic, have them first do a concept map in which they recollect specific details they wish to share. Explain that their point of view about the experience, whether humorous or serious, should be reflected in the writer's voice.

▶ **DRAMA**

Have students form groups of four or five and follow these steps to create a puppet show.

- Consider the tone, vocabulary level, characters, plot, and structure of your puppet show.
- Write a puppet show script of up to ten minutes.
- Storyboard the plot by sketching pictures to depict the action.
- Assign characters to group members.
- Gather materials, and then create hand puppets and a simple stage.
- Rehearse and perform the show.

Choices **199**

RESOURCES

Finding and Reporting Information

Assessment

- *Assessment Package*
  —*Chapter Tests,* Ch. 5
  —*Chapter Tests in Standardized Test Formats,* Ch. 5
  —*Assessment Alternatives,* Ch. 5

- *Test Generator (One-Stop Planner CD-ROM)*

Choices

Rubrics

- *Assessment Package*
  —*Assessment Alternatives,* Ch. 5

CHAPTER 6

Convincing Others

Use this guide to create an instructional plan that suits the individual needs of your students. Assignments marked by an asterisk (*) may be completed out of class. Times given for pacing lessons are estimated. See pp. 200–201 for chapter-wide resources. Resources listed in this guide are point-of-use resources only.

Curriculum Connections

Choices *p. 231*
- Speech
- Art
- Crossing the Curriculum: Social Studies
- Writing

 GO TO: go.hrw.com
KEYWORD: EOLang 7-6

All resources for this chapter are available for preview on the *One-Stop Planner CD-ROM with Test Generator.* All worksheets and tests may be printed from the CD-ROM.

	Chapter Opener pp. 200–201	Reading Workshop: Reading a Persuasive Article pp. 202–210
DEVELOPMENTAL PROGRAM	**30 minutes** • Your Turn 1 *p. 201*	**100 minutes** • Preparing to Read *p. 202* • Reading Selection *pp. 203–204* • First Thoughts in groups *p. 205* • Point of View *pp. 205–206* • Your Turn 2 *p. 206* • Logical Support *pp. 206–208* • Your Turn 3 *p. 208* • Test Taking Mini-Lesson *p. 210*
CORE PROGRAM	**20 minutes** • Your Turn 1 *p. 201*	**75 minutes** • Preparing to Read *p. 202* • Reading Selection *pp. 203–204* • First Thoughts *p. 205* • Point of View *pp. 205–206* • Your Turn 2 *p. 206* • Logical Support *pp. 206–208* • Your Turn 3 *p. 208* • Vocabulary Mini-Lesson *p. 209* • Test Taking Mini-Lesson *p. 210*
ADVANCED PROGRAM	**15 minutes** • Your Turn 1 *p. 201*	**60 minutes** • Preparing to Read *p. 202* • Reading Selection *pp. 203–204* • First Thoughts *p. 205* • Point of View *pp. 205–206* • Your Turn 2 *p. 206* • Logical Support *pp. 206–208* • Your Turn 3 *p. 208* • Vocabulary Mini-Lesson *p. 209*
RESOURCES — PRINT	• *Communications,* TP. 45, WS. p. 115	• *Alternative Readings,* Ch. 6 • *Communications,* TPs. 46, 47, WS. pp. 116–123
RESOURCES — MEDIA	• *One-Stop Planner CD-ROM*	• *One-Stop Planner CD-ROM*

TP.=Transparency   WS.=Worksheet

Writing Workshop: Writing a Persuasive Essay
pp. 211–227

⏱ 220 minutes
- Choose an Issue *pp. 211–212*
- State Your Opinion; Your Turn 4 *pp. 212–213*
- Consider Your Audience; Your Turn 5 *p. 213*
- Putting Your Audience in Focus; Your Turn 6 *p. 214*
- Gather Support; Your Turn 7 *pp. 214–216*
- Critical-Thinking Mini-Lesson *p. 217*
- Framework; Models; Your Turn 8* *pp. 218–220*
- Test Taking Mini-Lesson *p. 221*
- Evaluate and Revise; Your Turn 9 *pp. 222–224*
- Proofreading, Publishing, and Reflecting *pp. 225–226*
- Grammar Link *p. 225*
- Your Turn 10 *p. 226*

⏱ 160 minutes
- Choose an Issue *pp. 211–212*
- State Your Opinion; Your Turn 4 *pp. 212–213*
- Consider Your Audience; Your Turn 5 *p. 213*
- Putting Your Audience in Focus; Your Turn 6 *p. 214*
- Gather Support; Your Turn 7 *pp. 214–216*
- Critical-Thinking Mini-Lesson *p. 217*
- Framework; Models; Your Turn 8* *pp. 218–220*
- Test Taking Mini-Lesson *p. 221*
- Evaluate and Revise *pp. 222–224*
- Focus on Word Choice *p. 224*
- Your Turn 9* *p. 224*
- Proofreading, Publishing, and Reflecting *pp. 225–226*
- Grammar Link *p. 225*
- Your Turn 10 *p. 226*
- Connections to Life; Your Turn 11* *p. 227*

⏱ 120 minutes
- Choose an Issue *pp. 211–212*
- State Your Opinion; Your Turn 4 *pp. 212–213*
- Consider Your Audience; Your Turn 5 *p. 213*
- Putting Your Audience in Focus; Your Turn 6 *p. 214*
- Gather Support; Your Turn 7 *pp. 214–216*
- Critical-Thinking Mini-Lesson *p. 217*
- Framework; Models; Your Turn 8* *pp. 218–220*
- Evaluate and Revise *pp. 222–224*
- Focus on Word Choice *p. 224*
- Your Turn 9* *p. 224*
- Proofreading, Publishing, and Reflecting *pp. 225–226*
- Your Turn 10 *p. 226*
- Connections to Life; Your Turn 11* *p. 227*

- *Communications,* 🔊
  TPs. 48–51,
  WS. pp. 124–136
- *Designing Your Writing*

- *One-Stop Planner CD-ROM* 💿

Focus on Viewing and Representing: Analyzing an Editorial Cartoon *pp. 228–230*

⏱ 60 minutes
- What Is an Editorial Cartoon? *p. 228*
- Symbolism *p. 229*
- Exaggeration/Caricature *p. 229*
- Analogy *p. 230*
- Your Turn 12 *p. 230*

⏱ 30 minutes
- What Is an Editorial Cartoon? *p. 228*
- Symbolism *p. 229*
- Exaggeration/Caricature *p. 229*
- Analogy *p. 230*
- Your Turn 12* *p. 230*

⏱ 20 minutes
- What Is an Editorial Cartoon? *p. 228*
- Symbolism *p. 229*
- Exaggeration/Caricature *p. 229*
- Analogy *p. 230*
- Your Turn 12* *p. 230*

- *Media Literacy and Communication* 🔊
  Skills
  —*Support and Practice,* Ch. 6
  —*A How-to Handbook*
  —*A Teacher's Guide,* Ch. 6

- *One-Stop Planner CD-ROM* 💿

CHAPTER 6

Convincing Others

CHAPTER OBJECTIVES

- To read a persuasive magazine article and identify the author's point of view and logical appeals

- To write a persuasive essay

- To analyze persuasive techniques in editorial cartoons

Chapter Overview

Persuasion is present in every part of students' lives. This chapter is designed to help students recognize and use persuasive techniques when they are reading, writing, and viewing. The Reading Workshop (pp. 202–210) provides a magazine article in which students can identify the point of view and the use of logical appeals. In the Writing Workshop (pp. 211–227), students will follow steps to write a persuasive essay. The Focus on Viewing and Representing (pp. 228–230) offers an explanation of persuasive techniques in editorial cartoons, enabling students to analyze a political cartoon. The three sections of the chapter can be taught independently, but taught together they can give students a broad-based understanding of persuasion.

Why Study Persuasion?

Because students encounter persuasion daily—at school, on television, and in magazines and newspapers—it is important for them to recognize when someone is trying to convince them to accept a point of view or to take an action. Understanding persuasive techniques will help students to evaluate persuasive arguments and discriminate between fact and opinion. These skills will help students become informed readers and listeners who can make up their own minds about issues.

Teaching the Chapter

Option 1: Begin with Literature

If literature is the focus in your classroom, you might introduce this chapter after studying the use of persuasion in novels and short stories. As students read, encourage them to focus on characters who try to persuade others through their actions or words. Then, have students read the article in this chapter (pp. 203–204), noting the ways that the writer tries to persuade readers. Once students have read and analyzed the use of persuasive techniques, they will be ready to write their own persuasive essays in the Writing Workshop (pp. 211–227).

Option 2: Begin with Nonfiction and Writing

You might begin with the nonfiction reading and the information in this chapter. The article in the Reading Workshop and its accompanying instruction (pp. 202–210) explains how to identify point of view and persuasive techniques. The Writing Workshop (pp. 211–227) leads students through the steps to writing their own essay. When they return to literature, students may be better able to identify persuasion and evaluate its effectiveness.

Making Connections

■ To the Literature Curriculum

In literature, characters make use of a variety of persuasive techniques through their words or actions. For example, the urban legend "The Dinner Party," retold by Mona Gardner, shows readers how actions can be more persuasive than words. In Rudyard Kipling's short story "Rikki-tikki-tavi," characters use both persuasive words and actions to convince a cobra not to hurt a human family.

Lesson Idea: Persuasion in "Rikki-tikki-tavi" by Rudyard Kipling

1. Have students read "Rikki-tikki-tavi," noting ways in which Rikki-tikki and Darzee's wife use persuasion to keep Nagaina away from Teddy's family.

2. Have students work in small groups to analyze the use of persuasion in "Rikki-tikki-tavi" by filling in a chart like the one below, indicating the use of both persuasive actions and persuasive words. Possible responses follow.

	Rikki-tikki	**Darzee's Wife**
Persuasive Actions and Purpose	Holds one of Nagaina's eggs to show that he will crush it if she harms the family	Flutters nearby so that Nagaina will chase her, leaving behind her eggs
Persuasive Words and Purpose	Reminds Nagaina he has killed Nag to anger her into leaving Teddy and fighting him instead	Calls out that her wing is broken to entice Nagaina to leave her eggs and chase her

3. Discuss students' responses, encouraging them to explain their conclusions. Point out that nonfiction authors also rely on persuasive techniques to convince readers to accept an opinion or to take a course of action.

4. After discussion, introduce students to the magazine article in this chapter (pp. 203–204). Use the chart on p. 207 and the instruction on pp. 206–207 to help students understand the reasons and evidence the writer uses to persuade readers that children should not play video games frequently.

■ To Careers

Explain to students that what they are learning about persuasion applies to many careers. Point out that while careers in sales and advertising focus on selling ideas or products, many other careers involve persuasion in less obvious ways. Brainstorm with students a list of such careers, which might include teaching, nursing, or waiting on tables. Then, have students working in small groups role-play a scene in which a person in one of these careers convinces someone to believe or do something. Encourage groups to play their scenes for the class, and then discuss together what students have learned about the uses of persuasion in the working world. See also **Connections to Life** on p. 227.

■ To the Community

Help students understand that what they are learning in the classroom has meaning in the broader world. Invite a member of the community, such as a newspaper columnist, city employee, or member of your school's parent-teacher association to talk with the class about a time he or she tried to persuade someone to think or do something. Have the speaker describe any persuasive techniques used and possible ways he or she could have been more persuasive.

■ To the Social Studies Curriculum

Leaders in history had to be adept at convincing others about their ideas and plans for action. Have pairs of students research how a historical figure used persuasion. You might ask a history or social studies teacher for help in developing a list of historical leaders. Possibilities include Abraham Lincoln, Susan B. Anthony, and Martin Luther King, Jr. Partners might use encyclopedias, biographies, or primary sources to determine what persuasive techniques were used by the historical figure they selected. Have partners report their findings to the class.

CHAPTER

6

Convincing Others

SUPPORT AFTER-SCHOOL PROGRAMS

PREVIEWING THE CHAPTER

■ The three workshops in this chapter discuss persuasion. Each workshop may be taught separately, but when taught together, the workshops reinforce one another and help students gain a complete understanding of the techniques used to persuade others. For help in integrating this chapter with grammar, usage, and mechanics chapters, see pp. T311A–T311B.

INTRODUCING THE CHAPTER

■ To introduce the chapter, use the Journal Warm-up, Transparency 45, in *Communications*.

VIEWING THE ILLUSTRATION

■ This illustration shows five colorful human figures in the act of communicating persuasively. Have students identify all the ways messages are being conveyed in the illustration. [Newspaper, flag, computer, book, television, hand gestures, sign/banner, speech, pamphlets, hat, applause.] Ask students how the lines and shapes guide their eyes around to all the details and help contribute to the piece's meaning. [The curving road, horizon, and banner lead the viewer's eyes in a clockwise fashion around the illustration, giving equal treatment to each person's opinion in the piece.]

Representing. Invite students to design representations of the communication process that are not included in the illustration.

CHAPTER RESOURCES

Planning
■ *Lesson Planner, ELL Strategies,* Ch. 6
■ Block Scheduling, p. T199A (this book)
■ *One-Stop Planner CD-ROM*

Practice
■ *Communications,* Ch. 6
■ *Media Literacy and Communication Skills*

Extension
■ *Designing Your Writing*

Reinforcement
■ *Communications,* Ch. 6
■ *Alternative Readings,* Ch. 6
■ *Daily Language Activity Transparencies*
■ *Vocabulary Workshop* and *Tests*
■ *Spelling*

Reading Workshop

Reading a Persuasive Article

Writing Workshop

Writing a Persuasive Essay

Viewing and Representing

Analyzing an Editorial Cartoon

"Wait until you grow up." "You can do that when you're an adult." Do these comments sound familiar? Sometimes it must seem as if you have little or no say in the issues that affect your life. This can be frustrating, especially when you have a strong opinion. Fortunately, there *is* a way you can express your opinion effectively: through *persuasion*.

Persuasion is a type of communication that offers an opinion and supports it with reasons and evidence. Some persuasive communication even asks readers or listeners to take a specific action. You have probably come across persuasion in newspapers and magazines, or on TV or the radio. You can use persuasion to try to make a change in your world—begin by writing your own persuasive piece.

Informational Text

Persuasion

YOUR TURN 1 Discovering Persuasion

In your local newspaper or in a magazine, find an example of persuasive writing. Share the article you find with a few classmates, and discuss these questions:

- Why do you think the article is an example of persuasion?
- What reasons or examples does the author use to try to persuade you to share his or her opinion?
- Which article in your group is most persuasive? Why?

internetconnect

GO TO: go.hrw.com
KEYWORD: EOLang 7-6

Motivate

Ask students to list one or two things they have recently attempted to convince their teacher, parent, or guardian to let them do. Then, ask students to discuss *how* they tried to convince their audience.

ELEMENTS OF *Literature*

Persuasion in Literature. In *Elements of Literature,* First Course, see "The Frog Who Wanted to Be a Singer," by Linda Goss, pp. 172–177, and "The Origin of the Seasons," retold by Olivia Coolidge, pp. 501–508, for examples of characters who attempt persuasion.

YOUR TURN 1

- Answers will vary. After each student shares his or her ideas and insights about his or her examples, have another group member summarize that student's message. You might want to assess the productivity of students' discussions using the following guidelines:
- As they listen, students understand the speaker's major ideas and supporting evidence, interpret the speaker's overall message, and ask questions for clarification.
- As they speak, students support ideas with evidence, elaboration, and examples, and clarify those ideas if asked.

Evaluation and Assessment

- *Test Generator (One-Stop Planner CD-ROM)*
- *Assessment Package*
  —*Chapter Tests,* Ch. 6
  —*Chapter Tests in Standardized Test Formats,* Ch. 6
  —*Assessment Alternatives,* Ch. 6

Internet

- go.hrw.com (keyword: EOLang 7–6)

OBJECTIVES

Reading and Writing Connection

- To read a persuasive article in preparation for writing a persuasive essay

- To map out the logical appeals writers use to persuade their audiences

Reading Skills

- To identify the author's point of view or opinion on an issue

- To use context clues, word structure, word sounds, and a dictionary to figure out the meaning of unfamiliar words

Quotation for the Day

"I dearly love to persuade people. There can hardly be a greater pleasure (of a selfish kind) than to feel you have brought another person around to your way of thinking."

(James Hinton, 1822–1875, English philosopher)

Write the quotation on the chalkboard, and ask students to discuss it. Then, explain that you can be persuaded by something you have read just as easily as by something you have heard. Have students freewrite about a time when their minds were changed by something they read. Invite them to explore why the argument was convincing.

TEACHING TIP

Preparing to Read
This page discusses point of view and logical support, which are the instructional focuses of the Reading Workshop. Both concepts appear in the selection **"A Veto on Video Games."**

RESOURCES

Reading Workshop Reinforcement
- *Alternative Readings,* Ch. 6

Reading a Persuasive Article

WHAT'S AHEAD?

In this section you will read a persuasive article. You will also learn how to

- identify the author's point of view or opinion on an issue

- map out the logical appeals writers use to persuade their audiences

They cause young people to huddle over their game pads for hours. They mean big business for software developers. They ping, zap, and explode in arcades across the country. What are they? You guessed it: video games—the topic of the persuasive article on the next page. If you have an opinion about video games, you probably find reasons to back it up. Do you try to convince people to share your opinion? Or do you talk with those who already share it? As you read the article, remember the author's purpose: to persuade you to accept his point of view. Will he succeed? Read on and find out.

Preparing to Read

READING SKILL

Point of View   A **point of view** is a person's opinion on an issue. The author of the following article, Lloyd Garver, has a very definite point of view on video games. He may not announce it in the first paragraph, but he does provide certain clues that will help you figure it out.

READING FOCUS

Logical Support   Mr. Garver does not just expect people to accept his point of view without question. He supports his opinion. As you read, think about how *well* he supports it. If he wants to persuade a thoughtful reader—like you—he will use *logical appeals.* That means he will support his point of view with *reasons* and *evidence.* **Logical appeals** can include stories, facts, and expert opinions—support you can weigh carefully and confirm.

202   Chapter 6   **Persuasion:** Convincing Others

READING PROCESS

PREREADING
Set a Purpose. The **Preparing to Read** section gives students a purpose for reading the Reading Selection: to recognize the author's point of view and the appeals he uses to support it. Explain to students that reading with

goals in mind tends to improve comprehension and helps readers retain what they read longer.

Tell students that in their independent reading they will need to set their own purposes for reading. One way to identify a

Read the following article. In a notebook, jot down answers to the numbered active-reading questions in the shaded boxes. Underlined words will be discussed in the Vocabulary Mini-Lesson on page 209.

from Newsweek®

A Veto on Video Games

A parent speaks out on why he has barred TV video games from his home.

BY LLOYD GARVER

My wife and I are the kind of mean parents whom kids grumble about on the playground. We're among that ever-shrinking group of parents known as video game holdouts. We refuse to buy a video game set. Around Christmastime, my son made a wish list, and I noticed that Nintendo was No. 1. I said, "You know you're not going to get Nintendo." He said, "I know I'm not going to get it from *you*. But I might get it from *him*." Alas, Santa, too, let him down.

I don't think that playing a video game now and then is really harmful to children. But the children I know are so obsessed with these games that they have prompted at least one second-grade teacher (my son's) to ban the word *Nintendo* from the classroom. When I asked my seven-year-old if the teacher wouldn't let the kids talk about the games because that's all they were *talking* about, he said, "No. That's all we were *thinking* about."

Our society is already so computerized and dehumanized that kids don't need one more reason to avoid playing outside or going for a walk or talking with a friend. I'd still feel this way even if there were nothing wrong with games whose objectives are to kill and destroy.

I know, I know. There are games other than those like Rampage, Robocop, Motor Cross Maniacs, Bionic Commando, Dr. Doom's Revenge, Guerrilla War, and Super Street Fighter. But aren't the violent games the ones the kids love to play for hours? And hours. And hours. My son told me he likes the "killing games" the best, hasn't had much experience with

> **1. What is the author for or against? What specific words tell you?**

> **2. Why does the author tell us this story about his son's teacher?**

> **3. Why do you think the author quotes his young son?**

---

purpose for reading is to preview questions that accompany a text. Have students read the active-reading questions before they read the selection. This will help them discover what they need to know about the article and set their own purpose for reading.

4. If some students are still confused by the quotation after reading the next paragraph, ask a student to paraphrase the quotation for the class. [One possible paraphrase: Game makers create games that change the way players think and cause them to become completely involved in a game.]

5. Children are more familiar with electronic sports games than real-life sports.

6. The author clearly states his point of view in the second sentence of the paragraph: "Kids do play and talk about these games too much."

Critical Thinking

Analysis. To help students understand how an author uses style to establish a point of view, have them answer the following:

- What does the author's use of words such as *dehumanized* tell you about the author's point of view, or bias? [Such slanted or loaded language reveals that the author believes video games are harmful to children.] What other language in the article reveals the author's point of view? [the description of video games as "lifeless electronic images" and the concern that video games are "dominating children's lives"] Explain.

- Keeping in mind the author's point of view, how would you describe the tone in the following sentence? "And then there's the game with my favorite title . . . Skate or Die."

- Is the tone serious or sarcastic? How do you know?

- Do you think the author's style of writing—his language and tone—would be convincing to the primary audience (parents) of this essay? Explain.

"sports games," and likes "learning games" the least because they are "too easy." (Manufacturers take note.) My five-year-old daughter told me she enjoyed playing Duck Hunt at a friend's house. The beauty of this game is that even very young players can have the fun of <u>vicariously</u> shooting animals. And then there's the game with my favorite title—an obvious attempt to combine a graceful sport with exciting action—Skate or Die.

'Promote habituation'[1]: The January issue of the Journal of the American Academy of Child and Adolescent Psychiatry featured an article entitled "Pathological Preoccupation with[2] Video Games." The author believes that some game manufacturers try to develop programs that "deliberately promote habituation," and the goal of some of the people who make up these games is "to <u>induce</u> an altered level of concentration and focus of attention in the gamester."

> **4. Are you confused by the last quotation in this paragraph? Try reading on to the next paragraph for an explanation.**

If you have children, or know any, doesn't this "altered level of concentration and focus" sound familiar? If not, try talking to a child while he is staring at that screen, pushing buttons. He won't hear you unless the words you

---

1. **'Promote habituation':** cause addiction.
2. **"Pathological Preoccupation with . . .":** total focus of attention on, to the point of obsession.

---

happen to be saying are, "I just bought a new game for you."

In case you couldn't tell, I'm worried that electronic games are dominating children's lives. There are games that <u>simulate</u> sports like baseball and basketball, and that's all some kids know about the sports. Someday soon, a young couple will take their children to their first baseball game and hear the kids exclaim, "This is great. It's almost like the *real baseball* we play on our home screen." When I took my son to a recent Lakers basketball game, the thing that seemed to excite him most was a video game in the lobby. You see, if a kid didn't want to be bored watching some of the greatest athletes in the world play, he could just put a quarter in the machine and watch lifeless electronic images instead.

> **5. What is the main point of this paragraph?**

My son's teacher was right. Kids do play and talk about these games too much. They even have books and magazines that kids can study and classes so they can get better at the games. And that's what's got me worried. I'm just concerned that this activity is so <u>absorbing</u>, kids are going to grow up thinking that the first people to fly that airplane at Kitty Hawk were the Super Mario Brothers.

> **6. In this paragraph, where does the author's point of view come across most strongly?**

I don't like to discourage children from doing something they're good at; in this case, I must. ∎

READING PROCESS

READING

Ask Questions. Explain to students that understanding question-answer relationships can help them tackle reading questions and figure out the meaning of a text by focusing on what is important. Articles by T. E.

Raphael discuss two categories into which reading questions may be placed. Tell students that reading questions are either *In the Book* questions (answers to these questions can be found right in the text) or *In My Head* questions (these questions require

Point of View

READING SKILL

What Does the Author *Really* Think?

One step in understanding persuasive writing is figuring out the author's point of view on the issue. Sometimes persuasive writers announce their point of view in an *opinion statement*. An **opinion statement** is made up of an issue plus the writer's point of view on the issue.

Example: **Issue:** video games on library computers

    + **Point of view:** they should be included
    _____

    Opinion statement: Video games should be included on the library's computers.

Unfortunately, writers don't always include an opinion statement—especially if they think you will disagree with it. You can figure out the writer's point of view on an issue, though, from clues in the article.

Try figuring out the point of view in the paragraph below. The issue is video games as learning tools. The steps on the next page will help you if you get stuck.

From the Game Room to the Operating Room

There is a lot of talk about violence in some video games. Few people, however, stop to think about the positive benefits of the games. The workers of the future will need to know how to operate computers, concentrate on complicated tasks, and do several tasks at once. Does this sound familiar? I, for one, have marveled at the concentration of a child playing a video game. Last night, watching a documentary about microsurgery, I could not help noticing how much the surgeon's skilled movements resembled those of a child playing a video game. . . .

TIP Notice that the sentence containing the word *violence* is followed by a sentence containing the word *however*. A sentence that includes *however* tends to weaken the meaning of what came before. That means the impact of the word *violence* is not so negative after all.

First Thoughts on Your Reading

ANSWERS

Possible answers follow.

1. The author's main point is that video games are bad for children.

2. *Convincing:* children are obsessed with video games; video games are habit-forming. *Not convincing:* all children like violent games simply because the author's son does; children who play sports video games will prefer them to the physical games or will confuse the games with reality.

Critical Thinking

Analyzing Problems and Solutions. Use the following questions to help students analyze the problem and solution implicitly addressed in the article "A Veto on Video Games":

• What problem do you think inspired the author to write this article?

• What examples does the author give as evidence of the problem?

• What does the author think the solution is? What makes you say so?

Reading Workshop   **205**

independent thought).

As students read **"A Veto on Video Games,"** ask them to identify each of the accompanying active-reading questions as either *In the Book* or *In My Head* questions. [*In the Book:* 1, 4, 5, and 6; *In My Head:* 2 and 3]

Next, have students create their own examples of each of these types of questions based on the Reading Selection.

THINKING IT THROUGH ● Identifying Point of View

▶ **STEP 1** Scan the title and the first few sentences. Look for positive and negative words and comments related to the issue.

Positive: positive benefits, marveled, skilled
Negative: violence

▶ **STEP 2** Look for patterns. Are the words and comments you identified mostly positive or mostly negative?

Most of the words are positive. Also, the author compares a video game player to a surgeon—that has to be good.

▶ **STEP 3** Based on what you have found, make a decision about the author's point of view.

The author thinks video games are good learning tools.

YOUR TURN 2 Identifying the Author's Point of View

Using the three steps shown above, figure out the author's point of view in "A Veto on Video Games." Then complete this sentence:

The author's point of view is _____.

READING FOCUS

Logical Support

A Show of Support We all need a little support now and then, and so does a point of view. As a critical reader, you should always look at how well a writer supports his or her point of view in a persuasive article.

Remember, good writers always support their points of view logically, using *reasons* and *evidence*. Using this kind of support is called making a **logical appeal**. Logical appeals require readers to use their heads (that is, their logic) to decide whether they agree or disagree with the author.

Reasons A **reason** explains *why* the writer takes a certain point of view. In a persuasive article, the main point of each body paragraph is likely to be a reason. In "A Veto on Video Games" the first body paragraph begins this way:

> I don't think that playing a video game now and then is really harmful to children. But the children I know are so obsessed with these games that they have prompted at least one second-grade teacher (my son's) to ban the word *Nintendo* from the classroom....

The author begins by saying that video games played "now and then" are not harmful. Is that his main point in this paragraph, though? He goes on to say that children are obsessed with the games. That is the author's reason for having the point of view on video games that he does—and the main point of the paragraph.

Evidence   Since reasons alone are not always convincing, persuasive writers support them with evidence. There are several different kinds of evidence a writer can use. (One example from the following chart comes from "A Veto on Video Games." Can you identify it?)

Types of Evidence	Definition	Example
Fact	a statement that can be proven true	"While playing a video game, a person's heart rate, blood pressure, and oxygen intake all increase."
Anecdote	a brief story that illustrates a point	"When I asked my seven-year-old if the teacher wouldn't let the kids talk about the [video] games because that's all they were *talking* about, he said, 'No. That's all we were *thinking* about.'"
Expert Opinion	the opinion of someone with expert knowledge	"Psychologists say that playing video games helps children learn skills that will prepare them for the work force."

TIP   Persuasive writers often try to capture their readers' *hearts* as well as their *heads*. They choose support that has **emotional appeal** as well as logical appeal.

Example:
Today's video game players could be tomorrow's lifesavers. Many young surgeons who grew up playing video games show incredible skill in microsurgery.

?   Why would the example above appeal to readers' emotions?

Mapping the Logical Appeal Sorting out the reasons and evidence as you read a persuasive essay is hard work. You can keep track of a writer's support in a conceptual map like the one below. Think of the map as a mental filing cabinet: each space represents a folder in which you can file information. Mapping the information will help you in two ways: It will (1) help you think critically about the author's point of view and (2) help you learn how to organize a persuasive essay of your own.

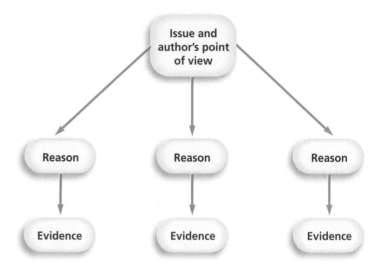

YOUR TURN 3 — Mapping the Logical Appeal

- Re-read the selection "A Veto on Video Games" on pages 203–204. Then, fill in a map like the one above with the issue, the author's point of view, and the reasons and evidence from the article. Identify each piece of evidence you find as a fact, an anecdote, or an expert opinion. (**Hint:** Look for reasons near the beginning of each body paragraph. Look for supporting evidence in those same paragraphs.)

- Now that you have had a chance to think carefully about the author's views on video games, do you agree with him? Why or why not? Explain your answer in a sentence or two.

READING PROCESS

EXTENDING
Apply What You Read. Remind students that they were given a set purpose for reading **"A Veto on Video Games"**: to identify point of view and logical support. Ask students to create additional facts, examples, or expert opinions to further develop the author's point of view. Invite students to develop an opposing point of view to claim that video games are not harmful to young children.

Wordbusting Strategy (CSSD)

Words have power—power to persuade. It is important, then, to understand the words you read. **Wordbusting** is a strategy for figuring out the meanings of unfamiliar words. The strategy has four parts, but you only need to use as many as it takes to understand a word. The letters *CSSD* can help you remember the parts of the strategy.

- **Context** You may get clues to an unfamiliar word's meaning from its context—

the words, sentences, or paragraphs around the unfamiliar word.

- **Structure** Look at the word to see if you recognize any roots, prefixes, or suffixes.
- **Sound** Say the word aloud; you may hear a root or another word part you recognize and can define.
- **Dictionary** If necessary, look up the word.

THINKING IT THROUGH — Using the Wordbusting Strategy

Here is an example of Wordbusting, using a word from "A Veto on Video Games."

Word: simulate

▶ **STEP 1** **Context:** "There are games that *simulate* sports like baseball and basketball, and that's all some kids know about the sports."

▶ **STEP 2** **Structure:** sim + u + late

▶ **STEP 3** **Sound:** sim′ yo͞o lāt′

My Best Guess:

The author says "that's all some kids know about the sports." I think those words have something to do with the meaning, but I'm not sure.

I know a <u>simile</u> is a comparison using "like" or "as." Maybe <u>sim</u> means the same thing in both words.

Sounds like <u>similar</u>, which means "kind of like." Based on all of these clues, I think <u>simulate</u> means "to be like something else."

PRACTICE

Figure out the meanings of the words on the right. The words are underlined in "A Veto on Video Games," so you can see each word's context. Write the steps of CSSD that you actually use to define each word, using the example above as a model.

1. dehumanized (page 203)
2. objectives (page 203)
3. vicariously (page 204)
4. induce (page 204)
5. absorbing (page 204)

Wordbusting Strategy (CSSD)

ANSWERS
Possible answers are given below.

1. The phrase about kids not wanting to play or talk with friends makes me think that *dehumanized* means "not human." The prefix *de–* means "to remove" and the word *human* refers to people. *Dehumanized* means "having the human qualities removed."

2. When the author mentions "games whose *objectives* are to kill and destroy," it sounds like he is describing the goals of a game. The root word *object* refers to something you can touch or aim for. I think *objectives* means "goals or aims."

3. The context implies that this word explains *how* someone shoots animals. The dictionary says that *vicariously* means "experienced through imaginative participation in the experience of someone else."

4. Since players focus on video games, *induce* may mean "to cause." The dictionary confirms this.

5. The word *absorbing* sounds like *absorbent*. Commercials describe paper towels as absorbent—they soak up liquids. I think that *absorbing* means "soaking up all your thoughts."

Taking a Second Look

Wordbusting Strategy (CSSD). Have students use dictionaries to explore the etymologies of the words in this lesson. Then, discuss how the history of each word relates to its present meaning.

RESOURCES

Your Turn 3
Practice
- *Communications,* WS. p. 118
Reinforcement
- *Communications,* TP. 47, WS. p. 119

Vocabulary
Practice
- *Communications,* WS. p. 120

Identifying Author's Purpose and Point of View

When you read a selection on a reading test, you may be asked to identify the author's point of view. You may also be asked to identify the author's *purpose:* to inform, to entertain, or to persuade the reader. Suppose the following passage and test item were on a reading test. How would you approach them?

Educational software, or kidware, grabs a child's attention through color, sound, and motion. In this way, kidware is like many video games. Many video games, however, are violent. Kidware, on the other hand, involves children in acts of learning, not in acts of destruction.

The author probably wrote this passage to

A. inform readers about a new video game on the market

B. tell a funny story about kidware and video games

C. explain how to use both kidware and video games

D. convince readers that kidware is better than video games

TIP Most writing in which the author has a strong point of view is *persuasive.* If you find a strong point of view in a test passage, the **author's purpose** is probably to persuade.

THINKING IT THROUGH — Identifying Author's Purpose

▶ **STEP 1** Turn the first part of the item into a question.

"The author probably wrote this passage to" means the same as "Why did the author write this passage?" ("What was the author's purpose?")

▶ **STEP 2** Try to answer the question in your own words.

The author uses negative words to describe video games. However, he or she says you can learn from kidware. I think the author wants to show that kidware is good.

▶ **STEP 3** Eliminate answer choices that are clearly wrong. Look for a choice that best matches your own answer.

Answer A is wrong because the author does not mention a particular video game. The author is not telling a story, so Answer B is not right. Answer C is wrong because the author is not giving an explanation. Answer D sounds most like my answer. This is the right choice.

Looking Ahead to Writing

In the Writing Workshop (pp. 211–226), students will be asked to write their own persuasive essays. As they prepare to write, students will need to provide reasons and evidence to support their opinions. Have students refer to the Reading Selection and consider what support they found most convincing and how they can model their writing to be as convincing. Remind students to refer to the evidence chart on p. 207 as they gather support for their essays.

RESOURCES

Test Taking
Practice
■ *Communications,* WS. pp. 121–123

Writing a Persuasive Essay

"That is *not* fair!" "We shouldn't let that happen!" Have you ever said those words? When you feel strongly about an issue, you want to *do* something about it. One way you might change a situation is to write about it. You can write something that might persuade other people to share your opinion. You may even convince people to help you bring about the change you want.

Here is your chance to make the world a better place. In this workshop you will write a persuasive essay on an issue about which you feel strongly. Using reasons and evidence, you will try to convince your readers to share your opinion.

WHAT'S AHEAD?

In this workshop you will write a persuasive essay. You will also learn how to

- **take a stand on an issue**
- **use reasons and evidence effectively**
- **distinguish between fact and opinion**
- **eliminate clichés from your writing**
- **use comparatives correctly**

Writing Workshop

OBJECTIVES

- To use the writing process to write a persuasive essay
- To take a stand on an issue
- To use reasons and evidence effectively
- To distinguish between fact and opinion
- To eliminate clichés from writing
- To use comparatives correctly

Quotation for the Day

"The act of writing is an act of optimism. You would not take the trouble to do it if you felt that it didn't matter."

(Edward Albee, 1928–   , American playwright)

Write the quotation on the chalkboard. Ask students to discuss whether they agree with Albee's statement. Then, as students begin work on their persuasive papers, use the quotation to encourage students to select topics about which they feel strongly.

Prewriting

Choose an Issue

Picking Your Battles Persuasive writing is about convincing your readers to share your point of view on an issue. So, the first step in writing a persuasive essay is to choose an issue. **An issue is a subject, situation, or idea about which people disagree,** such as the best way to raise money for the band trip, or whether television is harmful to children.

> KEY CONCEPT

Your issue should be important to you. It should also be important enough for other people to have strong feelings and opinions about it. Avoid matters of personal preference, such as clothing styles or food. **Focus on issues that have a real impact on people's lives,** such as school rules or current social issues.

> KEY CONCEPT

Writing Workshop **211**

THINKING IT THROUGH   **Choosing an Issue**

Here is how to choose an issue for your persuasive essay.

▶ **STEP 1** Brainstorm several issues about which you feel strongly. To come up with an issue, you may **quickwrite** using the starter sentences below. You won't use these sentences in your essay, but you may use the ideas they help you generate.

If I were president, the first thing I'd change is _____.

One thing that really bothers me about _____ is _____.

▶ **STEP 2** Decide which issues are most important to you. Discuss with a partner which issues create strong feelings and opinions in others.

▶ **STEP 3** Check off the single issue you want to address.

> **Issues**
>
> ✓ having to pay for athletes' autographs
> chores—should parents pay kids?
> bad-tasting school lunches

State Your Opinion

Taking a Stand   Every issue has at least two sides—for it and against it. What is your point of view? As a writer, you need to take a stand and tell your reader which side of the issue you support. In other words, **state your point of view clearly in an opinion statement.**

An **opinion statement** is made up of an issue plus a writer's point of view on the issue.

| KEY CONCEPT

TIP An opinion statement serves the same purpose as a **main idea statement,** or **thesis.** It tells your readers the topic of your essay and what you are going to say about the topic.

> **Issue:** having to pay for athletes' autographs
> + **Point of view:** fans shouldn't have to
> _____
> **Opinion statement:** Fans shouldn't have to pay for athletes' autographs.

Use the Thinking It Through steps on page 212 to choose an issue for your persuasive essay. Then, write an opinion statement. Make sure your opinion statement shows your readers the stand you have taken—for or against the issue.

Consider Your Audience

Who Cares?   You probably would not write a persuasive essay about the school cafeteria to your college-age brother. Since problems with the school cafeteria don't affect his life, he probably would not be very interested in them. Persuasive writing works best when it is directed at the right group, or audience. You can identify the audience for your persuasive essay in two steps.

1. Figure out what groups of people are interested in your issue.

2. Choose one group to focus on, and analyze that group.

Finding Your Audience   To identify the right audience for your essay, think about the issue you have chosen. Remember that any issue is likely to affect more than one group of people. Ask yourself these questions.

■ **Who is interested in this issue?**

After identifying at least two of the groups who might care about your issue, ask,

■ **For which group do I want to write?**

The student writing about athletes charging for autographs identified baseball card collectors and professional baseball players as groups interested in that issue. She then decided to write to baseball card collectors. As a collector herself, she feels she understands them and knows what is important to them.

To identify your general audience,

■ think of at least two groups interested in your issue

■ choose a group to address

> **TIP**   Your **voice** shows your attitude about the issue in your persuasive essay. Not all attitudes are right for all audiences, so take your audience into account when you choose a writing voice.
>
> For example, it might be okay to use humor and a lighthearted tone in a school newspaper piece about outdated science lab equipment. However, if you wrote to your principal or the school board on the same issue, your tone would have to be more serious and formal.

Have students read aloud their opinion statements. Class members will benefit from hearing a variety of opinions and issues, and you can quickly gauge students' mastery of the exercise.

Meeting INDIVIDUAL NEEDS

LEARNERS HAVING DIFFICULTY

To assist students who are having difficulty finding an audience, put the following opinion statements on the chalkboard. Ask students to work with a partner to brainstorm at least three groups who might be interested in each issue.

1. Teenagers should be able to work part-time. [audiences: parents, teachers, business leaders]

2. Students should have at least one all-school assembly per month that covers topics of interest to students. [audiences: principals, teachers, members of the school board]

To help you assess students' choices, have students meet in small groups and identify their two possible audience groups. Have them explain why they would like to address the group of their choice.

Writing Workshop   **213**

RESOURCES

Your Turn 4
Practice
■ *Communications*, WS. p. 124

Your Turn 5
Practice
■ *Communications*, WS. p. 125

YOUR TURN 6

To help students evaluate specific audience choices, ask them to exchange papers with partners. Partners who disagree with any response should write an explanation or suggestion on a separate sheet of paper. Have students submit both papers for your review.

TEACHING TIP

Gather Support
To help students find support for their opinions, you might want to teach research skills. Organize a library session to help students use periodical indexes to locate information in newspapers and magazines. If your school library has a computerized periodical index or a CD-ROM database, you may need to explain how to conduct an electronic search. Remind students to document any sources from which they gather information, including Internet sources, and to quote accurately people they may interview. You may want to obtain permission from parents and guardians and from parties students contact before beginning work on this assignment. *You should be aware that Internet resources are sometimes public forums and their content can be unpredictable.*

KEY CONCEPT

Putting Your Audience in Focus   Now you can zero in on the group you picked. **Focus on the members of that group who might be undecided or might disagree with you, because they are the ones you have to convince.** (You don't need to convince people who already share your opinion.) To get them on your side, you will have to understand their concerns.

TIP Addressing **counterarguments,** or the reasons why people might disagree with you, is persuasive. When you show your audience that you have considered their concerns, they may take your argument more seriously, even if they disagree.

> **The group I'm addressing:** baseball card collectors
>
> **Why might people in this group disagree with me?** They might think that signed cards aren't that expensive. Some collectors my age get a bigger allowance than I do, so the price of the cards won't matter.
>
> **How old are people in this group?** They are all ages, but I know more about the ones my age.
>
> **What else do I know about this group?** They all have their favorite players, but most of them love Hank Aaron.
>
> **Specific audience:** baseball card collectors my age who admire Hank Aaron and think it's okay for athletes to charge money for autographs

YOUR TURN 6   Identifying Your Specific Audience

Zero in on your audience by answering the questions that appear in the example above. Then, identify your specific audience by completing this sentence:

My specific audience is _____.

Gather Support

Putting Your Money Where Your Mouth Is   It is not enough to state your opinion on an issue. You also have to convince your reader that your opinion is logical, or that it makes sense. To do this, **you must provide support, reasons, and evidence that back up your opinion. Reasons** tell why you believe as you do. **Evidence**—in the form of anecdotes, facts, or expert opinions—backs up each reason.

KEY CONCEPT

RESOURCES

Your Turn 6
Practice
■ *Communications,* WS. p. 126

Prewriting
Extension
■ *Designing Your Writing*

Opinion Statement: The school lunchroom should offer vegetarian meals.

Reason: Many students at King Middle School are vegetarians.

Reason with Evidence: Many students at King Middle School are vegetarians. A poll shows that 30% of the students here do not eat meat. (fact)

To find support for your opinion, try the following sources:

- **Interview experts, friends, or other people who are interested in the issue.** For example, if you are writing about the school lunchroom, you might interview students, teachers, cafeteria workers, or the cafeteria manager.

- **Research the issue.** For example, find magazine articles, Web pages, or electronic newsgroup postings about other young people who are vegetarians. Taking a poll—to see how many students at a school are vegetarian, for instance—is another way to do research.

Designing Your Writing

Using Numbers **Statistical evidence**—numbers—can be very persuasive. You can create visuals to show graphically the statistical evidence in your essay. A pie chart is a good choice when you want to show how a whole breaks down into percentages or parts. For example, the writer who created the pie chart below wanted to show the percentages of all students at King Middle School who do and do not eat meat.

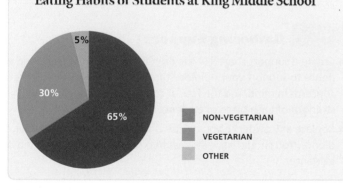

Eating Habits of Students at King Middle School

5%
30%
65%

NON-VEGETARIAN
VEGETARIAN
OTHER

TIP Reasons that appeal to a reader's logic, or intelligence, are called **logical appeals.** Logical appeals show why it makes sense to accept the writer's point of view.

Reference Note

For more on **reasons,** see page 206. For more on **evidence,** see page 207.

COMPUTER TIP

Many software programs allow you to create visuals such as pie charts on your computer. If you have access to a color printer, you can make each section of your pie chart a different color. This will help your reader see the different amounts represented by each part of the chart.

Meeting INDIVIDUAL NEEDS

INCLUSION

In persuasive writing, some students will benefit from visual-motor processing. Use the following dialogue and listing technique.

Ask the student to work with a helper to choose interesting topics, such as environmental issues or sports. Have the inclusion student pick one side of the issue and the helper take the opposing stand. As helper and student discuss the two sides, the helper should direct the student to write the opposing viewpoints in a two-column list. The list will help students gather support for the important points in their persuasive composition.

TECHNOLOGY TIP

Tell students that if their word-processing programs do not have the capability of creating graphs or charts, they can use a spreadsheet program. Almost all spreadsheet programs have charting abilities, and students can import the chart into their word-processing document. Most word-processing programs will allow students to view and print imported graphics, but they may not be able to edit this material. If computers are not available, remind students that hand-drawn graphs and charts can also improve their essays.

Writing Workshop **215**

Cooperative Learning

Consensus-Building Activity.
Consensus-building activities give students an opportunity to evaluate and influence other students' reasoning. After students complete their support charts and rate the strength of each piece of evidence, have them trade papers with a partner. Without looking at the student's initial ratings, the partner should evaluate the strength of each piece of evidence. If the partner comes up with a different rating or thinks that one of the pieces of evidence is too weak, students should work together until they reach a consensus about whether to change the rating or replace the piece of evidence.

This procedure should be followed for both students' support charts.

In the support chart below, a student lists several reasons why professional athletes should not charge fans for autographs. In the second column, she gives evidence to support each reason. In the third column, the writer evaluates her evidence, and in the fourth column, she rates the strength of each item ("Good," "Best," "Okay"), based on her audience's concerns. Knowing which evidence is strongest will help you organize your support before you write.

Support Chart

Reasons	Supporting Evidence	How Strong?	Rating
Players should be grateful for their fans' interest.	**Expert Opinion:** Hank Aaron's biographer says he was flattered to have kids look up to him.	Pretty strong. My audience still thinks of Hank Aaron as the greatest.	Good
The fans help the players get huge salaries.	**Fact:** The most popular major league baseball players earn millions of dollars a year in salaries.	Very strong. This example will make readers think, "Players already make so much money. They shouldn't take any more from us."	Best
Kids don't have enough money to spend on things like autographs.	**Anecdote:** A friend of mine spent his entire month's allowance on one card.	Not as strong as the other support—it depends on who's paying for the card.	Okay

YOUR TURN 7

To help you assess that students have considered the strengths and weaknesses of their reasons and evidence, have students meet with a partner to discuss their ratings. Have them discuss whether they agree and then sign off on the support chart.

YOUR TURN 7 Gathering Support

- Create a support chart like the one above, listing **reasons** and **evidence** to support your opinion statement. With your audience's concerns in mind, use the fourth column to rate the overall strength of each piece of evidence.

- Replace any evidence you decide is too weak to convince your audience. You should have at least two reasons, each supported by evidence.

RESOURCES

Your Turn 7
Practice
- *Communications,* WS. p. 127

Critical Thinking
Practice
- *Communications,* WS. p. 128

Telling the Difference Between Facts and Opinions

Picture this: A student you have never met tells you that you should buy a can of popcorn for a cheerleading fund-raiser.

"Why should I?" you ask.

"Because the cheerleaders need new uniforms," she says.

"What makes you say that?" you ask.

"Well, their old uniforms look really sad!" the student replies.

Are you persuaded? Probably not. The student stated her opinion and gave you a reason. What she did not do was support her reason with convincing evidence. Where she could have given you facts, she only gave you another opinion (". . . their old uniforms look really sad!"). In most cases, opinions do not make persuasive evidence.

Persuasive evidence should be based on fact, not on an opinion. An **opinion** expresses a personal belief. It can't be proved true or false. It may be *reasonable*, but it is not a fact.

> **Opinion:** The uniforms we want to buy are more attractive than those we have currently.

Words that evaluate—*greatest*, *best*, *worst*, and of course, *sad*—often signal an opinion.

> **Opinion:** Cotton is the *best* fabric for athletic wear.

When a writer begins *I believe, I feel, I think*, an opinion usually follows. Opinions may also contain words like *should* and *ought to*.

> **Opinion:** *I think* the cheerleaders *should* wear the school colors.

A **fact**, on the other hand, can be proved true. You can look it up, ask witnesses, or measure it yourself.

> **Fact:** The cheerleaders' current uniforms are blue and white.

> **Fact:** Blue and red are our school colors.

> **Fact:** In the majority of the middle schools in our district, the cheerleaders wear their school colors.

> **TIP** The only opinions you should use as evidence are *expert opinions*. An **expert opinion** comes from someone with expert knowledge in his or her field.

PRACTICE

Identify each of the following statements as either a fact or an opinion. Explain your answers in a sentence.

1. Every student should have a locker.

2. Taft Middle School has 500 students and 450 lockers.

3. The U.S. women's ice hockey team won gold in the 1998 Olympics.

4. Michael Jordan is the greatest basketball player of all time.

5. Figure skating requires more talent than gymnastics does.

Meeting
INDIVIDUAL NEEDS

MODALITY

Visual Learners. Some students may benefit from using colored pens as they draft their persuasive essays. Students might change colors as they begin writing a new section of the framework. For example, the attention-grabbing opening could be written in blue ink, the opinion statement in red ink, and so on.

YOUR TURN 8

If you wish to assign a length to the students' writing assignment, 500 to 700 words is an appropriate length. For assessment, make sure students follow the outline in the framework.

Timesaver

Ask students to label the right margins of their drafts with the corresponding framework terminology. You can quickly assess students' use of the framework in the organization of their papers. Labeling will also give students a visual way to check their papers' structures.

Persuasive Essay

Framework	Directions and Explanations

Introduction
- Attention-grabbing opening
- Opinion statement

Grab your reader's attention with an **interesting beginning.** Also include a **clear opinion statement** so your audience knows what you are supporting. (For more on writing **interesting beginnings,** see page 795 in the Quick Reference Handbook.)

Body
- Reason #1
  (evidence supporting reason #1)
- Reason #2
  (evidence supporting reason #2)
  and so on

Choose the most convincing reasons and evidence from your support chart. Here is one effective way to organize your reasons:

- Start with your **second strongest reason** to attract your reader to your side.
- Leave your audience with a strong impression by using your **strongest reason last.**
- Sandwich any **other reasons in the middle.**

This organization makes the most of your strongest support and downplays your weaker support.

Conclusion
- Restatement of opinion
- Summary of reasons and/or call to action

Leave your audience convinced that you are right. **Restate your opinion** in a new way. Then, **summarize your reasons** in a single sentence or **call on your audience** to take some kind of action. (You can do either or both).

YOUR TURN 8 **Writing Your Persuasive Essay**

Now it is your turn to write a persuasive essay. As you write,
- keep your audience in mind
- use the strongest reasons and evidence from your chart
- refer to the framework above and the Writer's Model on page 219

RESOURCES

Writing
Writing Prompts
- *Communications,* TP. 48, WS. p. 129

Your Turn 8
Practice
- *Communications,* TP. 49, WS. p. 130

A Writer's Model

The final draft below closely follows the framework for a persuasive essay on the previous page.

What Is a Fan's Loyalty Worth?

Last week at a baseball card show, I asked a well-known baseball player for his autograph. Imagine my surprise when his agent said I would have to pay fifteen dollars before the player would sign his name! Fans should not have to pay to get a baseball player's autograph.

Baseball players should be satisfied that their fans love them. Hank Aaron's biographer states that Aaron was flattered just to have kids look up to him. He would not have dreamed of asking people to pay for his autograph. Today's players should follow Hank Aaron's example.

Kids, who might grow up to be lifelong fans of a player, cannot afford to pay fifteen dollars for an autograph. A friend of mine spent his entire month's allowance on a single autographed card. His experience is not unusual. The average allowance of the twenty-five Eagle Middle School students I surveyed is five dollars a week. For these students, buying one card would leave little money for any other recreation for the month.

Athletes should not charge fans for autographs. After all, the fans help many athletes receive huge salaries in the first place. Popular players—the ones fans ask for autographs most—already make millions. In 2000, according to *USA Today*'s Internet site, these were the salaries of some popular players: Mike Piazza, $12,000,000; Pedro Martinez, $11,500,000; and Sammy Sosa, $11,000,000. Top players make more in a year than most of us will make in a lifetime.

Instead of taking our money, athletes should repay our loyalty by freely signing their beloved names to our tattered cards. Do not pay for autographs. Show players that an autograph should be a way of saying "thank you" to a loyal fan, and thank yous should not cost money.

Attention-grabbing opener

Opinion statement

Reason #1
Evidence (expert opinion)

Reason #2
Evidence (anecdote)

Reason #3

Evidence (fact)

Restatement of opinion

Call to action

Critical Thinking

Analysis. Remind students that **A Writer's Model** was written to persuade a specific audience: young baseball card collectors. As students read the model, have them analyze how the author uses language and evidence to appeal to the audience. [language: simple diction that most middle-school readers can understand; evidence: a detail about Hank Aaron and an anecdote about allowances for middle-school students]

Connecting Reading and Writing

Compare **A Writer's Model** to the Reading Selection on pp. 203–204. Ask students what audience the author of **"A Veto on Video Games"** had in mind and how students can determine who is the audience. [audience: most likely adults with children; the reader knows this because the author refers to himself as a parent, he tells stories about his young children to which other parents can relate, he quotes a journal of child psychiatry to impress parents, and he uses sophisticated language to match the reading level of his adult audience]

Meeting INDIVIDUAL NEEDS

MULTIPLE INTELLIGENCES: Linguistic Intelligence.

To help students emphasize a point in their essays, explain that they may choose to use humor. In order for students to understand the humor in the last sentence of the model, you might tell students that "Let us eat cake" is a reference to a historical remark, "Let them eat cake," supposedly spoken by Marie Antoinette, the wife of King Louis XVI of France, in response to the hungry people's pleas for bread. Marie Antoinette went to the guillotine on October 16, 1793, in the midst of the French Revolution.

Connecting Reading and Writing

Ask students what characteristics of persuasive writing the Reading Selection, **A Writer's Model,** and **A Student's Model** all share. [Students may notice the following: each has a definite point of view; each gives reasons and evidence to support the opinion statement; each attempts to persuade the reader to accept the point of view.] Remind students to think about these elements as they draft their persuasive essays.

A Student's Model

When you write a persuasive essay, remember to pick a topic about which you feel strongly. There is no doubt where David Stamas, a junior high school student from Oak Bluffs, Massachusetts, stands on the issue of snack time in school.

Hungry Students Can't Study

Opinion statement

"Grrr! Oh, I'm hungry! When is lunch?" If you have ever walked down the junior high halls, this is something you will definitely hear. All kids should be able to have a snack time, or at least be allowed to keep food in their lockers.

Reason #1

When I asked why we couldn't have a snack time, one teacher I asked just said, "Why? You're not little kids anymore." That is just the point; we need food because we are growing now more than we ever will in our lives. Being hungry can have a big effect on the performance of a student. We just can't work or concentrate when all we can hear is the rumbling of our stomachs. We count down the seconds till lunch.

Reason #2

Getting a snack time really wouldn't change things all that much. All we need is five minutes. Trust me, if we can cram blueberry muffins down our throats in a two-minute hall period, we can definitely do it in five. All we have to do is take off a minute from each class and we will have more than enough time to eat.

Reason #3

No one can work on an empty stomach and be focused at the same time. Teachers certainly have figured that out. That is why they have a vending machine in the teachers' room, and why you will find a box of crackers in almost every teacher's desk. . . .

Restatement of opinion

It is not that we just want a snack time; it is that we need a snack time to keep us focused in class. The way I feel is that kids aren't looked upon as regular people the way we should be. We need a snack during the day just as much as everyone else. As I say, "Let us eat cake!"

220   Chapter 6   **Persuasion:** Convincing Others

220   Persuasion: Convincing Others

Writing a Position Paper

A position paper is similar to a persuasive essay. Both require you to state your opinion and convince readers to take action. In a **position paper,** though, you discuss the benefits of both sides of an issue *before* you state your position and request that your readers take action. If the prompt to the right appeared on a writing test, how would you approach it?

> Your school is overcrowded. The school board is debating whether it is better to enlarge your school or build a new one that half the students would attend. Write a letter to your school board president discussing both sides of the issue. Then, state your position and give convincing support for it.

THINKING IT THROUGH   Writing a Position Paper

▶ **STEP 1** Read the prompt and identify the issue, the two options, the purpose, and the audience.

Issue: crowded school; Option #1: enlarge our school; Option #2: build a new school; Purpose: to persuade; Audience: school board president

▶ **STEP 2** To generate a list of the benefits of each option, use the memory strategy THEMES: **t**ime, **h**ealth, **e**ducation, **m**oney, **e**nvironment, and **s**afety.

Option 1: friends will continue to go to the same school, our community will not be divided, the school will look better since some parts will be new

Option 2: will still know everyone since the school will not be that big, traffic will be better since students will attend two different schools

▶ **STEP 3** Decide which option you support. Then, using THEMES again, list the drawbacks of the option you do not support.

I do not want a new school. These are the drawbacks: Friendships may be broken. A new school would cost a lot. Competition between the "old school" and the "new school" may cause problems.

▶ **STEP 4** Write your essay, elaborating on each benefit and drawback.

Introduction: Identify the issue and the two choices.
Body Paragraph #1: Discuss benefits of the first option.
Body Paragraph #2: Discuss benefits of the second option.
Body Paragraph #3: State position; give drawbacks of other option.
Conclusion: Restate position; ask audience to act.

TEACHING   TIP

Writing a Position Paper
Here are some additional prompts for extra practice. Students' answers should have the basic ingredients of a persuasive essay: an appropriate format as dictated by the publication, an attention-grabbing opening, a clear opinion statement, sound reasons and evidence, and perhaps some suitable emotional appeal.

1. The local newspaper ran an article about some middle schools cutting all art and music programs. What is your opinion about this action? Write a letter to your school board stating your opinion and supporting it with convincing reasons. Explain your reasons in detail.

2. Your school board is considering a proposal to require that students volunteer ten hours a year performing community service. Consider your opinion about this proposal. Then, write a letter to your school board to persuade them that they should or should not implement mandatory community service. Be sure to support your opinion.

RESOURCES

Test Taking
Practice
■ *Communications,* WS. p. 131

Quotation for the Day

"Great writers leave us not just their works, but a way of looking at things."

(Elizabeth Janeway, 1913– , American author and editor)

Write the quotation on the chalkboard, and ask students to form small groups to discuss how books, stories, television programs, or newspapers have changed their ways of looking at things. Encourage students as they revise their pieces to evaluate the impact their essays will have on an audience.

TEACHING TIP

▶ **Elaboration**
To help students elaborate on details in the bodies of their papers, show them the technique of adding a comparison to paragraphs that need to be developed. Put the following example on the chalkboard.

"Teens who drive are more independent. They can, for instance, drive to the library when they need to do research. Teens who don't drive, on the other hand, are always dependent on a parent, guardian, older sibling, or classmate for rides, and often are not able to do library research when they need to."

Point out that such a comparison about what life is like for teens who do not drive adds considerable support to the opinion that teens who drive are more independent. You may have to work individually with students who cannot see a way to use this elaboration technique in their essays.

Revising

Evaluate and Revise Content, Organization, and Style

Giving Your Essay the Twice Over As you evaluate a peer's paper or evaluate and revise your own draft, you should do at least two readings. In the first reading, consider the content and organization of your draft, using the guidelines below. In your second reading, get down to the sentence level, using the Focus on Word Choice on page 224.

▶ **First Reading: Content and Organization** Use this chart to evaluate and revise your paper so your message is persuasive.

Guidelines for Self-Evaluation and Peer Evaluation

Evaluation Questions	Tips	Revision Techniques
❶ Does the introduction grab the audience's attention?	**Put stars** next to questions, anecdotes, or statements that would interest the audience.	If needed, **add** an attention-grabber to the beginning of the introduction.
❷ Does the introduction have a clear opinion statement?	**Underline** the opinion statement. Ask a friend to read it and to identify the point of view.	**Add** an opinion statement, or, if necessary, **replace** the opinion statement with a clearer one.
❸ Does the essay include at least two reasons that logically support the opinion statement?	With a colored marker, **highlight** the reasons that support the opinion statement.	**Add** reasons that support the opinion statement as needed.
❹ Does at least one piece of evidence support each reason?	**Circle** evidence that supports each reason in the essay. **Draw a line** from the evidence to the reason it supports.	If necessary, **add** evidence to support each of the reasons. **Elaborate** evidence by adding details or explaining its meaning.
❺ Does the conclusion include a restatement of the opinion?	**Put a check mark** next to the restatement.	**Add** a restatement of the opinion if it is missing.
❻ Does the conclusion include a summary of reasons or a call to action?	**Draw a wavy line** under the summary of reasons or call to action.	**Add** a summary of reasons, a call to action, or both.

222   Chapter 6   **Persuasion:** Convincing Others

ONE WRITER'S REVISIONS This revision is an early draft of the essay on page 219.

> *Baseball players should be satisfied that their fans love them.*
> ^Hank Aaron's biographer states that Aaron was flattered just to have kids look up to him. He would not have dreamed of asking people to pay for his autograph. Today's players should follow Hank Aaron's example.
>
> Kids, who might grow up to be lifelong fans of a player, cannot afford to pay fifteen dollars for an autograph. A friend of mine spent his entire month's allowance on a single autographed card. His experience is not unusual. The average allowance of ^*the twenty-five* Eagle Middle School students ^*I surveyed* is ~~pretty low.~~ ^*five dollars a week.* For these students, buying one card would leave little money for any other recreation for the month.

add

elaborate

Responding to the Revision Process

1. Why did the writer add a sentence to the first paragraph?
2. How did elaborating the evidence improve the writing?

PEER REVIEW

As you evaluate a peer's persuasive essay, ask yourself these questions:

- What is the *most* convincing part of this essay? Why?
- What is the *least* convincing part? Why?

Second Reading: Style Now you will look at *how* you say what you say, and that means looking closely at each of your sentences. One way to improve sentence style is to eliminate **clichés,** or overused expressions.

When you evaluate your essay for style, ask yourself whether you have used any expressions that you have heard many times. As you re-read your essay, mark an *X* through every word or phrase that you think is a cliché. Then, delete each cliché and replace it with your own original words. The Focus on Word Choice on the next page can help you learn to identify and revise clichés.

Meeting INDIVIDUAL NEEDS

ENGLISH-LANGUAGE LEARNERS

General Strategies. Some students may need assistance with self-evaluation. Suggest that students work with English-proficient partners who can lead them through their first reading. Have partners read aloud each evaluation question and tip in the chart on p. 222, and then stop to help students follow the tips and work on necessary revisions.

Responding to the Revision Process

ANSWERS

Sample answers appear below.

1. The first paragraph needed a topic sentence to introduce the first supporting reason to the reader.
2. The changes add evidence (amount of average allowance) to support the author's point that kids cannot afford to pay for autographs.

Cooperative Learning

Replacing Clichés. You may want to give students an opportunity to practice improving sentences by replacing clichés. Have students form randomly selected groups of four. Ask each group to brainstorm four clichés and together compose a sentence for each one. Then, have each member replace one of the clichés with simple, forceful words or with a vivid simile or metaphor. After each group has finished, ask members to share their results with the class.

Responding to the Revision Process

ANSWER

Here is a possible answer: The new phrase is more descriptive, creating a vivid picture in the reader's mind.

YOUR TURN 9

To assess quickly whether students have followed the guidelines on page 222, check their papers for the appropriate proofreading markings. Ask students to underline one revision they made as a result of their peer or self-evaluation.

Evaluating Student Writing

The ancillary *Assessment Alternatives* contains a variety of assessment forms, including Inventories and Evaluation Forms and rubrics: Six-Point Scales, Four-Point Scales, and Six Trait Scales.

Focus On

Word Choice

Clichés

When you are writing persuasively, it is easy to reach for a familiar expression—called a **cliché**—to help you make your point. Clichés, though, are expressions that have been used so many times they have lost their meaning and freshness. If you use clichés in a persuasive paper, you run the risk of weakening the effect of your ideas on your audience.

Examples: cool as a cucumber   tough as nails
                  to run like the wind   on top of your game

You probably know many more overused expressions.

Replacing clichés with your own original, forceful words will help you get your opinion across in a more convincing way. Remember: *that* is the purpose of persuasive writing.

ONE WRITER'S REVISIONS

Instead of taking our money, athletes should repay
our loyalty by freely signing their ~~John Hancocks.~~ *beloved names to our tattered cards.*

Responding to the Revision Process

How did replacing "John Hancocks" with another phrase improve the sentence above?

YOUR TURN 9 **Evaluating and Revising Your Essay**

■ First, evaluate and revise the content and organization of your essay, using the guidelines on page 222.

■ Next, use the Focus on Word Choice above to see if you need to eliminate any clichés from your paper.

■ If a peer evaluated your paper, think carefully about each of your peer's comments as you revise.

RESOURCES

Focus on Word Choice
Practice
■ *Communications,* WS. p. 135

Grammar Link
Practice
■ *Communications,* WS. p. 136

Publishing

Proofread Your Essay

A Finishing Touch   Errors in your final essay will distract your reader from the persuasive point you are trying to make. If you have another person proofread your essay, you'll be much less likely to miss mistakes.

Reference Note

For more on **proofreading,** see page 13.

Grammar Link

Using Comparatives

When you write a persuasive paper, you sometimes want to compare one thing with another. For example, you may want to convince your readers that your candidate for class president is *more experienced* than other candidates.

Most one-syllable words and many two-syllable modifiers form the comparative by adding *–er.*

> closer   cheaper   likelier

Some two-syllable modifiers (and all modifiers with more than two syllables) form the comparative by using *more.*

> more polite   more recklessly

Do not use the word *more* if the modifier is already in the comparative form.

Incorrect   Powermax batteries last **more longer** than batteries from other companies. [The word *longer* doesn't need *more* added to it, because *longer* already means "more long."]

Correct   Powermax batteries last **longer** than batteries from other companies.

Some words, such as *good* and *bad*, have special comparative forms.

> good ➤ better   bad ➤ worse

PRACTICE

For each of the following sentences, identify the incorrect modifier. Then, give the correct form of the modifier.

Example:
1. Video games are more cheaper than ever.
1. cheaper

1. Some video games are more harder than others.
2. Is a video game more bad than a TV crime drama?
3. Playing real basketball is more slower than playing the video game version.
4. The more I play this video game, the more better I get.
5. The more I play real sports, the more good I get.

For more information and practice on **comparatives,** see page 532.

Quotation for the Day

"A writer doesn't know what his intentions are until he's done writing."

(Robert Penn Warren, 1905–1989, American author and poet)

As students begin proofreading and publishing, write the quotation on the chalkboard or on an overhead transparency. You may wish to ask them to discuss the truth of this statement. [Students might explain what they have learned while writing persuasively, or they might discuss whether their opinions have changed or grown stronger while working on their papers.]

Grammar Link

Using Comparatives

ANSWERS

1. more harder; harder
2. more bad; worse
3. more slower; slower
4. more better; better
5. more good; better

Meeting INDIVIDUAL NEEDS

ENGLISH-LANGUAGE LEARNERS
General Strategies. English-language learners may have difficulties in forming comparatives, as many languages form comparisons differently than in English. Help your students by reviewing the forms and rules for comparison

Publish Your Essay

Get the Word Out   Now is the time for your essay to do what it was written to do—persuade people. Think about the audience you identified before you wrote your first draft. What are some ways to get your persuasive essay in front of that audience?

- Send your essay to the opinion page editor of a magazine, your local or school newspaper, or another publication.
- Think about other ways to go public with your work. You might convert your essay to a speech and present it to your audience directly. (For more on **formal speaking,** see page 758.)

 **PORTFOLIO**

Reflect on Your Essay

Building Your Portfolio   Take time to reflect on your essay. Think about *what* you wrote and *how* you wrote. Reflecting will help you improve your next persuasive essay.

- What was the strongest piece of support in your essay? Why was it the strongest?
- What was your purpose for writing your essay? Do you think you achieved your purpose? Why or why not?

YOUR TURN 10 **Proofreading, Publishing, and Reflecting on Your Essay**

- Correct grammar, usage, and mechanics errors.
- Publish your essay to your target audience.
- Record your responses to the Reflect on Your Essay questions above in a learning log, or include them in your portfolio.

Calvin & Hobbes © 1993 Watterson. Reprinted with permission of Universal Press Syndicate. All rights reserved.

Connections to Life

Evaluating a Persuasive Speech

When you listen to a friend give advice or watch a TV ad, you are listening to persuasive messages. When you evaluate a persuasive speech, consider these basic elements:

- **Content** A persuasive speech contains an opinion and support for that opinion. A speaker may try to convince listeners by using *persuasive techniques,* such as the bandwagon approach. (For more on **persuasive techniques,** see page 246.) Try to identify a speaker's opinion, and do not confuse it with fact. (For more on **fact and opinion,** see page 217.) Pay attention to the connotations of words the speaker uses. (For more on **denotation** and **connotation,** see page 89.) Listen actively by asking questions. You may bring up points with which you agree, or challenge in an appropriate way those with which you disagree. Responding in this way will help you understand the speaker's message.

- **Delivery** The speaker's delivery contributes to the persuasiveness of the speech. To evaluate delivery, consider whether the speaker's voice has good volume, rate, and clarity. Also, notice gestures and eye contact.

- **Believability** Both content and delivery contribute to a speaker's believability. You should also analyze the speaker's purpose and perspective, or **bias**—the beliefs that affect his or her thinking.

To evaluate a persuasive speech, first develop **criteria,** using the steps below.

1. **Look at the main elements of a persuasive speech**—content, delivery, believability. Ask yourself how the speaker could persuade using each element. Ask, for example, "What makes a persuasive voice?" You might decide that a loud, clear speech would persuade more effectively than soft, mumbled speech.

2. **Make a chart with your criteria in one column and space for notes in the other.** Make thorough notes as you listen to the speech. You will use these notes to plan your evaluation. For more on **taking notes while you listen,** see page 775.

YOUR TURN 11 Evaluating a Persuasive Speech

Develop criteria for the content, delivery, and believability of a speech. Then, listen to a persuasive speech and take notes about how well the speaker meets your criteria. In a short presentation, evaluate the speech. Explain why you were or were not persuaded based on your criteria.

TEACHING TIP

Evaluating a Persuasive Speech

Point out to students that they can use this same method of generating criteria to evaluate the speeches they give. The only difference is that they will have to audiotape or videotape their performances to get critical distance on them. If students select **Choice 1** on p. 231, giving a persuasive speech, challenge them to generate and use criteria to evaluate their speeches. Students can review a tape of their speech and turn in a completed chart for part of their grade.

YOUR TURN 11

Before students listen to speeches, check their criteria lists. The following are some possible criteria:

- Content: What is the speaker's purpose and perspective? Is the speaker's opinion supported by evidence—facts and examples?

- Delivery: Is the speaker's voice clear? Does he or she speak slowly enough to be understood but rapidly enough to be stimulating? Do the speaker's tone and gestures match his or her words?

- Believability: Does the speaker provide evidence or rely on persuasive techniques to support his or her opinion? If so, does the speaker mention reliable sources for the evidence used to support the opinion?

Then, have students submit their evaluation charts, with detailed notes, when they make their presentations.

OBJECTIVES

- To analyze an editorial cartoon
- To identify symbolism
- To demonstrate an understanding of exaggeration and caricature
- To find and interpret analogies

Quotation for the Day

"**Those who stand for nothing fall for anything.**"

(Alex Hamilton, 1939–   , British writer and editor)

Write the quotation on the chalkboard, and discuss with students how the quotation applies to persuasion. Lead students to see the importance of being an informed reader. In addition, point out that there are other ways of expressing an opinion. Ask students to brainstorm other ways in which one might express an opinion. [persuasive speech, letter, song, photograph, cartoon, painting]

Critical Thinking

Evaluation

To further students' understanding of editorials and to develop comparative skills, find at least one editorial cartoon and one newspaper editorial covering the same event, idea, or person. Have students compare the purposes of the two media. [Both media aim to persuade or influence, one through words and the other through images.] Then, have students look at *how* each medium achieves its purpose. Students may need help analyzing a political cartoon. Remind them of the elements on this page and also discuss the cartoonists' style (exaggerated or realistic, for example). Finally, have students compare the effect of each medium. Does each succeed in persuading? Does one rely more on humor to persuade than the other?

WHAT'S AHEAD?

In this section you will analyze an editorial cartoon. You will also learn how to

- identify symbolism
- understand exaggeration and caricature
- find and interpret analogies

Analyzing an Editorial Cartoon

"**W**here are the funnies?" This question is heard the moment the newspaper arrives in homes. Reading the "funnies" or the comics page of your newspaper may be your favorite way to start the day. Have you ever noticed that the comics page is not the only place in the newspaper where you can find cartoons? On the editorial page of most newspapers you will find a special type of cartoon, known as an **editorial** or **political cartoon**.

What Is an Editorial Cartoon?

Editorial cartoons are different from the cartoons you find in a comic book. These cartoons are designed to persuade their readers. They reflect the cartoonist's opinion on an issue or current event.

To make their points, editorial cartoonists use several techniques in their words and images. To understand the cartoonist's point, you need to understand these tools of the trade.

Symbolism	using a concrete picture or idea to stand for a more abstract one
Exaggeration/ Caricature	overstating a problem or issue to draw attention to it, or exaggerating someone's physical features to make sure viewers will recognize that person
Analogy	a comparison of two things (in editorial cartoons, directly or indirectly comparing a situation or event with a historical or fictional event)

RESOURCES

**Focus on Viewing and Representing
Practice**

- *Media Literacy and Communication Skills*
  —*Support and Practice,* Ch. 6
  —*A How-to Handbook*

Teaching Notes

- *Media Literacy and Communication Skills*
  —*A Teacher's Guide,* Ch. 6

Symbolism

The cartoon at the right uses symbolism to make its point. Uncle Sam, the symbol of the United States, is in a stalled car that symbolizes the troubled economy. The elephant (the symbol of the Republican political party) and the donkey (the symbol of the Democratic political party) are both claiming that they can fix Uncle Sam's car. However, we see that they are about to pull the car apart. The cartoonist uses symbols to persuade readers that the two political parties have conflicting goals that could hurt the country.

Exaggeration/Caricature

The cartoon at the bottom of this page uses exaggeration to make its point. The cartoonist is exaggerating the trend in professional basketball for high school players to go straight into professional sports instead of going to college first. What statement do you think the cartoonist is trying to make about this trend?

Frequently, cartoons also exaggerate the physical characteristics of famous people. This kind of exaggeration is called caricature. Caricatures add humor and help readers to recognize the cartoon's subject. On the right is a caricature of President George Washington. Presidents and political leaders are often the subjects of caricature.

MODALITY

Visual Learners. To reinforce the concept of symbolism, draw some symbols that students will easily recognize on the chalkboard or on an overhead transparency. [a thought bubble, a flag, an equal sign, or an up or down arrow] Ask students to identify each symbol. Then, have volunteers draw on the chalkboard pictures of additional objects that are well-known symbols for the class to identify.

TEACHING TIP

Exaggeration/Caricature

Discuss the question about the cartoonist's intended statement. After studying the cartoon, students should see that the cartoonist feels that kids who enter professional basketball right after high school are too young and aren't socially ready for its demands. This idea is shown through sarcasm when the student in the cartoon talks of skipping middle school to play professionally.

Ask students to think about what physical characteristics cartoonists exaggerate when they draw caricatures of famous people. Students should notice that cartoonists exaggerate distinguishing features, making the subject more recognizable.

Analogy

Allow students to answer the questions about the cartoon analogy. Here is a possible answer: The tax cuts will unbalance, or sink, the budget again. The ship has risen from the ocean, just as the U.S. budget has been balanced. The ship heads for another iceberg, symbolizing the tax cuts that may result in another unbalanced budget. The cartoonist wants to persuade his readers that tax cuts are a bad thing.

YOUR TURN 12

For assessment, ask students to attach a copy of their cartoons to their answers. Then, have a representative of each group share with the class what they discovered about similarities and differences in their cartoons.

Wrap It Up

Metacognition. After students have completed their analyses of editorial cartoons, have them answer this question:

1. What skills have you developed that now make you a more informed reader of editorial cartoons? [Students may indicate that they recognize symbolism, exaggeration/caricature, and analogy in cartoons, and understand how these features contribute to the persuasive aspect of editorial cartoons.]

Then, have students answer this question:

2. What is an analogy, and how are analogies made in cartoons? [A comparison; cartoonists use visual symbols to make the comparison.]

Analogy

By using an analogy, a cartoonist can say a lot with very few words. The cartoon above makes an analogy, or a comparison, between the effort to balance the budget and the *Titanic*, the "unsinkable" ship that sank on its first voyage after it hit an iceberg. What is the cartoonist's opinion about the effect tax cuts will have on the balanced budget? (Notice that the iceberg is labeled "tax cuts.") Does the cartoonist want to persuade his readers that tax cuts are a good thing or a bad thing?

YOUR TURN 12   Looking at an Editorial Cartoon

Find an editorial cartoon that you would like to analyze. You might look in a newspaper or newsmagazine from home or the school library. Then, ask yourself the following questions about your cartoon.

- What is the issue or topic the cartoon addresses?
- What symbols, if any, are used in the cartoon? What do they represent?
- What exaggeration or caricature, if any, is used in the cartoon?
- What effect does the exaggeration or caricature have?
- What analogies, if any, are used in the cartoon? How do the analogies help tell the story?
- What do you think is the cartoonist's opinion on the issue or current event?

Write down your answers and be prepared to share them with a few classmates. Try to find similarities and differences in the topics, attitudes, and techniques of the cartoonists each of you chose.

RESOURCES

Your Turn 12
Practice and Reinforcement

- *Media Literacy and Communication Skills* —*Support and Practice,* Ch. 6, transparencies and worksheets

6 *Choices*

Choose one of the following activities to complete.

► **SPEECH**

1. Lay It on the Line Write a **persuasive speech** on an issue that is important to you. You might explore an interesting new issue, or you might discuss the issue you explored in the Writing Workshop. Compare and contrast different viewpoints on the topic as you make your case. (Your speech's audience may not be the same as your essay's audience—you may have to adapt your reasons and evidence.)

► **CAREERS**

2. Tools of the Trade Law, politics, advertising: These are just a few career fields that use persuasion. Research one of these fields or a different field. Then, write a **paragraph** describing a specific example of how a person in that field uses persuasion.

► **ART**

3. See You in the Funny Papers Create a cartoon reflecting the issue you wrote about in your essay. You may want to use it as an illustration to accompany your essay, but your cartoon's message should also be able to stand alone.

► **CROSSING THE CURRICULUM: SOCIAL STUDIES**

4. Time Traveling Write a **persuasive letter** from the point of view of someone living in the time and place you are studying in social studies. For example, if you were studying the pyramids of ancient Egypt, you could write a letter to the Pharaoh trying to convince him that your workers need more food and better living conditions.

► **WRITING**

5. What Is Your Problem? Think of a problem in your school or community—perhaps an overcrowded school or a lack of bike trails. Then, come up with a solution to the problem. You may need to brainstorm and write about several solutions before you decide which is best. Then, write a **problem-solution** composition in the form of an **editorial.**

PORTFOLIO

PORTFOLIO

► **ART**
Direct students to use at least one of the techniques they learned about in the Focus on Viewing and Representing (pp. 228–230) in their cartoons. Students should explain how the use of symbolism, exaggeration, or analogy contributes to their cartoon's message.

► **CROSSING THE CURRICULUM: SOCIAL STUDIES**
Remind students to evaluate their audiences. Someone in ancient times might not be convinced by the same reasons and evidence as someone today. You may arrange to work with the students' social studies teachers to check this assignment.

►**WRITING**
Provide students with examples of newspaper editorials that define problems and propose solutions. Remind students to think about their purpose [persuasion] and audience [the readers of a class newspaper, for example] to focus their editorials. Help students focus their editorials further by making sure their opinion statements—or theses—define the problem and propose a solution.

In the bodies of their editorials, the students' task is to persuade their audience that their solution is best. Urge students to provide two or three reasons that will be relevant to their audience, and to support each reason with evidence, including anecdotes.

Choices **231**

RESOURCES

Convincing Others
Assessment

■ *Assessment Package*
　—Chapter Tests, Ch. 6
　—*Chapter Tests in Standardized Test Formats,* Ch. 6
　—*Assessment Alternatives,* Ch. 6

■ *Test Generator (One-Stop Planner CD-ROM)*

Choices
Rubrics

■ *Assessment Package*
　—*Assessment Alternatives,* Ch. 6

CHAPTER 7

Advertising

Use this guide to create an instructional plan that suits the individual needs of your students. Assignments marked by an asterisk (*) may be completed out of class. Times given for pacing lessons are estimated. See pp. 232–233 for chapter-wide resources. Resources listed in this guide are point-of-use resources only.

Curriculum Connections

Choices *p. 265*
- Crossing the Curriculum: Math
- Crossing the Curriculum: Social Studies

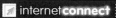

internet**connect**

 GO TO: go.hrw.com
KEYWORD: EOLang 7-7

 All resources for this chapter are available for preview on the *One-Stop Planner CD-ROM with Test Generator.* All worksheets and tests may be printed from the CD-ROM.

	Chapter Opener *pp. 232–233*	Reading Workshop: Reading a Print Advertisement *pp. 234–241*
DEVELOPMENTAL PROGRAM	⏱ **30 minutes** • Your Turn 1 *p. 233*	⏱ **90 minutes** • Preparing to Read *p. 234* • Reading Selection *p. 235* • First Thoughts in groups *p. 236* • Making Inferences: Forming Generalizations *pp. 236–238* • Your Turn 2 *p. 238* • Persuasive Techniques *pp. 238–239* • Your Turn 3 *p. 239* • Test Taking Mini-Lesson *p. 241*
CORE PROGRAM	⏱ **20 minutes** • Your Turn 1 *p. 233*	⏱ **75 minutes** • Preparing to Read *p. 234* • Reading Selection *p. 235* • First Thoughts *p. 236* • Making Inferences: Forming Generalizations *pp. 236–238* • Your Turn 2 *p. 238* • Persuasive Techniques *pp. 238–239* • Your Turn 3 *p. 239* • Vocabulary Mini-Lesson *p. 240* • Test Taking Mini-Lesson *p. 241*
ADVANCED PROGRAM	⏱ **15 minutes** • Your Turn 1 *p. 233*	⏱ **60 minutes** • Preparing to Read *p. 234* • Reading Selection *p. 235* • First Thoughts *p. 236* • Making Inferences: Forming Generalizations *pp. 236–238* • Your Turn 2 *p. 238* • Persuasive Techniques *pp. 238–239* • Your Turn 3 *p. 239* • Vocabulary Mini-Lesson *p. 240*
RESOURCES — PRINT	• *Communications,* TP. 52, WS. p. 137	• *Alternative Readings,* Ch. 7 • *Communications,* TPs. 53, 54, WS. pp. 138–145
RESOURCES — MEDIA	• *One-Stop Planner CD-ROM*	• *One-Stop Planner CD-ROM*

TP.=Transparency   WS.=Worksheet

Writing Workshop: Creating a Print Advertisement
pp. 242–260

🕐 130 minutes
- Pick a Product or Service *pp. 242–243*
- Find a Target Market; Your Turn 4 *p. 243*
- Analyze Your Target Market; Your Turn 5 *p. 246*
- Persuasive Technique; Your Turn 6 *pp. 246–247*
- Think About a Slogan; Your Turn 7 *p. 248*
- Choose an Image; Your Turn 8 *pp. 248–249*
- Plan the Text; Your Turn 9 *p. 249*
- Framework; Models; Your Turn 10* *pp. 250–252*
- Evaluate and Revise *pp. 253–255*
- Focus on Word Choice in groups; Your Turn 11 *p. 255*
- Proofread, Publish, and Reflect on Your Ad *pp. 256–258*
- Grammar Link; Your Turn 12 *pp. 256, 258*

🕐 160 minutes
- Pick a Product or Service *pp. 242–243*
- Find a Target Market; Your Turn 4 *p. 243*
- Critical-Thinking Mini-Lesson in groups *pp. 244–245*
- Analyze Your Target Market; Your Turn 5 *p. 246*
- Persuasive Technique; Your Turn 6; *pp. 246–247*
- Think About a Slogan; Your Turn 7 *p. 248*
- Choose an Image; Your Turn 8 *pp. 248–249*
- Plan the Text; Your Turn 9 *p. 249*
- Framework; Models; Your Turn 10* *pp. 250–252*
- Evaluate and Revise *pp. 253–255*
- Focus on Word Choice; Your Turn 11* *p. 255*
- Proofread, Publish, and Reflect on Your Ad *pp. 256–258*
- Grammar Link; Your Turn 12 *pp. 256, 258*
- Connections to Life; Your Turn 13* *pp. 259–260*

🕐 120 minutes
- Pick a Product or Service *pp. 242–243*
- Find a Target Market; Your Turn 4 *p. 243*
- Critical-Thinking Mini-Lesson *pp. 244–245*
- Analyze Your Target Market; Your Turn 5 *p. 246*
- Persuasive Technique; Your Turn 6 *pp. 246–247*
- Think About a Slogan; Your Turn 7 *p. 248*
- Choose an Image; Your Turn 8 *pp. 248–249*
- Plan the Text; Your Turn 9 *p. 249*
- Framework; Models; Your Turn 10* *pp. 250–252*
- Evaluate and Revise *pp. 253–255*
- Focus on Word Choice; Your Turn 11* *p. 255*
- Proofread, Publish, and Reflect on Your Ad *pp. 256–258*
- Your Turn 12 *p. 258*
- Connections to Life; Your Turn 13* *pp. 259–260*

- *Communications,* 🖐
  TPs. 55–58,
  WS. pp. 146–159
- *Designing Your Writing*

- *One-Stop Planner CD-ROM* 💿

Focus on Viewing and Representing: Analyzing Visual Effects in Ads *pp. 261–264*

🕐 45 minutes
- The Purpose of Visual Effects *p. 261*
- Types of Visual Effects *pp. 261–262*
- Analyze Visual Effects in Advertisements *pp. 263–264*
- Your Turn 14 *p. 264*

🕐 40 minutes
- The Purpose of Visual Effects *p. 261*
- Types of Visual Effects *pp. 261–262*
- Analyze Visual Effects in Advertisements *pp. 263–264*
- Your Turn 14 *p. 264*

🕐 30 minutes
- The Purpose of Visual Effects *p. 261*
- Types of Visual Effects *pp. 261–262*
- Analyze Visual Effects in Advertisements *pp. 263–264*
- Your Turn 14 *p. 264*

- *Media Literacy and Communication* 🖐
  Skills
  —*Support and Practice,* Ch. 7
  —*A How-to Handbook*
  —*A Teacher's Guide,* Ch. 7

- *Media Literacy and Communication Skills* 📼
  —Videocassette 2, Segment E
- *One-Stop Planner CD-ROM* 💿

Advertising

CHAPTER OBJECTIVES

- To read a print advertisement and analyze its persuasive techniques

- To create a print advertisement

- To analyze visual effects in advertisements

Chapter Overview

Students are constantly bombarded by advertisements in various media. This chapter is designed to help students recognize and analyze persuasive techniques in both print and nonprint advertisements. The Reading Workshop (pp. 234–241) provides students with a print advertisement in which they will identify and evaluate common persuasive techniques and then think about the generalizations the advertiser suggests. The

Writing Workshop (pp. 242–260) guides students to use their understanding of persuasive techniques to create product advertisements. The Focus on Viewing and Representing (pp. 261–264) offers information about analyzing visual effects in ads. While the sections of the chapter can be taught independently, they also work together to help students gain a solid understanding of persuasive techniques and how they are used.

Why Study Advertisements?

Being able to identify and analyze persuasive techniques used in advertisements will help make students more knowledgeable consumers, better equipped to make good choices about products and services. Students who are then able to apply the analysis of persuasive techniques in ads to other influences in their lives may have an advantage in making decisions that promote their own health and welfare.

Teaching the Chapter

Option 1: Begin with Literature

You might introduce the chapter by having students study persuasive messages in essays, plays, and fiction. Such messages might appear in a speech given by a character or in

the influence one character exerts on another. Ask students to identify the purpose of persuasive messages in their reading and then to examine the ways in which writers make their messages appealing. Afterward, have students read the print advertisement from this chapter (p. 235) and discuss the persuasive methods that are used. Encourage students to draw parallels between the methods used in literature and those used in the advertisement.

Option 2: Begin with Nonfiction and Writing

Introduce the persuasive techniques used in advertisements by beginning with the material in this chapter. The advertisement in the Reading Workshop and its accompanying activities (pp. 234–241) give students a solid basis for understanding both the persuasive techniques in advertising and the methods for analyzing them. The Writing Workshop (pp. 242–260) guides students in creating their own print ads. When students apply what they have learned about ads to literature, they will realize how often persuasive techniques are used in literature.

Making Connections

■ To the Literature Curriculum

Literature is full of examples of persuasion. For example, Shel Silverstein's poem "Sarah Cynthia Sylvia Stout Would Not Take the Garbage Out" uses humor to make a persuasive point. The short story "Four Skinny Trees" by Sandra Cisneros can be studied to show how a writer can change a reader's point of view.

Lesson Idea: Support for writer's point of view in "Four Skinny Trees" by Sandra Cisneros

1. Work with students to identify the meaning the four trees have for the speaker in the poem.

2. Have students make a cluster diagram of the meanings the trees have for the speaker. Students should fill in their diagrams with quotations from the work. A sample diagram appears below.

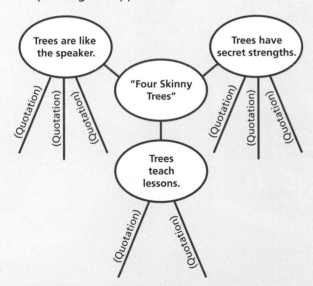

3. Have students think of ways that the speaker conveys these meanings. Ask students how the speaker convinces them that the trees are not ordinary. Invite students to share examples from the story of effective strong language and imagery.

4. After discussion, direct students to the advertisement in this chapter (p. 235). Point out that the ad uses powerful language and imagery to convince readers of something, just as the poem does. Help students identify the specific techniques used in the ad and the literary work.

■ To Careers

Invite one or more speakers who work in the fields of advertising or marketing to come to your class. Possible speakers include a small-business owner, a copywriter at an advertising agency, or a marketing executive of a nonprofit organization. Ask speakers to show material from a specific marketing or ad campaign for their business or organization and to explain the strategy behind it. Such presentations will help students understand that what they are learning about advertising applies to the wider world. See also **Connections to Life** on pp. 259–260.

■ To the Community

The print advertisement in this chapter promotes pharmaceutical companies' efforts to fight leukemia. It is similar to public service announcements. You may want to provide examples of public service announcements for students to discuss, along with ones that they recall hearing on the radio, seeing on television or on billboards, or reading in newspapers and magazines. Students should make the connection between the persuasive nature of the announcements and the effect they are designed to have on individuals and on the community. Emphasize that persuasive messages are always designed to have an effect on a specific audience of viewers or readers.

■ To the Health Curriculum

Many health-related issues, such as exercise, diet, and sports safety, are important in the lives of students. Have students work in small groups to identify health issues and find information about them in health and science textbooks. Have each group choose an issue and design an advertisement that includes a persuasive slogan and an illustration or photograph regarding the issue. Remind students that their ads should be aimed at convincing their fellow students of their message. You might wish to display the final advertisements on the class bulletin board.

Advertising

PREVIEWING THE CHAPTER

■ The three workshops in this chapter explore the primary persuasive techniques used in advertising. The workshops can be taught separately, but, taught together, they reinforce one another and help students understand the purposes and power of advertisements. Reading an advertisement can help students to write effective advertisements of their own. After both reading and writing advertisements, students will be better prepared to analyze the visual techniques used in advertisements. To integrate this chapter with grammar, usage, and mechanics chapters, see pp. T311A–T311B.

INTRODUCING THE CHAPTER

■ To introduce the chapter, use the Journal Warm-up, Transparency 52, in *Communications*.

VIEWING THE ILLUSTRATION

■ As students study this digitally-produced photo shoot of a bar of soap, ask them to guess why the artist "spotlighted" the bar of soap. Then, ask students how this illustration relates to the topic of the chapter. [Advertisements often "glamorize" mundane things to make these things look special and to persuade viewers that they need them.]

Representing. Invite students to find examples of advertisements that use effects such as lighting to spotlight a product or service. Ask students how the effects enhance or improve the appearance of the product.

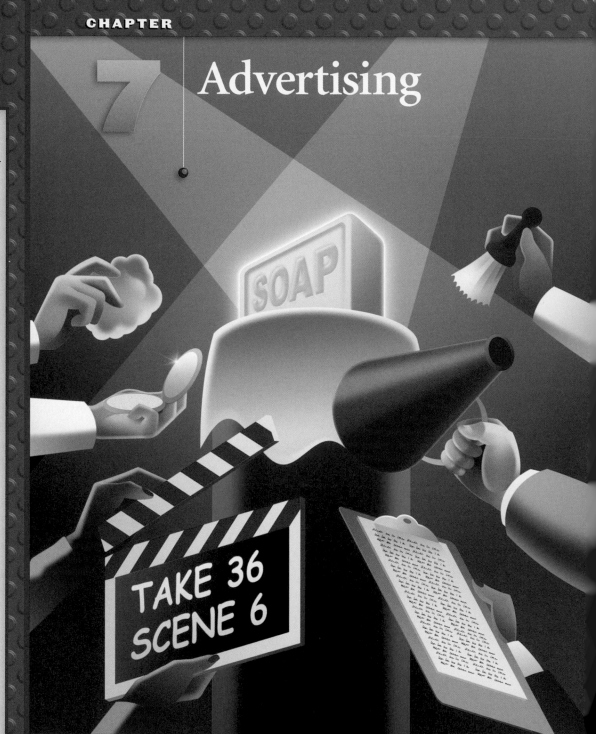

CHAPTER RESOURCES

Planning
■ *Lesson Planner, ELL Strategies,* Ch. 7
■ Block Scheduling, p. T231A (this book)
■ *One-Stop Planner CD-ROM*

Practice
■ *Communications,* Ch. 7
■ *Media Literacy and Communication Skills*

Extension
■ *Designing Your Writing*

Reinforcement
■ *Communications,* Ch. 7
■ *Alternative Readings,* Ch. 7
■ *Daily Language Activity Transparencies*
■ *Vocabulary Workshop* and *Tests*
■ *Spelling*

Reading Workshop

Reading a Print Advertisement

Writing Workshop

Creating a Print Advertisement

Viewing and Representing

Analyzing Visual Effects in Ads

A giant face looms on a billboard, smiling and suggesting that a particular brand of bread will make you happy, too. The scent of a flowery perfume drifts up as you open a magazine. Colorful signs on taxis and buses tell you to eat at certain restaurants.

Print advertisements are everywhere. These ads combine words, images, and sometimes even smells to convince people to buy or support a product or service. Print ads persuade people by appealing to their wants and needs. They often interest readers by using clever slogans and attractive images.

Informational Text

Persuasion

YOUR TURN 1 Exploring Advertising

Think about memorable print advertisements you have seen. Make a list of three or four advertisements you have seen on a billboard or in a newspaper or magazine, and answer these questions about them.

- Where did you see the advertisement?
- What product or service was being advertised?
- What in the advertisement caught your attention?
- Did the ad make you interested in buying the product or service? If so, how did it persuade you?

Then, share your list in a small group and decide what made each advertisement so memorable.

internet connect

go. hrw .com

GO TO: go.hrw.com
KEYWORD: EOLang 7-7

Connecting Reading and Writing **233**

OBJECTIVES

**Reading and Writing
Connection**

- To read a print advertisement in preparation for writing one

Reading Skills

- To form generalizations
- To identify persuasive techniques
- To use a dictionary to determine the definition of a word in context

Quotation for the Day

"Every time a message seems to grab us, and we think, 'I just might try it,' we are at the nexus of choice and persuasion that is advertising."

(Andrew Hacker, 1929–   ,
American political scientist and author)

Explain that *nexus* means "connection." Discuss the quotation with students. Ask them to explain the difference between choice and persuasion. [Persuasion is trying to convince someone to act or accept an opinion or belief; choice is making a decision.] Then, ask students to explain the connection between persuasion and choice in advertisements. [An ad attempts to persuade consumers to choose a particular product or service.]

TEACHING TIP

Preparing to Read
The material on this page introduces concepts that will be discussed on pp. 236–239. Making generalizations and identifying persuasive techniques are the focuses of the Reading Workshop. The Reading Selection on p. 235 illustrates both concepts.

RESOURCES

**Reading Workshop
Reinforcement**

- *Alternative Readings*, Ch. 7

WHAT'S AHEAD?

In this section you will read a print advertisement. You will also learn how to

- form generalizations
- identify persuasive techniques

Reading a Print Advertisement

Companies that share a common goal, such as fighting a dangerous illness, sometimes band together to create a joint advertising campaign. These companies have more than one goal for their advertising. They want to get the public's support for their efforts, and they want to enhance their images in the public's eye. Advertising is one way that organizations can work toward these goals. Ads like the one on the next page are designed to persuade the public that there is more to business than simply selling products or services.

Preparing to Read

READING SKILL

Making Inferences: Forming Generalizations   A **generalization** is a statement that applies to many different individuals or situations. When you form a generalization, you combine what you know with specific information you read to make a judgment about the world in general. The following advertisement contains information from which you can make several generalizations. As you read, think about what generalizations the advertisers are leading you to make.

READING FOCUS

Persuasive Techniques   Advertisers aim to persuade an audience to buy a product, support a cause, or view an organization in a certain way. They do this through *persuasive techniques*. **Persuasive techniques** are ways of adding to the appeal of information presented to support a persuasive argument. An advertiser may try to choose the one persuasive technique that best fits the audience for an ad. The advertisement on the following page uses persuasive techniques to convince readers to support pharmaceutical companies' efforts to fight leukemia, a type of cancer that often strikes children.

234   Chapter 7   **Persuasion:** Advertising

READING PROCESS

PREREADING
Activate Prior Knowledge. To prepare students to read the advertisement on the following page, ask them what they know about the disease leukemia. What kind of disease is it? Is it a serious condition? Do students know how leukemia is treated? If necessary, explain that leukemia is a kind of cancer that affects white blood cells and that it is the most common form of cancer in children; leukemia is usually treated with drugs (chemotherapy).

Read the following advertisement. In a notebook, answer the numbered active-reading questions located in the shaded boxes. The underlined words will be used in the Vocabulary Mini-Lesson on page 240.

LEUKEMIA MADE HIM A PATIENT. WE HELPED HIM BECOME A KID AGAIN.

"Your child has leukemia." The most <u>devastating</u> news a parent could hear. It used to mean there was little chance of survival. Now, 80 percent of kids <u>diagnosed</u> with leukemia not only survive—but lead normal lives. How? New <u>breakthrough</u> medicines, discovered and developed by <u>pharmaceutical</u> company researchers, have given many leukemia patients and their parents a second chance. The new medicines our researchers are discovering are giving families hope—and patients a chance to be kids again.

America's Pharmaceutical Companies

Leading the way in the search for <u>cures</u>

1. How does the picture contrast with the word *leukemia*?

2. Why do you think the advertiser used a dog in this ad?

3. What does the ad mean by "become a kid again"?

4. To what emotion does the first sentence below the picture appeal?

5. Why do you think the text below the picture repeats "be kids again" at the end?

6. Who are the advertisers trying to persuade? Why do you think so?

Reading Workshop **235**

Active-Reading Questions

The purpose of the active-reading questions is to encourage students to form generalizations and to think about advertisers' use of persuasive techniques as they explore the content of the Reading Selection. Use students' answers as an informal assessment of both their comprehension and their grasp of persuasive techniques. Possible answers are suggested below.

ANSWERS

1. The picture suggests warmth and happiness; the word *leukemia* is frightening and threatening.

2. Since many kids play with dogs, including a dog in the photograph suggests the idea of playing and being a kid.

3. "Become a kid again" implies being able to play and not having to worry about problems such as leukemia.

4. The first sentence appeals to the emotions of fear and sympathy. Most parents fear that their child could develop cancer; they feel sympathetic to all children and families who have to deal with this illness.

5. Repeating the words "be kids again" in the advertisement leaves the reader with a positive feeling and emphasizes that medicines can cure kids.

6. The aim is to persuade adults that pharmaceutical companies are developing drugs to make lives—especially children's lives—better. The picture of a happy, healthy-looking child and the large, overprinted type strongly convey this message.

READING / PROCESS

READING

Ask Questions. Remind students that every part of the advertisement is designed to have an effect on the reader. Tell students that as they read the text of the advertisement and view the picture, they should ask themselves why the creators of the ad decided on these specific words and pictures. They might ask why *kids* is used instead of *children,* or *devastating* instead of *awful.* Asking such questions will help students read actively and critically.

1. Students may say that the ad makes them feel happy for people who are able to lead normal lives despite having life-threatening diseases, or it makes them thankful for the ways that modern medicine can help people.

2. Students may say that the ad makes them think of the drug companies as friendly and helpful because they work to give sick people hope.

READING SKILL

TIP Generalizations tend to use clue words such as *most, many, often, generally, overall,* and *usually.*

What clue word does the generalization in the example to the right use?

Faulty generalizations may use clue words such as *none, no one, never, always, everyone, every,* and *all.*

Example:

Rivers *always* flood houses near their banks during heavy rains.

First Thoughts on Your Reading

1. What emotions does this advertisement make you feel?

2. What does this ad make you feel about the group of drug manufacturers who developed it?

Making Inferences: Forming Generalizations

Generally Speaking   As you read new information, you constantly make *inferences*. An **inference** is an educated guess based on what you read plus what you already know about the subject. One specific type of inference is a *generalization*. **Generalizations** are statements that apply to many individuals or situations.

Example: **What you read:** The Guadalupe River flooded several houses near its banks during recent heavy rains.

+   **What you know:** The Mississippi River also flooded houses near its banks during heavy rains a few years ago.

Generalization: Rivers often flood houses near their banks during heavy rains.

Advertisers expect the reader to make generalizations about the kinds of people who use their products and about what those products will do. Frequently, the generalizations that a reader makes from an ad are faulty. **Faulty generalizations** are either not true or do not apply in all cases. Questions like these can help you evaluate a generalization.

■ What would *really* happen if you did or did not use this product or service?

■ Do the people in the ad represent *everyone* who uses this product or service, or do they represent just *some* people?

■ Do the claims in the ad make sense?

Study the advertisement on the following page. What generalization does the ad lead you to make about the product and the people who buy it? Is that generalization a sound one, or is it faulty? If you need help answering these questions, use the Thinking It Through steps that follow the ad.

X-treme
The Power to Play

You work hard when you play. So when you drink, get the minerals your body craves. Soft drinks won't give you the essential nutrients you need to keep playing and winning. **X-treme** gives you what you need to be a winner.

Meeting
INDIVIDUAL NEEDS

MODALITIES

Visual Learners. As students think through the steps in forming and evaluating a generalization, point out that images often convey as much meaning as the text. Suggest to students that they may want to begin thinking about advertisements by first focusing on the images used. This approach may help them then evaluate the text.

THINKING IT THROUGH

Forming and Evaluating Generalizations from Advertisements

▶ **STEP 1** Look at the text and image in the advertisement. What does the ad *say* about the product or company? What does the ad *suggest*?

The ad <u>says</u> that the drink gives you the nutrients you need to be a winner. It <u>suggests</u> that the drink made the people in the picture more energetic.

▶ **STEP 2** Consider what you already know about the topic.

The football team drinks a special sports drink during games.

▶ **STEP 3** Make a generalization that extends to individuals or situations outside the ad.

Generalization: People who drink sports drinks will have more energy and be better athletes.

▶ **STEP 4** Evaluate the generalization you have made to see if it is faulty or not. You may use the questions on page 236.

I think this is a faulty generalization. You could drink all the sports drinks in the world and still not be a better athlete.

YOUR TURN 2

ANSWERS

Here is a sample answer to the second bulleted item.

The ad says that leukemia made the boy a patient, but the pharmaceutical companies made him a kid again. This suggests that the boy was not a kid when he was a patient. A possible generalization is *Children who are sick do not lead normal lives.* I think this is a faulty generalization. I have a friend who has asthma, but she leads a normal life.

Check that students' generalizations are derived from what the ads imply as well as what they state. Emphasize that evaluating generalizations involves thinking about whether the statements apply in all or most cases. Facilitate students' searches for ads by providing a variety of magazines in the classroom.

Meeting INDIVIDUAL NEEDS

INCLUSION

Have a helper work with students who have difficulty forming and evaluating generalizations from ads. The helper can use questions similar to the following ones about a car ad to elicit generalizations implicit in the ad.

- The ad says that this car lets people escape from their everyday lives. Is there any idea in this ad that seems to apply to all people? [All people want to escape from their everyday lives.]

- What does this make you think about most people's everyday lives? [They are boring; people need to escape from their daily routines.]

- How can this idea be expressed as a generalization? [People want to get away from their daily activities.]

- Do you think that statement is always true? [No, because many people enjoy their daily lives.]

The X-treme Sports Drink ad led the reader to form the faulty generalization that sports drinks will improve the performance and energy levels of people who drink them. Even though the generalization is not true, the ad may still accomplish its purpose: to persuade the reader to buy the product. As a reader, you should evaluate the generalizations you make from advertisements so that you do not buy a product or service based on a faulty generalization.

YOUR TURN 2 — Forming and Evaluating Generalizations from Advertisements

Look again at the advertisement on page 235. Use the Thinking It Through steps on page 237 to form and evaluate a generalization about

- the pharmaceutical companies that sponsored the ad

- the children who use those companies' treatments for leukemia

Then, find a print ad in a magazine. Form and evaluate a generalization about the company or product advertised.

READING FOCUS

Persuasive Techniques

Jump on the Bandwagon   Advertisers aim to get their audiences to believe in something or to take some action. The way ads accomplish this is by using specific **persuasive techniques.** Some people call these techniques *propaganda techniques.* **Propaganda** is a systematic approach to influencing many people at once. Propaganda is not only used in advertising, however. You may find propaganda in speeches, editorials, or any other form of persuasive communication.

Many people have negative feelings about propaganda. History is full of examples of how individuals, governments, or companies have used propaganda to deceive others. For example, advertisers might use propaganda to get the public to support an unworthy cause or to buy a product out of fear.

Still, propaganda is also used for good purposes. For example, a public service announcement could convince people to exercise more often. In that case, propaganda is being used to help people lead healthier lives.

The chart on the next page shows common persuasive techniques. You can find these techniques in all types of persuasive messages.

238   Chapter 7   Persuasion: Advertising

RESOURCES

Your Turn 2
Practice
- *Communications,* WS. p. 138
Reinforcement
- *Communications,* TP. 53, WS. p. 139

Your Turn 3
Practice
- *Communications,* WS. p. 140
Reinforcement
- *Communications,* TP. 54, WS. p. 141

Common Persuasive Techniques

Bandwagon	You are urged to do or believe something because everyone else does.	"Be where the action is. Shop at Hangout Mall."
Testimonial	Famous people endorse a product or idea.	"I'm professional football player Marcus Browning, and I use Wash Out window cleaner."
Emotional Appeal	Words or images that appeal to the audience's emotions are used. The appeal may be to positive emotions, such as desire for success, or to negative ones, such as fear.	"What would you do if all your possessions were lost in a fire? Get the Save-All fireproof safe and protect your valuables."
Plain Folks	Ordinary people sell a message. You are to believe that because these people are like you, they can be trusted.	"As a construction worker, I often get headaches on the job. That's why I use PainAway aspirin."
Snob Appeal	This technique suggests that you can be like the expensively dressed, perfectly shaped people who use this product.	"I accept only the best, and that's why I buy Aloft perfume."

When you read an advertisement, think about how the advertiser is trying to persuade you. Ask yourself these questions.

- What is the ad trying to persuade me to do, think, or feel?
- What persuasive words and images appear in the ad?
- Which technique would use those types of words and images?

Finally, ask yourself whether the ad gives any logical or concrete support that can persuade you. An ad that relies solely on the persuasive techniques above may not persuade a critical reader at all. For example, the X-treme Sports Drink ad says the drink gives you the nutrients you need to be a winner, but it doesn't name any specific nutrients. Should you really be persuaded by such an ad?

TIP Ads may use more than one persuasive technique at a time. The ad for X-treme Sports Drink on page 237 uses a bandwagon approach by showing a group of active teenagers who supposedly drink X-treme. The ad also uses an emotional appeal—"X-treme gives you what you need to be a winner"—which makes readers feel good about the product.

YOUR TURN 3 Identifying Persuasive Techniques

Re-read the pharmaceutical company advertisement on page 235. Ask yourself the questions above to identify how the advertiser is trying to convince you. Write your responses on a piece of paper, and provide examples from the ad to support your answers.

Cooperative Learning

Identifying Persuasive Techniques. Arrange students into small groups. Supply magazines and newspapers for groups to use as they find and discuss ads that use each of the persuasive techniques listed in the chart. Have groups share with the class some of the examples of persuasive techniques that they find.

Wrap It Up

Metacognition. Ask students to reflect on their reading processes by answering the following questions:

1. What was the most interesting thing you learned about persuasive techniques in advertisements? Why was this interesting to you?

Then, ask students the following question:

2. What clues help you know whether a generalization is valid or faulty? [Generalization clue words: valid ones include *most, many, often, usually;* faulty ones include *none, never, always*]

YOUR TURN 3

ANSWER
A sample answer appears below.

The ad uses emotional appeals, such as the picture of a boy with a dog and the words *leukemia* and *kid,* to convince readers that pharmaceutical companies help children.

READING PROCESS

EXTENDING
Connect to the World. Remind students that persuasive techniques are used in television and radio commercials, newspaper editorials, and speeches. Students should choose an example from one of those sources and then form a generalization based on that example. Finally, students should evaluate that generalization.

MINI-LESSON   VOCABULARY

Dictionaries, Glossaries, and Other References

ANSWERS

For items 1, 2, and 4, remind students to drop the endings –*ing*, –*d*, and –*s* when looking up each word. They should add these endings to their definitions. Possible answers are given below.

1. The dictionary definitions for the word *devastate* are "overwhelm" and "ruin or destroy completely." Only the first meaning works in context: "The most overwhelming news a parent could hear." Sample sentence: The farmers suffered devastating crop losses.

2. The dictionary defines the word *diagnose* as "recognize as having a disease, judging by signs and symptoms" and "analyze for the cause and nature of." Only the first meaning works in context: "Now, 80 percent of the kids recognized as having a disease, judging by signs and symptoms, not only survive . . ." Sample sentence: People diagnosed with flu need plenty of rest.

3. The dictionary definitions for the word *pharmaceutical* are "of and by drugs" and "involved in the manufacture and sale of medicinal drugs." Only the second meaning works in context: "New breakthrough medicines, discovered and developed by company researchers involved in the manufacture and sale of medicinal drugs . . ." Sample sentence: The pharmaceutical workers sealed the medicine containers.

4. The dictionary defines the word *cure* as "process or method to keep meat from spoiling" and "complete or permanent solution or remedy." Only the second meaning works in context: "Leading the way in the search for complete or permanent solutions or remedies." Sample sentence: Antibiotics are cures for many diseases caused by bacteria.

MINI-LESSON   VOCABULARY

Dictionaries, Glossaries, and Other References

A print ad may contain words that you do not understand. You can use many types of reference sources to find the meanings of unfamiliar words in print ads and other written works.

- **Dictionary:** Dictionaries tell how to pronounce a word, explain the word's usage, define all of the word's meanings, provide synonyms, and give information about a word's history.

- **Thesaurus:** A thesaurus lists **synonyms,** or words that have the same meaning, and **antonyms,** words with the opposite meaning of a word.

- **Glossary:** Glossaries list the important or difficult words used in a textbook. They only include the meaning of the word as it is used in the book.

- **Software:** Some computer software programs include an electronic dictionary or thesaurus. These resources list only the most common definitions or synonyms of each word.

Using a dictionary can be particularly challenging because dictionaries list several definitions for each word. You may have to decide which definition fits the word's context. The steps below can help.

THINKING IT THROUGH   Choosing the Right Definition

Here is an example using the word *breakthrough* from the reading selection on page 235.

▶ **STEP 1** Look up the unfamiliar word in the dictionary. Read the entire definition.

▶ **STEP 2** Use each of the meanings in the context of the reading selection. Decide which meaning makes the most sense.

Breakthrough: 1. the act of breaking through resistance 2. an important discovery

"New breaking through resistance medicines. . . ." That doesn't sound right. "New important discovery medicines. . . ." That sounds better. The second definition is correct here.

PRACTICE

Use a dictionary to look up these words from the reading selection on page 235. Write the correct definition of each word as it is used in the ad, and write a sentence using each word. The words are underlined in the ad.

1. devastating   2. diagnosed   3. pharmaceutical   4. cures

RESOURCES

Vocabulary
Practice
- *Communications,* WS. p. 142

Test Taking
Practice
- *Communications,* WS. pp. 143–145

Identifying Causes and Effects

Advertisements are built on cause-and-effect relationships. Readers are supposed to believe that a certain cause, such as buying a specific brand of toothpaste, will lead to a certain effect, such as having many friends.

When you read a selection on a reading test, you may be asked to identify a cause-and-effect relationship within the passage. Read the following text and question. How would you answer the question?

Cancer can attack many parts of the human body. Cancer of the white blood cells is known as leukemia. Human blood contains both red and white blood cells. Normally, the body produces white blood cells only to replace those that die off. In patients with leukemia, however, the body produces abnormal white blood cells at an increased rate. Leukemia negatively affects the function of organs such as the liver, spleen, and brain. Eventually, leukemia can cause serious infections and even death.

What effect does leukemia have on the body?

A. increases the number of red blood cells

B. harms the liver, spleen, and brain

C. causes sore throats and fever

D. decreases the number of white blood cells

Looking Ahead to Writing

In the Writing Workshop for this chapter (pp. 242–260), students will be writing their own advertisements. Have them refer to the reading selection and point out to students that the techniques they find most persuasive as readers might be the ones they would want to use as writers. Have students also refer to the chart of persuasive techniques on p. 239 as they think about persuasive techniques and plan their advertisements.

THINKING IT THROUGH — Answering a Cause-and-Effect Question

▶ **STEP 1** Read the question. Does it ask about a cause or an effect?

The question is asking about the effect of leukemia.

▶ **STEP 2** Look in the passage for clue words such as *cause, effect, affect, because, impact, influences, leads to,* or *results in.*

The passage says that leukemia "negatively affects the function of organs" and can "cause serious infections and even death."

▶ **STEP 3** Make a cluster diagram or a conceptual map that shows which event caused the other.

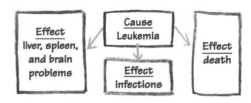

▶ **STEP 4** Choose an answer choice that closely matches your diagram.

Answer B matches one part of my diagram. The other answer choices aren't mentioned in the passage. I'll choose answer B.

OBJECTIVES

- To use the writing process to write and revise a print advertisement
- To identify a target market for an ad
- To analyze ads for their target markets
- To choose a persuasive technique
- To use emotional words
- To correctly punctuate possessive nouns

Quotation for the Day

"I take the family shopping round/ The markets of the world."

(Edgar A. Guest, 1881–1959, American poet and journalist, on the cover of a 1934 Sears, Roebuck catalogue)

Discuss with students how the quotation evokes some of the adventure and excitement that may be involved in shopping. Ask students what effect advertisements have on their shopping. [An ad may make them decide to go shopping for a certain product.]

Critical Thinking

Analyzing Problems and Solutions. To help students identify products to advertise, have them use the problem-solution process. Have students brainstorm in small groups problems that might lead to products. Examples include

1. People who often lose keys could solve the problem with a beeping key chain.
2. Students who want to hang posters in their lockers could solve the problem of not being allowed to use tape on the walls by using magnetic hangers that clip onto the corners of a poster.

WHAT'S AHEAD?

In this workshop you will create a print advertisement. You will also learn how to

- **identify a target market for your ad**
- **analyze ads for their target markets**
- **choose a persuasive technique**
- **use emotional words**
- **correctly punctuate possessive nouns**

Creating a Print Advertisement

After a hard day at school, you head home, hit the couch, and flip open your favorite magazine. Turning the pages, you see an advertisement that shows your favorite actor eating a sandwich. Suddenly you realize how hungry you are. You amble off to the kitchen for something, but as you peer into the refrigerator, you wish you had that big sandwich instead.

There is no doubt about it. Advertisements are persuasive. Print ads in magazines and newspapers influence what readers buy, how they vote, and even what social causes they support. Now is your chance to create an advertisement that will persuade a specific audience to buy a product or service of your own creation.

Prewriting

Pick a Product or Service

TIP A **product** is a thing, such as blue jeans, bottled fruit juice, or ballpoint pens. **Services** are tasks, such as housecleaning, car washing, or lawn mowing, done for another person.

Something You Can't Live Without   Brainstorm a product or service for your print advertisement. Try one of these methods to help you choose.

- Think of an improvement for an existing product or service, such as a computer program, a pair of shoes, or a pencil. How could you improve the way it works or looks? Create a new product based on your ideas for improving an existing one.
- Come up with a totally new product or service. Think about chores you do by hand that could be done with a machine. Invent a new snack. Offer a service for a task others might not like to do.

242   Chapter 7   **Persuasion:** Advertising

Once you have a product or service in mind, you can think of a name for it. You can think of a catchy, memorable name, or you can use a descriptive name that explains a key feature of the product or service. Either way, be careful not to choose a name that already exists.

Find a Target Market

Who Will Buy It? In any ad, the advertiser focuses on a specific group of people called the *target market*. **A target market is made up of the people who *might* use or buy a certain product or service.** For example, the target market for a new dog food would only include people who own a dog. The advertiser's job is to convince those people who *might* need the product that they *do* need it. To determine your target market, ask yourself these questions.

- Who might use the product or service?
- Who might actually buy the product or service?

The people who might use the product or service and the people who might actually buy it are not always the same. For example, small children ride tricycles, but adults buy them. In that case, decide which group to focus on in your ad. Here is how one student identified the target market for his product, an improved organizer for school lockers.

> KEY CONCEPT

> **TIP** *Target market* is a special advertising term. Choosing a **target market** in an advertisement is similar to considering your **audience** in other types of writing.

Product: Magnetic Attraction Locker Organizer

Who will use the product? My locker organizers are for middle school and high school students.

Who will buy it? Parents will most likely buy the organizers, but probably only when the students pick them out.

Who is the focus? Students should be the focus. Even if they don't buy the organizers, they do tell their parents what they need.

YOUR TURN 4 Choosing a Product and Finding a Target Market

- Identify a product or service for your advertisement.
- Name your new product or service by thinking of a catchy name or a descriptive name that highlights a key feature.
- Answer the questions above to determine your target market.

MINI-LESSON CRITICAL THINKING

Analyzing Target Markets in Advertisements

Imagine picking up your favorite music magazine and seeing an advertisement for baby food. You would probably think "Wow! That ad is sure out of place!" The target market for baby food is probably not the same as the audience for the music magazine.

Every advertisement has a target market. If you can determine who the target market is, you can begin to analyze that ad. The more you analyze advertising, the smarter you will be as a consumer. To determine the target market of an advertisement, ask questions about these four parts of the ad.

Product or service
Who would use this product or service? Who would buy it?

People
What people are shown using the product or service? How old are they? Are they male or female?

Other images
Aside from the people using the product, what other pictures are in the ad? Who would be interested in these types of pictures?

Text
Does the ad address certain people? Does it use language that would appeal to a particular group?

If these questions have different answers, you will need to look closely at people, im-ages, and text in the ad to figure out whom it really targets.

The following ad seems to target more than one group. Use the questions in the chart on the left side of the page to determine the real target market of the Dino Pockets ad.

Packs a Dinosaur Punch!

Dino Pockets take only 30 seconds to make in your microwave. These hot, flaky, dinosaur-shaped pocket sandwiches are filled with vitamins and minerals for the most important snackers in your house — your children.

Now, compare your answers to the questions on product, people, other images, and text to the answers below. Did you identify the correct target market?

- **Product** Pocket sandwiches shaped like dinosaurs are designed to be eaten by children. However, the people who will buy these sandwiches at the grocery store are parents.
- **People** The people pictured in the ad are a father and his two children. They represent two different age groups. The father represents the parents who buy the sandwiches. The two children represent the people who eat the sandwiches.
- **Other images** Besides the people, the ad shows a sunny kitchen and a neat table. This setting would appeal to parents who want a safe, orderly home for their children.

- **Text** The large text "Packs a Dinosaur Punch" probably appeals more to children. However, the smaller text addresses parents directly by saying "your house—your children."

The target market of this ad is not obvious at first. Looking only at the product and people, you might conclude the market is either parents or children. The other images and the text, though, suggest that the primary, or main, target market is parents. It is possible that the slogan "Packs a Dinosaur Punch" is an attempt to get children's attention. However, that slogan would also capture the attention of the parents whose children are interested in anything to do with dinosaurs. An ad like this might appear in a magazine geared towards parents and families.

PRACTICE

Use the questions on page 244 to help you identify the target market of each advertisement part shown below.

1.

2.

CRASH! BAM!
Be cool with our new high-top sneaker that makes crashing noises with every step.

3.

Oatmeal

MINI-LESSON — **CRITICAL THINKING**

Analyzing Target Markets in Advertisements

ANSWERS
Here are some possible responses.

1. older adults, retired people

2. teenagers

3. children

Analyze Your Target Market

Give 'Em What They Want   To convince your target market to spend hard-earned pay (or allowance) on your product or service, you have to give them a good reason.

To analyze your target market and what your product or service can do for them, you will brainstorm a list of this group's needs and wants, as in the example below.

TIP   The two most important questions you must answer before you can create your ad are
- What do people need from my product?
- What do they want, even if they do not need it?

> Product: locker organizer
>
> Target market: students who use lockers
>
> Needs: to be more organized
>   to have more room in their lockers
>   to find things fast and have more time between classes
>
> Wants: to have other students admire their lockers
>
> I think the most important need or want that my locker organizer can help fulfill is the need to be organized.

TIP   People use products to satisfy a variety of needs. One need ads often seem to target is the need to be liked by others. In a magazine, try to find an ad that appeals to this need.
> **?**   How do you feel about the ad?

YOUR TURN 5
You may wish to have students work in pairs. After students brainstorm their lists, they can exchange lists with their partners. Partners can add any additional needs and wants that occur to them. Then, students can review their partner's additions and choose the most important need.

YOUR TURN 5   Analyzing the Target Market

Analyze your target market by brainstorming a list of their needs and wants. Pick the most important need to focus on in your advertisement and circle it. You will use the most important need to choose your persuasive technique in the next section.

Choose a Persuasive Technique

Make Your Pitch   Advertisers use persuasive techniques to influence their audience. **Persuasive techniques can help convince people to buy the product or service.** Although some advertisements use more than one technique, they usually choose a single technique as the main focus. As you choose the main persuasive technique for your print advertisement, pick one that will appeal to your target market's wants and needs. The chart on the next page summarizes the most common persuasive techniques: bandwagon, testimonial, emotional appeal, plain folks, and snob appeal.

KEY CONCEPT

Reference Note
For more on **persuasive techniques,** see page 238.

RESOURCES

Your Turn 5
Practice
- *Communications,* WS. p. 148

Your Turn 6
Practice
- *Communications,* WS. p. 149

Common Persuasive Techniques	
Technique	**Example**
Bandwagon—says that everyone else is buying the product or service	"More people buy our basketball shoes than buy any other brand."
Testimonial—uses famous people to support the product or service	"Even basketball superstar Bob Tallman wears our shoes."
Emotional Appeal—promotes fear, hope, or other emotions	"Are you getting left behind on the courts? Our shoes can help."
Plain Folks—shows people like you	"My basketball shoes helped me make the basketball team at my school."
Snob Appeal—suggests you will be fashionable or trendy	"Our shoes are for the athletes who want only the best."

THINKING IT THROUGH

Choosing a Persuasive Technique

Here is how to choose a persuasive technique for your print ad.

▶ **STEP 1** Pick a persuasive technique to address the main need of your target market.

Students' main need is to be organized. I'll use an emotional appeal. The use of an emotional situation, such as the frustration of having a messy locker, might make students think they need my product.

▶ **STEP 2** Test the persuasive technique by filling in these blanks: "Will (technique) make the target market believe they will (need)?"

Will an emotional appeal make the target market believe they will be more organized? Yes. Showing a frustrated student with a messy locker will show students that they need to buy my product to get organized.

TIP Test several persuasive techniques to make sure you choose the one that best matches the needs of your target market.

YOUR TURN 6 Choosing a Persuasive Technique

Use the chart and Thinking It Through steps above to choose a persuasive technique to use in your advertisement.

Meeting INDIVIDUAL NEEDS

INTELLIGENCES

Intrapersonal Intelligence. Persuasive techniques are most effective when they reflect a keen understanding of people's emotional responses to an ad. Have students look at the advertisements in this chapter and identify and express their emotional responses to each. Then, ask students to discuss and identify which of the persuasive techniques listed in the chart on this page is used in each ad. Students should think about their emotional responses as they decide which persuasive techniques to use in their own ads.

YOUR TURN 6

Remind students that if the first technique they choose fails when they do Step 2, then they should use Step 2 to examine another technique. As a final check, partners can read each other's question and answer from Step 2 and discuss whether the persuasive technique satisfies the target market's need.

TEACHING TIP

Writing a Slogan

Refer students to a rhyming dictionary, a regular dictionary, and a thesaurus to use when revising and editing their slogans. Tell students that these resources will help them find specific language to use in their slogans.

YOUR TURN 7

The effect of alliteration, rhyme, and rhythm may be easier for students to identify when a slogan is read aloud. As students present their slogans orally, ask other students to identify the technique or combination of techniques they hear in the slogan.

TECHNOLOGY TIP

Students with access to appropriate technology can use computers to create visuals for their ads. For example, students can draw pictures by using illustration programs. They might also scan photographs or include clip art.

Think About a Slogan

Stuck on You   What do you think of when you hear, "Got milk?®" You may think of famous faces sporting milk mustaches. This is just one example of the power of *slogans.*

KEY CONCEPT ➤

A **slogan** is a short, catchy phrase or motto that attracts attention. **Slogans help advertising stick in the minds of the target market.** Think about your product or service. How can you tell something about it while using the persuasive technique you have chosen? Here is how one student thought of his slogan.

> Since I am using an emotional appeal, I want to point out what a difference my locker organizer will make in students' lives when they have more time between classes to talk to friends. My slogan will be: "What a difference three shelves make!"

TIP   Many slogans use rhyme or alliteration (the repetition of an initial consonant sound). Rhyming slogans like "For the best construction tools, buy Ruhl" create a singsong rhythm that is easy for people to remember. Alliteration such as "Cecil's serves sandwiches with a smile" repeats the *s* sound to make the slogan memorable. Also, active verbs are more effective than passive verbs in slogans.

YOUR TURN 7 Writing a Slogan

Keeping the persuasive technique that you have chosen in mind, write a catchy slogan for your product or service. You might use alliteration or rhyme to make your slogan easy to remember.

Choose an Image

Get the Picture   The most persuasive elements of a print advertisement are often the images that accompany the words, so to illustrate your ad, select a visual that stands out from the crowd. You may draw your own art, create pictures on a computer, take a photograph, cut out magazine photos, or trace other illustrations and adjust them for your advertisement.

As you choose a **subject** for your image, remember to make it match the persuasive technique you chose. If you picked a plain folks approach, you should not choose a person wearing expensive clothes as your subject. Also, choose your colors carefully. In general, bright, **warm colors** stir strong emotions, and light, **cool colors** create calm feelings. Tie your use of color to the type of emotion you want to create in your reader.

TIP   Use professional ads as a **resource** to get ideas about images, colors, and arrangement of subjects. Other resources such as a dictionary or thesaurus will help you write and revise the text of your ad.

248   Chapter 7   **Persuasion:** Advertising

RESOURCES

Your Turn 7
Practice
■ *Communications,* WS. p. 150

Your Turn 8
Practice
■ *Communications,* WS. p. 151

Your Turn 9
Practice
■ *Communications,* WS. p. 152

YOUR TURN 8 — Choosing an Image

Choose an image for your print ad that fits the persuasive technique you have chosen. Sketch a draft of the image after you

- choose a subject and decide what the subject will be doing
- decide what else will be included in the image with the subject
- choose colors to convey strong or soothing emotions

Plan the Text

The Ad Game   You have already planned parts of your ad, but you still need to write the main text. The chart below explains the three main parts of an ad's text and shows a student's example.

Description Describe the product or service completely. Give basic information, such as sizes, colors, business hours, or key features. Also explain what makes your product special.	The Magnetic Attraction Locker Organizer features ■ three sturdy metal shelves ■ adjustable widths to fit any locker ■ magnets for hanging pictures and notes
Reasons to Buy Mention any reasons to buy your product or service that you have not already included in your slogan or description.	Why spend the entire break between classes looking for homework in a messy locker? Get Magnetic Attraction and get organized!
Action Finally, your print advertisement needs to tell your target market what they should do. Where can they buy the product or service? What is their next step?	The Magnetic Attraction Locker Organizer is available wherever school supplies are sold. Get our organizer before <u>your</u> locker becomes a disaster.

Play Fair   In the Reading Workshop, you learned how to avoid being persuaded by persuasive techniques alone. Assume that your target market knows enough to demand **logical support** and **concrete evidence.** Give important facts about your product or service in your product description. Be sure the reasons you give are logical.

> **TIP**   Use a voice that fits your **purpose,** which is to persuade. One way to win over your audience is to use vivid language, including precise adjectives and verbs. Instead of saying a pen "writes smoothly," say it "glides like silk across the page."

YOUR TURN 9 — Planning the Text

Plan the text of your ad by using the chart and example above. Be sure to include a description of your product or service, reasons to buy it, and information that tells readers what action they should take.

To help you evaluate each student's image idea more quickly, have the student write one sentence at the bottom of his or her draft explaining how the image persuades the target audience. Check that the image satisfies this goal.

TEACHING TIP

Plan the Text
Point out the competition advertisers face. Suggest that students look through the first ten or twenty pages of a magazine to discover how many ads there are. Ask them how they would get a reader's attention if they were to place an ad against so much competition. For example, an ad might use a black page with only three words on it to counteract all the color in the other ads. Suggest that students keep in mind the competition for readers' attention as they plan their ads.

YOUR TURN 9

Suggest that students divide their paper into three columns corresponding to the three main parts of an advertisement's text: description, reasons to buy, and action. If students plan their texts by filling in the columns, it will allow you to check each plan more quickly.

Writing

Advertisement

Framework	Directions and Explanations
Slogan	**Slogans** should be short, catchy, and to the point. Since you want people to remember your slogan, **write it in large print** at the top of your ad.
Image	The most noticeable part of your ad should be an **attractive image** geared toward your target market. Use an **interesting subject** that supports your persuasive technique, and choose **colors** thoughtfully.
Text ■ Tie-in ■ Description ■ Reasons ■ Action	■ Start out with a statement that **ties the product or service to the persuasive technique** you use. ■ Include the **name** of your product or service at the beginning. ■ **Describe the product or service vividly.** Use words with punch and impact. ■ **Give logical reasons** to buy the product or service. ■ Provide **important facts** about your product or service. ■ Tell the customer **where to buy** the product or service.

 YOUR TURN 10 **Drafting Your Print Advertisement**

Now it is your turn to write a first draft of your print advertisement. As you draft,

- keep your persuasive technique in mind
- use vivid, precise language and important facts in the description
- refer to the framework above and the Writer's Model on page 251

RESOURCES

Writing	Your Turn 10
Writing Prompts	**Practice**
■ *Communications,* TP. 55, WS. p. 153	■ *Communications,* TP. 56, WS. p. 154

A Writer's Model

The final draft below closely follows the framework for a print advertisement on the previous page.

Slogan

Image

Tie-in

Do you want more time to talk to friends between classes? The Magnetic Attraction Locker Organizer can help.

Description

The Magnetic Attraction Locker Organizer features
- three sturdy metal shelves
- adjustable widths to fit any locker
- magnets for hanging pictures and notes

Reasons

Why spend the entire break between classes looking for homework in a messy locker? Get Magnetic Attraction and get organized!

Action

The Magnetic Attraction Locker Organizer is available wherever school supplies are sold. Get our organizer before <u>your</u> locker becomes a disaster.

Writing Workshop **251**

After students have read **A Writer's Model,** ask them to review the **Common Persuasive Techniques** chart on p. 247. Then, ask students to identify which of those persuasive techniques are used in **A Writer's Model** and to explain how they further the advertiser's goal. [Possible response: By using words like *messy* and *disaster,* the ad for the Magnetic Attraction Locker Organizer uses emotional appeals for persuasion. This technique furthers the advertiser's goal by appealing to students' fears that without the Magnetic Attraction Locker Organizer their lockers will become disorganized.]

Connecting Reading and Writing

After students read **A Student's Model,** have them review the instruction on forming generalizations on pp. 236–238. Then, ask students what generalization the ad makes about students who wear Logo-Matic shoes and whether this is a valid or faulty generalization. [The ad implies that students who wear Logo-Matic shoes will be popular with other students. This is a faulty generalization. The brand of shoes you wear will not make you popular.]

A Student's Model

Chris Cheung, a student at Davidson Middle School in Crestview, Florida, created the following print ad. His ad achieves most of the goals of the framework plus something else: It makes a funny comment about advertising and logos. What is that comment?

Revising

Evaluate and Revise Content, Organization, and Style

Once Is Not Enough   When you evaluate a classmate's advertisement or revise your own, you should always read the entire advertisement at least twice. The first reading gives you an opportunity to evaluate the content and organization of the advertisement. Use the guidelines below to help you during your first reading. In your second reading, use the Focus on Word Choice on page 255 to improve your style.

▶ **First Reading: Content and Organization**   Use this chart to evaluate and revise your advertisement so that it is more persuasive. If you need help answering the questions, use the tips in the center column. Then, use the revision techniques in the right-hand column to make necessary changes.

Guidelines for Self-Evaluation and Peer Evaluation

Evaluation Questions	Tips	Revision Techniques
❶ Would the image catch a reader's attention?	**Note** two things about the image that would make a reader look at it, such as color or subject.	**Delete** the image and replace it with one that is more visually interesting, unusual, or colorful, if needed.
❷ Is the slogan catchy and memorable?	**Underline** words that have rhyme, alliteration, or some other catchy element.	If necessary, **add** words that are memorable, or that use rhyme or alliteration.
❸ Does the ad have a clearly defined target market?	**Write down** two specific things that point to the ad's target market.	If needed, **add** to the image, slogan, or text to identify clearly the target market.
❹ Does the ad provide a clear description of the product or service?	**Put a number** next to each fact about the product or service.	**Elaborate** by adding facts about the product or service, if needed.
❺ Does the ad clearly tell readers what action to take to buy the product or service?	**Place a check mark** by the information that tells the readers what action to take.	**Add** an action or clarify what the reader should do.

Writing Workshop   **253**

Quotation for the Day

❝If it sounds like writing, I rewrite it.❞

(Elmore Leonard, 1925–   , American crime-fiction author)

Begin a discussion of the quotation with the students by asking them what they think it means. Lead them to understand that the language in writing should sound natural. The reader should not be aware of the writer, but, rather, of the writer's message. This is especially important in advertising. The best persuasive techniques convince readers that they want to buy a product or service without the reader being aware of the techniques.

TEACHING TIP

▶ **Elaboration**
To help students elaborate on the features of the products or services they are advertising, have them imagine that they are telling a friend about the products or services. Students should make a list of the features that they would point out to their friends. They can then check to make sure that the ads effectively present those features.

Critical Thinking

Metacognition. As students evaluate and revise their own ads, have them answer the following questions about their revision processes.

- What parts of the ad did you change? Why?
- What parts stayed the same?
- How did your revisions improve your ad?

Responding to the Revision Process

ANSWERS

1. The writer added the words to make the sentence more clearly identify the target market for the product.

2. The writer added a line to describe the product in more detail and to answer a question the target market might have about the product.

3. The writer added the sentences to provide more information about where the product can be purchased and to persuade the target market to take action.

Cooperative Learning

Peer Evaluation. Arrange students in randomly selected small groups for peer evaluation. Give each group some ads to evaluate that were created by students outside the group. For assessment criteria, the group members should use the evaluation questions in the **Guidelines for Self-Evaluation and Peer Evaluation** on p. 253. One member of the group can record the group's comments and turn in these assessment sheets to you. Give the comment sheets to the writer of the ad. When the students pass in their revised ads, they should also hand in the comment sheets for you to review.

ONE WRITER'S REVISIONS This revision is from an early draft of the print advertisement on page 251.

> *between classes*
> add
> Do you want more time to talk to friends? The
>
> Magnetic Attraction Locker Organizer can help.
>
> The Magnetic Attraction Locker Organizer features
>
> - three sturdy metal shelves
> elaborate ∧ - *adjustable widths to fit any locker*
> - magnets for hanging pictures and notes
>
> Why spend the entire break between classes looking for
>
> homework in a messy locker? Get Magnetic Attraction and
>
> get organized!
> add ∧ *The Magnetic Attraction Locker Organizer is available wherever school supplies are sold. Get our organizer before your locker becomes a disaster.*

PEER REVIEW

As you evaluate a peer's print advertisement, ask yourself these questions:
- What is the most persuasive part of this advertisement? What is the least persuasive? Why?

Responding to the Revision Process

1. Why did the writer add words to the first sentence?
2. Why did the writer elaborate on the description?
3. Why do you think the writer added the last two sentences?

Second Reading: Style During your first reading, you revised what you said and the order in which you said it. The second reading focuses on your style, or the way you say things in your advertisement. One method of improving your style is to make sure you use words that have a strong emotional impact on your readers.

When you evaluate your advertisement for style, ask yourself whether your writing uses emotional language. As you re-read your advertisement, circle words that create an emotional response. If the ad contains only a few emotional words, delete some ordinary words and replace them with ones that will draw a more intense response.

Using Emotional Language

When you write an advertisement, you should make your product or service descriptions create an emotional response in your target audience. Consider the following two descriptions.

The Abracadab Circus will be fun!

The Abracadab Circus will make you giggle and gasp!

The second sentence, which would probably appeal to a young audience, is more emotional than the first one. You feel more interested in the circus because the description suggests an emotional response. You want to go to the circus and see what will make you giggle and gasp.

You can find more emotional words by looking in a thesaurus or by brainstorming a whole new way of describing your subject. You should think carefully about your ad's descriptions and determine what type of emotional response you want your reader to have.

Focus on
Word Choice

ONE WRITER'S REVISIONS

> Get our organizer before your locker becomes ~~cluttered~~. *a disaster*

Responding to the Revision Process

Why do you think the writer changed a word? Do you think the change improves the advertisement? Why or why not?

YOUR TURN 11 **Evaluating and Revising Your Ad**

- First, evaluate and revise the content and organization of your advertisement by using the guidelines on page 253.

- Next, use the Focus on Word Choice above to add emotional impact to your words.

- If a peer evaluated your print ad, carefully consider each of your peer's comments as you revise.

RESOURCES

Focus on Word Choice
Practice
- *Communications,* WS. p. 158

Meeting
INDIVIDUAL NEEDS

MODALITY
Visual and Kinesthetic Learners.
Students may find it easier to use emotional language in their ads if they clearly envision their products or services in use. Pair students and have each partner use words, gestures, and role-playing to demonstrate using his or her product or service. Students can then discuss elements in each other's presentations that most affect them and choose emotional language to describe these elements.

Responding to the Revision Process
ANSWER

The writer changed to the word *disaster* because it is more emotionally charged than the word *cluttered.* The change works because it creates a powerful picture in the reader's mind.

YOUR TURN 11

Suggest that students use highlighters to mark emotional language in their final advertisements. You can use these highlighted phrases to evaluate the amount and content of descriptive language in the students' writing.

Evaluating Student Writing

The ancillary *Assessment Alternatives* contains a variety of assessment forms, including Inventories and Evaluation Forms and rubrics: Six-Point Scales, Four-Point Scales, and Six Trait Scales.

Publishing

Proofread Your Ad

Reference Note

For information on **proofreading guidelines,** see page 13.

Getting It Right Before you create the final draft of your ad, have someone else **edit,** or proofread, it for you. Mistakes in your advertisement might make your target market wonder whether your product is also flawed.

Grammar Link

Punctuating Possessives

Advertisements often talk about the features of certain products. For example, an ad for a vacuum cleaner might list its attachments. To explain these features, you will use the possessive form of a noun.

To form the possessive of a singular noun, add an apostrophe and an *s.*

Examples:
the computer**'s** software
the vacuum cleaner**'s** brushes

If the noun ends in *s,* it will still take both the apostrophe and the *s.* If the extra *s* would make the noun awkward to say, you may use only the apostrophe.

Examples:
Jonas**'s** house [*Jonas's* is not awkward to say.]
the Netherlands**'** exports [*Netherlands's* is awkward to say.]

To form the possessive of a plural noun, add only an apostrophe if the noun ends in an *s.*

Examples:
the brushes**'** bristles
four days**'** work

If the plural noun does not end in an *s,* add an apostrophe and an *s.*

Examples:
the teeth**'s** enamel
children**'s** games

Make sure nouns are possessive, not simply plural, before adding apostrophes.

Incorrect	The girl's left their bicycles.
Correct	The girls left their bicycles.

PRACTICE

For each sentence, identify the word that needs an apostrophe. Then, write the word correctly.

Example:
1. The beanbags stuffing is nontoxic.
1. beanbag's

1. Remove the air conditioners filter.

2. The two quilts stitching is excellent.

3. The womens team won both races.

4. Mrs. Rogers garden is blooming.

5. Everyone believed the four girls story.

For more information and practice on **punctuating possessives,** see page 638.

Sixteen-year-old swimmer Kristin Ziemke learned how to perform CPR for her

other buddies on the swim team. But little did she know that during one meet,

the one who needed it would be a spectator up in the stands. He collapsed

with a heart attack, and Kristin climbed into the bleachers and saved his life.

The American Red Cross gives a helping hand to people who urgently need it.

We are not a government agency. We depend on you. Please give us

your time and support. Because help can't wait.

+
American
Red Cross

Adding a Background
In this ad for the American Red Cross, the words are printed in white over the illustration. This "reverse" type over a background of the girl's face draws the reader's attention right away.

Look at your print advertisement. Can you use a background behind your text? If you use a computer, you can format the background as a color or as a simple pattern. If your background is dark, use reverse type to keep your words readable. Look for these options under the format menu, or use drawing tools if they are available. If you are drawing your ad by hand, use colored pencils to color in a light background.

Writing Workshop   **257**

Publish Your Ad

Students who do not use computers may choose to write in cursive style or in manuscript. In either case, emphasize to students that their writing should be legible and neat. If their writing is unclear, they will lose the benefit of their hard work. Writing that is not clear will not be persuasive.

Reflect on Your Ad

To help students analyze their writing portfolios to discover their strengths and weaknesses, have them make a three-column chart with the following headings: *Writing Strengths, Writing Weaknesses,* and *Plan.* Then, they can go through their writing and jot notes in the appropriate columns. Plans might include such things as using a dictionary or spellchecking feature to improve spelling, using a thesaurus to find more vivid verbs, or engaging in peer editing to improve proofreading skills.

YOUR TURN 12

Remind students to use specific examples from their ads when answering the reflection questions. Suggest that they comment on what they might do differently when writing their next ad.

Wrap It Up

Metacognition. Have students answer the following question about their ads:

1. How did you evaluate whether your techniques would target a specific market?

Then, ask students to answer the following question:

2. What are the five common persuasive techniques used in advertising? [bandwagon, testimonial, emotional appeal, plain folks, and snob appeal]

COMPUTER TIP

Use word-processing commands to make some words in your ad stand out. You can use font commands to make your slogan larger or to change its design. You can also use style buttons to print important words in boldface or italics. Avoid overusing these features, though, or your ad may look cluttered.

PORTFOLIO

Publish Your Ad

Showing Your Stuff   Now it is time to see whether your advertisement works. Will your target audience really be influenced by your ad? Try one of these methods to share your powers of persuasion.

- Create a class magazine with all of your print advertisements. You might even group advertisements together by the type of product or service.

- Show your ad to a member of the ad's target market. Would this person be persuaded to buy your product or service? Ask for comments about the techniques you used.

- Show your print ad to friends and family. What do they like about the product or service you advertised? What do they think are the most effective parts of your advertisement?

Reflect on Your Ad

Building Your Portfolio   Take some time now to reflect on your advertisement. Think about *what* you wrote and *how* you wrote it. As you reflect on your print advertisement, consider what skills you can improve for future assignments.

- What was the most difficult task you faced in creating an advertisement? Why do you think so?

- How did analyzing your target market help you create your advertisement? Do you think learning about your readers could help you on other writing assignments?

- Examine all the written works in your portfolio to set goals for yourself as a writer. What are three things you could do to improve your writing?

YOUR TURN 12   **Proofreading, Publishing, and Reflecting on Your Ad**

- Correct grammar, usage, and mechanics errors in your ad.
- Publish your ad by following one of the suggestions above.
- Answer the questions from Reflect on Your Ad above. Record your responses in a learning log, or include them in your portfolio.

Connections to Life

Creating Your Own Commercial

Now that you have created a print advertisement, bring it to life in a commercial. In this section you will adapt your print ad to create a television commercial.

Making a Plan   Follow these steps to convert a print ad into a commercial.

Fill in the Details   Many effective commercials are like little stories—stories in which a problem is solved by buying a product. Brainstorm a story for your own ad by answering the following questions.

Characters: Who will be in your commercial? How will they appeal to your target audience?

Setting: Where and when will your commercial take place?

Action: What will your characters do? How will that action tie in with your persuasive technique? How will the action appeal to your target audience?

Draw a Storyboard   A storyboard is like a graphic organizer for your commercial. It includes the **dialogue, narration,** and images showing the **major actions** that will take place in your commercial. Your storyboard will help you plan all of the props and other supplies you will need.

To make a storyboard, sketch the basic action of each scene in your commercial. Below each sketch, write the dialogue for your characters. Look at the following example.

GIRL 1: I never get a chance to talk to anybody between classes! And now I can't find my math homework!
GIRL 2: Your locker is out of control. Haven't you heard of the Magnetic Attraction Locker Organizer?
GIRL 1: The what?
GIRL 2: Look at MY locker.

GIRL 1: Wow! How did you manage that?
GIRL 2: Easy. I just installed the adjustable Magnetic Attraction Locker Organizer. It comes with three shelves and these cool little magnets to hang pictures with. Now I have all the time I need between classes.

GIRL 1: What a difference three shelves make!

Creating a TV Commercial

Have students evaluate the language, medium, presentation, and overall impression of their ads by using the following questions:

- How do the dialogue and narration work together to tell a story that involves the viewer?

- Why is the medium of TV appropriate for the story?

- How was the presentation made clear and direct?

- How could the commercial be improved in terms of language, medium, or presentation?

Students should record their responses and turn them in with their work.

YOUR TURN 13

You may want to set aside one class period for students to perform their commercials live or to present their videotaped versions. For assessment, check that students' commercials follow their storyboards and effectively reach their target audiences.

Prepare Your Commercial Before you can rehearse your commercial, you must pick out the scenery, the actors, and the props the actors will use. Once these are in place, rehearse your commercial all the way through several times. Doing a complete run-through will help you see problems in the script and adjust your commercial to run more smoothly.

Lights, Camera, Action If you have access to a video camera, you can tape your commercial for all to see. By using a process called "in-camera editing," you can create a commercial by taping each shot in the correct order so that special editing equipment is not necessary.

First, use your storyboard to plan each shot. Then, tape your shots in the order they happen according to your storyboard. If you make a mistake, stop, rewind, and try it again. Once you finish a shot exactly the way you want it, stop or pause the camera and set up the next shot. Repeat the process until your commercial is complete.

The suggestions in the next column can also help as you videotape your TV commercial.

- Watch the lighting of your scenes. The light should be bright enough for the action to show up well on camera. It should not come from behind the actors.

- Eliminate background clutter from your scenes. Extra furniture, backdrops, or people will only distract your viewers.

- Use a tripod if possible so the camera will not shake during recording. If you do not have access to a tripod, make sure the cameraperson practices holding the camera still.

- Remind your actors to face partway toward the camera. If your actors face each other, your audience will not be able to hear their voices or see their facial expressions as well.

- Your actors should speak clearly and slowly. Many people speak quickly when they get nervous, so have the actors talk more slowly than they normally would.

If you do not have access to a video camera, perform your commercial live. Once you get up in front of your audience, all of your hard work will pay off as you convince the whole class that your product is better than anything they could buy in a store.

YOUR TURN 13 Creating a TV Commercial

Use the suggestions on pages 259–260 to turn your print advertisement into a TV commercial. Remember to

- create a storyboard
- choose characters and props
- videotape your commercial or perform it live

Analyzing Visual Effects in Ads

Has a television commercial ever made you say, "Wow, did you see that?" Perhaps a three-dimensional object seemed to hurtle out of the screen. A dog might have dunked a basketball like a pro. Advertisers will do anything they can to keep potential customers from turning the page or changing the channel when an advertisement appears. One of their most powerful weapons is the *visual effect*. **Visual effects** are ways of changing an image to add to its message or create a certain impression in a viewer's mind.

The Purpose of Visual Effects

Not only are visual effects fun and interesting, but they also keep viewers looking at an advertisement. The longer a viewer looks at an ad, the more likely the product or service being advertised will stick in the viewer's mind. Visual effects naturally hold our attention because they combine reality with the fantastic. Which image would be more likely to grab your attention: a giant bug invading a house or a real bug walking across a kitchen floor?

Visual effects also help shape a viewer's feelings about the product or service in the ad. For example, if an ad shows the giant bug retreating and finally dying after being sprayed with bug spray, the viewer might feel confident that the product can get rid of *any* insect. After all, the bug spray successfully killed the giant bug.

Types of Visual Effects

Print advertisements and television commercials each use unique visual effects. These effects make an ad more interesting so it can attract the most readers or viewers possible.

WHAT'S AHEAD?

In this section you will analyze visual effects used in mass-media advertising. You will also learn how to

- recognize the visual effects used by print and television ads
- compare the ways effects are used
- find examples of print and television ads with visual effects

---

OBJECTIVES

- To analyze visual effects used in mass-media advertising
- To recognize visual effects used by print and television ads
- To compare the ways visual effects are used
- To find examples of print and television ads with visual effects

Quotation for the Day

" All television is educational television. The only question is what is it teaching? "

(Nicholas Johnson, 1934– , American lawyer and professor, Federal Communications Commission commissioner)

Read the quotation and ask students if they think commercials teach us anything. [We learn things from commercials, even if it is nothing more than the features of a new product. Through their visuals, commercials often give us subtle messages as well.] As a class, discuss how the visual aspects of commercials might contribute subtly to their messages. If an advertisement for a hotel shows the hotel brightly lit in contrast to the darkness outside, what is the nonverbal message? [The hotel is inviting, warm, and safe.]

Focus on Viewing and Representing **261**

RESOURCES

Focus on Viewing and Representing

Practice

- *Media Literacy and Communication Skills*
  —*Support and Practice*, Ch. 7
  —*A How-to Handbook*

Teaching Notes

- *Media Literacy and Communication Skills*
  —*A Teacher's Guide*, Ch. 7

Group Project. Divide the class into seven groups at random and assign one of the seven visual effects to each group. Group members can work together to find examples of their visual effect in magazine print ads. These examples can be cut out and then arranged on poster board to be displayed in the classroom.

TIP Visual effects also hold viewers' attention in film, television shows, newspapers, magazines, and news programs.

A print ad can include a collage of images and text—words and pictures that, when combined, create an overall effect on the readers. Unless a print ad runs for several pages, it usually focuses on one image which creates an unfinished story. Important information about what happened before the product was used or what happened afterward is missing. The readers become involved because they must fill in the blanks to finish the story.

Television commercials contain movement. They can fade in and out or dissolve from one scene to another. Instead of one primary image to develop, a television commercial has many. Action sequences can tell a story.

While some effects are limited to either television or print advertisements, most of the visual effects advertisers use are available to both. Visual effects can be divided into two catagories: **photographic** (made with a camera) or **digital** (made with a computer).

Common Visual Effects	
Photographic Effects	
Camera Angle (point of view)	■ Tilting the camera up makes the subject seem large and dominating. ■ Tilting the camera down makes the subject seem small.
Lighting	■ Dark, shadowy lighting can add mystery or gloom. ■ Bright lighting can create a shiny, happy appearance. ■ Soft lighting suggests pleasant feelings.
Filters	■ Filters alter the image as it gets to the camera, making it fuzzy, sharp, dull, or sparkling.
Digital Effects	
Digital Editing	■ Images can be converted to digital computer versions and then altered.
Digital Reality	■ Images such as babies that dance and animals that talk can be made completely by computer animation.
Both	
Miniaturization	■ Small models of props or settings can be used to make a subject a giant in comparison.
Superimposing	■ Two images can be cut or digitally placed on top of each other, making people look as if they are in a jungle or in the air, for example.

Analyze Visual Effects in Advertisements

As a viewer of print ads and commercials, you should know that visual effects are used to capture your attention and to convince you to think a certain way. Just flip through any magazine or watch a TV commercial, and see how advertisers use visual effects. When you create your own advertisements, you should know that visual effects are a valuable tool to help you persuade a target market. Whether you are a viewer or a creator of advertisements, you can become more aware of visual effects by analyzing the different ways they are used.

The following print ad and the television commercial storyboard on the next page use the same visual effect. As you read these ads, identify the visual effect and determine how the effect is used differently in the two different media.

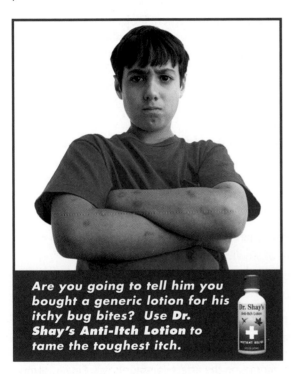

Are you going to tell him you bought a generic lotion for his itchy bug bites? Use **Dr. Shay's Anti-Itch Lotion** to tame the toughest itch.

Evaluation. Suggest that students compare the two advertisements for Dr. Shay's lotion—print ad and television commercial storyboard—to determine which uses the camera-angle technique more effectively. Each student should explain why his or her choice is the more effective presentation. [Most students will probably decide that the storyboard, which uses different camera angles rather than one angle, is more effective than the print ad because it shows contrasting sizes.]

NARRATOR:
Tell HIM you plan to use generic lotion on his bug bites.

NARRATOR:
Dr. Shay's Anti-Itch Lotion soothes and calms itches caused by most bites and rashes.

NARRATOR:
Bring the toughest itches down to size with Dr. Shay's Anti-Itch Lotion.

Wrap It Up

Metacognition. Have students reflect on their experience of analyzing ads by writing brief answers to the following question:

1. How do you think this experience of examining visual effects might affect how you view advertisements in the future?

Then, ask the following questions:

2. What are some examples of visual effects? [camera angle, lighting, filters, miniaturization, superimposing, computerization]

3. What are some of the purposes of visual effects in advertising? [attract viewer's attention, create visual association with the product, set the tone for the ad]

YOUR TURN 14

You may need to videotape some commercials and provide in-class viewing time for those students who do not have access to television at home.

In their answers, students should tell whether the effect is photographic, digital, or a combination of both. Also, have them point to specific examples that show the effectiveness of each ad.

TIP Some commercials deliberately omit information so that you become involved filling in the rest of the story.

? Can you think of a commercial for which you have to fill in the missing action?

The visual effect used in both of these ads is **camera angle.** Notice that in the print ad and in the first TV storyboard, the boy looks large and imposing because the camera looks up into his face, making him seem huge. However, the print ad could only hint that the lotion would bring the boy back down to size, but the television ad was able to tell the whole story. In the storyboard, you can see the boy getting the lotion and then returning to a more normal size through the use of a different camera angle.

YOUR TURN 14 Analyzing Print and Television Ads

Find a print ad and a television commercial that both use at least one of the following visual effects. You may choose an ad and a commercial that use the same visual effects or different effects. The effects are explained in the chart on page 262.

- camera angle
  (point of view)
- lighting
- filters
- digital editing
- digital reality
- miniaturization
- superimposing

Record the commercial, if possible, or draw a storyboard for it. Cut out the print advertisement if you have permission. Then, identify the visual effect used in each advertisement and explain what message or impression the effect communicates. Finally, compare the overall effectiveness of both ads.

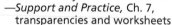

RESOURCES

Your Turn 14

Practice and Reinforcement

- *Media Literacy and Communication Skills*
  —*Support and Practice,* Ch. 7, transparencies and worksheets
  —Videocassette 2, Segment E

Choices

Choose one of the following activities to complete.

▶ COMMUNITY SERVICE

1. For a Good Cause A little publicity can help good causes. Choose a cause that is important to you, such as a tutoring or recycling program. Create a **poster,** or record a **TV or radio ad** to advertise this cause to your classmates. Include information telling how your friends and teachers can get involved with this issue to make a difference.

▶ CROSSING THE CURRICULUM: MATH

2. Charting the Course With two classmates, collect twelve print ads. Then, identify the main persuasive technique used in each ad. (See chart on page 239.) Make a **record** for each ad on a sheet of paper or in a database that has separate fields for a description of the ad and the technique. Then, make a **pie chart** that shows what percentage of the ads used each persuasive technique. Which techniques are the most common? Present your results to your class.

▶ CROSSING THE CURRICULUM: SOCIAL STUDIES

3. History Hall of Fame Use your new knowledge of advertising to create an entire advertising campaign for a historical figure you admire. Design a **campaign** of three or four **print and TV ads** nominating him or her for the History Hall of Fame. If you have access to a video camera, you can even record a television commercial to share with the rest of your class.

▶ CAREERS

4. The Ad Game The fields of advertising, marketing, and public relations are rapidly growing. Find out more about these careers by contacting companies such as advertising and public relations firms. Develop a list of questions and schedule a phone interview to get information about these career fields. Use your interview notes to write a **report** of your findings.

PORTFOLIO

Choices **265**

▶ COMMUNITY SERVICE

Provide students with examples of professionally developed material for community causes. Have students identify persuasive techniques used in these promotions and consider how they might use some of the same techniques. If students are having difficulty, refer them to the chart of common persuasive techniques on p. 247. Students who are creating a TV ad can follow the steps in **Connections to Life** on pp. 259–260. Those students creating a radio ad should begin with an introduction that catches the listener's attention and include a statement that tells the listener what action to take.

▶ CROSSING THE CURRICULUM: MATH

Students can work collaboratively in groups of three to analyze and compare the persuasive techniques they identify in their ads. Then, have students create a form or database record for each ad by using a template. A possible template might include the heading *Name of Product* and a field for each of the persuasive techniques: *bandwagon, testimonial, emotional appeals, plain folks,* and *snob appeal.* Students can fill out each field for the product, save the record, and use the template again for the next ad they analyze. Using a database program, students should be able to retrieve all the records by field, making it easy to analyze how often a particular persuasive technique is used.

▶ CROSSING THE CURRICULUM: SOCIAL STUDIES

Tell students to use the same process for their campaigns that they followed for the Writing Workshop. They will have to research their chosen figures. Remind students to identify the sources of their information.

RESOURCES

Advertising
Assessment

- *Assessment Package*
  —*Chapter Tests,* Ch. 7
  —*Chapter Tests in Standardized Test Formats,* Ch. 7
  —*Assessments Alternatives,* Ch. 7

- *Test Generator (One-Stop Planner CD-ROM)*

Choices
Rubrics

- *Assessment Package*
  —*Assessment Alternatives,* Ch. 7

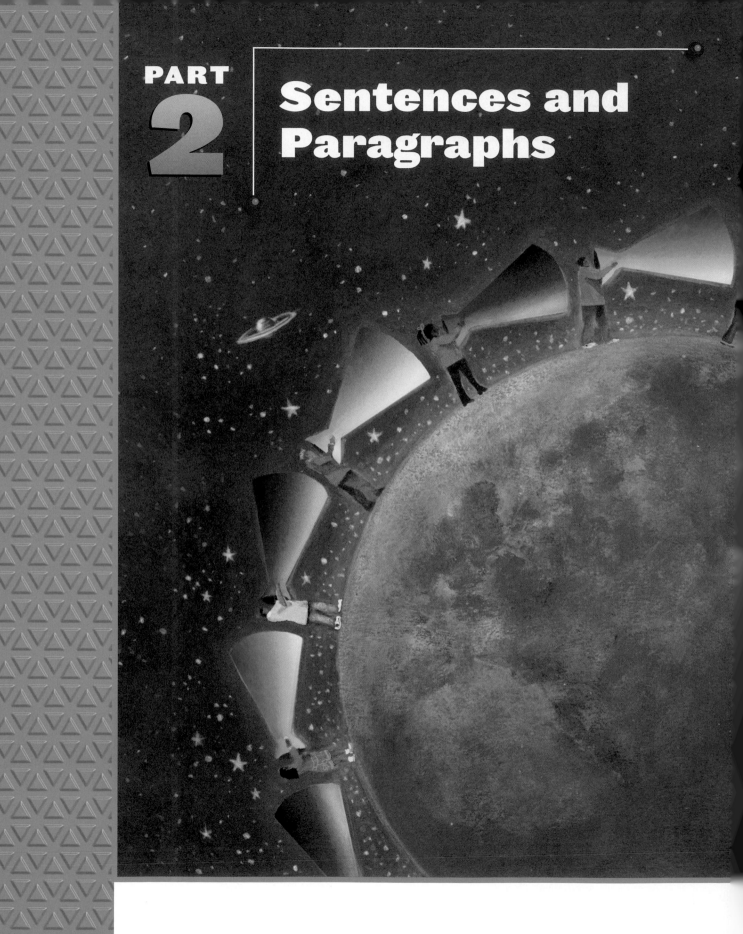

PART
2

Sentences and Paragraphs

8 Writing Effective Sentences

9 Learning About Paragraphs

CHAPTER

Writing Effective Sentences

internetconnect

go.
hrw
.com
GO TO: go.hrw.com
KEYWORD: EOLang

Writing Complete Sentences

One of the best ways to make your writing clear is to use complete sentences. A *complete sentence*

- has a subject
- has a verb
- expresses a complete thought

EXAMPLES   Trees help absorb excess carbon dioxide in the atmosphere.

Some species are in danger of dying out.

Get involved!

Each of the example word groups above expresses a complete thought. Each has a verb. The last example may not appear to have a subject in it, but it actually has the understood subject *you:* (You) Get involved!

Two common errors get in the way of writing complete sentences: *sentence fragments* and *run-on sentences*. Once you learn how to recognize fragments and run-ons in your writing, you can revise them to form clear, complete sentences.

Sentence Fragments

A *sentence fragment* is a word group that has been capitalized and punctuated as if it were a complete sentence. Because it is incomplete, a sentence fragment can confuse your reader.

FRAGMENT   Was the first African American man to win the Wimbledon tennis championship. [The subject is missing. *Who* was the first African American man to win Wimbledon?]

SENTENCE   Arthur Ashe was the first African American man to win the Wimbledon tennis championship.

FRAGMENT   Ashe the Wimbledon singles title in 1975. [The verb is missing. What is the connection between Ashe and the singles title?]

SENTENCE   Ashe won the Wimbledon singles title in 1975.

FRAGMENT   While he was a student at the University of California. [This group of words has a subject and a verb, but it does not express a complete thought. *What happened* while Ashe was a student?]

SENTENCE   Ashe also won several championships in college tennis while he was a student at the University of California.

As you can see from the first two examples, you can correct some sentence fragments by adding a subject or verb. Other times a sentence fragment just needs to be attached to the sentence next to it.

NOTE   Be careful not to create a fragment by putting in a period and a capital letter too soon.

FRAGMENT   The crowd cheered wildly. When Leon scored the winning touchdown. [The second word group is a fragment and belongs with the sentence before it.]

SENTENCE   The crowd cheered wildly when Leon scored the winning touchdown.

Exercise 1   Identifying Sentence Fragments

Decide whether the following groups of words are sentence fragments or complete sentences. If the word group is a

---

TIPS & TRICKS

Some words look like verbs but really aren't. These "fake" verbs can fool you into thinking a group of words is a sentence when it is really a fragment. A word that ends in *–ing* cannot stand as a verb unless it has a helping verb (such as *is, are,* or *were*) with it.

FRAGMENT
The children playing on the swings. [Without the helping verb, this is not a complete thought.]

SENTENCE
The children **were playing** on the swings.

Writing Complete Sentences

OBJECTIVES

■ To identify and revise sentence fragments

■ To identify and revise run-on sentences

Quotation for the Day

"**When people will not weed their own minds, they are set up to be overrun with nettles.**"

(Horace Walpole, 1717–1797, British writer)

Write the quotation on the chalkboard, and explain that nettles are weeds. Discuss the quotation with students, leading them to conclude that sentences also need to be weeded or they, too, become full of useless material.

TEACHING TIP

Sentence Fragments

You may want to use **Exercise 1** orally as an informal assessment of students' mastery. If students have trouble identifying fragments in the exercise, you may want to do some reteaching before moving on to **Exercise 2**. If you need material for sentence fragments for reteaching, use the examples of clauses that appear in Chapter 15.

Internet

■ go.hrw.com (keyword: EOLang)

RESOURCES

Writing Complete Sentences
Practice

■ *Sentences and Paragraphs,*
WS. pp. 1, 2, 3, 4, 5, 6, 7, 8

Relating to Literature

Consider using a selection such as Anne McCaffrey's "The Smallest Dragonboy," in which the author intentionally uses sentence fragments in dialogue. Ask students to locate pieces of dialogue that are not complete sentences. Then, ask them why the author might have chosen to write these sentence fragments. [*The fragments reflect the way a person or character naturally speaks.*] Explain that while experienced writers, such as novelists or poets, may use fragments for effect, students should not use fragments in their formal writing for school.

fragment, write *F*. If it is a sentence, write *S*. Remember that a complete sentence meets three requirements: It has a subject, it has a verb, and it expresses a complete thought.

F **1.** A flying squirrel a squirrel that can gracefully glide through the air.

F **2.** Some Asian flying squirrels three feet long.

F **3.** Skillfully leaps from one tree to another.

S **4.** The squirrel glides downward, then straight, and finally upward.

F **5.** Some flying squirrels more than fifty feet.

F **6.** If they use a higher starting point.

S **7.** Flying squirrels live in the forests of Asia, Europe, and North America.

F **8.** To eat berries, birds' eggs, insects, and nuts.

F **9.** Nesting in the hollows of trees.

S **10.** Notice how this squirrel stretches out its legs to help it glide.

Exercise 2 Finding and Revising Fragments

Some of the following groups of words are sentence fragments. Revise each fragment by (1) adding a subject, (2) adding a verb, or (3) attaching the fragment to a complete sentence. You may need to change the punctuation and capitalization, too. If an item is already a complete sentence, write *S*.

EXAMPLE   **1.** As soon as we finished eating breakfast.

        1. We left for our camping trip as soon as we finished eating breakfast.

Possible revisions follow.

1. The storm began just

2. S

3. , we unpacked⊙

4. ran

5. We

6. S

7. We didn't catch any fish

8. S

9. was

10. , we set up the picnic table⊙

1. As the whole family loaded into the car.

2. We traveled for hours.

3. When we arrived at the campground,

4. My sister and I down to the river.

5. Took our fishing gear with us.

6. We cast our lines the way our aunt had taught us.

7. Because we didn't have the best bait.

8. We headed back to the campsite at sunset.

9. Dad cooking bean soup over the fire.

10. While Mom and my sister pitched the tent,

MINI-LESSON   *Continued on pp. 271–272*

Cloze: Filling in the Missing Pieces. A cloze activity provides students with the opportunity to make meaning from sentences that lack essential pieces of information. Students use context and prior knowledge to fill in the gaps and make sense of the sentences. Because sentence fragments are word groups that are missing subjects or verbs or both, students may benefit from using a cloze activity. Work as a class, or have students work in randomly assigned groups of two or three to complete

Run-on Sentences

A *run-on sentence* is actually two complete sentences punctuated like one sentence. In a run-on, two separate thoughts run into each other. The reader cannot tell where one idea ends and another one begins.

RUN-ON   Researchers have created a "virtual frog" it will allow students to see the inside of a frog on the computer.

CORRECT   Researchers have created a "virtual frog." It will allow students to see the inside of a frog on the computer.

RUN-ON   The software allows students to peel back the frog's muscles, another option makes the skin invisible.

CORRECT   The software allows students to peel back the frog's muscles. Another option makes the skin invisible.

> **NOTE** A comma does mark a brief pause in a sentence, but it does not show the end of a sentence. If you use just a comma between two sentences, you create a run-on sentence.

RUN-ON   Scientists have discovered ice on the moon, the discovery is great news for people who study space exploration.

CORRECT   Scientists have discovered ice on the moon. The discovery is great news for people who study space exploration.

Revising Run-on Sentences

Here are two ways you can revise run-on sentences.

1. You can make two sentences.

RUN-ON   Asteroids are tiny planets they arc sometimes called planetoids.

CORRECT   Asteroids are tiny planets. They are sometimes called planetoids.

2. You can use a comma and a coordinating conjunction such as *and*, *but*, or *or*.

RUN-ON   Some asteroids shine with a steady light, others keep changing in brightness.

CORRECT   Some asteroids shine with a steady light, **but** others keep changing in brightness.

Reference Note

For more information and practice on **coordinating conjunctions**, see page 374.

Writing Complete Sentences   **271**

---

the cloze activity that follows. After students complete the exercise, explain that only subjects and verbs are missing from the sentences and that each item is actually a sentence fragment. Possible answers appear in brackets.

1. This _____ a story about Claudia. [*is*]

2. _____ was walking to school one rainy day. [*Claudia*]

3. She _____ an amazing thing. [*saw*]

4. _____ unbelievable! [*It was*]

ADVANCED LEARNERS

Some students might practice correcting run-on sentences in more sophisticated ways than those shown on p. 271. For example, a semicolon can replace a comma and coordinating conjunction to join two independent clauses. In addition, if two independent clauses are joined by a conjunctive adverb, such as *however, therefore,* or *consequently,* the correct punctuation is a semicolon before the conjunctive adverb and a comma after it.

EXAMPLE:
I enjoyed the game; however, it was only the first time I had played it.

Encourage students to revise some of the sentences in **Exercise 3** by using semicolons and conjunctive adverbs.

Exercise 3 **Identifying and Revising Run-on Sentences**

Decide which of the following groups of words are run-on sentences. Then, revise each run-on by (1) making it into two separate sentences or (2) using a comma and *and, but,* or *or.* If the group of words is already correct, write *C.* Sample revisions follow.

1. Saturn is a huge planet it is more than nine times larger than Earth. **1. ⊙**
2. Saturn is covered by clouds, it is circled by bands of color. **2. and**
3. Some of the clouds are yellow, others are off-white. **3. but**
4. Saturn has about twenty moons Titan is the largest. **4. ⊙**
5. Many of Saturn's moons have large craters the crater on Mimas covers one third of its diameter. **5. ⊙**
6. Saturn's most striking feature is a group of rings that circles the planet. **6. C**
7. The rings of Saturn are less than two miles thick, they spread out from the planet for a great distance. **7. and**
8. The rings are made up of billions of tiny particles. **8. C**
9. Some of the rings are dark, but others are brighter. **9. C**
10. You can use a telescope to view Saturn, you can visit a planetarium. **10. or**

Review A **Correcting Sentence Fragments and Run-on Sentences**

The following paragraph is confusing because it contains some sentence fragments and run-on sentences. First, identify the sentence fragments and run-on sentences. Then, revise each sentence fragment and run-on sentence to make the paragraph clearer. Here is a possible revision.

> Many deserts have no plant life, but some desert regions have a variety of plants. Many plants can survive. Where the climate is hot and dry. Cacti, Joshua trees, palm trees, and wild-flowers grow in deserts those plants ⊙ do not grow close together. They are spread out, each plant gets water and so minerals from a large area.

MINI-LESSON

5. Because her glasses were streaked with rain, _____ couldn't see clearly. [*Claudia*]
6. Then she _____ more closely. [*looked*]
7. _____ a dog wearing a red hat and carrying a basket of flowers. [*It was/Claudia saw*]
8. She _____ a friend, "What's going on?" [*asked*]
9. _____ was also confused. [*The friend*]
10. Actually, _____ the team mascot raising money for school. [*it was*]

Combining Sentences

Although short sentences can sometimes express your ideas well, using only short sentences will make your writing sound choppy and dull. For example, read the following paragraph, which has only short sentences.

> Thomas Edison invented the phonograph. He also experimented with mechanical toys. Many people do not know this. Edison created a talking doll. He created the talking doll in 1894. The doll would recite a nursery rhyme or poem. It said the words when a crank in its back was turned. The talking doll was very popular. Edison opened a factory. The factory made five hundred of the dolls every day.

Now read the revised paragraph. Notice how the writer has combined some of the short sentences to make longer, smoother sentences.

> Thomas Edison invented the phonograph. Many people do not know that he also experimented with mechanical toys. Edison created a talking doll in 1894. When a crank in its back was turned, the doll would recite a nursery rhyme or poem. The talking doll was very popular, and Edison opened a factory that made five hundred of the dolls every day.

Sentence combining also helps to reduce the number of repeated words and ideas. The revised paragraph is clearer, shorter, and more interesting to read. The following pages contain strategies for combining sentences. Once you learn these strategies, you can apply them to your own writing.

Combining Sentences

OBJECTIVES

- To combine sentences by inserting words and phrases
- To combine sentences by creating compound subjects and verbs and by forming compound sentences
- To combine sentences by using subordinate clauses

Quotation for the Day

"Real writers revise to make their meaning come through the form in the best possible way."

(Marian M. Mohr, 1933– , American author and teacher/consultant with the Northern Virginia Writing Project)

Ask students to discuss why revising their writing is important. They will probably talk about the value of having people understand their meaning. To make this point relevant, ask one or two students to volunteer accounts of situations that caused misunderstanding when they wrote unclear statements, such as in a note to a friend or family member. Have them show how they could have made the statements clearer.

RESOURCES

Combining Sentences
Practice
- *Sentences and Paragraphs,* WS. pp. 9–20

Extension
- *Combining Sentences,* WS. pp. 1–20

Combining Sentences by Inserting Words

One way to combine short sentences is to take a key word from one sentence and insert it into another sentence. Sometimes you will need to change the form of the key word before you can insert it. You can change the forms of some words by adding an ending such as *–ed, –ing, –ful,* or *–ly.* In its new form, the key word can describe or explain another word in the sentence.

ORIGINAL   Easter lily plants have leaves. The leaves have points.

COMBINED   Easter lily plants have **pointed** leaves.

Exercise 4 **Combining Sentences by Inserting Words**

Each of the following items contains two sentences. To combine the two sentences, take the italicized key word from the second sentence and insert it into the first sentence. The directions in parentheses will tell you how to change the form of the key word if you need to do so.

EXAMPLE   1. Peanuts are the tiny fruit of the peanut plant. They have a good *taste.* (Change *taste* to *tasty.*)

1. *Peanuts are the tiny, tasty fruit of the peanut plant.*

1. This picture shows peanuts underground. They *grow* underground. (Add *–ing.*)   **1.** growing

2. Peanuts are a crop of many warm regions. They are a *major* crop.   **2.** major

3. Peanuts are a food for snacking. Peanuts are good for your *health.* (Add *–ful.*)   **3.** healthful

4. The oil from peanuts is used in many dressings. The dressings are for *salad.*   **4.** salad

5. Grades of peanut oil are used to make soap and shampoo. The *low* grades are used for these products.   **5.** Low

6. Many countries grow peanuts solely for their oil. This oil is *versatile.*   **6.** versatile

7. The peanut-producing countries include China, India, and the United States. These countries *lead* the world in peanut production. (Add *–ing.*)   **7.** leading

8. Some soils will stain the peanut shells. *Dark* soils are responsible for the stains.   **8.** dark

Learning for Life

Students are probably at a stage in their lives when they have only vague ideas of what jobs or careers they might want to pursue when they are older, and they probably have no idea that many jobs have a writing component. Ask volunteers to name the careers that sound interesting to them. Then, take time to discuss whether those jobs will

9. After peanuts are harvested, the plants are used for feed.
   ~~The feed is for~~ *~~livestock.~~*   **9.** livestock

10. Peanuts are a good source of vitamins. ~~Peanuts contain~~
    B ~~vitamins.~~   **10.** B

Combining Sentences by Inserting Phrases

A *phrase* is a group of words that acts as a single part of speech and that does not have both a subject and a verb. You can combine sentences by taking a phrase from one sentence and inserting it into another sentence.

ORIGINAL   Arachne is a famous figure. She is a figure in Greek mythology.

COMBINED   Arachne is a famous figure **in Greek mythology.**

> **NOTE** Some phrases need to be set off by commas. Before you insert a phrase into a sentence, ask yourself whether the phrase renames or identifies a noun or pronoun. If it does, it is an **appositive phrase,** and you may need to set it off with a comma (or two commas if the phrase is in the middle of the sentence).
>
> ORIGINAL   Arachne challenged Athena to a weaving contest. Athena was the goddess of wisdom.
>
> COMBINED   Arachne challenged Athena**, the goddess of wisdom,** to a weaving contest. [The phrase in boldface type renames the noun *Athena.*]

Reference Note

For more information and practice on using commas to set off **appositive phrases,** see page 609.

Another way to combine sentences is to change the verb and create a new phrase. Just add *–ing* or *–ed* to the verb, or put the word *to* in front of it. You can then use the new phrase to describe a noun, verb, or pronoun in a related sentence.

ORIGINAL   The name *Inuit* refers to several groups of people. These people live in and near the Arctic.

COMBINED   The name *Inuit* refers to several groups of people **living in and near the Arctic.**

Meeting

ENGLISH-LANGUAGE LEARNERS
General Strategies. To assist students with sentence combining, explain that the easiest phrases to use in sentence combining are prepositional phrases. Point out that students may find it helpful to identify prepositional phrases by first picking out the prepositions. Since English-language learners often have trouble identifying prepositions in English, you may want to take time to review with them a list of the most common ones. Refer students to Chapter 12 for more information about prepositions.

require them to write effectively. Remind students that jobs in the fields of police work, journalism, medicine, consulting, business, social work, customer service, and law all demand good writing in the forms of formal reports, letters, memos, or public statements.

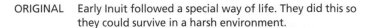

Meeting
INDIVIDUAL
NEEDS

MULTIPLE INTELLIGENCES

Spatial Intelligence. Students may need help understanding that a written sentence is not a rigid unit but a relatively flexible chain of words that may be grouped and regrouped. Have students write both example sentences in **Exercise 5** in large letters on a sheet of paper, using a different color ink for each sentence. Then, have them cut up the sentences into individual words. Now, demonstrate how words or phrases from one sentence can move into another by manipulating the cut pieces of paper. The colors will show more clearly how one sentence is combined with another. Challenge students to create other new sentences by moving the pieces of paper around on their desks.

ORIGINAL	Early Inuit followed a special way of life. They did this so they could survive in a harsh environment.
COMBINED	**To survive in a harsh environment,** early Inuit followed a special way of life.

NOTE When you combine sentences by adding a word or phrase from one sentence to another sentence, the resulting sentence may contain a compound phrase. Be sure to keep the compound elements **parallel,** or matching in form. Otherwise, instead of making your writing smoother, combining may actually make it more awkward.

ORIGINAL	Ana likes to hike. Ana also likes cycling.
NOT PARALLEL	Ana likes to hike and cycling. [*To hike* is an infinitive; *cycling* is a gerund.]
PARALLEL	Ana likes hiking and cycling. [*Hiking* and *cycling* are both gerunds.]

Exercise 5 Combining Sentences by Inserting Phrases

Each of the following items contains two sentences. Combine the sentences by taking the italicized word group from the second sentence and inserting it into the first sentence. The hints in parentheses tell you how to change the forms of words if you need to do so. Remember to insert commas where they are needed.

EXAMPLE
1. The Inuit followed their traditional way of life. They followed this way of life *for thousands of years.*

1. *The Inuit followed their traditional way of life for thousands of years.*

1. The Inuit built winter shelters in a few hours. They *stacked blocks of snow.* (Change *stacked* to *stacking.*)   **1.** Stacking blocks of snow,

2. They used harpoons. This is how they *hunted seals.* (Change *hunted* to *to hunt.*)   **2.** to hunt seals ⊙

3. The Inuit also hunted and ate caribou. Caribou are *a type of deer.*   **3.** , a type of deer ⊙

4. Whalers and fur traders came to the region and affected the Inuit way of life. They arrived *in the 1800s.*   **4.** in the 1800s

5. The Inuit often moved several times a year. ~~They moved so that they could~~ *find food.* (Change *find* to *to find.*)
6. During the summer, traditional Inuit lived in tents. ~~The tents were~~ *made from animal skin.*
7. In the 1800s, many Inuit began to trap animals. ~~They trapped animals~~ *for European fur traders.*
8. Some Inuit worked on whaling ships. ~~They~~ *needed to find other ways to provide for their families.* (Change *need* to *needing.*)
9. The Inuit have survived for thousands of years. ~~They have survived~~ *in the harsh Arctic climate.*
10. Most Inuit today follow a modern way of life. ~~They are~~ *like the Canadian Inuit seen in the photo on the opposite page.*

Combining Sentences Using *And, But,* or *Or*

You can also use the coordinating conjunctions *and, but,* and *or* to combine sentences. With these connecting words, you can make a *compound subject,* a *compound verb,* or a *compound sentence.*

Compound Subjects and Verbs

Sometimes two sentences have the same verb with different subjects. You can combine the sentences by linking the two subjects with *and* or *or* to make a **compound subject.**

ORIGINAL	Dolphins look a little like fish. Porpoises look a little like fish.
COMBINED	**Dolphins and porpoises** look a little like fish.

Two sentences can also have the same subject with different verbs. You can use *and, but,* or *or* to connect the two verbs. The result is a **compound verb.**

ORIGINAL	Dolphins live in water like fish. They breathe like other mammals.
COMBINED	Dolphins **live** in water like fish **but breathe** like other mammals.

---

5. to find food.
6. made from animal skin.
7. for European fur traders.
8. Needing to find other ways to provide for their families,
9. in the harsh Arctic climate.
10. Like the Canadian Inuit seen in the photo on the opposite page,

---

TIPS & TRICKS

When you use the coordinating conjunction *and* to link two subjects, your new compound subject will be a plural subject. Remember to make the verb agree with the subject in number.

ORIGINAL
Zach likes watching the sea mammals. Briana likes watching the sea mammals.

COMBINED
Zach and Briana like watching the sea mammals. [The plural verb *like* is needed with the plural subject *Zach and Briana.*]

For more information and practice on **agreement of subjects and verbs,** see page 458.

Crossing the Curriculum

Science. To help students understand how two sentences may combine to form a new sentence, ask a science teacher to draw a parallel between sentence combining and the way molecules of different elements bond and form new compounds. Simple examples, such as how oxygen and hydrogen join to create water or how carbon and oxygen create carbon dioxide and carbon monoxide, may help students see how components of one molecule may fill the gaps in another.

Relating to Usage

One way that students can make sure that they have correctly used plural verbs with compound subjects joined by *and* is to substitute the word *they* for any compound subject. If the verb agrees in number with the subject *they,* then the verb is correct.

When deciding whether to use *and, but,* or *or,* follow these rules.

- *And* shows equality. Use it if you mean *both.*

  Katie **and** Tyrone are my friends.

- *But* shows contrast. Use it to point out something *different.*

  Katie likes to play tennis, **but** Tyrone does not.

- *Or* shows a choice. Use it if you have *options.*

  Usually either Katie **or** Tyrone waits for me after school.

Exercise 6 Combining Sentences by Creating Compound Subjects and Verbs

Combine each of the following pairs of short, choppy sentences by using *and, but,* or *or.* If the two sentences have the same verb, make a compound subject. If they have the same subject, make a compound verb. Remember to keep the ideas in parallel forms.

EXAMPLE   1. Dolphins belong to a group of mammals called cetaceans. Porpoises belong to a group of mammals called cetaceans.

   1. *Dolphins and porpoises belong to a group of mammals called cetaceans.*

       1. and porpoises

1. Dolphins are warm-blooded. ~~Porpoises are warm-blooded.~~
2. Common dolphins live in warm waters. ~~Common dolphins swim in large schools.~~   2. and swim in large schools.
3. Porpoises are similar to dolphins. ~~Porpoises~~ generally live in cooler water.   3. but
4. Dolphins have beak-like snouts. ~~Dolphins~~ use sonar to locate objects under water.   4. and
5. Dolphins hunt fish. ~~Dolphins eat fish.~~   5. and eat
6. Dolphins swim by moving their tails up and down. ~~Porpoises swim by moving their tails up and down.~~   6. and porpoises
7. Porpoises can swim fast. ~~Dolphins can swim fast.~~
8. A porpoise could outswim most sharks. ~~A tuna could outswim most sharks.~~   7. and dolphins   8. or a tuna
9. Bottle-nosed dolphins can measure up to fifteen feet in length. ~~Bottle-nosed dolphins can weigh over four hundred pounds.~~   9. and can weigh over four hundred pounds.
10. Sharks sometimes attack porpoises. ~~Sharks sometimes kill porpoises.~~   10. and kill

Compound Sentences

Sometimes you will want to combine two sentences that express equally important ideas. You can connect two closely related, equally important sentences by using a comma plus the coordinating conjunction *and, but,* or *or.* Doing so creates a ***compound sentence.***

ORIGINAL   My brother entered the Annual Chili Cook-off. His chili won a prize.

COMBINED   My brother entered the Annual Chili Cook-off**, and** his chili won a prize.

Relating to Grammar

Remind students that when they combine two sentences into a compound sentence, they have to consider the tense of the verbs. For example, two sentences like "My cousins arrived" and "We go skating" cannot be easily combined, because the verb tenses differ. Point out that verb tense should be consistent—events that happen in the present take present-tense verbs, and events that occurred in the past take past-tense verbs.

| ORIGINAL | I did not help him cook the chili. I helped him clean up the kitchen. |
| COMBINED | I did not help him cook the chili**,** **but** I helped him clean up the kitchen. |

NOTE A compound sentence tells the reader that the two ideas are closely related. If you combine two short sentences that are not closely related, you may confuse your reader.

| UNRELATED | Fernando mowed the grass, and I brought a broom. |
| RELATED | Fernando mowed the grass, and I swept the sidewalk. |

Exercise 7 Combining Sentences by Forming a Compound Sentence

Each of the following pairs of sentences is closely related. Make each pair into a compound sentence by adding a comma and a coordinating conjunction such as *and* or *but*.

EXAMPLE
1. The Pueblos have lived in the same location for a long time. They have strong ties to their homeland.

1. *The Pueblos have lived in the same location for a long time, and they have strong ties to their homeland.*

Here are possible combinations.
1. Some Pueblos built villages in the valleys. Others settled in desert and mountain areas. **1. , but**
2. Desert surrounded many of the valleys. The people grew crops with the help of irrigation systems.
3. Women gathered berries and other foods. Men hunted game. **2. , but** **3. , and**
4. Their adobe homes had several stories. The people used ladders to reach the upper levels. **4. , and**
5. Today, each Pueblo village has its own government. The Pueblo people still share many customs. **5. , but**

Combining Sentences Using Subordinate Clauses

A *clause* is a group of words that contains a subject and a verb. *Independent clauses* can stand alone as a sentence. *Subordinate* (or *dependent*) *clauses* cannot stand alone because they do not express a complete thought.

Relating to Usage

As they create complex sentences by combining with subordinate clauses, students may benefit from your pointing out the distinctions between the relative pronouns *who, which,* and *that.* Explain that *who* refers to people only, *which* refers to things only, and *that* refers to people or things. Point out that the category *things* includes animals, organizations, and places. Write the following examples on the chalkboard and ask students to determine to what each underlined relative pronoun refers.

- Fernando is the man <u>who</u> installed the modem for our computer. [*man*]

- He had to move the computer, <u>which</u> needed to be connected to a cable line. [*computer*]

- Media Global, <u>which</u> is the local cable company, gave us the modem. [*Media Global*]

- Sue is the technician <u>that</u> trained my family to use the Internet. [*technician*]

- My mother designed a Web site <u>that</u> will help her at-home business grow. [*Web site*]

Timesaver

You can save some time reviewing subordinate clauses by pointing out the list of subordinating conjunctions on page 431. Students may use this list to find the words they need to combine sentences.

Reference Note

For more information and practice on **independent clauses** and **subordinate clauses,** see page 424.

Reference Note

For more information and practice on **complex sentences,** see page 445.

Reference Note

For more information and practice on the use of **commas with introductory clauses,** see page 613.

| INDEPENDENT CLAUSE | Gertrude Ederle swam the English Channel. [This clause can stand alone.] |
| SUBORDINATE CLAUSE | when she was nineteen years old [This clause cannot stand alone.] |

If two sentences are related, you can combine them by using a subordinate clause. The resulting sentence is called a ***complex sentence.*** The subordinate clause in a complex sentence will give information about a word or idea in the independent clause.

| TWO SIMPLE SENTENCES | Theresa traveled to Rome. She saw the Sistine Chapel. |
| ONE COMPLEX SENTENCE | Theresa traveled to Rome, **where she saw the Sistine Chapel.** |

Making Clauses That Begin with *Who, Which,* or *That*

You can make a short sentence into a subordinate clause by inserting *who, which,* or *that* in place of the subject.

| ORIGINAL | The Everglades is an area of swamps. It covers the southern part of Florida. |
| COMBINED | The Everglades is an area of swamps **that covers the southern part of Florida.** |

Making Clauses with Words of Time or Place

Another way to turn a sentence into a subordinate clause is to add a word that tells time or place. Words that begin this type of clause include *after, before, where, wherever, when, whenever,* and *while.* You may need to delete some words to insert the clause into another sentence.

| ORIGINAL | No humans lived in the Everglades until 1842. In 1842, Seminoles fled to the area. |
| COMBINED | No humans lived in the Everglades until 1842, **when Seminoles fled to the area.** |

NOTE If you put your time or place clause at the beginning of the sentence, use a comma after the clause.

| ORIGINAL | People began draining the swamps to make farmland. The Everglades was in danger. |
| COMBINED | **When people began draining the swamps to make farmland,** the Everglades was in danger. |

Exercise 8 Combining Sentences by Using Subordinate Clauses

Combine each sentence pair by making the second sentence into a subordinate clause and attaching it to the first sentence. You may need to cut a word or two from the second sentence.

1. The pearl is a gem. It is made by certain kinds of oysters and clams. (Use *that.*)   **1.** that
2. Beautiful pearls are found in tropical seas. The best pearl oysters live there. (Use *where.*)   **2.** , where/⊙
3. A valuable pearl has a shine. The shine comes from below its surface. (Use *that.*)   **3.** that
4. A pearl becomes round. It is formed in the soft part of the oyster. (Use *after.*)   **4.** after
5. Pearls should be wiped clean with a soft cloth. They are worn as jewelry. (Use *after.*)   **5.** after

Review B Revising a Paragraph by Combining Sentences

The following paragraph sounds choppy because it has too many short sentences. Use the methods you have learned in this section to combine sentences in the paragraph.   A sample revision follows.

```
 ∧Dr. James Naismith invented the game     When
of basketball over one hundred years ago∧
He probably never guessed the sport would
become so popular. He just wanted a new
game that could be played indoors. The
original basketball teams started in
1891∧ They had nine players instead of    and
five. The first basket was a peach bas-
ket∧ ∧A player had to climb up and        and
retrieve the ball after each score. Some
parts of the game have stayed the same.
Players still cannot hold the ball while
they run∧ ∧They must dribble. Thousands of   but
teams across the world now play Dr.
Naismith's game.
```

Improving Sentence Style

OBJECTIVES

- To identify and revise stringy sentences
- To identify and revise wordy sentences
- To add variety to sentences

Quotation for the Day

"This is one of the most important things a teacher can share with students: that a piece of writing can be manipulated and molded like clay."

(Meredith Sue Willis, 1946– , American author and teacher)

Share this quotation with students, and ask them to discuss how clay and writing are similar. Lead students to see that both clay and words are flexible and can be used to build something. Explain that a piece of writing, like a sculpture, goes through many stages before it is finished.

Meeting INDIVIDUAL NEEDS

MULTIPLE INTELLIGENCES
Bodily-Kinesthetic Intelligence. Students may benefit from a concrete model of a stringy sentence. Bring in long pieces of yarn or string, and give them to students. Then, write the following sentence on the chalkboard and read it aloud.

The fire alarm bell rang, and everyone started to file out of school, but then our principal came down the hall, and he said the bell was a mistake.

For every complete thought in the sentence, the students should tie a knot in the yarn or string. [*four in all*] Explain that a sentence that generates more than three knots is probably stringy.

Improving Sentence Style

In addition to combining some sentences, you can also make your writing more effective by revising *stringy* and *wordy sentences* to make them shorter and clearer. Your reader will stay involved if you mix long and short sentences and include simple, compound, and complex sentences in your writing.

Revising Stringy Sentences

A **stringy sentence** is made up of several complete thoughts strung together with words like *and* or *but*. Stringy sentences just ramble on and on. They don't give the reader a chance to pause before each new idea.

To fix a stringy sentence, you can

- break the sentence into two or more sentences
- turn some of the complete thoughts into phrases or subordinate clauses

STRINGY Martina climbed the stairs of the haunted house, and she knocked on the door several times, but no one answered, and she braced herself, and then she opened the door.

REVISED Martina climbed the stairs of the haunted house. She knocked on the door several times, but no one answered. Bracing herself, she opened the door.

Reference Note

For more information and practice on **compound sentences,** see page 441.

NOTE   When you revise a stringy sentence, you may decide to keep *and* or *but* between two closely related independent clauses. If you do this, be sure to use a comma before the *and* or *but*.

EXAMPLE   She knocked on the door several times**,** **but** no one answered.

Exercise 9   Revising Stringy Sentences

Some of the following sentences are stringy and need to be improved. First, identify the stringy sentences. Then, revise them by (1) breaking each sentence into two or more sentences or (2) turning some of the complete thoughts into phrases or subordinate clauses. If the sentence is effective and does not need to be improved, write *C* for *correct*.   Possible revisions follow.

1. Mercedes O. Cubría was born in Cuba,~~but~~ her mother died, ~~and~~ she moved to the United States,~~and she moved~~ with her two sisters.   1. ⊙ When   2. After working/⊙

2.~~She worked~~ as a nurse, ~~and then~~ she joined the Women's Army Corps,~~and~~ she soon became an officer in the army.

3. Cubría was the first Cuban-born woman to become an officer in the U.S. Army.   3. C

4. Her job during World War II was to translate important government papers into a secret code.   4. C

5.The war ended, ~~and~~ she was promoted to captain, ~~and~~ later her official rank rose to major.   5. After/⊙

6.~~Then there was~~ the Korean War, ~~and~~ she worked as an intelligence officer,~~and she studied~~ information about the enemy.

7. Cubría retired from the army in 1953 but was called to duty again in 1962.   6. During/studying   7. C

8. After the Castro revolution, thousands of Cubans fled to the United States,~~and~~ Cubría interviewed many of these refugees,~~and she~~ also prepared reports on Cuba.   8. ⊙

9. In her spare time, she helped people from Cuba find jobs and housing.   9. C   10. ⊙/where

10. She retired again in 1973,~~and~~ she settled in Miami, Florida, ~~and~~ she was surrounded by friends and family ~~there.~~

Revising Wordy Sentences

Sometimes you use more words in a sentence than you really need. Extra words do not make writing sound better and, in fact, they can even interfere with your message. Revise *wordy sentences* in these three ways.

1. Replace a phrase with one word.

WORDY   **In a state of exhaustion,** Tony slumped across the bus seat and fell asleep.

REVISED   **Exhausted,** Tony slumped across the bus seat and fell asleep.

WORDY   **As a result of what happened when** the tire went flat, we were late.

REVISED   **Because** the tire went flat, we were late.

─HELP─

As you revise these sentences, keep in mind that there is often more than one correct way to revise a sentence.

COMPUTER TIP

The grammar-checking option on a computer will often alert you if you have written a sentence that is too long. Review the sentence and see if you can break it into parts or edit out unnecessary words.

Exercise 9

ALTERNATIVE LESSON
Consider using **Exercise 9** as an exercise in summarizing skills. After students complete the exercise as it is presented, ask them to write two or three sentences summarizing the information presented in the exercise. Guide students toward understanding that summarizing is similar to sentence combining—both skills require them to see the essential information in a series of sentences and to restate it succinctly.

TEACHING TIP

Revising Wordy Sentences
As students learn to identify and revise wordy sentences, it may help them to have a list of words and phrases that can make sentences wordy. Start students with a list of items, such as *quite, really, a lot of,* and *in spite of the fact that.* Post the list in a prominent place as the class works on this section of the chapter, and encourage students to add other words and phrases to the list as they encounter more examples.

2. Take out *who is* or *which is.*

WORDY   Yesterday I went for a long hike with Sonya, **who is my best friend.**

REVISED   Yesterday I went for a long hike with Sonya, **my best friend.**

WORDY   Afterward, we drank some apple juice, **which is a good thirst quencher.**

REVISED   Afterward, we drank some apple juice, **a good thirst quencher.**

3. Take out a whole group of unnecessary words.

WORDY   I spent a lot of time writing this report because I **really** want people to learn about manatees **so they can know all about them.**

REVISED   I spent a lot of time writing this report because I want people to learn about manatees.

Exercise 10 **Revising Wordy Sentences**

Some of the following sentences are wordy and need improvement. Decide which of the sentences are wordy; then, revise them. You can (1) replace a phrase with one word, (2) take out *who is* or *which is,* or (3) take out a whole group of unnecessary words. If a sentence is effective as it is, write *C* for *correct.*

Here are possible revisions.
1. Our science class has been learning about the starfish, ~~which is~~ a strange and beautiful animal.
2. ~~What I want to say is that~~ starfish are fascinating creatures.
3. A starfish has little feet tipped with ∧suction cups ∧~~that have suction power.~~   **3.** powerful/⊙
4. At the end of each arm is a sensitive eyespot.   **4.** C
5. ∧~~In spite of the fact that~~ the eyespot cannot really see things, it can tell light from dark.   **5.** Although
6. The starfish's mouth is in the middle of its body. **6.** C
7. ∧~~When it uses~~ its arms, it can pull at the shells of clams.
8. ∧~~At the point at which~~ the clam's shell opens, the starfish can feed on the clam.   **7.** Using   **8.** When
9. Starfish come in a variety of colors, shapes, and sizes ∧~~and some are bigger than others.~~   **9.** ⊙
10. This photograph shows a blue sea star holding onto a soft coral ~~by holding it~~ with its suction cups.

Varying Sentence Structure

An important way to keep your readers' attention is to mix sentences of different lengths and structures. Think like a movie director. If you were making a movie, you would include long, complex scenes; but you would mix those scenes with shorter, simpler scenes to keep your audience's attention. A movie made up entirely of long scenes or short scenes would be difficult for your audience to follow. Apply the same ideas to your writing.

For example, the writer of the following paragraph uses only short sentences.

> Jim Knaub lost the use of his legs in a motorcycle accident. He decided he would not let that slow him down. He started racing wheelchairs. All the other racers were using standard wheelchairs. Those wheelchairs were not fast enough for Jim. He began to design his own. Soon, his light-weight, ultrafast wheelchair was winning races. He became a well-known wheelchair-racing champion. Jim now designs wheelchairs for others to use.

Now read the revised paragraph. Notice how the writer has varied the sentence structure to include different sentence lengths and a mixture of simple, compound, and complex sentences.

> When Jim Knaub lost the use of his legs in a motorcycle accident, he decided he would not let that slow him down. He started racing wheelchairs. All the other racers were using standard wheelchairs, but those wheelchairs were not fast enough for Jim. He began to design his own. Soon, his light-weight, ultrafast wheelchair was winning races. He became a well-known wheelchair-racing champion and began to design wheelchairs for others to use.

─HELP─

When adding variety to sentences in a paragraph, first look for words that are repeated. Sentences with repeated words can often be combined or rewritten to improve the paragraph.

Varying sentence length keeps the reader interested in the story. By changing the sentence structure, the writer avoids starting each sentence the same way, which would make the paragraph boring and repetitive.

Exercise 11   Adding Variety to Sentences

The following paragraph is uninteresting because it includes only compound sentences. Rewrite the paragraph to include a variety of sentence structures. Mix short, simple sentences; compound sentences; and longer sentences with subordinate clauses in your version. Remember, you are the director of this piece of writing. Use variety to keep your audience involved.

Here is a sample revision.

My friends and I have ^been talking, and we have made a decision. We should have a day off. and we could go on a class picnic. We could do it right before winter break, or we could go near the end of the school year. We could each bring a sack lunch, or we could each bring something to share with the rest of the class. The park near the school has picnic tables, and it has playing fields ^and a pool. ^We don't Since all know how to swim, so the students who can't swim can play soccer or baseball instead. It might seem bad to take a free day, but we work hard the rest of the year. We would enjoy the picnic, and we would have a fun day. We would return to school, ^and we would have smiles on our with faces.

Review C   Revising a Paragraph by Improving Sentence Style

The paragraph on the following page is hard to read because it contains stringy and wordy sentences. Identify the stringy and wordy sentences, and use the methods you have learned to revise them. Try to mix simple, compound, and complex sentences in your improved version.   A sample revision follows.

The movie *Anastasia* is based on a real story about ~~a real girl from history. Her name was~~ Anastasia Romanov ~~and she~~ was born in 1901 and , who lived in Russia. The movie is about **Although** ~~some historical~~ events in Russia's history, ~~and~~ many things in the movie are not true. For example, the movie says that Anastasia was eight years old when the revolutionaries ~~came to~~ overthrew ~~overthrow and defeat~~ her father, ~~who was~~ the czar, ~~but~~ the real Anastasia was a teenager, ~~in real life.~~ The movie shows Anastasia and her grandmother, ~~who was~~ the Grand Duchess Marie, escaping together, ~~but~~ in reality her grandmother was already safely in Denmark when the family was ~~seized and~~ captured. Unlike the character in the movie, the real Anastasia did not get away, her remains were found with her family's ~~remains when they were found~~ in 1991. Although *Anastasia* is an interesting movie, people who see it should also know the real story. ~~that happened.~~

STYLE **TIP**

When planning your own writing assignments, save time to edit your composition for style. Many writers revise first for content and organization; then they look at style elements like sentence variety.

RESOURCES

Writing Effective Sentences
Assessment

- *Assessment Package*
  —*Chapter Tests,* Ch. 8
  —*Chapter Tests in Standardized Test Formats,* Ch. 8
- *Test Generator (One-Stop Planner CD-ROM)*

CHAPTER

Learning About Paragraphs

internet connect

go. hrw .com

GO TO: go.hrw.com
KEYWORD: EOLang

What Is a Paragraph?

A *paragraph* is a section of text focused on a *main idea*. Usually a paragraph is part of a longer piece of writing. In an essay about summer camp, for example, one paragraph might focus just on the meals. Other paragraphs in the essay would each focus on another aspect of camp, such as the outdoor activities, adding up to create an overall picture of the experience.

Why Use Paragraphs?

As writers and readers, we often seem to take paragraphs for granted. Imagine, though, a piece of writing with no paragraphs. As a reader, you would face huge blocks of uninterrupted text, giving your eyes no chance for a break until the end. As a writer, you might think it would be nice not to worry about where to start a new paragraph or when to indent; however, paragraphs help you get your message across to readers. They show readers that you are moving from one idea (or setting, or speaker) to another. Showing where paragraphs begin and end is like holding the reader's hand and walking him or her through your piece. Paragraphs make it easier for readers to get where you want to take them.

CHAPTER RESOURCES

Planning
■ *One-Stop Planner CD-ROM*

Practice and Extension
■ *Sentences and Paragraphs,* for Ch. 9

Internet
■ go.hrw.com (keyword: EOLang) **go. hrw .com**

Evaluation and Assessment
■ *Assessment Package*
　—Chapter Tests, Ch. 9
　—Chapter Tests in Standardized Test Formats, Ch. 9

■ *Test Generator (One-Stop Planner CD-ROM)*

What Are the Parts of a Paragraph?

Most paragraphs that focus on a *main idea* have a *topic sentence* and *supporting sentences*. Many also include a *clincher sentence*.

The Main Idea

Whether they stand alone or are part of a longer piece of writing, paragraphs usually have a main idea. The **main idea** is the overall point of the paragraph. The following paragraph is from an article about the United States 2000 census, on which nearly seven million people identified themselves as belonging to more than one race. In this paragraph the main idea is in the first sentence.

> Many multiracial kids glide easily between their mixed cultures. Kelly Dubé, 12, of Los Angeles is half Korean and half French Canadian. His mother takes him to a Buddhist temple, where he has learned how to meditate. He can understand and speak some Korean and knows a little French. Most of the time, though, he doesn't think about his bi-racial status: "If anything, I think I'm more American."
>
> Ritu Upadhyay, "We, the People…,"
> *TIME for Kids*

The Topic Sentence

Location of the Topic Sentence

The main idea of a paragraph is often stated in a **topic sentence.** You may find it at the beginning of the paragraph, in the middle, or even at the end. In the paragraph above, the topic sentence is the first sentence: *Many multiracial kids glide easily between their mixed cultures.*

In the following paragraph, the topic sentence is last. This sentence makes clear that the villagers are preparing for a battle. The other sentences lead up to that point.

Positioning a Topic Sentence. To reinforce the concept of locating a topic sentence effectively, place students of different abilities in groups of three. Ask each group to find a short paragraph that has a topic sentence and to write each sentence in the paragraph on a separate index card. Ask group members to scramble the cards, clip them together with a paper clip, and pass them to another group. Next, ask students to look at all the sentence cards and to identify the topic sentence. Then, let students reconstruct the paragraph, experimenting with the placement of the topic sentence. Finally, discuss as a class how changing the position of a topic sentence affects the paragraph.

> Quickly, quickly we gathered the sheep into the pens. Dogs barked, and people shouted out orders to one another. Children rushed through the village gathering firewood to pile inside the homes. Men and women scooped up pots and pots of water, filling cisterns and containers as rapidly as possible. People pulled the last ears of corn from the fields and turned their backs on the dry stalks. Finally, we all stood together in the plaza in the center of the village for just a moment before the fighters went to stand near the walls and the wide-eyed children were coaxed inside the houses. We were prepared for the coming battle.

Importance of a Topic Sentence

Although not all paragraphs have topic sentences, it is helpful to use them when you are writing. Topic sentences may help you focus on your main idea. They also help the reader find the main idea and know what to expect from the paragraph. However, paragraphs that relate a series of events or that tell a story often lack a topic sentence. When a paragraph has no topic sentence, the reader must figure out the main idea by determining what all of the sentences have in common. Read the following paragraph. Although it has no topic sentence, all the sentences are about one main idea—the unexpected reactions of a poor woman toward her wealthy friend.

> "Oh, Lottie, it's good to see you," Bess said, but saying nothing about Lottie's splendid appearance. Upstairs Bess, putting down her shabby suitcase, said, "I'll sleep like a rock tonight," without a word of praise for her lovely room. At the lavish table, top-heavy with turkey, Bess said, "I'll take light and dark both," with no marveling at the size of the bird, or that there was turkey for two elderly women, one of them too poor to buy her own bread.
>
> Dorothy West, *The Richer, the Poorer*

Learning for Life

Writing Paragraphs. Students whose skills include the ability to write well-constructed paragraphs are better prepared for achievement outside of school. For instance, application forms often ask for a short paragraph in answer to a prompt or for a brief biographical sketch. Many jobs also require employees to write brief reports about their work activities. Ask students to write a single paragraph that describes the classroom.

When a writer includes no topic sentence, readers must determine the main idea of a paragraph from its supporting details. In paragraphs like the one from *The Richer, the Poorer*, the main idea is *implied*, rather than directly stated.

Exercise 1 Identifying Main Ideas and Topic Sentences

Finding a main idea is like detective work: Both require a keen eye for detail. Look for the main idea in each of the following paragraphs by looking for a topic sentence and by studying the paragraph's details. Remember that the main idea is the overall point of the paragraph. If the selection has a <u>topic sentence</u>, write it down. If the paragraph has no topic sentence, write the <u>main</u> idea of the paragraph in your own words, using details from the paragraph.

1.   He turned and looked back at the stand of raspberries. The bear was gone; the birds were singing; he saw nothing that could hurt him. <u>There was no danger here that he could sense, could feel.</u> In the city, at night, there was sometimes danger. You could not be in the park at night, after dark, because of the danger. But here, the bear had looked at him and had moved on and—this filled his thoughts—the berries were so good.

Gary Paulsen, *Hatchet*

2. m.i.—In spite of the disabilities associated with spina bifida, Auralea Moore leads an active life.

2.   Like lots of other kids her age, eight-year-old Auralea Moore plays baseball, swims, and skis. She also has a favorite plaything: a 19-inch doll named Susan, who was handcrafted to look like her. Auralea was born with spina bifida, a birth defect that has left her paralyzed from the waist down. Her look-alike doll, equipped with a pair of blue and silver "designer" braces, helps her remember that although she may be handicapped, she is definitely not out of the action.

"A Doll Made to Order," *Newsweek*

3. Personally, I thought Maxwell was just about the homeliest dog I'd ever seen in my entire life. He looked like a little old man draped in a piece of brown velvet that was too long, with the leftover cloth hanging in thick folds under his chin. Not only that, his long droopy ears dragged on the ground; he had sad wet eyes and huge thick paws with splayed toes. I mean, who could love a dog like that, except my brother Joji, aged nine, who is a bit on the homely side himself.

Yoshiko Uchida, *A Jar of Dreams*

COMPUTER TIP

Use a word-processing program's cut and paste commands to find the best placement of a topic sentence within a paragraph. You can always move or replace the sentence if you change your mind.

Exercise 2 **Writing a Topic Sentence**

For each of the following paragraphs, write a topic sentence that communicates the main idea.

1. A bottle of nail polish can cost as little as a dollar and last for months, depending on how much you use. You can find it in every color in nature and any unnatural color you can imagine. Best of all, if you get tired of a color, you can easily change it.

2. This movie is packed with action. I have never seen so many chases and explosions before. It also has an important lesson about friendship. The two main characters always look out for each other. Maybe the best thing about it is the music. The soundtrack will certainly be a bestseller.

3. First, you need some supplies. These include a roller or brush, a ladder tall enough to reach the roof, and enough paint to cover the whole house. You should have already scraped off the old paint. Start at the top of a section and work your way down to avoid dripping wet paint on a finished part.

Supporting Sentences

Supporting sentences are the details that expand on, explain, or prove a paragraph's main idea. These details can include *sensory details, facts,* or *examples.*

- *Sensory details* are what we experience through our five senses—sight, hearing, touch, taste, and smell.

- *Facts* give information that can be proved true by direct observation or by checking a reliable reference source. For instance, it is a fact that great herds of buffalo once roamed the western plains. You can prove this fact by checking an encyclopedia or history book.

- *Examples* give typical instances of an idea. An example of a creature with protective coloration is a chameleon, a lizard whose coloring changes with its surroundings.

The following chart shows the kinds of details you can use to support the main idea of a paragraph.

Kinds of Details	Supporting Sentences
Sensory Details	
Sight	The bright sun glared off the front windshield of the car.
Hearing	Thunder boomed down the canyon, echoing off the walls.
Touch	My hands felt frozen to the cold, steel handlebars.
Taste	Thirstily, she gulped down the sweet orange juice.
Smell	The sharp, unpleasant odor of asphalt met his nose.
Facts	In 1998, Mark McGwire slammed seventy home runs in one season to break the record of sixty-one held by Roger Maris.
Examples	Fierce windstorms occur worldwide. For example, tornadoes have wind speeds over 200 miles per hour.

Reference Note

Supporting details help you elaborate on your ideas. For more information and practice on **elaboration,** see page 304.

Critical Thinking

Evaluation. Ask students to look at the same paragraphs in their writing portfolio that they evaluated earlier for main ideas or topic sentences and to number the supporting details they find there. Then, have them answer another set of questions.

- Are all the supporting sentences about the main idea?

- Do the supporting details provide enough information? If not, what is missing?

Relating to Literature

After students have studied the material on sensory details on this page, read to them excerpts from poems such as James Weldon Johnson's "The Creation" or Alfred Noyes's "The Highwayman." After reading the excerpts, have students jot down the sensory details they remember. If you have time, read the excerpts a second time while students listen and fill in a chart like the one below.

Sensory Details in "The Highwayman"	Examples
Sight	road like a ribbon
Hearing	
Touch	
Taste	
Smell	

Exercise 3 Collecting Supporting Details

ANSWERS

Here are sample details.

1. We get together at the bowling alley, which smells of floor wax and popcorn. We yell at each other over the sound of the balls crashing into the pins, and we have a great time.

2. I would look in all the shop windows filled with displays of clothes, CDs, and books. Then, I would eat in the food court and sleep in the mattress store.

3. Joining an organization that teaches people to read is one way to make a difference. Volunteering for a community project is another.

4. Tamales are my favorite meal. Our house smells of the meat and *masa* steaming in papery corn husks. We serve the tamales with rice and tangy salsa.

TEACHING TIP

The Clincher Sentence

It may help students who are just learning about clincher sentences to have a short list of words or phrases that convey a sense of summing up, such as *in short, clearly, in other words, so,* and *finally.* Explain that not all clincher sentences contain these words or phrases, but that using them may help students bring their paragraphs to a close.

ALTERNATIVE LESSON

After students complete the section on clincher sentences on pp. 294–295, have them return to **Exercise 3** and add clincher sentences to the supporting sentences they provided earlier. Ask students to notice that with a topic sentence, supporting sentences, and a clincher sentence, they have created a complete paragraph.

Exercise 3 Collecting Supporting Details

When you write paragraphs, you have to collect details that support your main idea. You can practice with the following topic sentences. List at least two details to support each topic sentence.

EXAMPLE 1. The appliance that toasts our bread has changed over the years.

1. *Details: It originated in the early 1900s. It consisted of bare wires with no thermostat. The first pop-up toaster appeared in 1926.*

1. The time I spend with my friends on Saturday nights is my favorite time of the week.
2. My dream is to spend two days in a shopping mall.
3. One person's actions can make a difference in the lives of others.
4. When I feel hungry, I can just imagine my favorite meal.

The Clincher Sentence

Once you have written a topic sentence and developed well-organized details that support your main idea, the only thing left to do is to wrap it all up. Some writers do this by using a ***clincher sentence,*** also known as a ***concluding sentence.*** Notice how the last sentence of the following paragraph pulls together the preceding information by echoing the topic sentence.

> Helping the homeless helps the community. When homeless people are given housing assistance and job training, they can become our neighbors, co-workers, and friends. Not only do they find work and learn to support themselves, but they also pay taxes and share their skills with others. Every person we help out of homelessness is one more person who can enrich our neighborhood and community.

Although many paragraphs have no clincher sentence, you may want to use one to cement your main idea in readers' minds.

For each of the following short paragraphs, write a sentence that can serve as its clincher, wrapping up the information presented in the paragraph, but not repeating it.

EXAMPLE   **1.** Even though ferns grow everywhere in the forest, I can't seem to keep them alive at home. My shriveled brown ferns have the benefits of frequent waterings, plant food, and careful lighting. Nothing seems to help.

         1. *Clincher: I guess nature knows how to take care of ferns better than people do.*

1.   Eating food in the library is a bad idea. Crumbs get on the floor and between pages when you eat, even if you are careful. These tiny bits of food may be impossible for you to see, but insects know they are there and will raid the books to find them. These insects will eventually harm the pages.

2.   Computers have made getting information faster and easier. Almost all schools use them now, and they are very helpful in doing homework or typing papers. Before computers were available, most students had to do research by going to libraries, which might not be open. Now students can use computers any time of day in their own homes or at a friend's house.

What Makes a Good Paragraph?

Unity

A paragraph has *unity* when all the sentences support, or tell something about, one main idea. A paragraph that does not have unity may confuse your readers. For example, in a paragraph about Bonnie St. John Deane, you might tell how she became a skiing champion despite losing a leg. However, if

People Weekly/Time Inc., ©1986 Richard Howard.

Exercise 4 Developing a Clincher Sentence

ANSWERS
Here are sample clincher sentences.

1. Clearly, by not snacking in the library, we actually help preserve the books.
2. Today, computers are as much a part of learning as books or pens.

What Makes a Good Paragraph?

OBJECTIVES

- **To identify sentences that destroy unity**
- **To arrange details by using chronological, spatial, and logical order**
- **To identify transitional words and phrases in writing**
- **To elaborate by adding details to writing**

TEACHING (TIP)

Unity
As students write their own compositions, you might want to provide the following strategies for creating unity:

- Before drafting, organize ideas using a cluster diagram and cross out ideas that are not related to the main idea.

- Insert transitions between ideas as you write your paragraph, using the chart on pages 302–303. If you can't connect all of your ideas using transitions from a particular group (i.e., transitions for showing place in a description of a place), then your ideas may not be unified.

- Use precise words, and use them consistently. In a paragraph about different types of canoes, you probably should not see the world *sailboat*.

Read the quotation aloud and discuss its meaning with students. Point out that writers must often discipline themselves to keep their paragraphs organized and focused on their subject, or main idea, in order to present that subject clearly to the reader.

Meeting
INDIVIDUAL
NEEDS

ENGLISH-LANGUAGE LEARNERS

Spanish. To assist students who are not familiar with the concept of unity, explain that the English word *unity* is similar to the Spanish word *unidad*. On the chalkboard, write the definition of *unity*. [*a combination or ordering of parts so that each contributes to a single effect; the relevance of all parts in a literary work to a single main idea*] Then, ask students to give examples of related words [*united* and *unite*] and to suggest examples of unity or of things that are united. [*Students may mention the unity of members of a family, the United States, or the United Nations.*]

—HELP—

The first step in completing Exercise 5 is to decide what the main idea is. Next, find the sentence that is not closely connected to the main idea.

you mentioned a friend who is also a skier, you would destroy the unity. The information about the friend is not related to your main idea.

Notice how all the sentences in the following paragraph tell something more about the paragraph's main idea.

> Technology has changed the ways of the ranch. While cowboys continue to drive cattle to the corral on horseback, a pickup truck—air-conditioned, of course—also helps. And though they don't plug branding irons into electrical outlets, propane tanks make lighting fires and heating branding irons easier. Computers log inventory and keep track of wildlife. Hal Hawkins, King Ranch's animal physiologist, monitors herd research and development with a laptop computer.
>
> Johnny D. Boggs, "Home on the Range," *Boys' Life*

Exercise 5 **Identifying Sentences That Destroy Unity**

Each of the following paragraphs has one sentence that destroys the unity. Try your skill at finding the unrelated sentences.

1. It felt like an oven to Tamara as she walked up the street toward the park. It was a hot day for baseball practice. She wondered if the Cardinals game would be on television that evening. Tamara told herself she couldn't let the heat slow her down, though. Today the coach would be deciding who would start in the season's first game. Tamara wanted to be playing third base.

2. Canoes are made for many purposes. White-water canoes are made for use in fast, rock-filled streams. They can turn quickly to avoid obstacles. Other canoes are made for lakes and quiet rivers. Unable to turn quickly, they are poor

```
choices for use on a river with lots of
rapids. On the other hand, they are easy
to paddle in a straight line. White-water
canoes can be very expensive. Before
choosing a canoe, think about what kind of
water you will ride.
```

Coherence

What goes into a paragraph is only part of the picture.
Supporting details need to be clearly connected and
arranged. A paragraph has *coherence* when readers can tell
how and why ideas are connected. To create coherence you
can do two things. First, you can arrange your details in an
order that makes sense to the reader. Then, you can link
those ideas together with transitional words or phrases (like *first*
and *then* in this paragraph).

Order of Details

To help your readers follow your ideas, use one of the following
patterns to organize your ideas.

- *Chronological order* presents details in the order in which
  they happen.
- *Spatial order* presents details according to their location.
- *Logical order* groups related ideas together.

Chronological Order   What happens when a character
lost in the Arctic wilderness cannot build a fire? How is soccer
played? To answer these questions, you must tell about an event
or an action as it changes over time. To tell about changes in
time, you usually use chronological, or time, order.

You can use chronological order to tell a story (what happens
to the character in the Arctic), to explain a process (how to play
soccer), or to explain causes and effects (why the *Titanic* sank).

- **Using chronological order to tell a story**   On the following
  page is a story, passed down from one generation to the next,
  about some curious escapes from slavery before the Civil War.

What Makes a Good Paragraph?   **297**

Crossing the Curriculum

Social Studies. On the day you plan
to discuss chronological order, ask a
school librarian to bring to your classroom books that contain time lines.
After students read the section on
chronological order, ask a volunteer to
explain how a time line is read. [*from
left to right*] Point out how each slash
mark in the line denotes a particular
time period, which is marked below
the line. Above the mark is an important event that took place at that
time. Explain that a time line provides
an abbreviated history of events in
chronological order without any
transitions.

Then, have students make a time line
of a recent week's events. Ask them to
"translate" the time line into an
account of the events in chronological
order and to share it orally with a
partner.

Ask students where they are likely to read paragraphs that use chronological order to tell a story, to explain a process, or to explain causes and effects. [*All three, but particularly the last two, appear regularly in social studies and science textbooks.*] Ask students to think about how they read their social studies and science textbooks. They will probably say they look for facts and dates, but you can suggest that now they should pay closer attention to the patterns of chronological order. For more about writing to explain a process, see Chapter 2 in this book.

Uncle Mingo's forehead wrinkled like a mask in the moonlight. "Don't make light of what old folks tell you, son," he warned. "If the old folks say they seen slaves pick up and fly back to Africa, like birds, just don't you dispute them. If they tell you about a slave preacher what led his whole flock to the beach and sat down on the sand with them, looking across the ocean toward home, don't ask no questions. Next morning nobody could find trace of that preacher or his people. And no boat had been there neither. One day when I was chopping cotton in the field, I looked up and the old fellow working in the row next to mine was gone. He was too feeble to run away, and I couldn't see no place for him to hide. None of the others in the field saw him leave either, but later on an old woman drinking water at a well told us she noticed something pass in front of the sun about that time, like a hawk or a buzzard maybe, but she didn't pay it much mind."

Arna Bontemps, *Chariot in the Sky: A Story of the Jubilee Singers*

- **Using chronological order to explain a process**   When you tell how to do something or how something works, you are explaining a process. Often, this means telling how to do something step by step—what is done first, then next, and so on. The following paragraph tells how kites may have developed.

No one is quite sure how kite flying started. Perhaps an ancient Chinese first noticed big leaves of certain plants fluttering at the end of long vines. Then, after watching "leaf-kites" for a while, he tied his straw hat to a string just for fun and happily found that the wind kept it flying. Later, he may have stretched a piece of animal skin over a bamboo frame and flown that from the end of a line.

Dan Carlinsky, "Kites," *Boys' Life*

- **Using chronological order to explain causes and effects**

Chronological order is also used to explain a *cause-and-effect chain*. A **cause-and-effect chain** is a set of events that starts with a cause, and the effect that follows causes yet another event to occur. The chain continues with each event triggering yet another event, just as a stone thrown in the water causes a series of ripples. The following paragraph shows a cause-and-effect chain that started with some dogs getting sick.

> Dogs may be man's best friend. But to the lions of Serengeti National Park in Tanzania, dogs unintentionally have been worst enemies. In 1994, distemper, a deadly disease, started spreading to the lions from pet dogs living in villages near the park. Then it spread to lions in nearby Masai Mara Reserve in Kenya. Eventually distemper killed about 1,200 lions, reports biologist Craig Packer, who studies lions in Africa. In response, wildlife agents inoculated thousands of dogs against distemper. Now few animals catch the disease. Packer happily reports that the area's lion population has rebounded to 3,000, about as many as there were before the epidemic began.
>
> Scott Stuckey, "Lions Recover from Dog Disease," *National Geographic*

Cause

Effect/Cause

Effect/Cause

Effect/Cause

Effect/Cause
Effect

Exercise 6 **Arranging Details by Using Chronological Order**

Follow the directions for each item on the next page to practice telling about events in the order in which they happen.

A N S W E R S
Here are three sample responses.

1b. A tall, shy, new student enters your school.

- The new student showed up in October after all the other new kids had found friends.

- Every day I saw him eating by himself at lunch but ignored him.

- Then one day, some older kids threw my gym sneakers up into the basketball hoop so I couldn't reach them.

- The new kid came and pulled the sneakers down for me. He was so tall he could reach them easily.

- After that we became good friends.

2d. how to clean up your room

- First, set aside at least an hour to clean your room.

- Then, start making piles of clothes, books and magazines, CDs, and towels.

- Get rid of anything not needed.

- Wash dirty clothes and towels.

- Make your bed.

3e. missing the school bus

- I forgot to set the alarm so I overslept.

- I was so distracted from oversleeping that I left home without locking the door. I ran back to lock the door so I lost even more time, and I missed the school bus.

- I ended up walking two miles to school. When I got there, I noticed a big blister on my toe.

1. **Tell a story.** Select one of the following topics, and make up three or more events to include in a story about it. Arrange the events in chronological order.
   a. A mysterious light follows you down an empty street one night.
   b. A tall, shy new student enters your school. He has trouble fitting in at first, but soon the situation changes.
2. **Explain a process.** Pick one of the following activities. Then, list three or more steps involved in performing this activity. Arrange the steps in chronological order—that is, the order in which they should happen.
   c. how to wash a car
   d. how to clean up your room
3. **Explain cause and effect.** Create a cause-and-effect chain for one of the following situations.
   e. missing the school bus
   f. finding a litter of puppies

Spatial Order When you describe something, you often use *spatial order.* Spatial order organizes details according to their location. Think of a video camera shooting a scene. The camera acts as a roving eye, beginning in one place, then moving around to show viewers other parts of the scene. Writers use spatial order in much the same way. In the following paragraph, notice how the writer uses spatial order to describe her father's farm.

> The farm my father grew up on, where Grandpa Welty and Grandma lived, was in southern Ohio in the rolling hills of Hocking County, near the small town of Logan. It was one of the neat, narrow-porched, two-story farmhouses, painted white, of the Pennsylvania-German country. Across its front grew feathery cosmos and barrel-sized peony bushes with stripy heavy-scented blooms pushing out of the leaves. There was a springhouse to one side, down a little walk only one brick in width, and an old apple orchard in front, the barn and the pasture and fields of corn
>
> *(continued)*

(continued)

and wheat behind. Periodically there came sounds from the barn, and you could hear the crows, but everything else was still.

Eudora Welty, *One Writer's Beginnings*

Exercise 7 **Arranging Details by Using Spatial Order**

How would you describe an insect, a rock star, or a movie set? Working with one or two others, choose a subject below, and list details that describe it. Arrange the details in spatial order.

1. the most unusual animal you have ever seen
2. your favorite car
3. the best setting for a science fiction movie
4. your classroom, moments before a vacation break

Logical Order When you write about information that fits into categories, you will use *logical order.* For example, an informative paragraph about sea otters might group together details about where they live, then explain what they eat, and finally tell how they act. When you *compare and contrast,* it is logical to group related ideas together.

It is easy to confuse frogs with toads. After all, they have a similar body shape and are basically the same size, and both are amphibious. There are some observable differences, though, that can help you tell them apart. The first is their skin texture. Frogs have smooth skin, while toads' skin is more bumpy. Their body shapes are slightly different, too. Frogs look leaner and sleeker than toads. Finally, they move differently. Most frogs can leap long distances, while toads will usually take only small hops.

Comparison

Contrast

What Makes a Good Paragraph? **301**

ANSWER
Students should list details in a specific spatial order such as from far away to near, from left to right, or from top to bottom. Here are sample details.
3. the best setting . . .

- In the bank lobby, a huge revolving globe hangs under the skylight.
- An octagon-shaped elevator made of mirrors runs up to that globe.
- The floor is glass and robots work at the teller counter.

Meeting INDIVIDUAL NEEDS

LEARNERS HAVING DIFFICULTY
To help students who may be confused by the concept of comparing and contrasting, put a Venn diagram on the chalkboard. Leave the circles empty and label them *frogs* and *toads*. Have students complete the diagram with information from the paragraph on this page. Before you write their responses, ask students to consider if the information applies only to frogs or toads or to both frogs and toads. Remind students that the information in the center of the diagram shows how the two animals compare, and the information in the outer circles shows how they contrast.

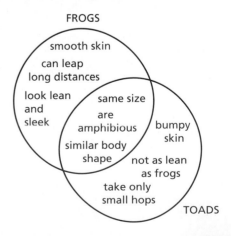

ANSWER

Students may benefit from placing
their answers in a Venn diagram or in
a chart. Here are possible points of
comparison and contrast for item 3.

**3. living in a large city and living
in a small community**

- In the city, you usually travel around
  by taxi, subway, or bus. In a small
  town, you usually drive or ride a
  bike. You can walk in both places.

- In the city, you usually see many
  people you don't know. In a town,
  you may see the same people all the
  time, so you may get to know most
  of them. In both cities and towns,
  you make some special friends.

- In the city, nights are bright and
  noisy. In a town, nights are usually
  dark and quiet. In both cities and
  towns, you can spend the evening
  in a restaurant.

Exercise 8 Arranging Details by Using Logical Order

Think about two subjects that are alike enough to be compared
yet different enough to be interesting. Write down three ways
that these subjects are alike and three ways that they are different. You might compare and contrast the following items:

1. being a child and being a teenager
2. live-action movies and animated movies
3. living in a large city and living in a small community

Transitional Words and Phrases

The second way of creating coherence in paragraphs is to use
transitional words or *phrases* to connect ideas. These are words
and phrases such as *for example, mainly,* and *in addition.* They
connect ideas and tell why and how they are related.

The following chart shows examples of some of the common
transitional words and phrases that help to create coherence.

Transitional Words and Phrases			
Comparing and Contrasting Ideas	also although and another but	however in the same way like likewise moreover	on the other hand similarly too unlike yet
Showing Cause and Effect	as a result because	consequently since	so therefore
Showing Time	about after at at last before during eventually	finally first, second, etc. immediately later meanwhile next	often soon then thereafter until when while

Transitional Words and Phrases			
Showing Place	above	beneath	into
	across	beside	near
	among	between	next
	around	by	over
	before	down	there
	behind	here	under
	below	in	
Showing Support	for example	for instance	in fact

The following paragraph tells how American Indians are recognized everywhere they go. The writer uses transitional words to show how ideas are connected. Notice, for example, how "at first" kids pretend not to see him. "Then," they turn and look.

> When I go someplace, most of the time those little people see me. At <u>first</u> they'll pretend not to see me. They go past me a little ways, and <u>then</u> they will turn back and look at me. <u>Then</u> they'll nudge their mama or daddy or grandma or grandpa, and I'll hear them say, "There's an Indian back there." So the Indians are still here. We never phased away. We didn't just blend into society and vanish. <u>In fact</u>, we're appearing more and more and more.
>
> Wallace H. Black Elk and William S. Lyon,
> *Black Elk: The Sacred Ways of a Lakota*

Exercise 9 Identifying Transitional Words and Phrases

Using the chart on pages 302–303 as a guide, make a list of all the <u>transitional words and phrases</u> in the paragraph that follows on the next page.

⎡STYLE ✏ TIP⎤

Another way to create coherence is to repeat key or similar words and phrases in your writing. For example, in the first few sentences of the paragraph to the left, the writer uses the words *look* and *see* to create a clear connection between ideas.

Meeting
INDIVIDUAL
NEEDS

INCLUSION

To assist students with transitions, have them use the example paragraphs on pages 303 and 304 to practice identifying transitions. Suggest that a helper read a paragraph aloud and then re-read it. During the second reading, the student should signal when he or she hears a transition. An alternative might be for the student to read silently beside the helper and to underline or point to the transitions.

⎡TECHNOLOGY TIP⎤

If you have access to computers, let students use word-processing programs to make final drafts of paragraphs they write. Then, help students see the structures of their paragraphs by using the program to underscore their topic sentences and to boldface all the transitional words or phrases. Also, encourage students to use the copy and paste features to reorder details, if necessary. You might wish to have students work in pairs, with one student at the keyboard and the other pointing out which sentences need reordering and which words require underscoring or boldface type.

Relating to Speaking

Explain to students that elaboration is essential to public speaking. A speaker cannot simply stand in front of people and deliver main ideas or topic sentences. Instead, the speaker must provide supporting details and elaboration to explain the ideas fully. Through the addition of details, facts, and examples, elaboration provides the audience with the information needed to make a decision about what the speaker is saying; and elaboration keeps the audience's interest, so it will listen to everything the speaker has to say. You might suggest that as students write paragraphs, they imagine that they will soon be reading them aloud to an audience. They can ask themselves what would help their audience stay engaged and interested.

When she was elected principal chief of the Cherokee Nation in 1987, Wilma Mankiller took on a huge job. She was used to challenges, though. For example, she had developed many needed projects for Cherokees in rural Oklahoma in 1976. First, she taught people how to build their own homes. Next, she installed new water supply lines. Finally, she started new rural health clinics. Then, she had to overcome serious injuries she suffered in an auto accident in late 1979. While others were impressed with the new chief's dedication, no one who really knew her well found her leadership ability surprising. Once elected chief, Mankiller continued her work to improve Cherokee communities. She focused on housing and education needs, and she encouraged her people to be proud of their language and culture. After serving two terms as chief, Wilma Mankiller continued to work for the Cherokee Nation by speaking across the country.

Reference Note

For more information and practice on adding **supporting details,** see page 293.

Elaboration

A good paragraph does not give just bare facts. It *elaborates,* or expands, on the supporting details so that readers get enough information to understand the subject. To elaborate, you must expand an idea by using *details, facts,* or *examples.* A writer who does not elaborate risks leaving the reader with an unclear or incomplete picture of the subject.

The paragraph below has a main idea and supporting details, but the supporting details need more elaboration.

```
Cheetahs are the fastest animals
on land. A typical cheetah runs faster
than a car moving at average speed.
Cheetahs can sprint so well because their
bodies are adapted for speed. Cheetahs
use this incredible speed to hunt prey
and to outrun predators.
```

MINI-LESSON

Elaborating with Adjective and Adverb Phrases. Explain that students can further elaborate supporting details by using adjective and adverb phrases. Remind them that an adjective phrase modifies a noun or a pronoun. An adverb phrase modifies a verb, an adjective, or another adverb. Write the following paragraph on the chalkboard. Ask students to underline each adjective or adverb phrase, identify the type of phrase, and tell what word it modifies.

Now read the elaborated paragraph. Notice how the writer has expanded on the supporting details by adding several new facts, a new example, and a new detail. Does this new information give you a clearer picture of the subject?

Cheetahs are the fastest animals on land. A typical cheetah runs faster than a car moving at average speed. In **New fact** fact, cheetahs can move from a standstill to 45 miles per **New fact** hour in two seconds. Their top speed has been clocked at 70 miles per hour, as fast as many highway speed limits. Cheetahs can sprint so well because their bodies are adapted for speed. They have **New** small heads, short ears, and **example** long sleek bodies. Unlike other cats, they also have **New detail** claws that do not retract. Their nonretractable claws **New fact** enable them to turn corners quickly and maintain good traction. Cheetahs use this incredible speed to hunt prey and to outrun predators.

Exercise 10 **Elaborating Details**

The following paragraph does not have enough elaboration. Add details, facts, or examples to improve the paragraph. Be ready to explain the elaboration strategies you used.

Getting to school on time is not easy. I usually have to wait in line to get in the bathroom. Then, I have to pick out something to wear. Finally, I have to make my own breakfast. Sometimes I think school should start an hour later.

Exercise 10 **Elaborating Details**

ANSWER
Here is a sample answer. The elaboration is italicized and labeled in brackets.

Getting to school on time is not easy. *Since there are three other kids in the family,* I usually have to wait in line to get in the bathroom. [*fact*] Then, I have to pick out something to wear, *which isn't easy either, because in Texas, it can be hot or freezing in January.* [*detail*] Finally, I have to make my own breakfast. *My choices are toast and eggs, which take time, or cold cereal.* [*example*] Sometimes I think school should start an hour later *because I am always rushing to catch the bus, which usually arrives at 7:30 A.M.* [*fact*]

My dog Tippy's brown eyes sparkle <u>with friendliness</u>. [*adverb:* sparkle] She has a pointed snout <u>with a few whiskers</u>. [*adjective:* snout] The triangular tip <u>of her left ear</u> always flops down slightly. [*adjective:* tip] Tippy weighs forty-five pounds and stands <u>about eighteen inches high</u>. [*adverb:* stands] Tippy wags her tail, which is the sign <u>of a happy dog</u>. [*adjective:* sign]

For more information about adjective and adverb phrases, see pp. 404–407.

What Are
the Types of
Paragraphs?

OBJECTIVES

■ To identify four types of paragraphs

■ To divide a longer piece of writing
into paragraphs

Quotation for the Day

❝You are just a puzzled man making
notes about what you think.❞

(Walter Lippmann, 1899–1974,
American journalist)

Write the quotation on the chalkboard
and explain that Lippmann was a journalist. While Lippmann may have been
talking about himself and his own
writing as a process of exploration
and questioning, his comment can
apply to students' writings. Ask students to discuss how they use questions in the process of writing and
what kinds of questions they are trying to answer in their writing.

Reference Note

For more information
and practice on
chronological order,
see page 297.

What Are the Types of
Paragraphs?

There are four different types of paragraphs.

Narrative	used to tell a story or a sequence of events
Descriptive	used to describe a scene or an object
Expository	used to provide information, including facts, instructions, and definitions
Persuasive	used to share opinions and convince others to agree or take action

The type of paragraph you use will depend on your *purpose
for writing.* To **entertain** readers or **express** themselves, writers
use narration or description. Exposition and narration are used
to **inform** readers about something. Writers use persuasion to
influence people. Several paragraphs written about the same
subject might be very different, depending on why the writers
wrote them. The four paragraphs that follow all talk about roller
coasters, but in different ways.

Narrative paragraphs tell about an event or series of events,
usually in chronological order. Most short stories and newspaper
articles are examples of narrative writing.

> Your knuckles are white, your palms are
> drenched, and it feels like your dentist has just
> switched on the drill. Worse still, as the click of the
> chain pulls the train skyward, you glance back at
> the gum-chewing guy who strapped you in and
> wonder what possessed you to put your life in the
> hands of a kid you wouldn't trust to wrap your
> sandwich. That's when you realize: This is all a big
> mistake. Only now you're at the top, staring into
> the air, the track seems to have vanished, and the
> car teeters on the edge of nothingness. Then grav-
> ity takes hold and whooooaa . . . you're hurtling
>
> *(continued)*

RESOURCES

What Are the Types of Paragraphs?
Practice

■ *Sentences and Paragraphs,* WS. pp. 39, 40

(continued)

earthward. Faster, faster. Suddenly you're upside down, spinning around corners, praying for it all to end. Minutes later the shoulder bar rises, you stagger out on wobbly knees . . . and hey, where's that kid? Maybe he'll let us ride up front this time.

Anne-Marie O'Neill, "On a Roll," *People Weekly*

Descriptive paragraphs do exactly what you think they do; they describe a person, an object, or a scene in detail.

> Rising ominously from the frozen Muskegon landscape, it is a sight both exhilarating and unnerving, this man-made mountain range of wood. Under a cold grey sky, the soul of this creation waits in silent hibernation for the warmth of spring. Then, when the clouds part, the snows melt, and the earth awakens, *it shall be silent no more.* A gorgeous, textbook example of the classic "out-and-back" roller coaster, Shivering Timbers will be Michigan's largest coaster. Even more, this humongous lumber wonder will rank as the third longest wooden coaster in the United States.
>
> "1998 Preview," Thrillride! Web site

Expository paragraphs are used for explanation. They can list facts, give directions, or explain ideas. Writers also use expository paragraphs to define terms, make comparisons, and show cause and effect. Since information in expository writing can usually be put into categories, it often uses logical order.

> In the Nickel Empire, attractions grew bigger, faster, weirder: horses diving from platforms; "guess men" who guessed your weight, age, occupation; clowns with cattle prods who mildly shocked innocent bystanders. Every amusement park had its Ferris wheel, but only Coney Island
>
> *(continued)*

Reference Note

For more information and practice on **spatial order,** see page 300.

Reference Note

For more information and practice on **logical order,** see page 301.

What Are the Types of Paragraphs? **307**

Critical Thinking

Analysis. Have students of different abilities work in groups of four to analyze the characteristics of each of the types of paragraphs. Assign each group one of the paragraphs about roller coasters on pp. 306–308. Have students read the paragraph at least twice before they answer the following questions.

- What kind of paragraph is it?

- What is the paragraph about? [*Each discusses roller coasters.*]

- Does the author use formal or informal language? Are all the sentences complete? Is there slang? [*Narrative: informal; no; yes Descriptive: informal; yes; yes Expository: informal; yes; no Persuasive: formal; yes; no*]

- Does the paragraph tell a story? [*Narrative only*]

- Does the author include sensory details? [*yes in Narrative, Descriptive, Expository*]

- Does the paragraph include many facts, dates, statistics, and examples? [*yes in Expository, Persuasive*]

- Is the paragraph trying to convince you to do or to think something? What? [*yes in Persuasive; to ride the roller coaster*]

After students have completed the questions, discuss their answers as a class.

(continued)

had the Wonder Wheel, with cages that rocked and slid along tracks inside the 135-foot disk. In 1920 the Wonder Wheel replaced the Statue of Liberty as the first sight immigrants saw as they sailed into New York Harbor. Pumping up the adrenaline, Coney's showmen built roller coasters with hair-raising names like the Tornado, the Thunderbolt, and in 1927, the Cyclone. With its 60-mile-per-hour plunge, the Cyclone soon drew lines five hours long. Charles Lindbergh has been quoted as calling the coaster "a greater thrill than flying an airplane at top speed."

Bruce Watson, "Three's a Crowd, They Say, But Not at Coney Island!" *Smithsonian*

Persuasive paragraphs are used to share an opinion about a particular subject. Writers of persuasive paragraphs try to convince readers to agree with the opinions in the paragraphs and, sometimes, to take action. A persuasive paragraph often uses *order of importance.*

Reference Note

For more on **order of importance,** see page 218.

Going on amusement park rides is one of the safest forms of recreation. According to the International Association of Amusement Park Attractions, you are more likely to be injured when you play sports, ride a horse, or even ride a bicycle. Statistics show the occurrence of death to be approximately one in 250 million riders. This group's statistics are supported by those of the National Consumer Product Safety Commission. It estimates that more than 270 million people visit amusement parks each year, and that 7,000 people out of those 270 million go to emergency rooms for injuries they receive on amusement park rides—that's only 0.00259 percent of riders.

"Amusement Park Physics," *Learner on Line* Web site

With two or three other students, find an example of each of the four paragraph types in magazines, newspapers, books, or on Web sites. Then, answer the following questions for each paragraph.

1. Do you think the paragraph is narrative, descriptive, expository, or persuasive? How can you tell?
2. How are the details organized in each paragraph (chronologically, spatially, logically)? How do you know? Could the information have been organized in a different way? How?
3. What was the writer's purpose for writing each piece (to entertain, inform, influence, express)? Does your group feel that the writer achieved his or her purpose? Why?

How Are Paragraphs Used in Longer Pieces of Writing?

So far, you have had practice with paragraphs that can stand on their own or are part of the body of a longer piece of writing. There are two other kinds of paragraphs you will need to use in your writing: *introduction* and *conclusion* paragraphs. The body paragraphs in a composition are like the supporting details in a paragraph—they serve as the filling for your "idea sandwich." Introduction and conclusion paragraphs are the bread for that sandwich. They are like larger versions of your topic and clincher sentences.

Dividing a Piece into Paragraphs

When you write a longer piece, you need to divide the body into paragraphs to give your readers' eyes a rest and to switch to a new main idea. To help your readers understand changes in a longer piece of writing, start a new paragraph when

- you express a new or different main idea
- you explain another part of your subject or step in a process
- you provide another kind of support for your opinion
- the setting—time or location—of your piece changes
- a different person or character speaks

Reference Note

For more on **introductions** and **conclusions,** see "Writing" in the Quick Reference Handbook.

Exercise 11 Identifying Types of Paragraphs

Ask students to submit their paragraphs with their comments and the pertinent material labeled and highlighted or underlined. Have students also submit a list of names of those in their group.

Meeting
INDIVIDUAL NEEDS

MULTIPLE INTELLIGENCES
Intrapersonal Intelligence. To help students understand the role of paragraphs in a longer piece of writing, have them sit quietly with their eyes closed or covered. Now, ask them to imagine that they are going to build a house of cards or blocks, or a human pyramid. Tell them to imagine how they would carefully arrange the cards, blocks, or acrobats, first creating a strong foundation and then slowly building upward. After students visualize the completed structure, ask them to imagine that one of the cards, blocks, or acrobats is pulled out. What happens? [*The structure falls down.*] Discuss with students how paragraphs in a composition are like the individual cards, blocks, or acrobats; all the pieces need to work together to support the structure of the whole.

Exercise 12 **Dividing a Piece into Paragraphs**

ANSWER

Here are suggested paragraph breaks, which create three paragraphs.

- "It was . . . one leg.'"

- "The students abandoned . . . seriously deformed."

- "Their discovery generated . . . affect us."

TECHNOLOGY TIP

If your classroom has an Internet connection, log on to the Holt, Rinehart and Winston Web site (http://www.hrw.com). Show a few of the pages on the site and ask students to notice how the text appears and to comment on the use of paragraphs. Students should recognize that because there is so much information on a Web page, paragraphs are essential for organizing the information. Without paragraphs, screens of uninterrupted text would overwhelm users. *You need to be aware that Internet resources are sometimes public forums, and their content can be unpredictable.*

Review A **Writing a Narrative Paragraph**

Students' narrative paragraphs should include the following features:

- a topic sentence that introduces the events of the narrative

- supporting sentences that describe events in chronological order

- a clincher sentence that sums up the narrative

┌HELP─

As you complete Exercise 12, keep in mind that there may be more than one correct way to divide the piece into paragraphs.

Exercise 12 **Dividing a Piece into Paragraphs**

The paragraph indentations from the following selection have been removed. Read the selection with a small group of classmates and decide where to start and end each paragraph.

> It was supposed to be a simple nature walk. In August 1995, eight middle school students and their teacher were hiking in a field near Henderson, Minnesota, as part of their study of the region's environment. But then they saw the frogs. "At first, when we saw that some of their back legs were twisted and bent or sticking straight out, we thought we had broken their legs," says Jack Bovee, now 16. "Then we found three or four that were missing one leg." The students abandoned their planned walk and headed to nearby Ney Pond to search for more frogs. "It seemed like the closer we got to the pond, the grosser the deformities," Jack says. "We saw one with three legs. It was like, Great, there's a problem here. Cool." By the end of the day, the students had caught twenty-two frogs. Half of them were seriously deformed. Their discovery generated much more than a couple of freaky frog jokes. The case of the deformed frogs has alarmed scientists across the country and turned into one of the nation's greatest environmental mysteries. Scientists want to know what happened to the frogs, and whether what's affecting them could affect us.
>
> Susan Hayes, "The Celebrated Deformed Frogs of Le Sueur County," *Scholastic Update*

Review A **Writing a Narrative Paragraph**

Write a narrative paragraph on one of the following topics. Use chronological (time) order to organize details in your supporting sentences.

- an event you saw recently

- a story you have heard before

Review B · Writing a Descriptive Paragraph

Apply what you have learned to write a descriptive paragraph on one of the following topics. Use plenty of sensory details to describe what your subject looks like, sounds like, smells like, and so on. Organize the details using spatial (place) order.

- a favorite pet or place
- a park you have visited

Review C · Writing an Expository Paragraph

This is the type of writing you will use most often, whether answering an essay test question or sharing your favorite recipe. Use an expository paragraph to explain what you know about a topic. Remember to support your main idea using facts, examples, and sensory details. Here are some ways you might approach your expository paragraph.

- Explain how to do something simple, such as tying shoelaces. (Use time order.)
- Compare and contrast two things, for example, dogs and cats. (Use logical order.)
- Provide information about a topic you know well, such as the history of hip-hop music or types of aquarium fish. (Use chronological order for history topics and logical order when explaining types of things.)

Review D · Writing a Persuasive Paragraph

You have probably used spoken persuasion since you were old enough to talk. Putting persuasion into writing gives you an edge, because you can better plan what you want to say. Remember that the supporting sentences of your persuasive paragraph should give good *reasons* for your opinion. Choose one of the following prompts and write a persuasive paragraph.

- Express your opinion about a school or community issue. For example, you might propose making passing periods between classes longer or building a new city park.
- Ask a parent for a privilege, such as a later bedtime.

Review B · Writing a Descriptive Paragraph

Students' descriptive paragraphs should include the following features:

- a topic sentence that states what is being described
- supporting sentences elaborated with sensory details and arranged in spatial order
- a clincher sentence that effectively ends the description

Review C · Writing an Expository Paragraph

Students' expository paragraphs should include the following features:

- a topic sentence that makes clear what is being explained
- supporting sentences elaborated with details, facts, and examples
- chronological order with appropriate transition words or phrases for either a process or cause and effect; or logical order with appropriate transition words or phrases to show comparison and contrast
- a clincher sentence that restates or confirms the topic sentence and sums up the entire explanation

Review D · Writing a Persuasive Paragraph

Students' paragraphs should include the following features:

- a topic sentence that includes an argument or opinion
- supporting sentences that provide reasons, facts, or examples
- a clincher sentence that reinforces the argument or opinion

RESOURCES

Learning About Paragraphs
Assessment

- *Assessment Package*
  —*Chapter Tests,* Ch. 9
  —*Chapter Tests in Standardized Test Formats,* Ch. 9
- *Test Generator (One-Stop Planner CD-ROM)*

Teaching Strands

This teaching-strand chart shows you a few of the possibilities for connecting grammar instruction more closely to the writing assignments in Part 1 of this textbook.

The *Elements of Language* grammar handbook is designed to be a flexible teaching tool that accommodates many teaching philosophies and styles. For example, some teachers will prefer to use the handbook as a reference source, having students refer to it only as the need for explicit grammar instruction arises. Others will use the handbook as a teaching text, having their classes work through the instruction, examples, and exercises in a more methodical fashion. Your personal teaching style and the needs of your students will determine the best way for you to teach this material.

 GO TO: go.hrw.com
KEYWORD: EOLang

 All resources for this chapter are available for preview on the *One-Stop Planner CD-ROM with Test Generator.* All worksheets and tests may be printed from the CD-ROM.

Writing Assignments	Rationale
EYEWITNESS ACCOUNT (Chapter 1)	To be exact, an eyewitness description should include proper pronoun use, strong verbs, vivid adjectives, precise adverbs, and correctly capitalized and punctuated supporting quotations.
INSTRUCTIONS (Chapter 2)	A paper that leads a reader through a process relies on use of adverbs indicating sequence, prepositions or subordinating conjunctions in transitional phrases, and clauses correctly punctuated.
ADVANTAGES/ DISADVANTAGES ESSAY (Chapter 3)	Effectively discussing two sides of an issue requires an understanding of adverbs such as *also, however,* and *therefore.* Using semicolons with independent clauses means understanding sentence structure as well as how semicolons, clauses, and conjunctions function.
BOOK JACKET (Chapter 4)	Book-jacket copy needs proper nouns to identify characters and setting and correctly punctuated quotations for the back cover. Working within the confines of a book-jacket margin means using hyphens correctly.
REPORT OF INFORMATION (Chapter 5)	An effective research report depends on clear language and credible information correctly spelled, quoted, and cited. Showing relationships between main ideas and supporting information may require using compound and complex sentences and conjunctive adverbs.
PERSUASIVE ARTICLE (Chapter 6)	An effective persuasive article makes skillful use of clear, exact adjectives and adverbs. Exclamatory sentences with strong active-voice verbs may be used to convey emotion; interrogative sentences may direct a line of thought.
PRINT ADVERTISEMENT (Chapter 7)	Advertisements often use interrogative, exclamatory, and imperative sentences. Pronouns may be used to speak directly to the customer. Comparative adjectives and adverbs such as *better* and *best* or *worse* and *worst* are common, as are testimonials that require proper use of quotation marks, dashes, and underlining (italics).

Links to Grammar	Links to Usage	Links to Mechanics
pronouns, adjectives (Ch. 11); adverbs (Ch. 12)	pronoun-antecedent agreement (Ch. 17); pronoun case (Ch. 19); comparison (Ch. 20)	quotation marks (Ch. 24)
verbs (Ch. 12)	verb tense, active voice (Ch. 18)	commas in a series (Ch. 23)
adverbs (Ch. 12)	comparison of modifiers (Ch. 20)	commas with introductory words and phrases (Ch. 23)
prepositional phrases (Ch. 14); subordinating conjunctions, subordinate clauses (Ch. 15)	placement of modifiers (Ch. 20)	commas with clauses (Ch. 23)
adverbs, conjunctions (Ch. 12); sentence structure (Ch. 16)		end punctuation, semicolons (Ch. 23)
clauses (Ch. 15)	placement of subordinate clauses, (Ch. 20); pronoun case with relative pronouns (Ch. 19)	commas with nonrestrictive clauses (Ch. 23)
proper nouns (Ch. 11); complements (Ch. 13)	subject-verb agreement with book titles (Ch. 17)	capital letters (Ch. 22)
varying sentence structure (Ch. 16)		quotation marks, hyphens (Ch. 24)
parts of speech (Ch. 11 & Ch. 12)	common errors (Ch. 21)	spelling words often confused (Ch. 25)
clauses (Ch. 15); sentence structure (Ch. 16)	correct placement of prepositional phrases and adjective clauses (Ch. 20)	underlining (italics), quotation marks (Ch. 24)
adjectives (Ch. 11); adverbs (Ch. 12)	comparison of adjectives and adverbs (Ch. 20)	commas in a series (Ch. 23)
kinds of sentences (Ch. 10)	subject-verb agreement with indefinite pronouns (Ch. 17)	question marks and exclamation marks (Ch. 23)
verbs (Ch. 12)	active voice (Ch. 18)	
kinds of sentences (Ch. 10)	subject-verb agreement with product names and indefinite pronouns (Ch. 17)	capital letters (Ch. 22); question marks, exclamation points (Ch. 23)
pronouns, adjectives (Ch. 11); adverbs (Ch. 12)	pronoun case (Ch. 19); comparison of adjectives and adverbs (Ch. 20)	quotation marks, underlining (italics), dashes (Ch. 24)

Grammar, Usage, and Mechanics

Grammar

Usage

Mechanics

internet **connect**

GO TO: go.hrw.com
KEYWORD: EOLang

Grammar, Usage, and Mechanics   313

The Sentence
Subject and Predicate, Kinds of Sentences

Diagnostic Preview

A. Identifying Sentences

Identify each of the following word groups as a *sentence* or a *sentence fragment*. If a word group is a sentence, write it in the correct form, using a capital letter at the beginning and adding the appropriate punctuation mark at the end.

EXAMPLES   **1.** having forgotten their homework
   1. sentence fragment

   2. how strong the wind is
   2. sentence—How strong the wind is!

1. after we visit the library and gather information for the research paper   **1.** frag.
2. are you ready for the big game next week?
3. listen closely to our guest speaker.
4. have read the first draft of my paper   **4.** frag.
5. an excellent short story, "The Medicine Bag," is in that book.
6. that we helped Habitat for Humanity to build   **6.** frag.
7. Mrs. Chin, our math teacher this year   **7.** frag.
8. be prepared to give your speech tomorrow.
9. fishing, skiing, and swimming in the lake   **9.** frag.
10. what a good idea you have, Amy!

314

B. Identifying Simple Subjects and Simple Predicates

Write the simple subject and the simple predicate in each of the following sentences.

EXAMPLE   1. A computer can be a wonderful tool for people with disabilities.

         1. *computer—simple subject; can be—simple predicate*

11. Specially designed machines have been developed in the past several years.
12. Have you ever seen a talking computer?
13. It is used mainly by people with visual impairments.
14. Most computers display writing on a screen.
15. However, these special models can give information by voice.
16. Closed-captioned television is another interesting and fairly recent invention.
17. Subtitles appear on the television screens of many hearing-impaired viewers.
18. These viewers can read the subtitles and enjoy their favorite television shows.
19. With a teletypewriter (TTY), people can type messages over phone lines.
20. Many new inventions and devices make life easier.

C. Punctuating and Classifying Sentences

Copy the last word of each of the following sentences, and then punctuate each sentence with the correct end mark. Classify each sentence as *declarative, interrogative, imperative,* or *exclamatory.*

EXAMPLE   1. Flowers and insects depend on one another for life

         1. *life.—declarative*

21. Have you ever watched a honeybee or a bumblebee in a garden?
22. The bee flies busily from one flower to another, drinking nectar.
23. Notice the yellow pollen that collects on the legs and body of the bee.
24. The bee carries pollen from flower to flower, helping the plants to make seeds.
25. What a remarkable insect the bee is!

21. int.
22. dec.
23. imp.
24. dec.
25. exc.

The Sentence

Rule 10a *(pp. 316–317)*

OBJECTIVES

- To identify sentences and sentence fragments
- To add capital letters to the beginnings of sentences
- To add correct punctuation to the ends of sentences

Relating to Writing

Explain to students that sentence fragments can sometimes go unnoticed in paragraphs because of the way in which information flows from one sentence to the next. However, when taken out of context, sentence fragments become more evident.

Ask students to locate a piece of their own writing to analyze for sentence completeness. First, have students highlight or circle each end mark. Then, ask them to consider each sentence separately—stopping at each highlighted end mark—to determine if the thought is complete. If not, they should revise the fragment to complete the sentence.

Meeting
INDIVIDUAL NEEDS

MODALITIES

Auditory Learners. To help students distinguish complete sentences from sentence fragments in **Exercise 1,** read aloud the examples.

Reference Note

For information on the use of **capital letters,** see page 572. For information on **end marks,** see page 598.

Reference Note

For information on **the understood subject,** see page 331.

STYLE TIP

Sentence fragments are common and acceptable in informal situations. However, in formal writing, you should avoid using sentence fragments.

COMPUTER TIP

Many grammar-checking software programs can help you identify sentence fragments. If you have access to such a program, use it to help you evaluate your writing.

Reference Note

For information on **revising sentence fragments,** see pages 269 and 685.

The Sentence

10a. A *sentence* is a word or word group that contains a subject and a verb and that expresses a complete thought.

A sentence begins with a capital letter and ends with a period, a question mark, or an exclamation point.

EXAMPLES   **S**he won a prize for her book**.**

Why did you stop running**?**

Wait**!** [The understood subject is *you*.]

Sentence or Sentence Fragment?

A *sentence fragment* is a group of words that looks like a sentence but does not contain both a subject and a verb or does not express a complete thought.

SENTENCE FRAGMENT	Sailing around the world. [The word group lacks a subject.]
SENTENCE	They are sailing around the world.
SENTENCE FRAGMENT	The hike through the Grand Canyon. [The word group lacks a verb.]
SENTENCE	The hike through the Grand Canyon was long and hard.
SENTENCE FRAGMENT	After they pitched the tent. [The word group contains a subject and a verb, but does not express a complete thought.]
SENTENCE	After they pitched the tent, they rested.

Exercise 1 **Identifying Sentences**

Identify each of the following word groups as a *sentence* or a *sentence fragment*. If a word group is a sentence, write it in the correct form, using a capital letter at the beginning and adding the appropriate punctuation mark at the end.

EXAMPLES   1. during her vacation last summer
1. *sentence fragment*

2. my friend Michelle visited Colorado
2. *sentence—My friend Michelle visited Colorado.*

RESOURCES

The Sentence

Practice

- *Grammar, Usage, and Mechanics,* pp. 2–4
- *Language Workshop CD-ROM,* Lessons 35, 36

1. <u>d</u>o you know what happened during Michelle's boat trip**?**
2. <u>d</u>own the rapids on the Colorado River
3. <u>a</u>t first her boat drifted calmly through the Grand Canyon**.**
4. <u>t</u>hen the river dropped suddenly**.**
5. and became foaming rapids full of dangerous boulders
6. many of which can break a boat
7. Michelle's boat was small**.**
8. with one guide and four passengers
9. <u>s</u>ome passengers prefer large inflatable boats with outboard motors**.**
10. carrying eighteen people

1. sent.
2. frag.
3. sent.
4. sent.
5. frag.
6. frag.
7. sent.
8. frag.
9. sent.

10. frag.

Subject and Predicate

Sentences consist of two basic parts: subjects and predicates.

The Subject

10b. The *subject* tells *whom* or *what* the sentence is about.

EXAMPLES   **Nicholasa Mohr** is a writer and an artist.

                The girls on the team were all good students.

                He shared his lunch with the boy on the other team.

                Swimming is good exercise.

To find the subject, ask *who* or *what* is doing something or *whom* or *what* is being talked about. The subject may come at the beginning, middle, or end of a sentence.

EXAMPLES   **The pitcher** struck Felicia out. [*Who* struck Felicia out? *The pitcher* did.]

                After practicing for hours, **Timmy** bowled two strikes. [*Who* bowled two strikes? *Timmy* did.]

                How kind **you** are! [*Who* is kind? *You* are.]

                When will **the afternoon train** arrive? [*What* will arrive? *The afternoon train* will.]

                Hiding in the tall grass was **a baby rabbit.** [*What* was hiding? *A baby rabbit* was.]

Reference Note

A compound noun, such as *Nicholasa Mohr,* is considered one noun. For information on **compound nouns,** see page 337.

Subject and Predicate   **317**

GRAMMAR

Subject and Predicate

Rules 10b–e *(pp. 317–325)*

OBJECTIVES

■ To complete sentences by adding subjects and end marks and by capitalizing first words

■ To identify the subjects of sentences

■ To identify simple and complete subjects in sentences

■ To identify verbs, verb phrases, and complete predicates in sentences

■ To complete sentences by adding predicates

Meeting
INDIVIDUAL
NEEDS

ENGLISH-LANGUAGE LEARNERS
General Strategies. In many languages other than English, the meaning of a sentence does not depend on word order. Consequently, sentence structure is much less restrictive than it is in English. Point out to students that, in most cases, the simple subject comes before the simple predicate in English declarative sentences.

Japanese and Korean. In Japanese, the subject is always followed by *wa* or *ga.* In Korean, the subject is always followed by *i* (pronounced "ee") or *ga.* When identifying the subject of a sentence, Japanese and Korean speakers may benefit by finding which English word(s) would be followed by a subject particle in their native languages.

Relating to Writing

Varying the position of the subject can add interest to students' writing. Have students select a story or poem that they have written. Then, ask them to circle the subject of each sentence and, using the following chart, to tally the position of each subject.

POSITION	TALLY
First word in sentence	
Following modifiers but preceding verb	
Following verb	
Surrounded by verbs (question)	

Suggest that students try revising selected sentences to vary the subject's position. Then, have students exchange papers to evaluate the changes.

Writing Subjects and Punctuating Sentences

Add subjects to fill in the blanks in the following sentences. Use a different subject in each sentence. Begin each sentence with a capital letter, and end it with a punctuation mark.   Answers will vary.

EXAMPLE   1. _____ is very heavy
        1. *This is very heavy.*

1. _____ is a difficult game to play.   **1.** Soccer
2. _____ works in the post office.   **2.** Jack
3. Luckily for me, _____ was easy to read.   **3.** this book
4. Tied to the end of the rope was _____.   **4.** a calf
5. Did _____ help you?   **5.** anyone
6. _____ eventually became President of the United States.   **6.** He
7. Have _____ always wanted to visit Peru?   **7.** the Millers
8. Luis, _____ was the score?   **8.** what
9. Before the game, _____ will meet in the gym.   **9.** Jo and Han
10. _____ has always been one of my favorite books.   **10.** That
11. What a great basketball player _____ is!   **11.** Amber
12. Has _____ called you yet?   **12.** your mother
13. In the afternoon _____ takes a nap.   **13.** my cat
14. _____ is playing at the theater this weekend?   **14.** What
15. When did _____ start making that sound?   **15.** the car
16. In a minute _____ will feed you, Spot.   **16.** I
17. Under the pile of leaves in the front yard was _____.   **17.** the ball
18. _____ is the group's best-known song?   **18.** What
19. In my opinion _____ is a better goalie than Alex.   **19.** she
20. Where in the world did _____ get that hat?   **20.** Michael

---

Simple Subject and Complete Subject

10c. The *simple subject* is the main word or word group that tells *whom* or *what* the sentence is about.

The *complete subject* consists of all the words that tell *whom* or *what* a sentence is about.

EXAMPLES   The four new students arrived early.

Complete subject	The four new students
Simple subject	students

⌐TIPS & TRICKS⌐

Here is a test you can use to find the simple subject of most sentences: If you leave out the simple subject, a sentence does not make sense.

EXAMPLE
The four new . . . arrived early.

MINI-LESSON

Spelling Compound Nouns. Explain to students that a simple subject could be composed of more than one word if the words are part of a compound noun. Some compound nouns are spelled as one word (*newspaper*); some are spelled as two or more words (*space station*); and some are hyphenated (*self-confidence*). Explain to students that a dictionary can be used to check the spelling of compound nouns.

Is the winner of the go-cart race present?

| Complete subject | the winner of the go-cart race |
| Simple subject | winner |

A round walnut table with five legs stood in the middle of the dining room.

| Complete subject | A round walnut table with five legs |
| Simple subject | table |

A simple subject may consist of one word or several words.

EXAMPLES **Jets** often break the sound barrier. [one word]

Does **Aunt Carmen** own a grocery store? [two words]

On the library shelf was ***The Island of the Blue Dolphins.*** [six words]

NOTE In this book, the simple subject is usually referred to as the *subject*.

Exercise 3   Identifying Subjects

Write the <u>subject</u> of each of the following sentences.

EXAMPLE **1.** A book by N. Scott Momaday is on the table.

    1. book

1. Born in 1934 in Oklahoma, <u>Momaday</u> lived on Navajo and Apache reservations in the Southwest.
2. Momaday's <u>father</u> was a Kiowa.
3. As a young man, <u>Momaday</u> attended the University of New Mexico and Stanford University.
4. In *The Way to Rainy Mountain*, <u>he</u> tells about the myths and history of the Kiowa people.
5. The <u>book</u> includes poems, an essay, and stories about the Kiowa people.
6. *<u>The Way to Rainy Mountain</u>* was published in 1969.
7. After Momaday's book came <u>works</u> by other modern American Indian writers.
8. <u>William Least Heat-Moon</u> traveled in a van across the United States and wrote about his journey.
9. Was <u>he</u> inspired to write by his travels?
10. <u>Readers</u> of this Osage writer enjoy his beautiful descriptions of nature.

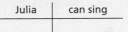 Link to Literature

Subject and Predicate **319**

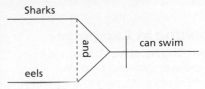
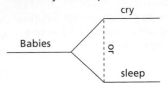
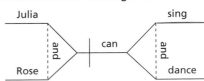
Subject and Predicate **319**

Cooperative Learning

To help students identify complete subjects and predicates, write complete subjects and complete predicates on separate strips of paper.

Divide the class into two equal groups, distributing complete-subject strips to one group and complete-predicate strips to the other. Make sure each student has a strip.

Have a student from the complete-subject group stand at the front of the class and display his or her strip. Then, have the complete-predicate group decide which of them holds a matching strip. After that student joins his or her counterpart at the front of the class, have the students arrange themselves to make a complete sentence.

As you continue, have the two groups take turns being the first in front of the class.

Looking at Language

Word Origins. Have students look up the word *predicate* in an unabridged dictionary and identify the word's origin (Latin) and original meaning (to proclaim or preach). Point out that the predicate "proclaims" something about the noun. If students do not know the definition of *proclaim,* point out the use of *tell* in **Rule 10d.**

Link to Literature

Exercise 4 **Identifying Complete Subjects and Simple Subjects**

Write the complete subject in each of the following sentences. Then, underline the simple subject.

EXAMPLES
1. Stories about time travel make exciting reading.
   1. *Stories about time travel*

2. Samuel Delany writes great science fiction.
   2. *Samuel Delany*

1. Ray Bradbury is also a writer of science fiction.
2. The Golden Apples of the Sun is a collection of Bradbury's short stories.
3. Is your favorite story in that book "A Sound of Thunder"?
4. The main character in the story is called Mr. Eckels.
5. For ten thousand dollars, Mr. Eckels joins Time Safari, Inc.
6. He is looking for the dinosaur *Tyrannosaurus rex.*
7. With four other men, Bradbury's hero travels more than sixty million years back in time.
8. On the safari, trouble develops.
9. Because of one mistake, the past is changed.
10. Do the results of that mistake affect the future?

The Predicate

10d. The *predicate* of a sentence tells something about the subject.

EXAMPLES   The phone **rang.**

Old Faithful **is a giant geyser in Yellowstone National Park.**

Jade Snow Wong **wrote about growing up in San Francisco's Chinatown.**

Like the subject, the predicate may be found anywhere in a sentence.

EXAMPLES   **Outside the tent was** a baby bear.

Late in the night we **heard a noise.** [The predicate in this sentence is divided by the subject, *we.*]

Has the dough **risen enough**? [The predicate is divided by the subject, *the dough*.]

Stop right there! [The subject in this sentence is understood to be *you*.]

Exercise 5 **Identifying Predicates**

Write the predicate in each of the following sentences.

EXAMPLES
    1. My favorite sports poster is this one of Roberto Clemente.
      1. *is this one of Roberto Clemente*

    2. Have you heard of this famous sports hero?
      2. *Have heard of this famous sports hero*

1. Also among my baseball treasures is a book about Clemente's life and career.
2. Clemente played right field for the Pittsburgh Pirates, my favorite team.
3. During his amazing career, he won four National League batting titles.
4. In 1966, he was named the league's Most Valuable Player.
5. Twice Clemente helped lead the Pirates to World Series victories.
6. In fourteen World Series games, Clemente never went without a hit.
7. Roberto Clemente died in a plane crash off the coast of his homeland, Puerto Rico.
8. The plane crash occurred on a flight to Nicaragua to aid earthquake victims.
9. After his death, Clemente was elected to the National Baseball Hall of Fame.
10. In New York, a park has been named for this beloved ballplayer.

Subject and Predicate   **321**

Exercise 5

ALTERNATIVE LESSON
After students have completed this exercise, have them identify the complete subject in sentences 1, 3, 5, and 10. [1. *a book about Clemente's life and career;* 3. *he;* 5. *Clemente;* 10. *a park*] Emphasize that any word not included in the complete subject is part of the complete predicate. Students can use this information to check their answers for the exercise.

Crossing the Curriculum

Science. Tell students that the simple subject and simple predicate of a sentence are sometimes called its *skeleton*. Like the body's skeleton, the subject and predicate form a framework—a base that supports everything else. Lead a discussion about how other parts of the sentence are like other body systems.

Exercise 6 Writing Predicates

Make a sentence out of each of the following word groups by adding a predicate to fill the blank or blanks.   Answers will vary.

EXAMPLES   1. A flock of geese ____
            1. *A flock of geese flew high overhead.*

            2. ____ a poster of Nelson Mandela.
            2. *Over Kim's desk hung a poster of Nelson Mandela.*

1. My favorite food ____.   1. is spinach
2. A course in first aid ____.   2. is offered here
3. ____ our car ____?   3. Does, look purple
4. Rock climbing ____.   4. is fun   5. were looking for gold
5. Spanish explorers in the Americas ____.
6. Several computers ____.   6. were given to our school
7. ____ a new pair of roller skates.   7. In the box was
8. The skyscrapers of New York City ____.   8. loomed above us
9. Some dogs ____.   9. chase cars
10. ____ my family ____.   10. In June, is going to Mexico
11. Winning the championship ____.   11. is his dream
12. ____ all sorts of birds ____.   12. At night, roost there
13. The new store at the mall ____.   13. opened last week
14. ____ a small, brown toad.   14. There is
15. The flowers in Mr. Alvarez's garden ____.   15. bloom in spring
16. ____ my chores ____.   16. Now, are finished
17. Gerry's allowance ____.   17. has been spent
18. ____ we ____?   18. Where are, going
19. The cool of the morning ____.   19. was soothing
20. The tiny kittens ____.   20. crawled out of the basket

Simple Predicate and Complete Predicate

10e. The *simple predicate*, or *verb*, is the main word or word group that tells something about the subject.

The *complete predicate* consists of a verb and all the words that describe the verb and complete its meaning.

EXAMPLES   The pilot broke the sound barrier.

            Complete predicate   broke the sound barrier
            Simple predicate (verb)   broke

Learning for Life

Letters to the Editor. Clear writing relies on complete sentences. To show students examples of clear, complete sentences, bring to class some letters to the editor. Try to include a variety of sources: school, neighborhood, city, and national newspapers as well as various magazines.

Have students work in small groups to compile lists of guidelines for such a letter. As each group shares its guidelines with the rest of the class, write on the chalkboard the following list:

We should have visited the diamond field in Arkansas.

Complete predicate	should have visited the diamond field in Arkansas
Simple predicate (verb)	should have visited

The telephone on the table rang.

Complete predicate	rang
Simple predicate (verb)	rang

NOTE In this book, the simple predicate is usually referred to as the *verb*.

Exercise 7 **Identifying Complete Predicates and Verbs**

Write the complete predicate of each of the following sentences. Then, underline the verb.

EXAMPLE 1. Who created the U.S. flag?
1. *created the U.S. flag*

1. Many scholars are unsure about the history of the Stars and Stripes.
2. The Continental Congress approved a design for the flag.
3. The flag's design included thirteen red stripes and thirteen white stripes.
4. The top inner quarter of the flag was a blue field with thirteen white stars.
5. The name of the designer has remained a mystery.
6. During the American Revolution, the colonists needed a symbol of their independence.
7. George Washington wanted flags for the army.
8. Unfortunately, the flags did not arrive until the end of the Revolutionary War.
9. According to legend, Betsy Ross made the first flag.
10. However, most historians doubt the Betsy Ross story.

The Verb Phrase

Some simple predicates, or verbs, consist of more than one word. Such verbs are called *verb phrases* (verbs that include one or more helping verbs).

EXAMPLE Kathy **is riding** the Ferris wheel.

Reference Note
For information on **helping verbs,** see page 361.

Relating to Literature

If your literature textbook contains the Randall Jarrell poem "The Chipmunk's Day," have students read the poem and identify the simple predicate of each sentence. Then, ask what effect is created in the first three stanzas by placing the simple predicates at the ends of the lines where they appear. [*The placement emphasizes the chipmunk's rapid movements.*] Ask students what shift in emphasis is produced by placing the simple predicates in the last stanza at the beginning of the lines where they appear. [*The focus shifts from the chipmunk's quick activity to its burrow.*]

- is brief
- has a strong, clear opinion statement
- has supporting information that is organized logically
- has emotional appeal
- has a strong ending

Then, ask students to work individually to write letters to the editor. Encourage them to focus on issues about which they feel strongly and to target specific publications. Remind students to check their letters for sentence completeness.

ENGLISH-LANGUAGE LEARNERS

General Strategies. In some languages, verbs always appear at the ends of sentences. Consequently, speakers of such languages might expect to find verbs at the end of English sentences.

Make sure students know that verbs in English can appear anywhere in English sentences. You may want to share the following examples:

1. Beginning: *Listen to the rain.*

2. Middle: *Most of the players scored in last night's basketball game.*

3. End: *Please go.*

Reference Note

For information on **adverbs,** see page 366.

EXAMPLES   The carnival **has been** in town for two weeks.

Should Imelda **have gotten** here sooner?

NOTE   The words *not* and *never* are not verbs; they are adverbs. They are never part of a verb or verb phrase.

EXAMPLES   She **has** not **written** to me recently.

I **will** never **forget** her.

They **do**n't **know** my cousins. [*Don't* is the contraction of *do* and *not*. The *n't* is not part of the verb phrase *do know.*]

Exercise 8   **Identifying Verbs and Verb Phrases**

Write the verb or verb phrase in each of the following sentences.

EXAMPLES   1. Look at these beautiful pictures of Hawaii.
    1. Look

    2. They were taken by our science teacher.
    2. were taken

1. Hawaii is called the Aloha State.
2. It was settled by Polynesians about 2,000 years ago.
3. The musical heritage and rich culture of the original Hawaiians have contributed to the islands' popularity.
4. Have you ever seen a traditional Hawaiian dance, one with drums and chants?
5. The Hawaiian islands are also known for their lush, exotic scenery.
6. I can certainly not imagine anything more spectacular than an active volcano at night.
7. Would you like a helicopter ride over misty waterfalls like those in Hawaii?
8. What an incredible sight that surely is!
9. Those Hawaiian dancers must have been practicing for years.
10. Save me a place on the next flight!

Finding the Subject

To find the subject of a sentence, find the verb first. Then, ask "Who?" or "What?" before the verb.

EXAMPLES   In high school we will have more homework. [The verb is *will have. Who* will have? *We* will have. *We* is the subject of the sentence.]

Can you untie this knot? [*Can untie* is the verb. *Who* can untie? *You* can untie. *You* is the subject of the sentence.]

The peak of Mount Everest was first reached by Sir Edmund Hillary and Tenzing Norgay. [The verb is *was reached. What* was reached? *Peak* was reached. *Peak* is the subject of the sentence.]

Ahead of the explorers lay a vast wilderness. [The verb is *lay. What* lay? *Wilderness* lay. *Wilderness* is the subject of the sentence.]

Where are the Canary Islands located? [*Are located* is the verb. *What* are located? *Canary Islands* are located. *Canary Islands* is the subject of the sentence.]

Pass the salad, please. [*Pass* is the verb. *Who* should pass? *You* pass. Understood *you* is the subject of the sentence.]

Compound Subjects and Compound Verbs

Compound Subjects

10f. A *compound subject* consists of two or more subjects that are joined by a conjunction and that have the same verb.

The conjunctions most commonly used to connect the words of a compound subject are *and* and *or.*

EXAMPLES   **Paris** and **London** remain favorite tourist attractions. [The two parts of the compound subject have the same verb, *remain.*]

Nelson Mandela or **Archbishop Desmond Tutu** will speak at the conference. [The two parts of the compound subject have the same verb, *will speak.*]

Among my hobbies are **reading, snorkeling,** and **painting.** [The three parts of the compound subject have the same verb, *are.*]

┌─ TIPS & TRICKS ─┐

When you are looking for the subject of a sentence, remember that the subject is never part of a prepositional phrase. Cross through any prepositional phrases; the subject will be one of the remaining words.

EXAMPLE
Several ~~of the puzzle pieces~~ are ~~under the sofa.~~

SUBJECT
Several

VERB
are

Reference Note
For information on **prepositional phrases,** see page 371.

Reference Note
For information on **conjunctions,** see page 374.

Subject and Predicate   **325**

Compound Subjects and Compound Verbs
Rules 10f, g *(pp. 325–330)*

OBJECTIVES

■ **To identify compound subjects, compound verbs, and verb phrases in sentences**

■ **To create sentences by adding compound subjects to predicates**

TEACHING TIP

Activity. To help students visualize the concept of compound subjects and compound verbs, give magazines to students and ask them to find photographs that depict actions involving several things or people. Then, work with students to write sentences using compound subjects and compound verbs that describe the photographs. Encourage students to vary the connecting words they use. Suggest that students read their sentences aloud and listen to determine whether they have used compound subjects and compound verbs correctly.

Relating to Literature

If the E. E. Cummings selection "maggie and milly and molly and may" appears in your literature textbook, have your students read the poem and identify the compound subjects [*maggie and milly and molly and may*]. Ask students to explain how Cummings treats the compound subjects. [*He places* an *and* between *each name.*] Ask students what might be inferred from this treatment. [*Students might suggest that the girls know each other.*]

Ask students to write sentences about things they have done with their friends and to create a compound subject as E. E. Cummings does. Remind students that poems sometimes take liberties with the rules of standard (or formal) English and that they should keep in mind the difference between creative and standard, formal usage.

⌐ TIPS & TRICKS ⌐

In sentences with a compound subject joined by *or,* the verb agrees with the subject closest to it. Here is a quick test you can use. (1) Cover the part of the subject that is farther from the verb. (2) Decide whether the remaining part of the compound subject agrees with the verb.

EXAMPLE
Janie or her parents (is, are) coming. [*Her parents is coming* or *her parents are coming? Her parents are coming* is correct.]

ANSWER
Janie or her parents **are** coming.

Exercise 9 **Identifying Compound Subjects**

Write the compound subject in each of the following sentences.

EXAMPLE 1. The shapes and sizes of sand dunes are determined by the wind.

    1. shapes, sizes

1. The national <u>parks</u> and <u>monuments</u> of the United States include many of the world's most spectacular landforms.
2. The <u>Grand Canyon</u> and the <u>waterfalls</u> of Yosemite are examples of landforms shaped by erosion.
3. <u>Water</u>, <u>wind</u>, and other natural <u>forces</u> are continuing the age-old erosion of landforms.
4. On the Colorado Plateau, for example, natural <u>bridges</u> and <u>arches</u>, like the one in the photograph on the left, have been produced by erosion.
5. Likewise, <u>Skyline Arch</u> and <u>Landscape Arch</u> in Utah are two natural arches formed by erosion.
6. Underground, <u>caves</u> and immense <u>caverns</u> are created by rushing streams and waterfalls.
7. <u>Stalagmites</u> and <u>stalactites</u>, such as the ones in the photograph on the right, are formed by lime deposits from drops of water seeping into these caverns.

8. In river systems throughout the world, <u>canyons</u> and <u>gorges</u> are cut into the earth by erosion.
9. Many <u>rapids</u> and <u>waterfalls</u> have also originated through the process of erosion.
10. Do steep <u>areas</u> with heavy rainfall or dry <u>regions</u> with few trees suffer more from erosion?

326 **Chapter 10** The Sentence

Exercise 10   Writing Compound Subjects

Add a compound subject to each of the following predicates. Use *and* or *or* to join the parts of your compound subjects.

EXAMPLE   1. ____ were at the bottom of my locker.

   1. *My bus pass and a pair of gym socks were at the bottom of my locker.*

1. Yesterday ____ arrived in the mail.
2. ____ make loyal pets.
3. On the beach ____ spotted a dolphin.
4. ____ will present their report on the adventures of Álvar Núñez Cabeza de Vaca.
5. In the attic were piled ____ .
6. Ever since first grade, ____ have been friends and neighbors.
7. Is ____ coaching the tennis team this year?
8. For Indian food, ____ always go to the Bombay Cafe in the shopping center nearby.
9. To our great surprise, out of my little brother's pockets spilled ____ .
10. Both ____ may be seen on the African plains.

Compound Verbs

10g. A *compound verb* consists of two or more verbs that are joined by a conjunction and that have the same subject.

The conjunctions most commonly used to connect the words of a compound verb are *and*, *or*, and *but*.

EXAMPLES   The rain **has fallen** for days and **is** still **falling.**

   The team **played** well but **lost** the game anyway.

   Will Rolando **mop** the floor or **wash** the dishes?

   A sentence may contain both a *compound subject* and a *compound verb*. Notice in the following example that both subjects carry out the action of both verbs.

EXAMPLE   A few **vegetables** and many **flowers sprouted** and **grew** in the rich soil. [The vegetables sprouted and grew, and the flowers sprouted and grew.]

Answers
Exercise 10
Compound subjects will vary. Here are some possibilities:
1. four letters and a magazine
2. Dogs and birds
3. Daniel or Chandra
4. My sister and her friend
5. suitcases and picture albums
6. Kerry, Steven, and I
7. Hector or Alicia
8. Kimrey and I
9. a compass, six coins, and a toad
10. lions and zebras

| S T Y L E | T I P |

Using compound subjects and verbs, you can combine ideas to make your writing less wordy. Compare the examples below.

WORDY
   Orville and Wilbur Wright built one of the first airplanes. Orville and Wilbur Wright flew it near Kitty Hawk, North Carolina.

REVISED
   Orville and Wilbur Wright **built** one of the first airplanes and **flew** it near Kitty Hawk, North Carolina.

Relating to Writing

Have students volunteer examples of verbs, and make a list of the suggestions on the board. Tell students they will write a four-line poem using at least two combinations of verbs from the list as compound verbs. To get started, have the class compose a poem together orally while you or a helper transcribes the work in progress on the chalkboard or a transparency.

Subject and Predicate   **327**

MINI-LESSON   *Continued on pp. 328–329*

Compound Verb or Compound Sentence? Because of the punctuation needed in a compound sentence, students should distinguish between compound sentences and simple sentences with compound verbs.

Write the following examples on the chalkboard:

   Eric runs track and plays soccer.

   Maurice writes poetry in his spare time, and Elayne paints portraits.

Critical Thinking

Metacognition. After students have completed **Exercise 12,** ask the following questions:

• When identifying subjects and verbs, which do you look for first? Why? Does identifying one help you find the other?

• How do you know whether a subject or verb is compound?

Exercise 11 | Identifying Compound Verbs

Write each compound verb or verb phrase in the following sentences.

EXAMPLE   1. Have you heard of the game Serpent or learned the game Senet?
            1. *have heard, learned*

1. Just like children today, children in ancient Egypt played games and enjoyed toys.
2. For the Egyptian board game Serpent, players found or carved a serpent-shaped stone.
3. Players placed the serpent in the center of the board and then began the game.
4. They used place markers and threw bones or sticks as dice.
5. The players took turns and competed with one another in a race to the center.
6. Senet was another ancient Egyptian board game and was played by children and adults alike.
7. Senet looked like an easy game but was actually difficult.
8. Players moved their playing pieces toward the ends of three rows of squares but sometimes were stopped by their opponents.
9. Senet boards were complex and had certain squares for good luck and bad luck.
10. These squares could help players or could block their pieces.

Exercise 12 | Identifying Subjects and Verbs

Identify the subject and verb in each of the following sentences.

EXAMPLE   1. American pioneers left their homes and traveled to the West.
            1. *pioneers—subject; left, traveled—verbs*

1. Settlers faced and overcame many dangers.
2. Mount McKinley and Mount Whitney are two very high mountains.
3. Sacagawea of the Shoshone people helped open the West to explorers and settlers.
4. Every winter many skiers rush to the Grand Tetons.

MINI-LESSON

Explain that if a sentence is compound, a comma generally precedes a coordinating conjunction such as *and, but, or, nor, for, so,* or *yet.* No commas, however, are needed for compound verbs.

Ask students to write the following sentences and exchange their papers with partners to check for correct structure and punctuation:

• A simple sentence with one subject and one verb

• A simple sentence with one subject and a

5. Did <u>all</u> of the mountaineers successfully <u>ascend</u> and <u>descend</u> Mount Everest?
6. <u>Valleys</u> and dense <u>forests</u> <u>cool</u> and <u>refresh</u> travelers in the Appalachian Mountains.
7. On Beartooth Highway in Montana, excellent <u>campgrounds</u> and scenic <u>overlooks</u> <u>provide</u> many views of distant glaciers.
8. <u>Mount Evans</u> <u>is</u> west of Denver and <u>can be</u> <u>reached</u> by the highest paved road in the United States.
9. Is the <u>view</u> from the top slopes of Mount Evans breathtaking?
10. Thick <u>forests</u> <u>cover</u> the Great Smoky Mountains and <u>help form</u> the peaks' smoky mist.

| Review A | **Identifying Subjects and Predicates** |

Write the <u>simple subject</u> and the <u>verb or verb phrase</u> in each of the following sentences.

EXAMPLE   1. Even the ancient Incas and the Aztecs paid and collected taxes.
       1. *Incas, Aztecs; paid, collected*

1. Among the obligations of citizens in large cities <u>is</u> the prompt <u>payment</u> of taxes.
2. The ancient <u>citizens</u> of Mesoamerica <u>were</u> no exception to this rule.
3. <u>Are</u> some of these taxes also <u>known</u> today as "tribute"?
4. <u>Bowls</u>, <u>blankets</u>, <u>honey</u>, or even warriors' <u>shields</u> <u>were given</u> and <u>accepted</u> as tribute.
5. High <u>officials</u> and the <u>sick</u> <u>did</u> not, however, <u>pay</u> taxes.
6. In the interest of fairness, <u>taxes</u> <u>must be counted</u> and <u>recorded</u> in some way by accountants.
7. As a record, <u>Incas</u> <u>knotted</u> a string or cord and <u>counted</u> the number of knots.
8. The <u>Codex Mendoza</u> <u>is</u> a formal record of the Aztecs' taxes.
9. Both the <u>Incas</u> and the <u>Aztecs</u> <u>used</u> the number *20* as the base of their mathematics.
10. <u>Might</u> <u>roads</u>, <u>buildings</u>, or emergency <u>supplies</u> <u>have been</u> <u>paid</u> for with the tribute, or taxes?

┌─HELP─┐
Some of the subjects and verbs in Review A are compound.

Cooperative Learning
Divide the class into groups of three, and have each student number off within the group. Write the first sentence from **Review A** on the chalkboard, and ask students to find the complete subject, simple subject, complete predicate, and verb. Have students consult within their groups to make sure that everyone knows the answer. Then, call out one of the three numbers. Students with that number can raise their hands to respond. Continue with the remaining sentences in the exercise, making sure to call each number.

Subject and Predicate   **329**

compound verb
• A simple sentence with a compound subject and a compound verb
• A compound sentence

Ask students to check any compound sentences in pieces of their own writing for

correct punctuation. Suggest that students highlight coordinating conjunctions and examine how they are used.
For more about compound sentences, see p. 441. For more about using commas in compound sentences, see p. 605.

GRAMMAR

Review B **Identifying Subjects and Predicates**

Write the following sentences. Underline the complete subjects once and the complete predicates twice. Then, circle each simple subject and each verb.

EXAMPLES 1. The entire continent of Australia is occupied by a single country.

1. *The entire* (continent) *of Australia* (is occupied) *by a single country.*

2. What do you know about this continent?

2. *What* (do) (you) (know) *about this continent?*

1. It (is located) within the Southern Hemisphere.
2. Can you name the capital of Australia?
3. Australia is a federation of six states and two territories.
4. The continent of Australia was claimed for Britain by Captain James Cook.
5. The native people of Australia live mainly in the desert regions and, traditionally, have a very close bond with their environment.
6. A large number of British colonists settled in cities and towns on the coast.
7. Many ranchers raise sheep and export wool.
8. In addition, large quantities of gold and uranium are mined in Australia.
9. The country is also highly industrialized and produces a variety of goods, ranging from shoes to airplanes.
10. Among Australia's most unusual animals are the platypus and the anteater.

Kinds of Sentences

10h. A *declarative sentence* makes a statement and ends with a period.

EXAMPLES   Amy Tan was born in Oakland, California.

I couldn't hear what Jason said.

10i. An *imperative sentence* gives a command or makes a request. Most imperative sentences end with a period. A strong command ends with an exclamation point.

Reference Note

For information about how **sentences can be classified according to their structure,** see Chapter 16.

Kinds of Sentences

Rules 10h–k *(pp. 330–332)*

OBJECTIVE

■ To classify sentences as declarative, imperative, interrogative, or exclamatory

Meeting
│INDIVIDUAL│
══**NEEDS**

MODALITIES

Auditory Learners. Read the example sentences for **Rules 10h, 10i, 10j,** and **10k** aloud to students. Inflect your voice to indicate the purpose of each sentence.

RESOURCES

Kinds of Sentences

Practice

■ *Grammar, Usage, and Mechanics,* pp. 15–16
■ *Language Workshop CD-ROM,* Lesson 35

EXAMPLES   Be quiet during the play. [command]

Please give me another piece of melon. [request]

Stop! [strong command]

The subject of a command or a request is always *you*, even if *you* doesn't appear in the sentence. In such cases, *you* is called the **understood subject.**

EXAMPLES   (You) Be quiet during the play.

(You) Please give me another piece of melon.

(You) Stop!

The word *you* is the understood subject even when the person spoken to is addressed by name.

EXAMPLE   Miguel, (you) please answer the phone.

10j. An *interrogative sentence* asks a question and ends with a question mark.

EXAMPLES   When did you return from your camping trip?

Did the surfboard cost much?

10k. An *exclamatory sentence* shows excitement or expresses strong feeling and ends with an exclamation point.

EXAMPLES   Gabriella won the match!

How terrifying that movie was!

Exercise 13 **Classifying Sentences by Purpose**

Label each of the following sentences *declarative, imperative, interrogative,* or *exclamatory.*

EXAMPLE   1. Ask Yoshiko for the address.
   1. *imperative*

1. Will your grandfather compete in the Kansas City Marathon again this year?   1. int.
2. Our school's project, cleaning up the Silver River Nature Preserve, was a success.   2. dec.
3. Bring more sandbags over here now!   3. imp.
4. Is the Rig-Veda the oldest of the Hindu scriptures?   4. int.
5. Read this poem by Naomi Shihab Nye.   5. imp.

Meeting
INDIVIDUAL
NEEDS

ENGLISH-LANGUAGE LEARNERS
Spanish. In Spanish, questions are preceded by an inverted question mark and followed by a regular question mark; exclamations are preceded by an inverted exclamation point and followed by a regular exclamation point. Explain to your Spanish-speaking students that a single question mark or exclamation point is used at the end of an English sentence and that neither is inverted.

TEACHING **TIP**

Exercise 13 To help students recognize the differences between the types of sentences, give students a declarative sentence and ask them to convert it to the other three types of sentences. For example, *The test was hard* could become *Was the test hard?* (interrogative); *Please tell me if the test was hard* (imperative); and *What a hard test that was!* (exclamatory).

6. How huge this library is! **6.** excl.

7. Origami is the fascinating Japanese folk art of folding paper into shapes. **7.** dec.

8. How did you make that paper crane? **8.** int.

9. Please line up alphabetically. **9.** imp.

10. After we eat supper, we're going to my aunt's house down the block. **10.** dec.

Review C **Classifying and Punctuating Sentences**

Write the last word of each of the following sentences, adding the correct end mark. Then, label each sentence as *declarative*, *imperative*, *interrogative*, or *exclamatory*.

EXAMPLE   **1.** Are prairie dogs social creatures

         1. creatures?—interrogative

1. dec.

1. Many of these small mammals live together in underground "towns" like the one shown below.

2. imp.

2. Look at how prairie dogs dig family burrows. *or* !

3. int.

3. How large are the burrows?

4. dec.

4. The burrows sometimes cover several acres.

5. dec.

5. These creatures can usually be seen at night or in the early morning.

6. exc.

6. What alert animals prairie dogs are!

7. dec.

7. At least one prairie dog always keeps a lookout for threats to the community.

8. imp.

8. Look at how it sits up to see better. *or* !

9. dec.

9. It then dives headfirst into the burrow and alerts the colony.

10. exc.

10. How shrill the prairie dog's whistle of alarm is!

10

Chapter Review

A. Identifying Sentences

Identify each of the following groups of words as a *sentence* or a *sentence fragment*.

1. Trying a double somersault.   **1.** frag.
2. She barely caught her partner's hands!   **2.** sent.
3. As she began the triple.   **3.** frag.
4. She fell into the net.   **4.** sent.
5. The crowd gasped.   **5.** sent.
6. Even the clowns turned and looked.   **6.** sent.
7. Was she hurt?   **7.** sent.
8. Rolled off the net to the ground.   **8.** frag.
9. Smiling as she waved to the crowd.   **9.** frag.
10. She was fine!   **10.** sent.

B. Identifying Subjects

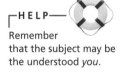

┌HELP─┐

Remember
that the subject may be
the understood *you*.

Identify the [complete subject] of the following sentences. Then, underline the simple subject. The simple subject may be compound.

11. [Foods and beverages with large amounts of sugar] can contribute to tooth decay.
12. [The lava from a volcano] hardens when it cools.
13. [The earthquake survivors] camped on blankets in the rubble.
14. In Beijing, [bicyclists] weave through the busy streets.
15. By 1899, [many gold prospectors] had rushed to Alaska.
16. [The weather during an Alaskan summer] can be hot.
17. Have [you] read this collection of Claude McKay's poems?
18. In the center of the table was [a huge bowl of fruit].
19. Linked forever in legend are [Paul Bunyan and Babe the Blue Ox].
20. Have [many famous racehorses] been trained in Kentucky?
21. [The bright lights and the tall buildings] amaze and delight most visitors to New York City.

Chapter Review   **333**

Using the Chapter Review

To assess student progress, you may want to compare the types of items missed on the **Diagnostic Preview** to those missed on the **Chapter Review**. You could then work out specific goals for mastering essential information with individual students who are still having difficulty.

22. Are [Lita and Marisa] going to give their presentation?
23. After soccer practice tomorrow afternoon, please come to my house for dinner.   23. (you)
24. Inside the box were [letters and postcards written around the turn of the century].
25. [The book *Come a Stranger*] was written by the award-winning author Cynthia Voigt.

C. Identifying Predicates

Identify the [complete predicate] of the following sentences. Then, underline the simple predicate (verb or verb phrase). The simple predicate may be compound.

26. Teenagers [need a balanced diet for good health].
27. A balanced diet [improves student performance in school].
28. Students [are sometimes in a hurry and skip breakfast].
29. [For a nutritious breakfast,] they [can eat cereal and fruit].
30. Cheese and juice [also provide good nutrition].
31. The cheese [contains calcium, an important mineral].
32. People [need protein as well].
33. Protein [builds body tissue].
34. Protein [can be supplied by eggs, dried beans, red meat, fish, and poultry].
35. Carbohydrates [include whole grains, vegetables, and fruits].
36. Junk foods [can ruin your appetite].
37. Sweets [cause tooth decay and contain many calories].
38. [According to nutritionists,] sweets [are low in nutrients and fill the body with "empty" calories].
39. Good eating habits [keep you healthy and help you live longer].
40. [Start eating right]!

D. Classifying and Punctuating Sentences

Classify each of the following sentences as *declarative, interrogative, imperative,* or *exclamatory.* Then, write each sentence with the correct end punctuation.

41. In ancient times, the Julian calendar was used.   41. dec.

RESOURCES

The Sentence
Review
■ *Grammar, Usage, and Mechanics,* pp. 17, 18, 19, 20

Assessment
■ *Assessment Package*
  —*Chapter Tests,* Ch. 10
  —*Chapter Tests in Standardized Test Formats,* Ch. 10
■ *Test Generator (One-Stop Planner CD-ROM)*

42. Why was it called Julian? **42.** int.

43. It was named after the Roman leader Julius Caesar. **43.** dec.

44. I thought so! *or* . **44.** exc. *or* dec.

45. Because the Julian calendar was not perfect, the Gregorian calendar was invented. **45.** dec.

46. In 1752, the calendar was changed in England. **46.** dec.

47. Tell me the result. **47.** imp.

48. Eleven days in September were lost. **48.** dec.

49. That's the strangest thing I've ever heard! *or* . **49.** exc. *or* dec.

50. Were those days lost forever? **50.** int.

Writing Application
Writing a Letter

Using Complete Sentences   Yesterday, you went to a birthday party. Write a letter describing the party to a friend or relative who lives far away. Include details about the activities you enjoyed and about the other people who were there. Use complete sentences to make sure your thoughts are clear.

Prewriting   Make a list of the details that you would like to include in your letter. At this stage, you do not have to use complete sentences. Simply jot down your thoughts.

Writing   Use your prewriting list of details as you write your rough draft. Choose details that would be interesting to your friend or relative. You might organize your letter chronologically (describing events in the order in which they occurred).

Revising   Read your letter aloud. As you read, mark any parts of the letter that seem unclear. Add, cut, or rearrange details to make your letter clear and interesting to your reader.

Publishing   Check your work to make sure you have used only complete sentences. Read your letter for any errors in spelling and punctuation. You and your classmates may want to collect the letters in a booklet. Make a copy for each member of the class.

Reference Note

For information on **writing a letter,** see "Writing" in the Quick Reference Handbook.

Chapter Review   **335**

Writing Application
(p. 335)

O B J E C T I V E

■ **To write a letter using complete sentences**

Writing Application

Tip. Because some students may not have had the experience of going to a birthday party, you may want to provide alternative topics for students' descriptive letters.

Scoring Rubric. While you will want to pay particular attention to students' use of complete sentences, you will also want to evaluate overall writing performance. You may want to give a split score to indicate development and clarity of the composition as well as grammar skills.

RESOURCES

Writing Application
Extension

■ *Grammar, Usage, and Mechanics,* p. 23
■ *Language Workshop CD-ROM,* Lessons 29, 30, 35, 36

Parts of Speech Overview

Noun, Pronoun, Adjective

Diagnostic Preview

Identifying Nouns, Pronouns, and Adjectives

Identify each italicized word in the following paragraphs as a *noun*, a *pronoun,* or an *adjective*.

EXAMPLES   The [1] *achievements* of the [2] *native* peoples of North America have sometimes been overlooked.

1. noun
2. adjective

Recent [1] *studies* show that the Winnebago people developed a [2] *calendar* based on careful observation of the [3] *heavens*. An [4] *archaeologist* has found that markings on an old [5] *calendar* stick are the precise records of a [6] *lunar* year and a solar year. These records are remarkably accurate, considering that at the time the [7] *Winnebagos* had neither a [8] *written* language nor a system of [9] *mathematics*.

[10] *The* calendar stick is a carved [11] *hickory* branch with [12] *four* sides. [13] *It* is worn along the [14] *edges* and shows other signs of frequent use. A [15] *similar* stick appears in a portrait of an early chief of the Winnebagos. In the portrait, the chief holds a calendar stick in [16] *his* right hand. [17] *One* current theory is that the chief went out at [18] *sunrise* and

the stick what he saw. According to one researcher, this calendar is the [20] *oldest* indication we have that native North American peoples recorded the year day by day.

The Noun

11a. A *noun* is a word or word group that is used to name a person, a place, a thing, or an idea.

Persons	Jessye Norman, teacher, chef, Dr. Ling
Places	Grand Canyon, city, Namibia, kitchen
Things	lamp, granite, Nobel Prize, Golden Gate Bridge
ideas	happiness, self-control, liberty, bravery

Notice that some nouns are made up of more than one word. A *compound noun* is a single noun made up of two or more words used together. The compound noun may be written as one word, as a hyphenated word, or as two or more words.

One Word	grandmother, basketball
Hyphenated Word	mother-in-law, light-year
Two Words	grand piano, jumping jack

┌ TIPS & TRICKS ┐
To find the correct spelling of a compound noun, look it up in a recent dictionary.

Exercise 1 Identifying Nouns

Identify the nouns in the following sentences.

EXAMPLE
1. We have been reading about patriotic heroines in our textbook.
   1. heroines, textbook

┌HELP┐
In Exercise 1,
some nouns are used more than once.

1. Rebecca Motte was a great patriot.
2. During the Revolutionary War, British soldiers seized her mansion in South Carolina.
3. General Harry Lee told Motte that the Americans would have to burn her home to smoke out the enemy.

The Noun **337**

RESOURCES

The Noun
Practice
- *Grammar, Usage, and Mechanics,* pp. 25, 26, 27, 28
- *Language Workshop CD-ROM,* Lesson 1

GRAMMAR

The Noun
Rule 11a *(pp. 337–341)*

OBJECTIVES

- To identify nouns in sentences
- To classify nouns as common or proper
- To revise sentences by substituting proper nouns for common nouns
- To classify nouns as concrete or abstract and to use each type in a sentence

TEACHING TIP

Motivation. Explain to students that grammar, just like various sports and hobbies, has special terminology that all participants must understand in order to communicate effectively. For example, if a soccer player were instructed by the coach to "dribble the ball to the penalty area and make a through pass to the left striker," that player would need to be familiar with the terminology in order to complete the tasks.

Ask students to come up with examples of terminology from their activities or hobbies. On the chalkboard, list activities or hobbies and the corresponding terminology for each. Explain that if a peer reviewer or teacher suggests that a student use specific kinds of nouns or make sure that pronouns agree with their antecedents, the student must be familiar with the terminology in order to complete the tasks.

LEARNERS HAVING DIFFICULTY
To give students additional instruction on common and proper nouns, list on the chalkboard some common nouns that name people or things related to the classroom. Then, ask students to name the same people or things as proper nouns. Some examples include book/*Elements of Language;* teacher/Mr. Fuentes; school/Ezra Middle School; girl/Devon Defoyd.

ENGLISH-LANGUAGE LEARNERS
Spanish. Months of the year; days of the week; languages and nationalities; and the first-person singular pronoun, *yo* (I), are not capitalized in Spanish. Emphasize to Spanish-speaking students that these words must be capitalized in English.

Looking at Language
Share with students the fact that some common nouns were originally proper nouns. For example, the sandwich was named after the man who reputedly came up with the concept of layering bread and meat to make a meal—John Montagu, the fourth Earl of Sandwich. Other examples include *cardigan* (after the seventh Earl of Cardigan) and *denim* (from the French, meaning "from Nîmes," where it was first made). Interested students could research these or other examples and present their findings to the class.

Reference Note
For more information about **capitalizing proper nouns,** see page 574.

4. <u>Motte</u> supported the <u>plan</u> and was glad to help her <u>country</u>.
5. She even supplied flaming <u>arrows</u> and a <u>bow</u> for the <u>attack</u>.
6. The <u>house</u> was saved after the <u>enemy</u> raised the white <u>flag</u> of surrender.
7. Other <u>people</u> might not have been so generous or patriotic.
8. Afterward, <u>Motte</u> invited <u>soldiers</u> from both <u>sides</u> to <u>dinner</u>.
9. How their <u>laughter</u> must have filled the air!
10. The <u>colonies</u> and all <u>citizens</u> of the <u>United States</u> are in her <u>debt</u>.

Proper Nouns and Common Nouns

A **proper noun** names a particular person, place, thing, or idea and begins with a capital letter. A **common noun** names any one of a group of persons, places, things, or ideas and is generally not capitalized.

Common Nouns	Proper Nouns
girl	Kay O'Neill
writer	Octavio Paz
country	Morocco
monument	Eiffel Tower
compact disc	*A Long Way Home*
book	*Tiger Eyes*
religion	Buddhism
language	Arabic
city	Ottawa

Exercise 2 **Identifying Common Nouns and Proper Nouns**

—HELP—

In Exercise 2, some nouns are used more than once.

Write the nouns in each of the following sentences. Then, identify each noun as a *common noun* or *proper noun*.

EXAMPLE 1. Mark visited an interesting museum in Colorado last month.

1. *Mark—proper; museum—common; Colorado—proper; month—common*

338 | Chapter 11 | Parts of Speech Overview

MINI-LESSON *Continued on pp. 339–340*

Capitalizing Proper Nouns. You may want to take this opportunity to discuss capitalization rules with students. Explain that a common noun is not capitalized unless it begins a sentence or is part of a title. Proper nouns are always capitalized. Some proper nouns, however, consist of more than one word, such as *Statue of Liberty.* In these names, articles, conjunctions, and prepositions of fewer than five

1. <u>Mark</u> and his <u>parents</u> went to the <u>Black American West Museum and Heritage Center</u> in <u>Denver</u>.
2. The <u>museum</u> displays many <u>items</u> that <u>cowboys</u> used.
3. These <u>items</u> are from the <u>collection</u> of <u>Paul Stewart</u>, the <u>man</u> who founded the <u>museum</u>.
4. <u>Mark</u> saw <u>saddles</u>, <u>knives</u>, <u>hats</u>, and <u>lariats</u>.
5. He also saw many <u>pictures</u> of African American <u>cowboys</u>.
6. The <u>museum</u> is located in an old <u>house</u> that is listed in the <u>National Register of Historic Places</u>.
7. The <u>house</u> once belonged to <u>Dr. Justina L. Ford</u>.
8. She was the first black female <u>physician</u> in <u>Colorado</u>.
9. <u>Mark</u> was amazed by all of the old medical <u>instruments</u> in one <u>display</u>.
10. He said he was glad <u>doctors</u> don't use <u>equipment</u> like that anymore.

Exercise 3 Revising Sentences by Using Proper Nouns

Revise the following sentences by substituting a proper noun for each common noun. You might have to change some other words in each sentence. You may make up proper names.

EXAMPLE
    1. An ambassador visited a local school and spoke about his country.
       1. *Ambassador Rios visited Jackson High School and spoke about Brazil.*

1. That painting is in a famous museum.
2. The police officer cheerfully directed us to the building on that street.
3. My relatives, who are originally from a small town, now live in a large city.
4. The librarian asked my classmate to return the book as soon as possible.
5. That newspaper is published daily; this magazine is published weekly.
6. The girl read a poem for the teacher.
7. That state borders the ocean.
8. The owner of that store visited two countries during a spring month.
9. A man flew to a northern city one day.
10. Last week the mayor visited our school and talked about the history of our city.

Exercise 3 Revising Sentences by Using Proper Nouns

ANSWERS
Proper nouns will vary. Here are some possibilities:

1. The *Mona Lisa* is in the Louvre.
2. Officer Martinez cheerfully directed us to the Clark Building on Main Street.
3. Aunt Sally and Uncle Bill, who are originally from Butte, now live in Chicago.
4. Mr. Ellman asked Jerry to return *A Wizard of Earthsea* as soon as possible.
5. The *Daily Bugle* is published daily; *Newsweek* is published weekly.
6. Iris read "The Highwayman" for Mr. Hodge.
7. Maine borders the Atlantic Ocean.
8. Ms. Jensen, owner of Jensen's Dive Shop, visited Vietnam and China during the month of May.
9. Mr. Anoki flew to New York City last Friday.
10. Last week, Mayor Arlene James visited Lincoln Middle School and talked about the history of Andersonville, New Jersey.

letters are not capitalized.
    Write the following items on the chalkboard, and have students work in small groups to correct the capitalization. For additional help or practice, refer students

to p. 574.
1. winfield middle school
2. isle of pines
3. "madam and the rent man"
4. lost creek boulevard

ENGLISH-LANGUAGE LEARNERS

Spanish. In Spanish, both concrete and abstract nouns are always accompanied by definite articles. Examples of abstract nouns include *la democracia* (democracy), *la justicia* (justice), and *la inflación* (inflation). Therefore, students might construct sentences such as "The freedom is our goal." Scan student writing for this type of construction, and offer extra practice if necessary.

INCLUSION

Students might understand the distinction between abstract nouns and concrete nouns more easily if they associate the terms with familiar words. Put the following charts on the chalkboard (without the sample answers). Then, ask students to supply words to fill in the charts.

CONCRETE NOUNS

PERSON	PLACE	THING
teacher	school	book

ABSTRACT NOUNS

IDEA	FEELING	CHARACTERISTIC
freedom	joy	courage

Students might need help filling in the abstract nouns.

Exercise 4 — Identifying and Classifying Nouns

Identify the nouns in the following sentences, and label each noun as a *common noun* or a *proper noun*.

EXAMPLE   [1] Lillian Evanti performed in Europe, Latin America, and Africa.

     1. *Lillian Evanti—proper noun; Europe—proper noun; Latin America—proper noun; Africa—proper noun*

[1] Evanti was the first African American woman to sing opera professionally. [2] Her talent was recognized early; when she was a child, she gave a solo concert in Washington, D.C. [3] As an adult, she performed in a special concert at the White House for President Franklin Roosevelt and his wife, Eleanor. [4] Evanti also composed a musical piece titled "Himno Panamericano," which was a great success. [5] Her career inspired many other African American singers.

[6] A few years later Marian Anderson stepped into the limelight. [7] Always a champion of the arts, Mrs. Roosevelt again aided a great performer. [8] With the assistance and encouragement of the former First Lady, Anderson sang at a most appropriate site—the Lincoln Memorial. [9] Like Evanti, Anderson broke barriers, for before her, no other African American had sung at the famous Metropolitan Opera House in New York City. [10] Honors Anderson earned include a place in the National Arts Hall of Fame.

Concrete Nouns and Abstract Nouns

A *concrete noun* names a person, place, or thing that can be perceived by one or more of the senses (sight, hearing, taste, touch, smell). An *abstract noun* names an idea, a feeling, a quality, or a characteristic.

Concrete Nouns	photograph, music, pears, filmmaker, sandpaper, rose, Brooklyn Bridge
Abstract Nouns	love, fun, freedom, self-esteem, beauty, honor, wisdom, Buddhism

---

MINI-LESSON

5. thanksgiving day
6. washington monument
7. nobel prize

8. mayor gernhardt
9. *the wizard of oz*
10. *webster's new world dictionary*

Exercise 5 Writing Sentences with Concrete and Abstract Nouns

Identify each noun in the following list as *concrete* or *abstract*. Then, use each noun in an original sentence.

EXAMPLE   **1.** truth
     1. abstract—People should always tell the truth.

1. soy sauce   **4.** ice   **7.** motor   **9.** pillow
2. brotherhood   **5.** excitement   **8.** health   **10.** honor
3. laughter   **6.** kindness

Collective Nouns

A *collective noun* is a word that names a group.

audience	committee	herd	quartet
batch	crew	jury	swarm
class	family	litter	team

Review A Using the Different Kinds of Nouns

Complete the following poem, which is based on this painting. Add common, proper, concrete, abstract, or collective nouns as directed. For proper nouns, you'll need to make up names of people and places. Be sure you capitalize all proper nouns.

Meet my [1] (*common*), the really amazing,
Truly tremendous [2] (*proper*), that's who.
You can see what [3] (*abstract*) he gives
The [4] (*collective*) of fans who hang on him
   like glue.

The walls of his gym on [5] (*proper*)
Are covered with [6] (*concrete*) that show
The muscled, tussled [7] (*common*) aplenty,
Who work out there, come rain or come snow.

Eduardo, [8] (*proper*), and I really enjoy
The [9] (*abstract*) of hanging on tight
Way above the [10] (*concrete*) and swinging,
Held up by the muscleman's might.

Reference Note
For more information about **collective nouns,** see pages 468 and 477.

Jacob Lawrence, *Strong Man.* Gouache on paper, 22" x 17". Photo by Chris Eden, Francine Seders Gallery.

The Noun   **341**

Exercise 5 Writing Sentences with Concrete and Abstract Nouns

ANSWERS
Sentences will vary. Here are some possibilities.

1. concrete—Do you want soy sauce on your rice?
2. abstract—A spirit of brotherhood among peoples of the earth might bring world peace.
3. concrete—Laughter is contagious.
4. concrete—I like to put ice in my water.
5. abstract—The crowd's excitement mounted as the players were introduced.
6. abstract—Her kindness is extraordinary.
7. concrete—The motor is electric.
8. abstract—His health is improving.
9. concrete—That pillow belongs on the sofa.
10. abstract—She served her country with honor.

Review A Using the Different Kinds of Nouns

ANSWERS
Nouns will vary. Here are some possibilities.

1. friend
2. Lou
3. joy
4. group
5. Sycamore Street
6. posters
7. athletes
8. Jan
9. thrill
10. sidewalk

The Pronoun

Rule 11b *(pp. 342–346)*

OBJECTIVES

- To identify pronouns and their antecedents
- To rewrite sentences by replacing nouns with pronouns

TEACHING TIP

Activity. Write the following awkwardly written paragraph on the chalkboard or on a transparency:

> The boys and girls were excited about the boys' and girls' first day in junior high. The boys and girls got lost and wandered around the huge building. To find the boys' and girls' way to class, the boys and girls asked some ninth-graders to help the boys and girls.

Ask students to revise the paragraph by replacing the repeated nouns with the appropriate personal pronouns.

> [Possible answer: *The boys and girls were excited about **their** first day in junior high. **They** got lost and wandered around the huge building. To find **their** way to class, the boys and girls asked some ninth-graders to help **them**.*]

Reference Note

For information about choosing **pronouns that agree with their antecedents,** see page 475.

┌HELP──

When you use a pronoun, be sure that its antecedent is clear. If two or more nouns in the sentence could be the antecedent, the reader may not be able to tell what the sentence means. Rewording the sentence to change the position of the pronoun can make the meaning clearer.

EXAMPLES
Randy saw Mike as he left the field. [Who left the field, Randy or Mike?]

As Randy left the field, **he** saw Mike. [The pronoun *he* now clearly refers to the antecedent *Randy*.]

As Mike left the field, Randy saw **him**. [The pronoun *him* now clearly refers to the antecedent *Mike*.]

┌HELP──

Some authorities prefer to call possessive pronouns (such as *my, your,* and *their*) possessive adjectives. Follow your teacher's directions when you are labeling these words.

The Pronoun

11b. A *pronoun* is a word that is used in place of one or more nouns or pronouns.

EXAMPLES   Ask Dan if Dan has done Dan's homework.

Ask Dan if **he** has done **his** homework.

Both of Lois's friends said both would help Lois find Lois's missing books.

Both of Lois's friends said **they** would help **her** find **her** missing books.

The word or word group that a pronoun stands for (or refers to) is called its *antecedent.*

          antecedent   pronoun   pronoun

EXAMPLES   **Frederick,** have **you** turned in **your** report?

           antecedent   pronoun

Walking the dog is fun, and **it** is good exercise.

Sometimes the antecedent is not stated.

EXAMPLES   **Who** asked that question?

I did not understand what **you** said.

Someone will have to clean up the mess.

Personal Pronouns

A *personal pronoun* refers to the one speaking (*first person*), the one spoken to (*second person*), or the one spoken about (*third person*).

Personal Pronouns		
	Singular	**Plural**
First Person	I, me, my, mine	we, us, our, ours
Second Person	you, your, yours	you, your, yours
Third Person	he, him, his, she, her, hers, it, its	they, them, their, theirs

---

RESOURCES

The Pronoun

Practice

- *Grammar, Usage, and Mechanics,* pp. 29, 30, 31, 32, 33
- *Language Workshop CD-ROM,* Lesson 2

Reflexive and Intensive Pronouns

A *reflexive pronoun* refers to the subject and is necessary to the meaning of the sentence. An *intensive pronoun* emphasizes a noun or another pronoun and is unnecessary to the meaning of the sentence.

Reflexive and Intensive Pronouns	
First Person	myself, ourselves
Second Person	yourself, yourselves
Third Person	himself, herself, itself, themselves

REFLEXIVE   Tara enjoyed **herself** at the party.
              The team prided **themselves** on their victory.

INTENSIVE   I **myself** cooked that delicious dinner.
              Did you redecorate the room **yourself**?

Demonstrative Pronouns

A *demonstrative pronoun* points out a person, a place, a thing, or an idea.

Demonstrative Pronouns			
this	that	these	those

EXAMPLES   **This** is the book I bought for my sister.

             Are **those** the kinds of plants that bloom at night?

NOTE *This, that, these,* and *those* can also be used as adjectives. When they are used in this way, they are called *demonstrative adjectives.*

DEMONSTRATIVE PRONOUN   **Those** are very sturdy shoes.
DEMONSTRATIVE ADJECTIVE   **Those** shoes are very sturdy.

DEMONSTRATIVE PRONOUN   Did you order **this**?
DEMONSTRATIVE ADJECTIVE   Did you order **this** salad?

TIPS & TRICKS

If you are not sure whether a pronoun is reflexive or intensive, use this test: Read the sentence aloud, omitting the pronoun. If the basic meaning of the sentence stays the same, the pronoun is intensive. If the meaning changes, the pronoun is reflexive.

EXAMPLES
The children amused **themselves** all morning. [Without *themselves,* the sentence doesn't make sense. The pronoun is reflexive.]

Mark repaired the car **himself.** [Without *himself,* the meaning stays the same. The pronoun is intensive.]

Reference Note

For more about **demonstrative adjectives,** see page 348.

Meeting
INDIVIDUAL NEEDS

ENGLISH-LANGUAGE LEARNERS
Spanish. The English possessive pronouns *your, his, her, its,* and *their* all can be written in Spanish as *su* (or *sus* if more than one thing is possessed). *Yourself, himself, herself, itself,* and *themselves* can all be translated as *se.* Watch for any difficulties students may have distinguishing among these pronouns.

Asian Languages. Many Asian languages—such as Indonesian, Japanese, and Vietnamese—have a variety of possessive pronouns that mean *you.* Consequently, some English-language learners might avoid using *you* because it seems impolite or awkward to use the same word to address respected elders, peers, both men and women, and animals. Remind students that in English it is acceptable to use *you* in all of these situations.

MODALITIES
Kinesthetic Learners. You may want to have the class perform exercises that require physically connecting pronouns with their antecedents. Having students circle pronouns and draw lines to their antecedents may help them understand the relationship between the two words.

GRAMMAR

Interrogative Pronouns

An *interrogative pronoun* introduces a question.

Interrogative Pronouns				
what	which	who	whom	whose

EXAMPLES   **What** is the best brand of frozen yogurt?

Who wrote *Barrio Boy*?

Indefinite Pronouns

An *indefinite pronoun* refers to a person, a place, a thing, or an idea that may or may not be specifically named.

Common Indefinite Pronouns				
all	each	many	nobody	other
any	either	more	none	several
anyone	everything	most	no one	some
both	few	much	one	somebody

EXAMPLES   **Both** of the girls forgot their lines.

I would like **some** of that chow mein.

NOTE   Most indefinite pronouns can also be used as adjectives.

PRONOUN   **Some** are bored by this movie.
ADJECTIVE   **Some** people are bored by this movie.

Relative Pronouns

A *relative pronoun* introduces a subordinate clause.

Common Relative Pronouns				
that	which	who	whom	whose

EXAMPLES   Thomas Jefferson, **who** wrote the Declaration of Independence, was our country's third president.

Exercise is something **that** many people enjoy.

344   **Chapter 11**   Parts of Speech Overview

⌐ TIPS & TRICKS ⌐

The indefinite pronouns *some, any, none, all, more,* and *most* may be singular or plural. Look closely at any prepositional phrase that follows these pronouns. The object of the preposition determines whether the pronoun is singular or plural.

SINGULAR
None of the milk **is** sour. [*Milk* is singular.]

PLURAL
None of the grapes **are** sweet. [*Grapes* is plural.]

Reference Note
For information on **indefinite pronouns and subject-verb agreement,** see page 463.

Reference Note
For information on **subordinate clauses,** see page 424.

Meeting
| INDIVIDUAL |
NEEDS

ENGLISH-LANGUAGE LEARNERS
Spanish. Because the Spanish relative pronoun *que* can be translated as *that, which, who,* or *whom,* Spanish speakers may use *which* in cases where *who* would sound natural in English. Show students some sentences containing *that, who,* and *which* in adjective clauses, allowing them to investigate situations in which each is used. Once they seem to understand the distinctions, have them practice inserting the proper relative pronoun into sentences.

MINI-LESSON

Subject-Verb Agreement. You may want to provide students with some instruction to help with subject-verb agreement when the subject of a sentence is an indefinite pronoun, as in *Neither of the girls wants her ears pierced.* Explain to students that the following pronouns are always singular and need a singular verb: *each, either, neither, one, everyone, everybody, no one, nobody, anyone, anybody, someone,* and *somebody.* Point out that prepositional phrases following the singular indefinite

Exercise 6 Identifying Pronouns

Identify each <u>pronoun</u> in the following sentences. Then, tell what type of pronoun each one is.

EXAMPLES   1. The drama coach said he would postpone the rehearsal.

           1. he—personal

         2. Does Pamela, who is traveling to Thailand, have her passport and ticket?

           2. who—relative; her—personal

1. "I want <u>you</u> to study," Ms. Gaines said to the class.
2. The firefighter carefully adjusted <u>her</u> oxygen mask.
3. The children made lunch <u>themselves</u>.
4. Jenny and Rosa decided <u>they</u> would get popcorn, but Amy didn't want <u>any</u>.
5. <u>Who</u> will be the next president of the school board?
6. Mr. Yoshira, <u>this</u> is Mrs. Volt, a neighbor of <u>yours</u>.
7. Ralph Bunche, <u>who</u> was awarded the Nobel Peace Prize, was a diplomat for <u>his</u> country at the United Nations.
8. Of all United States Olympic victories, perhaps <u>none</u> were more satisfying than Jesse Owens's 1936 triumphs in the 200-meter dash and broad jump.
9. Oh, yes, the puppy taught <u>itself</u> how to open the gate.
10. Only <u>one</u> of seventy-five fine boys and girls will win the grand prize.

―HELP―

Some sentences in Exercise 6 have more than one pronoun.

1. personal/personal
2. personal
3. intensive
4. personal/indefinite
5. interrogative
6. demonstrative/ personal
7. relative/personal
8. indefinite
9. reflexive
10. indefinite

Exercise 7 Writing Appropriate Pronouns

Rewrite each sentence, replacing the repeated nouns with pronouns.

EXAMPLE   1. The boy forgot the boy's homework.

           1. The boy forgot his homework.

1. Put the flowers in water before ~~the flowers'~~ petals droop.
2. The canoe capsized as ~~the canoe~~ neared the shore.
3. The players convinced ~~the players~~ that ~~the players~~ would win the game.
4. Lorraine oiled the bicycle before ~~Lorraine~~ put ~~the bicycle~~ in the garage.
5. Tim said, "~~Tim~~ answered all six questions on the quiz."
6. Ben folded the newspapers for Ms. Glinsmann, and then ~~Ben~~ stuffed ~~the newspapers~~ in plastic bags for ~~Ms. Glinsmann~~.

1. their
2. it
3. themselves/they
4. she/it
5. I
6. he/ them/her

The Pronoun   **345**

pronoun may contain plural objects, but the verb must be singular.

   Write the following sentences on the chalkboard, and ask students to indicate which are correct:

• <u>One</u> of these dogs <u>eats</u> too much! [correct]

• <u>Each</u> of the boys <u>know</u> the answer. [incorrect]

   For additional instruction and practice, refer students to p. 457.

7. we

8. it

9. he

10. his/
    them

7. Sarah, Keith, and I arrived early so that ~~Sarah, Keith, and I~~ could get good seats.

8. Her wheelchair was amazingly fast, and ~~her wheelchair~~ was lightweight, too.

9. Grandpa just graduated from college, and ~~Grandpa~~ is now working as a computer programmer.

10. Because Japan fascinates Ron and ~~Ron's~~ brother, this film will interest ~~Ron and Ron's brother.~~

The Adjective

Rule 11c *(pp. 346–351)*

OBJECTIVES

- To identify adjectives and the words they modify in sentences

- To complete a story by inserting appropriate adjectives

- To identify common and proper adjectives in sentences

- To convert proper nouns into proper adjectives

Crossing the Curriculum

Music. In addition to the notes being played, music includes the key signature, which can add sharps and flats to the notes. This device can be seen as the adjective for the music because it modifies the notes.

COMPUTER TIP

Using a software program's thesaurus can help you choose appropriate adjectives. To make sure that an adjective has exactly the connotation you intend, check the word in a dictionary.

Reference Note

For more about **predicate adjectives,** see page 393.

The Adjective

11c. An *adjective* is a word that is used to modify a noun or a pronoun.

To *modify* a word means to describe the word or to make its meaning more definite. An adjective modifies a noun or a pronoun by telling *what kind*, *which one*, *how much*, or *how many*.

What Kind?	Which One or Ones?	How Much or How Many?
Korean children	**seventh** grade	**several** days
busy dentist	**these** countries	**five** dollars
braided hair	**any** book	**no** marbles

Sometimes an adjective comes after the word it modifies.

EXAMPLES   A woman, **kind** and **helpful,** gave us directions.
[The adjectives *kind* and *helpful* modify *woman.*]

The box is **empty.** [The predicate adjective *empty* modifies *box.*]

LOOK, HOBBES! DAD FIXED MY BEANIE!

WELL? HOW'S IT LOOK?

ADJECTIVES FAIL ME.

I'M TURNING IT ON. READY? HERE GOES.

I DON'T SEEM TO BE LIFTING OFF. THIS IS VERY PECULIAR.

THAT'S THE WORD I WAS LOOKING FOR.

THBBTPTH88

CALVIN & HOBBES ©1989 Watterson. Reprinted with permission of Universal Press Syndicate. All rights reserved.

346   Chapter 11   Parts of Speech Overview

RESOURCES

The Adjective

Practice

- *Grammar, Usage, and Mechanics,* pp. 34, 35, 36, 37, 38

- *Language Workshop CD-ROM,* Lesson 3

Articles

The most commonly used adjectives are *a*, *an*, and *the*. These adjectives are called **articles.** *A* and *an* are called **indefinite articles** because they refer to any member of a general group. *A* is used before a word beginning with a consonant sound. *An* is used before a word beginning with a vowel sound.

EXAMPLES   **A** frog croaked.

An orange is **a** good source of vitamin C.

My cousin Jimmy wears **a** uniform to school. [Even though *u* is a vowel, the word *uniform* begins with a consonant sound.]

This is **an** honor. [Even though *h* is a consonant, the word *honor* begins with a vowel sound. The *h* is not pronounced.]

The is called the **definite article** because it refers to someone or something in particular.

EXAMPLES   **The** frog croaked.

Where is **the** orange?

Nouns or Adjectives?

Many words that can stand alone as nouns can also be used as adjectives modifying nouns or pronouns.

Nouns	Adjectives
bean	**bean** soup
spring	**spring** weather
gold	**gold** coin
football	**football** game
Labor Day	**Labor Day** weekend
Super Bowl	**Super Bowl** party
Milan	**Milan** fashions
White House	**White House** security
Persian Gulf	**Persian Gulf** pearls

Reference Note

For more about **words used as different parts of speech,** see pages 351 and 379.

Critical Thinking

Evaluation. Tell students that well-chosen adjectives can make their writing more colorful and descriptive. Write the following phrases on the chalkboard:

<u>hot</u> sun   <u>nice</u> girl
<u>cute</u> monkey   <u>pretty</u> day

Ask students to evaluate the adjectives in terms of their effectiveness, considering what sorts of images they bring to mind. [*Students may say the words are overused or not very descriptive.*] Add words to the expressions above to create the sentences below, and have students substitute adjectives that create a more vivid mental picture.

1. The <u>hot</u> sun had made us thirsty. [*blazing, scorching*]

2. We saw a <u>cute</u> monkey at the zoo. [*playful, charming*]

3. Everybody thinks she is such a <u>nice</u> girl. [*polite, thoughtful*]

4. What a <u>pretty</u> day this is! [*glorious, splendid*]

Reference Note

For more about **demonstrative pronouns,** see page 343.

Demonstrative Adjectives

This, that, these, and *those* can be used both as adjectives and as pronouns. When they modify a noun or pronoun, they are called ***demonstrative adjectives.*** When they are used alone, they are called ***demonstrative pronouns.***

DEMONSTRATIVE ADJECTIVES	**This** drawing is mine, and **that** drawing is his.
	These soccer balls are much more expensive than **those** soccer balls are.
DEMONSTRATIVE PRONOUNS	**This** is mine and **that** is his.
	These are much more expensive than **those** are.

Exercise 8 Identifying Adjectives

Identify the <u>adjectives</u> in the following sentences, and give the <u>noun or pronoun each modifies</u>. Do not include the articles *a, an,* and *the.*

EXAMPLE 1. Why don't you take the local bus home from school on cold days?
   1. *local—bus; cold—days*

1. On <u>winter</u> <u>afternoons</u>, I sometimes walk home after <u>band</u> <u>practice</u> rather than ride on a <u>crowded</u>, <u>noisy</u> <u>bus</u>.
2. I hardly even notice the <u>heavy</u> <u>traffic</u> that streams past me on the street.
3. The <u>wet</u> <u>sidewalk</u> glistens in the <u>bright</u> <u>lights</u> from the windows of stores.
4. The stoplights throw <u>green</u>, <u>yellow</u>, and <u>red</u> <u>splashes</u> on the pavement.
5. After I turn the corner away from the <u>busy</u> <u>avenue</u>, I am on a <u>quiet</u> <u>street</u>, where a <u>jolly</u> <u>snowman</u> often stands next to one of the <u>neighborhood</u> <u>houses</u>.
6. At last, I reach my <u>peaceful</u> <u>home</u>.
7. There I am often greeted by my <u>older</u> <u>brother</u>, Kenny, and my <u>sister</u>, Natalie.
8. I know <u>they</u> are <u>glad</u> to see me.
9. <u>Delicious</u> <u>smells</u> come from the kitchen where Mom and Dad are cooking dinner.
10. <u>This</u> <u>quiet</u>, <u>private</u> <u>walk</u> always makes <u>me</u> feel a little <u>tired</u> but also <u>happy</u>.

348   Chapter 11   Parts of Speech Overview

Learning for Life

Writing a Classified Ad. Explain to students that using vivid, descriptive language will enable them to communicate their ideas effectively. Tell students to choose an item— a bicycle, a baseball trading card, a music box, or something else—they might sell by using a classified ad. An accurate description will help potential buyers to get a clear picture of the object and also will help to ward off unnecessary phone calls that may result from misleading information.

First, ask students to describe in paragraph

Exercise 9 Writing Appropriate Adjectives

Complete the following story by writing an appropriate adjective to fill each blank.   Adjectives will vary.

EXAMPLES   [1] _____ parks have [2] _____ trails for hikers.
1. Many
2. wooded

The hikers went exploring in the [1] _____ forest. Sometimes they had difficulty getting through the [2] _____ undergrowth. On [3] _____ occasions they almost turned back. They kept going and were rewarded for their [4] _____ effort. During the [5] _____ hike through the woods, they discovered [6] _____ kinds of [7] _____ animals. In the afternoon the [8] _____ hikers pitched camp in a [9] _____ clearing. They were [10] _____ for supper and rest.

1. dark
2. thick
3. several
4. huge   5. long
6. ten
7. small   8. tired
9. beautiful   10. ready

Proper Adjectives

A *proper adjective* is formed from a proper noun.

Proper Nouns	Proper Adjectives
Thanksgiving	**Thanksgiving** dinner
Catholicism	**Catholic** priest
Middle East	**Middle Eastern** country
Africa	**African** continent

Notice that a proper adjective, like a proper noun, is capitalized. Common adjectives are generally not capitalized.

NOTE Some proper nouns, such as *Thanksgiving,* do not change spelling when they are used as adjectives.

Exercise 10 Identifying Common and Proper Adjectives

Identify the adjectives in the sentences on the next page. Then, tell whether each is a *common* or *proper* adjective. Do not include the articles *a, an,* and *the.*

Reference Note

For more about **capitalizing proper adjectives,** see page 584.

Meeting INDIVIDUAL NEEDS

ENGLISH-LANGUAGE LEARNERS
Spanish. Adjectives derived from names of languages, races, peoples, and nationalities are capitalized in English but not in Spanish.

TECHNOLOGY TIP

Many word-processing programs have a thesaurus in addition to spellchecking features. If your school has the facilities and the appropriate software for computer-assisted instruction, encourage students to use the thesaurus to find synonyms for overused adjectives. Caution students to check the meanings of words in a dictionary to avoid using a word with inappropriate connotations.

The Adjective   **349**

form a real or imagined item for sale, including all necessary details. Explain that specific nouns and vivid adjectives will enhance their descriptions. Then, have students use classified ads in newspapers as models when they adapt their paragraphs to the abbreviated form used in advertisements.

Provide bulletin board space for students to post their ads (with their parents' permission). Your local newspaper's classified department might even be willing to donate column space to the project.

Exercise 10

ALTERNATIVE LESSON
Students who had trouble with **Exercise 8** (identifying adjectives and the nouns or pronouns they modify) might benefit from a reversal of the adjectives-first strategy. Have students identify the nouns in sentences 1, 4, and 8 of **Exercise 10**. [1. *animals, ways;* 4. *armor;* 8. *residents, citizens, creatures*] Point out that after identifying the nouns, students can more easily find the adjectives that "color" them.

TEACHING TIP

Exercise 10 Depending on what students have been taught, they may identify *their* in sentences 3, 4, and 10 as an adjective.

Also, in sentence 8 the word *these* functions as a demonstrative adjective. Remind students that *these* can also function as a demonstrative pronoun, depending on its use.

Exercise 11 Writing Proper Adjectives

ANSWERS

1. Roman

2. Victorian

3. Memorial Day (no change)

4. Korean

5. Congressional *or* congressional

6. New Year's Day (no change) *or* New Years'

7. Incan

8. Shakespearean

9. Jewish *or* Judaic *or* Judaistic

10. Celtic

EXAMPLE   1. We have been studying how various animals protect themselves.
    1. *various—common*

1. Many small animals defend themselves in unusual ways.
2. For example, South American armadillos wear suits of armor that consist of small, bony scales.
3. Armadillos seem delicate, with their narrow faces.
4. However, their tough armor protects them well.
5. Likewise, the Asian anteater has scales that overlap like the shingles on a roof.
6. Unlike anteaters, armadillos are a New World animal.
7. *Armadillo* is a Spanish word that can be translated as "little armor."
8. Texas and Florida residents as well as Mexican citizens are familiar with these shy creatures.
9. At early twilight, look for armadillos, energetic and ready for a meal of unlucky spiders or insects.
10. Like tortoises, armadillos can pull in their noses and all four of their feet for better protection.

Exercise 11 Writing Proper Adjectives

Change the following proper nouns into proper adjectives.

EXAMPLE   1. Spain
    1. *Spanish*

1. Rome	6. New Year's Day
2. Victoria	7. Inca
3. Memorial Day	8. Shakespeare
4. Korea	9. Judaism
5. Congress	10. Celt

Review B Identifying Nouns, Pronouns, and Adjectives

Identify each italicized word in the following paragraph as a *noun*, a *pronoun,* or an *adjective.*

EXAMPLE   Four [1] *forces* govern the flight of an aircraft.
    1. *noun*

┌HELP─
Use a dictionary to help you spell the adjectives in Exercise 11.

MINI-LESSON

Punctuating Adjectives Before Nouns.
Explain to students that a comma is used to separate two or more adjectives that come before a noun, as in *I rode a gentle, intelligent horse.* A comma should never be used between an adjective and the noun immediately following it.

Sometimes, when the final adjective in a series is closely linked to the noun, a comma is not needed before the final adjective:

Lift and thrust must overcome [1] *drag* and weight. If an airplane is very [2] *heavy*, it cannot lift off unless it has great thrust or speed. If the craft is slow, [3] *it* may not have enough thrust to achieve lift. By 1783, the [4] *French* Montgolfiers had learned how to beat gravity and achieve lift in their hot-air balloon. However, it had little thrust and didn't steer well. Nevertheless, [5] *Parisians* didn't mind the unpredictability. In fact, everybody [6] *who* was anybody wanted to hitch a ride on a balloon. With a rudder and propellers, airships (also known as blimps, dirigibles, and Zeppelins) achieved enough thrust to be steered but became unpopular after the [7] *Hindenburg* met [8] *its* fiery fate. Not until Orville and [9] *Wilbur Wright* put an engine on their famous craft and made its wings slightly [10] *movable* was the quest for thrust and lift achieved. As you know, the rest is history.

Determining Parts of Speech

Remember, the way a word is used in a sentence determines what part of speech it is. Some words may be used as nouns or as adjectives.

NOUN   The helmet is made of **steel.**
ADJECTIVE   It is a **steel** helmet.

Some words may be used as pronouns or as adjectives.

PRONOUN   **That** is a surprise.
ADJECTIVE   **That** problem is difficult.

Determining Parts of Speech   **351**

Meeting INDIVIDUAL NEEDS

ADVANCED LEARNERS

A few words can be used as nouns, adjectives, *and* verbs. Challenge students to think of as many such words as possible (individually or in small groups) and to share their lists with the class. [Possibilities include *calm, cut, marble, quiet, silver, snap,* and *yellow.*]

Cooperative Learning

Divide the class into groups of three. Have each group pick from the list they created in the preceding activity three or four words to use in writing a story. Have the first student in each group write a sentence using one of the words as a noun. The second student will write a sentence using the same word as an adjective, and the third student will write a sentence using the word as a verb. As each group moves on to the next word, have them change the order so that each student works with a different part of speech. Volunteers can read their stories to the class.

Maya is a respected broadcast journalist.
If students aren't sure whether the final adjective and the noun are linked, have them use this test. Insert the word *and* between the adjectives. If the use of *and* makes sense, students should use a comma.
For further instruction and practice, refer students to **Chapter 23: Punctuation.**

Meeting INDIVIDUAL NEEDS

MULTIPLE INTELLIGENCES
Intrapersonal Intelligence. Have interested students make a list of five nouns and five adjectives to describe themselves. (Remind students not to write anything they are not willing to share.) Ask them to use this list and to add pronouns as needed to write a short autobiography. If necessary, have them consult the pronoun charts on p. 342 and p. 343.

Review C Identifying Nouns, Pronouns, and Adjectives

Identify the nouns, pronouns, and adjectives in the following sentences. Do not include the articles *a*, *an*, and *the*.

EXAMPLE   1. We walked along the empty beach at sundown.

1. *We—pronoun; empty—adjective; beach—noun; sundown—noun*

1. When the tide comes in, it brings a variety of interesting items from the sea.
2. When the tide ebbs, it leaves behind wonderful treasures for watchful beachcombers.
3. Few large creatures live here, but you almost certainly will find several small animals if you try.
4. Some live in shallow burrows under the wet sand and emerge in the cool evening to dine on bits of plants and other matter.
5. A number of different species of beetle like this part of the beach.
6. Around them you can find bristly flies and tiny worms.
7. You might also come across old pieces of wood with round holes and tunnels in them.
8. These holes are produced by shipworms.
9. If you watch the shoreline carefully, you will see many signs of life that casual strollers miss.
10. Low tide is a marvelous time to search along the shore.

"Now! ... *That* should clear up a few things around here!"

Chapter Review

A. Identifying Types of Nouns

For each of the following sentences, identify the underlined noun of the type indicated in parentheses. There may be more than one type of noun in the sentence.

1. No one understands why <u>whales</u> sometimes strand themselves. (*common*)
2. Since 1985, people in a group called <u>Project Jonah</u> have used an inflatable pontoon to rescue stranded whales and other marine mammals. (*proper*)
3. The people in Project Jonah find <u>fulfillment</u> in helping stranded mammals. (*abstract*)
4. More than two thousand marine <u>mammals</u> have been helped in recent years. (*concrete*)
5. The <u>group</u> has rescued mammals ranging in size from dolphins to whales. (*collective*)

B. Identifying Types of Pronouns

For each of the following sentences, identify the underlined pronoun of the type indicated in parentheses. There may be more than one type of pronoun in the sentence.

6. <u>Which</u> of all the animals do you think has the worst reputation? (*interrogative*)
7. I believe the skunk is the animal <u>that</u> most people want to avoid. (*relative*)
8. The skunk can easily protect <u>itself</u> from others. (*reflexive*)
9. <u>It</u> can spray those nearby with a bad-smelling liquid. (*personal*)
10. <u>This</u> is a repellant that drives away predators. (*demonstrative*)
11. <u>What</u> do you think a skunk uses as its warning? (*interrogative*)
12. It warns possible predators by stamping its feet, <u>which</u> is intended to frighten the predator. (*relative*)
13. When the skunk needs to "attack" some other animal, <u>it</u> sprays in the direction of the victim. (*personal*)

Using the Chapter Review

To assess student progress, you may want to compare the types of items missed on the **Diagnostic Preview** to those missed on the **Chapter Review**. You may want to work out specific goals for mastering essential information with individual students who are still having difficulty.

GRAMMAR

14. <u>Anyone</u> who has ever been sprayed by a skunk will never forget the smell. (*indefinite*)

15. I <u>myself</u> would prefer never to upset a skunk. (*intensive*)

C. Identifying Adjectives

Identify the <u>adjectives</u> in each of the following sentences. Then, write the <u>word the adjective modifies</u>. Do not include the articles *a*, *an*, and *the*. A sentence may have more than one adjective.

16. Chapultepec is the name of a <u>historic</u> <u>castle</u> on a hill in Mexico City.

17. <u>This</u> <u>word</u> means "hill of the grasshopper" in the language of the <u>early</u> <u>Aztecs</u>.

18. <u>Aztec</u> <u>emperors</u> used the <u>park</u> <u>area</u> for hunting and relaxation.

19. In 1783, the hilltop was chosen as the location for the castle of the <u>Spanish</u> <u>viceroy</u>.

20. Even though the castle was never finished, it was used as a fortress during the <u>colonial</u> <u>period</u> of <u>Mexican</u> <u>history</u>.

21. After <u>several</u> <u>decades</u> of neglect, the <u>unfinished</u> <u>castle</u> became the home of the National Military Academy in 1842.

22. In 1847, during a war with the United States, <u>this</u> <u>castle</u> was captured by <u>enemy</u> <u>troops</u>.

23. The emperor of Mexico, Maximilian, converted the castle into an <u>imperial</u> <u>residence</u>.

24. After the downfall of Maximilian in 1867, it became the <u>summer</u> <u>residence</u> of <u>Mexican</u> <u>presidents</u>.

25. In 1937, the property was converted into a <u>national</u> <u>museum</u>.

D. Identifying Nouns, Pronouns, and Adjectives

The following paragraph contains twenty numbered, italicized words. Identify each italicized word as a <u>noun</u>, a ⟨pronoun,⟩ or an <u>adjective</u>.

In [**26**] *this* country [**27**] *mangroves* grow along the coasts of [**28**] *Florida*. [**29**] ⟨*They*⟩ form a [**30**] *wonderland* where land, water, and [**31**] *sky* blend. [**32**] *The* lush, green [**33**] *mangrove* islands and [**34**] *shoreline* are both beautiful and valuable. Mangroves are important to [**35**] ⟨*our*⟩ [**36**] *environment*. They

RESOURCES

Parts of Speech Overview

Review

■ *Grammar, Usage, and Mechanics,* pp. 39, 40, 41

Assessment

■ *Assessment Package*
—*Chapter Tests,* Ch. 11
—*Chapter Tests in Standardized Test Formats,* Ch. 11
■ *Test Generator (One-Stop Planner CD-ROM)*

produce [37] _tons_ of valuable [38] _vegetable_ matter and are an [39] _essential_ part of [40] _tropical_ biology. So far as [41] (we) know, the [42] _first_ reference to mangroves dates back to [43] _Egyptian_ times. A [44] _South African_ expert has also discovered evidence of mangrove islands along the [45] _Red Sea._

Writing Application
Using Pronouns in a Report

Clear Pronoun Reference Your class is creating a bulletin board display for the school's Special People Day. For the display, write a brief report about someone you think is special. Tell why you think so. Be sure that the pronouns you use refer clearly to their antecedents.

Prewriting First, you will need to select your subject. Make a list of the different people you know. Which of these people do you find really remarkable? After you choose a subject, jot down notes about this person. Tell what this person has done to earn your respect and admiration.

Writing As you write your first draft, refer to your notes. Your thesis statement should briefly state what is special about your subject. In the rest of your paragraphs, give specific examples that illustrate why the person is special.

Revising Now, read through your report and imagine that you do not know the subject. What do you think about him or her? Does the person sound special? If not, you may want to add or cut details or rearrange your report. Read your report aloud. Combine short, related sentences by inserting prepositional phrases or appositive phrases.

Publishing Look closely at your use of pronouns. Be sure that each pronoun has a clear antecedent. You may need to correct some sentences to make the antecedents clear. You and your classmates may want to use your reports to make a classroom bulletin board display. If possible, include pictures or drawings of your subjects. You may also wish to send a copy of your report to the special person.

Reference Note

For more about **combining sentences,** see page 273.

Writing Application
(p. 355)

OBJECTIVE

■ To write a brief report about a person, using pronouns that refer clearly to their antecedents

Writing Application

Tip. Remind students that when they use pronouns, they will need to modify the structure of their sentences to ensure clarity of reference.

Scoring Rubric. While you will want to pay particular attention to students' use of pronouns, you will also want to evaluate overall writing performance. You may want to give a split score to indicate development and clarity of the composition as well as grammar skills.

Chapter Review   **355**

CHAPTER

12 Parts of Speech Overview
Verb, Adverb, Preposition, Conjunction, Interjection

Diagnostic Preview

Identifying Verbs, Adverbs, Prepositions, Conjunctions, and Interjections

Identify each italicized word or word group in the following paragraphs as a *verb*, an *adverb*, a *preposition*, a *conjunction*, or an *interjection*.

EXAMPLES   Some [1] *very* unusual words [2] *are used* [3] *in* crossword puzzles.

1. adverb
2. verb
3. preposition

1. prep.	
2. v.	**3.** prep.
4. conj.	**5.** adv.
6. v.	**7.** prep.
8. adv.	**9.** adv.
	10. adv.
	11. adv.
	12. v.

The first crossword puzzle was published [1] *in* 1913. It [2] *appeared* on the Fun Page [3] *of* a New York City newspaper, [4] *and* readers [5] *immediately* [6] *asked* the editors [7] *for* more. [8] *Almost* every newspaper in the United States [9] *now* publishes a daily crossword puzzle.

Every day, millions of Americans [10] *faithfully* work crossword puzzles. Many people take puzzles [11] *quite* seriously. For many, solving puzzles [12] *is* a competitive game.

I [13] *do* puzzles [14] *strictly* for fun. Best of all, I can work on them [15] *by* myself. That way, no one knows whether I succeed [16] *or* fail. I [17] *occasionally* [18] *brag* about my successes. [19] "*Aha!*" I exclaim. "That was a tough one, [20] *but* I filled in every space."

13. v.	**14.** adv.	
15. prep.		
16. conj.	**17.** adv.	**18.** v.
19. int.	**20.** conj.	

The Verb

12a. A ***verb*** is a word that expresses action or a state of being.

EXAMPLES   We **celebrated** the Chinese New Year yesterday.

              The holiday **is** usually in February.

NOTE   In this book, verbs are classified as action or linking verbs, as helping or main verbs, and as transitive or intransitive verbs.

Action Verbs

12b. An ***action verb*** is a verb that expresses either physical or mental activity.

EXAMPLES   The owls **hooted** all night. [physical action]

              Gloria **plays** volleyball. [physical action]

              She **thought** about the problem. [mental action]

              I **believe** you. [mental action]

NOTE   Action verbs may be transitive or intransitive.

Reference Note

For more information about **transitive and intransitive verbs,** see page 364.

Exercise 1   **Classifying Verbs**

Tell whether each of the following action verbs expresses <u>physical</u> or <u>mental</u> action.

EXAMPLE   **1.** visualize

            1. mental

1. pounce   **1.** phys.
2. consider   **2.** ment.
3. wish   **3.** ment.
4. want   **4.** ment.
5. rest   **5.** phys.
6. remember   **6.** ment.
7. dash   **7.** phys.
8. anticipate   **8.** ment.
9. shout   **9.** phys.
10. nibble   **10.** phys.

The Verb   **357**

The Verb
Rules 12a–f *(pp. 357–365)*

OBJECTIVES

■ To classify verbs according to physical or mental action

■ To identify action verbs in sentences

■ To identify linking verbs in sentences

■ To identify verb phrases and helping verbs in sentences

■ To identify verbs in sentences as transitive or intransitive

■ To write sentences that use given verbs as both transitive and intransitive

TEACHING TIP

Activity. To introduce the concept of action verbs, have the class play a game of charades. In advance, prepare strips of paper with one action verb written on each strip. Have volunteers act out the words as the rest of the class tries to guess the action verb. To end the game, write the following commands on the chalkboard: **Stop! Listen. Hurry!** Tell students that verbs are such an important part of our language that they are the only part of speech that can stand alone as a complete sentence.

Meeting
INDIVIDUAL
NEEDS

INCLUSION
This chapter includes many terms. It might help students to have a helper review important ideas frequently with them. Students could benefit from beginning each lesson with a summary of material previously covered. This repetition will help students who have poor recall.

┌─HELP─

Sentences in Exercise 2 may contain more than one action verb.

Reference Note

For more information about **transitive and intransitive verbs,** see page 364.

Exercise 2 **Identifying Action Verbs**

Identify each action verb in the following sentences.

EXAMPLE   **1.** I saw that movie last week.

   1. *saw*

1. For a science project, Elena built a sundial.
2. Mr. Santos carefully explained the word problem to each of the students.
3. I enjoy soccer more than any other sport.
4. This waterfall drops two hundred feet.
5. Mike's bicycle suddenly skidded and fell hard on the wet pavement.
6. Mrs. Karras showed us the way to Johnson City.
7. Mix the ingredients slowly.
8. The heavy traffic delayed us.
9. For the Jewish holiday of Purim, Rachel and her sister Elizabeth gave a party.
10. The early Aztecs worshiped the sun.

Linking Verbs

12c. A *linking verb* is a verb that expresses a state of being. A linking verb connects, or links, the subject to a word or word group that identifies or describes the subject.

EXAMPLES   Denzel Washington **is** an actor. [The verb *is* connects *actor* with the subject *Denzel Washington*.]

The children **remained** quiet. [The verb *remained* links *quiet* with the subject *children*.]

NOTE   Linking verbs never have objects (words that tell who or what receives the action of the verb). Therefore, linking verbs are always intransitive.

Some Forms of the Verb *Be*			
am	were	will be	can be
is	has been	shall be	should be
are	have been	may be	would have been
was	had been	might be	

Other Linking Verbs			
appear	grow	seem	stay
become	look	smell	taste
feel	remain	sound	turn

NOTE *Be* is not always a linking verb. *Be* can express a state of being without having a complement (a word or word group that identifies or describes the subject). In the following sentences, forms of *be* are followed by words or word groups that tell *where*.

EXAMPLES   We **will be** there.

The apples **are** in the bowl.

Some words may be either action verbs or linking verbs, depending on how they are used.

ACTION   Amy **looked** through the telescope.
LINKING   Amy **looked** pale. [The verb *looked* links *pale* with the subject *Amy*.]

ACTION   **Stay** in your seats until the bell rings.
LINKING   **Stay** calm. [The verb *stay* links *calm* with the understood subject *you*.]

Reference Note

For information about **complements,** see Chapter 13.

Exercise 3 Identifying Linking Verbs

Identify the <u>linking verb</u> in each of the following sentences.

EXAMPLE   **1.** A radio station can be the voice of a community.
    1. can be

1. This <u>is</u> Roberto Martínez, your weather forecaster.
2. Unfortunately, the forecast <u>looks</u> bad today.
3. Outside the window here at Station WOLF, the skies <u>appear</u> cloudy.
4. It certainly <u>felt</u> rainy earlier this morning.
5. According to the latest information, it <u>should be</u> a damp, drizzly day with an 85 percent chance of rainfall.
6. Our sportscaster this morning <u>is</u> Marta Segal.
7. Things <u>have been</u> quiet here around Arlington for the past few days.

Reference Note

For more about **understood subjects** in imperative sentences, see page 331.

Critical Thinking

Synthesis. Integrate the study of linking verbs with that of metaphors. Explain to students that a metaphor is an imaginative comparison between two unlike things in which one thing is said to be another thing. A metaphor often uses a linking verb to connect the two things being compared, as in *The night is a black cape* or *The stars are glittering jewels.*

Have students use the chart below to help them create original metaphors. Students can use the noun suggestions in the left-hand column or devise their own.

NOUN	LINKING VERB	METAPHOR
night	is	black cape
stars	are	glittering jewels
eyes		
city		
house		

Exercise 3

ALTERNATIVE LESSON
To remind students that nouns can be both common and proper, have them identify the proper nouns in **Exercise 3** and replace each with an equivalent common noun. [1. *Roberto Martínez—weather forecaster;* 3. *Station WOLF—radio station;* 6. *Marta Segal—sportscaster;* 7. *Arlington—city;* 9. *Arlington Angels—sports team, Jackson City— city, Jackson City Dodgers—sports team*]

Point out that in sentence 6, the proper noun and its common-noun equivalent are actually the items being connected by the linking verb.

GRAMMAR

Meeting

INDIVIDUAL NEEDS

MULTIPLE INTELLIGENCES

Logical-Mathematical Intelligence. Point out that linking verbs are the language equivalent of equal signs. Any verb that can be replaced with *is, am, are, be, become,* or *becomes* to create a sentence with nearly the same meaning is a linking verb. ("The sky looks blue" passes this test, but "I walked home" does not.) If the replacement produces an unintelligible sentence or one with a substantially different meaning, then the original verb is an action verb.

Relating to Writing

Point out that overusing the linking verb *be* can make writing seem dull and lifeless. Replacing overused *be* verbs with well-chosen action verbs can add life to writing.

Ask students to locate pieces of their own writing. Have them work in pairs to circle all forms of *be* that are used as linking verbs. Then, ask the pairs to determine which sentences would seem more lively using action verbs and to rewrite those sentences. Make sure students understand that there is nothing necessarily wrong with using forms of *be*. Have pairs of students share their changes with the rest of the class.

TECHNOLOGY TIP

Tell students that a computer's search function can help them locate and highlight forms of *be* in their writing. Then, students can determine whether the highlighted verb should be replaced with an action verb for greater impact.

8. <u>Stay</u> alert for sports action tonight.
9. It <u>should be</u> an exciting game between our own Arlington Angels and the visiting Jackson City Dodgers.
10. The team <u>looked</u> great at practice today, and I predict a hometown victory.

Review A **Identifying Action Verbs and Linking Verbs**

Identify the verbs in the following sentences. Then, label each verb as either an *action verb* or a *linking verb*.

EXAMPLE **1.** I always enjoy field trips.
  1. enjoy—action verb

—HELP—

Sentences in Review A may contain more than one verb.

1. Last spring, our earth science class <u>visited</u> the Hayden Planetarium.
2. It <u>is</u> a wonderful place, full of amazing sights.
3. We <u>wandered</u> slowly through the various displays and <u>saw</u> a collection of fascinating exhibits.
4. One space vehicle <u>seemed</u> like something from a science fiction movie.
5. Another amazing and interesting display <u>showed</u> a thirty-four-ton meteorite.
6. When this meteorite <u>fell</u> to earth many years ago, it <u>made</u> a huge crater.
7. After a delicious lunch, we <u>stayed</u> for the show in the observatory.
8. As the room <u>became</u> darker, the picture of a galaxy <u>appeared</u> on the ceiling of the dome above us.
9. The lecturer <u>said</u> that the galaxy <u>is</u> so far away from here that its light <u>reaches</u> us centuries after its first appearance.
10. When we <u>look</u> at such stars, we actually <u>see</u> the ancient past!

Exercise 4 **Identifying Action Verbs and Linking Verbs**

Identify the verb in each of the following sentences. Then, label each verb as either an *action verb* or a *linking verb*. If the verb is a linking verb, give the words that it connects.

EXAMPLES   **1.** We sent our dog to obedience school.

      1. sent—action verb

      2. Some breeds are extremely nervous.

      2. are—linking verb; breeds, nervous

1. Everyone felt sorry about the misunderstanding.   **1.** l.v.
2. In daylight, we looked for the lost ring.   **2.** a.v.
3. The temperature plunged to ten degrees below zero.   **3.** a.v.
4. The local museum exhibited beautiful Inuit sculptures.   **4.** a.v.
5. Loretta felt her way carefully through the dark, quiet room.   **5.** a.v.
6. The city almost always smells musty after a heavy summer thunderstorm.   **6.** l.v.
7. Dakar is the capital of Senegal.   **7.** l.v.
8. The firefighter cautiously smelled the burned rags.   **8.** a.v.
9. Antonia Novello was the first female surgeon general of the United States.   **9.** l.v.
10. They looked handsome in their party clothes.   **10.** l.v.

Helping Verbs and Main Verbs

12d. A *helping verb* (*auxiliary verb*) helps the main verb express action or a state of being.

EXAMPLES   **can** speak   **has been** named

          were sent   **should have been** caught

A *verb phrase* contains one main verb and one or more helping verbs.

EXAMPLES   Many people in Africa **can speak** more than one language.

          The packages **were sent** to 401 Maple Street.

          Kansas **has been named** the Sunflower State.

          The ball **should have been caught** by the nearest player.

Relating to Literature

Have students read Alfred Noyes's poem "The Highwayman" if it is available in your literature textbook. Ask students to identify action verbs and linking verbs in several stanzas of the poem. Then, ask students what effect the verb types have on the rhythm and meaning of the poem. [*For example, the repetitive use of the linking verb* was *in the first stanza creates rhythm and a sense of eerie stillness. The sharp onomatopoeic action verbs (*clattered, clashed, *and* creaked) *along with other action verbs (*tapped *and* whistled) *in the third and fourth stanzas break that stillness.*]

Meeting
INDIVIDUAL
NEEDS

LEARNERS HAVING DIFFICULTY

To give students additional assistance with helping verbs, provide examples that can also be used as main verbs, either action or linking. Beginning with *am* in the **Commonly Used Helping Verbs** chart, write these sentence pairs on the chalkboard:

Main verb: I <u>am</u> a teacher.
Helping verb: I <u>am writing</u> a letter.

Main verb: We <u>are</u> hungry.
Helping verb: The girls <u>are playing</u> ball.

Have students volunteer sentences as you continue working through the chart. Make sure students realize that not all helping verbs can be used as main verbs.

ENGLISH-LANGUAGE LEARNERS

Spanish. In Spanish, helping verbs are not used as frequently as they are in English. Consequently, students might need extra help identifying and using helping verbs. You may want to have students write sentences using each of the helping verbs listed in the chart.

Commonly Used Helping Verbs			
Forms of *Be*	am are be	been being is	was were
Forms of *Do*	do	does	did
Forms of *Have*	have	has	had
Other Helping Verbs	can could may	might must will	would shall should

Some verbs can be used as either helping verbs or main verbs.

HELPING VERB   **Do** you like green beans?
  MAIN VERB   Did you **do** this math problem?

HELPING VERB   She **is** arriving at noon.
  MAIN VERB   Her luggage **is** over there.

HELPING VERB   **Have** they arrived yet?
  MAIN VERB   They **have** a dog.

HELPING VERB   Where **has** he gone?
  MAIN VERB   He **has** his homework in his backpack.

Sometimes a verb phrase is interrupted by another part of speech. Often the interrupter is an adverb. In a question, however, the subject often interrupts the verb phrase.

EXAMPLES   Our school **has** always **held** a victory celebration when our team wins.

          Did you **hear** Jimmy Smits's speech?

          Should Anita **bring** her model airplane to class?

          Ken **does** not [*or* **does**n't] **have** a new desk.

Notice in the last example that the adverb *not* [or its contraction *–n't*] is not included in the verb phrase.

Exercise 5 Identifying Verb Phrases and Helping Verbs

Identify the verb phrases in the following sentences. Underline the helping verbs.

EXAMPLE
1. You can recognize redwoods and sequoias by their bark.

1. *can recognize*

1. Have you ever visited Redwood National Park?
2. The giant trees there can be an awesome sight.
3. For centuries, these trees have been an important part of the environment of the northwest United States.
4. Surely, these rare trees must be saved for future generations.
5. More than 85 percent of the original redwood forest has been destroyed over the years.
6. Because of this destruction, the survival of the redwood forest is being threatened.
7. With proper planning years ago, more of the forest might already have been saved.
8. Unfortunately, redwood forests are still shrinking rapidly.
9. According to some scientists, redwood forests outside the park will disappear within our lifetime.
10. However, according to other experts, the redwood forests can still be saved!

Review B Identifying Action Verbs and Linking Verbs

Identify the verbs in the following sentences. Then, label each verb as an *action verb* or a *linking verb*.

EXAMPLE
1. Have you ever seen a play in Spanish?

1. *Have seen—action verb*

1. The Puerto Rican Traveling Theatre performs plays about Hispanic life in the United States.
2. Over the past twenty years, this group has grown into a famous Hispanic theater group.
3. Sometimes, a production has two casts—one that speaks in English and one that speaks in Spanish.
4. In this way, speakers of both languages can enjoy the play.
5. In recent years many young Hispanic playwrights, directors, and actors have begun their careers at the Traveling Theatre.

—HELP—

Some sentences in Review B contain more than one verb. Also, be sure to include all parts of each verb phrase.

The Verb   **363**

Cooperative Learning

To review this segment on verbs, write the following story segment on the chalkboard.

One bright, sunny day a frog (_intransitive_) onto a lily pad. "A frog's life (_linking_) so exciting!" he croaked. "I (_intransitive verb phrase_) all morning, and then I (_transitive_) tasty bugs for lunch."

Have the students supply the correct type of verb or verb phrase for each blank in the story. Then, divide the class into groups of three to continue the story or make up a segment of their own. They should supply only the verb labels instead of the verbs. Their choices are _transitive, transitive verb phrase, intransitive, intransitive verb phrase, linking,_ and _linking verb phrase._ Then, ask groups to exchange papers and fill in the blanks. Circulate throughout the room to help students who are having problems.

Meeting
INDIVIDUAL NEEDS

ENGLISH-LANGUAGE LEARNERS
Spanish. In Spanish, there is not always a distinction between transitive and intransitive verbs as in English. Verbs that are intransitive in English are often used with a reflexive pronoun in Spanish. (_Me bañé antes de salir_ = "I bathed myself before going out.") Point out to your Spanish speakers that when the object of the verb seems to them to be the same as the subject of the verb, the verb is likely considered intransitive in English (unless the verb is followed by a pronoun ending in _–self_ or _–selves_).

6. Some became well-known at the Puerto Rican Traveling Theatre and then moved on to Broadway or Hollywood.
7. Others remain happy at the Traveling Theatre, where they enjoy the warm, supportive atmosphere.
8. Each production by the Traveling Theatre has its own style.
9. Some shows are musicals, full of song and dance, while other plays seem more serious.
10. Light or serious, Puerto Rican Traveling Theatre productions present a lively picture of Hispanic life today.

Transitive and Intransitive Verbs

12e. A _transitive verb_ is a verb that expresses an action directed toward a person, a place, a thing, or an idea.

With transitive verbs, the action passes from the doer—the subject—to the receiver of the action. Words that receive the action of a transitive verb are called _objects._

Reference Note
For more about **objects** and their uses in **sentences,** see page 386.

EXAMPLES   Derrick **greeted** the visitors. [The action of the verb _greeted_ is directed toward the object _visitors._]

When **will** Felicia **paint** her room? [The action of the verb _will paint_ is directed toward the object _room._]

12f. An _intransitive verb_ expresses action (or tells something about the subject) without the action passing to a receiver, or object.

EXAMPLES   The train **stopped.**

Last night we **ate** on the patio.

A verb may be transitive in one sentence and intransitive in another.

EXAMPLES   The children **play** checkers. [transitive]
The children **play** quietly. [intransitive]

Mr. Lopez **is baking** bread. [transitive]
Mr. Lopez **is baking** this afternoon. [intransitive]

Have Roland and Tracy **left** their coats? [transitive]
Have Roland and Tracy **left** yet? [intransitive]

MINI-LESSON

Prepositional Phrases. Recognizing and eliminating prepositional phrases from sentences should make finding objects easier for students. Write the following sentences on the chalkboard.

1. Ally swam across the pool.

2. He kicked the ball over the fence.

3. Will Tony go with us?

Explain that the receiver of the action of a transitive verb is almost always a noun or pronoun and will never be in a preposi-

Exercise 6 — Identifying Transitive and Intransitive Verbs

Identify the italicized verb in each of the following sentences as either *transitive* or *intransitive*.

EXAMPLE
1. She *runs* early in the morning.
1. intransitive

1. If you do different kinds of exercises, you *are exercising* in the correct way.
2. When you exercise to improve endurance, flexibility, and strength, your body *develops*.
3. Aerobic exercise *builds* endurance and strengthens the heart and lungs.
4. When you *walk* quickly, you exercise aerobically.
5. Many active people in the United States *attend* classes in aerobics.
6. They *enjoy* the fun of exercising to popular music.
7. Exercises that *improve* flexibility require you to bend and stretch.
8. *Perform* these exercises slowly to gain the maximum benefit from them.
9. Through isometric and isotonic exercises, your muscle strength *increases*.
10. These exercises *contract* your muscles.

Exercise 7 — Writing Sentences with Transitive and Intransitive Verbs

For each verb given below, write two sentences. In one sentence, use the verb as a *transitive* verb and underline its object. In the other, use the verb as an *intransitive* verb. You may use different tenses of the verb.

EXAMPLE
1. write
1. Alex is writing a research report. (transitive)
   Alex writes in his journal every day. (intransitive)

1. fly	5. drive	9. climb	13. turn	17. skip
2. leave	6. jump	10. watch	14. pay	18. read
3. return	7. hear	11. visit	15. row	19. help
4. draw	8. answer	12. shout	16. run	20. sing

Meeting INDIVIDUAL NEEDS

MODALITIES
Kinesthetic and Visual Learners. To help students better understand transitive and intransitive verbs, write the following sentences on the chalkboard.

1. Melanie ate a baked potato.
2. Hector and Tom are reading.
3. They painted the house.
4. Did you carry his suitcase?
5. My plant grows quickly.

Ask volunteers to go to the chalkboard and draw arrows from the verbs in the sentences to the persons or things that receive the actions of the verbs. Students will find that this can be done only for sentences 1, 3, and 4. Tell students that sentences 1, 3, and 4 contain transitive verbs, while sentences 2 and 5 contain intransitive verbs.

Exercise 7 — Writing Sentences with Transitive and Intransitive Verbs

ANSWERS
Sentences will vary. Here are some possibilities for numbers 1 through 5:

1. I flew a <u>kite</u>.
   The kite flew overhead.
2. She left the <u>meeting</u>.
   We left yesterday.
3. Sharika returns library <u>books</u>.
   Sharika returns from her trip tomorrow.
4. Draw a <u>monster</u>.
   You draw very well.
5. Gabriel drives a <u>convertible</u>.
   Gabriel drove here.

tional phrase. Then, use colored chalk to mark through the prepositional phrases on the chalkboard. Ask volunteers to determine whether the verbs are transitive or intransitive and to explain why. Discuss how eliminating the prepositional phrases made looking for an object in the sentences easier. Suggest that students try to locate all prepositional phrases in **Exercise 6** before determining whether the verb is transitive or intransitive.

The Adverb

Rule 12g *(pp. 366–370)*

OBJECTIVES

- To identify adverbs and the words they modify in sentences
- To supply adverbs to complete a paragraph

Meeting INDIVIDUAL NEEDS

ENGLISH-LANGUAGE LEARNERS
General Strategies. Students may mistakenly use the adverbs *very* and *too* interchangeably. Explain that *very* means "extremely," whereas *too* means "excessively."

For extra practice, have students complete the following sentences by supplying either *very* + an adjective or *too* + an adjective.

1. Vegetarian pizza is _____.
2. I find English class _____.
3. My best friend is _____.
4. Rock music is _____.
5. Summer weather can be _____.

Spanish. Point out to your Spanish-speaking students that the English *–ly* suffix is equivalent to the Spanish *–mente* suffix. Both convert adjectives to adverbs. (In Portuguese the suffix is also *–mente;* in French, it is *–ment.*)

The Adverb

12g. An *adverb* is a word that modifies a verb, an adjective, or another adverb.

Just as an adjective makes the meaning of a noun or a pronoun more definite, an adverb makes the meaning of a verb, an adjective, or another adverb more definite.

Adverbs answer the following questions:

Where?	How often? *or* How long?
When?	To what extent?
How?	*or* How much?

EXAMPLES The sprinter ran **swiftly.** [The adverb *swiftly* modifies the verb *ran* and tells *how.*]

I read the funny pages **early** on Sunday morning. [The adverb *early* modifies the verb *read* and tells *when.*]

Jolene was comforting a **very** small child. [The adverb *very* modifies the adjective *small* and tells *to what extent.*]

The fire blazed **too wildly** for anyone to enter. [The adverb *too* modifies the adverb *wildly* and tells *to what extent.* The adverb *wildly* modifies the verb *blazed* and tells *how.*]

Dad will **sometimes** quote from Archbishop Desmond Tutu's speech. [The adverb *sometimes* modifies the verb *will quote* and tells *how often.*]

Put the apples **there,** and we will eat them **later.** [The adverb *there* modifies the verb *put* and tells *where.* The adverb *later* modifies the verb *will eat* and tells *when.*]

Words Often Used as Adverbs	
Where?	away, here, inside, there, up
When?	later, now, soon, then, tomorrow
How?	clearly, easily, quietly, slowly

RESOURCES

The Adverb

Practice

- *Grammar, Usage, and Mechanics*, pp. 52, 53, 54
- *Language Workshop CD-ROM*, Lesson 5

Words Often Used as Adverbs	
How often? or *How long?*	always, usually, continuously, never, forever, briefly
To what extent? or *How much?*	almost, so, too, more, least, extremely, quite, very, not

NOTE The word *not* is nearly always used as an adverb modifying a verb. When *not* is part of a contraction, as in *hadn't, aren't,* and *didn't,* the *–n't* is still an adverb and is not part of the verb.

Adverb or Adjective?

Many adverbs end in *–ly.* These adverbs are generally formed by adding *–ly* to adjectives.

Adjective	+	–ly	=	Adverb
clear	+	–ly	=	clearly
quiet	+	–ly	=	quietly
convincing	+	–ly	=	convincingly

However, some words ending in *–ly* are used as adjectives.

Adjectives Ending in *–ly*		
daily	friendly	lonely
early	kindly	timely

NOTE The adverb *very* is often overused. In your writing, try to use adverbs other than *very* to modify adjectives. You can also revise sentences so that other words carry more of the descriptive meaning.

EXAMPLE Chloe is **very** tall.
REVISED Chloe is **amazingly** tall.
or
Chloe is **5'11" tall** and **is a guard on the varsity basketball team.**

Reference Note
For more about **contractions,** see page 641.

TIPS & TRICKS

If you aren't sure whether a word is an adjective or an adverb, ask yourself what it modifies. If a word modifies a noun or a pronoun, it is an adjective.

EXAMPLE
She gave us a **friendly** hello. [*Friendly* modifies the noun *hello* and is used as an adjective.]

If a word modifies a verb, an adjective, or an adverb, then it is an adverb.

EXAMPLE
People from many nations have come to the United States **recently.** [The adverb *recently* modifies the verb *have come.*]

Reference Note
For more about **adjectives,** see page 346.

The Adverb **367**

Cooperative Learning

Explain to students that some words can be used either as adjectives or as adverbs. To reinforce the concept, divide students into groups of four, which will then split off into two pairs. Give each pair the following list of words: *close, next, far, late, more, most, low, light, deep,* and *first.* Have each pair work together to generate two sentences for each word—one using the word as an adjective [*That was a* close *call*] and one using the word as an adverb [*The bird flew* close *to the window*]. Then, ask the two pairs in each group to exchange sentences and label the words as adjectives or adverbs.

Use the **Mini-Lesson** that begins at the bottom of this page to help students who have difficulty distinguishing between adjectives and adverbs.

MINI-LESSON *Continued on pp. 368–369*

Adverb or Adjective? In their writing, students will often have to decide whether to use the adjective or the adverb form of a word. Write the following sentences on the chalkboard. Answers are underlined.

1. I am having a (*real, really*) good time.

2. Tim arrived (*safe, safely*).

3. He spoke too (*quiet, quietly*).

Ask volunteers to determine which of

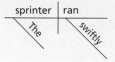
Meeting INDIVIDUAL NEEDS

MULTIPLE INTELLIGENCES

Spatial Intelligence. Some students—especially visual, spatial, and logical learners—may find sentence diagramming useful in understanding adverbs. Include the information about adjectives on p. 367 to help students differentiate between adjectives and adverbs.

You may want to use several example sentences from p. 366 to illustrate diagramming.

The sprinter ran swiftly.

sprinter	ran
The	swiftly

Jolene was comforting a very small child.

Jolene	was comforting	child
		a / small / very

Statue of Cherokee mourning those who died on the Trail of Tears.

Exercise 8 Identifying Adverbs

Identify each <u>adverb</u> and the <u>word or words it modifies</u> in each of the following sentences.

EXAMPLE 1. Today, many Cherokee people make their homes in Oklahoma.

1. *Today—make*

1. Oklahoma is <u>not</u> the Cherokees' original home.
2. The Cherokees <u>once</u> lived in Georgia, North Carolina, Alabama, and Tennessee.
3. A number of Cherokees <u>still</u> live in the Great Smoky Mountains of North Carolina.
4. Settlers <u>often</u> ignored the Cherokees' right to the land.
5. Feeling threatened by the settlers, the Cherokees <u>readily</u> supported the British during the Revolutionary War.
6. In 1829, people hurried <u>excitedly</u> to northern Georgia for the first gold rush in the United States.
7. Many white settlers of the region were <u>extremely</u> eager to find gold.
8. <u>Later</u>, the Cherokees were forced by the United States government to leave their land.
9. The Cherokee people were <u>hardly</u> given a chance to collect their belongings.
10. Many Cherokees will <u>never</u> forget the Trail of Tears, which led their ancestors to Oklahoma.

The Position of Adverbs

One of the characteristics of adverbs is that they may appear at various places in a sentence. Adverbs may come before, after, or between the words they modify.

EXAMPLES   We **often** study together.

We study together **often.**

Often we study together.

When an adverb modifies a verb phrase, it frequently comes in the middle of the phrase.

EXAMPLE   We have **often** studied together.

MINI-LESSON

the answers are correct, and explain why. Remind students to ask themselves two questions:

• What does the word modify?

• What question does the word answer? (Refer students to p. 346 for a list of ways that adjectives modify nouns and pronouns and to p. 366 for a list of questions that adverbs answer.)

An adverb that introduces a question, however, appears at the beginning of a sentence.

EXAMPLES   **When** does your school start? [The adverb *When* modifies the verb phrase *does start.*]

          How did you spend your vacation? [The adverb *How* modifies the verb phrase *did spend.*]

Exercise 9   Identifying Adverbs

Identify the <u>adverbs</u> and the <u>words they modify</u> in the following sentences.

—HELP—
Some sentences in Exercise 9 contain more than one adverb.

EXAMPLE   1. "To Build a Fire" is a dramatically suspenseful short story.

          1. dramatically—suspenseful

1. In this story, a nameless character <u>goes</u> <u>outdoors</u> on a <u>terribly</u> <u>cold</u> day in the Yukon.
2. Except for a dog, he is traveling completely alone.
3. <u>Soon</u> both the dog's muzzle and the man's beard <u>are frosted</u> with ice.
4. Along the way, the man <u>accidentally</u> <u>falls</u> into a stream.
5. Soaked and chilled, he <u>desperately</u> <u>builds</u> a fire under a tree.
6. The flames <u>slowly</u> <u>grow</u> stronger.
7. <u>Unfortunately</u>, he <u>has built</u> his fire in the wrong place.
8. A pile of snow <u>suddenly</u> <u>falls</u> from a tree limb and kills the small fire.
9. Unable to relight the fire, the man <u>again</u> <u>finds</u> himself in serious trouble.
10. Based on what you <u>now</u> <u>know</u> about the story, what kind of ending would you write <u>for</u> "To Build a Fire"?

2. completely—alone/alone is traveling

Link to   Literature

Exercise 10   Writing Adverbs

Write ten different adverbs to fill the blanks in the following sentences.

EXAMPLE   I have **[1]** _____ been a music lover.

          1. always

Every Friday I **[1]** _____ go to the record store. I can **[2]** _____ wait to see what new cassettes and CDs have arrived. As soon as

The Adverb   **369**

Exercise 10   Writing Adverbs

ANSWERS
Responses will vary. Only adverbs that answer certain questions can go in each blank.

  1. how *or* how often
  2. to what extent *or* how often

To extend the lesson, ask students to locate pieces of their own writing and circle all adjectives and adverbs to see whether the words have been used correctly.

Exercise 10 Writing Adverbs

ANSWERS continued

3. where *or* how
4. to what extent *or* how
5. how *or* when *or* how often
6. how *or* to what extent
7. how
8. how *or* when
9. where *or* how
10. how *or* to what extent

The Preposition

Rule 12h (*pp. 370–373*)

OBJECTIVES

■ **To supply prepositions in order to complete sentences**

■ **To identify prepositional phrases in sentences**

■ **To identify prepositions and their objects in prepositional phrases**

■ **To identify words in sentences as adverbs or as prepositions**

Meeting
INDIVIDUAL NEEDS

ENGLISH-LANGUAGE LEARNERS
General Strategies. There is no clear correspondence between English prepositions and prepositions in other languages. Using the list of **Commonly Used Prepositions**, pair English-language learners with native speakers to write down an example of each preposition used in a sentence and then to define the preposition. Be prepared to help struggling students define the less familiar prepositions.

STYLE TIP

In formal writing, it is often considered best to avoid ending a sentence with a preposition. However, this usage is becoming more accepted in casual speech and informal writing. You should follow your teacher's instructions on sentences ending with prepositions.

---

school is out, I bicycle [**3**] _____ to the store and join the other [**4**] _____ enthusiastic customers. [**5**] _____ I stroll through the aisles and [**6**] _____ study the selections. I listen [**7**] _____ as the loudspeaker announces the day's specials. When I have decided what I want, I [**8**] _____ figure out which items I can afford. Then I walk [**9**] _____ to the cash register. I grin [**10**] _____ as I think of how much I will enjoy the music.

The Preposition

12h. A *preposition* is a word that shows the relationship of a noun or pronoun to another word.

Notice how changing the preposition in these sentences changes the relationship of *walked* to *door* and *kite* to *tree*.

> The cat walked **through** the door.
> The cat walked **toward** the door.
> The cat walked **past** the door.

> The kite **in** the tree is mine.
> The kite **beside** the tree is mine.
> The kite **in front of** the tree is mine. [Notice that a preposition may be made up of more than one word. Such a preposition is called a *compound preposition*.]

Commonly Used Prepositions				
aboard	before	for	off	toward
about	behind	from	on	under
above	below	in	out	underneath
across	beneath	in front of	out of	unlike
after	beside	inside	over	until
against	between	instead	past	up
along	beyond	into	since	up to
among	by	like	through	upon
around	down	near	throughout	with
as	during	next to	till	within
at	except	of	to	without

RESOURCES

The Preposition
Practice

■ *Grammar, Usage, and Mechanics,* pp. 55, 56, 57
■ *Language Workshop CD-ROM,* Lesson 6

Exercise 11 Writing Prepositions

Write two prepositions for each blank in the following sentences. Be prepared to tell how the meanings of the two resulting sentences differ.

EXAMPLE   1. The car raced _____ the highway.
           1. *along, across*

1. We practiced karate _____ dinner.
2. She jumped up and ran _____ the park.
3. A boat with red sails sailed _____ the river.
4. The hungry dog crawled _____ the fence.
5. The marathon runner jogged easily _____ the track at the stadium.
6. Put the speakers _____ the stage, Cody.
7. Brightly colored confetti streamed _____ the piñata when it burst open.
8. Why does Roseanne always sit _____ the door?
9. Excuse me, but the blue fountain pen _____ your chair is mine, I believe.
10. Parrots _____ the South American jungle squawked all through the hot afternoon.

The Prepositional Phrase

A *prepositional phrase* includes a preposition, a noun or pronoun called the *object of the preposition,* and any modifiers of that object.

EXAMPLES   You can press those leaves **under glass.** [The noun *glass* is the object of the preposition *under.*]

Fred stood **in front of us.** [The pronoun *us* is the object of the compound preposition *in front of.*]

The books **in my new pack** are heavy. [The noun *pack* is the object of the preposition *in.* The words *my* and *new* modify *pack.*]

A preposition may have more than one object.

EXAMPLES   Thelma's telegram to **Nina** and **Ralph** contained good news. [The preposition *to* relates its objects, *Nina* and *Ralph,* to *telegram.*]

┌HELP─

In the example for Exercise 11, the car was on the highway. In the second sentence, the car crossed the highway.

OVERBOARD © 1993 Universal Press Syndicate. Reprinted with permission. All rights reserved.

The Preposition   **371**

Exercise 11 Writing Prepositions

ANSWERS
Responses will vary. Here are some possibilities:
1. before, after
2. by, to
3. down, along
4. under, through
5. around, near
6. above, on
7. from, out of
8. near, by
9. on, near
10. in, from

TEACHING TIP

Activity. Find or draw a large picture of a dangerous animal such as a shark. Post it in the room, and write the following sentence on the chalkboard.

I don't want to be _____ the [*name of animal*].

Have students suggest prepositions that tell where (in relationship to the animal) they don't want to be. [*Possible answers:* around, in, near, on, under, *and so on.*]

GRAMMAR

Learning for Life

Continued on pp. 372–373

Thank-you Notes. The instructions and exercises that help students identify parts of speech are simply stepping stones to the real objective: actually using the various parts of speech effectively in writing and speaking. Explain to students that they will incorporate what they have learned in **Chapter 12** in writing a thank-you note. Ask students to think of a reason—either real or imagined—to thank someone for taking the time, trouble, or expense to do something nice for them. Refer students to

ENGLISH-LANGUAGE LEARNERS
Spanish. In Spanish, the preposition *a* can be used to denote *in, on,* and *at* (as well as other prepositions). To help students decide which of these three English prepositions is appropriate, define the prepositions and give examples of them that can be demonstrated in the classroom, such as *in the desk, on the desk,* and *at the chalkboard.*

Looking at Language

Dialects. Explain that prepositions are especially subject to dialect variations, which depend partly on where we live, how old we are, and to what ethnic or social group we belong. Ask students to tell which of the following choices sound most familiar. Ask whether they have heard the others used as well.

1. I feel sick (to, at, in, on) my stomach.

2. The time is a quarter (of, till, to) ten.

3. We will stay (at, to) home this weekend.

Reference Note

For more about **infinitives,** see page 414.

— HELP —

Some sentences in Exercise 12 contain more than one prepositional phrase.

The objects of prepositions may have modifiers.

EXAMPLE   It happened during **the last** examination. [*The* and *last* are adjectives modifying *examination,* which is the object of the preposition *during.*]

NOTE   Be careful not to confuse a prepositional phrase beginning with *to* (*to the park, to him*) with an infinitive beginning with *to* (*to sing, to be heard*).

Exercise 12 **Identifying Prepositional Phrases**

Identify the prepositional phrases in the following sentences. Underline the preposition once and its object twice.

EXAMPLES   1. Commander Robert Peary claimed that he reached the North Pole in 1909.

   1. *in 1909*

   2. Peary and Matthew Henson searched for the North Pole for many years.

   2. *for the North Pole, for many years*

1. Henson traveled with Peary on every expedition except the first one.

2. However, for a long time, Henson received no credit at all for his role.

3. Peary had hired Henson as an assistant on a trip Peary made to Nicaragua.

4. There, Peary discovered that Henson had sailing experience and could also chart a path through the jungle.

5. As a result, Peary asked Henson to join his Arctic expedition shown in the photograph on this page.

6. The two explorers became friends during their travels in the North.

7. On the last three miles to the North Pole, Henson did not go with Peary.

8. Because he was the leader of the trip, Peary received the credit for the achievement.

9. Finally, after many years, Henson was honored by Congress, Maryland's state government, and two U.S. presidents.

10. Both Peary and Henson wrote books about their experiences.

Learning for Life

the **Quick Reference Handbook** for the appropriate letter form.

Before students write their rough drafts, explain that their notes should say more than simply "Thank you for the lovely sweater." Students should tell why the

gift or gesture was special to them.

Upon completion, have students exchange papers and check for the appropriate use of the parts of speech. Peer reviewers might use the following questions:

Preposition or Adverb?

Some words may be used either as prepositions or as adverbs. Remember that a preposition always has an object. An adverb never does. If you can't tell whether a word is used as an adverb or a preposition, look for an object.

ADVERB	I haven't seen him **since.**
PREPOSITION	I haven't seen him **since** Thursday. [*Thursday* is the object of the preposition *since.*]

ADVERBS	The bear walked **around** and then went **inside.**
PREPOSITIONS	The bear walked **around** the yard and then went **inside** the cabin. [*Yard* is the object of the preposition *around. Cabin* is the object of *inside.*]

Exercise 13 Identifying Adverbs and Prepositions

Identify the italicized word in each of the following sentences as either an *adverb* or a *preposition*.

EXAMPLE   **1.** He watches uneasily as the hunter slowly brings the pistol *up.*

  1. *up—adverb*

1. "The Most Dangerous Game" is the story of Rainsford, a famous hunter who falls *off* a boat and comes ashore on a strange island.
2. Rainsford knows that this island is feared by every sailor who passes *by.*
3. In fact, *among* sailors, the place is known as Ship-Trap Island.
4. After looking *around* for several hours, Rainsford can't understand why the island is considered so dangerous.
5. Finally, he discovers a big house *on* a high bluff.
6. A man with a pistol *in* his hand answers the door.
7. Putting his pistol *down*, the man introduces Rainsford to the famous hunter General Zaroff.
8. Zaroff invites Rainsford *inside.*
9. Soon, however, Rainsford wishes he could get *out* and never see Zaroff again.
10. Rainsford has finally discovered the secret *about* the island—Zaroff likes to hunt human beings!

TIPS & TRICKS

When you are looking for the object of a preposition, be careful. Sometimes the object comes before, not after, the preposition.

EXAMPLES
Here is the CD **that** I was looking for yesterday. [*That* is the object of the preposition *for.*]

She is the speaker **whom** we enjoyed listening to so much. [*Whom* is the object of the preposition *to.*]

Link to Literature

The Preposition   **373**

---

1. Could any linking verbs be replaced with action verbs to make the writing more lively?
2. Would well-chosen adverbs add interest?
3. Could any subjects, verbs, or sentences be joined by conjunctions to improve the note?

Students may choose to mail their thank-you notes, or you could display the notes in the classroom.

The Conjunction

Rule 12i *(pp. 374–377)*

OBJECTIVES

- To identify conjunctions and the words they join in sentences
- To complete sentences by providing appropriate conjunctions
- To write sentences that contain conjunctions used in specified ways

TEACHING TIP

Activity. To reinforce the concept of conjunctions as joining words, diagram some of the examples on this page, adding additional words to make complete sentences. Diagramming could prove particularly helpful for visual, spatial, and logical-mathematical learners. Refer students to the **Diagramming Appendix** for more examples.

Jill or Anna is going.

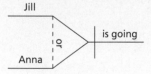

Our strict but fair teacher is leaving.

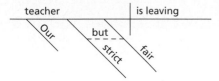

I must go over the river and through the woods.

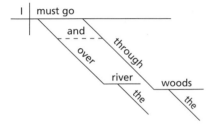

STYLE TIP

The conjunction *so* is often overused. In your writing, revise sentences as needed to avoid overusing *so*.

EXAMPLE
Traffic is bad, so we'll probably be late.

REVISED
Because traffic is bad, we'll probably be late.

TIPS & TRICKS

You can remember the seven coordinating conjunctions as FANBOYS:

For
And
Nor
But
Or
Yet
So

Reference Note

For more about **using commas between independent clauses,** see page 605.

The Conjunction

12i. A *conjunction* is a word that joins words or word groups.

(1) *Coordinating conjunctions* join words or word groups that are used in the same way.

Coordinating Conjunctions						
and	but	for	nor	or	so	yet

EXAMPLES   Jill **or** Anna [*Or* joins two nouns.]

strict **but** fair [*But* joins two adjectives.]

over the river **and** through the woods [*And* joins two prepositional phrases.]

Alice Walker wrote the book, **yet** she did not write the movie script. [*Yet* joins two independent clauses.]

The word *for* may be used either as a conjunction or as a preposition. When *for* joins word groups that are independent clauses, it is used as a conjunction. Otherwise, it is used as a preposition.

CONJUNCTION   He waited patiently, **for** he knew his ride would be along soon.

PREPOSITION   He waited patiently **for** his ride.

NOTE   Coordinating conjunctions that join independent clauses are almost always preceded by a comma. When *for* is used as a conjunction, there should always be a comma in front of it.

EXAMPLES   She has read the book**,** **but** she has not seen the movie.

We can bathe the dog**,** **or** you can do it when you get home from school.

Did Nazir call her**,** **and** has she called him back?

We asked Jim to be on time**,** **yet** he isn't here.

I'll be home late**,** **for** I have basketball practice until 4:30 or 5:00 today.

RESOURCES

The Conjunction

Practice

- *Grammar, Usage, and Mechanics,* pp. 58–59
- *Language Workshop CD-ROM,* Lesson 7

---

(2) *Correlative conjunctions* are pairs of conjunctions that join words or word groups that are used in the same way.

Correlative Conjunctions	
both . . . . and	not only . . . . but also
either . . . . or	whether . . . . or
neither . . . . nor	

EXAMPLES   **Both** Bill Russell **and** Larry Bird played for the team. [The pair of conjunctions joins two nouns.]

She looked **neither** to the left **nor** to the right. [The pair of conjunctions joins two prepositional phrases.]

Not only did Wilma Rudolph overcome her illness, **but** she **also** became an Olympic athlete. [The pair of conjunctions joins two independent clauses.]

NOTE A third kind of conjunction—the *subordinating conjunction*—introduces an adverb clause.

EXAMPLES Meet me in the park **after** the bell chimes.

Before I washed the dishes, I let them soak in the sudsy water.

Reference Note

For more information about **subordinating conjunctions,** see page 431. For more on **adverb clauses,** see page 430.

Exercise 14 Identifying Conjunctions

Identify the conjunction or conjunctions in each of the following sentences. Be prepared to tell what words or word groups each conjunction or pair of conjunctions joins.

EXAMPLE   **1.** Both she and her mother enjoy sailing.
      1. *Both . . . and*

1. I wanted to see Los Lobos in concert, but I didn't have the money.
2. Our class is recycling not only newspapers but also glass bottles and aluminum cans.
3. He set the table with chopsticks and rice bowls.
4. Have you seen either LeAnn Rimes or Janet Jackson in person?

HELP

In the example in Exercise 14, the conjunction joins *she* and *her mother*.

The Conjunction   **375**

Crossing the Curriculum

Physical Science. In addition to its meaning in grammar, the word *conjunction* has a scientific meaning as well: the apparent meeting or passing of two or more celestial bodies. For example, the moon is in conjunction with the sun when the moon moves between the sun and the earth. In this way, the celestial bodies are "joined together" by the imaginary straight line that connects them.

Meeting
INDIVIDUAL
NEEDS

MULTIPLE INTELLIGENCES
Logical-Mathematical Intelligence. Draw a Venn diagram on the chalkboard with the following labels: (a) months whose names start with *m,* (b) months whose names end with *y,* and (c) months whose names start with *m and* end with *y*:

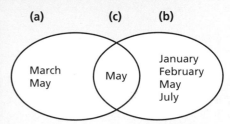

(a) March May **(c)** May **(b)** January February May July

The activity can be expanded to include other conjunctions besides *and,* such as *or* (months whose names start with *m or* end with *y*) and *neither . . . nor* (months whose names *neither* start with *m nor* end with *y*).

MINI-LESSON   *Continued on p. 376*

Subject-Verb Agreement. Explain to students that subjects and verbs must agree in number. When a subject is compound, the conjunction that connects the subjects affects number. Write the following sentences on the chalkboard.

1. The train **and** the bus leave in five minutes.
2. **Neither** the train **nor** the bus leaves on time.
3. The conductor **or** the passengers need assistance.

5. We learned to use <u>neither</u> too many adjectives <u>nor</u> too few.
6. That diet is dangerous, <u>for</u> it does not adequately meet the body's needs.
7. Both the Mohawk <u>and</u> the Oneida are part of the famous Iroquois Confederacy.
8. It rained all day, <u>yet</u> we enjoyed the trip.
9. Shall we walk home <u>or</u> take the bus?
10. Revise your paper, <u>and</u> proofread it carefully.

Exercise 15 Writing Conjunctions

POSSIBLE ANSWERS

1. either...or *or* both...and
2. and
3. but
4. both...and *or* not only...but also
5. Either...or
6. so
7. or
8. whether...or
9. neither...nor
10. yet

PEANUTS reprinted by permission of United Feature Syndicate, Inc.

Exercise 15 Writing Conjunctions

Provide an appropriate conjunction for each blank in the following sentences.

EXAMPLES
1. _____ solve the problem yourself, _____ ask your teacher for help.
1. *Either . . . or*

2. Would she prefer juice _____ iced tea?
2. *or*

1. We will visit _____ the Johnson Space Center _____ Astroworld in Houston, Texas.
2. Alaska _____ Hawaii were the last two states admitted to the Union.
3. Those two students are twin sisters, _____ they do not dress alike.
4. They were _____ hungry _____ thirsty.
5. _____ turn that radio down, _____ take it into your room while I'm studying.
6. These nails aren't long enough, _____ I'm going to buy some others.
7. You could put the chair in the living room, in your bedroom, _____ even in the dining room.
8. Their weather forecaster isn't sure _____ it will rain _____ not.
9. In the delicate ecosystem of the river, _____ motorboats _____ personal watercraft are allowed.
10. His bike is old, _____ it takes him anywhere he needs to go.

MINI-LESSON

The first sentence shows that subjects joined by *and* usually take a plural verb. The second sentence illustrates that singular subjects joined by *or* or *nor* take a singular verb. When a singular subject and a plural subject are joined by *or* or *nor,* the verb agrees with the subject nearer the verb, as in the third sentence. For additional information and practice, refer students to p. 458.

Exercise 16 Writing Sentences with Conjunctions

Follow the directions given below to write sentences using conjunctions.

EXAMPLE   **1.** Use *and* to join two verbs.

        1. Jessye Norman smiled at the audience and bowed.

1. Use *and* to join two adverbs.
2. Use *or* to join two prepositional phrases.
3. Use *for* to join word groups that are sentences.
4. Use *but* to join two linking verbs.
5. Use *either . . . or* in an imperative sentence.
6. Use *or* to join two nouns.
7. Use *both . . . and* to join two subjects.
8. Use *neither . . . nor* to join two adverbs.
9. Use *yet* to join two adjectives.
10. Use *whether . . . or* in an interrogative sentence.

The Interjection

12j. An ***interjection*** **is a word that expresses emotion.**

Commonly Used Interjections			
aha	my	ouch	wow
hey	oh	rats	yikes
hurray	oops	well	yippee

An interjection has no grammatical relationship to the rest of the sentence.

     Usually an interjection is followed by an exclamation point.

EXAMPLES   **Ouch!** That hurts!

            Goodness! What a haircut!

            Aha! I know the answer.

     Sometimes an interjection is set off by a comma.

EXAMPLES   **Oh,** I wish it were Friday.

            Well, what have you been doing?

The Interjection   **377**

Exercise 16 Writing Sentences with Conjunctions

ANSWERS
Sentences will vary. Here are some possibilities:

1. He sang merrily and loudly.
2. The spy may be hiding in the attic or behind the curtains.
3. I will run to school, for I am late.
4. He seems frightening but is actually very sweet.
5. Either wash the dishes or sweep the floor.
6. Katrina or Joey will win the contest.
7. Both oranges and grapefruits are good sources of vitamin C.
8. Her efforts were performed neither promptly nor satisfactorily.
9. I found that book interesting yet lengthy.
10. Do you know whether our team won or lost the game?

The Interjection
Rule 12j *(pp. 377–378)*

OBJECTIVE

■ **To complete sentences using interjections**

RESOURCES

The Interjection
Practice
■ *Grammar, Usage, and Mechanics,* pp. 60, 61
■ *Language Workshop CD-ROM,* Lesson 8

Exercise 17 Writing Interjections

ANSWERS
Answers will vary.

TEACHING TIP

Activity. Have students create comic strips that include interjections. Students can create their own characters or use existing comic strip characters. Students should use the conventional word-bubble format for dialogue and include several interjections.

Meeting
INDIVIDUAL
NEEDS

ENGLISH-LANGUAGE LEARNERS
General Strategies. Most languages include interjections. Ask students who speak other languages to share appropriate interjections from their languages with the class. Often, interjections such as *ouch* are similar in many different languages.

STYLE TIP

Interjections are common in casual conversation. In writing, however, they're usually used only in dialogue meant to represent such conversation. When you use interjections in dialogue, use an exclamation point to indicate strong emotion and a comma to indicate mild emotion.

EXAMPLES
Hey! Watch out for that wire!

I like that outfit, but, **wow,** it's really expensive.

Notice in the second example above that commas are used both before and after an interjection that interrupts a sentence.

Exercise 17 Writing Interjections

Choose an appropriate interjection for each blank in the following sentences. Use a variety of interjections.

EXAMPLE   1. _____ , I'd love to go to your party.
          1. *Hey, I'd love to go to your party.*

1. _____! The heel just fell off my shoe.
2. There's, _____, about seven dollars in the piggy bank.
3. _____, finally we're finished raking those leaves.
4. _____! You squirrels, stop eating the birds' food!
5. Young Eric, _____, you certainly have grown!
6. _____! I sprained my ankle during the obstacle course!
7. Weren't the special effects in the movie amazing? _____!
8. _____, there's only one round left in the tournament.
9. _____! I knew you were planning a surprise!
10. _____, what a relief it is to have that term paper finished.

Review C Identifying Parts of Speech

Label each italicized word or word group in the following sentences as a *verb*, an *adverb*, a *preposition*, a *conjunction*, or an *interjection*.

EXAMPLE   1. *Both* otters *and* owls hunt *from* dusk to dawn.
          1. *Both . . . and—conjunction; from—preposition*

1. int./adv.   1. *Oh!* I *just* spilled tomato soup on the new white tablecloth!
2. adv./prep.   2. Luis Alvarez *closely* studied atomic particles *for* many years.
3. v./conj.   3. *Did* Toni Morrison *or* Toni Cade Bambara write the book that you are reading?
4. v./prep.   4. The Inuit hunters *ate* their meal *inside* the igloo.
5. conj./adv.   5. They were tired, *yet* they did *not* quit working.
6. v./conj.   6. I *like* Persian carpets, *for* they are beautiful and wear well.
7. v./prep.   7. The plane from Venezuela *nears* the terminal and taxis *down* the runway.
8. conj./adv.   8. *Either* geraniums *or* daisies would grow *well* in that sunny corner of the garden.
9. adv./prep.   9. Put your pencils *down,* class, *during* the instructions for this test.
10. int./adv.   10. Computers and, *oh,* all that electronic stuff seem *so* easy for you, Brittany.

Determining Parts of Speech

12k. The way a word is used in a sentence determines what part of speech it is.

The same word may be used as different parts of speech.

NOUN	The **play** had a happy ending.
VERB	The actors **play** their roles.

NOUN	The **outside** of the house needs paint.
ADVERB	Let's go **outside** for a while.
PREPOSITION	I saw the birds' nest **outside** my window.

NOUN	The **well** has run dry.
ADVERB	Did you do **well** on the quiz?
ADJECTIVE	I don't feel **well** today.
INTERJECTION	**Well,** that's a relief.

Review D **Identifying Verbs, Adverbs, Prepositions, Conjunctions, and Interjections**

For each of the following sentences, identify the italicized, numbered word or word group as a *verb*, an *adverb*, a *preposition*, a *conjunction*, or an *interjection*.

EXAMPLE   [1] *Hey,* I recognize that place!

       1. interjection

Though you might recognize the scene at right from the movies, it is [1] *not* a fake movie set. Khasneh al Faroun, or the "Pharaoh's Treasury," is the name of this magnificent structure, and it is [2] *quite* real. Located south of Jerusalem [3] *and* west of the Jordan River, the Pharaoh's Treasury is one of many sites in the ancient city of Petra. The word *Petra* [4] *means* "rock," and the city is carved out of solid sandstone. Petra served as a busy center of trade, and thousands of people strolled its streets [5] *or* sat in its outdoor theater. The theater seats [6] *about* four thousand people and is so old that the Romans had to repair it in A.D. 106. After a short occupation by Crusaders, the city was forbidden to Europeans [7] *for* about seven hundred years.

Determining Parts of Speech   **379**

Review D **Identifying Verbs, Adverbs, Prepositions, Conjunctions, and Interjections**

ANSWERS

1. adv.
2. adv.
3. conj.
4. v.
5. conj.
6. adv.
7. prep.

Review D Identifying Verbs, Adverbs, Prepositions, Conjunctions, and Interjections

ANSWERS continued

8. int.
9. v.
10. v.

Review E Writing Sentences

ANSWERS

Sentences will vary. Here are some possibilities:

1. Don't *walk* on the grass.—verb
   The *walk* helped her headache.
   —noun

2. That smells *like* spaghetti.
   —preposition
   I *like* fresh vegetables.—verb

3. That *well* has been dry for
   years.—noun
   Are you feeling *well*?—adjective

4. I'm staying *inside*.—adverb
   He keeps his marbles *inside* a jar.
   —preposition

5. Who needs a *fast* car?—adjective
   He drives too *fast*.—adverb

[8] *Well*, you're probably wondering about the "treasury" part of the name. For many years, the large urn atop the dome over the statue [9] *was believed* to be full of gold. However, as Bedouin treasure hunters [10] *discovered* long ago, the urn is just rock.

Review E Writing Sentences

Write ten sentences, following the directions given below. Underline the given word in each sentence, and identify how it is used.

EXAMPLE
1. Use *yet* as an adverb and as a conjunction.
   1. Are we there *yet*?—adverb
      The sky grew somewhat brighter, *yet* the rain continued falling.—conjunction

1. Use *walk* as a verb and as a noun.
2. Use *like* as a preposition and as a verb.
3. Use *well* as a noun and as an adjective.
4. Use *inside* as an adverb and as a preposition.
5. Use *fast* as an adjective and as an adverb.

Chapter Review

A. Identifying Types of Verbs

Identify each <u>italicized verb</u> in the following sentences as a *linking verb*, a *transitive action verb*, or an *intransitive action verb*.

1. l.v.
2. t.a.v.
3. l.v.
4. l.v.
5. t.a.v.
6. t.a.v.
7. i.a.v.
8. t.a.v.
9. i.a.v.
10. l.v.

1. A land survey *is* a method of measuring land.

2. When he was cutting lumber, my father *used* a table saw.

3. Each concert in the series *was* an hour long.

4. The water *became* ice when the temperature dropped.

5. *Hang* the banner from the ceiling.

6. The astronomer *calculated* the distance to the galaxy.

7. Mr. Lurie and Ms. Modeski *walked* hand in hand.

8. The cook *multiplied* the ingredients of the stew by three.

9. Substitute teachers *work* hard!

10. *Are* they weary at the end of the day?

B. Identifying Verb Phrases

Identify the <u>verb phrase</u> in each of the following sentences, and underline the (helping verb).

11. (Have) you ever <u>heard</u> of a mongoose?

12. (Do) these small carnivores <u>inhabit</u> parts of Africa and Asia?

13. In captivity they (have) <u>lived</u> for more than twenty years.

14. They (will) <u>attack</u> even the largest snakes.

15. The mongoose (was) <u>made</u> famous by a Rudyard Kipling story.

C. Identifying Adverbs

┌HELP─

There may be more than one adverb in each sentence in Chapter Review C.

Identify the <u>adverb</u> in each of the following sentences. Then, write the <u>word it modifies</u>.

16. The lonely boy <u>looked</u> <u>longingly</u> across the street.

17. "I'm <u>going</u> <u>there</u> after I've graduated," Rochelle <u>said</u> <u>decisively</u>, as she pointed to a map of Malaysia.

18. It is <u>always</u> <u>easier</u> for a child than for an adult to learn a second language.

Using the Chapter Review

To assess student progress, you may want to compare the types of items missed on the **Diagnostic Preview** to those missed on the **Chapter Review.** You may want to work out specific goals with individual students who are still having difficulty mastering essential information.

19. I <u>unfailingly</u> <u>read</u> the newspaper at breakfast.

20. <u>Did</u> Joni <u>remember</u> the details of the accident <u>later</u>?

D. Identifying Prepositions and Prepositional Phrases

Identify the prepositional phrases in each of the following sentences. Underline the preposition once and its object twice. A sentence may have more than one prepositional phrase.

21. Will I find the broom beside the refrigerator?

22. My cat Sam likes to sit upon the television.

23. Mr. Takei used tofu in the recipe instead of chicken.

24. My mom gets upset when people talk throughout the film.

25. During the storm the windowpane streamed with rain.

E. Identifying Conjunctions

Identify the <u>conjunctions</u> in each of the following sentences.

26. Are you coming to the party, <u>or</u> are you staying home?

27. <u>Not only</u> did he produce the film, <u>but</u> he <u>also</u> wrote it.

28. I didn't finish the *Odyssey,* <u>but</u> I enjoyed what I did read.

29. We will have beans <u>and</u> rice for dinner.

30. <u>Both</u> Taj Mahal <u>and</u> B.B. King performed at the blues festival.

F. Identifying Verbs, Adverbs, Prepositions, Conjunctions, and Interjections

The following paragraphs contain twenty numbered, italicized words and word groups. Identify each of these italicized words as a *verb,* an *adverb,* a *preposition,* a *conjunction,* or an *interjection.*

31. v.	32. prep.
	33. v.
	34. v.
35. conj.	36. v.
37. v.	
38. prep.	
39. adv.	

Have you ever [31] *hiked* into the wilderness [32] *with* a pack on your back? Have you ever [33] *camped* under the stars? Backpacking [34] *was* once popular only with mountaineers, [35] *but* now almost anyone who loves the outdoors [36] *can become* a backpacker.

First, however, you [37] *must be* able to carry a heavy pack long distances [38] *over* mountain trails. To get in shape, start with short walks and [39] *gradually* increase them to several

RESOURCES

Parts of Speech Overview
Review
- *Grammar, Usage, and Mechanics,* pp. 62, 63, 64

Assessment
- *Assessment Package*
 —*Chapter Tests,* Ch. 12
 —*Chapter Tests in Standardized Test Formats,* Ch. 12
- *Test Generator (One-Stop Planner CD-ROM)*

miles. Exercising [**40**] *and* going on practice hikes can [**41**] *further* build your strength. [**42**] *After* a few short hikes, you [**43**] *should* be ready for a longer one.

    [**44**] *Oh*, you [**45**] *may be thinking*, what equipment and food should I take? Write [**46**] *to* the International Backpackers Association [**47**] *for* a checklist. The first item on the list will [**48**] *usually* be shoes with rubber [**49**] *or* synthetic soles. The second item on the list will [**50**] *certainly* be a sturdy backpack.

40. conj.	41. adv.
42. prep.	43. v.
44. int.	45. v.
46. prep.	
47. prep.	
48. adv.	49. conj.
50. adv.	

Writing Application
Using Prepositions in Directions

Prepositional Phrases   Your class has decided to provide a "how-to" manual for seventh-graders. The manual will have chapters on crafts and hobbies, personal skills, school skills, and other topics. Write an entry for the manual, telling someone how to do a particular activity. In your entry, be sure to use prepositional phrases to make your directions clear and complete. Underline the prepositional phrases that you use.

Prewriting   First, picture yourself doing the activity you are describing. As you imagine doing the activity, jot down each step. Then, put each step in the order it is done.

Writing   Refer to your prewriting notes as you write your first draft. You may find it necessary to add or rearrange steps to make your directions clear and complete.

Revising   Ask a friend or a classmate to read your paragraph. Then, have your reader repeat the directions in his or her own words. If any part of the directions is unclear, revise your work. Make sure you have used prepositional phrases correctly.

Publishing   Read your entry again to check your spelling, grammar, and punctuation. You may want to share your how-to hints with other students.

Reference Note

See page 540 for more about the **correct placement of phrase modifiers.**

Chapter Review   **383**

Writing Application

Tip. Before students begin the Writing Application, you may want to review adverbs that indicate the sequence of events (first, next, then, afterward, and so on).

Scoring Rubric. While you will want to pay particular attention to students' use of the parts of speech, you will also want to evaluate overall writing performance. You may want to give a split score to indicate development and clarity of the composition as well as grammar skills.

Critical Thinking

Analysis. Tell students that to avoid skipping a necessary stage, they should break down their processes into as many steps as possible. To illustrate the importance of this advice, have a student give you oral directions for performing an activity, such as tying your shoe. Assume that you have never tied a shoe before, and follow the student's directions precisely. It is likely that students will see the importance of including all necessary steps.

RESOURCES

Writing Application
Extension
- *Grammar, Usage, and Mechanics*, p. 67
- *Language Workshop CD-ROM*, Lessons 4–8

CHAPTER

13

Complements
Direct and Indirect Objects, Subject Complements

Diagnostic Preview

Identifying Complements

Identify the <u>complement</u> or <u>complements</u> in each of the following sentences. Then, label each complement as a *direct object*, an *indirect object*, a *predicate nominative*, or a *predicate adjective*.

EXAMPLE 1. A respirator pumps oxygen into the lungs.
            1. *oxygen—direct object*

1. d.o./d.o.   1. Our cat avoids <u>skunks</u> and <u>raccoons</u>.
2. p.n.   2. Jim Thorpe was an American Indian <u>athlete</u>.
3. i.o./d.o.   3. The teacher showed <u>us</u> a <u>film</u> about the Revolutionary War.
4. p.a.   4. The television commercials for that new product sound <u>silly</u>.
5. d.o.   5. Who put the <u>tangerines</u> in that basket?
6. i.o./d.o.   6. I sent my <u>grandparents</u> a <u>gift</u> for their anniversary.
7. p.a./p.a.   7. During her interview on television, Zina Garrison-Jackson appeared <u>relaxed</u> and <u>confident</u>.
8. p.a.   8. At first the colt seemed <u>frightened</u>.
9. i.o./d.o./d.o. 9. Mrs. Constantine offered <u>us</u> <u>olives</u> and stuffed grape <u>leaves</u>.
10. d.o.   10. The DJ played <u>songs</u> by Will Smith, Shania Twain, and Paula Cole.
11. d.o.   11. The newspaper story prompted an <u>investigation</u> by the mayor's office.
12. p.n.   12. My sister has become a computer-repair <u>technician</u>.
13. d.o./d.o.   13. Write your <u>name</u> and <u>address</u> on the envelope.

Pam left the **waiter** a tip. [The noun *waiter* is the indirect object of the verb *left.* It answers the question "For whom did she leave a tip?"]

Did she tip **him** five dollars? [The pronoun *him* is the indirect object of the verb *Did tip.* It answers the question "For whom did she tip five dollars?"]

If the word *to* or *for* is used, the noun or pronoun following it is part of a prepositional phrase and cannot be an indirect object.

OBJECTS OF PREPOSITIONS	The ship's captain gave orders to the **crew.**
	Vinnie made some lasagna for **us.**
INDIRECT OBJECTS	The ship's captain gave the **crew** orders.
	Vinnie made **us** some lasagna.

Like a direct object, an indirect object can be a compound of two or more objects.

EXAMPLE   Felicia threw **David, Jane,** and **Paula** slow curveballs. [The compound indirect object *David, Jane,* and *Paula* tells to whom Felicia threw curveballs.]

MOTHER GOOSE & GRIMM © Tribune Media Services, Inc. All rights reserved. Reprinted with permission.

Exercise 3   Identifying Direct Objects and Indirect Objects

Identify and label the direct objects and the indirect objects in the following sentences. Make sure that you include all parts of compound objects.

EXAMPLE   1. Did you buy Mom a calculator for her birthday?
              1. *Mom—indirect object; calculator—direct object*

1. The usher found us seats near the stage.
2. I'll gladly lend you my new Garth Brooks CD.

Reference Note
For information on **prepositional phrases** and **objects of prepositions,** see page 371.

HELP

In Exercise 3, you may find it easier to identify the direct object first and then to look for the indirect object.

GRAMMAR

Critical Thinking

Metacognition. Ask students to think about the processes they use to identify indirect objects in sentences. Do they first look for the verb or do they eliminate prepositional phrases? Do they always remind themselves that in order to have an indirect object, a sentence must have a direct object? What further steps do they follow? Suggest that students use a sequence chain like the one below to chart their steps.

SAMPLE

| verb | → | prep. phrase | → | direct object |

Encourage students to evaluate the effectiveness of their personal strategies and to consider more effective alternatives as needed.

RESOURCES

Indirect Objects

Practice

- *Grammar, Usage, and Mechanics,* pp. 71, 72–73
- *Language Workshop CD-ROM,* Lesson 32

Meeting
INDIVIDUAL
NEEDS

ENGLISH-LANGUAGE LEARNERS
General Strategies. Because a pronoun used as a direct or indirect object comes before the verb in some languages, students might have difficulty positioning direct and indirect object pronouns within the sentence. For example, *Lalo gave me it* is translated in Spanish as *Lalo me lo dio* (Lalo me it gave). A small group activity can reinforce the sentence order used in English. Ask students to sit in a circle; next, hand a book to one student. Then, ask another "Did I give Delia the book?" The student should respond, "Yes, you gave her the book." Finally, hand the book to the student who just spoke and ask him or her "Did I give you the book?" He or she should respond "Yes, you gave me the book." Continue with other variations as needed.

MODALITIES

Auditory Learners. It might be easier for some students to hear direct and indirect objects than to recognize them visually. Have groups of students take turns reading aloud the example sentences and the sentences in the exercises, stressing the direct and indirect objects.

3. The Nobel Foundation awarded Octavio Paz the Nobel Prize in literature.
4. Please show me your beaded moccasins.
5. They owe you and me an apology.
6. Our teacher taught us some English words of American Indian origin.
7. After the ride to Laramic, I fed the horse and the mule some hay and oats.
8. My secret pal sent me a birthday card.
9. Mai told the children stories about her family's escape from Vietnam.
10. Will you please save Ricardo a seat?

—HELP—

Some sentences in Review A do not contain an indirect object.

Review A   Identifying Objects of Verbs

Identify and label the direct objects and the indirect objects in the following sentences. Make sure that you include all parts of compound objects.

EXAMPLES   1. Did you bring the map?
            1. *map—direct object*

            2. My parents gave me a choice of places to go on our camping vacation.
            2. *me—indirect object; choice—direct object*

1. I told them my answer quickly.
2. I had recently read a magazine article about the Flathead Reservation in Montana.
3. A Salishan people known as the Flatheads governs the huge reservation.
4. We spent five days of our vacation there.
5. We liked the friendly people and the rugged land.
6. I especially liked the beautiful mountains and twenty-eight-mile-long Flathead Lake.
7. My sister and I made camp beside the lake.
8. Someone gave my father a map and some directions to the National Bison Range, and we went there one day.
9. We also attended the Standing Arrow Pow-Wow, which was the highlight of our stay.
10. The performers showed visitors traditional Flathead dances and games.

Subject Complements

13d. A *subject complement* is a word or word group in the predicate that identifies or describes the subject.

EXAMPLES   Julio has been **president** of his class since October. [*President* identifies the subject *Julio.*]

Was the masked stranger **you**? [*You* identifies the subject *stranger.*]

The racetrack looks **slippery.** [*Slippery* describes the subject *racetrack.*]

A subject complement is connected to the subject by a linking verb.

Common Linking Verbs					
appear	become	grow	remain	smell	stay
be	feel	look	seem	sound	taste

There are two kinds of subject complements—*predicate nominatives* and *predicate adjectives.*

Predicate Nominatives

13e. A *predicate nominative* is a word or word group in the predicate that identifies the subject.

A predicate nominative may be a noun, a pronoun, or a word group that functions as a noun. A predicate nominative is connected to its subject by a linking verb.

EXAMPLES   A dictionary is a valuable **tool.** [*Tool* is a predicate nominative that identifies the subject *dictionary.*]

This piece of flint could be an old **arrowhead.** [*Arrowhead* is a predicate nominative that identifies the subject *piece.*]

The winner of the race was **she.** [*She* is a predicate nominative that identifies the subject *winner.*]

Is that **what you ordered**? [*What you ordered* is a predicate nominative that identifies the subject *that.*]

┌ TIPS & TRICKS ┐

To find the subject complement in a question, rearrange the sentence to make a statement.

EXAMPLE
Is Reagan the drummer in the band?

Reagan is the **drummer** in the band.

Reference Note
For more about **linking verbs,** see page 358.

┌ STYLE TIP ┐

Expressions such as *It is I* and *That was he* may sound awkward even though they are correct. In conversation, many people say *It's me* and *That was him.* Such expressions may one day become acceptable in formal writing and speaking as well as in informal situations. For now, however, it is best to follow the rules of standard, formal English, especially in your writing.

Subject Complements
Rules 13d–f *(pp. 391–396)*

OBJECTIVES

■ To identify linking verbs and predicate nominatives in sentences

■ To identify linking verbs and predicate adjectives in sentences

Meeting
INDIVIDUAL
NEEDS

LEARNERS HAVING DIFFICULTY
Students might need to review linking verbs before studying subject complements. Assign articles from provided newspapers, asking students to underline linking verbs. Have students write the sentences with linking verbs on the chalkboard. Using these examples, explain that any noun, pronoun, or adjective that follows a linking verb and identifies or describes the subject is a subject complement. Have volunteers circle the subject complements.

Subject Complements   **391**

RESOURCES

Subject Complements
Practice

■ *Grammar, Usage, and Mechanics,* pp. 74, 75, 76, 77–78

■ *Language Workshop CD-ROM,* Lesson 33

Crossing the Curriculum

Art. Color pigments can be divided into two basic groups: primary (red, blue, and yellow) and secondary (purple, green, and orange). Secondary colors are created by combining two primary colors; for example, blue and yellow make green. When all three primary colors are mixed in equal amounts, the result is the color black. The relationships between the colors can be illustrated using a *color wheel.*

SAMPLE

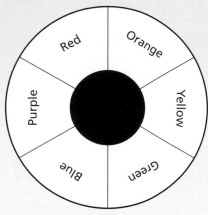

Any two colors that lie directly opposite each other on the color wheel are called *complementary colors;* note that complementary colors are always a primary color and a second color that results from combining the other two primary colors. Point out that complementary colors, when combined, "complete" the color black, just as complements "complete" the meaning of verbs in a sentence.

Reference Note

For more information about **prepositional phrases,** see page 371.

┌─HELP─
Sentences in Exercise 4 may contain a compound predicate nominative.

Like other sentence complements, a predicate nominative may be compound.

EXAMPLES   The discoverers of radium were **Pierre Curie** and **Marie Sklodowska Curie.**

The yearbook editors will be **Maggie, Imelda,** and **Clay.**

Be careful not to confuse a predicate nominative with a direct object. A predicate nominative always completes a linking verb. A direct object always completes an action verb.

PREDICATE   We are the **delegates** from our school.
NOMINATIVE

DIRECT OBJECT   We elected the **delegates** from our school.

A predicate nominative is never part of a prepositional phrase.

PREPOSITIONAL   Bill Russell became famous **as a basketball player.**
PHRASE

PREDICATE   Bill Russell became a famous basketball **player.**
NOMINATIVE

Exercise 4 Identifying Predicate Nominatives

Identify the <u>linking verb</u> and the <u>predicate nominative</u> in each of the following sentences.

EXAMPLE   1. Are whales mammals?

1. Are—mammals

1. Kilimanjaro is the tallest mountain in Africa.
2. The kingdom of Siam became modern-day Thailand.
3. Dandelions can be a problem for gardeners.
4. Sue Mishima should be a lawyer or a stockbroker when she grows up.
5. When will a woman be president of the United States?
6. Reuben has become a fine pianist.
7. The team captains are Daniel, Mark, and Hannah.
8. At the moment, she remains our choice as candidate for mayor.
9. Is Alaska the largest state in the United States?
10. According to my teacher, *philately* is another name for stamp collecting.

MINI-LESSON

Nominative Case Pronouns. To explain sentences such as *It is I* and *That was he*—which are standard English but probably not part of students' everyday speech—tell students that pronouns used as subjects or predicate nominatives should be in the nominative case. Use the following sentences to illustrate the rules:

1. He is the winner. (subject)

2. The winner is he. (predicate nominative)

Predicate Adjectives

13f. A *predicate adjective* is an adjective that is in the predicate and that describes the subject.

A predicate adjective is connected to the subject by a linking verb.

EXAMPLES   Cold milk tastes **good** on a hot day. [*Good* is a predicate adjective that describes the subject *milk*.]

The pita bread was **light** and **delicious.** [*Light* and *delicious* form a compound predicate adjective that describes the subject *bread*.]

How **kind** you are! [*Kind* is a predicate adjective that describes the subject *you*.]

Exercise 5   Identifying Predicate Adjectives

Identify the linking verbs and the predicate adjectives in the following sentences.

EXAMPLES   1. The crowd became restless.
    1. *became—restless*

    2. Do the waves seem high and rough today?
    2. *Do seem—high, rough*

1. Everyone felt good about the decision.
2. The milk in this container smells sour.
3. Don't the black beans mixed with rice and onions taste delicious?
4. The situation appears dangerous and complicated.
5. Everyone remained calm during the emergency.
6. Why does the water in that pond look green?
7. During Annie Dillard's speech, the audience grew thoughtful and then enthusiastic.
8. Jan stays cheerful most of the time.
9. She must be happy with her excellent results on the science midterm.
10. From my seat in the stadium, I thought the big bass drums sounded too loud.

Subject Complements   **393**

| STYLE TIP |

As you review your writing, you may get the feeling that nothing is *happening*, that nobody is *doing* anything. That feeling is one sign that your writing may contain too many *be* verbs. Wherever possible, replace a dull *be* verb with a verb that expresses action.

BE VERB
    Behind the door **was** a hideous monster.

ACTION VERB
    Behind the door **lurked** a hideous monster.

┌HELP─

Sentences in Exercise 5 may contain a compound predicate adjective.

Relating to Writing

Point out to students that overusing vague predicate adjectives such as *nice, pretty,* and *neat* can deaden their writing. Give students the following sentence, and ask them to replace the vague adjective *good* with alternatives that are more precise.

The apples look good.
[*delicious, ripe, refreshing*]

Then, write the following sentences on the chalkboard. Have students work in pairs to think of vivid, precise adjectives to replace the underlined vague ones. Tell students to list as many vivid adjectives as they can for each sentence. Have them share their answers.

1. These drawings are <u>neat</u>.
   [*eye-catching, colorful, marketable*]

2. Your dress is <u>pretty</u>.
   [*fashionable, elegant, chic*]

3. The concert was <u>bad</u>.
   [*boring, substandard, amateurish*]

To extend the activity, suggest that students check a piece of their own writing for overuse of vague predicate adjectives.

To extend the lesson, ask students to locate a piece of their own writing—either from their language arts portfolios or from another class—and to check for the correct use of pronouns as subjects and predicate nominatives. For additional instruction, refer students to p. 391.

Meeting INDIVIDUAL NEEDS

LEARNERS HAVING DIFFICULTY

To help students visualize the relationship of a predicate nominative or predicate adjective to the subject, write the following sentences on the chalkboard:

1. The two families were proud of their heritage.

2. The long road was hazardous.

3. She might be the winner.

Have students draw an arrow from each subject complement to the subject.

1. The two families were proud of their heritage.

2. The long road was hazardous.

3. She might be the winner.

HELP

Complements in Review B may be compound.

COMPUTER TIP

The overuse of *be* verbs is a problem that a computer can help you solve. Use the computer's search function to highlight each occurrence of *am, are, is, was, were, be, been,* and *being.* For each case, decide whether the *be* verb can be replaced with an action verb for greater variety.

Answers will vary. Possible answers are given.

1. sergeant—p.n.
2. doctor—p.n.
3. sweet—p.a.
4. difficult—p.a.
5. happy—p.a.
6. Mexico—p.n.
7. spring—p.n.
8. delicious—p.a.
9. surprised—p.a.
10. shark—p.n.

Review B   **Identifying Predicate Nominatives and Predicate Adjectives**

Identify each subject complement in the following sentences. Then, label each complement as a *predicate nominative* or a *predicate adjective.*

EXAMPLE   1. Are these your shoes, Janelle?
1. *shoes—predicate nominative*

1. This tasty eggplant dish is a favorite in Greece.   1. p.n.
2. The twins are tired after the long flight.   2. p.a.
3. How beautiful that kimono is, Keiko!   3. p.a.
4. This perfume smells sweet and almost lemony.   4. p.a./p.a.
5. When will the piñata be ready?   5. p.a.
6. The winners of the race are Don, Shelby, and she.   6. p.n./p.n./p.n.
7. Vijay Singh is a professional golfer.   7. p.n.
8. What good dogs they are!   8. p.n.
9. Why is your little brother acting so shy?   9. p.a.
10. Loyal and true are the royal bodyguards.   10. p.a./p.a.

Review C   **Writing Predicate Nominatives and Predicate Adjectives**

Choose an appropriate predicate nominative or predicate adjective for each blank in the following sentences. Then, label each answer as a *predicate adjective* or *predicate nominative.*

EXAMPLES   1. The currents looked _____ than they were.
1. *slower—predicate adjective*

2. Should I become a _____?
2. *veterinarian—predicate nominative*

1. He remained a _____ in the army for more than twenty years.
2. My sister became a _____ after many years of study.
3. In the night air, the jasmine smelled _____.
4. The Navajo way of life was sometimes _____.
5. Peggy seemed _____ with her new kitten.
6. For many travelers, a popular vacation spot is _____.
7. My favorite season has been _____ ever since I was five.
8. Don't these Japanese plums taste _____, Alex?
9. How _____ Grandpa will be to see us!
10. One of the most dangerous animals in the ocean is the _____.

Learning for Life

Introductions. Most students have had or will have opportunities to introduce people to each other. In doing so, students will use complements. Provide the following examples:

1. Hi! I'm Ms. King. I teach Language Arts at Carson Middle School.
2. Maria, this is Tom Jones. Tom is new to our school. Tom, this is Maria Gomez. Maria is my best friend.

Review D — Identifying Complements

Identify the complement or complements in each of the following sentences. Then, label each complement as a *direct object*, an *indirect object*, a *predicate nominative*, or a *predicate adjective*.

EXAMPLES
   1. Our teacher read us stories from *The Leather-Stocking Tales.*

    1. us—indirect object; stories—direct object

   2. James Fenimore Cooper is the author of these tales.

    2. author—predicate nominative

1. Leather-Stocking is a fictional scout in Cooper's popular novels. **1.** p.n.   **2.** p.n./p.n.
2. He is also a woodsman and a trapper.
3. He cannot read, but he understands the lore of the woods. **3.** d.o.
4. To generations of readers, this character has been a hero. **4.** p.n.   **5.** d.o.
5. He can face any emergency. **6.** p.a./p.a.
6. He always remains faithful and fearless.
7. Leather-Stocking loves the forest and the open country. **7.** d.o./d.o.
8. In later years he grows miserable. **8.** p.a.
9. The destruction of the wilderness by settlers and others greatly disturbs him.
10. He tells no one his views and retreats from civilization.

    9. d.o.   **10.** i.o./d.o.

---HELP---

Complements in Review D may be compound.

Link to **Literature**

Review E — Identifying Complements

Identify the complement or complements in each of the following sentences. Then, label each complement as a *direct object*, an *indirect object*, a *predicate nominative*, or a *predicate adjective*.

EXAMPLES
   1. Sean, my brother, won three medals at the Special Olympics.

    1. medals—direct object

   2. Are the Special Olympics an annual event?

    2. event—predicate nominative

1. Sean was one of more than one hundred special-education students who competed in the regional Special Olympics.

   1. p.n.

---HELP---

Complements in Review E may be compound.

Cooperative Learning

To review the various sentence patterns presented in this chapter, pair students and ask them to write two sentences illustrating each of the following five sentence patterns: S-V; S-AV-DO; S-AV-IO-DO; S-LV-PN; S-LV-PA. Encourage students to add modifiers and prepositional phrases to their sentences.

After students have completed the sentences, combine student pairs into groups of four. Have one pair present each of its sentences to the other pair, who must discuss and identify the pattern that each sentence illustrates. Ask pairs to reverse roles. Be prepared to help students who have difficulty.

In formal situations, students should first introduce the person who has achieved higher status or who is older. When the people being introduced are of similar status or age, students should start the introductions by naming the more familiar person first.

Have students work in groups of three to make introductions. Suggest that students assume other identities to practice the status and age rules. Remind students to be aware of the complements they use.

2. The games brought <u>students</u> from many schools to our city. **2.** d.o.
3. The highlights of the games included track <u>events</u> such as sprints and relay races. **3.** d.o.
4. These were the closest <u>contests</u>. **4.** p.n.
5. Sean's excellent performance in the relays gave <u>him</u> <u>confidence</u>. **5.** i.o./d.o.
6. The softball throw and high jump were especially challenging <u>events</u>. **6.** p.n.
7. Sean looked <u>relaxed</u> but <u>determined</u> as he prepared for the broad jump. **7.** p.a./p.a.
8. He certainly felt <u>great</u> after his winning jump, shown in the top photograph. **8.** p.a.
9. Mrs. Duffy, one of the coaches, told <u>us</u> the <u>history</u> of the Special Olympics. **9.** i.o./d.o. **10.** d.o.
10. Eunice Kennedy Shriver founded the <u>program</u> in 1968.
11. To begin with, the program was a five-week <u>camp</u>. **11.** p.n.
12. Several years later, the camp became an international sports <u>event</u> with contestants from twenty-six states and Canada.
13. Today, the organizers of the Special Olympics sponsor **12.** p.n. regional and international <u>games</u>. **13.** d.o.
14. The Special Olympics are <u>exciting</u> and <u>inspiring</u>. **14.** p.a./p.a.
15. Many of the contestants have physical <u>impairments</u>; some cannot walk or see. **15.** d.o.
16. Teachers and volunteers train <u>contestants</u> in the different events. **16.** d.o.
17. However, the young athletes themselves are the <u>force</u> behind the program. **17.** p.n.
18. The pictures on the left give <u>you</u> a <u>glimpse</u> of the excitement at the Special Olympics. **18.** i.o./d.o. **19.** d.o.
19. In the middle photograph, a volunteer guides a <u>runner</u>.
20. In the photo on the left, this determined boy prepares <u>himself</u> for the wheelchair race. **20.** d.o.

Chapter Review

A. Classifying Complements

Classify each italicized complement in the following sentences as a *direct object*, an *indirect object*, a *predicate adjective*, or a *predicate nominative*.

1. Pamela was the *star* of the play.   **1.** p.n.
2. The guidebook gave the lost *tourists* the wrong directions.   **2.** i.o.
3. Monet is *famous* for the way his paintings captured light.   **3.** p.a.
4. Manuel offered *Anita* some good advice.   **4.** i.o.
5. Ms. Benton is our next-door *neighbor*.   **5.** p.n.
6. Bring *me* the cutting board, please.   **6.** i.o.
7. The box was *big* and awkward to handle.   **7.** p.a.
8. The library receives many new *books* each week.   **8.** d.o.
9. Mexico celebrates its *independence* on September 16.   **9.** d.o.
10. The new president of the bank will be *Ms. Morales*.   **10.** p.n.
11. Angel became a professional jai alai *player*.   **11.** p.n.
12. Amelia Earhart flew her *plane* across the Atlantic in 1932.   **12.** d.o.
13. The glow from the diamond is *dazzling*!   **13.** p.a.
14. Thomas Edison provided *people* with electric light bulbs.   **14.** d.o.
15. New York City was briefly the *capital* of the United States.   **15.** p.n.
16. The Simpsons showed *him* slides of China.   **16.** i.o.
17. My chair was hard and *uncomfortable*.   **17.** p.a.
18. The machine can produce two *crates* a day.   **18.** d.o.
19. Have you seen Akiho's yellow *sweater*?   **19.** d.o.
20. The house appeared *empty*.   **20.** p.a.

B. Identifying Complements

Write the complement or complements in each sentence. Then, identify each complement as a *direct object*, an *indirect object*, a *predicate adjective*, or a *predicate nominative*. Write *none* if the sentence does not contain a complement.

21. American Indian peoples taught the English colonists many useful skills for survival.   **21.** i.o./d.o.

Using the Chapter Review

The **Chapter Review** requires students to identify direct objects, indirect objects, predicate nominatives, and predicate adjectives in sentences. The results of this review can be compared to those of the **Diagnostic Preview** (p. 384) to assess student progress.

Meeting INDIVIDUAL NEEDS

LEARNERS HAVING DIFFICULTY
You may want to provide students with an organizational strategy for the **Chapter Review**. List the following steps on the chalkboard, and suggest that students follow this sequence to analyze each sentence in the exercise:

1. Bracket the prepositional phrases (as a reminder that essential parts of sentences cannot be within the brackets).
2. Find the verb.
3. Find the subject.
4. Find the complement that receives the action or identifies or describes the subject.

22. Steven Spielberg is a famous <u>director</u> and <u>producer</u> of motion pictures.   **22.** p.n./p.n.

23. A hurricane of immense power lashed the Florida <u>coast</u> a few years ago.   **23.** d.o.

24. The fans became very <u>anxious</u> during the final minutes of the game.   **24.** p.a.

25. This winter was <u>colder</u> and <u>drier</u> than most.   **25.** p.a./p.a.

26. Nora sent <u>postcards</u> from Argentina to her friends.   **26.** d.o.

27. The new homeowners found some rare <u>photographs</u> in the back of the attic.   **27.** d.o.

28. Although many eggshells are <u>white</u>, others are <u>brown</u>, and still others are light <u>green</u>.   **28.** p.a./p.a./p.a.

29. Lita and Trenell studied until seven o'clock.   **29.** none

30. During this month, Mars is too <u>close</u> to the sun to be seen easily from Earth.   **30.** p.a.

31. Both the House and the Senate gave the <u>President</u> their <u>support</u> on the bill.   **31.** i.o./d.o.

32. The movers carried the <u>sofa</u> and dining room <u>table</u> up the front stairs.   **32.** d.o./d.o.

33. Armand worked all day with his grandfather.   **33.** none

34. That gigantic reflector is considered the world's most powerful <u>telescope</u>.   **34.** p.n.

35. Our dog Spike is both a good <u>watchdog</u> and an affectionate family <u>pet</u>.   **35.** p.n./p.n.

36. *A Raisin in the Sun* was certainly Lorraine Hansberry's most successful <u>play</u>.   **36.** p.n.

37. Why do animals seem <u>nervous</u> during a storm?   **37.** p.a.

38. The theater manager will pay each <u>usher</u> an extra five <u>dollars</u> this week.   **38.** i.o./d.o.

39. Luis Alvarez won a <u>Nobel Prize</u> for his important research in nuclear power.   **39.** d.o.

40. Our neighbor has offered my <u>mother</u> and <u>father</u> a good <u>price</u> for their car.   **40.** i.o./i.o./d.o.

RESOURCES

Complements
Review
- *Grammar, Usage, and Mechanics,* pp. 79, 80, 81

Assessment
- *Assessment Package*
  — *Chapter Tests,* Ch. 13
  — *Chapter Tests in Standardized Test Formats,* Ch. 13
- *Test Generator (One-Stop Planner CD-ROM)*

Writing Application
Using Subject Complements to Write Riddles

Predicate Nominatives and Predicate Adjectives

A magazine for young people is sponsoring a riddle-writing contest. Whoever writes the best riddle will win the most advanced computer game on the market. You are determined to write the best riddle and win. Write two riddles to enter in the contest. In each one, use at least two subject complements.

Prewriting The best way to make up a riddle is to begin with the answer. List some animals, places, and things that suggest funny or hidden meanings. For each animal, place, or thing, jot down a description based on the funny or hidden meaning. Then, choose the two topics that you think will make the best riddles.

Writing Use your prewriting notes as you write your first draft. In each riddle, make sure that your clues will help your audience guess the answer. Be sure that you use a subject complement (a predicate nominative or a predicate adjective) in the riddle.

Revising Ask a friend to read your riddles. If the riddles are too difficult or too simple, revise them. You may want to add details that appeal to the senses. Linking verbs such as *appear, feel, smell, sound,* and *taste* can help you add such details.

Publishing Read through your riddles again to check for errors in spelling, punctuation, and capitalization. Pay special attention to the capitalization of proper nouns. You and your classmates may want to publish a book of riddles. Collect your riddles and draw or cut out pictures as illustrations. Make photocopies for all the members of the class.

Reference Note

For a longer **list of linking verbs,** see page 359.

Chapter Review   **399**

Writing Application
(p. 399)

OBJECTIVE

- To write riddles using subject complements

Writing Application

Tip. You may want to stress the importance of brainstorming for riddle ideas before students begin jotting down descriptions. Explain to students that brainstorming is a necessary part of prewriting because it allows them to think of many ideas and to choose the best ones for their riddles.

Scoring Rubric. While you will want to pay particular attention to students' use of subject complements, you will also want to evaluate the students' overall writing performance. You may want to give a split score to indicate development and clarity of the composition as well as grammar skills.

Critical Thinking

Synthesis. Students will be applying critical-thinking skills to create riddles. They must decide what characteristics of the persons, places, or things described by the riddles can be used cleverly to keep the audience guessing. You may want to discuss with students how riddles often rely on wordplay to divert the listeners. Encourage students to use plays on words to describe their subjects accurately but in such a way that the audience will have to think of all possible word meanings to solve the riddles.

14 | The Phrase
Prepositional and Verbal Phrases

Diagnostic Preview

A. Identifying and Classifying Prepositional Phrases

Identify the prepositional phrase in each of the following sentences. Then, classify each phrase as an *adjective phrase* or an
adverb phrase, and write the word that the phrase modifies.

EXAMPLE   1. The chairs in the kitchen need new cushions.

      1. in the kitchen—adjective phrase—chairs

1. adv.	1. I wish I were better at tennis.
2. adj.	2. The Rio Grande is the boundary between Texas and Mexico.
3. adv.	3. Those apples come from Washington State.
4. adj.	4. The most popular name for the United States flag is the Stars and Stripes.
5. adj.	5. The pony with a white forelock is Sally's.
6. adv.	6. Through the window crashed the baseball.
7. adj.	7. Cathy Guisewite is the creator of that comic strip.
8. adv.	8. During the last presidential election, we watched the national news often.
9. adv.	9. The first United States space shuttle was launched in 1981.
10. adv.	10. Outside the door the hungry cat waited patiently.

B. Identifying and Classifying Verbal Phrases

Identify the <u>verbal phrase</u> in each of the following sentences. Then, classify each phrase as a *participial phrase* or an *infinitive phrase*.

EXAMPLE   **1.** The snow, falling steadily, formed huge drifts.
        1. falling steadily—participial phrase

11. We expect <u>to do well on the test.</u>	**11.** inf.
12. The bus, <u>slowed by heavy traffic</u>, arrived at our stop later than it usually does.	**12.** part.
13. <u>Breaking the eggs into the wok</u>, he made egg foo yong.	**13.** part.
14. <u>To remain calm</u> is not always easy.	**14.** inf.
15. She wants <u>to study Japanese in high school.</u>	**15.** inf.
16. The magazine <u>featuring that article</u> is in the school library.	**16.** part.
17. <u>Chilled to the bone</u>, the children finally went inside.	**17.** part.
18. Who are the candidates that they plan <u>to support in the election?</u>	**18.** inf.
19. Bethune-Cookman College, <u>founded by Mary McLeod Bethune</u>, is in Daytona Beach, Florida.	**19.** part.
20. Teresa called <u>to ask about tonight's homework assignment.</u>	**20.** inf.

What Is a Phrase?

14a. A ***phrase*** is a group of related words that is used as a single part of speech and that does not contain both a verb and its subject.

> VERB PHRASE   could have been hiding [no subject]
>
> PREPOSITIONAL PHRASE   in the kitchen [no subject or verb]
>
> INFINITIVE PHRASE   to go with them [no subject or verb]

NOTE If a word group has both a subject and a verb, it is called a ***clause.***

EXAMPLES   The wind howled. [*Wind* is the subject of the verb *howled.*]

           when the Wilsons left [*Wilsons* is the subject of the verb *left.*]

Reference Note

For information on **clauses,** see Chapter 15.

What Is a Phrase?

Rule 14a *(pp. 401–402)*

OBJECTIVE

■ **To determine whether or not given groups of words are phrases**

RESOURCES

What Is a Phrase?

Practice

■ *Grammar, Usage, and Mechanics,* p. 86

■ *Language Workshop CD-ROM,* Lesson 23

Prepositional Phrases

Rule 14b *(pp. 402–403)*

OBJECTIVE

- To identify prepositional phrases in sentences

Meeting
INDIVIDUAL
NEEDS

ENGLISH-LANGUAGE LEARNERS
General Strategies. The use of prepositions varies from language to language. If you notice the incorrect use of prepositions in students' writing, help them understand the correct uses of both the prepositions they used and the prepositions they should have used, providing examples and a simple definition of each one.

Reference Note

For a list of commonly used **prepositions,** see page 370.

Reference Note

For more about the **object of a preposition,** see page 371.

Exercise 1 **Identifying Phrases**

Identify each of the following word groups as a *phrase* or *not a phrase*.

EXAMPLES   **1.** on the paper   **2.** after we eat
            1. phrase   *2. not a phrase*

1. when you know   **1.** not phr.   **6.** smiling brightly   **6.** phr.
2. as they walked in **2.** not phr.   **7.** to the supermarket **7.** phr.
3. in the garden   **3.** phr.   **8.** where the car is   **8.** not phr.
4. is sleeping   **4.** phr.   **9.** to laugh at myself   **9.** phr.
5. how she remembered   **10.** if he says so   **10.** not phr.
                         5. not phr.

Prepositional Phrases

14b. A *prepositional phrase* includes a preposition, the object of the preposition, and any modifiers of that object.

EXAMPLES   under the umbrella   for ourselves
            among good friends   next to them

Notice that an article or another modifier may appear in a prepositional phrase. The first example above contains the article *the*. In the second example, *good* modifies *friends*.

The noun or pronoun that completes a prepositional phrase is called the **object of the preposition.**

EXAMPLES   Linh Phan has the lead in the school **play.** [The noun *play* is the object of the preposition *in*.]

            Standing between **them** was the Russian chess champion. [The pronoun *them* is the object of the preposition *between*.]

Any modifier that comes between the preposition and its object is part of the prepositional phrase.

EXAMPLE   **Into the thick mist** vanished the carriage. [The adjectives *the* and *thick* modify the object *mist*.]

An object of a preposition may be compound.

EXAMPLE   Come with **Rick** and **me** to the concert. [Both *Rick* and *me* are objects of the preposition *with*.]

RESOURCES

Prepositional Phrases
Practice

- *Grammar, Usage, and Mechanics,* p. 87
- *Language Workshop CD-ROM,* Lesson 23

NOTE Be careful not to confuse an infinitive with a prepositional phrase beginning with *to*. A prepositional phrase always has an object that is a noun or a pronoun. An infinitive is a verbal that usually begins with *to*.

PREPOSITIONAL PHRASE   Send the package **to them.**
INFINITIVE   Are you ready **to go**?

Reference Note
For more information about **infinitives,** see page 414.

Exercise 2 **Identifying Prepositional Phrases**

Identify the prepositional phrases in each of the following sentences.

EXAMPLE   1. Many soldiers fought bravely during the Vietnam War.
    1. *during the Vietnam War*

1. One of these soldiers was Jan C. Scruggs.
2. When the war was over, he and other veterans wondered why there was no national memorial honoring those who had served in Vietnam.
3. Scruggs decided he would raise funds for a Vietnam Veterans Memorial.
4. The memorial would include the names of all American men and women who were missing in action or who had died.
5. Organizing the project took years of great effort.
6. Many different people contributed their talents to the project.
7. Maya Ying Lin, a college student, designed the memorial that now stands in Washington, D.C.
8. This picture shows the V-shaped, black granite wall that was built from Lin's design.
9. A glass company from Memphis, Tennessee, engraved each name on the shiny granite.
10. Now the names of those who died in Vietnam will never be forgotten by the American people.

HELP

The sentences in Exercise 2 may contain more than one prepositional phrase apiece.

TEACHING **TIP**

Activity. To show students the important role that prepositions play in our language, write on a transparency or on the chalkboard a "What am I?" riddle that describes an object in your classroom. Use as many prepositional phrases as possible, and underline them. For example: "I hang above the chalkboard in the center of the front wall. Students glance at me throughout class. My hands move in a circle. What am I?" Ask students to guess the answer to the riddle. [*a clock*]

Then, have students take turns creating similar riddles for the rest of the class to answer. Refer students to the list of prepositions on p. 370.

Prepositional Phrases   **403**

Adjective Phrases

Rule 14c *(pp. 404–406)*

OBJECTIVES

- To identify adjective phrases and the words they modify
- To complete sentences by supplying adjective phrases

Relating to Writing

Point out to students that using too many short, choppy sentences can make their writing seem dull. Use the following examples to show students how prepositional phrases can be used to combine sentences.

Two sentences: This shirt has colorful buttons. It is my favorite.
Revision: This shirt <u>with colorful buttons</u> is my favorite.

Two sentences: Put your bottle in the recycle bin. The recycle bin is behind the garage.
Revision: Put your bottle in the recycle bin <u>behind the garage.</u>

Suggest that students examine their own writing for opportunities to use prepositional phrases to combine sentences.

Adjective Phrases

A prepositional phrase used as an adjective is called an *adjective phrase.*

ADJECTIVE	Rosa chose the **blue** one.
ADJECTIVE PHRASE	Rosa chose the one **with blue stripes.**

14c. An *adjective phrase* modifies a noun or a pronoun.

Adjective phrases generally come after the words they modify and answer the same questions that single-word adjectives answer.

> What kind? Which one?
> How many? How much?

EXAMPLES The store **with the neon sign** is open. [The prepositional phrase *with the neon sign* is used as an adjective modifying the noun *store.* The phrase answers the question *Which one?*]

We bought a CD **by Janet Jackson.** [*By Janet Jackson* is used as an adjective modifying the noun *CD.* The phrase answers the question *What kind?*]

Exercise 3 **Identifying Adjective Phrases**

Identify the <u>adjective phrase</u> in each of the following sentences, and write the <u>word that each phrase modifies</u>.

EXAMPLE 1. Marie Sklodowska Curie, a scientist from Poland, was awarded the Nobel Prize in 1911.

1. *from Poland—scientist*

1. While she was a <u>student</u> <u>in France</u>, Marie met Pierre Curie.
2. Pierre had already gained <u>fame</u> <u>as a scientist</u>.
3. Paris was where the <u>two</u> <u>of them</u> became friends.
4. Their <u>enthusiasm</u> <u>for science</u> brought them together.
5. The <u>marriage</u> <u>between the two scientists</u> was a true partnership.
6. The <u>year</u> <u>after their marriage</u> another scientist discovered natural radioactivity.
7. The Curies began researching the <u>radioactivity</u> <u>of certain substances</u>.
8. Their <u>theories</u> <u>about a new element</u> were proved to be true.

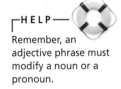

┌HELP──
Remember, an adjective phrase must modify a noun or a pronoun.

RESOURCES

Adjective Phrases

Practice

- *Grammar, Usage, and Mechanics*, p. 88
- *Language Workshop CD-ROM*, Lesson 23

9. Their <u>research on the mineral pitchblende</u> uncovered a new radioactive element, radium.

10. In 1903, the Curies and another scientist shared a <u>Nobel Prize</u> for their discovery.

More than one adjective phrase may modify the same noun or pronoun.

EXAMPLE   Here's a gift **for you from Uncle Steve.** [The prepositional phrases *for you* and *from Uncle Steve* both modify the noun *gift.*]

An adjective phrase may also modify the object in another adjective phrase.

EXAMPLE   A majority **of the mammals in the world** sleep during the day. [The adjective phrase *of the mammals* modifies the noun *majority.* The adjective phrase *in the world* modifies the noun *mammals,* which is the object of the preposition in the first phrase.]

Exercise 4 **Identifying Adjective Phrases**

Identify the <u>adjective phrases</u> in the following sentences. Then, write the <u>word that each phrase modifies</u>.

EXAMPLE   1. R.I.C.E. is the recommended treatment for minor sports injuries.
           1. *for minor sports injuries—treatment*

1. The first <u>letters</u> of the words *Rest, Ice, Compression,* and *Elevation* form the abbreviation *R.I.C.E.*
2. Total bed rest is not necessary, just <u>rest</u> for the injured <u>part</u> of the body.
3. Ice helps because it deadens pain and slows the <u>loss</u> of blood.
4. Ice also reduces <u>swelling</u> of the injured area.
5. <u>Compression</u> with a tight bandage of elastic <u>cloth</u> prevents further <u>strain</u> on the injury.
6. This photograph shows an ice pack treating the injured <u>knee</u> of the athlete Robert Horry.
7. The last <u>step</u> in the treatment is <u>elevation</u> of the injured area.
8. The <u>effect</u> of gravity helps fluid drain away.

┌HELP┐
The sentences in Exercise 4 may contain more than one adjective phrase apiece.

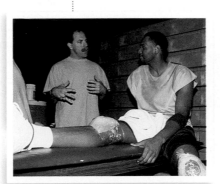

Meeting
INDIVIDUAL
NEEDS

INCLUSION
To help students become confident in using prepositional phrases, have them add adjective phrases to short, simple sentences. On separate index cards, write sentences like the following ones that the students can complete with their own phrases. Possible prepositions for the phrases are indicated in parentheses.

1. The house (by) _____ sat on a hill.
2. The girl (with) _____ became involved in sports.
3. Mike's trip (to) _____ was exhausting.
4. Uncle Joe liked gardening (in) _____.

Have students continue the activity by working in groups to create sentences like the models. Then, groups can trade sentences and fill in the blanks.

GRAMMAR

Exercise 5 Using Adjective Phrases

ANSWERS

Phrases will vary. Here are some possibilities:

1. from the stereo—sound

2. across the street—theater

3. of the bagels—more

4. in the Blue Ridge Mountains—vacation

5. of a blue whale—photograph

6. to her question—answer

7. on the table—vase

8. in a serape—boy

9. of the old oak tree—branch

10. in the front—Someone

Adverb Phrases

Rule 14d *(pp. 406–409)*

OBJECTIVES

■ **To identify adverb phrases and the words they modify**

■ **To distinguish between adverb phrases and adjective phrases**

HELP

Remember, an adjective phrase must modify a noun or a pronoun.

---

9. If pain continues, <u>someone</u> with medical training should be called to examine the injured person.

10. Even <u>injuries of a minor nature</u> need proper attention.

Exercise 5 **Using Adjective Phrases**

Write an adjective phrase for each blank in the following sentences. Then, write the word that the phrase modifies.

EXAMPLE   1. A flock _____ flew overhead.

 1. *of small gray birds—flock*

1. The sound _____ suddenly filled the air.
2. The theater _____ often shows kung-fu movies.
3. May I have some more _____?
4. Our vacation _____ was relaxing.
5. Her photograph _____ looks like a prizewinner.
6. Andrea found the answer _____.
7. He put the flowers in a vase _____.
8. A boy _____ hung a piñata in the tree.
9. The nest is in the top branch _____.
10. Someone _____ shouted for quiet.

Adverb Phrases

A prepositional phrase used as an adverb is called an ***adverb phrase.***

      ADVERB   The cavalry will reach the fort **soon.**

ADVERB PHRASE   The cavalry will reach the fort **by noon.**

14d. An ***adverb phrase*** modifies a verb, an adjective, or an adverb.

Adverb phrases answer the same questions that single-word adverbs answer: *When? Where? How? Why? How often? How long? To what extent?*

EXAMPLES   We got our new puppy **at the animal shelter.** [The adverb phrase *at the animal shelter* modifies the verb *got,* telling *where.*]

    A puppy is always ready **for a game.** [The adverb phrase *for a game* modifies the adjective *ready,* telling *how.*]

    He barks loudly **for a puppy.** [The adverb phrase *for a puppy* modifies the adverb *loudly,* telling *to what extent.*]

RESOURCES

Adverb Phrases

Practice

■ *Grammar, Usage, and Mechanics,* pp. 89, 90–91

■ *Language Workshop CD-ROM,* Lesson 23

Unlike adjective phrases, which generally follow the word or words they modify, adverb phrases may appear at various places in sentences.

EXAMPLES   **At dusk,** we went inside to eat dinner.

We went inside **at dusk** to eat dinner.

We went inside to eat dinner **at dusk.**

Exercise 6   **Identifying Adverb Phrases**

Identify the <u>adverb phrase</u> in each of the following sentences. Then, write the <u>word that each phrase modifies</u>. Do not list adjective phrases.

EXAMPLE   1. Pecos Bill will live forever in the many legends about him.

     1. *in the many legends—will live*

1. When he was only a baby, Pecos Bill <u>fell</u> <u>into the Pecos River</u>.
2. His parents <u>searched</u> <u>for him</u> but couldn't find him.
3. He was <u>saved</u> <u>by coyotes</u>, who raised him.
4. He <u>thought</u> <u>for many years</u> that he was a coyote.
5. <u>After a long argument</u>, a cowboy <u>convinced</u> Bill that he was not a coyote.
6. <u>During a drought</u>, Bill <u>dug</u> the bed of the Rio Grande.
7. <u>On one occasion</u> he <u>rode</u> a cyclone.
8. A mountain lion once <u>leaped</u> <u>from a ledge</u> above Bill's head.
9. Bill was always <u>ready</u> <u>for trouble</u> and soon had the mountain lion tamed.
10. Stories like these about Pecos Bill are <u>common</u> <u>in the West</u>.

Like adjective phrases, more than one adverb phrase may modify the same word.

EXAMPLES   She drove **for hours through the storm.** [Both adverb phrases, *for hours* and *through the storm,* modify the verb *drove.*]

The library is open **during the day on weekends.** [Both adverb phrases, *during the day* and *on weekends,* modify the adjective *open.*]

On Saturday we will rehearse our drill routine **before the game.** [Both adverb phrases, *On Saturday* and *before the game,* modify the verb phrase *will rehearse.*]

TIPS & TRICKS

If you are not sure whether a prepositional phrase is an adjective phrase or an adverb phrase, remember that an adjective phrase almost always follows the word it modifies. If you can move the phrase without changing the meaning of the sentence, the phrase is probably an adverb phrase.

Link to Literature

Meeting
INDIVIDUAL
NEEDS

MULTIPLE INTELLIGENCES
Spatial Intelligence. It might be easier for students to understand how placement of adverb phrases can be varied if they see two versions of the same sentence with an adverb phrase placed differently in each. Copy sentences 5, 6, and 7 of **Exercise 6** onto the chalkboard. Have student volunteers rewrite the sentences on the chalkboard by moving each adverb phrase to a new location. Point out that adverb phrases, unlike adjective phrases, do not always need to be next to the words they modify to be clear.

Crossing the Curriculum

Math. To show students that concepts learned in language arts apply to other subjects as well, discuss the use of prepositional phrases in mathematical language. For example, *six divided by two equals three; ten percent of sixty is six; two into eight is four.*

Ask students to volunteer other examples. [*One half of ten is five; four goes into twenty five times; the circumference of the circle is fifteen inches; three subtracted from ten equals seven; two multiplied by four equals eight.*]

┌HELP┐
The sentences in Exercise 7 may contain more than one adverb phrase apiece.

NOTE An adverb phrase may be followed by an adjective phrase that modifies the object in the adverb phrase.

EXAMPLE The boat landed **on an island near the coast.** [The adverb phrase *on an island* modifies the verb *landed.* The adjective phrase *near the coast* modifies the noun *island.*]

Exercise 7 Identifying Adverb Phrases

Identify the adverb phrases in the following sentences. Then, write the word or words that each phrase modifies. Do not list adjective phrases.

EXAMPLE 1. Never before had a blizzard struck the coastal area with such force.
1. *with such force—had struck*

1. Andrea saw the dark clouds and turned toward home.
2. The raging wind blew the eleven-year-old over a sea wall near the shore.
3. She found herself trapped in a deep snowdrift.
4. No one could hear her shouts over the howling wind.
5. Andrea's dog charged through the snow toward the beach.
6. He plunged into the snow around Andrea and licked her face, warming the skin.
7. Then the huge dog walked around Andrea until the snow was packed down.
8. The dog pulled her to an open area on the beach.
9. With great effort, Andrea and her dog made their way home.
10. Grateful to their dog, Andrea's family served him a special steak dinner.

Review A Identifying and Classifying Prepositional Phrases

Identify the prepositional phrase in each of the following sentences, and classify it as an *adjective phrase* or an *adverb phrase.* Then, write the word or words the phrase modifies.

EXAMPLE 1. Here is some information about sharks.
1. *about sharks—adjective phrase; information*

Misplaced Modifiers. To illustrate the confusion caused by misplaced modifiers, write the following sentences on the chalkboard:

1. I borrowed a radio from my sister with a weather band.

2. We read about the thieves who were captured in today's paper.

Ask volunteers to revise the sentences by repositioning the misplaced prepositional phrases. [*From my sister I borrowed a radio*

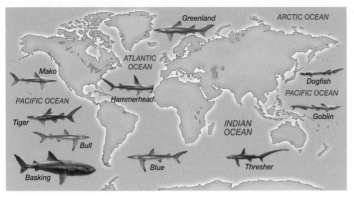

1. Did you know that there are <u>hundreds of shark species</u>?
2. Scientists group these species <u>into twenty-eight families</u>.
3. Sharks <u>within the same family</u> share many traits.
4. <u>The body shape, tail shape, and teeth</u> determine the differences <u>among families</u>.
5. Sharks are found <u>throughout the world's oceans</u>.
6. As the <u>map shows</u>, some sharks prefer cold waters, and others live mostly <u>in warm tropical oceans</u>.
7. Only thirty <u>kinds of sharks</u> are dangerous.
8. The huge <u>whale shark</u>, however, <u>falls</u> under the "not dangerous" category.
9. Divers can even hitch a <u>ride on its fins</u>.
10. Beautiful yet <u>frightening to most people</u>, sharks are perhaps the world's most awesome creatures.

1. adj.
2. adv.
3. adj.
4. adj.

5. adv.
6. adv.

7. adj.
8. adv.

9. adj.
10. adv.

Review B | **Writing Sentences with Prepositional Phrases**

For each of the following items, write a sentence using the given prepositional phrase. Then, tell whether you have used each phrase as an *adjective phrase* or an *adverb phrase*.

EXAMPLE   **1.** through the tollbooth
         1. A car passed through the tollbooth.—adverb phrase

1. in the movie theater
2. for the party
3. along the water's edge
4. about Madeleine
5. into the department store
6. underneath the bed
7. with chopsticks
8. of the equipment
9. in front of city hall
10. at the campsite

TEACHING **TIP**

Extension. To emphasize map reading skills, you may want to use the exercise below as an oral activity or to write the question on the board for students to answer in writing.

1. Does the tiger shark live in cold waters or warm tropical oceans? [*tropical*]

2. Which shark species live in the Atlantic Ocean, according to the map? [*hammerhead, blue*]

3. Which shark species live off of the western coast of South America? [*tiger, bull, basking*]

4. Where is the dogfish shark found, according to the map? [*eastern Pacific*]

Review B   **Writing Sentences with Prepositional Phrases**

ANSWERS
Answers will vary, but students should be particularly careful to place adjective phrases next to the words modified.

with a weather band. In today's paper we read about the thieves who were captured.]

     Explain to students that an adjective phrase generally should be placed directly after the word it modifies; an adverb phrase should generally be placed near the word it modifies. For additional instruction and practice, refer students to **Chapter 20: Using Modifiers Correctly.**

The Participle

Rules 14e, f *(pp. 410–414)*

OBJECTIVES

- To identify present and past participles and the words they modify

- To identify participial phrases and the words they modify

- To write sentences containing given participial phrases

Meeting
INDIVIDUAL NEEDS

ENGLISH-LANGUAGE LEARNERS

Spanish. The English present participle suffix *–ing* is equivalent to the Spanish *–ando* and *–iendo* (e.g., *hablando,* "speaking," from *hablar,* "to speak," and *comiendo,* "eating," from *comer,* "to eat"). The English past participle suffix *–(e)d* is equivalent to the Spanish *–ado* and *–ido* (e.g., *marcado,* "marked," and *adquirido,* "acquired"). In English and in Spanish, past participles can be used as adjectives.

Portuguese and French. The English *–ing* suffix corresponds to *–ando, –endo,* and *–indo* in Portuguese and *–ant* in French; the English *–(e)d* suffix corresponds to *–ado* and *–ido* in Portuguese and *–é(e)* in French.

Reference Note

For a list of **irregular past participles,** see page 489.

Verbals and Verbal Phrases

A ***verbal*** is a word that is formed from a verb but is used as a noun, an adjective, or an adverb.

The Participle

14e. A ***participle*** is a verb form that can be used as an adjective.

Two kinds of participles are *present participles* and *past participles.*

(1) *Present participles* end in *–ing.*

EXAMPLES   Mr. Sanchez rescued three people from the **burning** building. [*Burning* is the present participle of the verb *burn.* The participle modifies the noun *building.*]

Chasing the cat, the dog ran down the street. [*Chasing* is the present participle of the verb *chase.* The participle modifies the noun *dog.*]

(2) *Past participles* usually end in *–d* or *–ed.* Some past participles are formed irregularly.

EXAMPLES   Well **trained,** the soldier successfully carried out her mission. [The past participle *trained* modifies the noun *soldier.*]

We skated on the **frozen** pond. [The irregular past participle *frozen* modifies the noun *pond.*]

NOTE Be careful not to confuse participles used as adjectives with participles used in verb phrases. Remember that the participle in a verb phrase is part of the verb.

ADJECTIVE   **Discouraged,** the fans went home.
VERB PHRASE   The fans **were discouraged** by the string of losses.

ADJECTIVE   **Singing** cheerfully, the birds perched among the branches of the trees.
VERB PHRASE   The birds **were singing** cheerfully among the branches of the trees.

Exercise 8 Identifying Participles and the Nouns They Modify

Identify the <u>participles used as adjectives</u> in the following sentences. Then, write the <u>noun that each participle modifies</u>.

EXAMPLE   1. The deserted cities of the Anasazi are found in the Four Corners area of the United States.

      1. deserted—cities

1. Utah, Colorado, New Mexico, and Arizona are the <u>bordering</u> <u>states</u> that make up the Four Corners.
2. Because of its natural beauty, Chaco Canyon is one of the most <u>visited</u> <u>sights</u> in this region of the Southwest.
3. Among the <u>remaining</u> <u>ruins</u> in Chaco Canyon are the houses, public buildings, and plazas of the Anasazi.
4. What <u>alarming</u> <u>event</u> may have caused these people to leave their valley?
5. Historians are studying the <u>scattered</u> <u>remains</u> of the Anasazi culture to learn more about these mysterious people.
6. <u>Woven</u> <u>baskets</u> were important to the earliest Anasazi people, who were excellent basket weavers.
7. On the floors of some caves are pits for <u>stored</u> <u>food</u> and other vital supplies.
8. <u>Surviving</u> <u>descendants</u> of the Anasazi include today's Zuni, Hopi, and some of the Pueblo peoples.
9. <u>Programs</u> <u>protecting</u> archaeological sites help ensure the preservation of our nation's heritage.
10. There are several national <u>parks</u> and <u>monuments</u> <u>commemorating</u> the Pueblo's past.

Exercise 9 Identifying Participles and the Words They Modify

Identify the <u>participles used as adjectives</u> in the following sentences. Then, write the <u>noun or pronoun each participle modifies</u>.

EXAMPLE   1. Buzzing mosquitoes swarmed around me.

      1. Buzzing—mosquitoes

1. <u>Annoyed</u>, <u>I</u> went inside to watch TV.
2. I woke my <u>sleeping</u> <u>father</u> to ask about mosquitoes.
3. <u>Irritated</u>, <u>he</u> directed me to an encyclopedia.

Verbals and Verbal Phrases   **411**

Relating to Vocabulary Skills

The grammatical rule requiring adjectives to be alongside the words they modify can offer students valuable clues to an unfamiliar word's meaning. For example, write the following sentence on the chalkboard and ask students to use the above-mentioned rule as a context clue for the underlined participle: *The colored light <u>emanating</u> from the stained-glass windows dazzled our eyes.* [Emanating *must be something light can do.*]

In addition, point out to students that all the information within the participial phrase can offer context clues. [From the stained-glass windows *suggests shining, coming through.* Emanate *means "to come forth" or "to issue, as from a source."*]

Meeting
INDIVIDUAL
NEEDS

LEARNERS HAVING DIFFICULTY

The following activity may help students who are having difficulty identifying and using participles.

First, list the verbs *jump, howl, march, polish, iron,* and *trust* on the chalkboard. Ask students to add *ing* to the first three verbs and *ed* to the last three verbs and to use these newly formed participles to modify nouns of their own choosing. [*jumping frogs, howling dogs, marching band, polished floor, ironed shirt, trusted friend*]

Cooperative Learning

To give students additional practice with participles, pair students for this flashcard game. Make three signs: one saying *verb phrase,* one saying *participle,* and one saying *participial phrase.* Then, write the word *missing* on the chalkboard, and ask each pair to write a sentence using the word as instructed by the sign you hold up. For example, if you show the *participle* sign, students might write *The missing photo is mine.*

Give students time to discuss their sentence while they are writing; then, call upon pairs at random to share their sentences. Continue with such words as *locked, running, dancing, broken,* and *startled.*

Reference Note

For information on **modifiers,** see Chapter 20. For information on **complements,** see Chapter 13.

Reference Note

For information on **how to place participial phrases correctly,** see page 544.

4. I learned that some flying insects carry diseases.
5. Biting mosquitoes can spread malaria.
6. Bites make the skin swell, and the swollen skin itches.
7. Sucking blood for food, mosquitoes survive in many different climates.
8. Sometimes you can hear mosquitoes buzzing.
9. Their beating wings make the sound.
10. Mosquitoes, living only a few weeks, may go through as many as twelve generations in a year.

The Participial Phrase

14f. A *participial phrase* consists of a participle together with its modifiers and complements. The entire phrase is used as an adjective.

EXAMPLES   **Stretching slowly,** the cat jumped down from the windowsill. [The participle *Stretching* is modified by the adverb *slowly.* The phrase modifies *cat.*]

The tornado **predicted by the meteorologist** did not hit our area. [The participle *predicted* is modified by the prepositional phrase *by the meteorologist.* The whole participial phrase modifies *tornado.*]

Reading the assignment, she took notes carefully. [The participle *Reading* has the direct object *assignment.* The phrase modifies *she.*]

A participial phrase should be placed close to the word it modifies. Otherwise, the phrase may appear to modify another word, and the sentence may not make sense.

MISPLACED   Hopping along the fence, I saw a rabbit. [Was *I* hopping along the fence?]

CORRECTED   I saw a rabbit **hopping along the fence.**

Exercise 10   Identifying Participial Phrases and the Words They Modify

Identify the participial phrases in the following sentences. Then, write the word or words each phrase modifies.

MINI-LESSON

Participles in Sentence Fragments.
Students might create sentence fragments by mistaking a participle for a verb. Write the following groups of words on the chalkboard, and ask students to explain why the word groups are not complete

sentences. [*Each needs a helping verb.*]

1. The bird singing cheerfully

2. The game scheduled for tonight

3. Branches tapping on the roof

EXAMPLE   1. Living over four hundred years ago, Leonardo da Vinci
               kept journals of his ideas and inventions.

           1. *Living over four hundred years ago—Leonardo da
               Vinci*

1. The journals, written backwards in "mirror writing," are
    more than five thousand pages long.
2. Leonardo drew many pictures showing birds in flight.
3. He hoped that machines based on his sketches of birds would
    enable humans to fly.
4. Shown here, his design for a
    helicopter was the first one
    in history.
5. Studying the eye, Leonardo
    understood the sense of sight.
6. He worked hard, filling his
    journals with sketches like
    the ones on this page for a
    movable bridge.
7. The solutions reached in
    his journals often helped
    Leonardo when he created his artworks.
8. He used the hands sketched in the journals as models
    when he painted the hands in the *Mona Lisa.*
9. Painting on a large wall, Leonardo created
    The Last Supper.
10. Leonardo, experimenting continually, had little time
    to paint in his later years.

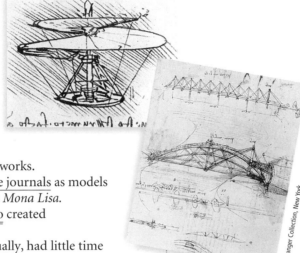

The Granger Collection, New York.

Exercise 11 **Writing Sentences with Participial Phrases**

For each of the following items, write a sentence using the given
participial phrase. Make sure the participial phrase modifies a
noun or pronoun.

EXAMPLE   1. cheering for the team
           1. *Cheering for the team, we celebrated the victory.*

1. confused by the directions
2. gathering information on the Hopi
3. practicing my part in the play
4. followed closely by my younger brother

┌─HELP─
In Exercise 11,
place a comma after a participial phrase that begins
a sentence.

Reference Note

For more information
about **punctuating
participial phrases,** see
pages 607 and 613.

Verbals and Verbal Phrases   **413**

Exercise 10

ALTERNATIVE LESSON
Have students identify the prepositional phrases in sentences 3 and 4.
[3. *on his sketches, of birds;* 4. *for a
helicopter, in history*] Point out that
in sentence 3 the prepositional
phrases are part of the participial
phrase, whereas in sentence 4 they
are not.

Exercise 11   **Writing Sentences
with Participial Phrases**

ANSWERS
Sentences will vary. Here are some
possibilities:

1. Confused by the directions, we
    couldn't locate the street.

2. The boy gathering information on
    the Hopi went to the library.

3. Practicing my part in the play, I
    bowed to the imaginary audience.

4. Followed closely by my younger
    brother, the cat climbed the tree.

    Explain to students that the word groups
on p. 412 can become sentences if a helping
verb is added to the participle to complete
the thought. [*The bird was singing cheerfully. The game is scheduled for tonight.
Branches are tapping on the roof.*]

    Encourage students to locate a piece of
their own writing and to circle all present
and past participles. Then, have students
determine whether they have included a
helping verb with participles used as verbs.

GRAMMAR

Exercise 11 Writing Sentences with Participial Phrases

ANSWERS continued

5. The drummer, searching through the crowd, located the singer.

6. Shaped by wind and water, the sandbar changes daily.

7. Your car, freshly painted at the shop, will be ready tomorrow.

8. Born in Tahiti, she moved here last year.

9. Reading a book by the window, I saw my carpool arrive.

10. The mover holding the Ming vase walked carefully across the room.

The Infinitive

Rules 14g, h *(pp. 414–417)*

OBJECTIVES

■ To identify infinitives and infinitive phrases in sentences

■ To write sentences using given infinitive phrases

Relating to Literature

If your literature textbook contains Charles Dickens's *A Christmas Carol,* select several paragraphs that illustrate how extensively Dickens uses descriptive phrases. Explain to students that many nineteenth-century writers used elaborate descriptions containing many phrases. The more descriptive the passages were, the more easily readers could visualize the scenes. Literature was the television of their day.

Ask students to analyze other paragraphs in *A Christmas Carol* for the author's use of descriptive phrases. Tell them to find at least one adjective prepositional phrase, one adverb prepositional phrase, one participial phrase, and one infinitive phrase.

5. searching through the crowd

6. shaped by wind and water

7. freshly painted at the shop

8. born in Tahiti

9. reading a book by the window

10. holding the Ming vase

The Infinitive

14g. An *infinitive* is a verb form that can be used as a noun, an adjective, or an adverb. Most infinitives begin with *to*.

Infinitives	
Used as	**Examples**
Nouns	**To succeed** is my goal. [*To succeed* is the subject of the sentence.] My ambition is **to teach** Spanish. [*To teach* is a predicate nominative.] She tried **to win.** [*To win* is the direct object of the verb *tried*.]
Adjectives	The place **to meet** tomorrow is the library. [*To meet* modifies the noun *place*.] She is the one **to call.** [*To call* modifies the pronoun *one*.]
Adverbs	Tamara claims she was born **to surf.** [*To surf* modifies the verb *was born*.] This math problem will be hard **to solve** without a calculator. [*To solve* modifies the adjective *hard*.]

NOTE *To* plus a noun or a pronoun (*to Washington, to her*) is a prepositional phrase, not an infinitive.

PREPOSITIONAL PHRASE   I am going **to the mall** today.

INFINITIVE   I am going **to shop** for new shoes.

Reference Note
For more information about **prepositional phrases,** see page 371.

RESOURCES

The Infinitive

Practice

■ *Grammar, Usage, and Mechanics,* pp. 96, 97, 98–99, 100–101

■ *Language Workshop CD-ROM,* Lesson 25

Exercise 12 Identifying Infinitives

Identify the underlined infinitives in the following sentences. If a sentence does not contain an infinitive, write *none*.

EXAMPLE   **1.** I would like to go to New York City someday.
              1. to go

1. My first stop would be to visit the Statue of Liberty.
2. Thousands of people go to see the statue every day.
3. They take a boat to Liberty Island.   **3.** none
4. The statue holds a torch to symbolize freedom.
5. The idea of a statue to represent freedom came from a French historian.
6. France gave the statue to the United States in 1884.   **6.** none
7. The statue was shipped to this country in 214 cases.   **7.** none
8. It was a gift to express the friendship between the two nations.
9. In the 1980s, many people helped to raise money for repairs to the statue.
10. The repairs were completed in time to celebrate the statue's hundredth anniversary on October 28, 1986.

The Infinitive Phrase

14h. An *infinitive phrase* consists of an infinitive together with its modifiers and complements. The entire phrase may be used as a noun, an adjective, or an adverb.

EXAMPLES   **To be a good gymnast** takes hard work. [The infinitive phrase is used as a noun. The infinitive *To be* has a complement, *a good gymnast*.]

The first person **to fly over both the North Pole and the South Pole** was Richard Byrd. [The infinitive phrase is used as an adjective modifying the noun *person*. The infinitive *to fly* is modified by the prepositional phrase *over both the North Pole and the South Pole*.]

Are you ready **to go to the gym now**? [The infinitive phrase is used as an adverb modifying the adjective *ready*. The infinitive *to go* is modified by the prepositional phrase *to the gym* and by the adverb *now*.]

Reference Note

For information on **modifiers,** see Chapter 20. For information on **complements,** see Chapter 13.

Meeting INDIVIDUAL NEEDS

ENGLISH-LANGUAGE LEARNERS
Spanish and Portuguese. Point out to students that the word *to* in English infinitives (*to speak, to sell, to part*) corresponds to the Spanish and Portuguese infinitive endings *–ar, –er,* or *–ir* (*hablar, vender,* and *partir* in Spanish; *falar, vender,* and *partir* in Portuguese).

French. In French, the infinitive ends in *–er, –ir, –oir,* or *–re* (for example, *aimer, finir, reçevoir, rompre*).

TEACHING TIP

Activity. To emphasize the different uses of infinitive phrases, use the same infinitive in three different ways—as a noun, adjective, and adverb—in three different sentences. Write the sentences on the chalkboard, and ask students to pick out the infinitive phrases. Then, discuss whether these phrases are used as nouns, adjectives, or adverbs. Here are some examples using the infinitive *to keep*:

1. To keep the peace is the role of the military. [*To keep the peace—noun*]

2. A locker is a place to keep books and pencils. [*to keep books and pencils—adjective*]

3. To keep his desk in order, John needs an extra drawer. [*To keep his desk in order—adverb*]

Verbals and Verbal Phrases   **415**

Exercise 13 **Identifying Infinitive Phrases**

Identify the infinitive phrase in each of the following sentences.

EXAMPLE   **1.** We went to the park to watch birds.

     1. to watch birds

1. A bird is able to control many of its feathers individually.
2. Birds use their feathers to push their bodies through the air.
3. Human beings learned to build aircraft by carefully studying the way birds fly.
4. A bird sings to claim its territory.
5. To recognize the songs of different birds takes many hours of practice.
6. By molting (or gradual shedding), birds are able to replace their feathers.
7. Eagles use their feet to catch small animals.
8. Since they have no teeth, many birds have to swallow their food whole.
9. In many cases both parents help to build a nest.
10. Most birds feed their young until the young are ready to fly from the nest.

Exercise 14 **Writing Sentences with Infinitive Phrases**

For each of the following items, write a sentence using the given infinitive phrase. Try to vary your sentences as much as possible.

EXAMPLE   **1.** to see the carved masks of the Haida people

     1. Terry wants to see the carved masks of the Haida people.

1. to sing with the Boys Choir of Harlem
2. to ask a question about the test
3. to write a poem to his girlfriend
4. to understand the assignment
5. to give a report on the Spanish exploration of California
6. to learn a little Japanese over the summer
7. to predict accurately the weather patterns
8. to imitate that style
9. to be the best at everything
10. to dry in the sun

Exercise 14 **Writing Sentences with Infinitive Phrases**

POSSIBLE ANSWERS

1. His goal is to sing with the Boys Choir of Harlem.
2. She wants to ask a question about the test.
3. Rusty is too shy to write a poem to his girlfriend.
4. They learned that it was important to understand the assignment before starting to work on it.
5. To give a report on the Spanish exploration of California will take some research.
6. In order to learn a little Japanese over the summer, she traveled to Tokyo.
7. My grandmother is able to predict accurately the weather patterns for our area.
8. It would be better to develop your own ideas than to imitate that style.
9. It is impossible to be the best at everything.
10. We left our beach towels to dry in the sun.

Learning for Life

Giving Directions. To review the various types of phrases in **Chapter 14,** write the following directions on a transparency or on the chalkboard. You may want to adapt the example to apply to your school. The prepositional phrases are underlined once, the participial phrases are bracketed, and the infinitive phrases are underlined twice.

     To find the principal's office, go out the door and turn to your left. Walk down the hall until you see an orange banner [hanging above the lockers on your

Review C Identifying and Classifying Participial Phrases and Infinitive Phrases

Identify the <u>participial phrase</u> or the <u>infinitive phrase</u> in each sentence of the following paragraph. Classify each phrase as a *participial phrase* or an *infinitive phrase*.

EXAMPLES
[1] My family is proud to celebrate our Jewish holidays.

1. *to celebrate our Jewish holidays—infinitive phrase*

[2] Observing Jewish traditions, we celebrate each holiday in a special way.

2. *Observing Jewish traditions—participial phrase*

[1] During Rosh Hashana we hear writings from the Torah <u>read in our synagogue</u>. [2] <u>Celebrated in September or October</u>, Rosh Hashana is the Jewish New Year. [3] On this holiday, our rabbi chooses <u>to wear white robes instead of the usual black robes</u>. [4] <u>Representing newness and purity</u>, the white robes symbolize the new year. [5] My favorite food of Rosh Hashana is the honey cake <u>baked by my grandmother</u>. [6] During this holiday everyone eats a lot, <u>knowing that Yom Kippur, a day of fasting, is only ten days away</u>. [7] Yom Kippur, <u>considered the holiest day of the Jewish year</u>, is a serious holiday. [8] <u>To attend services like the one you see here</u> is part of my family's Yom Kippur tradition. [9] I am always pleased <u>to see many of my friends and neighbors there</u>. [10] Sunset, <u>marking the end of the day</u>, brings Yom Kippur to a peaceful close.

1. part.
2. part.
3. inf.

4. part.
5. part.
6. part.

7. part.
8. inf.

9. inf.
10. part.

right]. Turn right <u>into the next hallway</u>. The principal's office is the third door <u>on the right</u>.

Next, ask students to write directions for a location of their choice in or around the school. Suggest that they try to use at least one example of each kind of phrase covered in this chapter. Then, ask students to read their directions aloud while the rest of the class guesses the destinations.

For each of the following sentences, write the kind of phrase that is called for in parentheses.   Answers will vary.

EXAMPLE   **1.** _____, the audience cheered Yo-Yo Ma's performance. (participial phrase)

1. *Clapping loudly, the audience cheered Yo-Yo Ma's performance.*

1. toward the car

2. in the auditorium

3. of fire ants

4. from the faucet

5. On our trip

6. Trying to catch his breath

7. using all his strength

8. to go to the movies

9. To help end world hunger

10. praising her mother

1. We walked slowly _____. (adverb phrase)

2. The people _____ applauded Mayor Garza's speech. (adjective phrase)

3. My little brother is afraid _____. (adverb phrase)

4. The water _____ dripped steadily. (adjective phrase)

5. _____ we saw many beautiful Navajo rugs. (adverb phrase)

6. _____, the principal entered the classroom. (participial phrase)

7. Suddenly, _____, the lion pounced. (participial phrase)

8. My friends and I like _____. (infinitive phrase)

9. _____ is my greatest ambition. (infinitive phrase)

10. She wrote a poem _____. (participial phrase)

Chapter Review

A. Identifying Prepositional Phrases

Identify each <u>prepositional phrase</u> in the following sentences. Then, write the <u>word each phrase modifies</u>. There may be more than one prepositional phrase in a sentence.

1. The <u>view</u> <u>from Mount Fuji</u> is spectacular.
2. Boulder Dam was the original <u>name</u> <u>of Hoover Dam</u>.
3. <u>Eat</u> something <u>before the game</u>.
4. We heard <u>stories</u> <u>about our Cherokee ancestors</u>.
5. The coach <u>paced</u> nervously <u>on the sidelines</u>.
6. The second-longest <u>river</u> <u>in Africa</u> is the Congo.
7. <u>For the costume party</u>, Jody <u>dressed</u> <u>as a lion tamer</u>.
8. Has the hiking party <u>returned</u> <u>to the campsite</u>?
9. The Hudson River was once the chief trading <u>route</u> <u>for the western frontier</u>.
10. Hearing a loud noise, Rita stopped the car and <u>looked</u> <u>underneath it</u>.

B. Identifying Adjective and Adverb Phrases

Classify each italicized prepositional phrase in the following sentences as an *adjective phrase* or an *adverb phrase*. Then, write the <u>word the phrase modifies</u>.

11. adj.   **11.** The <u>jacket</u> *with the gray stripes* is mine.
12. adj.   **12.** The <u>man</u> *across the aisle* is sleeping.
13. adv.   **13.** Mai <u>spoke</u> *with confidence* at the leadership conference.
14. adj.   **14.** A young <u>woman</u> *in a blue uniform* answered the phone.
15. adj.   **15.** <u>Nobody</u> *except Alicia* was amazed at the sudden downpour.
16. adv.   **16.** Were you <u>upset</u> *about the delay*?
17. adv.   **17.** Does your doctor <u>work</u> *at Emerson Hospital*?
18. adv.   **18.** *Along the Appalachian National Scenic Trail*, you will <u>find</u> painted rocks that indicate the route.
19. adj.   **19.** Masud's <u>friends</u> *from New Jersey* are coming to visit.
20. adv.   **20.** He is <u>tall</u> *for his age*.

Using the Chapter Review

To assess student progress, you may want to compare the types of items missed on the **Diagnostic Preview** to those missed on the **Chapter Review.** You may want to work out specific goals with individual students who are still having difficulty mastering essential information.

GRAMMAR

C. Classifying Verbal Phrases

Identify each italicized verbal phrase in the following sentences as an *infinitive phrase* or a *participial phrase*.

21. part.	**21.** *Returning her library books,* Janelle chose two more.
22. part.	**22.** Commander Scott, *chilled by the brisk wind,* pulled on her gloves.
23. inf.	**23.** *To become a park ranger* is Keisha's dream.
24. part.	**24.** The awards dinner *planned for this evening* has been canceled because of a snowstorm.
25. inf.	**25.** A soufflé can be difficult *to prepare properly.*
26. part.	**26.** *Organized in 1884,* the first African American professional baseball team was the Cuban Giants.
27. inf.	**27.** Guillermo hopes *to visit us soon.*
28. inf.	**28.** My brother was the first person *to see a meteor* last evening.
29. part.	**29.** Stella did not disturb the cat *sleeping in the window.*
30. inf.	**30.** How do you plan *to tell the story?*

D. Identifying Verbal Phrases

Identify the verbal phrase in each of the following sentences. Then, classify each phrase as an *infinitive phrase* or a *participial phrase.*

31. inf.	**31.** To skate around the neighborhood was Lee's favorite pastime.
32. part.	**32.** Racing around on his in-line skates, he felt as if he were flying.
33. part.	**33.** Then one afternoon, prevented from skating by the rain, Lee wondered about the history of skates.
34. inf.	**34.** He decided to search the Internet for information.
35. inf.	**35.** Lee learned that Joseph Merlin, an eighteenth-century Dutchman, was the first person to adapt ice skates for use on dry land.
36. inf.	**36.** Merlin's idea was to attach wooden spools to a plate that supported them.
37. part.	**37.** First fashioned in 1763, skates with metal wheels were in use for a century.
38. part.	**38.** Appearing in 1863, the first modern skates were invented by an American.

RESOURCES

The Phrase

Review

- *Grammar, Usage, and Mechanics,* pp. 102, 103, 104

Assessment

- *Assessment Package*
  —*Chapter Tests,* Ch. 14
  —*Chapter Tests in Standardized Test Formats,* Ch. 14
- *Test Generator (One-Stop Planner CD-ROM)*

39. Skates with more durable ball-bearing wheels, <u>introduced later in the nineteenth century</u>, popularized roller skating.

40. At the end of the afternoon, Lee exclaimed, "It's fun <u>to know the history of skates!</u>"

39. part.

40. inf.

Writing Application

Using Prepositional Phrases in a Note

Adjective and Adverb Phrases   You are writing a note to a friend explaining how to care for your pet while you are away on vacation. In your note, use a combined total of at least ten adjective phrases and adverb phrases to give detailed instructions to your friend.

Prewriting   Begin by thinking about a pet you have or would like to have. Then, make a chart or list of the pet's needs. If you need more information about a particular pet, ask a friend or someone else who owns such a pet.

Writing   As you write your first draft, focus on giving information about each of your pet's needs. Tell your friend everything he or she needs to know to care for your pet properly.

Revising   Ask a family member or friend to read your note. Add any missing information and take out any unnecessary instructions. Be sure that you have used both adjective phrases and adverb phrases and that you have used a total of at least ten phrases.

Publishing   Read over your note again to check the grammar, punctuation, and spelling. You and your classmates may wish to create a pet care guide. Gather your notes in a three-ring binder and group your instructions by type of pet.

Chapter Review   **421**

RESOURCES

Writing Application

Extension

- *Grammar, Usage, and Mechanics,* p. 107
- *Language Workshop CD-ROM,* Lessons 23–25

Writing Application

(p. 421)

OBJECTIVE

- To use both adjective and adverb phrases to write instructions

Writing Application

Tip. Tell students to visualize themselves going through the procedure. They should stop after each imagined action and write exactly what they did. Then, before they begin writing, they should look at their lists of steps to make sure that all steps are in the correct sequence.

Scoring Rubric. While you will want to pay particular attention to students' uses of adjective and adverb phrases, you may also want to evaluate the students' overall writing performance. You may want to give a split score to indicate development and clarity of the composition as well as grammar skills.

Critical Thinking

Evaluation. In prewriting, students might include more information than is necessary for writing the instructions. Tell students that in the writing stage, they should omit any procedures not essential to accomplishing the task. For example, while they will need to tell where to find can openers or food and water dishes, it is not necessary to include instructions for opening the can or placing the contents in a dish.

Tell students to keep in mind what information their friends will need and what knowledge a person would already have.

CHAPTER

15 The Clause
Independent and Subordinate Clauses

PREVIEWING THE CHAPTER

- The first part of the chapter explains the difference between independent and subordinate clauses and asks students to write sentences using subordinate clauses. The rest of the chapter discusses adjective and adverb clauses.

- The chapter closes with a **Chapter Review**, which includes a **Writing Application** feature that asks students to write a safety manual. Students must use subordinating conjunctions to show the relationships between ideas.

- For help in integrating this chapter with composition chapters, use the **Teaching Strands** chart on pp. T311A–T311B.

USING THE DIAGNOSTIC PREVIEW

- You may want to use this informal **Diagnostic Preview** to determine students' understanding of clauses, especially if you are working on combining sentences in the revision stage of compositions. You also will be able to assess students' comprehension of adjective and adverb clauses.

Diagnostic Preview

A. Identifying and Classifying Independent and Subordinate Clauses

Identify each of the following clauses as either *independent* or *subordinate*.

EXAMPLE   **1.** when I was eleven years old

       1. subordinate

1. sub.	**1.** because I have lived in Chile and Ecuador
2. ind.	**2.** his writing has improved
3. sub.	**3.** although Gullah is still spoken on South Carolina's Sea Islands
4. sub.	**4.** when the Philadelphia Phillies baseball team won the National League pennant
5. ind.	**5.** she served as secretary of labor
6. sub.	**6.** which we brought to the Juneteenth picnic
7. ind.	**7.** everyone laughed
8. sub.	**8.** whose mother you met yesterday
9. ind.	**9.** during the storm the power failed
10. sub.	**10.** to whom his mother explained the reason for the delay

CHAPTER RESOURCES

Planning
- *One-Stop Planner CD-ROM*

Practice and Extension
- *Grammar, Usage, and Mechanics*, p. 108
- *Developmental Language Skills*, pp. 47–52

Internet
- go.hrw.com (keyword: EOLang) **go.hrw.com**

Evaluation and Assessment
- *Chapter Tests*, Ch. 15
- *Chapter Tests in Standardized Test Formats*, Ch. 15
- *Test Generator (One-Stop Planner)*

B. Identifying and Classifying Subordinate Clauses

Identify the subordinate clause in each of the following sentences. Then, classify each as either an *adjective clause* or an *adverb clause*.

EXAMPLES
1. Today is the day that you are eating at my house.
   1. *that you are eating at my house—adjective clause*

2. I will give you a map so that you can find my house.
   2. *so that you can find my house—adverb clause*

11. If you have never had Caribbean food, you are in for a treat.
12. My mother, who was born and raised in Jamaica, really knows how to cook.
13. Whenever I have a chance, I try to learn her secrets.
14. My grandmother, whose cooking is spectacular, is making her special sweet potato pone for dessert.
15. Some of the fruits and vegetables that grow in Jamaica are hard to find in the markets around here.
16. Today we are shopping for coconuts, avocados, and callaloo greens, which were introduced to the Caribbean by Africans.
17. We must also remember to buy the fresh hot peppers, onions, and spices that are needed for seasoning the meat.
18. Although my mother never uses measuring spoons, she seems to know just how much of each spice to add.
19. As soon as we pay for these items, let's take them home.
20. Part of your treat will be to smell the delicious aroma from the kitchen before you even begin eating.

11. adv.
12. adj.
13. adv.
14. adj.
15. adj.
16. adj.
17. adj.
18. adv.
19. adv.
20. adv.

What Is a Clause?

15a. A *clause* is a word group that contains a verb and its subject and that is used as a sentence or as part of a sentence.

Every clause contains a subject and a verb. However, not all clauses express complete thoughts. A clause that does express a complete thought is called an *independent clause*. A clause that does not make sense by itself is called a *subordinate clause*.

NOTE A subordinate clause that is capitalized and punctuated as if it were a sentence is a **sentence fragment.**

Reference Note

For information about **correcting sentence fragments,** see page 269.

What Is a Clause? **423**

Independent and Subordinate Clauses

Rules 15a–c *(pp. 423–427)*

OBJECTIVES

- To identify independent and subordinate clauses in sentences

- To complete sentences by adding independent clauses to subordinate clauses

Meeting INDIVIDUAL NEEDS

MULTIPLE INTELLIGENCES
Interpersonal Intelligence.
Students with strong interpersonal intelligence are sensitive to the moods, motivations, and desires of others. You might want to train these students to be "clause tutors." They can be available with help for other students who might need assistance throughout the lessons on clauses.

Looking at Language

Remind students about the meanings of the prefixes *in–* ("not") and *sub–* ("below" or "under"). *Independent,* or "not dependent," clauses can stand by themselves as sentences; *subordinate,* or "ranked below," clauses must be accompanied in sentences by an independent clause. Knowing these prefixes can help students distinguish between the two types of clauses.

Reference Note

For information on using **commas and coordinating conjunctions to join two independent clauses,** see page 605. For information about **using commas to join independent and subordinate clauses,** see page 607.

The Independent Clause

15b. An *independent* (or *main*) *clause* expresses a complete thought and can stand by itself as a sentence.

EXAMPLES   I woke up late this morning.

Do you know Joseph?

When an independent clause stands alone, it is called a sentence. Usually, the term *independent clause* is used only when such a clause is joined with another clause.

EXAMPLES   **My mother drove me to school.** [This entire sentence is an independent clause.]

My mother drove me to school, but **my brother rode his bicycle.** [This sentence contains two independent clauses.]

Since I missed the bus, **my mother drove me to school.** [This sentence contains one subordinate clause and one independent clause.]

The Subordinate Clause

15c. A *subordinate* (or *dependent*) *clause* does not express a complete thought and cannot stand by itself as a complete sentence.

Words such as *because, if, since, that, until, which,* and *whom* signal that the clauses following them may be subordinate. *Subordinate* means "lesser in rank or importance." A subordinate clause must be joined with at least one independent clause to make a sentence and express a complete thought.

SUBORDINATE CLAUSES   **if** the dress is too long

that the veterinarian recommended

SENTENCES   **If the dress is too long,** we will hem it.

The new food **that the veterinarian recommended** is good for our hamster.

Subordinate clauses may appear at the beginning, in the middle, or at the end of a sentence.

RESOURCES

Independent and Subordinate Clauses
Practice

- *Grammar, Usage, and Mechanics,* pp. 109, 110, 111, 112–113
- *Language Workshop CD-ROM,* Lesson 26

Exercise 1 **Identifying Independent and Subordinate Clauses**

Identify the italicized clause in each of the following sentences as *independent* or *subordinate*.

EXAMPLE **1.** *If you know any modern music history,* then you are probably familiar with the Motown sound.

  1. *subordinate*

1. Do you recognize the entertainers *who are shown in the photographs on this page and the next*?

2. These performers had hit records in the 1950s and 1960s *when the music business in Detroit (the Motor City, or "Motown") was booming.*

3. Berry Gordy, *who founded the Motown record label,* began his business in a small office in Detroit.

4. He was a songwriter and producer, and *he was able to spot talent.*

5. Gordy went to clubs to hear local groups *whose sound he liked.*

6. The Miracles, *which was the first group discovered by Gordy,* had a lead singer named Smokey Robinson.

7. *Robinson was also a songwriter,* and Gordy included him in the Motown team of writers and musicians.

MODALITIES

Auditory Learners. Some students may find it easier to hear the difference between a complete and an incomplete thought than to recognize the difference visually. You or a student helper could read aloud the examples in this lesson and the italicized clauses in **Exercise 1**. Have volunteers explain why each example is either an independent clause or a subordinate clause.

Crossing the Curriculum

Social Studies. Students may be most familiar with the word *independent* and the idea of independence as it relates to United States history (Independence Day, the Declaration of Independence). Point out that before the Revolutionary War, the thirteen colonies were subordinate to England; after winning the war, the former colonies became a country equal in status to England.

The Subordinate Clause   **425**

 Continued on p. 426

Sentence Structure. Sentences can be classified by the kinds of clauses they contain.

• A simple sentence has one independent clause and no subordinate clauses.

The **girls** on our team **want** new uniforms.

• A compound sentence has more than one independent clause and no subordinate clauses.

We ordered new uniforms last year, but **they were** the wrong colors.

Cooperative Learning

To give students additional practice distinguishing between phrases, subordinate clauses, and independent clauses, divide the class into small groups. Provide each group with three signs: one that says *phrase,* one that says *independent clause,* and one that says *subordinate clause.* Then, write on the chalkboard or on a transparency the following group of words: *because I lost my book.*

Ask group members to confer and then to hold up the sign that correctly identifies the word group. Check to see that all groups have the right answer. [*subordinate clause*] Continue the activity with the following word groups. Then, have the members of each group take turns adding words to the phrases and subordinate clauses to make complete sentences.

1. around the beautiful, fragrant garden [*phrase*]

2. that I really want [*subordinate clause*]

3. any student can join [*independent clause*]

4. thinking about tonight's game [*phrase*]

5. as soon as the bell rings [*subordinate clause*]

S T Y L E ✏ T I P

Although short sentences can be effective, a variety of sentence structures is usually more effective. To revise choppy sentences into smoother writing, combine shorter sentences by changing some into subordinate clauses.

CHOPPY
This is our dog, Skippy. He is five years old. He is a Yorkshire terrier.

SMOOTH
This is our dog, Skippy, who is a five-year-old Yorkshire terrier.

In the example above, two of the short sentences are combined into a single subordinate clause.

---

8. Gordy carefully managed all aspects of the Motown sound, *which is a special combination of rhythm and blues and soul.*

9. Diana Ross and the Supremes, Stevie Wonder, Marvin Gaye, the Four Tops, the Temptations, Gladys Knight and the Pips, and Michael Jackson are just some of the performers *that Gordy discovered.*

10. As you look carefully at the photographs again, *can you and your classmates recognize these music legends*?

Exercise 2 Identifying Subordinate Clauses

Identify the subordinate clause in each of the following sentences.

EXAMPLE   **1.** When you get up in the morning, do you look at your sleepy face in a mirror?

   1. When you get up in the morning

1. A mirror is a piece of polished metal or glass that is coated with a substance such as silver.

2. The most common type of mirror is the plane mirror, which is flat.

3. The image that is reflected in a plane mirror is reversed.

4. As you look into a mirror, your left hand seems to be the image's right hand.

5. When an image is reversed, it is called a mirror image.

6. A sailor who looks through the periscope of a submarine is using a system of lenses and mirrors in a tube to see above the water's surface.

7. Right-hand rearview mirrors on cars, which show a wide area of the road behind, are usually convex, or curved outward.

8. Drivers must be careful because convex mirrors make reflected objects appear far away.

9. Because the mirror in a flashlight is concave, or curved inward, it strengthens the light from a small lightbulb.

10. When you look in a concave mirror, you sometimes see a magnified reflection of yourself.

MINI-LESSON

- A complex sentence has one independent clause and at least one subordinate clause.

  If **we order** now, our **uniforms will arrive** in time for the first game.

Discuss with students how using a variety of sentence types can add interest to their writing. To extend the activity, ask students to locate a piece of their own writing and to count how many times they used each type of sentence.

Exercise 3 Writing Sentences with Subordinate Clauses

Write ten sentences by adding an independent clause to each of the following subordinate clauses. Underline the independent clause in each of your sentences. Make your sentences interesting by using a variety of independent clauses.

EXAMPLES   **1.** who lives next door to us

     1. <u>Have you or Peggy met the woman</u> who lives next door to us?

     2. that Alexander bought

     2. <u>The sleeping bag</u> that Alexander bought <u>was on sale</u>.

1. when I bought the CD
2. who won the contest
3. if my parents agree
4. as Jessye Norman began to sing
5. because we are going to a concert
6. that you made
7. who built the pyramids
8. for which this musician is famous
9. since the introduction of the telephone
10. whose paintings are now famous

The Adjective Clause

15d. An *adjective clause* is a subordinate clause that modifies a noun or a pronoun.

Like an adjective or an adjective phrase, an adjective clause may modify a noun or a pronoun. Unlike an adjective phrase, an adjective clause contains both a verb and its subject.

ADJECTIVE	a **blue** flower
ADJECTIVE PHRASE	a flower **with blue petals** [The phrase does not have a verb and its subject.]
ADJECTIVE CLAUSE	a flower **that has blue petals** [The clause does have a verb and its subject.]

An adjective clause usually follows the word or words it modifies and tells *which one* or *what kind*.

The Subordinate Clause   **427**

Exercise 3 Writing Sentences with Subordinate Clauses

ANSWERS
Sentences will vary. You may want to require that students vary the position of the subordinate clauses in their sentences.

The Adjective Clause
Rule 15d (pp. 427–429)

OBJECTIVES

- **To identify adjective clauses and relative pronouns in sentences**

- **To complete sentences by supplying appropriate adjective clauses**

Meeting
INDIVIDUAL
NEEDS

ENGLISH-LANGUAGE LEARNERS
General Strategies. Students may have difficulty with adjective clauses that end with a verb, such as "I like the book *that Maria is reading*." In some languages, it is considered awkward to end a clause with a verb. For instance, a Spanish speaker will invert the subject and the verb, as in the following sentence: "Me gusta el libro *que lee Maria*." English-language learners may invert the word order in this manner when writing in English.

Relating to Writing

Discuss with students that unnecessary adjective clauses can contribute to wordiness in their writing. Use the following examples to show students how sentences can be revised to eliminate unnecessary adjective clauses.

1. This is the car <u>that I want</u>.
   Revision: I want this car.

2. My house has a door <u>that is red</u>.
   Revision: My house has a red door.

3. She wore a floral dress, <u>which was lovely</u>.
   Revision: She wore a lovely floral dress.

Ask students to highlight any adjective clauses in a piece of their own writing. Have students decide whether any of the sentences containing adjective clauses could be revised to reduce wordiness. Check students' revisions.

Meeting
INDIVIDUAL
NEEDS

ADVANCED LEARNERS

A relative pronoun can perform various functions within the adjective clause it introduces. Write the following examples on the chalkboard, and ask students to give additional examples.

1. **Subject:** Elsa is a good friend *who listens to my problems.*

2. **Direct Object:** Have you read the story *that I wrote?*

3. **Object of a Preposition:** She is the woman *from whom we bought the car.*

4. **Modifier:** She is the artist *whose painting took first place.*

| S T Y L E | | T I P |

The relative pronoun *that* is used to refer both to people and to things. The relative pronoun *which* is used to refer to things.

EXAMPLES
She is the person **that** I met yesterday.

This is the CD **that** you should buy.

The bus, **which** is behind schedule, stops at the next corner.

Reference Note

For information about **when to use commas to set off adjective clauses,** see page 607.

EXAMPLES Emma Willard was the one **who founded the first women's college in the United States.** [The adjective clause modifies the pronoun *one*, telling *which one*.]

I want a bicycle **that I can ride over rough ground.** [The adjective clause modifies the noun *bicycle*, telling *what kind*.]

The Relative Pronoun

An adjective clause is usually introduced by a *relative pronoun*.

Commonly Used Relative Pronouns				
that	which	who	whom	whose

These words are called ***relative pronouns*** because they *relate* an adjective clause to the noun or pronoun that the clause modifies.

EXAMPLES A snorkel is a hollow tube **that lets a diver breathe underwater.** [The relative pronoun *that* begins the adjective clause and relates it to the noun *tube*.]

The team's mascot, **which is a horse,** is called Renegade. [The relative pronoun *which* begins the adjective clause and relates it to the noun *mascot*.]

Gwendolyn Brooks is the writer **who is the poet laureate of Illinois.** [The relative pronoun *who* begins the adjective clause and relates it to the noun *writer*.]

Those **whose library books are overdue** must pay fines. [The relative pronoun *whose* begins the adjective clause and relates it to the pronoun *Those*.]

NOTE In some cases, the relative pronoun can be omitted.

EXAMPLE   The person [**that** *or* **whom**] **we met at the market** was Mrs. Herrera.

Exercise 4 **Identifying Adjective Clauses**

Identify the <u>adjective clause</u> in each of the sentences on the next page. Underline the <u>relative pronoun</u> that begins the clause.

EXAMPLE   1. The person who wrote the Declaration of
               Independence was Thomas Jefferson.

           1. *who wrote the Declaration of Independence*

1. In his later years, Jefferson lived at his home, Monticello,
   which he designed.
2. Jefferson planned a daily schedule that kept him busy all day.
3. He began each day by writing himself a note that recorded
   the morning temperature.
4. Then he did his writing, which included letters to friends and
   businesspeople.
5. Afterward, he ate breakfast, which was served around
   9:00 A.M.
6. Jefferson, whose property included stables as well as farm
   fields, went horseback riding at noon.
7. Dinner, which began about 4:00 P.M., was a big meal.
8. From dinner until dark, he talked to friends and neighbors
   who came to visit.
9. His large family, whom he often spent time with, included
   twelve grandchildren.
10. Jefferson, whose interests ranged from art and architecture to
    biology and mathematics, read each night.

Exercise 5 Writing Appropriate Adjective Clauses

Complete each of the following sentences with an adjective
clause. Then, underline the relative pronoun.

EXAMPLE   1. We read the Greek legend ____.

           1. We read the Greek legend *that tells the story
               of the Trojan horse.*

1. You should proofread every composition ____.
2. My best friend, ____, is a good student.
3. Mrs. Rivera, ____, was my fifth-grade teacher.
4. We heard a sound ____.
5. Our neighbors ____ are from Fez, Morocco.
6. The ship, ____, carried bananas.
7. Anyone ____ is excused from the final exam.
8. Carmen, can you tell us about the scientist ____?
9. Is Victor Hugo the author ____?
10. Wow! I didn't know you had a dog ____.

┌─HELP─
Remember,
to be a clause, a word
group must contain both
a verb and its subject.

Relating to Literature

If the Edgar Allan Poe poem
"Annabel Lee" is in your literature
textbook, you could use the poem
to give students practice identifying
subordinate clauses and the words
they modify. As a class, discuss the
effects of Poe's use of clauses in this
poem. [*Poe's use of the word* that
*and his placement of adjective
clauses help sustain the poem's
rhythm.*]

Exercise 5   Writing
Appropriate Adjective Clauses

ANSWERS
Sentences will vary. You may want
students to label the subjects and
verbs of their clauses and to draw
arrows from the adjective clauses
to the words they modify.

The Adverb Clause

Rule 15e *(pp. 430–434)*

OBJECTIVES

- To identify adverb clauses in sentences
- To complete sentences by writing adverb clauses

Meeting
INDIVIDUAL
NEEDS

ADVANCED LEARNERS

To help students see how adverb clauses clarify relationships between ideas and give coherence to paragraphs, write the following paragraph on the chalkboard:

> Last year we visited several antique shops. We were looking for an old radio to use in the spring play. We came to a small shop. We were sure it didn't have what we wanted. It had one radio—just the radio we needed.

Ask students to revise the sentences, using adverb clauses to subordinate some of the ideas. [*Possible revision: Last year we visited several antique shops because we were looking for an old radio to use in the spring play. When we came to a small shop, although we were sure it didn't have what we wanted, it had just the radio we needed.*]

| S T Y L E | T I P |

In most cases, deciding where to place an adverb clause is a matter of style, not correctness.

As he leapt across the gorge, Rex glanced back at his alien pursuers.

Rex glanced back at his alien pursuers **as he leapt across the gorge.**

Which sentence might you use in a science fiction story? The sentence to choose would be the one that looks and sounds better in context—the rest of the paragraph to which the sentence belongs.

Reference Note
For more information on **punctuating introductory adverb clauses,** see page 613.

The Adverb Clause

15e. An *adverb clause* is a subordinate clause that modifies a verb, an adjective, or an adverb.

Like an adverb or an adverb phrase, an adverb clause can modify a verb, an adjective, or an adverb. Unlike an adverb phrase, an adverb clause contains both a verb and its subject.

ADVERB	**Bravely,** Jason battled a fierce dragon.
ADVERB PHRASE	**With great bravery,** Jason battled a fierce dragon. [The phrase does not have both a verb and its subject.]
ADVERB CLAUSE	**Because Jason was brave,** he battled a fierce dragon. [The clause does have a verb and its subject.]

Adverb clauses answer the following questions: *How? When? Where? Why? To what extent? How much? How long?* and *Under what condition?*

EXAMPLES   I feel **as though I will never catch up.** [The adverb clause tells *how* I feel.]

After I finish painting my bookcases, I will call you. [The adverb clause tells *when* I will call you.]

I paint **where there is plenty of fresh air.** [The adverb clause tells *where* I paint.]

I have more work to do today **because I didn't paint yesterday.** [The adverb clause tells *why* I have more work to do.]

Jennifer can run faster **than Victor can.** [The adverb clause tells *to what extent* Jennifer can run faster.]

I will paint **until Mom comes home;** then I will clean my brushes and set the table for supper. [The adverb clause tells *how long* I will paint.]

If I paint for two more hours, I should be able to finish. [The adverb clause tells *under what condition* I should be able to finish.]

Notice in the preceding examples that adverb clauses may be placed in various positions in sentences. When an adverb clause comes at the beginning, it is usually followed by a comma.

430   Chapter 15   The Clause

RESOURCES

The Adverb Clause
Practice

- *Grammar, Usage, and Mechanics,* pp. 117–118, 119, 120–121
- *Language Workshop CD-ROM,* Lesson 28

Subordinating Conjunctions

Adverb clauses begin with *subordinating conjunctions*.

Some words that are used as subordinating conjunctions, such as *after, as, before, since,* and *until,* can also be used as prepositions.

PREPOSITION	**Before** sunrise, we left for the cabin.
SUBORDINATING CONJUNCTION	**Before** the sun had risen, we left for the cabin.

PREPOSITION	In the nineteenth century, buffalo skins were used **as** blankets and clothing.
SUBORDINATING CONJUNCTION	Around 1900, **as** the buffalo became nearly extinct, conservationists fought for its protection.

Exercise 6 **Identifying Adverb Clauses**

Identify the adverb clause in each of the following sentences.

EXAMPLE **1.** As long as they have been a people, the Chinese have been making kites.

　　　 1. *As long as they have been a people*

1. Although the following story is only a legend, many people believe that a kite like the one pictured on the next page may have saved the people of China's Han dynasty.
2. The Chinese were about to be attacked by an enemy army when an advisor to the emperor came up with a plan.
3. As the advisor stood beside an open window, his hat was lifted off by a strong wind.
4. He immediately called for a number of kites to be made so that they might be used to frighten the enemy.

COMPUTER TIP

A computer can help you proofread your writing. Use the computer's search function to highlight any uses of the words *after, as, before, since,* and *until.* Look at the use of such words at the beginnings of sentences. Decide whether the word begins a prepositional phrase or a subordinate clause. In most cases an introductory prepositional phrase is not set off by a comma. An introductory adverb clause, though, should be followed by a comma.

Exercise 6

ALTERNATIVE LESSON
Have students identify the past participle used as an adjective in sentence 1 [*pictured*], then tell which word or words it modifies [*one*].

5. The kite makers had no trouble finding lightweight bamboo for their kite frames <u>because bamboo grows widely in China</u>.

6. <u>As each frame was completed</u>, silk was stretched over it.

7. The emperor's advisor attached noisemakers to the kites <u>so that they would produce an eerie sound</u>.

8. He ordered his men to fly the kites in the darkest hour of night <u>because then the enemy would hear the kites but would not be able to see them</u>.

9. <u>Unless the advisor was wrong</u>, the enemy would think that the kites were gods warning them to retreat.

10. According to the legend, the enemy retreated <u>as if they were being chased by a fire-breathing dragon</u>.

David F. Jue, *Chinese Kites, How to Make and Fly Them*. Charles E. Tuttle Co. Inc., of Tokyo, Japan.

Exercise 7 Writing Adverb Clauses

Complete each of the following sentences with an adverb clause. Then, underline the subordinating conjunction.

EXAMPLE   1. _____, digital cameras will become quite popular.

　　　　　1. *If I'm right, digital cameras will become quite popular.*

1. _____, everything seemed fresh and new.

2. The gears jammed _____.

3. _____, the African dancers began their routine.

─HELP─

Remember, a clause contains both a verb and its subject.

Exercise 7　Writing Adverb Clauses

ANSWERS

Clauses will vary. You may want students to label the subjects and verbs of their clauses and to draw arrows from the adverb clauses to the words they modify.

Learning for Life

Essay Questions. Throughout their school years (and possibly beyond), students will be asked to write essays, generally in a testing situation. Ask students to respond to one of the following questions by writing a short one- or two-paragraph essay.

1. Describe what you see yourself doing ten years from now.

2. Explain how studying language arts helps you in other subjects.

3. Summarize your favorite movie.

4. From the trees, a Bengal tiger watched the herd ____.
5. ____, maybe he'll help you clean your room.
6. Call us ____.
7. ____, the cement mixer backed up to the wooden frame.
8. The buses have been running on time ____.
9. ____, street sweepers rolled slowly next to the curb.
10. His map looked ____.

Review A Identifying and Classifying Subordinate Clauses

Identify the subordinate clause in each of the following sentences. Then, classify each clause as an *adjective clause* or an *adverb clause*.

EXAMPLES
1. American history is filled with stories of people who performed heroic deeds.
   1. *who performed heroic deeds—adjective clause*

2. As the American colonists struggled for independence, women played important roles.
   2. *As the American colonists struggled for independence—adverb clause*

1. When you study the American Revolution, you may learn about the adventures of a woman known as Molly Pitcher.
2. Molly Pitcher, whose real name was Mary, was the daughter of farmers.
3. Although she was born in New Jersey, she moved to the Pennsylvania colony.
4. There she married William Hays, who was a barber.
5. Hays joined the colonial army when the Revolution began.
6. Mary Hays went to be with her husband in Monmouth, New Jersey, which was the site of a battle on a hot June day in 1778.
7. At first, she carried water to the soldiers so that they would not be overcome by the intense heat.
8. The soldiers nicknamed her "Molly Pitcher" because she carried the water in pitchers.
9. Later, when her husband collapsed from the heat, she took over his cannon.
10. George Washington, who was the commander of the Continental Army, made Molly an honorary sergeant.

┌─HELP─
You have learned about two kinds of subordinate clauses: adjective clauses and adverb clauses. Another kind of subordinate clause is the **noun clause.** Noun clauses can be used as nouns in sentences.

EXAMPLES
That they played our song on the radio delighted us. [The noun clause *That they played our song on the radio* acts as the subject of this sentence.]

Sarah liked **what you said.** [The noun clause *what you said* acts as the direct object of *liked.*]

Review A You may want to use the first five items in **Review A** as guided practice. Then, have students complete the exercise as independent practice.

Critical Thinking

Evaluation. As students work through **Review A**, encourage them to write down questions that come up as they search for and label the subordinate clauses. You may want to write the example sentence on the chalkboard and model the process.

After students have completed the exercise, place them in small groups and have them share their methods for finding subordinate clauses. Suggest that each group develop a technique that they can share with the rest of the class.

Remind students that subordinate clauses can help them show relationships between ideas and add variety to their writing. Ask students to underline any subordinate clauses they use in their essays.

You may want students to exchange essays and have their peers review the essays for correct subordinate clause usage. Encourage students to keep their essays in their portfolios for future reference.

Review B **Writing Sentences with Subordinate Clauses**

ANSWERS
Sentences will vary. You may want students to label the subjects and verbs of their clauses and to draw arrows to the words the clauses modify.

Review B **Writing Sentences with Subordinate Clauses**

Write twenty different sentences of your own. In each sentence, include a subordinate clause that begins with one of the following words or word groups. Underline the subordinate clause. After the sentence, classify the subordinate clause as an *adjective clause* or an *adverb clause*.

EXAMPLES **1.** so that

1. *We hurried <u>so that we wouldn't miss the bus going downtown</u>.—adverb clause*

2. whom

2. *Jim Nakamura, <u>whom I met at summer camp</u>, is now my pen pal.—adjective clause*

1. which	**11.** because
2. before	**12.** unless
3. since	**13.** as soon as
4. who	**14.** whom
5. than	**15.** while
6. whose	**16.** whenever
7. as though	**17.** after
8. although	**18.** where
9. that	**19.** as much as
10. if	**20.** wherever

Chapter Review

GRAMMAR

A. Identifying Independent and Subordinate Clauses

Identify the italicized clause in each of the following sentences as an *independent* or a *subordinate clause.*

1. As Jawan walked to school, *he saw a strange sight.*
2. *If you go to the library*, you should take a look at the young adult section.
3. The book *that I read last night* was very scary!
4. Long after the rain had stopped, *the ground was still wet.*
5. If the trip is cancelled, *we can play tennis.*
6. *When the spin cycle stops*, please take the laundry out of the washing machine.
7. The shells *that they found* are still in the closet.
8. *Most people are asleep* when the morning newspaper is delivered.
9. Was the movie *that the reviewers liked* sold out?
10. Since we moved here from Chile, *we have met many people.*

B. Identifying Adjective and Adverb Clauses

Identify each italicized clause in the following sentences as an *adjective clause* or an *adverb clause.* Then, write the word each clause modifies.

11. We camped near Lake Arrowhead *when we went fishing last year.*   **11.** adv.
12. *Because the weather was cold*, I wore a sweater under my jacket.   **12.** adv.
13. The coat *that my mother bought for me* was blue.   **13.** adj.
14. *As she left her office*, Cletha heard the phone.   **14.** adv.
15. Vince hit the home run *that won the game*!   **15.** adj.
16. Everyone *who signed up for the marathon* should meet at 8:00 A.M. tomorrow in the school parking lot.   **16.** adj.
17. On Tuesday the Chavez family went to the Rex parade, *which is held every year in New Orleans during Mardi Gras.*   **17.** adj.

18. Larry is a little <u>taller</u> *than Dana is.*   **18.** adv.

19. The <u>CD</u> *that Rita wanted to buy* was out of stock.   **19.** adj.

20. Louise <u>stayed</u> home today *because she has a bad case of the flu.*   **20.** adv.

21. <u>Play</u> soccer *if you need more exercise.*   **21.** adv.

22. The turtle moves <u>faster</u> *than I expected.*   **22.** adv.

23. My older <u>sister</u>, *who is on the varsity basketball team,* practices after school every day.   **23.** adj.

24. *Since it was such a beautiful evening,* we <u>decided</u> to take a long walk.   **24.** adv.

25. Will the <u>students</u> *whose families observe the Jewish Sabbath* be excused early on Friday?   **25.** adj.

C. Identifying Subordinate Clauses

Identify the subordinate clause in each sentence. Then, classify the clause as an *adjective clause* or an *adverb clause*. Write *none* if the sentence does not contain a subordinate clause.

26. The denim blue jeans <u>that are known as Levi's</u> have an interesting history.

27. none   **27.** They were created in 1873 by Levi Strauss.

28. Strauss, <u>who had immigrated to the United States from Bavaria</u>, founded a clothing company called Levi Strauss & Co.

29. Six years after his arrival in the United States, he sailed to San Francisco <u>because his sister and brother-in-law had a dry goods business there.</u>

30. In 1872, Strauss had received a letter from Jacob Davis, a tailor in Nevada <u>who was one of his regular customers.</u>

31. Davis told Strauss about riveting the pocket corners of work pants <u>so that the pants would be more durable.</u>

32. <u>Since Davis lacked the money to patent this invention</u>, he asked Strauss to be his partner.

33. none   **33.** Both men were named as patent holders in 1873.

34. The copper-riveted overalls were popular with working people <u>who needed tough but comfortable pants.</u>

35. In 1880, the company, <u>whose sales had reached $2.4 million,</u> was selling denim pants to retailers for about $1.50 a pair.

RESOURCES

The Clause

Review

- *Grammar, Usage, and Mechanics,* pp. 122, 123, 124

Assessment

- *Assessment Package*
  —*Chapter Tests,* Ch. 15
  —*Chapter Tests in Standardized Test Formats,* Ch. 15
- *Test Generator (One-Stop Planner CD-ROM)*

36. Strauss died in 1902, four years before an earthquake and fire in San Francisco destroyed his company's factories.

37. After the earthquake, the company built a new factory that is still operating today.

38. The company suffered financially, as did many other businesses, during the Great Depression of the 1930s.

39. Since the 1940s, the pants have become increasingly fashionable among young people.

39. none

40. In the 1950s, when actors such as James Dean wore them in film roles, the jeans skyrocketed in popularity.

 ## Writing Application
Using Clauses in a Manual

Subordinate Clauses Your class project for National Safety Week is to write a safety manual. Each class member will write one page of instructions telling what to do in a particular emergency. Use subordinating conjunctions to show the relationships between your ideas.

Prewriting Think of a specific emergency that you know how to handle. List the steps that someone should follow in this emergency. Number the steps in order. If you aren't sure of the order or don't know a particular step, stop writing and get the information you need.

Writing Use your prewriting list to begin your first draft. As you write, make your instructions as clear as possible. Define or explain terms that might be unfamiliar to your readers. Be sure that your instructions are in the right order.

Revising Read over your instructions to be sure that you've included all necessary information. Add, cut, or rearrange steps to make the instructions easy to follow. Be sure to use appropriate subordinating conjunctions to make the order of the steps clear.

Publishing Check your work carefully for any errors in grammar, punctuation, and spelling. To publish your class safety manual, gather all the pages and make booklets out of printouts or photocopies. Organize your topics alphabetically, or group them by kinds of emergencies.

┌─ **HELP** ─
A health teacher, the school nurse, or an organization such as the Red Cross should be able to provide information.

Reference Note
For information about **punctuating introductory adverb clauses,** see page 613.

Writing Application
(p. 437)

OBJECTIVE

■ To write a safety manual

Writing Application

Tip. This writing assignment gives students practice in clarifying the relationships between clauses and the logical order of ideas within sentences. Because students will be writing to inform other students of a process, you may wish to review the guidelines in **Chapter 2: Explaining a Process.**

Scoring Rubric. While you will want to pay particular attention to students' use of the subordinating conjunctions, you will also want to evaluate the students' overall writing performance. You may want to give a split score to indicate development and clarity of the composition as well as grammar skills.

Critical Thinking

Synthesis. Ask students to design posters that highlight important safety tips based on their instructions. For example, if a student writes instructions explaining how to vacate one's home during a fire, the student's poster might illustrate the importance of each family's planning an evacuation route in advance. During the publishing stage of the writing process, students can present their posters with their instructions.

CHAPTER

16 Kinds of Sentence Structure

Simple, Compound, Complex, and Compound-Complex Sentences

Diagnostic Preview

A. Identifying and Classifying Clauses

Identify each clause in the following sentences. Then, classify each clause as an *independent clause* or a *subordinate clause*.

EXAMPLE   **1.** Students who are interested in attending the science fair at the community college should sign up now.

     1. Students should sign up now—independent clause; who are interested in attending the science fair at the community college—subordinate clause

1. We did warm-up exercises before we practiced the routine.

2. The musical *West Side Story* is a modern version of the story of Romeo and Juliet.

3. The first poem in the book is about spring, and the second one is about autumn.

4. Molasses, which is made from sugar cane, is a thick brown liquid used for human food and animal feed.

5. Before the test we studied the chapter and did the chapter review exercises.

6. While our teacher discussed the formation of the African nation of Liberia, we took notes.

7. It rained Saturday morning, but the sun came out in time for the opening of the Special Olympics.

8. The player whose performance is judged the best receives the Most Valuable Player Award.

9. Not all stringed instruments sound alike, for their shapes and the number of their strings vary.

10. The tourists that we saw wandering up Esplanade Avenue went to the Japanese ceramics exhibit after they had reached the museum.

B. Identifying Simple, Compound, Complex, and Compound-Complex Sentences

Identify each of the following sentences as *simple*, *compound*, *complex*, or *compound-complex*.

EXAMPLE 1. The Museum of Science and Industry, which is in Chicago, features a German submarine captured during World War II.

   1. *complex*

11. Either Ana or Lee will sing the opening song for the fair. **11.** s.
12. We visit the Liberty Bell whenever we go to Philadelphia. **12.** cx.
13. Have you chosen a topic for your report yet, or are you still making your decision? **13.** cd.
14. When George Washington Carver was working on soil improvement and plant diseases, the South was recovering from the Civil War, and his discoveries gave planters a competitive edge. **14.** cc.
15. *A Tree Grows in Brooklyn,* which was written by Betty Smith, is one of my favorite books. **15.** cx.
16. The call of a peacock sounds very much like that of a person in distress. **16.** s.
17. Although it was warm enough to go swimming on Monday, snow fell the next day. **17.** cx.
18. The student whose photographs of American Indian cliff dwellings won the contest was interviewed on the local news. **18.** cx.
19. The house looked completely empty when I first saw it, yet a party was going on in the backyard. **19.** cc.
20. The game was tied at the top of the ninth inning, but then Earlene hit a home run. **20.** cd.

TEACHING TIP

Motivation. To demonstrate that a variety of sentence types is needed to make writing interesting, read the following paragraph to students.

I am nervous and excited. The championship game is tomorrow. Our team is ready. We have been practicing for months. The other team is good. We are better. We will win. I know it.

Explain to students that the repetitive use of short, simple sentences can make writing seem monotonous. Write the above paragraph on the chalkboard, and ask students to help you revise it. Upon completion, point out the use of different sentence types. [*Possible revision: I am nervous and excited because the championship game is tomorrow. Our team is ready, as we have been practicing for months. The other team is good, but we are better. I know that we will win.*]

The Simple Sentence

Rule 16a (pp. 440–441)

OBJECTIVE

■ To identify subjects and verbs in simple sentences

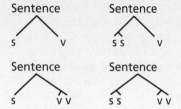

Meeting INDIVIDUAL NEEDS

MODALITIES

Visual Learners. To illustrate the relationship of subjects and verbs in simple sentences, draw the following tree diagrams for students.

You could point to the different parts of the diagram as you discuss the example sentences on this page. In addition, students can use the diagrams to analyze sentences.

Exercise 1

ALTERNATIVE LESSON

Have students locate the prepositional phrases in sentences 1, 8, and 10. [1. *from city life, of Central Park, in New York City*; 8. *of purple finches, along the pond*; 10. *In Central Park, of nature, in the middle of a bustling city*]

Reference Note

For information on **independent and subordinate clauses,** see Chapter 15.

Reference Note

For information on the **understood subject,** see page 331.

┌HELP─

Some sentences in Exercise 1 have a compound subject, a compound verb, or both.

The Simple Sentence

16a. A *simple sentence* contains one independent clause and no subordinate clauses.

EXAMPLES

            S   V
A good rain will help the farmers.

                  V   S
Up for the rebound leaped Reggie.

        V   S
Where are my keys?

        V
Please put that down near the table in the corner.
[The understood subject is *you*.]

A simple sentence may have a compound subject, a compound verb, or both.

EXAMPLES

        S   S   V
Chalupas and **fajitas are** two popular Mexican dishes.
[compound subject]

        S   V   V
Kelly read *The Planet of Junior Brown* and **reported** on it last week. [compound verb]

          S   S   V   V
The **dog** and the **kitten lay** there and **napped.**
[compound subject and compound verb]

Exercise 1   **Identifying Subjects and Verbs in Simple Sentences**

Identify the subjects and the verbs in each of the following sentences.

EXAMPLE   **1.** I enjoy urban life but need to escape from the city once in a while.

           1. I—subject; enjoy, need—verbs

1. My favorite escape from city life is the green world of Central Park in New York City.

2. Its beautiful woods and relaxing outdoor activities are just a few minutes from our apartment.

RESOURCES

The Simple Sentence

Practice

■ *Grammar, Usage, and Mechanics*, p. 129
■ *Language Workshop CD-ROM*, Lesson 34

3. The enormous <u>size</u> of the park, however, <u>can</u> sometimes be a problem.
4. Often, <u>I</u> <u>take</u> this map with me for guidance.
5. Using the map, <u>I</u> <u>can</u> easily <u>find</u> the zoo, the band shell, and the Lost Waterfall.
6. In the summertime my <u>brothers</u> and <u>I</u> <u>row</u> boats on the lake, <u>climb</u> huge rock slabs, and <u>have</u> picnics in the Sheep Meadow.
7. <u>I</u> also <u>watch</u> birds and often <u>wander</u> around the park in search of my favorite species.
8. Last month a <u>pair</u> of purple finches <u>followed</u> me along the pond.
9. Near Heckscher Playground, the <u>birds</u> <u>tired</u> of the game and <u>flew</u> off.
10. In Central Park my <u>family</u> and <u>I</u> <u>can enjoy</u> a little bit of nature in the middle of a bustling city.

The Compound Sentence

16b. A *compound sentence* contains two or more independent clauses and no subordinate clauses.

INDEPENDENT CLAUSE	Melvina wrote about her mother's aunt
INDEPENDENT CLAUSE	Leroy wrote about his cousin from Jamaica
COMPOUND SENTENCE	Melvina wrote about her mother's aunt, and Leroy wrote about his cousin from Jamaica.

The independent clauses of a compound sentence are usually joined by a comma and a coordinating conjunction (*and, but, for, nor, or, so,* or *yet*).

EXAMPLES A variety of fruits and vegetables should be a part of everyone's diet, **for** they supply many important vitamins.

Kathryn's scene is in the last act of the play, **so** she must wait in the wings for her cue.

No one was injured in the fire, **but** several homes were destroyed, **and** many trees burned down.

Douglass Circle — Frawley Circle
Central Park North
Boathouse
Harlem Meer
Great Hill
Loch
The Pool
North Meadow
East Meadow
Tennis Court
Jacqueline Kennedy Onassis Reservoir
South Gate House
Summit Rock
The Great Lawn
Metropolitan Museum of Art
Belvedere Castle
Belvedere Lake
Shakespeare Garden
Lost Waterfall
Loeb Boathouse
The Lake
Naumberg Bandshell
Sheep Meadow
Ballfields
Zoo
Wollman Rink
Heckscher Playground
The Pond
Central Park South
Columbus Circle

- ▦ Bridge   F Food
- • Monument   R Restroom
- ▪ Building   P Playground

Reference Note
For more about using **commas in compound sentences,** see page 605.

The Compound Sentence **441**

TEACHING TIP

Extension. You may wish to extend students' map-reading skills by asking these questions orally or by writing them on the chalkboard for students to write answers.

1. The Central Park Zoo is near what street corner, according to the map? *[the corner of Fifth Ave. and E. 64th St.]*

2. Would you find the Lost Waterfall near The Pond, The Lake, or The Reservoir? [*The Lake*]

3. What building is near the corner of Fifth Ave. and E. 84th St.? [*the Metropolitan Museum of Art*]

4. Would you find more monuments near Central Park North or Central Park South? [*Central Park South*]

The Compound Sentence

Rule 16b (pp. 441–444)

OBJECTIVES

- To identify subjects, verbs, and coordinating conjunctions in compound sentences

- To distinguish compound sentences from simple sentences with compound subjects or compound verbs

RESOURCES

The Compound Sentence
Practice
- *Grammar, Usage, and Mechanics,* pp. 130, 131
- *Language Workshop CD-ROM,* Lesson 34

ENGLISH-LANGUAGE LEARNERS
General Strategies. In many languages, the ordering of sentence elements is much less restricted than it is in English. Consequently, English-language learners may have problems identifying subjects and verbs in sentences. Start by having students identify subjects and verbs in simple sentences. Once students have mastered doing so, have them move on to compound sentences.

Crossing the Curriculum

Science. Just as a compound sentence is formed by joining two or more independent clauses, most matter is made of two or more elements joined together to form a compound. For example, water is made of two parts hydrogen and one part oxygen (H_2O). Ask students if they know of any other compounds. [salt—*sodium and chlorine (NaCl)*; baking soda—*sodium, hydrogen, carbon, and oxygen (NaHCO$_3$)*; sugar—*carbon, hydrogen, and oxygen ($C_{12}H_{22}O_{11}$)*; carbon dioxide—*carbon and oxygen (CO_2)*]

Reference Note
For more about using **semicolons in compound sentences,** see page 618.

The independent clauses of a compound sentence may be joined by a semicolon.

EXAMPLES   Pedro Menéndez de Avilés founded St. Augustine, the first permanent European settlement in the United States; he also established six other colonies in the Southeast.

My favorite places are Miami, Florida, and Aspen, Colorado; Bernie's favorites are San Diego, California, and Seattle, Washington.

Exercise 2 **Identifying Subjects and Verbs in Compound Sentences**

Identify the subject and verb in each independent clause. Then, give the punctuation mark and coordinating conjunction (if there is one) that join the clauses.

EXAMPLE   1. A newspaper reporter will speak to our class next week, and we will learn about careers in journalism.

1. *reporter—subject; will speak—verb; we—subject; will learn—verb; comma + and*

1. Ruth Benedict was a respected anthropologist, and Margaret Mead was one of her students. **1.** comma + *and*
2. An area's weather may change rapidly, but its climate changes very slowly. **2.** comma + *but*
3. Linh Phan lived in Vietnam for many years, so he could tell us about Vietnamese foods such as *nuoc mam*. **3.** comma + *so*
4. Students may prepare their reports on the computer, or they may write them neatly. **4.** comma + *or*
5. Our apartment manager is kind, yet she will not allow pets in the building. **5.** comma + *yet*
6. Daniel Boone had no formal education, but he could read and write. **6.** comma + *but*
7. Sofia's favorite dance is the samba; Elena enjoys the merengue. **7.** semicolon
8. Benjamin Franklin is known for his inventions, and he should also be remembered for his work during the Constitutional Convention. **8.** comma + *and*
9. Sheena did not play soccer; she had sprained her ankle. **9.** semicolon
10. They did not watch the shuttle take off, nor did they watch it land. **10.** comma + *nor*

MINI-LESSON

Commas in Compound Sentences.
Correct comma usage depends upon students' ability to distinguish compound sentences from simple sentences with compound verbs. Write the following sentences on the chalkboard, and work with the class to punctuate them correctly.

1. Maureen stepped up to the plate but she looked back at the bench for encouragement.
2. The ball soared through the air and

Simple Sentence or Compound Sentence?

A simple sentence has only one independent clause. It may have a compound subject or a compound verb or both.

A compound sentence has two or more independent clauses. Each independent clause has its own subject and verb. Any of the independent clauses in a compound sentence may have a compound subject, a compound verb, or both.

	S S V
SIMPLE SENTENCE	Kim and Maureen read each other's short stories

V
and made many suggestions for improvements.
[compound subject and compound verb]

	S S V
COMPOUND SENTENCE	Kim and Maureen read each other's stories,

S   V
and they gave each other suggestions for improvements. [The first independent clause has a compound subject and a single verb. The second independent clause has a single subject and a single verb.]

NOTE When a subject is repeated after a coordinating conjunction, the sentence is not simple.

	S V
SIMPLE SENTENCE	**We studied** the artist Romare Bearden and

V
went to an exhibit of his paintings.

	S V
COMPOUND SENTENCE	**We studied** the artist Romare Bearden, and

S   V
we went to an exhibit of his paintings.

Exercise 3 **Distinguishing Compound Sentences from Sentences with Compound Subjects or Compound Verbs**

Identify the subjects and verbs in each of the sentences on the following page. Then, identify each sentence as either *simple* or *compound*.

landed just short of the fence.

Explain that the first sentence has two independent clauses and is a compound sentence; therefore, a comma is needed before the coordinating conjunction. The second sentence is not compound; the second verb has the same subject as the first. Therefore, no comma is needed.

Ask students to locate pieces of their own writing and, using this method, to evaluate comma usage in any compound sentences.

TECHNOLOGY **TIP**

If possible, have students use a computer program designed to check for grammatical and stylistic errors. Such programs can identify such relevant errors as comma splices, run-on sentences, and sentence fragments. Common mistakes—for example, forgetting commas before coordinating conjunctions or joining two subordinate clauses to form a fragment—will be highlighted immediately for the student.

Some programs also evaluate students' ability to vary sentence types and, therefore, help to increase the readability of writing. If possible, have students run such a program on samples of their writing.

Looking at Language

Compound Nouns. In many dictionaries, *rain forest* (sentence 8) and *raw materials* (sentence 10) are classified as compound nouns. You may want to remind students that a compound noun is two or more words used together as a single noun. Have students find *rain forest* and *raw material* in a dictionary.

EXAMPLES
1. A rain forest is a tropical evergreen forest and has heavy rains throughout the year.
   1. *rain forest—subject; is, has—verbs; simple*

2. The trees and other plants in a rain forest grow close together, and they rise to different heights.
   2. *trees, plants—subjects; grow—verb; they—subject; rise—verb; compound*

1. The Amazon River is located in South America and is one of the longest rivers in the world. **1.** simp.
2. The Amazon begins in Peru, and it flows across Brazil to the Atlantic Ocean. **2.** comp.
3. This river carries more water than any other river and drains about one fifth of the earth's entire freshwater supply. **3.** simp.

4. The Amazon is actually a network of several rivers, but most people think of these combined rivers as only one river. **4.** comp.
5. These rivers drain the largest rainy area in the world, and during the flood season, the main river often overflows its banks. **5.** comp. **6.** simp.
6. In the photo at the left, the Amazon does twist and curve.
7. Generally, it follows a fairly straight course and flows at an average rate of about one and one-half miles an hour during the dry season. **7.** simp.
8. The Amazon rain forest is only two hundred miles wide along the Atlantic, but it stretches to twelve hundred miles wide at the foot of the Andes Mountains in Peru. **8.** comp.
9. The variety of plant life in the Amazon rain forest is remarkable; in fact, of all rain forests in the world, this area may contain the greatest number of plant species. **9.** comp.
10. Raw materials are shipped directly from ports deep in the rain forest, for oceangoing ships can sail more than two thousand miles up the Amazon. **10.** comp.

The Complex Sentence

16c. A *complex sentence* contains one independent clause and at least one subordinate clause.

Two kinds of subordinate clauses are adjective clauses and adverb clauses. Adjective clauses usually begin with relative pronouns such as *who, whom, whose, which,* and *that.* Adverb clauses begin with subordinating conjunctions such as *after, as, because, if, since,* and *when.*

EXAMPLES   Patricia Roberts Harris, **who served as President Carter's secretary of housing and urban development,** was the first African American woman to be a Cabinet member. [complex sentence with adjective clause]

         When I hear classical music, I think of Aunt Sofia. [complex sentence with adverb clause]

         One interesting annual event **that is held in the Southwest** is the Inter-Tribal Indian Ceremonial, **which involves many different American Indian peoples.** [complex sentence with two adjective clauses]

Reference Note

For more information on **adjective clauses,** see page 427. For more about **adverb clauses,** see page 430. For more about **relative pronouns,** see page 344. For more about **subordinating conjunctions,** see page 431.

Reference Note

For information on using **commas with subordinate clauses,** see page 607.

Exercise 4   **Identifying Subordinate Clauses**

Identify the subordinate clause in each of the following sentences. Then, underline the relative pronoun or the subordinating conjunction that begins the subordinate clause.

EXAMPLES   1. Helen Keller, who overcame severe physical impairments, showed great determination.
         1. *who overcame severe physical impairments*

         2. Keller was fortunate because she had such a skillful and loving teacher.
         2. *because she had such a skillful and loving teacher*

1. Helen Keller, who is shown in the photograph at right, became very ill as a small child.
2. After she recovered from the illness, she could no longer see or hear.
3. Because she could not hear, she also lost her ability to speak.

The Complex Sentence   **445**

RESOURCES

The Complex Sentence

Practice

■ *Grammar, Usage, and Mechanics,* pp. 132, 133

■ *Language Workshop CD-ROM,* Lesson 34

GRAMMAR

The Complex Sentence

Rule 16c *(pp. 445–447)*

OBJECTIVE

■ To identify subordinate clauses, subordinating conjunctions, and relative pronouns

TEACHING TIP

Activity. To help students understand the structure of a complex sentence, diagram on the chalkboard several of the example sentences on this page.

When I hear classical music, I think of Aunt Sophia.

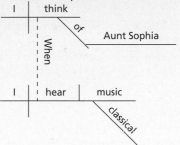

Have students diagram other sentences on this page. For additional instruction and practice in sentence diagramming, refer students to the **Diagramming Appendix.**

Cooperative Learning

Writers often adjust the complexity of their language and sentence structure so that it is appropriate to their audience. To illustrate, divide the class into small mixed-ability groups and ask each group to rewrite a simple children's story, gearing the revision to an audience of their peers. You may want to provide a stack of children's books for students or ask students to bring the books in advance. Because children's stories are often written in short, simple sentences, ask students to use a mixture of simple, compound, and complex sentences in their revisions. Then, ask volunteers from each group to read aloud both versions of their stories.

TEACHING TIP

Review A You may want to use the first five items in **Review A** as guided practice. Then, have students complete the exercise as independent practice.

4. Helen's parents asked Alexander Graham Bell, who trained teachers of people with hearing impairments, for his advice about the child's education.
5. Upon Bell's suggestion, a special teacher, whose name was Anne Sullivan, stayed at the Kellers' home to teach Helen.
6. Sullivan spelled words into Helen's hand as the child touched the object represented by the word.
7. From this basic understanding of language, Helen went on to learn Braille, which is the alphabet used by people with visual impairments.
8. Sullivan, whose own vision had been partly restored by surgery, remained with Helen for many years.
9. Because she had triumphed over her impairments, Helen Keller was awarded the Medal of Freedom.
10. Keller's autobiography, which is titled *The Story of My Life*, tells about her remarkable achievements.

Review A Classifying Simple, Compound, and Complex Sentences

Classify each of the following sentences as *simple*, *compound*, or *complex*.

EXAMPLE
1. The Mississippi River, which begins in the town of Lake Itasca, Minnesota, is the setting for many of Mark Twain's stories.

1. *complex*

1. I drew an illustration for a poem that was written by Robert Hayden. **1.** cx.
2. The Olympic skaters felt anxious, but they still performed their routine perfectly. **2.** comp.
3. Kamehameha Day is an American holiday that honors the king who united the islands of Hawaii. **3.** cx.
4. For the first time in his life, Luke saw the ocean. **4.** simp.
5. If you had a choice, would you rather visit China or Japan? **5.** cx.
6. The bull was donated to the children's zoo by the people who bought it at the auction. **6.** cx.
7. Lookout Mountain, which is in Tennessee, was the site of a battle during the Civil War. **7.** cx.
8. The guide led us through Mammoth Cave; she explained the difference between stalactites and stalagmites. **8.** comp.
9. Wilhelm Steinitz of Austria became famous after he was officially recognized as the first world champion of chess. **9.** cx.
10. Amy Tan is the author of the book *The Joy Luck Club*. **10.** simp.

The Compound-Complex Sentence

16d. A *compound-complex sentence* contains two or more independent clauses and at least one subordinate clause.

In the examples below, independent clauses are underlined once. Subordinate clauses are underlined twice.

EXAMPLES

The band began to play, and Clarissa was pulled onto the floor for a dance that was starting. [compound-complex sentence with adjective clause]

Whenever we go on vacation, our neighbors mow our yard, and they collect our mail. [compound-complex sentence with adverb clause]

STYLE TIP

Simple sentences are best used to express single ideas. To describe more complicated ideas and to show how the ideas fit together, use compound and complex sentences.

SIMPLE SENTENCES
We went camping in the national park. Darla saw a snake. At first she was afraid. Then she looked more closely at it. [The sentences are choppy, and the ideas seem unrelated.]

COMPLEX AND COMPOUND SENTENCES
When we went camping in the national park, Darla saw a snake. At first she was afraid, but then she looked more closely at it.

Reference Note
For more about **adjective and adverb clauses,** see pages 427 and 430.

The Compound-Complex Sentence   **447**

The Compound-Complex Sentence
Rule 16d *(pp. 447–450)*

OBJECTIVE

■ To identify compound, complex, and compound-complex sentences

Relating to Listening

The more familiar students are with the various sentence structures, the easier it will be for them to identify complete sentences. To give students additional practice with sentence structures, read aloud several paragraphs from an interesting article or story. As you read, have students tally the number of simple, compound, complex, and compound-complex sentences they hear. Then, provide students with copies of the paragraphs so that they can visually check their tallies.

Crossing the Curriculum

Math. To show students how math and grammar concepts can be related, ask students to make a bar graph showing the breakdown of their use of the various sentence structures. Coordinate with math teachers to be sure that students are comfortable figuring percentages and making bar graphs.

First, have students count the total number of sentences in a recent essay. Then, ask students to count the number of each type of sentence structure they used and to compute the percentage of each type. (An example follows.)

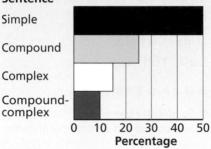

Type of Sentence

Suggest that students keep their graphs in their portfolios and periodically include data from new pieces of writing to see if their percentages are changing. Students interested in math and statistics could create other types of graphs to show their own progress with other grammar, usage, and mechanics skills.

COMPUTER TIP

A computer can help you focus on sentence length and structure in your writing. Programs are now available that can tell you the average number of words in your sentences. Such programs can also tell you how many different kinds of sentences you used. You can compare your numbers with the averages for students at your grade level. Using these programs, you can easily see which sentence structures you have mastered and which ones need work.

Exercise 5 Identifying Compound, Complex, and Compound-Complex Sentences

Identify each of the following sentences as either *compound*, *complex*, or *compound-complex*.

EXAMPLE   **1.** I'll sweep the porch, and Ben will start supper before Mom gets home.

　　　　　　1. compound-complex

1. If you've never tried Indian curry, try some of Usha's. **1.** cx.
2. The disk drive light went on, and the drive motor whirred, but the computer would not read the disk. **2.** cd.
3. Although the river appeared calm, crocodiles lay motionless beneath the surface. **3.** cx.
4. Several small herds of mustangs roam these hills; we're going to find them. **4.** cd.
5. An antique wagon, whose wheels once rolled along the Chisholm Trail, stood next to the barn. **5.** cx.
6. You can talk to me whenever you have a problem, or you can talk to your mom. **6.** cc.
7. Since daylight saving time started, the sky doesn't get dark until late, and that just doesn't seem right to me. **7.** cc.
8. The plaster, which had been given a rough texture, cast shadows on itself. **8.** cx. 　　　　　　　　　　**9.** cc.
9. They don't have the book that we need, so let's go to the library.
10. Did you really live in Nairobi, or are you just kidding? **10.** cd.

Review B Classifying Simple, Compound, Complex, and Compound-Complex Sentences

Classify each of the following sentences as *simple*, *compound*, *complex*, or *compound-complex*.

EXAMPLE   **1.** The Iroquois people traditionally held a Green Corn Festival in August when their crops were ready for harvesting.

　　　　　　1. complex

　　　　　　　　　　　　　　　　　　　　　　　1. cc.
1. For the early Iroquois, the Green Corn Festival was a celebration that included many events, so it often lasted several days.
2. During the celebration, all children who had been born since midwinter received their names. **2.** cx.

Learning for Life 　　　*Continued on pp. 449–450*

Anecdotes. This activity will focus on including a variety of sentence structures to add interest to anecdotes.

Explain to students that although anecdotes—brief, sometimes amusing retellings of events—are common to everyday con-

versation, they also play an important part in compositions and speeches. Anecdotes can catch an audience's attention in an introduction, elaborate on a main idea in the body of the speech or composition, or tie material together in the closing.

3. Iroquois leaders made speeches, and adults and children listened to them carefully. **3.** cd.

4. In one traditional speech, the leader would give thanks for the harvest. **4.** s.

5. cx.

5. After they had heard the speeches, the people sang and danced.

6. On the second day of the festival, the people performed a special dance; during the dance they gave thanks for the sun, the moon, and the stars. **6.** cd.

7. On the third day, the Iroquois gave thanks for the helpfulness of their neighbors and for good luck. **7.** s.

8. The festival ended on the fourth day when teams of young people would play a bowling game. **8.** cx.

9. During the festival the people renewed their friendships, and they rejoiced in their harmony with nature. **9.** cd.

10. cx.

10. This Iroquois festival resembles the U.S. Thanksgiving holiday, which has its roots in similar American Indian celebrations.

The Corn Dance

Review C **Writing Simple, Compound, Complex, and Compound-Complex Sentences**

Write ten sentences of your own, following the guidelines given below.

EXAMPLE **1.** Write a simple sentence with a compound subject.

1. *Jorge and Pilar gave me their recipe for guacamole.*

1. Write a simple sentence with a compound verb.

Cooperative Learning

To give students more practice with compound-complex sentences, divide the class into groups of three students each. One student will write a simple sentence, such as "My dog has fleas," and pass the piece of paper with this sentence to the next student. The second student will add a subordinate clause such as "because he sleeps outside." This student will pass the paper along to the third group member, who will add a comma, a coordinating conjunction, and another independent clause such as "he scratches all the time." The final compound-complex sentence would read "Because he sleeps outside, my dog has fleas, and he scratches all the time." Have the group work together to correct punctuation in the final sentence. Each group can repeat this exercise after switching roles.

Ask each student to write a brief anecdote that illustrates a point. You might want to provide the following topic sentences for students having trouble getting started.

1. Small acts of kindness can spread joy.

2. The traffic in the school halls is getting worse every day.

3. The ability to read can save lives.

4. My young cousin does the cutest things.

2. Write a simple sentence with a compound subject and a compound verb.

3. Write a compound sentence with two independent clauses joined by a comma and the coordinating conjunction *and*.

4. Write a compound sentence with two independent clauses joined by a comma and the coordinating conjunction *but*.

5. Write a compound sentence with two independent clauses joined by a semicolon.

6. Write a compound sentence with three independent clauses.

7. Write a complex sentence with an adjective clause.

8. Write a complex sentence with an adverb clause.

9. Write a compound-complex sentence with an adjective clause.

10. Write a compound-complex sentence with an adverb clause.

Answers

Review C

Sentences will vary. Here are some possibilities:

1. Emilia sang and danced at the talent show.

2. Juan and Kim went to the dance and met Steve.

3. Silvia found the scissors, and Lily searched for paper.

4. I wanted to go to the show, but he wanted to stay home.

5. Alex played tennis after school; Mia went to soccer practice.

6. Eric sliced tomatoes, Maria cut bell peppers, and Selena cleared the table.

7. Some of the sailors who took part in the mutiny on the British ship *Bounty* settled Pitcairn Island.

8. When I watch Martha Graham's performances, I feel like studying dance.

9. I have read several novels this month and the one that I like best is *Animal Farm*.

10. When Bill left, he locked the door, but he forgot to turn off the lights.

Learning for Life

Encourage students to include a variety of sentence structures in their anecdotes. You might want to share the following model.

The traffic in the school halls is getting worse every day. Just yesterday when I had an appointment to see the principal, I was running late. People were shoulder-to-shoulder in one hall, so I tried another to save time. What a mistake that was!

Chapter Review

A. Identifying Independent and Subordinate Clauses

Identify each clause in the following sentences. Then, classify each clause as an *independent clause* or a *subordinate clause*.

1. Yvette raked the leaves, and Tito mowed the lawn.
2. Lupe and Ben went to the park so that they could watch the fireworks display.
3. Carl and I chose enchiladas instead of sandwiches from the cafeteria's menu.
4. The new camp that offers instruction in computer programming will be in session from August 17 through August 28.
5. The rain changed to snow that was mixed with sleet.
6. Practice your tai chi exercises when you go to the beach.
7. My grandparents, who enjoy exciting vacations, visited Nepal last year.
8. Since last year Simone has grown three inches, but she still can't reach the top shelf in the kitchen.
9. Will Martin loan me this book by Jamaica Kincaid when he is through with it?
10. Aretha hopes to be a veterinarian because she likes to be around animals.

B. Identifying Simple and Compound Sentences

Classify each of the following sentences as *simple* or *compound*.

11. Do Nathan and Shenille read only science fiction or fantasy short stories? **11.** s.
12. My sister and brother-in-law live in Colorado, and they raise sheep and grow fruit trees. **12.** cd.
13. Chai wants to walk to the theater, but I want to take the bus. **13.** cd.
14. Aunt Evelyn and Uncle Michael are both surgeons and work at Riverside Hospital. **14.** s.
15. The good queen pardoned the jester, for he had meant no real harm. **15.** cd.

Chapter Review **451**

16. Taking the train, Mei-Ling and her parents can be in Chicago in two hours. **16.** s.

17. Blair is interested in becoming an astronaut, so she wrote to NASA for information. **17.** cd.

18. Tate laid out the patio and built it himself. **18.** s.

19. s.

19. After eating, Marcia's cat Bartinka likes to take a long nap.

20. Mike designed and contructed the sets for the play, and Mary Anne designed the costumes and makeup. **20.** cd.

C. Identifying Compound and Complex Sentences

Identify each of the following sentences as *compound* or *complex*. If the sentence is compound, write the comma and coordinating conjunction or the semicolon that joins the clauses. If the sentence is complex, write the relative pronoun or subordinating conjunction that joins the clauses.

21. cx. — which

21. Nineteenth-century shopkeepers often attracted customers by placing a carved wooden figure, which was called a shop figure, outside their shops.

22. cx. — who

22. The shop figures were usually carved by ship carvers, who had learned to carve figures by creating ship figureheads.

23. cd. — comma + *and*

23. The figures cost a great deal to make, and they were expensive to maintain.

24. cx. — because

24. Many shopkeepers were upset because the figures were so very costly.

25. cd. — semicolon

25. Many of the wooden figures were of politicians and baseball players; others represented American Indians.

26. cd. — comma + *and*

26. One surviving figure represents Father Time, and another one represents a New York City firefighter.

27. cx. — which

27. The firefighter, which commemorates Columbian Engine Company 14, now stands in the New York City Fire Museum.

28. cd. — comma + *and*

28. The figures were popular between the 1840s and the 1890s, and during that time they actually became a fad.

29. cx. — since

29. By the end of the century, the carved shop figure was no longer widely used since new types of advertising had become available.

30. cd. — comma + *so*

30. People saw shop figures as old-fashioned, so shopkeepers stopped using them.

D. Classifying Compound, Complex, and Compound-Complex Sentences

Classify each of the following sentences as *compound*, *complex*, or *compound-complex*.

31. Islam, which originated in Arabia, is the religion of the Muslims, and it is based on a belief in one God.   **31.** cc.

32. Most Muslims live in Africa, the Middle East, and Malaysia; in recent years many have come to the United States and have brought their religion with them. **32.** cd.

33. Some American Muslims are members of the Nation of Islam, which was founded in the United States after World War II. **33.** cx.

34. When a mosque was opened in New York in May 1991, religious leaders and other Muslims went there to pray.   **34.** cx.

35. Some worshipers wore the traditional clothing of their **35.** cd. homelands; others were dressed in typical American clothes.

36. Muslims were particularly pleased that the new mosque opened in the spring.   **36.** cx.

37. The Muslim month of fasting, which is called Ramadan, had just ended, so the holiday after Ramadan could be celebrated in the new house of worship.   **37.** cc.

38. Although Muslims share a common religion, their languages differ.   **38.** cx.

39. Many Muslims speak Arabic, but those in Iran, Turkey, and neighboring countries, for example, speak other languages as well.   **39.** cd.

40. Of course, Muslims who were born in the United States generally speak English, and many Muslims who are recent immigrants are learning it as a new language.   **40.** cc.

E. Classifying Sentences by Structure

Classify each of the following sentences as *simple*, *compound*, *complex*, or *compound-complex*.

41. Easter Island, which is also known as Rapa Nui, is a small Polynesian island in the South Pacific.   **41.** cx.

42. s.

42. The island is the most remote inhabited place on the planet.

43. The Polynesians were among the most accomplished sailors in the world; they are especially known for their skill at navigation. **43.** cd.

44. The earliest evidence of people on Easter Island dates from around A.D. 700, but the island may have been inhabited earlier than that. **44.** cd.

45. The island is best known for its giant stone statues with long noses and pursed lips. **45.** s.

46. The statues, which are called *moai,* were carved out of volcanic rock, and some of them were placed upright on platforms called *ahu.* **46.** cc.

47. The *moai* that were set up on platforms were transported as far as six miles from the quarry, but no one knows for certain how the islanders moved them. **47.** cc.

48. Several theories have been proposed, yet no single theory explains all the evidence. **48.** cd.

49. When the British explorer Captain Cook visited the island in 1774, he noticed that many of the statues had been overturned. **49.** cx.

50. The oral tradition of the islanders speaks of a civil war that broke out between two peoples on the island, the Hanau Eepe and the Hanau Momko. **50.** cx.

Writing Application
Writing a Letter

Using a Variety of Sentence Structures   Anyone can enter the "Win Your Dream House" Contest. All you have to do is describe your ideal house. Write a letter to the contest judges, describing where your dream house would be and what it would look like. Use a variety of sentence structures to make your letter interesting for the judges to read.

RESOURCES

Kinds of Sentence Structure

Review

■ *Grammar, Usage, and Mechanics,* pp. 136, 137, 138

Assessment

■ *Assessment Package*
    — *Chapter Tests,* Ch. 16
    — *Chapter Tests in Standardized Test Formats,* Ch. 16
■ *Test Generator (One-Stop Planner CD-ROM)* 💿

Prewriting Make a list of the special features of the house you want to describe. To help you think of ideas, you may want to look through magazines or books to find pictures of interesting homes. You may also find it helpful to draw a rough diagram of the rooms, yard, and other features you would want to add. Take notes on the details you want to include.

Writing As you write your first draft, use your notes to include vivid details that will give the contest judges a clear picture of your dream house.

Revising Read your letter to make sure it is interesting and clear. Also, check to see whether you can combine similar ideas by using either compound or complex sentences. Ask an adult to read your letter. Does he or she think your description would impress the contest judges?

Publishing Check the grammar and spelling in your letter. Also, make sure that you have used commas correctly in compound sentences and complex sentences. You and your classmates may want to create a bulletin board display of the pictures or diagrams you used in designing your dream house and to post your descriptions next to the display.

Reference Note

For information on **using commas,** see page 602.

Writing Application
(p. 454)

OBJECTIVE

■ **To use a variety of sentence structures to write a letter**

Writing Application

Tip. You could have students develop lists of things they dislike about houses as well as lists of things they like. Because their letters must be about the good things in their dream houses, tell them that they should identify the opposites of the things they dislike about houses.

Scoring Rubric. While you will want to pay particular attention to students' use of a variety of sentence structures, you will also want to evaluate overall writing performance. You may want to give a split score to indicate development and clarity of the composition as well as grammar skills.

Critical Thinking

Synthesis. Have students list adjectives or short descriptions next to the features they identify in the prewriting stage. Then, have students look over their lists of adjectives to brainstorm about what kinds of images those adjectives or descriptions might give to a judge. [*Students might find that a bright, happy, open, and green house could be compared to an open field or a clear ocean.*] Encourage students to describe their houses in terms of these images.

RESOURCES

Writing Application

Extension

■ *Grammar, Usage, and Mechanics*, p. 141
■ *Language Workshop CD-ROM*, Lesson 34

CHAPTER

17

Agreement
Subject and Verb, Pronoun and Antecedent

Diagnostic Preview

A. Identifying Correct Subject-Verb Agreement and Pronoun-Antecedent Agreement

Choose the correct word or word group in parentheses in each of the following sentences.

EXAMPLE **1.** Some of the paintings (*is, are*) dry now.
   1. are

1. Three hours of work (*is, are*) needed to finish the charcoal drawing for art class.
2. Everybody has offered (*his or her, their*) advice.
3. *Harlem Shadows* (*is, are*) a collection of poems by the writer Claude McKay.
4. Either Stu or Ryan can volunteer (*his, their*) skill in the kitchen.
5. Black beans, rice, and onions (*tastes, taste*) good together.
6. Not one of them has offered (*his or her, their*) help.
7. Sometimes my family (*disagrees, disagree*) with one another, but usually we all get along fairly well.
8. Five dollars (*is, are*) all you will need for the matinee.
9. (*Doesn't, Don't*) too many cooks spoil the broth?
10. One of my aunts gave me (*her, their*) silk kimono.

CHAPTER RESOURCES

Planning
■ *One-Stop Planner CD-ROM*

Practice and Extension
■ *Grammar, Usage, and Mechanics,* p. 142
■ *Developmental Language Skills,* pp. 57–66

Internet

■ go.hrw.com (keyword: EOLang)

Evaluation and Assessment
■ *Chapter Tests,* Ch. 17
■ *Chapter Tests in Standardized Test Formats,* Ch. 17
■ *Test Generator (One-Stop Planner)*

B. Proofreading for Subject-Verb Agreement and Pronoun-Antecedent Agreement

Most of the following sentences contain an agreement error. Write the incorrect verb or pronoun. Then, write the correct form. If the sentence is already correct, write *C*.

EXAMPLE **1.** Most stargazers has seen points of light shooting across the night sky.

  1. has—have

11. These points of light is commonly called shooting stars. **11.** are

12. Scientists who study our solar system calls these points of light *meteors*. **12.** call

13. C

13. Some meteors are pieces of asteroids that exploded long ago.

14. Each of these pieces are still flying through space on the path of the original asteroid. **14.** is

15. Most nights, a person is lucky if they can see a single meteor now and then. **15.** he or she

16. are

16. Throughout the year, however, there is meteor "showers."

17. None of these showers are as big as the ones that come each year in August and November. **17.** C

18. Either Katie or Carla once saw a spectacular meteor shower on their birthday. **18.** her

19. In November 1833, one of the largest meteor showers in history were recorded. **19.** was

20. Two hundred forty thousand meteors observed in just a few hours are a record that has never been matched! **20.** is

Number

Number is the form a word takes to indicate whether the word is singular or plural.

17a. When a word refers to one person, place, thing, or idea, it is *singular* in number. When a word refers to more than one, it is *plural* in number.

Reference Note

For more about **forming plurals,** see page 663.

Singular	igloo	she	one	child	class
Plural	igloos	they	many	children	classes

Number **457**

Exercise 1 You may want to use the first ten items in **Exercise 1** as guided practice. Then, have students complete the exercise as independent practice.

Meeting INDIVIDUAL NEEDS

ENGLISH-LANGUAGE LEARNERS

General Strategies. Speakers of languages that do not show number in nouns or verbs might have difficulty with the concept of agreement. Students should be reminded that in written English, proper agreement is essential.

Spanish. The Spanish word for people (*la gente*) is a singular noun, so Spanish-speaking students might use sentences such as *The people is going to the game*. Emphasize that *people* is plural in English, and provide some practice in subject-verb agreement using *people* as the subject.

1. s.	11. s.
2. p.	12. p.
3. p.	13. s.
4. s.	14. s.
5. p.	15. p.
6. p.	16. s.
7. p.	17. p.
8. p.	18. s.
9. s.	19. p.
10. p.	20. s.

TIPS & TRICKS

Most nouns ending in *–s* are plural (*cheetahs, families*). Most verbs that end in *–s* are singular (*fills, begins*). However, verbs used with the singular pronouns *I* and *you* do not end in *–s*.

EXAMPLES
Ed takes the bus.

I take the train.

You ride your bike.

Reference Note

The plurals of some nouns do not end in *–s* (*mice, teeth, deer*). For more about **irregularly formed plurals,** see page 664.

Exercise 1 Classifying Nouns and Pronouns by Number

Classify each of the following words as *singular* or *plural*.

EXAMPLES
1. girl 2. rivers
1. *singular* 2. *plural*

1. evening	6. teeth	11. hoof	16. magazine
2. wolves	7. tacos	12. mice	17. oxen
3. women	8. we	13. I	18. he
4. leaf	9. thief	14. shelf	19. cities
5. they	10. armies	15. geese	20. cargo

Agreement of Subject and Verb

17b. A verb should agree in number with its subject.

Two words *agree* when they have the same number. The number of a verb should agree with the number of its subject.

(1) Singular subjects take singular verbs.

EXAMPLES
The **lightning fills** the sky. [The singular verb *fills* agrees with the singular subject *lightning*.]

Jan begins her vacation today. [The singular verb *begins* agrees with the singular subject *Jan*.]

(2) Plural subjects take plural verbs.

EXAMPLES
Cheetahs run fast. [The plural verb *run* agrees with the plural subject *Cheetahs*.]

New **families move** into our neighborhood often. [The plural verb *move* agrees with the plural subject *families*.]

When a sentence contains a verb phrase, the first helping verb in the verb phrase agrees with the subject.

EXAMPLES
The **motor is** running.
The **motors are** running.

The **girl has** been delayed.
The **girls have** been delayed.

Is anyone filling the aquarium?
Are any **students** filling the aquarium?

MINI-LESSON

Finding the Subject. To determine correct agreement of the subject and verb, students must be able to locate the subject of a sentence. Write the following sentences on the chalkboard, and have volunteers find the subjects by asking *Who?* or *What?* before the verbs. This exercise will be particularly helpful with sentences containing prepositional phrases between the subjects and verbs (see p. 460) and with sentences with inverted word order (see p. 470).

Exercise 2 Identifying Verbs That Agree in Number with Their Subjects

Identify the <u>form of the verb</u> in parentheses that agrees with its subject.

EXAMPLE
   1. wind (*howls, howl*)

     1. howls

1. people (*talks, <u>talk</u>*)
2. rain (*<u>splashes</u>, splash*)
3. birds (*flies, <u>fly</u>*)
4. we (*helps, <u>help</u>*)
5. it (*<u>appears</u>, appear*)
6. geese (*hisses, <u>hiss</u>*)
7. night (*<u>falls</u>, fall*)
8. roofs (*leaks, <u>leak</u>*)
9. baby (*<u>smiles</u>, smile*)
10. tooth (*<u>aches</u>, ache*)

Exercise 3 Identifying Verbs That Agree in Number with Their Subjects

Identify the <u>form of the verb</u> in parentheses that agrees with its subject.

EXAMPLE
   1. Special tours (*is, are*) offered at the National Air and Space Museum in Washington, D.C.

     1. are

1. This museum (*<u>has</u>, have*) been called the best of all the Smithsonian museums.
2. This enormous building (*<u>covers</u>, cover*) three blocks.
3. Twenty-three galleries (*offers, <u>offer</u>*) visitors information and entertainment.
4. The different showrooms (*deals, <u>deal</u>*) with various aspects of air and space travel.
5. As you can see, the exhibits (*features, <u>feature</u>*) antique aircraft as well as modern spacecraft.
6. In another area, a theater (*<u>shows</u>, show*) films on a five-story-high screen.
7. A planetarium (*<u>is</u>, are*) located on the second floor.
8. Projectors (*casts, <u>cast</u>*) realistic images of stars on the ceiling.
9. Some tours (*is, <u>are</u>*) conducted by pilots.
10. In addition, the museum (*<u>houses</u>, house*) a large research library.

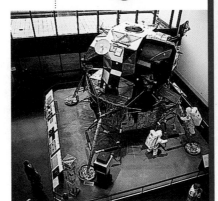

Looking at Language

Dialects. Some dialects of U.S. English frequently omit the *–s* ending from verbs. [*He work hard. She like mysteries.*] Suggest that students take turns reading aloud the following subjects and verbs to hear examples of standard English. You may want to have students work together to expand the list and then read aloud their subjects and verbs.

1. horse jumps
2. girls leave
3. apple tastes
4. Marie talks
5. telephone rings
6. soldier waits
7. sisters want
8. teacher gives
9. car stops
10. Bill works

Exercise 3

ALTERNATIVE LESSON
Ask students to identify the prepositional phrases in sentences 4, 6, and 8. [4. *with various aspects of air and space travel, of air and space travel;* 6. *In another area, on a five-story-high screen;* 8. *of stars, on the ceiling*] Students who have difficulty identifying prepositional phrases might need assistance with the next section, **Problems in Agreement: Phrases Between Subject and Verb.**

1. The tired <u>campers</u> built a campfire.
2. <u>Leonie</u> enjoyed her hike through the canyon.
3. On the calm waters, the <u>boat</u> rocked gently.
4. The <u>cabin</u> in the valley offered shelter from the rain.

For additional information and practice, refer students to **Chapter 10: The Sentence.**

Exercise 4 Proofreading for Errors in Subject-Verb Agreement

Most of the following sentences contain errors in subject-verb agreement. If a verb does not agree with its subject, write the correct form of the verb. If a sentence is already correct, write *C*.

EXAMPLE **1.** More than fifteen million people lives in and around Mexico's capital.

1. *live*

1. Located in an ancient lake bed, Mexico City have been built on Aztec ruins. **1.** has

2. Visitors admire the colorful paintings of Diego Rivera at the National Palace. **2.** C

3. In one of the city's many subway stations, an Aztec pyramid still stand. **3.** stands

4. Sculptures grace the Alameda, which is Mexico City's main park. **4.** C

5. Atop the Latin American Tower, an observatory offer a great view on a clear day. **5.** offers

6. At the National Autonomous University of Mexico, the library's outer walls is famous as works of art. **6.** are

7. Juan O'Gorman's huge mosaics shows the cultural history of Mexico. **7.** show

8. Usually, tourists is quite fascinated by the Great Temple of the Aztecs. **8.** are

9. Many fiestas fills Mexico City's social calendar. **9.** fill

10. In addition, the city has one of the largest soccer stadiums in the world. **10.** C

Problems in Agreement

Phrases Between Subject and Verb

17c. The number of a subject is not changed by a phrase following the subject.

EXAMPLES The **hero** of those folk tales **is** Coyote. [The verb *is* agrees with the subject *hero,* not with *tales.*]

The successful **candidate,** along with two of her aides, **has entered** the auditorium. [The helping verb *has* agrees with the subject *candidate,* not with *aides.*]

Problems in Agreement

Rule 17c *(pp. 460–461)*

OBJECTIVE

■ To choose verb forms that agree in number with subjects

RESOURCES

Problems in Agreement
Practice

■ *Grammar, Usage, and Mechanics,* p.146
■ *Language Workshop CD-ROM,* Lesson 10

Scientists from all over the world **have gathered** in Geneva. [The helping verb *have* agrees with the subject *Scientists*, not with *world*.]

The crystal **pitcher,** oozing water droplets, **was cracked** along the base. [The helping verb *was* agrees with the subject *pitcher*, not with *droplets*.]

NOTE If the subject is the indefinite pronoun *all, any, more, most, none,* or *some,* its number may be determined by the object of a prepositional phrase that follows it.

EXAMPLES **Most** of the essays **were** graded. [*Most* refers to the plural word *essays*.]

Most of this essay **is** illegible. [*Most* refers to the singular word *essay*.]

Reference Note

For more about **indefinite pronouns,** see Rules 17d–17f on page 462.

Exercise 5 **Identifying Verbs That Agree in Number with Their Subjects**

Identify the form of the verb in parentheses that agrees with its subject.

EXAMPLE 1. The water in the earth's oceans (*cover, covers*) much of the planet's surface.

1. *covers*

1. A tidal wave, despite its name, (*is, are*) not caused by the tides.
2. Earthquakes beneath the sea (*causes, cause*) most tidal waves.
3. A network of warning signals (*alert, alerts*) people in coastal areas of an approaching tidal wave.
4. The tremendous force of tidal waves sometimes (*causes, cause*) great destruction.
5. Walls of earth and stone along the shore (*is, are*) often too weak to protect coastal villages.
6. Some tidal waves, according to this encyclopedia article, (*travel, travels*) more than five hundred miles an hour.
7. Tidal waves in the open ocean generally (*do, does*) not cause much interest.
8. The height of tidal waves there often (*remain, remains*) low.
9. However, waves up to one hundred feet high (*occur, occurs*) when tidal waves hit land.
10. The scientific name for tidal waves (*are, is*) tsunamis.

Meeting INDIVIDUAL NEEDS

USAGE

ENGLISH-LANGUAGE LEARNERS

Japanese and Korean. In these languages, objects often appear before their verbs. For example, the English sentence "Mary sees the boys often" would have the order "Boys often Mary sees" or "Often Mary boys sees." Some English-language learners may try to write English sentences in one of these orders and, thus, try to make the verb agree with the object. Stress that students should concentrate primarily on writing English sentences in subject-verb-object order until they feel more comfortable with English. Remind them that the verb agrees with the subject, not the object.

MULTIPLE INTELLIGENCES

Spatial Intelligence. Some students may find diagramming helpful in understanding prepositional phrases as modifiers. Diagram several of the example sentences from **Rule 17c** (one is shown here).

Most of this essay is illegible.

Indefinite Pronouns

Rules 17d–f *(pp. 462–465)*

OBJECTIVE

- To identify verb forms that agree in number with their subjects

⌈ TIPS & TRICKS ⌉

The words *one, thing,* and *body* are singular. The indefinite pronouns that contain these words are singular, too.

EXAMPLES

Was [every]**one** there?

[Some]**body has** answered.

[No]**thing works** better.

⌐HELP─

Remember that the subject is never part of a prepositional phrase.

Indefinite Pronouns

You may recall that personal pronouns refer to specific people, places, things, or ideas. A pronoun that does not refer to a definite person, place, thing, or idea is called an *indefinite pronoun.*

Personal Pronouns	Indefinite Pronouns
she	anybody
them	both
we	either
you	everyone

17d. The following indefinite pronouns are singular: *anybody, anyone, anything, each, either, everybody, everyone, everything, neither, nobody, no one, nothing, one, somebody, someone,* and *something.*

EXAMPLES   **Each** of the newcomers **was welcomed** to the city.

        Neither of these papayas **is** ripe.

        Does anybody on the bus **speak** Arabic?

Exercise 6 **Identify Verbs That Agree in Number with Their Subjects**

Choose the form of the verb in parentheses that agrees with its subject.

EXAMPLE   **1.** One of these books (*is, are*) yours.

          1. is

1. Neither of the movies (*were,* <u>*was*</u>) especially funny.
2. Everybody in those classes (<u>*gets*</u>, *get*) to leave early.
3. Someone among the store owners (<u>*donates*</u>, *donate*) the big trophy each year.
4. Each of the Jackson brothers (*study,* <u>*studies*</u>) dance.
5. No one on either team (<u>*was*</u>, *were*) ever in a playoff before.
6. Everyone with an interest in sports (*are,* <u>*is*</u>) at the tryouts.
7. Anybody with binoculars (*are,* <u>*is*</u>) popular at a large stadium.
8. Each of our neighbors (*have,* <u>*has*</u>) helped us plant the new community garden.

RESOURCES

Indefinite Pronouns

Practice

- *Grammar, Usage, and Mechanics,* pp. 147–148
- *Language Workshop CD-ROM,* Lesson 11

9. One of the new Spanish teachers (*supervises*, *supervise*) the language lab.

10. Nobody in our family (*speak*, *speaks*) Greek well, but we all can speak a little bit.

17e. The following indefinite pronouns are plural: *both, few, many, several.*

EXAMPLES   **Few** of our neighbors **have** parakeets.

            Many of them **keep** dogs as pets.

17f. The indefinite pronouns *all, any, more, most, none,* and *some* may be either singular or plural, depending on their meaning in a sentence.

The number of the pronouns *all, any, more, most, none,* and *some* is often determined by the number of the object in a prepositional phrase following the subject. These pronouns are singular when they refer to a singular word and are plural when they refer to a plural word.

EXAMPLES   **All** of the fruit **is** ripe. [*All* is singular because it refers to the singular word *fruit.* The verb *is* is singular to agree with the subject *All.*]

            All of the pears **are** ripe. [*All* is plural because it refers to the plural word *pears.* The verb *are* is plural to agree with the subject *All.*]

            Some of the harvest **has been sold.** [*Some* is singular because it refers to the singular word *harvest.* The helping verb *has* is singular to agree with the subject *Some.*]

            Some of the apples **have been sold.** [*Some* is plural because it refers to the plural word *apples.* The helping verb *have* is plural to agree with the subject *Some.*]

NOTE The pronouns listed in Rule 17f aren't always followed by prepositional phrases.

EXAMPLES   **All are** here.

            Some has spilled.

In such cases you should look at the **context**—the sentences before and after the pronoun—to see if the pronoun refers to a singular or a plural word.

┌HELP───

Some indefinite pronouns, such as *both, each,* and *some,* can also be used as adjectives. When an indefinite adjective comes before the subject of a sentence, the verb agrees with the subject as it normally would.

Just as you would write
  Children love playing in the park.
     or
  The **child loves** playing in the park.

you would write
  Both children love playing in the park.
     or
  Each child loves playing in the park.

USAGE

Problems in Agreement   **463**

Cooperative Learning

Divide the class into groups of four. Give each group twenty-six index cards, and ask students to write on each card one of the twenty-six indefinite pronouns listed in **Rules 17d–f.** On the back of each card, students should indicate whether the pronoun is *singular, plural,* or *either singular or plural.*

Have students take turns being the card holder, holding up a card while the other members each write a sentence using the pronoun on the card as the subject of the sentence. Specify that the sentences must contain prepositional phrases modifying the subject. Ask the card holder to repeat the process several times with different cards, and then have the groups check all of the sentences for correct subject-verb agreement. The notations on the back of the cards should help with evaluation. Have students change roles until everyone in the group has had a chance to be the card holder.

Exercise 7 **Identifying Verbs That Agree in Number with Their Subjects**

Identify the <u>verb form</u> in parentheses that agrees with its subject.

EXAMPLE   1. Somebody in the club (*want, wants*) the meetings held on a different day.

      1. wants

1. "Both of the tapes (*sound, sounds*) good to me," Gregory said.
2. If anyone (*know, knows*) a better way to get to Washington Square, please tell me.
3. Each of the problems (*are, is*) easy to solve if you know the correct formulas.
4. Probably everyone in the class (*remember, remembers*) how to boil an egg.
5. All of the new research on dreams (*is, are*) fascinating.
6. Most of our dreams (*occur, occurs*) toward morning.
7. Few of us really (*understand, understands*) the four cycles of sleep.
8. Most of the research (*focus, focuses*) on the cycle known as rapid eye movement, or REM.
9. None of last night's dream (*is, are*) clear to me.
10. Many of our dreams at night (*is, are*) about that day's events.

Review A **Identifying Verbs That Agree in Number with Their Subjects**

Identify the <u>verb form</u> in parentheses that agrees with its subject.

EXAMPLE   1. The flying object shown on the next page probably (*look, looks*) familiar to you.

      1. looks

1. Many people throughout the world (*claims, claim*) to have seen objects like this.
2. However, no one (*know, knows*) for sure what they are.
3. They (*resembles, resemble*) huge plates or saucers.
4. Not surprisingly, people (*call, calls*) them flying saucers.
5. Since 1947, they (*has, have*) been officially called unidentified flying objects, or UFOs.
6. The U.S. government (*has, have*) investigated many unusual UFO sightings.

Critical Thinking

Metacognition. As students work through **Review A,** ask them to think about the process they use to ensure correct subject-verb agreement. Do they first eliminate prepositional phrases? Do they ask *Who?* or *What?* before the verb? Once they locate the subject, how do they determine its number? Do they read aloud the subject and verb to determine what sounds right? Encourage students to evaluate the effectiveness of their personal strategies and to consider more effective alternatives as needed.

USAGE

7. The U.S. Air Force (*was, were*) responsible for conducting these investigations.
8. Government records (*shows, show*) that more than twelve thousand sightings were reported between 1948 and 1969.
9. Most reported sightings (*has, have*) turned out to be fakes, but others remain unexplained.
10. None of the official reports positively (*proves, prove*) that UFOs come from outer space.

Compound Subjects

17g. Subjects joined by *and* usually take a plural verb.

EXAMPLES   Our **dog and cat get** baths in the summer.

Mr. Duffy and his **daughter have gone** fishing.

A compound subject that names only one person or thing takes a singular verb.

EXAMPLES   **A famous singer and dancer is going** to speak at our drama club meeting. [One person is meant.]

Macaroni and cheese is my favorite supper. [One dish is meant.]

Compound Subjects

Rules 17g–i *(pp. 465–468)*

O B J E C T I V E

■ **To choose verbs that agree with their compound subjects**

RESOURCES

Compound Subjects

Practice

■ *Grammar, Usage, and Mechanics,* p. 149
■ *Language Workshop CD-ROM,* Lesson 11

Crossing the Curriculum

Math. You may want to use the concept of a math equation to help students determine correct subject-verb agreement with compound subjects. Write the following equations on the chalkboard or a transparency, and have students volunteer examples for each. If possible, keep the equations and examples on display as students work through the exercises in this segment.

1. subject + *and* + subject = plural verb

2. $\dfrac{\text{singular}}{\text{subject}}$ + *or/nor* + $\dfrac{\text{singular}}{\text{subject}}$ = $\dfrac{\text{singular}}{\text{verb}}$

3. $\dfrac{\text{singular}}{\text{subject}}$ + *or/nor* + $\dfrac{\text{plural}}{\text{subject}}$ = $\dfrac{\text{plural}}{\text{verb}}$

4. $\dfrac{\text{plural}}{\text{subject}}$ + *or/nor* + $\dfrac{\text{singular}}{\text{subject}}$ = $\dfrac{\text{singular}}{\text{verb}}$

Meeting INDIVIDUAL NEEDS

ENGLISH-LANGUAGE LEARNERS

Spanish. The rules for agreement with compound subjects in Spanish are complex. The number of the Spanish verb can be influenced by three things: the applicability of the verb to both elements of the compound subject, the relative distance of the subject and the object from the verb, and the importance of the predicate nominative, if there is one. You may want to emphasize the agreement rules for compound subjects in English and to give extra practice to any students who have trouble with agreement.

3. One person is meant.

8. One combination is meant.

| STYLE TIP |

Compound subjects that have both singular and plural parts can sound awkward even though they are correct. Whenever possible, revise sentences to avoid such constructions.

AWKWARD
Two small boards or one large one is what we need to patch that hole.

REVISED
We need two small boards or one large one to patch that hole.

Exercise 8 **Identifying Verbs That Agree in Number with Their Subjects**

Identify the <u>correct form of the verb</u> in parentheses. If you choose a singular verb with any of these compound subjects, be prepared to explain why.

EXAMPLE   **1.** Chris and her sister (*is, are*) in the school band.

       1.   *are*

1. (*Is, <u>Are</u>*) the brown bear and the polar bear related?
2. Wind and water (*erodes, <u>erode</u>*) valuable farmland throughout the United States.
3. My guide and companion in Bolivia (*<u>was</u>, were*) Pilar.
4. New words and new meanings for old words (*is, <u>are</u>*) included in a good dictionary.
5. Mrs. Chang and her daughter (*rents, <u>rent</u>*) an apartment.
6. Iron and calcium (*needs, <u>need</u>*) to be included in a good diet.
7. Mr. Marley and his class (*has, <u>have</u>*) painted a wall-size map.
8. A horse and buggy (*<u>was</u>, were*) once a common way to travel.
9. Tornadoes and hurricanes (*is, <u>are</u>*) dangerous storms.
10. Fruit and cheese (*tastes, <u>taste</u>*) good together.

17h. Singular subjects joined by *or* or *nor* take a singular verb.

EXAMPLES   The chief **geologist or** her **assistant is** due to arrive tonight. [Either one *is* due, not both.]

           Neither a **rabbit nor** a **mole does** that kind of damage. [Neither one *does* the damage.]

Plural subjects joined by *or* or *nor* take a plural verb.

EXAMPLES   Either **mice or squirrels are** living in our attic.

           Neither the **senators nor** the **representatives want** the bill to be vetoed by the president.

17i. When a singular subject and a plural subject are joined by *or* or *nor*, the verb agrees with the subject nearer the verb.

EXAMPLES   A **book or flowers** usually **make** an appropriate gift. [The verb agrees with the nearer subject, *flowers.*]

           Flowers or a **book** usually **makes** an appropriate gift. [The verb agrees with the nearer subject, *book.*]

Exercise 9 Identifying Verbs That Agree in Number with Their Subjects

Identify the <u>correct form of the verb</u> in parentheses in each of the following sentences. Be prepared to explain the reason for your choice.

┌HELP┐

In the example, the verb *meet* agrees with the nearer subject, *officers*.

EXAMPLE   1. The club president or the officers (*meets, meet*) regularly with the sponsors.

     1. *meet*

1. Neither pens nor pencils (*is, <u>are</u>*) needed to mark the ballots.
2. Either my aunt or my uncle (<u>*is*</u>, *are*) going to drive us.
3. That table or this chair (<u>*was*</u>, *were*) made by hand in Portugal.
4. (*Has*, <u>*Have*</u>) the sandwiches or other refreshments been served yet?
5. Index cards or a small tablet (<u>*is*</u>, *are*) handy for taking notes.
6. Neither that clock nor my wristwatch (<u>*shows*</u>, *show*) the correct time.
7. One boy or girl (<u>*takes*</u>, *take*) the part of the narrator.
8. During our last visit to Jamaica, a map or a guidebook (<u>*was*</u>, *were*) my constant companion.
9. The dentist or her assistant (<u>*checks*</u>, *check*) my braces.
10. Either Japanese poetry or Inuit myths (*is*, <u>*are*</u>) going to be the focus of my report.

Review B Proofreading for Subject-Verb Agreement

Identify each verb that does not agree with its subject in the following sentences. Then, write the correct form of each verb.

EXAMPLE   1. The players in the photograph on the next page is competing in the most popular sport in the world— soccer.

     1. *is—are*

1. One expert in the field of sports͵have described soccer as the world's favorite type of football. **1. has**
2. Some sports writers͵has estimated that there are over thirty million registered soccer players around the globe. **2. have**
3. Youth leagues and coaching clinics͵has helped make amateur soccer the fastest-growing team sport in the United States. **3. have**
4. In Dallas, Texas, neither baseball nor American football ͵attract as many young players as soccer does. **4. attracts**

Meeting
|INDIVIDUAL|
NEEDS

MODALITIES

Auditory Learners. You may want to use **Review B** as an oral activity. Hearing the sentences read aloud could help some students determine subject-verb agreement. In addition, have volunteers read aloud each corrected sentence.

TEACHING TIP

Activity. Have your students write an expressive paragraph together using compound subjects. Have the first student at the head of each row or group write a topic sentence with a compound subject. If students have trouble getting started, suggest topics for paragraphs, such as snow, football, or summer vacation. As the first writer finishes writing, he or she will pass the paper to the next student in line, who will compose a sentence with another compound subject and verb and then pass the paper to the next student. Encourage students to use *or* and *nor* as well as *and* to connect their subjects. Encourage students who are having difficulty to ask questions. When all students have added their contributions, the students who began the writing will read the paragraphs aloud.

Other Problems in Subject-Verb Agreement

Rules 17j–o *(pp. 468–474)*

OBJECTIVES

- To identify subjects of sentences and the verbs that agree with them

- To choose correct verb forms in sentences

- To practice using correct forms of *don't* and *doesn't* orally

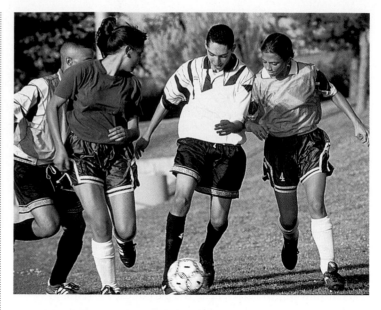

5. Also, more colleges now ~~has~~ varsity soccer teams than have football teams. **5.** have

6. This increase in soccer fans ~~are~~ a trend that started in 1967, when professional teams began playing in the United States. **6.** is

7. Additional interest ~~were~~ generated when the U.S. Youth Soccer Association was formed. **7.** was

8. Both males and females ~~enjoys~~ playing this sport. **8.** enjoy

9. In fact, by the 1980s, many of the soccer teams in the country ~~was~~ women's teams. **9.** were

10. In the past, professional soccer ~~were~~ more popular abroad, but the United States hosted the World Cup in 1994. **10.** was

Reference Note

For more information about **collective nouns,** see page 341.

Other Problems in Subject-Verb Agreement

17j. A collective noun may be either singular or plural, depending on its meaning in a sentence.

A *collective noun* is singular in form but names a group of persons, animals, or things.

RESOURCES

Other Problems in Subject-Verb Agreement
Practice

- *Grammar, Usage, and Mechanics,* pp. 150, 151, 152, 153, 154
- *Language Workshop CD-ROM,* Lesson 12

Common Collective Nouns		
People	**Animals**	**Things**
audience	brood	batch
chorus	flock	bundle
committee	gaggle	cluster
crew	herd	collection
faculty	litter	fleet
family	pack	set
jury	pod	squadron

A collective noun takes a singular verb when the noun refers to the group as a unit. A collective noun takes a plural verb when the noun refers to the individual parts or members of the group.

EXAMPLES   The **class has decided** to have a science fair in November. [The class as a unit has decided.]

The **class were divided** in their opinions of the play. [The members of the class were divided in their opinions.]

My **family plans** to attend Beth's graduation. [The family as a unit plans to attend.]

My **family are coming** from all over the state for the reunion. [The members of the family are coming.]

17k. When the subject follows the verb, find the subject and make sure that the verb agrees with it.

The subject usually follows the verb in questions and in sentences beginning with *here* or *there*.

EXAMPLES   Where **was** the **cat**?
Where **were** the **cats**?

Does Jim know the Chens?
Do the **Chens** know Jim?

Here **is** my **umbrella.**
Here **are** our **umbrellas.**

There **is** a scary **movie** on TV.
There **are** scary **movies** on TV.

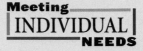

Meeting
INDIVIDUAL
NEEDS

MODALITIES

Visual Learners. Helping students to picture the number of the subject may clarify collective nouns. Write the following sentences on the chalkboard.

1. The herd of horses in the south pasture runs together.

2. Ten dollars is the fee.

3. The basketball team differ in their opinions of the new uniforms.

Ask volunteers to draw pictures illustrating these sentences. Then, ask students to label each subject as acting as *one group* or as *several individuals.* Finally, have the class tell whether the verbs are correct.

[1. *subject—herd (one group), singular; verb—runs, singular; 2. subject—dollars (one group), singular; verb—is, singular; 3. subject—team (several individuals), plural; verb—differ, plural*]

If any students can think of other example sentences to label, have them come to the chalkboard to write the sentences.

NOTE When the subject of a sentence follows part or all of the verb, the word order is said to be ***inverted.*** To find the subject of a sentence with inverted order, restate the sentence in normal subject-verb word order.

INVERTED   Here **are** your **gloves.**
NORMAL   Your **gloves are** here.

INVERTED   **Were you arriving** late, too?
NORMAL   **You were arriving** late, too.

INVERTED   In the pond **swim** large **goldfish.**
NORMAL   Large **goldfish swim** in the pond.

Reference Note

For more information about **contractions,** see page 641.

The contractions *here's, there's,* and *where's* contain the verb *is* and should be used only with singular subjects.

NONSTANDARD   There's our new neighbors.
STANDARD   There**'s** our new **neighbor.**
STANDARD   There **are** our new **neighbors.**

Exercise 10 Identifying Verbs That Agree in Number with Their Subjects

Identify <u>the subject</u> in each of the following sentences. Then, write <u>the correct form of the verb</u> in parentheses.

EXAMPLE   1. That flock of geese (*migrates, migrate*) each year.
           1. *flock—migrates*

1. There (*is, <u>are</u>*) at least two <u>solutions</u> to this complicated Chinese puzzle.
2. The soccer <u>team</u> (*was, <u>were</u>*) all getting on different buses.
3. (*Is, <u>Are</u>*) <u>both</u> of your parents from Korea?
4. Here (*comes, <u>come</u>*) the six <u>members</u> of the decorations committee for the dance.
5. Here (*is, <u>are</u>*) some <u>apples</u> and <u>bananas</u> for the picnic basket.
6. There (*<u>is</u>, are*) neither <u>time</u> nor <u>money</u> for that project.
7. (*Here's, <u>Here are</u>*) the social studies <u>notes</u> I took.
8. At the press conference, there (*was, <u>were</u>*) several <u>candidates</u> for mayor and two for governor.

9. The <u>family</u> (*has*, *have*) invited us over for a dinner to celebrate Grandma's promotion.

10. Here (*is*, <u>*are*</u>) some <u>masks</u> carved by the Haida people.

17l. Some nouns that are plural in form take singular verbs.

EXAMPLES   **Electronics is** a branch of physics.

                    Civics is being taught by Ms. Gutierrez.

                    Measles is the most unpleasant disease I've ever had.

                    The **news was** not encouraging.

17m. An expression of an amount (a measurement, a percentage, or a fraction, for example) may be singular or plural, depending on how it is used.

A word or phrase stating an amount is singular when the amount is thought of as a unit.

EXAMPLES   Fifteen **dollars is** enough for that CD.

                    Sixteen **ounces equals** one pound.

                    Is two **weeks** long enough for a hiking trip?

Sometimes, however, the amount is thought of as individual pieces or parts. If so, a plural verb is used.

EXAMPLES   **Ten** of the dollars **were borrowed.**

                    Two of the hours **were spent** at the theater.

A fraction or a percentage is singular when it refers to a singular word and plural when it refers to a plural word.

EXAMPLES   One fourth of the **salad is** gone.

                    Forty percent of the **students are** new.

NOTE Expressions of measurement (such as length, weight, and area) are usually singular.

EXAMPLES   Ten **feet is** the height of a regulation basketball hoop.

                    Seventy-five **pounds is** the maximum baggage weight for this airline.

17n. Even when plural in form, the title of a creative work (such as a book, song, film, or painting), the name of an organization, or the name of a country or city generally takes a singular verb.

EXAMPLES   ***World Tales*** **is** a collection of folk tales retold by Idries Shah. [one book]

Tonya's painting ***Sunflowers*** **was inspired** by the natural beauty of rural Iowa. [one painting]

Friends of the Earth was founded in 1969. [one organization]

The **Philippines is** an island country in the southwest Pacific Ocean. [one country]

Is Marble Falls a city in central Texas? [one city]

Exercise 11   **Identifying Verbs That Agree in Number with Their Subjects**

Identify the correct form of the verb in parentheses in each of the following sentences.

EXAMPLE   1. Three inches in height (*is, are*) a great deal to grow in one year.

        1. *is*

1. *The Friends* (*is, are*) a book about a girl from the West Indies and a girl from Harlem.
2. Two cups of broth (*seems, seem*) right for that recipe.
3. Fifteen feet (*was, were*) the length of the winning long jump.
4. Navarro and Company (*is, are*) selling those jackets.
5. The National Council of Teachers of English (*is, are*) holding its convention in our city this year.
6. Mumps (*is, are*) a highly infectious disease.
7. Three hours of practice (*is, are*) not unusual for the band.
8. *Arctic Dreams* (*was, were*) written by Barry Lopez.
9. Two weeks of preparation (*has, have*) been enough.
10. A dollar and a half (*is, are*) the cost of a subway ride.

17o. *Don't* and *doesn't* should agree in number with their subjects.

The word *don't* is a contraction of *do not.* Use *don't* with plural subjects and with the pronouns *I* and *you.*

EXAMPLES   The **children don't** seem nervous.

I **don't** understand.

Don't you remember?

The word *doesn't* is a contraction of *does not*. Use *doesn't* with singular subjects except the pronouns *I* and *you*.

EXAMPLES   **Kim doesn't** ride the bus.

He doesn't play tennis.

It doesn't snow here.

Oral Practice 1 Using *Don't* and *Doesn't*

Read the following sentences aloud, stressing the italicized words.

1. My friend *doesn't* understand the problem.
2. *Doesn't* she want to play soccer?
3. The tomatoes *don't* look ripe.
4. Our school *doesn't* have a gymnasium.
5. Italy *doesn't* border Germany.
6. The geese *don't* hiss at Mr. Waverly.
7. Our Muslim neighbors, the Nassers, *don't* eat pork.
8. He *doesn't* play chess.

Review C Identifying Verbs That Agree in Number with Their Subjects

Write the verb form in parentheses that agrees with its subject.

EXAMPLE   1. Wheelchairs with lifts (*help, helps*) many people.
1. *help*

1. Twenty-five cents (*is, are*) not enough to buy the Sunday newspaper.
2. Everyone in her family (*prefers, prefer*) to drink water.
3. Allen and his parents (*enjoy, enjoys*) basketball.
4. Jan (*don't, doesn't*) know the rules of volleyball.
5. Neither the cassette player nor the speakers (*work, works*) as well as we had hoped.
6. There (*is, are*) 132 islands in the state of Hawaii.
7. Many California place names (*comes, come*) from Spanish.

USAGE

Meeting
INDIVIDUAL
NEEDS

LEARNERS HAVING DIFFICULTY
To give students additional help with **Review C,** indicate which subject-verb agreement rule applies to each sentence. Then, students can review the rules and the examples before completing each sentence.

1. 17m	**6.** 17k
2. 17d	**7.** 17e
3. 17g	**8.** 17h
4. 17o	**9.** 17l
5. 17i	**10.** 17j

8. The principal or her assistant (*is, are*) the one who can help you.

9. Home economics (*is, are*) a required course in many schools.

10. A flock of sheep (*was, were*) grazing on the hill.

Review D **Proofreading for Subject-Verb Agreement**

Most of the following sentences contain errors in subject-verb agreement. If a verb does not agree with its subject, write the correct form of the verb. If a sentence is already correct, write *C*.

EXAMPLE   **1.** Here is two pictures of Wang Yani and her artwork.

       1. are

1. There surely is few young artists as successful as Yani. **1.** are

2. In fact, the People's Republic of China regard her as a national treasure. **2.** regards

3. She has shown her paintings throughout the world. **3.** C

4. Yani don't paint in just one style. **4.** doesn't

5. Her ideas and her art naturally changes over the years. **5.** change

6. The painting below shows one of Yani's favorite childhood subjects. **6.** C

7. Many of her early paintings features monkeys. **7.** feature

8. In fact, one of her large works portray 112 monkeys. **8.** portrays

9. However, most of her later paintings is of landscapes, other animals, and people. **9.** are

10. As her smile suggests, Yani fill her paintings with energy. **10.** fills

Agreement of Pronoun and Antecedent

A pronoun usually refers to a noun or another pronoun called its ***antecedent.*** Whenever you use a pronoun, make sure that it agrees with its antecedent.

17p. A pronoun should agree in number and gender with its antecedent.

Some singular pronouns have forms that indicate gender. Feminine pronouns refer to females. Masculine pronouns refer to males. Neuter pronouns refer to things (neither male nor female) and sometimes to animals.

Feminine	she	her	hers	herself
Masculine	he	him	his	himself
Neuter	it	it	its	itself

EXAMPLES **Carlotta** said that **she** found **her** book.

Aaron brought **his** skates with **him.**

The **plant** with mold on **it** is losing **its** leaves.

The antecedent of a pronoun can be another kind of pronoun. In such cases, you may need to look in a phrase that follows the antecedent to determine which personal pronoun to use.

EXAMPLES **Each** of the **girls** has offered **her** ideas. [*Each* is the antecedent of *her*. The word *girls* tells you to use the feminine pronoun to refer to *Each*.]

One of the **men** lost **his** key. [*One* is the antecedent of *his.* The word *men* tells you to use the masculine pronoun to refer to *One*.]

Some antecedents may be either masculine or feminine. In such cases, use both the masculine and the feminine forms.

EXAMPLES Every **one** of the parents praised **his or her** child's efforts that day.

No one in the senior play forgot **his or her** lines on opening night.

Reference Note

For more information on **antecedents,** see page 342.

STYLE TIP

In conversation, people often use a plural personal pronoun to refer to a singular antecedent that may be either masculine or feminine. This nonstandard usage is becoming more common in writing, too.

NONSTANDARD
Everybody brought their swimsuit.

Every member of the club sold their tickets.

For now, however, it is best to follow the rules of standard usage in formal situations.

STYLE TIP

To avoid the awkward use of *his or her,* try to rephrase the sentence.

EXAMPLES
Everybody brought **a** swimsuit.

All the members of the club sold **their** tickets.

Agreement of Pronoun and Antecedent

Rules 17p–x *(pp. 475–480)*

OBJECTIVES

- **To complete sentences by adding pronouns and to identify the pronouns' antecedents**
- **To choose correct pronouns in sentences**

Meeting INDIVIDUAL NEEDS

ENGLISH-LANGUAGE LEARNERS

Asian Languages. English-language learners whose native languages use pronouns differently from the way English uses them may have difficulty with pronoun-antecedent agreement in English. In Korean, for example, pronouns do not refer to gender. Japanese has no number agreement, and the languages of Vietnam and Laos have no neuter pronouns. To prevent confusion, you can explain which personal pronouns refer to which sorts of antecedents, with special emphasis on the use of *he, she,* and *it.*

RESOURCES

Agreement of Pronoun and Antecedent

Practice

- *Grammar, Usage, and Mechanics,* pp. 155, 156, 157, 158, 159
- *Language Workshop CD-ROM,* Lesson 13

Relating to Writing

Explain to students that using unclear pronouns will cause confusion in their writing. Write the following sentences on the chalkboard to show how sentences can be revised to correct unclear pronouns.

Unclear: Colleen called Alicia while she was doing her homework. [*The antecedent of* she *and* her *is unclear. Who was doing her homework, Colleen or Alicia?*]

Clear: While Colleen was doing her homework, she called Alicia.

Clear: While Alicia was doing her homework, Colleen called her.

Have students take out pieces of their own writing and work in pairs to revise any sentences that have unclear pronouns. Suggest that students highlight all pronouns and then identify the antecedents to which the pronouns refer. Remind students that pronouns often refer to antecedents in previous sentences.

│ S T Y L E   T I P │

Sentences with singular antecedents joined by *or* or *nor* can sound awkward if the antecedents are of different genders. If a sentence sounds awkward, revise it to avoid the problem.

AWKWARD
Odessa or Raymond will bring her or his road map.

REVISED
Odessa will bring **her** road map, or **Raymond** will bring **his.**

17q. Use a singular pronoun to refer to *anybody, anyone, anything, each, either, everybody, everyone, everything, neither, nobody, no one, nothing, one, somebody, someone,* or *something.*

EXAMPLES   **Each** of the snakes escaped from **its** cage.

Someone in the class left behind **his or her** pencil.

17r. Use a plural pronoun to refer to *both, few, many,* or *several.*

EXAMPLES   **Both** of the sailors asked **their** captain for shore leave.

Many among the others waiting below deck hoped that **they** could go, too.

17s. The indefinite pronouns *all, any, more, most, none,* and *some* may be singular or plural, depending on how they are used in a sentence.

EXAMPLES   **All** of the book is interesting, isn't **it**?
All of the books are interesting, aren't **they**?

None of the casserole is left; **it** was terrific!
None of the casseroles are left; **they** were terrific!

17t. Use a singular pronoun to refer to two or more singular antecedents joined by *or* or *nor.*

EXAMPLES   Either **Ralph or Carlos** will display **his** baseball cards.

Neither **Nina nor Mary** will bring **her** CD player.

17u. Use a plural pronoun to refer to two or more antecedents joined by *and.*

EXAMPLES   **Isaac and Jerome** told me that **they** were coming.

Elena and Roberto sent letters to **their** cousin.

Exercise 12   **Using Pronouns in Sentences**

For each of the following sentences, write a pronoun or a pair of pronouns that will correctly complete the sentence.

EXAMPLE   1. Dominic or Martin will show _____ slides.

1. *his*

Answers may vary.

1. A writer should proofread _____ work carefully. **1.** his or her
2. One of the boys had finished _____ homework. **2.** his
3. No, Joyce has not given me _____ answer. **3.** her
4. The store sent Paula and Eric the posters that _____ had ordered last week. **4.** they
5. Mark or Hector will arrive early so that _____ can help us. **5.** he
6. Everyone read one of _____ poems aloud. **6.** his or her
7. One of the students raised _____ hand. **7.** his or her
8. _____ of the tennis rackets were damaged by the water leak. **8.** Many
9. The dogs had eaten none of _____ food. **9.** their
10. Each of the dogs ate the scraps that we gave _____ . **10.** it
11. The principal and the Spanish teacher announced _____ plans for the Cinco de Mayo fiesta. **11.** their
12. All of the bowling pins were on _____ sides. **12.** their
13. The movie made sense to _____ of the audience members. **13.** none
14. Everyone in my class has _____ own writer's journal. **14.** his or her
15. Neither recalled the name of _____ first-grade teacher. **15.** his or her
16. _____ of the players, Sharon and P. J., agreed that the game was a draw. **16.** Each
17. Ms. Levine said _____ was proud of the students. **17.** she
18. Frank had tried on all of the hats before _____ chose one. **18.** he
19. Anyone may join if _____ collects stamps. **19.** he or she
20. Either Vanessa or Marilyn was honored for _____ design. **20.** her

17v. A pronoun that refers to a collective noun has the same number as the noun.

A collective noun is singular when it refers to the group as a unit and plural when it refers to the individual members of the group.

EXAMPLES   The **cast** is giving **its** final performance tonight. [The cast as a unit is giving its final performance.]

The **cast** are trying on **their** costumes. [The members of the cast are trying on their individual costumes.]

The **faculty** has prepared **its** report. [The faculty as a unit has prepared its report.]

The **faculty** are returning to **their** classrooms. [The members of the faculty are returning to their separate classrooms.]

COMPUTER TIP

Using indefinite pronouns correctly can be tricky. To help yourself, you may want to create an indefinite pronoun guide. First, summarize the information in Rules 17d–17f and 17q–17s.

Then, choose several examples to illustrate the rules. If you use a computer, you can create a Help file in which to store this information.

Call up your Help file whenever you run into difficulty with indefinite pronouns in your writing. If you don't use a computer, you can keep your guide in a writing notebook.

Relating to Literature

May Swenson uses many pronouns but only a few antecedents in her poem "Cat & the Weather." If the selection is in your literature book, ask students to read the poem carefully and to examine closely how all the pronouns and their antecedents are used.

Ask students to tell you how the poem uses gender and placement to avoid confusing the reader with so many pronouns. [*All pronouns referring to the cat are masculine; other pronouns are placed near their antecedents.*] The pronoun *it* in the contraction *it's* (line 26) does not have a stated antecedent. Ask students if they know what the pronoun refers to [*personal world, life*].

You may want to have students write short poems in which they use pronouns. Like Swenson, they may want to incorporate several pronouns and only a few antecedents. Ask for volunteers to read their poems in class.

USAGE

17w. An expression of an amount may take a singular or plural pronoun, depending on how the expression is used.

EXAMPLES **Five dollars** is all I need. I hope my sister will lend **it** to me. [The amount is thought of as a unit.]

Two dollars are torn. The vending machine won't take **them.** [The amount is thought of as individual pieces or parts.]

17x. Even when plural in form, the title of a creative work (such as a book, song, film, or painting), the name of an organization, or the name of a country or city usually takes a singular pronoun.

EXAMPLES Have you read ***Great Expectations***? **It** is on our summer reading list.

The **United Nations,** which has **its** headquarters in New York, also has offices in Geneva and Vienna.

My grandmother, who is from the **Maldives,** told us of **its** coral reefs and lagoons.

Exercise 13 Choosing Pronouns That Agree with Their Antecedents

Choose the <u>correct word or words</u> in parentheses in the following sentences.

EXAMPLE 1. Even a trio can have a big sound if (*it, they*) can arrange the score properly.

   1. *it*

1. They are asking two hundred dollars, but (*it, they*) should be a lower price because there is no chair with the desk.
2. Darla, *The Hero and the Crown* has been checked out; however, (*it, they*) should be back next Wednesday.
3. If the high school band doesn't show up soon, (*it, they*) won't lead the parade.
4. These plans call for ten feet of African ebony, and although (*it, they*) would look great, I have no idea where we could even find ebony.
5. Seven points may not seem like much, but in jai alai, (*it, they*) can be enough to decide the game.
6. The unit took up (*its, their*) position on the hill.

Learning for Life

Continued on pp. 479–480

Informal vs. Formal Language. Explain to students that in casual conversation, most people frequently use informal, sometimes even nonstandard, English. However, in formal writing and speaking situations, standard English—including correct agreement—is required.

Ask each student to imagine that he or she is applying for a summer scholarship to a camp or other summer program. In a letter to the camp or program, each student should explain why he or she is the best

7. "Sixteen Tons" has always been one of my favorite songs, and (*it, they*) always will be.
8. Six of the sales teams exceeded (*its, their*) goals.
9. Will the board of directors alter (*its, their*) decision?
10. Try Harper Brothers Appliances first; if (*it, they*) happens to be closed, go up the street to Smith's Hardware.

Review E **Proofreading Sentences for Correct Pronoun-Antecedent Agreement**

Most of the following sentences contain errors in pronoun-antecedent agreement. Identify each error, and write the correct pronoun or pronouns. If a sentence is already correct, write *C*.

EXAMPLE   1. At the meeting, each member of the Small Business Council spoke about their concerns.
            1. *their—his or her*

1. Everybody had a chance to express their opinion about the new shopping mall. **1.** his or her
2. Mrs. Gomez and Mr. Franklin are happy about his or her new business locations at the mall. **2.** their   **3.** their
3. Both said that his or her profits have increased significantly.
4. Neither Mr. Chen nor Mr. Cooper, however, feels that his or her customers can find convenient parking.
5. Anyone shopping at the mall has to park their car too far from the main shopping area. **5.** his or her
6. Several members of the council said that the mall has taken away many of their customers. **6.** C
7. One of the women on the council then presented their own idea about creating a farmers' market on weekends.   **7.** her

Agreement of Pronoun and Antecedent   **479**

Meeting
INDIVIDUAL
NEEDS

LEARNERS HAVING DIFFICULTY
To give students additional practice on pronoun-antecedent agreement, form study groups of two or three students each, and assign the even-numbered items in **Review E**. Go over the answers orally to identify students who are having difficulty with the material, and offer reteaching as neccesary. Then, assign the odd-numbered items for students to complete on their own.

USAGE

recipient for the scholarship. For example, an athlete might apply to a sports camp for a week of training, or an artist might apply for a summer art class at a local museum.
    Remind students that making a good impression is important, so they must check

their letters for correct subject-verb and pronoun-antecedent agreement. Because the information could be somewhat personal, students might not feel comfortable sharing their letters; therefore, suggest that students keep their letters in their port-

Review F — Writing Sentences That Demonstrate Correct Subject-Verb and Pronoun-Antecedent Agreement

POSSIBLE ANSWERS

1. Both Jed and Bob <u>found</u> their lost books in the office.

2. None of the puppies <u>has</u> eaten today.

3. Los Angeles <u>is</u> known as the "city of angels."

4. Fifty cents <u>is</u> not very much money these days.

5. *Anne of Green Gables* <u>is</u> my sister's favorite book; she has read <u>it</u> four times.

6. What good news <u>is</u> in today's paper?

7. Either the teacher or the students <u>need</u> to return the permission slips.

8. <u>Has</u> the litter of kittens <u>been fed</u>?

9. Neither Nancy nor Tim <u>remembers</u> who ate the last apple.

10. Everyone <u>wants</u> to help.

11. *The Adventures of Tom Sawyer* <u>was</u> written by Mark Twain, and <u>it</u> is still a very popular book.

12. The football team <u>hopes</u> to win the championship this year.

13. Each of the chairs <u>has</u> been repainted.

14. Athletics <u>is</u> her favorite activity, but I don't like <u>it</u> as much as I like singing in the choir.

15. The Masters tournament <u>becomes</u> more exciting every year.

16. Few armadillos <u>like</u> dogs.

17. Most of the apple <u>is</u> red.

18. Several days <u>is</u> too long to wait.

19. <u>Is</u> any of the orange juice left?

20. None of the pizza <u>is</u> left.

---

8. Many members said ~~he or she~~ favored the plan, and a proposal was discussed. **8.** they

9. Each farmer could have ~~their~~ own spot near the town hall. **9.** his or her

10. The Small Business Council then agreed to take ~~their~~ proposal to the mayor. **10.** its

Review F — Writing Sentences That Demonstrate Correct Subject-Verb and Pronoun-Antecedent Agreement

Using the following words or word groups as subjects, write twenty sentences. In each sentence, underline the verb that agrees with the subject. Then, underline twice any pronoun that agrees with the subject.

—HELP—

Not every sentence in Review F needs to have a pronoun that agrees with the subject.

EXAMPLE 1. all of the players

1. *All of the players <u>were</u> tired; <u>they</u> had had a long practice.*

1. both Jed and Bob
2. none of the puppies
3. Los Angeles
4. fifty cents
5. *Anne of Green Gables*
6. news
7. either the teacher or the students
8. the litter of kittens
9. neither Nancy nor Tim
10. everyone
11. *The Adventures of Tom Sawyer*
12. the football team
13. each of the chairs
14. athletics
15. the Masters tournament
16. few armadillos
17. most of the apple
18. several days
19. any of the orange juice
20. none of the pizza

Learning for Life

folios for future reference.

If students need guidance with persuasive writing, refer them to **Chapter 6: Convincing Others.**

Chapter Review

A. Determining Subject and Verb Agreement

Identify the <u>correct form of the verb</u> given in parentheses in each of the following sentences. Base your answers on the rules of standard, formal usage.

1. Elephants (*has*, <u>*have*</u>) worked with people for centuries.
2. A blue vase (<u>*is*</u>, *are*) the only thing in the room.
3. (<u>*Doesn't*</u>, *Don't*) Midori come here every afternoon?
4. The exhibit of drawings by John James Audubon (<u>*was*</u>, *were*) fascinating, don't you think?
5. Civics (<u>*was*</u>, *were*) only one of the classes that challenged me.
6. Since Mom repaired them, both of the radios (<u>*work*</u>, *works*).
7. Everyone (<u>*calls*</u>, *call*) Latisha by her nickname, Tish.
8. Fifty cents (<u>*was*</u>, *were*) a lot of money in 1910!
9. Ms. Sakata's former neighbor and best friend, Ms. Chang, (<u>*writes*</u>, *write*) poetry.
10. (*Is*, <u>*Are*</u>) there any other blacksmiths in town?
11. I'm sorry, but somebody (<u>*has*</u>, *have*) checked out that book.
12. (*Was*, <u>*Were*</u>) the geese in the cornfield again?
13. All of the shells in my collection (*was*, <u>*were*</u>) displayed.
14. Neither Cindy nor her cousins (*knows*, <u>*know*</u>) how to sew.
15. Outside the back door (*is*, <u>*are*</u>) a few of your friends.
16. My brother and my uncles (*plays*, <u>*play*</u>) rugby.
17. The Netherlands (<u>*has*</u>, *have*) a coastline on the North Sea.
18. Here (*is*, <u>*are*</u>) several subjects for you to consider.
19. The team (*has*, <u>*have*</u>) all received their jerseys and hats.
20. Some of Ernest Hemingway's writings (*was*, <u>*were*</u>) autobiographical.
21. This news (<u>*was*</u>, *were*) just what Barb wanted to hear.
22. *Giants of Jazz* (<u>*is*</u>, *are*) an interesting book.
23. Everyone (<u>*is*</u>, *are*) expected to attend.
24. Most of our reading (<u>*was*</u>, *were*) done on weekends.
25. Either Gordon or Ruben (<u>*knows*</u>, *know*) the right answer.

Using the Chapter Review

To assess student progress, you may want to compare the types of items missed on the **Diagnostic Preview** to those missed on the **Chapter Review**. If students have not made significant progress, you may want to refer them to **Exercises 8–13** of **Chapter 26: Correcting Common Errors** for additional practice.

B. Determining Pronoun and Antecedent Agreement

If the italicized pronoun in each of the following sentences does not agree with its antecedent, write the correct form of the pronoun. If the pronoun does agree with its antecedent, write *C*. Base your answers on the rules of standard, formal usage.

26. Everyone put ∧ *their* suitcases on the bus. **26.** his or her

27. Either Marcia or Christina will bring *her* serving platter to the dinner party. **27.** C

28. Both Sarah and Sue agreed with ∧ *her* counselor. **28.** their

29. Several of my friends do ∧ *his or her* homework after school. **29.** their

30. One of the boys used ∧ *their* bat in the game. **30.** his

31. My grandfather's favorite television show is The Honeymooners. He watches ∧ *them* every night on cable. **31.** it

32. All of the horses received ∧ *its* vaccinations. **32.** their

33. Either Maria or Louise will receive ∧ *their* award today. **33.** her

34. Everybody should know ∧ *their* ZIP Code. **34.** his or her

35. Each student in the class has given ∧ *their* report on an African American folktale. **35.** his or her

36. Every one of the dogs obeyed *its* owner. **36.** C

37. I found twenty dollars in my sock drawer. Do you think I should spend ∧ *them* on Christmas presents? **37.** it

38. Will either Hector or Tony read *his* paper aloud? **38.** C

39. Not one of the students had finished ∧ *their* science project on time this semester. **39.** his or her

40. After Celia finished her solo, the audience roared ∧ *their* approval for five minutes. **40.** its

Writing Application
Using Agreement in a Composition

Subject-Verb Agreement   If you could be any person in history, who would you be? Why? Your social studies teacher has asked you to answer these questions in a short composition. Be sure to use correct subject-verb agreement in explaining your choice.

Prewriting   First, decide what historical person you would like to be, and freewrite about that person. As you write, think about why the person is noteworthy and why you would want to be him or her.

Writing   Use your freewriting ideas to write your first draft. Begin with a sentence that states the purpose of your composition and identifies your historical figure. Then, give your main reasons for wanting to be that person. Summarize your main points in a conclusion.

Revising   Read through your composition, and then answer these questions: (1) Is it clear what person from history I want to be? If not, revise your main idea statement. (2) Is it clear why I want to be that person? If not, explain your reasons in more detail.

Publishing   Make sure that all subjects and verbs agree in number. Check your composition for errors in spelling, capitalization, and punctuation. Your class may want to create a display using the compositions and pictures of the historical figures chosen.

Chapter Review   **483**

USAGE

Writing Application

Tip. This writing assignment gives students an opportunity to develop essays using correct subject-verb agreement. To help students develop strategies for writing, you may want to review **Chapter 6: Convincing Others** before the students begin to write.

Scoring Rubric. While you will want to pay particular attention to students' use of subject-verb and pronoun-antecedent agreement, you will also want to evaluate overall writing performance. You may want to give a split score to indicate development and clarity of the composition as well as usage skills.

Critical Thinking

Analysis. Students may list more information in the prewriting stage than they can use in their essays. Suggest that students' main ideas focus on why they admire the individuals they have selected. Then, have students analyze the information they have listed and decide what supports their main ideas and what is irrelevant and should be left out.

RESOURCES

Writing Application

Extension

■ *Grammar, Usage, and Mechanics,* p. 167
■ *Language Workshop CD-ROM,* Lesson 10–13

CHAPTER

PREVIEWING THE CHAPTER

- This chapter explains the use of regular and irregular verbs and emphasizes past and past participle forms. The chapter also discusses the use of active and passive voice. Also covered are tense and consistent use of tense as well as six verbs that are often used incorrectly.

- The chapter closes with a **Chapter Review**, which includes a **Writing Application** feature that asks students to write an exciting paragraph to serve as the cliffhanger opening of an adventure story. Students should use at least five verbs from the lists of **Common Irregular Verbs** on pp. 489–492.

- For help in integrating this chapter with composition chapters, use the **Teaching Strands** chart on pp. T311A–T311B.

▼

USING THE DIAGNOSTIC PREVIEW

- This preview will show you which students have problems using correct verb forms. Some students may make errors because they do not recognize how helping verbs show tense. Others may have problems using the correct forms of irregular verbs and of the six troublesome verbs discussed in this chapter.

18 # Using Verbs Correctly

Principal Parts, Regular and Irregular Verbs, Tense, Voice

Diagnostic Preview

Proofreading Sentences for Correct Verb Forms

If a sentence contains an ~~incorrect past or past participle form~~ of a verb, write the correct form. If a sentence is already correct, write *C*.

EXAMPLE   **1.** Melissa drunk the medicine in one gulp.

      1. drank

1. We ~~swum~~ in the lake last weekend.   **1.** swam
2. Carlos ~~come~~ from the Dominican Republic.   **2.** came
3. The crow just ~~set~~ there on the wire fence.   **3.** sat
4. The balloon burst with a loud pop.   **4.** C
5. I ~~seen~~ that magician on television.   **5.** saw
6. The leader raised his tambourine to begin the dance.   **6.** C
7. You should have ~~went~~ with Thomas to the game.   **7.** gone
8. The ice cube has ~~shrinked~~ to half its original size.   **8.** shrunk
9. Meanwhile, the water level has ~~rose~~.   **9.** risen
10. I would have ~~wrote~~ to you much sooner, but I lost your address after you moved.   **10.** written
11. Sandra ~~throwed~~ the ball to the shortstop.   **11.** threw
12. Ms. López has ~~spoke~~ before many civic groups.   **12.** spoken

CHAPTER RESOURCES

Planning
- *One-Stop Planner CD-ROM*

Practice and Extension
- *Grammar, Usage, and Mechanics,* p. 168
- *Developmental Language Skills,* pp. 67–72

Internet

- go.hrw.com (keyword: EOLang)

Evaluation and Assessment
- *Chapter Tests,* Ch. 18
- *Chapter Tests in Standardized Test Formats,* Ch. 18
- *Test Generator (One-Stop Planner)*

13. All of these photographs were taken in Florida's Everglades National Park.   **13. C**
14. The bell has ~~rang~~ for fourth period.   **14. rung**
15. While visiting Los Angeles last August, I ~~run~~ into an old friend in the city's Little Tokyo district.   **15. ran**
16. I ~~laid~~ down under a tree to rest.   **16. lay**
17. I ~~done~~ everything asked of me.   **17. did**
18. It ~~begun~~ to rain shortly after dusk.   **18. began**
19. Some of the saucers were broken.   **19. C**
20. Sue ~~lay~~ her pen down and studied the question again.   **20. laid**

Principal Parts of Verbs

The four basic forms of a verb are called the *principal parts* of the verb.

18a. The principal parts of a verb are the *base form,* the *present participle,* the *past,* and the *past participle.*

When they are used to form tenses, the present participle and the past participle forms require helping verbs (forms of *be* and *have*).

┌HELP──
Some teachers refer to the base form as the *infinitive.* Follow your teacher's directions when you are labeling this form.

Base Form	Present Participle	Past	Past Participle
talk	[is] talking	talked	[have] talked
draw	[is] drawing	drew	[have] drawn

Because *talk* forms its past and past participle by adding *–ed,* it is called a *regular verb. Draw* forms its past and past participle differently, so it is called an *irregular verb.*

The principal parts of a verb are used to express time.

Reference Note

For information on **participles used as adjectives,** see page 410. For information on **helping verbs,** see page 361.

PRESENT TIME   He **draws** excellent pictures.
                       Susan **is drawing** one now.

PAST TIME   Last week they **drew** two maps.
                  She **has** often **drawn** cartoons.

FUTURE TIME   Perhaps she **will draw** one for you.
                   By Thursday, we **will have drawn** two more.

TEACHING **TIP**

Motivation. To help students practice using correct verb forms, prepare a set of flashcards with one of the following verbs on each card: *begun, done, eaten, gone, grown, known, lain, seen, swum,* and *sung.*

Ask students to write a sentence with each verb as you show a card. After all the cards have been used, let students work in groups of four to compare sentences. Encourage groups to ask questions if they encounter difficulties. Students will probably discover that in sentences such as "We had gone to the game," each of these verbs needs a helping verb; clarify this point for groups who do not come to this realization. (Some students may find uses for the verbs as participial modifiers.)

Regular Verbs

Rule 18b *(pp. 486–487)*

OBJECTIVES

- To read aloud sentences containing the past tense forms of regular verbs

- To supply the present participle, past, and past participle forms of given regular verbs

Meeting INDIVIDUAL NEEDS

ENGLISH-LANGUAGE LEARNERS
General Strategies. Adding the past tense suffix *–d* or *–ed* creates a final consonant sound that does not occur in many other languages. Speakers of these languages often simplify words ending in *–d* or *–ed* by omitting the last sound, a practice that might lead to omitting the final consonant in writing as well. You could model **Oral Practice 1** for students to emphasize the past tense suffix sound.

┌─**HELP**─

Most regular verbs that end in *e* drop the *e* before adding *–ing*. Some regular verbs double the final consonant before adding *–ing* or *–ed.*

EXAMPLES
shake—shak**ing**
hug—hu**gged**

Reference Note

For more about **spelling rules,** see Chapter 25. For information on **standard and nonstandard English,** see page 553.

Regular Verbs

18b. A *regular verb* forms its past and past participle by adding *–d* or *–ed* to the base form.

Base Form	Present Participle	Past	Past Participle
clean	[is] cleaning	cleaned	[have] cleaned
hope	[is] hoping	hoped	[have] hoped
inspect	[is] inspecting	inspected	[have] inspected
slip	[is] slipping	slipped	[have] slipped

One common error in forming the past or the past participle of a regular verb is to leave off the *–d* or *–ed* ending.

NONSTANDARD	Our street use to be quieter.
STANDARD	Our street **used** to be quieter.

Another common error is to add unnecessary letters.

NONSTANDARD	The swimmer almost drownded in the riptide.
STANDARD	The swimmer almost **drowned** in the riptide.

NONSTANDARD	The kitten attackted that paper bag.
STANDARD	The kitten **attacked** that paper bag.

Oral Practice 1 Using Regular Verbs

Read each of the following sentences aloud, stressing the italicized verbs.

1. We are *supposed* to meet at the track after school.
2. The twins *happened* to buy the same shirt.
3. They have already *called* me about the party.
4. Do you know who *used* to live in this house?
5. I had *hoped* they could go to the concert with us.

WOOF
WOOFS
WOOFING
WOOFED

© 1992 by Sidney Harris.

RESOURCES

Regular Verbs

Practice

- *Grammar, Usage, and Mechanics,* pp. 169, 170
- *Language Workshop CD-ROM,* Lesson 14

6. The chairs have been *moved* into the hall for the dance.
7. That salesclerk has *helped* my mother before.
8. Eli may not have *looked* under the table for the cat.

Exercise 1 Writing the Forms of Regular Verbs

Write the correct present participle, past, or past participle form of the italicized verb given before each of the following sentences.

EXAMPLES
  1. *learn*   Many people today are _____ folk dances from a variety of countries.

  1. *learning*

  2. *hope*   Dad and I had _____ to take lessons in folk dancing this summer.

  2. *hoped*

1. *practice* These Spanish folk dancers must have _____ for a long time.
2. *perform* Notice that they are _____ in their colorful native costumes.
3. *wish* Have you ever _____ that you knew how to do any folk dances?
4. *use* Virginia reels _____ to be popular dances in the United States.
5. *promise* Mrs. Stamos, who is from Greece, _____ to teach her daughter the Greek chain dance.
6. *lean* The young Jamaican dancer _____ backward before he went under the pole during the limbo dance competition.
7. *start* The group from Estonia is _____ a dance about a spinning wheel.
8. *request* Someone in the audience has _____ an Irish square dance called "Sweets of May."
9. *dance* During the Mexican hat dance, the woman _____ around the brim of the sombrero.
10. *fill* The Jewish wedding dance _____ the room with both music and movement.

ANSWERS
1. practiced
2. performing
3. wished
4. used
5. promised
6. leaned
7. starting
8. requested
9. danced
10. filled

Meeting INDIVIDUAL NEEDS

ENGLISH-LANGUAGE LEARNERS

Spanish. Remind Spanish speakers that the English suffix *–ing* is equivalent to the Spanish *–ando* and *–iendo.* For example, *hablando* (speaking) comes from *hablar* (to speak), and *comiendo* (eating) comes from *comer* (to eat). Also, the English suffix *–d* or *–ed* is equivalent to the Spanish *–ado* and *–ido,* as in *abandonado* (abandoned) and *adquirido* (acquired). As in English, the past participle in Spanish may also function as an adjective.

USAGE

USAGE

Irregular Verbs

Rule 18c *(pp. 488–496)*

OBJECTIVES

- To read aloud sentences containing principal parts of irregular verbs
- To supply the past and past participle forms of given irregular verbs

Meeting INDIVIDUAL NEEDS

ENGLISH-LANGUAGE LEARNERS
General Strategies. Some English-language learners might not understand the use of irregular verbs if their native languages have few or no irregular verbs. To give students practice using the base form, the past form, and the past participle form of irregular verbs, suggest that students read aloud the following sentences, filling in the blanks with verbs from the charts on pp. 488–492.

1. Today I _____.

2. Yesterday I _____.

3. Often I have _____.

┌─HELP─
If you are not sure about the principal parts of a verb, look in a dictionary. Entries for irregular verbs list the principal parts of the verb. If the principal parts are not given, the verb is a regular verb.

Irregular Verbs

18c. An *irregular verb* forms its past and past participle in some way other than by adding –d or –ed to the base form.

Irregular verbs form their past and past participle in various ways:

- by changing vowels

Base Form	Past	Past Participle
sing	sang	[have] sung
become	became	[have] become
drink	drank	[have] drunk

- by changing consonants

Base Form	Past	Past Participle
make	made	[have] made
build	built	[have] built
lend	lent	[have] lent

- by changing vowels *and* consonants

Base Form	Past	Past Participle
do	did	[have] done
go	went	[have] gone
buy	bought	[have] bought

- by making no changes

Base Form	Past	Past Participle
hurt	hurt	[have] hurt
put	put	[have] put
let	let	[have] let

RESOURCES

Irregular Verbs

Practice

- *Grammar, Usage, and Mechanics,* pp. 171–175
- *Language Workshop CD-ROM,* Lesson 14

Common Irregular Verbs			
Base Form	Present Participle	Past	Past Participle
begin	[is] beginning	began	[have] begun
bite	[is] biting	bit	[have] bitten or bit
blow	[is] blowing	blew	[have] blown
break	[is] breaking	broke	[have] broken
bring	[is] bringing	brought	[have] brought
build	[is] building	built	[have] built
burst	[is] bursting	burst	[have] burst
buy	[is] buying	bought	[have] bought
catch	[is] catching	caught	[have] caught
choose	[is] choosing	chose	[have] chosen
come	[is] coming	came	[have] come
cost	[is] costing	cost	[have] cost
cut	[is] cutting	cut	[have] cut
do	[is] doing	did	[have] done
draw	[is] drawing	drew	[have] drawn
drink	[is] drinking	drank	[have] drunk
drive	[is] driving	drove	[have] driven
eat	[is] eating	ate	[have] eaten
fall	[is] falling	fell	[have] fallen
feel	[is] feeling	felt	[have] felt
fight	[is] fighting	fought	[have] fought
find	[is] finding	found	[have] found
fly	[is] flying	flew	[have] flown
forgive	[is] forgiving	forgave	[have] forgiven
freeze	[is] freezing	froze	[have] frozen
get	[is] getting	got	[have] got or gotten
give	[is] giving	gave	[have] given
go	[is] going	went	[have] gone
grow	[is] growing	grew	[have] grown

(continued)

Relating to Spelling

Point out to students that when they have questions about the principal parts of irregular verbs, they can look up the verbs in a dictionary. Explain that the entry word in a dictionary is the base form and that the past, past participle, and present participle forms are listed following the entry word. For example, if they look up *sing,* they will also find *sang, sung,* and *singing* listed. Ask each student to look up two or three irregular verbs in a dictionary and to compare the principal parts listed in the dictionary with those on the chart in the textbook.

USAGE

Continued on p. 490

Participles as Modifiers. Use the following sentences to illustrate to students that the present participle and past participle forms of many verbs can be used as adjectives to modify nouns or pronouns. Point out that a participle used as a verb must have a helping verb (a form of *be* or *have*).

Verb: Snow is falling outside.
Adjective: The falling snow looks beautiful.
Verb: I have broken a saucer.
Adjective: That broken glass is sharp.

Cooperative Learning

To give students practice using the principal parts of verbs, divide the class into groups of three. Give each group six index cards with the base form of one irregular verb written on each card.

Ask group members to take turns drawing cards. The student who draws the first card will confer with group members to write on the card four sentences—one using each of the four principal parts of that verb. For example, if the card says *eat*, the student might write the following:

1. I eat cereal for breakfast every day.

2. She is eating her lunch.

3. We ate at a new restaurant.

4. I have not eaten any fruit today.

If a group is unsure of a verb form, have the members use a dictionary rather than the charts in their textbooks. Groups should repeat the process until all students have had a turn writing sentences and all cards have been used. Then, have groups exchange their cards with other groups to check for sentence correctness.

TEACHING TIP

Exercise 2 You may want to use the first ten items in **Exercise 2** as guided practice. Then, have students complete the exercise as independent practice.

(continued)

Common Irregular Verbs			
Base Form	Present Participle	Past	Past Participle
have	[is] having	had	[have] had
hear	[is] hearing	heard	[have] heard
hide	[is] hiding	hid	[have] hid *or* hidden
hit	[is] hitting	hit	[have] hit
hold	[is] holding	held	[have] held
know	[is] knowing	knew	[have] known
lead	[is] leading	led	[have] led

Oral Practice 2 Using Irregular Verbs

Read the following sentences aloud, stressing the italicized verbs.

1. Edward's sister *drove* him to the mall this afternoon.
2. My parents *came* to the spelling bee last year.
3. I should have *known* the test would be difficult.
4. He's *going* to Cape Canaveral this summer.
5. Maya has been *chosen* to play on our team.
6. The water pipe *burst* during the ice storm.
7. *Did* you see the northern lights last night?
8. Wyatt *brought* his new computer game to the slumber party at Alexander's house.

Exercise 2 Writing the Past and Past Participle Forms of Irregular Verbs

Write the correct past or past participle form of the italicized verb given before each of the following sentences.

EXAMPLE **1.** *choose* Sara has _____ her song for the piano recital next week.

1. chosen

1. drove

1. *drive* Last summer we _____ to Denver, where we visited the U.S. Mint.

2. began

2. *begin* The concert _____ an hour ago.

MINI-LESSON

Have students work in pairs to write two sentences with each of the following words. As in the models, the word should first be used as a verb and then as an adjective. Have pairs exchange their sentences to check for correctness.

1. beginning
2. fallen
3. lost
4. written

For additional instruction and practice, refer students to **Chapter 14: The Phrase.**

3. *break* Mike Powell ____ the world long-jump record by jumping 29 feet 4½ inches.

4. *blow* The wind has ____ the tent down.

5. *get* We ____ tickets to ride *The Silverton*.

6. *fall* Several people have ____ over that log.

7. *do* Mother ____ her best, and she got a promotion.

8. *drink* According to legend, the Aztec emperor Montezuma ____ chocolate.

9. *build* People in Africa ____ large cities hundreds, even thousands, of years ago.

10. *go* You've never ____ to Puerto Rico, have you?

11. *bite* I think that Roseanne ____ into a green chile!

12. *grow* Well, nephew, you surely have ____!

13. *catch* You look like you just ____ the brass ring!

14. *give* Mom had already ____ us a color copy of her grandmother's journal.

15. *eat* The Japanese have box lunches, too, but they call them *obentos*; we have ____ them several times.

16. *feel* They ____ better after taking a short nap.

17. *cost* Those tickets shouldn't have ____ so much.

18. *buy* Have you ever ____ a Greek sandwich called a *gyro*?

19. *find* My cousin said that she has ____ a new canyon trail.

20. *freeze* The pond ____ last winter, and we went skating.

3. broke

4. blown

5. got

6. fallen

7. did

8. drank

9. built

10. gone

11. bit

12. grown

13. caught

14. given

15. eaten

16. felt

17. cost

18. bought

19. found

20. froze

More Common Irregular Verbs			
Base Form	Present Participle	Past	Past Participle
leave	[is] leaving	left	[have] left
lend	[is] lending	lent	[have] lent
let	[is] letting	let	[have] let
light	[is] lighting	lighted *or* lit	[have] lighted *or* lit
lose	[is] losing	lost	[have] lost
make	[is] making	made	[have] made
meet	[is] meeting	met	[have] met
pay	[is] paying	paid	[have] paid

(continued)

S T Y L E   T I P

Some verbs have two correct past or past participle forms. However, these forms are not always interchangeable.

EXAMPLES

I **shone** the flashlight into the woods. [*Shined* also would be correct in this usage.]

I **shined** my shoes. [*Shone* would be incorrect in this usage.]

If you are unsure about which past participle form to use, check an up-to-date dictionary.

Relating to Writing

To help students improve their writing, explain that they should choose vivid verbs whenever possible. Offer the following sentences as examples of vivid verbs that could be used for *run*.

1. I <u>raced</u> down the street.

2. I <u>dashed</u> down the street.

3. I <u>sprinted</u> down the street.

Have the class work in groups of three to create a class word bank of vivid verbs. Ask each group to choose five common verbs and, using a thesaurus or dictionary, to list interesting synonyms for each verb. Then, have groups compile their lists on a poster or bulletin board to be displayed in the classroom.

To extend the activity or to challenge advanced students, suggest that students explore the shades of meaning of the synonymous verbs. For example, students might write the following definitions for the *run* example above.

1. race—to rush at top speed

2. dash—to move with sudden speed

3. sprint—to run at top speed for a short distance

(continued)

TEACHING TIP

Activity. As students work through the exercises in this chapter, have them make lists of irregular verbs that are problematic for them. For example, students might be unaccustomed to using or hearing *have swum* or *have drunk.* Ask students to take one verb at a time from their lists and to try to incorporate its unfamiliar form into their vocabulary.

Critical Thinking

Metacognition. Ask students to think about the process that works best for them in trying to incorporate a new word or a new usage into their vocabulary. Is writing the word in a number of different sentences the best method? Does speaking it aloud repeatedly work best? Does hearing the word used correctly help? Encourage students to evaluate the effectiveness of their personal strategies and to consider more effective alternatives as needed.

More Common Irregular Verbs

Base Form	Present Participle	Past	Past Participle
put	[is] putting	put	[have] put
read	[is] reading	read	[have] read
ride	[is] riding	rode	[have] ridden
ring	[is] ringing	rang	[have] rung
run	[is] running	ran	[have] run
say	[is] saying	said	[have] said
see	[is] seeing	saw	[have] seen
seek	[is] seeking	sought	[have] sought
sell	[is] selling	sold	[have] sold
send	[is] sending	sent	[have] sent
shrink	[is] shrinking	shrank *or* shrunk	[have] shrunk
sing	[is] singing	sang	[have] sung
sink	[is] sinking	sank *or* sunk	[have] sunk
speak	[is] speaking	spoke	[have] spoken
spend	[is] spending	spent	[have] spent
stand	[is] standing	stood	[have] stood
steal	[is] stealing	stole	[have] stolen
swim	[is] swimming	swam	[have] swum
swing	[is] swinging	swung	[have] swung
take	[is] taking	took	[have] taken
teach	[is] teaching	taught	[have] taught
tear	[is] tearing	tore	[have] torn
tell	[is] telling	told	[have] told
think	[is] thinking	thought	[have] thought
throw	[is] throwing	threw	[have] thrown
wear	[is] wearing	wore	[have] worn
win	[is] winning	won	[have] won
write	[is] writing	wrote	[have] written

Oral Practice 3 Using Irregular Verbs

Read the following sentences aloud, stressing the italicized verbs.

1. When the bell *rang,* we hurried out of the building.
2. The audience was quiet as the acrobats *swung* from the trapeze.
3. That dress had already *shrunk* before I washed it.
4. Otherwise, Lily would have *worn* it to the dance.
5. Have you *met* the new foreign exchange student?
6. We were late to the picnic because I *lost* the map.
7. My father *lent* me the money to buy a new watch.
8. Would you believe that Raymond *took* singing lessons?

Exercise 3 Writing the Past and Past Participle Forms of Irregular Verbs

Write the correct past or past participle form of the italicized verb given before each of the following sentences.

EXAMPLE   **1.** *see*   I have _____ that movie twice already.
           1. *seen*

1. *run*	Michael _____ the 100-meter dash in excellent time.	**1.** ran
2. *sell*	My aunt has _____ more houses than any other real estate agent in the city.	**2.** sold
3. *speak*	The director of the state health department _____ to our class today.	**3.** spoke
4. *win*	The Mexican poet Octavio Paz _____ the Nobel Prize in literature.	**4.** won
5. *write*	I have _____ some poems, but I am shy about showing them to anyone.	**5.** written
6. *ride*	Tamisha's whole family _____ mules to the bottom of the Grand Canyon.	**6.** rode
7. *sing*	At the concert, the group _____ my favorite song.	**7.** sang
8. *throw*	Someone must have _____ this trash from a car.	**8.** thrown
9. *swim*	Within minutes, the two beautiful swans had _____ across the lake.	**9.** swum
10. *sink*	King Arthur's sword Excalibur had _____ slowly to the bottom of the lake.	**10.** sunk
11. *send*	My aunt in South America _____ me a fabulous sweater made from the wool of an alpaca, which is an animal similar to a llama.	**11.** sent

Looking at Language

Explain to students that the English language is constantly changing as meanings, pronunciations, and usages are added or updated. For example, some verbs have alternate past tense forms such as *dived* or *dove, shone* or *shined, rang* or *rung,* and *shrank* or *shrunk.* Ask students to check a dictionary to see how these alternative verb forms are listed.

Crossing the Curriculum

Multidisciplinary. Use this activity to show students that correct verb usage carries over to subjects other than language arts. The activity will also give students additional practice with verb forms.

Divide the class into groups of three or four. Have each group list the subjects they take in school besides language arts. Next, have the groups brainstorm five verbs that could be associated with each of the listed subjects. For example, verbs used in art class might include *feel, make, teach, think,* and *draw.*

Then, ask the groups to write sentences using the past or past participle forms of each of the verbs they listed, such as the following examples:

1. I have never <u>felt</u> such an interesting texture.
2. I have <u>made</u> a beautiful sculpture!
3. Mrs. Alt <u>taught</u> us about the color wheel.
4. I <u>thought</u> about using bright colors.
5. Have you ever <u>drawn</u> with charcoal?

If time permits, have each group read its sentences aloud.

12. told	**12.** *tell*	Mr. Noguchi ____ us that *R.S.V.P.* at the bottom of an invitation means that you should let the host know whether you are coming or not.
13. lent	**13.** *lend*	Before the softball game, my friend Gabriela ____ me her glove.
14. worn	**14.** *wear*	Shouldn't you have ____ a warmer jacket for the hike this morning?
15. swam	**15.** *swim*	Soon-hee, who is training for a triathlon, ____ two miles on Saturday.
16. rung	**16.** *ring*	I have ____ the doorbell several times, but no one has come to the door.
17. lost	**17.** *lose*	The swan living in the pond ____ many large feathers; Tony says it must be molting.
18. taken	**18.** *take*	It has ____ more than four hours to find the last item for the scavenger hunt.
19. sung	**19.** *sing*	Gerald, Annie, and Trish have ____ the national anthem at assembly.
20. said	**20.** *say*	The weather forecast this morning ____ to expect snow flurries.

Review A **Writing the Past and Past Participle Forms of Irregular Verbs**

Write the correct past or past participle form of the italicized verb given before each of the following sentences.

EXAMPLE **1.** *tell*   Has Alameda ____ you about the book *The Indian Tipi: Its History, Construction, and Use*?

     1. told

1. *write*   Reginald and Gladys Laubin ____ that book and others about American Indian culture.   **1.** wrote

2. *build*   The Laubins ____ their own tepee.   **2.** built

3. *stand*   Tepees of various sizes once ____ all across the Great Plains.   **3.** stood

4. *see*   I have ____ pictures of camps full of beautifully decorated tepees.   **4.** seen

5. *make*   For many years, American Indians have ____ tepees out of cloth rather than buffalo hides.   **5.** made

6. *come*   The word *tepee,* or *tipi,* has ____ into English from the Sioux language.   **6.** come

7. *draw* On the outside of their tepees, the Sioux and Cheyenne peoples ____ designs like the ones shown on the previous page.   **7.** drew

8. *take* Because the Plains Indians followed animal herds, they needed shelter that could be easily ____ from place to place.   **8.** taken

9. *know* Even before reading the book, I ____ that the inside of a tepee cover was rarely painted.   **9.** knew

10. *do* Traditionally, women ____ all the work of making tepees and putting them up.   **10.** did

Review B   **Writing the Past and Past Participle Forms of Irregular Verbs**

Write the correct past or past participle form of the italicized verb given before each of the following sentences.

EXAMPLE   **1.** *write*   I ____ a report on Jim Thorpe.

   1. wrote

1. *blow* Yesterday the wind ____ the leaves into our yard.   **1.** blew

2. *break* My pen pal from Australia has never ____ his promise to write once a week.   **2.** broken

3. *bring* I ____ the wrong book to class.   **3.** brought

4. *burst* The children almost ____ with excitement.   **4.** burst

5. *choose* The director ____ James Earl Jones for the role.   **5.** chose

6. *come* My aunt and her friend ____ to dinner last night.   **6.** came

7. *do* I have always ____ my homework right after supper.   **7.** done

8. *drink* The guests ____ four quarts of fruit punch.   **8.** drank

9. *fall* One of Julian's Russian nesting dolls has ____ off the shelf.   **9.** fallen

10. *freeze* Has the pond ____ yet?   **10.** frozen

11. *go* We have never ____ to see the Parthenon in Nashville.   **11.** gone

12. *know* Had I ____, I would have called you sooner.   **12.** known

13. *ring* Suddenly the fire alarm ____.   **13.** rang

14. *run* Joan Samuelson certainly ____ a good race.   **14.** ran

15. *see* I ____ you in line at the movies.   **15.** saw

16. *shrink* The apples we dried in the sun have ____.   **16.** shrunk

17. *speak* After we had ____ to George Takei, who played Mr. Sulu, we went to the *Star Trek* convention banquet.   **17.** spoken

18. *swim* We ____ out to the float and back.   **18.** swam

Principal Parts of Verbs   **495**

19. written
20. thrown

19. *write* She has _____ me several long letters.
20. *throw* You shouldn't have _____ the ball to second base.

Tense

Rules 18d, e *(pp. 496–499)*

OBJECTIVE

■ To revise a paragraph to make the tenses of verbs consistent

MULTIPLE INTELLIGENCES

Musical Intelligence. Because students with musical intelligence often enjoy speaking and hearing rhythm, you may want to have students conjugate selected verbs to a musical beat. Suggest that they first practice with the conjugation of the verb *see* on p. 497. Then, have them choose other irregular verbs to conjugate.

Tense

18d. The *tense* of a verb indicates the time of the action or of the state of being that is expressed by the verb.

EXAMPLES   Yesterday, Denise **served** lox and bagels for breakfast.

Randy **has played** bass guitar for the band, but now he **plays** drums.

Once they **have painted** the signs, Jill and Cody **will finish** the decorations for the dance.

Verbs in English have six tenses.

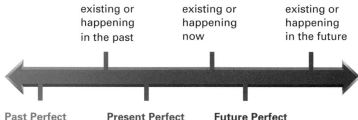

Present	Past	Future
Present Perfect	Past Perfect	Future Perfect

The following time line shows the relationship between the six tenses.

Past
existing or
happening
in the past

Present
existing or
happening
now

Future
existing or
happening
in the future

Past Perfect
existing or
happening
before a
specific time
in the past

Present Perfect
existing or
happening
sometime
before now;
may be
continuing now

Future Perfect
existing or
happening
before a
specific time
in the future

Listing the different forms of a verb is called *conjugating* the verb.

496 Chapter 18   Using Verbs Correctly

RESOURCES

Tense

Practice

■ *Grammar, Usage, and Mechanics,* pp. 176, 177
■ *Language Workshop CD-ROM,* Lesson 15

Conjugation of the Verb *See*	
Present Tense	
Singular	**Plural**
I see	we see
you see	you see
he, she, *or* it sees	they see
Past Tense	
Singular	**Plural**
I saw	we saw
you saw	you saw
he, she, *or* it saw	they saw
Future Tense	
Singular	**Plural**
I will (shall) see	we will (shall) see
you will (shall) see	you will (shall) see
he, she, *or* it will (shall) see	they will (shall) see
Present Perfect Tense	
Singular	**Plural**
I have seen	we have seen
you have seen	you have seen
he, she, *or* it has seen	they have seen
Past Perfect Tense	
Singular	**Plural**
I had seen	we had seen
you had seen	you had seen
he, she, *or* it had seen	they had seen
Future Perfect Tense	
Singular	**Plural**
I will (shall) have seen	we will (shall) have seen
you will (shall) have seen	you will (shall) have seen
he, she, *or* it will (shall) have seen	they will (shall) have seen

STYLE TIP

Traditionally, the helping verbs *shall* and *will* were used to mean different things. Now, however, *shall* can be used almost interchangeably with *will*.

Meeting INDIVIDUAL NEEDS

ENGLISH-LANGUAGE LEARNERS

General Strategies. Some languages do not use verb tenses to indicate time. The idea of specifying tense repeatedly in every sentence might seem redundant to some students; therefore, they might use only the present tense. Emphasize that in English the appropriate tense must be used in every sentence.

Spanish. Spanish speakers face a number of difficulties when attempting to master conjugating verbs in English.

- Spanish makes a distinction between the past that is habitual or ongoing (imperfect tense) and the past that is completed (preterite tense).

- Spanish frequently uses the subjunctive mood.

- Spanish verb tenses usually have a different form for each combination of person and number.

- Two different verbs (*ser* and *estar*) split both the meanings and the duties of the English verb *be*.

Challenge your English-language learners to learn the listed English conjugations perfectly, encouraging them to look for patterns that will make the task easier.

USAGE

Tense **497**

Relating to Literature

If the A. B. Guthrie story "Bargain" is in your literature textbook, have students read it. Explain to students that the character Mr. Baumer sometimes simplifies his verb tenses and omits words that are grammatically necessary. Ask students why they think the author chose to have Baumer speak in this manner. [*Baumer emigrated from a foreign country, so his speech includes nonstandard English. Writers often use nonstandard English to make dialogue sound natural—to reflect the speech patterns of real people.*]

Exercise 4 Making Tenses of Verbs Consistent

ANSWERS

Students can choose either present or past tense, but they must be consistent throughout their paragraphs. Verbs in direct quotations and in statements of general truth (an example of which is *what lightning is* in sentence 6) should not be changed. In the following answers, the present tense is given first and the past tense is in parentheses.

┌HELP─

The progressive form is not a separate tense but an additional form of each of the six tenses.

┌HELP─

When you rewrite Exercise 4, either tense is correct, as long as you are consistent.

NOTE Each tense has an additional form called the *progressive form,* which expresses continuing action or state of being. In each tense, the progressive form of a verb consists of the appropriate tense of *be* plus the verb's present participle.

Present Progressive	am, is, are seeing
Past Progressive	was, were seeing
Future Progressive	will (shall) be seeing
Present Perfect Progressive	has been seeing, have been seeing
Past Perfect Progressive	had been seeing
Future Perfect Progressive	will (shall) have been seeing

Consistency of Tense

18e. Do not change needlessly from one tense to another.

When writing about events that take place at the same time, use verbs that are in the same tense. When writing about events that occur at different times, use verbs that are in the different tenses.

INCONSISTENT   When we go to the movies, we bought some popcorn. [The events occur at the same time, but *go* is in the present tense and *bought* is in the past tense.]

CONSISTENT   When we **go** to the movies, we **buy** some popcorn. [Both *go* and *buy* are in the present tense.]

CONSISTENT   When we **went** to the movies, we **bought** some popcorn. [Both *went* and *bought* are in the past tense.]

Exercise 4 Making Tenses of Verbs Consistent

Read the following sentences, and choose whether to rewrite them in the present or past tense. Then, rewrite the sentences, changing the verb forms to correct any needless changes.

EXAMPLE   [1] I picked up the telephone receiver quickly, but the line is still dead.

1. *I picked up the telephone receiver quickly, but the line was still dead.*

or

I pick up the telephone receiver quickly, but the line is still dead.

[**1**] Lightning struck our house, and I run straight for cover. [**2**] "Oh, no!" I exclaim. [**3**] The electricity was out! [**4**] My parents get out the flashlights, and we played a game. [**5**] Later, since the stove, oven, and microwave didn't work without electricity, we have a cold supper in the living room—picnic style! [**6**] My younger brother asks me what lightning is. [**7**] "Lightning is a big spark of electricity from a thundercloud," I tell him. [**8**] He nods. [**9**] I started to tell him about positive and negative charges creating lightning, but he doesn't understand what I'm talking about and walks away. [**10**] In the morning, we were all glad when the sun shone and our electricity is on again.

Active and Passive Voice

A verb in the ***active voice*** expresses an action done *by* its subject. A verb in the ***passive voice*** expresses an action done *to* its subject. In passive voice, the verb phrase always includes a form of *be* and the past participle of the main verb. Other helping verbs may also be included. Compare the following sentences:

ACTIVE VOICE	The pilot **instructed** us. [The subject, *pilot,* performs the action.]
PASSIVE VOICE	We **were instructed** by the pilot. [The subject, *we,* receives the action.]
ACTIVE VOICE	Alice **caught** a fly ball. [The subject, *Alice,* performs the action.]
PASSIVE VOICE	A fly ball **was caught** by Alice. [The subject, *ball,* receives the action.]
ACTIVE VOICE	The firefighters **have put** out the blaze. [The subject, *firefighters,* performs the action.]
PASSIVE VOICE	The blaze **has been put** out by the firefighters. [The subject, *blaze,* receives the action.]

Exercise 5 **Identifying Active and Passive Voice**

Tell whether the verb is in the *active voice* or *passive voice* in each of the following sentences.

EXAMPLE **1.** The 10K race was won by Mikki.
  1. passive voice

Reference Note

For more about **helping verbs,** see page 361.

STYLE	TIP

In general, you should avoid using the passive voice because it can make your writing sound weak and awkward. Using the active voice helps make your writing direct and forceful.

PASSIVE VOICE
  A no-hitter **was pitched** by Valerie, and the game **was won** by her team.

ACTIVE VOICE
  Valerie **pitched** a no-hitter, and her team **won** the game.

RESOURCES

Active and Passive Voice
Practice

- *Grammar, Usage, and Mechanics,* p. 178

USAGE

Exercise 4 **Making Tenses of Verbs Consistent**

ANSWERS continued

1. strikes, run (struck, ran)
2. exclaim (exclaimed)
3. is (was)
4. get, play (got, played)
5. do work, have (did work, had)
6. asks (asked)
7. tell (told)
8. nods (nodded)
9. start, does, am talking, walks (started, did, was talking, walked)
10. are, shines, is (were, shone or shined, was)

Active and Passive Voice

(pp. 499–500)

OBJECTIVE

- **To identify active voice and passive voice in sentences**

Exercise 5

ALTERNATIVE LESSON
Have students identify the prepositional phrases in sentence 5 [*of the yearbook photos, by Adrienne*]. Point out that if students follow the directions found in the **Style Tip** on p. 499, the object of the preposition in *by Adrienne* becomes the subject in the revised sentence, and the subject *many* becomes the direct object in the revised sentence. [*Adrienne took many of the yearbook photos.*]

1. active	**1.** On Sunday afternoon we painted the den.
2. passive	**2.** Brianne was elected to the student council.
3. passive	**3.** The CD has been misplaced by my cousin.
4. active	**4.** The new animation software creates vivid images.
5. passive	**5.** Many of the yearbook photos were taken by Adrienne.
6. passive	**6.** Shoddy work was done on the building.
7. active	**7.** Mike and I don't understand this algebra problem.
8. active	**8.** I am unloading the food and supplies at the campsite.
9. passive	**9.** The tickets had been sold months before the concert.
10. passive	**10.** Andre was awarded the certificate for his service to the community.

Six Troublesome Verbs

(pp. 500–506)

OBJECTIVES

- To read aloud sentences containing six troublesome verbs

- To supply the correct forms of *sit* or *set* to complete sentences

- To choose the correct forms of *rise* or *raise* in sentences

- To choose the correct forms of *lie* or *lay* in sentences

Meeting
INDIVIDUAL
NEEDS

MODALITIES

Kinesthetic Learners. Acting out the verbs might help students to differentiate between the troublesome verb pairs presented in this lesson. Have students work in pairs to act out the following sentences. Point out to students that the second verb in each pair requires a direct object that receives the action.

1. I <u>sit</u> in the chair.

2. I <u>set</u> the book on the table.

3. I <u>rise</u> from my chair.

4. I <u>raise</u> this book in the air.

5. I <u>lie</u> on the floor.

6. I <u>lay</u> this pencil on the desk.

STYLE	TIP

You may know that the word *set* has more meanings than the two given here. Check in a dictionary to see if the meaning you intend requires an object.

EXAMPLE
The sun **sets** in the West. [Here, *sets* does not take an object.]

Six Troublesome Verbs

Sit and *Set*

The verb *sit* means "to be seated" or "to rest." *Sit* seldom takes an object. The verb *set* usually means "to place (something somewhere)" or "to put (something somewhere)." *Set* usually takes an object. Notice that *set* has the same form for the base form, past, and past participle.

Base Form	Present Participle	Past	Past Participle
sit	[is] sitting	sat	[have] sat
set	[is] setting	set	[have] set

EXAMPLES

Who **is sitting** on the blanket by the pool? [no object]
Theresa **is setting** the lawn chairs by the pool. [Theresa is setting what? *Chairs* is the object.]

Three boys **sat** on the platform. [no object]
The boys **set** the instruments on the platform. [The boys set what? *Instruments* is the object.]

We **had sat** on the pier for an hour before Suzanne arrived with the bait. [no object]
I **had set** the bucket of bait on the pier. [I had set what? *Bucket* is the object.]

RESOURCES

Six Troublesome Verbs
Practice

- *Grammar, Usage, and Mechanics*, pp. 179, 180, 181, 182
- *Language Workshop CD-ROM*, Lesson 16

Oral Practice 4 — Using the Forms of *Sit* and *Set* Correctly

Read each of the following sentences aloud, stressing the italicized verbs.

1. Darnell and I *sat* down to play a game of chess.
2. After we had been *sitting* for a while, he decided to make bread.
3. I *set* the pan on the table.
4. After Darnell had *set* out the ingredients, he mixed them.
5. We returned to our game but could not *sit* still for long.
6. We had not *set* the pan in the oven.
7. Then, we almost *sat* too long.
8. If it had *sat* in the oven much longer, it would have burned.

Exercise 6 — Writing the Forms of *Sit* and *Set* Correctly

Write the correct form of *sit* or *set* for each blank in the following sentences.

EXAMPLE 1. I _____ my suitcase on the rack.
         1. *set*

1. On the train to Boston, I _____ next to a woman wearing a shawl.
2. She _____ a large covered basket on the floor by her feet.
3. When the conductor asked her if she would like to _____ it in the baggage rack, she refused.
4. She insisted that the basket must _____ by her feet.
5. As I _____ beside her, I wondered what was in the basket.
6. I _____ my book down and tried to see inside the tightly woven basket.
7. Perhaps I was _____ next to a woman with a picnic lunch.
8. Maybe she had _____ next to me because I looked hungry.
9. As the woman _____ her packages down, I watched the basket.
10. A sudden movement of the train caused the basket to open, and inside it _____ a small, white rabbit.

1. sat
2. set
3. set
4. sit
5. sat
6. set
7. sitting
8. sat
9. set
10. sat

Rise and *Raise*

The verb *rise* means "to move upward" or "to go up." *Rise* does not take an object. The verb *raise* means "to lift (something) up." *Raise* usually takes an object.

Meeting INDIVIDUAL NEEDS

ENGLISH-LANGUAGE LEARNERS
General Strategies. Some English-language learners will use the troublesome verbs incorrectly because spoken, casual English is not as precise as formal, written English. Students may therefore think that standard usage sounds incorrect. You could emphasize that writers use standard English because it is clear, and speakers can use either formal or informal English depending on the audience.

TEACHING TIP

Mnemonics. Place students in groups of four to create short poems that will help them remember the correct usage of the six troublesome verbs. An example follows:

> The bread has <u>risen</u>,
> And it's time to bake it.
> I <u>raised</u> my hand
> And asked to taste it.

Encourage students to recite their poems or to put them on posters.

USAGE

MINI-LESSON

Continued on p. 502

Direct Objects. You may want to review direct objects with students since one verb in each troublesome verb pair usually takes a direct object. Explain to students that a direct object is a noun or pronoun that receives the action of the verb; a direct object is never in a prepositional phrase. Write the following sentences on the chalkboard or on a transparency. Bracket the prepositional phrases, and circle the direct objects. Point out to students that remembering which verb in each pair takes a direct object will help them with

Meeting INDIVIDUAL NEEDS

ENGLISH-LANGUAGE LEARNERS

General Strategies. The vowel sounds in the six verbs in this section sound rather similar—especially to students who speak languages other than English. This similarity can cause confusion for students whose languages do not have these sounds. You could pronounce the words for any students who have difficulty, and students could write down these words to help with memorization. Be sure to emphasize the vowel sounds.

LEARNERS HAVING DIFFICULTY

Have each student choose two television shows to view and analyze. Tell each student to watch one scene and to write down the verbs that one of the characters uses. Students should then repeat this process with another scene and character. Have students use the following questions as the basis for a summary of their findings.

1. Were the characters' verb choices standard or nonstandard?

2. Are these characters appealing? If so, why?

3. Describe the scenes in which these verbs were used.

4. Is there a connection between each scene and the choice of language?

| S T Y L E | T I P |

You may know that the verb *raise* has more meanings than the one given here.

EXAMPLE
The Nelsons **raise** geese.
[*Raise* does not mean "lift up" here, but it still takes an object.]

Base Form	Present Participle	Past	Past Participle
rise	[is] rising	rose	[have] risen
raise	[is] raising	raised	[have] raised

EXAMPLES   The fans **were rising** to sing the national anthem. [no object]

Fans **were raising** signs and banners. [Fans were raising what? *Signs* and *banners* are the objects.]

The student **rose** to ask a question. [no object]
The student **raised** a good question. [The student raised what? *Question* is the object.]

Prices **had risen.** [no object]
The store **had raised** prices. [The store had raised what? *Prices* is the object.]

Oral Practice 5 Using Forms of *Rise* and *Raise* Correctly

Read the following sentences aloud, stressing the italicized verbs.

1. Mount Everest *rises* over 29,000 feet.
2. He *raises* the flag at sunrise.
3. The TV reporter *raised* her voice to be heard.
4. She *rose* from her seat and looked out the window.
5. The constellation Orion had not yet *risen* in the southern sky.
6. They had *raised* the piñata high in the tree.
7. I hope the bread is *rising*.
8. He will be *raising* the bucket from the well.

Exercise 7 Identifying the Correct Forms of *Rise* and *Raise*

Identify the correct verb of the two given in parentheses in each of the following sentences.

EXAMPLE   1. After the storm, Diana (*rose, raised*) the window.
   1. *raised*

1. The entire audience quickly (*rose*, *raised*) to their feet to sing the "Hallelujah Chorus."

MINI-LESSON

correct verb usage. For additional information and practice, refer students to **Chapter 13: Complements.**

1. The tourists <u>sat</u> [on benches].

2. We <u>set</u> the (dishes) [on the table].

3. The full moon <u>rose</u> [through the clouds].

4. The cheering crowd <u>raised</u> (banners).

5. The deer <u>lay</u> very still.

6. The senator <u>laid</u> her (notes) aside.

2. They used a jack to (*rise*, *raise*) the car so that they could change the tire.

3. The fire juggler is (*rising*, *raising*) two flaming batons over his head to signal the start of the show.

4. Some people have trouble remembering that the sun always (*rises*, *raises*) in the east.

5. He gently (*rose*, *raised*) the injured duckling from the lake.

6. Only half of Mauna Kea, a volcano on the island of Hawaii, (*rises*, *raises*) above the ocean.

7. The proud winner has (*risen*, *raised*) her trophy so that everyone can see it.

8. The guests have (*risen*, *raised*) from their seats to see the bride enter.

9. Yeast makes the dough for pizza and other baked goods, such as bread and rolls, (*rise*, *raise*).

10. They will (*rise*, *raise*) the couch while I look under it.

Lie and *Lay*

The verb *lie* generally means "to recline," "to be in a place," or "to remain lying down." *Lie* does not take an object. The verb *lay* generally means "to put (something) down" or "to place (something somewhere)." *Lay* usually takes an object.

Base Form	Present Participle	Past	Past Participle
lie	[is] lying	lay	[have] lain
lay	[is] laying	laid	[have] laid

EXAMPLES

The silverware **is lying** on the table. [no object]
The waiter **is laying** silverware beside each plate.
[The waiter is laying what? *Silverware* is the object.]

The apple dolls **lay** drying in the sun. [no object]
Aunt Martha **laid** her apple dolls in the sun to dry. [Aunt Martha laid what? *Dolls* is the object.]

That bicycle **had lain** in the driveway for a week.
[no object]
Bill **had laid** that bicycle in the driveway. [Bill had laid what? *Bicycle* is the object.]

| STYLE   TIP |

The verb *lie* can also mean "to tell an untruth." Used in this way, *lie* still does not take an object.

EXAMPLE
Don't **lie** to her, Beth.

The past and past participle forms of this meaning of *lie* are *lied* and [have] *lied*.

TEACHING TIP

Activity. You may want to make the following tic-tac-toe game available to pairs of students who complete assignments early or who need extra practice with troublesome verbs. To make the game, you will need nine one-inch squares of paper. On the front of five of the squares, write *lie, sit, rose, lain,* and *lay;* on the back of each of the squares, write *needs no object.* On the front of the remaining four squares, write *lay, set, raised,* and *laid;* on the back of each of these squares, write *needs an object.* Make a game board by dividing a nine-by-nine inch paper into one-inch squares.

To play the game, one student draws a square, reads the verb, and uses it in a sentence according to the description on the back of the square. If the sentence is correct, the player puts the square anywhere on the board, verb side down. If the sentence is wrong, the player returns the square to the pile. Then, the second player takes a turn. The winner is the first to get three *needs no object* cards or three *needs an object* cards in a row in any direction.

 Learning for Life

Continued on pp. 504–505

Telling a Story. Students will probably encounter times when they will be asked to describe a firsthand experience—to give an eyewitness report. For example, a friend might have missed the end of last night's game and wants to hear all about it or a parent might ask how the vase in the living room *really* broke.

For this activity, tell students to imagine that they are reporters for the *Good News Gazette,* a local newspaper that reports on positive happenings. Their assignment is to

Oral Practice 6 Using Forms of *Lie* and *Lay* Correctly

Read the following sentences aloud, stressing the italicized verbs.

1. If you are tired, *lie* down for a while.
2. *Lay* your pencils down, please.
3. Two huge dogs *lay* by the fire last night.
4. The cat has been *lying* on the new bedspread.
5. Mr. Cortez *laid* the map of Puerto Rico on the table.
6. In our state, snow usually *lies* on the ground until late March or the first weeks of April.
7. He had *laid* your coats on the bed in my room.
8. After the baby had *lain* down for a nap, she still wanted to play with her new toy.

COMPUTER TIP

Most word processors can help you check your writing to be sure that you've used verbs correctly. For example, a spellchecker will highlight misspelled verb forms such as *attackted* or *drownded*.

Grammar-checking software can point out inconsistent verb tense, and it may also highlight questionable uses of problem verb pairs such as *lie* and *lay* or *rise* and *raise*. Some programs can also identify verbs in the passive voice.

Remember, though, that the computer is just a tool. As a writer, you are responsible for making all the style and content choices that affect your writing.

Exercise 8 Identifying the Correct Forms of *Lie* and *Lay*

Identify the correct verb of the two in parentheses for each of the following sentences.

EXAMPLE 1. Marc (*lay, laid*) his new tennis shoes on the floor.
       1. laid

1. The islands of American Samoa (*lie, lay*) about 4,800 miles southwest of San Francisco.
2. Dad quickly (*lay, laid*) the hermit crab down when it began to pinch him.
3. I don't know where I have (*lain, laid*) my copy of *Chinese Proverbs* by Ruthanne Lum McCunn.
4. I have often (*lain, laid*) under the oak tree and napped.
5. Many visitors (*lie, lay*) flowers and wreaths at the Vietnam Veterans Memorial in Washington, D.C.
6. My brother, who is sick, has been (*lying, laying*) in bed all day.
7. The clerk (*lay, laid*) the small package on the scale.
8. (*Lie, Lay*) your backpack down, and come see the new comic books I bought yesterday.
9. Those clothes will (*lie, lay*) on the floor until you pick them up.
10. After he had circled several times, the puppy (*lay, laid*) down and slept.

Learning for Life

write a brief eyewitness report about a true or imagined good-news event in their school or neighborhood. Because proper sequence is necessary in the accurate retelling of an event, tell students to be particularly careful in their choice of tense

and the use of verb forms.

You may want to share the following model with students.

Dog Returns Home
After several days of wandering, Zelda finally found her way back home early this

Review C **Identifying the Correct Forms of *Sit* and *Set*, *Rise* and *Raise*, and *Lie* and *Lay***

Identify the <u>correct verb</u> of the two given in parentheses in each of the following sentences.

EXAMPLE   1. The bricklayer (*rose, raised*) from the patio floor and dusted himself off.

          1. *rose*

1. These rocks have (*<u>lain</u>, laid*) here for centuries.
2. Please (*<u>sit</u>, set*) there until your name is called.
3. The nurse (*lay, <u>laid</u>*) her cool hand on the sick child's brow and decided to take his temperature.
4. The horses are (*<u>lying</u>, laying*) in the pasture.
5. The senator and her advisors had (*<u>sat</u>, set*) around the huge conference table.
6. After the picnic, everyone (*<u>lay</u>, laid*) on blankets to rest in the shade of the oak tree.
7. Smoke (*<u>rose</u>, raised*) from the chimney.
8. The farmhands (*sat, <u>set</u>*) their lunch boxes under a tree to keep them cool.
9. Have you been (*<u>sitting</u>, setting*) there all afternoon?
10. The sun has already (*<u>risen</u>, raised*).
11. Why has the stage manager (*rose, <u>raised</u>*) the curtains before the second act has begun?
12. A gust of hot air caused the enormous balloon to (*<u>rise</u>, raise*) out of sight of the spectators.
13. Be sure to (*lie, <u>lay</u>*) these windowpanes down carefully.
14. When the queen enters, each guest should (*<u>rise</u>, raise*) from his or her chair.
15. Who (*sat, <u>set</u>*) the glasses on my chair?
16. "(*<u>Lie</u>, Lay*) down!" the trainer sharply ordered the puppy, but the puppy didn't obey him.
17. If we had a pulley, we could (*rise, <u>raise</u>*) that stone.
18. Just (*sit, <u>set</u>*) those green beans by the sink; I'll get to them in a minute.
19. Mom and Aunt Opal must have been (*lying, <u>laying</u>*) tile in the kitchen all night.
20. You (*rise, <u>raise</u>*) the garage door, and I'll bring the bikes in out of the rain.

TEACHING TIP

Review C You may want to use the first ten items in **Review C** as guided practice. Then, have students complete the exercise as independent practice.

Meeting
INDIVIDUAL
NEEDS

ADVANCED LEARNERS
You may want to have students develop rules for using additional verb pairs that frequently cause problems, such as *learn/teach* and *leave/let*. Ask students to write explanations of each of the verbs and to include sentences as examples of the correct usage. Then, have the students present the material to the rest of the class.

USAGE

morning. Sporting muddy fur and several small scratches, Zelda was sitting on her family's doorstep when they awoke. Her family, the Murrays of 2601 Bowman Drive, had been frantic ever since Monday morning, when they discovered her missing.

Everyone, Zelda included, seems happy to be reunited.

As a publication option, students can compile their own class newspaper. Volunteers can also read aloud their features.

TEACHING TIP

Activity. Have students work in pairs to use the troublesome verbs in original cartoon strips. One person in each pair could be the illustrator, while the other partner could write the dialogue. These comic strips could be displayed on a bulletin board as a reminder of the correct usage of the troublesome verbs.

Review D Proofreading Sentences for Correct Verb Forms

Most of the following sentences contain ~~incorrect verb forms~~. If a sentence contains the wrong form of a verb, write the correct form. If a sentence is already correct, write *C*.

EXAMPLE   1. During the 1800s, many German settlers choosed to live in the Hill Country of central Texas.
   1. *chose*

1. built   1. These hardy, determined pioneers ~~builded~~ towns and cleared land for farming.

2. gone   2. I have ~~went~~ to the town of Fredericksburg several times with my family.

3. lies   3. This interesting town ~~lays~~ about 80 miles west of Austin.

4. used   4. Fredericksburg ~~use~~ to be in Comanche territory.

5. C   5. Early on, German settlers made peace with neighboring Comanche chiefs.

6. grew   6. The town then ~~growed~~ rapidly.

7. German-style churches, public buildings, and houses like the

7. rose   one shown here ~~raised~~ along the town's central street.

8. sat   8. On one of our visits, my family ~~set~~ and talked about the town with a woman who had been born there.

9. spoken   9. She said that she had ~~spoke~~ German all her life.

10. C   10. When we left, she raised a hand and said, *"Auf Wiedersehen"* (until we meet again).

Chapter Review

A. Using Irregular Verbs

Write the correct past or past participle form of the italicized irregular verb provided before each sentence.

1. broke	**1.** *break*	The thunder ____ the silence.
2. rang	**2.** *ring*	Who ____ the fire alarm so quickly?
3. shrunk	**3.** *shrink*	Either my jeans have ____ or I've put on weight.
4. thrown	**4.** *throw*	You've ____ the ball out of bounds!
5. led	**5.** *lead*	Julio ____ the parade last year, so now it's my turn.
6. rose	**6.** *rise*	The sun ____ over the pyramids of Giza in Egypt.
7. swum	**7.** *swim*	We have ____ only three laps.
8. chosen	**8.** *choose*	Vera was ____ as captain of the volleyball team.
9. gone	**9.** *go*	I have ____ to visit the Grand Canyon twice.
10. sat	**10.** *sit*	The tiny tree frog ____ motionless.
11. written	**11.** *write*	Joan has ____ a story about aliens from the Andromeda galaxy.
12. did	**12.** *do*	During lunch, Jorge ____ his impersonation of Rubén Blades.
13. stole	**13.** *steal*	Three runners ____ bases during the first inning.
14. broken	**14.** *break*	This summer's heat wave has ____ all records.
15. drunk	**15.** *drink*	Have you ____ all of the tomato juice?
16. sunk	**16.** *sink*	The log had slowly ____ into the quicksand.
17. lain	**17.** *lie*	The old postcards have ____ in the box for years.
18. driven	**18.** *drive*	Have you ever ____ across the state of Texas?
19. began	**19.** *begin*	Our local PBS station ____ its fund-raising drive.
20. set	**20.** *set*	Have you ____ the paper plates and napkins on the picnic table?
21. threw	**21.** *throw*	Who ____ the ball to first base?
22. known	**22.** *know*	I have ____ some of my classmates for six years.
23. took	**23.** *take*	Kadeem ____ the role of Frederick Douglass.
24. tore	**24.** *tear*	My mother ____ the tag off the mattress.
25. came	**25.** *come*	We ____ close to winning the tournament.

Chapter Review **507**

Using the Chapter Review

To assess student progress, you may want to compare the types of items missed on the **Diagnostic Preview** to those missed on the **Chapter Review**. If students have not made significant progress, you may want to refer them to **Exercises 14–17** in **Chapter 26: Correcting Common Errors** for additional practice.

USAGE

B. Changing Tenses of Verbs

Rewrite each of the following sentences to change the verb or verbs to the tense indicated in *italics*.

26. has come/has brought

26. *present perfect*   Every time Roger ~~comes~~ to visit me, he ~~brings~~ his dog Zip with him.

27. had slept

27. *past perfect*   The dog ~~will sleep~~ on the kitchen floor for the entire visit.

28. moves/hears

28. *present*   Zip ~~moved~~ only if he ~~heard~~ the sounds of food being prepared.

29. will have

29. *future perfect*   Zip ~~has~~ broken all records for a dog not moving a muscle.

30. knew/grew

30. *past*   We ~~had known~~ Zip before he ~~had grown~~ old.

C. Making Verb Tenses Consistent

Read the following sentences, and choose whether to rewrite them in the present or past tense. Then, rewrite the sentences, changing the verb forms to make the verb tense consistent.

31. comes/drives *or* came/drove

31. My uncle ~~comes~~ back to Michigan for Christmas, and he ~~drove~~ his vintage sports car.

32. finishes/forgets *or* finished/forgot

32. Ava ~~finished~~ her assignment, but she ~~forgets~~ to put a title page on it.

33. drop/climbs *or* dropped/climbed

33. The stages of the booster rocket ~~dropped~~ away as the space shuttle ~~climbs~~ into the sky.

34. jumps/cheers/ makes *or* jumped/ cheered/made

34. Aunt Maureen ~~jumped~~ to her feet and ~~cheers~~ when Mia ~~made~~ the winning basket.

35. presents/are *or* presented/were

35. When Barbara ~~presents~~ her science fair project, all the judges ~~were~~ very impressed.

D. Identifying Active and Passive Voice

Tell whether the italicized verb is in the *active voice* or the *passive voice* in each of the following sentences.

36. passive

36. The grass clippings and the kitchen scraps *were placed* on the compost pile.

37. active

37. Most of the class *had* already *gone* to see that movie.

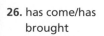

RESOURCES

Using Verbs Correctly

Review

■ *Grammar, Usage, and Mechanics,* pp. 183, 184, 185, 186, 187

Assessment

■ *Assessment Package*
  —*Chapter Tests,* Ch. 18
  —*Chapter Tests in Standardized Test Formats,* Ch. 18
■ *Test Generator (One-Stop Planner CD-ROM)*

38. All of the pencils *were sharpened* by Erica and Austin before the test began.

39. My father *was asked* for his advice on repairing the old playground equipment.

40. Every Friday night the Lopez family *invites* us to their house for dinner.

38. passive

39. passive

40. active

Writing Application
Using Verbs in a Story

Verb Forms and Tenses   A local writers' club is sponsoring a contest for the best "cliffhanger" opening of an adventure story. Write an exciting paragraph to enter in the contest. Your paragraph should leave readers wondering, "What happens next?" In your paragraph, use at least five verbs from the lists of Common Irregular Verbs in this chapter.

Prewriting   First, you will need to imagine a suspenseful situation to describe. Jot down several ideas for your story opening. Then, choose the one you like best. With that situation in mind, scan the lists of irregular verbs. Note at least ten verbs you can use. Include some lively action verbs like *burst*, *swing*, and *throw*.

Writing   As you write your rough draft, think of your readers. Choose words that create a suspenseful, believable scene. Remember that you have only one paragraph to catch your readers' interest.

Revising   Ask a friend to read your paragraph. Does your friend find it interesting? Can he or she picture the scene clearly? If not, you may want to add, delete, or revise some details.

Publishing   Check your spelling, usage, punctuation, and grammar. Check to make sure the forms of verbs are correct and the tenses are consistent. You may want to exchange your cliffhanger with a partner, and complete each other's stories. With your teacher's permission, you can then read the completed stories aloud to the class.

Writing Application
(p. 509)

OBJECTIVE
■ **To write an exciting paragraph to serve as the cliffhanger opening of an adventure story**

Writing Application

Tip. Review short stories that students have read from the literature textbook to give students some examples and ideas for story openers. Tell students to visualize their scenes before they begin writing to help them think of descriptive words.

Scoring Rubric. While you will want to pay particular attention to students' use of regular and irregular verbs, tense, and voice, you will also want to evaluate overall writing performance. You may want to give a split score to indicate development and clarity of the composition as well as usage skills.

Critical Thinking

Synthesis. To help students use irregular verbs in their assignments, have them choose which words they think they will use. Then, tell each student to write three sentences with each verb and to use a different tense for each sentence. Next, explain that these sentences can be used as prewriting and may be included in the paragraphs.

USAGE

RESOURCES

Writing Application
Extension
■ *Grammar, Usage, and Mechanics*, p. 190
■ *Language Workshop CD-ROM*, Lessons 14–16

CHAPTER

19 Using Pronouns Correctly

Nominative and Objective Case Forms

PREVIEWING THE CHAPTER

- This chapter concentrates on the specific uses of the nominative and objective cases of personal pronouns. Also included are lessons on three special pronoun problems: the use of *who* and *whom,* the use of pronouns with appositives, and the use of reflexive pronouns.

- The chapter closes with a **Chapter Review,** which includes a **Writing Application** feature that asks students to write a letter to the manager of a radio station, using a variety of pronouns in the nominative and objective cases.

- For help integrating the chapter with writing chapters, use the **Teaching Strands** chart on pp. T311A–T311B.

USING THE DIAGNOSTIC PREVIEW

- You could use the **Diagnostic Preview** in conjunction with assessments of students' writing to gauge their understanding of correct pronoun usage. The **Diagnostic Preview** will help you pinpoint error patterns and specific strengths and weaknesses.

Diagnostic Preview

Correcting Errors in Pronoun Forms

Most of the following sentences contain errors in the use of pronoun forms. Identify the error, and give the correct pronoun form for each of the following sentences. If a sentence is already correct, write *C.*

EXAMPLE   1. The Garcia children and them grew up together in East Texas.

   1. *them—they*

1. he

1. Omar and him offered us some pita, a Middle Eastern bread.

2. We

2. Us basketball players know the value of warming up.

3. she

3. The computer experts in our class are Rosalinda and her.

4. me

4. There's more than a three-year age difference between Edward and I.

5. I

5. Pablo and me are planning to visit the Andes Mountains someday.

6. C

6. At Passover, my grandparents make gefilte fish and other traditional foods for my cousins and me.

7. C

7. Give Sue and him this invitation to the Japanese tea ceremony.

CHAPTER RESOURCES

Planning
- *One-Stop Planner CD-ROM*

Practice and Extension
- *Grammar, Usage, and Mechanics,* p. 191
- *Developmental Language Skills,* pp. 73–80

Internet
- go.hrw.com (keyword: EOLang)

Evaluation and Assessment
- *Chapter Tests,* Ch. 19
- *Chapter Tests in Standardized Test Formats,* Ch. 19
- *Test Generator (One-Stop Planner)*

8. Josh made ~~hisself~~ a bookcase in industrial arts class.
9. Two angry hornets chased Earline and ~~she~~ all the way home.
10. The first actors on stage were Jesse and ~~him~~.
11. Mr. Mendez and ~~us~~ organized a debate about the rights of students.
12. Will you attend the rally with Dominick and me?
13. I helped Kimberly and ~~they~~ with their play about Hiawatha.
14. Jeannette and ~~her~~ know a great deal about Greek myths.
15. The hickory smoke smelled good to ~~we~~ campers.
16. The only seventh-graders in the marching band this year are Bianca and ~~me~~.
17. Liang was telling them and me about his home in Hong Kong.
18. Julia and ~~them~~ learned how to use hot wax to make batik patterns on cloth.
19. During the marathon, Lionel ran just behind Jim and ~~she~~.
20. Thomas asked Marvella and ~~he~~ if they wanted to join a gospel chorus.

8. himself
9. her
10. he
11. we

12. C
13. them
14. she
15. us
16. I

17. C
18. they

19. her
20. him

Case

19a. *Case* is the form that a noun or pronoun takes to show its relationship to other words in a sentence.

English has three cases for nouns and pronouns:

- nominative
- objective
- possessive

The form of a noun is the same for both the nominative and the objective cases. For example, a noun used as a subject (nominative case) will have the same form when used as a direct object (objective case).

| NOMINATIVE CASE | That Ming **vase** is very old. [subject] |
| OBJECTIVE CASE | Who bought the **vase**? [direct object] |

A noun changes its form only in the possessive case, usually by adding an apostrophe and an *s*.

| POSSESSIVE CASE | The Ming **vase's** new owner is pleased. |

┌HELP──

The nominative case is sometimes referred to as the subject form. The objective case is sometimes referred to as the object form. Follow your teacher's instructions when using these terms.

Reference Note

For more about **forming the possessive case of nouns,** see page 638.

Case **511**

USAGE

TEACHING **TIP**

Motivation. Have students bring articles from their favorite magazines or newspapers to class. Ask students to identify the pronouns used in the articles. As you proceed through the chapter, have students return to the articles to identify the case of the pronouns.

Case
Rules 19a–e (pp. 511–521)

OBJECTIVES

- To read sentences aloud stressing personal pronouns
- To choose the correct forms of pronouns in sentences
- To complete sentences by adding the correct forms of pronouns

Unlike nouns, most personal pronouns have different forms for all three cases.

Personal Pronouns		
Nominative Case	**Objective Case**	**Possessive Case**
Singular		
I	me	my, mine
you	you	your, yours
he, she, it	him, her, it	his, her, hers, its
Plural		
we	us	our, ours
you	you	your, yours
they	them	their, theirs

NOTE The personal pronouns in the possessive case—*my, mine, your, yours, his, her, hers, its, our, ours, their, theirs*—are used to show ownership or relationship.

The possessive pronouns *mine, yours, his, hers, its, ours,* and *theirs* are used as parts of sentences in the same ways in which the pronouns in the nominative and the objective cases are used.

EXAMPLES   His book and **mine** are overdue.

                This desk is **his.**

                We completed **ours** this morning.

The possessive pronouns *my, your, his, her, its, our,* and *their* are used as adjectives before nouns.

EXAMPLES   **My** shoes need to be cleaned.

                Have you proofread **her** report for her yet?

                There goes **their** dog Rex.

NOTE Some authorities prefer to call these words adjectives. Follow your teacher's instructions regarding these possessive forms.

Review A   Writing Sentences
That Contain Pronouns in the
Nominative Case

ANSWERS continued

8. Yes, she and the baby are having a good time.

9. No, that is not he.

10. The one now looking at the picture of the birthday party is I.

MODALITIES
Kinesthetic and Visual Learners.
Have students write each of the sixteen personal pronouns in the nominative and objective cases on separate sheets of paper or on index cards. Then, write a sentence on the chalkboard and leave a blank where a personal pronoun should go. Ask students to hold up a card with a pronoun that would correctly fill the blank. Write all of the correct choices in the blank. Repeat the process until all pronouns have been used.

Relating to Literature

If the Edgar Allan Poe poem "Annabel Lee" is in your literature textbook, have students read it and discuss Poe's use of personal pronouns. Ask students why they think the poet repeated the pronoun *me* so often. [Me *rhymes with* Annabel Lee; *in the first four stanzas, every other line ends with the long* e *sound.*]

You may want to discuss the use of pronouns in comparisons, as in line 28, ". . . older than we," and line 29, ". . . wiser than we." Explain to students that the nominative case pronoun is used because *we* functions as a subject, but the verb has been omitted. With the missing verbs added, the lines would read "older than we were" and "wiser than we were."

8. Are the baby and his mother near the table having a good time? (*Use* the baby *and a singular personal pronoun as the compound subject.*)

9. Is Carmen's father the man holding the piñata rope? (*Use a singular personal pronoun as a predicate nominative.*)

10. Who is the one now looking at the picture of Carmen Lomas Garza's birthday party? (*Use a singular personal pronoun as a predicate nominative.*)

Reprinted by permission of GRM Associates, Inc., Agents for Children's Book Press, from the book *Family Pictures* by Carmen Lomas Garza, copyright 1990 by Carmen Lomas Garza.

The Objective Case

19d. *Direct objects* and *indirect objects* of verbs should be in the objective case.

A *direct object* is a noun, pronoun, or word group that tells *who* or *what* receives the action of the verb.

EXAMPLES   Mom called **me** to the phone. [*Me* tells *whom* Mom called.]

Julia bought sweet potatoes and used **them** to make filling for the empanadas. [*Them* tells *what* she used.]

Reference Note
For more about **direct and indirect objects,** see pages 386 and 388.

2. The volunteers must be (*them*, *they*).
3. Is the last performer (*she*, *her*)?
4. The next speaker will be (*him*, *he*).
5. The guests of honor are Luther and (*us*, *we*).
6. I knew the one in red was (*she*, *her*), of course.
7. The hardest workers are Susan, Tranh, and (*me*, *I*).
8. Can that be (*she*, *her*) in the Indian sari?
9. The next batter should be (*she*, *her*).
10. Our newest neighbors are the Blumenthals and (*them*, *they*).

Review A **Writing Sentences That Contain Pronouns in the Nominative Case**

The busy scene you see on the next page was painted by the Mexican American artist Carmen Lomas Garza. It shows one of her childhood birthday parties. The fish-shaped object is a piñata, full of treats for the children. Carmen is getting ready to take a swing at the piñata. Answer each of the following questions by writing a sentence. Follow the directions after each question.

EXAMPLE   1. What are the kneeling boys in the lower right-hand corner doing? (*Use a plural personal pronoun as the subject.*)

   1. *They are getting ready to play marbles.*

1. What is Carmen using to hit the piñata? (*Use a singular personal pronoun as the subject.*)
2. For whom are the presents on the table? (*Use a plural personal pronoun as the subject.*)
3. Who will get the gifts and treats inside the piñata? (*Use a person's name and a plural personal pronoun as the compound subject.*)
4. Have you and your classmates ever played a game that requires a blindfold? (*Use a plural and a singular personal pronoun as the compound subject.*)
5. Why does the boy at the far left have presents in his hand? (*Use a singular personal pronoun as the subject.*)
6. What would Carmen say if you asked her, "Who's the birthday girl?" (*Use a singular personal pronoun as a predicate nominative.*)
7. Did Carmen's parents and her grandmother plan the party? (*Use a plural and a singular personal pronoun as a compound predicate nominative.*)

Case   **515**

Review A   **Writing Sentences That Contain Pronouns in the Nominative Case**

POSSIBLE ANSWERS

1. She is using a bat.
2. They are for Carmen.
3. Carmen and they will get the gifts and treats.
4. They and I have played a game that requires a blindfold.
5. He is going to give the presents to Carmen.
6. "The birthday girl is I."
7. Yes, it was they and she.

USAGE

4. I'm (I am) happy to see you.

   Have students work in pairs to use the following contractions in sentences: *I'm, I'd, you've, you're, he's, she'll, it's, they've, we're,* and *we've.* As in the models, have students identify the words that are combined to form the contractions.

   Upon completion, have pairs exchange sentences to check for correctness. For additional information and practice, refer students to **Chapter 24: Punctuation,** p. 641.

Relating to Writing

Although using nominative case pronouns as predicate nominatives is considered standard usage, it may sound awkward to most students. Tell students that they can rewrite sentences to make them sound more natural by using the predicate nominatives as subjects. For example, the second sentence in **Oral Practice 2** can be rephrased as "She could have been the caller."

6. I told Mother that I thought (_she, her_) would enjoy the trail.
7. To my surprise, (_she, her_) wanted to walk part of the trail then.
8. Lou and (_she, her_) immediately started hiking down the trail.
9. (_They, Them_) knew that I would follow.
10. (_Us, We_) had fun but were ready to ride instead of walk home!

19c. A _predicate nominative_ should be in the nominative case.

A _predicate nominative_ is a word or word group that is in the predicate and that identifies or refers to the subject of the verb. A pronoun used as a predicate nominative completes the meaning of a linking verb, usually a form of the verb _be_ (such as _am, are, is, was, were, be, been,_ or _being_).

EXAMPLES   The candidates should have been **he** and **she.** [_He_ and _she_ follow the linking verb _should have been_ and identify the subject _candidates._]

         The members of the team are **they.** [_They_ follows the linking verb _are_ and identifies the subject _members._]

Oral Practice 2 **Using Pronouns as Predicate Nominatives**

Read each of the following sentences aloud, stressing the italicized pronouns.

1. Were the only Spanish-speaking people you and _they_?
2. The caller could have been _she._
3. The leaders will be my mother and _he._
4. The three candidates for class president are _she_ and _we._
5. That must be the pilot and _he_ on the runway.
6. The three winners were Eduardo, Maya, and _I._
7. The first ones on the scene were our neighbors and _they._
8. The speakers at the rally were _she_ and Jesse Jackson.

Exercise 2 **Identifying Correct Pronoun Forms**

Choose the <u>correct form of the pronoun</u> in parentheses in each of the following sentences.

EXAMPLE   1. Were the ones who left early (_they, them_)?
           1. _they_

1. Two witnesses claimed that the burglar was (_him, he_).

STYLE TIP

Expressions such as _It's me_ and _That's her_ are acceptable in everyday speaking. However, these expressions contain the objective case pronouns _me_ and _her_ used incorrectly as predicate nominatives. Such expressions should be avoided in formal writing and speaking.

Reference Note

For more about **predicate nominatives,** see page 391.

TIPS & TRICKS

To choose the correct form of a pronoun used as a predicate nominative, try reversing the order of the sentence.

EXAMPLE
The fastest runner is (_he, him_).

REVERSED
(_He, Him_) is the fastest runner.

ANSWER
The fastest runner is **he.**

MINI-LESSON

Contractions. You may want to discuss with students that pronouns in the nominative case can combine with helping or linking verbs to form contractions. Write the following sentences on the chalkboard to show that the apostrophe takes the place of omitted letters.

1. I've (I have) never eaten tofu.
2. They're (They are) arriving tomorrow.
3. We'll (We will) be home early.

The Nominative Case

19b. The *subject* of a verb should be in the nominative case.

EXAMPLES   **He** and **I** mowed lawns. [*He* and *I* are used together as the compound subject of *mowed.*]

Did **they** craft candles from antique molds? [*They* is the subject of *Did craft.*]

She took orders while **we** made change. [*She* is the subject of *took. We* is the subject of *made.*]

Oral Practice 1   Using Pronouns as Subjects

Read each of the following sentences aloud, stressing the italicized pronouns.

1. Dr. Chen and *they* discussed the usefulness of herbal medicines.
2. *He* and *I* live next door to each other.
3. *They* should try to get along better.
4. Yesterday *she* and *they* gave their reports on modern African American poets.
5. *You* and *she* left the party early.
6. Since the third grade, *we* have been friends.
7. *He* and his family are moving to Puerto Rico.
8. *I* will miss them.

Exercise 1   Identifying Correct Pronoun Forms

Choose the correct form of the pronoun in parentheses in each of the following sentences.

EXAMPLE   **1.** My friends and (*I, me*) like to spend time outdoors.
     1. *I*

1. Lou and (*me, I*) asked my mother to drive us to a nearby state park.
2. There (*he and I, him and me*) set out on a marked trail through the woods.
3. Before long, (*he and I, him and me*) were exploring a snowy area off the beaten track.
4. At midday Lou and (*me, I*) reluctantly followed our tracks back to the path.
5. (*Us, We*) had had the best time of our lives.

Reference Note

For more about **subjects,** see page 317.

TIPS & TRICKS

To help you choose the correct pronoun in a compound subject, try each form of the pronoun separately.

EXAMPLE
(*She, Her*) and (*I, me*) found them. [*She found* or *Her found? I found* or *Me found?*]

ANSWER
She and **I** found them.

USAGE

Unlike nouns, most personal pronouns have different forms for all three cases.

Personal Pronouns		
Nominative Case	**Objective Case**	**Possessive Case**
Singular		
I	me	my, mine
you	you	your, yours
he, she, it	him, her, it	his, her, hers, its
Plural		
we	us	our, ours
you	you	your, yours
they	them	their, theirs

NOTE The personal pronouns in the possessive case—*my, mine, your, yours, his, her, hers, its, our, ours, their, theirs*—are used to show ownership or relationship.

The possessive pronouns *mine, yours, his, hers, its, ours,* and *theirs* are used as parts of sentences in the same ways in which the pronouns in the nominative and the objective cases are used.

EXAMPLES   His book and **mine** are overdue.

This desk is **his.**

We completed **ours** this morning.

The possessive pronouns *my, your, his, her, its, our,* and *their* are used as adjectives before nouns.

EXAMPLES   **My** shoes need to be cleaned.

Have you proofread **her** report for her yet?

There goes **their** dog Rex.

NOTE Some authorities prefer to call these words adjectives. Follow your teacher's instructions regarding these possessive forms.

8. Josh made ~~hisself~~ a bookcase in industrial arts class.
9. Two angry hornets chased Earline and ~~she~~ all the way home.
10. The first actors on stage were Jesse and ~~him~~.
11. Mr. Mendez and ~~us~~ organized a debate about the rights of students.
12. Will you attend the rally with Dominick and me?
13. I helped Kimberly and ~~they~~ with their play about Hiawatha.
14. Jeannette and ~~her~~ know a great deal about Greek myths.
15. The hickory smoke smelled good to ~~we~~ campers.
16. The only seventh-graders in the marching band this year are Bianca and ~~me~~.
17. Liang was telling them and me about his home in Hong Kong.
18. Julia and ~~them~~ learned how to use hot wax to make batik patterns on cloth.
19. During the marathon, Lionel ran just behind Jim and ~~she~~.
20. Thomas asked Marvella and ~~he~~ if they wanted to join a gospel chorus.

8. himself
9. her
10. he
11. we

12. C
13. them
14. she
15. us
16. I

17. C
18. they

19. her
20. him

Case

19a. *Case* is the form that a noun or pronoun takes to show its relationship to other words in a sentence.

English has three cases for nouns and pronouns:

- nominative
- objective
- possessive

The form of a noun is the same for both the nominative and the objective cases. For example, a noun used as a subject (nominative case) will have the same form when used as a direct object (objective case).

| NOMINATIVE CASE | That Ming **vase** is very old. [subject] |
| OBJECTIVE CASE | Who bought the **vase**? [direct object] |

A noun changes its form only in the possessive case, usually by adding an apostrophe and an *s*.

POSSESSIVE CASE The Ming **vase's** new owner is pleased.

┌─ **HELP** ─

The nominative case is sometimes referred to as the subject form. The objective case is sometimes referred to as the object form. Follow your teacher's instructions when using these terms.

Reference Note

For more about **forming the possessive case of nouns,** see page 638.

Case **511**

RESOURCES

Case

Practice

- *Grammar, Usage, and Mechanics,* pp. 192, 193, 194–195, 196–197, 198–199
- *Language Workshop CD-ROM,* Lessons 17, 18

TEACHING TIP

Motivation. Have students bring articles from their favorite magazines or newspapers to class. Ask students to identify the pronouns used in the articles. As you proceed through the chapter, have students return to the articles to identify the case of the pronouns.

Case
Rules 19a–e *(pp. 511–521)*

OBJECTIVES

- To read sentences aloud stressing personal pronouns

- To choose the correct forms of pronouns in sentences

- To complete sentences by adding the correct forms of pronouns

An ***indirect object*** is a noun, pronoun, or word group that often appears in sentences containing direct objects. An indirect object tells *to whom* or *to what* or *for whom* or *for what* the action of the verb is done.

An indirect object generally comes between an action verb and its direct object.

EXAMPLES The hostess handed **her** a name tag. [*Her* tells *to whom* the hostess handed the name tag.]

Mr. Tanaka raises large goldfish; he often feeds **them** rice. [*Them* tells *to what* Mr. Tanaka feeds rice.]

NOTE Indirect objects do not follow prepositions. If *to* or *for* precedes a pronoun, the pronoun is an object of a preposition, not an indirect object.

OBJECT OF A PREPOSITION Send a letter to **me**.
INDIRECT OBJECT Send **me** a letter.

Oral Practice 3 Using Pronouns as Direct Objects and Indirect Objects

Read each of the following sentences aloud, stressing the italicized pronouns.

1. I took Joe and *her* to a performance by French mimes.
2. The bus driver let Melba, Joe, and *me* off at the next corner.
3. An usher gave *us* programs.
4. Another usher showed *them* and *me* our seats.
5. The performers fascinated Melba and *me*.
6. Their costumes delighted the crowd and *her*.
7. No one else impressed Joe and *me* as much as the youngest mime did.
8. We watched *her* exploring the walls of an invisible room.

Exercise 3 Writing Pronouns Used as Direct Objects and Indirect Objects

Write an appropriate pronoun for each blank in the sentences on the following page. Use a variety of pronouns, but do not use *you* or *it*. Responses will vary.

EXAMPLE **1.** Have you seen Kim and _____?
    1. her

Case **517**

USAGE

ALTERNATIVE LESSON
In each of the sentences in **Exercise 3,** the added pronoun completes a compound object. Point out to students the similarities between this use of *compound* and other uses they may have already encountered: compound subjects and compound verbs **(Chapter 10: The Sentence),** compound nouns **(Chapter 12: Parts of Speech Overview),** and compound sentences **(Chapter 16: Kinds of Sentence Structure).**

Possible answers:
1. me
2. them/us
3. her

4. them/me
5. him

6. me
7. her/him
8. her/me
9. her
10. me

1. The manager hired Susana and ____.
2. Lana sent ____ and ____ invitations.
3. We gave Grandpa López and ____ round-trip tickets to Mexico City.
4. The firefighters rescued ____ and ____.
5. Aunt Coretta showed my cousins and ____ a carved mask from Nigeria.
6. The show entertained the children and ____.
7. The waiter served ____ and ____ a variety of dumplings.
8. Our team chose ____ and ____ as representatives.
9. The election committee nominated Gerry and ____.
10. The clerk gave Misako and ____ the receipt for the paper lanterns.

Review B **Identifying Correct Pronoun Forms**

Choose the correct form of each pronoun in parentheses in the following sentences.

EXAMPLE 1. Paul told Ms. Esteban that (*he, him*) and (*I, me*) need a topic for our report.

1. *he, I*

1. In our American history class, some of the other students and (*he, him*) thought that there should be more reports on women.
2. We were interested in Amelia Earhart and wanted to give (*she, her*) the recognition she deserves.
3. The picture on the left, showing Amelia Earhart looking relaxed and confident, interested Paul and (*I, me*).
4. Both (*he, him*) and (*I, me*) were eager to find out more about her contribution to aviation.
5. We learned that it was (*she, her*) who made the first solo flight by a woman across the Atlantic.
6. The fact that Amelia Earhart was the first pilot to fly from Hawaii to California surprised the rest of the class and (*we, us*), too.
7. In 1937, her navigator and (*she, her*) took off in a twin-engine plane for a trip around the world.
8. After (*they, them*) had completed two thirds of the trip, Earhart and her navigator lost contact with radio operators.

9. No one ever saw (*they, them*) or the airplane again.

10. Ms. Esteban and (*we, us*) are among the many people still puzzling over this mystery.

19e. The *object of a preposition* should be in the objective case.

A noun or pronoun that follows a preposition is called the *object of a preposition.* Together, the preposition, its object, and any modifiers of the object make a *prepositional phrase.*

EXAMPLES   Before **us** lay rows of green cornstalks. [*Us* is the object of the preposition *Before.*]

The secret is between **him** and **me.** [*Him* and *me* are the compound object of the preposition *between.*]

Please stand next to **her.** [*Her* is the object of the compound preposition *next to.*]

Reference Note

For a list of commonly used **prepositions,** see page 370. For more about **prepositional phrases,** see page 402.

Oral Practice 4 **Using Pronouns as Objects of Prepositions**

Read each of the following sentences aloud, stressing the italicized prepositions and pronouns.

1. Mr. Torres divided the burritos *among them* and *us.*
2. At the game Maria sat *near him* and *her.*
3. Rose walked *toward* Nell and *me.*
4. Sam stood *between him* and *me.*
5. Mom ordered sandwiches *for* Hannah and *her.*
6. "*Without* Squanto and *me,* the Pilgrims won't last another winter," thought Samoset.
7. I have read biographies *about him* and Martin Luther.
8. David's parents gave a bar mitzvah party *for him.*

┌ TIPS & TRICKS ┐

To determine the correct pronoun form when the object of a preposition is compound, use each pronoun separately in the prepositional phrase.

EXAMPLE
Maria sent a postcard to (*she, her*) and (*I, me*). [*To she* or *to her*? *To I* or *to me*?]

ANSWER
Maria sent a postcard to **her** and **me.**

Exercise 4 **Choosing Pronouns Used as Objects of Prepositions**

Choose the <u>correct form of the pronoun</u> in parentheses in each of the sentences on the following page.

EXAMPLE   **1.** Of all the people who traveled with Lewis and Clark, Sacagawea was particularly helpful to (*them, they*).

    1. them

Cooperative Learning

To give students additional practice with correct pronoun usage, divide the class into groups of four. Prepare a sheet of paper in advance with the following instructions:

1. Use *I* as a predicate nominative.

2. Use *he* in a compound subject.

3. Use *them* in a compound object of a preposition.

4. Use *us* as an indirect object.

5. Use *me* in a compound object of a preposition.

6. Use *she* as a subject.

7. Use *her* in a compound indirect object.

8. Use *they* in a compound predicate nominative.

9. Use *we* in a compound subject.

10. Use *us* in a compound object of a preposition.

Help each group work out a method to ensure that each member participates and that the group functions cooperatively. Along with their sentences, ask each group to include a brief summary of how their group cooperated to complete the assignment and what each individual's role was.

USAGE

Exercises You may wish to use **Exercise 4** as guided practice and then have students complete **Review C** as independent practice.

Critical Thinking

Metacognition. Ask students to think about the process they use to determine a pronoun's function in a sentence. Do they locate the verb first, find the subject, and then identify any complements? Do they draw a mental diagram to visualize the sentence parts? Do they first identify and eliminate prepositional phrases, since the skeleton of the sentence does not include prepositional phrases? Encourage students to evaluate the effectiveness of their personal strategies and to consider more effective alternatives as needed.

S T Y L E   T I P

Just as there are good manners in behavior, there are also good manners in language. In English it is considered polite to put first-person pronouns (*I, me, my, mine, we, us, our, ours*) last in compound constructions.

EXAMPLE
Please return the photos to **Bill, Ellen,** or **me** [not *me, Bill, or Ellen*].

1. Sacagawea's husband, a guide named Toussaint Charbonneau, joined the expedition with (*her, she*) and their newborn baby.
2. The Shoshone were Sacagawea's people, and she longed to return to (*them, they*).
3. Captain Clark soon realized how important she would be to Lewis and (*he, him*).
4. The land they were exploring was familiar to (*she, her*).
5. Luckily for (*she, her*) and the expedition, they met a group of friendly Shoshone.
6. From (*them, they*), Sacagawea obtained the ponies that Lewis and Clark needed.
7. Sacagawea's baby boy delighted the expedition's leaders, and they took good care of (*he, him*).
8. In fact, Captain Clark made a promise to (*she, her*) and Charbonneau that he would give the boy a good education.
9. At the age of eighteen, the boy befriended a prince and traveled with (*him, he*) in Europe.
10. Although sources disagree about when Sacagawea died, a gravestone for (*she, her*) in Wyoming bears the date April 9, 1884.

Review C **Identifying Correct Pronoun Forms**

Choose the correct form of the pronoun in parentheses in each of the following sentences. Then, tell what part of the sentence each pronoun is: subject, predicate nominative, direct object, indirect object, or object of a preposition.

EXAMPLE   1. My brother Pete and (*I, me*) wanted to know more about Elizabeth Blackwell.

            1. *I—subject*

1. Mom told Pete and (*I, me*) the story of Elizabeth Blackwell, the first woman to graduate from medical school in the United States. **1.** i.o.
2. Geneva College granted (*she, her*) a degree in 1849. **2.** i.o.
3. At first, because she was a woman, no male doctor would let her work for (*he, him*). **3.** o.p.
4. Pete and (*I, me*) admire Elizabeth Blackwell for not giving up. **4.** s.
5. She wanted to help the poor and opened her own clinic for (*they, them*). **5.** o.p.

6. Wealthy citizens were soon supporting (*she*, *her*) and the clinic with donations. **6.** d.o.

7. Before long, one of the most talked-about topics in medical circles was (*she*, *her*) and the excellent work she was doing for the poor. **7.** p.n.

8. Mom and (*we*, *us*) read more about Dr. Blackwell, and we learned that she opened a medical school just for women. **8.** s.

9. Dr. Blackwell set high standards for students and gave (*they*, *them*) hard courses of study to complete. **9.** i.o.

10. Her teaching prepared (*they*, *them*) well, and many went on to become successful physicians. **10.** d.o.

Special Pronoun Problems

Who and *Whom*

The pronoun *who* has different forms in the nominative and objective cases. *Who* is the nominative form; *whom* is the objective form.

When you need to decide whether to use *who* or *whom* in a question, follow these steps:

STEP 1 Rephrase the question as a statement.

STEP 2 Decide how the pronoun is used in the statement—as a subject, a predicate nominative, a direct or an indirect object, or an object of a preposition.

STEP 3 Determine the case of the pronoun according to the rules of formal, standard English.

STEP 4 Select the correct form of the pronoun.

EXAMPLE (*Who, Whom*) is she?

STEP 1 The statement is *She is (who, whom)*.

STEP 2 The pronoun is a predicate nominative that refers to the subject *She*.

STEP 3 A pronoun used as a predicate nominative should be in the nominative case.

STEP 4 The nominative form is *who*.

ANSWER: **Who** is she?

┌─ STYLE   TIP ─┐

In informal English, the use of *whom* is becoming less common. In fact, in informal situations, you may correctly begin any question with *who* regardless of the grammar of the sentence. In formal English, however, you should distinguish between *who* and *whom*.

Special Pronoun Problems

(pp. 521–526)

OBJECTIVES

- To reinforce the correct use of *who* and *whom* by reading sentences aloud

- To choose the correct forms of pronouns in sentences

- To choose the correct forms of reflexive pronouns

RESOURCES

Special Pronoun Problems

Practice

- *Grammar, Usage, and Mechanics*, pp. 200, 201, 202
- *Language Workshop CD-ROM,* Lesson 19

EXAMPLE (*Who, Whom*) will you invite to the dance?

STEP 1   The statement is *You will invite (who, whom) to the dance.*

STEP 2   The pronoun is the direct object of the verb *will invite.*

STEP 3   A pronoun used as a direct object should be in the objective case.

STEP 4   The objective form is *whom.*

ANSWER: **Whom** will you invite to the dance?

Oral Practice 5   Using Who and Whom

Read each of the following sentences aloud, stressing the italicized pronouns.

1. *Who* is captain of the football team this year?
2. To *whom* did you give your old skateboard?
3. *Whom* will you call to come and pick us up after band practice?
4. *Who* were the first Americans?
5. In the last play of the game, *who* passed the ball to *whom*?
6. *Who*'s that woman in the green sari?
7. For *whom* did you buy those flowers?
8. *Who* painted that beautiful picture?

Exercise 5   Choosing *Who* or *Whom*

Choose the correct form of the pronoun in parentheses in each of the following sentences.

EXAMPLE   1. (*Who, Whom*) helped load the hay on the wagon this morning?

1. *Who*

2. To (*who, whom*) are you going to give the award?

2. *whom*

1. (*Who, Whom*) will your brother invite to his birthday party?
2. (*Who, Whom*) will be our substitute teacher while Mr. Chen is away?
3. (*Who, Whom*) has Ms. Spears appointed?
4. Of the three candidates, in (*who, whom*) do you have the most confidence?
5. To (*who, whom*) do you wish these balloons sent?
6. For (*who, whom*) is the package that was delivered?

Meeting INDIVIDUAL NEEDS

ENGLISH-LANGUAGE LEARNERS
Spanish. In Spanish, *who* does not change form when used as an object, so Spanish-speaking students may be confused by the pronoun *whom.* As a supplement to **Oral Practice 5,** have students work in pairs to create original sentences using *who* and *whom.* After you check for correct usage, suggest that students read the sentences aloud.

TEACHING TIP

Oral Practice 5 To help students decide when to use *who* or *whom* in their speaking and writing, share the following tip. Ask students to substitute other nominative case pronouns such as *I, she,* or *they* for the word *who* or *whom.* If the nominative case substitution is not correct, then the objective form *whom* is needed.

Use **Oral Practice 5** to demonstrate this process. Model the process for the first sentence. Then, have students work alone or in pairs to continue.

1. Can *She* correctly replace *Who?*

2. If so, the nominative case *Who* is correct. If not, *Whom* is needed.

Learning for Life   *Continued on pp. 523–524*

Speaking on the Telephone. Although most students have used a telephone since early childhood, they can always practice and improve telephone skills. The following activity will focus on skills that include correct pronoun usage.

Write on the chalkboard or on a transparency the following beginnings of telephone conversations. Ask volunteers to read aloud parts #1 and #2 of each scenario.

7. (*Who*, *Whom*) is the architect of the new library building?
8. With (*who*, *whom*) would you most like to talk?
9. Among your friends, (*who*, *whom*) has the quickest smile?
10. (*Who*, *Whom*) have the students elected class president?

Pronouns with Appositives

Sometimes a pronoun is followed directly by a noun that identifies the pronoun. Such a noun is called an ***appositive.*** To help you choose which pronoun to use before an appositive, omit the appositive and try each form of the pronoun separately.

Reference Note

For more about **appositives,** see page 609.

EXAMPLE On Saturdays, (*we, us*) cyclists ride to Mount McCabe and back. [*Cyclists* is the appositive identifying the pronoun.]
We ride or *Us ride*?

ANSWER On Saturdays, **we** cyclists ride to Mount McCabe and back.

EXAMPLE The speaker praised (*we, us*) volunteers. [*Volunteers* is the appositive identifying the pronoun.]
The speaker praised we or *The speaker praised us*?

ANSWER The speaker praised **us** volunteers.

Exercise 6 **Choosing Correct Pronouns**

Choose the correct form of the pronoun in parentheses in each of the following sentences.

EXAMPLE 1. Hanukkah is always an exciting holiday for (*we, us*) Feldmans.

1. *us*

1. Tiger Woods is a role model for (*we, us*) golfers.
2. Miss Jefferson, (*we, us*) students want to thank you for all your help.
3. (*We, Us*) contestants shook hands warmly.
4. The woman gave (*we, us*) girls five dollars for shoveling the snow.
5. The attorneys politely answered the questions from (*we, us*) reporters.
6. For (*we, us*) volunteers, service is its own reward.
7. Frank loaned (*we, us*) fans two classical tapes.

Special Pronoun Problems **523**

---

1. #1 Hello.
   #2 Is Leah there?
   #1 This is she.

2. #1 Hello.
   #2 May I please speak with Paul?
   #1 Who is speaking, please?

3. #1 Hello.
   #2 Is Mrs. Tays there?
   #1 Yes, she is. May I say who is calling?

4. #1 Hello.
   #2 Congratulations! Are you ready to hear about a once-in-a-lifetime offer?

8. The huge dog knocked (*we*, *us*) joggers off the sidewalk.
9. (*We*, *Us*) actors need to rehearse again before Friday night.
10. The new team members were (*we*, *us*) boys.

┌HELP───

The pronouns *himself* and *themselves* can also be used as intensive pronouns.

EXAMPLES
Daniel **himself** will lead the parade.

They **themselves** traveled only twenty miles to get here.

Reference Note
For more about **reflexive and intensive pronouns,** see page 343.

Reflexive Pronouns

Do not use the nonstandard forms *hisself* and *theirselfs* or *theirselves* in place of *himself* and *themselves.*

| NONSTANDARD | The secretary voted for hisself in the last election. |
| STANDARD | The secretary voted for **himself** in the last election. |

| NONSTANDARD | The cooks served theirselves some of the hot won-ton soup. |
| STANDARD | The cooks served **themselves** some of the hot won-ton soup. |

Exercise 7 Identifying Correct Pronoun Forms

Choose the correct form of the pronoun in parentheses in each of the following sentences.

EXAMPLE   1. The contestants promised (*theirselves, themselves*) it would be a friendly competition.
1. themselves

1. Before he started to read, Zack asked (*hisself, himself*) three questions to set his purpose.
2. My little brother often falls down, but he never seems to hurt (*himself, hisself*).
3. The guests helped (*theirselves, themselves*) to the nuts and raisins.
4. John Yellowtail enjoys (*himself, hisself*) when he is making fine silver jewelry.
5. When the early settlers wanted cloth, they had to spin it (*theirselves, themselves*).
6. My brother was upset with (*hisself, himself*) for being rude.
7. Andrew gave (*himself, hisself*) an early birthday present— a new CD.
8. The Sartens talked (*theirselves, themselves*) out of buying a second vehicle.

Learning for Life

#1 With whom would you like to speak?

Then, have students work in pairs to incorporate the following lines into imaginary telephone conversations.

1. This is she (he).
2. Who is speaking, please?
3. May I say who is calling?
4. With whom would you like to speak?

9. Uncle Allen took the last potatoes for (*hisself*, *himself*) and passed the onions to me.

10. Bart and Una consider (*theirself*, *themselves*) authorities on stamp collecting.

DRABBLE reprinted by permission of United Feature Syndicate, Inc.

Review D **Identifying Correct Pronoun Forms**

Choose the <u>correct form of the pronoun</u> in parentheses in each of the following sentences.

EXAMPLE   **1.** To me, the two most interesting explorers are (*he, him*) and Vasco da Gama.

   1. he

1. The team captains will be Jack and (*he*, *him*).

2. The finalists in the local talent contest are Alfredo, Sylvia, and (*I*, *me*).

3. We were warned by our parents and (*they*, *them*).

4. The Washington twins and (*I*, *me*) belong to the same club.

5. Both (*he and she*, *her and him*) have promised to write us this summer.

6. Pelé and (*he*, *him*) both played soccer for the New York Cosmos.

7. "What do you think of (*he and I*, *him and me*)?" I asked.

8. "You and (*he*, *him*) are improving," they replied.

9. When Miriam Makeba and the troupe of African musicians arrived, we gave (*she and they*, *her and them*) a party.

10. Do you remember my sister and (*I*, *me*)?

11. The coach spoke to (*we*, *us*) players before the game.

12. Was the joke played on you and (*he*, *him*)?

13. Are you and (*she*, *her*) going to celebrate Kwanzaa this year?

14. Père Toussaint taught my brother and (*I*, *me*) several French phrases.

15. Mom, Andy gave (*himself*, *hisself*) the biggest piece of banana bread.
16. Who are (*they*, *them*), Travis?
17. They congratulated (*themselves*, *theirselves*) on a difficult job well done.
18. Don't leave without (*he and I*, *him and me*).
19. (*We*, *Us*) skiers had a beautiful view from the lift.
20. (*Who*, *Whom*) were you expecting?
21. When we met at the auditions for the school play last year, (*he and I*, *him and me*) got along very well right away.
22. (*Who*, *Whom*) recommended that book about the history of Ireland to you?
23. When Dawna, Sharon, and (*I*, *me*) work on homework together, we always get through it faster and remember it better.
24. (*Who*, *Whom*) will you be tutoring from the elementary school, Margaret Tanaka or Billy Worthington?
25. Everyone agreed that the science project designed by Shannon and (*him*, *he*) was the best one in the show.

Chapter Review

A. Identifying Correct Pronoun Forms

Identify the <u>correct form of the pronoun</u> in parentheses in each of the following sentences.

1. One hot afternoon Mabel and (*I, me*) walked to the old mill.
2. Grandma sent a crate of apples to my family and (*I, me*).
3. The counselor chose (*we, us*) eighth-graders to give the school tour.
4. Don't worry; my stepmother will take you and (*I, me*) home.
5. Ms. Chavez sat between Kareem and (*I, me*) at the assembly.
6. It's a shame that the boys hurt (*themselves, theirselves*) last night.
7. Will you and (*I, me*) be able to reach them in time?
8. Mayor Petrakis asked my mom and (*she, her*) to help.
9. After I mailed the letter, Willie and (*they, them*) arrived.
10. Is this (*she, her*) to whom we spoke yesterday?
11. The senator (*himself, hisself*) sent me a reply.
12. Our coach sent e-mails to (*we, us*) marathon runners about the race tomorrow.
13. The fastest typists in class are Gene and (*they, them*).
14. Will you and (*she, her*) please come to my house this Wednesday?
15. While we were at the store, we saw my cousin and (*she, her*).
16. Our dog Piper will bring the ball to (*he, him*) or (*she, her*).
17. Last night Dad told Canditha and (*I, me*) a story.
18. (*Whom, Who*) wrote *The Wind in the Willows*?
19. (*We, Us*) students were not expecting the pop quiz.
20. The referee told (*we, us*) players that the game would go into overtime.
21. The best calligrapher in the school is (*she, her*).
22. (*Whom, Who*) is the better candidate?
23. To (*who, whom*) is the letter addressed?
24. Roger and (*I, me*) are studying for our lifeguard certificates.
25. Derek looked at (*hisself, himself*) in the mirror.

Chapter Review   **527**

Using the Chapter Review

The **Chapter Review** asks students to identify the correct use of pronouns in sentences. The results can be compared to those of the **Diagnostic Preview** (p. 510) to assess student progress. If students need additional practice, refer them to **Exercises 18–20** in **Chapter 26: Correcting Common Errors.**

Meeting INDIVIDUAL NEEDS

INCLUSION

Students with visual-processing deficits such as dyslexia might have trouble reading the sentences in the **Chapter Review** in a limited amount of time. To ensure that the testing situation is fair to these students, have student helpers read the sentences aloud. Student helpers should read the sentences slowly and pause after each sentence to allow their partners to record their answers.

USAGE

B. Correcting Errors in Pronoun Forms

Most of the following sentences contain an error in the use of pronoun forms. Identify the error, and give the correct form for each of the following sentences. If a sentence is already correct, write *C*.

26. him

26. The closing procession of the powwow will be led by ~~he~~ and the other Dakota dancers.

27. we

27. May ~~us~~ choir members leave science class early today?

28. whom

28. To ~~who~~ are you sending the flowers?

29. C

29. Please give these copies of Consuela's report to her and the committee members.

30. He

30. ~~Him~~ and his best friend watched *Antz* for the third time.

31. himself

31. Darnell enjoyed ~~hisself~~ at the African Heritage Festival.

32. she

32. The last tennis player to beat my sister in straight sets was ~~her.~~

33. Whom

33. ~~Who~~ have you asked for help with your math homework?

34. me

34. Tell Jennifer and ~~I~~ what your science project will be this year.

35. C

35. Whom did you invite to the awards ceremony?

36. We

36. ~~Us~~ science fiction fans are going to see *Forbidden Planet.*

37. Whom

37. ~~Who~~ will we see at the mosque?

38. us

38. Mario's mother will be driving Elena and ~~we~~ to the stadium.

39. he

39. Emilio and ~~him~~ volunteered to decorate the cafeteria.

40. C

40. The perfect person to play Lady Macbeth in the school play is she.

41. C

41. Neither Kevin nor I can decide which of Ray Bradbury's stories we like best.

42. Who

42. ~~Whom~~ are the most famous inventors in history?

43. her

43. Last year, the best piñata was designed by the twins and ~~she.~~

44. themselves

44. They really outdid ~~theirselves~~!

45. C

45. You should hear the fight song written by us four fans this year!

46. I

46. My father and ~~me~~ watched *The Man Who Would Be King* on video last night.

47. me

47. Between you and ~~I,~~ I don't think Bill will finish his Web page in time for the contest.

48. C

48. The state trooper gave her a ticket for an illegal left turn.

49. he

49. The last people to arrive at the party were Cordelia and ~~him.~~

50. C

50. Mom, will you take us tired yard workers out for dinner?

RESOURCES

Using Pronouns Correctly

Review

- *Grammar, Usage, and Mechanics,* pp. 203, 204, 205, 206

Assessment

- *Assessment Package*
  —*Chapter Tests,* Ch. 19
  —*Chapter Tests in Standardized Test Formats,* Ch. 19
- *Test Generator (One-Stop Planner CD-ROM)* 💿

Writing Application
Using Pronouns in a Letter

Nominative and Objective Case Your favorite radio station is having a "Create a Radio Show" contest. Write a letter to the manager of the station explaining what you would like to include in a half-hour weekly radio show. In your letter, use a variety of pronouns in the nominative case and the objective case. Be sure to include enough nouns so that the meaning of all your pronouns is clear.

Prewriting Discuss your ideas for a radio program with a group of your classmates. List the kinds of entertainment and information you could present. Above all, think about what you would like to hear on the radio.

Writing As you write your first draft, follow the format for a business letter. Give specific examples of what you want to do on the show, and give reasons for your choices. Remember that even though your ideas may be very creative, your writing must be formal.

Revising Ask the other group members to read your letter to see if your ideas sound interesting and are clearly stated. Ask them if the relationship between each pronoun and its antecedent is clear. If your meaning is not clear, revise your letter.

Publishing Re-read your letter, and correct any remaining errors in usage, spelling, punctuation, or capitalization. Be sure that you have followed the correct format for a business letter. Also, make sure that you have used all pronouns according to the rules for standard written English. Your class might want to create a bulletin board display of the letters. With your teacher's permission, the class might vote on the best idea for a show and then produce and tape the pilot episode.

Reference Note

For information about **business letters,** see "Writing" in the Quick Reference Handbook.

Writing Application
(p. 529)

OBJECTIVE

■ To use nominative and objective case pronouns in a letter to the manager of a radio station

Writing Application

Tip. Explain that every pronoun refers to or stands for a noun or pronoun that is called its antecedent. You may want to write on the chalkboard some sentences that contain pronouns and guide students through the process of identifying each pronoun's antecedent.

Scoring Rubric. While you will want to pay particular attention to students' use of nominative and objective case pronouns, you will also want to evaluate overall writing performance. You may want to give a split score to indicate development and clarity of the composition as well as usage skills.

Critical Thinking

Analysis. A successful radio show must address the concerns and interests of its intended audience. Explain that to write proposals for radio shows that young people will enjoy, students will need to analyze the concerns and interests of young people.

RESOURCES

Writing Application

Extension

■ *Grammar, Usage, and Mechanics,* p. 209
■ *Language Workshop CD-ROM,* Lessons 17–19

PREVIEWING THE CHAPTER

- The chapter begins with an explanation of what modifiers are, discussing one-word modifiers, adjectives and adverbs, as well as phrases and clauses used as modifiers. Positive, comparative, and superlative forms of adjectives and adverbs are discussed. Lessons on special problems in using modifiers and the placement of modifiers conclude the chapter.

- The chapter closes with a **Chapter Review** that includes a **Writing Application** feature asking students to write a letter to their school's administrators describing improvements they would like to see at their school. Students should use at least three comparative and two superlative forms of adjectives and adverbs.

- For help in integrating this chapter with writing chapters, use the **Teaching Strands** chart on pp. T311A–T311B.

USING THE DIAGNOSTIC PREVIEW

- If students are using modifiers incorrectly in their writing, you can use the **Diagnostic Preview** to pinpoint error patterns and specific strengths and weaknesses. Your assessment of students' performances on the **Diagnostic Preview** may indicate the need for more review of certain parts of the chapter than of others.

Using Modifiers Correctly
Comparison and Placement

Diagnostic Preview

Revising Sentences by Correcting Errors in the Use of Modifiers

Most of the following sentences contain errors in the use, form, or placement of modifiers. Revise each incorrect sentence to eliminate the error. If a sentence is already correct, write *C*.

┌─HELP─

Although two possible answers are shown, you need to give only one answer for each item in the Diagnostic Preview.

1. heavier
2. we watched as
3. in the newspaper

4. C
5. Walking to school,
6. C
7. While I was

9. When the balloons burst, they

EXAMPLE   1. There wasn't nothing missing.
            1. *There wasn't anything missing.*
                            or
            There was nothing missing.
                                    Answers may vary.

1. Please weigh both packages to see which of them is heaviest.
2. Alarmed, the wildfire started to spread quickly to our camp.
3. Did you read that Eduardo Mata received an award in the newspaper?
4. The bean soup tasted good.
5. We pass my aunt and uncle's restaurant walking to school.
6. I think the play *Fiddler on the Roof* is better than the movie.
7. Reading a magazine, my cat jumped up in my lap.
8. Jason tried to push the huge desk but couldn't scarcely move it.
9. The balloons startled the young children when they burst.
10. A jet taking off can sound more noisier than a jackhammer.

CHAPTER RESOURCES

Planning
- *One-Stop Planner CD-ROM*

Practice and Extension
- *Grammar, Usage, and Mechanics,* p. 210
- *Developmental Language Skills,* pp. 81–90

Internet

- go.hrw.com (keyword: EOLang)

Evaluation and Assessment
- *Chapter Tests,* Ch. 20
- *Chapter Tests in Standardized Test Formats,* Ch. 20
- *Test Generator (One-Stop Planner)*

11. Surprised, my coin collection interested a local coin dealer.
12. He examined two old Greek coins but couldn't see no date.
13. The shinier of those two coins looked newer.
14. That coin turned out to be the oldest of the two, however.
15. I showed one coin to the dealer valued at nearly twenty dollars.
16. He said he couldn't hardly pay more than fifteen dollars for it.
17. If I had bargained good, I might have gotten more for it.
18. Those two coins come from Ireland that have images of harps on them.
19. Collecting coins, my knowledge about other countries and peoples increases.
20. I polished my Saudi Arabian fifty-halala piece careful so that I could see the Arabic writing on it.

11. I was/when

13. C
14. older
15. the dealer

17. well
18. come from Ireland

19. increases

20. carefully

What Is a Modifier?

A *modifier* is a word, a phrase, or a clause that makes the meaning of a word or word group more specific. The two kinds of modifiers are *adjectives* and *adverbs*.

One-Word Modifiers

Adjectives

20a. *Adjectives* make the meanings of nouns and pronouns more specific.

ADJECTIVES Andy gave a **loud** cheer. [The adjective *loud* tells *what kind* of cheer.]

The one I made is **blue**. [The adjective *blue* tells *which one*.]

Adverbs

20b. *Adverbs* make the meanings of verbs, adjectives, and other adverbs more specific.

ADVERBS Andy cheered **loudly.** [The adverb *loudly* makes the meaning of the verb *cheered* more specific.]

Reference Note

For more about **adjectives,** see page 346. For more about **adverbs,** see page 366.

TIPS & TRICKS

Many adverbs end in *–ly,* but many others do not. Furthermore, not all words with the *–ly* ending are adverbs. Some adjectives end in *–ly.*

ADVERBS
quickly   soon
calmly   not

ADJECTIVES
elderly   holy
curly   silly

To decide whether a word is an adjective or an adverb, look at how the word is used in the sentence.

What Is a Modifier?   **531**

TEACHING TIP

Activity. To help students understand how adjectives and adverbs are compared, divide the class into four groups and give each group one of the following lists of modifiers:

- tall, taller, tallest
- thick, thicker, thickest
- happily, more happily, most happily
- tasty, less tasty, least tasty

Have each group demonstrate its modifier list without using words. Groups can use objects in the classroom (including themselves), draw pictures, or act out the concepts. As each group presents its demonstration, the rest of the class can guess which words are being demonstrated by using words and phrases alone or using the words in complete sentences.

Comparison of Adjectives and Adverbs

Rule 20c *(pp. 532–536)*

OBJECTIVE

- To form the degrees of comparison of modifiers correctly

Reference Note

For more about different kinds of **phrases,** see Chapter 14.

Reference Note

For more about **clauses,** see Chapter 15.

The design is **very** modern. [The adverb *very* makes the meaning of the adjective *modern* more specific.]

The crocodile moved **surprisingly** quickly. [The adverb *surprisingly* makes the meaning of the adverb *quickly* more specific.]

Phrases Used as Modifiers

Like one-word modifiers, phrases can also be used as adjectives and adverbs.

EXAMPLES **Leaping from the step,** the toddler flapped his arms in the air. [The participial phrase *Leaping from the step* acts as an adjective that modifies the noun *toddler.*]

The Greek salad is the one **to try.** [The infinitive phrase *to try* acts as an adjective that modifies the pronoun *one.*]

Ms. Elizondo planted rosebushes **along the fence.** [The prepositional phrase *along the fence* acts as an adverb that modifies the verb *planted.*]

Clauses Used as Modifiers

Like words and phrases, clauses can also be used as modifiers.

EXAMPLES Italian is the language **that I like best.** [The adjective clause *that I like best* modifies the noun *language.*]

Before Albert went to school, he took the trash to the curb. [The adverb clause *Before Albert went to school* modifies the verb *took.*]

Comparison of Adjectives and Adverbs

When adjectives and adverbs are used in comparisons, they take different forms. The specific form they take depends upon how many things are being compared. The different forms of comparison are called *degrees of comparison.*

RESOURCES

Comparison of Adjectives and Adverbs
Practice

- *Grammar, Usage, and Mechanics,* pp. 211, 212, 213, 214, 215, 216, 217, 218–219, 220–222
- *Language Workshop CD-ROM,* Lesson 20

20c. The three degrees of comparison of modifiers are the *positive,* the *comparative,* and the *superlative.*

(1) The ***positive degree*** is used when at least one thing is being described.

EXAMPLES   This suitcase is **heavy.**

Luís **cheerfully** began the job.

Those murals are **colorful.**

(2) The ***comparative degree*** is used when two things or groups of things are being compared.

EXAMPLES   My suitcase is **heavier** than yours.

Luís talked **more cheerfully** than Albert.

Those murals are **more colorful** than these.

(3) The ***superlative degree*** is used when three or more things or groups of things are being compared.

EXAMPLES   Sylvia's suitcase is the **heaviest** of all.

Of the four boys, Luís worked at the task **most cheerfully.**

Those murals are the **most colorful** that I've seen.

Regular Comparison

Most one-syllable modifiers form the comparative degree by adding *–er* and the superlative degree by adding *–est.*

Positive	Comparative	Superlative
close	clos**er**	clos**est**
slow	slow**er**	slow**est**
soon	soon**er**	soon**est**
straight	straight**er**	straight**est**

Notice that both adjectives and adverbs form their degrees of comparison in the same way.

STYLE TIP

In conversation, you may hear and use expressions such as *Put your best foot forward* and *May the best team win.* Such uses of the superlative are acceptable in spoken English. However, in your writing for school and other formal occasions, you should generally use superlatives only when three or more things are compared.

Reference Note

For guidelines on how to spell words when **adding –er or –est,** see page 661.

TIPS & TRICKS

Here is a way to remember which form of a modifier to use. When comparing two things, use *–er* (the two-letter ending). When comparing three or more things, use *–est* (the three-letter ending).

Meeting INDIVIDUAL NEEDS

ENGLISH-LANGUAGE LEARNERS
General Strategies. The practice of counting the syllables of an adjective in order to determine how to form its comparative and superlative degrees (see p. 534) is found in few, if any, other languages. Some of your English-language learners may be unaccustomed to thinking about syllables or may be unsure what syllables are. If students have trouble with the comparative forms of two- and three-syllable modifiers, be sure they know how to consult a dictionary to check syllabication.

Spanish. Spanish speakers may need extra practice adding *–er* and *–est* to words to form comparatives and superlatives, because suffixes are not used to form most comparatives or superlatives in Spanish. For example, the English words *fast, faster, fastest* are translated in Spanish as *rápido* (fast), *más rápido* (more fast), and *el más rápido* (the most fast).

Relating to Literature

If the Robert Frost poem "Stopping by Woods on a Snowy Evening" is in your literature textbook, have students read it to analyze Frost's use of modifiers. Ask students how the use of *darkest* in the eighth line affects the mood of the poem. [*The phrase the darkest evening of the year creates a strong image of how dark it is and contributes to the feeling of quiet and solitude in the poem.*]

Exercise 1 Forming the Degrees of Comparison of Modifiers

ANSWERS

1. nearer, nearest
2. prouder, proudest
3. more carefully, most carefully
4. more honestly, most honestly
5. smaller, smallest
6. tinier, tiniest (*or*) more tiny, most tiny
7. more timidly, most timidly
8. more loyal, most loyal
9. safer, safest
10. shadier, shadiest (*or*) more shady, most shady
11. healthier, healthiest (*or*) more healthy, most healthy
12. taller, tallest
13. more grateful, most grateful
14. quicker, quickest
15. easier, easiest (*or*) more easy, most easy
16. more confident, most confident
17. more enthusiastically, most enthusiastically
18. drier, driest
19. tastier, tastiest (*or*) more tasty, most tasty
20. more generous, most generous

STYLE TIP

Many two-syllable modifiers can correctly form the comparative and superlative degrees using either the suffixes *–er* and *–est* or the words *more* and *most*. If adding *–er* or *–est* sounds awkward, use *more* or *most*.

AWKWARD
  bitterer
  comicest

BETTER
  more bitter
  most comic

Two-syllable modifiers form the comparative degree by adding *–er* or by using *more*. They form the superlative degree by adding *–est* or by using *most*.

Positive	Comparative	Superlative
simple	simpl**er**	simpl**est**
easy	easi**er**	easi**est**
jealous	**more** jealous	**most** jealous
swiftly	**more** swiftly	**most** swiftly

Modifiers that have three or more syllables form the comparative degree by using *more* and the superlative degree by using *most*.

Positive	Comparative	Superlative
powerful	**more** powerful	**most** powerful
illegible	**more** illegible	**most** illegible
joyfully	**more** joyfully	**most** joyfully
attractively	**more** attractively	**most** attractively

Exercise 1 Forming the Degrees of Comparison of Modifiers

Give the forms for the comparative and superlative degrees of the following modifiers.

EXAMPLE   1. light

    1. *lighter; lightest*

1. near
2. proud
3. carefully
4. honestly
5. small
6. tiny
7. timidly
8. loyal
9. safe
10. shady
11. healthy
12. tall
13. grateful
14. quick
15. easy
16. confident
17. enthusiastically
18. dry
19. tasty
20. generous

Decreasing Comparison

To show decreasing comparisons, modifiers form the comparative degree by using *less* and the superlative degree by using *least*.

Positive	Comparative	Superlative
sharp	**less** sharp	**least** sharp
costly	**less** costly	**least** costly
often	**less** often	**least** often
frequently	**less** frequently	**least** frequently

Irregular Comparison

The comparative and superlative degrees of some modifiers are irregular in form.

Positive	Comparative	Superlative
bad	worse	worst
far	farther *or* further	farthest *or* furthest
good	better	best
well	better	best
many	more	most
much	more	most

Review A **Writing Comparative and Superlative Forms of Modifiers**

Correctly complete each of the following sentences with the comparative or superlative form of the italicized adjective or adverb given.

EXAMPLE   **1.** *unusual*   The Corn Palace in Mitchell, South Dakota, is one of the _____ buildings in the United States.

    1. *most unusual*

1. *big*   The Corn Palace is _____ than I thought it would be.

2. *pretty*   People in Mitchell try to make each year's Corn Palace decorations _____ than the ones before.

3. *fresh*   The building looks the _____ in September after new corn and grasses are put on it.

4. *easy*   Some workers find it _____ to saw and nail the corn to panels, while others prefer to hang the finished panels on the building.

1. bigger
2. prettier [*or* more pretty]
3. freshest
4. easier [*or* more easy]

USAGE

USAGE

Cooperative Learning

Divide the class into groups of three. Ask students to consider the ways in which using comparative and superlative words is important in the area of social studies. [*Comparisons might be made between the sizes of two countries, their populations, their gross national products, and/or the amounts of specific items they produce (agricultural or manufactured goods, natural resources).*]

Each student could research one country (you may want to provide a list of choices); then, students could divide the tasks of defining categories for comparison, creating a chart, and presenting the group's findings to the class. Students could then compare the countries based on each group's findings.

5. best	**5.** *well*
6. most mysterious	**6.** *mysterious*
7. most famous	**7.** *famous*
8. most interesting	**8.** *interesting*
9. more slowly	**9.** *slowly*
10. farther	**10.** *far*

I could not decide which of the many corn murals on the Corn Palace I liked ____.

The mural of the dancing figure was the ____ one to me.

Until his death in 1983, Mitchell's ____ artist, Oscar Howe, helped to design and paint these murals.

The life of this Sioux artist is the ____ story I've ever heard.

My parents walked ____ around the Corn Palace than I did and studied every design.

I met a family from Mexico who had traveled ____ than we had to see the Corn Palace.

Special Problems in Using Modifiers

Rules 20d–g *(pp. 536–540)*

OBJECTIVES

- **To decide when to use adjectives and when to use adverbs in sentences**

- **To revise sentences to eliminate double comparisons**

- **To revise sentences to eliminate double negatives**

Reference Note

For more about **using good** and **well**, see page 557.

Special Problems in Using Modifiers

20d. Use *good* to modify a noun or a pronoun in most cases. Use *well* to modify a verb.

EXAMPLES   The weather was **good** on the day of the match. [*Good* modifies the noun *weather*.]

If you want a pear, here is a **good** one. [*Good* modifies the pronoun *one*.]

The trees are producing **well** this fall. [*Well* modifies the verb phrase *are producing*.]

RESOURCES

Special Problems in Using Modifiers
Practice
- *Grammar, Usage, and Mechanics,* pp. 223, 224, 225, 226
- *Language Workshop CD-ROM,* Lesson 21

Good should not be used to modify a verb.

NONSTANDARD   Both teams played good.

    STANDARD   Both teams played **well.**

Although *well* is usually used as an adverb, *well* may also be used as an adjective meaning "in good health" or "in good condition."

EXAMPLE   Mom feels quite **well** today. [Meaning "in good health," *well* modifies *Mom.*]

20e. Use adjectives, not adverbs, after linking verbs.

Linking verbs are often followed by predicate adjectives modifying the subject.

EXAMPLES   Ingrid looked **sleepy** [not *sleepily*] this morning. [The predicate adjective *sleepy* modifies the subject *Ingrid.*]

    Christina felt **uncertain** [not *uncertainly*] about running in the relay race. [The predicate adjective *uncertain* modifies the subject *Christina.*]

NOTE   Some verbs can be used as either linking or action verbs. As action verbs, they may be modified by adverbs.

EXAMPLES   Ingrid looked **sleepily** at the clock. [*Sleepily* modifies the action verb *looked.*]

    Christina **uncertainly** felt her way along the hall. [*Uncertainly* modifies the action verb *felt.*]

Exercise 2 **Using Adjectives and Adverbs Correctly**

Choose the adjective or adverb that will make each sentence correct.

EXAMPLE   **1.** John seems (*nervous, nervously*) about his speech.

    1. nervous

1. When we came into the house after ice-skating, the fire felt (*good, well*).
2. The wind sounds (*fierce, fiercely*) at night.
3. Tino looked (*good, well*) after recovering from his operation.
4. After all, it doesn't taste (*bad, badly*).
5. Venus looks (*beautiful, beautifully*) tonight.
6. Liang cooked a (*good, well*) meal of vegetables and shrimp.

Reference Note

For a discussion of **standard and nonstandard English,** see page 553.

Reference Note

For a list of **linking verbs,** see page 359.

Relating to Literature

At the beginning of *Flowers for Algernon,* the main character, Charlie, mistakenly uses *good* to modify a verb. After the experiment begins to work, however, Charlie makes fewer and fewer mistakes in his writing. He even learns to use *well* rather than *good,* when appropriate. If *Flowers for Algernon* is in your literature textbook, have students read it (or selections from it) and discuss how the changes in Charlie's language arts skills contribute to plot and character development in the story.

USAGE

7. Is the sick child feeling (*good*, *well*) enough to eat something?
8. We looked (*close*, *closely*) at the fragile cocoon.
9. A cup of soup tastes (*good*, *well*) on a cold day.
10. Kudzu grows (*rapid*, *rapidly*) in the South.

20f. Avoid using double comparisons.

A ***double comparison*** is the use of both –*er* and *more* (or *less*) or –*est* and *most* (or *least*) to form a comparison. When you make a comparison, use only one form, not both.

| NONSTANDARD | This is Kathleen Battle's most finest performance. |
| STANDARD | This is Kathleen Battle's **finest** performance. |

| NONSTANDARD | His hair is more curlier than his sister's. |
| STANDARD | His hair is **curlier** than his sister's. |

| NONSTANDARD | The baby is less fussier in the morning than in the evening. |
| STANDARD | The baby is **less fussy** in the morning than in the evening. |

Exercise 3 Correcting Double Comparisons

Identify the incorrect modifier in each of the following sentences. Then, give the correct form of the modifier.

EXAMPLES
1. I have been studying more harder lately.
   1. *more harder—harder*

2. Frederick Douglass was one of the most brilliantest speakers against slavery.
   2. *most brilliantest—most brilliant*

1. Sunday was less ~~rainier~~ than Saturday.   1. rainy
2. That is the ~~most~~ saddest story I have ever heard.
3. Are you exercising more ~~oftener~~ than you used to?
4. That evening was the least ~~cloudiest~~ one in weeks.   4. cloudy
5. Native arctic peoples have learned to survive in the ~~most~~ coldest weather.
6. Please show me the ~~most~~ finest tennis racket in the shop.
7. It is ~~more~~ farther from New York to Montreal than from New York to Boston.
8. Grumpkins was less ~~jollier~~ than the other elves.   8. jolly

USAGE

9. Your suitcase is ~~more~~ lighter since you took out the boots.
10. Is Venus the ~~most~~ brightest object in the sky tonight?

Double Negatives

20g. Avoid using double negatives.

A *double negative* is the use of two or more negative words to express one negative idea. Most of the negative words in the chart below are adjectives or adverbs.

Common Negative Words			
barely	never	none	nothing
hardly	no	no one	nowhere
neither	nobody	not (–n't)	scarcely

NONSTANDARD	We couldn't hardly move in the subway car.
STANDARD	We **could hardly** move in the subway car.

NONSTANDARD	Yolanda didn't eat no breakfast this morning.
STANDARD	Yolanda **didn't** eat **any** breakfast this morning.
STANDARD	Yolanda **ate no** breakfast this morning.

NONSTANDARD	Didn't she get you nothing for your birthday?
STANDARD	**Didn't** she get you **anything** for your birthday?
STANDARD	Did she get you **nothing** for your birthday?

Exercise 4 Correcting Double Negatives

Revise each of the following sentences to eliminate the double negative.   Revisions may vary.

EXAMPLE   **1.** I couldn't find no one to go camping with me.
    1. I couldn't find anyone to go camping with me.
                        or
    I could find no one to go camping with me.

1. I didn't see ~~no one~~ I knew at the game.
2. Early Spanish explorers searched that area of Florida for gold, but they didn't find ~~none~~.

4. anything

3. We could~~n't~~ hardly hear the guest speaker.
4. The cafeteria didn't serve ~~nothing~~ I like today. ∧
5. Double negatives ~~don't~~ have no place in standard English.

6. any

6. The bird-watchers saw scarcely ~~no~~ bald eagles this year. ∧

7. any

7. The club officers never do ~~none~~ of the work themselves. ∧
8. We would~~n't~~ never need three tractors on our small farm.
9. Jesse could~~n't~~ barely see the top of the waterfalls.

10. anywhere

10. The Paynes didn't go ~~nowhere~~ special during the three-day ∧ holiday weekend.

Review B Using Modifiers Correctly

Most of the following sentences contain errors in the use of modifiers. Revise each incorrect sentence to eliminate the error. If a sentence is already correct, write *C*.   Revisions may vary.

EXAMPLES

1. My cold is worst today than it was yesterday.

   1. *My cold is worse today than it was yesterday.*

2. There wasn't nobody willing to go into that house alone.

   2. *There wasn't anybody willing to go into that house alone.*

1. C

1. She is the funnier of the two comedians.
2. Kendo, a Japanese martial art, is more gracefu~~ller~~ than many other sports.

3. well

3. No one in our class can play volleyball as ~~good~~ as Sylvia Yee. ∧

4. really

4. Time passes ~~real~~ slowly during the summer. ∧

5. C [*or* well]

5. After a long swim, she felt good.
6. I was~~n't~~ scarcely able to hear you.

7. stronger

7. Which of the Rogers twins is ~~strongest~~? ∧

8. any

8. Some people don't seem to have ~~no~~ control over their tempers. ∧

9. visits

9. He hardly ever ~~visit~~ us.

10. [*or* most simple]

10. Of all the folk dances my grandfather taught me, the polka is the ~~most~~ simplest.

Placement of Modifiers

20h. Place modifying words, phrases, and clauses as close as possible to the words they modify.

Placement of Modifiers

Rule 20h *(pp. 540–548)*

OBJECTIVES

- To revise sentences to eliminate misplaced or dangling modifiers

- To add prepositional phrases correctly to sentences

- To revise sentences to place participles and participial phrases correctly

- To revise sentences to eliminate misplaced or dangling participial phrases

- To revise sentences to eliminate misplaced clause modifiers

RESOURCES

Placement of Modifiers

Practice

- *Grammar, Usage, and Mechanics,* pp. 227, 228, 229, 230–231
- *Language Workshop CD-ROM,* Lesson 22

Notice how the meaning of the following sentence changes when the position of the phrase *from Cincinnati* changes.

EXAMPLES   The basketball player **from Cincinnati** gave a TV interview for his fans. [The phrase modifies *player*.]

The basketball player gave a TV interview for his fans **from Cincinnati.** [The phrase modifies *fans*.]

From Cincinnati the basketball player gave a TV interview for his fans. [The phrase modifies *gave*.]

A modifier that seems to modify the wrong word in a sentence is called a ***misplaced modifier.*** A modifier that does not clearly modify another word in a sentence is called a ***dangling modifier.***

MISPLACED   Ringing, everyone glared at the man with the cell phone.

CORRECT   Everyone glared at the man with the **ringing** cell phone.

DANGLING   Before moving to Philadelphia, Mexico City was their home.

CORRECT   **Before moving to Philadelphia,** they lived in Mexico City.

Prepositional Phrases

A ***prepositional phrase*** consists of a preposition, a noun or a pronoun called the *object of the preposition*, and any modifiers of that object.

A prepositional phrase used as an adjective generally should be placed directly after the word it modifies.

MISPLACED   The hat belongs to that girl with the feathers.

CLEAR   The hat **with the feathers** belongs to that girl.

A prepositional phrase used as an adverb should be placed near the word it modifies.

MISPLACED   She read that a new restaurant had opened in today's newspaper.

CLEAR   She read **in today's newspaper** that a new restaurant had opened.

| STYLE   TIP |

Be sure to place modifiers correctly to show clearly the meaning you intend.

EXAMPLES

Only Mrs. Garza teaches Spanish. [Mrs. Garza, not anybody else, teaches Spanish.]

Mrs. Garza **only** teaches Spanish. [Mrs. Garza teaches Spanish; she does not research Spanish texts.]

Mrs. Garza teaches **only** Spanish. [Mrs. Garza does not teach any other subjects.]

Reference Note

For more about **prepositions,** see page 370. For more about **prepositional phrases,** see page 371.

USAGE

Activity. Students (especially visual learners and students with strong logical-mathematical intelligence) might benefit from a diagramming example taken from **Exercise 5.** Have the class help you diagram the following sentence after you write it on the chalkboard.

Incorrect: The poster caught my eye on the wall.
Correct: The poster on the wall caught my eye.

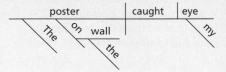

Explain to students that diagramming helps to clarify the relationship between modifiers and the words they modify. Explain that students can try diagramming if they are having trouble analyzing or correcting sentences. For further practice in diagramming to show the placement of modifiers, have students diagram more of the sentences in **Exercise 5,** or refer to them to the **Diagramming Appendix.**

COMPUTER TIP

A computer can help you find and correct problems with modifiers. For example, a spell-checker can easily find nonstandard forms such as *baddest, expensiver,* and *mostest.* However, you will need to examine the placement of phrase and clause modifiers yourself.

HELP

Although some items in Exercise 5 can be revised in more than one way, you need to give only one revision for each. You may need to add, delete, or rearrange words.

Avoid placing a prepositional phrase so that it seems to modify either of two words. Place the phrase so that it clearly modifies the word you intend it to modify.

MISPLACED   Manuel said in the afternoon he would call Janet.
[Does *in the afternoon* modify *said* or *would call*?]

CLEAR   Manuel said he would call Janet **in the afternoon.**
[The phrase modifies *would call.*]

CLEAR   **In the afternoon** Manuel said he would call Janet.
[The phrase modifies *said.*]

Exercise 5 Revising Sentences with Misplaced Prepositional Phrases

Each of the following sentences contains a misplaced prepositional phrase. Decide where the prepositional phrase belongs; then, revise the sentence.   Revisions will vary.

EXAMPLES   1. In the United States, Zora Neale Hurston grew up in the first self-governed black township.

1. *Zora Neale Hurston grew up in the first self-governed black township in the United States.*

2. The cat toy rolled down the hall with a clatter.

2. *With a clatter, the cat toy rolled down the hall.*

1. Joshua and Reginald heard that there was a destructive hailstorm on the news.
2. The poster caught my eye on the wall.
3. In the tiny bird's nest, we thought there might be eggs.
4. Our teacher said on Monday the class would put on a play.
5. Don't forget to take the box to the store with the empty bottles.
6. We saw José Clemente Orozco's beautiful murals on vacation in Guadalajara.
7. Tranh read that a wasp larva spins a cocoon in the encyclopedia.
8. A beautiful Bolivian weaving hangs on our living room wall from the town of Trinidad.
9. Did you find the kimonos worn by your grandmother in that old trunk?
10. In confusion, they watched with amusement as the puppies scrambled all over each other.

    Continued on pp. 543–544

Comma Usage. If students are having trouble revising sentences due to uncertainty about comma usage, give them the following rules:

1. When a clause or phrase is not essential to the meaning of a sentence—that is, if the basic meaning of the sentence is the same without it—the clause or phrase should be set off by commas; for example, "My brother, who is a vegetarian, loves tofu."

Placing Prepositional Phrases Correctly

Rewrite each of the following sentences, adding the prepositional phrase given in parentheses.   Answers may vary.

EXAMPLE   **1.** Many paintings show strange, fantastical scenes. (*by Marc Chagall*)

1. *Many paintings by Marc Chagall show strange, fantastical scenes.*

1. Chagall's *The Green Violinist* contains many delightful mysteries and surprises. (*for the eye and mind*)
2. As you can see in the painting, a gigantic violinist sits among the buildings of a small village. (*with a green face and hand*)
3. Dark windows look just like the windows of the houses. (*on the musician's pants*)
4. A man waves to the violinist, and a dog taller than a house seems to smile at the music it hears. (*above the clouds*)
5. As you look at the painting's bright colors, perhaps you can almost hear the enchanting music. (*of the green violinist*)
6. You may be surprised to learn that the fiddler is found in many of Chagall's other works. (*in this painting*)
7. Chagall enjoyed listening to his uncle play the violin. (*during his childhood*)
8. *The Green Violinist* and other paintings of the fiddler are tributes. (*to Chagall's uncle*)
9. In a painting titled *Violinist*, Chagall painted himself standing. (*beside the violinist*)
10. In that unusual painting, Chagall has three heads turned to show enjoyment of the music. (*toward the uncle*)

┌ H E L P ─

Be careful to place each prepositional phrase in Exercise 6 near the word or words it modifies.

The Granger Collection, New York

USAGE

Viewing the Art

The Green Violinist. Marc Chagall's choice of subject matter was influenced by his love for Russian and Jewish folklore, and he was also inspired by the Fauvists to use bright colors and by the Cubists to experiment with space. Chagall often ignored traditional treatment of perspective in his paintings. In *The Green Violinist,* for example, the houses in the background are roughly the same size as those in the foreground (traditional artists draw background figures smaller and foreground figures larger to give the illusion of depth), and the animal at the bottom left of the painting is as large as the dwelling by its side.

Placement of Modifiers   **543**

---

2. An introductory phrase is usually followed by a comma; for example, "Feeling excited about the first day of cool weather, she decided to take her dog for a walk."

Write the following sentences on the chalkboard without commas, and ask students to copy the sentences and to add commas:

My mother, who was born in Georgia, is an attorney.

Reference Note

For more information about **participles,** see page 410. For more about **participial phrases,** see page 412.

┌─────────────────────────┐
│ S T Y L E   T I P │
└─────────────────────────┘

A dangling modifier often occurs when a sentence is in the passive voice. Rewriting sentences in the active voice not only eliminates many dangling modifiers but also makes your writing more interesting and lively.

PASSIVE VOICE
   Having just waxed the car, a trip to the fair was planned. [*Having just waxed the car* is a dangling modifier.]

ACTIVE VOICE
   Having just waxed the car, I planned a trip to the fair. [*Having just washed the car* modifies *I.*]

Reference Note

For more about **active voice and passive voice,** see page 499.

Reference Note

For more information on **using commas with participial phrases,** see pages 607 and 613.

Participial Phrases

A *participial phrase* consists of a present participle or a past participle and its modifiers and complements. A participial phrase is used as an adjective to modify a noun or a pronoun. Like a prepositional phrase, a participial phrase should be placed as close as possible to the word it modifies.

EXAMPLES **Walking to school,** Celia and James found a wallet. [The participial phrase modifies *Celia* and *James.*]

I. M. Pei, **born in China,** is a gifted architect. [The participial phrase modifies *I. M. Pei.*]

A participial phrase that is not placed near the noun or pronoun that it modifies is a *misplaced modifier.*

MISPLACED Stolen from the media center, the deputies found the videocassette recorder. [Were the deputies stolen from the media center?]

CLEAR The deputies found the videocassette recorder **stolen from the media center.**

MISPLACED Sleeping on the roof, I saw the neighbor's cat. [Was I sleeping on the roof?]

CLEAR I saw the neighbor's cat **sleeping on the roof.**

MISPLACED We're used to the noise living by the airport. [Is the noise living by the airport?]

CLEAR **Living by the airport,** we're used to the noise.

A participial phrase that does not clearly and logically modify a word in the sentence is a *dangling modifier.*

DANGLING Cleaning the attic, an old trunk was found. [Who was cleaning the attic?]

CLEAR **Cleaning the attic,** we found an old trunk.

(**Exercise 7**) **Placing Participial Phrases Correctly**

Rewrite each of the following sentences, adding the participial phrases given in parentheses. Be sure to use commas to set off participial phrases that begin or interrupt your sentences.

Answers may vary.

┌─────────┐
│ MINI-   │
│ LESSON │
└─────────┘

Walking home from school, we found a lost puppy.

For more information on comma usage, refer students to **Chapter 23: Punctuation.**

EXAMPLES

   1. Finn and Darcy searched for their younger sister. (*scanning the crowd*)

   1. Scanning the crowd, Finn and Darcy searched for their younger sister.

   2. The sea turtle ducked back into its shell. (*startled by the sound of the boat's engine*)

   2. Startled by the sound of the boat's engine, the sea turtle ducked back into its shell.

1. My older sister will be working at the garden center near my house. (*beginning next week*)

2. Our new kitten crawled under the sofa. (*exploring the house*)

3. By mistake, we sat on the swings. (*freshly painted*)

4. Lucy helped her brother find the books. (*lost somewhere in his messy room*)

5. Josie and Fred passed the playground. (*walking through the park*)

6. Ms. Surat told us about Sri Lanka and its people. (*pointing to the map*)

7. The two girls yelled loudly. (*surprised by their little brother*)

8. The horse likes to watch people. (*munching on grass*)

9. Andrea picked up the pencil and waited for the test to begin. (*sharpened moments earlier*)

10. On the beach this morning, the children found a mysterious note. (*folded in a blue bottle*)

Exercise 8   **Revising Sentences to Correct Misplaced and Dangling Participial Phrases**

Revise all sentences that contain misplaced or dangling participial phrases. If a sentence is already correct, write *C*.

EXAMPLE   **1.** Made from matzo meal, Rachel cooks tasty dumplings.

    1. Rachel cooks tasty dumplings made from matzo meal.

1. Pacing in its cage, I watched the lion.

2. Talking on the telephone, Amanda did not hear the doorbell ringing.

3. Exploring the cave, a new tunnel was discovered.

┌HELP─

Although some items in Exercise 7 can be revised in more than one way, you need to give only one revision for each.

┌HELP─

You will need to add, delete, or rearrange some words in your revisions for Exercise 8.

Exercise 7

ALTERNATIVE LESSON
Ask students to name the two types of participles introduced in **Chapter 14: The Phrase** [*present participles and past participles*]. Next, have them identify the type of participle to be added to sentences 1, 2, 5, 6, and 8. [*present*] Finally, have them identify the type of participle to be added to sentences 3, 4, 7, 9, and 10. [*past*] Remind students that present participles end in –*ing* and regular past participles end in –*d* or –*ed*.

Exercise 8   **Revising Sentences to Correct Misplaced and Dangling Participial Phrases**

ANSWERS
Revisions may vary.

  1. I watched the lion pacing in its cage.

  2. C

  3. Exploring the cave, we discovered a new tunnel.

Exercise 8 Revising Sentences to Correct Misplaced and Dangling Participial Phrases

ANSWERS continued

4. The circus featured a clown wearing a bright orange suit and floppy yellow shoes.

5. The two young girls walked slowly through the field filled with countless daisies.

6. While he was reading his part, his nervousness was hard to overcome.

7. The turkey, stuffed with sage and bread crumbs, was large enough for three families.

8. Tired from the long walk through the snow, we welcomed food and rest.

9. C

10. Selling the old farm, she felt sadness well up inside.

Meeting INDIVIDUAL NEEDS

MODALITIES

Visual and Kinesthetic Learners. Write on the chalkboard four sentences containing adjective clauses. Have student volunteers come to the chalkboard, circle the adjective clauses, and draw arrows from the clauses to the words they modify. Possible sentences:

1. Akeem, who is very good at math, helped me study.

2. I enjoyed the movie that we saw.

3. The man whose books you borrowed wants them back.

4. The bicycle that she rides to school is broken.

4. Wearing a bright orange suit and floppy yellow shoes, the circus featured a clown.

5. Filled with countless daisies, the two young girls walked slowly through the field.

6. Reading his part, the nervousness was hard to overcome.

7. The turkey was large enough for three families stuffed with sage and bread crumbs.

8. Tired from the long walk through the snow, food and rest were welcomed.

9. Checking the shelves, Judy found all the reference books she needed.

10. Selling the old farm, sadness welled up inside.

Adjective Clauses

An *adjective clause* modifies a noun or a pronoun. Most adjective clauses begin with a relative pronoun—*that, which, who, whom,* or *whose.* Like an adjective phrase, an adjective clause should generally be placed directly after the word it modifies.

MISPLACED   The Labor Day picnic in the park that we had was fun. [Did we have the park?]

CLEAR   The Labor Day picnic **that we had** in the park was fun.

MISPLACED   The girls thanked their coach who had won the relay race. [Did the coach win the relay race?]

CLEAR   The girls **who had won the relay race** thanked their coach.

Exercise 9 Revising Sentences with Misplaced Clause Modifiers

Revise each of the following sentences by placing the adjective clause near the word it should modify.

EXAMPLE   1. My friend Beverly visited me who lives in Sarasota, Florida.

1. *My friend Beverly, who lives in Sarasota, Florida, visited me.*

1. The students received an A who made the first presentation.

2. The kitten belongs to my neighbor that is on the branch.

Reference Note

For more about **adjective clauses,** see page 427.

┌─HELP─
Be sure to use commas to set off nonessential adjective clauses.

Reference Note

For information on using commas to set off **nonessential adjective clauses,** see page 607.

Learning for Life

Continued on pp. 547–548

Comparison Shopping. Every day, students are bombarded with advertisements claiming that some company's products are the best—or at least better than the competition's. Ask students to compare three different brands of a product, such as a video game. Students should use a rating chart like the one on p. 547.

3. I showed the colorful cotton fabric ʌ to my sister. ~~that was made in Kenya.~~

4. The doctor ʌ said that the triplets were quite healthy. ~~who examined them.~~

5. The cleanup program ʌ was supported by all of the students. ~~that the president of the seventh-grade class suggested.~~

6. The flight attendant ʌ welcomed us aboard the plane. ~~whose brother I know.~~

7. The friend ʌ has a broken leg. ~~whom I called.~~

8. Donald's package ʌ is from his mother. ~~which came in the mail.~~

9. Quasars ʌ fascinate me. ~~which many astronomers throughout the world study.~~

10. The dog ʌ barked at the letter carrier. ~~that has been running loose in the neighborhood.~~

Review C **Correcting Errors in the Use of Modifiers**

Each of the following sentences contains an error in the use, form, or placement of a modifier. Revise each sentence by changing the form of a modifier or by adding, deleting, or rearranging words. Answers may vary.

EXAMPLE **1.** I have never been more happier in my life.

    1. I have never been happier in my life.

1. My stepsister plays both soccer and softball, but she likes soccer ~~best.~~ **1.** better

2. The waiter brought plates ~~to Terrell and me~~ piled high with spaghetti and meat sauce ʌ. **2.** to Terrell and me.

3. Very frustrated ʌ her locker ~~just would not open~~! **3.** she just could not open

4. Barking and growling loudly ʌ the stranger ~~was frightened by the dogs.~~ **4.** the dogs frightened

5. The antique German cuckoo clock still runs ʌ ~~good~~ after all these years. **5.** well

6. I didn't do too ʌ ~~bad~~ on the geography quiz this morning. **6.** badly

7. Our puppy is much more playful ~~ler~~ than our older dog is.

8. We drove ʌ ~~slow~~ past the duck pond to see if any new ducklings had hatched. **8.** slowly

9. They never did find ʌ ~~no~~ sponsor for their team. **9.** a

10. The CD ʌ is the soundtrack of my favorite movie. ~~that we heard.~~ **10.** that we heard

┌HELP─

Although some sentences in Review C can be correctly revised in more than one way, you need to give only one revision for each sentence.

TEACHING **TIP**

Reviews You may wish to use **Review C** as guided practice, then have students complete **Review D** as independent practice.

USAGE

Placement of Modifiers **547**

	PRICE	FEATURE 1	FEATURE 2	FEATURE 3
Brand A				
Brand B				
Brand C				

Placement of Modifiers **547**

Review D Proofreading Sentences for Correct Use of Modifiers

ANSWERS
Revisions may vary.

1. Her mother thought that a law career would offer her daughter the brightest future.
2. Ms. Atencio always knew she would become a lawyer, but she never expected to be so successful.
3. Looking ahead to college and law school, she made excellent grades in high school.
4. Along with two other Hispanic women, she helped to launch Denver's first bilingual radio station in 1985.
5. Ms. Atencio felt quite proud about helping to organize Colorado's first minority women lawyers' conference.
6. Receiving encouragement from a friend, she decided to run for president of the Hispanic National Bar Association (HNBA).
7. Serving as president of HNBA, she made the legal rights of Hispanics her main focus.
8. In 1991, *Hispanic Business Magazine* named her one of the most outstanding Hispanic women.
9. For all the time she had devoted to community service, she also was given the Outstanding Young Woman Award from the city of Denver.
10. In addition to enjoying community service, Ms. Atencio feels really good when she is spending time with her family.

Review D Proofreading Sentences for Correct Use of Modifiers

Each of the following sentences contains an error in the use, form, or placement of a modifier. Revise each sentence by changing the form of a modifier or by adding, deleting, or rearranging words.

EXAMPLE
1. Of all the important women featured in this book, Dolores S. Atencio is the one I admire more.
   1. *Of all the important women featured in this book, Dolores S. Atencio is the one I admire most.*

1. Her mother thought that a law career would offer her daughter the most brightest future.
2. Ms. Atencio always knew she would become a lawyer, but she didn't never expect to be so successful.
3. Looking ahead to college and law school, her grades in high school were excellent.
4. Along with two other Hispanic women, her efforts helped to launch Denver's first bilingual radio station in 1985.
5. Ms. Atencio felt quite proudly about helping to organize Colorado's first minority women lawyers' conference.
6. She decided to run for president of the Hispanic National Bar Association (HNBA) receiving encouragement from a friend.
7. Serving as president of HNBA, the legal rights of Hispanics were her main focus.
8. In 1991, she was named one of the most outstanding Hispanic women in *Hispanic Business Magazine.*
9. She also was given the Outstanding Young Woman Award from the city of Denver, which she received for all the time she had devoted to community service.
10. In addition to enjoying community service, Ms. Atencio feels really well when she is spending time with her family.

Learning for Life

Then, have each student write a testimonial to the company that makes the best brand, in his or her opinion. Letters should list the good qualities of the favorite brand and provide specific comparisons with features of the other two brands. Have students pay particular attention to their use of comparative and superlative forms and to the placement of their phrase and clause modifiers. Students could post their letters in class or compile a consumer's guide using the charts and letters of the entire class.

Chapter Review

A. Using the Correct Modifier

Identify the word in parentheses that will make each sentence correct.

1. I have to admit that this recording sounds (*bad, badly*).

2. Our Irish setter came (*shy, shyly*) toward the new puppy.

3. Yoki was anxious, but she appeared (*calm, calmly*).

4. Must the twins play so (*noisy, noisily*)?

5. We're pleased that you did so (*good, well*).

6. The storm ended as (*sudden, suddenly*) as it began.

7. With a little oil, the engine started (*easy, easily*).

8. Their performance is now (*good, well*) enough for any stage.

9. The kitchen counter looks (*clean, cleanly*).

10. It is (*good, well*) to be alive on a beautiful day like today.

11. Of the five designs, which one do you like (*better, best*)?

12. José Canseco played (*good, well*).

13. This ring is the (*more, most*) expensive of the two.

14. That striped tie would go (*good, well*) with your green shirt.

15. Choose the (*larger, largest*) of the two poodles.

B. Writing Comparative and Superlative Forms of Modifiers

Write the comparative or superlative form of the italicized adjective or adverb in each of the following sentences.

16. *dry*	The towels felt ____ after an afternoon on the clothesline than they had felt coming out of the washer.
17. *grateful*	We were ____ for Mr. Chang's advice than we could say.
18. *small*	The screwdriver my father used to repair my glasses was the ____ one he had.
19. *proud*	After the awards ceremony, Kerry seemed ____ of her son than she ever had before.
20. *slow*	The ____ horse of them all finished last in the race.

16. drier

17. more grateful

18. smallest

19. prouder

20. slowest

Using the Chapter Review

The **Chapter Review** asks students to identify the correct use of modifiers in sentences. The results can be compared to those of the **Diagnostic Preview** to assess student progress. If students are still having difficulty, refer them to **Exercises 21–24** in **Chapter 26: Correcting Common Errors** for additional practice.

USAGE

21. most enthusiastically

22. tastier [*or* more tasty]

23. most loyal

24. more easily

25. tallest

21. *enthusiastically* — Pleased by all the performances, the audience applauded ____ for the dancers.

22. *tasty* — Since Dad started taking cooking classes, each dinner is ____ than the previous one.

23. *loyal* — Tadger is the ____ of our three dogs.

24. *easily* — With more practice, we solved the second puzzle ____ than the first one.

25. *tall* — Which of the five Romine girls do you think is ____?

C. Correcting Double Comparisons and Double Negatives

Rewrite the following sentences to correct errors in the use of modifiers.   Revisions may vary.

26. These Hawaiian shirts don't have ~~no~~ pockets.   26. any

27. Pineapple juice tastes ~~more~~ sweeter than orange juice to me.

28. What is the ~~most~~ funniest thing that ever happened to you?

29. I can~~'t~~ hardly take another step.

30. Sakima could~~n't~~ barely catch her breath after running so far.

D. Correcting Misplaced and Dangling Modifiers

Each sentence below contains a misplaced or dangling modifier. Rewrite the sentences so that they are clear. You may need to add, delete, or rearrange words.   Revisions may vary.

31. bruised by the storm
32. that you heard
33. we left
34. When I opened
35. As my brother was / him
36. , born in Virginia,
37. While I was
38. , are using fish ladders

31. The fruit was marked for quick sale ~~bruised by the storm.~~

32. Those tapes came from the library ~~that you heard.~~

33. After ~~leaving~~ India, Singapore was the next destination.

34. ~~Opening~~ a savings account, a form of identification was required.

35. Skateboarding down the street, a large dog chased ~~my brother.~~

36. Black Hawk was a chief of the Sauk people ~~born in Virginia.~~

37. Trying to study, the noise from the chainsaw was distracting.

38. These salmon ~~are using fish ladders,~~ which are returning to spawn.

USAGE

39. Sifting carefully through the sand, an old Spanish coin called a doubloon,~~was found.~~

40. I saw the gazelles jumping,~~through the binoculars.~~

39. she found

40. Through the binoculars,

Writing Application
Using Comparisons in a Letter

Comparative and Superlative Forms   An anonymous donor has given a large sum of money for improvements to your school. Write a letter to the administrators describing the improvements you would like to see. Use at least three comparative and two superlative forms of adjectives and adverbs in your writing.

Prewriting   What facilities, equipment, or supplies would make your school a better place? List your improvement ideas. You may want to discuss your ideas with a classmate or a teacher before you select the ones to include in your letter. Also, note why the improvements are needed.

Writing   As you write your first draft, use your list to help you make clear and accurate comparisons. Keep your audience in mind. The administrators need practical suggestions for how to spend the money, so let them know exactly what improvements your school needs and why.

Revising   Read your letter to a parent or other adult to see if your arguments are convincing. Add, delete, or rearrange details to make your letter more interesting and effective.

Publishing   Be sure you have used the correct comparative and superlative forms of adjectives and adverbs. Check the form of your letter to make sure it follows the guidelines for business letters. Read through your letter a final time to catch any errors in spelling, grammar, usage, or punctuation. Share your ideas for improving the school with the rest of the class, and make a chart displaying the most popular suggestions.

Reference Note

See "Writing" in the Quick Reference Handbook for guidelines on **writing business letters.**

OBJECTIVE

- To write a letter to the school's administrators, using comparative and superlative adjectives and adverbs

Writing Application

Tip. This assignment gives students practice writing business letters. Students must consider their audience (the school administrators) and their purpose (to influence administrators' decisions about how the money given to the school should be spent).

If students need help with persuasive writing, refer them to **Chapter 6: Convincing Others.**

Scoring Rubric. While you will want to pay particular attention to students' use of modifiers, you will also want to evaluate overall writing performance. You may want to give a split score to indicate development and clarity of the composition as well as usage skills.

RESOURCES

Writing Application

Extension

- *Grammar, Usage, and Mechanics,* p. 239
- *Language Workshop CD-ROM,* Lessons 20–22

CHAPTER

21

A Glossary of Usage
Common Usage Problems

Diagnostic Preview

Correcting Errors in Usage

Each of the following sentences contains an error in the use of formal, standard English. Revise each sentence to correct the error.

EXAMPLE   1. They did they're best to help.

           1. *They did their best to help.*

1. all ready
2. among
3. bring
4. well

6. teach

8. have
9. used
10. who
11. all right
12. that
13. They're
14. burst
15. unless
16. than

1. We are ~~already~~ for our trip to Washington, D.C.
2. They divided the crackers equally ~~between~~ the four toddlers.
3. Please ~~take~~ those packages here to me.
4. Elena had a cold, but she is feeling ~~good~~ now.
5. Mr. Chang ~~he~~ is my tai chi instructor.
6. Will you ~~learn~~ me how to play chess?
7. May I borrow that ~~there~~ collection of Cheyenne folk tales?
8. Tara might ~~of~~ come with us, but she had to baby-sit.
9. We ~~use~~ to live in Karachi, Pakistan.
10. She is the woman ~~which~~ owns the Great Dane.
11. I dropped the pictures, but I think they're ~~alright~~.
12. I read ~~where~~ Mayor Alvarez will visit our school.
13. ~~Their~~ the best players on the team this season.
14. The pipes ~~busted~~ last winter during a hard freeze.
15. We cannot go sailing ~~without~~ we wear life jackets.
16. Her new apartment is bigger ~~then~~ her last one.

17. The group went ~~everywheres~~ together.
18. Lydia acted ~~like~~ she was bored.
19. *Antonyms* are ~~when~~ words are opposite in meaning.
20. I hope that you will ~~except~~ my apology.

17. everywhere
18. as if
19. that
20. accept

About the Glossary

This chapter contains an alphabetical list, or ***glossary,*** of many common problems in English usage. You will notice throughout the chapter that some examples are labeled *nonstandard, standard, formal,* or *informal.* **Nonstandard English** is language that does not follow the rules and guidelines of standard English. **Standard English** is language that is grammatically correct and appropriate in formal and informal situations. **Formal** identifies usage that is appropriate in serious speaking and writing situations (such as in speeches and compositions for school). The label **informal** indicates standard usage common in conversation and in everyday writing such as personal letters.

The following are examples of formal and informal English.

Formal	Informal
angry	steamed
unpleasant	yucky
agreeable	cool
very impressive	totally awesome

a, an Use *a* before words beginning with a consonant sound. Use *an* before words beginning with a vowel sound. Keep in mind that the sound, not the actual letter, that a word begins with determines whether *a* or *an* should be used.

EXAMPLES They are building **a** hospital near our house.

I bought **a** one-way ticket. [Even though *o* is a vowel, the word *one* begins with a consonant sound.]

I would like **an** orange.

We worked for **an** hour. [Although *h* is a consonant, the word *hour* begins with a vowel sound. The *h* is not pronounced.]

Reference Note

For a list of **words often confused,** see page 666.

COMPUTER TIP

The spellchecker on a computer will help you catch misspelled words such as *anywheres* and *nowheres.* The grammar checker may help you catch errors such as double negatives. However, in the case of words that are often misused, such as *than* and *then* and *between* and *among,* you will have to check your work yourself for correct usage.

HELP

In doing the exercises in this chapter, be sure to use only standard English.

A Glossary of Usage   **553**

A, An—Had Ought, Hadn't Ought

(pp. 553–559)

OBJECTIVES

■ To identify correct usage in sentences

■ To recognize nonstandard usage and to select correct formal, standard usage

Meeting INDIVIDUAL NEEDS

ENGLISH-LANGUAGE LEARNERS
General Strategies. Korean and Russian do not have articles, and Arabic does not have indefinite articles. Few languages other than English have articles that vary in form depending on the following sound. You may need to remind students that in English the use of *a* or *an* is determined by the sound of the following word.

Activity. To help students learn to replace *ain't* with standard contractions, write the following list on the chalkboard:

> you are not
>
> he is not
>
> we are not
>
> they are not
>
> I am not

Guide students through forming contractions with each of the groups of words. [*you're not, you aren't; he's not, he isn't; we're not, we aren't; they're not, they aren't; I'm not*] Ask for a student volunteer to write the contractions on the chalkboard as members of the class call them out. Stress to students that the bracketed answers are the only possible standard contractions for the given word groups; the use of *ain't* is nonstandard.

Activity. To inspire students to use alternatives for the overused *a lot,* bring in a copy of *An Exaltation of Larks* by James Lipton. This illustrated book lists traditional names for groups of animals, such as a "pride of lions." Lipton then coins a series of modern group names such as a "slouch of models" or a "wince of dentists." Have students work in small groups to come up with collective terms for numerous items or groupings in their world: books, teachers, homework, music videos, and so on.

STYLE **TIP**

Many writers overuse *a lot.* Whenever you run across *a lot* as you revise your own writing, try to replace it with a more exact word or phrase.

ACCEPTABLE
Emily Dickinson wrote a lot of poems.

BETTER
Emily Dickinson wrote **hundreds** of poems.

accept, except   *Accept* is a verb; it means "to receive." *Except* may be used as either a verb or a preposition. As a verb, it means "to leave out." As a preposition, *except* means "excluding."

EXAMPLES   Ann **accepted** the gift. [verb]

No one will be **excepted** from writing a research paper. [verb]

All my friends will be there **except** Jorge. [preposition]

ain't   Do not use this nonstandard word in formal situations.

all right   Used as an adjective, *all right* means "satisfactory" or "unhurt." Used as an adverb, *all right* means "well enough." *All right* should be written as two words.

EXAMPLES   Your science project looks **all right** to me. [adjective]

Judy cut her toe, but she is **all right** now. [adjective]

I did **all right** in the drama club tryouts. [adverb]

a lot   *A lot* should be written as two words.

EXAMPLE   I have read **a lot** of American Indian folk tales.

already, all ready   *Already* means "previously." *All ready* means "completely prepared."

EXAMPLES   By 5:00 P.M., I had **already** cooked dinner.

The students were **all ready** for the trip.

among   See **between, among.**

anyways, anywheres, everywheres, nowheres, somewheres   These words should have no final *s.*

EXAMPLE   I looked **everywhere** [not *everywheres*] for it!

as   See **like, as.**

as if, as though   See **like, as if, as though.**

at   Do not use *at* after *where.*

NONSTANDARD   Where are the Persian miniatures at?
STANDARD   Where are the Persian miniatures?

bad, badly   *Bad* is an adjective. It modifies nouns and pronouns. *Badly* is an adverb. It modifies verbs, adjectives, and adverbs.

EXAMPLES   The fruit tastes **bad.** [The predicate adjective *bad*
            modifies *fruit.*]

            Don't treat him **badly.** [The adverb *badly* modifies
            the verb *Do treat.*]

Exercise 1 Identifying Correct Usage

For each of the following sentences, choose the word or word
group in parentheses that is correct according to the rules of
formal, standard usage.

EXAMPLE   1. Navajo people came to the American Southwest from
              (*somewhere, somewheres*) in the North.

           1. *somewhere*

1. One group of Navajos settled in the region where the Pueblo
   people (*lived, lived at*).
2. The Pueblo people were (*already, all ready*) farming and living in permanent dwellings by the time the Navajos arrived.
3. The Navajos may have (*excepted, accepted*) the practice of
   sand painting from the Pueblos and adapted it to fit their
   own customs.
4. When the Navajo artists are
   (*all ready, already*) to begin a sand
   painting, they gather in a circle, as
   shown in the picture here.
5. When creating a sand painting,
   (*a, an*) artist receives directions
   from the singer, who leads the
   ceremony.
6. The painter might make a certain
   design when things are not (*all
   right, allright*) in the community.
7. The Navajo sand painter may also
   use this art to help someone who
   is injured or feeling (*badly, bad*).
8. Because sand paintings used in healing ceremonies are swept
   away at the end of each ceremony, the designs are recorded
   nowhere (*accept, except*) in the artist's imagination.
9. However, the patterns used in sand painting (*ain't, aren't*)
   limited to this art form.
10. Variations of the sacred designs can be found almost
    (*anywheres, anywhere*) on items that the Navajos make.

⌐S T Y L E   T I P⌐

The expression *feel badly*
has become acceptable
in informal situations
although it is not strictly
grammatical English.

INFORMAL
   Carl felt badly about
   losing the race.

FORMAL
   Carl felt **bad** about losing
   the race.

Meeting
|INDIVIDUAL|
NEEDS

MODALITIES
Visual Learners. Tell students that
they will create an illustrated book
to teach the words in this glossary.
Assign pairs of students to brainstorm visual ways to teach one of
the glossary entries. Students might
create cartoon drawings, three-
dimensional clay figures, or even a
tableau or computer-graphics presentation to illustrate the concepts. Be
sure that each important entry is covered, but allow more than one pair
of students to work on a specific
entry, if necessary. Assign a student
to photograph any display that cannot be pasted directly into a book.
Assign a volunteer to compile the
materials into an alphabetical book
to be kept in the classroom for easy
reference.

USAGE

MODALITIES

Auditory Learners. Auditory learners may have difficulty with *could of, should of,* and so on because the standard construction *could have* is often spoken quickly or even shortened to the contraction *could've;* to the ear it is virtually indistinguishable from *could of.* To reinforce the use of *have* instead of *of,* have students recite aloud sentences containing constructions that include *have* while dramatically exaggerating and emphasizing the *have's.* You could write the following sentences on the chalkboard for students to recite in sequence three or four times.

We should *have* stopped for gas.

You could *have* told me you weren't going.

She must *have* gone on that trip.

They ought to *have* worn their costumes.

He might *have* told you my secret.

I would *have* been sad if they had stayed home.

---

beside, besides   *Beside* is a preposition that means "by the side of" someone or something. *Besides,* when used as a preposition, means "in addition to." As an adverb, *besides* means "moreover."

EXAMPLES   That lamp should be placed **beside** the sofa.

Besides Marcia and Tom, who was cast in the play?

It's too cold to run outside. **Besides,** the track is still muddy.

between, among   Use *between* when referring to two items at a time, even when they are part of a group consisting of more than two.

EXAMPLES   Who was standing **between** you and Sue?

Between the season's track meets, I trained very hard. [Although there may have been more than two meets, the training occurred between any two of them.]

There isn't much difference **between** these three brands of juice. [Although there are more than two brands, each one is being compared with the others separately.]

Use *among* when referring to a group rather than individuals.

EXAMPLES   We divided the burritos **among** the five of us.

There was much discussion **among** the governors. [The governors are thought of as a group.]

bring, take   *Bring* means "to come carrying something." *Take* means "to go carrying something." Think of *bring* as related to *come* (*to*), *take* as related to *go* (*from*).

EXAMPLES   Please **bring** that chair here.

Now **take** this one over there.

bust, busted   Avoid using these words as verbs in formal English. Use a form of either *burst* or *break* or *catch* or *arrest.*

EXAMPLES   The pipe **burst** [not *busted*] after the storm.

The Japanese raku vase **broke** [not *busted*] when it fell.

Mom **caught** [not *busted*] our dog Pepper digging in the garden.

Did the police **arrest** [not *bust*] the burglar?

can't hardly, can't scarcely   The words *hardly* and *scarcely* are negative words. They should not be used with another negative word.

EXAMPLES   I **can** [not *can't*] **hardly** wait to hear your new CD.

We **had** [not *hadn't*] **scarcely** enough paper.

could of   Do not write *of* with the helping verb *could*. Write *could have*. Also avoid *ought to of, should of, would of, might of,* and *must of*.

EXAMPLES   Abdullah **could have** [not *could of*] helped us.

You **should have** [not *should of*] left sooner.

don't, doesn't   See page 472.

except   See **accept, except**.

fewer, less   *Fewer* is used with plural words. *Less* is used with singular words. *Fewer* tells "how many"; *less* tells "how much."

EXAMPLES   We had expected **fewer** guests.

Please use **less** salt.

good, well   *Good* is an adjective. Do not use *good* to modify a verb; use *well*, which can be used as an adverb.

NONSTANDARD   The steel-drum band played good.
STANDARD   The steel-drum band played **well**.

Although it is usually an adverb, *well* is also used as an adjective to mean "healthy."

EXAMPLE   I did not feel **well** yesterday.

had ought, hadn't ought   The verb *ought* should not be used with *had*.

NONSTANDARD   You had ought to learn to dance the polka.
You hadn't ought to be late for class.
STANDARD   You **ought** to learn to dance the polka.
or
You **should** learn to dance the polka.
You **oughtn't** to be late for class.
or
You **shouldn't** be late for class.

Reference Note

For more about **double negatives,** see page 539.

Reference Note

For more information about **using good and well,** see page 536.

┌**H E L P**

Feel good and *feel well* mean different things. *Feel good* means "to feel happy or pleased." *Feel well* simply means "to feel healthy."

EXAMPLES
Helping others makes me feel **good**.

I went home because I didn't feel **well**.

Cooperative Learning
Tell students that a simple way to know when to use *fewer* or *less* is to remember that *fewer* is used with things that can be counted.

For practice with this concept, have students work in groups of four. Have pairs of students within the groups work together to create a list of twenty nouns to be modified by *fewer* or *less*. Then, have each pair trade lists with the other pair and the individuals in each pair take turns adding *fewer* or *less* to each of the nouns on the list they have been given. Finally, have all four students go over the nouns together until they all agree on the standard usage of *fewer* or *less* with each noun from their lists.

USAGE

Looking at Language

Dialect. Most of the nonstandard forms studied in this chapter appear in various regional and ethnic dialects. These nonstandard forms are used in such spoken sentences as "Have a apple," "She don't like spinach," and "You did good." Tell your students that standard English is the dialect of business, government, schools, and colleges. To succeed in any of these settings, it is useful to be fluent in standard English.

Exercise 2 Identifying Correct Usage

For each of the following sentences, choose the word or word group in parentheses that is correct according to the rules of formal, standard usage.

EXAMPLE   1. Bike riders (*had ought, ought*) to know some simple rules of safety.
   1. *ought*

1. Just about (*everywheres, everywhere*) you go these days, you see people riding bikes.
2. Riders who wear helmets have (*fewer, less*) major injuries than riders who don't.
3. When Aunt Shirley came for a visit, she (*brought, took*) her bicycle with her.
4. In choosing clothes, cyclists (*can hardly, can't hardly*) go wrong by wearing bright, easy-to-see colors.
5. On busy streets, groups of cyclists should ride in single file and leave space (*among, between*) their bikes in case of sudden stops.

6. Members of cycling clubs decide (*between, among*) themselves on special communication signals.
7. A cyclist who is involved in an accident should not try to ride home, even if he or she seems to feel (*well, good*).
8. The cyclist should call a family member or friend who can (*bring, take*) both the rider and the bike home.
9. A tire that is punctured can usually be patched, but you may not be able to fix one that has (*burst, busted*).
10. Many of the cycling accidents that have happened over the years (*could of, could have*) been avoided if cyclists and motorists had been more careful.

Review A Proofreading for Correct Usage

Each of the following sentences contains an error in formal, standard English usage. Identify each error. Then, write the correct word or words.

EXAMPLE   1. Don't almonds grow somewheres in Africa?
   1. *somewheres—somewhere*

1. burst
2. fewer

1. Check the hoses to see whether a seal has ~~busted~~.
2. When rainfall is low here, there are ~~less~~ rabbits because there are not as many plants for them to eat.

3. I didn't know you could program computers that ~~good~~.

4. Except for the spelling errors, you could ~~of~~ gotten an A.

5. Tracy's new hamster has ~~all ready~~ escaped.

6. Even a ten-ton truck ~~can't~~ hardly haul a load this size.

7. That bull ~~ain't~~ likely to appreciate anybody trespassing on his property.

8. ~~Bring~~ a glass of ice water outside to your father.

9. *Chutzpah* is a term applied to people who have ~~alot~~ of nerve.

10. You really ~~had~~ ought to hear Thelonious Monk's music.

3. well
4. have
5. already
6. can
7. isn't

8. Take
9. a lot

he, she, they   Do not use a pronoun along with its antecedent as the subject of a verb. This error is called the *double subject.*

NONSTANDARD   Michael Jordan he was named Most Valuable Player.

STANDARD   Michael Jordan was named Most Valuable Player.

hisself, theirself, theirselves   These words are nonstandard English. Use *himself* and *themselves*.

EXAMPLES   Bob hurt **himself** [not *hisself*] during the game.

They served **themselves** [not *theirselves*] last.

how come   In informal English, *how come* is often used instead of *why*. In formal English, *why* is preferred.

INFORMAL   How come caribou migrate?

FORMAL   **Why** do caribou migrate?

its, it's   *Its* is a personal pronoun in the possessive case. *It's* is a contraction of *it is* or *it has*.

EXAMPLES   The kitten likes **its** new home. [possessive pronoun]

We have Monday off because **it's** Rosh Hashana. [contraction of *it is*]

It's been a long day. [contraction of *It has*]

kind, sort, type   The words *this, that, these*, and *those* should agree in number with the words *kind, sort*, and *type*. *This* and *that* are singular. *These* and *those* are plural.

EXAMPLES   **That kind** of watch is expensive. [singular]

Those kinds of jokes are silly. [plural]

A Glossary of Usage   **559**

He, She, They— Nowheres

(*pp. 559–562*)

OBJECTIVES

- To identify standard usage of words and expressions in sentences

- To recognize nonstandard usage and to select correct formal, standard usage

USAGE

Meeting
INDIVIDUAL
NEEDS

ENGLISH-LANGUAGE LEARNERS
General Strategies. Many languages, such as Spanish and Portuguese, do not require a subject pronoun in a sentence when there is no noun subject. Languages such as Korean and Japanese make a point of avoiding the use of subject pronouns. Learning that subject pronouns are necessary in English, as in "He went there" instead of "Went there," students might think subject pronouns are necessary in all English sentences and try to use them when a subject noun is present, as in "That man he went there." Remind students that in English, a subject pronoun is used in place of, not in addition to, a noun subject.

RESOURCES

He, She, They—Nowheres
Practice
- *Grammar, Usage, and Mechanics*, pp. 242, 243
- *Language Workshop CD-ROM*, Lesson 60

kind of, sort of   In informal English, *kind of* and *sort of* are often used to mean "somewhat" or "rather." In formal English, *somewhat* or *rather* is preferred.

INFORMAL   I feel kind of tired.
FORMAL   I feel **somewhat** tired.

learn, teach   *Learn* means "to acquire knowledge." *Teach* means "to instruct" or "to show how."

EXAMPLES   My brother is **learning** how to drive.

The driving instructor is **teaching** him.

leave, let   *Leave* means "to go away" or "to depart from." *Let* means "to allow" or "to permit."

NONSTANDARD   Leave her go to the movie.
STANDARD   **Let** her go to the movie.
STANDARD   Let's **leave** on time for the movie.

less   See **fewer, less.**

lie, lay   See page 503.

Reference Note

For more about **prepositional phrases,** see page 402. For more about **clauses,** see Chapter 15.

like, as   *Like* is a preposition; it introduces a prepositional phrase. In informal English, *like* is often used before a clause as a conjunction meaning "as." In formal English, *as* is preferred.

EXAMPLES   Your uncle's hat looked **like** a sombrero. [*Like* introduces the phrase *like a sombrero.*]

Marcia trained every day **as** the coach had suggested. [*As the coach had suggested* is a clause and needs the conjunction *as,* not the preposition *like,* to introduce it.]

like, as if, as though   In formal, standard English, *like* should not be used for the subordinating conjunction *as if* or *as though.*

EXAMPLES   The Swedish limpa bread looks **as if** [not *like*] it is ready.

The car looks **as though** [not *like*] it needs to be washed.

might of, must of   See **could of.**

nowheres   See **anyways,** etc.

MINI-LESSON

Apostrophes. The use of *it's* instead of *its* as a possessive pronoun may stem from students' confusing possessive nouns, which do take an apostrophe [*the* dog's *toy*], with possessive personal pronouns, which do not [*its* toy].

Write on the chalkboard the following list of word groups. Do not include bracketed answers.

- the book that belongs to me [*my book*]
- the chair that belongs to you [*your chair*]

Exercise 3 Identifying Correct Usage

For each of the following sentences, choose the word or word group in parentheses that is correct according to the rules of formal, standard usage.

EXAMPLE   **1.** Young rattlesnakes (*learn, teach*) themselves to make a rattling noise by imitating their parents.

          1. teach

1. (*Its, It's*) a sound that most people have learned to dread.
2. The snake's rattle consists of "buttons" of flesh at the end of (*its, it's*) tail, which are shaken against rings of loose skin.
3. The rings of skin (*themselves, theirselves*) are fragile.
4. (*Like, As*) zookeepers have discovered, snakes that rattle at visitors all day may damage their rattles.
5. (*This kind, These kind*) of snake delivers a poisonous bite, but rattlesnakes do not attack unless threatened.
6. Not all scientists agree about (*how come, why*) certain snakes have rattles.
7. According to many scientists, rattlesnakes (*they use, use*) the rattling sound to frighten enemies.
8. Some scientists believe that snakes use the rattles (*as, like*) other animals use different sounds—to communicate with each other.
9. Snakes don't have ears; however, they are (*sort of, rather*) sensitive to sound vibrations.
10. When people hear a rattlesnake, they may react (*like, as if*) the situation is an emergency—and it often is.

Review B Proofreading for Correct Usage

Each of the following sentences contains an error in formal, standard English usage. Identify each error. Then, write the correct word or words.

EXAMPLE   **1.** I should of known that the painting on the next page was done by Grandma Moses.

          1. should of—should have

1. My art teacher gave me a assignment to write a report about any artist I chose.

2. ~~Between~~ all the artists that I considered, Grandma Moses appealed to me the most.

1. an

2. Among

- the lizard's eyes [*its eyes*]
- Bob's shoes [*his shoes*]
- Karina's grades [*her grades*]
- the flowers we bought [*our flowers*]
- Lee's and Maria's project [*their project*]

Have students rewrite the phrases, using possessive pronouns to transform each of these word groups. For more about possessive pronouns, direct students to **Chapter 19: Using Pronouns Correctly.**

USAGE

Viewing the Art

Rockabye. Art critics refer to Grandma Moses as a modern primitive or folk artist. She first began expressing herself artistically by doing needlework, but arthritis in her hands forced her to abandon her thread pictures. She then began painting with oils.

Grandma Moses, *Rockabye*. Copyright © 1987, Grandma Moses Properties Co., New York.

3. I went to the library and looked for a quiet place where I could do my research ~~at~~.
4. I learned that Anna Mary Robertson Moses didn't start painting until she was ~~all ready~~ in her seventies.
5. By then, her children were grown, and she had ~~less~~ responsibilities.
6. Grandma Moses had no art teacher ~~accept~~ herself.
7. As you can see in the self-portrait *Rockabye*, Grandma Moses felt ~~well~~ about her role as a grandmother.
8. You can't ~~hardly~~ help feeling that Grandma Moses really loves these children.
9. My sister Kim likes this painting ~~alot~~.
10. My report is ~~already~~ for class now, and I can't wait to tell my classmates about Grandma Moses.

4. already
5. fewer
6. except
7. good
9. a lot
10. all ready

Of—Type

(*pp. 562–566*)

OBJECTIVES

- **To identify correct formal, standard usage of words in sentences**
- **To correct errors in usage by rewriting sentences**

of   Do not use *of* with prepositions such as *inside, off,* and *outside.*

EXAMPLES   We waited **outside** [not *outside of*] the theater for the ticket window to open.

The glass fell **off** [not *off of*] the table.

Only Muslims are allowed **inside** [not *inside of*] the city of Mecca in Saudi Arabia.

Of is also unnecessary with the verb *had.*

EXAMPLE   If we **had** [not *had of*] tried harder, we would have won.

ought to of   See **could of.**

real   In informal English, the adjective *real* is often used as an adverb meaning "very" or "extremely." In formal English, *very, extremely,* or another adverb is preferred.

INFORMAL   The new car is real quiet.
  FORMAL   The new car is **very** quiet.

562   Chapter 21   A Glossary of Usage

RESOURCES

Of—Type
Practice
- *Grammar, Usage, and Mechanics,* p. 244
- *Language Workshop CD-ROM,* Lessons 60, 61

562   **A Glossary of Usage**

rise, raise   See page 501.

she, he, they   See **he,** etc.

should of   See **could of.**

sit, set   See page 500.

some, somewhat   Do not use *some* for the adverb *somewhat.*

NONSTANDARD	I like classical music some.
STANDARD	I like classical music **somewhat.**

somewheres   See **anyways,** etc.

sort   See **kind,** etc.

sort of   See **kind of,** etc.

take   See **bring, take.**

teach   See **learn, teach.**

than, then   *Than* is a subordinating conjunction used in making comparisons. *Then* is an adverb meaning "next" or "after that."

EXAMPLES   I sing better **than** I act.

We'll eat first, and **then** we'll ride our bikes.

that   See **who,** etc.

that there   See **this here, that there.**

their, there, they're   *Their* is the possessive form of *they. There* is used to mean "at that place" or to begin a sentence. *They're* is a contraction of *they are.*

EXAMPLES   Do you have **their** CDs?

The lake is over **there.**

There are five movie theaters in town. [*There* begins the sentence but does not add to its meaning.]

They're writing a report on the poet Américo Paredes.

theirself, theirselves   See **hisself,** etc.

them   *Them* should not be used as an adjective. Use *these* or *those.*

EXAMPLE   Where did you put **those** [not *them*] papers?

they   See **he,** etc.

Reference Note

For information about **subordinating conjunctions,** see page 431. For more about **adverbs,** see page 366.

Meeting INDIVIDUAL NEEDS

ADVANCED LEARNERS

Explain to students that while *of* is unnecessary and nonstandard following prepositions such as *outside, inside,* and *off,* some compound prepositions (such as *out of, because of,* and *in spite of*) do end in *of.*

Have pairs of students brainstorm a list of compound prepositions ending in *of.* Students may want to search literature books, magazines, or other sources. Ask students to devise a rule explaining when *of* is standard as part of a compound preposition and when it is unnecessary. [*If the preposition makes sense or has the same meaning without* of, *as with* inside, of *is unnecessary. If the preposition does not make sense or does not have the same meaning without* of, *it is necessary. For example, "Get out here" has a different meaning from "Get out of here."*]

Have pairs present their findings to the rest of the class and then post their lists on a classroom bulletin board. [*Possible answers include* as of, because of, by means of, in front of, in place of, in spite of, instead of, *and* on account of.]

USAGE

this here, that there   The words *here* and *there* are not needed after *this* and *that*.

EXAMPLE   I like **this** [not *this here*] Chinese dragon kite, but I like **that** [not *that there*] one better.

this kind, sort, type   See **kind,** etc.

try and   In informal English, *try and* is often used for *try to*. In formal English, *try to* is preferred.

INFORMAL   I will try and be there early.

  FORMAL   I will **try to** be there early.

type   See **kind,** etc.

Exercise 4 **Identifying Correct Usage**

For each of the following sentences, choose the word or word group in parentheses that is correct according to the rules of formal, standard usage.

EXAMPLE   1. The Amish people (*try and, try to*) maintain a simple, traditional way of life.

       1. *try to*

1. In the early 1700s, the Amish were not allowed to practice (*their, they're, there*) religion in Germany and Switzerland.
2. Hearing that there was more freedom in the Americas (*than, then*) in Europe, the Amish left their homes and settled in North America.
3. Since that time, they have remained (*outside of, outside*) the mainstream of American life.
4. The Amish work (*real, very*) hard at producing organically grown crops.
5. In Amish communities such as (*this, this here*) one, modern conveniences such as telephones, cars, and televisions are not used.
6. The closeness of Amish family life is evident in the way (*these, them*) people build their homes.
7. (*They're, There, Their*) are often three generations—grandparents, parents, and children—living in a large residence made up of several houses.

8. Pictures and photographs are not allowed (*inside of, inside*) Amish homes, but the Amish brighten their plain houses with colorful pillows, quilts, and rugs.
9. If an Amish person gets sick, he or she is almost always cared for by family members rather (*than, then*) by a doctor.
10. The Amish way of life might surprise you (*somewhat, some*), yet Amish communities have thrived in North America for nearly three hundred years.

Review C Proofreading for Correct Usage

Each of the following sentences contains an error in the use of formal, standard English. Identify each error. Then, rewrite the sentence to correct the error.

EXAMPLE　　**1.** It was real cold that spring!
　　　　　　　1. *real—It was extremely cold that spring!*

1. Few people commanded more respect and admiration‸then Mother Teresa did.
2. Nobody can dance‸like you do, Ariel.
3. These‸sort of questions can be found on every standardized test.
4. Oh, no! The baby's gotten oatmeal all over‸hisself.
5. The structure of molecules like these,‸it can most easily be understood by building a model.
6. What I want to know is‸how come we can't go to the concert.
7. Who‸learned your dog all those tricks?

1. than

2. as

3. sorts [*or* This sort of question]

4. himself

6. why
7. taught

USAGE

Viewing the Illustration

Representing. After students have completed **Exercise 4,** have them pretend that they have been invited to spend a weekend with an Amish family on their farm. Ask students to write an expressive/descriptive paragraph about the visit. Have students find more information in the library first. They can explain what work they may have observed, what they ate, what their hosts wore, what recreational activities they may have experienced, and how many generations of family members may have lived at the farm.

Critical Thinking

Metacognition. After students complete **Review C,** ask them to think about how they identified and corrected the errors.

- Did they compare words in the sentences to items in the glossary?

- Did they read sentences out loud or to themselves to hear what "sounded wrong"?

- Were some errors more obvious than others? If so, why?

Encourage students to share their strategies with the class and to adapt their own strategies as needed.

Use to, Used to— Your, You're

(pp. 566–568)

OBJECTIVES

- To identify correct usage of words and expressions in sentences
- To correct errors in usage by rewriting sentences

Meeting
INDIVIDUAL
NEEDS

ENGLISH-LANGUAGE LEARNERS
General Strategies. Many of the points of usage covered in this chapter are problems that native English speakers have, such as using *ways* for *way* or *like* for *as.* English-proficient speakers will be familiar with such usages, while English-language learners might wonder why certain points of usage are emphasized. Explain that many of the problems outlined in this chapter arise from the differences in usage between regional or ethnic dialects in the United States and standard English.

---

8. those

8. A *howdah* is one of ~~them~~ seats that have a canopy and that sit on a camel or an elephant.

9. The RV campsite is just outside ~~of~~ town.

10. to

10. Mrs. Whitfield will try ~~and~~ explain how the European Economic Community is organized.

use to, used to Don't leave off the *d* when you write *used to.* The same advice applies to *supposed to.*

EXAMPLE   Gail **used to** [not *use to*] be on the softball team.

way, ways Use *way*, not *ways*, in referring to a distance.

EXAMPLE   Do we have a long **way** [not *ways*] to drive?

well   See **good, well.**

when, where Do not use *when* or *where* incorrectly to begin a definition.

NONSTANDARD   A *homophone* is when a word sounds like another word but has a different meaning and spelling.

STANDARD   A *homophone* is a word that sounds like another word but has a different meaning and spelling.

where   Do not use *where* for *that.*

EXAMPLE   Did you read in the newsletter **that** [not *where*] the teen center is closing?

who, which, that The relative pronoun *who* refers to people only. *Which* refers to things only. *That* refers to either people or things.

EXAMPLES   Jolene is the one **who** called. [person]

Here is the salad, **which** is my favorite part of the meal. [thing]

The book **that** you want is here. [thing]

This is the salesperson **that** helped me choose the gift. [person]

who, whom   See page 521.

whose, who's *Whose* is used as the possessive form of *who* and as an interrogative pronoun. *Who's* is a contraction of *who is* or *who has.*

RESOURCES

Use to, Used to—Your, You're
Practice
- *Grammar, Usage, and Mechanics*, p. 245
- *Language Workshop CD-ROM*, Lesson 61

EXAMPLES   **Whose** book is this? [possessive pronoun]

Whose is this? [interrogative pronoun]

Who's the new student? [contraction of *who is*]

Who's read "A Walk to the Jetty"? [contraction of *who has*]

without, unless   Do not use the preposition *without* in place of the conjunction *unless*.

EXAMPLE   I can't go **unless** [not *without*] I ask Dad.

would of   See **could of.**

your, you're   *Your* is the possessive form of *you. You're* is the contraction of *you are.*

EXAMPLES   **Your** Saint Patrick's Day party was great!

You're a good friend.

Exercise 5   **Identifying Correct Usage**

For each of the following sentences, choose <u>the word or word group in parentheses that is correct</u> according to the rules of formal, standard usage.

EXAMPLE   **1.** Last week I received a letter from Sandra Joyce, (*who's, whose*) a good friend of mine.

1. who's

1. When I opened the envelope, I saw (*where,* <u>*that*</u>) she had sent me chopsticks and these instructions.
2. "I thought you'd like (*you're,* <u>*your*</u>) own pair of chopsticks, with instructions showing how to use them," Sandra wrote.
3. Instructions like the ones Sandra sent me are helpful because chopsticks can be hard to use (<u>*unless,*</u> *without*) you are shown how.
4. In the letter, Sandra told me (<u>*that,*</u> *where*) she and her family had been to New York.
5. Because Sandra lives in a small town, she wasn't (*use,* <u>*used*</u>) to the crowds.

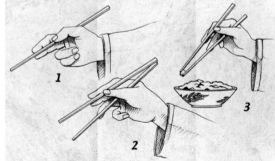

A Glossary of Usage   **567**

Relating to Literature

If the Marjorie Kinnan Rawlings story "A Mother in Mannville" is in your literature textbook, have students read it and discuss the author's use of formal and informal English. Ask students to identify situations in which the author uses informal or nonstandard English. [*She does so when she is quoting the boy, Jerry.*] Ask students to cite passages in which she uses standard English. [*She does so when quoting the narrator and in the narrative portions of her story.*] Why did she not correct Jerry's usage in her story? [*His speech would have seemed stilted and unnatural.*]

1. your
2. there
3. unless
4. who [*or that*]
5. When a plane flies low and fast over the runway, it is "buzzing the runway."
6. that
7. why do I win every time I wear it?
8. used
9. to
10. it's

6. She enjoyed visiting her grandparents, (*who's, whose*) home is near Chinatown, on Manhattan Island.
7. While her family was eating in a Chinese restaurant, one of the servers, (*which, who*) was very helpful, showed her how to use chopsticks.
8. "(*Your, You're*) not going to believe this," she wrote, "but by the end of the meal, I was using chopsticks quite well."
9. Etiquette is (*when you use good manners, the use of good manners*); Sandra wondered whether using chopsticks to eat Chinese food was a matter of etiquette or of skill.
10. I'll write Sandra that I have a long (*ways, way*) to go before I'm an expert in using chopsticks.

Review D Proofreading for Correct Usage

Each of the following sentences contains an error in the use of formal, standard English. Rewrite each sentence to correct the error. Answers may vary.

EXAMPLE 1. If the quarterback can't play, whose the backup?
1. If the quarterback can't play, who's the backup?

1. Are you selling you're old bike or one of theirs?
2. If they're not their, you can have their seats.
3. Don't go outside without you wear those galoshes!
4. Is Alfonso García Robles the man which was awarded the 1982 Nobel Peace Prize?
5. "Buzzing the runway" is when a plane flies low and fast over the runway.
6. I read where the word *Nippon* means "where the sun rises."
7. If this hat isn't lucky, then how come every time I wear it, I win?
8. Yes, I use to live in Madrid.
9. Please try and be ready on time tonight.
10. Listen to Lydia's new poem; its dedicated to Queen Liliuokalani.

Chapter Review

A. Identifying Correct Usage

For each of the following sentences, choose the word or word group in parentheses that is correct according to the rules of formal, standard English usage.

1. Helene made (*fewer*, *less*) mistakes this time.
2. That restaurant looks (*as if*, *like*) it might be expensive.
3. Those (*kind*, *kinds*) of games are easy to learn.
4. Terrance felt (*badly*, *bad*) about losing the house key.
5. Leticia practiced an hour every day (*like*, *as*) her teacher had recommended.
6. Divide the sheet music (*among*, *between*) the three musicians.
7. We brought the juice, but (*it's*, *its*) still in the car.
8. Both cars had pinstripes painted on (*their*, *there*) hoods.
9. The rice will feed more people (*then*, *than*) the bread will.
10. "(*Your*, *You're*) a polite young man," Aunt Henrietta told Jason.
11. There's the police officer (*which*, *who*) helped me yesterday.
12. Did you see in the newspaper (*that*, *where*) farmers are losing their crops because of the drought?
13. Chika is the woman (*whose*, *who's*) going to be my math tutor.
14. The child cried out when her balloon (*busted*, *burst*).
15. Vincent van Gogh did not receive (*a lot*, *alot*) of recognition during his lifetime.
16. Just do your best, and everything will be (*allright*, *all right*).
17. Will you (*take*, *bring*) that *National Geographic* to me?
18. Elyssa must (*of*, *have*) left her wallet here.
19. Petra likes salsa music (*somewhat*, *some*).
20. Can your brother (*learn*, *teach*) me how to play the drums?
21. Let the bread rise for (*a*, *an*) hour, and then put it in the oven.
22. Is Emily coming to the party, or (*ain't*, *isn't*) she?
23. (*Leave*, *Let*) me walk to the concert by myself.
24. We (*should not*, *hadn't ought to*) let the cat eat whatever it wants.
25. Where did you (*sit*, *set*) the bag of groceries?

Using the Chapter Review

The **Chapter Review** asks students to identify and correct common usage errors. The results of this review can be compared to the results of the **Diagnostic Preview** on pp. 552–553 to assess student progress.

If students need additional practice, refer them to **Exercises 25–27** in **Chapter 26: Correcting Common Errors.**

USAGE

B. Proofreading for Correct Usage

Read each sentence below, and decide whether it contains an error in the use of formal, standard English. If the sentence contains an error in usage, rewrite the sentence correctly. If the sentence is already correct, write *C*. Answers may vary.

26. very	**26.** Try to be real quiet while you are inside the library.
27. unless	**27.** We cannot ride our bikes without it stops raining.
	28. Be careful not to knock the lamp off of the table.
29. C	**29.** The cartoon page looks as if it got wet.
30. to	**30.** I told Gretchen to try and keep still.
	31. Where's the salt shaker at?
32. broken	**32.** Robbie said that the lock on the back door is busted.
33. C	**33.** Andrea thought we should have turned right at the stop sign.
34. rather	**34.** Mr. Funicello seems kind of uncomfortable.
	35. This here poem would be easier to memorize than that one.
36. used	**36.** Before 1920, farmers use to grow strawberries here.
	37. My grandmother she worked in a factory when she was my age.
38. why	**38.** Sakura knows how come the play was canceled.
39. somewhere	**39.** Those game tickets are somewheres in this drawer.
40. C	**40.** Before our trip, we ought to buy a map.
41. those	**41.** Where did Rory put them CDs?
42. There	**42.** Their are two bridges downriver.
43. accept	**43.** The tollbooth will except quarters and dimes but not pennies.
44. that	**44.** A pronoun is when a word is used in place of a noun.
45. already	**45.** By noon we had all ready seen Mr. Kerr's film.
46. can	**46.** The class can't hardly wait to go on the field trip to the power plant.
47. way	**47.** The Immerguts have a long ways to drive to visit their grandparents.
48. C	**48.** My older sister is doing very well in law school.
49. himself	**49.** In the final seconds of the game, Lee tripped hisself and missed the winning basket.
50. C	**50.** It's true: Mimi doesn't want to come to the New Year's Eve party.

RESOURCES

A Glossary of Usage
Review
- *Grammar, Usage, and Mechanics,* pp. 246, 247, 248, 249

Assessment
- *Assessment Package*
  —*Chapter Tests,* Ch. 21
  —*Chapter Tests in Standardized Test Formats,* Ch. 21
- *Test Generator (One-Stop Planner CD-ROM)*

Writing Application
Writing a Speech

Using Formal English   A local television station has started a new program called *Sound-Off*. Each speaker on the program gets five minutes on the air to express an opinion about a community issue. Choose a topic that you think is important, and write a speech to submit to the TV station. Use only formal, standard English in your speech.

Prewriting   First, choose a specific topic that interests you. List important facts and information about the issue. Do you have all the information you need? If not, do some research at your school or local library. Also, be sure to include your own feelings and opinions about your topic. Finally, make a rough outline of what you want to say.

Writing   Use your notes and outline to help you write a draft of your speech. Try to write a lively introduction that will grab your listeners' attention. In your introduction, give a clear statement of opinion. Then, discuss each supporting point in a paragraph or two. Conclude your speech by restating your main point.

Revising   Ask a friend to time you as you read your speech aloud. Then, ask your friend the following questions:

- Is the main idea clear?
- Does the speech give useful information?

Publishing   Proofread your speech for errors in grammar or formal, standard usage. You and your classmates may want to present your speeches to the class. You might also want to investigate whether a local TV or radio program would allow you to give your speeches on the air.

Reference Note

For more about **statements of opinion**, see page 212.

Chapter Review   **571**

Capital Letters
Rules for Capitalization

Diagnostic Preview

Proofreading Sentences for Correct Capitalization

Write each word that requires capitalization in the following sentences. If a sentence is already correct, write *C.*

EXAMPLE　　1.　Next saturday rachel and i will get to watch the taping of our favorite TV show.

　　　　　　1.　*Saturday, Rachel, I*

1. The curtiss soap corporation sponsors the television show called *three is two too many.*
2. The show's theme song is "you and i might get by."
3. My favorite actor on the show is joe fontana, jr., who plays the lovable dr. mullins.
4. The female lead, janelle bledsoe, used to go to our junior high school right here in houston, texas.
5. The action is set in the west just after the civil war.
6. The program is on monday nights, except during the summer.
7. One episode took place at a fourth of july picnic, at which dr. mullins challenged the sheriff to a grapefruit-eating contest.

8. [or President]

8. Ms. Bledsoe plays a teacher who is married to Mr. reginald wilson foster II, president of the flintsville National bank.
9. Mrs. foster teaches latin, home economics, and arithmetic I at flintsville's one-room school.

CHAPTER RESOURCES

Planning
- *One-Stop Planner CD-ROM*

Practice and Extension
- *Grammar, Usage, and Mechanics,* p. 253
- *Developmental Language Skills,* pp. 97–108

Internet
- go.hrw.com (keyword: EOLang)

Evaluation and Assessment
- *Chapter Tests,* Ch. 22
- *Chapter Tests in Standardized Test Formats,* Ch. 22
- *Test Generator (One-Stop Planner)*

10. One local character, uncle ramón, once played a practical joke on judge grimsby right outside the mayor's office.

10. [or Mayor's]

11. Some people, including my mother, think that the program is silly, but my father enjoys watching it occasionally. **11. C**

12. Even i don't think it will receive an emmy from the academy of television arts and sciences.

13. When grandma murray and aunt edna from mobile, alabama, visited us, they watched the program.

14. In that monday night's show, an alien named romax from the planet zarko stayed at the sidewinder hotel.

15. The alien, who looked like president zachary taylor, spoke english perfectly and could read people's minds.

16. He settled a dispute between the union pacific railroad and the flintsville ranchers' association.

17. In another show a united states senator and romax discussed their views of justice.

17. [or Senator]

18. In the silliest show, the people in the next town, longview, thought that a sea monster was living in lake cranberry and reported it to the department of the interior.

19. A week later, mayor murdstone lost the only copy of his secret recipe for irish stew and saw the recipe in the next issue of the *flintsville weekly gazette.*

20. One time a mysterious stranger appeared, claiming he had sailed around cape horn on the ship *the gem of the ocean.*

21. Another time, the wealthy landowner mabel platt hired the law firm of crumbley, lockwood, and starr to sue mayor murdstone and threatened to take the case all the way to the united states supreme court.

22. In the next episode, a buddhist priest who just happened to be traveling through the west on his way back to china stopped off in flintsville.

23. Once, when someone mistakenly thought he had found gold down at cutter's creek, thousands of prospectors flocked to flintsville, including three bank-robbing members of the feared gumley Gang.

24. The programs are taped before a live audience in the metro theater in los angeles, california.

25. You can get tickets to be in the audience by writing to curtiss soap corporation, 151 holly avenue, deerfield, mi 49238.

25. [*MI* should be written with two capitals.]

First Words, Pronoun *I*, Proper Nouns

Rules 22a–d *(pp. 574–584)*

OBJECTIVES

- To write proper nouns from given common nouns

- To proofread and revise sentences for correct capitalization of the first words of sentences, quotations, and salutations in letters; the pronoun *I*; and proper nouns

Meeting
|INDIVIDUAL|
NEEDS

ENGLISH-LANGUAGE LEARNERS

General Strategies. Because many languages have no capital letters, native speakers of such languages may have trouble learning and remembering how to use capital letters in English. Acknowledge to these students that the use of capitalization in English is different from that in their native language, but emphasize that in English, use of capital letters is important. Have these students focus especially on capitalization when they are proofreading their writing. You may want to provide these students with partners who can serve as their capitalization helpers.

MECHANICS

Reference Note

For more about using **capital letters** in **quotations,** see page 631.

Reference Note

For more about **writing letters,** see "Writing" in the Quick Reference Handbook. For information on using **colons in letters,** see page 620. For information on using **commas in letters,** see page 615.

Reference Note

For more about **common nouns** and **proper nouns,** see page 338.

Using Capital Letters Correctly

22a. Capitalize the first word in every sentence.

EXAMPLES **M**y dog knows several tricks. **D**oes yours?

The first word of a directly quoted sentence should begin with a capital letter.

EXAMPLE Mrs. Hernandez said, "**D**on't forget to bring your contributions for the bake sale."

Traditionally, the first word of every line of poetry begins with a capital letter.

EXAMPLE **I**n the night
The rain comes down.
Yonder at the edge of the earth
There is a sound like cracking,
There is a sound like falling.
Down yonder it goes on slowly rumbling.
It goes on shaking.

A Papago poem, "In the Night"

NOTE Some modern poets do not follow this style. If you are using a quotation from a poem, be sure to use the capitalization that the poet uses.

22b. Capitalize the first word in both the salutation and the closing of a letter.

SALUTATIONS **D**ear Service Manager:
Dear Emily,

CLOSINGS **S**incerely,
Yours truly,

22c. Capitalize the pronoun *I*.

EXAMPLE This week **I** have to write two essays.

22d. Capitalize proper nouns.

A *proper noun* names a particular person, place, thing, or idea. Proper nouns are capitalized. A *common noun* names a kind or type of person, place, thing, or idea. A common noun generally is not capitalized unless it begins a sentence or is part of a title.

RESOURCES

First Words, Pronoun *I*, Proper Nouns
Practice

- *Grammar, Usage, and Mechanics,*
  pp. 254, 255, 256, 257, 258, 259, 260, 261

- *Language Workshop CD-ROM,* Lessons 53, 54

Proper Nouns	Common Nouns
Central **H**igh **S**chool	high school
Saturday	day
Rigoberta **M**enchú	woman
Cambodia	country
Smokey	bear
USS **N**autilus	submarine

Some proper nouns consist of more than one word. In these names, short words such as prepositions (those of fewer than five letters) and articles (*a, an, the*) are generally not capitalized.

EXAMPLES   House **o**f Representatives

Ivan **t**he Terrible

(1) Capitalize the names of persons and animals.

Persons	**M**onica **S**one	**A**aron **N**eville
	Charlayne **H**unter-**G**ault	**M**ohandas **K.** **G**andhi
Animals	**S**hamu	**T**rigger
	Socks	**R**ikki-tikki-tavi

(2) Capitalize geographical names.

Type of Name	Examples	
Continents	**E**urope **A**ntarctica	**S**outh **A**merica **A**sia
Countries	**A**ustralia **E**l **S**alvador	**E**gypt **S**audi **A**rabia
Cities, Towns	**M**iami **L**os **A**ngeles	**I**ndianapolis **M**anila
States	**T**ennessee **R**hode **I**sland	**D**elaware **W**yoming

(continued)

Reference Note

Abbreviations of the names of states are capitalized. See page 599 for more about using and punctuating such abbreviations.

STYLE   TIP

Some names consist of more than one part. The different parts may begin with capital letters only or with a combination of capital and lowercase letters. If you are not sure about the spelling of a name, ask the person with that name or check a reference source.

EXAMPLES
Van **d**en **A**kker,
van **G**ogh, **M**c**E**nroe,
La **F**ontaine, **d**e **l**a **G**arza,
Ibn **S**aud

COMPUTER TIP

If you use a computer, you may be able to use a spellchecker to help you capitalize names correctly. Make a list of the names you write most often. Be sure that you have spelled and capitalized each name correctly. Then, add this list to your computer's dictionary or spellchecker.

TEACHING   TIP

Activity. To give students practice in capitalizing proper nouns, have them play a game called Capital Cap. First, have students in groups of four brainstorm categories (such as holidays) that require items to be capitalized. Then, have each group write five categories on five slips of paper to be mixed in a baseball cap or some other type of cap. Have each group in turn draw a slip from the cap and give a proper noun that exemplifies the category on the card [*for example,* Memorial Day *for the category* holidays]. While categories may be duplicated, the proper nouns must always be different from ones given previously. Continue passing the cap until all slips have been drawn and answered.

Crossing the Curriculum

Geography. To give students practice in capitalization of geographical names, provide them with state and local maps for your area. Have each student use the maps to write the name of one of each of the following items: a street, a river, a lake, a highway, a town or city, and a county. Then, ask a student to list the examples of each category on the chalkboard or a transparency as students give their answers aloud, noting which letters require capitalization.

MECHANICS

Using Capital Letters Correctly   **575**

Using Capital Letters Correctly   575

Relating to Literature

You may want to give students some examples of poems that begin every line with a capital letter and other poems that do not. You can find many suitable examples in literature anthologies. For example, Anna Lee Walters begins each line in "I Am of the Earth" with a capital letter, while Gogisgi/Carroll Arnett does not begin each line in "Early Song" with a capital letter. Ask students if they think such a style difference matters, and discuss how the flow of a poem such as "Early Song" would be different if each line did begin with a capital letter. [*Capitalizing the first word in each line of a poem can give the poem a more formal tone. In "Early Song," not capitalizing the first word of each line focuses attention on the sentences in the poem rather than on the poem's structure.*]

Timesaver

If students have a good understanding of the basic rules of capitalization, you may want to have them review the rules on their own so that you can devote class time to discussing the **Notes** included with rules. For example, for the second subrule of **Rule 22d,** you could discuss the capitalization of words such as *east, west, north,* or *south;* for the tenth subrule, you could discuss capitalization of the word *god.*

STYLE TIP

A two-letter state abbreviation without periods is used only when it is followed by a ZIP Code. Both letters of the abbreviation are capitalized. No mark of punctuation is used between the abbreviation and the ZIP Code.

EXAMPLES

New Orleans, **LA** 70131-5140

New York, **NY** 10003-6981

Reference Note

In addresses, abbreviations such as *St., Blvd., Ave., Dr.,* and *Ln.* are **capitalized.** For more about punctuating abbreviations, see page 599.

(continued)

Type of Name	Examples	
Islands	**A**leutian **I**slands **C**rete	**L**ong **I**sland **I**sle of **P**ines
Bodies of Water	**A**mazon **R**iver **C**hesapeake **B**ay **S**uez **C**anal	**L**ake **O**ntario **J**ackson's **P**ond **I**ndian **O**cean
Other Geographical Names	**M**ayon **V**olcano **P**ainted **D**esert	**S**inai **P**eninsula **M**eteor **C**rater
Streets, Highways	**M**ain **S**treet **E**ighth **A**venue	**C**anary **L**ane **H**ighway 71

NOTE In a hyphenated street number, the second part of the number is not capitalized.

EXAMPLE   West Thirty-**f**ourth Street

Type of Name	Examples	
Parks and Forests	**S**herwood **F**orest **B**rechtel **P**ark	**E**verglades **N**ational **P**ark
Mountains	**C**atskills **M**ount **F**uji	**M**ount **E**verest the **A**lps
Regions	the **M**iddle **E**ast **N**ew **E**ngland the **W**est	**S**outhern Hemisphere **C**orn **B**elt the **S**outheast

NOTE Words such as *east, west, northern,* or *southerly* are not capitalized when the words merely indicate direction. However, they are capitalized when they name a particular region.

EXAMPLES   A car was going **s**outh on Oak Street. [direction]

The **S**outh has produced some of America's great writers. [region of the country]

MINI-LESSON

Capitalizing Direct Quotations. To help students capitalize dialogue correctly, explain that a direct quotation begins with a capital letter, but when the speaker tag (the expression identifying the speaker) interrupts a quoted sentence, the second part of the quotation begins with a lowercase letter. When the second part of a divided quotation is a complete sentence, however, it begins with a capital letter. Write the following sentences on the chalkboard:

Exercise 1 — Writing Proper Nouns

For each common noun given below, write two proper nouns. You may need to use a dictionary and an atlas. Be sure to use capital letters correctly. **Answers will vary.**

EXAMPLE   1. country

          1. Canada, Japan

1. lake
2. continent
3. president
4. highway
5. teacher
6. athlete
7. park
8. ocean
9. city
10. region

Possible answers:
1. Lake Michigan, Town Lake
2. Asia, Africa
3. George Washington, John Tyler
4. Loop 410, Redwood Highway
5. Mr. Ferguson, Mrs. Longstreth
6. Mark McGwire, Randy Johnson
7. Zilker Park, Central Park
8. Indian Ocean, Pacific Ocean
9. Duluth, Memphis
10. Midwest, East Coast

Exercise 2 — Correcting Errors in Capitalization

Each of the following sentences contains at least one capitalization error. Correct these errors by writing the <u>words that are incorrectly capitalized</u> and either changing capital letters to lowercase letters or changing lowercase letters to capital letters.

EXAMPLE   1. The original Settlers of hawaii came from the marquesas islands and tahiti.

          1. settlers, Hawaii, Marquesas Islands, Tahiti

Words that should be capitalized or lowercased are underscored.

1. <u>our</u> <u>Class</u> is studying <u>hawaii</u>.
2. The Hawaiian <u>islands</u> are located in the <u>pacific</u> <u>ocean</u>, nearly twenty-four hundred miles <u>West</u> of <u>san</u> <u>francisco</u>, <u>california</u>.
3. Hawaii officially became the fiftieth <u>State</u> in the <u>united</u> <u>states</u> in 1959.
4. Our teacher, <u>ms.</u> Jackson, explained that the <u>Capital City</u> is <u>honolulu</u>; she said that it is located on the southeast <u>Coast</u> of <u>oahu</u> <u>island</u>.
5. The largest of the <u>Islands</u> is <u>hawaii</u>.
6. On the southeast shore of <u>hawaii</u> <u>island</u> is <u>hawaii</u> <u>volcanoes</u> <u>national</u> <u>park</u>.
7. Ms. Jackson asked, "<u>can</u> anyone name one of the <u>Volcanoes</u> there?"
8. Since <u>i</u> had been reading about <u>National</u> <u>Parks</u>, <u>i</u> raised my hand.
9. "The <u>Park</u> has two active volcanoes, <u>mauna</u> Loa and <u>kilauea</u>," I answered.

Halima asked, "Where are my in-line skates?"

"Your in-line skates," answered Tonya, "are not in my room."

"I saw them yesterday," called Mia. "They were in the basement."

Have students look through stories or books containing dialogue to find examples of each of these three types of quotations. For more information on capitalizing words in direct quotations, refer students to **Chapter 23: Punctuation.**

MECHANICS

LEARNERS HAVING DIFFICULTY

Provide students with a questionnaire that personalizes the application of the capitalization rules for proper nouns. Here are some questions that you could include.

1. What is the name of your favorite television personality?

2. What high school do you plan to attend?

3. In what city, county, and state do you live?

4. What is the full address of your current school?

5. What are the names of some shops, museums, parks, or restaurants that you like to visit?

6. What is your birth date?

7. What brands of cereal do you like?

8. What day of the week is today?

10. "These pictures show how lava from kilauea's eruption threatened everything in its path in 1989," I added.

11. Its crater, halemaumau crater, is the largest active crater in the World.

12. "we'll go into much more detail about volcanoes tomorrow," ms. jackson said.

13. then ms. jackson told us that honolulu is probably the most important business center in the pacific ocean.

14. Ever since captain William Brown sailed into the harbor in 1794, Hawaii has played an increasingly important role in business.

15. It's easy to see why—Hawaii is midway between Continents.

16. hawaii's largest city has a fine seaport; it links japan, china, and even australia with North and south America.

17. Cultural and academic studies thrive there in places such as the university of hawaii and the east-west center.

18. You can even get a look at the iolani palace where the Rulers of hawaii once lived.

19. Perhaps best of all, hawaii offers Tourists a day in the sun at waikiki beach.

20. Suddenly, i blurted out, "wouldn't it be great if we could all go there now!"

(3) Capitalize names of organizations, teams, institutions, and government bodies.

Type of Name	Examples	
Organizations	Clark Drama Club Junior League	Modern Language Association
Teams	Boston Celtics Dallas Cowboys	Los Angeles Dodgers Hutto Hippos
Institutions	Westside Regional Hospital	Roosevelt Junior High School
Government Bodies	United Nations Peace Corps	Congress York City Council

(4) Capitalize the names of historical events and periods, special events, calendar items, and holidays.

Type of Name	Examples	
Historical Events and Periods	Revolutionary War Bronze Age Holocaust	United States Bicentennial Age of Reason
Special Events	Texas State Fair Special Olympics	Super Bowl Festival of States
Calendar Items and Holidays	Monday Memorial Day	February Thanksgiving Day

NOTE Do not capitalize the name of a season unless it is part of a proper name.

EXAMPLES   the winter holidays   the Quebec Winter Carnival

(5) Capitalize the names of nationalities, races, and peoples.

EXAMPLES   Mexican   Nigerian

        African American   Iroquois

┌HELP─

The names of organizations, businesses, and government bodies are often abbreviated to a series of capital letters.

EXAMPLES

National Organization for Women	NOW
American Telephone & Telegraph	AT&T
National Science Foundation	NSF

Usually the letters in such abbreviations are not followed by periods, but always check an up-to-date dictionary or other reliable source to be sure.

┌STYLE   TIP│

The words *black* and *white* may or may not be capitalized when they refer to races. Either way is correct.

EXAMPLE

In the 1960s, both Blacks and Whites [or blacks and whites] worked to end segregation.

Within each piece of writing, be sure to be consistent in your use of capitals or lowercase letters for these words.

Cooperative Learning

Divide the class into eleven groups, and assign each group one of the eleven subrules of **Rule 22d**. Give each group a slip of paper with the subrule written on it. Then, have each group compile a list of at least five properly capitalized words that exemplify the subrule of **Rule 22d** that the group represents. Have each group choose a student to write down the words, while group members take turns supplying words. Circulate among the groups to observe and to offer support. Students may consult a dictionary or an encyclopedia if they run out of ideas. After the lists are completed, have a student from each group read the group's list to the rest of the class.

MECHANICS

Activity. Make up some categories based on the eleven subrules of **Rule 22d,** such as names of female singers, businesses in a well-known mall, holidays, and heavenly bodies. Divide the class into two teams and, at random, choose one of the categories. Then, tell one of the teams to select a specific, capitalized name to fit the category, and write that name on the chalkboard. The next team does the same, and play using that category continues until one team cannot give a name. The team with the last answer gets a point. Then, at random, choose another category. The game can continue as long as time and categories permit; the team with the most points wins.

Reference Note

For information on **using italics in names,** see page 628.

(6) Capitalize the names of businesses and the brand names of business products.

Type of Name	Examples	
Businesses	**S**ears, **R**oebuck and **C**o.	**F**ields **D**epartment **S**tore
	Thirfty **D**ry **C**leaners	**F**irst **N**ational **B**ank
Business Products	**S**chwinn **M**esa	**A**pple **M**acintosh
	GMC Jimmy	**C**allaway **B**ig **B**ertha

NOTE   Names of types of products are not capitalized.

EXAMPLES   Schwinn **b**icycle, Apple **c**omputer, Callaway **g**olf **c**lub

(7) Capitalize the names of ships, trains, aircraft, and spacecraft.

Type of Name	Examples	
Ships	*Queen Elizabeth 2*	*Kon Tiki*
Trains	*City of New Orleans*	*Silver Meteor*
Aircraft	*Memphis Belle*	*Spruce Goose*
Spacecraft	*Voyager 2*	*Sputnik*

(8) Capitalize the names of buildings and other structures.

EXAMPLES   **S**ydney **O**pera **H**ouse, **S**t. **L**ouis **C**athedral, **A**swan **D**am, **E**iffel **T**ower, **B**rooklyn **B**ridge

NOTE   Do not capitalize such words as *hotel, theater,* or *high school* unless they are part of the name of a particular building or institution.

EXAMPLES   **C**apital **T**heater   a theater

Lane **H**otel   the hotel

Taft **H**igh **S**chool   this high school

Learning for Life

Writing a Press Release. Correct use of capitalization is important in any formal writing that will be shared publicly. Have students write press releases about an event they want to advertise, such as a play, sports event, recital, dance performance, or fund-raiser. Information in the press release, which will go to all the area radio and television stations and newspapers, should include the following items:

• title and description of the event

(9) Capitalize the names of monuments, memorials, and awards.

Type of Name	Examples	
Monuments	**G**reat **S**phinx **N**avajo **N**ational **M**onument	**W**ashington **M**onument
Memorials	**L**incoln **M**emorial the **C**oronado **M**emorial	**T**omb of the **U**nknown **S**oldier
Awards	**E**mmy **A**ward **C**ongressional **M**edal of **H**onor	**N**obel **P**rize **P**ulitzer **P**rize

(10) Capitalize the names of religions and their followers, holy days and celebrations, sacred writings, and specific deities.

Type of Name	Examples	
Religions and Followers	**J**udaism **H**induism	**C**hristian **M**uslim
Holy Days and Celebrations	**E**aster **A**ll **S**aints' **D**ay	**Y**om **K**ippur **C**hristmas **E**ve
Sacred Writings	**K**oran **B**ible	**D**ead **S**ea **S**crolls **U**panishads
Specific Deities	**G**od **A**llah	**J**ehovah **K**rishna

NOTE The words *god* and *goddess* are not capitalized when they refer to a deity of ancient mythology. However, the names of specific gods and goddesses are capitalized.

EXAMPLES   The king of the Norse **g**ods was **O**din.

Athena was the Greek **g**oddess of wisdom and warfare.

ADVANCED LEARNERS

Students who have a firm grasp of **Rules 22a–22d** may want to analyze the effect of creative punctuation and capitalization. Students might analyze E. E. Cummings's use of capitalization or punctuation in a poem like "maggie and milly and molly and may" and that of Shel Silverstein in "Sarah Cynthia Sylvia Stout Would Not Take the Garbage Out." Tell students to write short analyses that give their opinions about the effects created by the creative uses of capitalization and punctuation.

- date, time, place, address
- names of five participants
- name of person writing the press release
- sponsoring organizations
- phone number to call for more information

Press releases should be written just as they are to be printed in newspapers and read aloud on the air. Have students pay special attention to their use of capitalization.

(11) Capitalize the names of planets, stars, constellations, and other heavenly bodies.

Type of Name	Examples	
Planets	**M**ercury	**V**enus
Stars	**R**igel	**P**roxima **C**entauri
Constellations	**U**rsa **M**ajor	**A**ndromeda
Other Heavenly Bodies	**M**ilky **W**ay	**C**omet **K**ohoutek

| STYLE | TIP |

The word *earth* is not capitalized unless it is used along with the names of other heavenly bodies that are capitalized. The words *sun* and *moon* are generally not capitalized.

EXAMPLES

Oceans cover three fourths of the **e**arth's surface.

Which is larger—Saturn or **E**arth?

How many **m**oons does **J**upiter have?

TEACHING TIP

Exercises You may wish to use **Exercise 3** as guided practice, and then have students complete **Review A** as independent practice.

Exercise 3 **Proofreading Sentences for Correct Capitalization**

Supply capital letters wherever they are needed in each of the following sentences. Words that should be capitalized are underscored.

EXAMPLE 1. Each arbor day the students at franklin junior high school plant a tree.

1. *Arbor Day, Franklin Junior High School*

1. The <u>golden gate bridge</u> spans the entrance of <u>san francisco</u> bay.
2. Our <u>muslim</u> neighbors, the Rashads, fast during the month of <u>ramadan</u>.
3. The <u>peace corps</u> became a government agency by an act of <u>congress</u>.
4. Do you think the <u>henderson hornets</u> will win the play-offs?
5. Thousands of <u>cherokee</u> people live in the Smoky Mountains in and around North Carolina.
6. To stop flooding in the South, the <u>tennessee valley authority</u>, a government agency, built thirty-nine dams on the Tennessee River and the streams that flow into it.
7. Which biographer won the <u>pulitzer prize</u> this year?
8. On <u>new year's day</u>, many fans crowd into football stadiums for annual bowl games such as the <u>rose bowl</u>.
9. Can you see <u>neptune</u> or any of its moons through your telescope?
10. Have you read any myths about <u>apollo</u>, a god once worshiped by the <u>greeks</u>?

Rewrite the following sentences, using capital letters wherever they are needed.   Words that should be capitalized are underscored.

EXAMPLE   1. according to my sister, i'm a mall rat.
           1. *According to my sister, I'm a mall rat.*

1. the branford mall is the largest in melville county.
2. It is on jefferson parkway, two miles north of duck lake state park and the big bridge that crosses duck lake.
3. Across the parkway from the mall is our new local high school with its parking lots, playing fields, and stadium, home of the branford panthers.
4. Near the mall are the american legion hall, bowlarama, and king skating rink.
5. The mall includes two jewelry stores, nicholson's department store, the palace cinema, and thirty-five other businesses.
6. They range from small stationery stores to one of the finest restaurants in the midwest.
7. The restaurant larue is run by marie and jean larue, who are from france.
8. Also in the mall is the american paper box company, which sells boxes for every packaging need.
9. My friends sharon and earl always shop at gene's jeans, which specializes in denim clothing.
10. An outlet store for northwestern leather goods of chicago sells uffizi purses and wallets.

Review B **Correcting Errors in Capitalization**

Each of the following sentences contains errors in capitalization. Correct these errors by changing incorrect capital letters to lowercase letters and incorrect lowercase letters to capital letters.
Words that should be capitalized or lowercased are underscored.
EXAMPLE   1. African americans in massachusetts have played an important part in American history.

           1. *Americans, Massachusetts*

1. In Boston, the Crispus attucks monument is a memorial to attucks and the other men who died in the boston Massacre.
2. According to many Historians, attucks was a former slave who fought against the british in the american Revolution.

STYLE TIP

Misusing a capital letter or a lowercase letter at the beginning of a word can confuse the meaning of a sentence.

EXAMPLE

I'd like to see inside the **w**hite **h**ouse. [The sentence means I'd like to see inside a particular house that is white.]

I'd like to see inside the **W**hite **H**ouse. [The sentence means I'd like to see inside the home of the president of the United States.]

You may be able to use double meanings effectively in poetry or in other creative writing. In formal writing, though, you should follow the rules of standard capitalization.

Using Capital Letters Correctly   **583**

Jan Ernst Matzeliger

W.E.B. DuBois

Crispus Attucks

MECHANICS

Proper Adjectives, Course Names

Rules 22e, f *(pp. 584–586)*

OBJECTIVE

■ **To proofread and revise sentences for correct capitalization of proper adjectives and the names of school subjects**

Reference Note

For more about **proper adjectives,** see page 349.

3. The department of the Interior has made the Home of maria baldwin a historic building in cambridge.
4. Baldwin was a Leader in the league for Community Service, an Organization to help the Needy.
5. One of the founders of the National association for the Advancement of colored people, w.e.b. DuBois, was born in great Barrington, Massachusetts.
6. A marker stands on the Spot where DuBois lived.
7. Jan ernst matzeliger, who lived in lynn, invented a machine that made Shoes easier and cheaper to manufacture.
8. The nantucket whaling Museum has information about Peter green, a Sailor on the ship *john Adams.*
9. During a storm at sea, Green saved the Ship and crew.
10. Use the Map of Massachusetts shown above to locate the Towns and Cities in which these notable african Americans lived.

22e. Capitalize proper adjectives.

A ***proper adjective*** is formed from a proper noun and is capitalized.

RESOURCES

Proper Adjectives, Course Names
Practice

■ *Grammar, Usage, and Mechanics,* pp. 262, 263–264
■ *Language Workshop CD-ROM,* Lesson 54

Proper Noun	Proper Adjective
Greece	**G**reek theater
Mars	**M**artian moons
Darwin	**D**arwinian theory
Japan	**J**apanese tea ceremony

22f. Do not capitalize the names of school subjects, except course names followed by numerals and names of language classes.

EXAMPLES   **h**istory, **t**yping, **a**lgebra, **E**nglish, **S**panish, **L**atin, **H**istory 101, **M**usic III, **A**rt **A**ppreciation I

Exercise 4 **Proofreading Sentences for Correct Capitalization**

Supply capital letters where they are needed in each of the following sentences.   Words that should be capitalized are underscored.

EXAMPLE   **1.** Rosa said we were eating mexican bread.
                 1. Mexican

1. The program featured <u>russian</u> ballet dancers.
2. The <u>european</u> Common Market improves international trade.
3. The <u>scandinavian</u> countries include both Norway and Sweden.
4. In geography, we learned about the platypus and the koala, two <u>australian</u> animals.
5. We read several <u>english</u> plays in my literature class.
6. I am planning to take <u>computers</u> I next year.
7. On the floor was a large <u>persian</u> rug.
8. England, France, Scotland, Russia, and the United States played important roles in <u>canadian</u> history.
9. The backyard was decorated with <u>chinese</u> lanterns.
10. Are you taking <u>french</u> or <u>art</u> II?

Review C **Correcting Errors in Capitalization**

Each of the sentences on the following page contains errors in capitalization. Correct these errors by writing the <u>words that are incorrectly capitalized</u> and changing capital letters to lowercase letters or changing lowercase letters to capital letters.

MECHANICS

MECHANICS

Titles

Rule 22g *(pp. 586–592)*

OBJECTIVE

- To proofread and revise sentences for correct capitalization of titles

Meeting
INDIVIDUAL
NEEDS

ENGLISH-LANGUAGE LEARNERS
General Strategies. Some languages may vary from English in how the words in the title of a book, article, or movie are capitalized. Consequently, when using English, students might have difficulty determining which words in titles to capitalize. Help students by showing them a variety of titles so that they get a sense of which words in titles are capitalized in English.

Reference Note

For information about **punctuating abbreviations,** see page 599.

STYLE TIP

For special emphasis or clarity, writers sometimes capitalize a title used alone or following a person's name.

EXAMPLES
At the ceremony, the **Q**ueen honored the Royal Navy.

Mr. Biden, the **S**enator from Delaware, called for a committee vote.

EXAMPLE
1. "what do you know about Modern architecture at the beginning of the Century, sean?"

1. *What, modern, century, Sean*

Words that should be capitalized or lowercased are underscored.

1. In Social Studies, i learned about the famous Architect Frank Lloyd Wright.
2. One of wright's best-known works is his house, fallingwater, in bear run, Pennsylvania.
3. "Yes, wright still may be the best-known american architect," Mrs. Lee said.
4. Louis sullivan (1856–1924) was among the first Builders in the united States to use a steel frame.
5. A german architect helped design the Seagram Building, an early Skyscraper in the east.
6. Both architects and the Public wanted new ideas after world war II, according to my architecture 101 teacher.
7. the use of reinforced Concrete made possible large, thin roofs such as the one at the Massachusetts institute of technology.
8. Next tuesday we will see a Film about inventive designs in the brazilian capital.
9. I imagine that brazilian Citizens are proud of the architect Oscar niemeyer.
10. Hear my report on the israeli architect Moshe Safdie during History today.

22g. Capitalize titles.

(1) Capitalize the title of a person when the title comes before a name.

EXAMPLES **P**resident Lincoln   **M**rs. Oliver Wendell

Mayor Bradley   **C**ommissioner Rodriguez

Generally, a title that is used alone or following a person's name is not capitalized, especially if the title is preceded by *a* or *the.*

EXAMPLES   The **s**ecretary of **d**efense held a news conference.

Lien Fong, our class **s**ecretary, read the minutes.

However, a title used by itself in direct address is usually capitalized.

RESOURCES

Titles
Practice

- *Grammar, Usage, and Mechanics,* pp. 265, 266, 267–268
- *Language Workshop CD-ROM,* Lesson 54

EXAMPLES   Is it very serious, **D**octor?

How do you do, **S**ir [or **s**ir]?

(2) Capitalize a word showing a family relationship when the word is used before or in place of a person's name.

EXAMPLES   We expect **U**ncle Fred and **A**unt Helen soon.

Both **M**om and **D**ad work at the hospital.

However, do not capitalize a word showing a family relationship when a possessive comes before the word.

EXAMPLE   We asked Pedro's **m**other and his **a**unt Celia to be chaperons.

(3) Capitalize the first and last words and all important words in titles and subtitles.

Unimportant words in titles include

- articles (*a, an, the*)
- coordinating conjunctions (*and, but, for, nor, or, so, yet*)
- prepositions of fewer than five letters (such as *by, for, on, with*)

Type of Name	Examples	
Books	*The **M**ask of **A**pollo* *Mules and Men*	*Long **C**laws: **A**n Arctic Adventure*
Chapters and Other Parts of Books	"**T**he **C**irculatory **S**ystem" "**L**anguage **H**andbook"	"**T**he **C**ivil **W**ar **B**egins" "**E**pilogue"
Magazines	*Popular **M**echanics* *Ebony*	*Seventeen* *Sports **I**llustrated*
Newspapers	*The **T**ennessean* the *Boston **G**lobe*	*The **W**all **S**treet Journal*
Poems	"**S**eason at the **S**hore"	*Evangeline* "**B**irches"

(continued)

Reference Note

For more about **articles,** see page 347. For more about **coordinating conjunctions,** see page 374. For more about **prepositions,** see page 370.

Reference Note

For guidelines on **what titles are italicized,** see page 628. For guidelines on **what titles are enclosed in quotation marks,** see page 635.

MULTIPLE INTELLIGENCES
Interpersonal Intelligence. Have interested students interview at least five people to get answers to the following questions.

1. What is your favorite book?

2. What is your favorite magazine?

3. What is your favorite movie?

4. What is your least favorite CD?

5. What is your favorite television show?

Ask students to write short summaries of their findings, reminding them to capitalize titles correctly as they record responses and write their summaries. Then, ask volunteers to read their summaries to the class, and post all the summaries on a bulletin board.

TECHNOLOGY

If students have access to a tape recorder or a computer with audio-recording capability, encourage them to use it while conducting interviews for the activity above. The recorded answers can be used to confirm responses to interview questions or to fill in any gaps students may have in their notes.

MECHANICS

(continued)

Type of Name	Examples	
Short Stories	"**T**he **P**urloined **L**etter"	"**Z**lateh the **G**oat" "**B**roken **C**hain"
Plays	*The Three Sisters* *A Midsummer Night's Dream*	*A Doll's House* *I Never Sang for My Father*
Movies and Videos	*Fairy Tale: A True Story* *Babe*	*It's a Wonderful Life* *The Wizard of Oz*
Television Series	*Home Improvement* *Kratt's Creatures*	*Star Trek: The Next Generation*
Cartoons and Comic Strips	*Jump Start* *Cathy*	*Scooby Doo* *Dilbert*
Audiotapes and CDs	*Butterfly* *Falling into You*	*Dos Mundos* *Spirit*
Computer Games and Video Games	*Sonic the Hedgehog* *Math Blaster* *Rockett's New School*	*Logical Journey* *SimCity* *Space Kids*
Works of Art	*Mona Lisa* *David*	*The Night Watch* *Mankind's Struggle*
Musical Compositions	*The Marriage of Figaro*	"*America the Beautiful*"
Historical Documents	**M**agna **C**arta **T**reaty of **P**aris	**T**he **D**eclaration of **I**ndependence

┌HELP─

The official title of a book is found on the title page. The official title of a newspaper or periodical is found on the masthead, which usually appears on the editorial page or the table of contents.

NOTE The article *the* at the beginning of a title is not capitalized unless it is the first word of the official title.

EXAMPLES My father reads *The Wall Street Journal.*

Does she work for **t**he *Texas Review*?

MINI-LESSON

***The* in Titles.** Capitalizing and italicizing the word *the* when it is the first word in the title of a periodical or newspaper can be confusing. *The* is italicized and capitalized only when it is part of the official title. Ask students to refer to a reference work that contains titles of periodicals and newspapers and to make a list of five titles containing *the* and five titles that don't contain *the.* Students can ask at the reference desk of the library for help finding the appropriate reference books, or they could

Exercise 5 Correcting Sentences by Capitalizing Words

Most of the following sentences contain at least one word that should be capitalized but is not. Correctly write each incorrect word. If a sentence is already correct, write *C*.

EXAMPLE   1. Ms. Chang is meeting with principal Hodges.
            1. *Principal*

1. Tom Hanks' career really took off after he starred in the movie *big*.
2. In 1998, John Glenn, a former senator, became the oldest person to travel in space.   **2. C [or Senator]**
3. The assignment is to compare and contrast Amy Tan's story "Two kinds" with Bernard Malamud's "The first seven years."
4. Rummaging through the pile of used books, Marcia found a copy of *the Complete Poems Of Stephen Crane*.
5. Our English teacher, mrs. Fernandez, has a small sculpture of the globe theatre sitting on her desk.
6. Isn't it a coincidence that your aunt Jenny and my uncle Herbert work for the same company?   **6. C**
7. Which do you prefer, Bob Dylan's CD *Nashville skyline* or his son's *The wallflowers*?
8. Some of my friends claim that *The Empire strikes back* is the best movie of the series.
9. Did you remember to clip that article we read yesterday in *The Washington post*?
10. Mom and dad always chuckle when they read *Hagar the Horrible*.

Review D Proofreading Sentences for Correct Capitalization

Write the sentences on the following page, using capital letters wherever they are needed.   Words that should be capitalized are underscored.

EXAMPLE   1. The series *all creatures great and small* is being rerun on public television.

            1. *The series* All Creatures Great and Small *is being rerun on public television.*

MODALITIES
Visual and Kinesthetic Learners.
Have students search newspapers and magazines to find capitalized words that illustrate each of the rules and subrules in this chapter. Ask students to cut out sentences or phrases containing the words that illustrate the rules and to label the words with the rules that apply. Then, allow students, in groups of three, to share their work. The projects could be displayed in the classroom.

MECHANICS

Timesaver

Since **Reviews D–G** and the **Chapter Review** cover the same material **(Rules 22a–22g),** you may not want to assign all of the exercises. You could make assignments based on students' understanding and their application of the rules in previous exercises and activities.

conduct a search on the Internet. Explain to students that whenever they are in doubt about whether *the* is part of the title of a periodical or newspaper, they can find the answer by consulting a reference work or a copy of the periodical or newspaper.

Critical Thinking

Metacognition. After students have completed **Review D,** have them analyze the process they use to correct errors in capitalization. Do they check a word at a time, a sentence at a time, or read the entire exercise before starting to make corrections? Do they note areas of difficulty and go back to those after finishing the corrections for which they know the answers? Do they recheck their work to see if they may have overlooked a correction? How effective do they think their strategies are? What might they change to make their strategies more effective? Have students work in pairs to ask these questions and analyze their processes.

1. While waiting to interview <u>mayor</u> <u>ward</u>, I read an article in *newsweek*.
2. Have you read <u>leslie</u> <u>marmon</u> <u>silko</u>'s poem "<u>story</u> from <u>bear</u> <u>country</u>"?
3. You have probably seen a picture of *the thinker*, one of <u>rodin</u>'s best-known sculptures.
4. On television last night, we saw the movie *the return of the native*.
5. Every four years voters elect a president and several <u>united</u> <u>states</u> senators.
6. Uncle <u>nick</u> read aloud from <u>francisco</u> <u>jiménez</u>'s short story "<u>the</u> <u>circuit</u>."
7. The reporter asked, "Can you tell us, <u>senator</u> <u>inouye</u>, when you plan to announce the committee's final decision?"
8. The main speaker was <u>dr.</u> <u>andrew</u> <u>holt</u>, a former president of the <u>university</u> of <u>tennessee</u>.
9. Besides <u>uncle</u> <u>don</u>, our visitors included <u>aunt</u> <u>pat</u>, <u>aunt</u> <u>jean</u>, both of my grandmothers, and my great-grandfather.
10. The soccer players listened to <u>coach</u> Daly as he outlined defensive strategy.

Review E Proofreading Sentences for Correct Capitalization

The following sentences each contain at least one capitalization error. Correctly write the <u>words that require capital letters</u>.

EXAMPLE   1. The waters of the caribbean are pleasantly warm.
1. *Caribbean*

1. The <u>greeks</u> believed that <u>zeus</u>, the king of the gods, lived on <u>mount</u> <u>olympus</u>.
2. The *titanic* sank after hitting an iceberg off the coast of <u>newfoundland</u>.
3. My cousin collects <u>scandinavian</u> pottery.
4. Stephanie is taking <u>english</u>, <u>math</u> II, and biology.
5. On <u>friday</u> we were cheered by the thought that <u>monday</u>, <u>memorial</u> <u>day</u>, would be a holiday.
6. My picture is in today's *austin American-Statesman*.
7. The <u>quaker</u> <u>oats</u> <u>company</u> has introduced a new corn cereal.
8. In *roots*, <u>alex</u> <u>haley</u>, a famous author, traces the history of his family.
9. She usually travels to <u>boston</u> on <u>american</u> <u>airlines</u>.

MINI-LESSON

Punctuating Titles. If students are confused about when to use underlining (italics) with titles and when to use quotation marks with titles, write the following titles on the chalkboard without punctuation. Have students add either underlining or quotation marks to each.

The Borrowers [The Borrowers]

Row, Row, Row Your Boat ["Row, Row, Row Your Boat"]

Jabberwocky ["Jabberwocky"]

10. I wanted to name my <u>persian</u> cat after one of the justices on the <u>supreme court</u>.

Review F — Proofreading a Paragraph for Correct Capitalization

Each sentence in the following paragraph contains at least one error in capitalization. Correctly write the <u>words that require capital letters</u>.

EXAMPLE   **[1]** Before thanksgiving, i learned some interesting facts about africa in my history II class.

    1. Thanksgiving, I, Africa, History II

[1] My teacher, <u>mr. davidson</u>, told us about the mighty kingdoms and empires that existed for hundreds of years in <u>africa</u>. [2] <u>some</u> of these kingdoms dated back to the time of the <u>roman empire</u>. [3] Others rose to power during the period known as the <u>middle ages</u> in <u>europe</u>. [4] For many years, the people in the kingdom of <u>cush</u> did ironwork and traded along the <u>nile river</u>. [5] Later, the <u>cush</u> were defeated by the people of <u>axum</u>, led by <u>king ezana</u>. [6] As you can see in the map below, several kingdoms in <u>africa</u> developed between <u>lake chad</u> and the <u>atlantic ocean</u>. [7] Three of these kingdoms were <u>ghana</u>, <u>mali</u>, and <u>songhai</u>. [8] These kingdoms established important trade routes across the <u>sahara</u>. [9] Tombouctou's famous university attracted <u>egyptian</u> and other <u>arab</u> students. [10] I read more about these <u>african</u> kingdoms and empires in our textbook, *<u>world history: people and nations</u>*.

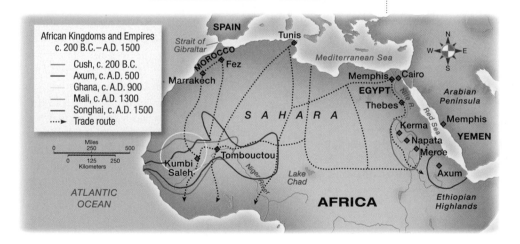

Looking at Language

Redundancy. Point out to students that in formal usage, one would say "the Sahara" without using the term *desert,* as in sentence 8 of **Review F**. In informal usage, "Sahara Desert" is acceptable. This distinction is made because *sahara* is Arabic for *desert,* making the word *desert* redundant after "the Sahara." Similarly, the word *sierra* in Spanish means a range of hills or mountains; in formal usage, one would say "the Sierra Nevada" rather than "the Sierra Nevada Mountains." However, the latter term is common in informal usage.

TEACHING **TIP**

Extension. You may wish to extend students' study of the map by asking these questions orally or by writing them on the chalkboard and having students write answers to them.

1. What river is near Lake Chad, according to the map? [*the Niger River*]

2. What city was within the kingdom of Ghana? [*Kumbi Saleh*]

3. Was the kingdom of Songhai located in West Africa or East Africa? [*West Africa*]

4. The Cush and Axum kingdoms were near what sea? [*the Red Sea*]

5. What city is on the Mediterranean Sea? [*Tunis*]

MECHANICS

Be sure that students understand that they should use underlining for titles of books, periodicals, movies, television programs, and works of art, and that they should use quotation marks to enclose the titles of short works such as articles, short stories, poems, and songs.

For more information on punctuating titles, refer students to **Chapter 23: Punctuation.**

Viewing the Art

Battle of the Little Bighorn.

Kicking Bear was a Sioux medicine man as well as an artist. He was also a preacher of the Ghost Dance religion. The Ghost Dance is a religious dance performed with the belief that Native Americans' former, traditional way of life will be restored to them.

Exploring the Subject. With long yellow hair and a mustache, General George Armstrong Custer was a fearless, flamboyant leader. In the battle popularly known as "Custer's Last Stand," Custer led his troops to the Little Bighorn River in Montana. Custer's cavalry numbered more than 200 men; the Sioux and Cheyenne numbered more than 2,000. Leaders of the American Indians included the great Sioux warriors Crazy Horse and Sitting Bull. It took less than an hour for the Sioux and the Cheyenne to defeat Custer's troops.

Review G **Correcting Errors in Capitalization**

Each of the following sentences contains at least one error in capitalization. Correctly write each underlined word, changing capital letters to lowercase letters or changing lowercase letters to capital letters.

EXAMPLE   1. On june 25, 1876, sioux and cheyenne warriors defeated general george a. Custer and his Troops.

    1. *June, Sioux, Cheyenne, General George A., troops*

1. The Defeat of general custer occurred at the battle of the little bighorn.
2. In december of 1890, many Sioux were killed by Soldiers in a battle at wounded Knee creek in south Dakota.
3. Depicted by artists, writers, and filmmakers, both Battles have become part of american History.
4. In the late nineteenth century, the sioux Artist Kicking bear painted the *Battle Of the little Bighorn.*
5. The painting, done on muslin Cloth, is shown below.
6. Kicking bear, who himself fought in the Battle, painted at the pine Ridge agency in south Dakota, where he lived.
7. soldiers who fought against kicking Bear described him as courageous.
8. The well-known American Poet Stephen vincent benét wrote about the battle of wounded knee in a Poem called "american names."

Battle of Little Bighorn by Kicking Bear (Sioux), 1898. Courtesy of the Southwest Museum, Los Angeles

9. More recently, the author Dee brown wrote about the american indians of the west in his book *bury my Heart at Wounded knee.*
10. In 1970, the movie *Little big Man* told the story of a fictional 121-year-old character who had survived the Battle against general Custer.

Chapter Review

A. Correcting Errors in Capitalization

Each of the following sentences contains at least one error in capitalization. Correct the errors either by changing capital letters to lowercase letters or by changing lowercase letters to capital letters. Words that should be capitalized or lowercased are underscored.

1. Please pick up a box of Tide <u>Detergent</u> at the store.
2. The "Battle Hymn <u>Of The</u> Republic" was written by Julia <u>ward</u> Howe.
3. Are we going to <u>uncle</u> Ted's house for Thanksgiving again?
4. Charing <u>cross book shop</u> is on Thirty-<u>Second</u> Street.
5. Ms. <u>wong</u> always stays at the Four Seasons <u>hotel</u> when she's in New York <u>city</u> on business.
6. Do you know if <u>professor</u> Ezekiel will be teaching <u>Creative Writing</u> during the spring semester?
7. In what year was the <u>battle</u> of <u>gettysburg</u> fought?
8. My aunt remembers when Mother Teresa won the Nobel Peace <u>prize</u>.
9. Every winter my <u>Grandparents</u> travel to the <u>southwest</u>.
10. My <u>Uncle</u> <u>sid</u> once met <u>sir</u> Winston Churchill.
11. Mr. Salter often remembers his old house on <u>vine street</u> in McAllen, Texas.
12. Father and <u>mother</u> traveled all over the <u>World</u> when they were buying furniture for their antique store.
13. The principal asked me, "<u>how</u> would you like to study <u>Geography</u> next semester?"
14. When Jim went back to New York for Christmas, he left his dog, <u>piper</u>, at the kennel.
15. Sometimes my <u>Mother</u> works at home on <u>friday</u>.
16. Grand Canyon National <u>park</u> was closed this weekend because of heavy snow.
17. Shall we renew our subscription to <u>national geographic</u>?
18. This <u>june</u> we plan to welcome a <u>swedish</u> exchange student to our home.

Using the Chapter Review

To assess student progress, you may want to compare the types of items missed on the **Diagnostic Preview** to those missed on the **Chapter Review.** If students have not made significant progress, you may want to refer them to **Exercises 28, 29, 33, and 34,** and **Sections 1** and **2** of the **Mechanics Test** in **Chapter 26: Correcting Common Errors** for additional practice.

Meeting INDIVIDUAL NEEDS

LEARNERS HAVING DIFFICULTY
The twenty-five lengthy sentences in **Part A** of this **Chapter Review** might be overwhelming to some students. Here are some steps you can take to make the text more manageable.

1. Isolate each sentence so that students can focus on one sentence at a time.
2. Have helpers read the sentences aloud to students with visual-processing deficits.
3. Suggest that students first check for errors in the application of **Rule 22a** only. Next, students should look for errors in the application of **Rule 22b,** and so on.

19. We're going to Washington, D.C., to see the <u>white</u> <u>house</u>.

20. At the Henry Ford Museum in Dearborn, Michigan, you can see a replica of the *<u>spirit</u> <u>of</u> <u>st.</u> <u>louis</u>*, the plane that Charles Lindbergh used to fly solo across the <u>atlantic</u>.

21. At the Crossbay Market, <u>i</u> bought a can of <u>progresso</u> soup.

22. My <u>Aunt</u> Janice visited Petrified Forest National Park.

23. The Rosenbach <u>museum</u> and <u>library</u> in Philadelphia is open Tuesday through Sunday.

24. <u>dear</u> Mr. Boylan:

    I enjoyed your book enormously.

    <u>sincerely</u> yours,

    Jimmy Connolly

25. In <u>History</u> class, we learned about <u>queen</u> Elizabeth I.

B. Proofreading Sentences for Correct Capitalization

Write the following sentences, and correct errors in capitalization either by changing capital letters to lowercase letters or by changing lowercase letters to capital letters.

Words that should be capitalized or lowercased are underscored.

26. Mars, Venus, and Jupiter were <u>roman</u> gods.

27. *The <u>wind</u> <u>in</u> <u>the</u> <u>willows</u>* is my <u>Mother's</u> favorite book.

28. Davis Housewares <u>emporium</u> has moved to Fifth <u>street</u>.

29. The <u>lozi</u> people in Africa live near the Zambezi <u>river</u>.

30. "Stopping <u>By</u> Woods <u>On</u> a Snowy Evening" is by Robert Frost, a <u>Poet</u> from New England.

31. Do you know when David Souter was appointed to the <u>supreme</u> <u>court</u>?

32. Next Monday is <u>memorial</u> <u>day</u>.

33. When we traveled through the <u>south</u>, we visited the Antietam National Battlefield.

34. Ms. Ling is teaching us about <u>chinese</u> culture.

35. Cayuga <u>lake</u> stretches <u>North</u> from Ithaca, New York.

36. The main religion in Indonesia is <u>islam</u>, but there are also many Indonesian <u>buddhists</u>.

37. My older sister is taking Spanish, <u>Science</u>, Mathematics II, and <u>Art</u>.

RESOURCES

Capital Letters
Review
- *Grammar, Usage, and Mechanics,* pp. 269, 270, 271, 272

Assessment
- *Assessment Package*
  —*Chapter Tests,* Ch. 22
  —*Chapter Tests in Standardized Test Formats,* Ch. 22
- *Test Generator (One-Stop Planner CD-ROM)*

38. Carlos and I had turkey sandwiches made with <u>german</u> mustard on <u>french</u> bread.

39. We turned west onto <u>route</u> 95 and stayed on it for five miles.

40. George Copway, who was born in Canada, wrote about his people, the <u>ojibwa</u>.

Writing Application
Using Capital Letters in a Letter

Proper Nouns   Students in your class have become pen pals with students in another country. You have been given the name of someone to write. Write your pen pal a letter introducing yourself and telling about your school and your community. In your letter, be sure to use capitalization correctly.

Prewriting   Note the information you want to give in your letter. You may wish to include information such as your age; a description of yourself; your favorite books, movies, actors, or musicians; some clubs, organizations, or special activities you participate in; some special places, events, or attractions in your community or state.

Writing   As you write your draft, keep in mind that your pen pal may not recognize names of some people, places, and things in the United States. For example, he or she may not recognize the names of your favorite movies or musical groups. Be sure to use correct capitalization to show which names are proper nouns.

Revising   Read through your letter carefully. Have you left out any important information? Are any parts of your letter confusing? If so, you may want to add, cut, or revise some details. Is the tone of your letter friendly? Have you followed the correct form for a personal letter?

Publishing   Read your letter carefully to check for any errors in grammar, spelling, and punctuation. Use the rules in this chapter to help you double-check your capitalization. With your teacher's permission, post a map of the world on the classroom wall and display the letters around the map.

Reference Note

For more about writing **personal letters,** see "Writing" in the Quick Reference Handbook.

Writing Application

Tip. If students are unsure about the form for a personal letter, refer them to **Writing** in the **Quick Reference Handbook.** If students are interested in writing letters to pen pals, they could find the addresses of pen-pal services at the library. Alternatively, they could search for Internet pen pals at monitored, youth-oriented Web sites.

Scoring Rubric. While paying particular attention to students' use of correct capitalization, you will also want to evaluate overall writing performance. You may want to give a split score to indicate development and clarity of the composition as well as mechanics skills.

MECHANICS

CHAPTER

23

Punctuation

End Marks, Commas, Semicolons, and Colons

Diagnostic Preview

Using End Marks, Commas, Semicolons, and Colons

The following sentences lack necessary periods, question marks, exclamation points, commas, semicolons, and colons. Rewrite each sentence, inserting the correct punctuation.
Optional commas are underlined.

EXAMPLE   1. Snakes lizards crocodiles and turtles are reptiles

1. *Snakes, lizards, crocodiles, and turtles are reptiles.*

┌HELP┐

All of the punctuation marks that are already in the sentences in the Diagnostic Preview are correct.

1. Toads and frogs on the other hand are amphibians
2. Some turtles live on land others live in lakes streams or oceans
3. Turtles have no teeth but you should watch out for their strong hard beaks
4. The words *turtle* and *tortoise* are similar in meaning but *tortoise* usually refers to a land dweller
5. The African pancake tortoise which has a flat flexible shell uses an unusual means of defense
6. Faced with a threat it crawls into a narrow crack in a rock takes a deep breath and wedges itself in tightly
7. Because some species of tortoises are endangered they cannot be sold as pets

8. Three species of tortoises that can be found in the United States are as follows: the desert tortoise, the gopher tortoise, and the Texas tortoise.

9. The gopher tortoise lives in the Southeast, and the desert tortoise comes from the Southwest.

10. Is the Indian star tortoise, which is now an endangered species, very rare?

11. As this kind of tortoise grows older, its shell grows larger, the number of stars on the shell increases, and their pattern becomes more complex.

12. The Indian star tortoise requires warmth, sunlight, and a diet of green vegetables.

13. Living in fresh water, soft-shelled turtles have long, flexible beaks and fleshy lips.

14. Their shells are not really soft, however, but are covered by smooth skin.

15. Sea turtles are the fastest turtles; the green turtle can swim at speeds of almost twenty miles per hour.

16. Most turtles can pull their head, legs, and tail into their shell; however, sea turtles cannot do so.

17. Mr. Kim, my neighbor up the street, has several turtles in his backyard pond.

18. Come to my house at 4:30 in the afternoon, and I'll show you our turtle.

19. At 7:00 P.M., we can watch that new PBS documentary about sea turtles.

20. Wanda, may I introduce you to Pokey, my pet turtle?

21. Pokey, who has been part of our family for years, is a red-eared turtle.

22. The book *Turtles: A Complete Pet Owner's Manual* has helped me learn how to take care of Pokey.

23. Pokey has been in my family for fifteen years, and my parents say that he could easily live to be fifty if he is cared for properly.

24. What a great pet Pokey is! [*or* .]

25. Don't you agree with me, Wanda, that a turtle makes a good pet?

End Marks

End Marks

Rules 23a–e *(pp. 598–601)*

OBJECTIVES

- To rewrite sentences by adding the appropriate end marks
- To punctuate abbreviations correctly

TEACHING **TIP**

Activity. To give students practice in identifying sentence types and supplying appropriate end marks, have volunteers add end marks to the following nursery rhyme. Write the nursery rhyme on the chalkboard or on a transparency, or have students copy the nursery rhyme and work in groups to add one question mark, two exclamation points, and one period.

The north wind doth blow,
we soon shall have snow,
and what will poor robin do then [?]
Poor thing [!]
He'll sit in the barn
to keep himself warm,
and hide his head under his wing [.]
Poor thing [!]

Meeting
INDIVIDUAL
NEEDS

LEARNERS HAVING DIFFICULTY

Point out to students that sentences beginning with *what* and *how* that are obviously not questions are usually exclamations, as in "What a beautiful day we're having!" or "How beautiful that flower is!" Then, work with students to write both exclamations and questions that begin with the words *what* or *how*. Have students illustrate the sentences. The illustrations could then be displayed on a bulletin board.

┌─HELP─
Periods (decimal points) are also used to separate dollars from cents and whole numbers from tenths, hundredths, and so forth.

EXAMPLES
$10.23 [ten dollars and twenty-three cents]
5.7 [five and seven tenths]

An ***end mark*** is a mark of punctuation placed at the end of a sentence. *Periods, question marks,* and *exclamation points* are end marks.

23a. **Use a period at the end of a statement.**

EXAMPLE　　Tea is grown in Sri Lanka.

23b. **Use a question mark at the end of a question.**

EXAMPLE　　Did you see the exhibit about lightning?

23c. **Use an exclamation point at the end of an exclamation.**

EXAMPLE　　What a high bridge that was!

23d. **Use either a period or an exclamation point at the end of a request or a command.**

When an imperative sentence makes a request, it is generally followed by a period. When an imperative sentence expresses a strong command, an exclamation point is generally used.

EXAMPLES　　Please call the dog. [a request]
　　　　　　Call the dog! [a command]

Exercise 1 **Adding End Marks to Sentences**

Rewrite each of the following sentences, adding the necessary end marks.

EXAMPLE　　1. Did you know that a choreographer is a person who creates dance steps

　　　　　　1. Did you know that a choreographer is a person who creates dance steps?

1. Why is Katherine Dunham called the mother of African American dance?
2. She studied anthropology in college and won a scholarship to visit the Caribbean.
3. How inspiring the dances she saw in Haiti were!
4. When Dunham returned to the United States, she toured the country with her own professional dance company.
5. How I admire such a talented person!
6. Ask me anything about Katherine Dunham.

RESOURCES

End Marks
Practice

- *Grammar, Usage, and Mechanics,* pp. 277, 278, 279
- *Language Workshop CD-ROM,* Lesson 46

MECHANICS

7. How many honors has Dunham's creativity won her?
8. She was named to the Hall of Fame of the National Museum of Dance in Saratoga, New York.
9. She was also given the National Medal of Arts for exploring Caribbean and African dance.
10. The editors of *Essence* magazine praised Dunham for helping to break down racial barriers.

23e. Many abbreviations are followed by a period.

Types of Abbreviations	Examples
Personal Names	A. B. Guthrie W.E.B. DuBois Livie I. Durán
Titles Used with Names	Mr. Mrs. Ms. Jr. Sr. Dr.
Organizations and Companies	Co. Inc. Corp. Assn.

NOTE Abbreviations for government agencies and other widely used abbreviations are written without periods. Each letter of the abbreviation is capitalized.

EXAMPLES	FBI	NAACP	NIH	NPR
	PTA	TV	UN	YWCA

Types of Abbreviations	Examples
Addresses	Ave. St. Rd. Blvd. P.O. Box
States	Tex. Penn. Ariz. Wash. N.C.
Times	A.M. (*ante meridiem,* used with times from midnight to noon) P.M. (*post meridiem,* used with times from noon to midnight) B.C. (before Christ) A.D. (*anno Domini,* in the year of the Lord)

STYLE TIP

When writing the initials of someone's name, place a space between two initials (S. E. Hinton). Do not place spaces between three initials (M.F.K. Fisher).

STYLE TIP

An **acronym** is a word formed from the first (or first few) letters of a series of words. Acronyms are written without periods.

EXAMPLES
  UNICEF (**U**nited **N**ations **I**nternational **C**hildren's **E**mergency **F**und)

  VISTA (**V**olunteers **i**n **S**ervice **t**o **A**merica)

End Marks **599**

Learning for Life   *Continued on pp. 600–601*

Everyday Abbreviations. To demonstrate to students the common occurrence of abbreviations in daily life, write the following paragraph on the chalkboard or on a transparency.

Today I went to the store and bought 5 lbs of potatoes; then, I stopped by the library to borrow a book of poems by E. E. Cummings. After that, I made it to the post office before it closed at 5:30 P.M. and mailed my tax

Meeting INDIVIDUAL NEEDS

ADVANCED LEARNERS

Tell students that some abbreviations commonly used in English have no periods. Ask students to consult a dictionary or reference book that deals specifically with abbreviations and to create a list of abbreviations that do not use periods. Ask students to suggest guidelines that explain when periods can be left out of abbreviations. [*Abbreviations used without periods are usually the names of government agencies (CIA), organizations (PTA), or job titles (CEO)*]

Crossing the Curriculum

Math. Pose the following question to students: How does a period in a decimal function differently from a period in a sentence? You may want to have students in small groups brainstorm the possibilities or have them puzzle over the answers overnight and discuss the possibilities with family members or others. [*Students may conclude that in a sentence, the period signals a stop—the end of a sentence—while in a decimal, the period means* and *(for example, 4.6 is interpreted as "four and six tenths"). Also, when reading amounts of money, the period means* and *(for example, $1.98 is read as "one dollar and ninety-eight cents").*]

STYLE TIP

The abbreviations *A.D.* and *B.C.* need special attention. Place *A.D.* before the numeral and *B.C.* after the numeral.

EXAMPLES
 A.D. 760   54 **B.C.**

However, for centuries expressed in words, place both *A.D.* and *B.C.* after the century.

EXAMPLES
 seventh century **B.C.**

 fourth century **A.D.**

HELP

If you are not sure whether you should use a period with an abbreviation, look up the abbreviation in a dictionary.

NOTE A two-letter state abbreviation without periods is used only when it is followed by a ZIP Code. Both letters of such abbreviations are capitalized.

EXAMPLE   Orlando, **FL** 32819

Abbreviations for units of measure are usually written without periods and are not capitalized.

EXAMPLES   mm   kg   dl   oz   lb   ft   yd   mi

However, to avoid confusion with the word *in*, you should use a period with the abbreviation for *inch* (*in.*).

NOTE When an abbreviation with a period ends a sentence, another period is not needed. However, a question mark or an exclamation point is used as needed.

EXAMPLES   We will arrive by 3:00 P.M.

Can you meet us at 3:30 P.M.?

Oh no! It's already 3:30 P.M.!

Exercise 2 Punctuating Abbreviations

Some of the following sentences contain abbreviations that have not been correctly punctuated. Correct each error. If a sentence is already correct, write *C*. Carets indicate where periods should be inserted.

EXAMPLE   1. Of course, we watch P.B.S.; we love the science shows it broadcasts.

   1. *PBS*

1. Not everyone knows that WEB DuBois eventually became a Ghanaian citizen.
2. The writing isn't clear, but I think it says *10 ft 6 in* or *10 ft 5 in.*
3. Write me in care of Mrs. Audrey Coppola, 10 Watson Ave.
4. Yes, that's in California—Novato, CA 94949.
5. Were those clay statues made as far back as 500 B.C?
6. Send your check or money order to Lester's Low-Cost Computer Chips, Inc Duluth, Minn and receive your new chips in two days!
7. Could you be there at 7:00 P.M.?   7. C

Learning for Life

forms to the IRS office in Austin, Tex. Now I won't be panicking when the April 15 deadline comes. Finally, I drove home to my house on Harcourt Dr. for an evening of old movies on TV.

Ask a student volunteer to read the paragraph aloud, then have another student underline all the abbreviations in the paragraph. Discuss with students which types of abbreviations are contained in the paragraph. Then, ask students to work in groups of three to list abbreviations they

---

8. I would never do business with a company whose only address was a PO box.
9. Miss Finch, Dr. Bledsoe will see you now.
10. His full name is Marvin French Little Hawk, Jr., but everyone calls him Junior.   **10.** C

Review A **Adding Periods, Question Marks, and Exclamation Points to Sentences**

Rewrite each of the following sentences, adding the necessary periods, question marks, and exclamation points.

EXAMPLE   1. Do you ever think about how electricity is produced

    1. *Do you ever think about how electricity is produced?*

1. Electricity can come from large hydroelectric power stations.
2. Wow, these stations certainly do create a lot of power!
3. How do hydroelectric power stations work?
4. Look at the diagram to gain a better understanding.
5. Falling water from natural falls or artificial dams provides the initial power in the process.
6. Have you ever been to Niagara Falls, New York, to see the famous falls?
7. From 12:00 A.M. to 12:00 A.M.—constantly, in other words—the falls are a tremendous power source.
8. As you can see, rushing water turns turbines, which then drive generators.
9. What exactly are generators, and what do they do?
10. Dr. D. explained that generators are the machines that turn the motion of the turbines into electricity.

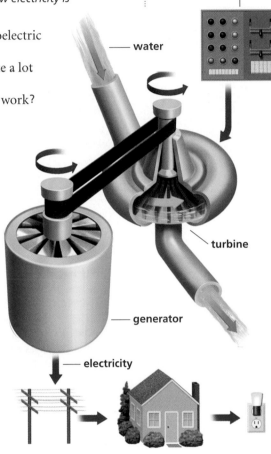

controls

water

turbine

generator

electricity

use in their daily lives. Remind them that in school they use weights and measurements in home economics, science, geography, health, and PE. They may use acronyms that relate to social studies, organizations to which they belong, TV networks they watch, and communication on the Internet. They probably use abbreviations when writing names, addresses, and times of the day; and they may use personal abbreviations in lists and informal notes.

MECHANICS

Commas

Rules 23f–k *(pp. 602–617)*

OBJECTIVES

- To proofread sentences for the correct use of commas

- To correct compound sentences by adding commas

- To add commas to sentences with nonessential phrases and clauses

- To proofread for the correct use of commas with appositives and appositive phrases

- To correct sentences by using commas with words of direct address

- To correct sentences by using commas to set off parenthetical expressions

- To edit sentences for the correct use of commas with introductory elements

- To edit sentences for the correct use of commas in conventional situations

Meeting

INDIVIDUAL

NEEDS

ENGLISH-LANGUAGE LEARNERS

General Strategies. Discuss with students the uses of commas in various languages. In Japanese, Persian, and Arabic, for example, the comma is raised above the line of writing and reversed. If any of your students are native speakers and writers of these languages, perhaps they could share with the class some examples of what commas look like in sentences in their languages.

Reference Note

For information about using **semicolons**, see page 618.

Commas

End marks are used to separate complete thoughts. *Commas,* however, are generally used to separate words or groups of words within a complete thought.

23f. Use commas to separate items in a series.

A *series* is a group of three or more items in a row. Words, phrases, and clauses may appear in a series.

Words in a Series
January, February, and March are all summer months in the Southern Hemisphere. [nouns]
The engine rattled, coughed, and stalled. [verbs]
The baby was happy, alert, playful, and active. [adjectives]

Phrases in a Series
There were fingerprints at the top, on the sides, and on the bottom. [prepositional phrases]
Cut into pieces, aged for a year, and well dried, the wood was ready to burn. [participial phrases]
To pitch in a World Series game, to practice medicine, and to run for mayor are all things I hope to do someday. [infinitive phrases]

Clauses in a Series
We sang, we danced, and we played trivia games. [short independent clauses]
I knew that we were late, that the ice cream was melting, and that the car was nearly out of gas. [short subordinate clauses]

NOTE Only short independent clauses in a series may be separated by commas. A series of independent clauses that are long or that contain commas should be separated by semicolons.

EXAMPLE   Yawning, Mother closed the curtains; Father, who had just come in, turned on the porch lights; and my little sister, Christina, put on her pajamas.

RESOURCES

Commas

Practice

- *Grammar, Usage, and Mechanics,* pp. 280, 281, 282, 283, 284, 285–286, 287, 288–289

- *Language Workshop CD-ROM,* Lessons 42–45

Always be sure that there are at least three items in the series; two items generally do not need a comma between them.

INCORRECT   You will need a pencil, and plenty of paper.

CORRECT   You will need a pencil and plenty of paper.

When all the items in the series are joined by *and* or *or*, do not use commas to separate them.

EXAMPLES   Take water **and** food **and** matches with you.

Stephen will take a class in karate **or** judo **or** aikido next year.

Exercise 3 Proofreading Sentences for the Correct Use of Commas

Some of the following sentences need commas; others do not. If a sentence needs any commas, write the word before each missing comma and add the comma. If a sentence is already correct, write *C*.   Optional commas are underlined.

EXAMPLES   **1.** Seal the envelope stamp it and mail the letter.

1. envelope, it,

2. You should swing the club with your knees bent and your back straight and your elbows tucked.

2. C

1. The mountains and valleys of southern Appalachia were once home to the Cherokee people.   **1. C**
2. Cleveland, Cincinnati, Toledo, and Dayton are four large cities in Ohio.
3. The captain entered the cockpit, checked the instruments, and prepared for takeoff.
4. Luisa bought mangos and papayas and oranges.   **4. C**
5. The speaker took a deep breath and read the report.   **5. C**
6. Rover can roll over, walk on his hind feet, and catch a tennis ball.
7. The neighbors searched behind the garages, in the bushes, and along the highway.
8. Rubén Blades is an attorney, an actor, and a singer.
9. Eleanor Roosevelt's courage, her humanity, and her service to the nation will always be remembered.
10. Tate dusted, I vacuumed, and Blair washed the dishes.

23g. Use a comma to separate two or more adjectives that come before a noun.

EXAMPLES   A white dwarf is a tiny, dense star.

                 Venus Williams played a powerful, brilliant game.

Do not place a comma between an adjective and the noun immediately following it.

INCORRECT   My spaniel is a fat, sassy, puppy.

CORRECT   My spaniel is a fat, sassy puppy.

Sometimes the final adjective in a series is thought of as part of the noun. When the adjective and the noun are linked in such a way, do not use a comma before the final adjective.

EXAMPLES   A huge **horned owl** lives in those woods.
[not *huge, horned owl*]

                 An unshaded **electric light** hung from the ceiling.
[not *unshaded, electric light*]

NOTE   When an adjective and a noun are closely linked, they may be thought of as a unit. Such a unit is called a **compound noun.**

EXAMPLES   Persian cat   Black Sea   French bread

Review B Proofreading Sentences for the Correct Use of Commas

Most of the following sentences need commas. If a sentence needs any commas, write the word before each missing comma and add the comma. If a sentence is already correct, write *C.*
Optional commas are underlined.

EXAMPLE   **1.** Chen participated in debate volleyball and drama.

         1. debate, volleyball,

1. Carla sneaked in and left a huge gorgeous fragrant bouquet of flowers on the desk.
2. I chose the gift Michael wrapped it and Charley gave it to Gina and Kelly.
3. Smoking is a costly dangerous habit.
4. In the human ear, the hammer anvil and stirrup carry sound waves to the brain.
5. Buffalo Bill was a Pony Express rider a scout and a touring stunt performer.

TIPS & TRICKS

To see whether a comma is needed between two adjectives, insert *and* between the adjectives (*unshaded and electric,* for example). If *and* sounds awkward there, do not use a comma.
   Another test you can use is to switch the order of the adjectives. If the sentence still makes sense when you switch them, use a comma.

Reference Note

For more information about **compound nouns,** see page 337.

Continued on pp. 605–606

Punctuating Compound Nouns Preceded by Adjectives. Students may become confused about using commas when an adjective precedes a compound noun that is written as two words. To give students practice using commas with adjec-

tives that precede compound nouns, write the following two columns of word sets on the chalkboard, leaving out the adjectives in brackets. Tell students that only one word set in each row is a compound noun.

6. "The Masque of the Red Death" is a famous horror story by Edgar Allan Poe.　**6. C**
7. According to Greek mythology, the three Fates spin the thread of life, measure it, and cut it.
8. LeVar Burton played the intelligent, likable character Geordi on *Star Trek: The Next Generation*.
9. The fluffy kitten with the brown, white, and black spots is my favorite.
10. Falstaff begged for mercy in a fight, ran away, and later bragged about his bravery in battle.

Compound Sentences

23h. Use a comma before *and, but, for, nor, or, so,* or *yet* when it joins independent clauses in a compound sentence.

EXAMPLES　Tamisha offered me a ticket, and I accepted.

They had been working very hard, but they didn't seem especially tired.

The Mullaney twins were excited, for they were going to day care for the first time.

When the independent clauses are very short and there is no chance of misunderstanding, the comma before *and, but,* or *or* is sometimes omitted.

EXAMPLES　It rained and it rained.

Come with us or meet us there.

NOTE　Always use a comma before *for, nor, so,* or *yet* when joining independent clauses.

EXAMPLE　I was tired, yet I stayed.

Do not be misled by a simple sentence that contains a compound verb. A simple sentence has only one independent clause.

SIMPLE SENTENCE WITH COMPOUND VERB　Usually we **study** in the morning and **play** basketball in the afternoon.

COMPOUND SENTENCE　Usually we study in the morning, and we play basketball in the afternoon. [two independent clauses]

STYLE　　**TIP**

The word *so* is often overused. If possible, try to reword a sentence to avoid using *so*.

EXAMPLE
It was late, so we went home.

REVISED
Because it was late, we went home.

Reference Note

For more information about **compound sentences,** see page 441. For more about **simple sentences** with **compound verbs,** see page 327.

Commas　**605**

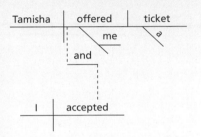
MECHANICS

---

grand piano	new piano	[*beautiful*]
green tree	pecan tree	[*giant*]
lawn chair	white chair	[*new*]
cold juice	apple juice	[*refreshing*]

Guide students through placing adjectives before each word set and then punctuating each set. Help them to identify the sets of words that are compound nouns, which do not require a comma after the added adjective [*grand piano, pecan tree,*

Exercise 4 Correcting Compound Sentences by Adding Commas

If a sentence needs a comma, write the <u>word before the missing comma</u> and add the comma. If a comma is unnecessary, write the words <u>before and after the comma</u> and omit the comma. If the sentence is already correct, write *C*.

EXAMPLE   **1.** American Indian artists have a heritage dating back thousands of years and many of them draw on this heritage, to create modern works.

     1. years, heritage to

1. Today's artists sometimes work with nontraditional <u>materials</u> but they often use traditional techniques.
2. In the photograph below, you can see the work of the Tohono O'odham artist Mary <u>Thomas, and</u> begin to appreciate this basket weaver's skill.
3. The baskets in the photograph are woven in the "friendship design" and show a circle of human figures in a traditional prayer ceremony.   **3.** C
4. Yucca and devil's claw are used to make these <u>baskets</u> and each plant's leaves are a different color.
5. The Navajo artist Danny Randeau Tsosie listened to his grandmother's <u>stories, and</u> learned about his family's heritage.
6. Tsosie's works show her influence but also express his own point of view.   **6.** C
7. Christine Nofchissey McHorse learned the skill of pottery making from her <u>grandmother</u> and now McHorse can make beautiful bowls.
8. McHorse has an unusual <u>style</u> for her designs combine traditional Navajo and Pueblo images.

MINI-LESSON

lawn chair, and *apple juice*], and the sets that include a simple noun and adjective and therefore might require a comma between the adjectives [*new piano, green tree, white chair,* and *cold juice*]. If a word group is read aloud with the word *and*

between the adjectives and *and* sounds awkward (for example, *giant and pecan tree*), no comma is needed.

For more information on compound nouns, refer students to **Chapter 11: Parts of Speech Overview.**

9. American Indian jewelry makers often use pieces of turquoise and coral found in <u>North America</u>,and they also use other stones from around the world.

10. American Indian art often looks very <u>modern</u>,yet some of its symbols and patterns are quite old.

Interrupters

23i. Use commas to set off an expression that interrupts a sentence.

Two commas are needed if the expression to be set off comes in the middle of the sentence. One comma is needed if the expression comes first or last.

EXAMPLES   Ann Myers, **our neighbor,** is a fine golfer.

Naturally, we expect to win.

My answer is correct, **I think.**

(1) Use commas to set off nonessential participial phrases and nonessential subordinate clauses.

A *nonessential* (or *nonrestrictive*) phrase or clause adds information that is not needed to understand the basic meaning of the sentence. Such a phrase or clause can be omitted without changing the main idea of the sentence.

NONESSENTIAL   My sister, **listening to her radio,** did not
PHRASES   hear me.
    Paul, **thrilled by the applause,** took a bow.

NONESSENTIAL   *The Wizard of Oz,* **which I saw again last**
CLAUSES   **week,** is my favorite movie.
    I reported on *Secret of the Andes,* **which was written by Ann Nolan Clark.**

Each boldface clause or phrase above can be omitted because it is not essential to identify the word or phrase it modifies. Omitting such a clause or phrase will not change the meaning of the sentence.

EXAMPLES   Paul took a bow.

I reported on *Secret of the Andes.*

PEANUTS reprinted by permission of United Feature Syndicate, Inc.

Relating to Writing

Caution your students against overusing adjective clauses, as this tendency leads to wordiness. Here are two examples of sentences that overuse adjective clauses, along with revisions that make the sentences more concise. Write the sentences on the chalkboard, and guide students through the revisions.

1. The day, which was rainy and cold, dampened their spirits. [*The rainy, cold day dampened their spirits.*]

2. The girl, who was smart, helped the new boy in class. [*The smart girl helped the new boy in class.*]

Ask students to choose completed writing assignments from their portfolios or from another class and to proofread their writing for overuse of adjective clauses. Ask students to revise sentences containing wordy adjective clauses and to share their revisions with a partner. If some students don't find any sentences to revise, write the following sentences on the chalkboard and ask students to revise them.

1. The leaves, which were crimson, orange, and gold, caught the late afternoon fall sun and glowed radiantly. [*The crimson, orange, and gold leaves caught the late afternoon fall sun and glowed radiantly.*]

2. I lost my sweater, which is made of green wool. [*I lost my green wool sweater.*]

Cooperative Learning

Separate the class into groups of three or four students. Give each group a set of index cards containing a list of phrases and clauses. Have each group write a correctly punctuated short story using all the phrases and clauses. One member of each group should read the group's story to the class. Here are some possible clauses:

1. who stole a million dollars

2. while they had nothing to lose

3. with no hope in sight

4. putting on her makeup

5. which made them scream

After each group has presented its story to the class, have groups exchange stories to check each other's use of commas with phrases and clauses.

Reference Note

For more about **phrases,** see Chapter 14. For more about **subordinate clauses,** see page 424.

Do not set off an *essential* (or *restrictive*) phrase or clause. Since such a phrase or clause tells *which one(s)*, it cannot be omitted without changing the basic meaning of the sentence.

ESSENTIAL PHRASES The people **waiting to see Michael Jordan** whistled and cheered. [Which people?]

A bowl **made by Maria Martínez** is a collector's item. [Which bowl?]

ESSENTIAL CLAUSES The dress **that I liked** has been sold. [Which dress?]

The man **who tells Navajo folk tales** is Mr. Platero. [Which man?]

Notice how the meaning changes when an essential phrase or clause is omitted.

EXAMPLES The people whistled and cheered.

A bowl is a collector's item.

The dress has been sold.

The man is Mr. Platero.

NOTE A clause beginning with *that* is usually essential.

EXAMPLE This is the birdhouse **that I made.**

Exercise 5 **Adding Commas to Sentences with Nonessential Phrases and Clauses**

Some of the following sentences need commas to set off nonessential phrases and clauses. Other sentences are correct without commas. If a sentence needs commas, write the word that comes before each missing comma and add the comma. If the sentence is already correct, write *C.*

EXAMPLE 1. My grandfather's favorite photograph which was taken near Ellis Island shows his family after their arrival from Eastern Europe.

1. *photograph, Island,*

1. Millions of immigrants who came to the United States between about 1892 and 1954 stopped at Ellis Island‚which is in Upper New York Bay.

2. Families arriving from Europe were interviewed there.   **2. C**

3. The island and its buildings,which were closed to the public for many years,are now part of the Statue of Liberty National Monument.

4. In 1990, Ellis Island,rebuilt as a museum,was officially opened to the public.

5. Visitors who wish to see the museum can take a ferry ride from Manhattan Island.   **5. C**

6. The museum's lobby,crowded with steamer trunks and other old baggage, is the visitors' first sight.

7. One special attraction in the museum consists of audiotapes and videotapes that describe the immigrants' experiences.   **7. C**

8. The Registry Room,which is on the second floor,sometimes held as many as five thousand people.

9. The immigrants,who came from many countries,hoped to find freedom and a happier life in America.

10. Immigrants who came to the United States brought with them a strong work ethic and a variety of skills that helped to make our country great.   **10. C**

The Granger Collection, New York.

(2) Use commas to set off nonessential appositives and nonessential appositive phrases.

An *appositive* is a noun or a pronoun used to identify or describe another noun or pronoun.

NONESSENTIAL APPOSITIVE	My oldest sister, **Alicia,** will be at basketball practice until 6:00 P.M.
NONESSENTIAL APPOSITIVE PHRASES	Jamaica, **a popular island for tourists,** is in the Caribbean Sea.
	May I introduce you to Vernon, **my cousin from Jamaica**?

Meeting INDIVIDUAL NEEDS

MECHANICS

Commas   **609**

TEACHING **TIP**

Rule 23i. When an appositive naming someone is preceded by a possessive and a noun signifying a relationship, it is difficult to know whether the appositive is essential or nonessential without knowing something about the situation. Explain to students that they always have to ask in such cases, "Is this person the only one?" For example, if Alicia is my only sister, her name is set off with commas and is nonessential. If, however, I have other sisters, Alicia's name is essential to identifying which sister I mean and is not set off with commas. Write on the chalkboard the following phrases:

Lilly's friend Elena
Mike's cousin Haman
my dog Pinta
your gerbil Fred
their sister Sky

Have students work in pairs to write two sentences with each phrase: one sentence with an essential appositive and one with a nonessential appositive. Have students explain the situation in each sentence. Then, have pairs trade sentences to check each other's identification of essential and nonessential appositives and correct use of commas.

┌─HELP─
Not all of the appositives in Exercise 6 require commas.

Do not use commas to set off an appositive that is essential to the meaning of a sentence.

ESSENTIAL APPOSITIVES

My sister **Alicia** is at basketball practice. [The speaker has more than one sister and must give a name to identify which sister.]

The planet **Mercury** is closer to the Sun than any other planet in our solar system. [The solar system contains more than one planet. The name is needed to identify which planet.]

Exercise 6 Proofreading for the Correct Use of Commas with Appositives and Appositive Phrases

Rewrite each of the following sentences, and underline the appositive or appositive phrase. Then, supply commas where needed.

EXAMPLE
1. Mars one of the planets closest to Earth can be seen without a telescope.

1. *Mars, one of the planets closest to Earth, can be seen without a telescope.*

1. The whole class has read the novel *Old Yeller*.
2. Shana Alexander a former editor of a popular magazine was the main speaker at the conference.
3. The character Sabrina is Josie's favorite.
4. The Galápagos Islands a group of volcanic islands in the Pacific Ocean were named for the Spanish word that means "tortoise."
5. Rubber an elastic substance quickly restores itself to its original size and shape.
6. This bowl is made of clay found on Kilimanjaro the highest mountain in Africa.
7. The North Sea an arm of the Atlantic Ocean is rich in fish, natural gas, and oil.
8. Jamake Highwater a Blackfoot/Eastern Band Cherokee author writes about the history of his people.
9. At Gettysburg a town in Pennsylvania an important battle of the Civil War was fought.
10. My friend Imelda is teaching me how to make empanadas.

(3) Use commas to set off words that are used in direct address.

EXAMPLES   **Ben,** please answer the doorbell.

           Mom needs you, **Francine.**

           Would you show me, **ma'am,** where the craft store is?

Exercise 7   Correcting Sentences by Using Commas with Words of Direct Address

Identify the words used in <u>direct address</u> in the following sentences. Then, rewrite each sentence, inserting commas before, after, or both before and after the words, as needed.

EXAMPLE   1. Listen folks to this amazing announcement!

           1. *folks—Listen, folks, to this amazing announcement!*

1. Andrea when are you leaving for Detroit?
2. Pay attention now class.
3. Let us my sisters and brothers give thanks.
4. Please Dad may I use your computer?
5. Senator please summarize your tax proposal.
6. Help me move this table Marlene.
7. "Tell me both of you what movie you want to see," Jo said.
8. Hurry William and give me the phone number!
9. Mrs. Larson where is Zion National Park?
10. I'm just not sure friends that I agree with you.

(4) Use commas to set off parenthetical expressions.

A *parenthetical expression* is a side remark that adds information or shows a relationship between ideas.

EXAMPLES   Carl, **on the contrary,** prefers soccer to baseball.

           To tell the truth, Jan is one of my best friends.

Common Parenthetical Expressions		
by the way	in fact	of course
for example	in my opinion	on the contrary
however	I suppose	on the other hand
I believe	nevertheless	to tell the truth

MECHANICS

Commas   **611**

Some of these expressions are not always used parenthetically.

EXAMPLES   **Of course** it is true. [not parenthetical]

That is, **of course,** an Indian teakwood screen. [parenthetical]

I suppose we ought to go home now. [not parenthetical]

He'll want a ride, **I suppose.** [parenthetical]

Exercise 8 **Correcting Sentences by Using Commas to Set Off Parenthetical Expressions**

The following sentences contain parenthetical expressions that require commas. Write the parenthetical expressions, inserting commas before, after, or both before and after the expressions, as needed.

EXAMPLES   1. Everyone I suppose has heard of the Hubble Space Telescope.

1. , I suppose,

2. As a matter of fact even a small refracting telescope gives a good view of Saturn's rings.

2. As a matter of fact,

1. You don't need a telescope, however, to see all the beautiful sights in the night sky.
2. For instance, on a summer night you might be able to view Scorpio, Serpens, and the Serpent Bearer.
3. By the way, you should not overlook the Milky Way.
4. The Milky Way, in fact, is more impressive in the summer than at any other time of year.
5. Hercules, of course, is an interesting constellation.
6. Studying the constellations is, in my opinion, a most interesting hobby.
7. It takes an active imagination, however, to spot some constellations.
8. Sagittarius, for example, is hard to see unless you're familiar with a constellation map.
9. Scorpio, on the other hand, is quite clearly outlined.
10. Astronomy is a fascinating science, I think.

MECHANICS

Introductory Words, Phrases, and Clauses

23j. Use a comma after certain introductory elements.

(1) Use a comma after *yes, no,* or any mild exclamation such as *well* or *why* at the beginning of a sentence.

EXAMPLES   **Yes,** you may borrow my bicycle.

             Why, it's Lena!

             Well, I think you are wrong.

(2) Use a comma after an introductory participial phrase.

EXAMPLES   **Beginning a new school year,** Zelda felt somewhat nervous.

             Greeted with applause from the fans, Rashid ran out onto the field.

> **Reference Note**
>
> For information about **participial phrases,** see page 412.

(3) Use a comma after two or more introductory prepositional phrases.

EXAMPLES   **At the bottom of the hill,** you will see the baseball field.

             Until the end of the song, just keep strumming that chord.

> **Reference Note**
>
> For information about **prepositional phrases,** see page 402.

Use a comma after a single introductory prepositional phrase when the comma is necessary to make the meaning of the sentence clear.

EXAMPLES   In the morning they left. [clear without a comma]

             In the morning, sunlight streamed through the window. [The comma is needed so that the reader does not read "morning sunlight."]

(4) Use a comma after an introductory adverb clause.

EXAMPLES   **After I finish my homework,** I will go to the park.

             When you go to the store, could you please pick up a gallon of milk?

> **Reference Note**
>
> For information about **adverb clauses,** see page 430.

NOTE An adverb clause that comes at the end of a sentence does not usually need a comma.

EXAMPLE   I will go to the park **after I finish my homework.**

MECHANICS

Commas   **613**

Exercise 9 Using Commas with Introductory Elements

If a comma is needed in a sentence, write the <u>word before the missing comma</u> and add the comma. If a sentence is already punctuated correctly, write *C*.

EXAMPLE   1. Walking among the tigers and lions the trainer seemed unafraid.

      1. lions,

1. Because pemmican remained good to eat for several <u>years</u>ᴧit was a practical food for many American Indians.
2. Although Jesse did not win the student council <u>election</u>ᴧhe raised many important issues.
3. On the desk in the <u>den</u>ᴧyou will find your book.
4. <u>Yes</u>ᴧI enjoyed the fajitas that Ruben made.
5. Walking home from <u>school</u>ᴧRosa saw her brother.
6. When I go to bed <u>late</u>ᴧI sometimes have trouble waking up in the morning.
7. <u>Well</u>ᴧwe can watch television or play checkers.
8. Attracted by the computer games in the store <u>window</u>ᴧ George decided to go in and buy one.
9. At the stoplight on the corner of the next <u>block</u>ᴧthey made a right turn.
10. After <u>eating</u>ᴧthe chickens settled down.

Conventional Situations

23k. Use commas in certain conventional situations.

(1) Use commas to separate items in dates and addresses.

EXAMPLES   She was born on January 26, 1988, in Cheshire, Connecticut.

          A letter dated November 26, 1888, was found in the old house at 980 West Street, Davenport, Iowa, yesterday.

Notice that a comma separates the last item in a date or in an address from the words that follow it. However, a comma does not separate a month from a day (*January 26*) or a house number from a street name (*980 West Street*).

┌─HELP─
Commas are also used in numbers over 999. Use a comma before every third digit to the left of the decimal point.

EXAMPLE
3,147,425.00

(2) Use a comma after the salutation of a personal letter and after the closing of any letter.

EXAMPLES   Dear Dad,   Dear Sharon,

With love,   Yours truly,

Reference Note

For information about using **colons for salutations in business letters,** see page 620.

Relating to Writing

Students may be interested in writing letters to pen pals. (You can get the names of appropriate pen-pal organizations from your school library.) Remind students to use the correct format for a personal letter—using a comma after the salutation and after the closing of the letter. Also, remind your students to use commas appropriately when addressing the envelopes to their pen pals.

Exercise 10 Using Commas Correctly

Rewrite the following sentences, inserting commas wherever they are needed.

EXAMPLE   1. I received a package from my friend who lives in Irving Texas.

1. *I received a package from my friend who lives in Irving, Texas.*

1. On May 25, 1935, the runner Jesse Owens tied or broke six world track records.
2. The American Saddle Horse Museum is located at 4093 Iron Works Pike, Lexington, KY 40511-8462.
3. Marian Anderson was born on February 27, 1902, in Philadelphia, Pennsylvania.
4. Our new address will be 1808 Jackson Drive, Ames, IA 50010-4437.
5. Ocean City, New Jersey, is a popular seaside resort.
6. October 15, 1988, is an important date because I was born then.
7. Have you ever been to Paisley, Scotland?
8. We adopted our dog, King Barnabus IV, in Lee's Summit, Missouri, on May 9, 1995.
9. The national headquarters of the Environmental Defense Fund is located at 257 Park Avenue South, New York, NY 10010-7304.
10. Dear Lynn,
      I am fine. How are you and your family?

Commas   **615**

┌─HELP─

Too much punctuation is just as confusing as not enough punctuation, especially where the use of commas is concerned.

CONFUSING
My uncle, Doug, said he would take me fishing, this weekend, but now, he tells me, he will be out of town.

CLEAR
My uncle Doug said he would take me fishing this weekend, but now he tells me he will be out of town.

Have a reason for every comma or other mark of punctuation that you use. When there is no rule requiring punctuation and the meaning of the sentence is clear without it, do not use any punctuation mark.

Review C **Proofreading Sentences for the Correct Use of Commas**

For the following sentences, write each <u>word that should be followed by a comma</u> and add the comma after the word.

EXAMPLE   1. The substitute's name is Mr. Fowler I think.
           1. *Fowler,*

1. What time is your <u>appointment</u>ᴧKevin?
2. My aunt said to forward her mail to 302 Lancelot <u>Drive</u>ᴧ <u>Simpsonville</u>ᴧSC 29681-5749.
3. George Washington <u>Carver</u>ᴧa famous <u>scientist</u>ᴧhad to work hard to afford to go to school.
4. <u>Quick</u>ᴧviolent flashes of lightning cause an average of 14,300 forest fires a year in the United States.
5. My oldest <u>sister</u>ᴧ<u>Kim</u>ᴧsent a postcard from <u>Ewa</u>ᴧHawaii.
6. A single branch stuck out of the <u>water</u>ᴧand the beaver grasped it in its paws.
7. The <u>beaver</u>ᴧby the <u>way</u>ᴧis a rodent.
8. This hard-working mammal builds <u>dams</u>ᴧ<u>lodges</u>ᴧand canals.
9. Built with their entrances <u>underwater</u>ᴧthe lodges of American beavers are marvels of engineering.
10. The beaver uses its large <u>tail</u>ᴧwhich is <u>flat</u>ᴧto steer.

Review D **Proofreading Sentences for the Correct Use of Commas**

Each of the following sentences contains at least one error in the use of commas. Write each <u>word that should be followed by a comma</u>, and add the comma. Optional commas are underlined.

EXAMPLES   1. Kyoto's palaces shrines and temples remind visitors of this city's importance in Japanese history.
            1. *palaces, shrines,*

            2. In Japanese Kyoto means "capital city" which is what Emperor Kammu made Kyoto in A.D. 794.
            2. *Japanese, city,*

1. <u>Kyoto</u>ᴧa beautiful <u>city</u>ᴧwas Japan's capital for more than one thousand years.

2. It still may be called the cultural capital of Japan,for it contains many Shinto shrines,Buddhist temples,the Kyoto National Museum, and wonderful gardens.

3. Yes,Kyoto,which was called Heian-kyo during the ninth century,was so important that an entire period of Japanese history, the Heian period, is named for it.

4. Originating from the monasteries outside ancient Kyoto,the magnificent mandala paintings feature universal themes.

5. Oh,haven't you seen the wonderful *ukiyo-e* paintings of vast mountains and tiny people?

6. Believe it or not,readers,there are now more than twenty colleges and universities in this treasured city.

7. Its people,historic landmarks,and art are respected across the globe.

8. With attractions like these,it's no surprise that Kyoto is a popular tourist stop.

9. Used in industries around the world,the tools of fine crafts are made in Kyoto.

10. Kyoto manufactures silk for the fashion industry,copper for artists and electricians,and machines for businesses.

11. Fine,delicate porcelain from Kyoto graces many tables around the world.

12. The Procession of the Eras,celebrated every autumn,takes place in Kyoto.

13. The Procession of the Eras festival,which celebrates Kyoto's history,begins on October 22.

14. The beautiful,solemn procession is a remarkable sight.

15. At the beginning of the festival,priests offer special prayers.

16. Portable shrines are carried through the streets,and thousands of costumed marchers follow.

17. Elaborate headgear and armor,for example,are worn by marchers dressed as ancient warriors.

18. Because the marchers near the front represent recent history, they wear costumes from the nineteenth-century Royal Army Era.

19. Marching at the end of the procession,archers wear costumes from the eighth-century Warrior Era.

20. The procession is,in fact,a rich memorial to Kyoto's long and varied history.

Semicolons

Rules 23l, m *(pp. 618–619)*

OBJECTIVE

- To proofread sentences for correct semicolon use

Relating to Literature

If your literature textbook contains the Paul Annixter short story "Last Cover," have your students read the selection. "Last Cover" begins with a one-sentence paragraph containing a semicolon. That sentence introduces the two most important characters in the story: the narrator's brother and a fox. Analyze with students how the drama of that one-sentence paragraph sets the reader up for an equally dramatic story. Discuss why the semicolon is necessary both for the sentence and for the sense of foreshadowing in the story. [*Students may not be familiar with a semicolon preceding a coordinating conjunction. Explain that the semicolon is used for clarity because of the comma that separates the second part of the sentence into two independent clauses. Students may also notice that the semicolon divides two major themes in the story: the brother's acceptance in the family and the search for the fox. Like the parts of the compound sentence, the person and the animal are of equal importance in the story. The semicolon may suggest that while the boy and the fox are separate beings, like the parts of the sentence, they form a whole.*]

STYLE   TIP

Semicolons are most effective when they are not overused. Sometimes it is better to separate a compound sentence or a heavily punctuated sentence into two sentences rather than to use a semicolon.

ACCEPTABLE
Garden visitors include butterflies, bats, and ladybugs; such creatures benefit gardens in various ways, some by adding color, some by controlling pests, and all by pollinating plants.

BETTER
Garden visitors include butterflies, bats, and ladybugs. Such creatures benefit gardens in various ways, some by adding color, some by controlling pests, and all by pollinating plants.

Semicolons

A *semicolon* looks like a combination of a period and a comma, and that is just what it is. A semicolon can separate complete thoughts much as a period does. A semicolon can also separate items within a sentence much as a comma does.

23l. Use a semicolon between independent clauses if they are not joined by *and, but, for, nor, or, so,* or *yet.*

EXAMPLES   Jimmy took my suitcase upstairs; he left his own travel bag in the car.

After school, I went to band practice; then I studied in the library for an hour.

Use a semicolon to link clauses only if the clauses are closely related in meaning.

INCORRECT   Uncle Ray likes sweet potatoes; Aunt Janie prefers the beach.

CORRECT   Uncle Ray likes sweet potatoes; Aunt Janie prefers peas and carrots.

or

Uncle Ray likes the mountains; Aunt Janie prefers the beach.

23m. Use a semicolon rather than a comma before a coordinating conjunction to join independent clauses that contain commas.

CONFUSING   I wrote to Ann, Ramona, and Mai, and Jean notified Charles, Latoya, and Sue.

CLEAR   I wrote to Ann, Ramona, and Mai; and Jean notified Charles, Latoya, and Sue.

NOTE   Semicolons are also used between items in a series when the items contain commas.

EXAMPLES   They visited Phoenix, Arizona; Santa Fe, New Mexico; and San Antonio, Texas.

Mr. Schultz, my science teacher; Ms. O'Hara, my English teacher; Mrs. Gomez, my math teacher; and Mr. Kim, my social studies teacher, attended the seventh-grade picnic.

RESOURCES

Semicolons

Practice

- *Grammar, Usage, and Mechanics,* pp. 290–291
- *Language Workshop CD-ROM,* Lesson 45

Exercise 11 **Using Semicolons Correctly**

Most of the following sentences have a comma where there should be a semicolon. If the sentence needs a semicolon, write the <u>words before and after the missing semicolon</u> and insert the punctuation mark. If the sentence does not need a semicolon, write *C*.

Carets indicate placement of semicolons.

EXAMPLE   **1.** Human beings have walked on the moon, they have not yet walked on any planet but earth.

     1. moon; they

1. Miyoko finished her <u>homework, then</u> she decided to go to Sally's house.   **2.** C
2. Each January some people try to predict the major events of the upcoming year, but their predictions are seldom accurate.
3. Tie these newspapers together with <u>string, put</u> the aluminum cans in a bag.
4. I called Tom, Paul, and <u>Francine, and</u> Fred called Amy, Luis, Carlos, and Brad.
5. Reading is my favorite <u>pastime, I</u> love to begin a new book.
6. In 1991, Wellington Webb was elected mayor of <u>Denver, he</u> was the first African American to hold that office.
7. The two companies merged, and they became the largest consumer goods firm in the nation.   **7.** C
8. Your grades have definitely <u>improved, you</u> will easily pass the course.
9. Paris, <u>France, Cairo, Egypt, and</u> Copenhagen, Denmark, are all places that I would like to visit someday.
10. We haven't seen the movie, for it hasn't come to our town yet.   **10.** C

Colons

23n. **Use a colon before a list of items, especially after expressions such as *the following* or *as follows*.**

EXAMPLES   You will need these items for map work**:** a ruler, colored pencils, and tracing paper.

    Jack's pocket contained the following items**:** a key, a note from a friend, a button, and two quarters.

    The primary colors are as follows**:** red, blue, and yellow.

Colons   **619**

Colons

Rules 23n–q *(pp. 619–622)*

OBJECTIVE

- To use colons correctly before lists and in times of day, titles with subtitles, and salutations in business letters

ENGLISH-LANGUAGE LEARNERS
General Strategies. The colon is used infrequently in most languages. Some of your English-language learners might have had few chances to see colons used in English. They might need some extra explanation as to why anyone would need or want to use a colon.

LEARNERS HAVING DIFFICULTY
Some students may try to put a comma after a salutation in all letter types. Tell students that a comma after a salutation can be compared to a waved hand; people don't usually wave to strangers. In a business letter, students should use a colon after the salutation, but after the salutation of a personal letter, they can use a comma—a wave.

STYLE TIP

Use a comma after the salutation of a personal letter.

EXAMPLES
Dear Kim,
Dear Uncle Remy,

Reference Note
For information about **writing letters,** see "Writing" in the Quick Reference Handbook.

Do not use a colon between a verb and its object or between a preposition and its object. Omit the colon, or reword the sentence.

INCORRECT	Your heading should contain: your name, the date, and the title of your essay.
CORRECT	Your heading should contain your name, the date, and the title of your essay.
CORRECT	Your heading should contain the following information: your name, the date, and the title of your essay.

INCORRECT	This marinara sauce is made of: tomatoes, onions, oregano, and garlic.
CORRECT	This marinara sauce is made of tomatoes, onions, oregano, and garlic.
CORRECT	This marinara sauce is made of the following ingredients: tomatoes, onions, oregano, and garlic.

NOTE Colons are also often used before long formal statements or quotations.

EXAMPLE My opinion of beauty is clearly expressed by Margaret Wolfe Hungerford in *Molly Bawn*: "Beauty is in the eye of the beholder."

Conventional Situations

23o. Use a colon between the hour and the minute.

EXAMPLE 8:30 A.M.   10:00 P.M.

23p. Use a colon after the salutation of a business letter.

EXAMPLES   Dear Sir or Madam: Dear Mrs. Foster:

To Whom It May Concern: Dear Dr. Christiano:

23q. Use a colon between chapter and verse in Biblical references and between all titles and subtitles.

EXAMPLES   I Chronicles 22:6–19

"Oral Storytelling: Making the Winter Shorter"

Exercise 12 Using Colons and Commas Correctly

Make each of the following word groups into a complete sentence by supplying the item called for in the brackets. Insert colons and commas where they are needed.

EXAMPLE　　1. The test will begin at [time].
　　　　　　　1. The test will begin at 9:30 A.M.

1. So far, the class has studied the following topics [list].
2. You will need these supplies for your science-fair experiment [list].
3. If I were writing a book about my friends and me, I would call it [title and subtitle].
4. Meet me at the mall at [time].
5. My classes this year are the following [list].
6. You should begin your business letter with [salutation].
7. The concert begins at [time].
8. I need the following from the hardware store [list].
9. Three countries I would like to visit are [list].
10. The alarm is set to go off at [time].

Review E Using End Marks, Commas, Semicolons, and Colons Correctly

The sentences in the following paragraph lack necessary end marks, commas, semicolons, and colons. Write each sentence, inserting the correct punctuation. Optional commas are underlined.

EXAMPLE　　**[1]** What an unusual clever caring way to help animals that is
　　　　　　　1. What an unusual, clever, caring way to help animals that is!

[1] Animal lovers, have you heard about the Sanctuary for Animals? [2] Founded by Leonard and Bunny Brook, the sanctuary is a safe home for all kinds of animals. [3] Through the years, hundreds of stray, unwanted, and abused animals have found a home at the sanctuary. [4] It is located on the Brooks' land in Westtown, New York. [5] On their two hundred acres, the Brooks take care of the following animals: dogs, cats, camels, elephants, lions, and even an Australian kangaroo. [6] Of course, Mr. and

Answers will vary. Optional commas are underlined.

1. : periods, commas, semicolons, and colons
2. : paper, glue, and scissors
3. *The Best Days: The Adventures of Kim, Eddie, Fran, and Julio*
4. 4:15 this afternoon
5. : geometry, biology, English, American history, and gym
6. *Dear Sir or Madam:*
7. 8:00 tonight
8. : nails, wood glue, and a c-clamp
9. Austria, India, and Argentina
10. 6:30 A.M.

Mrs. Brook also raise chickens keep horses and look after their other farm animals [7] The Brooks their family and their friends care for animals like this young cougar they also let the animals work for themselves [8] How do the animals work? [9] The Brooks formed the Dawn Animal Agency and their animals became actors and models [10] You may have seen a camel or some of the other animals in magazines movies television shows and commercials

23

Chapter Review

A. Using End Marks, Commas, Semicolons, and Colons Correctly

The following sentences lack necessary periods, question marks, exclamation points, commas, semicolons, and colons. Write each sentence, inserting the correct punctuation.
Optional commas are underlined.

1. The following students gave reports: Carlos, Sue, and Alan.
2. Tanay carved this beautiful soapstone cooking pot.
3. Walter, this is Ellen, who has transferred to our school.
4. Calling Simon's name, I ran to the door.
5. The Wilsons' new address is 3100 DeSoto St., New Orleans, LA 70119-3251.
6. Have you listened to that Bill Cosby tape, Felix?
7. Let me know, of course, if you can't attend.
8. Joy, our club president, will conduct the meeting, and Gary, our recently elected secretary, will take notes.
9. Looking at the harsh, bright glare, Mai closed the blinds.
10. Carlos Montoya picked up the guitar, positioned his fingers, and strummed a few chords of a flamenco song.
11. If you hurry, you can get home before 9:00.
12. Help! This is an emergency!
13. By the way, Rosa, have you seen any of Alfred Hitchcock's movies?
14. Dave hit a long fly ball, but Phil was there to catch it.
15. Flooding rapidly, the gully quickly became a tremendous torrent.
16. *The Grapes of Wrath,* which is one of my favorite movies, is about a family's struggles during the Great Depression.
17. Nicaragua, Panama, and Honduras are in Central America, and Colombia, Peru, and Chile are in South America.
18. One of our cats, Gypsy, scooted through the door, across the room, and out the window.
19. The Lock Museum of America, a fascinating place in Terryville, Conn., has more than twenty thousand locks.
20. Could the surprise gift be in-line skates, a new football, or tickets to a concert?

Chapter Review   **623**

B. Proofreading a Business Letter

The following business letter lacks periods, commas, semicolons, and colons. Correct each error. If a sentence is already correct, write C.

```
        Gable Books
        387 Monocle Lane
        Bozeman, MT  59715
        June 28, 2001
```

[21] Dear Mr. Gable:

[22] Please find enclosed a copy of *Edith Wharton: A Biography* by R. W. B. Lewis. **[23]** I purchased this book recently at your book shop, but I have since discovered that several pages are missing. **[24]** I am not happy with the book; please send me a new copy.

[25] Sincerely,

E. Frome

E. Frome

C. Proofreading for Correct Punctuation

Most of the following sentences lack at least one period, question mark, exclamation point, comma, semicolon, or colon. Correct each error. If a sentence is already correctly punctuated, write C. Optional commas are underlined.

26. He went shopping, cooked dinner, and washed the dishes. **26.** C

27. For the good of us all, please think before you act next time.

28. Mr. T. E. Hawk, a friend of my mother's, helps me with math.

29. Caroline, have your relatives arrived?

30. Yes, Mario, they came just last week.

31. At the center of a map of Texas, you will find Brady.

32. Our new address is 72 Maple Ave., Rochester, NY 14612.

33. Inger designs the clothes; her mother sews them.

34. We followed the trail; it led around the garage.

35. The world record in the long jump was held by Jesse Owens for several years, but the record is now held by another outstanding athlete.

RESOURCES

Punctuation

Review

■ *Grammar, Usage, and Mechanics,* pp. 293, 294, 295, 296, 297

Assessment

■ *Assessment Package*
   —*Chapter Tests,* Ch. 23
   —*Chapter Tests in Standardized Test Formats,* Ch. 23
■ *Test Generator (One-Stop Planner CD-ROM)*

36. On June 15, 1983, my father opened his first florist shop.

37. Your use of materials, for example, is very artistic. **37. C**

38. My hobbies are as follows: baseball, ballet, and magic tricks.

39. After I carry the groceries into the house, my sister puts them away.

40. Stop that now, Veronica!

 Writing Application

Using Punctuation in an Announcement

Correct Punctuation   Your class is sponsoring a carwash to raise money for a special project or trip. You have been chosen to write an announcement about the carwash for publication in a community newsletter. Write a brief announcement telling when and where the carwash will be, how much it will cost, what the money will be used for, and any other important details. Be sure to use end marks, commas, semicolons, and colons correctly in your announcement.

Prewriting   List the information that you will include in your announcement. Make sure you have included all the facts people will need to know about the purpose, time, location, and cost of the carwash.

Writing   As you write, remember that the purpose of your announcement is to attract customers. Start with an attention-grabbing first sentence that explains the purpose of the carwash. Be sure to present all your information in clear, complete sentences. Add any important details that you did not list earlier.

Revising   Ask a friend to read your announcement. Is it clear and straightforward? Does it convince your friend that the carwash is for a good cause? If not, revise, rearrange, or add details.

Publishing   As you proofread your announcement, pay special attention to your use of punctuation. Remember to check the placement of colons in expressions of time. You may wish to offer your announcement-writing services to a club or service organization at your school.

Writing Application

(p. 625)

OBJECTIVE

■ To write a brief announcement that uses end marks, commas, semicolons, and colons correctly

Writing Application

Tip. Announcements must include enough information to be clear about the event. You may want to specify how many sentences students should write.

Scoring Rubric. While paying particular attention to students' use of punctuation, you will also want to evaluate overall writing performance. You may want to give a split score to indicate development and clarity of the composition as well as punctuation skills.

MECHANICS

RESOURCES

Writing Application
Extension

■ *Grammar, Usage, and Mechanics*, p. 300
■ *Language Workshop CD-ROM*, Lessons 42–46, 51

CHAPTER

24 Punctuation
Underlining (Italics), Quotation Marks, Apostrophes, Hyphens, Parentheses, Brackets, and Dashes

Diagnostic Preview

A. Proofreading Sentences for the Correct Use of Underlining (Italics), Quotation Marks, Apostrophes, Hyphens, Parentheses, Brackets, and Dashes

Revise each of the following sentences so that underlining, quotation marks, apostrophes, hyphens, parentheses, brackets, and dashes are used correctly. Hyphens are indicated by the - symbol.

┌─HELP─┐
Sentences in the Diagnostic Preview, Part A, may contain more than one error.

EXAMPLE
1. "May I borrow your copy of 'Life' magazine?" Phil asked Alan.

1. "May I borrow your copy of <u>Life</u> magazine?" Phil asked Alan.

1. Boris Karloff (his real name was William Henry Pratt)played the monster in the original movie version of <u>Frankenstein</u>.

2. "I've never known—do you? what the word *kith* means," Paul said.   **2. dash**

3. "It (the new version of the software) corrects that problem," said Steve.   **3. brackets**

4. I've heard that the program's announcer and interviewer will be Connie Chung, a favorite of mine.

CHAPTER RESOURCES

Planning
- *One-Stop Planner CD-ROM*

Practice and Extension
- *Grammar, Usage, and Mechanics*, p. 301
- *Developmental Language Skills*, pp. 115–124

Internet
- go.hrw.com (keyword: EOLang)   go. hrw .com

Evaluation and Assessment
- *Chapter Tests*, Ch. 24
- *Chapter Tests in Standardized Test Formats*, Ch. 24
- *Test Generator (One-Stop Planner)*

5. Anne said that "Norma couldn't understand why twenty-two people had voted against having the dance on a Friday night.

6. "A two-thirds majority said they didn't want to have it then," Shawn said.

7. Fred said, "This magazine article titled "Luxury Liners of the Past" is interesting."

8. "Does the public library have copies of The Seminole Tribune or any other American Indian newspapers"? Tanya asked.

9. My sisters' enjoy reading folk tales like the stories in Two Ways to Count to Ten by Ruby Dee.

10. "The Garcia's cat is I don't think they know living in our garage," Mary said.   10. dash/dash [*or* parentheses]

B. Punctuating Quotations Correctly

Add quotation marks where they are needed in each of the following sentences.

EXAMPLE   1. I wonder why so many people enjoy collecting things, said J. D.

   1. *"I wonder why so many people enjoy collecting things," said J. D.*

11. "I know I do! Julia exclaimed.

12. Tomás said, "My grandmother said, "It's the thrill of the hunt."

13. "Do you collect anything as a hobby? Josh asked Marsha.

14. "No, Marsha answered, "but I know a person who collects old cameras and antique costume jewelry."

15. "My aunt collects John McCormack's records, Kevin said. "Do you know who he is?"

16. "I'm not sure, Julia said, "but I think that he was an Irish singer."

17. "Yes, he sang in the opera; he also sang popular Irish songs such as "The Rose of Tralee, Kevin said.

18. "My stepbrother has a collection of arrowheads. He hasn't been collecting them very long, Sydney said.

19. "You should see Mrs. Kominek's collection of Chinese jade carvings, J. D. said. "It's great!"

20. "Some people—I'm sure you know—have odd collections, Josh said. "For instance, my aunt collects old shoelaces."

Underlining (Italics)

Rules 24a–c (pp. 628–630)

OBJECTIVE

■ To identify words that should be italicized and to underline them

TEACHING TIP

Rules 24a, m. Remembering which titles require underlining (italics) and which require quotation marks can be confusing for students. It might be helpful to teach the rule for using quotation marks with titles **(24m)** with the rule for using underlining (italics) with titles **(24a)**. Point out to students that titles requiring quotation marks are often titles of a work that is a part of a larger work—for example, a story or article in a magazine; a song on a CD; or an episode in a television series. Titles requiring italics are titles of things that stand alone or contain the smaller parts: the magazine itself, the CD, or the television series.

COMPUTER TIP

If you use a personal computer, you can probably set words in italics yourself. Most word-processing software and many printers can produce italic type.

Reference Note

For examples of **titles** that are not italicized but are **enclosed in quotation marks,** see page 635.

Underlining (Italics)

Italics are printed letters that lean to the right—*like this*. When you write or type, you show that a word should be italicized by underlining it. If your composition were printed, the typesetter would set the underlined words in italics. For example, if you typed

    Gary Soto wrote <u>Pacific Crossing</u>.

the sentence would be printed like this:

Gary Soto wrote *Pacific Crossing.*

24a. Use underlining (italics) for titles and subtitles of books, plays, periodicals, films, television series, works of art, and long musical works.

Type of Name	Examples	
Books	*My Life and Hard Times*	*Life on the Mississippi*
	To Kill a Mockingbird	*Maud Martha*
Plays	*Our Town*	*I Never Sang for My Father*
	Hamlet	
Periodicals	the *Daily News*	*National Geographic*
	Essence	
Films	*The Maltese Falcon*	*Stand and Deliver*
Television Series	*Nova*	*Bill Nye the Science Guy*
	Sesame Street	
Works of Art	*Starry Night*	*The Dream*
	American Gothic	*View of Toledo*
Long Musical Works	*Carmen*	*Don Giovanni*
	An American in Paris	*Music for the Royal Fireworks*

RESOURCES

Underlining (Italics)

Practice

■ *Grammar, Usage, and Mechanics,* pp. 302, 303, 304
■ *Language Workshop CD-ROM,* Lessons 49, 52

24b. Use underlining (italics) for the names of ships, trains, aircraft, and spacecraft.

Type of Name	Examples	
Ships	HMS *Titanic* the *Pequod*	the USS *Eisenhower*
Trains	the *City of New Orleans*	the *Orient Express* *Golden Arrow*
Aircraft	the *Silver Dart*	the *Hindenburg*
Spacecraft	*Soyuz XI*	*Atlantis*

NOTE Underline (italicize) an article at the beginning of a title only if it is the first word of the official title. Check the table of contents or the masthead to find the preferred style for the title.

EXAMPLES   Would you like to subscribe to **the** *San Francisco Chronicle*?

The *Seattle Times* is a daily newspaper.

24c. Use underlining (italics) for words, letters, and numerals referred to as such.

EXAMPLES   Double the final *n* before you add *–ing* in words like *running.*

If your *Z's* look like *2's,* your reader may see *200* when you meant *zoo.*

Exercise 1 **Using Underlining (Italics) Correctly**

For each of the following sentences, write and underline each word or item that should be italicized.

EXAMPLE   1. Does Dave Barry write a humor column for The Miami Herald?

1. *The Miami Herald*

1. The British spell the word <u>humor</u> with a <u>u</u> after the <u>o</u>.
2. In Denmark, you might see the spelling *triatlon* for the word <u>triathlon</u>.

STYLE TIP

Now and then, writers will use underlining (italics) for emphasis, especially in written dialogue. Read the following sentences aloud. Notice that by italicizing different words, the writer can change the meaning of the sentence.

EXAMPLES

"Are you going to buy the *green* shirt?" asked Ellen. [Will you buy the green shirt, not the blue one?]

"Are you going to buy the green *shirt*?" asked Ellen. [Will you buy the green shirt, not the green pants?]

"Are *you* going to buy the green shirt?" asked Ellen. [Will you, not your brother, buy it?]

"Are you going to *buy* the green shirt?" asked Ellen. [Will you buy it, or are you just trying it on?]

MECHANICS

Underlining (Italics)   **629**

3. The current <u>Newsweek</u> has an informative article on the famine in Africa.
4. Our school paper, the <u>Norwalk Valley News</u>, is published weekly.
5. Luis Valdez wrote and directed <u>La Bamba</u>, a movie about the life of the singer Ritchie Valens.
6. Mr. Weyer said that the <u>Oceanic</u> is one of the ocean liners that sail to the Caribbean.
7. I think the movie <u>The Sound of Music</u> has some of the most beautiful photography that I have ever seen and some of the most memorable songs.
8. Our local theater group is presenting <u>The Time of Your Life</u>, a comedy by William Saroyan.
9. Charles Lindbergh's <u>Spirit of St. Louis</u> is on display at the museum, along with the Wright brothers' <u>Flyer</u> and NASA's <u>Gemini IV</u>.
10. The best novel that I read during vacation was <u>The Summer of the Swans</u>.

Quotation Marks

24d. Use quotation marks to enclose a *direct quotation*—a person's exact words.

Be sure to place quotation marks both before and after a person's exact words.

EXAMPLES   The sonnet containing the words **"**Give me your tired, your poor, /Your huddled masses/ . . .**"** is inscribed on the Statue of Liberty.

"When the bell rings,**"** said the teacher, **"**leave the room quietly.**"**

Do not use quotation marks for an *indirect quotation*—a rewording of a direct quotation.

DIRECT QUOTATION   Tom predicted, **"**It will be a close game.**"** [Tom's exact words]

INDIRECT QUOTATION   Tom predicted that it would be a close game. [not Tom's exact words]

Meeting INDIVIDUAL NEEDS

ENGLISH-LANGUAGE LEARNERS
General Strategies. Many languages do not use the Roman alphabet, from which most modern European alphabets, including English, are derived. For speakers of such languages (for example, many Asian languages, Greek, Russian, and Arabic), italics might be totally unfamiliar. Show students several examples of italics and underlining and, if necessary, give students extra practice using underlining in writing.

Quotation Marks
Rules 24d–m (pp. 630–637)

OBJECTIVES

- To proofread and revise sentences for the correct use of quotation marks, commas, end marks, and capital letters

- To revise indirect quotations to create direct quotations

RESOURCES
Quotation Marks
Practice
- *Grammar, Usage, and Mechanics,* pp. 305, 306, 307–308, 309, 310
- *Language Workshop CD-ROM,* Lessons 49, 50

24e. A direct quotation generally begins with a capital letter.

EXAMPLES   Lisa said, **"T**he *carne asada* isn't ready yet, but please help yourself to the guacamole.**"**

While he was in prison, Richard Lovelace wrote a poem containing the well-known line **"S**tone walls do not a prison make.**"**

24f. When an expression identifying the speaker interrupts a quoted sentence, the second part of the quotation begins with a lowercase letter.

EXAMPLE   "Lightning has always awed people," explained Mrs. Worthington, "**a**nd many of us are still quite frightened by it."

A quoted sentence that is divided in this way is called a *broken quotation.* Notice that each part of a broken quotation is enclosed in a set of quotation marks.

When the second part of a divided quotation is a complete sentence, it begins with a capital letter.

EXAMPLE   "I can't go today," I said. "**A**sk me tomorrow."

24g. A direct quotation can be set off from the rest of the sentence by one or more commas or by a question mark or an exclamation point, but not by a period.

To set off means "to separate." If a quotation begins a sentence, a comma follows it. If a quotation ends a sentence, a comma comes before it. If a quoted sentence is interrupted, a comma follows the first part and comes before the second part.

EXAMPLES   "I think science is more interesting than history**,**" said Bernie.

Velma commented**,** "I especially like to do the experiments."

"Yes**,**" Juan added**,** "Bernie loves experiments, too."

When a quotation at the beginning of a sentence ends with a question mark or an exclamation point, no comma is needed.

EXAMPLES   "Is that a good video game**?**" Jane wanted to know.

"I'll say it is**!**" Debbie exclaimed.

MECHANICS

Relating to Literature

From your literature textbook, select a story that contains plenty of dialogue (for example, Shirley Jackson's "Charles"), and have students read the story. During a class discussion of the story, ask students to consider how difficult it would be to read the story without correct use of quotation marks. To illustrate this point, ask a student volunteer to copy a portion of dialogue from the story on the chalkboard and to omit quotation marks.

MODALITIES

Auditory Learners. Designate sounds to represent each punctuation mark. For example, quotation marks could be represented by the sound *blip*, commas by *ping*, and periods by *pop*. Write the punctuation marks and their corresponding sounds on the chalkboard. Then, ask student volunteers to read their answers for **Exercise 2** aloud. Have them indicate the appropriate punctuation marks as they read by making the designated sounds. The example sentence for **Exercise 2** would sound like this: *blip* Let's go to a movie this afternoon *ping blip* said Bob *pop*

24h. A comma or a period should be placed inside the closing quotation marks.

EXAMPLES   "The Ramses exhibit begins over there**.**" said the museum guide.

                 Darnell replied, "I'm ready to see some ancient Egyptian jewelry and artwork**.**"

24i. A question mark or an exclamation point should be placed inside the closing quotation marks when the quotation itself is a question or an exclamation. Otherwise, it should be placed outside.

EXAMPLES   "How far have we come**?**" asked the exhausted man. [The quotation is a question.]

                 Who said, "Give me liberty or give me death"**?** [The sentence, not the quotation, is a question.]

                 "Jump**!**" ordered the firefighter. [The quotation is an exclamation.]

                 I couldn't believe it when he said, "No, thank you"**!** [The sentence, not the quotation, is an exclamation.]

When both the sentence and the quotation at the end of the sentence are questions (or exclamations), only one question mark (or exclamation point) is used. It is placed inside the closing quotation marks.

EXAMPLE   Did Josh really say, "What's Cinco de Mayo**?**"

Exercise 2   Punctuating and Capitalizing Quotations

Use commas, quotation marks, and capital letters where they are needed in each of the following sentences. If a sentence is already correct, write *C*.

EXAMPLE   1. Let's go to a movie this afternoon, said Bob.
              1. "Let's go to a movie this afternoon," said Bob.

1. When I shrieked in fear, the usher warned me to be quiet. **1.** C
2. At the same time, Bob whispered it's only a movie—calm down.
3. He pointed out that the people around us were getting annoyed. **3.** C

Learning for Life

Continued on pp. 633–635

Testimonials in Advertising. Point out to students that testimonials used in advertising—whether on television or radio or in print—are direct quotations. Write the following example testimonials on the chalkboard.

"I laughed, I cried, and I was deeply moved by this play." —Fran Ellison, Centerville Junior High

Alan Whittle, a junior at Lincoln High School, says, "This is definitely the most

4. I quietly replied "I'm sorry."
5. "You shouldn't have screamed," he complained.
6. "From now on" I said to him "I promise I'll try to be quiet."
7. When the lights came on, Bob said "it's time to go."
8. Outside the theater he muttered something about people
   who shouldn't go to scary movies.   8. C
9. "I just couldn't help it" I explained.
10. "You were even afraid" Bob protested "during the credits!"

Exercise 3 — Punctuating and Capitalizing Quotations

Use capital letters, quotation marks, and other punctuation
marks where they are needed in each of the following sentences.

EXAMPLE   1. Ashley Bryan wore traditional African clothes when he
              came to our school Elton said.

           1. *"Ashley Bryan wore traditional African clothes when
              he came to our school," Elton said.*

1. "Oh, like the clothes Mr. Johnson showed us in class!" Janell
   exclaimed.
2. Elton asked "have you read any of Ashley Bryan's books
   about African culture?"
3. "I've read" Janell quickly replied "the one titled *Beat the Story-
   Drum, Pum-Pum.*"
4. "I'd like to read that again" Elton said "those African folk tales
   are wonderful."
5. "Mrs. Ray thinks *Walk Together Children* is excellent" Janell said.
6. "Isn't that" Elton asked "about
   African American spirituals?"
7. "You're right" Janell answered "and
   Bryan wrote that spirituals are
   America's greatest contribution
   to world music."
8. She added "he grew up in New York
   City and" began writing stories and
   drawing when he was still in
   kindergarten."
9. "Did you know" Elton asked "that
   he illustrated his own books?"
10. "Bryan made woodcuts to
    illustrate *Walk Together Children*"
    he added.

Reprinted with the permission of Atheneum Books for Young Readers, an imprint of Simon & Schuster Children's Publishing Division from *Walk Together Children,* selected and illustrated by Ashley Bryan.

Quotation Marks   **633**

Meeting
INDIVIDUAL
NEEDS

INCLUSION
Some students may find it difficult to
use quotation marks in conjunction
with other punctuation marks. To
give students modified practice in
writing quotations, write visual cues
on the chalkboard. For example, a
cue for a statement could be presented like this.
    ___ said, "___."

Similarly, the cue for a question and
exclamation could be presented like
this.
    ___ asked, "___ ?" and ___
exclaimed, "___!"

Viewing the Art
About the Artist. Folklorist Ashley
Bryan (1923–   ) was educated at
Cooper Union and Columbia
University. He is professor emeritus of
art and visual studies at Dartmouth
College.

Several of Bryan's collections contain
stories that explain how certain animals, such as dogs and cats, became
natural enemies.

MECHANICS

exciting adventure book I've ever read. I
was on the edge of my chair the whole
time."

"I couldn't believe how soft and silky my
hair felt," says Miana Brown of Fairfax

Middle School. "This is my shampoo from
now on!"

Have students work in pairs, conducting
brief interviews of other students to gather
testimonials for something they want to

Exercise 4 **Creating Direct Quotations**

MECHANICS

A N S W E R S

1. Mayor Alaniz announced, "I will lead the parade this year."

2. Ms. Feldman asked me, "What are your plans for the big parade?"

3. I answered, "My brother and I are building a float."

4. She exclaimed, "That's terrific!"

5. Ron remarked, "Your float probably has something to do with sports."

6. I told Ron, "You are exactly right."

7. Alinda asked me, "What sports will be represented on the float?"

8. I replied, "The float will salute swimming, soccer, and tennis."

9. Ron said excitedly, "I would love to help!"

10. Ms. Feldman said, "You and your brother would probably be glad to have help."

Exercise 4 **Creating Direct Quotations**

Revise each of the following sentences by changing the indirect quotation to a direct quotation. Be sure to use capital letters and punctuation wherever necessary.

EXAMPLE   1. I asked my grandmother whether she would like to help us paint our float.

      1. *"Grandma," I asked, "would you like to help us paint our float?"*

1. Mayor Alaniz announced that he would lead the parade this year.
2. Ms. Feldman asked me what my plans for the big parade were.
3. I answered that my brother and I were building a float.
4. She exclaimed that she thought that was terrific.
5. Ron remarked that our float probably had something to do with sports.
6. I told Ron that he was exactly right.
7. Alinda asked me what sports will be represented on the float.
8. I replied that the float will salute swimming, soccer, and tennis.
9. Ron said excitedly that he would love to help.
10. Ms. Feldman said that my brother and I would probably be glad to have help.

24j. When you write dialogue (a conversation), begin a new paragraph every time the speaker changes.

EXAMPLE   The young man smiled, and said, "My old master, now let me tell you the truth. My home is not so far away. It is quite near your temple. We have been old neighbors for many years."

    The old monk was very surprised. "I don't believe it. You, young man, will have your joke. Where is there another house round here?"

    "My master, would I lie to you? I live right beside your temple. The Green Pond is my home."

    "You live in the pond?" The old monk was even more astonished.

    "That's right. In fact," said Li Aiqi, in a perfectly serious tone, "I'm not a man at all. I am a dragon."

"Green Dragon Pond," a Bai folk tale

Learning for Life

advertise: a performance they're involved in, a service they want to market (such as baby-sitting, mowing lawns, or computer work), or a speech or presentation on an issue that interests them. Ask the student pairs to take notes carefully during the interviews. If they have access to a tape recorder, they could tape the interviews and transcribe them later. (Students should get permission from the interviewees before taping.) They will want to choose the most enthusiastic testimonials for their ads.

24k. When a quotation consists of several sentences, put quotation marks only at the beginning and the end of the whole quotation.

EXAMPLE   "Mary Elizabeth and I will wait for you at Robertson's Drugstore. Please try to get there as soon as you can. We don't want to be late for the concert," Jerome said.

24l. Use single quotation marks to enclose a quotation within a quotation.

EXAMPLES   Brandon added, "My mom always says, 'Look before you leap.'"

"Did Ms. Neuman really say, 'It's all right to use your books and your notes during the test'?" asked Sakura.

24m. Use quotation marks to enclose the titles of short works such as short stories, poems, songs, episodes of television series, essays, articles, and chapters and other parts of books.

Reference Note

For examples of **titles that are italicized,** see page 628.

Type of Name	Examples
Short Stories	"A Day's Wait" "The Medicine Bag"
Poems	"In Time of Silver Rain" "Birdfoot's Grampa"
Songs	"The Star-Spangled Banner" "Swing Low, Sweet Chariot"
Episodes of Television Series	"This Side of Paradise" "Growing Up Hispanic"
Essays	"Self-Reliance" "The Creative Process"
Articles	"Rooting for the Home Team" "Annie Leibovitz: Behind the Images"
Chapters and Other Parts of Books	"The Natural World" "The Myths of Greece and Rome" "The Double Task of Language"

MECHANICS

As students design their ads, have them pay particular attention to the use of quotation marks, commas, and end marks in their testimonials. Have each pair exchange ads with another pair to check for correct punctuation.

┌─ TIPS & TRICKS ─┐

In general, the title of a work that can stand alone (for instance, a novel, a movie, or a newspaper) is in italics. The title of a work that is usually part of a collection or series (for instance, a short story, an episode of a television series, or a poem) is in quotation marks.

NOTE Titles that are usually set in quotation marks are set in single quotation marks when they appear within a quotation.

EXAMPLE   James said, "We learned 'The Star-Spangled Banner' in music class today."

Exercise 5 Using Quotation Marks

Insert quotation marks where they are needed in each of the following items. If a sentence is already correct, write *C*.

EXAMPLE   1. Let's sing 'The Ballad of Gregorio Cortez,' suggested Jim.

   1. *"Let's sing 'The Ballad of Gregorio Cortez,'" suggested Jim.*

1. "Lani, have you seen my clarinet?" asked Rob. "It was on this table. I need it for my lesson this afternoon."
2. The most interesting chapter in *The Sea Around Us* is "The Birth of an Island."
3. "Didn't Benjamin Franklin once say, 'Time is money'?" asked Myra impatiently.
4. "I believe my favorite Langston Hughes poem is 'As I Grew Older,'" said Mom.
5. Lea Evans said, "One of the greatest changes in architecture has been in the design of churches. They no longer necessarily follow traditional forms. Churches have been built that are shaped like stars, fish, and ships."
6. The latest issue of *Discover* magazine has a fascinating picture of a shark that swallowed an anchor.   **6.** C
7. "Do you know which character asked 'What's in a name?' in *Romeo and Juliet?*" I asked.
8. "Yes, that was Juliet," answered Li. "My mother used to say that to me when I was a little girl. That's how I first heard of Shakespeare."
9. "A human hand has more than twenty-seven bones and thirty-five muscles!" exclaimed Marcus. "No wonder it can do so much."
10. There is an article titled "The Customers Always Write" in today's newspaper.

Review A Punctuating Paragraphs

Revise the following paragraphs, adding quotation marks and other marks of punctuation wherever necessary. Remember to begin a new paragraph each time the speaker changes. If a sentence is already correct, write *C*.   Carets (∧) indicate paragraph breaks.

EXAMPLES   **[1]**   Mr. Brown asked Can you baby-sit tonight?

1.   *Mr. Brown asked, "Can you baby-sit tonight?"*

[2]   Sure I said I'd be happy to.

2.   *"Sure," I said. "I'd be happy to."*

[1] Last night I baby-sat for the Browns, a new family on our block. [2] Come in Mrs. Brown greeted me. [3] You must be Lisa. [4] Hello, Mrs. Brown I replied. [5] I'm looking forward to meeting the children. [6] First Mrs. Brown explained I want you to meet Ludwig. [7] Is he a member of the family I asked. [8] In a way replied Mrs. Brown as she led me to the kitchen and pointed to an aging dachshund. [9] That is Ludwig. [10] He rules this house and everyone in it.

[11] Mr. Brown entered the kitchen and introduced himself. [12] I see that you've met Ludwig he said. [13] Yes Mrs. Brown answered for me. [14] Why don't you give Lisa her instructions while I go find the children?

[15] If Ludwig whines said Mr. Brown give him a dog biscuit. [16] Should I take him for a walk I asked. [17] No replied Mr. Brown. [18] Just let him out into the yard.

[19] Mrs. Brown came back into the kitchen with the children. [20] Did my husband remind you to cover Ludwig when he falls asleep she asked. [21] I'll remember I promised. [22] Also, what should I do for the children? [23] Don't worry said Mr. Brown. [24] They'll behave themselves and go to bed when they're supposed to. [25] As I told you laughed Mrs. Brown Ludwig rules this house and everyone in it, even the sitter!

HELP

The marks of punctuation that are already included in Review A are correct.

1. C

6. ∧ (before "First")

11. C

19. C

Apostrophes

Rules 24n–t (pp. 638–645)

OBJECTIVES

- To add apostrophes to singular possessives
- To rewrite expressions using the possessive case
- To write possessives of indefinite pronouns
- To add apostrophes to contractions
- To complete sentences by adding suitable contractions
- To create contractions from given pronouns and verbs

Meeting
INDIVIDUAL
NEEDS

ENGLISH-LANGUAGE LEARNERS
General Strategies. There are many ways to express possession in the world's many languages. English-language learners may be completely unfamiliar with showing possession by using an apostrophe and an *s*. Ask students to tell you how possession is indicated in their languages, and discuss with students the differences between those methods and the English method of showing possession with punctuation.

MECHANICS

Apostrophes

Possessive Case

The *possessive case* of a noun or a pronoun shows ownership or possession.

EXAMPLES	**Kathleen's** desk	**anybody's** guess
	his bat	an **hour's** time
	their car	those **horses'** manes

24n. To form the possessive case of a singular noun, add an apostrophe and an *s*.

| EXAMPLES | a boy**'s** cap | Cleon**'s** pen |
| | the baby**'s** toy | Charles**'s** opinion |

NOTE A proper noun ending in *s* may take only an apostrophe to form the possessive case if the addition of an apostrophe and an *s* would make the name awkward to say.

| EXAMPLES | the Philippine**s'** government |
| | Ms. Rodger**s'** cat |

Exercise 6 Using Apostrophes for Singular Possessives

Identify the word that needs an apostrophe in each of the following sentences. Then, write the word correctly punctuated.

EXAMPLE
1. The Prado in Madrid, Spain, is one of the worlds greatest museums.

1. worlds—world's

1. Shown on the next page is one of the Prados paintings by Diego Velázquez, *Las Meninas.*
2. Velázquezs painting is known in English as *The Maids of Honor.*
3. In the center of the canvas is Princess Margarita, the royal couples daughter.
4. To the princesss right, a kneeling maid of honor offers her something to drink.

RESOURCES

Apostrophes

Practice

- *Grammar, Usage, and Mechanics,* pp. 311, 312, 313, 314, 315, 316
- *Language Workshop CD-ROM,* Lessons 47, 48

5. To the royal child's left, another maid of honor curtsies.
6. On the far left of the canvas, you can see the artist's own image, for he has painted himself!
7. The palace's other important people, such as the chamberlain and a court jester, also appear.
8. The faces of Margarita's parents are reflected in the mirror on the back wall.
9. In the foreground, the royal dog ignores a young guest's invitation to play.
10. This painting's fame has grown since it was painted in 1656, and each year millions of people see it when they visit the Prado.

The Granger Collection, New York

24o. To form the possessive case of a plural noun that does not end in *s,* add an apostrophe and an *s.*

EXAMPLES

mice**'s** tracks	men**'s** hats
children**'s** games	teeth**'s** enamel
women**'s** shoes	Sioux**'s** land

24p. To form the possessive case of a plural noun ending in *s,* add only the apostrophe.

EXAMPLES

cat**s'** basket	four day**s'** delay
brushe**s'** bristles	the Carson**s'** bungalow

NOTE In general, you should not use an apostrophe to form the plural of a noun.

INCORRECT	Three girl's lost their tickets.
CORRECT	Three **girls** lost their tickets. [plural]
CORRECT	Three **girls'** tickets were lost. [plural possessive]

Reference Note

For information on **using apostrophes to form the plurals of letters, numerals, and symbols and of words used as words,** see page 645.

Apostrophes **639**

MECHANICS

Apostrophes **639**

Exercise 7 Writing Possessives

ANSWERS

1. the party's nominee
2. the babies' clothes
3. my sister's grades
4. the guests' name tags
5. the cat's dish
6. Mr. Granger's yard
7. my foot's muscles
8. the oxen's strength
9. James's computer
10. the teams' members

Reference Note

For more information about **possessive personal pronouns,** see page 342.

Reference Note

For a list of **words that are often confused,** see Chapter 25.

Reference Note

For more information about **indefinite pronouns,** see page 344.

Exercise 7 Writing Possessives

Using the possessive case, rewrite each of the following word groups. Be sure to insert an apostrophe in the correct place.

EXAMPLE 1. food for the dog
1. *the dog's food*

1. the nominee of the party
2. the clothes of the babies
3. the grades of my sister
4. the name tags of the guests
5. the dish for the cat
6. the yard of Mr. Granger
7. the muscles of my foot
8. the strength of the oxen
9. the computer of James
10. the members of the teams

24q. Do not use an apostrophe with possessive personal pronouns.

EXAMPLES Is that sticker **yours** or **mine**?

Our cat is friendlier than **theirs.**

His report on Cherokee folk tales was as good as **hers.**

NOTE Do not confuse the possessive pronoun *its* with the contraction *it's.* The possessive pronoun *its* means *belonging to it.* The expression *it's* is a contraction of the words *it is* or *it has.*

POSSESSIVE PRONOUN Please give the cat **its** rubber ball.

CONTRACTIONS **It's** time for the soccer tournament.

It's taken three hours.

24r. To form the possessive case of some indefinite pronouns, add an apostrophe and an *s.*

EXAMPLES neither**'s** homework

everyone**'s** choice

somebody**'s** jacket

Exercise 8 Writing Possessives of Personal and Indefinite Pronouns

Rewrite each of the following expressions, using the possessive case of each pronoun.

EXAMPLE 1. the park for everyone
1. *everyone's park*

Continued on pp. 641–642

Contractions and Possessive Personal Pronouns. Because some contractions and possessive personal pronouns sound alike—*it's* and *its,* for example—students sometimes confuse such words in their writing.

Tell students that if they are having trouble deciding which word in these confusing pairs to use, they should try saying the word as two words (for *it's/its,* substitute *it is*). If the sentence makes sense with the

1. the opinion of them
2. the footprints of anyone
3. the fault of nobody
4. the turn of either
5. the stereo that belongs to you
6. the logo of it
7. the idea of neither
8. the backpack of someone
9. the guess of anybody
10. the land owned by no one

Contractions

24s. Use an apostrophe to show where letters, words, or numerals have been omitted (left out) in a contraction.

A *contraction* is a shortened form of a word, a numeral, or a word group. The apostrophe in a contraction shows where letters or numerals have been left out. Contractions are acceptable in informal writing, but in formal writing, you should generally avoid using them.

Common Contractions	
I am .... I'm	they had .... they'd
1999 .... '99	where is .... where's
let us .... let's	we are .... we're
of the clock .... o'clock	he is .... he's
she would .... she'd	you will .... you'll
we have .... we've	what is .... what's
they are .... they're	I would .... I'd

The word *not* can be shortened to *n't* and added to a verb, usually without any change in the spelling of the verb.

EXAMPLES

is not .... isn't
are not .... aren't
does not .... doesn't
do not .... don't
was not .... wasn't
were not .... weren't

has not .... hasn't
have not .... haven't
had not .... hadn't
should not .. shouldn't
would not .... wouldn't
could not ...... couldn't

EXCEPTIONS

will not .... won't

cannot .... can't

STYLE | TIP

In formal writing, avoid using a contraction of a year. In informal writing, if the reader cannot determine the time period from the context of the sentence, it is best to write out the year.

EXAMPLE
The famous tenor toured Europe in '01. [Did the tenor tour in 1801, 1901, or 2001?]

The famous tenor toured Europe in **2001**.

Apostrophes **641**

MECHANICS

Meeting
INDIVIDUAL
NEEDS

MODALITIES

Kinesthetic Learners. Have students write on strips of paper word combinations that can be made into contractions, such as *cannot, have not, they would, we have,* and *who is.* Students should also write apostrophes on several strips. Have students cut and rearrange the strips to change the words and phrases into contractions. Then, have students consult a dictionary to check their contractions.

Be careful not to confuse contractions with possessive pronouns.

Contractions	Possessive Pronouns
It's Friday. [*It is*]	**Its** nest is over there.
It's been a pleasure. [*It has*]	
Who's your server? [*Who is*]	**Whose** backpack is this?
Who's been practicing the piano? [*Who has*]	
They're arriving soon. [*They are*]	**Their** parakeet is friendly.
There's the path. [*There is*]	That rosebush is **theirs**.

Exercise 9　Using Apostrophes Correctly

Correct each error in the use of possessive forms and contractions in the following sentences. If a sentence is already correct, write *C.*

HELP

Some sentences in Exercise 9 contain more than one error.

EXAMPLE　　**1.** Arent you going with us at one oclock?

　　　　　　　1. *Aren't; o'clock*

1. We'd better chain our bicycles to the rack.
2. You're old cars seen better days, hasn't it?　**2.** Your
3. She wasn't too happy to see us.
4. Whose ringing the doorbell?　**4.** Who's
5. We won't forget how helpful you've been.
6. I'm certain you'll be invited.
7. Whose turn is it to take attendance?　**7.** C
8. Ann's an excellent swimmer, but she can't dive.
9. They're turning in their's now.　**9.** theirs
10. She's sure they'll show up before it's over.

Exercise 10　Punctuating Contractions

For each of the following sentences, identify the word that needs an apostrophe to indicate a contraction. Then, write the word correctly.

EXAMPLE　　**1.** Whats the best route from Lawrenceville, New Jersey, to Newtown, Pennsylvania?

　　　　　　　1. *What's*

MINI-LESSON

It's my turn now.
There's your little sister.
That ball is theirs.

Have students exchange papers. Read the sentences again, and write the underlined words on the chalkboard. Students who are having problems may want to write in their grammar logs sentences using the confusing words. For a chart showing the possessive personal pronouns, refer students to **Chapter 19: Using Pronouns Correctly**.

1. There's one especially pretty route you can take to get there.
2. I think you'll enjoy the drive.
3. You shouldn't go due west directly.
4. You've got to go north or south first.
5. It's easier to go south on Route 206 to Route U.S. 1, cross the Delaware River, and then go north on Route 32 to Yardley.
6. From Yardley, turn left on Route 322, and in a little while I'm sure you will find yourself in Newtown.
7. If you'd prefer a different route, go south on Route 206 to Route 546 and make a right turn to go west.
8. After you cross the Delaware River and the road becomes 532, don't turn until Linton Hill Road.
9. When you turn left onto Linton Hill Road, it won't be long before you arrive in Newtown.
10. Here's a map you can use to help you find your way.

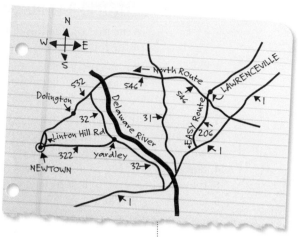

Exercise 11 Writing Contractions

Write a suitable contraction to correctly complete each of the following sentences.   Answers may vary.

EXAMPLE   **1.** Do you know _____ for supper?

　　　　　　 1. *what's*

1. _____ my sweater?   **1.** Where's
2. _____ lying on the beach.   **2.** It's
3. We _____ help you right now.   **3.** can't
4. _____ dinner ready?   **4.** Isn't
5. They _____ played that game before.   **5.** haven't
6. She was in the class of _____.   **6.** '01
7. _____ go to the museum.   **7.** Let's
8. I _____ know that game.   **8.** don't
9. _____ rather order the salad.   **9.** He'd
10. Is it nine _____ yet?   **10.** o'clock

TEACHING TIP

Extension. You may wish to extend students' study of the map by asking these questions orally or by writing them on the board, then having students provide answers.

1. Lawrenceville, New Jersey, is near what intersection, according to the map? [*intersection of Easy Route 206 and North Route 546*]

2. Is Newtown, Pennsylvania, to the west or the east of the Delaware River? [*west*]

3. Does Linton Hill Road run east to west? [*No, it makes a north-south curve.*]

4. What route runs alongside the Delaware River? [*Route 32*]

5. At what intersection would you find Yardley, Pennsylvania? [*intersection of 32 and 322*]

MECHANICS

Apostrophes   **643**

Cooperative Learning

To help students become more familiar with the correct use of apostrophes, have them find and graph the use of apostrophes in print material. Divide the class into groups of four. Have each group assemble some written sources—comics, newspapers, books, and magazines. Then, have each group designate two students to find examples of apostrophe use, one student to record each use, and one to match apostrophe rules in this chapter to the examples the group finds. Each entry should include the source, the page number, the word containing an apostrophe, and the rule number that applies. Have students switch tasks until each student has had a chance to complete each task, and encourage the groups to use a variety of sources. Have each group make a graph like the one below to illustrate their findings.

RULE

24n				
24o				
24p				
24q				
24r				
24s				
24t				
	5	10	15	20

NUMBER OF USES

Then, have each group present its graph to the rest of the class.

Exercise 12 **Writing Contractions**

Write the contraction of the underlined word or words in each of the following sentences.

EXAMPLE   1. If you think it <u>should have</u> been easy to visit the building shown below, guess again!

   1. *should've*

1. It's
2. couldn't
3. who's
4. don't
5. they've
6. can't

1. <u>It is</u> the Potala Palace in Lhasa, Tibet, which my parents and I visited last year.
2. The city of Lhasa is two miles high in the Himalaya Mountains, and we <u>could not</u> move around much because the lack of oxygen made us tired.
3. The Potala Palace is the former residence of the Tibetan spiritual leader, <u>who has</u> been living in exile in India.
4. Because this palace is a holy shrine, pilgrims <u>do not</u> mind traveling on foot from all over the country to worship there.

5. After <u>they have</u> bought yak butter in the city square, they take it to the palace as an offering.
6. From the photograph, you <u>cannot</u> imagine how steep those stairs on the right are!
7. Because it <u>would have</u> taken a long time to climb them, our bus driver took us directly to the rear entrance on the left.
8. Once inside, we spent hours exploring the palace, but we <u>were not</u> able to visit most of its more than one thousand rooms!

7. would've
8. weren't
9. I'm
10. wasn't

9. <u>I am</u> sure we would never have found our way out without our guide, who led us to an exit on the right.
10. Walking down the stairs <u>was not</u> too hard, and soon we were in the beautiful central square in the Himalayan sunshine!

Plurals

24t. Use an apostrophe and an *s* to form the plurals of letters, numerals, and symbols, and of words referred to as words.

EXAMPLES   Your *o*'s look like *a*'s, and your *u*'s look like *n*'s.

There are three *5*'s and two *8*'s in his telephone number.

Place *$*'s before monetary amounts and *¢*'s after.

One sign of immature writing is too many *and*'s.

Review B   **Using Underlining (Italics) and Apostrophes Correctly**

For each of the following sentences, add underlining or apostrophes as necessary. The punctuation already supplied is correct.

EXAMPLE   1. One of my oldest brothers college textbooks is History of Art by H. W. Janson.

      1. *brother's; History of Art*

1. Who's the painter who inspired the musical play <u>Sunday in the Park with George</u>?
2. He's Georges Seurat, one of France's greatest painters.
3. "The young children's reactions to Jacob Lawrence's paintings were surprising," Angie said.
4. Didn't you read the review in <u>Entertainment Weekly</u> of the movie <u>Vincent & Theo</u>?
5. It's about Vincent van Gogh and his brother, who often supported him.
6. "I like Jasper Johns," Rick said, "but I can't tell if that is one of Johns's paintings."
7. Have you ever tried counting all the 2's or 4's in his painting <u>Numbers in Color</u>?
8. On a class trip to Chicago, we saw a bronze statue titled <u>Horse</u>, by Duchamp-Villon.
9. In our group, everybody's favorite painting is <u>Cow's Skull: Red, White and Blue</u>, by Georgia O'Keeffe.
10. "On PBS, I've seen an <u>American Playhouse</u> program about O'Keeffe's life," Joyce said.

MECHANICS

Apostrophes   **645**

Hyphens

Rules 24u–w *(pp. 646–648)*

OBJECTIVE

■ To use hyphens correctly when writing numbers

TEACHING **TIP**

Activity. To reinforce the practice of looking up words to check for syllable divisions, give each student a dictionary. (If there are not enough dictionaries available to give one to each student, divide the class into groups based on the number of available dictionaries.) Then, call out words one by one from the dictionary. As you call out a word, students should find the word in the dictionary and write the word with hyphens dividing the syllables. If there is a wide range of spelling and dictionary skills among your students, you may also want to write each word on the chalkboard as you call it out so that students can take longer to complete the exercise if needed.

After the class has completed the exercise, ask a student volunteer to rewrite the words on the chalkboard and to put hyphens between the syllables. (You may want to check the volunteer's work first.) Then, students can check their own lists.

MECHANICS

COMPUTER TIP

Some word-processing programs will automatically divide a word at the end of a line and insert a hyphen. Sometimes, such hyphenation will violate one of the rules given here.

Always check a printout of your writing to see how the computer has hyphenated words at the ends of lines. If a hyphen is used incorrectly, revise the line by moving the word or by dividing the word yourself and inserting a "hard" hyphen (one that the computer cannot move).

STYLE **TIP**

Hyphens are often used in compound names. In such cases, the hyphen is thought of as part of the name's spelling.

EXAMPLES
Jackie Joyner-Kersee [person]

Rikki-tikki-tavi [animal]

Wilkes-Barre [city]

If you are not sure whether a compound name is hyphenated, ask the person with that name, or look in a reference source.

Hyphens

24u. Use a hyphen to divide a word at the end of a line.

EXAMPLE   Will you and Marguerite help me put the silver-ware on the table?

When dividing a word at the end of a line, remember the following rules:

(1) Divide a word only between syllables.

INCORRECT   The man in the pinstriped suit sat bes-ide the tree, looking bewildered.

CORRECT   The man in the pinstriped suit sat be-side the tree, looking bewildered.

(2) Do not divide a one-syllable word.

INCORRECT   Exercises like push-ups help to develop stren-gth of the arm muscles.

CORRECT   Exercises like push-ups help to develop strength of the arm muscles.

(3) Do not divide a word so that one letter stands alone.

INCORRECT   The seating capacity of the new stadium is e-normous.

CORRECT   The seating capacity of the new stadium is enor-mous.

24v. Use a hyphen with compound numbers from *twenty-one* to *ninety-nine* and with fractions used as modifiers.

EXAMPLES   During a leap year, there are twenty-nine days in February.

Thirty-two species of birds are known to live in the area.

Did you know that Congress may override a president's veto by a two-thirds majority? [*Two-thirds* is an adjective that modifies *majority.*]

The pumpkin pie was so good that only one sixth of it is left. [*One sixth* is not used as a modifier. Instead, *sixth* is a noun modified by the adjective *one.* Fractions used as nouns do not have hyphens.]

RESOURCES

Hyphens
Practice

■ *Grammar, Usage, and Mechanics,* p. 317
■ *Language Workshop CD-ROM,* Lesson 52

24w. Use a hyphen with the prefixes *ex–, self–, all–, and great–* and with the suffixes *–elect* and *–free*.

EXAMPLES
ex-coach   president-elect   all-star

great-uncle   self-propelled   fat-free

Exercise 13   Using Hyphens Correctly

Write an expression—using words, not numerals—to fit the blank in each of the following sentences. Use hyphens where they are needed with compound numbers or fractions.

EXAMPLE   1. The sum of ten and fifteen is ____.
1. *twenty-five*

1. January, March, May, July, August, October, and December are the months that have ____ days.
2. ____ of the moon is visible from the earth, but the other half can be seen only from outer space.
3. In twenty years I will be ____ years old.
4. I used ____ cup, which is 25 percent of the original one cup.
5. Our seventh-grade class has ____ students.
6. The train ride is short; the route is only ____ miles long.
7. The doctor said that the heel of my shoe needs to be raised ____ of an inch.
8. Who decided that there should be ____ hours in a day?
9. ____ teaspoon of vanilla is not enough in the cake batter.
10. Only about ____ of the expected people actually attended.

Review C   Punctuating Sentences Correctly

Rewrite the following sentences, correcting any errors in the use of underlining, quotation marks, commas, apostrophes, and hyphens.   Hyphens are indicated by the – symbol.

EXAMPLE   1. For the talent show, Leila is planning to recite Poes poem The Raven.
1. *For the talent show, Leila is planning to recite Poe's poem "The Raven."*

1. Queen Hatshepsut seized the throne of Egypt in 1503 B.C. and ruled for twenty-one years.
2. Whos borrowed my scissors? demanded Jean.
3. Its hard to decide which authors story I should read first.
4. A weeks vacation never seems long enough.

MECHANICS

5. After we'd eaten supper, we decided to watch an old episode of <u>Star Trek</u>.

6. The driver shouted "Move to the rear of the bus!"

7. We didn't eat any salmon at all during our visit to O-regon.   **7.** Or-egon *or* Ore-gon *or* Oregon

8. "I wasn't very sorry," admitted the clerk, "to see those picky customers leave."

9. "Very Short on Law and Order" is my favorite chapter in <u>Tough Trip Through Paradise</u>.   **9.** Tough

10. Our new phone number starts with two 6's and ends with two 4's.

Parentheses, Brackets, and Dashes

Rules 24x–z *(pp. 648–650)*

OBJECTIVES

- To correct sentences by adding parentheses
- To correct sentences by adding dashes and brackets

Relating to Writing

You may want to emphasize to students that the use of parentheses and dashes to set off parenthetical expressions should be limited in formal writing.

┌─────────────────────┐
│ S T Y L E   T I P │
└─────────────────────┘

Too many parenthetical expressions in a piece of writing can keep readers from seeing the main idea. Keep your meaning clear by limiting the number of parenthetical expressions you use.

Parentheses

24x. Use parentheses to enclose material that is added to a sentence but is not considered of major importance.

EXAMPLES   Emilio Aguinaldo (1869–1964) was a Filipino patriot and statesman.

Mom and Dad bought a kilim (pronounced ki • lēm′) rug from our Turkish friend Ali.

Material enclosed in parentheses may be as short as a single word or as long as a short sentence. A short sentence in parentheses may stand alone or be contained within another sentence. Notice that a parenthetical sentence within a sentence is not capitalized and has no end mark.

EXAMPLES   Please be quiet during the performance. (Take crying babies to the lobby.)

Jack Echohawk (he's Ben's cousin) told us about growing up on a reservation.

Exercise 14 Correcting Sentences by Adding Parentheses

Insert parentheses where they are needed in the following sentences.

EXAMPLE   **1.** My bicycle I've had it for three years is a ten-speed.

    1. My bicycle (I've had it for three years) is a ten-speed.

RESOURCES

Parentheses, Brackets, and Dashes

Practice

- *Grammar, Usage, and Mechanics,* p. 318
- *Language Workshop CD-ROM,* Lesson 52

1. At the age of fourteen, Martina Hingis began playing tennis (my favorite sport) professionally.
2. Elijah McCoy (1843–1929) invented a way to oil moving machinery.
3. I bought a new calculator (my old one stopped working) and a notebook.
4. Charlemagne (pronounced shär′lə • mān′) was one of Europe's most famous rulers.
5. Lian Young (she's a friend of mine) told our class about her school in China.

Brackets

24y. Use brackets to enclose an explanation added to quoted or parenthetical material.

EXAMPLES   Elena said in her acceptance speech, "I am honored by this [the award], and I would like to thank the students who volunteered to help with the Special Olympics this year." [The words are enclosed in brackets to show that they have been inserted into the quotation and are not the words of the speaker.]

By a vote of 6 to 1, the council approved the petition to build a nature preserve. (See next page for a map [Diagram A] of the proposed reserve.)

Dashes

A *parenthetical expression* is a word or phrase that breaks into the main thought of a sentence. Parenthetical expressions are usually set off by commas or parentheses.

EXAMPLES   Grandma Moses, **for example,** started painting in her seventies.

In the first act of the play, the butler **(Theo Karras)** was the detective's prime suspect.

Some parenthetical elements need stronger emphasis. In such cases, a dash is used.

Reference Note

For more about using **commas with parenthetical expressions,** see page 611. For more about **using parentheses,** see page 648.

24z. Use a dash to indicate an abrupt break in thought or speech.

EXAMPLES   The right thing to do—I know it'll be hard—is to apologize.

"Do you think Ann will mind—I really hope she won't—if I borrow her sunglasses?" asked Melody.

Exercise 15 Correcting Sentences by Adding Dashes and Brackets

Insert dashes or brackets where they are needed in the following sentences.   Carets indicate placement of dashes.

EXAMPLE   1. The school lunchroom it was a dull green has been painted a cheery yellow.

          1. The school lunchroom—it was a dull green—has been painted a cheery yellow.

1. Fireflies I can't remember where I read this make what is called cold light.
2. Roberto has always wanted to be can't you guess? an astronaut.
3. Shania Twain I really want to see her concert has a great new song out.
4. Do you mind I don't if Jill and Marcus go to the mall with us tomorrow?
5. The best way to learn how to swim that is, after you've learned the basic strokes is to practice.
6. (See page 8[Box A]of the school yearbook for a list of the drama club's best performers.)
7. Where is the computer game I've looked everywhere for it that I borrowed from Alex?
8. Please hand me if you don't mind the stack of magazines on the table behind you.
9. The newspaper quoted our principal as saying, "The girls' volleyball team took both the district[District 14–5A]and regional championships."
10. The class trip to Chicago I've never been there will include a visit to the Art Institute.

Chapter Review

A. Using Underlining (Italics), Quotation Marks, Dashes, Parentheses, and Brackets

The following sentences contain errors in the use of underlining (italics), quotation marks, dashes, parentheses, and brackets. Rewrite the sentences correctly.   Carets indicate placement of dashes.

1. The song Amazing Grace has been sung for many years.
2. Garth Brooks I love his music is giving a benefit concert.
3. Did you see the article called Yogamania that appeared in last month's <u>Seventeen</u> magazine?
4. The poet Wallace Stevens (1879–1955) won a Pulitzer Prize.
5. (See the map of Normandy [Figure D] for the deployment of the German forces on June 6.)
6. The reading list included the novel <u>Great Expectations</u>.
7. Sharon she's my youngest cousin asked me to tell her a story.
8. The bearded man you probably guessed this is really the thief in disguise.
9. He misspelled the word <u>accommodate</u> by leaving out one <u>c</u>.
10. Aunt Rosie the aunt I told you about went to Mexico on the cruise ship <u>Princess</u>.

B. Proofreading for the Correct Use of Punctuation and Capitalization in Quotations

The following sentences contain errors in the use of punctuation and capitalization in quotations. Rewrite the sentences correctly. If a sentence is already correct, write *C*.

11. "Did you read Robert Hayden's poem "Those Winter Sundays"? asked Jorge.
12. "Who's your favorite baseball player." asked Don?
13. "Meet me at 2:30 sharp," my sister's note read.
14. Why did Ms. Redfeather say, "I need to see a doctor"?
15. Ms. Liu said, Turn to Chapter 7, 'Fractions,' now.
16. "Did you know," Katrina said, "That Robin Williams organizes fund-raisers for the homeless"?

Using the Chapter Review

To assess student progress, you may want to compare the types of items missed on the **Diagnostic Preview** to those missed on the **Chapter Review**. If students have not made significant progress, you may want to refer them to **Exercises 33–35** in **Chapter 26: Correcting Common Errors** for additional practice.

Chapter Review

B. Proofreading for the Correct Use of Punctuation and Capitalization in Quotations

ANSWERS

11. "Did you read Robert Hayden's poem 'Those Winter Sundays'?" asked Jorge.
12. "Who's your favorite baseball player?" asked Don.
13. C
14. C
15. Ms. Liu said, "Turn to Chapter 7, 'Fractions,' now."
16. "Did you know," Katrina said, "that Robin Williams organizes fund-raisers for the homeless?"

Chapter Review

B. Proofreading for the Correct Use of Punctuation and Capitalization in Quotations

ANSWERS continued

17. C

18. "Are the Echols Eagles playing tomorrow?" Lorraine asked Ted.

19. Chang predicted that it would be a rainy summer.

20. "He can work ten hours a week," said Liang.

Chapter Review

C. Writing Dialogue Correctly

ANSWERS

21. "A few of us are starting a reading group," said Michael.

22. "Would you like to join us?"

23. ¶"That sounds like fun," replied Audra.

24. "Who is in the group?"

25. ¶"Well, I am, of course," Michael said, "and Stephanie, Jeff, and Kerry.

26. I've asked Megan to join, too, but she may be too busy.

27. She's going to let me know tomorrow."

28. ¶"What books are you going to read," asked Audra, "or haven't you decided that yet?"

29. ¶"I'm going to suggest that we start with <u>The Owl Service</u>, by Alan Garner," said Michael, "but only if it is everyone's choice."

30. ¶"I'd love to join!" said Audra.

---

17. Akeem exclaimed, "Those giant redwoods are more than three hundred feet tall!"

18. "Are the La Vernia Bears playing tomorrow? Lorraine asked Ted.

19. Chang predicted that "it would be a rainy summer."

20. "he can work ten hours a week", said Liang.

C. Writing Dialogue Correctly

Revise the following paragraphs, adding quotation marks and other punctuation marks wherever necessary. Begin a new paragraph each time the speaker changes.

[**21**] A few of us are starting a reading group said Michael. [**22**] Would you like to join us? [**23**] That sounds like fun replied Audra. [**24**] Who is in the group? [**25**] Well, I am, of course Michael said and Stephanie, Jeff, and Kerry. [**26**] I've asked Megan to join, too, but she may be too busy. [**27**] She's going to let me know tomorrow.

[**28**] What books are you going to read asked Audra or haven't you decided that yet? [**29**] I'm going to suggest that we start with The Owl Service, by Alan Garner, said Michael but only if it is everyones choice. [**30**] I'd love to join! said Audra.

D. Using Apostrophes and Hyphens

The following sentences contain errors in the use of apostrophes and hyphens. Correctly write each incorrectly punctuated word. Hyphens are indicated by the - symbol.

31. The test includes twenty͜two questions.

32. It̷s easy to see that you like to use &̷s instead of writing out the word *and* each time.

33. One fourth of the children̷s toys were broken.

34. My two sisters̷bicycles are sporty, but neither̷s is as sport-y as mine.   **34.** sporty

35. Isn̷t this play often considered one of Shakespeare̷s best wo-rks, Stephanie?   **35.** works

36. What̷s the lowest common denominator of these two numbers?

37. Are those lawn chairs our's or the Millers̷?   **37.** ours

38. They̷re drawings of Augusta Savage̷s sculptures.

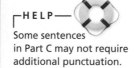

─HELP─
Some sentences in Part C may not require additional punctuation.

---

39. My baby brother's a good sleeper; he should have a mobile made of Z's instead of airplanes over his crib.

40. Who's going to help repaint the club's float for the parade?

Writing Application
Using Quotations in Reports

Direct Quotations   Your social studies class is taking a survey of people's attitudes toward recycling. Interview at least three people from different households in your community. Ask them specific questions to find out whether they think recycling is important; what items, if any, they recycle; and how they think recycling could be made easier for people in the community. Based on the information you gather, write a brief report about recycling in your community. In your report, quote several people's exact words.

Prewriting   First, think of several questions to ask. Next, decide whom you want to interview. Begin each interview by recording the person's name, age, and occupation. When all your interviews are completed, compare your interviewees' responses. What conclusions can you draw about attitudes toward recycling in your community? Jot down some notes to help you organize your information.

Writing   In the first paragraph of your draft, give a statement that sums up the main idea of your report. Then, use your interviewees' answers to support your main idea.

Revising   Re-read your first draft. Does the body of your report support your main idea? If not, you may need to rethink and revise your main idea.

Publishing   As you proofread your report, check your quotations against your notes. Make sure that you have put quotation marks around direct quotations and that you have capitalized and punctuated all quotations correctly. Your class may want to combine the information from all the reports and create a wall chart showing the community's attitudes toward recycling.

Chapter Review   **653**

O B J E C T I V E

■ **To use direct quotations in a brief report based on interviews**

Writing Application

Tip. You may want to videotape a couple of sample television interviews to show to your class. After students have watched the interviews, use the questions at the end of **Prewriting** to initiate discussion.

You could also allow students to videotape their own interviews and show them to the class. (Be sure students obtain permission from the interviewees before taping the interviews.) However, students who videotape interviews should still be required to complete written reports.

Scoring Rubric. While paying particular attention to students' use of quotation marks, you will also want to evaluate overall writing performance. You may want to give a split score to indicate development and clarity of the composition as well as punctuation skills.

MECHANICS

RESOURCES

Writing Application
Extension

■ *Grammar, Usage, and Mechanics,* p. 325
■ *Language Workshop CD-ROM,* Lessons 47–50, 52

25 Spelling
Improving Your Spelling

Diagnostic Preview

Proofreading Sentences for Correct Spelling

Write correctly all of the <u>misspelled words</u> in the following
sentences.

EXAMPLE   **1.** Andrew carefully lifted the massive lid and peekked
inside the trunk.

    1. carefully, peeked

1. tomatoes/
strawberries

2. daily/training

3. led

4. laid/knives

5. scissors

6. two/nieces

7. benches/
freezing

8. studies/swimming

9. *Weaving*

10. piece/proceed

1. Do you have any fresh <u>tomatos</u> or <u>strawberrys</u>?

2. Alex rides her bicycle forty miles <u>dayly</u> when she is in <u>trainning</u>.

3. The experienced tour guide <u>lead</u> the students to the base of
the Mayan pyramid.

4. My sister made the salad while I <u>layed</u> the spoons and <u>knifes</u>
on the table for dinner.

5. Would you please hand me the <u>scissor's</u>?

6. Mr. Escobar's <u>too</u> <u>neices</u> went to the annual family reunion.

7. Icicles formed on the park <u>benchs</u> when the temperature
dropped below <u>freezeing</u>.

8. Angela's favorite classes are social <u>studys</u> and <u>swiming</u>.

9. On Wednesday our science class watched *<u>Weavving Ants</u>*, a
film about the insect world.

10. Take out a <u>peice</u> of paper, and then <u>prosede</u> with the test.

Good Spelling Habits

Practicing the following techniques can help you spell words correctly.

1. **To learn the spelling of a word, pronounce it, study it, and write it.** Pronounce words carefully. Mispronunciation can lead to misspelling. For instance, if you say *ath•a•lete* instead of *ath•lete,* you will be more likely to spell the word incorrectly.

   - First, make sure that you know how to pronounce the word correctly, and then practice saying it.

   - Second, study the word. Notice especially any parts that might be hard to remember.

   - Third, write the word from memory. Check your spelling.

   - If you misspelled the word, repeat the three steps of this process.

2. **Use a dictionary.** When you find that you have misspelled a word, look it up in a dictionary. Do not guess about the correct spelling.

3. **Spell by syllables.** A *syllable* is a word part that is pronounced as one uninterrupted sound.

   EXAMPLES   thor•ough [two syllables]

                   sep•a•rate [three syllables]

   Instead of trying to learn how to pronounce and spell a whole word, break it up into its syllables whenever possible.

Exercise 1   Spelling by Syllables

Look up the following words in a dictionary, and divide each one into syllables. Pronounce each syllable correctly, and learn to spell the word by syllables.

1. legislature	8. definition	15. separate
2. perspire	9. recognize	16. opportunity
3. modern	10. awkward	17. eliminate
4. temperature	11. accept	18. government
5. probably	12. interest	19. business
6. similar	13. temperament	20. appreciation
7. library	14. conscious	

┌**HELP**──

If you are not sure how to pronounce a word, look it up in an up-to-date dictionary. In the dictionary, you will usually find the pronunciation given in parentheses after the word. The information in parentheses will show you the sounds used, the syllable breaks, and any accented syllables. A guide to the pronunciation symbols is usually found at the front of the dictionary.

┌**STYLE** ✏ **TIP**┐

In some names, marks that show how to pronounce a word are considered part of the spelling.

PEOPLE
Díaz   Rölvaag   Žižka

PLACES
Aswân   Cádiz

Compiègne

If you are not sure about the spelling of a name, ask the person with that name or look it up in a dictionary or other reference source.

Answers may vary according to the dictionary used. These answers are from *Webster's New World College Dictionary,* Third Edition.

Good Spelling Habits and Spelling Rules
Rules 25a–h *(pp. 655–663)*

OBJECTIVES

- **To divide words correctly into syllables**

- **To spell correctly words that contain the letters** *ie* **or** *ei*

- **To proofread sentences to correct spelling errors**

- **To add prefixes and suffixes to words correctly**

Internet

- go.hrw.com (keyword: EOLang)

RESOURCES

Good Spelling Habits and Spelling Rules

Practice

- *Grammar, Usage, and Mechanics,* pp. 327, 328, 329, 330, 331, 332, 333, 334, 335
- *Language Workshop CD-ROM,* Lesson 55 🎵

Activity. The following word riddle game can help students learn spelling while having fun. Have each student work with a partner of similar spelling ability. Each person should choose five spelling words from memory or from somewhere in this chapter. Then, have students make up and write out several clues, such as

- starts with an *s*
- ends with an *n*
- has two syllables
- is a kind of doctor

[*Answer: surgeon*]

Ask student pairs to take turns presenting clues and guessing words. As students guess the words, they could write them down and check their spellings at the end of the game against their partners' correct spellings. If students misspell familiar or commonly used words, they could add the words to their spelling notebooks or writing logs, using the format presented on pp. 655–656.

| COMPUTER TIP

A computer can help you catch spelling mistakes. Use the computer's spellchecker whenever you proofread your writing. Remember, though, that a computer's spellchecker points out misspellings but not misused homonyms. For example, if you use *their* when you should use *there,* a spellchecker won't catch the mistake. Always double-check your writing to make sure that your spelling is error-free.

4. **Proofread for careless spelling errors.** Re-read your writing carefully, and correct any mistakes and unclear letters. For example, make sure that your *i*'s are dotted, that your *t*'s are crossed, and that your *g*'s don't look like *q*'s.

5. **Keep a spelling notebook.** Divide each page into four columns:

COLUMN 1　Correctly spell any word you missed. (Never enter a misspelling.)

COLUMN 2　Write the word again, dividing it into syllables and indicating which syllables are accented or stressed.

COLUMN 3　Write the word once more, circling the spot that gives you trouble.

COLUMN 4　Jot down any comments that might help you remember the correct spelling.

Here is an example of how you might make entries for two words that are often misspelled.

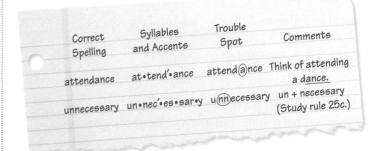

Correct Spelling	Syllables and Accents	Trouble Spot	Comments
attendance	at•tend′•ance	attend@nce	Think of attending a d*a*nce.
unnecessary	un•nec′•es•sar•y	u(nn)ecessary	un + necessary (Study rule 25c.)

Spelling Rules

ie and *ei*

25a. Write *ie* when the sound is long *e*, except after *c*.

EXAMPLES　ch**ie**f, br**ie**f, bel**ie**ve, y**ie**ld, rec**ei**ve, dec**ei**ve

EXCEPTIONS　s**ei**ze, l**ei**sure, **ei**ther, n**ei**ther, prot**ei**n

Write *ei* when the sound is not long *e*, especially when the sound is long *a*.

EXAMPLES sl**ei**gh, v**ei**l, fr**ei**ght, w**ei**ght, h**ei**ght, for**ei**gn

EXCEPTIONS fr**ie**nd, misch**ie**f, anc**ie**nt, p**ie**

Exercise 2 Writing Words with *ie and ei*

Rewrite the following words, adding the letters *ie* or *ei*.

EXAMPLE   **1.** conc . . . t
         1. conceit

1. dec . **ei** . ve
2. n . **ei** . ther
3. rec . **ei** . ve
4. h . **ei** . ght
5. fr . **ie** . nd
6. l . **ei** . sure
7. misch . **ie** . f
8. w . **ei** . ght
9. . **ei** . ght
10. sl . **ei** . gh

11. fr . **ei** . ght
12. n . **ei** . ghbor
13. c . **ei** . ling
14. shr . **ie** . k
15. rec . **ei** . pt
16. p . **ie** . ce
17. r . **ei** . gn
18. th . **ei** . r
19. s . **ei** . ze
20. br . **ie** . f

Exercise 3 Proofreading Sentences to Correct Spelling Errors

Most of the following sentences contain a spelling error involving the use of *ie* or *ei*. Write each misspelled word correctly. If a sentence has no spelling error, write *C*.

EXAMPLE   **1.** Last summer I recieved an airline ticket as a birthday gift.
         1. received

1. I used the ticket to fly to Puerto Rico with my freind Alicia to see my grandmother and other relatives.

2. We flew to San Juan, where my grandmother's nieghbor, Mr. Sanchez, met us and drove us to my grandmother's house.

3. When we got there, all of my relatives—aunts, uncles, cousins, neices, nephews—came to welcome us.

4. They couldn't believe that niether of us had ever been to Puerto Rico before, so they took us sightseeing the next day.

1. ie

2. ei

3. ie
4. ei

┌─────────────────────┐
│ TIPS & TRICKS │
└─────────────────────┘

You may find this time-tested verse a help in remembering the *ie* rule.

I before *e*
Except after *c*
Or when sounded like *a,*
As in *neighbor* and
weigh.

If you use this rhyme, remember that "*i* before *e*" refers only to words in which these two letters are in the same syllable and stand for the sound of long *e*, as in the examples under Rule 25a.

MECHANICS

Meeting INDIVIDUAL NEEDS

MODALITIES

Auditory Learners. You may want to conduct a modified spelling bee for students by asking them to pronounce and spell the words below. Call out a word (enunciate normally), and ask a student to pronounce it syllable by syllable, pausing slightly after each syllable, and then to spell the word.

To continue this activity beyond the provided words, ask other students to use a dictionary to find challenging words. Give everyone in the class a chance to participate.

1. stripe [*stripe*]

2. clearance [*clear•ance*]

3. examination [*ex•am•i•na•tion*]

4. improbable [*im•prob•a•ble*]

5. characteristic [*char•ac•ter•is•tic*]

6. dilate [*di•late*]

7. powerful [*pow•er•ful*]

TEACHING TIP

Extension. To emphasize map-reading skills, you may want to use the exercise below as an oral activity or to write the questions on the chalkboard for students to answer in writing.

1. Humacao is between which two mountain ranges, according to the map? [*the Sierra de Cayey and the Sierra de Luquillo*]

2. What town lies approximately halfway between Arecibo and Ponce? [*Utuado*]

3. What town is on the northwestern tip of the island? [*Aguadilla*]

4. Where is the Cordillera Central? [*It extends from the center to the southwest of the island*]

---

5. C **5.** First, we walked through a field in Humacao, which is located on the Caribbean Sea.

6. ie **6.** Then, we drove along the coast to Ponce, the island's cheif city after San Juan.

7. ei **7.** Continuing north from Ponce, we thought that we'd take a liesurely drive on the mountain road *Ruta Panoramica*, which means "Panoramic Road."

8. However, the road turned and twisted so much that I was relieved to get back on the main road.

8. ie

9. ie **9.** After we had a breif rest that afternoon, we explored the western part of the island.

10. ei **10.** Within a week, Puerto Rico no longer seemed foriegn to us.

–cede, –ceed, and –sede

25b. The only English word ending in *–sede* is *supersede*. The only English words ending in *–ceed* are *exceed*, *proceed*, and *succeed*. Most other words with this sound end in *–cede*.

EXAMPLES   con**cede**   re**cede**

               pre**cede**   se**cede**

Prefixes and Suffixes

A **prefix** is a letter or a group of letters added to the beginning of a word to change its meaning. A **suffix** is a letter or a group of letters added to the end of a word to change its meaning.

25c. When adding a prefix to a word, do not change the spelling of the word itself.

EXAMPLES   il + legal = il**legal**

un + natural = un**natural**

dis + appear = dis**appear**

mis + spent = mis**spent**

Exercise 4 **Spelling Words with Prefixes**

Spell each of the following words, adding the given prefix.

EXAMPLE   **1.** semi + circle

    1. semicircle

1. il + legible	**6.** mis + spell	**1.** illegible	**6.** misspell
2. un + necessary	**7.** dis + satisfy	**2.** unnecessary	**7.** dissatisfy
3. im + partial	**8.** dis + approve	**3.** impartial	**8.** disapprove
4. in + offensive	**9.** mis + understand	**4.** inoffensive	**9.** misunderstand
5. im + mortal	**10.** over + rule	**5.** immortal	**10.** overrule

25d. When adding the suffix *–ness* or *–ly* to a word, do not change the spelling of the word itself.

EXAMPLES   sudden + ness = **sudden**ness

truthful + ly = **truthful**ly

EXCEPTION   For most words that end in *y,* change the *y* to *i* before adding *–ly* or *–ness.*

kindly + ness = kindl**iness**   day + ly = da**ily**

25e. Drop the final silent *e* before adding a suffix beginning with a vowel.

EXAMPLES   nice + est = **nic**est

love + ing = **lov**ing

EXCEPTION   Keep the silent *e* in words ending in *ce* and *ge* before a suffix beginning with *a* or *o.*

notice + able = notic**eable**

courage + ous = courag**eous**

┌─ H E L P ───
Vowels are the letters *a, e, i, o, u,* and sometimes *y.* The other letters of the alphabet are consonants.

Relating to Vocabulary Skills

Explain to students that base words (*part, take*) can stand alone or combine with other word parts (*partly, mistake*). Word roots (*–dict–, –vis–*), like prefixes and suffixes, cannot stand alone and are combined with other word parts to form words (*dictionary, visible*).

Write on the chalkboard or a transparency the following base words and word roots.

base words: *verse, cycle, graph, gram*

word roots: *–loc–, –gest–, –crit–, –fer–*

Ask students to take a base word or word root and add a prefix, a suffix, or both to form a word. They should continue until they have at least five words.

When the whole class has finished, ask a few student volunteers to read their words out loud while you write the words on the chalkboard or a transparency. If any students have additional words, add them to the list on the chalkboard. Then, students can check the spelling of their own words.

MECHANICS

Relating to Literature

If Shel Silverstein's poem "Sarah Cynthia Sylvia Stout Would Not Take the Garbage Out" is available in students' literature textbooks, ask students to read the poem aloud and to look at the word at the end of each line. Ask students if any of these words conform to the spelling rules they have studied in this chapter [*ceilings, pie*]. Next, ask students to look at the words at the ends of lines 40 through 45; ask if a pronunciation rule could be derived from the spellings of these words. [*An a followed by a single consonant will usually have a long sound if that consonant is followed by an* e.]

To test the rule, divide the class into two teams and give each a dictionary. Ask one team to list as many words as it can find that follow the rule [*made, ace*], and ask the other to find as many exceptions as it can [*cadet, panel*]. If the team looking for exceptions finds as many or almost as many words as the other team, the rule must be declared invalid or must be further qualified.

FRANK & ERNEST reprinted by permission of Newspaper Enterprise Association, Inc.

25f. Keep the final silent e before adding a suffix that begins with a consonant.

EXAMPLES care + less = car**eless**

plate + ful = plat**eful**

false + hood = fals**ehood**

EXCEPTIONS argue + ment = argu**ment**

true + ly = tru**ly**

Exercise 5 Spelling Words with Suffixes

Spell each of the following words, adding the given suffix.

EXAMPLE **1.** like + able

　　　　　　1. likable

1. awful + ly	**8.** advance + ment	**15.** value + able
2. care + ful	**9.** true + ly	**16.** hope + ful
3. sincere + ly	**10.** courage + ous	**17.** grateful + ly
4. write + ing	**11.** notice + able	**18.** pleasant + ness
5. desire + able	**12.** brave + est	**19.** sore + est
6. change + able	**13.** accidental + ly	**20.** final + ly
7. cross + ing	**14.** pace + ing	

25g. For words ending in *y* preceded by a consonant, change the *y* to *i* before any suffix that does not begin with *i*.

EXAMPLES beauty + ful = beaut**iful**　mystery + ous = myster**ious**

carry + ing = carr**ying**　envy + able = env**iable**

EXCEPTIONS dry + ness = dr**yness**　fry + er = fr**yer**

Words ending in *y* preceded by a vowel do not change their spelling before a suffix.

EXAMPLES   key + ed = ke**yed**   buy + er = bu**yer**

                    pay + ment = pa**yment**   enjoy + ing = enjo**ying**

EXCEPTIONS   lay + ed = la**id**   say + ed = sa**id**   day + ly = da**ily**

25h. Double the final consonant before adding *–ing, –ed, –er,* or *–est* to a one-syllable word that ends in a single consonant preceded by a single vowel.

EXAMPLES   sit + ing = si**tt**ing   can + er = ca**nn**er

                    hop + ed = ho**pp**ed   flat + est = fla**tt**est

EXCEPTIONS   Do not double the final consonant in words ending in *w* or *x*.

                    mow + ed = mo**w**ed   tax + ing = ta**x**ing

For a one-syllable word ending in a single consonant that is not preceded by a single vowel, do not double the consonant before adding *–ing, –ed, –er,* or *–est.*

EXAMPLES   reap + ed = rea**p**ed   neat + est = nea**t**est

                    cold + er = col**d**er   hold + ing = hol**d**ing

In words of more than one syllable, the final consonant is usually not doubled before a suffix beginning with a vowel.

EXAMPLES   final + ist = fina**l**ist   center + ed = cente**r**ed

NOTE   In some cases, the final consonant may or may not be doubled.

EXAMPLES   cancel + ed = cance**l**ed *or* cance**ll**ed

                    travel + er = trave**l**er *or* trave**ll**er

Most dictionaries list both spellings for each word as correct.

Exercise 6   **Spelling Words with Suffixes**

Spell each of the twenty words on the following page, adding the given suffix.

EXAMPLE   **1.** beauty + ful

              1. beautiful

┌HELP─

When you are not sure about the spelling of a word, it is best to look it up in an up-to-date dictionary.

Spelling Words with Suffixes

ANSWERS

1. baying	11. swimmer
2. showed	12. tidier
3. dropped	13. hurried
4. denying	14. tapping
5. pitiless	15. cleaner
6. qualifier	16. folded
7. tripped	17. daily
8. employment	18. bountiful
9. happiest	19. fixing
10. hitting	20. helpful

Meeting INDIVIDUAL NEEDS

INCLUSION

Some students may benefit from three special techniques to identify spelling errors in their writing. The first strategy is to have students use rulers or pieces of paper to cover all but the sentences on which they are working. The second strategy is for the student to read through the selection, moving his or her fingers along under the words to check for words that do not sound or look right. A third strategy is for students to read passages backward to help them spot incorrect spellings.

Crossing the Curriculum

Social Studies. Point out to students that knowing how to spell correctly is important in any of their studies that involve writing. Ask the social studies teacher to provide you with a list of terms or place names that are frequently misspelled by students. Then, have students apply the spelling techniques they are learning to these words.

1. bay + ing	8. employ + ment	15. clean + er
2. show + ed	9. happy + est	16. fold + ed
3. drop + ed	10. hit + ing	17. day + ly
4. deny + ing	11. swim + er	18. bounty + ful
5. pity + less	12. tidy + er	19. fix + ing
6. qualify + er	13. hurry + ed	20. help + ful
7. trip + ed	14. tap + ing	

Review A **Proofreading Sentences for Correct Spelling**

Most of the following sentences contain a word that has been misspelled. Write each misspelled word correctly. If a sentence is already correct, write *C*.

EXAMPLE　　1. Have you seen the beautyful bonsai trees on display in the new garden center?

　　　　　　1. *beautiful*

1. C

2. proceed

3. inexpensive

4. choosing

5. careful

1. These trees can live to be hundreds of years old, yet you can quickly create one of your own in an afternoon.
2. Simply use these pictures to help you as you <u>procede</u> through the following steps.
3. First, you will need an <u>inxpensive</u> plant (such as a juniper), some soil, some moss, and a shallow bowl.
4. When you are <u>chooseing</u> a plant, try to get one with a trunk that has some of its roots showing above the soil so that your tree will look old.
5. Make a <u>carful</u> study of your plant, and decide how you want the bonsai to look in the bowl.

6. Then, cut or pinch away <u>undesireable</u> branches and leaves until the plant looks like a tree.

7. After <u>triming</u> your plant, remove most of the large roots so that the plant can stand in the bowl.

8. Cover the remaining roots with soil, and if the weather is mild, put your bonsai in a shaded place outside.

9. You don't have to water your plant <u>dayly</u>, but you should keep the soil moist.

10. After your plant has healed, you will have <u>succeded</u> in creating your very own bonsai.

6. undesirable

7. trimming

8. C

9. daily

10. succeeded

Forming the Plurals of Nouns

25i. Observe the following rules for spelling the plurals of nouns.

(1) To form the plurals of most nouns, add –s.

SINGULAR	girl	cheese	task	oat	banana
PLURAL	girl**s**	cheese**s**	task**s**	oat**s**	banana**s**

NOTE Make sure that you do not confuse the plural form of a noun with its possessive form. Generally, you should not use an apostrophe to form the plural of a word.

INCORRECT   The girl's raced to the stadium for soccer practice.

CORRECT   The **girls** raced to the stadium for soccer practice. [plural]

CORRECT   The **girls'** soccer team has practice today. [possessive]

(2) Form the plurals of nouns ending in s, x, z, ch, or sh by adding –es.

SINGULAR	moss	wax	Sanchez	birch	dish
PLURAL	moss**es**	wax**es**	Sanchez**es**	birch**es**	dish**es**

NOTE Some one-syllable words ending in z double the final consonant when forming plurals.

EXAMPLES	quiz	fez
	qui**zz**es	fe**zz**es

Reference Note

For a discussion of the **possessive forms of nouns,** see page 638. For information about **using an apostrophe and an s to form the plural of a letter, a numeral, a symbol, or a word used as a word,** see page 645.

Spelling Rules   **663**

RESOURCES

Forming the Plurals of Nouns
Practice
- *Grammar, Usage, and Mechanics*, pp. 336, 337, 338, 339, 340
- *Language Workshop CD-ROM*, Lesson 56

Forming the Plurals of Nouns

Rule 25i *(pp. 663–666)*

OBJECTIVE

■ To spell the plural forms of nouns

Meeting
INDIVIDUAL
NEEDS

ENGLISH-LANGUAGE LEARNERS
General Strategies. Some of your English-language learners might speak languages that have no plural forms or that have very regular plural forms. Periodically remind students of the importance of the rules by reviewing different rules on different days.

Looking at Language

Dialects. In some regional and ethnic dialects of English, the –s ending of plurals is not pronounced. If you have students who speak such dialects, remind them that standard English is used in business, mass media, and academia. Being able to switch between their native dialects and standard English will enable students to move easily in different segments of United States culture. You could ask students to read aloud a portion of text containing many plurals and to emphasize the –s endings on plurals, pronouncing them normally like the s sound in *lights* or the z sound in *phones*.

MECHANICS

MECHANICS

Critical Thinking

Evaluation. Point out to students that in some situations—especially in product labeling and advertising—phonetic, nonstandard spellings of words are used. For example, highway signs display the phonetic spelling of *through,* as in *thruway* and *thru street,* because the simplified version is easier and quicker to read from a moving vehicle. Similarly, in the names of many products, *lite* is substituted for *light* to make the name more catchy. Write on the chalkboard or a transparency the following list of words, and have students write possible phonetic spellings of the words: though, highway, tough, night, cheese, knight, rough, right [*tho, hiway, tuff, nite, cheez, nite, ruff, rite*]. Then, ask students if any of these phonetically spelled words would be confusing for the reader. [*Ruff* for rough *could be confusing because* ruff *is already a word.* Nite *for* knight *would be confusing because most people would think of* night *when they see* nite.]

┌─HELP─

When you are not sure about how to spell the plural of a noun ending in *f* or *fe,* look up the word in a dictionary.

Exercise 7 **Spelling the Plurals of Nouns**

Spell the plural form of each of the following nouns.

EXAMPLE   1. match
          1. matches

1. box es
2. crash es
3. sneeze s
4. address es
5. church es
6. tax es
7. Gómez es
8. ditch es
9. miss es
10. mask s
11. mix es
12. clip s
13. gym s
14. coach es
15. dash es
16. plate s
17. key s
18. pass es
19. Walsh es
20. business es

(3) Form the plurals of nouns ending in *y* preceded by a consonant by changing the *y* to *i* and adding *–es.*

| SINGULAR | lady | hobby | county | strawberry |
| PLURAL | lad**ies** | hobb**ies** | count**ies** | strawberr**ies** |

EXCEPTION   With proper nouns, simply add *s.*

the Appleby**s**   the Trilby**s**

(4) Form the plurals of nouns ending in *y* preceded by a vowel by adding *–s.*

| SINGULAR | toy | journey | highway | Wednesday |
| PLURAL | toy**s** | journey**s** | highway**s** | Wednesday**s** |

(5) Form the plurals of most nouns ending in *f* by adding *–s.* The plural form of some nouns ending in *f* or *fe* is formed by changing the *f* to *v* and adding *–es.*

| SINGULAR | gulf | belief | knife | loaf | wolf |
| PLURAL | gulf**s** | belief**s** | kni**ves** | loa**ves** | wol**ves** |

(6) Form the plurals of nouns ending in *o* preceded by a vowel by adding *–s.*

| SINGULAR | video | ratio | patio | Romeo |
| PLURAL | video**s** | ratio**s** | patio**s** | Romeo**s** |

(7) The plural form of many nouns ending in *o* preceded by a consonant is formed by adding *–es.*

| SINGULAR | veto | hero | tomato | potato |
| PLURAL | veto**es** | hero**es** | tomato**es** | potato**es** |

EXCEPTION   silo—silo**s**

MINI-LESSON

Spelling and Agreement. Remind students that when they make a subject noun plural in a sentence by adding an *s,* they often must remove an *s* from the verb to make the verb plural. For example, *The*

horse gallops becomes *The horses gallop.*

Write the following sentences on the chalkboard or a transparency. Ask students to rewrite each sentence, making the subject noun plural and changing the form of

NOTE With proper nouns, simply add –s.

EXAMPLES the Sato**s** the Korolenko**s**

However, you should form the plural of most musical terms ending in *o* preceded by a consonant by adding –s.

SINGULAR	piano	alto	solo	trio
PLURAL	piano**s**	alto**s**	solo**s**	trio**s**

NOTE To form the plural of some nouns ending in *o* preceded by a consonant, you may add either –*s* or –*es*.

SINGULAR	banjo	mosquito	flamingo
PLURAL	banjo**s**	mosquito**s**	flamingo**s**
	or	*or*	*or*
	banjo**es**	mosquito**es**	flamingo**es**

The best way to determine the plural forms of words ending in *o* preceded by a consonant is to check their spelling in an up-to-date dictionary.

(8) The plurals of some nouns are formed in irregular ways.

SINGULAR	man	mouse	foot	ox	child
PLURAL	m**en**	m**ice**	f**eet**	ox**en**	child**ren**

Exercise 8 Spelling the Plurals of Nouns

Spell the plural form of each of the following nouns.

EXAMPLE　**1.** industry
　　　　　1. industries

1. turkey͜s
2. studio͜s
3. chief͜s
4. soprano͜s
5. pupp͜ies
6. sel͜ves
7. chimney͜s
8. bab͜ies
9. tomato͜es
10. echo͜es
11. ferr͜ies
12. joy͜s
13. li͜ves
14. hero͜es
15. bluff͜s
16. radio͜s
17. lobb͜ies
18. wi͜ves
19. f͜eet
20. Whitby͜s

STYLE TIP

When it refers to the computer device, the word *mouse* can form a plural in two ways: *mouses* or *mice*. Someday one form may be the preferred style. For now, either is correct.

the verb to agree with the subject. Then, ask volunteers to provide answers.
　The thief has escaped. [*thieves have*]
　The kitty you found belongs to my sister. [*kitties belong*]

The fax I sent you doesn't have all the information. [*faxes don't*]
　Our dog gets out of the yard often. [*dogs get*]

TEACHING TIP

Review B You may wish to use the first ten items in **Review B** as guided practice. Then, have students complete the review as independent practice.

Review B **Spelling the Plurals of Nouns**

ANSWERS

1. side-wheelers
2. deer *or* deers
3. mothers-in-law
4. *A*'s
5. *hello*'s
6. thirteen-year-olds
7. aircraft
8. governors-elect
9. *O*'s
10. commanders in chief
11. maids of honor
12. runners-up
13. bookshelves
14. vice-presidents
15. *x*'s
16. lean-tos
17. Swiss
18. *$*'s
19. Japanese
20. *M*'s

Words Often Confused

(pp. 666–678)

OBJECTIVE

- To choose between words often confused

Reference Note

For more information on **compound nouns,** see page 337.

STYLE TIP

In your reading you may notice that some writers do not use apostrophes to form the plurals of numerals, letters, symbols, and words referred to as words. However, an apostrophe is not wrong, and it may be needed for clarity. Therefore, it is best to use the apostrophe.

---

(9) For most compound nouns written as one word, form the plural by adding *–s* or *–es.*

SINGULAR	textbook	grandfather	toothbrush
PLURAL	textbook**s**	grandfather**s**	toothbrush**es**

(10) For compound nouns in which one word is modified by the other word or words, form the plural of the word modified.

SINGULAR	sister-in-law	coat of arms	editor in chief
PLURAL	sister**s**-in-law	coat**s** of arms	editor**s** in chief

(11) Some nouns are the same in the singular and the plural.

SINGULAR AND PLURAL	moose	sheep	salmon
	Sioux	Chinese	spacecraft

(12) Form the plurals of numerals, letters, symbols, and words referred to as words by adding an apostrophe and *s.*

SINGULAR	1800	*B*	*i*	*&*	*that*
PLURAL	1800**'s**	*B***'s**	*i***'s**	*&***'s**	*that***'s**

Review B **Spelling the Plurals of Nouns**

Spell the plural form of each of the following nouns.

EXAMPLE 1. push-up
1. push-ups

1. side-wheeler	8. governor-elect	15. *x*
2. deer	9. *0*	16. lean-to
3. mother-in-law	10. commander in chief	17. Swiss
4. *A*	11. maid of honor	18. *$*
5. *hello*	12. runner-up	19. Japanese
6. thirteen-year-old	13. bookshelf	20. *M*
7. aircraft	14. vice-president	

Words Often Confused

People often confuse the words in each of the following groups. Some of these words are *homonyms*—that is, their pronunciations are the same. However, these words have different meanings and spellings. Other words in the following groups have the same or similar spellings yet have different meanings.

RESOURCES

Words Often Confused

Practice

- *Grammar, Usage, and Mechanics,* pp. 341, 342, 343, 344, 345
- *Language Workshop CD-ROM,* Lessons 57, 58

accept	[verb] *to receive; to agree to* The Lanfords would not *accept* our gift.
except	[preposition] *with the exclusion of; but* Everyone *except* Lauren agreed with Selena.
advice	[noun] *a recommendation for action* What is your mother's *advice*?
advise	[verb] *to recommend a course of action* She *advises* me to take the job.
affect	[verb] *to act upon; to change* Does bad weather *affect* your health?
effect	[noun] *result; consequence* What *effect* does the weather have on your health?
already	[adverb] *previously* We have *already* studied the customs of the Navajo people.
all ready	[adjective] *all prepared; in readiness* The crew is *all ready* to set sail.
all right	[adjective] *correct; satisfactory; safe;* [adverb] *adequately* Jesse will be *all right* when his injury heals. We did *all right,* didn't we?

┌─HELP─

All right is the only acceptable spelling. The spelling *alright* is not considered standard usage.

Exercise 9 **Choosing Between Words Often Confused**

From each pair in parentheses, choose the word or words that will make the sentence correct.

EXAMPLE   **1.** All of us (*accept, except*) Josh forgot our tickets.
   1. except

1. By the time Melba arrived, Roscoe had (*already, all ready*) baked the sweet potatoes.
2. One duty of the Cabinet is to (*advice, advise*) the president.
3. The soft music had a soothing (*affect, effect*) on the child.
4. The girls were (*already, all ready*) for the sleigh ride.
5. The (*affect, effect*) of Buddhism on Japanese culture was huge.
6. By this time of year, the snow has melted everywhere (*accept, except*) in the mountains.

MECHANICS

Critical Thinking

Metacognition. Using the following questions, have students analyze the process they used in the **English-Language Learners** activity on p. 667.

- How did you begin looking for a homonym if one didn't come immediately to mind?

- Did you think about all the different ways the sounds in the word could be spelled?

- Did you write down the different possibilities as you thought of them?

- At what point, if ever, did you refer to a dictionary?

- Did you use the dictionary to find homonyms or to check possibilities you had thought of already?

- Are there some things you weren't aware of (for example, different possible spellings for particular sounds) that would have been useful?

- How did your strategies work?

- Would you do the exercise differently now? If so, how?

7. The doctor's (*advice, advise*) was to drink plenty of fluids and get a lot of rest.
8. Sarita was happy to (*accept, except*) the invitation to the party.
9. Reading the newspaper usually (*affects, effects*) my ideas about current events.
10. Do you think it would be (*alright, all right*) to leave before the end of the movie?

Reference Note

In the Glossary of Usage (Chapter 21), you can find many other words that are often confused or misused, or you can look them up in an up-to-date dictionary.

⌐ TIPS & TRICKS ⌐

Here is a sentence to help you remember the difference between *capital* and *capitol:* There is a d**o**me on the capit**o**l.

altar	[noun] *a table or stand at which religious rites are performed* There was a bowl of flowers on the *altar*.
alter	[verb] *to change* Another hurricane may *alter* the shoreline near our town.
altogether	[adverb] *entirely* It is *altogether* too cold for swimming.
all together	[adjective] *in the same place;* [adverb] *at the same time* *All together,* the class looked bigger than it was. Sing *all together* now.
brake	[noun] *a device to stop a machine* I used the emergency *brake* to prevent the car from rolling downhill.
break	[verb] *to fracture; to shatter* Don't *break* that mirror!
capital	[noun] *a city; the location of a government* What is the *capital* of this state?
capitol	[noun] *a building; statehouse* The *capitol* is on Congress Avenue.
choose	[verb, rhymes with *lose*] *to select* We *choose* activities today in gym class.
chose	[verb, past tense of *choose*] We *chose* activities yesterday.
cloths	[noun] *pieces of cloth* I need some more cleaning *cloths*.
clothes	[noun] *wearing apparel* I decided to put on warm *clothes*.

Exercise 10 Choosing Between Words Often Confused

From each pair in parentheses, choose the <u>word or words that</u> <u>will make the sentence correct.</u>

EXAMPLE **1.** If it rains, we will (*altar, alter*) our plans.

1. *alter*

1. My summer (*cloths,* <u>*clothes*</u>) are loose and light.
2. In England, you can still see remains of (*altars, alters*) built by ancient peoples.
3. A bicyclist can wear out a set of (<u>*brakes,*</u> *breaks*) quickly.
4. You should use soft (<u>*cloths,*</u> *clothes*) to clean silver.
5. The cold weather did not (*altar,* <u>*alter*</u>) Ling's plans for the Chinese New Year celebration.
6. Accra is the (<u>*capital,*</u> *capitol*) of Ghana.
7. Keep the pieces of the vase (*altogether,* <u>*all together*</u>), and I will try to repair it.
8. Did he (<u>*choose,*</u> *chose*) a partner during class yesterday?
9. On the dome of the (*capital,* <u>*capitol*</u>) stands a large statue.
10. The audience was (<u>*altogether,*</u> *all together*) charmed by the mime's performance.

coarse	[adjective] *rough; crude; not fine* The *coarse* sand acts as a filter.
course	[noun] *path of action; series of studies;* [also used in the expression *of course*] What is the best *course* for me to take? You may change your mind, of *course*.
complement	[verb] *to make complete;* [noun] *some-* *thing that completes* The piano music *complemented* Ardene's violin solo. Red shoes are a good *complement* to that outfit.
compliment	[verb] *to praise someone;* [noun] *praise* *from someone* Mrs. Katz *complimented* Jean on her persuasive speech. Thank you for the *compliment*.

(continued)

Timesaver

After students have completed any of the exercises, you may want to have them exchange papers to mark corrections as you write on the chalkboard or a transparency the answers to the exercises.

Meeting INDIVIDUAL NEEDS

LEARNERS HAVING DIFFICULTY

Students might need extra help to become proficient with homonyms. Write the following pairs of words on the chalkboard, and ask volunteers to circle the letter or letters that differentiate each pair. Next, ask students to copy the words, circling the differentiating letter or letters, and to write the definitions of the words next to them. (Definitions are available in this chapter in alphabetical order.)

1. altar, alter [*a, e*]

2. stationary, stationery [*a, e*]

3. their, there [*ir, re*]

4. threw, through [*ew, ough*]

5. weak, week [*a, e*]

6. capital, capitol [*a, o*]

MECHANICS

Relating to Vocabulary Skills

Students can sometimes improve their spelling skills and expand their vocabularies by building related words from a word they are learning. To model this process, ask the class to think of words related to *popular* and list the words on the chalkboard [*population, popularity, populous, populate, populace, unpopular, depopulate*]. If students run out of ideas, show them how to add prefixes and suffixes and to consult a dictionary to build and find more related words. Ask the class to tell you the word root and meaning that all these words have in common [*–popul–* <L *popularis, populus,* "people"]. Have student volunteers tell in their own words the meanings of all the related words and how they relate to the root word.

Then, write on the chalkboard or a transparency the following list of words: *advice, alter, break, jury.* Ask students to work in groups of three to brainstorm related words and to write down each word's root or base word and its meaning. One member of the group should serve as scribe. Students may consult dictionaries. After the groups are finished, appoint a class member to record student responses on kraft paper. Then, read aloud a word from the list and have a student volunteer give the word root or base word and its meaning. Have each group in turn call out one of the words related to the base or root. Continue until all the related words are listed, and then post the list in the classroom.

(continued)

council	[noun] *a group called together to accomplish a job* The mayor's *council* has seven members.
counsel	[noun] *advice;* [verb] *to give advice* He needs legal *counsel* on this matter. His attorney will *counsel* him before the hearing.
councilor	[noun] *a member of a council* The mayor appointed seven *councilors*.
counselor	[noun] *one who advises* Mr. Jackson is the guidance *counselor* for the seventh grade.
desert	[noun, pronounced des'•ert] *a dry, barren, sandy region; a wilderness* This cactus grows only in the *desert*.
desert	[verb, pronounced de•sert'] *to abandon; to leave* A good sport does not *desert* his or her teammates.
dessert	[noun, pronounced des•sert'] *a sweet, final course of a meal* Let's have fresh peaches for *dessert*.

Exercise 11 Choosing Between Words Often Confused

From each pair in parentheses, choose the word that will make the sentence correct.

EXAMPLE **1.** At the end of dinner, we ate a (*desert, dessert*) made of fresh fruits and berries mixed with frozen yogurt.

     1. dessert

1. The city (*council, counsel*) will not meet unless seven of the ten (*councilors, counselors*) are present.
2. The patient received (*council, counsel*) from the doctor on the best (*coarse, course*) to a speedy recovery.
3. Chutney and yogurt (*complement, compliment*) an Indian meal very well.
4. When we were staying in Cairo last year, we saw the Nile River, of (*coarse, course*).

5. Edward is preparing the enchiladas, and I'm making empanadas for (*desert*, *dessert*) tonight.
6. Marilyn made a hand puppet out of (*coarse*, *course*) burlap, buttons, and felt.
7. We all know the major would not (*desert*, *dessert*) her regiment for any reason.
8. Please, I am asking for your (*council*, *counsel*), not your (*complements*, *compliments*).
9. My mother and father both took part in the (*dessert*, *desert*) hiking trip last week.
10. What did you think when our camp (*councilor*, *counselor*) (*complemented*, *complimented*) us on our endurance?

formally	[adverb] *with dignity; following strict rules or procedures* We must behave *formally* at the reception.
formerly	[adverb] *previously; at an earlier date* *Formerly,* people thought travel to the moon was impossible.
hear	[verb] *to receive sounds through the ears* You can *hear* a whisper through these walls.
here	[adverb] *in this place* How long have you lived *here*?
its	[possessive form of the pronoun *it*] *belonging to it* That book has lost *its* cover.
it's	[contraction of *it is* or *it has*] *It's* [It is] the coldest winter I can remember. *It's* [It has] been a long time.
lead	[verb, rhymes with *feed*] *to go first; to be a leader* Can she *lead* us out of this tunnel?
led	[verb, past tense of *lead*] *went first* Elizabeth Blackwell *led* the movement for hospital reform.
lead	[noun, rhymes with *red*] *a heavy metal; graphite used in a pencil* There is no longer any *lead* in lead pencils.

(continued)

Words Often Confused   **671**

Cooperative Learning

The following exercise gives students an opportunity to create a game with often-confused words. Divide the class into groups of three students each, and assign each team confusing words from this chapter.

Among the groups, divide up the list of words often confused from pp. 667–677. Leave out any word that contains apostrophes. Make sure each group has at least eight words. Students in each group will work together to make a grid of one hundred squares, with ten squares going down and ten across. They will write their words in the grid, with one letter in each square, fill in the remaining squares with random letters, and write short clues for each hidden word. The words can be placed in any direction, including diagonally. Groups should check their words against the spelling in the textbook. Have each group make three copies of its puzzle, and then have groups exchange puzzles so that each student has a puzzle to work. Ask students to study the clues and to draw a circle around each word they find. After students have finished working the puzzles, you could post the original unworked puzzles with their clues on a bulletin board.

(continued)

loose	[adjective, rhymes with *moose*] *not tight* This belt is too *loose.*
lose	[verb, rhymes with the verb *use*] *to suffer loss* Fran will *lose* the race if she panics.
passed	[verb, past tense of *pass*] *went by* He *passed* us five minutes ago.
past	[noun] *time that has gone by;* [preposition] *beyond;* [adjective] *ended* Good historians make the *past* come alive. We rode *past* your house. That era is *past.*

Exercise 12 **Choosing Between Words Often Confused**

From each pair in parentheses, choose the word that will make the sentence correct.

EXAMPLE 1. Kaya (*lead, led*) us to the ceremonial lodge.

1. *led*

1. The woman who (*formally, formerly*) (*lead, led*) the band now teaches music in Alaska.
2. We do not expect to (*loose, lose*) any of our backfield players this year.
3. We (*passed, past*) three stalled cars this morning on our way to school.
4. "Why did you (*lead, led*) us (*hear, here*)?" the bewildered tourist demanded.
5. Can you (*hear, here*) the difference between the CD and the digital audio tape?
6. The workers removed the (*lead, led*) pipes from the old house and replaced them with copper ones.
7. Has the (*loose, lose*) bolt lost (*its, it's*) washer and nut?
8. The guests are to dress (*formally, formerly*) for the governor's inauguration ball.
9. "I think (*it's, its*) time for a pop spelling quiz," announced Mrs. Ferrari.
10. Has the last school bus of the morning already gone (*passed, past*) our street, Tiffany?

peace	[noun] *quiet order and security* World *peace* is the goal of the United Nations.
piece	[noun] *a part of something* Lian bought that *piece* of silk in Hong Kong.
plain	[adjective] *unadorned, simple, common;* [noun] *flat area of land* Jeans were part of his *plain* appearance. A broad, treeless *plain* stretched before them.
plane	[noun] *a flat surface; a tool; an airplane* The movers pushed the couch up an inclined *plane* and into the truck. I have just used a carpenter's *plane*. Have you ever flown in a *plane*?
principal	[noun] *the head of a school;* [adjective] *chief, main* Our *principal* spoke of his *principal* duties. I outlined the *principal* ideas.
principle	[noun] *a rule of conduct; a fundamental truth* Action should be guided by *principles*.
quiet	[adjective] *still and peaceful; without noise* The forest was very *quiet*.
quite	[adverb] *wholly or entirely; to a great extent* Some students are already *quite* sure of their career plans.
shone	[verb, past tense of *shine*] *gleamed; glowed* The moon *shone* softly over the grass in the silent meadow.
shown	[verb, past participle of *show*] *revealed; demonstrated* Tamisha has *shown* me how to crochet.

NOTE *Shine* can mean "to direct the light of" or "to polish," but the preferred past tense form for these meanings is *shined,* not *shone.*

EXAMPLES   The firefighters **shined** a light into the attic.

Elton **shined** his shoes before the dance.

| TIPS & TRICKS |

Here is a way to remember the difference between *peace* and *piece.* You eat a p**ie**ce of p**ie**.

| TIPS & TRICKS |

To remember the spelling of *principal,* use this sentence: The princi**pal** is your **pal.**

Relating to Dictionary Skills

The activity described here gives students an opportunity to practice their spelling techniques by playing a game with a dictionary. Model the game for students by opening a student dictionary to any page and picking a fairly common word. Tell students the guide words listed at the top of the page, and give some hints about the word, such as what part of speech it is or what it means. For example, for *suspect* you could say, "The guide words are *surprisedly* and *suspend.* A verb, this word means 'to believe without real proof that someone is bad, wrong, or guilty.' What's the word?" You can keep giving more clues, such as how many letters are in the word, until someone guesses the word and spells it. Then, have students pair up and play the game. They should switch roles with each new word, with one student presenting the clue and the other giving the answer.

MECHANICS

Viewing the Art

Portrait of an Old Man
About the Artist. Rembrandt (whose full name was Rembrandt Harmensz van Rijn) was born in 1606 in Leiden, the Netherlands.

Rembrandt learned how to paint and draw by serving as an apprentice to several successful artists, including Jacob van Swanenburgh and master artist Pieter Lastman.

Rembrandt moved to Amsterdam at the age of twenty-five and lived there until he died in 1669. His paintings are highly prized by museums and collectors, and reproductions of them appear in many books.

Exercise 13 Choosing Between Words Often Confused

From each pair in parentheses, choose the word that will make the sentence correct.

EXAMPLE   1. Mr. Ramírez used a (*plain, plane*) to smooth the board.
   1. *plane*

1. Each drop of water (*shone, shown*) like crystal.
2. Motor vehicles are one of the (*principal, principle*) sources of air pollution in our cities.
3. If you don't hurry, you will miss your (*plain, plane*).
4. The (*principals, principles*) of justice and trust can lead to world (*peace, piece*).
5. Jan has (*shone, shown*) me how to change a tire.
6. It is clear that Luisa is acting on (*principal, principle*), not from a personal motive.
7. On Christmas Eve we each have a (*peace, piece*) of fruitcake.
8. "The bake sale was (*quiet, quite*) successful," said Gloria.
9. "For once," the (*principal, principle*) announced with a smile, "you do not have to be (*quiet, quite*)."
10. (*Plain, Plane*) fruits and vegetables can be delicious.

—HELP—
Some sentences in Review C contain more than one spelling error.

Review C Proofreading for Words Often Confused

Identify the misspelled words in the following sentences. Then, give the correct spelling of each word.

EXAMPLE   1. Portraits of people do not have to be plane.
   1. *plane—plain*

1. Some portraits have a striking affect. **1.** effect
2. A vivid portrait can often make people from the passed seem alive. **2.** past
3. The painting on the left is by Rembrandt, one of the principle painters of the seventeenth century. **3.** principal
4. The portrait, probably of a rabbi in the city of Amsterdam, is quiet lovely. **4.** quite
5. It's detail shows why Rembrandt was such a popular portrait artist. **5.** Its
6. The painting illustrates one of Rembrandt's main artistic principals, the strong contrast between light and dark. **6.** principles
7. Light has shown only on the rabbi's face, hands, and a peace of his clothing. **7.** shone/piece

8. The rest of the painting is <u>quiet</u> dark, highlighting these lighted features. **8.** quite

9. The rabbi is <u>shone</u> in a state of <u>piece</u>, and the lack of detail in the painting gives an impression of <u>quite</u> elegance.

9. shown, peace, quiet

10. Rembrandt is <u>excepted</u> as a great artist because of his ability to give life to the human form. **10.** accepted

stationary	[adjective] *in a fixed position* Is that chalkboard *stationary*?
stationery	[noun] *writing paper* Do you have any white *stationery*?
than	[conjunction used in comparisons] Alaska is bigger *than* Texas.
then	[adverb] *at that time* If we meet, we can talk about it *then*.
their	[possessive form of the pronoun *they*] *belonging to them* Can you understand *their* message?
there	[adverb] *at or to that place;* [also used to begin a sentence] Let's meet *there*. *There* are toys hidden inside the piñata.
they're	[contraction of *they are*] *They're* all from Guam.
threw	[verb, past tense of *throw*] *hurled; tossed* Ted *threw* me the mitt.
through	[preposition] *in one side and out the opposite side* I can't see *through* the lens.

┌─────────────────┐
| TIPS & TRICKS |
└─────────────────┘

Here is an easy way to remember the difference between *stationary* and *stationery:* You write a lett**er** on station**er**y.

MECHANICS

Exercise 14 **Choosing Between Words Often Confused**

From each pair or group in parentheses, choose the <u>word that will make the sentence correct</u>.

EXAMPLE   **1.** (*Their, They're, There*) first rehearsal is after school.

        1. Their

1. The stars appear to be (*stationary, stationery*), but we know that (*their, there, they're*) moving at very high speeds.
2. Thailand is much larger (*than, then*) South Korea.

Words Often Confused   **675**

ENGLISH-LANGUAGE LEARNERS
General Strategies. English-language learners might be unsure of how to spell a word they hear or how to pronounce a word they see. English-proficient speakers who have not memorized spellings will make educated guesses based on the usual spellings of certain sounds or on similarities to other words they know. Some English-language learners, however, might not be able to distinguish subtle differences between some English sounds, know which spellings are more usual, or have the vocabularies to make analogies. Pointing out the various ways to spell certain sounds and giving practice with comparing similar words may help students minimize mistakes.

3. That noise is from a jet plane going (*threw*, *through*) the sound barrier.
4. The pitcher (*threw*, *through*) a curveball.
5. A (*stationary*, *stationery*) store usually sells paper, pencils, and other writing supplies.
6. We started our trip in Barcelona and (*than*, *then*) traveled west to Madrid.
7. The girls completed (*their*, *there*, *they're*) displays for the science fair.
8. Is a moving target much harder to hit (*than*, *then*) a (*stationary*, *stationery*) one?
9. Each time Chris got a free throw, he lobbed the ball neatly (*threw*, *through*) the net to score one point.
10. The children in the back seat kept asking, "When will we get (*their*, *they're*, *there*)?"

to	[preposition] *in the direction of; toward* [also used before the base form of a verb] We are going *to* Mexico *to* visit Gabriel.
too	[adverb] *also; more than enough* Audrey is going, *too.* Kazuo used *too* much miso, so the soup was salty.
two	[adjective or noun] *one plus one* We bought *two* sets of chopsticks before we left the restaurant.
waist	[noun] *the midsection of the body* The anchor of the tug-of-war team wrapped the rope around her *waist.*
waste	[verb] *to use foolishly;* [noun] *a needless expense* Try not to *waste* all your film now. Rodney did not agree that golf is a *waste* of time.
weak	[adjective] *feeble; not strong* Melinda's illness has left her very *weak.*
week	[noun] *seven days* We'll wait for at least a *week.*

weather	[noun] *the condition of the atmosphere* The *weather* seems to be changing.
whether	[conjunction] *if* We do not know *whether* we should expect rain.
who's	[contraction of *who is* or *who has*] *Who's* [Who is] going to the museum? "*Who's* [Who has] been eating my porridge?" asked Papa Bear.
whose	[possessive form of the pronoun *who*] *belonging to whom* *Whose* report was the most original?
your	[possessive form of the pronoun *you*] *belonging to you* What is *your* middle name?
you're	[contraction of *you are*] *You're* my best friend.

Exercise 15   Choosing Between Words Often Confused

From each pair or group in parentheses, choose the <u>word that will make the sentence correct</u>.

EXAMPLE   **1.** What are (*your, you're*) plans for celebrating Juneteenth?

     1. *your*

1. (*Who's, Whose*) the present secretary of state of the United States, Elaine?
2. My stepsister and I built (*to, too, two*) snow forts on our front lawn yesterday.
3. "(*Your, You're*) late," my friend complained.
4. Would you be able to stand the (*weather, whether*) in Alaska?
5. That sounds like a (*weak, week*) excuse to me.
6. (*Your, You're*) dog is (*to, too, two*) sleepy to learn any new tricks today.
7. "(*Who's, Whose*) boots are these?" Mrs. Allen asked.
8. The pilot must decide very quickly (*weather, whether*) she should parachute to safety or try to land the crippled plane.

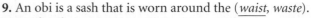

9. An obi is a sash that is worn around the (*waist, waste*).

10. My family is going (*to, too, two*) New Orleans.

Review D **Choosing Between Words Often Confused**

From each pair or group in parentheses, choose the word that will make the sentence correct.

EXAMPLE   My parents asked my **[1]** (*advice, advise*) about where we should spend our vacation.

      1. advice

My family could not decide **[1]** (*weather, whether*) to visit Boston or Philadelphia. Finally, we all agreed on Boston, the **[2]** (*capital, capitol*) of Massachusetts. We drove **[3]** (*to, too, two*) the city one week later. Even my parents could not conceal **[4]** (*their, there, they're*) excitement. We did not **[5]** (*loose, lose*) a moment. Boston **[6]** (*formally, formerly*) was "the hub of the universe," and we discovered that **[7]** (*it's, its*) still a truly fascinating city.

Everyone in my family **[8]** (*accept, except*) me had eaten lobster, and I ate it for the first time there in Boston. I was not **[9]** (*altogether, all together*) certain how to eat the lobster, but my doubt did not **[10]** (*affect, effect*) my appetite. My parents insisted that pear yogurt was a strange **[11]** (*desert, dessert*) to follow lobster, but I would not **[12]** (*altar, alter*) my order. After the pear yogurt, I thought about ordering a small **[13]** (*peace, piece*) of pie, but I decided to keep **[14]** (*quiet, quite*).

While in Boston, we walked up and down the streets just to **[15]** (*hear, here*) the Bostonians' accents. **[16]** (*Their, There, They're*) especially noted for **[17]** (*their, there, they're*) pronunciation of *a*'s and *r*'s.

We had been in Boston for only a week or so when the **[18]** (*weather, whether*) bureau predicted a big snowstorm for the area. Since we had not taken the proper **[19]** (*cloths, clothes*) for snow, we decided to return home. On the way back, we were **[20]** (*already, all ready*) making plans for another visit to Boston.

MECHANICS

Chapter Review

A. Identifying Misspelled Words

Identify the misspelled word in each of the following groups of words. Then, write the correct spelling of the word.

1. height, weight, <u>cheif</u> **1.** chief
2. succeed, <u>supercede</u>, proceed **2.** supersede
3. <u>unecessary</u>, unavailable, unusual **3.** unnecessary
4. <u>happyly</u>, finally, truly **4.** happily
5. said, paid, <u>keyd</u> **5.** keyed
6. cleaner, tapping, <u>driped</u> **6.** dripped
7. taxes, buzzes, <u>foxs</u> **7.** foxes
8. switches, <u>mixs</u>, keys **8.** mixes
9. <u>knifes</u>, tomatoes, solos **9.** knives
10. mothers-in-law, <u>father-in-laws</u>, drive-ins **10.** fathers-in-law
11. achieve, <u>feirce</u>, friend **11.** fierce
12. <u>mowwer</u>, followed, staying **12.** mower
13. acquire, <u>arguement</u>, always **13.** argument
14. tired, <u>trys</u>, guess **14.** tries
15. <u>noticable</u>, yield, daily **15.** noticeable
16. staying, priceless, <u>easyer</u> **16.** easier
17. <u>halfs</u>, coughs, princesses **17.** halves
18. heating, <u>hiting</u>, trying **18.** hitting
19. <u>changable</u>, drinkable, smiling **19.** changeable
20. misspell, <u>ilegible</u>, unnoticed **20.** illegible

B. Writing the Correct Plural Form

Write the correct plural form of each of the following words.

21. boss‸es
22. thief‸ves
23. sheep [no change]
24. wom‸en

25. freeway‸s
26. ten-year-old‸s
27. Vietnamese [no change]

28. 3‸'s
29. cit‸ies
30. soprano‸s

Using the Chapter Review

To assess student progress, you may want to compare the types of items missed on the **Diagnostic Preview** to those missed on the **Chapter Review**. If students have not made significant progress, you may want to refer them to **Exercises 36–37** in **Chapter 26: Correcting Common Errors** for additional practice.

MECHANICS

C. Choosing Between Words Often Confused

In each of the following sentences, choose the underlined correct word from the pair in parentheses.

31. Have you (*already*, *all ready*) adopted a kitten from the animal shelter?

32. Although it's only July, the store already has a display of winter (*cloths*, *clothes*).

33. "I believe that both candidates for senator have very high (*principals*, *principles*)," my aunt said.

34. The sophomore (*councilor*, *counselor*) is working on next year's class schedules.

35. The moon is (*quiet*, *quite*) bright this evening.

36. Not getting enough exercise can (*effect*, *affect*) your health.

37. You must (*formally*, *formerly*) declare your interest in joining the club by filling out the membership card.

38. My (*advise*, *advice*) is that you buy a mountain bike.

39. (*Its*, *It's*) hard to believe that the leatherback turtle can grow to be seven feet long!

40. The fabric on the couch in Dr. Alexander's waiting room is (*course*, *coarse*) and scratchy.

D. Identifying Misused Words

In many of the following sentences, one word has been misused because it has been confused for another word. Write each underlined incorrectly used word. Then, write the word that should have been used. If a sentence is already correct, write *C*.

41. alter	**41.** An editor will <u>altar</u> this manuscript.
42. dessert	**42.** We had fruit and sherbet for <u>desert</u>.
43. C	**43.** I thanked Mr. Chu for the compliment.
44. here	**44.** While you are <u>hear</u>, use this towel.
45. passed	**45.** Eventually, winter <u>past</u> and spring arrived.
46. C	**46.** Maria received a box of stationery for her birthday.
47. than	**47.** The blue chair is more comfortable <u>then</u> the green one.
48. weather	**48.** The <u>whether</u> report comes on right after the news.
49. Who's	**49.** <u>Whose</u> the man speaking to Officer Grant?
50. accept	**50.** The town voted to <u>except</u> the gift of a new library wing.

RESOURCES

Spelling

Review

- *Grammar, Usage, and Mechanics,* pp. 346, 347, 348, 349, 350

Assessment

- *Assessment Package*
  —*Chapter Tests,* Ch. 25
  —*Chapter Tests in Standardized Test Formats,* Ch. 25
- *Test Generator (One-Stop Planner CD-ROM)*

Writing Application
Using Correct Spelling in a Review

Spelling Words Correctly   Write a one- or two-paragraph review of your favorite book or movie. Be sure to use at least five of the words listed as Words Often Confused in this chapter.

Prewriting   Pick a favorite book or movie and make a list of the reasons that you prefer it over other books or movies. If you decide to write about a book, for example, you may want to compare it to a film that is based on that book.

Writing   As you write your first draft, be sure to include information about the book or film, such as who wrote it, who directed it, and who stars in it. Remember to use a dictionary to help with correct spelling.

Revising   Evaluate your draft and revise it to improve its content, organization, and style. Add sensory details that make the story come alive for the reader. Replace clichés and worn-out verbs and nouns with fresher, more precise words.

Publishing   Check your paragraph for spelling mistakes. Use a computer spellchecker if one is available, but remember that spellcheckers will not recognize a misused word (for example, *piece* for *peace*), as opposed to a misspelled word. Also, pay attention to the spelling of words in languages other than English, and consult a dictionary if you have any doubt. Exchange your report with a partner, and check each other's spelling.

You and your classmates may want to gather the class's reviews and create a bulletin board display of favorite books and movies.

Writing Application
(p. 681)

OBJECTIVE

- To write a book review correctly using five words from the list of words often confused

Writing Application

Tip. You may wish to have students make a list of the words they most often confuse and consider if those words would be appropriate to include in their reviews.

Scoring Rubric. While you will want to pay particular attention to students' use of words often confused, you will also want to evaluate overall writing performance. You may want to give a split score to indicate development and clarity of the review as well as spelling skills.

MECHANICS

RESOURCES

Writing Application
Extension
- *Grammar, Usage, and Mechanics,* p. 353
- *Language Workshop CD-ROM,* Lessons 55–58

TEACHING TIP

The number of each word group in the **Spelling Words** list corresponds to a lesson number in the *Spelling* workbook.

Lesson 1: OBJECTIVE
- To spell compound words

Lesson 2: OBJECTIVE
- To spell pairs of homophones

Lesson 3: OBJECTIVE
- To spell verb forms with *–ed* and *–ing* endings

Lesson 4: OBJECTIVE
- To spell English words that come from Spanish

Lesson 5: OBJECTIVE
- To spell words related to the field of music

Lesson 7: OBJECTIVE
- To spell words with the prefixes *en–* and *ex–*

Lesson 8: OBJECTIVE
- To spell words with the prefixes *de–* and *dis–*

Lesson 9: OBJECTIVE
- To spell the names of countries and continents and words derived from them

Lesson 10: OBJECTIVE
- To spell words that begin with forms of the prefix *ad–*

Lesson 11: OBJECTIVE
- To spell words with the adjective suffixes *–some, –ish, –ine,* and *–ward*

Lesson 12: OBJECTIVE
- To spell words that contain sounds often omitted in speech

Lesson 14: OBJECTIVE
- To spell words with the noun suffixes *–ary, –ory, –ery,* and *–ury*

Lesson 15: OBJECTIVE
- To spell multisyllabic words that include double consonants

Lesson 16: OBJECTIVE
- To spell word pairs that end with the suffixes *–ar* and *–ation* or *–le* and *–ular*

Spelling Words

1
- offshore
  strawberry
  daylight
  seaweed
  wildlife
  grandparents
  moonlight
  chairperson
  killer whale
  watermelon
  headache
  typewrite

2
- shoot
  mist
  birth
  swayed
  shown
  tied
  pane
  shone
  reel
  berth
  chute
  suede

3
- gathered
  hammered
  controlling
  bothering
  ruined
  listening
  studying
  swallowed
  permitting
  carrying
  compelled
  groaned

4
- cafeteria
  alligator
  corral
  vanilla
  mosquito
  stampede
  guitar
  coyote
  jaguar
  chili

cocoa
tortillas

5
- classical
  conductor
  concert
  instrument
  clarinet
  banjo
  bugle
  harmony
  pianist
  performance
  violin
  rehearsal

7
- express
  envelope
  extend
  excitement
  exceed
  explode
  enthusiasm
  enclose
  expand
  exclaim
  exclude
  excel

8
- defeat
  destroyed
  decline
  defects
  disabled
  disappeared
  disappointment
  dependent
  deduction
  disadvantages
  disguised
  dissolved

9
- Spanish
  Greek
  England
  African
  French
  Spain
  Vietnam

Australia
Japanese
Greece
Australian
Vietnamese

10
- arrange
  accommodate
  announced
  approaching
  accepted
  appoint
  accompanying
  array
  arrangements
  accomplish
  accelerate
  annoy

11
- selfish
  marine
  greenish
  awkward
  wholesome
  grayish
  childish
  masculine
  feminine
  reddish
  genuine
  awesome

12
- temperature
  strength
  length
  vegetable
  arctic
  twelfth
  probably
  jewelry
  literature
  boundary
  reference
  beverage

14
- machinery
  discovery
  nursery
  dictionary
  century
  injury
  missionary
  territory
  scenery
  revolutionary
  treasury
  luxury

15
- barrier
  corridor
  umbrella
  buffalo
  gorilla
  pinnacle
  syllable
  tobacco
  massacre
  opossum
  moccasins
  cinnamon

16
- muscular
  triangle
  muscle
  circular
  regulation
  particles
  particular
  rectangle
  vehicles
  rectangular
  triangular
  vehicular

17
- doubtful
  specialist
  misfortune
  fortunate
  unfortunate
  especially
  specific
  specifications
  judicial
  judgment

Lesson 17: OBJECTIVE
- To spell words with the Latin roots *–dub–/–doubt–, –jud–/–judg–, –fors–/–fort–,* and *–spec–*

Lesson 18: OBJECTIVE
- To spell words with the verb-forming suffixes *–ize, –ate, –yze,* and *–ise*

prejudice
undoubtedly

18 • organize
cooperate
congratulate
exercise
calculate
illustrate
recognize
compromise
memorize
paralyze
criticize
inaugurate

20 • depositing
recess
televised
revised
position
constructing
composition
opposite
structures
destruction
vision
necessary

21 • existence
incident
frequent
endurance
balance
intelligent
influence
reluctant
magnificent
experience
confidence
elegant

22 • transmission
contracted
commitment
attract
submit
references
offered
omit
admits

distract
subtraction
refer

23 • portrait
buffet
ballet
bouquet
dialogue
antique
unique
vague
fatigue
technique
plaque
camouflage

24 • fantasy
fantastic
company
companion
editor
editorial
colony
colonial
strategy
strategic
diplomacy
diplomatic

25 • hasten
autumn
autumnal
softly
heritage
designated
designed
reception
signature
haste
sign
resign

27 • diameter
graph
meters
astronomer
barometer
biography
astronaut
kilometers

astronomy
photography
centimeters
autograph

28 • trio
monopoly
quartet
tricycle
decade
octopus
decimal
quarters
triangles
binoculars
triple
monotonous

29 • desperate
lightning
adjective
penetrate
aspirin
athletes
identity
disastrous
ecstatic
platinum
incidentally
tentatively

30 • caravan
luncheon
champion
gymnasium
laboratory
mathematics
parachute
submarine
teenagers
memorandum
limousine
examination

32 • logic
biology
monologue
hydrant
technology
analogy
mythology

apologizing
periscope
telescope
dehydrated
psychology

33 • agricultural
identification
encyclopedia
possibility
exceptionally
responsibilities
characteristic
recommendation
rehabilitation
acceleration
simultaneously
accumulation

34 • inspired
convention
formula
adventure
depends
uniform
inventor
pending
invention
transformed
perform
suspended

35 • civilian
historian
guardian
scientist
biologist
volunteer
musician
engineer
physician
technician
politician
psychiatrist

MECHANICS

Lesson 22: O B J E C T I V E
■ To spell words with the Latin roots –*mit*– or –*miss*–, –*tract*–, and –*fer*–

Lesson 23: O B J E C T I V E
■ To spell words of French derivation, especially those ending in –*que*, –*gue*, –*et*, and –*age*

Lesson 24: O B J E C T I V E
■ To spell related words in which a suffix is added to a base word, changing the vowel sound but not the vowel spelling near the end of the base word

Lesson 25: O B J E C T I V E
■ To spell related words with sounded and unsounded consonants

Lesson 27: O B J E C T I V E
■ To spell words that have the Greek word parts –*ast(e)r*–, –*graph*–, and –*meter*–

Lesson 28: O B J E C T I V E
■ To spell words that have the number prefixes and combining forms *mon*– or *mono*–, *bi*–, *tri*–, *quadr*– or *quart*–, *oct*–, and *dec*– or *deci*–

Lesson 29: O B J E C T I V E
■ To spell words that are commonly mispronounced

Lesson 30: O B J E C T I V E
■ To spell words that are often clipped to form shorter words

Lesson 32: O B J E C T I V E
■ To spell words with the Greek word parts –*hydr*–, –*log*–, –*ology*, and –*scop*–

Lesson 33: O B J E C T I V E
■ To spell words with five or six syllables

Lesson 34: O B J E C T I V E
■ To spell words with the Latin roots –*ven*–, –*spir*–, –*form*–, and –*pend*–

Lesson 35: O B J E C T I V E
■ To spell words with the suffixes –*ian*, –*eer*, –*ist*, and –*ie*

Lesson 20: O B J E C T I V E
■ To spell words with the Latin roots –*struct*–, –*vis*–, –*pos(i)t*–, and –*cess*– or –*ceed*–

Lesson 21: O B J E C T I V E
■ To spell words with the unstressed endings –*ant* or –*ent* and –*ance* or –*ence*

Correcting
Common Errors

Key Language Skills Review

This chapter reviews key skills and concepts that pose special
problems for writers.

- **Sentence Fragments and Run-on Sentences**
- **Subject-Verb and Pronoun-Antecedent Agreement**
- **Verb Forms and Pronoun Forms**
- **Comparison of Modifiers**
- **Misplaced Modifiers**
- **Standard Usage**
- **Capitalization**
- **Punctuation—End Marks, Commas, Semicolons, Colons,
  Quotation Marks, and Apostrophes**
- **Spelling**

Most of the exercises in this chapter follow the same format
as the exercises found throughout the grammar, usage, and
mechanics sections of this book. You will notice, however, that
two sets of review exercises are presented in standardized test
formats. These exercises are designed to provide you with practice not only in solving usage and mechanics problems but also
in dealing with these kinds of problems on standardized tests.

Exercise 1 Finding and Revising Sentence Fragments

Most of the following groups of words are sentence fragments. Revise each fragment by (1) adding a subject, (2) adding a verb, or (3) attaching the fragment to a complete sentence. You may need to change the punctuation and capitalization, too. If the word group is already a complete sentence, write *S*.

Reference Note
For information about **correcting sentence fragments,** see page 269.

EXAMPLE 1. Because she likes Chihuahuas.
1. *My mother bought a book about dogs because she likes Chihuahuas.*

1. Wanted to study the history of Chihuahuas.
2. Small dogs with big, pointed ears.
3. When my mother's Chihuahuas begin their shrill, high-pitched barking.
4. Chihuahuas lived in ancient Mexico.
5. Ancient stone carvings showing that the Toltecs raised Chihuahuas during the eighth or ninth century A.D.
6. Are related to dogs of the Middle East.
7. Travelers may have brought Chihuahuas to the Americas as companions.
8. That Chihuahuas score poorly on canine intelligence tests.
9. However, can be trained to assist people who have hearing impairments.
10. If you want a Chihuahua.

Exercise 2 Revising Sentence Fragments

Identify each of the following groups of words as a sentence fragment or a complete sentence. Write *F* if it is a sentence fragment and *S* if it is a sentence. Then, revise each sentence fragment by (1) adding a subject, (2) adding a verb, or (3) attaching the fragment to a complete sentence. You may need to change the punctuation and capitalization, too.

Reference Note
For information about **correcting sentence fragments,** see page 269.

EXAMPLE 1. Juggling a fascinating hobby.
1. *F—Juggling is a fascinating hobby.*

1. If you would like to be able to juggle. **1.** F
2. You might start with a good, simple how-to book. **2.** S
3. Most people can learn the basic moves. **3.** S
4. Within a fairly short period of time. **4.** F

OBJECTIVE

- To identify complete sentences and sentence fragments and revise the sentence fragments to make complete sentences

Exercise 1 Finding and Revising Sentence Fragments

POSSIBLE ANSWERS

1. She wanted to study the history of Chihuahuas.
2. They are small dogs with big, pointed ears.
3. I cover my ears when my mother's Chihuahuas begin their shrill, high-pitched barking.
4. S
5. Ancient stone carvings show that the Toltecs raised Chihuahuas during the eighth or ninth century A.D.
6. Chihuahuas are related to dogs of the Middle East.
7. S
8. I was surprised to learn that Chihuahuas score poorly on canine intelligence tests.
9. However, Chihuahuas can be trained to assist people who have hearing impairments.
10. If you want a Chihuahua, I suggest that you read about the breed's history and characteristics.

Exercise 2 Revising Sentence Fragments

POSSIBLE ANSWERS

1. If you would like to be able to juggle, you might take a class.
4. Within a fairly short period of time, you may be entertaining your friends.

Exercise 2 Revising Sentence Fragments

ANSWERS continued

5. While beginners first develop a sense of how to hold one juggling bag, they also practice tossing it up and letting it drop on the floor.
7. Next, the juggler must master the ability to toss one bag back and forth.
8. Then, the next step is learning the right way to throw two bags.
10. Before they move up to three bags, beginning jugglers must be competent juggling two bags.

Exercise 3 Finding and Revising Sentence Fragments

POSSIBLE ANSWERS

1. Eventually, the idea of dinosaurs started taking root in the imaginations of many people.
2. Considering this fascination, it is no wonder people flock to films about dinosaurs.
3. S
4. S
5. I saw a picture of the place where the first dinosaur eggs were found.
6. For example, people interested in dinosaurs can see magnificent, full skeletons in museums, lifelike animations, television documentaries, and even children's toys and cartoons.
7. What can explain the sudden disappearance of these mighty creatures?
8. The remarkable work of physicists Dr. Luis Alvarez and his son Walter sheds some light on this mystery.
9. Their theory is based on the idea of a meteor hitting the earth.
10. According to the theory, the meteor destroyed the dinosaurs by sending a huge, dark cloud around the earth, killing many plants and destroying the dinosaurs' food sources.

Reference Note

For information about **correcting sentence fragments,** see page 269.

HELP

Although the example for Exercise 3 shows two possible answers, you need to give only one for each item.

5. While beginners first develop a sense of how to hold one juggling bag. **5.** F
6. They also practice standing in the proper, relaxed way. **6.** S
7. Next, must master the ability to toss one bag back and forth. **7.** F
8. Then learning the right way to throw two bags. **8.** F
9. Beginners often need to practice juggling with two bags for some time. **9.** S
10. Before they move up to three bags. **10.** F

Exercise 3 Finding and Revising Sentence Fragments

Some of the following groups of words are sentence fragments. Revise each sentence fragment by (1) adding a subject, (2) adding a verb, or (3) attaching the sentence fragment to a complete sentence. You may need to change the punctuation and capitalization, too. If the word group is already a complete sentence, write *S*.

EXAMPLE   1. Could have been the source of the world's legends of dragons.

1. *Could dinosaur fossils have been the source of the world's legends of dragons?*

or

Large lizards, such as monitors, could have been the source of the world's legends of dragons.

1. Eventually, taking root in the imaginations of many people.
2. Considering this.
3. The word *dinosaur* was first used around one hundred and fifty years ago.
4. That fact surprises many people.
5. Where the first dinosaur eggs were found.
6. For example, magnificent, full skeletons in museums, lifelike animations, television documentaries, and even children's toys and cartoons.
7. Can explain the sudden disappearance of these mighty creatures.
8. The remarkable work of physicists Dr. Luis Alvarez and his son Walter on this mystery.
9. Their theory based on the idea of a meteor hitting the earth.
10. Sending a huge, dark cloud around the earth, killing many plants and destroying the dinosaurs' food sources.

COMMON ERRORS

Revising Run-on Sentences

Each of the following items is a run-on sentence. Revise each sentence by following the italicized instructions in parentheses. Remember to use correct punctuation and capitalization.

EXAMPLE

1. The study of shells is called malacology, shell collections are particularly popular in Japan. (*Make two sentences.*)

   1. *The study of shells is called malacology. Shell collections are particularly popular in Japan.*

Answers may vary. Sample responses are given.

1. At four feet in diameter, the shell of the giant clam is the largest shell today. during prehistoric times, the shell of the Nautiloidea sometimes grew to eight feet across. (*Make two sentences.*)

2. From the Mediterranean to Japan, shells have played an important part in everyday life. they have functioned as money, as decoration, and even as magic charms. (*Make two sentences.*)

3. American Indians used wampum, beads cut from shells, as money. West Africans and Arabs used the cowrie shell in the same way. (*Use a comma and a coordinating conjunction.*)

4. Africans prized the shell as jewelry. shells are still sold as jewelry. (*Use a comma and a coordinating conjunction.*)

5. Jewelry, buttons, figurines, and all kinds of decorative objects can be purchased at tourist shops along the coasts. shells are plentiful nearby. (*Make two sentences.*)

6. The ancient Greeks boiled mollusks and created a valuable purple dye. cloth treated with this dye may retain its color for hundreds of years. (*Make two sentences.*)

7. Perhaps because of their great beauty, shells have also played important parts in religious life. they may be found in several belief systems. (*Make two sentences.*)

8. Quetzalcoatl, god of the Mayans, Toltecs, and Aztecs, was born from a seashell. the chank shell is associated with the Hindu god Vishnu. (*Make two sentences.*)

9. Shells can be free for the taking. their rarity can make them quite valuable. (*Use a comma and a coordinating conjunction.*)

10. Shells are regularly exported from the United States to Europe. Japan and the United States also ship shells back and forth. (*Make two sentences.*)

Reference Note

For information about **correcting run-on sentences,** see page 271.

3. , and
4. , and

9. , or

Exercise 4

OBJECTIVE

■ To revise run-on sentences

COMMON ERRORS

Exercise 5

OBJECTIVE

■ To revise run-on sentences

Exercise 6

OBJECTIVE

■ To revise run-on sentences

Reference Note

For information about **correcting run-on sentences,** see page 271.

Exercise 5 **Correcting Run-on Sentences**

Correct each of the following run-on sentences by (1) making it into two separate sentences or (2) using a comma and a coordinating conjunction to make a compound sentence. Remember to use correct punctuation and capitalization.

EXAMPLE   **1.** Anthony uses chopsticks skillfully I have trouble with them.

      1. *Anthony uses chopsticks skillfully, but I have trouble with them.*

Answers may vary. Sample responses are given.

1. The large crane lifted the ten-ton boxes it set them on the concrete deck.

2. My dad does not know much about computers he has learned to surf the Internet.   **2.** , but

3. Allen Say wrote *The Ink-Keeper's Apprentice* the events in the story are based on his boyhood in Japan.

4. Two robins landed on the ice in the birdbath one of them drank water from around the thawed edges.

5. Egyptian hieroglyphics may be written from left to right   **5.** or or from right to left they may be written from top to bottom.

6. John is my youngest brother Levy is my oldest brother. **6.** , and

7. The nature preserve was beautiful some people had littered.

8. Grandma believes in keeping a positive attitude she says that   **7.** , but thinking positively is the key to a happy life.

9. Let's see that new movie from Korea I have never seen a Korean movie.

10. All my friends like to shop for bargains at the downtown mall I do, too.   **10.** and

Reference Note

For information about **correcting run-on sentences,** see page 271.

Exercise 6 **Revising Run-on Sentences**

Revise each of the following run-on sentences by (1) making it into two separate sentences or (2) using a comma and a coordinating conjunction to make a compound sentence. Remember to use correct punctuation and capitalization.   Answers may vary. Sample responses are given.

EXAMPLE   **1.** James Earl Jones is a famous actor he has been in movies and plays.

      1. *James Earl Jones is a famous actor. He has been in movies and plays.*

1. You may not remember seeing James Earl Jones, you would probably recognize his voice.   **1.** but
2. Jones provided the voice of Darth Vader in the *Star Wars* movies. Jones's deep voice helped make the character forceful and frightening.
3. Jones has a distinctive voice he has even won a medal for his vocal delivery.   **3.** , and
4. The prize was given by the American Academy of Arts and Letters, is that the organization that gives the Academy Awards?
5. Jones's autobiography was published in 1993, it is, quite appropriately, titled *Voices and Silences*.
6. Jones was born in Mississippi in 1931, he was raised by his grandparents on a farm in Michigan.   **6.** and
7. His father was a prizefighter and an actor. Jones decided to be an actor, too, and studied in New York City.
8. He portrayed a boxing champion in *The Great White Hope*, he starred in both the Broadway production and the movie version of the play.
9. Jones won a Tony Award for his Broadway performance he was nominated for an Academy Award for his role in the movie.

9. , and

10. Another of Jones's movies is *The Man*, in that movie he plays the first African American to be elected president of the United States.

Exercise 7 Revising Sentence Fragments and Run-on Sentences

Identify each of the following word groups by writing *F* if it is a sentence fragment, *R* if it is a run-on sentence, and *S* if it is a complete sentence. Revise each fragment to make it into a complete sentence. Revise each run-on to make it into one or more complete sentences. Remember to use correct capitalization and punctuation.

EXAMPLE   **1.** Because my ancestors were Scandinavian.

1. *F—I have heard many stories about Vikings because my ancestors were Scandinavian.*

1. The Viking Age lasted three centuries, it started at the end of the eighth century A.D.   **1.** R

Reference Note

For information on **correcting sentence fragments,** see page 269. For information on **correcting run-on sentences,** see page 271.

Exercise 7

OBJECTIVE

■ To identify and correct sentence fragments and run-on sentences

Exercise 7 Revising Sentence Fragments and Run-on Sentences

ANSWERS
Revisions will vary. Sample responses are given.

1. The Viking Age, which started at the end of the eighth century A.D., lasted three centuries.

COMMON ERRORS

Grammar and Usage   **689**

690

COMMON ERRORS

Correcting Common Errors

Exercise 7   Revising Sentence Fragments and Run-on Sentences

ANSWERS continued

2. Vikings came from Scandinavian countries known today as Sweden, Denmark, and Norway.
4. The range of influence of the Vikings was enormous. The Vikings developed trade routes in western Europe and in the Middle East.
5. Vikings also were skilled at fishing and farming.
6. All Vikings spoke the language called Old Norse and shared similar religious beliefs.
7. Odin was the chief god of the Vikings, but Odin's son Thor was worshiped more widely.
9. Viking society was divided into three main social classes—royal families, free citizens, and slaves.
10. Viking women held several important rights; they could own property and land, for example.

Exercise 8

OBJECTIVE

■ To choose verbs that agree with their subjects

TEACHING TIP

To give students extra practice with subject-verb agreement, you could write a list of subjects and a list of verbs on the chalkboard. Ask students to compose sentences showing combinations of various subjects and verbs, changing verb forms to agree with their subjects. You can change the directions from time to time to have students write each of the following types of sentences: sentences with compound subjects, sentences with phrases between the subjects and verbs, and sentences with the subjects following the verbs.

Reference Note

For information about **subject-verb agreement**, see page 458.

---

2. Vikings from Scandinavian countries known today as Sweden, Denmark, and Norway.   **2.** F
3. Since the Vikings lived along the sea, they often became boatbuilders, sailors, and explorers.   **3.** S
4. The range of influence of the Vikings was enormous the Vikings developed trade routes in western Europe and also in the Middle East.   **4.** R
5. Also were skilled at fishing and farming.   **5.** F
6. All Vikings spoke the language called Old Norse they shared similar religious beliefs.   **6.** R
7. Odin was the chief god of the Vikings, Odin's son Thor was worshiped more widely.   **7.** R
8. After they were converted to Christianity, the Vikings built many wooden churches.   **8.** S
9. Was divided into three main social classes—royal families, free citizens, and slaves.   **9.** F
10. Viking women held several important rights, they could own property and land, for example.   **10.** R

Exercise 8   Identifying Verbs That Agree in Number with Their Subjects

For each of the following sentences, choose <u>the form of the verb in parentheses that agrees with the subject.</u>

EXAMPLE   1. The band (*play, plays*) mostly reggae.
   1. plays

1. Samantha and Matthew (*take, takes*) art classes at the museum on weekends.
2. The card table or the folding chairs (*belong, belongs*) in that closet by the front door.
3. Earlene (*don't, doesn't*) know the exact time because her watch stopped working last week.
4. Both the stalagmites and the stalactites (*was, were*) casting eerie shadows on the cave walls.
5. Several of the exchange students at our school (*speak, speaks*) Portuguese.
6. Neither an emu nor an ostrich (*lay, lays*) eggs that look like that.

7. The members of the audience always (*clap*, *claps*) as soon as the star appears onstage.
8. Mike said that either the main herd or the stragglers (*is*, *are*) in the near canyon.
9. The coaches on the visiting team (*agree*, *agrees*) with the referee's decision.
10. Some of the fruit baskets (*sell*, *sells*) for less than three and a half dollars each.

Exercise 9 **Identifying Verbs That Agree in Number with Their Subjects**

For each of the following sentences, choose the form of the verb in parentheses that agrees with the subject.

EXAMPLE   1. (*Do, Does*) you know what a powwow is?

    1. *Do*

Reference Note

For information about **subject-verb agreement**, see page 458.

1. Each of us in my class (*has*, *have*) given a report about powwows, which are ceremonies or gatherings of American Indians.
2. Dancing and feasting (*is*, *are*) very important activities at powwows.
3. People in my family (*come*, *comes*) from around the country to attend the Crow Fair, which is held every August in Montana.
4. Many of the people at the powwow (*has*, *have*) come here from Canada.
5. Everyone here (*know*, *knows*) that it is the largest powwow in North America.
6. Peoples represented at the fair (*include*, *includes*) the Crow, Lakota, Ojibwa, Blackfoot, and Cheyenne.
7. Only one of my relatives (*dance*, *dances*) all four of the main kinds of dances at powwows.
8. Both skill and practice (*go*, *goes*) into the Traditional, Fancy, Grass, and Jingle-dress dances.
9. Last year, all of the costumes of the Fancy dancers (*was*, *were*) extremely colorful.
10. Either a row of porcupine quills or a band of beads (*go*, *goes*) all the way around some of the dancers' headdresses.

COMMON ERRORS

Reference Note

For information about **subject-verb agreement,** see page 458.

Exercise 10

OBJECTIVE

■ To correct errors in subject-verb agreement

Meeting

INDIVIDUAL

NEEDS

ENGLISH-LANGUAGE LEARNERS
General Strategies. Speakers of Chinese, Vietnamese, and other languages that do not show number in nouns or verbs might have difficulty with the concept of agreement. Students should be reminded that in written English, proper agreement is essential in every sentence.

Exercise 11

OBJECTIVE

■ To select pronouns that agree in number with their antecedents

Reference Note

For information on **using pronouns correctly,** see Chapter 19.

Exercise 10 **Correcting Errors in Subject-Verb Agreement**

Most of the following sentences contain errors in subject-verb agreement. Identify each error, and give the correct form of the verb. If a sentence is already correct, write *C*.

EXAMPLE   1. All of us is very excited about our Drama Club's next play.

     1. *is—are*

1. *Six Friends and One Dog* are the title of the play we are performing this fall.   **1.** is
2. The director and producer of the play are Mark Taylor.   **2.** is
3. Neither our sponsor nor the actors have ever staged a production like this.   **3.** C
4. Most of the actors was chosen last week.   **4.** were
5. Of course, the cast don't know their lines yet.   **5.** C
6. Many of the costumes is still being made.   **6.** are
7. Either Lauren or Kawanda's older brother is painting the backdrops.   **7.** C
8. Are five dollars too much for a ticket?   **8.** Is
9. My friends and the crew hopes not, because the tickets are already printed!   **9.** hope
10. Channel 6 News have promised to cover our opening night, so we'll all be famous, at least for a little while.   **10.** has

Exercise 11 **Choosing Correct Pronoun Forms**

Choose the correct pronoun or pronouns in parentheses in each of the following sentences.

EXAMPLE   1. Tell anyone with an idea to take (*their, his or her*) suggestion to the vice-principal.

     1. *his or her*

1. Everyone on the field trip must bring (*their, his or her*) own sack lunch.
2. When my sister or mother comes back from the bakery, (*they, she*) will bring fresh-baked bread.
3. No, neither of the cowboys ever takes off (*their, his*) hat.
4. The United States was proud when (*its, their*) astronauts landed on the moon.

5. If Doug or Simon is in the clear downfield, pass (*them*, <u>*him*</u>) the ball.
6. Usually Rosita or Paula plays (<u>*her*</u>, *their*) guitar at our picnics.
7. If anybody is still in the gym, tell (*them*, <u>*him or her*</u>) to turn out the lights and shut the door.
8. The colonists and Governor William Bradford depended on Squanto as (*his or her*, <u>*their*</u>) interpreter.
9. This is a very large company, but (*they*, <u>*it*</u>) treats the employees with respect.
10. Ask Jennie or Sara what (<u>*her*</u>, *their*) middle name is.

Exercise 12 **Proofreading Sentences for Correct Pronoun-Antecedent Agreement**

Most of the following sentences contain errors in pronoun-antecedent agreement. Identify <u>each error</u>, and give the correct form of the pronoun. If a sentence is already correct, write *C*.

EXAMPLE   1. Jesse and Michael enjoyed his Kwanzaa activities.
         1. *his—their*

1. During Kwanzaa, which lasts from December 26 through January 1, several of our friends and neighbors celebrate <u>his or her</u> African heritage.   **1.** their
2. African American families affirm traditional values and principles during their Kwanzaa activities.   **2.** C
3. This year, both of my sisters made storybooks as <u>her</u> *zawadi*, or Kwanzaa gifts.   **3.** their
4. Either Uncle Willis or Uncle Roland will bring <u>their</u> candles for the observance.   **4.** his
5. One of them will bring <u>their</u> wooden candleholder, called a *kinara*.   **5.** his
6. The joyful celebration of Kwanzaa has its origins in African harvest festivals.   **6.** C
7. Each of my parents will discuss his or her own individual ideas about Kwanzaa.   **7.** C
8. Either Lily or Charlotte mentioned in <u>their</u> speech that Kwanzaa was created in 1966.   **8.** her
9. Nobody in our family likes to miss <u>their</u> turn to make up dances on the sixth day of Kwanzaa.   **9.** his or her
10. Jerry and Charles will volunteer <u>his</u> time on the third day of Kwanzaa, when collective work is celebrated.   **10.** their

Reference Note

For information about **pronoun-antecedent agreement,** see page 475.

COMMON ERRORS

Exercise 13

OBJECTIVE

■ To identify and correct errors in subject-verb and pronoun-antecedent agreement

Meeting INDIVIDUAL NEEDS

LEARNERS HAVING DIFFICULTY

If your students need additional review before attempting **Exercise 13,** you may want to give them some guided practice. Form study groups of two or three students each, and assign the even-numbered items. Go over the answers orally to identify students who are struggling with the material, and reteach concepts as needed. Then, assign the odd-numbered items for students to complete as independent practice.

Exercise 14

OBJECTIVE

■ To supply the correct forms of given regular and irregular verbs to complete sentences

Reference Note

For information about **subject-verb agreement,** see page 458. For information about **pronoun-antecedent agreement,** see page 475.

Reference Note

For information about **using verbs correctly,** see Chapter 18.

Exercise 13 **Proofreading Sentences for Correct Subject-Verb and Pronoun-Antecedent Agreement**

Most of the following sentences contain <u>agreement errors</u>. For each error, identify the incorrect verb or pronoun and supply the correct form. If a sentence is already correct, write *C*.

EXAMPLE 1. Every animal, including humans, need water to survive.

  1. *need—needs*

1. The human body <u>consist</u> mostly of water.   1. consists
2. You and I, along with everyone else, <u>is</u> about 65 percent water.   2. are
3. Everybody in my family tries to drink at least eight glasses of water a day.   3. C
4. "<u>Don't</u> Carlos usually drink more than that?" Janet asked.   4. Doesn't
5. Either Angie or Ramona said that <u>their</u> family usually drinks bottled water.   5. her
6. Evidence shows that drinking water helps our bodies keep <u>its</u> proper temperature.   6. their
7. Ian or Calinda <u>have</u> studied the mineral content of our local water supply.   7. has
8. Industry and agriculture depend on a good water supply for <u>its</u> success.   8. their
9. Most of the world's fresh water is frozen in polar icecaps and glaciers.   9. C
10. While more than 70 percent of the earth's surface <u>are</u> covered by water, only 3 percent of that water is not salty.   10. is

Exercise 14 **Writing the Forms of Regular and Irregular Verbs**

Provide the correct present participle, past, or past participle form of the given verb to complete each of the following sentences.

EXAMPLE 1. *eat*   Angela has already _____ her serving of acorn squash.

  1. *eaten*

1. *install*   The shopping mall has _____ wheelchair ramps at all of the entrances.   1. installed

2. *send* We have already ___ for a new crossword-puzzle magazine. **2.** sent
3. *see* Have you ___ the koalas at the Australian wildlife exhibit? **3.** seen
4. *put* Marianna is ___ together a colorful mobile. **4.** putting
5. *grow* My uncle ___ the largest pumpkin in the United States this year. **5.** grew
6. *draw* Anthony has ___ two different self-portraits. **6.** drawn
7. *run* Both of my stepbrothers have ___ in the Cowtown Marathon. **7.** run
8. *jump* Have the cats ___ out of the tree? **8.** jumped
9. *write* Murasaki Shikibu of Japan ___ what may be the world's first novel. **9.** wrote
10. *go* More than half of my friends ___ to the May Day parade. **10.** went

Exercise 15 **Proofreading Sentences for Correct Verb Forms**

Identify any <u>incorrect past or past participle verb forms</u> in the following sentences, and write the correct forms. If a sentence is already correct, write *C*.

EXAMPLE   **1.** Many African American women maked names for themselves during the pioneer days.

         1. made

1. A friend of mine <u>lended</u> me a book called *Black Women of the Old West*. **1.** lent
2. It contains many biographies of African American women who <u>leaded</u> difficult but exciting lives. **2.** led
3. For example, May B. Mason <u>gone</u> to the Yukon to mine gold during the Klondike Gold Rush. **3.** went
4. Journalist Era Bell Thompson <u>writed</u> articles about the West for a Chicago newspaper. **4.** wrote
5. In *American Daughter* she <u>telled</u> about her youth in North Dakota. **5.** told
6. Our teacher has <u>spoke</u> highly of Dr. Susan McKinney Stewart, a pioneer physician. **6.** spoken
7. During the 1800s, Cathy Williams wore men's clothes and served under the name William Cathay as a Buffalo Soldier. **7.** C
8. I <u>seen</u> a picture of Williams at work on her farm. **8.** saw

Reference Note

For information about **using verbs correctly,** see Chapter 18.

COMMON ERRORS

9. Mary Fields <u>choosed</u> an exciting but sometimes hard life in the West.　**9.** chose
10. Nicknamed "Stagecoach Mary," she <u>drived</u> freight wagons and stagecoaches in Montana.　**10.** drove

Reference Note

For information about **using verbs correctly,** see Chapter 18.

Exercise 16 Proofreading Sentences for Correct Verb Forms

If any of the following sentences contains an <u>incorrect past or past participle form</u> of a verb, write the correct form. If a sentence is already correct, write *C*.

EXAMPLE　**1.** When I was ten, I begun to collect stamps.
　　　　　1. began

1. Over the years, my collection has <u>growed</u> large enough to fill three binders.　**1.** grown
2. I have <u>went</u> to several stamp shows.　**2.** gone
3. At nearly every show, I <u>seen</u> many rare and valuable stamps.　**3.** saw
4. I <u>told</u> my friend Warren that I aim to own some of those stamps one day.　**4.** told
5. I once saw a picture of a rare two-cent stamp that cost one collector $1.1 million in 1987.　**5.** C
6. As you might imagine, that price <u>setted</u> a world record!　**6.** set
7. Stamps have <u>appear</u> in many shapes.　**7.** appeared
8. My uncle, a mail carrier, <u>sended</u> me a banana-shaped stamp.　**8.** sent
9. He also has <u>give</u> me a book about the history of stamp collecting.　**9.** given
10. It <u>sayed</u> that stamp collecting was already a popular hobby by the 1860s.　**10.** said

Exercise 17 Choosing Correct Verb Forms

Choose the <u>correct verb form in parentheses</u> in each of the following sentences.

EXAMPLE　**1.** (*Set, Sit*) those packages down, and come help me catch these kittens.
　　　　　1. Set

1. Did Keefe (*rise, raise*) the flag for the ceremony?
2. The crowd roared when Sheila (*sit, set*) a new track record for the fifty-yard dash.
3. A giant lobster was (*laying, lying*) motionless on the seabed.

Reference Note

For information about using *rise* and *raise*, *sit* and *set*, and *lie* and *lay*, see page 500.

COMMON ERRORS

Exercise 16

OBJECTIVE

■ To identify and correct verb forms

Cooperative Learning

You may want to pair students for **Exercise 16.** One student will be responsible for the even-numbered sentences, and the other student will work with the odd-numbered sentences. Tell them to write the sentences in sequence but to answer alternately. They should then check each other's work.

Exercise 17

OBJECTIVE

■ To select correct verb forms

4. The incoming tide (*rose*, *raised*) the boat that had been beached on the sandbar.

5. An heirloom quilt (*lays*, *lies*) neatly folded on the bed.

6. Why is the price of housing (*rising*, *raising*) in this area?

7. Someone had (*laid*, *lain*) a row of stones carefully on either side of the path.

8. Freshly washed and brushed, the mare walked out to the corral, (*lay*, *laid*) down in the dust, and rolled over three or four times.

9. By noon, the fog had (*risen*, *raised*) and the sun had come out.

10. In the old photograph, five Sioux warriors (*sat*, *set*) and stared with dignity into the camera.

Exercise 18 Identifying Correct Pronoun Forms

Choose the correct form of the pronoun in parentheses in each of the following sentences.

EXAMPLE   **1.** Doris and (*me*, *I*) are planning a trip to Vietnam.

        1. I

1. Will you take the first-aid class with (*we*, *us*)?

2. The principal gave (*he*, *him*) the key to the trophy case.

3. The minister gave (*they*, *them*) a wedding present.

4. Ulani and (*he*, *him*) greeted their guests with "Aloha!"

5. Mr. Galvez saved the comics especially for (*I*, *me*).

6. (*They*, *Them*) are learning how to draw with pastels.

7. R. J. asked (*she*, *her*) for a new CD.

8. Stan's jokes amused Martha and (*I*, *me*).

9. The person who called you last night was (*I*, *me*).

10. The captain of the debate team is (*she*, *her*).

Exercise 19 Identifying Correct Pronoun Forms

Choose the correct form of the pronoun in parentheses in each of the following sentences.

EXAMPLE   **1.** The guest speaker told (*us*, *we*) students many facts about Hispanic Americans in the arts.

        1. us

1. Mrs. Ramirez picked out some poems by Jimmy Santiago Baca and read (*they*, *them*) to us.

Reference Note

For information on **using pronouns correctly,** see Chapter 19.

Reference Note

For information about **using pronouns correctly,** see Chapter 19.

Grammar and Usage   **697**

Exercises 18–19

O B J E C T I V E

■ To identify correct pronoun forms

T E A C H I N G   TIP

Activity. For review and practice of pronoun use, create flashcards that state the number, person, and form of a personal pronoun on one side and the corresponding pronoun on the reverse side. (For example, one side of the flashcard might read "First Person Singular—Nominative Case," while the other side reads *I*.) Prepare sixteen cards, one for each nominative and objective case personal pronoun form (*I, you, he, she, it, we, you, they, me, you, him, her, it, us, you, them*). Be sure to include the gender of third-person pronouns in your descriptions.

Show the descriptive sides of the cards, and have student volunteers name the correct pronouns. Then, to increase students' understanding of how these pronouns are used, have student teams compose sentences in which the pronouns are replaced with blanks. Let other student teams then attempt to describe the type of pronoun that would have to go into the blank to complete each sentence and then name the pronoun. (For example, *The gatekeeper helped Gwen and me by giving _____ a key to the lock.* The pronoun would be described as "First Person Plural—Objective" and the pronoun itself would be *us*.)

COMMON ERRORS

2. Jan and (*he, him*) agree that Barbara Carrasco's murals are outstanding.

3. Between you and (*I, me*), Gaspar Perez de Villagra's account of an early expedition to the American Southwest sounds interesting.

4. (*He, Him*) wrote the first book to have been written in what is now the United States.

5. Our teacher showed (*we, us*) pictures of the work of the Puerto Rican artist Arnaldo Roche.

6. (*Who, Whom*) is your favorite artist?

7. The writings of Christina Garcia appeal to (*we, us*).

8. In Luz's opinion, the best writer is (*she, her*).

9. Tito Puente has recorded at least one hundred albums and has appeared in several movies; we saw (*he, him*) in *Radio Days*.

10. (*Who, Whom*) did you research for your report?

Exercise 20

OBJECTIVE

■ To identify and correct errors in the use of pronouns

Reference Note

For information about **using pronouns correctly,** see Chapter 19.

Exercise 20 **Proofreading for Correct Pronoun Usage**

Most of the following sentences contain errors in pronoun usage. Identify each error, and give the correct pronoun. If a sentence is already correct, write *C*.

EXAMPLE   **1.** Who did the student council appoint?

    1. Who—Whom

1. Let me know whom will be in charge of decorating. **1.** who

2. Mr. Rodriguez gave Nicole and we shop students a handout on using the jigsaw safely. **2.** us

3. Waiting for us at the door were Grandma and they. **3.** C

4. For Ron and myself, geometry is easy. **4.** me

5. Gina, us girls are going to the park to fly our kites; come along with us! **5.** we

6. Mr. Chin, his wife, and me are going to the Mayan exhibit at the museum next weekend. **6.** I

7. The big dog always keeps the bowl of food for hisself, so we feed the little dog on the porch. **7.** himself

8. From who could we borrow a map? **8.** whom

9. Yes, the team did all the planning and production of the video by theirselves. **9.** themselves

10. The only ones who can speak French are us boys from Miss LaRouche's class. **10.** we

Exercise 21 Choosing Correct Forms of Modifiers

Choose the correct form of the modifier in parentheses in each of the following sentences.

EXAMPLE   **1.** Many people think that of all pets, Siamese cats are the (*better, best*).

      1. best

1. The boys thought that they were (*stronger, strongest*), but the girls beat them in the tug of war.
2. The (*simplest, simpler*) way to attract birds to a yard is by having water available for them.
3. Jovita is the (*most intelligent, intelligentest*) student in the seventh grade.
4. I worry about my grades (*least often, less often*) now that I do my homework every night.
5. Kim Lee has traveled (*farthest, farther*) on her bicycle than anyone else in our class has.
6. Hasn't this year's quiz-bowl team won (*more, most*) local competitions than last year's team?
7. Grandfather says that this winter is the (*colder, coldest*) one he remembers.
8. Wynton Marsalis was born in the city (*more, most*) associated with jazz—New Orleans.
9. Bicyclists who wear helmets are injured (*least, less*) often than those who do not.
10. Louisiana has (*fewer, fewest*) wetlands than it once had.

Exercise 22 Proofreading for Correct Modifiers

Most of the following sentences contain errors in the use of modifiers. Identify each incorrect modifier, and supply the correct form. If the sentence is already correct, write *C*.

EXAMPLE   **1.** Low, green hills roll gentle in the dawn mist.

      1. gentle—gently

1. The tourists looked uncomfortably as they rode the elephant along the beach.   **1.** uncomfortable
2. An Indian elephant calmly carried a surfboard with its trunk and did the job good, too.   **2.** well
3. The white waves of the Bay of Bengal smell quite well to us. **3.** good

Reference Note

For information on **using modifiers correctly,** see Chapter 20.

Reference Note

For information about **using modifiers correctly,** see Chapter 20.

Exercise 21

OBJECTIVE

- To select the correct comparative or superlative forms of modifiers

Exercise 22

OBJECTIVE

- To identify and correct misused modifiers

COMMON ERRORS

Exercise 23

OBJECTIVE

- To revise sentences with double comparisons or double negatives

Meeting
INDIVIDUAL NEEDS

ENGLISH-LANGUAGE LEARNERS

Spanish. The double negative is perfectly acceptable in Spanish (as it is in Russian and a number of other languages). Your observation of your students will help you identify those who are transferring this usage to English, especially with words such as *nothing, none,* or *nobody.* Ask questions that call for the negative form. Give additional written practice to students who are having trouble.

Reference Note

For information about **double comparisons,** see page 538. For information about **double negatives,** see page 539.

4. The island of Sri Lanka was once known as Ceylon, and tea grows <u>good</u> there.   **4.** well

5. At first, I felt bad for the workers up to their waists in mud.   **5.** C

6. I thought they had the <u>worstest</u> job in the world.   **6.** worst

7. They were searching for rubies and garnets that might appear <u>sudden</u> in their muddy baskets.   **7.** suddenly

8. I couldn't recognize a raw gem very well; could you?   **8.** C

9. I thought the highlands, especially Sri Pada and World's End, looked <u>beautifully</u>.   **9.** beautiful

10. You can live <u>simple</u> when you are in Sri Lanka.   **10.** simply

Exercise 23 Revising Sentences to Correct Double Comparisons and Double Negatives

Revise each of the following sentences to correct each double comparison or double negative.   Answers may vary.

EXAMPLES   1. Of the three games, the first was the least funnest.
    1. *Of the three games, the first was the least fun.*

    2. There are not hardly any stores near the ranch.
    2. *There are hardly any stores near the ranch.*

1. The recycling center is much ~~more~~ busier than it used to be.

2. Sometimes even indoor water pipes freeze if they do not have ~~no~~ insulation around them.

3. I think that our dog Sammy is ~~most~~ happiest when the weather is cold.

4. I haven't received a birthday card from ~~neither~~ of my grandmothers yet.   **4.** either

5. Almost any circle that you draw by hand will be less ~~rounder~~ than one you draw with a compass.   **5.** round

6. Wearing sunscreen with a high sun-protection factor can make being in the sun ~~more~~ safer.

7. My second-oldest cousin, Giovanni, is not like ~~nobody~~ else I know.   **7.** anybody

8. We never went ~~nowhere~~ during spring vacation this year.   **8.** anywhere

9. That was probably the most ~~cleverest~~ chess move I've ever seen you use, Elise.   **9.** clever

10. When I'm old enough to vote, I'm ~~not~~ never going to miss a chance to do so.

Exercise 24 Revising Sentences by Correcting the Placement of Modifiers

The following sentences contain errors in the placement of modifiers. Revise each sentence by adding or rearranging words or by doing both to correct the placement of each modifier.

EXAMPLE 1. My grandmother and I saw a horse on the way to the movie.

1. *On the way to the movie, my grandmother and I saw a horse.*

1. The party was held in the park celebrating Mary's birthday.
2. With wind-filled sails, I saw a ship approaching the harbor.
3. The tree was struck by lightning that we had pruned.
4. The Yamamotos enjoyed planting the iris that arrived from their Japanese relatives in a box.
5. The softball team is from my hometown that won the district championship.
6. Trying to steal home, the catcher tagged the runner.
7. Jaime told Katya about the kitten playing in a happy voice.
8. Painted bright colors, Kamal saw many houses.
9. Hanging from a clothes rack, the drama students finally found the costumes.
10. Recently picked from the orchard, the bowl was full of fruit.

Exercise 25 Identifying Correct Usage

From the word or words in parentheses in each of the following sentences, choose the answer that is correct according to the rules of formal, standard English.

EXAMPLE 1. The boys carried the new recycling containers (*themselves, theirselves*).

1. *themselves*

1. This orange marmalade smells (*bad, badly*).
2. In science class last week, we learned (*how come, why*) water expands when it freezes.
3. The dam (*busted, burst*) because of the rising floodwaters.
4. Mario should plant (*fewer, less*) bulbs in that small flower bed.
5. This button looks (*as if, like*) it will match the material.
6. Let's (*try and, try to*) arrive at the concert early so that we can get good seats.

Reference Note

For information about the **correct placement of modifiers,** see page 540.

Reference Note

For information on **common usage errors,** see Chapter 21. For information on **formal, standard English,** see page 553.

Exercise 24

OBJECTIVE

■ To revise sentences with errors in the placement of modifiers

Exercise 24 Revising Sentences by Correcting the Placement of Modifiers

ANSWERS

Answers may vary. Accept reasonable responses.

1. The party celebrating Mary's birthday was held in the park.
2. I saw a ship with wind-filled sails approaching the harbor.
3. The tree that we had pruned was struck by lightning.
4. The Yamamotos enjoyed planting the iris that arrived in a box from their Japanese relatives.
5. The softball team that won the district championship is from my hometown.
6. The catcher tagged the runner who was trying to steal home.
7. In a happy voice, Jaime told Katya about the kitten playing.
8. Kamal saw many houses painted bright colors.
9. The drama students finally found the costumes hanging from a clothes rack.
10. The bowl was full of fruit recently picked from the orchard.

Exercise 25

OBJECTIVE

■ To identify correct usage

COMMON ERRORS

7. The defending champion played (*good*, *well*) during the chess tournament.

8. Yes, our nearest neighbor lives a long (*way*, *ways*) from us.

9. Those (*kind*, *kinds*) of fabrics are made in Madras, India.

10. Did you share the leftover chop suey (*among*, *between*) the three of you?

Reference Note

For information about **common usage errors,** see Chapter 21. For information about **formal, standard English,** see page 553.

Exercise 26 Identifying Correct Usage

From the word or words in parentheses in each of the following sentences, choose the answer that is correct according to the rules of formal, standard English.

EXAMPLE   **1.** Mrs. Lawrence is (*learning*, *teaching*) us about the Hohokam culture.

        1. teaching

1. The Hohokam civilization (*might of*, *might have*) begun around 300 B.C.

2. Where did the Hohokam people (*live*, *live at*)?

3. The Hohokam (*use to*, *used to*) live in the American Southwest.

4. Hohokam farmers grew their crops in a climate that was (*real*, *extremely*) dry.

5. The Hohokam irrigated the land by using (*alot*, *a lot*) of canals—more than six hundred miles of them!

6. (*Them*, *These*) canals sometimes changed the courses of rivers.

7. The Hohokam were also skilled artisans (*who's*, *whose*) work included jewelry, bowls, and figurines.

8. I (*can*, *can't*) hardly imagine what caused the culture to change so much around A.D. 1450.

9. (*Their*, *They're*) descendants are the Papago and the Pima peoples.

10. We read (*that*, *where*) one Hohokam site is known as Snaketown.

Reference Note

For information about **common usage errors,** see Chapter 21. For information about **formal, standard English,** see page 553.

Exercise 27 Proofreading Sentences for Correct Usage

Each of the following sentences contains an error in the use of formal, standard English. Identify each error. Then, write the correct usage.

EXAMPLE   **1.** If that ain't the proper first aid for heat exhaustion, what is?

        1. ain't—isn't

Left margin column

Exercise 26

OBJECTIVE

- To identify correct usage

TECHNOLOGY TIP

Have students check for proper grammar and usage within their writing by using a computer program. Grammar-checking programs will readily catch a number of mistakes, including double subjects, double negatives, and nonstandard usage such as *anywheres* and *being that.* Emphasize that such programs are not foolproof. Often a program will do no more than ask the user, "Is this word used correctly?" It is up to the user of the program to understand the rules of grammar and usage.

Exercise 27

OBJECTIVE

- To proofread sentences for correct usage

1. During the track meet last Saturday, we used <u>a</u> American Red Cross guidebook for first aid.   **1.** an
2. Fortunately, <u>their</u> was a handy section that was about treating heat exhaustion.   **2.** there
3. The day of the meet, the temperature was hotter <u>then</u> it had been all summer.   **3.** than
4. The athletes were <u>all ready</u> hot by the time that the track meet began.   **4.** already
5. Some of the runners <u>should of</u> been drinking more water than they were.   **5.** should have
6. Several of the athletes <u>which</u> were not used to running in such high temperatures needed medical treatment for heat exhaustion.   **6.** who [*or* that]
7. We volunteers helped the runners <u>like</u> the first-aid guidebook instructed.   **7.** as
8. They soon felt <u>alright</u> after we led them out of the heat and helped them cool down.   **8.** all right
9. The doctor on duty at the meet examined them and checked <u>they're</u> vital signs.   **9.** their
10. According to the doctor, even athletes in good condition must protect <u>theirselves</u> against heat exhaustion and heatstroke.   **10.** themselves

Meeting INDIVIDUAL NEEDS

ADVANCED LEARNERS

Some students will benefit from exposure to usage rules not covered in **Exercises 25, 26,** and **27.** Have students review manuals of style such as Strunk and White's *The Elements of Style.* Encourage students to identify additional usage rules that might help them or their classmates.

Students can then present the rules they discover by providing examples or explanations of them. These rules, examples, and the explanations can be collected in a notebook, indexed, and updated continuously as a reference work—a type of linguistic legacy—for their class and other classes that come after theirs.

COMMON ERRORS

COMMON ERRORS

Grammar and Usage Test: Section 1

DIRECTIONS   Read the paragraph that follows. For each numbered blank, select the word or word group that best completes the sentence.

EXAMPLE   1. The platypus is one of __(1)__ mammals that lays eggs.

 (A) to
 (B) too
 (C) two
 (D) 2

ANSWER   1. (A) (B) (C) (D)

> The platypus is __(1)__ very unusual mammal. It __(2)__ external ears, __(3)__ feet are webbed, and it has thick fur. A broad tail and a fleshy bill __(4)__ to the platypus's odd appearance. Platypuses use __(5)__ bills to catch water worms and insects. Besides having a bill like a duck's, a platypus is __(6)__ like a bird than a mammal in another important way. Like a duck, the platypus __(7)__ eggs. The mother deposits __(8)__ in a nest, __(9)__ she has dug in a riverbank. If you get to Australia, you may see a platypus making its nest __(10)__ a burrow.

1. (A) an   1. B
 (B) a
 (C) the
 (D) some

2. (A) don't have no   2. D
 (B) doesn't have no
 (C) has any
 (D) has no

3. (A) its   3. A
 (B) it's
 (C) its'
 (D) their

4. (A) adds   4. B
 (B) add
 (C) added
 (D) adding

5. (A) its   5. D
 (B) it's
 (C) they're
 (D) their

6. (A) more   6. A
 (B) most
 (C) mostly
 (D) least

7. (A) lays   7. A
 (B) lies
 (C) is lying
 (D) has lain

8. (A) it   8. C
 (B) they
 (C) them
 (D) their

9. **(A)** which   **9.** A
  (B) it
  (C) who
  (D) whom

10. **(A)** inside of   **10.** D
  (B) outside of
  (C) a ways from
  (D) inside

Grammar and Usage Test: Section 2

DIRECTIONS   Part or all of each of the following items is underlined. Using the rules of formal, standard English, choose the revision that most clearly expresses the meaning of the item. If there is no error, choose *A*.

EXAMPLE   1. The chopsticks that my aunt sent us made of
bamboo.

    (A) The chopsticks that my aunt sent us made of
bamboo.
    (B) The chopsticks that my aunt sent us are made
of bamboo.
    (C) The chopsticks are made of bamboo, that my
aunt sent us.
    (D) That my aunt sent us chopsticks made of bamboo.

ANSWER   1.   A   B   C   D

1. Don't buy none of that ripe fruit if you don't plan to eat it soon.   **1.** D
  (A) Don't buy none of that ripe fruit if you don't plan to eat
it soon.
  (B) Do buy none of that ripe fruit if you don't plan to eat
it soon.
  (C) Don't buy none of that ripe fruit if you do plan to eat
it soon.
  (D) Don't buy any of that ripe fruit if you don't plan to eat
it soon.

2. The study group meeting in the library on Wednesday?   **2.** C
  (A) The study group meeting in the library on Wednesday?
  (B) The study group that will be meeting in the library on Wednesday?
  (C) Is the study group meeting in the library on Wednesday?
  (D) Will the study group meeting in the library on Wednesday?

3. Some visitors to the park enjoy rock <u>climbing others prefer kayaking</u>.

3. D

    (A) climbing others prefer kayaking

    (B) climbing, others prefer kayaking

    (C) climbing, others, who prefer kayaking

    (D) climbing, and others prefer kayaking

4. Martin <u>prepares the salad, Justine sets the table</u>.   **4.** B

    (A) prepares the salad, Justine sets the table

    (B) prepares the salad, and Justine sets the table

    (C) prepares the salad Justine sets the table

    (D) preparing the salad, and Justine sets the table

5. Many Cherokee now live in Oklahoma, but <u>this area were not their</u> <u>original home</u>.   **5.** B

    (A) this area were not their original home

    (B) this area was not their original home

    (C) this area was not they're original home

    (D) this area were not they're original home

6. <u>Pulling weeds in the garden, a tiny toad was discovered by Ernie.</u>   **6.** D

    (A) Pulling weeds in the garden, a tiny toad was discovered by Ernie.

    (B) A tiny toad was discovered pulling weeds in the garden by Ernie.

    (C) While pulling weeds in the garden, a tiny toad was discovered by Ernie.

    (D) Pulling weeds in the garden, Ernie discovered a tiny toad.

7. <u>Will rehearse together for the class play.</u>   **7.** C

    (A) Will rehearse together for the class play.

    (B) Will be rehearsing together for the class play.

    (C) We will rehearse together for the class play.

    (D) Because we will rehearse together for the class play.

8. Some people are <u>more afraider</u> of snakes than of any other kind of animal.   **8.** C

(**A**) more afraider

(**B**) afraider

(**C**) more afraid

(**D**) most afraid

9. <u>Several important African kingdoms developed between Lake Chad and the Atlantic Ocean.</u>   **9.** A

(**A**) Several important African kingdoms developed between Lake Chad and the Atlantic Ocean.

(**B**) Several important African kingdoms that developed between Lake Chad and the Atlantic Ocean.

(**C**) Several important African kingdoms between Lake Chad and the Atlantic Ocean.

(**D**) Several important African kingdoms developing between Lake Chad and the Atlantic Ocean.

10. <u>The singer waved to some people he knew in the audience from the stage.</u>   **10.** D

(**A**) The singer waved to some people he knew in the audience from the stage.

(**B**) The singer waved to some people from the stage he knew in the audience.

(**C**) The singer waved to some people from the stage in the audience he knew.

(**D**) The singer waved from the stage to some people he knew in the audience.

YEAH, I'M WORRIED ALL THE TIME, TOO -- I WISH WE'D NEVER INVENTED THE FUTURE TENSE!

FRANK & ERNEST reprinted by permission of Newspaper Enterprise Association, Inc.

THAVES

Exercise 28

OBJECTIVE

- To correct errors in capitalization

Exercise 29

OBJECTIVE

- To correct sentences with errors in capitalization

─HELP─

Some capital letters in Exercise 28 are already used correctly.

Reference Note

For information on **capital letters,** see Chapter 22.

Reference Note

For information on **capital letters,** see Chapter 22.

Exercise 28 **Correcting Errors in Capitalization**

The following groups of words contain errors in capitalization. Correct the errors either by changing capital letters to lowercase letters or by changing lowercase letters to capital letters.

EXAMPLE 1. a buddhist temple

1. *a Buddhist temple*

1. appalachian state university
2. world history and math 101
3. tuesday, May 1
4. senator williams
5. Summer In texas
6. Thirty-Fifth avenue
7. saturn and the moon
8. a korean Restaurant
9. empire state building
10. will rogers turnpike

Exercise 29 **Proofreading Sentences for Correct Capitalization**

For each of the following sentences, find the words that should be capitalized but are not. Then, write the words correctly.

EXAMPLE 1. American indians gave the name Buffalo Soldiers to African American troops who served in the West during the civil war.

1. *Indians, Civil War*

1. Thirteen Buffalo Soldiers won the congressional medal of honor, which is the highest military award in the United States.
2. *Black frontiers: A history of African american heroes in the Old west,* by Lillian Schlissel, was published in 1995.
3. A chapter about mary fields tells the story of a woman known as Stagecoach Mary who drove freight wagons and stagecoaches in the west.
4. One of the museums listed in the back of the book is the great plains black museum in Omaha, Nebraska.
5. The book also tells about benjamin singleton, who was born into slavery.

6. After the Civil War, he and some others bought land and founded the communities of Nicodemus and d͟u͟nlap, k͟a͟nsas.

7. The exciting story of the cowboy Nat Love is told in his autobiography, *t͟h͟e life a͟n͟d a͟d͟ventures of Nat Love.*

8. b͟i͟ll p͟i͟ckett, who was of black, white, and American Indian ancestry, was one of the most famous rodeo competitors of all time. **8.** *or* B͟lack, W͟hite

9. Pickett's biography was published by the u͟niversity of o͟klahoma p͟ress in 1977.

10. The businessman and gold miner Barney Ford became very wealthy and built f͟ord's h͟otel on f͟ifteenth s͟treet in d͟enver, Colorado.

Exercise 30 **Proofreading Sentences for the Correct Use of Commas**

For each of the following sentences, write <u>each word or numeral that should be followed by a comma</u> and then add the comma.

EXAMPLE   **1.** The colors of the French flag are red white and blue.

           1. red, white,   Optional commas are underscored.

1. No‚the mountain dulcimer is not the same as the hammered dulcimer‚but both of them are stringed instruments.

2. Abraham Lincoln‚who was the sixteenth president of the United States‚died on April 15‚1865.

3. If you want to knit a sweater‚you will need to get knitting needles‚yarn‚and a pattern.

4. After oiling the wheels on his sister's wagon‚Tyrel oiled the wheels on his skates and on his bicycle.

5. Competing in the 10K race‚Nathan found that he could run faster than his friends.

6. In my opinion‚a person should be fined if loose trash in the back of his or her pickup truck blows out and litters the road.

7. Lupe‚please show us how to use the new computer program.

8. Although Cody is afraid of heights‚he rescued a cat that was stuck high in a tree.

9. I hope that Amy Tan‚my favorite author‚will write another book soon.

10. Many people want to conserve resources‚yet some of these people overlook simple ways to conserve.

Reference Note

For information about **using commas correctly,** see page 602.

COMMON ERRORS

Exercise 31

OBJECTIVE

- To correct sentences with errors in the use of end marks and commas

Cooperative Learning

To review the use of end marks and commas, have students write short, informative paragraphs about topics that interest them. Tell students that their paragraphs should include at least one question and one exclamation. Then, pair students and have them dictate their paragraphs to each other. When they have finished, have the pairs compare their use of commas and end marks in both the original and the dictated version of each paragraph. If there are any discrepancies, have students decide cooperatively which version is correct.

Exercise 32

OBJECTIVE

- To correct sentences with errors in the use of semicolons and colons

Reference Note

For information about **end marks,** see page 598. For information about **commas,** see page 602.

Reference Note

For information about **semicolons and colons,** see page 618.

Exercise 31 **Using Periods, Question Marks, Exclamation Points, and Commas Correctly**

The following sentences lack necessary periods, question marks, exclamation points, and commas. Write the <u>word before each missing punctuation mark</u>, and insert the correct punctuation.

EXAMPLE   1. When will Anita Luís Martina and Sam be back from the mall

   1. *Anita, Luís, Martina, mall?*

Answers may vary. Optional commas are underscored.
1. <u>Wow</u>, look at the size of that <u>alligator</u>!   [*or* Wow! . . . alligator.]
2. Leaning against the <u>mast</u>, I could feel the sails catch the <u>wind</u>.
3. Won't these new colorful curtains brighten this <u>room</u>?
4. By the <u>way</u>, that stack of newspapers should be <u>recycled</u>.
5. Oil <u>paints</u>, whether used for art projects or home <u>improvement</u>, should be used only in well-ventilated <u>areas</u>.
6. <u>Hidiko</u>, watch out for that <u>cactus</u>!   [*or* . . . cactus.]
7. Was Uncle Jesse born in <u>Cincinnati</u>, <u>Ohio</u>, or <u>Louisville</u>, <u>Kentucky</u>?
8. As far as I am <u>concerned</u>, the most interesting parts of the lecture were about the life of <u>W.</u> <u>E.</u> <u>B.</u> <u>DuBois</u>.
9. <u>Monday</u>, <u>Tuesday</u>, or Wednesday will be fine for our next <u>meeting</u>.
10. Would you like to watch a movie <u>tonight</u>, or should I bring over the model-plane kit to work on <u>together</u>?

Exercise 32 **Using Semicolons and Colons Correctly**

The following sentences lack necessary semicolons and colons. Write the <u>words or numerals that come before and after the needed punctuation</u>, and insert the correct punctuation.

EXAMPLE   1. Elena learned Spanish and English at home she learned French and German at school.

   1. *home; she*

1. They should be here before <u>9</u>:<u>30</u> this morning.
2. Our recycling center accepts the following <u>materials</u>: <u>glass</u>, newspaper, cardboard, and aluminum cans.
3. The landscape designer planted bushes around the school last <u>fall</u>; <u>she</u> will plant flowers this spring.
4. Please be at the station by <u>2</u>:<u>15</u> P.M.

5. The children wanted to see bears, lions, and elephants; but parrots, snakes, tortoises, and goats were the only animals there.
6. The sermon was based on Isaiah 61:1.
7. To refinish this dresser, we will need some supplies: varnish remover, sandpaper, steel wool, wood stain, and a clear polyurethane sealant.
8. Walking is terrific exercise; it improves both your stamina and your muscle tone.
9. Many children's books have beautiful illustrations; some are worth having just for the art.
10. Many palaces in Europe are spectacular; Linderhof in Bavaria is my favorite.

Exercise 33 Punctuating and Capitalizing Quotations and Titles

For each of the following sentences, correct any capitalization errors and add or change quotation marks and other marks of punctuation where needed.

Reference Note

For information about **punctuating and capitalizing quotations,** see page 630.

EXAMPLE
1. I learned how to play a new virtual-reality game today Pat said.

1. *"I learned how to play a new virtual-reality game today," Pat said.*

1. The most helpful chapter in my computer manual is "Search Tips" I explained to her.
2. Do Asian cobras look like African cobras Shawn asked.
3. I want to go to the fair after school Ivan said but my trumpet lesson is today.
4. The pilot said we are now beginning our descent into Orlando. Please fasten your seat belts, and return your seats to the upright position.
5. Goodness! what a surprise Taka exclaimed
6. Did some famous person say A smile is contagious
7. Cyclists should always wear helmets said the safety officer
8. Was it he who said a penny saved is a penny earned Troy asked
9. Carlos shouted, look at that dolphin near our boat!
10. During his speech at our school, the mayor said Our children are our future

Exercise 33

OBJECTIVE

■ To correctly punctuate and capitalize quotations and titles

Exercise 33 Punctuating and Capitalizing Quotations and Titles

ANSWERS
Answers may vary slightly. Accept reasonable responses.

1. "The most helpful chapter in my computer manual is 'Search Tips,'" I explained to her.
2. "Do Asian cobras look like African cobras?" Shawn asked.
3. "I want to go to the fair after school," Ivan said, "but my trumpet lesson is today."
4. The pilot said, "We are now beginning our descent into Orlando. Please fasten your seat belts, and return your seats to the upright position."
5. "Goodness! What a surprise!" Taka exclaimed.
6. Did some famous person say, "A smile is contagious"?
7. "Cyclists should always wear helmets," said the safety officer.
8. "Was it he who said, 'A penny saved is a penny earned'?" Troy asked.
9. Carlos shouted, "Look at that dolphin near our boat!"
10. During his speech at our school, the mayor said, "Our children are our future."

COMMON ERRORS

Exercise 34

OBJECTIVE

■ To correctly punctuate and capitalize quotations and titles

Exercise 34 Punctuating and Capitalizing Quotations and Titles

ANSWERS

Answers may vary slightly. Accept reasonable responses.

1. "She has lived a remarkable life," Ernesto said, "and I admire her very much."

2. Angela exclaimed, "Yes, I know about Menchú!"

3. "Menchú is from Guatemala," said Mrs. Harper. "She won the Nobel Peace Prize in 1992."

4. "I once wrote about Menchú in a poem called 'The Heart of a Peacemaker,' " Gale said.

5. "I think Rigoberta Menchú is a great role model," Carla said.

6. "Menchú has tried to make life better for the laborers. Her own family is of Quiché heritage," explained Mark.

7. "Did Stephanie say, 'My dream is to meet Rigoberta Menchú'?" asked Ryan.

8. "Yes, and I'd like to meet her too!" exclaimed Emilio.

9. Mark continued, "Menchú worked long hours on cotton and coffee plantations when she was a child."

10. "Menchú's autobiography is *I . . . Rigoberta Menchú*," said Mrs. Harper.

Reference Note

For information about **using quotation marks,** see page 630.

Reference Note

For information on **using apostrophes,** see page 638.

Exercise 34 Punctuating and Capitalizing Quotations and Titles

For each of the following sentences, correct any capitalization errors and add or change quotation marks and other marks of punctuation where needed.

EXAMPLE 1. Sheila asked have you read about Rigoberta Menchú?

1. *Sheila asked, "Have you read about Rigoberta Menchú?"*

1. She has lived a remarkable life Ernesto said and I admire her very much

2. Angela exclaimed yes, I know about Menchú!

3. Menchú is from Guatemala said Mrs. Harper She won the Nobel Peace Prize in 1992.

4. I once wrote about Menchú in a poem called "The Heart of a Peacemaker" Gale said.

5. I think Rigoberta Menchú is a great role model Carla said.

6. Menchú has tried to make life better for the laborers. Her own family is of Quiché heritage explained Mark

7. Did Stephanie say My dream is to meet Rigoberta Menchú asked Ryan

8. Yes, and I'd like to meet her too exclaimed Emilio.

9. Mark continued Menchú worked long hours on cotton and coffee plantations when she was a child.

10. Menchú's autobiography is *I . . . Rigoberta Menchú* said Mrs. Harper.

Exercise 35 Using Apostrophes Correctly

Add, delete, or move apostrophes where needed in the following word groups. If a word group is already correct, write *C*.

EXAMPLE 1. both boys shoes

1. *boys'*

1. somebodys lunch
2. cant play
3. Neals motorcycle
4. better than theirs 4. C
5. womens volleyball
6. too many letter *u*s
7. its engine   7. C
8. Betsy Rosss flag
9. no more *if*s
10. the bushes branches

Exercise 35

OBJECTIVE

■ To use apostrophes correctly

Exercise 36   Correcting Spelling Errors

Most of the following words are misspelled. If a word is spelled incorrectly, write the correct spelling. If a word is already spelled correctly, write *C*.

EXAMPLE   **1.** succede

  1. succeed

1. taxs	**8.** stathood	**15.** improper
2. vien	**9.** lovelyer	**16.** fancifuly
3. supercede	**10.** clearest	**17.** dryest
4. disallow	**11.** wolfs	**18.** cluless
5. countrys	**12.** sheild	**19.** overjoied
6. emptyness	**13.** preceed	**20.** skiping
7. tracable	**14.** father-in-laws	

Reference Note

For information on **spelling rules,** see page 656.

Exercise 37   Choosing Between Words Often Confused

From each pair in parentheses, choose the word or words that make the sentence correct.

EXAMPLE   **1.** The school plans to (*except, accept*) the new computer company's offer.

  1. accept

1. Did Coach Jefferson (*advise, advice*) you to take the first-aid course at the community center?
2. My cousins and I are (*all ready, already*) to enter the marathon.
3. Sacramento became the (*capital, capitol*) of California in 1854.
4. When garden hoses (*brake, break*), they sometimes can be mended with waterproof tape.
5. Avoid wearing (*loose, lose*) clothing when operating that equipment.
6. Many people know Mr. Perez, but I think he should be (*formerly, formally*) introduced.
7. My grandfather threw the football (*passed, past*) the trees and over the creek.
8. (*Its, It's*) a good idea to test home smoke detectors frequently to make sure the batteries are still working.
9. One basic (*principle, principal*) of our Constitution is the right to free speech.
10. Some cats are called bobtails because of (*their, there*) very short tails.

Reference Note

For information on **words often confused,** see page 666.

Mechanics   **713**

Exercise 36

OBJECTIVE

- To correct spelling errors

Exercise 36   Correcting Spelling Errors

ANSWERS

1. taxes	**11.** wolves
2. vein	**12.** shield
3. supersede	**13.** precede
4. C	**14.** fathers-in-law
5. countries	**15.** C
6. emptiness	**16.** fancifully
7. traceable	**17.** driest
8. statehood	**18.** clueless
9. lovelier	**19.** overjoyed
10. C	**20.** skipping

Exercise 37

OBJECTIVE

- To choose correctly between words often confused

COMMON ERRORS

COMMON ERRORS

Mechanics Test: Section 1

DIRECTIONS Each numbered item below consists of an underlined word or word group. Choose the answer that shows the correct capitalization, punctuation, and spelling of the underlined part. If there is no error, choose D (Correct as is).

EXAMPLE   **[1]** 29 South Maple street

      (A) 29 south Maple Street

      (B) 29 South Maple Street

      (C) Twenty Nine South Maple Street

      (D) Correct as is

ANSWER   1.    Ⓐ Ⓑ Ⓒ Ⓓ

---

29 South Maple Street
Philadelphia, PA 19107

[1] <u>January 15 2001</u>

Mail-Order Sales Manager
[2] <u>Direct Electronics, Inc.</u>
214-C Billings Boulevard
[3] <u>New Castle, Ken. 40050</u>

[4] <u>Dear Sales Manager,</u>

The modem that I ordered from your company arrived today in **[5]** <u>peices.</u> The package was **[6]** <u>open, and appeared</u> not to have been sealed properly. **[7]** <u>In addition I</u> have not yet received the computer game that I also ordered. Please send me a new **[8]** <u>modem the</u> broken modem is enclosed.

I appreciate **[9]** <u>you're</u> prompt attention to both of these matters.

[10] <u>Sincerely yours,</u>

Cameron Scott

Cameron Scott

---

1. **(A)** January 15, 2001   **1.** A
   (B) January, 15 2001
   (C) January 15th 2001
   (D) Correct as is

2. **(A)** direct electronics, inc.   **2.** D
   (B) Direct electronics, inc.
   (C) Direct Electronics, inc.
   (D) Correct as is

3. **(A)** New Castle Ken. 40050   **3.** B
   (B) New Castle, KY 40050
   (C) New Castle KY, 40050
   (D) Correct as is

4. **(A)** Dear sales manager,   **4.** C
   (B) dear sales manager:
   (C) Dear Sales Manager:
   (D) Correct as is

5. **(A)** pieces   **5.** A
   (B) piece's
   (C) peaces
   (D) Correct as is

6. **(A)** open and appeared   **6.** A
   (B) open; and appeared
   (C) open, and, appeared
   (D) Correct as is

7. **(A)** In addition, I   **7.** A
   (B) In addition i
   (C) In addition, i
   (D) Correct as is

8. **(A)** modem, the   **8.** B
   (B) modem; the
   (C) modem: the
   (D) Correct as is

9. **(A)** youre   **9.** C
   (B) your,
   (C) your
   (D) Correct as is

10. **(A)** Sincerely Yours',   **10.** D
    (B) Sincerely your's,
    (C) Sincerely yours:
    (D) Correct as is

Mechanics Test: Section 2

DIRECTIONS   Each of the following sentences contains an underlined word or word group. Choose the answer that shows the correct capitalization, punctuation, and spelling of the underlined part. If there is no error, choose D (Correct as is).

EXAMPLE   1.   Rosie said that her cousin sent her that <u>soft colorful fabric</u> from Kenya.

   (A) soft, colorful, fabric
   (B) soft, colorful fabric
   (C) soft; colorful fabric
   (D) Correct as is

ANSWER   1.   Ⓐ **Ⓑ** Ⓒ Ⓓ

Mechanics   **715**

1. C   **1.** The following people have volunteered to make <u>enchiladas, Manuel,</u> Shawn, and Anita.

      (A) enchiladas; Manuel   **(C)** enchiladas: Manuel

      (B) enchiladas. Manuel   **(D)** Correct as is

2. A   **2.** Our school's <u>recycling program which</u> is now three years old, has been quite successful.

      (A) recycling program, which   **(C)** recycling program; which

      (B) Recycling Program, which   **(D)** Correct as is

3. C   **3.** <u>Looking at the astronomical map in my science book I</u> spotted the constellations Orion, Taurus, and Pisces.

      (A) Looking at the astronomical map, in my science book I

      (B) Looking at the astronomical map, in my science book, I

      (C) Looking at the astronomical map in my science book, I

      (D) Correct as is

4. A   **4.** Donna <u>asked, "who</u> plans to work as a baby sitter over the summer?"

      (A) asked, "Who   **(C)** asked, Who

      (B) asked "who   **(D)** Correct as is

5. D   **5.** Angela and Wanda painted the <u>mural, and Jamal</u> attached it to the wall in the gym.

      (A) mural and Jamal   **(C)** mural, and jamal

      (B) mural: and Jamal   **(D)** Correct as is

6. C   **6.** Many television programs have closed captioning for <u>people who cant</u> hear.

      (A) people, who cant   **(C)** people who can't

      (B) people, who can't   **(D)** Correct as is

7. B   **7.** "What a great time we had at the <u>park"! Sandy</u> exclaimed as she got into the car.

      (A) Park"! Sandy   **(C)** park", Sandy

      (B) park!" Sandy   **(D)** Correct as is

8. D   **8.** "<u>Your aunt Helen</u> certainly is a fascinating person," Carla said.

      (A) "Your Aunt Helen   **(C)** Your aunt Helen

      (B) "Your aunt, Helen   **(D)** Correct as is

RESOURCES

Correcting Common Errors

Review

- *Grammar, Usage, and Mechanics,* pp. 387, 388, 389, 390

Assessment

- *Assessment Package*
  —*Chapter Tests,* Ch. 26
  —*Chapter Tests in Standardized Test Formats,* Ch. 26
- *Test Generator (One-Stop Planner CD-ROM)*

9. "Many of us would have gone to the picnic if we had known about <u>it</u>" Alan said.

    (A) it",
    (B) it,"
    (C) it,
    (D) Correct as is

10. The Zunigas have a new <u>puppy; its</u> a cocker spaniel.

    (A) puppy; Its   **(C)** puppy, its
    (B) puppy; it's   **(D)** Correct as is

11. The ants <u>carried large leafs</u> across John Henry's backyard.

    (A) carryed large leafs   **(C)** carried large leaves
    (B) carryed large leaves   **(D)** Correct as is

12. Has the guide <u>all ready led</u> the hikers to the top of the mesa?

    (A) all ready lead   **(C)** already led
    (B) already lead   **(D)** Correct as is

13. If Carlos wants to play the role of Eddie in the <u>musical, he'll have too practice</u> the solos.

    (A) musical, he'll have to practice
    (B) musical; he'll have to practice
    (C) musical he'll have too practice
    (D) Correct as is

14. <u>Sara said that the big guppy in the class aquarium is going to have babies.</u>

    (A) Sara said "That the big guppy in the class aquarium is going to have babies."
    (B) Sara said "that the big guppy in the class aquarium is going to have babies."
    (C) Sara said "That the big guppy in the class aquarium is going to have babies".
    (D) Correct as is

15. On <u>October 1 1960</u> Nigeria became an independent nation.

    (A) October, 1 1960   **(C)** October 1, 1960
    (B) October 1, 1960,   **(D)** Correct as is

COMMON ERRORS

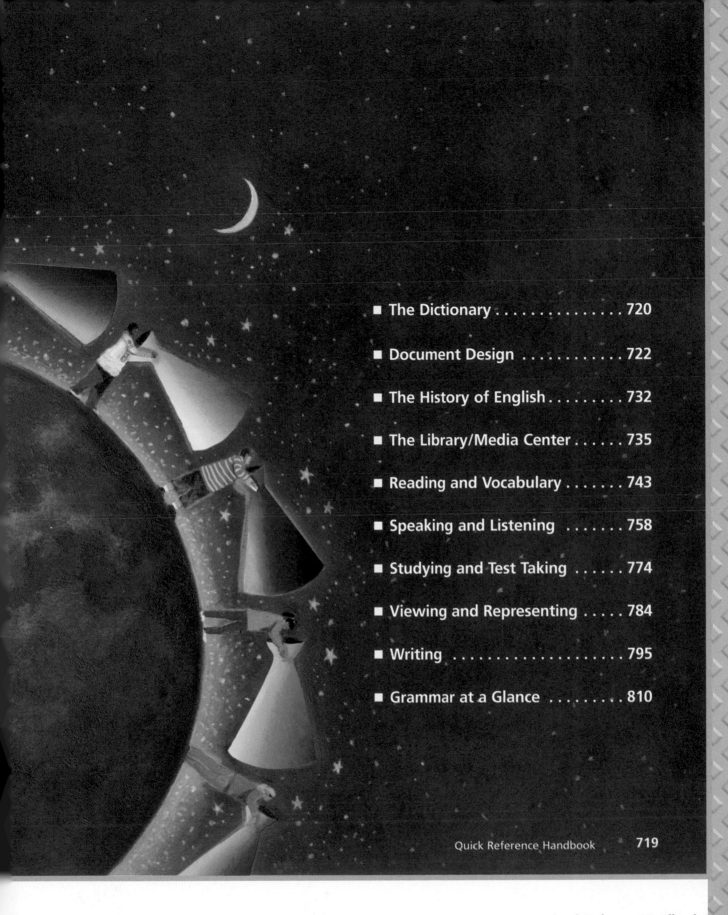

Quick Reference Handbook **719**

The Dictionary

Types and Contents

Types of Dictionaries   Different types of dictionaries provide different kinds of information. You should choose a dictionary based on the kind of information that you need. The chart below explains the differences among three types of dictionaries; abridged, specialized, and unabridged. It also provides an example of each type of dictionary.

Dictionary Entry   A dictionary entry gives more than just the meaning of a word. A sample entry from an abridged dictionary appears on the next page. The callout explanations that follow the entry explain what kinds of information an entry provides.

Types of Dictionaries

Type	Example
An **abridged** dictionary is the most common type of dictionary. The word *abridged* means "shortened" or "condensed." An abridged dictionary contains most of the words you are likely to use or encounter in your writing or reading.	*Merriam-Webster's Collegiate Dictionary, Tenth Edition*
A **specialized** dictionary defines words or terms that are used in a particular profession, field, or area of interest.	*Stedman's Medical Dictionary*
An **unabridged** dictionary contains nearly all the words in use in a language.	*Webster's Third New International Dictionary*

QUICK REFERENCE HANDBOOK

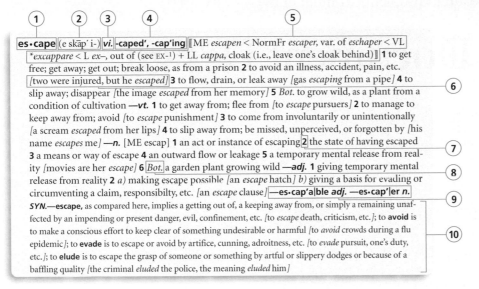

1. **Entry word** The *entry word* shows the correct spelling of a word. An alternate spelling may also be shown. The entry word shows how the word should be divided into syllables, and it may show whether the word should be capitalized.

2. **Pronunciation** The pronunciation of a word is shown using accent marks, phonetic symbols, and diacritical marks. *Accent marks* show stress. Each *phonetic symbol* represents a specific sound. *Diacritical marks* are symbols placed above letters to show how they sound.

3. **Part-of-speech labels** These labels are usually abbreviated and show how the entry word should be used in a sentence. Some words may be used as more than one part of speech.

4. **Other forms** A dictionary may show spellings of plural forms of nouns, tenses of verbs, or the comparative forms of adjectives and adverbs.

5. **Etymology** The *etymology* tells how a word (or its parts) entered the English language. The etymology also shows how the word has changed over time.

6. **Examples** A dictionary may demonstrate how a word may be used by giving phrases or sentences containing that word.

7. **Definitions** If there is more than one meaning for a word, the definitions are separated by numbers or letters.

8. **Special usage labels** These labels identify the fields in which a word has a special meaning, such as *Bot.* (botany), or how it is used in special ways, such as *Slang* or *Rare*.

9. **Related word forms** These are other forms of the entry word, such as another form of the word that is created by adding suffixes or prefixes, or a common phrase in which the entry word appears.

10. **Synonyms and antonyms** Words that are similar in meaning are *synonyms*. Words that are opposite in meaning are *antonyms*. Dictionaries may list synonyms and antonyms at the end of some word entries.

Document Design

Manuscript Style

Whether you write a paper by hand or use a word-processing program, your teacher will want you to set up your paper in a certain way. Use the following guidelines to prepare a typed or handwritten paper that is neat and easy to read.

Guidelines for Manuscript Style

1. Use only one side of each sheet of paper.

2. Type your paper using a word processor, or write it neatly in blue or black ink.

3. For handwritten papers, ask your teacher if he or she wants you to skip lines. For typed papers or word-processed papers, many teachers prefer that you double-space your assignment.

4. Leave one-inch margins at the top, bottom, and sides of your paper.

5. The first line of every paragraph should be indented five spaces. You can set a **tab** on a word processor to indent five spaces automatically.

6. Number all pages in the top right-hand corner. Do not number the first page.

7. Make sure your pages look neat and clean. For handwritten papers, you may want to use correction fluid to correct your mistakes. If you have several mistakes on one page, however, write out the page again. For papers typed on a word processor, you can make corrections and print out a clean copy.

8. Use the heading your teacher prefers for your name, your class, the date, and the title of your paper. Your teacher may prefer that you list this information on a title page. If so, use a separate sheet of paper and place the information your teacher requests in the center of the sheet. Put only one piece of information on each line, and center-align the text. (See page 723.)

Desktop Publishing

Which would you be more likely to read: a report that contains page after page of poorly arranged text, or one that contains both neatly arranged text and eye-catching graphics? You can create attractive reports, newsletters, and other documents by using *desktop publishing*. **Desktop publishing** is a way of using a personal computer to create attractive documents that contain both text and graphics. However, even if you do not have access to a computer, you can use many of the ideas discussed below to help you design a better-looking handwritten paper.

The information in the following section will help you arrange the text of your document. For information about how you can use graphics to make your ideas clearer to readers, see also **Graphics** on page 728.

Page Layout

Page layout refers to how a page is arranged. To create an effective page layout, you must decide the best way to arrange text and graphics on the page. As you prepare to lay out the design of your page, consider the following page layout features.

Alignment   The term *alignment* refers to the arrangement of lines of text on the page. Text can be *left-*, *right-*, or *center-aligned*. Alignment can also be *ragged* or *justified*. Aligning your text properly can help you produce a neat, easy-to-read document.

- **Left-aligned**   When a section of text is *left-aligned,* each line begins at the left margin of the page or column. Since

English is read from left to right, most blocks of text are left-aligned.

EXAMPLE

These lines of text are left-aligned. Notice that each line begins at the left margin of the column.

- **Right-aligned**   Text that is *right-aligned* lines up against the right margin of the page or column. In reports, your name, the date, and page numbers may be right-aligned. Usually, only small amounts of text are right-aligned, because right-aligned text is difficult to read. Quotes pulled from poetry or other writing are sometimes right-aligned to make them stand out more. (See also **Pull-quote** on page 725.)

EXAMPLE

These lines of text are right-aligned. All of the text is lined up against the right margin of the column.

- **Center-aligned**   Text that is *center-aligned* is centered on an invisible line down the middle of the page or column. Centered text is frequently used for titles or other information, especially in posters, advertisements, and cards.

EXAMPLE

These lines are center-aligned. They are centered on an imaginary line down the middle of the column.

■ **Justified**   Text that is *justified* forms a straight edge along the right and left margins. However, spaces must be added to the lines to make sure each edge lines up. (The last line in justified text may be shorter than the other lines.) Justified text can give your document a neat, clean look.

EXAMPLE

This text is justified. The text forms a straight edge along the right and left margins of the column.

■ **Ragged**   Text that is *ragged* does not line up on both sides. When ragged text is right-aligned, each line forms a neat edge on the right but not on the left. When ragged text is left-aligned, each line forms a neat edge on the left but not on the right.

EXAMPLE

These lines are left-aligned and ragged. Each line forms a neat edge on the left but not on the right.

Bullet   A *bullet* (•) is a large dot or other symbol used to call attention to information. Brief, important pieces of information, such as instructions or lists, are easier to read when listed with bullets. The following bulleted list gives some guidelines for using bullets.

■ Make sure your bulleted list contains at least two items.

■ Be sure that each item in your list begins with the same type of wording. For example, each item in this bullet list begins with an imperative sentence, which is a sentence that gives a command.

■ Line up text within a bulleted item beneath the first letter of the first word, not beneath the bullet itself. For example, all of the text after the first line of this bulleted item lines up beneath the word *Line.*

Contrast   The balance of light and dark areas on a page is called *contrast.* Light areas have very little text and few, if any, pictures. Dark areas contain lots of text and perhaps pictures or other graphics. Pages with high contrast—or a good mix of both light and dark areas—are easier to read than pages with low contrast.

Emphasis   *Emphasis* is a designer's way of showing readers the most important information on a page. You can create emphasis by putting a box around important information or by experimenting with text size or style. Emphasis can also be created by using color and graphics. All of these techniques are used in the sample newspaper layout shown below.

THE WEEKLY TRUMPET
The Voice of Miller Middle School
January 30, 2001

Teen Triathlete Triumphs!

Millersville

What is a Triathlon?

Gutter   A *gutter* is the inner margin of space from the printed area of a page to the book's binding.

Headers and Footers   A writer uses *headers* and *footers* to provide information about a document. Headers appear in the top margin of a page, and footers appear in the bottom margin of a page. Headers and footers frequently contain information such as the following:

- author's name
- publication's name
- publication date
- chapter or section title
- page numbers

Headings and Subheadings   Titles within the sections of a document are called *headings* and *subheadings.* Headings and subheadings (also called *heads* and *sub-heads*) show readers how information in a document is organized.

- **Headings** are titles for major sections of text. A heading appears at the beginning of the section of text and is often in large, bold, or capital letters. (See also **Type** on page 726.)

- **Subheadings** are more specific headings within a major section. A writer uses subheadings to break a section into smaller sections so that readers can easily find the information they need. To make a subheading stand out, it may be set in a different size or design of type than that of the main text.

EXAMPLE

Information Just ——(heading)
a Click Away
The Internet Is Changing——(subheading)
How We Get the Weather
Forecast

Not so long ago, if you wanted ——(text) to find out the weather forecast, you had to flip on the television at the right time. If you turned it on five minutes too early, you had to wait; if you turned it on five minutes too late, you were out of luck. Now, with the help of the Internet, you can go online any time during the day and find out the forecast.

Indentation   When you *indent* text, you move the text a few spaces to the right of the left margin. The standard amount of indentation for beginning a new paragraph is five spaces or half an inch.

Margins   The *margin* on a page is the blank space that surrounds the text on the sides, the top, and bottom. Many word-processing programs commonly set margins at 1.25 inches for the sides and 1 inch for the top and bottom. However, you can change the margins to fit more or less text on the page. Make sure you check with your teacher before changing your margins on an assignment.

Pull-quote   A *pull-quote* is a direct quotation pulled out of a text and made into a graphic within the story. For example, an important quote may be taken from a magazine article and set in the margin of that article to attract a reader's attention. Pull-quotes should be short. They may even be just part of a sentence instead of a complete one.

EXAMPLE

> Microbes, the tiny forms of life that many think of as "germs" or "bugs," are everywhere. They have been discovered living in sediments found over five hundred meters beneath the ocean bed. They even exist inside of rocks. Microbes indeed surround us.
>
> ***Microbes indeed surround us.***

Rules   A *rule* is a vertical or horizontal line used to set off text from other elements such as headlines and graphics. Vertical rules can separate columns on a page.

Titles and Subtitles   The *title* of a document is its name. A *subtitle* is usually longer and more descriptive than a title. You may find a title followed by a colon and a subtitle, but if the title appears on its own line, no colon is necessary. Titles and subtitles of books appear on a title page at the beginning of the book.

EXAMPLE

Going to the Extreme
A Guide to Snowboarding, Skateboarding, and Other Extreme Sports

White Space   On a page, any area where there is no text or graphics is called *white space.* Proper use of white space can make a page look neater; it can also make a page easier to read. Usually, white space is limited to the margins; the gutter; and the spaces between words, lines, and columns. (See also **Contrast** on page 724.)

Type

Type refers to the characters that make up printed text. When you create a document, you must make several decisions about type. For example, you must decide which size and design of type is best for your document. Making thoughtful decisions about type can help you produce an eye-catching, easy-to-read document.

Font   The term *font* is used to describe a set of characters (such as numbers, letters, and punctuation marks) of a particular design and size. For example, 12-point Times Roman is a font. The font size is twelve points (see below); the font design is Times Roman. Many different computer fonts are available. A font design is also called a *typeface.*

Font Size   The size of type in a document is known as the *font size,* or *point size.* The size of type is measured in points, each of which is $\frac{1}{72}$ of an inch. School assignments are usually printed in twelve-point type. Captions for pictures are usually printed in smaller sizes. Titles may be printed in point sizes that are larger than the point size of the main text.

EXAMPLE

Title ————— (24 point)
Text text text text —— (12 point)
Caption caption caption —— (9 point)

Font Style   The *font style* refers to the way the type is printed. A different font style may be used to emphasize words or phrases. For example, important words in a passage are frequently printed in *italics.* Other styles of font, such as **boldface,** can be used to set off headings, subheadings, subtitles, or other parts from the main text. Look at the examples of font styles below.

- **Boldface**   A *boldface* word is written in thick, heavy type. Boldface can be used to emphasize information.

  EXAMPLE
  This sentence is written in boldface type.

- **Capital letters**   A *capital* (or *uppercase*) *letter* signals a proper name, the beginning of a sentence, a title, and so on. Headings and subheadings may appear in all capital letters. For emphasis, a writer will sometimes put a word or a sentence in all capital letters. However, this strategy should not be overused.

- **Condensed**   When type is *condensed,* the letters in a word have less space between them. Writers may use condensed type to save space.

  EXAMPLE
  This sentence is written in condensed type.

- **Expanded**   When type is *expanded,* the letters in a word have more space between them. Writers may use expanded type to fill up space.

  EXAMPLE
  This sentence is written in expanded type.

- **Italics**   Type that is *italic* has a slanted style. Italic type can be used to emphasize information. It is also used to cite titles in text and in other conventional situations. (For more on **italics,** see page 628.)

EXAMPLE
This sentence is written in italic type.

- **Lowercase letters**   A *lowercase letter* is not a capital or a small capital. (See **Small capitals** below.) Lowercase letters are the most frequently used letters.

- **Shadow**   A word written in *shadow* style appears to cast shadows. Shadow style may be used for titles and headings.

  EXAMPLE
  This sentence is written in shadow style.

- **Small capitals**   When writing abbreviations referring to time, use *small capitals.* For example, when typing the time *12:05 P.M.* and year A.D. *1066,* you should use small capitals.

Leading   Another word for *line spacing,* or the distance between lines of text, is *leading* (rhymes with *wedding*). Most word-processing programs allow you to adjust the amount of space between each line. Most formal documents you create for your teacher are double-spaced. Double-spaced papers make it easier for your teacher to read your assignment and make corrections or comments on the page. Books, magazines, and newspapers, which are meant for a general audience, are single-spaced.

Legibility   A *legible* document has text and graphics that are clear and easily recognizable. A document with high legibility uses a simple, easy-to-read font size and design for the main text.

Typeface   See **Font** on page 726.

Graphics

Graphics can often communicate information more quickly and effectively than words. Graphics you can use in your documents include *charts, diagrams, graphs, illustrations,* and *tables.* Graphics can

- show information
- explain how to do something
- show how something looks, works, or is organized
- show developments over a period of time

Graphics have the most impact when they support text information on the page where they appear. When designed carefully, graphics and text work together to communicate the same message clearly.

Arrangement and Design

The following arrangement and design ideas can help you create informative and effective graphics.

Accuracy   When creating your graphic, make sure the information it contains is *accurate.* In other words, make sure your graphic contains true information.

Color   Readers are attracted to colorful graphics. You can use color to do the following:

- get readers' attention
- emphasize certain information
- group items on a page
- help organize a page or document

Keep the following tips in mind when you choose colors for your graphics.

- *Create a color scheme.* A color scheme is a collection of two or more colors that work well together. Using only one color can make your document look dull.

- *Choose complementary colors.* Colors that are too close to each other on the color wheel (see below) will tend to blend together. Instead, use colors that are opposite each other on the wheel. Colors that are opposite each other are considered *complements.* Color schemes work best when they combine complementary colors.

- *Do not overuse warm colors.* Warm colors, such as red, orange, and yellow, seem to jump off the page. Using them less often creates a more dramatic effect when you do use them.

- *Use cool colors to create a softer effect.* Cool colors, such as blue and green, can work well as backgrounds because they will not overpower your text and graphics.

Color wheels, like the one below, show how colors relate to each other. The three

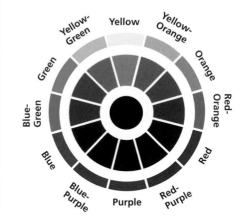

primary colors are red, blue, and yellow. All other colors are made by combining the primary colors or by mixing them with white or black.

Focus   The subject of a graphic is the graphic's *focus*. Answer these questions to make sure your graphic has a clear focus.

- *Is the graphic's subject clear?* Make sure your graphic has a clear title that describes the subject.

- *Does the graphic have any unnecessary details?* Any detail that does not make your idea clearer can be distracting. Crop or trim out the distracting details to make the graphic's focus clear.

- *Does the graphic show all of the subject, or are some parts hidden from view?* Make sure the reader can see all important parts of the subject.

- *Does the graphic need labels?* Labeling the graphic can help readers understand it better. Make sure not to use too many labels, however. Too many labels can confuse the reader and make the graphic look cluttered.

- *Is a source provided for the information in the graphic?* Telling readers where you found the facts in your visual can show that the information is trustworthy.

    Make sure that the focus of your graphic supports your text.

Labels and Captions   If your graphic needs explanation, add *labels* and *captions*. *Labels* either appear within the graphic or are connected to it by thin lines called *rules*. Labels identify important parts of a graphic. A **caption** is a sentence that explains a graphic. Photographs and illustrations often have captions. A caption appears directly beside, above, or under the graphic. If you do not use labels or captions in your graphic, make sure your graphic has a clear, descriptive title.

Types of Graphics

Use the definitions and examples that follow to choose graphics that will make your ideas clear to readers. Once you decide on the type of graphics you will use in your document, you can create the graphics by computer or by hand.

Chart   A *chart* helps show how pieces of information relate to each other. Two of the most common types of charts are flowcharts and pie charts.

- **Flowcharts**   *Flowcharts* show a sequence, or order, of events. The boxes in a flowchart contain text, and they are set in order from left to right or top to bottom. Many flowcharts contain arrows to show the direction to read.

EXAMPLE

Planning a Party

Choose a date and reason for your party.

↓

Plan the food, drinks, and activities.

↓

Make a list of guests and send out invitations.

↓

Buy supplies.

↓

Have fun!

Graphics   **729**

■ **Pie charts** *Pie charts* show percentages, or how parts of a whole relate to each other. Pie charts are often used to show comparisons. (For an example of a pie chart, see page 750.)

Diagram A *diagram* uses pictures and symbols, such as arrows or circles, to compare abstract ideas or to provide instruction. A diagram may show how to do something or how something works. Diagrams contain only the most important information, leaving out unnecessary details. They may be drawn by hand or by using a computer program.

EXAMPLE

The Greenhouse Effect

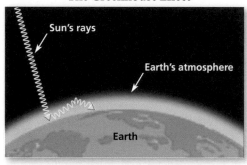

Graphs A *graph* can show changes over time in a way that allows readers to understand the changes at a glance. A line graph is often used to show the patterns of change, or trends. Bar graphs are usually used to show comparisons. The horizontal axis (the bottom line) in a line or bar graph usually shows periods or points in time. The vertical axis (the line to the left side of the graph) usually shows amounts.

EXAMPLES

Line Graph

Tree Planting Efforts in Chesterfield

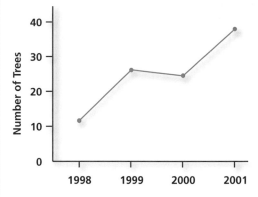

Bar Graph

Tree Planting Efforts in Chesterfield

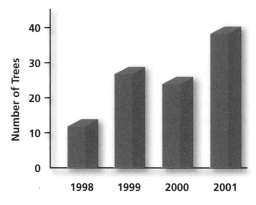

Illustration An *illustration* is a drawing or photograph that can show readers unfamiliar, new, or hard-to-describe items or events; the way something works; how to do something; or what something or someone looks like. (See also **Diagram** on this page; see also page 789.)

Storyboard A *storyboard* illustrates the different segments or scenes of an event or story. Storyboards are frequently used to map out a story or to plan a video. A storyboard contains several boxes, each representing one scene in the story. The boxes contain drawings and some text. If the storyboard will be used for a video, the narrator's or actors' words will appear as a caption outside the box. Most storyboards are drawn by hand, although the text may be typed. (See also page 259.)

Table A *table* provides raw information without showing trends or patterns. While readers of graphs can immediately see an increase or decrease, readers of tables must look at all of the information and draw their own conclusions. After studying the following tables, for example, a reader could conclude that teen volunteerism rose for three years in a row and that most of the volunteers were fifteen years old. A reader might also predict that teen volunteerism will continue to rise in the future.

EXAMPLES

Two-column Table

Number of Teen Volunteers in Hastings by Year	
Year	Number of Teen Volunteers
1999	15
2000	17
2001	27

Three-column Table

Number of Retirement Home Volunteers by Age and School		
Age of teens	Jamestown High	Boomer High
14	1	2
15	5	8
16	3	5
17	2	1

When making a table, be sure to organize information logically and label information clearly so that your readers will understand your point.

Time Line A *time line* shows events that happen over a period of time. The points along the horizontal axis of a time line show points in time. The events that happen during a specific year or period of years are described above or below the time line. Time lines may also include small illustrations.

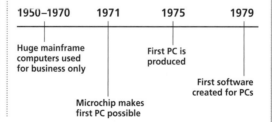

Events in the Creation of Personal Computers

1950–1970	1971	1975	1979

Huge mainframe computers used for business only

First PC is produced

Microchip makes first PC possible

First software created for PCs

The History of English

Origins and Uses

A Changing Language

A family tree shows the ancestors of a particular family. The English language has a family tree that sprang up thousands of years ago. A single early language grew into different branches. Each branch represented a different language, and one of these languages was English. No one knows exactly when English branched off as a separate language. However, we do know that a form of English was spoken by tribes of people who invaded the island of Britain in the fifth century. These tribes conquered the area that is now England, and the language they spoke was the ancestor of modern-day English.

English did not always look and sound the way it does today. The development of English into the language we use today took centuries. Speakers of English continued to change the language by adding new words and by changing the pronunciation, spelling, and meaning of existing words.

Changes in Spelling   Would you recognize the words *threo, sumor,* or *sceap*?

Believe it or not, you know the meanings of these common words, but their spelling has changed over time. The modern spellings are *three, summer,* and *sheep*. Time is not the only reason that a word's spelling changes. Different spellings of a word can be standard in different places. For example, in the United States standard spellings include *color, theater,* and *tire*. In Great Britain, these words are spelled *colour, theatre,* and *tyre*.

Changes in Pronunciation   By the 1300s, written English looked similar to the English we use now, but the words were pronounced differently. For example, *meek* was pronounced like *make, boot* like *boat,* and *mouse* like *moose*.

Changes in pronunciation explain why many English words are not spelled the way they sound. For example, the word *knight* used to begin with a strong *k* sound. The letter remained part of the spelling even though the *k* sound was eventually dropped.

Changes in Meaning   What if your mother accused you of being nice and your teacher complimented you for being awful? If you lived during the Middle Ages, you would understand that *awful* is appropriate for a compliment while being called *nice* would be an insult. During the Middle Ages, *nice* meant "lazy" or "foolish," and *awful* meant "very impressive." Today, these words have almost the opposite meanings.

Meanings of words are still changing today. Some words change their meaning as a result of their usage. For example, the word *cool* can mean "excellent" in informal English. Other words may change their meanings in different locations. A *bonnet* means "a hat" in the United States, but in Great Britain, it means "the hood of a car."

Word Origins   English is a multicultural language. Only about 15 percent of the words we use are native to English. The other 85 percent are words that we have borrowed from other languages and cultures. When you say you want to *munch* a *burrito* or *feast* on *chop suey,* you have borrowed words from other languages. Here are some other examples of words that English has borrowed in the past one thousand years.

AFRICAN LANGUAGES	gumbo, okra
FRENCH	beauty, dance, study
LATIN	area, candle, decorate, joke
NATIVE AMERICAN LANGUAGES	bayou, chipmunk, squash
NORSE	fellow, get, leg
SPANISH	chili, hurricane, mustang

Dialects of American English

You probably know people who pronounce words differently than you do or use words in unfamiliar ways. The variety of English comes from various **dialects,** which are the ways that different groups of people speak English. Although dialects vary widely, no dialect is better or worse than another. In this section, you will learn about two types of American English dialects, *ethnic dialects* and *regional dialects.*

Ethnic Dialects   People who share the same cultural heritage may share a dialect of English, too. The English used by a particular cultural group is called an ***ethnic dialect.*** Widely used American ethnic dialects include the English of many African Americans (called African American Vernacular English) and the Spanish-influenced English of many people whose families come from Mexico, Central America, Cuba, and Puerto Rico.

Many words that are now part of general English usage originally came from ethnic dialects. For example, the words *afro, jazz,* and *jukebox* were originally African American English dialect words, and *arroyo, mesa,* and *taco* were originally from Hispanic English.

Regional Dialects   Do you eat *lunch* or *dinner*? Do you *wash* (or *warsh*) the *car* (or *cah*)? Do you stand *on* line or *in* line? Where you come from can help determine what words you use, how you pronounce them, and how you put words together. A dialect shared by people from the same area of the United States is called a ***regional dialect.***

TEACHING TIP

Word Origins
Show students that the source language of a word can determine its spelling. Begin by pointing out other words from French that contain the pattern *ance* found in *dance,* including *romance* and *elegance.* Then, divide the class evenly into five groups and assign each group to research one of the following spelling patterns: *tio* (Latin) [relation, lotion], *ll* pronounced *y* (Spanish) [tortilla, llano], *ps/pt/pn* with silent *p* (Greek) [psychology, pteranodon, pneumonia], *gn* with a silent *g* (French) [campaign, gnome], and *sch* pronounced *sh* (German/Yiddish) [schnauzer, mensch]. Each group member should use a dictionary to search for three to five words from the source language. Then, group members should compile a list of all of the words found and try to identify two spelling patterns common to words from the source language. Finally, each group should present its findings in a poster that highlights the spelling patterns identified and lists all of the words found.

Not everyone who lives in a region uses that region's dialect. Someone from Alabama or Georgia might not say *y'all,* and someone from Boston may not pronounce *farm* like *fahm.* When people move from place to place, they often lose some of their old dialect and learn a new one.

Standard American English

Every variety of English has its own set of guidelines, but no variety is better or more correct than another. However, one form of English is more widely used and accepted than others in the United States. This variety is called ***standard American English.***

Standard American English is a variety that people from many different regions and cultures can understand. It is the variety you hear on radio and television and read in books and magazines, and it is the form people are expected to use in school and business situations.

Part 3: Grammar, Usage, and Mechanics in this textbook will help you understand the rules for using standard American English. The label *nonstandard* that appears next to some expressions in Part 3 indicates that the form is not considered *standard. Nonstandard* does not mean incorrect language. It identifies language that is inappropriate in situations where standard English is expected.

Formal and Informal English

The various dialects mentioned above account for some of the differences in the way people speak and write English.

Different situations also affect the way people speak or write, because you choose different words based on your purpose and audience. Look at the following sentences:

I really enjoyed that story about the men who climbed Mount Everest.

I really got into that story about the guys who climbed Mount Everest.

The sentences say the same things, but the first sentence uses *formal English,* and the other uses *informal English.* You might use the second sentence in a conversation with a friend. In a report, however, the formal English in the first sentence is more appropriate.

- **Colloquialisms** *Colloquialisms* are a common type of informal English that we use in everyday conversations. These colorful expressions have understood meanings that are different from the basic meanings of the words.

EXAMPLES
My parents **hit the ceiling** when I wrecked my bike.
The plot of that movie was **hard to swallow**.

- **Slang** *Slang* consists of made-up words or old words used in new ways. Slang is often the special language of specific groups, such as teenagers or athletes. Since slang changes very quickly, with expressions going out of style, some of the examples below may seem dated to you.

EXAMPLES
dis—to insult
my bad—an apology
weak—inadequate

The Library/Media Center

Using Print and Electronic Sources

Information is at your fingertips at your community or school library/media center. Libraries are not just for school assignments. You can find the statistics for your favorite sports team, research a place for a family vacation, or read the latest movie magazines. As long as you know how to use the library, it can bring you hours of enjoyment and information. Understanding the following terms will help you get the most out of the library.

Call Number   Every book in a library has a number and letter code known as its *call number*. The call number tells how a book has been classified and where it is shelved in the library. Most libraries use the *Dewey decimal system* to assign call numbers. (See also **Card Catalog** on this page.)

The *Dewey decimal system* assigns numbers to nonfiction books according to ten general subjects. However, biographies and autobiographies may be placed in a separate section from other nonfiction books and arranged alphabetically according to the last name of the book's subject. Fiction books are usually separated from nonfiction books, too. Novels and short stories are grouped together under *Fiction* and arranged alphabetically by the author's last name.

Card Catalog   The traditional *card catalog* is a cabinet of small drawers containing index cards that show information about a book and where to find it in the library. These cards are arranged in alphabetical order by title, author, and subject. You do not need to know all three forms of information. You can find a book using the card catalog even if you know only the subject or only the author's name. All books have a *title card* and an *author card.* Nonfiction books will have a third card, a *subject card.* The title card is placed in the card catalog alphabetically by the first

Information in the Card Catalog

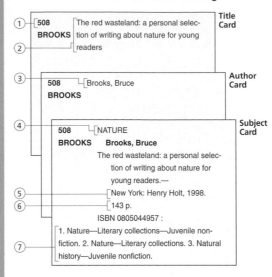

7. Cross-references to other headings or related topics under which you can find additional books

Many libraries now use electronic or online card catalogs instead of traditional card catalogs. (See also **Online Card Catalog** on page 737.) Even if a library has a card catalog, make sure it includes all of the books in the library. Many libraries no longer update the cards.

CD-ROMs (Compact Disc-Read Only Memory) A *CD-ROM* is like a giant book that you see and hear using a computer with a CD-ROM drive. CD-ROMs are a compact way to store many pages of text, so many encyclopedias, dictionaries, and indexes now use this format. One CD-ROM may contain the equivalent of 250,000 pages of printed text. In addition, CD-ROMs can perform searches, provide interactive graphics, and supply audio. (For some specific CD-ROM titles, see the **Reference Sources** chart on page 739.)

Indexes When researching, you might first consult an *index*, which lists topics, sources, and authors. The *Readers' Guide to Periodical Literature*, for example, helps readers find articles, poems, and stories from more than two hundred magazines and journals. Articles are listed alphabetically by author and by subject in boldface, capitalized headings. A key located in the front of the *Readers' Guide* explains the meanings of the abbreviations used in the entries. On the next page you will find examples of entries from the print and online versions of the *Readers' Guide*.

important word in the title. The author card is alphabetized by the author's last name. The subject card is alphabetized by the first letter of the subject category. Above are examples of the title, author, and subject cards for *The Red Wasteland* by Bruce Brooks. The features of each card are explained in the following list.

1. The **call number** assigned to a book by the Dewey decimal or Library of Congress classification system
2. The full **title** and **subtitle** of a book
3. The **author's full name,** last name first
4. The general **subject** of a book; a subject card may show specific headings
5. The place and date of **publication**
6. A **description** of the book, such as its size and number of pages, and whether it is illustrated

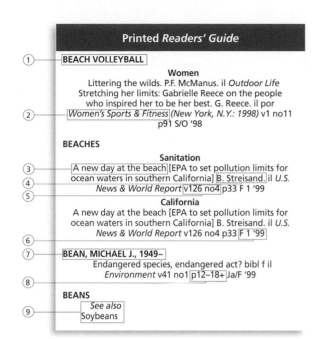

Printed *Readers' Guide*

(1) **BEACH VOLLEYBALL**

Women
Littering the wilds. P.F. McManus. il *Outdoor Life*
Stretching her limits: Gabrielle Reece on the people
who inspired her to be her best. G. Reece. il por
(2) *Women's Sports & Fitness* (New York, N.Y.: 1998) v1 no11
p91 S/O '98

BEACHES

Sanitation
(3) A new day at the beach [EPA to set pollution limits for
(4) ocean waters in southern California] B. Streisand. il *U.S.*
(5) *News & World Report* v126 no4 p33 F 1 '99

California
A new day at the beach [EPA to set pollution limits for
ocean waters in southern California] B. Streisand. il *U.S.*
(6) *News & World Report* v126 no4 p33 F 1 '99

(7) **BEAN, MICHAEL J., 1949–**
Endangered species, endangered act? bibl f il
(8) *Environment* v41 no1 p12–18+ Ja/F '99

BEANS
(9) *See also*
Soybeans

(1) **Subject entry**

(2) **Name of magazine**

(3) **Title of article**

(4) **Author of article**

(5) **Volume number of magazine**

(6) **Date of magazine**

(7) **Author entry**

(8) **Page reference**

(9) **Subject cross-reference**

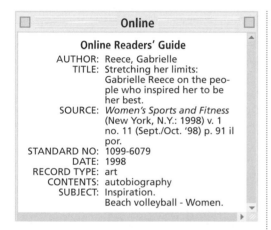

Online

Online Readers' Guide
AUTHOR: Reece, Gabrielle
TITLE: Stretching her limits:
Gabrielle Reece on the peo-
ple who inspired her to be
her best.
SOURCE: *Women's Sports and Fitness*
(New York, N.Y.: 1998) v. 1
no. 11 (Sept./Oct. '98) p. 91 il
por.
STANDARD NO: 1099-6079
DATE: 1998
RECORD TYPE: art
CONTENTS: autobiography
SUBJECT: Inspiration.
Beach volleyball - Women.

Internet   The *Internet* is an international network of computers. Using the Internet, a computer user can get information from other computers anywhere in the world. The Internet was first used by research scientists in the 1960s to share data with each other.

The Internet now contains information on almost any topic. To use the Internet, you need access to a computer and a modem.

Microforms   *Microforms* are pages from various newspapers and magazines that are reduced on film to miniature size. The two most common types are **microfilm** (a roll or reel of film) and **microfiche** (a sheet of film). You view them by using a special projector which enlarges the images to a readable size.

Online Card Catalog   An *online card catalog* is a card catalog stored on a computer. Instead of searching through individual cards, you may find a book by typing in the book's title, author, or subject. The computer will display the results of the search information, which you can then print out. On the next page is an example of an online card catalog entry.

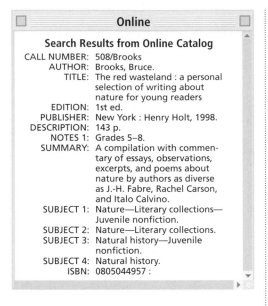

Online

Search Results from Online Catalog

CALL NUMBER: 508/Brooks
AUTHOR: Brooks, Bruce.
TITLE: The red wasteland : a personal selection of writing about nature for young readers
EDITION: 1st ed.
PUBLISHER: New York : Henry Holt, 1998.
DESCRIPTION: 143 p.
NOTES 1: Grades 5–8.
SUMMARY: A compilation with commentary of essays, observations, excerpts, and poems about nature by authors as diverse as J.-H. Fabre, Rachel Carson, and Italo Calvino.
SUBJECT 1: Nature—Literary collections—Juvenile nonfiction.
SUBJECT 2: Nature—Literary collections.
SUBJECT 3: Natural history—Juvenile nonfiction.
SUBJECT 4: Natural history.
ISBN: 0805044957 :

Online Databases An *online database* is a collection of information stored on a computer. Most databases are created for specific groups of people or organizations, such as universities, libraries, or businesses. Some databases require a subscription, and subscribers must pay to use the database. Other databases, including some encyclopedias, are free and may be accessed through the World Wide Web.

Online Sources Anytime you retrieve information using the Internet, you have used an *online source*. The term *online* refers to the telephone and fiber-optic lines or satellites that allow computers to send information to each other. When computers are linked, they form a *network*. Computer networks are what make the Internet and the World Wide Web possible.

Periodicals Magazines, journals, and newspapers are called *periodicals*. In a library, you can find a variety of periodicals, such as scientific journals, sports magazines, consumer-related periodicals, and national newspapers.

Radio, Television, Video, and Film
Radio and *television* may also be used as sources of information. News programs and documentaries are regular features on radio and TV. Documentaries and educational programs are also found on *film* or *video*. You can find listings that describe radio and television programs in newspapers and sometimes on the Internet. To look up existing films and videos, check indexes. *The Video Source Book* (Gale, 1999) is one index available at some libraries. Be sure to check the ratings provided for the films and videos before viewing them. (See also **Media Messages** on page 773 and **Critical Viewing** on page 787.)

Reference Books When you want to check facts or get information quickly, reference books are a good place to start. Reference books arrange information in a convenient format, such as alphabetical or chronological order. Encyclopedias give general information about subjects. Dictionaries and thesauruses focus on words, while atlases specialize in maps and geographical information. (See also the **Reference Sources** chart on the next page.)

Reference Sources Being familiar with the various kinds of reference sources can help you do research more efficiently. The chart on the next page describes common reference sources and gives examples.

Reference Sources

Types of Reference Sources	Description	Examples
Encyclopedias	• multiple volumes • articles arranged alphabetically by subject • source for general information	*Collier's Encyclopedia* *Compton's Encyclopedia* *The World Book Multimedia Encyclopedia*™
General Biographical References	• information about the lives and accomplishments of outstanding people	*Current Biography* *The International Who's Who* *World Biographical Index on CD-ROM*
Atlases	• maps and geographical information	*Atlas of World Cultures* *National Geographic Atlas of the World*
Almanacs	• up-to-date information about current events, facts, statistics, and dates	*The Information Please Almanac, Atlas & Yearbook* *The World Almanac and Book of Facts*
Books of Synonyms	• list more interesting or more exact words to express ideas	*Roget's International Thesaurus* *Webster's New Dictionary of Synonyms*

Vertical File A *vertical file* is a cabinet containing up-to-date materials. These materials may include newspaper clippings and government or information pamphlets.

World Wide Web (*WWW* or the *Web*) The *World Wide Web* is a large system of connected documents on the Internet. These documents are known as *Web sites* or *Web pages*. They contain text, graphics, video, and sometimes sound. (See also page 740.) Documents on the World Wide Web are connected by *hyperlinks*. Clicking on a hyperlink brings a new site to the computer screen. To navigate and view the World Wide Web, you must have access to a computer with browser software installed. The following terms will help you understand the workings of the World Wide Web.

■ **Browser** There are different ways to view material on the Internet, one of which includes using a *World Wide Web browser*. World Wide Web browsers provide access to files and documents, news and discussion groups, bulletin boards, e-mail, and the World Wide Web. The browser helps viewers to find, read, save, download, and explore Web sites and to use the links between sites.

TEACHING TIP

World Wide Web
You need to be aware that Internet resources are sometimes public forums and their content can be unpredictable.

World Wide Web
Let students know that the World Wide Web is a good resource for information on writing. As students write, revise, and edit their next writing project, you may want to have them visit and use some of the writing-related reference sites on *Elements of Language*'s Internet site. The address is given on the part opening spread for the **Quick Reference Handbook.**

- **Hyperlink**　Users click on *hyperlinks,* or *links,* to move from one site to another. On screen, hyperlinks are usually underlined and colored words.

- **Search Engine**　A search engine is a tool for finding specific information on the Web. (See also **World Wide Web, Searching** on this page.)

- **URL** (*Uniform Resource Locator*) All documents on the Web have an address called a *URL.* A typical URL includes words, abbreviations, numbers, and punctuation.

EXAMPLE

1	2	3

http://go.hrw.com/ndNSAPI.nd/gohrw_rls1/pHome

1. The type of Internet service. World Wide Web sites begin with *http.*
2. The **hostname** is a group of *domains.* A domain gives a computer broad or specific information about finding a Web site. In the example above, *com* tells the computer that the site is part of a commercial network, *hrw* identifies the company where the site is located, and *go* indicates which machine within the company contains the site.

Common Networks on the World Wide Web	
com	commercial or individual
edu	educational
gov	governmental
net	administrative
org	usually nonprofit organization

3. The specific request for the file or piece of information that you want. Not all addresses will have this part.

- **Web Site (or Web Page)**　Any location or document that you view on the Web is called a Web site or Web page. The *home page* is the first page on a Web site and usually gives an overview of the major areas in the site. It also lists hyperlinks, or related Web sites, and usually tells who created or sponsors the site. On the next page is a typical example of what you would see if you had located a Web site using a browser.

World Wide Web, Searching　In some ways, the World Wide Web is like a massive library. The information you want is there, but you must find it before you can use it. You can search the Internet by using a *search engine* or a *directory*.

- **Search Engines**　A *search engine* allows you to conduct a *keyword search* to find Web sites that contain key words or phrases. To do a keyword search, you must first decide which keyword or words to use in your search. Then, you type the keyword(s) in the search space and hit the return key or the search or find button. A list of sites will appear, with the most relevant matches at the top.

　A keyword search can sometimes result in a list of hundreds or thousands of Web sites. *Refining* your search can make a search more productive. Use the strategies on the next page to help you find a manageable number of matches. Keep in mind, though, that your search engine may use slightly different commands. Consult the help section of your search engine for specific commands.

1. **Toolbar** Click the toolbar to perform functions such as searching, printing, moving forward or back to different pages, and seeing or hiding images.
2. **Location window** This box provides the address, or the URL, of the site you are looking at.
3. **Content area** This section displays the text, images, hyperlinks, and other parts of a Web page.
4. **Hyperlinks** Click these buttons to connect to other Web pages within this same site.
5. **Scroll bar** Clicking along the horizontal or vertical scroll bar (or on the arrows at either end) allows you to move left to right or up and down in the image area.

① Back Forward Reload Home Search

Location: http://www.groverms.edu/~ldillard

② ③ **Welcome to Disc Doggies**

The Sports Page for High Flying Canines

Expand your backyard toss-and-fetch games by joining the fun at our Disc Doggie events. Check out our Web page for information about training. Look at our Club news and please sign our guestbook.

④ History of the Sport | Photo Gallery
Disc Doggie Club Events | Links
Disc Doggie Training | Guestbook

copyright © by Lamar Dillard
All rights reserved.

⑤

Refining a Keyword Search

Choose specific terms instead of general ones. A general keyword can produce many irrelevant matches.	EXAMPLE If you are interested in distance running, use *marathon* rather than *running* or *sports*.
Use quotation marks. Using quotation marks around your keyword or phrases will find sites that use those exact words.	EXAMPLE Enter *"Olympic gold medalists"* to find sites about medal winners rather than sites about the Olympics.
Use *AND* and *NOT*. Put the word *AND* between your keywords to narrow your search. The search engine will find only Web sites that contain all words connected by *AND*. Use *NOT* between keywords to make sure that the search engine does not pull up sites that deal with topics that are similar but unrelated.	EXAMPLE For sites that mention both the Atlanta and the Salt Lake City Olympics, enter *Atlanta AND Salt Lake City AND Olympics.* EXAMPLE Enter *Olympics NOT mountains* to avoid Web sites about the Olympic mountain range.
Use *OR*. To broaden your search, use *OR* to let the search engine know that you would accept sites that contain any of your keywords.	EXAMPLE If you want sites that discuss either the summer or the winter Olympics, enter *summer OR winter AND Olympics*.

QUICK REFERENCE HANDBOOK

■ **Directories** A directory provides you with organized lists of Web sites on the World Wide Web. A directory organizes the sites into broad categories, such as *Recreation* and *Health*. Each category can be broken down into subcategories, which can be broken down even more into sub-subcategories. You search a subject catalog by narrowing down a general topic to a specific one.

For example, to find information about Eileen Collins, the first woman space shuttle commander, you could start with the broad category *science*, then narrow your search to *space, astronauts*, and finally *Eileen Collins*. Many search engine sites include directories.

You should pare down the resulting list of sites in order to choose those most relevant to your search. Make predictions about the content of a site by considering its name and the design, images, and categories on its home page. Begin with those that seem most reliable. (See also **World Wide Web, Web Site Evaluation** below.)

World Wide Web, Web Site Evaluation Newspapers, books, and TV news shows must check and verify information to be sure it is accurate. The World Wide Web, however, does not have the same requirements. Therefore, you must *evaluate* a Web site and the accuracy of its information. Here are some questions to help you.

Evaluating Web Sites	
Who created or sponsored the Web site?	You can find the site's creator or sponsor on the site's home page. You should use Web sites that are created by trustworthy organizations, such as government agencies, universities, and museums. These organizations' Web sites usually are found in the *edu, gov,* or *org* networks. National news organizations are another source of reliable information on the Web.
When was the page first posted, and is it frequently updated?	A copyright notice will tell you when a page was created. The date of the most recent update will tell you how often the information is updated. These dates are usually at the bottom of the home page. They can help you see whether a site tries to keep up with recent developments.
To what other Web pages is the site linked?	Trustworthy sites will have links to respected organizations. These links add to a site's credibility.
Does the Web site present information objectively?	Check to see if the site covers both sides of an issue. If the site uses strong language or opinions, it might not be objective.
Is the Web site well designed?	A well-designed Web site is easy to read, understand, and use. The links work properly, and the text uses proper spelling, punctuation, and grammar.

Reading and Vocabulary

Reading

Skills and Strategies

You can use the following skills and strategies to become a more effective reader.

Author's Point of View, Determining
An author's attitude about a subject is called the **author's point of view.** Point of view is also called **bias.** Recognizing an author's point of view will help you evaluate how fair the author's conclusions are. (See also page 205.)

EXAMPLE   Basketball is the champion of all sports. With just five players on a team, basketball is more selective than football, baseball, or soccer. Basketball players must be better conditioned than other athletes because they are always running up and down the court playing offense and defense.

Author's point of view: Basketball is the best sport.

Author's Purpose, Determining
An author has a reason or **purpose** for writing a selection. To inform, to influence, to express oneself, and to entertain are the major purposes for writing. As a reader, determining the author's purpose will help you get more meaning from the text. (See also page 53.)

EXAMPLE   Learning to play music is one reason to join the school band, but it is not the only one. By joining the school band you will meet new friends, take fun trips for concerts, and be a part of a great team of musicians. Make the smart and fun choice by joining the school band.

Author's purpose: To persuade teenagers to join the school band.

Cause-Effect Relationships, Analyzing
A **cause** makes something happen. An **effect** is what happens as a result of that cause. When you ask "Why?" and "What happened because of this?" as you read, you are examining causes and effects. (See also page 241.)

EXAMPLE   Taking care of my new puppy has changed my schedule. Since the puppy has to go out first thing in the morning, I have to get up thirty minutes earlier. Then, I have to rush home from school to walk him.

Analysis: A new puppy is the *cause* that makes the following *effects* happen: getting up early and coming home quickly from school.

Clue Words, Using

Writers use certain *clue words* to connect their ideas within a text. You can use these clue words to identify the author's organizational pattern. (See also **text structures** on page 748.)

Clue Words	
Cause/effect	
as a result	because
consequently	if . . . then
since	so that
therefore	this led to
thus	
Chronological Order	
after	as
before	finally
first	not long after
now	second
then	when
Comparison/contrast	
although	as well as
but	either . . . or
however	not only . . . but also
on the other hand	similarly
unless	yet
Listing	
also	for example
in fact	most important
to begin with	

Problem/solution	
as a result	nevertheless
therefore	this led to
thus	

Conclusions, Drawing

A *conclusion* is a judgment you make by combining information in a text with information you already know. As you read, you gather information, connect it to your experiences, and then draw conclusions about the text. (See also page 87.)

EXAMPLE A flash of jagged light suddenly illuminated Keisha's bedroom. Loud booms and pelting water shook the windowpanes. Keisha sighed and covered her head with her pillow, hoping to get back to sleep.

Conclusion: A thunderstorm has awakened Keisha in the night.

Fact and Opinion, Distinguishing

A *fact* is information that can be proved true or false. An *opinion* expresses a personal belief or attitude, so it cannot be proved true or false. Facts are often used to support opinions. A reader who can tell the difference between a fact and an opinion is less likely to make false judgments. (See also page 217.)

EXAMPLE

Fact: Professional basketball player Dikembe Mutombo speaks seven languages and five African dialects.

Opinion: Americans should learn to speak more than one language.

Generalizations, Forming

A reader forms a *generalization* by combining information in a text with personal experience to make a judgment about the world in general. (See also page 236.)

EXAMPLE More and more students at Northshore Middle School are organizing and participating in activities that help the community and other people. The student council organized a food drive to benefit Helping Hands food bank, and the students in Ms. Shaw's science classes started a recycling program. Seventh-grader Leon Miller works as a volunteer at Memorial Hospital. He said, "You really feel good about yourself when you see that something you have done makes someone else happy."

Generalization: Many young people want to help others in their community.

Implied Main Idea, Identifying

Some writers do not directly state the main idea of the text. Instead, they choose to *imply,* or suggest it. In this case, you, the reader, have to analyze the details the writer provides and decide the overall meaning of these details. (See also page 22 and **Stated Main Idea** on page 747.)

EXAMPLE If you have Internet access, you can send an e-mail message. You do not need stationery, a pen, or a stamp. You do not have to find a post office or mailbox to send the letter. You just type in your message and hit the send button. The person will get your e-mail message, usually in minutes, rather than days.

Implied main idea: E-mail is easy to use.

Inferences, Making
An *inference* is an educated guess based on information in the text and on your prior knowledge and experience. *Conclusions, generalizations,* and *predictions* are three types of inferences. As you read, you make decisions about ideas and

details that writers do not directly reveal. (See also page 236.)

EXAMPLE "Oh, no," Mrs. Patel said into the phone. She sat down quickly and listened intently. "When?" she asked, swallowing hard. As she listened to the reply, tears filled her eyes.

Inference: Mrs. Patel's phone call brought very bad news.

Paraphrasing
When you *paraphrase,* you restate someone else's ideas in your own words. Paraphrasing a difficult piece of writing can help you better understand that writing. A paraphrase is usually about the same length as the original text. A *summary,* on the other hand, is much shorter than a paraphrase. When you summarize, you focus only on the key ideas in a passage. Be sure to avoid *plagiarism* when you write a paraphrase or a summary. Plagiarism happens when you copy an author's exact words without using quotation marks, and then publish these words as your own. (See the chart on page 776 for **paraphrasing guidelines.**)

EXAMPLE When Peggy Knight was just fourteen, she lost her hair due to alopecia areata, a disease of the immune system. Knight remembers the terrible teasing she got at a time when she desperately wanted to be like everyone else. Now she is helping children with the disorder by providing free, custom-made wigs of human hair. Knight's organization is called Locks of Love. People from all over the country donate their hair in ponytails, which must be at least ten inches long.

Paraphrasing: At age fourteen, Peggy Knight suffered from alopecia areata and lost all her hair. She didn't like the teasing and feeling left out. Her experience prompted her to start Locks of Love. This organization donates wigs of human hair to children with the same

Reading Log

Suggest that students use a reading log to help them keep track of the books they have read and reviewed. Aside from explaining the suggestions for using a reading log in the main entry, point out that students should develop a system for organizing the entries for each book. For example, students may want to divide their log for each book into four sections:

1. Book (title and author)

2. Prereading (predictions made before reading)

3. Reading (summaries, thoughts, predictions made while reading, important events, questions, and so on)

4. After Reading (final thoughts, overall impression, favorite moments, good points and bad points, and so on)

---

disease. The wigs are made from hair donated by people across America who want to help out. They must cut at least ten inches of their hair to donate it.

Persuasive Techniques, Analyzing

A writer uses **persuasive techniques** to convince readers to think or act in a certain way. Two types of persuasive techniques are *emotional appeals* and *faulty reasoning*. As you read persuasive writing, look for reasons and facts that are logical or make sense. (See also page 239.)

EXAMPLE   More students need to recycle by tossing their empty soda cans into the recycling bin. Our janitor, Mr. Saunders, says that he finds many soda cans in the four trash cans near the drink machines. That means that many students do not care about the environment or our school. A school that does not recycle is a school that has no pride!

Analysis: The second sentence contains a fact that supports the opinion in the first sentence. The second-to-last sentence contains faulty reasoning. (There is not enough evidence to support the conclusion in this sentence.) The last sentence contains an emotional appeal. (It appeals to the readers' pride.)

Predicting

Predicting is deciding what will happen next in a text. As you read, you use information from the text plus your own knowledge and experience to make predictions. As you read on, you can adjust or confirm your predictions. (See also page 124.)

EXAMPLE   The 200-meter freestyle relay was the next event in the swim meet, but Lauren was still not there. The coach paced nervously, trying to decide on a substitute. No one else could swim the anchor leg as well as Lauren, but the coach had no choice. "Reina!" he barked. "Take the anchor leg. Lauren has just let the team down for the last time."

Predictions: Lauren will lose her anchor position on the relay team. The coach may even kick her off the team. The team will probably not win the race.

Problem-Solution Relationships

A **problem** is an unanswered question. A **solution** is an attempt to answer that question. When an author writes about a problem, he or she may suggest one solution or several. To identify a problem, ask yourself these questions: *What is the problem? Who has the problem?* Then, look for the solution or solutions the author provides.

EXAMPLE   The music program's budget at Lincoln Middle School was cut in half. As a result, the school does not have the money to buy instruments for all fifty students in the program. Mr. Nguyen, the music teacher, placed an ad in the local newspaper asking people to donate used instruments. In addition, students organized a benefit concert to raise money to buy instruments.

Analysis: The problem is that Lincoln Middle School does not have money to buy instruments because the music program's budget was cut. Students who want to participate in the music program have the problem. One solution is asking people in the community to donate used instruments. The second solution is organizing a benefit concert to raise money.

Reading Log, Using a

A *reading log* is simply a notebook or journal in which a reader writes about reading. Before you read, use the log to write down ideas about the title and the pictures in the selection. As you read, write down your honest reactions to the text: Ask questions, make connections to your own experiences, and note important passages. Because readers have different experiences, interests, beliefs, and opinions, no two reading logs will be alike.

Reading Rates According To Purpose		
Reading Rate	**Purpose**	**Example**
Scanning	Reading for specific details	Searching for the age of a character in a short story
Skimming	Reading for main points	Reviewing the headlines in a newspaper to find an interesting article
Reading for mastery	Reading to understand and remember	Taking notes and making a time line of events while reading a chapter in your history textbook
Reading at your most comfortable speed	Reading for enjoyment	Reading a book written by your favorite author

Reading Rate, Adjusting Your *reading rate* is the speed at which you read a text. How quickly or how slowly you read depends upon your purpose for reading, the difficulty of the text, and your knowledge of the text's subject. The chart above explains four possible reading rates.

SQ3R *SQ3R,* a popular reading-study strategy, stands for a five-step process:

S *Survey* the entire text. Look briefly at each page—the headings, titles, illustrations, charts, and so on.

Q *Question* yourself as you survey the text. What should you know after completing your reading? Make a list of questions to be answered.

R *Read* the entire selection. Look for answers to your questions as you read.

R *Recite* in your own words the answers you find for each of your questions.

R *Review* the material by re-reading quickly, looking over the questions, and recalling the answers.

Stated Main Idea and Supporting Details, Identifying A *main idea* is the focus or central idea in a piece of writing. Main ideas often appear as topic sentences of paragraphs or in an introduction or conclusion of a composition. *Supporting details* support or explain the main idea. (See **Implied Main Idea** on page 745.)

EXAMPLE   The yo-yo has been a popular toy through many centuries and cultures. Invented in China about one thousand years ago, it appeared in England in the late eighteenth century. The troops of the French ruler Napoleon entertained themselves with the yo-yo in the nineteenth century. The yo-yo came to the United States from the Philippines in the 1920s and became a favorite toy of people of all ages.

Stated main idea: The yo-yo has appealed to many different cultures during different time periods.

Supporting details: The yo-yo was invented one thousand years ago in China. It became popular in England, France, and the United States.

Summarizing   A *summary* is a short restatement of the main points of a selection. Summarizing a long passage can help you understand it. When you summarize, you try to present the key ideas in a passage without repeating every detail. A *paraphrase,* though, restates almost all of the ideas in a passage. (See also **paraphrasing** on page 745. See chart on page 777 for **summarizing guidelines**.)

EXAMPLE   Middle school students in Japan take entrance exams to get into high school. The exams are very demanding, and students study every day, including weekends, for months before the test. Parents, teachers, students, and communities focus on the upcoming test. If students fail the test, they go to a "cram school" and retake the test the next year.

Summary: In Japan, entrance exams to high school are so difficult and important that students spend months preparing for them. Everyone gets involved, and students who fail go to a special school to prepare to take the test again.

Text Structures, Analyzing   A *text structure* is the pattern a writer uses to organize ideas or events. Writers commonly use five major patterns of organization: *cause-effect, chronological order, comparison-contrast, listing,* and *problem-solution.* Being able to recognize these structures will help you better understand the text and its ideas. Use the following guidelines to determine the structure of a text:

1. Search the text for the main idea.

2. Look for clue words that signal a specific pattern of organization and identify one pattern. (See also **Clue Words, Using** on page 744.)

3. Look for details that support the main idea, and think about how the details and the main idea are connected to one another. Use a **graphic organizer** to map the relationship between the main idea and the supporting details. Your graphic organizer may look like one of the four following examples.

- *Cause-effect pattern* shows the relationship between results and the ideas or events that cause the results. (See also page 241.) The following example shows how faulty bicycle brakes (cause) led to a bike accident, injuries, and doctor's bills (effects).

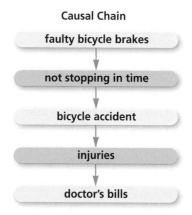

Causal Chain

faulty bicycle brakes
↓
not stopping in time
↓
bicycle accident
↓
injuries
↓
doctor's bills

- *Chronological order pattern* shows events or ideas in the order in which they happen. (See also page 55.) The example on the next page shows the sequence for washing a car.

Sequence Chain

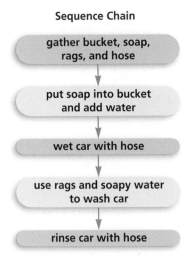

gather bucket, soap, rags, and hose

↓

put soap into bucket and add water

↓

wet car with hose

↓

use rags and soapy water to wash car

↓

rinse car with hose

- ***Comparison-contrast pattern*** points out similarities and/or differences. The example below compares the Mayan and Aztec people.
- ***Listing pattern*** presents material according to certain criteria such as size, location, or importance. The following example lists pets according to their size.

List

1. small: my guinea pig Little Bit

2. medium: my cat Bella

3. large: my horse Cleo

- ***Problem-solution pattern*** identifies at least one problem and offers one or more solutions to the problem. The example below shows how a school dealt with a locker shortage.

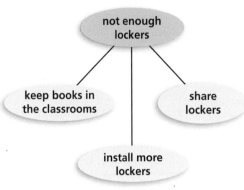

not enough lockers

keep books in the classrooms

share lockers

install more lockers

Venn Diagram

Differences   Similarities   Differences

Maya

- lived in Yucatán region
- skilled astronomers
- lived between A.D. 250–900
- civilization mysteriously disappeared

- Native Americans
- built impressive cities
- early inhabitants of Mexico

Aztec

- lived in central Mexico
- fierce warriors
- lived between A.D. 1200 and 1521
- conquered by the Spanish

Transitional Words and Phrases, Using *Transitions* are words or phrases that connect ideas. Transitions help you understand how all the ideas in a selection fit together. (See also the chart on **transitional words and phrases** on page 302.)

Visuals and Graphics, Interpreting *Visuals* and *graphics* give readers information using pictures or symbols.

- **Elements**   Effective visuals and graphics contain the following elements. (See also page 192.)
  1. A *title* identifies the subject or main idea of the graphic or visual.
  2. The *body* presents information in the form of a graph, chart, time line, diagram, or table. The body is specific to the type of information that is presented.
  3. *Labels* identify and give meaning to the information shown in the graphic or visual.
  4. A *legend* identifies special symbols, colors, scales, or other features readers need to know in order to read the information. The legend usually appears as a small box near the body.
  5. The *source* is where the information contained in the graphic or visual was found. Knowing the source helps readers judge whether the information in the graphic or visual is accurate.

- **Types**   The most common forms of visuals and graphics are *charts, diagrams, graphs, tables,* and *time lines.*
  1. *Charts* are a compact way to show information. In the following *pie chart,* notice that the segments show the per-

centage of hours, not the specific number of hours.

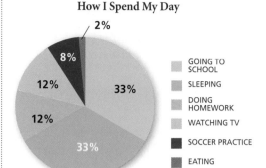

How I Spend My Day

2% — 8% — 12% — 12% — 33% — 33%

GOING TO SCHOOL
SLEEPING
DOING HOMEWORK
WATCHING TV
SOCCER PRACTICE
EATING

2. *Diagrams* use symbols (such as circles or arrows) or pictures to compare ideas, show a process, or provide instruction. The example below uses pictures to show the forces of action and reaction. A *Venn diagram* uses two overlapping circles to compare two ideas or things. (See page 749 for a **Venn diagram.**)

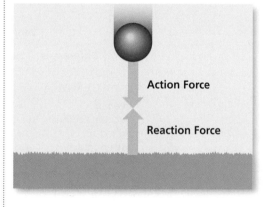

Action Force

Reaction Force

3. *Line graphs and bar graphs* show changes over time. On the next page is an example of a bar graph and a line graph. The horizontal line, or the line

that goes from left to right, shows different points in time. The vertical line, or the line that goes up and down, shows quantities.

Miles Run by Sean and Lisa

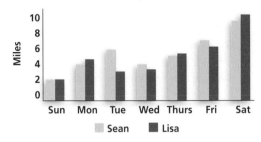

Miles Run by Sean and Lisa

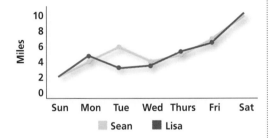

4. *Tables* provide information in a very simple way. Readers must draw their own conclusions about the information in a table.

Money Made Doing Extra Chores in the Month of June		
Date	Chore	Amount
6/4	mowed yard	$5.00
6/12	bathed dog	$2.00
6/19	washed car	$5.00
6/26	pulled weeds	$3.00

5. *Time lines* show the order of events. On a time line, you will see the event and the time in which the event happened.

Major Political Events, 1989–1995

■ **Tips**   Always read graphics or visuals carefully. Keep in mind these tips:

1. Always look at the title, labels, and legend of any visual or graphic before you start to interpret the information.
2. Draw your own conclusions about the information and compare them to those of the writer.
3. Think about information that is not included in the visual or graphic. Often, information is left out because it does not match the writer's conclusions.

Vocabulary

Skills and Strategies

You can use the following skills and strategies to become a more effective reader.

Context Clues Sometimes you can find clues to the meaning of an unfamiliar word by examining its *context,* the group of words or sentences surrounding the unfamiliar word. The following chart shows examples of some of the common types of context clues.

How to Use Context Clues
Type of Clue
Definitions and Restatements: Look for words that define the term or restate it in other words.   *The speaker was **eloquent,** persuading us with her moving stories.*
Examples: Look for examples used in context that reveal the meaning of an unfamiliar word.   *Ticks, fleas, and other **parasites** can make your pet miserable.*
Synonyms: Look for clues that indicate an unfamiliar word is similar in meaning to a familiar word or phrase.   *The eyewitness gave such **credible** testimony that it was easy to believe her account.*
Antonyms or Contrasts: Look for clues that indicate an unfamiliar word is opposite in meaning to a familiar word or phrase.

*His **placid** expression gave no sign of the panic he felt while taking the test.*

Cause and Effect: Look for clues that indicate an unfamiliar word is related to the cause or is the result of an action, feeling, or idea.

*Because most people use computers, type-writers have become almost **obsolete.***

Word Bank A *word bank* is a list of words that you gather from your reading, listening, and viewing. Storing new words in a word bank is a good way to increase your vocabulary. Check your dictionary for the meaning of each new word.

Word Meanings Words have layers of meanings that can change depending on how the word is used. Use the following definitions and examples to help you make sure that your words say what you mean.

■ **Clichés and tired words** *Clichés* are overused expressions that are no longer effective in writing.

EXAMPLES *sharp as a tack, cold as ice, home sweet home, easier said than done*

A *tired word* is one that has lost its freshness and force. It has been used so often and so carelessly that it has become worn-out and almost meaningless.

EXAMPLES *nice, good, pretty, wonderful, terrific,* and *great*

■ **Denotation and connotation**
The *denotation* of a word is its actual meaning—the one a dictionary lists. The *connotation* is the additional meaning or feeling suggested by the word. Because connotations often stir people's feelings, they can have powerful effects on the listener or reader.

EXAMPLES   The words *stubborn* and *determined* have similar denotative meanings, but they connote different ideas. *Stubborn* connotes someone headstrong and difficult. *Determined,* on the other hand, has positive connotations and suggests someone who is hardworking and refuses to give up.

■ **Euphemisms**   A *euphemism* is a word or phrase that is used in place of another word that might seem too direct or blunt. Some people use euphemisms to be polite and to avoid offending others. Euphemisms are also used to mislead people—to hide unpleasant truths or misrepresent the facts.

Euphemism	More Direct Term
laid to rest	buried
stretched the truth	lied
petite	short
correctional facility	jail

■ **Figurative language**   *Figurative language* consists of descriptive words and phrases that are not meant to be taken literally. The following chart shows the most common types of figurative language.

Type of Figurative Language	Example
A **metaphor** says that something *is* something else.	*Her smile is a neon sign.*
Personification gives human characteristics to nonhuman things.	*The ocean breeze whispered in my ears.*
A **simile** compares two basically unlike things, using the words *like* or *as.*	*The road was like a black ribbon winding through the mountains.*

■ **Idioms**   *Idioms* are phrases that mean something different from the literal meanings of the words. Idioms often can't be explained grammatically, and they may not make sense if translated word-for-word into another language.

EXAMPLES
The two girls wanted to *hang out* at Marina's house.
I was *glued to my seat* as I watched the game.
We *plugged away* at our homework.

■ **Jargon**   *Jargon* is a special language used by groups of people who share the same profession, occupation, hobby, or field of study. Jargon is effective only if the reader or listener is familiar with its special meaning. Note in the following example how the word *strike* can mean different things in different fields.

EXAMPLE strike

Baseball—a pitch thrown over home plate within a "strike zone" or a pitch that the batter swings at but misses.

Bowling—knocking down ten pins with the first ball of a frame

Labor—refusal to work due to a contract disagreement

Fishing—the fish's grab at hooked bait

- **Loaded words** *Loaded words* are intended to provoke strong feelings, either positive or negative. A writer or speaker who wants to persuade you to share his or her opinion may use loaded words that appeal to your emotions.

EXAMPLES

The coach looked *serious* as he *paced* up and down the sidelines.

The coach looked *grim* as he *stomped* up and down the sidelines.

- **Multiple meanings** Many English words have more than one meaning. When using a dictionary to find a word's meaning, look at all the definitions given. Keep in mind the context in which you read or heard the word. Then, try the various definitions in that context until you find the one that fits.

EXAMPLE

With his low *threshold* for pain, even a headache sends him straight to bed.

threshold (thre**th**ʹ ōld′) *n.* **1.** the piece of wood or stone placed beneath a door **2.** an entrance **3.** the place or point of beginning **4.** the lowest point or level at which an action can be felt (The fourth definition best fits the meaning in context.)

Word Origins See **The History of English.**

Word Parts Most English words can be broken into smaller units called **word parts**. The three types of word parts are **roots, prefixes,** and **suffixes**. Knowing the meanings of these word parts can help you determine the meanings of many unfamiliar words.

- **Roots** The **root** is the main part of a word. It carries the word's meaning, and it is the part to which prefixes and suffixes are added. (See also page 57.)

Commonly Used Roots		
Roots	**Meanings**	**Examples**
–act–	do	action, react
–biblio–, –bibli–	book	bibliography, biblical
–chron–	time	chronology, chronic
–fac–	make	manufacture, factory
–log–, –logue–, –logy–	study, word	logo, biology
–magni–	large	magnitude, magnify
–mal–	bad	malpractice, dismal
–mot–	move	motion, promote
–ped–	foot	pedal, quadruped
–phon–	sound	telephone, phonograph
–sym–, –syn–	with, together	sympathy, syndrome

■ **Prefixes** A *prefix* is a word part that is added before a root. (See also page 166.)

Commonly Used Prefixes

Prefixes	Meanings	Examples
de–	away from, off, down	decode, defend, defuse
dia–	through, across, between	dialogue, diameter
hemi–	half	hemicycle, hemisphere
inter–	between, among	interact, interstate
mis–	badly, not, wrongly	mislead, mistake
non–	not	nonfiction, nonstop
over–	above, excessive	overthrow, overtime
post–	after, following	postdated, postwar
pre–	before	prepare, preview
re–	back, backward, again	replay, return, reverse
sub–, suf–, sum–, sup–, sus–	under, beneath	subplot, suffocate, summon, support, suspend
trans–	across, beyond	translate, transport
un–	not, reverse of	uneven, unspoken

■ **Suffixes** A *suffix* is a word part that is added after a root. Adding or changing a suffix will often change both a word's meaning and its part of speech, as in *teach/teacher. Teach* is a verb. *Teacher* is a noun. (See also page 166.)

Commonly Used Suffixes

Suffixes	Meanings	Examples
–ate	to become, to cause	concentrate, vaccinate
–dom	state, condition	freedom, wisdom
–en	made of, to become	sharpen, wooden
–fy	to make, to cause	magnify, terrify
–hood	state, condition	neighborhood, sisterhood
–ible	able, likely	collectible, visible
–ish	tending to be, like	childish, smallish
–ity	state, condition	activity, flexibility
–ize	to make, to cause to be	dramatize, legalize
–ment	result, act of	appointment, payment
–ness	quality, state	darkness, sadness
–ous	characterized by	generous, joyous
–tion	act of, state	flirtation, protection

TEACHING TIP

Words to Learn
For more help with vocabulary instruction, see the *Vocabulary Workshop* program. *Vocabulary Workshop* includes vocabulary instruction and practice with the three hundred words that make up the Words to Learn list.

Words to Learn Use the 300 words in the list below to increase your vocabulary this year. Make it a habit to learn unfamiliar words from this list regularly.

abrupt
absolute
abstract
absurd
accord
acute
adhere
adopt
aerial
aggravate
alien
ally
alternate
anguish
anticipate
antiseptic
approximate
audible
authentic
avert

banish
barbarous
baron
barren
blemish

caliber
camouflage
cancel
candid
capacity
challenge
chaos
cherish
coincide
commit
comparable
compensate

competent
compute
confirm
conform
congregate
conifer
consequence
consistent
conspicuous
constitution
contemplate
controversial
credible
crisis
crucial
cultural

dashing
debris
defiant
deliberate
designate
destiny
dialogue
diaphragm
digital
diplomatic
discrimination
dismal
distort
distract
diversity
dual

economical
ecosystem
edible
editorial
effect

efficiency
elaborate
elective
eloquent
encounter
endurance
era
eventual
exceed
excel
excess
exotic
expand

faculty
fascinate
fatigue
financial
flaw
forbidding
formal
fortress
forum
frail
fugitive
fulfill
fundamental
futile

galaxy
geological
germinate
gesture
ghastly
glacial
glucose
grammatical
grandeur
gratify
grotesque
guarantee

habitat
hardy
haunt

hesitation
hover
humane
hypocrite
hysterical

idle
ignorance
illusion
illustrious
immature
immortal
immune
impact
indefinite
indirect
indispensable
inert
inferior
infinite
inhabit
initial
inquisitive
intellect
intermediate
interpret
intolerable
intricate
invade
involuntary
irritable

journal
judicial

kernel

leash
legendary
legible
legitimate
lenient
literary
logical
loiter

luminous
lure

magnitude
maintain
mammal
maneuver
manual
manuscript
mastery
maternal
maturity
mechanism
memorandum
mere
merit
metropolitan
minimum
minority
moderate
modest
monarchy
moral
mortal
motive
myth
mythology

narration
naturalist
navigable
nocturnal
notable
notorious
nutrition

obligation
obsolete
obstacle
obstinate
offend
officially
opponent
opposition
optical
optional

organism
originality
overture

pageant
parasite
partial
participant
participate
penetrate
percentage
perilous
perpetual
persuasion
phase
photosynthesis
pigment
placid
planetary
poach
porcelain
precaution
precise
preliminary
preservation
prestige
principally
probability
proclamation
profound
prompt
propel
proportion
prose
prudent
pursue

radiate
random
reality
reception
recognition
recoil
recommend
refrain

relinquish
repel
resolve
revise
ridicule
rival

satellite
scholarship
seasonal
segregation
self-conscious
serf
signify
speculate
spontaneous
stability
stationary
stationery
status
stellar
submerged
substantial
subtle
supervise
surplus
symbolic

tactics
technique
temperate
tendency
threshold
timid
tiresome
toil
tranquil
tributary
turmoil
tutor
tyrant

undergrowth
unison
universal
unpredictable

usage
utility

vague
valiant
velocity
vengeance
versatile
veto
via
vigor
vital

wretched

yield

zoology

Speaking and Listening

Speaking

Although you speak all the time without even thinking about it, you can learn to speak more effectively. Using the strategies in this section will help you get your ideas across to listeners more clearly, in formal speeches and oral interpretations as well as in informal speaking situations.

Formal Speaking

A formal speech is given at a specific time for a specific reason. Most formal speeches are given to provide information to listeners, though they can also be given to persuade, to entertain, or even to express.

Content of a Formal Speech A formal speech must be planned carefully ahead of time. To prepare your speech, use a process similar to the writing process. The following steps can help you write an effective speech.

1. **Select a topic.** If it is up to you to choose the topic of your speech, use one of the methods below to help you find a topic that will be interesting to both you and your audience.
   - Consider turning one of your written compositions into a speech.
   - Brainstorm a list of interesting topics.
   - Ask for suggestions from your teachers, friends, and classmates.
   - Look over past journal entries.
   - Read through sources such as magazines, newspapers, and books.
   - Search the World Wide Web for ideas. (See also page 740.)

2. **Identify purpose and occasion.** The *purpose* of your speech is the reason you are giving your speech. The purpose of most speeches is to inform or to persuade an audience to do or believe something. Knowing your purpose will help you decide what ideas and words to use in your speech to achieve that purpose. The chart on the next page describes some of the most common purposes for formal speeches.

Purposes for Giving a Speech

Purpose for Speech	Examples of Speech Titles
To inform gives facts or general information or explains how to do something	• Dinosaurs Once Lived in West Texas • How to Take Good Snapshots
To persuade attempts to change an opinion or attempts to get listeners to act	• Why Everyone Should Recycle • How Volunteering Can Make a Difference
To entertain relates an interesting or amusing story or incident	• My Most Embarrassing Moment • The Day I Met the President

The *occasion* of your speech is when and where it takes place. The occasion or event at which you are speaking will influence what you will say and how you will deliver your speech. Use the questions below to help you think about how the occasion of your speech will affect it.

- *Is the occasion formal or informal?* For a formal occasion, such as a school awards assembly, you will need to use **standard, formal English.** For an informal occasion, such as a friend's birthday party, you can worry less about formal language and word choice.
- *When will you give your speech?* Think about how the date and the time of day will affect your speech. Your speech may

be given on a certain anniversary or holiday, and its content may be connected to that observance. The time of day can also affect your speech. If you are speaking at a time when people may be tired, such as the early morning or after a meal, plan to include lots of attention-getting information.

- *Where will your speech be given?* The place where you are speaking affects your preparation, also. Find out whether you will be using a microphone to speak or whether you will have to speak loudly to be heard.
- *What other conditions might affect your speech?* How much time will you have to speak? Can you speak on any topic? Can you use notes? Will you be able to show pictures or charts? Find out about any restrictions that may be placed on your speech.

3. **Analyze the audience.** Your speech needs to appeal to your audience. Use a vocabulary and manner of speaking that they will understand. Avoid using technical terms or jargon in your speech. Also, organize your ideas in a way that will make sense to your listeners. If you are turning a written composition into a speech, you may need to reorganize ideas or change the way you explain some concepts. The audience you had in mind when you wrote the composition may not be the same audience that will listen to your speech. Use the chart on the next page to help you analyze your audience's needs and interests.

Analyzing Your Audience		
Questions about audience	**Answer**	**Your speech will need**
What does the audience already know about this subject?	very little	to give background details to listeners
	a little	to give at least some background details
	a lot	to focus on less well-known points
How interested will the audience be in this subject?	very interested	to keep your listeners' interest with surprising information
	only a little interested	to focus on aspects most interesting to your listeners
	uninterested	to convince your listeners that this topic is important

4. **Gather information.** Once you know about the topic, purpose, occasion, and audience of your speech, your next step is to find information. For information about how to use the library or media center for research, see page 735. For information on taking notes and preparing outlines, see pages 775 and 807. (If you are turning a written piece into a speech, you will already have gathered most of the information you need. You will simply need to turn that information into speech notes.)

5. **Organize your speech notes.** You will need to organize the information you have gathered to give an effective speech that will achieve your purpose. First, organize your major ideas in an outline. Then, create a note card for each major idea in your outline. When you give your speech, you will speak directly to the audience, not read from notes. You can glance at your note cards from time to time to remind yourself of the informa-

tion you want to share with your audience. The chart below can help you create note cards for an effective speech.

How to Create Speech Note Cards

- Write each main point or idea on its own note card, with notes to remind you of evidence, elaborations, or examples you will use to clarify and support each point.
- Make a separate note card for anything you want to read word-for-word, including quotations or facts that would be difficult to memorize.
- Include a special note card to remind you when to show or refer to a visual, such as a chart, diagram, model, or illustration.
- Number your completed cards to keep them in order.

6. **Use media.** Including media such as *audiovisuals* or *electronic media* in your

speech can make your ideas clearer for listeners or provide extra information in your speech. Here are some common forms of media you might use in a presentation.

- electronic media (graphic images, audio files, and text presentations)
- audio recordings (cassettes or compact discs)
- prerecorded videotapes or videodiscs
- short films
- slides or filmstrips
- visuals such as charts, graphs, illustrations, and diagrams

Use these questions to help you decide whether to use audiovisuals or electronic media in your presentation.

Evaluating the Use of Media in Presentations

1. *Will media help you make a point more clearly?* Some ideas need a visual to help explain them. Using a chart or poster can help get your idea across more easily and clearly.

2. *Will the media help the audience remember a point?* Some points in your speech are more important than others. You can use an audiovisual to help emphasize the most important points.

3. *Will the media distract the audience while you are speaking?* Use only media that are essential to your speech. As soon as the audience has something to concentrate on besides your words, you risk losing their attention. Too many audiovisuals can distract your audience and weaken your speech.

When you use media, make sure the materials are easy for your audience to see and hear. Have audio clips cued up and ready to play. Make sure posters, charts, and other visuals are large enough for your audience to read. (See also **Graphics** on page 728.)

Delivery of a Formal Speech

1. **Rehearse.** To do your best, rehearse your speech before you give it. These strategies can help you as you practice.
   - Create a situation as much like the actual speech situation as possible. Practice your speech in front of an audience of friends and family members, and ask for feedback.
   - Present your speech just as you hope to deliver it. Use hand gestures and eye contact. You might also practice in front of a mirror to see how you come across.
   - Evaluate your performance. Ask yourself how you did, and answer honestly. Then, use your answers to help yourself improve as you keep practicing. (See also **Listening to Evaluate** on page 771.)
   - Plan for improvement with additional rehearsals. Practice can make you more confident. Make sure you plan far enough in advance to be able to practice several times before you give your speech.

2. **Deliver the speech to your audience.** To give an effective speech, you will need to use your voice and your gestures to help express your meaning to your listeners. Here are some pointers to use when you are speaking.
   - *Be prepared.* Organize your material carefully. Make sure your note cards and

Delivery of a Formal Speech
Students may need help understanding how verbal elements can help make their spoken messages effective and appropriate for various audiences and settings. Make the concept vivid by having students imagine these audiences and settings: Toddlers in a day care center and a group of noisy campers in a camp group. Have eight different students act out the following line, in the role of someone responsible for each group. (Each student should focus on the verbal element of rate, volume, pitch, or tone for *one* of the audience-and-setting combinations described):

"OK, it's time to go to sleep."

How would the rate, volume, pitch, and tone vary for each of these audiences in each of these settings? Why? Have students explain their interpretations of the line.

QUICK REFERENCE HANDBOOK

Nonverbal Elements	Examples or Meanings	Functions
Eye Contact	Look directly into the eyes of your audience members	• Can communicate honesty or sincerity • Can keep audience attention
Facial Expression	Raise an eyebrow, smile, frown, or sneer	• Reveals your feelings • Can emphasize certain words or messages
Gesture	Give thumbs up (approval, encouragement), shrug (uncertainty), nod the head (agreement), shake the head (disagreement)	• Can sometimes replace words • Emphasizes words or phrases • Adds meaning to the speech
Posture	Stand tall and straight	• Gives an attitude of confidence and poise

other special information and visuals are ready before you speak.

- *Remember your purpose.* Focus on what you want to tell your audience and how you want them to react instead of worrying about your performance. Try to give your listeners a clear and accurate perspective about your topic.
- *Use nonverbal elements.* One way you communicate with your audience is by using nonverbal signals, sometimes called *body language.* The chart above lists some nonverbal elements you can use in your speech.
- *Use verbal elements.* When you make your speech, use your voice's expressive qualities to communicate with your audience. You may need to vary some or all of these elements depending on your audience and on the setting of your speech. Practice the tips in the Verbal Elements chart.

Verbal Elements	Definitions
Diction	Pronounce words clearly, or *enunciate.* Speak clearly and carefully so that your listeners can understand you.
Emphasis (or stress)	Your voice *inflections*—changes in pitch and tone—naturally put stress on some words or phrases and not others. Emphasize words that are important in your message.
Mood (or tone)	Your speech may make your listeners feel certain emotions. Mood usually applies to oral interpretations of literature, but it may also apply to a speech.

Verbal Elements	Definition
Pause	Pauses are the small silences in your speech. Pauses can emphasize a point that you are making or help listeners catch up.
Pitch	Your voice modulates, or changes pitch, when you speak. If you are nervous, your voice may get higher. To control your pitch, take deep breaths and stay calm as you give your speech.
Rate	In conversations, your rate, or tempo, of speaking may be fast. When you make a speech, you should talk more slowly than you normally would to help listeners understand you.
Volume	Even if you normally speak fairly quietly, you will need to speak loudly while giving a formal speech. Listeners at the back of the room should be able to hear you clearly when you speak.

Other Formal Speaking Situations

Here are tips for getting through some additional formal speaking situations.

- **Announcements** An announcement provides a short piece of information to many people at once. Write out the message you want to get across, keeping it brief and direct. Get your audience's attention, and then read the announce-ment slowly, clearly, and loudly enough that everyone can hear it.

- **Introductions** Before you introduce someone to an audience, you must find out a bit about him or her. Tell the audience the person's name and title, as well as a few important or interesting facts about the person. Be respectful, and welcome the person you are introducing.

- **Oral Summaries** To summarize a book or article you have read, tell your audience about the main idea and most important points or details included in the book or article. Retell these ideas in your own words, and make connections between these ideas and your own thoughts or experiences about the topic.

Informal Speaking

Group Discussion Group discussions happen when a group of people gets together for a particular purpose. In a group discussion, members share and build on information, ideas, experiences, and insights. The elements of a group discussion are listed below.

1. **Setting a Purpose** You probably work in groups in many of your classes. Successful group discussions have a specific purpose. This purpose may be
   - to discuss and share ideas
   - to cooperate in group learning
   - to solve a problem
   - to arrive at a group decision

   Once your group has chosen a purpose, find out how much discussion time will be allowed. Then, figure out what your group will be expected to accomplish within the time allowed.

TEACHING TIP

Group Discussion
Have students practice a group discussion to share ideas, insights, experiences, or information about communication in various cultures. Guide students in observing the guidelines for group discussion laid out in the Pupil's Edition.

Although one member of the group may be designated as the recorder, group members should collaborate on a record of the discussion. The recorder's role is to take notes during the discussion. Another group member can organize and condense the notes into a more formal summary of what each group member contributed to the discussion. The summary should identify at least one important contribution to the discussion made by each member and should summarize the outcome of the discussion. A third group member can revise the notes, reorganizing ideas in order of importance, for example, and proofread them.

Suggest students begin by discussing what communication looks like among their friends and relatives. What is dinner table conversation like? Is communication between older and younger family members formal or informal? Do you write notes to friends, talk on the phone, or talk in person? Then, have students identify which of these practices might be cultural, that is, based in the customary practices of ethnic or social groups. Finally, have students look for points of similarity and difference in the ways they communicate.

2. Understanding Roles and Responsibilities Everyone involved in a group discussion should have a specific role. Each role has special responsibilities. For example, your group may choose a chairperson to help keep the discussion moving smoothly. Someone else may be chosen as the recorder, who has the responsibility of taking notes during the discussion. Each member of the group should actively listen to the speaker. Listeners should consider how the speaker's ideas, information, and experience relate to their own.

Many groups begin by creating a plan or outline for the order of topics to follow in a discussion. The chairperson, or sometimes the entire group, may create the plan.

Impromptu Speaking At times you will need to speak to a group of people without having time to plan what you will say. This is called an *impromptu speech*. Here are some suggestions.

1. Think about your purpose. Do you want to give information to your audience? Do you want to persuade them?
2. Think about your topic. What is the main thing you need to say? If you have time, add details to explain your main points.
3. Think about your audience. Does what you are saying fit the time, the place, and the people you are addressing?

Speaking Socially Although you do not need to choose words as carefully when speaking socially as you do in more formal situations, you do need to think about how clearly you are communicating your ideas. Here are some guidelines for speaking effectively in common social situations.

1. Giving Directions or Instructions
- Divide the instructions or directions into a series of clear, logical steps.
- Tell your listener each of the steps in the process, one at a time, in order.
- Check to be sure your listener understands all of the instructions or directions.
- Repeat any instructions that are not clear.

2. Making Social Introductions
- Have confidence. If no one else introduces you, introduce yourself to other people.

Responsibilities of Group Members	
Chairperson	Announce the topic and set the plan.
	Follow the plan.
	Encourage each member to participate actively.
	Keep the discussion on track. Help the group avoid disagreements and distractions.
Recorder	Take notes about important information.
	Prepare a final report.
Participant	Participate actively in the discussion both when speaking and when listening.
	Ask questions and give full attention to others.
	Cooperate and share information.

- When you introduce others, identify them by name.
- When you are introducing others, it is customary to speak first to an older person before a younger person or to the person you know best.

3. Speaking on the Telephone
- Call people at times that are convenient for them. It may not be convenient for someone to speak to you early in the morning, late at night, or around mealtimes.
- Identify yourself; then, state your reason for calling.
- Be polite, speak clearly, and keep your call to a reasonable length.

Oral Interpretation *Oral interpretation* is more like acting in a play than giving a speech. When you give an oral interpretation, you read a piece of literature expressively to your listeners. To indicate the meaning of the selection, you use facial expressions, your voice, gestures, and movements to interpret the literary work for your listeners.

1. Selecting or Adapting Material The purpose of an oral interpretation is to entertain. As you choose your selection, think about who your audience is, how much time you will have, what the occasion or situation is, and how expressive you want to be in your interpretation.

To find a literary work for your oral interpretation, consider the following suggestions.

Selecting an Oral Interpretation	
Type of Literature	**Description of Possible Selection**
poem	a poem that tells a story, such as an epic poem
	a poem that has a speaker (using the word *I*) or a conversation between characters
	a poem that expresses a particular emotion
short story	a brief story, or portion of a story, that has
	- a beginning, middle, and end
	- either a narrator who tells the story (using *I*) or characters who talk to one another (using dialogue in quotation marks)
play	a short play, or one scene from a play, that has
	- a beginning, middle, and end
	- dialogue between two characters or a dramatic monologue
personal narrative	a piece you wrote about an experience or event in your life that has a beginning, middle, and end

You may be able to find just the right piece of literature. It may already be the perfect length. It may have just the right number of characters, with dialogue that tells the part of the story you want to tell. Sometimes, though, you need to shorten a short story, a long poem, or a play. This shortened version is called a *cutting*.

How to Make a Cutting

1. Decide where the part of the story you want to use should begin and where it should end, and follow that part of the story in time order.

2. From a short story, cut dialogue tags, such as *she whispered sadly.* Instead, use these clues to tell you how to act out the character's words.

3. Cut out parts that do not contribute to the portion of the story you are telling.

2. Presenting an Oral Interpretation

- *Prepare a reading script.* Once you have chosen a piece to interpret, create a *reading script*. A **reading script** is typed with double spacing, or written neatly with an extra space between each line. This space gives you a place to make marks that will help you with your reading. Underline words you want to emphasize, mark slashes where you will take a breath, or write a note to remind yourself of the emotion you want to convey.

- *Create an introduction.* You should plan to introduce your oral interpretation with a short introduction. Tell your listeners what has happened before your scene, explain whether the scene is told from the **point of view** of a certain character or an anonymous narrator, or describe the **setting** in which the action takes place.

- *Rehearse your presentation.* Rehearse in several different ways until you find the most effective way to present your scene. Practice in front of your mirror. Then, try out your reading on your friends, classmates, or relatives. Use your voice to emphasize your meaning. Vary your body movements and your voice to show that you are portraying different characters and to show important emotions.

Listening

Listening involves understanding the meaning of the sounds you hear. Listening can be especially challenging when you are listening to understand new information. This section focuses on the elements of listening.

Basics of the Listening Process

Like the reading process, the listening process includes skills you use before, during, and after you get the message.

Getting Ready to Listen   You will be a more effective listener if you take steps to get focused before you begin listening.

1. **Know Why You Are Listening**   Keeping your purpose in mind as you listen will help you to be a more effective listener. The way you take in information depends on your reason for listening. For example, if you are listening to the radio for enjoyment, you won't think carefully about the ideas in the songs, ads, or DJ comments. If you are listening to find out how to get tickets to see your favorite group, though, you will listen much more carefully and may even write down information you need to remember. Common purposes for listening are
   - for enjoyment or entertainment
   - to gain information or solve a problem
   - to understand information or an explanation
   - to evaluate or form an opinion

2. **Limit Distractions**   Listening can be difficult if you are not focused on the speaker. Before you listen, think about the steps below.

> ### Eliminating Barriers to Effective Listening
>
> **Keep a positive attitude, and focus your attention on the speaker.**
> Before you listen, make sure you feel rested and relaxed. As you sit down, remind yourself that you are going to focus on the speaker for the next few minutes. Put aside distracting thoughts, plans, or worries as you listen.
>
> **Think about the message.**
> As you listen to the speaker, focus on what he or she is saying. Try not to be distracted by any mannerisms or accent the speaker has.
>
> **Prepare for the setting.**
> Sometimes lecture halls and classrooms are too hot or cold. Wearing a sweater or jacket can help you adjust to the temperature. Also, choose a seat where you can see and hear the speaker well. Try to choose a place to sit that will minimize distractions.

Listening   Communication involves give and take, both speaking and listening. Nonverbal elements, such as your facial expressions and body language, can tell the speaker when you are listening and when you are not. Follow these guidelines to listen politely and effectively to a speaker.

- **Communicate respect and attention through your body language**   Look

Getting Ready to Listen
Tell students that their purposes for listening (to gain information, to solve problems, or to enjoy) will depend on to whom or what they are listening. It may be useful for students to ask themselves the following questions to help determine their purposes for listening:

- What reaction should I have to what I am hearing?

- What does the speaker expect me to do with what I am hearing?

Encourage students to suggest other questions that are useful for determining purpose and write them on the chalkboard.

directly at the speaker, and sit up straight.

- **Listen quietly** Do not interrupt the speaker or distract others in the audience. Wait until the speaker finishes before asking questions.

- **Keep an open mind** Do not rush to judge the speaker. Listen politely to the speaker even if you do not agree with him or her. Be respectful of such possible differences as the speaker's accent, race, religion, or customs.

- **Monitor yourself as you listen** Ask yourself questions to see if you understand what the speaker is saying.

- **Take notes** Note taking will help you remember the speaker's main points and other important information. Taking notes is a way of organizing your ideas. You should not try to write down every single word, but instead capture the main points as well as your own thoughts. You may choose to organize a speaker's ideas in a graphic organizer or an outline instead. Later, use your notes to help yourself ask questions or make comments. (See also **paraphrasing** and **summarizing** on page 776.)

Responding After you finish listening to a speech, you still have a role to play. Your response can help the speaker know how the speech went. Choose one or more of these ways to respond to a speaker.

- **Ask questions** If anything the speaker said was unclear to you, ask a question about it. By rephrasing the confusing information, the speaker can help you and others to understand it better.

- **Give positive feedback** Everybody needs a pat on the back. Compliment one or two specific things that the speaker did well. Even if you do not agree with the speaker, you can praise his or her clear explanations or well-designed graphics.

- **Offer constructive criticism** One way to help speakers improve is by offering constructive, or helpful, information. Politely identify something that the speaker can improve, and call his or her attention to it.

- **Remember the power of nonverbal feedback** Sometimes the most helpful feedback is given without words. To show your appreciation, stay in your seat until after the speech is completely over. Listen attentively to questions and answers. Remember that a smile can say more than words.

- **Discuss the speech with others** Compare your understanding of the speaker's message to that of other people around you. Find out what other audience members thought of the speech. You may find that someone else got something different from the speech than you did.

Listening with a Purpose

As you listen, keep your purpose in mind. Use the strategies that follow to help you listen effectively in specific situations.

Listening to Appreciate When you listen to poetry, drama, fiction, or stories passed down through generations, you generally listen for enjoyment. Here are some ways to increase your enjoyment and appreciation as you listen.

■ **Listening to Literature**   Listening to literature is like reading literature in some ways. Readers preview a piece of literature, read it, and think about it afterward. You can use a similar process for listening to literature by following the steps below.

Before you listen

- Ask questions about the literature you are about to hear. What is the selection about? What is its title? Who wrote it? What kind of literature is it (poetry, a short story, a play)?
- Use your questions to help you make predictions about what you will hear. Don't worry about whether your predictions are correct.

As you listen

- Create mental images or pictures of what you hear as you listen.
- Write down notes, questions, or ideas you have as you listen.
- Make connections to your own life. Think about similar experiences or feelings you have had.

After you listen

- Confirm or adjust the predictions you made before you listened. How did your predictions change as you listened?
- Think about your response to the selection. What did you like about the selection? Did you learn anything? What did you feel while listening?
- Think about the literary elements used in the literature. Did the selection use imagery, alliteration, foreshadowing, repetition, or rhyme? What was the theme or message of the selection? How did the literary elements add to the theme of the selection?

- Organize your ideas. Summarize what happened in the selection and what you learned from listening to it.

■ **Listening to Oral Tradition**   *Oral tradition* refers to the way people's culture and history are passed down verbally, usually through storytelling. When you listen to oral traditions such as fairy tales or folk tales, you are participating in the process of passing that story down to a new generation. As you listen to a folk tale or fairy tale, use the following tips to be an active listener.

Strategies for Listening to Oral Tradition

Compare elements of different stories.
Many folk tales and fairy tales have elements in common, such as characters, setting, themes or messages, or plots. As you listen, think about other stories you know that have similar elements. How are the two stories alike? How are they different?

Compare versions of the same story.
Every time a story is told, the storyteller changes it in some way. By emphasizing certain parts or changing the wording, a storyteller makes the story he or she tells unique. Compare the story you hear now with the story as you have read or heard it before. How are the two stories different?

Look for similarities and differences between the story and the storyteller's regional or cultural background.
Did you know that there are hundreds of versions of the Cinderella story?

(continued)

TEACHING TIP

■ **Listening to Oral Tradition**
Ask students if they say "faucet," "spigot," or "tap." Do they stand "in line" or "on line"? drink "soda" or "pop"? Point out to students that people in different regions sometimes have different terms for things. The same often holds true for different cultures. Tell students to be aware of this rich diversity of language when they are listening. You may want to challenge students to name examples from their own listening experiences of how language use reflects both region and culture.

TEACHING TIP

Strategies for Listening to Oral Tradition
Students may be able to identify similarities between stories from the oral traditions of various regions. Ask who in the class has come to your area from elsewhere in the country or state. Then, ask these students, as well as the students who are originally from your area, to recall a "tall tale" or another story they have heard (such as the kind told around campfires or at slumber parties). Look for similarities between two stories recounted by students from different areas. Once a similar pair has been identified, ask students to identify the variations between the two stories. In particular have students look for variations tied to region, such as references to local customs or place names.

TEACHING TIP

Listening to Comprehend
You may want to provide students with a "listening for information" activity. Select an informative text from Part 1 of this book or another text containing information you would like students to learn. To help them get ready to listen, have students think about what their purpose is. [Their purpose may vary, depending on what you want them to do with the text you read.] Review the strategies for listening for information in the chart. Also, remind students to eliminate distractions by facing the speaker, removing unnecessary items from their desktops, and so on.

Advise students to take notes in an organized way, using a graphic organizer or an outline. In their notes, students should identify the main ideas and supporting evidence. After reading each section, ask a different student to summarize the meaning of that section.

Strategies for Listening to Oral Tradition

Each version, however, is unique to its storyteller's culture of origin or region. For example, the Egyptian Cinderella story is different from the Vietnamese Cinderella story. Listen for ways that the story you are hearing seems to match or differ from the culture or region of the storyteller.

Identify labels or sayings from specific regions and cultures.
As you listen to the story, try to identify words or phrases that are used in specific regions or by people of specific cultures. What do these phrases add to the story?

Listening to Comprehend These steps and the strategies that follow them can help you listen to get information.

Strategies for Listening for Information

Find the main idea.
What is the most important point of the speech? Listen for clue words, such as *major, main, most important,* or similar words.

Identify significant details.
What dates, names, or facts does the speaker use to support main points of the speech? What kinds of examples or explanations are used to support the main idea?

Distinguish between facts and opinions.
A *fact* is a statement that can be proved to be true. (May is the fifth month.) An *opinion* is a belief or a judgment about something. It cannot be proved. (Strawberries are better than oranges.)

Identify the order of organization.
What order does the speaker use to present ideas—time order, spatial order, logical order?

Note comparisons and contrasts.
Are some details compared or contrasted with others?

Understand cause and effect.
Does the speaker say or hint that some events cause others to occur? Or does the speaker suggest that some events are the result of others?

Predict outcomes and draw conclusions.
What reasonable conclusions or predictions can you make from the facts and evidence you have gathered from the speech?

■ **LQ2R** The LQ2R study method is especially helpful when you are listening to a speaker who is giving information or instructions.

L *Listen* carefully to information as it is being presented.

Q *Question* yourself as you listen. Make a mental list of questions as they occur to you, or write down your questions.

R *Recite* mentally in your own words the answers to your questions as they are presented, or jot down notes as you listen.

R *Relisten* as the speaker concludes the presentation. The speaker may sum up, or repeat, major points of the presentation.

■ **5W-How? Questions**   When you listen for information, you need to listen for details that answer the basic *5W-How?* questions: *Who? What? When? Where? Why?* and *How?* For example, if you were listening to an invitation, you would make sure you understood these details.

- who is giving the party
- when and where the party will be held
- what kind of party it is
- how you can help with arrangements

■ **Listening to Instructions and Directions**   Instructions and directions are usually given in a series of steps. It is important to make sure you understand each step as you listen.

Guidelines for Listening to Instructions

1. *Listen for the order of steps.* Listen for clue words that tell you the order of steps, including *first, next, then,* and *last.*

2. *Identify the number of steps in the process.* If the process includes many steps, make notes to help you remember all of the steps.

3. *Picture each step.* Imagine yourself completing each step of the process in order.

4. *Review the steps.* Make sure you have all the instructions and understand them. Ask questions if you are unclear about any step. Repeat the instructions back to the speaker to make sure you understand them.

Listening to Evaluate   When you evaluate a speech, you judge its content, delivery, and impact on the audience. Usually when you listen to evaluate, you judge a persuasive or informative speech based on criteria that fit the type of speech. The questions in the chart below are a starting point for interpreting and evaluating a speech. Generate more criteria for evaluation, and add your own questions to those listed. You can use the criteria to evaluate not only speeches given by others, but also your own speeches.

Points to Interpret and Evaluate

Analyze the speaker's message
- Can you summarize the main idea of the speech?
- Can you explain why the message of the speech is important?

Identify the speaker's point of view
- Can you identify the speaker's perspective or attitude toward the subject?

Evaluate the clearness of the speech
- Is the speech organized in an order that makes sense?
- Can you identify each of the main points of the speech?

Analyze the speaker's believability
- Does the speaker refer to outside sources of information?
- Are the sources respectable or credible?

Evaluate the speaker's delivery
- Does the speaker speak loudly and clearly enough to be understood easily?
- Does the speaker use eye contact, gestures, and facial expressions well?
- Does the speaker use visual materials?

Identify nonverbal messages
- Does the speaker use nonverbal elements to emphasize points?

(continued)

Listening   **771**

Listening to Evaluate
Provide students with a persuasive message to evaluate. There are many persuasive messages on the radio, in the form of advertisements or editorials on news programs like *All Things Considered*. Review the information in the chart titled "Points to Interpret and Evaluate" as well as the chart on page 239. As students listen, have them answer these questions (divide responsibility for answering the questions among different students):

- What is the speaker's message? (What is the speaker's opinion? What facts support this opinion?)

- What is the speaker's purpose?

- What is his or her perspective? (What values, beliefs, or motives are driving the message? How can you tell?)

- What persuasive techniques does the speaker use?

- What, if anything, makes the speaker believable?

- Overall, how would you rate the speaker's content, delivery (in terms of volume, rate, pitch, and tone), and believability?

As students listen, encourage them to monitor their understanding and jot down what they don't understand. After listening, have students compare their responses to the questions.

(continued)

Points to Interpret and Evaluate

- Do the speaker's nonverbal gestures match his or her words?

Identify the speaker's purpose

- Why is the speaker giving the speech?
- Is the speech intended to inform, persuade, or entertain?

Identify the persuasive techniques

- Does the speaker try to convince you by using reasons and evidence, by appealing to your emotions, or both?
- Does the speaker use propaganda? For example, does the speaker try to make you feel that because everyone is doing something, you should, too? Does the speaker try to make you feel that he or she understands you?

Summarize the speaker's ideas

- Does the speech have a strong beginning and ending?

Special Listening Situations

In some situations, you will not only listen, but actively respond to the speaker's ideas and present new ideas or questions of your own.

Group Discussions See **Group Discussion** on page 763.

Interviews An interview is a one-on-one listening situation. You conduct interviews to gather information from someone who knows a great deal about a topic that interests you. This person is called the *interviewee*. Use the suggestions in the following chart to help you conduct a successful interview.

Strategies for Conducting an Interview

Before the Interview

- Decide what information you want to get from the interview.
- Make a list of questions to ask in the interview.
- Arrange an interview time and location with the person you will interview. Arrive on time.

During the Interview

- Take notes or tape-record the interview if the interviewee gives permission. If you will directly quote the person you interview, be sure you have his or her permission to do so.
- Be polite even if you disagree with the speaker's opinions. Make eye contact, and respond with facial expressions or gestures. Don't interrupt; give the interviewee time to thoroughly answer each of your questions. Then, ask follow-up questions that occur to you.
- If you do not understand an answer, ask questions to have the interviewee explain what he or she means, or repeat back to the speaker what you think he or she might have meant.
- Conclude by thanking the interviewee for his or her time.

After the Interview

- Review your notes, or make notes from your tape recording. Write a summary of the interview, and choose quotes you would like to use while the interview is still fresh in your mind.
- Send the interviewee a short note thanking him or her again for helping you gather the information you need.

Media Messages The term *media* refers to forms of communication such as television, radio, newspapers, magazines, and the Internet. These are often called mass communication because they reach a large audience. Media may be created to inform, to persuade, or to entertain. Sometimes it is difficult to tell whether a program was created to entertain, to inform, or to persuade. Listeners must carefully analyze the messages they hear in media.

■ **Analyzing Media Messages** In the media, persuasive messages may be disguised as entertainment or information. To understand the true purpose of a message, ask yourself the questions below.

Guidelines for Analyzing Media Messages

1. *What seems to be the purpose of the message?* Listen to the message. How is it presented? Is it presented by an authority? Does it sound true to you?

2. *Is the information in the message true and up-to-date?* Where does the information come from? If no sources are given, the information may not be trustworthy. Distinguish between facts and opinions, and watch out for fiction being presented as fact.

3. *What kind of language does the message contain?* Does it use language such as "you should . . ." to persuade you to do something? Does it compare two things using words such as *better* or *worse*?

4. *What are the underlying values or assumptions of the message?* Think about what the message is *not* saying. Sometimes what is not said in a message is as important as what is said. For exam-

---

ple, a program on nuclear power that tells only about its positive aspects while ignoring the dangers caused by malfunctions presents an uneven picture.

5. *What is your opinion of the message?* Use everything you know to form your own opinion about the message. If you think the message may not be accurate, you may want to find out more information on your own.

■ **Identifying Lack of Objectivity in the Media** The chart below contains terms that you need to understand to help you evaluate media messages. These terms describe ways in which a message can be less than objective or truthful.

Bias is a preference or inclination. A biased speaker may present only one side of an issue or may downplay information that supports an opposing view. A biased listener may not pay attention to information that does not support his or her opinion.

Misleading Information means bending facts to support an idea. A speaker may use misleading information to support a point, especially if the point is already popular with the audience.

Prejudice is a pre-judgment or belief based on preconceived notions, rather than on facts or reason. Prejudiced speakers or listeners will ignore facts that go against their beliefs.

Propaganda is a systematic approach to influencing many people at once. Propaganda is found in advertisements, speeches, and other forms of persuasion. (See also page 792.)

Listening **773**

Cooperative Learning

Discussion. Have students help each other understand how listening experiences vary depending on listening purpose. Divide your class into four discussion groups after they complete this two-part activity.

1. Have students tape-record themselves reading aloud a selection of their choice or a selection you have assigned. Randomly assign 1/4 of the class to record narratives, 1/4 to record drama or poetry, 1/4 to record persuasion (including ads), and 1/4 to record informational selections. Readings should be fairly short. As they read, students should use effective volume, rate, pitch, and tone. Arrange these recordings into four "listening stations" labeled with the type of reading.

2. Have students choose listening stations based on their interests. Each student should then choose a specific reading based on its title, author, or subject and consider the purpose for listening. (Have students review listening purposes on pp. 768–772 and the appropriate listening guidelines on pp. 768–773.)

Group students based on the type of selection they chose for listening. Have each group discuss the following questions about the selections they heard.

- What were the subjects of the readings in your listening category? Are these subjects similar to or different from the subjects of the pieces you read aloud? Why do you think that is?

- Did you achieve your listening purpose? Do you think other types of selections could have helped you fulfill your purpose? Explain.

Studying and Test Taking

Studying

Skills and Strategies

Studying helps you get good grades on assignments and tests, but good grades are not the only reason for studying. The real purpose of studying is to learn new information so that you can remember and use it later. The following section teaches skills and strategies you can use to study more effectively. (See also **Test Taking** on page 778.)

Making a Study Plan   Plan a study schedule that will help you study successfully. When you map out a schedule, stick to it. Here are some suggestions:

1. **Know your assignments.** Write down all your assignments and their due dates. Be sure you understand the instructions for each assignment.
2. **Make a plan.** Break large assignments into small steps. Keep track of when you should be finished with each step.
3. **Concentrate when you study.** Set aside time and find a quiet, well-lighted place to study. This will help you focus your attention on your assignments.

Organizing and Remembering Information   Various study skills and strategies are simply different ways of organizing and handling information. The following are some of the most common strategies that can help you organize and remember information as you study.

■ **Classifying**   *Classifying* is arranging information into categories or groups. All the items that are in a category or group are related to each other. The name or description of the category shows the relationship among the various items in the group. If you break your notes into categories, you will have an easier time learning the material. For example, if you were studying earthquakes, you might divide your notes into these categories: the causes of earthquakes, the effects of earthquakes, and measuring earthquakes.

■ **Graphic organizers** Sometimes, new information is easier to remember if you organize it visually. Using a graphic organizer, such as a map, diagram, or chart, can help you organize important details and understand their relationship to one another. Instead of trying to remember all the details in a long passage, you can simply remember the important ones you choose to include in your graphic organizer. (See also **Arranging Ideas** on page 806.)

■ **Memorization** When you take tests and quizzes, you sometimes need to *memorize* the information on which you will be tested. Trying to memorize all of the study material the night before a test will not be very effective. Frequent, short, focused sessions are more likely to help you remember information. The following chart provides you with hints for memorizing effectively.

How to Memorize

1. Memorize key concepts. Whenever possible, condense the material you need to remember.

2. Rehearse the material in different ways. Copy the material by hand or recite the material out loud.

3. Invent memory games. Form a word from the first letters of important terms, or make up rhymes to help you remember facts and details.

■ **Notes on reading or lectures** Taking accurate *notes* during a reading

assignment or in class is worth the extra effort. With detailed information recorded in your notebook, you will be ready to study for even the most challenging test. It is much easier to review your study notes before a test than to review a whole chapter or series of chapters in a textbook.

How to Take Study Notes

1. Identify and take note of the main ideas in class or in your reading. These main ideas should be the headings in your notes. In class, listen for key words and phrases, such as *first, most important,* or *therefore.* These words often introduce main ideas or key concepts. In a textbook, chapter headings and related subheadings usually contain key ideas.

2. Include brief examples or details, if you can. Important examples or details can help you recall the main ideas.

3. Keep your notes brief. Develop a system of abbreviations and use it consistently. Summarize material in your own words.

4. Review your notes soon after you have written them to make sure you have included all important information.

At the top of page 776 is an example of careful study notes about an article on the history of soccer. The notes show main ideas as headings. Underneath these main headings are important details that relate to each heading. Not every detail from the passage appears. These notes list only the most important details.

> **Soccer is a very old game.**
>   Evidence of games similar to soccer has been found in ancient Chinese, Mayan, Greek, and Egyptian cultures.
>   Modern soccer began in England in the 1800s.
>   "Football" was split into two games, soccer and rugby, in 1863.
>
> **The Growth of Professional Soccer**
>   Professional soccer was first played in England and was officially recognized by the Football Association in 1885.
>   The first international game was played between Scotland and England in 1872.
>   British citizens spread soccer throughout Europe and South America.

■ **Outlines**   An *outline* helps you organize ideas that you read or hear. Outlines group the ideas in an order and in a pattern that shows relationships among the ideas. (See also **Formal** and **Informal Outlines** on page 807.)

■ **Paraphrasing**   *Paraphrasing* involves putting someone else's ideas into your own words. Putting an idea that you read or hear into your own words helps you understand it better. When you write a paraphrase of something you read, it will usually be about the same length as the original. You will probably not use paraphrasing for long passages of writing. Instead, you might *summarize* or *outline* the passage. (See also **Paraphrasing** on page 745, **Outlines** above, and **Summarizing** in the next column.)

Follow these guidelines when you write a paraphrase.

> **How to Paraphrase**
>
> **1. Read the selection carefully** before you begin.
>
> **2. Be sure you understand the main idea of the selection.** Look up unfamiliar words in a dictionary.
>
> **3. Determine the tone of the selection.** (What is the writer's attitude toward the subject of the selection?)
>
> **4. Identify the speaker in fictional material.** (Is the writer speaking, or is a character in the selection?)
>
> **5. Write your paraphrase in your own words.** Shorten long sentences or stanzas. Use your own, familiar vocabulary, but follow the same order of events or ideas that is used in the selection.
>
> **6. Check to be sure that the ideas in your paraphrase match the ideas that are expressed in the original selection.**

■ **SQ3R**   *SQ3R* stands for *Survey, Question, Read, Recite,* and *Review.* This five-step method will help you read material more carefully and actively. When you read actively, you are more likely to remember what you read. (See also **SQ3R** on page 747.)

■ **Summarizing**   Like a paraphrase, a *summary* expresses another person's ideas in your own words. However, a summary shortens the original material by presenting only the most important points. (See also **Summarizing** on page 748.)

Use the following guidelines when you summarize.

How to Summarize

1. Skim the selection you wish to summarize.

2. Read the passage again closely. Look for the main ideas and notice all of the details that support each main idea.

3. Write your summary in your own words. Include only the main ideas and the most important supporting points.

4. Evaluate and revise your summary, checking to see that you have covered the most important points. Make sure you have clearly expressed the ideas in your passage.

The sample in the next column summarizes the reading selection on pages 83–85.

A recent study found that all-girl schools give girls more confidence in science and math, but not better test scores. Supporters of all-girl schools claim that girls get more attention and gain more confidence in all-girl schools. Opponents argue that all-girl schools discriminate against boys. They claim it is better to improve all schools so that girls and boys get equal, quality education in schools where they can learn to work together.

■ **Writing to learn** *Writing* can help you learn. When you write, you are forced to put your thoughts in order. For example, you can write to solve problems, record your observations, or work out the details of a plan. See the following chart for examples of different types of writing and their purposes.

Types of Writing for Different Purposes		
Type of Writing	**Purpose**	**Example**
Freewriting	To help you **focus** your thoughts	Writing for five minutes about a lecture you heard in history class
Autobiography	To help you **examine** the meaning of important events in your life	Writing about a personal experience that taught you to be thankful for what you have
Diary	To help you **recall** your impressions and **express** your feelings	Writing about your reactions to a field trip with your art class to a local art museum
Journal or Learning Log	To help you **record** your observations, descriptions, solutions, and questions	Writing down questions for your teacher as you watch a documentary on advances in math
	To help you **define** or **analyze** information, or **discover** a **solution** to a problem	Listing good and bad points of a proposed law you discussed in government class

TEACHING TIP

■ **Writing to Learn**
Suggest that students write a journal entry in order to discover something new about themselves. Remind students that journals are private, and they do not have to share this entry with anyone else. Before they write, ask students to think about an interesting interaction they have had with someone recently. Write this sentence starter on the board: *I recently had an interesting interaction with _____ about _____.*

Have students briefly summarize the interaction. Then, complete this sentence starter: *As a result of this interaction, I discovered _____.*

Encourage students to elaborate on what they discovered and how the discovery came about.

Test Taking

Studying for Tests

As you go through school, you will take many tests. Two of the most common types are essay tests and objective tests. The following information can help you prepare for these types of tests.

Essay tests   *Essay tests* measure how well you understand a subject. Essay answers are usually a paragraph or longer.

How to Study for Essay Tests

1. **Read assigned material carefully.**

2. **Make an outline of main points and important details.**

3. **Create your own essay questions and practice writing answers.**

4. **Evaluate and revise your practice answers.** Check your answers against the information in your notes and textbook. Also, use the Writing Workshops in this textbook for help in writing.

Objective tests   *Objective tests* ask you for specific information, such as names, terms, dates, or definitions. Most objective test questions have only one correct answer.

How to Study for Objective Tests

1. **Identify important terms, facts, or ideas** in your textbook or class notes.

2. **Review the information in more than one form.** For example, if you are responsible for defining literary terms, make flash cards. Practice identifying the definition from the term; then identify the term from its definition.

3. **Practice and rehearse factual information.** Go over the items you have had difficulty with until you know them well.

4. **If possible, briefly review all information shortly before the actual test.**

Types of Test Questions

This section describes the different types of questions you may find on a test. You can use the tips and strategies for each question type to improve your performance on tests.

Analogy questions   An *analogy question* requires you to do two things. First, you must recognize the relationship between two words. Then, you must identify two other words that have a similar relationship.

EXAMPLE

Directions: Select the appropriate pair of words to complete the analogy.

1. MUG : TEA :: _____
   A. plate : bowl
   B. ice : iced water
   C. glass : milk
   D. curtain : window

How to Answer Analogy Questions

1. **Create a sentence that expresses the relationship between the first pair of words.** For example, you could say, "A *mug* is used to hold *tea*."

2. **Use your sentence to find the answer choice with the same relationship.** Test each answer choice using your sentence. Does a *plate* hold a *bowl*? Does *ice* hold *iced water*? Continue with the remaining answer choices.

3. **Find the best available choice to complete the analogy.** In this example, the only reasonable choice is C, since a *glass* holds *milk* just as a *mug* holds *tea*.

Essay questions *Essay questions* require thoughtful, thorough answers that are usually several paragraphs long. Prepare your essay with a topic sentence, supporting details, and a conclusion. Follow these steps to answer essay questions.

1. **Plan your approach.** Read the directions carefully to determine how many questions you are expected to answer. Decide how much time to spend on each section. Stay with your schedule. You may run out of time if you spend too much time on one question.

2. **Read the question carefully.** You may be asked for an answer that contains several parts.

3. **Pay attention to important terms in the question.** Essay questions on tests usually require an answer that accomplishes specific tasks. Each task is expressed by a verb. If you become familiar with the key verbs and the kind of response each one calls for, you can write a more successful essay. See the chart below.

Key Verbs That Appear in Essay Questions

Key Verb	Task	Sample Question
analyze	Take something apart to see how each part works.	Analyze the water cycle.
compare	Point out likenesses.	Compare smoothies and juices.
contrast	Point out differences.	Contrast radio and TV news.
define	Give specific details that make something unique.	Define the word *culture* and give examples.
demonstrate	Provide examples to support a point.	Demonstrate the importance of voting in a democratic society.
describe	Give a picture in words.	Describe how a main character changes throughout a story.
discuss	Examine in detail.	Discuss the strategy of the Union army during the Battle of Shiloh.

(continued)

Key Verbs That Appear in Essay Questions

Key Verb	Task	Sample Question
explain	Give reasons.	Explain why a new computer lab is needed at your school.
identify	Point out specific characteristics.	Identify the different types of rock.
list	Give all steps in order or all details about a subject.	List the steps for finding the lowest common denominator of a group of numbers.
persuade	Form an opinion on an issue and give reasons to support it.	Persuade your principal that your school should or should not have vending machines.
summarize	Give a brief overview of the main points.	Summarize the tale of "Beauty and the Beast."

4. **Use prewriting strategies.** Consider the key verbs in the question. Then, jot down a few notes or an outline to help you decide what you want to say.

5. **Evaluate and revise as you write.** Look over what you have written, and find areas to improve your essay. Then, revise and edit it.

Matching questions   *Matching questions* ask you to match each item in one list with an item in another list.

EXAMPLE

Directions: Match the greeting in the left-hand column with its language in the right-hand column.

B	1. Guten Tag	A. Italian
D	2. Bonjour	B. German
A	3. Buon giorno	C. Spanish
C	4. Buenos días	D. French

These steps can help you answer matching questions.

How to Answer Matching Questions

1. Read the directions carefully. Sometimes you will not use all the items listed in one column. Other items may be used more than once.

2. Scan the columns. If you match items you know first, you'll have more time to evaluate items you are less sure about.

3. Complete the rest of the matching. Make your best guess on remaining items.

Multiple-choice questions   With a *multiple-choice question,* you select the best answer from a number of choices.

EXAMPLE

1. The majority of meteorites found on Earth are from
   A. Mars
   B. the asteroid belt
   C. the Moon
   D. Jupiter

The following guidelines can help you answer multiple-choice questions.

How to Answer Multiple-Choice Questions

1. Read the question or statement carefully. Make sure you understand the question or statement you are given before you look at the answer choices. Look for words such as *not* or *always*. These words limit your choice of answers.

2. Read all the choices before selecting an answer. Eliminate choices that you know are incorrect. This improves your chances of choosing correctly among the remaining choices. Think carefully about each remaining choice. Then, select the one that makes the most sense.

On-demand reading questions An on-demand test is one for which you cannot study in advance. One type of on-demand test requires reading. An *on-demand reading question* asks you to read a passage and answer questions about it. The answer may be found in the passage or may be based on your understanding of the passage.

EXAMPLE

Directions: Read the following passage and the questions after it.

People are not the only ones to get viruses. Computers also get viruses, or programs that are designed to "infect" one computer and be passed along to another. Viruses frequently scramble a computer's data. Some viruses, such as the Cascade virus, can produce spectacular effects. When the Cascade virus strikes, letters of a document appear to fall into a heap at the bottom of the screen.

1. In this passage, the author's purpose is to
   A. give information about computer viruses
   B. persuade people not to use computers
   C. compare different types of computers
   D. entertain with a story about viruses

These steps can help you answer on-demand reading questions.

How to Answer On-Demand Reading Questions

1. Read the passage carefully. As you read, identify the main idea of the passage, as well as important details. (See also **Stated Main Idea** on page 747.)

2. Read the questions that follow. Most questions after reading selections are multiple-choice.

3. Look for similar language in the questions and the reading passage. You can match words from the questions with a sentence in the reading passage and find the answer.

4. Draw your own conclusions. The example passage never states the purpose directly. However, you can tell that the author is giving information about computer viruses.

On-demand writing questions

On-demand writing questions are essay questions. You will frequently find them on state writing tests. You cannot study for the content of an on-demand writing question, but you can prepare by being familiar with different kinds of writing. These questions often ask you to write a persuasive, informative, narrative, or descriptive essay about a broad topic. Prepare by writing practice essays.

EXAMPLE

Fictional characters are often created from an author's real-life relationships. Think about a character in a book you have read. How is the character similar to someone you know? How is the character different? Write an essay comparing and contrasting a fictional character with a real-life friend or family member.

How to Answer On-Demand Writing Questions

1. Read the question carefully. Look for key terms in the question to help you determine what the question is asking. Decide whether your essay should be persuasive, informative, or descriptive. (See also **Key Verbs That Appear in Essay Questions** on page 779.)

2. Plan your answer. Use a prewriting technique to help you plan before you begin writing. (See also **Prewriting Techniques** on page 802.)

3. Evaluate and revise your answer as you write. Your essay should have a topic sentence, supporting details and examples, transitions, and a conclusion.

Reasoning or logic questions

Reasoning or *logic questions* test your reasoning abilities rather than your knowledge of a particular subject. Some reasoning questions ask you to identify the relationship among several items. For example, a reasoning question may ask you to predict the next item in a sequence.

EXAMPLE

What comes next?

In this sequence of three drawings, the front of the block is in a different corner of the box each time. Therefore, in its final position the front of the block must be in the lower right corner of the box.

How to Answer Reasoning or Logic Questions

1. Be sure you understand the instructions. Reasoning or logic questions are often multiple-choice. On some tests, however, you may need to write a word or phrase, complete a number sequence, or even draw a picture for your answer.

2. Analyze the relationship implied in the question. Study the question carefully to gather information about the relationship of the items.

3. Draw reasonable conclusions. Evaluate the relationship of the items to decide your answer.

Sentence-completion questions

Many *sentence-completion questions* test your understanding of vocabulary words used in a sentence.

EXAMPLE

1. Because of the dry weather conditions, the tree _____ will not be as colorful and spectacular this year.
   A. function   C. canopy
   B. foliage   D. yacht

   (B is circled)

How to Answer Sentence-Completion Questions

1. Read the sentence carefully. Make sure you understand the words in the sentence. Some sentences may contain clues to the meaning of the word or words that go in the blanks.

2. Rule out incorrect answer choices. If you can immediately rule out some answer choices, mark through them. In the previous example, the word *yacht* refers to a type of boat. You can immediately rule out this choice since you know the correct word has something to do with trees.

3. Fill in the blank with the remaining choices and choose the best answer. If you are not sure which choice is correct, use each one in the blank of the sentence.

Short-answer questions
Short-answer questions ask for short, precise responses. Instead of choosing from among a set of choices, you write the answer yourself. Some short-answer questions (such as labeling a map or diagram, or fill-in-the-blank questions) can be answered with one or a few words. Other types of short-answer questions require you to give a full, written response, usually one or two sentences in length.

EXAMPLE How are suspension bridges different from other types of bridges?

Answer: Suspension bridges are supported by cables. They can cover larger distances than other types of bridges because they do not need support in the middle. Suspension bridges use less metal so they can also be cheaper to build than other types of bridges.

How to Answer Short-Answer Questions

1. Read the question carefully. Some questions have more than one part. You must answer each part.

2. Plan your answer. Quickly decide what you need to include in the answer.

3. Be as specific as possible in your answers. Give a full, exact answer.

4. Budget your time. Begin by answering those questions you know.

True-false questions
In a *true-false question,* you are asked to decide whether a certain statement is true or false.

EXAMPLE

1. T (F) The Niagara Suspension Railway Bridge is the longest suspension bridge in the world.

How to Answer True-False Questions

1. Read the statement carefully. The statement is false if any part of it is false.

2. Look for word clues. Words such as *always* or *never* limit a statement. A statement is true only if it is always true.

Viewing and Representing

QUICK REFERENCE HANDBOOK

Critical Thinking

Evaluation. Suggest that students use a media log to help them keep track of the significant messages they hear and view in the mass media. Provide students with a framework for making records in their media logs. For example, students may want to divide their log for each message into four sections:

1. Name of message and its context (for example, "The Andy Griffith Show" viewed on cable TV one Saturday evening)

2. Before Viewing or Listening (predictions about what the media message will contain and what its purpose is)

3. Viewing or Listening (personal connections, determination of purpose, questions, interesting techniques, and so on)

4. After Viewing or Listening (summary, evaluation of how well message achieved its purpose, what its most successful effect was, and the technique used to create that effect, and so on)

Understanding Media Terms

Like people in many other professions, people who work in and write about the media often use *jargon*. **Jargon** is special language or terminology that helps a group of people with shared interests communicate quickly. Learning some media terms will help you analyze and evaluate the media messages you receive as well as those you create.

The terms in this section are divided into three lists: Electronic Media Terms, General Media Terms, and Print Media Terms. Terms that apply to both print media and electronic media are defined under Print Media Terms on pages 792–794. Terms relating to the Internet and the World Wide Web can be found in the "Library/Media Center" section beginning on page 735; terms relating to use of type and graphics can be found in "Document Design" beginning on page 722.

Electronic Media Terms

Advertising   See **Advertising** on page 792.

Animation   *Animation* is the technique of making photographs or drawings appear to move. Animators take a series of photographs of drawings or objects, or they generate a series of pictures on a computer. Each picture is called a frame, and each frame varies slightly from the ones before and after it. When the pictures are viewed at a rate of twenty-four frames per second, they create an illusion of movement. Many different types of media messages, including commercials and cartoons, use animation.

Broadcasting   *Broadcasting* is the sending of television or radio content over a wide area through the airwaves. *Commercial* *broadcasting* is done for profit. Advertisers pay broadcasters for airtime in which to persuade the audience to buy their products or services. *Public broadcasting* is not-for-profit broadcasting. In the United States, the Public Broadcasting Service (PBS) has more than three hundred member stations. The service is funded mostly by corporations and individual viewers and listeners. The federal government also provides some funds.

Byline   See **Byline** on page 792.

Cable Television   *Cable television* is a method of delivering television signals to homes and businesses through cables. A cable service provider receives the signals using powerful antennae. Viewers pay to receive the signals in their homes and offices.

Camera Angle   The *camera angle* is the angle at which a camera is pointed at its subject. A low angle makes the subject look tall and powerful, while a high angle makes the subject look small. A tilted angle suggests that the subject is not balanced.

Camera Shot   A *camera shot* is a single, continuous image in film or video. The following shots are some of the most common shots used in film and video production.

- **Close-up shot**   a shot showing the subject up close, for example, a person's face
- **Medium shot**   a shot showing the subject from a midrange distance, for example, a person and the top of the desk at which he or she sits

- **Long shot**   a shot showing the subject from a distance, for example, a city from an airplane

Commercial Broadcasting   See **Broadcasting** on page 784.

Copy   See **Copy** on page 792.

Credits   *Credits* list the names of people who worked on a presentation. They usually appear at the end of a television program, film, or video.

Demographics   See **Demographics** on page 792.

Digital Editing   See **Digital Editing** on page 792.

Documentary   A *documentary* is a type of film or television program that interprets actual events. A documentary usually includes interviews and footage of actual events. Some documentaries include reenactments of events as well as voice-over narration. The primary purpose of a documentary may be to inform, persuade, or entertain. The purpose of some documentaries is to make money. Documentaries may have more than one purpose. For instance, a documentary about lions may be both informative (telling where lions live and what they eat) and entertaining (showing lion cubs playing together).

Editor   See **Editor** on page 792.

QUICK REFERENCE HANDBOOK

Sound

Have students consider the effects of not only sound but also silence in a movie, TV show, or documentary. Have them begin by discussing with a partner times when there are pauses or silent periods in a program—in what situations is there silence? Why might a director include silent periods or pauses in a program? Remind students that no sound or silence is in a program by chance—everything is a result of choices the director has made.

Then, either show a scene from a program that includes a silent period or have students watch a program at home. Students should make notes on the following questions.

- What is the situation in the scene when the pause or silent period occurs? Who are the people involved? About how long does the silence last?

- Why do you think this silent period was included in the scene? What point do you think the director is making?

- How are the thoughts or emotions of the people in the scene communicated during the silent period? Do you think this method of communicating ideas is more or less effective than communicating through sound? Why?

Feature News   See **Feature News** on page 793.

Film   *Film* is a medium for recording sounds and images. On film, sounds and images are clearer than they are on videotape. Filmed images and sounds last a long time, and they can be presented on a large screen. However, film is more expensive to buy and develop than videotape. (See also **Videotape** on page 787.)

Hard News   See **Hard News** on page 793.

Internet   The *Internet* is a network of computers that allows computer users all over the world to communicate with each other. Using the Internet requires a computer equipped with a modem, a device that connects the computer with a telephone or cable line. Internet service providers (ISPs) provide access to the Internet for a monthly fee. (See also **"The Library/Media Center."**)

Lead   See **Lead** on page 793.

Marketing   See **Marketing** on page 793.

Medium   See **Medium** on page 793.

Message   See **Message** on page 791.

News   See **News** on page 793.

Newsmagazine   See **Newsmagazine** on page 794.

Photography   See **Photography** on page 794.

Producer   A *producer* is the person who oversees the production of a movie or a television or radio program. He or she develops the overall message and finds appropriate materials. The producer also organizes a crew or staff, finds funding, budgets, and keeps the production on schedule. (See also **Production** on page 794.)

Production   See **Production** on page 794.

Public Broadcasting   See **Broadcasting** on page 784.

Reporter   See **Reporter** on page 794.

Script   A *script* is the text to be spoken during a film, a play, or a television or radio program. It may include voice-over narration as well as dialogue. Film and television scripts also include information about the images to be shown. The script for a news broadcast is called *copy*.

Soft News   See **Soft News** on page 794.

Sound   In film and video, *sound* is all of the recorded material that you hear, including dialogue, music, and sound effects. Producers and filmmakers use sound to achieve various goals. One role of sound is to create an illusion. For example, you may watch a movie and think it is raining even though the rain is not visible. The sounds of rain falling on a roof and the cracking of thunder convince you that it is raining. Another role of sound is to create mood. For example, the music that a video producer selects to accompany visual images can tell the audience how to feel about those images.

Source See under **Print Media Terms**.

Storyboard A *storyboard* is a series of drawings showing the sequence of shots and scenes in a script. It may also include audio and visual cues. (See also page 259.)

Target Audience See **Target Audience** on page 794.

Text See **Text** on page 794.

Videotape *Videotape* is a medium used to record sounds and images. A videotape may be easier to make than a film because video equipment is cheaper and easier to use. However, images recorded on videotape tend to have poorer *resolution,* or less clarity, than filmed images, and videotape does not last as long as film. (See also **Film** on page 786.)

General Media Terms

Audience An *audience* is a group of people who receive a media message. Advertisers try to reach the audience they think is most likely to buy their products or services. (See also **Advertising** on page 792, **Demographics** on page 792, and **Target Audience** on page 794.)

Authority *Authority* refers to how knowledgeable and trustworthy the source of a message seems. When a message appears to come from an expert source, you find it authoritative. For example, a meteorologist would know more about tornadoes than a figure skater would, but a figure skater would know more about triple toe loops than a meteorologist would.

Bias A *bias* is a preference for one side of an issue, either for it or against it. A biased speaker or writer may ignore information that does not support his or her views. (See also **Point of View** on page 791.)

Context *Context* is the material that surrounds a media message. For example, the context of a magazine ad includes the other ads and the articles in that magazine. The context may influence how you interpret a message.

Credibility *Credibility* is the quality of being believable. A person's credibility is decided by the audience members. (For more on **evaluating credibility**, see page 771. See also **Message** on page 791.)

Critical Viewing *Critical viewing* means analyzing, interpreting, and evaluating visual messages in the mass media. Such messages may take a range of forms, from still photographs and editorial cartoons to films and television programs. Critical viewers keep the following five concepts in mind as they view messages in the media.

Media Concepts	
Concept 1: All messages are made by someone.	To create a visual message, an artist, photographer, or filmmaker must decide which elements (words, images, sounds) to include, which ones to leave out, and how to arrange and sequence the chosen elements. Knowing how

(continued)

Critical Thinking

Evaluation. After studying the **Media Concepts** chart, apply the **Evaluating Media Messages** questions to a media representation in a whole-class activity. Provide an example of a Web site, a news article, or an ad. After giving students time to examine media form, begin answering the questions. Keep in mind the critical thinking skill required for each question: The first three questions require identification or interpretation skill (such as interpreting purpose); the fourth and fifth require analysis; the sixth through tenth require evaluation (including evaluating the message's effectiveness and authenticity); and the last question requires synthesis.

After going through the process of analyzing and evaluating one media form, you may want to have students provide additional examples and present their own evaluations to the class.

You need to be aware that Internet resources are sometimes public forums and their content can be unpredictable.

(continued)

Media Concepts	
	visual messages are constructed will help you analyze the message. It will also help you appreciate the skill that went into creating the message.
Concept 2: Messages are reflections of reality.	A visual message is a version of reality, not reality itself. For a television broadcast of a baseball game, for example, everything from the camera angles to the amount of time set aside for commercials is carefully packaged. Realizing that a visual message is a version of reality will help you evaluate how authentic (true to life) the message seems.
Concept 3: Each person interprets messages differently.	The meaning a viewer draws from a visual message depends on the viewer's prior knowledge and experience. Since people's prior knowledge and experience vary, viewers may draw different meanings from the same message. Connecting the message to your own life experiences will help you interpret the message.
Concept 4: Messages have a wide range of purposes.	Every person who creates a visual message has a purpose. Usually, that purpose is to inform, persuade, entertain, or express thoughts and feelings. Most visual messages in the mass media also have another purpose: to make money. Being aware of the underlying commercial purpose of such messages will help you understand their effects on you.
Concept 5: The medium shapes the message.	Each type of visual medium has its own strengths and weaknesses. For example, film combines motion and sound, but the action flashes by quickly. A still photograph captures only a single moment, but it can be studied at length. People who create visual messages tailor their work to take full advantage of a particular medium's strengths. Knowing how the medium shapes the message will help you understand its creator's choice of medium and its effect on you.

Evaluating Media Messages The following questions will help you analyze, interpret, and evaluate messages in the mass media—radio, TV, film, newspapers, and magazines. The questions are based on the five media concepts explained above.

- Through what medium is the message delivered?

- Who created the message?

- What seems to be the purpose of the message? Is there also an underlying purpose? If so, what is it?

- What elements (words, images, or sounds) does the message include?

- How are those elements arranged and sequenced?

- How skillfully are the elements presented?
- What may have been left out of the message?
- How is the message's version of reality similar to or different from what you know from your own experience or from other sources?
- How authentic (true to life) does the message seem? Why?
- What does the message make you think of? How does it make you feel about the world? about yourself? about other people?
- How does the medium help shape the message?

Feedback   *Feedback* is a response from an audience to the sender of a message. It can be immediate or delayed. Applauding and asking questions are examples of immediate feedback. Writing a letter to an editor and filling out a questionnaire are examples of delayed feedback.

Formula   A *formula* is an established model or approach. In television and film, it refers to a typical way of combining characters or presenting material. Situation comedies, for example, often follow the formula of pairing characters with opposite personalities and interests.

Genre   A *genre* is a category of media products that share certain characteristics. Examples of genres common on television include
- children's programming
- documentary
- drama
- game show
- infomercial
- music video
- news broadcast
- sitcom (situation comedy)
- soap opera
- talk show

Illustration   An *illustration* is a drawing, painting, photograph, or computer-generated image. Illustrations are created to decorate or explain something. Consider the following elements as you create or evaluate illustrations (or any other visual art form).

- **Color**   Illustrators use color to create a specific mood or feeling, focus attention on a certain part of the illustration, or both. The quality of color is affected by its medium: felt-tip pens, powder, paints, and watercolors, for example, all create different effects.
- **Form**   Form is the three-dimensional look of an illustration. An illustration that appears to have depth and weight can look more realistic. Artists use color, line, and shape to give form to the objects they illustrate.
- **Line**   Line is the most basic element of illustration. Although real objects do not have lines around them, illustrators can create the illusion of reality through lines. Lines can be fine and delicate, showing texture, for example, or strong and bold. Artists also use line to show depth in an illustration and to show viewers the location of the horizon line.

Images

Using the following activity, have students consider the effects in the chart as well as other image effects found in a brief segment of a television program, movie, or documentary. Emphasize that nothing in the scene is there by chance—everything is a result of choices the director has made.

As you watch the video segment, make notes on the items in the chart and on the following:

- **movement** What people or objects in the scene move? What are these movements like? What do they tell you about the person or situation in the scene? What movements happen in response to other movements? What does this tell you about the relationship between the two moving things or people? What does not move? Do you think this is important? Why?

- **placement** Where are people and important objects in the scene in relation to each other? Is any object in a prominent position in the scene? Why? How close or far apart are people? Are they turned toward or away from each other? What does this tell you about their relationship? Why do you think the director chose to place the people and objects in the scene as they are?

■ **Shape** Lines come together to form a shape, or a two-dimensional outline of an object. An illustration may contain several shapes that are all connected to each other in some way.

Images An **image** is a visual representation of something. A painting, a photograph, a sculpture, and a moving picture are all examples of an image. Images may be *moving* or *still*.

■ A *still image,* such as a painting or a single frame of a film, allows viewers the time to notice details and consider the meaning of the image because the image does not move. Still images may also be easier to change—through cropping or digital editing, for example—than moving images.

■ A *moving image* is a series of still images projected quickly onto a television or film screen. Moving images that show actual events are called *documentary footage.* The evening news may include examples of documentary footage. Moving images that show an event arranged by a TV producer or filmmaker are called *dramatizations.* You can see a dramatization when you go to a movie theater. Both kinds of moving images can be incomplete or altered.

To analyze the effects of an image, consider the following techniques.

Creating Effects with Images	
Technique	**Definition/Effects**
Color	Color can create feelings or emphasize parts of an image. For example, filming a scene in black-and-white may have a sobering effect on the viewer. In a color photograph of a crowd, people wearing brightly colored clothes, such as red, orange, or yellow, will stand out compared to people wearing white or black.
Juxtaposition	Putting two or more images together creates a juxtaposition. Sometimes two images, still or moving, placed side-by-side can communicate more meaning than one image alone. For example, a detective show that cuts between images of a criminal opening a safe and a detective sneaking around a corner tells its viewers that the robbery will be interrupted by the detective.
Slow or fast motion	Moving images can be slowed down or sped up to create a certain effect. Making an image move slower than normal can create a dramatic effect, whereas speeding up an image can create a comic effect.

Media Law The First Amendment of the U.S. Constitution guarantees the freedom of the press. Therefore, except during wartime, the United States government rarely uses *censorship*. (*Censorship* refers to any attempt by a government or other group to control people's access to literature or the mass media.) Some media regulations, however, do exist. The Federal Communications Commission (FCC) enforces laws governing electronic media. Other laws protect individuals from the media. For example, a person whose reputation has been damaged by the publication of a false statement may sue the publisher. Copyright laws guard authors or publishers against *plagiarism,* or theft, of a message.

The growing use of the Internet has raised many new questions about regulation of the media. These questions will be the subject of debate for years to come.

Media Literacy *Media literacy* is the ability to access, analyze, evaluate, and communicate messages in a wide variety of forms. (See also **Critical Viewing** on page 787.)

Message A *message* is a communication sent to one or more people through language, gestures, images, or sounds. The *content* of a message is the information it presents. (See also **Credibility** on page 787, **Realism** on page 792, and **Source** on page 794.)

Multimedia Presentation *Multimedia presentations* involve the use of two or more forms of media. When you give an oral presentation that includes visuals—such as slides, video segments, or transparencies—you are giving a multimedia presentation. One medium is your voice; the other is the visuals you use. A multimedia presentation that involves the use of presentation software or Web sites is called a *technology presentation.*

Newsworthiness *Newsworthiness* is the quality of an event that makes it seem worth reporting. An event is considered newsworthy if it meets certain criteria (standards). News criteria include

- **impact** events or issues that make a difference in people's lives
- **timeliness** events or issues that are happening now
- **celebrity angle** stories about people who are famous or in power
- **human interest** stories that touch people's emotions

An event that meets several of these criteria is more likely to be covered by the news media.

Persuasion See **Propaganda** on page 792.

Point of View *Point of view* is the way a message sender approaches a topic. Everyone's point of view is shaped by his or her background and values. For example, in covering the opening of a new shopping center, one reporter might focus on the jobs the center has created. Another might focus on the locally owned stores that may lose business to the center.

In photography, point of view refers to the photographer's approach to his or her subject. The photographer's point of view

Understanding Media Terms **791**

TEACHING TIP

Media Law
Discuss the Children's Television Act, a federal law enforced by the FCC, which licenses broadcast media. To be eligible for a broadcast license, TV stations are obligated to air three hours per week of educational and informational programming for children under 16. Such programming must meet these criteria:

a) its purpose is educational

b) it airs between 7 A.M. and 10 P.M.

c) it is in a regularly scheduled weekly program

d) the program is at least thirty minutes in length

However, the FCC allows the TV stations it licenses to make "good faith judgments" about what each station considers educational children's programming. It also allows that, if a station does not air three hours per week of educational children's programming, it can deliver a package of "somewhat less" than the equivalent over a six-month period, in the form of specials, public service announcements, and so on.

After sharing this information with students, ask them to reflect on what they think "educational" programming should consist of. Invite students to watch a specific children's cartoon at home and keep a list of any educational concepts they encounter while watching. For example, early morning cartoons often make references to scientific concepts, to literature, or to famous events or people from history.

You may also choose to have students review the daily listings for several TV stations and identify how many deliver thirty minutes of educational children's programming per day. Have students debate whether TV stations should be required to air thirty minutes per day.

affects the selection of the subject and the camera angle. (See also **Bias** on page 787 and **Propaganda** below.)

Propaganda   *Propaganda* is a form of communication that influences an audience by using persuasive techniques. These techniques play on the audience's emotions and may be used to mislead audiences. You can find propaganda in television commercials, political speeches, and advertisements in magazines and newspapers. The persuasive techniques used in propaganda convince by leading the viewer to make a generalization about a person, product, or service. For instance, a commercial that shows a movie star with beautiful hair using a particular brand of shampoo may lead you to the conclusion that you can have beautiful hair if you use the shampoo, too. (See also **Advertising** below, **Bias** on page 787, and **Point of View** on page 791.)

Realism   *Realism* is representing people and things just as they appear in real life, without making them seem more pleasant or acceptable.

Stereotypes   *Stereotypes* are beliefs about all the members of a group. One common stereotype is that all Texans wear cowboy boots and ride horses. Such beliefs do not take into account the many differences between any two people. Usually, stereotypes are based on too little evidence or on false or misleading information.

Print Media Terms

Advertising   *Advertising* is the use of images, text, or both to persuade an audi-ence to buy, use, or accept a product, serv-ice, image, or idea. Advertisers pay the media for time or space in which to pro-mote their products and services. (See also **Marketing** on page 793.)

Byline   A *byline* is the name of the reporter or writer of a newspaper or magazine article or a television or radio presentation.

Copy   *Copy* is the text in a media mes-sage. (See also **Script** on page 786.)

Demographics   *Demographics* are the characteristics of a particular audience. They may include gender (male or female), age, education, cultural heritage, and income. Advertisers use demographics to target cer-tain audiences. For example, advertisers know that many women read the life and arts section of a newspaper, so they will advertise products and services in the life and arts section to capture that audience's attention. (See also **Audience** on page 787 and **Target Audience** on page 794.)

Digital Editing   *Digital editing* is the use of computer technology to change a digitalized (or online) image before it is presented to an audience. When an image is converted to a digital version, it is easy to add or delete people and objects or change the original background. For example, a photograph taken in a studio can be altered so that it appears it was taken on a beach.

Editor   An *editor* supervises reporters. Editors decide what news stories will appear, check facts for accuracy, and correct errors.

Editorial Cartoon   An *editorial cartoon* is a cartoon, usually found in the editorial section of a newspaper, that reflects the cartoonist's opinion on a current event. Editorial cartoonists use exaggeration and caricature to make their points in a humorous way.

Feature News   *Feature news* (also called *soft news*) refers to news stories whose primary purpose is to entertain. Such stories may or may not be timely. They may be about celebrities or ordinary people or about places, animals, events, or products. An article about a movie star's wedding would be an example of feature news. (See also **Hard News** below and **Soft News** on page 794.)

Font   A *font* is a style of lettering used for printing text. (See also **Font** on page 726.)

Hard News   *Hard news* is fact-based reporting of current events. Hard news answers the basic *5W-How?* questions about important subjects such as politics and social issues. For example, a story about factories dumping toxins into a river is hard news. (See also **Feature News** above and **Soft News** on page 794.)

Headline   A *headline* is the title of a newspaper article, usually set in large, boldface type. It has two purposes: to catch the reader's attention and to tell the reader what the article is about. (See also **Titles and Subtitles** on page 726.)

EXAMPLE   **Senator Seeks Second Term**

Lead   A *lead* is the opening words or paragraph of a news story. It may contain the major facts of the story, or it may use a surprising or unusual fact or idea to hook the audience's attention.

EXAMPLE   Nearly one hundred volunteers helped to ease the overcrowding at the Trevor County Animal Shelter. Volunteers worked nights and weekends for an entire month repairing fences and building new dog runs. Money for the project was donated by citizens and local businesses.

Marketing   *Marketing* is the process of moving goods or services from the producer to the consumer. It includes identifying consumer wants or needs; designing, packaging, and pricing a product; and arranging for locations where the product will be sold. It also includes promoting the product to a target audience through advertising or other means. (See also **Advertising** on page 792, **Demographics** on page 792, and **Target Audience** on page 794.)

Medium   The *medium* of a message is the means through which it is communicated. *Medium* is a singular noun; its plural form is *media.* Modern media can be grouped into two general categories: *print media,* such as newspapers and magazines; and *electronic media,* such as radio, television, audio and video recordings, film, and the Internet. The *mass media* are those that reach a large audience.

Message   See **Message** on page 791.

News   *News* is the presentation of current information that will interest or affect an audience. Local news organizations focus on news of regional interest. National news organizations cover national and world issues and events.

Newsmagazine   A *newsmagazine* is a publication, usually issued weekly, that focuses on recent events and issues. In television, the term is used for a news program that airs one or more times a week and analyzes and interprets the news.

Photography   *Photography* is the process of using a camera to record an image on film. Like all media messages, photographs are selective and incomplete. Before an image is photographed, a photographer makes many decisions, including what will be in the frame and from what angle the image will be shot. The photographer will also choose a specific speed of film depending on the amount of light available. Once the photograph is developed, a photographer or editor decides whether the photograph needs to be cropped, or cut, and whether it needs a caption. (See also **Digital Editing** on page 792 and **Point of View** on page 791.)

Political Cartoon   See **Editorial Cartoon** on page 793.

Production   *Production* is the process of creating a film, video, radio or television program, or publication. There are three stages to production.

- During *preproduction,* copy or scripts are obtained and polished, funds are raised and budgeted, staff and crew are hired, and schedules are planned.
- During *production,* the work is filmed, recorded, or printed.
- During *postproduction,* finishing touches are added. Films and tapes are edited, soundtracks are recorded, and sound and special effects are added. Books and newspapers are bound or gathered. Postproduction also includes marketing and distribution. (See also **Marketing** on page 793.)

Reporter   A *reporter* is a journalist who gathers information and works with editors to create electronic or print reports.

Soft News   *Soft news* is the presentation of general-interest material, such as consumer information and sports, in a news format. A story about a local basketball team competing at a state tournament is an example of soft news. The purpose of soft news is to inform and entertain. (See also **Feature News** on page 793 and **Hard News** on page 793.)

Source   A *source* is a person or publication that supplies information or ideas. Journalists rely on sources for much of the information they report. They try to select individuals they believe are credible and have authority. (See also **Credibility** on page 787 and **Message** on page 791.)

Target Audience   A *target audience* is a segment of the population for which a product or message is designed. Children are usually the target audience for Saturday morning TV commercials, and men are often the target audience for tool ads. (See also **Demographics** on page 792.)

Text   *Text* refers to the words used to create a message. (See also **Message** on page 791.)

Writing

Skills, Structures, and Techniques

You can use the following ideas and information to become a more effective writer.

Applications See **Forms** on page 797.

Composition A *composition* is a piece of writing with three basic parts: *introduction, body,* and *conclusion*. The introduction is like a topic sentence in a paragraph because it states the main idea. The body develops the main idea of the composition, and the conclusion ends the composition.

■ **Introduction** Your composition's *introduction* should do two things:

1. **Catch the readers' attention.** Your introduction should hook your readers and make them want to read more. To capture your readers' attention, try one of the following techniques. The examples show how you might use these techniques to write an introduction for a composition about summer camp.

> ### How to Catch Your Readers' Attention
>
> **Begin by asking a question.**
> *Do you find yourself bored during the summer? If so, you may want to find out what it would be like to go to summer camp.*
>
> **Begin with an anecdote or a funny story.**
> *I packed my bags, rolled up my sleeping bag, and said goodbye to my dog Max and my parents, too. I was on my way to having fun and meeting new friends. I was on my way to summer camp.*
>
> **Begin with a startling fact.**
> *For over one hundred years, YMCA camps have helped children of all ages learn new skills, make new friends, and have fun during the summer.*

2. **Present the main idea.** Include your *main idea statement,* or *thesis,* in your introduction. A *main idea statement* is

Skills, Structures, and Techniques **795**

one or two sentences that announce your topic and your main point about the topic. A main idea statement works in a composition the way a topic sentence works in a paragraph. You can use your main idea statement as a guide as you plan, write, and revise your paper. Here are some strategies for writing a main idea statement.

How to Write a Main Idea Statement

1. Ask yourself, "What is my topic?"
summer camp

2. Review your prewriting notes. Think about how the facts and details fit together. Identify the idea that connects the details to one another.
Summer camp taught me much more than tennis or swimming.

3. Use specific details to make the main idea clear. Zooming in on specific details will make the main idea more focused.
Summer camp taught me to get along with new people, challenge myself, and enjoy nature.

■ **Body** Every paragraph in the *body* supports the composition's main idea by developing a part of it. To help the body paragraphs work together, use the following guidelines.

1. The ideas in your composition should be easy to follow. Give your composition *coherence* by arranging your

information in an order that your readers will understand. (See also page 297.) To show how your ideas are connected, use *transitional words and phrases*. (See also pages 302–303.)

2. Give your paper *unity* by eliminating any details that do not support your thesis. (See also page 295.)

■ **Conclusion**   As the final part of your paper, the *conclusion* should do two things:

1. **Let the readers feel your composition is complete.** If your composition ends too suddenly, your readers may feel dissatisfied, as if they have been left hanging.

2. **Bring the readers back to the main idea.** The conclusion should tie your composition's supporting ideas together and flow once more into your main idea.

How to Write a Conclusion

Refer to your introduction.
The girl who got off the bus and ran to greet her puppy and her parents was not the same girl who had said goodbye a month earlier. Summer camp taught me much more than swimming. I learned many valuable lessons about life.

Restate your main idea.
I might forget the songs we sang around the campfire, and maybe I won't ever get on another sailboat. However, I will never forget the real lessons that camp taught me about myself, others, and nature.

Close with a final idea or example.

I enjoyed my time at summer camp so much that I decided to help others learn life lessons, too. By volunteering at YMCA day camps, I help motivate five-year-olds to make new friends, accept new challenges, and experience nature.

E-mail Electronic mail, or *e-mail,* comes by computer rather than by a letter carrier. E-mail can be used for both personal letters and business letters. When you write a personal e-mail, you do not have to follow the usual guidelines for writing letters. However, if you are using e-mail for business or research purposes, you should follow the guidelines listed below.

E-mail Guidelines

Make sure you enter the correct address. It is easy to send e-mails to the wrong person.

Always fill in the subject line before you send a message. This helps your readers to scan and decide which e-mail messages are most important.

When writing to someone you do not know, include salutations, such as *Dear Senator Costa.* It is also polite to include a closing, such as *Sincerely* or *Thank you,* followed by your full name.

Make your message short and to the point. Be considerate of your reader by limiting yourself to one full screen or less of text.

Make sure your spelling, grammar, and punctuation are correct.

Use bulleted lists and indentation to make the document easy to read. Bulleted lists are especially helpful if you are raising more than one question or point.

Be polite in your messages—even ones to people you know well.

Avoid capitalizing entire words in your messages. USING CAPITALS IN YOUR WRITING IS SIMILAR TO SHOUTING WHEN YOU SPEAK. Constant shouting is annoying even in cyberspace. If you want to emphasize a word, try placing asterisks (*) on either side of it. For example, "Did you remember to buy the game *tickets*?"

Never use *emoticons* in formal e-mails. *Emoticons* are combinations of symbols and letters that resemble faces. They are a kind of shorthand to communicate feelings or reactions. For example, the emoticon :-) suggests laughter or the statement "I'm just kidding." Emoticons should be used only in informal e-mails.

Ask permission of the original sender before forwarding an e-mail. Private e-mails are usually intended for your eyes only.

Forms There are many kinds of forms. For example, an *application* is a form you fill out to ask or apply for something. You might fill out an application to request membership in a school organization, to open a savings account, or to apply for a job. The form on the next page is an application for a library card.

**Whitehouse Public Library System
Youth Card Application**

Date __9/21/2001__

Name __Shawna Washington__

Address __5310 Rosemont Drive__

City __Whitehouse__ State __TX__

Zip __75791__

Home Phone __555-0121__

Birth date __4/30/90__

Parent or Guardian
Signature __Eleanor Washington__

When completing forms, use the following guidelines to help you give clear, complete information.

- Look over the entire form before you begin.

- Follow special instructions (such as "Type or print" or "Use a pencil").

- Supply all the information requested. If a question does not apply to you, write *does not apply*, the symbol *N/A*, which means "not applicable," or use a dash.

- Proofread your finished form, making sure nothing is left blank. Neatly correct any errors.

Letters *Letters* are an important form of communication. Everyone likes to get letters. To receive letters, however, you usually have to write your share. Keep in mind that each type of letter has a specific purpose and an intended audience. Therefore, it is important to know a few general rules about writing different types of letters. The following chart describes the purposes and audiences of different types of letters.

Types of Letters

Business

- The *purpose* of a business letter is to inform a business that you need its services or to tell how well or badly a service was performed.

- The *audience* of a business letter is a business or an organization.

Informal or Personal

- The *purpose* of an informal or personal letter is to express emotions, ideas, or appreciation, or to communicate information about a specific event.

- The *audience* of an informal or personal letter is a close friend, a relative, or a social acquaintance.

Letters, Business A *business letter* is a formal letter about a business-related matter, such as a request for a product or service or an application for a job. To be effective, a business letter must look and sound professional. That means you should type the letter or use your best handwriting, either print or cursive. You should also use your best English, and never use slang.

- **Envelopes** An envelope must be addressed correctly for it to arrive at its destination. Your address, or the return address, goes in the top left-hand corner of the envelope. The name and address of the person to whom you are writing go in the center of the envelope. For a business letter, the name and address on the envelope should exactly match the inside address of the letter. Use the two-letter state code on the envelope rather than writing out the state name, and always include the correct ZIP Code.

```
Tama Wuliton
2703 Bryant Road
Dana Point, CA 92629


    Clasprite Paper Clip Company
    1605 S. Noland Rd., Building 8
    San Diego, CA 92105
```

▪ **Parts** Business letters follow a particular form, which includes six parts.

1. The **heading** usually has three lines: your street address; your city, state, and ZIP Code; and the date the letter was written.

   EXAMPLE
   4516 Magnolia Drive
   Walpole, MA 02081
   November 8, 2001

2. The **inside address** gives the name and address of the person to whom you are writing. If you know the name of the person, use a courtesy title (such as *Mr.* or *Ms.*) or a professional title (such as *Dr.* or *Professor*). Include the person's business title after the name. If you do not have the person's name, use a business title or position title (such as *Store Manager* or *Complaints Department Manager*).

3. The **salutation** is your greeting to the person to whom you are writing. The salutation ends with a colon (such as in *Dear Mayor Williams:*). If you are writing to a specific person, use the person's name (such as *Dear Ms. Stokes:*). If you don't have the name of a specific person, use a general salutation (such as *Dear Sir or Madam:* or *Ladies and Gentlemen:*). You can also use a department or a position title (such as *Activity Director:* or *Head of Division:*), with or without the word *Dear*.

4. The **body** contains the message of your letter. Leave a blank line between paragraphs in the body of the letter.

5. The **closing** should end your letter politely. There are several standard phrases that are often used to close business letters, such as *Sincerely, Respectfully yours,* or *Yours truly*.

6. Your **signature** should be handwritten in ink, directly below the closing. Your name should be typed or printed neatly just below your signature.

▪ **Styles** The six parts of a letter are usually arranged in one of the two most common styles used for business letters.

The **block form** places each part of the letter at the left margin of the page. A blank space is left between each paragraph in the body of the letter. Paragraphs are not indented.

The **modified block form** arranges the heading, the closing, and your signature just to the right of the center of the page. The middle parts of the letter all begin at the left margin, and a blank space is left between each paragraph in the body of the letter. Each paragraph is indented.

Block Style

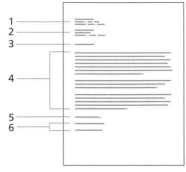

Modified Block Style

■ **Types**   Types of business letters include the following.

1. **Appreciation and commendation letters**   In an *appreciation* or *commendation letter,* you tell someone—a specific person, a group of people, a business, or an organization—that he, she, or they did a good job with a product or service. Be specific about exactly what action or idea of this person's you are praising. For example, if your city's mayor approved the construction of a skateboarding park that you and your friends enjoy, you might want to write an appreciation letter to thank him or her for being aware of what young people in your community need.
   Here is a sample appreciation letter.

Carey Middle School
12 Green Street
Chesters Corner, ME 01154
September 12, 2001

Marguerite Hong, Director
Chesters Corner Parks and
Recreation Department
251 Main Street
Chesters Corner, ME 01154

Dear Ms. Hong:

I am writing to let you know how much I enjoy the town's new skateboarding park. I have been reading the news stories about all the time and planning that went into the park. The new park shows this effort, and my friends and I think the park is definitely a winner! We are thrilled to have a place to practice our stunts.

Thank you for recognizing the need for such a park and for the work that went into creating it. I appreciate all your efforts.

Yours truly,

Benny McLean

Benny McLean

2. **Complaint and adjustment letters**   When you do not receive services or products that you expect, you may wish to write a *complaint* or *adjustment letter*. Remember these guidelines as you write.

Guidelines for Writing a Complaint or Adjustment Letter

Send your letter as soon as possible.

Be specific in your letter. Tell why you are unhappy, how you were affected, and what solution you believe will correct the problem.

Read over your letter to make sure its tone is calm and courteous.

EXAMPLE
The following is the body of a sample adjustment letter written about a faulty product.

> On April 12, I ordered the CD entitled "Hip-Hop's Greatest Hits" from your catalog. However, the CD does not work properly. It skips on the third song. I have tried cleaning it with a special CD cleaner, but it keeps skipping. The CD cost $14, plus $1.95 shipping and handling, for a total of $15.95. I am returning the CD. Please send a replacement CD or a refund. Thank you for your attention to this matter.

3. **Request and order letters**   In a *request letter,* you write to ask for a product or service. For example, you might write to an art museum to request a schedule of its exhibits. In an *order letter,* you ask for something specific, such as a free brochure advertised in a magazine. You may also need to write an order letter to ask for a product that appears in a magazine or advertisement without a printed order form. When you are writing a request or order letter, remember the following guidelines.

Guidelines for Writing a Request or Order Letter

State your request clearly.

If you need to receive information, enclose a stamped envelope addressed to yourself. You are asking a favor of the people to whom you are writing, so it is polite to pay for the cost of their reply yourself.

Make your request long before you need whatever you are requesting. Allow the persons to whom you have sent your request plenty of time to respond to you.

If you want to order something, include all necessary information. For example, give the size, color, brand name, or any other specific information about the item you want. If there are costs involved, add the amount carefully.

EXAMPLE
Here is an example of the salutation and body of a request letter.

> Dear Professor Mack:
>
> I would like to invite you to be one of our speakers at the Florida History Celebration at Lawton Chiles Middle Academy. This year's event will be held on October 11, from 9:00 A.M. to 12:00 noon.
>
> The Florida History Celebration is part of the seventh-grade study of Florida history. We would like for you to give a thirty-minute talk to about one

(continued)

> hundred seventh-graders about the
> history of citrus in our state.
> Your talk would take place at
> 10:30 A.M.
>
> Please let me know by September
> 30 whether you will be able to
> take part in this event. I look
> forward to hearing from you soon.

Letters, Informal or Personal

A *personal letter* is often a gesture of friendship containing a personal message from the sender to the receiver, such as best wishes for an upcoming holiday. When you are writing a personal letter, remember to write about things that interest you and the person you are writing.

■ **Types**   There are three common types of informal or personal letters.

1. **Invitations**   An *invitation* should contain specific information about the occasion, such as the time and place and other details your guest might need to know (such as that everyone may bring a friend, should dress casually, or is expected to bring food).

2. **Letters of regret**   You write a *letter of regret* when you receive an invitation to an event that you will not be able to attend. You should make a special effort to respond in writing to invitations that include the letters *R.S.V.P.* (an abbreviation for "please reply" in French). You should always respond quickly enough so that the person who is inviting you can prepare for the number of guests. If the planned event is very soon, you may want to telephone the person to say

that you can't come. Even if you telephone to say you won't attend, it is still polite to send a follow-up letter of regret.

EXAMPLE

> 5455 Blackford Street
> Chicago, IL 60615
> February 24, 2001
>
> Dear Felicia,
>
>   I was so happy to receive your invitation to your birthday slumber party next Friday evening. I really would like to be there. Unfortunately, my parents had already made plans for the whole family for that night.
>   Thank you very much for inviting me. I hope you have a happy birthday and a lot of fun at your party.
>
>   Your friend,
>
>   *Bianca*
>
>   Bianca

3. **Thank-you letters**   You write *thank-you letters* when you want to thank someone for taking the time, trouble, or expense to do something for you. Thank the person, and then try to add a personal note. For example, if you are thanking someone for a gift, tell why the gift is special to you.

Prewriting Techniques

You can use the following techniques to find a subject to write about, to gather information about a subject, or to organize your ideas before you begin to write. Although the prewriting techniques are listed separately, you may use more than one technique at a time. You may also find that you prefer some techniques to others.

Many of the prewriting techniques below involve the use of *graphic organizers*. A **graphic organizer** is a visual that helps you see the ideas and details you are generating or arranging as you prewrite.

1. **Generating Ideas**   The following techniques can help you draw ideas for writing out of your own imagination.

■ **Asking the *5W-How?* questions**
News reporters track down information by asking the *5W-How?* questions—*Who? What? When? Where? Why?* and *How?* You can ask the same questions to find information on a topic you have chosen. For some topics, some questions won't apply. With other topics, you may think of several good answers for one question.

EXAMPLE

Who are some local people who have worked for or performed in a circus?

What are the most dangerous jobs in the circus?

When are circus animals fed?

Where do circus performers and animal trainers learn their skills?

Why are there three rings in a circus performance?

How does a person join the circus?

■ **Asking "What if?" Questions**
"What if?" questions will help you find ideas for creative writing. The following are some "What if" questions you might ask to spark your imagination.

EXAMPLES

What if I could change one thing in my life? (What if I had an identical twin? What if I grew up in India?)

What if some common thing did not exist? (What if there were no telephones? What if Earth had no water?)

What if one situation in the world could be changed? (What if everyone spoke the same language? What if there were no diseases?)

What if I could meet a historical figure? (What if I could meet Martin Luther King, Jr.? What would I ask him?)

■ **Brainstorming**   You can *brainstorm* alone, but it is more fun with a partner or a group. In a group, you can bounce ideas off each other. Follow the guidelines below as you brainstorm.

How to Brainstorm

1. Write a subject at the top of a piece of paper or on a chalkboard.

2. Write down every single thought about the subject that comes to mind. Do not stop to judge ideas. (You can do that later.)

3. Keep going until you run out of ideas.

On the next page you will find some brainstorming notes on the subject *happiness.* The list contains more ideas than the writer will use, but it gives the writer a starting point.

EXAMPLE

> Happiness
> playing soccer
> if you could drive at 12
> making an A on a difficult test
> getting a raise in my allowance
> the dentist saying that I don't have any
>   cavities
> my little brother spending the night some-
>   where else
> splashing in a puddle of water
> getting to play my stereo really loud
> when my math class is not cold
> if the entire world could take a nap for one
>   hour every day

- **Clustering**   *Clustering* is sometimes called *webbing* or *making connections.* When you make a cluster diagram, you break a topic into its smaller parts. The guidelines below will help you.

How to Cluster

1. Write your subject in the center of your paper and circle it.

2. Around the subject, write related ideas as you think of them. Circle these ideas, and draw lines to connect them with the subject.

3. An idea may make you think of other ideas. Connect these with circles and lines, too.

The cluster diagram in the next column shows a writer's ideas related to the topic *Titanic.*

EXAMPLE

- **Cubing**   Visualize a cube with these six methods for investigating a subject written on each side: *(1) Describe it. (2) Compare it. (3) Associate it. (4) Analyze it. (5) Apply it. (6) Argue for or against it.* Think of a subject, and then write for three minutes about each suggestion on the cube. The example below shows a response to "associate it." (Tell what is similar to the subject.)

EXAMPLE
Rugby
Rugby is similar to American football. In both sports, you throw and kick a ball, tackle opposing players, and score by getting the ball behind the goal line.

- **Freewriting**   *Freewriting* is writing down whatever ideas pop into your head about a subject. Think of a word or topic that is important to you. Then, write for three to five minutes about whatever your subject makes you think of or remember. Don't worry about complete sentences, spelling, or punctuation. If you get stuck, write anything. Don't let your pen or pencil stop, just continue writing down all your ideas. Keep writing until the time is up.

EXAMPLE

Swim Meets: The starting whistle. Relays. My best stroke is backstroke. Wish I could make my turn faster. Like looking up and seeing the sky and clouds and then the flags that mean I'm almost to the end of the pool. Long practices with coach yelling "Go!" Swimmer's ear kept me out of one meet last year.

- **Using your five senses**   While you are awake, you receive steady input from each of your five senses (sight, hearing, smell, taste, touch). Most of the time, you ignore these sensory details. Paying attention to what your senses are telling you, however, can give you details for your writing.

EXAMPLE

Cuban New Year's Eve celebration
touch: warm night, breezes through open windows, embroidered tablecloth, paper plates and plastic forks and knives
sound: record player, singing, people talking, telling jokes, laughter, children's shouts, TV in living room
smell: spicy smells, ground coffee
taste: crisp barbecued pork, black beans and rice, yucca, guava pastries, sweet and bitter orange
sight: dark night, brightly lit house, about thirty family members and friends, children playing, men tending the backyard barbecue

- **Visualizing**   *Visualizing* means seeing something in your mind's eye. As you "see" your scene, try to use your other senses as well.

EXAMPLE

I'm walking down the beach on a hot afternoon. Brightly colored beach umbrellas dot the sand. A group of small children busily builds a sand castle with a collection of toy shovels and buckets. Sea gulls swoop and cry above me. The waves splash, and the foamy, cool water covers my feet.

- **Writer's notebook or journal**   A *writer's journal* is a notebook or folder where you can record your everyday thoughts, observations, questions, and experiences. Journal entries can be very short or go on for several pages. You can use your journal as a source for writing ideas. Another type of writing journal is a *learning log*. A learning log contains thoughts and questions about things you learn from reading and participating in school discussions. A learning log helps you make connections between what you learn and what you think.

2. **Gathering Information**   To find information from outside sources on your topic to include in your composition, you can use the following techniques.

- **Listening with a focus**   Some people learn better by listening than by reading. You can gather information on a specific topic by listening to speeches, interviews, radio and TV programs, audiotapes, and videotapes. Before you

Skills, Structures, and Techniques   **805**

begin to listen, think of questions you would like answered. These questions will give you a purpose for listening. Listen carefully with your questions in front of you, and take notes to help you remember the answers.

■ **Reading with a focus** Many people find ideas for writing by reading books, newspapers, or magazines. To find information in a book, newspaper, or magazine, check the table of contents or index. Go directly to the pages on your topic. Don't read everything. Skim the text quickly looking only for information on your topic. Don't forget to check photos and captions, too. When you find information on your topic, read the passage carefully. Then, take notes.

3. **Arranging Ideas** Once you have chosen a subject and gathered information, you can use one or more of the following strategies to organize and summarize your ideas. These strategies can be especially helpful for organizing ideas from a number of different sources.

■ **Charts** Dividing a subject into its logical parts can help you to better analyze the subject of your writing. Organizing the information into a *chart* then helps you to understand the categories quickly. In the following example, a writer uses a type of chart called a table to organize the information she found about the three branches of government. The chart will help the writer stay organized as she begins to write a composition about the United States government.

United States Government		
Branch	Main Job	Head of the Branch
Executive	Enforces the laws	President
Legislative	Makes the laws	Congress
Judicial	Makes decisions about the laws	Supreme Court

■ **Conceptual mapping** Mapping might look like clustering, but it is more like outlining because it shows the relationship between ideas. Mapping can help you know if you have

enough support for each main idea. Notice how the conceptual map on the previous page groups main ideas and supporting ideas.

- **Outlines** An *outline* helps you organize important information. In an outline, the ideas are arranged in a pattern that makes their relationship to one another clear. There are two types of outlines, *formal* and *informal.* You may need to make a formal outline for a research report. To make a formal outline like the one below, use Roman numerals for headings and capital letters for subheadings. (See also page 776.)

Formal Outline

```
Title: The Patter of Little Hooves
Main Idea: Pigs make great pets.

I. Benefits
   A. Characteristics
      1. Ease of housebreaking
      2. Lack of fur
      3. Friendliness
   B. Enjoyment of games
      1. Fetching
      2. Swimming
      3. Rolling over
II. Drawbacks
   A. Size
   B. Inability to protect
```

To organize your ideas quickly before you begin to write, you might want to make an informal outline (sometimes called an **early plan**). An informal outline groups ideas in a logical way.

Informal Outline

Topic: Pet Pigs	
Benefits	Drawbacks
easier to housebreak than some other animals	can get very large
	can get very lazy
don't shed	can be too playful
can communicate	not a good watch
easy to train	animal
will play and do tricks	
easy to feed	

- **Sequence chain** A *sequence chain* helps you see how one event leads to another. A sequence chain works well when you are narrating or explaining a process.

- **Time line** A *time line* puts events in order on a horizontal or vertical line, with the first or earliest events usually starting on the left (in a horizontal time line) or at the top (in a vertical time line). The most recent or latest events most often will be on the right (in a horizontal time line) or at the bottom (in a vertical time line).

Meeting INDIVIDUAL NEEDS

LEARNERS HAVING DIFFICULTY

Students may benefit from working together to practice determining an appropriate style. Arrange students in small groups and tell them they are writing about year-round school. For each box in the chart below, group members should decide on a style to fit that purpose and audience: formal (in which they use standard English and avoid slang), or informal (in which they might use slang, humor, or elements of informality). Group members should collaborate to compose example sentences for each style they select. Have groups share their results.

	Your peers	Your teachers
To persuade that year-round school is or is not a good idea		
To explain what year-round school would mean for your school		
To entertain by discussing possible problems		

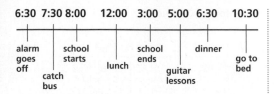

- **Venn diagram** A *Venn diagram* uses intersecting circles to show the similarities and differences between two subjects. The area where the two circles overlap shows how the two subjects are alike. The remaining areas show how they are different. (See also page 749.)

EXAMPLE

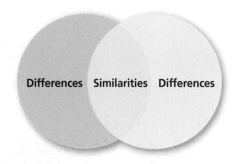

Differences   Similarities   Differences

Style From the way you dress to the way you act, every day you make choices that reveal your unique style. When you write, you also make choices—choices such as what words to use and how to arrange those words in sentences. The sum of these choices is your writing style. You do not make choices about writing style in a vacuum, though. Your style should be determined partly by you, partly by your purpose for writing, and partly by your audience.

- **Think about audience** In a book report for your teacher, you will probably use a formal style. For example, you would be careful about correct grammar, use longer sentences, and try to work in some of the new vocabulary words you have been learning. In an e-mail to a friend, though, your writing might include sentence fragments, slang, and nonstandard usage. These are the types of style adjustments you make for your audience.

- **Think about purpose** You also adjust your style according to your purpose for writing. Informative writing, for example, goes right to the point. Describing a character for a book report, you would choose precise language to paint a clear picture in the fewest words possible. If you were writing a journal entry about the same character, however, your purpose would be to express your feelings. You might sprinkle your entry with questions, describe your emotional response, and make connections between the character and yourself—all without much attention to how briefly you made your point. This informal style is appropriate for personal correspondence between friends.

Symbols for Revising and Proofreading

When you are revising and proofreading, you will add and remove letters, words, and sentences. By using standard revising and proofreading symbols, such as the ones in the chart on the next page, your revisions will be more consistent.

Symbols for Revising and Proofreading

Symbol	Example	Meaning of Symbol
≡	Tucker's homestyle Restaurant	Capitalize a lowercase letter.
/	the City of Raleigh	Lowercase a capital letter.
∧	a cupof milk	Insert a missing word, letter, or punctuation mark.
ℰ	How's the that apple?	Leave out a word, letter, or punctuation mark.
∽	frist	Change the order of letters or words.
¶	¶ "Go ahead," he said.	Begin a new paragraph.
⊙	She wept⊙	Add a period.
⋀	I still apologized however.	Add a comma.

Transitions When you want to show readers how ideas and details fit together, use transitions, or **transitional words and phrases**. (See page 302 for a chart of transitional words and phrases.)

Voice Voice is the way a piece of writing "sounds." In most writing assignments, your voice should sound like you and should communicate your ideas simply and naturally. You should take care to adjust your writing voice to fit your audience and purpose for writing. As you become more experienced with writing for a variety of purposes and audiences, you will eventually develop a voice that is yours alone.

■ **Think about audience** Writing instructions for a younger audience, you would probably want to use a friendly, reassuring voice. For example, your instructions might include easy vocabulary, examples that relate to a child's experience, and an enthusiastic conclusion. These elements would help your young readers feel confident that they can carry out the instructions you have explained. That same voice would not suit an older audience, however; they might feel that you were "talking down" to them. Your voice can go a long way toward drawing your audience in—or turning them off.

■ **Think about purpose** When writing to express your feelings, do not try to sound like anyone else. Your voice should come as close to "the real you" as possible. When writing to inform or persuade, however, you may need to pull the reins on "the real you": Even if you feel passionately about the topic of an informative or persuasive composition, your voice should sound reasonable, not hotheaded.

Skills, Structures, and Techniques   **809**

Meeting
INDIVIDUAL
NEEDS

LEARNERS HAVING DIFFICULTY
Students may benefit from working together to practice determining an appropriate voice. Arrange students in small groups and tell them they are writing about school uniforms. For each box in the chart below, group members should decide on a voice to fit that purpose and audience. Give students the following voice descriptions to use in their charts: *enthusiastic, helpful, reasonable, respectful, angry, ridiculing, polite,* and *humorous.* They may use more than one adjective for each box. Group members should collaborate to compose example sentences for each voice they select. Have groups share their results.

	Your peers	The school board
To persuade that school uniforms are or are not a good idea		
To explain what school uniforms would mean for your school		
To entertain by discussing possible problems		

QUICK REFERENCE HANDBOOK

Skills, Structures, and Techniques   **809**

Grammar at a Glance

─HELP─

Grammar at a Glance is an alphabetical list of special terms and expressions with examples and references to further information. When you encounter a grammar or usage problem in the revising or proofreading stage of your writing, look for help in this section first. You may find all you need to know right here. If you need more information, **Grammar at a Glance** will show you where in the book to turn for a more complete explanation. If you do not find what you are looking for in **Grammar at a Glance,** turn to the index on page 854.

abbreviation An abbreviation is a shortened form of a word or a phrase.

■ **capitalization of**

TITLES USED WITH NAMES	**M**rs.	**C**apt.	**S**r.	**M.D.**
KINDS OF ORGANIZATIONS	**A**ssn.	**I**nc.	**D**ept.	**C**orp.
PARTS OF ADDRESSES	**A**ve.	**S**t.	**B**lvd.	**P.O. B**ox
NAMES OF STATES	[without ZIP Codes]	**V**a.		**A**rk.
				Mass.	**N. M**ex.
	[with ZIP Codes]	**VA**		**AR**
		MA		**NM**
TIMES	**A.M.**	**P.M.**	**B.C.**	**A.D.**

■ **punctuation of** (See page 599.)

WITH PERIODS	(See preceding examples.)
WITHOUT PERIODS	CD-ROM NBC UFO FBI
	DC (D.C. without ZIP Code)
	mg qt tbsp cm yd
	[Exception: inch = in.]

action verb An action verb expresses physical or mental activity. (See page 357.)

EXAMPLE   Uncle Jim **drives** a school bus.

active voice Active voice is the voice a verb is in when it expresses an action done by its subject. (See page 499. See also **voice.**)

EXAMPLE   The dog **chased** the squirrel across the yard.

adjective An adjective modifies a noun or a pronoun. (See page 346.)

EXAMPLE Do you see **that beautiful, old wood** house over there?

adjective clause An adjective clause is a subordinate clause that modifies a noun or a pronoun. (See page 427.)

EXAMPLE We saw an advertisement for a car **that has aluminum wheels.** [The adjective clause modifies the noun *car.*]

adjective phrase A prepositional phrase that modifies a noun or a pronoun is called an adjective phrase. (See page 404.)

EXAMPLE Dana prefers the backpack **with large pockets.** [The adjective phrase modifies the noun *backpack.*]

adverb An adverb modifies a verb, an adjective, or another adverb. (See page 366.)

EXAMPLE Mom and Dad **often** drive us to the lake on weekends. [The adverb modifies the verb *drive.*]

adverb clause An adverb clause is a subordinate clause that modifies a verb, an adjective, or an adverb. (See page 430.)

EXAMPLE Trudy's grades have improved **since she cut back her TV viewing.** [The adverb clause modifies the verb *have improved.*]

adverb phrase A prepositional phrase that modifies a verb, an adjective, or an adverb is called an adverb phrase. (See page 406.)

EXAMPLE **After dark,** the carol singers went from house to house. [The adverb phrase modifies the verb *went.*]

agreement Agreement is the correspondence, or match, between grammatical forms. Grammatical forms agree when they have the same number and gender.

■ **of pronouns and antecedents** (See page 475.)

SINGULAR **Desmond** often rides **his** bicycle to school.

PLURAL Desmond's **classmates** ride **their** bicycles to school.

SINGULAR	Has **everyone** in the club paid **his** or **her** dues?
PLURAL	Have **all** of the club members paid **their** dues?
SINGULAR	Neither **Darleen** nor **Clarissa** was pleased with **her** audition.
PLURAL	**Darleen** and **Clarissa** were not pleased with **their** auditions.

■ **of subjects and verbs** (See page 458.)

SINGULAR	The music **teacher is composing** an opera.
	The music **teacher,** with the help of her students, **is composing** an opera.
PLURAL	The music **students are composing** an opera.
	The music **students,** with the help of their teacher, **are composing** an opera.

SINGULAR	**Each** of the students **is looking** forward to seeing the dinosaur exhibit.
PLURAL	**All** of the students **are looking** forward to seeing the dinosaur exhibit.

SINGULAR	Neither **Kevin** nor **I was** able to go to band camp last summer.
PLURAL	Needless to say, both **Kevin** and **I were** disappointed.

SINGULAR	Here **is** a **list** of topics from which you can choose.
PLURAL	Here **are** the **topics** from which you can choose.

SINGULAR	The social studies **class is watching** a video about the space program.
PLURAL	The social studies **class are writing** their essays on the space program.

SINGULAR	**Six dollars is** the price of the kite.
PLURAL	From this stack of bills, **six dollars are** missing.

SINGULAR	*Parallel Journeys* **was written** by Eleanor Ayer.
PLURAL	Early **journeys** to North America **were** risky.

SINGULAR	**Is measles** an infectious disease?
PLURAL	**Are** the **scissors** in your sewing basket?

antecedent An antecedent is the word or words that a pronoun stands for. (See page 342.)

EXAMPLE   **Tim** doesn't know how long his essay will be.
           [*His* refers to *Tim*.]

apostrophe
- **to form contractions** (See page 641.)
  EXAMPLES   wouldn'␣t   I'␣ll   o'␣clock   '␣99
- **to form plurals of letters, numerals, and words used as words** (See page 645.)
  EXAMPLES   *A*'s and *B*'s   *and*'s instead of &'s   5's and 10's
- **to show possession** (See page 638.)
  EXAMPLES   player's uniform

                  players' uniforms

                  children's literature

                  someone's backpack

                  Steven Spielberg's and George Lucas's movies

                  Batman and Robin's first adventure

appositive An appositive is a noun or a pronoun placed beside another noun or pronoun to identify or describe it. (See page 609.)

EXAMPLE   My friend **Désirée** recently moved to a new house.
           [*Désirée* identifies *friend*.]

appositive phrase An appositive phrase consists of an appositive and its modifiers. (See page 609.)

EXAMPLE   The first taxi in the line was driven by Stavros, **a gray-haired man with a mustache.**

article The articles, *a, an,* and *the,* are the most frequently used adjectives. (See page 347.)

EXAMPLES   **a** football   **the** farmhouse

              an antelope   **the** answer

              an honor

bad, badly (See page 554.)

NONSTANDARD   This green apple tastes badly.
STANDARD   This green apple tastes **bad.**

base form The base form, or infinitive, is one of the four principal parts of a verb. (See page 485.)

EXAMPLE   Can you help me to **find** this address?

brackets (See page 649.)

EXAMPLES   The movie critic wrote, "Leonardo DiCaprio's performance is a tour de force **[**an unusually skillful performance**].**"

Many of the Iroquois legends we know today might have been lost without the efforts of Kaiiontwa'ko (perhaps better known as Cornplanter **[**his Iroquois name means "by what one plants"**]**).

capitalization

■ **of abbreviations** (See **abbreviation.**)

■ **of first words** (See page 574.)

EXAMPLES   **M**y brother has started taking cello lessons.

Nick asked, "**W**hat does the French phrase *déjà vu* mean?"

Dear Ms. Neruda:

Yours truly,

■ **of proper nouns and proper adjectives** (See page 574.)

Proper Noun	Common Noun
North **A**merica	continent
El **S**alvador	country
Staten **I**sland	island
Chautauqua **L**ake	body of water
Jurassic **P**eriod	historical period
Mother's **D**ay	holiday

Proper Noun	Common Noun
Blue **R**idge **M**ountains	mountain chain
Saguaro **N**ational **P**ark	park
Bernheim **A**rboretum and **R**esearch **F**orest	forest
Mammoth **C**ave	cave
Kings **C**anyon	canyon
Southeast	region
Thirty-second **S**treet	street
National **U**rban League	organization
San **D**iego **P**adres	team
Bowling **G**reen **S**tate **U**niversity	institution
Democratic **P**arty (*or* **p**arty)	political party
Roth's **O**ptical	business firm
Super **B**owl	special event
Memorial **D**ay	holiday
February, **M**ay, **A**ugust, **N**ovember	calendar items
Yavapai-**A**pache	people
Christianity	religion
Buddhist	religious follower
God (*but* the **g**od **Z**eus)	deity
Passover	holy day
Torah	sacred writing
Jupiter	planet
Alpha **C**entauri	star
Ursa **M**ajor	constellation
Andrea Doria	ship
Enola Gay	aircraft
Atlantis	spacecraft
Biology **I** (*but* **b**iology)	school subject
Mandarin	language
Mount **R**ushmore **N**ational **M**emorial	monument
World **T**rade **C**enter	building
Heisman **T**rophy	award

■ **of titles** (See page 586.)

EXAMPLES	**S**enator Feinstein [preceding a name]
	Feinstein, a **s**enator from California [following a name]
	Thank you, **S**enator. [direct address]
	Uncle Alphonse (*but* my **u**ncle Alphonse)
	***A**nasazi: **A**ncient **P**eople of the **R**ock* [book]
	***M**ythic **W**arriors: **G**uardians of the **L**egend* [TV program]
	***A**rrangement in **B**lack and **G**ray: **T**he **A**rtist's **M**other* [work of art]
	***R**hapsody in **B**lue* [musical composition]
	"**T**he **F**rog **W**ho **W**anted to **B**e a **S**inger" [short story]
	"**I A**m of the **E**arth" [poem]
	***R**eader's **D**igest* [magazine]
	the ***O**rlando **S**entinel* [newspaper]
	***F**amily **C**ircus* [comic strip]
	***B**ack to **T**itanic* [audiotape or CD]

case of pronouns Case is the form a pronoun takes to show how it is used in a sentence. (See page 511.)

NOMINATIVE	**She** and **I** are taking tae kwon do lessons.
	Two of the award winners are Erica and **he.**
	Neither baby sitter, Brigitte nor **she,** is available this evening.
	We students are making animal characters from our favorite books.
	Is David Alfaro Siqueiros the artist **who** painted this?
	We don't know **who** she is.
OBJECTIVE	Did you see Jamaal and **her** at the Juneteenth festival?
	Kristen invited **him** and **me** to the Natalie Merchant concert.
	Are you going with **them** to the video arcade?
	The Earth Day festivities are being organized by two teachers, Mr. Zapata and **her.**

Our guide gave **us** spelunkers a map of the cave we would explore.

Ms. Jennings, **whom** everyone at school admires, will retire this year.

One of the candidates **whom** I will vote for is Tamisha.

POSSESSIVE   **Their** understanding of the rules differs from **ours.**

Her making the jump shot in the final seconds sent the game into overtime.

clause A clause is a group of words that contains a subject and a verb and is used as part of a sentence. (See page 423. See also **independent clause** and **subordinate clause.**)

EXAMPLES   she arrives at work on time [independent clause]
unless the bus is late [subordinate clause]

She arrives at work on time unless the bus is late.

colon (See page 619.)

■ **before lists**

EXAMPLES   To assemble the bookcase, you will need the following tools: a crescent wrench, a small hammer, and a Phillips screwdriver.

The Bookends Club is featuring books by these authors: A. A. Milne, Laura Ingalls Wilder, and Judy Blume.

■ **in conventional situations**

EXAMPLES   7:30 P.M.

Exodus 20:3–17

The Whole Internet: User's Guide & Catalog

Dear Sir:

comma (See page 602.)

■ **in a series**

EXAMPLES   Shandra, Seth, and I spent the summer working at the animal shelter.

Alonzo's hobbies include making wind chimes, working jigsaw puzzles, and writing limericks.

■ **in compound sentences**

EXAMPLES We seventh graders performed three plays this year, but my favorite was *Androcles and the Lion* by Bernard Shaw.

My friend Albert portrayed Androcles, and I played the part of the lion.

■ **with nonessential phrases and clauses**

EXAMPLES Yu the Great, a mythical Chinese king, possessed superhuman powers. [nonessential phrase]

Yu the Great, who possessed superhuman powers, could transform himself into different animals. [nonessential clause]

■ **with introductory elements**

EXAMPLES Sitting around the bonfire, the campers told ghost stories.

If you like to read books in which animals are the main characters, you may enjoy *The Long Patrol.*

■ **with interrupters**

EXAMPLES The Gila monster, for example, is a poisonous lizard.

Most other lizards, however, are harmless.

■ **in conventional situations**

EXAMPLES On Friday, July 17, 2000, we flew from Baltimore, Maryland, to Raleigh, North Carolina, to attend my brother's graduation.

Isn't your address 728 Lakewood Boulevard, Grand Rapids, MI 49501-0827?

comma splice A comma splice is a run-on sentence in which only a comma separates two complete sentences. (See **run-on sentence.**)

COMMA SPLICE In 1962, John H. Glenn, Jr., became the first American to orbit the earth, then in 1998, at the age of 77, Glenn made history again by becoming the oldest person to travel in space.

REVISED In 1962, John H. Glenn, Jr., became the first American to orbit the earth, **and** then in 1998, at the age of 77, Glenn made history again by becoming the oldest person to travel in space.

REVISED   In 1962, John H. Glenn, Jr., became the first American to orbit the earth; then in 1998, at the age of 77, Glenn made history again by becoming the oldest person to travel in space.

comparison of modifiers (See page 532.)

■ comparison of adjectives and adverbs

Positive	Comparative	Superlative
short	short**er**	short**est**
heavy	heav**ier**	heav**iest**
generous	**more (less)** generous	**most (least)** generous
slowly	**more (less)** slowly	**most (least)** slowly
bad/ill	**worse**	**worst**

■ comparing two

EXAMPLES   Of Mars and Venus, which planet is **closer** to Earth?

In the balloon, we flew **higher** and **farther** than we had thought we would.

China is **more populous** than **any other** country.

■ comparing more than two

EXAMPLES   Lake Superior is the **largest** of the five Great Lakes.

Of all of the figure skaters in the competition, I think that Michelle Kwan performed **most gracefully.**

complement A complement is a word or word group that completes the meaning of a verb. (See page 385. See also **direct object, indirect object, predicate nominative,** and **predicate adjective.**)

EXAMPLES   All of Ms. Lozano's students admire **her.**

Bring **us** the map, please.

Do you feel **thirsty**?

Angela, this is **Ramona.**

complex sentence A complex sentence has one independent clause and at least one subordinate clause. (See page 445.)

EXAMPLES My favorite animated film was *Cinderella* [independent clause], until I saw *Jungle Book* [subordinate clause].

When my little sister wrote a letter to Santa Claus [subordinate clause], she used the address North Pole, AK 99705 [independent clause], which, by the way, is the correct address. [subordinate clause]

compound-complex sentence A compound-complex sentence has two or more independent clauses and at least one subordinate clause. (See page 447.)

EXAMPLES The Taj Mahal, which is located near Agra, India [subordinate clause], is a beautiful structure made almost entirely of white marble [independent clause]; it was built in the seventeenth century by Shah Jahan as a tomb for his wife [independent clause].

When they publish their works [subordinate clause], some writers use pseudonyms, or pen names, instead of their real names [independent clause]; for example, Theodor Geisel published most of his books for children under the pen name Dr. Seuss [independent clause].

The sweater that I bought last week [subordinate clause] was on sale [independent clause], and it fits well, too [independent clause].

compound sentence A compound sentence has two or more independent clauses but no subordinate clauses. (See page 441.)

EXAMPLES Two of the kittens are gray [independent clause], but the third one is orange [independent clause].

Yuri was born on February 29 [independent clause]; consequently, each year, except in a leap year, he celebrates his birthday on February 28 [independent clause].

Last night, Dad and I made pizza primavera [independent clause]; he prepared the dough and the Parmesan-cheese sauce [independent clause], and I diced the green onions, red peppers, carrots, and broccoli [independent clause].

conjunction A conjunction joins words or groups of words. (See page 374.)

EXAMPLES   fish **or** fowl

            not only fair **but also** firm

            through the kitchen **and** up the stairs

            Although Boris had a cold, he insisted on performing.

            They stayed on the field, **for** the game was not over.

contraction A contraction is a shortened form of a word, a numeral, or a group of words. Apostrophes in contractions indicate where letters or numerals have been omitted. (See page 641. See also **apostrophe**.)

EXAMPLES   you're [you are]   there's [there is *or* there has]

            who's [who is *or* who has]   they're [they are]

            aren't [are not]   it's [it is *or* it has]

            can't [cannot]   won't [will not]

            '14–'18 war [1914–1918 war] o'clock [of the clock]

dangling modifier A dangling modifier is a modifying word, phrase, or clause that does not clearly and sensibly modify a word or a word group in a sentence. (See page 541.)

DANGLING   Digging a well near Xi'an, China, in 1974, thousands of ancient terra-cotta sculptures of warriors, horses, and chariots were uncovered. [Were thousands of sculptures digging a well?]

REVISED   Digging a well near Xi'an, China, in 1974, **workers** uncovered thousands of ancient terra-cotta sculptures of warriors, horses, and chariots.

dash (See page 649.)

EXAMPLE   The marine biologist spent several days—ten, I think— recording the movements of the manatee and her calf.

declarative sentence A declarative sentence makes a statement and is followed by a period. (See page 330.)

EXAMPLE   Edinburgh is the capital of Scotland.

direct object A direct object is a word or word group that receives the action of the verb or shows the result of the action. A direct object answers the question *Whom?* or *What?* after a transitive verb. (See page 386.)

EXAMPLE   Rashmi visited **them** Tuesday afternoon.

double comparison A double comparison is the nonstandard use of two comparative forms (usually *more* and *–er*) or two superlative forms (usually *most* and *–est*) to express comparison. In standard usage, the single comparative form is correct. (See page 538.)

NONSTANDARD   Olympus Mons, a volcano on Mars, is the most highest mountain in our solar system.

STANDARD   Olympus Mons, a volcano on Mars, is the **highest** mountain in our solar system.

double negative A double negative is the nonstandard use of two negative words when one is enough. (See page 539.)

NONSTANDARD   Alonzo is so very sleepy that he can't hardly keep his eyes open.

STANDARD   Alonzo is so very sleepy that he **can hardly** keep his eyes open.

NONSTANDARD   I haven't never ridden in an airplane.

STANDARD   I **have never** ridden in an airplane.

STANDARD   I **haven't ever** ridden in an airplane.

double subject A double subject occurs when an unnecessary pronoun is used after the subject of a sentence. (See page 559.)

NONSTANDARD   Abner Doubleday, contrary to popular belief, he did not create the game of baseball.

STANDARD   Abner Doubleday, contrary to popular belief, did not create the game of baseball.

E

end marks (See page 598.)

■ **with sentences**

EXAMPLES   In 1998, Mark McGwire broke Roger Maris's single-season home-run record**.** [declarative sentence]

How many home runs did Mark McGwire hit in 1998**?**
[interrogative sentence]

Wow**!** [interjection] McGwire hit seventy home runs**!**
[exclamatory sentence]

Don't forget that in 1998 Sammy Sosa also surpassed
Maris's record by hitting sixty-six home runs**.**
[imperative sentence]

■ **with abbreviations** (See page 599. See also **abbreviation.**)

EXAMPLES In 1964, the Nobel Peace Prize was awarded to
Dr**.** Martin Luther King, Jr**.**

In 1964, was the Nobel Peace Prize awarded to
Dr**.** Martin Luther King, Jr**.?**

essential clause/essential phrase An essential, or
restrictive, clause or phrase is necessary to the meaning of a
sentence and is not set off by commas. (See page 608.)

EXAMPLES The woman **who gives the lectures on Romanian art**
is Ms. Antonescu. [essential clause]

The animals **drinking at the water hole** gave the
elephants a wide berth. [essential phrase]

exclamation point (See **end marks.**)

exclamatory sentence An exclamatory sentence expresses
strong feeling and is followed by an exclamation point. (See page
331.)

EXAMPLE What a surprise this is**!**

fragment (See **sentence fragment.**)

F

fused sentence A fused sentence is a run-on sentence in
which no punctuation separates complete sentences. (See **run-on
sentence.**)

FUSED   Most totems, or images, carved into a totem pole are
symbolic usually the totem at the top of the pole represents
the family's guardian spirit.

REVISED   Most totems, or images, carved into a totem pole are
symbolic**;** usually the totem at the top of the pole
represents the family's guardian spirit.

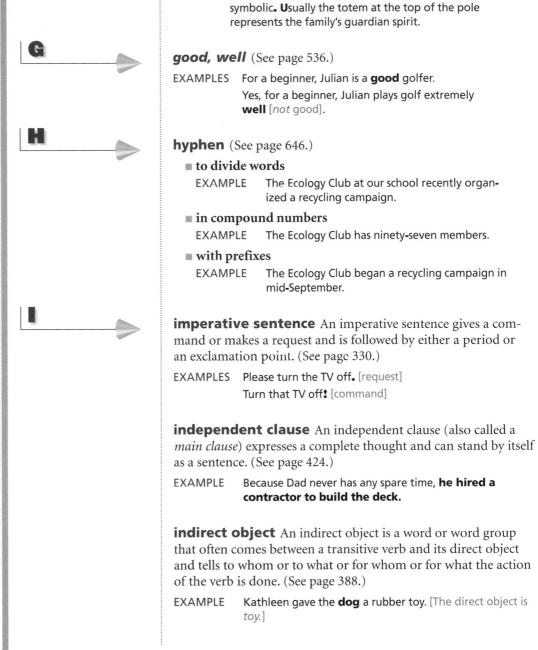

REVISED   Most totems, or images, carved into a totem pole are symbolic. Usually the totem at the top of the pole represents the family's guardian spirit.

G

good, well (See page 536.)

EXAMPLES   For a beginner, Julian is a **good** golfer.

Yes, for a beginner, Julian plays golf extremely **well** [*not* good].

H

hyphen (See page 646.)

- **to divide words**

EXAMPLE   The Ecology Club at our school recently organ-ized a recycling campaign.

- **in compound numbers**

EXAMPLE   The Ecology Club has ninety-seven members.

- **with prefixes**

EXAMPLE   The Ecology Club began a recycling campaign in mid-September.

I

imperative sentence An imperative sentence gives a command or makes a request and is followed by either a period or an exclamation point. (See page 330.)

EXAMPLES   Please turn the TV off. [request]

Turn that TV off! [command]

independent clause An independent clause (also called a *main clause*) expresses a complete thought and can stand by itself as a sentence. (See page 424.)

EXAMPLE   Because Dad never has any spare time, **he hired a contractor to build the deck.**

indirect object An indirect object is a word or word group that often comes between a transitive verb and its direct object and tells to whom or to what or for whom or for what the action of the verb is done. (See page 388.)

EXAMPLE   Kathleen gave the **dog** a rubber toy. [The direct object is *toy.*]

QUICK REFERENCE HANDBOOK

infinitive An infinitive is a verb form, usually preceded by *to*, that is used as a noun, an adjective, or an adverb. (See page 414.)

EXAMPLE   We all wanted **to swim,** so Mom took us to the pool.

infinitive phrase An infinitive phrase consists of an infinitive and its modifiers and complements. (See page 415.)

EXAMPLE   **To help one's fellow human beings** is an admirable goal, Ronny.

interjection An interjection expresses emotion and has no grammatical relation to the rest of the sentence. (See page 377.)

EXAMPLE   **Wow!** Look at those fireworks!

interrogative sentence An interrogative sentence asks a question and is followed by a question mark. (See page 331.)

EXAMPLE   Have you ever seen the Rockies**?**

intransitive verb An intransitive verb is a verb that does not take an object. (See page 364.)

EXAMPLE   The wind **howls** fiercely.

irregular verb An irregular verb is a verb that forms its past and past participle in some way other than by adding *–d* or *–ed* to the base form. (See page 488. See also **regular verb.**)

Base Form	Present Participle	Past	Past Participle
be	[is] being	was, were	[have] been
bring	[is] bringing	brought	[have] brought
choose	[is] choosing	chose	[have] chosen
cost	[is] costing	cost	[have] cost
eat	[is] eating	ate	[have] eaten
grow	[is] growing	grew	[have] grown
pay	[is] paying	paid	[have] paid
spread	[is] spreading	spread	[have] spread

italics (See **underlining [italics].**)

its, it's (See page 559.)

EXAMPLES **It's** [It is] your turn to clean **its** [the gerbil's] cage.

It's [It has] been a long time since **it's** [it has] been cleaned.

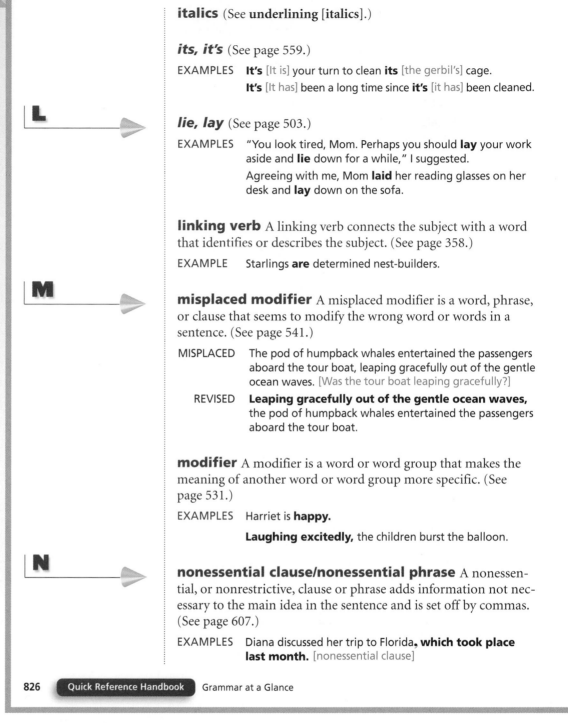

lie, lay (See page 503.)

EXAMPLES "You look tired, Mom. Perhaps you should **lay** your work aside and **lie** down for a while," I suggested.

Agreeing with me, Mom **laid** her reading glasses on her desk and **lay** down on the sofa.

linking verb A linking verb connects the subject with a word that identifies or describes the subject. (See page 358.)

EXAMPLE Starlings **are** determined nest-builders.

misplaced modifier A misplaced modifier is a word, phrase, or clause that seems to modify the wrong word or words in a sentence. (See page 541.)

MISPLACED The pod of humpback whales entertained the passengers aboard the tour boat, leaping gracefully out of the gentle ocean waves. [Was the tour boat leaping gracefully?]

REVISED **Leaping gracefully out of the gentle ocean waves,** the pod of humpback whales entertained the passengers aboard the tour boat.

modifier A modifier is a word or word group that makes the meaning of another word or word group more specific. (See page 531.)

EXAMPLES Harriet is **happy.**

Laughing excitedly, the children burst the balloon.

nonessential clause/nonessential phrase A nonessential, or nonrestrictive, clause or phrase adds information not necessary to the main idea in the sentence and is set off by commas. (See page 607.)

EXAMPLES Diana discussed her trip to Florida**, which took place last month.** [nonessential clause]

The twins, **sitting quietly for a change,** posed for the picture. [nonessential phrase]

noun A noun names a person, a place, a thing, or an idea. (See page 337.)

EXAMPLES   Elizabeth Peña   Paris   mountain   knowledge

number Number is the form a word takes to indicate whether the word is singular or plural. (See page 457.)

SINGULAR   child   man   leaf   town

PLURAL   children   men   leaves   towns

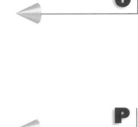

object of a preposition An object of a preposition is the noun or pronoun that ends a prepositional phrase. (See page 371.)

EXAMPLE   She heard a composition on the **radio** by her **music teacher.** [*On the radio* and *by her music teacher* are prepositional phrases.]

parentheses (See page 648.)

EXAMPLES   A praying mantis **(**see Illustration C**)** is the only insect that can turn its head from side to side.

A praying mantis is the only insect that can turn its head from side to side. **(**See Illustration C.**)**

participial phrase A participial phrase consists of a participle and any complements and modifiers it has. (See page 412.)

EXAMPLE   **Admired for his courage,** my cousin George is an impressive young man.

participle A participle is a verb form that can be used as an adjective. (See page 410.)

EXAMPLE   **Blushing,** Tina accepted the award.

passive voice The passive voice is the voice a verb is in when it expresses an action done to its subject. (See page 499. See also **voice.**)

EXAMPLE   The president **was reelected** with 60 percent of the vote.

period (See **end marks.**)

phrase A phrase is a group of related words that does not contain both a verb and its subject and that is used as a single part of speech. (See page 401.)

EXAMPLES Steve, **our champion swimmer,** will represent King Junior High **at the meet in Kansas City.** [*Our champion swimmer* is an appositive phrase. *At the meet* and *in Kansas City* are prepositional phrases.]

To make her own quilt is Maya's goal. [*To make her own quilt* is an infinitive phrase.]

The leaves, **pressed thoroughly and laminated,** will make beautiful coasters. [*Pressed thoroughly and laminated* is a participial phrase.]

predicate The predicate is the part of a sentence that says something about the subject. (See page 320.)

EXAMPLES **Will** she **perform a solo**?

Horace **may be responsible for that prank.**

predicate adjective A predicate adjective is an adjective that completes the meaning of a linking verb and modifies the subject of the verb. (See page 393.)

EXAMPLES The trees looked **red** in the evening light.

This rose smells **beautiful.**

predicate nominative A predicate nominative is a noun or pronoun that completes the meaning of a linking verb and identifies or refers to the subject of the verb. (See page 391.)

EXAMPLES A lizard is a **reptile.**

My sister will be a **lawyer** soon.

prefix A prefix is a word part that is added before a base word or root. (See page 658.)

EXAMPLES un + fair = **un**fair   il + legal = **il**legal

re + elect = **re**elect   pre + historic = **pre**historic

self + esteem =
self-esteem

ex + governor =
ex-governor

mid + April =
mid-April

post + Holocaust =
post-Holocaust

preposition A preposition shows the relationship of a noun or a pronoun to some other word in a sentence. (See page 370.)

EXAMPLE   Berlin, the capital **of** Germany, is located **in** the east.

prepositional phrase A prepositional phrase is a group of words beginning with a preposition and ending with its object. (See page 371. See also **object of a preposition.**)

EXAMPLE   **Before work,** Dan always feeds the birds.

pronoun A pronoun is used in place of one or more nouns or pronouns. (See page 342.)

EXAMPLES   **His** muscles ached, **she** was sunburned, and **their** feet were sore, but all in all **they** had had a wonderful day.

All of the guests helped **themselves** to **more** of the spinach salad.

question mark (See **end marks.**)

quotation marks (See page 630.)

- **for direct quotations**
  EXAMPLE   **"**Learning a few simple rules,**"** said the teacher, **"**will help you avoid many common spelling errors.**"**

- **with other marks of punctuation** (See also preceding example.)
  EXAMPLES   **"**Through which South American countries does the Amazon River flow**?"** asked Enrique.

  Which popular poem by Alfred Noyes begins with the line **"**The wind was a torrent of darkness among the gusty trees**"?**

  Cynthia asked, **"**Did Amy Tan write the short story **'**Fish Cheeks**'?"**

■ **for titles**

EXAMPLES   "Song of the Trees" [short story]

                "Mama Is a Sunrise" [short poem]

                "Many Rivers to Cross" [song]

regular verb A regular verb is a verb that forms its past and past participle by adding *–d* or *–ed* to the base form. (See page 486. See also **irregular verb.**)

Base Form	Present Participle	Past	Past Participle
ask	[is] asking	asked	[have] asked
attack	[is] attacking	attacked	[have] attacked
drown	[is] drowning	drowned	[have] drowned
suppose	[is] supposing	supposed	[have] supposed
use	[is] using	used	[have] used

rise, raise (See page 501.)

EXAMPLES   The river **rose** rapidly.

              The lieutenant **raised** a white flag to signal surrender.

run-on sentence A run-on sentence is two or more complete sentences run together as one. (See page 271. See also **comma splice** and **fused sentence.**)

RUN-ON   We were so impressed by the story that we said nothing he grew a little impatient.

REVISED   We were so impressed by the story that we said nothing**.** **H**e grew a little impatient.

REVISED   We were so impressed by the story that we said nothing**;** he grew a little impatient.

semicolon (See page 618.)

■ **in compound sentences with no conjunction**

EXAMPLE   My sister plays violin in her school's symphony orchestra**;** her goal is to become first chair.

- **in compound sentences with conjunctive adverbs**

  EXAMPLE   I play that movie's soundtrack nearly every day; consequently, I know the lyrics of all of its songs.

- **between items in a series when the items contain commas**

  EXAMPLE   The band's cross-country tour includes concerts in Seattle, Washington; Albuquerque, New Mexico; Cincinnati, Ohio; and Miami, Florida.

sentence A sentence is a group of words that contains a subject and a verb and expresses a complete thought. (See page 316.)

S   V

EXAMPLE   Mr. Holland will give his presentation in the auditorium.

sentence fragment A sentence fragment is a group of words that is punctuated as if it were a complete sentence but that does not contain both a subject and a verb or that does not express a complete thought. (See pages 269 and 316.)

FRAGMENT   In 2002, the Winter Olympic Games in Salt Lake City.

SENTENCE   In 2002, the Winter Olympic Games will be held in Salt Lake City.

FRAGMENT   To find more information about the Zapotec culture.

SENTENCE   To find more information about the Zapotec culture, we searched the Internet.

simple sentence A simple sentence has one independent clause and no subordinate clauses. (See page 440.)

EXAMPLES   Both the cheetah and the chimpanzee are endangered species.

How many other species of mammals are endangered?

sit, set (See page 500.)

EXAMPLES   The science students **sat** quietly, watching the televised launch of the space shuttle *Atlantis.*

On top of the television, the science teacher **set** her model of the space shuttle *Atlantis.*

stringy sentence A stringy sentence is a sentence that has too many independent clauses. Usually, the clauses are strung together with coordinating conjunctions like *and* or *but*. (See page 282.)

STRINGY   I remember that the first time I looked through binoculars at the night sky I was surprised that I could clearly see the craters of the moon and the satellites of Jupiter, but what amazed me most was a bright object shimmering with many different colors near the horizon, and I, of course, immediately thought that I had spotted a UFO, but I learned later that the colorful object was not a UFO but the planet Venus.

REVISED   I remember the first time I looked through binoculars at the night sky**.** **I** was surprised that I could clearly see the craters of the moon and the satellites of Jupiter**.** **W**hat amazed me most, however, was a bright object shimmering with many different colors near the horizon**.** **I,** of course, immediately thought that I had spotted a UFO**.** **I** learned later, though, that the colorful object was not a UFO but the planet Venus.

subject The subject tells whom or what a sentence is about. (See page 317.)

EXAMPLE   Finally, **the train** entered the station.

subject complement A subject complement is a word or word group that completes the meaning of a linking verb and identifies or describes the subject. (See page 391.)

EXAMPLE   Linus was **impressive** in the play last night.

subordinate clause A subordinate clause (also called a *dependent clause*) does not express a complete thought and cannot stand alone as a sentence. (See page 424. See also **adjective clause, adverb clause.**)

EXAMPLE   Margaret and Melanie are two six-year-old girls **who live in San Marcos, Texas.**

suffix A suffix is a word part that is added after a base word or root. (See page 658.)

EXAMPLES   safe + ly =safe**ly**   fair + ness =fair**ness**

busy + ly =busi**ly**   enjoy + ing = enjoy**ing**

active + ity = activ**ity**

knowledge + able = knowledge**able**

swim + er = swimm**er**

teach + er = teach**er**

tense of verbs The tense of verbs indicates the time of the action or state of being expressed by the verb. (See page 496.)

Present

I write	we write
you write	you write
he, she, it writes	they write

Past

I wrote	we wrote
you wrote	you wrote
he, she, it wrote	they wrote

Future

I will (shall) write	we will (shall) write
you will (shall) write	you will (shall) write
he, she, it will (shall) write	they will (shall) write

Present Perfect

I have written	we have written
you have written	you have written
he, she, it has written	they have written

Past Perfect

I had written	we had written
you had written	you had written
he, she, it had written	they had written

Future Perfect

I will (shall) have written	we will (shall) have written
you will (shall) have written	you will (shall) have written
he, she, it will (shall) have written	they will (shall) have written

Grammar at a Glance   **833**

transitive verb A transitive verb is an action verb that takes an object. (See page 364.)

EXAMPLE   Marcia **washed** her minivan yesterday.

underlining (italics) (See page 628.)

■ **for titles**

EXAMPLES   *Thurgood Marshall: American Revolutionary* [book]

Sports Illustrated for Kids [periodical]

American Gothic [work of art]

The Water Carrier [long musical composition]

■ **for words, letters, and symbols used as such and for foreign words**

EXAMPLES   Notice that the word *Mississippi* has four *i*'s, four *s*'s, and two *p*'s.

A *fait accompli* is anything that is done that cannot be undone.

verb A verb expresses an action or a state of being. (See page 357.)

EXAMPLES   We **walked** slowly down the steep hill.

The grasshopper **is** near the fence.

verbal A verbal is a form of a verb used as a noun, an adjective, or an adverb. (See page 410. See also **participle** and **infinitive.**)

EXAMPLES   The children were amazed by the **leaping** lemurs.

To leave was hard.

verbal phrase A verbal phrase consists of a verbal and any modifiers and complements it has. (See page 410. See also **participial phrase** and **infinitive phrase.**)

EXAMPLES   **Running fast,** the squirrel reached the safety of the tree.

I don't want **to say goodbye.**

verb phrase A verb phrase consists of a main verb and at least one helping verb. (See page 323.)

EXAMPLES **Have** you **seen** Rich today?

I **would be going** tomorrow, otherwise.

voice Voice is the form a transitive verb takes to indicate whether the subject of the verb performs or receives the action. (See page 499.)

ACTIVE VOICE   Patricia MacLachlan **wrote** the book *Sarah, Plain and Tall.*

PASSIVE VOICE   The book *Sarah, Plain and Tall* **was written** by Patricia MacLachlan.

well (See *good, well.*)

who, whom (See page 521.)

EXAMPLES   For two weeks last summer, I visited my pen pal Émile, **who** lives in Montreal, Quebec.

My pen pal Émile, **whom** I have known for five years, has taught me much about French Canadian traditions.

wordiness Wordiness is the use of more words than necessary or the use of fancy words where simple ones will do. (See page 283.)

WORDY   In the event that it rains, we will not cancel the party that we have planned in celebration of Cinco de Mayo but instead, as an alternative, will hold the party indoors, not outdoors.

REVISED   If it rains, we will hold our Cinco de Mayo party indoors.

Diagramming Appendix

Diagramming Sentences

A *sentence diagram* is a picture of how the parts of a sentence fit together. It shows how the words in the sentence are related.

Subjects and Verbs

Reference Note

For information on **subjects and verbs,** see page 317.

To diagram a sentence, first find the simple subject and the simple predicate, or verb, and write them on a horizontal line. Then, separate the subject and verb with a vertical line. Keep the capital letters, but leave out the punctuation marks, except in cases such as *Mr.* and *July 1, 1999.*

EXAMPLE   Horses gallop.

Horses	gallop

Questions

Reference Note

For information on **questions,** see page 331.

To diagram a question, first make the question into a statement. Then, diagram the sentence. Remember that in a diagram the subject always comes first, even if it does not come first in the sentence.

EXAMPLE   Are you going?

you	Are going

The examples on the previous page are easy because each sentence contains only a simple subject and a verb. Now, look at a longer sentence.

EXAMPLE   One quiet, always popular pet is the goldfish.

To diagram the simple subject and verb of this sentence, follow these steps.

Step 1:   Separate the complete subject from the complete predicate.

complete subject	complete predicate
One quiet, always popular pet	is the goldfish.

Step 2:   Find the simple subject and the verb.

simple subject	verb
pet	is

Step 3:   Draw the diagram.

pet	is

Understood Subjects

To diagram an imperative sentence, place the understood subject *you* in parentheses on the horizontal line.

EXAMPLE   Clean your room.

(you)	Clean

Reference Note

For information on **understood subjects,** see page 330.

Exercise 1 **Diagramming Simple Subjects and Verbs**

Diagram only the simple subject and verb in each of the following sentences.

EXAMPLE   **1.** Gwendolyn Brooks has been the poet laureate of Illinois.

1. | Gwendolyn Brooks | has been |
|---|---|

1. Angela just returned from Puerto Rico.
2. She was studying Spanish in San Juan.

⌐HELP⌐

Remember that simple subjects and verbs may consist of more than one word.

Exercise 1 Diagramming
Simple Subjects and Verbs

ANSWERS

1.
Angela	returned

2.
She	was studying

DIAGRAMMING

Exercise 1 **Diagramming Simple Subjects and Verbs**

Exercise 1 **Diagramming Simple Subjects and Verbs**

ANSWERS continued

3.

(you)	Listen

4.

She	enjoyed

5.

you	Have been

Reference Note
For information on **compound subjects,** see page 325. For information on **conjunctions,** see page 374.

Reference Note
For information on **compound verbs,** see page 327.

3. Listen to her stories about her host family.
4. She really enjoyed her trip.
5. Have you ever been to Puerto Rico?

Compound Subjects

To diagram a compound subject, put the subjects on parallel lines. Then, put the connecting word (the conjunction) on a dotted line that joins the subject lines.

EXAMPLE   **Sharks** and **eels** can be dangerous.

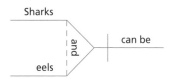

Compound Verbs

To diagram a compound verb, put the two verbs on parallel lines. Then, put the connecting word (the conjunction) on a dotted line that joins the verb lines.

EXAMPLE   The cowboy **swung** into the saddle and **rode** away.

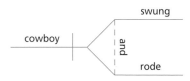

This is how a compound verb is diagrammed when it has a helping verb that is not repeated.

EXAMPLE   Ray Bradbury **has written** many books and **received** several prizes for them.

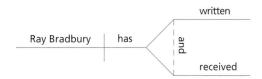

Compound Subjects and Compound Verbs

A sentence with both a compound subject and a compound verb combines the patterns for each.

EXAMPLE   **Rosa Parks** and **Dr. Martin Luther King, Jr., saw** a problem and **did** something about it.

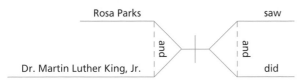

Sometimes parts of a compound subject or a compound verb are joined by correlative conjunctions, such as *both . . . and.* Correlatives are diagrammed like this:

EXAMPLE   **Both** Luisa **and** Miguel can sing.

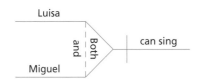

Exercise 2   Diagramming Compound Subjects and Compound Verbs

Diagram the simple subjects and the verbs in the following sentences. Include the conjunctions that join the compound subjects or the compound verbs.

EXAMPLE   **1.** Both LeAnn Rimes and Clint Black are going on tour and cutting new albums.

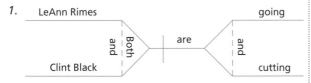

1. Everyone knows and likes Mr. Karras.
2. Hurricanes and tornadoes occur most often during the summer.
3. Julio and Rosa were cutting paper and tying string for the kites.

Diagramming Sentences   **839**

Reference Note

For information on **using compound subjects with compound verbs,** see page 327.

PEANUTS reprinted by permission of United Feature Syndicate, Inc.

Exercise 2   Diagramming Compound Subjects and Compound Verbs

ANSWERS

1.

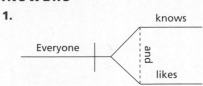

2.

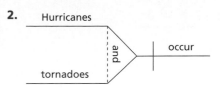

3.

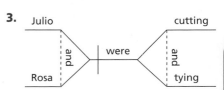

DIAGRAMMING

Diagramming Sentences   **839**

Exercise 2 Diagramming Compound Subjects and Compound Verbs

ANSWERS continued

4.

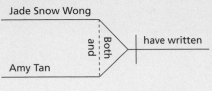

5.

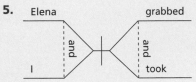

Exercise 3 Diagramming Sentences with Adjectives

ANSWERS

1.

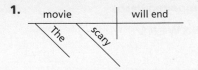

2.

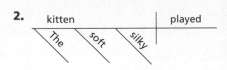

3.

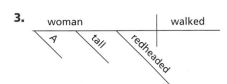

4.

5.

Reference Note

For information on **possessive pronouns,** see page 342.

Reference Note

For information on **adjectives,** see page 346.

4. Both Jade Snow Wong and Amy Tan have written books about their childhoods in San Francisco's Chinatown.
5. Elena and I grabbed our jackets and took the bus to the mall.

Adjectives and Adverbs

Adjectives and adverbs are written on slanted lines connected to the words they modify. Notice that possessive pronouns are diagrammed in the same way adjectives are.

Adjectives

EXAMPLES **dark** room **a lively** fish **my best** friend

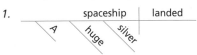

Exercise 3 Diagramming Sentences with Adjectives

Diagram the subjects, the verbs, and the adjectives that modify the subjects in the following sentences.

EXAMPLE 1. A huge silver spaceship landed in the field.

1.

1. The scary movie will soon end.
2. The soft, silky kitten played with a shoelace.
3. A tall redheaded woman walked into the room.
4. Actor John Lithgow starred in that popular television show.
5. A weird green light shone under the door.

Adverbs

EXAMPLES walks **briskly** arrived **here late**

Reference Note

For information on **adverbs,** see page 366.

DIAGRAMMING

When an adverb modifies an adjective or another adverb, it is placed on a line connected to the word it modifies.

EXAMPLES   a **very** happy child   drove **rather slowly**

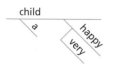

EXAMPLE   This **extremely** rare record will **almost certainly** cost a great deal.

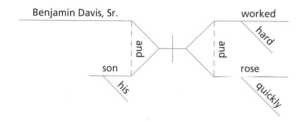

Conjunctions and Modifiers

When a modifier applies to only one part of a compound subject or compound verb, it is diagrammed like this:

EXAMPLE   Benjamin Davis, Sr., and **his** son worked **hard** and rose **quickly** through the military.

Reference Note

For information on **conjunctions,** see page 374. For information on **modifiers,** see Chapter 20.

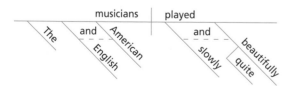

A conjunction joining two modifiers is diagrammed like this:

EXAMPLE   The **English** and **American** musicians played **slowly** and quite **beautifully.**

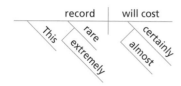

Exercise 4 Diagramming Sentences with Adjectives and Adverbs

ANSWERS

1.

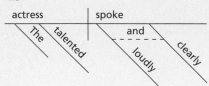

2.

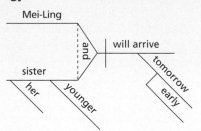

3.

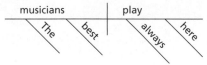

4.

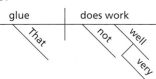

5.

Exercise 4 Diagramming Sentences with Adjectives and Adverbs

Diagram the subjects, verbs, adjectives, adverbs, and conjunctions in the following sentences.

EXAMPLE **1.** A relatively unknown candidate won the election easily and rather cheaply.

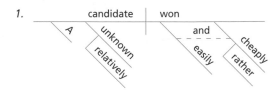

1. The determined young Frederick Douglass certainly worked hard.
2. The talented actress spoke loudly and clearly.
3. Mei-Ling and her younger sister will arrive early tomorrow.
4. The best musicians always play here.
5. That glue does not work very well.

Reference Note

For information on **objects,** see Chapter 13.

Reference Note

For information on **direct objects,** see page 386.

Objects

Direct Objects

A direct object is diagrammed on the horizontal line with the subject and verb. A vertical line separates the direct object from the verb. Notice that this vertical line does not cross the horizontal line.

EXAMPLES   We like **pizza.**

The robin caught a **worm.**

DIAGRAMMING

Compound Direct Objects

EXAMPLE   Lizards eat **flies** and **earthworms.**

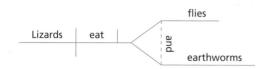

Reference Note

For information on **compound direct objects,** see page 387.

Indirect Objects

An indirect object is diagrammed on a horizontal line beneath the verb. The verb and the indirect object are joined by a slanting line.

EXAMPLE   Marisol brought **me** a piñata.

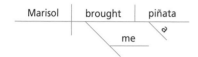

Reference Note

For information on **indirect objects,** see page 388.

Compound Indirect Objects

EXAMPLE   Tanya gave the **singer** and the **dancer** cues.

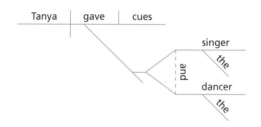

Reference Note

For information on **compound indirect objects,** see page 389.

Exercise 5   Diagramming Direct and Indirect Objects

Diagram the following sentences.

EXAMPLE   **1.** I gave the clerk a dollar.

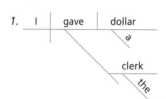

Exercise 5 Diagramming Direct and Indirect Objects

ANSWERS

1.

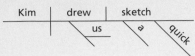

2.

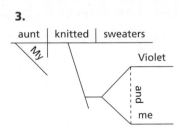

3.

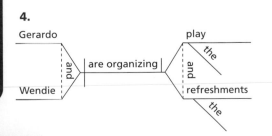

1. Kim drew us a quick sketch.
2. He sent the American Red Cross and Goodwill Industries his extra clothes.
3. My aunt knitted Violet and me sweaters.
4. Gerardo and Wendie are organizing the play and the refreshments.
5. Several businesses bought our school new computers.

Reference Note

For information on **subject complements,** see page 391.

Reference Note

For information on **predicate nominatives,** see page 391.

Subject Complements

A subject complement is diagrammed on the horizontal line with the subject and the verb. It comes after the verb. A line slanting toward the verb separates the subject complement from the verb.

Predicate Nominatives

EXAMPLES   Mariah Carey is a famous **singer.**

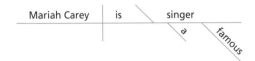

That bird is a female **cardinal.**

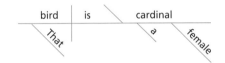

Compound Predicate Nominatives

EXAMPLE   Clara is a **student** and a volunteer **nurse.**

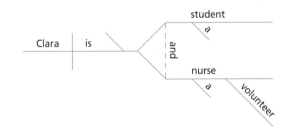

4.

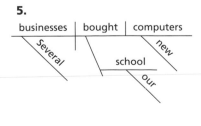

5.

Predicate Adjectives

EXAMPLE   She was extremely **nice**.

This juice tastes **great**.

Compound Predicate Adjectives

EXAMPLE   We were **tired** but very **happy**.

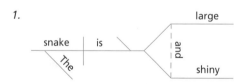

Reference Note

For information on **predicate adjectives,** see page 393.

Exercise 6   **Diagramming Sentences**

Diagram the following sentences.

EXAMPLE   **1.** The snake is large and shiny.

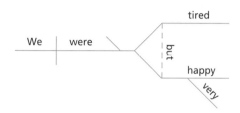

1. Turtles are reptiles.
2. Their tough beaks look sharp and strong.
3. Turtles may grow very old.
4. The alligator snapper is the largest freshwater turtle.
5. Few turtles are dangerous.

ANSWERS

1.

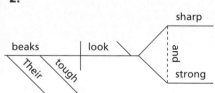

Turtles | are \ reptiles

2.

3.

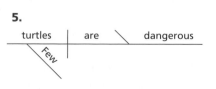

4.

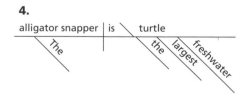

5.

DIAGRAMMING

Reference Note

For information on **prepositional phrases,** see page 402.

Reference Note

For information on **adjective phrases,** see page 404.

Reference Note

For information on **adverb phrases,** see page 406.

Prepositional Phrases

A prepositional phrase is diagrammed below the word it modifies. Write the preposition on a slanting line below the modified word. Then, write the object of the preposition on a horizontal line connected to the slanting line.

Adjective Phrases

EXAMPLES   traditions **of the Sioux**

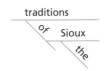

gifts **from Nadine and Chip**

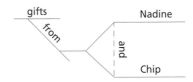

Adverb Phrases

EXAMPLES   awoke early **in the morning**

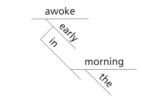

search **for the gerbil and the hamster**

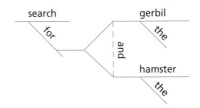

Two prepositional phrases may modify the same word.

EXAMPLE   The tour extends **across the country** and **around the world.**

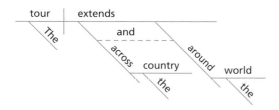

When a prepositional phrase modifies the object of another preposition, the diagram looks like this:

EXAMPLE   Richard Wright wrote one **of the books on that subject.**

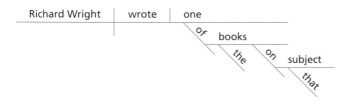

Exercise 7 **Diagramming Sentences with Prepositional Phrases**

Diagram the following sentences.

EXAMPLE   **1.** Our team practices **late in the afternoon.**

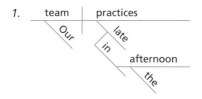

1. The scientist worked late into the night.
2. A play about Cleopatra will be performed tonight.
3. Leroy practices with his band and by himself.

ANSWERS

1.

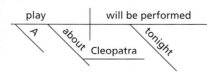

2.

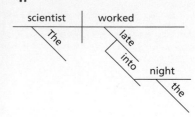

3.

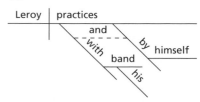

Reference Note

For information on **subordinate clauses,** see page 424.

Reference Note

For information on **adjective clauses,** see page 427.

Reference Note

For information on **relative pronouns,** see page 428.

Reference Note

For information on **adverb clauses,** see page 430.

4. Garth Brooks has written songs about love and freedom.
5. The director of that movie about the Civil War was chosen for an Academy Award.

Subordinate Clauses

Adjective Clauses

Diagram an adjective clause by connecting it with a broken line to the word it modifies. Draw the broken line between the relative pronoun and the word to which it relates.

NOTE The words *who, whom, whose, which,* and *that* are relative pronouns.

An adjective clause is diagrammed below the independent clause.

EXAMPLE   The students **whose projects are selected** will attend the regional contest.

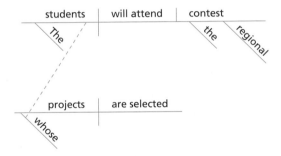

Adverb Clauses

Diagram an adverb clause by using a broken line to connect the adverb clause to the word it modifies. Place the subordinating conjunction that introduces the adverb clause on the broken line.

NOTE The words *after, because, if, since, unless, when,* and *while* are common subordinating conjunctions.

Exercise 7 **Diagramming Sentences with Prepositional Phrases**

ANSWERS continued

4.

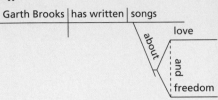

5.

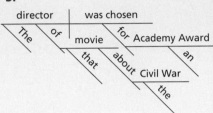

DIAGRAMMING

The adverb clause is diagrammed below the independent clause.

EXAMPLE   **If I study for two more hours,** I will finish my homework.

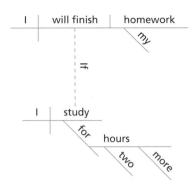

Reference Note

For information on **subordinating conjunctions,** see page 431.

Exercise 8 **Diagramming Sentences with Adjective Clauses and Adverb Clauses**

Diagram the following sentences.

EXAMPLE   1. Will you stop by my house after you go to the library?

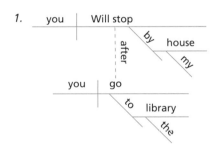

1. Most proverbs are sayings that give advice.
2. Because the day was very hot, the cool water felt good.
3. If it does not rain tomorrow, we will visit Crater Lake.
4. Janice and Linda found some empty seats as the movie started.
5. The problem that worries us now is the pollution of underground sources of water.

Exercise 8 **Diagramming Sentences with Adjective Clauses and Adverb Clauses**

ANSWERS

1.
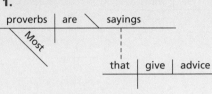

2.
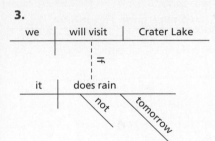

3.
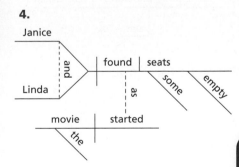

4.
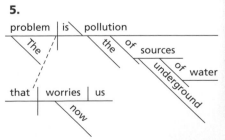

5.

DIAGRAMMING

Exercise 9 Diagramming Compound Sentences

ANSWERS

1.

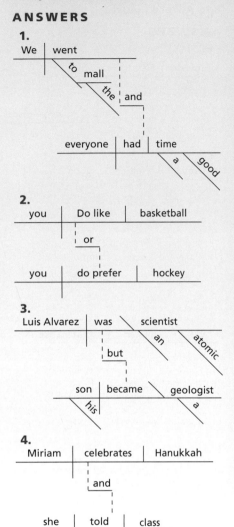

2.

3.

4.

5.

Reference Note

For information on the **kinds of sentence structure,** see Chapter 16.

Reference Note

For information on **simple sentences,** see page 440.

Reference Note

For information on **compound sentences,** see page 441.

The Kinds of Sentence Structure

Simple Sentences

EXAMPLE   Ray showed us his new bike. [one independent clause]

Compound Sentences

The second independent clause in a compound sentence is diagrammed below the first and usually is joined to it by a coordinating conjunction. A dotted line joins the clauses. The line is drawn between the verbs of the two clauses, and the conjunction is written on a solid horizontal line connecting the two parts of the dotted line.

EXAMPLE   Ossie Davis wrote the play, and Ruby Dee starred in it. [two independent clauses]

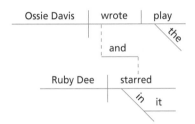

Exercise 9 Diagramming Compound Sentences

Diagram the following compound sentences.

EXAMPLE   **1.** Lucas likes that new CD, but I have not heard it.

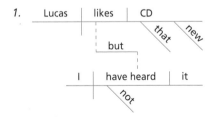

1. We went to the mall, and everyone had a good time.
2. Do you like basketball, or do you prefer hockey?
3. Luis Alvarez was an atomic scientist, but his son became a geologist.
4. Miriam celebrates Hanukkah, and she told our class about the holiday.
5. Sammy Sosa is my baseball hero, but my sister prefers Randy Johnson.

Complex Sentences

EXAMPLE   Altovise has a carving **that was made in Nigeria.** [one independent clause and one subordinate clause]

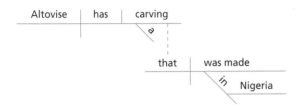

Reference Note

For information on **complex sentences,** see page 445.

Exercise 10 Diagramming Complex Sentences

Diagram the following complex sentences.

EXAMPLE   1. If you see Lola, you can give her this book.

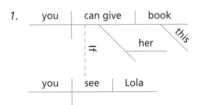

1. Valentina Tereshkova was the first woman who flew in space.
2. Because my cousins live in Toledo, they took a plane to the wedding.
3. Although Wilma Rudolph had been a very sick child, she became a top Olympic athlete.

1.

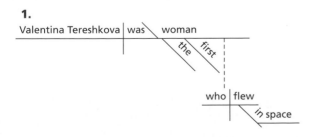

Exercise 10 Diagramming Complex Sentences

ANSWERS
(Answer to item 1. at bottom of page)

2.

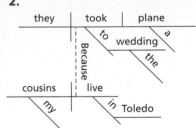

3.

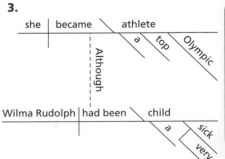

DIAGRAMMING

4.

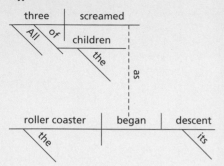

5.

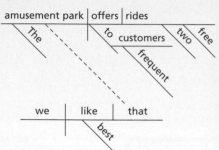

Reference Note

For information on
**compound-complex
sentences,** see page 447.

4. All three of the children screamed as the roller coaster began its descent.

5. The amusement park that we like best offers two free rides to frequent customers.

Compound-Complex Sentences

EXAMPLES   Soon-Yee, whose father is a sculptor, studies art, but
Mi-Kyung prefers the violin. [two independent clauses
and one subordinate clause]

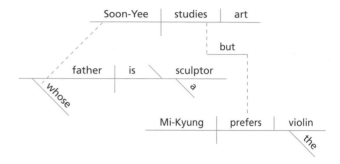

After the raccoon had fallen from the tree, it looked
injured, so we called the Humane Society.

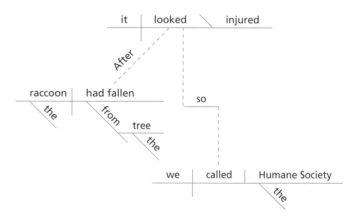

Exercise 11 Diagramming Compound-Complex Sentences

Diagram the following compound-complex sentences.

EXAMPLE   1. The room that Carla painted had been white, but she changed the color.

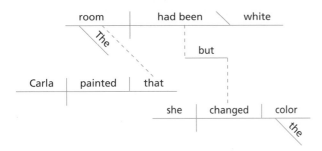

1. We have a game that we bought in Korea, but we do not understand the instructions.
2. Mariella wanted frozen yogurt after she won the tennis match, but Hector and I wanted sandwiches and milk.
3. When I returned to the store, the blue backpack had been sold, so I bought the green one.
4. The restaurant that we like best serves excellent seafood, and the chef has won many awards.
5. Before we conduct the experiment, we should ask for permission from the principal and we should prepare the science lab.

ANSWERS

1.

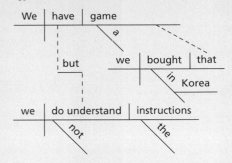

2.

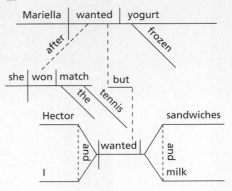

3.

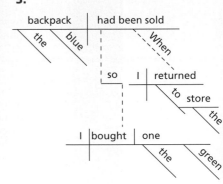

4.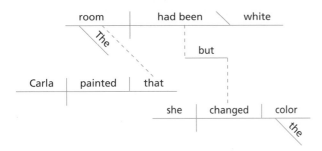

5.

DIAGRAMMING

types of, 800–802
Bust, busted, 556
Butterworth, W. E., IV, 7
Buy, **principal parts of,** 488, 489
Byline, definition of, 792

Cable television, 785. *See also* Television.
Call number, 735
Camera angles, 785
Camera lighting, 262
Camera shots, 785
Can't hardly, can't scarcely, 556
Capital, capitol, 668
Capitalization
    of abbreviations, 810
    of aircraft, 580
    of awards, 581
    of brand names/business products, 580
    of buildings/structures, 580
    of businesses, 580
    of calendar items, 579
    of common nouns, 574–75
    of constellations, 582
    in direct quotation, 39
    of *east, west, north, south,* 576
    of family relationship words, 587
    of first word of direct quotation, 574
    of first word of sentence, 574, 814
    of geographical names, 575–76
    of government bodies, 579
    of historical events/periods, 579
    of holidays, 579
    of holy days and celebrations, 581
    of institutions, 579
    of *I* pronoun, 574
    of memorials, 581
    of monuments, 581
    of names of animals, 575
    of names of persons, 575
    of nationalities/races/peoples, 579
    of organizations, 579
    of planets and heavenly bodies, 582
    in poetry, 574
    of proper adjectives, 584–85, 814
    of proper nouns, 574–75, 814
    proper nouns used as adjectives, 349
    in quoted sentences, 574, 631
    of races of people, 579
    of religions and sacred writings, 581
    rules for, 574–88
    of school subjects, 585
    of seasons, 579
    of sentence within sentence, 648

    of ships, 580
    of spacecraft, 580
    of special events, 579
    of specific deities, 581
    of stars, 582
    of teams, 579
    of titles, 586–88, 816
    of trains, 580
Capitol, capital, 668
Card catalog, 735–36
Career development activities
    collaborative news story, 47
    letter to an author, 79
    oral report on aspect of workplace, 115
    research and reporting on advertising careers, 265
    writing a journal entry about work activities, 199
    writing about professional uses of persuasion, 231
Case forms
    definition of, 511
    nominative case, 513–14, 816
    nouns and, 511
    objective case, 516–19, 816–17
    personal pronouns, 512
    possessive case, 511, 512, 817
    of pronouns, 816–17
Catch, **principal parts of,** 489
Categorizing ideas (writing). *See* Early plan, making an; Organization.
Cause-and-effect chain, 299
Cause-and-effect relationships
    analyzing, 743–44
    causal chain, 748
    identifying cause-and-effect relationships, 241
    pattern of, 748
    transitional words and phrases and, 302
CD-ROM, 736
–cede, –ceed, –sede, **spelling rule for,** 658
Celebrity angle in news, 45
Center-aligned text, 723
Central idea. *See* Main idea.
Characters
    analyzing, 155
    book jackets and, 148
    protagonist, 133
    in short stories, 144
Chariot in the Sky: A Story of the Jubilee Singers, 298
Chart, 115
Charts
    to arrange ideas, 806
    definition of, 729
    flowcharts, 729
    interpreting ideas from, 750
    pie charts, 730, 750
Choose, **principal parts of,** 489, 825
Choose, chose, 668
Choosing a topic. *See* Topics.

Chronological order
    cause-and-effect explanations and, 299
    chronological order pattern, 748
    definition of, 30
    explaining process with, 298
    in paragraphs, 297–99
    telling story in, 297–98

Classification
    advantages/disadvantages article and, 86
    classifying information, 774
    definition of, 81

Clauses. *See also* Independent clauses; Subordinate clauses.
    adjective clauses, 427–28, 546
    adverb clauses, 430–31, 445
    definition of, 279, 423, 817
    essential clauses, 608
    independent clauses, 423, 424
    kinds of, 423–31
    nonessential clauses, 607
    phrases distinguished from, 401
    punctuation of, 602, 605, 607–608, 613
    in series, 602
    subordinate clauses, 423, 424

Clean, **principal parts of,** 486

Clichés, 752
    definition of, 224
    elimination of, 223

Climax, 133

Clincher sentences, 294

Close, **comparison of,** 533

Closing, punctuating with comma, 615

Cloths, clothes, 668

Clue words. *See also* Context clues.
    advantages/disadvantages pattern and, 86
    cause-effect relationship, 744
    chronological order and, 744
    comparison/contrast structure, 744
    generalizations and, 236
    "how-to" explanations and, 55
    listing structure, 744
    problem/solution structure, 744

Clustering, how to, 804

Coarse, course, 669

Coherence. *See also* Order of ideas; Organization; Precise words; Rearranging (as revision strategy).
    chronological order and, 297–99
    compare and contrast in, 301
    logical order and, 301
    order of details and, 297–99
    order of information and, 796
    in paragraphs, 297–303
    revising to improve, 71
    spatial order and, 300–301
    transitional words and phrases and, 302–303
    in writing, 71

Cohesive. *See* Unity.

Collaborative writing (composing, organizing, and revising). *See also* Content and Organization Guidelines for Self-Evaluation and Peer Evaluation; Peer review.
    letter, 79
    records, 265
    news story, 47

Collection of works. *See* Portfolio building.

Collective nouns, 468–69, 477

Collins, Eileen, 742

Colloquialisms, definition of, 734

Colons
    in Biblical references, 620
    in conventional situations, 817
    in expressions of time, 620
    before lists, 817
    placement of, 619–20
    in salutations of letters, 620
    between titles/subtitles, 620

Colors
    cool colors and warm colors, 248, 728
    creating effects with, 790
    effect in, 149, 150, 248
    in illustrations, 149, 150, 728–29, 789

Combining (as revision strategy), 140–41, 273–80

Combining sentences
    into compound sentences, 278–79
    example of, 273
    by inserting phrases, 275–76
    by inserting words, 274
    as revision technique, 140–41
    using *and, but,* or *or,* 277–79
    using clauses beginning with *who, which,* or *that,* 280
    using clauses beginning with words of time or place, 280
    using compound subject, 277
    using compound verb, 277
    using subordinate clauses, 279–80

Come, **principal parts of,** 489

Commands, 330–31, 598

Commas
    in addresses, 614–15
    adverb clauses and, 430
    appositive/appositive phrases and, 609–610
    in compound sentences, 441, 605, 818
    conventional situations and, 614–15, 818
    coordinating conjunctions and, 271
    dates and, 614
    direct address and, 611
    independent clauses and, 602
    interjections and, 377
    with interrupters, 607–608, 818
    introductory elements and, 72, 280, 613, 818
    items in series and, 602–603, 817
    with multiple adjectives, 602, 604
    nonessential phrases/clauses and, 607, 818

creating family tree, 199
  writing persuasive letter from historical
    perspective, 231
Cubing, as prewriting technique, 804
Cursive writing, 75
Cut, **principal parts of,** 489

Dangling modifiers, 541, 544
  definition of, 821
Dashes, uses of, 649–50
Database records, 115
Databases
  on CD-ROM, 736
  online databases, 738
Declarative sentences, 330
  definition of, 821
Definite articles, 347
Definitions in dictionary, 721
Degrees of comparison, 532–35
Deleting (as revision strategy), 69, 102, 183, 223, 253,
  254
Delivery, of speech, 153–54, 191–92, 762–63
Demographics, definition of, 792
Demonstrative adjectives, 348
Demonstrative pronouns, 343, 348
Denotation, definition of, 89, 753
Dependent clauses. *See* Subordinate clauses.
Description (writing)
  essay, 41–42
  paragraphs, 47, 306, 307
  poem, 43
Descriptive essays, 41–42
Descriptive language
  definition of, 41
  in eyewitness account, 18–20
  figures of speech, 21, 31
  metaphors, 31, 146, 753
  precise words, 21
  sensory language, 21
  in short stories, 145
  similes, 31, 146, 753
Desert, dessert, 670
Designing your writing. *See* Document design.
Desktop publishing, page layout, 723–27
Details. *See also* Evidence; Sensory details; Support.
  elaboration and, 304
  eyewitness account and, 29
  irrelevant details, 68
  relevant details, 68
  using prepositional phrases to add, 421
  in writing, 293
Developing
  developing details, 41

writing to develop ideas, 79, 211–26
Developing ideas, writing to, 79, 211–26
Dewey, Jennifer Owings, 19–20
Diacritical marks, 721
Diagrams. *See also* Sentence diagrams.
  definition of, 730
  using diagrams, 750
Dialects, ethnic and regional, 733–34
Dialogue
  comparing television dialogue with real-life
    dialogue, 108–109
  new paragraphs and, 634
  punctuating dialogue, 39, 634
  to show character, 145
  writing for commercials, 259
Diary writing, 777
Diction, in formal speech, 762
Dictionary
  dictionary entry, 720–21
  function of, 240
  as spelling aid, 655
  types and contents of, 720–21
  wordbusting strategy and, 209
Digital editing, 262, 792
Digital effects, 262
Digital reality, 262
Direct address, capitalizing the title of person in,
  586–87
Direct objects
  action verbs and, 392
  as compound, 387
  definition of, 386, 516, 822
  diagram of, 842
  objective case and, 516
  predicate nominative distinguished from, 392
  prepositional phrases and, 386
  pronouns as, 386
Direct quotations
  capitalization of, 574, 631
  punctuating with commas, 631–32
  punctuating with end marks, 632
  quotation marks and, 630–35, 829
Directions
  following oral, 76–78
  giving oral and written, 75
Discover, writing to, 79, 155, 199
Discussion. *See* Group discussion, informal speaking.
Divided quotation. *See* Broken quotations.
Dividing words, hyphens and, 646
Do
  as helping verb, 362
  principal parts of, 488, 489
Document design. *See also* Graphics; Illustrations; Page
  layout.
  desktop publishing, 723–27
  guidelines for submitting papers, 722

Had of, 562
Had ought, hadn't ought, 557
Haiku, 43
Handwriting, 75
Handwritten papers, 722
Hanson-Harding, Alexandra, 83–85
Hard news, 44, 45, 793
Hatchet (Paulsen), 149–50, 291
Have
    as helping verb, 362, 485
    principal parts of, 490
Headings, 725
    in note taking, 175
Headlines, in media, 793
Hear, **principal parts of,** 490
Hear, here, 671
Helping verbs
    complete sentences and, 269
    list of, 362
    past participle and, 485
    present participle and, 485
    subject-verb agreement and, 458
Here's, 470
He, she, they, 559
Hide, **principal parts of,** 490
Himself, themselves, 524, 559
Hinton, S. E., 136–37
Hisself, theirselfs, theirselves, 524, 559
Hit, **principal parts of,** 490
Hold, **principal parts of,** 490
"Home on the Range," 296
Home page, 740
Homonyms, 666–77
Hooking the reader, in informative report, 178
Hope, **principal parts of,** 486
"Hopi Snake Ceremonies" (Dewey), 19–20
Hostname, 740
How come, 559
However, **as weakening sentence meaning,** 205
"How-to" writing
    chronological order and, 55, 62
    explanation of, 54
    writing "how-to" essay, 74
Hubbell, Patricia, 146
Humorous "how-to" poem, 79
Hurt, **principal parts of,** 488
Hyperlinks, 740
    definition of, 197
Hyphens
    in addresses, 576
    with compound numbers, 646, 824
    dividing words with, 824
    fractions and, 646

    with prefixes, 647, 824
    with suffixes, 647
    syllables and, 646
    word division and, 142, 646
Hypothesis, 155

Idioms, 753
ie **and** *ei,* **spelling rule for,** 656–57
Illegible, **comparison of,** 534
Illustrations. *See also* Art activities; Graphics; Visuals.
    analyzing illustrations for book cover image, 130
    clarifying instructions with, 73
    color and, 149, 150
    definition of, 148, 730, 789
    elements of, 149, 150, 789–90
    literal illustrations, 150
    media choices, 150
    style choices, 149, 150
    symbolic illustrations, 150
    type font and, 149, 150
Images
    creating effects with, 790
    moving images, 790
    still images, 790
Imperative sentences, 824
    definition of, 330
    punctuation of, 330–31
Implied main idea
    in eyewitness account, 18
    identifying implied main idea, 22–24, 745
    mapping of, 23–24
    in test taking, 26
Impromptu speaking, 764
Indefinite articles, 347
Indefinite pronouns
    context and, 463
    definition of, 462
    list of, 344
    number and, 461
    plural in number, 463
    possessive case, 640
    singular/plural in number, 462, 463
Indentation in text design, 725
Indentations, in citing sources, 186
Independent clauses, 279–80
    combining with semicolons, 105
    in compound sentences, 441–42
    definition of, 424, 824
    punctuation of, 602, 605, 618
    as sentences, 424
    transitional expressions and, 605
Index, 197, 736
Indirect objects

numbers and, 600
overuse of, 616
parentheses, 648
of parenthetical expressions, 649
periods, 598–600
of possessives, 256, 638–40
question mark, 598
quotation marks, 39, 630–36
of salutation of a personal letter, 615
semicolons, 618
Puppet show, 199
Purpose (listening), 193, 227, 767, 768–72
interpreting speaker's purpose, 227, 772
Purpose (reading), xxxii–xxxiii
identifying author's purpose, 50, 53–55, 210
Purpose (speaking), adapting word choice to, 191, 758
Purpose (viewing), evaluating, 44, 46, 110, 112
Purpose (writing)
in advantages/disadvantages essay, 92
evaluating achievement of, 143, 226
for book jacket, 129
definition of, 50
in eyewitness account, 29
in formal speech, 758–59
for informal speaking, 763–64
report of information, 169–70
of instructions, 61
Put, **principal parts of,** 488, 492

Questioning, predicting and, 124–25
Question marks
abbreviations and, 600
commas and, 39
as end mark, 316, 598
quotations and, 632
Quickwriting, 212
Quiet, quite, 673
Quotation marks
broken quotations and, 631
commas and, 632
dialogue and, 39
direct quotations and, 630–36, 829
exclamation points and, 632
indirect quotation and, 630
periods and, 39
question marks and, 632
quotation within quotation, 635
several sentences and, 635
single quotation marks, 635, 636
titles and, 830

for titles of short works, 635–36
Quotations
on book jackets, 131–32
capitalization of, 574, 631

Radio, as source of information, 738
Radio ad, 265
Ragged text, 724
Raise, **principal parts of,** 502
Raise, rise, 501–502
Rate, in speaking, 191, 763
Rawls, Wilson, 122, 124
Read, **principal parts of,** 492
Readers' Guide to Periodical Literature, The, 736
Reading for enjoyment, 747
Reading for mastery, 747
Reading log, 746
Reading process
after reading, xxxii–xxxiii
note taking, 746
patterns of organization and, 748–49
predicting, 746
prereading, xxxii–xxxiii
prior knowledge and, xxxii–xxxiii
purpose, xxxii–xxxiii
reading-writing connection, xxxii–xxxiii
scanning, 747
skimming, 747
steps in, xxxii–xxxiii
Reading scripts, 766
Reading skills and focuses
adjusting reading rate, 747
advantage/disadvantage pattern, 82, 86
analyzing cause-and-effect relationships, 743–44
analyzing text structures, 748–49
descriptive language, 18, 21–22
determining author's point of view, 202, 743
distinguishing fact and opinion, 217, 744
drawing conclusions, 82, 87–88, 744
forming generalizations, 234, 236–38, 744–45
identifying author's purpose, 50, 53–55, 210
identifying stated main idea and supporting details, 747
implied main idea, 18, 22–24, 26, 745
interpreting visuals and graphics, 750–51
logical support, 202, 206–208
making inferences, 745
order of a process, 50, 55–56
paraphrasing, 745, 776
persuasive techniques, 234, 238–39, 746
point of view, 202, 205–206
predicting, 118, 124–25, 746

Search engines, 740, 741
Second-person pronouns, 342
–sede, –cede, –ceed, **spelling rule for,** 658
See
 conjugation of, 497–98
 principal parts of, 492
Seek, **principal parts of,** 492
Sell, **principal parts of,** 492
Semicolons
 combining independent clauses with, 105
 in compound sentences, 442, 830
 with conjunctive adverbs, 831
 definition of, 618
 independent clauses and, 602, 618
 items in series and, 618, 831
Send, **principal parts of,** 492
Sensory details, in writing, 293, 805
Sensory language, definition of, 21
Sentence(s)
 abbreviation at end of, 600
 basic parts of, 317
 clincher sentences, 294
 combining sentences, 140–41
 complete sentences, 268–71
 complex sentences, 445, 820
 compound-complex sentences, 447, 820
 compound sentences, 441–43, 820
 declarative sentences, 330, 821
 definition of, 316
 diagrams of, 850–52
 distinguishing between simple and compound, 443, 605
 end marks and, 822–23
 exclamatory sentences, 316, 331, 823
 fragments, 269, 316
 fused sentences, 823–24
 imperative sentences, 330–31, 824
 improving style of, 282–86
 independent clauses used as, 424
 interrogative sentences, 331, 825
 inverted word order in, 470
 kinds of, 330–31
 punctuation of, 316, 330–31, 598
 run-on sentences, 105, 271, 830
 simple sentences, 831
 stringy sentences, 103–104, 282, 831–32
 supporting sentences, 293
 topic sentences, 289–90
 uses of, 447
 varying beginnings of, 185
 varying structure of, 285–86, 426
 wordy sentences, 283–84
Sentence-completion questions, 783
Sentence diagrams, 836–52
Sentence fragments, 269, 316
Sentence punctuation. *See* End marks.
Sentence structure

 adding variety to, 141, 185, 285–86
 complex sentences, 445, 820
 compound-complex sentences, 447, 820
 compound sentences, 441–43, 820
 simple sentences, 440, 443, 831
Sequence
 identifying sequence of events, 58
 sequence chain of organization, 749, 807
Sequence of ideas. *See* Order of ideas.
Sequential order. *See* Chronological order.
Services, in advertising, 242
Set, **principal parts of,** 500
Set, sit, 500
Setting (literary element)
 book covers and, 149
 description of, 145
 as element of fiction, 133
 in writing short stories, 144
Setting (of speech), adapting verbal elements to, 762–63
Sharp, **comparison of,** 535
She, he, they, 559
Shone, shown, 673
Short-answer questions, 783
Short stories
 dialogue in, 145
 elements of, 144
 suspense and, 145
 writing a short story, 144–45
Short story, oral interpretation of, 765–66
Should of, 557
Shrink, **principal parts of,** 492
Similes
 definition of, 31, 753
 in poetry, 146
Simple, **comparison of,** 534
Simple predicate, 322–23
Simple sentences
 compound sentences distinguished from, 443, 605
 definition of, 440, 831
 diagram of, 850
Simple subjects
 definition of, 318–19
 identification of, 318
Sing, **principal parts of,** 488, 492
Single quotation marks, 635
Singular, 457. *See also* Agreement (pronoun-antecedent); Agreement (subject-verb).
Sink, **principal parts of,** 492
Sit, **principal parts of,** 500
Sit, set, 500, 832
Skimming, 747
Slang, 734
Slip, **principal parts of,** 486
Slogan, in advertisements, 248
Slow, **comparison of,** 533

Syntax. *See* Sentence structure.

ACKNOWLEDGMENTS

For permission to reprint copyrighted material, grateful acknowledgment is made to the following sources:

Annenberg/CPB Project: From "Amusement Park Physics" from *The Annenberg/CPB Project Exhibits* Web site, accessed June 10, 2002, at http://www.learner.org/exhibits/parkphysics/ridesafety. html. Copyright © 1998–2002 by Annenberg/CPB .

Johnny D. Boggs: From "Home on the Range" by Johnny D. Boggs from *Boys' Life,* June 1998, published by the Boy Scouts of America. Copyright © 1998 by Johnny D. Boggs.

Boyds Mills Press, Inc.: From "Hopi Snake Ceremonies" from *Rattlesnake Dance: True Tales, Mysteries, and Rattlesnake Ceremonies* by Jennifer Owings Dewey. Copyright © 1997 by Jennifer Owings Dewey.

Carlinsky & Carlinsky, Inc.: From "Kites" by Dan Carlinsky from *Boys' Life*, May 1974. Copyright © 1974 by Dan Carlinsky.

Dell Publishing, a division of Random House, Inc.: Front cover, front flap text, and back cover text from *Where the Red Fern Grows* by Wilson Rawls. Copyright © 1961 by Sophie S. Rawls, Trustee, or successor for Trustee(s) of the Rawls Trust, dated July 31, 1991; copyright © 1961 by The Curtis Publishing Company.

Doubleday, a division of Random House, Inc.: From *The Richer, the Poorer* by Dorothy West. Copyright © 1995 by Dorothy West.

Farrar, Straus & Giroux, LLC: From "A Walk to the Jetty" from *Annie John* by Jamaica Kincaid. Copyright © 1985 by Jamaica Kincaid.

Lloyd Garver: From "My Turn: No, You Can't Have Nintendo" (retitled "A Veto on Video Games") by Lloyd Garver from *Newsweek*, June 11, 1990, p. 8. Copyright © 1990 by Lloyd Garver.

Harcourt, Inc.: From "The No-Guitar Blues" from *Baseball in April and Other Stories* by Gary Soto. Copyright © 1990 by Gary Soto.

HarperCollins Publishers, Inc.: From *Black Elk: The Sacred Ways of a Lakota* by Wallace H. Black Elk and William S. Lyon, Ph.D. Copyright © 1990 by Wallace H. Black Elk and William S. Lyon. From "Green Dragon Pond" from *The Spring of Butterflies,* translated by He Liyi. Copyright © 1985 by William Collins Sons & Co. Ltd.

Henry Holt and Company, LLC: From "A Runaway Slave" from *Chariot in the Sky: A Story of the Jubilee Singers* by Arna Bontemps. Copyright 1951 by Arna Bontemps; copyright © 1979 by Mrs. Arna (Alberta) Bontemps.

Alfred A. Knopf, Inc.: Front cover, text from front and back flaps, and back cover text from *Crash* by Jerry Spinelli. Copyright © 1996 by Jerry Spinelli; jacket illustration copyright © 1996 by Eleanor Hoyt.

Margaret K. McElderry Books, an imprint of Simon & Schuster Children's Publishing Division: From *A Jar of Dreams* by Yoshiko Uchida. Copyright © 1981 by Yoshiko Uchida.

Millbrook Press: From "The Voice in the Attic" from *Voice Magic: Secrets of Ventriloquism & Voice Conjuring* by Ormond McGill. Copyright © 1992 by Ormond McGill.

NASA: From "NASA'S Future: Online Multimedia Presentation" by Brian Dunbar from *NASA Homepage* Web site, accessed May, 1999 at http://www.nasa.gov/. Copyright © 1999 by NASA.

National Geographic Society: "Lions Recover from Dog Disease" by Scott Stuckey from "Geo News: Comebacks" from *National Geographic World,* February 1999. Copyright © 1999 by National Geographic Society.

Newsweek, Inc.: From "A Doll Made to Order" from *Newsweek*, December 9, 1985. Copyright © 1985 by Newsweek, Inc. All rights reserved.

People Magazine: From "On a Roll: Flipping, Flying and (Almost) Losing It on the 10 Scariest Roller Coasters in America" by Anne-Marie O'Neill from *People*, vol. 48, no. 1, July 7, 1997. Copyright © 1997 by Time Inc.

Marian Reiner for Patricia Hubbell: "Construction" from *8 A. M. Shadows* by Patricia Hubbell. Copyright © 1965, 1993 by Patricia Hubbell.

Ride Warrior, Inc.: From "ThrillRide! 98 Preview" from *ThrillRide!* Web site, at http://www.thrillride.com. Copyright © 1998 by Robert Coker–Ride Warrior, Inc.

Scholastic Inc.: Adaptation from "For Girls Only" by Alexandra Hanson-Harding from *Junior Scholastic,* April 27, 1998. Copyright © 1998 by Scholastic Inc. From "The Celebrated Deformed Frogs of Le Sueur County" by Susan Hayes from *Scholastic Update,* vol. 130, no. 13, April 13, 1998. Copyright © 1998 by Scholastic Inc.

Simon & Schuster Books for Young Readers, an imprint of Simon & Schuster Children's Publishing Division: From *Hatchet* by Gary Paulsen. Copyright © 1987 by Gary Paulsen.

TIME for Kids, a division of Time Inc.: From *"We the People"* by Ritu Upadhyay from *TIME for Kids,* March 23, 2001. Copyright © 2001 by Time Inc.

University of California Press: From "In the Night" from *Singing for Power: The Song Magic of the Papago Indians of Southern Arizona* by Ruth Murray Underhill. Copyright 1938, © 1966 by Ruth Murray Underhill.

Viking Penguin, a division of Penguin Putnam Inc.: From *The Outsiders* by S. E. Hinton. Copyright © 1967 by S. E. Hinton.

Wiley Publishing, Inc.: Entry for "escape" from *Webster's New World™ Dictionary,* Fourth Edition. Copyright © 2000, 1999 by Wiley Publishing, Inc.

PHOTO CREDITS

Abbreviations used: (tl)top left, (tc)top center, (tr)top right, (l)left, (cl)center left, (c)center, (cr)center right, (r)right, (bl)bottom left, (bc)bottom center, (br)bottom right.

COVER: Scott Van Osdol/HRW Photo.

TABLE OF CONTENTS: Page T15 (tl), Gambell/SuperStock; T15 (bl), Image Copyright © 2001 Photodisc, Inc.; T16, Ron Sefton/Bruce Coleman, Inc.; T17, Courtesy of Terry Dewald/Jerry Jacka Photography; T18, Tom Prettyman/PhotoEdit; T19, John Elk, III/Bruce Coleman, Inc.; T20, Image Copyright ©1998 Photodisc, Inc.; T21, Tony Arruza/Bruce Coleman, Inc.; T22, James Sugar/Black Star; T23, SuperStock; T24, Bettmann/CORBIS; T26, Image Club Graphics ©1998 Adobe Systems; T27, Sylvain Grandadam/Getty Images/Stone.

PART OPENERS: Page xxxii, 1, 266, 267, 312, 313, 718, 719, Kazu Nitta/The Stock Illustration Source, Inc.

TAKING TESTS: Page 2, Rob Gage/Getty Images/Stone; 4, Jim Zuckerman/CORBIS; 8, AFP/CORBIS.

CHAPTER 1: Page 19, MONA ©1996 d cube™ Cone Mill Corporation; 45, Reuters NewMedia Inc./CORBIS.

CHAPTER 2: Page 60, Wolfgang Kaehler/CORBIS.

CHAPTER 3: Page 85, Nina Berman/SIPA Press; 93, David Young-Wolff/PhotoEdit.

CHAPTER 4: Page 119, From CRASH by Jerry Spinelli/ Copyright ©1996 by Jerry Spinelli. Jacket Illustration/ Copyright ©1996 by Eleanor Hoyt. Reprinted by permission of Alfred A. Knopf, Inc.; 123, ©1989 by Robert McGinnis.; 134, The Kobal Collection/Warner Bros; 138, Victoria Smith/HRW Photo; 149 (tr), Photos by Michael Orton/Getty Images/Stone (trees) and Victoria Smith (eyes)/HRW Photo; jacket design by HRW; 149 (tc), Illustrations by Jerry Dadds/Deborah Wolfe Ltd.; jacket design by HRW; 149 (br), Illustration by Mike Wimmer/Mendola Ltd. Artists Representatives; jacket design by HRW; 150, Illustration by Bill Schmidt/Hankins & Tebenborg LTD; jacket design by HRW.

CHAPTER 5: Page 159, Diane Gentry/Black Star; 160, SuperStock; 181, Tom & Pat Lesson/Photo Researchers, Inc.; 197, NASA; 198, NASA/CORBIS.

CHAPTER 7: Page 235, American Pharmaceutical Companies; 237, John Langford/HRW Photo; 238, Victoria Smith/HRW; 244, John Langford/HRW Photo; 245, Dick Luria/Getty Images/FPG; 257, Courtesy of the American Red Cross; 263 (c), John Langford/HRW Photo; 263 (br), Sam Dudgeon/HRW Photo; 264, John Langford/HRW Photo.

CHAPTER 8: Page 270, Kim Taylor/Bruce Coleman, Inc.; 272, NASA/Nawrocki Stock Photo; 273, Image Copyright ©2001 Photodisc, Inc.; 275, SuperStock; 276, Gambell/SuperStock; 279, SuperStock; 281, Image Copyright ©2001 Photodisc, Inc.; 284, Ron Sefton/Bruce Coleman, Inc.; 285, Reuters/Mark Cardwell/Hulton Archive/Getty Images; 287, Bettmann/CORBIS.

CHAPTER 9: Page 289, Getty Images/Digital Vision; 291, Image Copyright ©2001 Photodisc, Inc.; 295, People Weekly ©1986 Richard Howard; 297, David R. Frazier Photolibrary; 299, Image Copyright ©2001 Photodisc, Inc.; 301 (cr), John Shaw/Bruce Coleman, Inc.; 301 (br), Michael P. Gadomski/ Bruce Coleman, Inc.; 304, Bettmann/CORBIS; 305, Tim Davis/Davis/Lynn Images; 308, Hulton Archive/ Getty Images.

CHAPTER 10: Page 321, Bettmann/CORBIS; 324 (cl), Paul Chesley/Getty Images/Taxi; 324 (bl), John Elk, III/Bruce Coleman, Inc.; 326 (bc), John Elk, III/Bruce Coleman, Inc.; 326 (bl), Tony Arruza/Bruce Coleman, Inc.; 329, Corbis Images; 335, David Young-Wolff/PhotoEdit.

CHAPTER 11: Page 341, Chris Eden/Francine Seders Gallery; 351, Corbis Images; 355, Brooklyn Productions/Getty Images/The Image Bank.

CHAPTER 12: Page 365, Image Copyright ©1998 Photodisc, Inc.; 368, Tony Kirves/Southern Exposure; 372, Culver Pictures, Inc.; 379, Fred Bruemmer/Peter Arnold, Inc.; 383, Michael Newman/PhotoEdit.

CHAPTER 13: Page 387, Vandystadt Agence de Presse/Allsport/Getty; 388, Nawrocki Stock Photo; 395, Image Copyright ©1998 Photodisc, Inc.; 396, (tl), Bob Daemmrich/Getty Images/Stone; 396 (cl), Jose Carrillo/ PhotoEdit; 396 (bl), Tom Prettyman/PhotoEdit; 399, Pictor International, Ltd./PictureQuest.

CHAPTER 14: Page 403, D. P. Hershkowitz/Bruce Coleman, Inc.; 405, Andrew Bernstein/Allsport/Getty; 411, CORBIS; 413 (c), Fielder Kownslar/IBM Corporation; 413 (cr), The Granger Collection, New York; 416, Image Copyright ©1998 Photodisc, Inc.; 417, Bill Aron/PhotoEdit; 421, David Young-Wolff/PhotoEdit.

CHAPTER 15: Page 425, 426, Michael Ochs Archives/ Venice, CA.

CHAPTER 16: Page 444, Getty Images/FPG International; 445, 446, Bettmann/CORBIS; 449, Culver Pictures, Inc.; 454, Eric Draper/AP/Wide World Photos.

CHAPTER 17: Page 459 (br), Paul S. Conklin/Nawrocki Stock Photo; 459 (cl), David R. Frazier Photolibrary; 460 (cl), Gerhard Gachelde/HRW Photo; 460 (tl), Image Club Graphics ©1998 Adobe Systems; 465, SuperStock; 468, David Young-Wolff/Getty Images/Stone; 483 (lc), (c), (rc), (br), Bettmann/CORBIS; 483 (bl), North Carolina Museum of Art/CORBIS.

CHAPTER 18: Page 487, SuperStock; 499, Image Copyright ©2001 Photodisc, Inc.; 506, Bob Daemmrich/The Image Works; 509, Original Art by Lloyd Mitchell, 1974. Used by permission from the Leanin' Tree Museum of Western Art, Boulder, Colorado.

Grade 7 ATE, Acknowledgments

For permission to reprint copyrighted material, grateful acknowledgment is made to the following source:

Milbrook Press: From "The Voice in the Attic" from *Voice Magic: Secrets of Ventriloquism & Voice Conjuring* by Ormond McGill. Copyright © 1992 by Ormond McGill.

Grade 7
Reading Selection Amendments

CHAPTER 1, PAGES 19–20
Excerpted, with some word and mechanics changes and internal deletions, as an example of an eyewitness account
CHAPTER 1, PAGE 42
Excerpted to focus on the concept of spatial description presented in this chapter
CHAPTER 2, PAGES 51–52
Excerpted, with some word and mechanics changes, as an example of process writing
CHAPTER 3, PAGES 83–85
Excerpted, with some mechanics changes and internal deletions, as an example of an advantage/disadvantage article
CHAPTER 4, PAGE 123
Excerpted, with some word changes and internal deletions, as an example of a dust jacket
CHAPTER 4, PAGE 132
Excerpted, with some internal deletions, to focus on the concept of identifying an interesting quotation presented in this chapter
CHAPTER 4, PAGE 144
Excerpted to focus on the concept of writing a short story presented in this chapter
CHAPTER 5, PAGES 159–161
Excerpted, with some internal deletions, as an example of giving information through research
CHAPTER 6, PAGES 203–204
Excerpted, with some word and mechanics changes and internal deletions, as an example of persuasive writing
CHAPTER 9, PAGE 289
Excerpted, with some word and mechanics changes, to focus on the concept of topic sentences presented in this chapter

CHAPTER 9, PAGE 290
Excerpted to focus on the concept of implied main idea presented in this chapter
CHAPTER 9, PAGE 291
Excerpted as a practice assignment for students to identify the main idea
CHAPTER 9, PAGE 291
Excerpted, with some mechanics changes, as a practice assignment for students to identify the main idea
CHAPTER 9, PAGE 292
Excerpted as a practice assignment for students to identify the main idea
CHAPTER 9, PAGE 296
Excerpted, with some internal deletions, to focus on the concept of unity within a paragraph presented in this chapter
CHAPTER 9, PAGE 298
Excerpted to focus on the concept of chronological order to tell a story presented in this chapter
CHAPTER 9, PAGE 298
Excerpted, with some internal deletions, to focus on the concept of chronological order to explain a process presented in this chapter
CHAPTER 9, PAGE 299
Excerpted, with some internal deletions, to focus on chronological order to explain causes and effects presented in this chapter
CHAPTER 9, PAGES 300–301
Excerpted to focus on the concept of spatial order presented in this chapter
CHAPTER 9, PAGE 303
Excerpted to focus on the concept of transitional words and phrases presented in this chapter

Grade 7
Reading Selection Amendments continued

CHAPTER 9, PAGES 306–307
Excerpted, with some word changes, to focus on the concept of narrative writing presented in this chapter

CHAPTER 9, PAGE 307
Excerpted, with some word changes and internal deletions, to focus on the concept of descriptive writing presented in this chapter

CHAPTER 9, PAGES 307–308
Excerpted to focus on the concept of expository writing presented in this chapter

CHAPTER 9, PAGE 308
Excerpted, with some internal deletions, to focus on the concept of persuasive writing presented in this chapter

CHAPTER 9, PAGE 310
Excerpted, with some word changes and internal deletions, as a practice assignment for students to break a story into paragraphs

CHAPTER 22, PAGE 574
Excerpted to focus on the concept of capitalization presented in this chapter

CHAPTER 24, PAGE 630
Excerpted to focus on the concept of quotation marks presented in this chapter

CHAPTER 24, PAGE 631
Excerpted to focus on the concept of quotation marks presented in this chapter

CHAPTER 24, PAGE 634
Excerpted to focus on the concept of quotation marks presented in this chapter